*Success seems to be largely
a matter of hanging on
after others have let go.*

— William Feather

# ENTREPRENEURSHIP
## —How to—
# Start & Operate a Small Business

**A Guide for**

**Tenth Revised Edition**

**STEVE MARIOTTI,**

*President and Founder of the National Foundation for Teaching Entrepreneurship, Inc. (NFTE)*

**with Seana Moran**

*plus Peter McBride, Jack Mariotti, Michael Caslin, Chris Meenan, and Alaire Mitchell*

*Edited by Tony Towle*

Copyright © 1987, 1994, 1997, 2001 & 2006 by
**The National Foundation for Teaching Entrepreneurship, Inc. (NFTE)**
120 Wall Street, 29th Floor, New York, NY 10005.

ISBN 1-890859-21-4

# Table of Contents

*The curriculum can be delivered in several ways to suit the needs of the district, school, teacher, or students: as one full-year course; as a semester-long or multi-quarter course; as two one-year courses; as a supplement or unit of study in other courses; as an "after-school" community-based program. Pacing and scheduling suggestions are provided on pages xii-xiii.*

# To the Teacher

**O**n behalf of the National Foundation for Teaching Entrepreneurship (NFTE — pronounced "Nifty"), we would like to thank and congratulate you for choosing to teach our curriculum. When young people participate in our programs, they begin to unlock their unique entrepreneurial creativity, develop a greater understanding of the free enterprise system, and improve the quality of their lives.

Through entrepreneurship education, NFTE teaches young people (ages 11 through 18) from low income communities to become economically productive members of society by improving their academic, business, technology, and life skills. NFTE is a recognized world leader in promoting entrepreneurial literacy among youth. In partnership with public schools, community-based organizations and other social service organizations, as well as some of our nation's most outstanding companies and corporate leaders, NFTE teaches its students how to start and maintain their own small businesses. In the process, they develop important understandings about business, about lifelong learning, about adult roles, and about themselves.

NFTE began in 1987 as a dropout-prevention and academic-performance improvement program for students who were at risk of failing or quitting school. Then as now, NFTE impacts basic academic and life skills through a hands-on and engaging entrepreneurship curriculum that reinforces math, reading and writing, and other literacy skills, and develops proficiencies in critical thinking, problem solving, teamwork, communication, and decision-making.

NFTE's results are well documented (see Harvard and Koch Foundation results later in this text) and prove that exposure to entrepreneurship can give hope, increase interest in educational pursuits, spur enterprise, and assist in the renewal of neighborhoods and communities. NFTE is helping young people to dare to dream for brighter futures and, by doing so, preparing a new generation of leaders — successful entrepreneurs, marketable employees, responsible family members, and conscientious members of their communities.

The curriculum text that this Teacher's Edition is meant to accompany, *How to Start and Operate a Small Business: A Guide for the Young Entrepreneur,* can be used as an independent introduction to entrepreneurship and basic business principles, or can be easily integrated into other courses. NFTE's curriculum also helps students meet academic and workplace readiness standards, including the U.S. Department of Labor Secretary's Commission on Achieving Necessary Skills (SCANS), the National Council of Teachers of Mathematics (NCTM) Curriculum and Evaluation Standards, the National Council of Teachers of English (NCTE) Standards, and NCSS Curriculum Standards for Social Studies, as well as state academic standards and benchmarks in math and English.

We wish you much success with the NFTE program. Please keep in touch with us through the contact information on the next page. It is through your ideas and feedback that NFTE is able to continually improve the program.

Sincerely,

Steve Mariotti
Founder and President, NFTE

# The NFTE Story

**S**teve Mariotti received an M.B.A. from the University of Michigan, Ann Arbor, and has studied at Harvard University, Stanford University, and Brooklyn College. His professional career began as a Treasury Analyst for Ford Venezuela, Mexico, Caribbean, Argentina, Peru, Chile, South Africa and the Export Division (1976-79). He introduced financial systems that saved the company over $5 million per annum via interest-expense reduction and improved cash management. After leaving Ford, Steve founded - and for the next three years operated - Mason Import/Export Services, in New York, eventually acting as sales representative and purchasing agent for 32 overseas firms.

In 1982, Steve Mariotti made a momentous career change and became a Special Education/Business Teacher in the New York City school system, choosing to teach in such at-risk neighborhoods as Bedford-Stuyvesant in Brooklyn and the "Fort Apache" section of the South Bronx. It was at Jane Addams Vocational High School in the Bronx that Steve Mariotti had the idea to bring entrepreneurial education to low-income youth. This inspiration led to the founding of the National Foundation for Teaching Entrepreneurship (NFTE) in 1987, and 501(c)(3) nonprofit status was granted by the IRS the following year.

From the Bronx, NFTE's mission has expanded into an international movement for teaching entrepreneurship, academic, and technology skills to young people worldwide, and NFTE has been recognized with many awards and honors. So, too, has Steve Mariotti, who has been honored with countless tributes and recognitions for his leadership and enabling contributions to the nation's disadvantaged youth.

Although still an emerging curriculum, entrepreneurship has enjoyed tremendous growth in acceptance by K-12 educators, and in popularity among young adults. NFTE believes that entrepreneurship could and should be profitably added to school programs nationwide.

To achieve its goals, NFTE

- partners with universities, schools and community-based organizations and leading businesses;
- creates innovative, experiential curricula;
- trains and supports teachers and youth workers through NFTE University and its regional offices;
- provides supportive alumni services for students.

NFTE's programs are offered in public schools; after-school programs at community-based organizations; and intensive summer business camps.

NFTE has developed specialized programs and tools for students that offer hands-on, interactive learning, including the use of technology, field trips to local businesses, and activities such as the Negotiation Game and the Trading Game. NFTE's curriculum covers a range of key topics such as return on investment, supply and demand, opportunity recognition, personal finance, cost/benefit analysis, sales and marketing, venture capital, business ethics, taxes, and much more.

All programs consistently emphasize the connections between personal motivation, succeeding in the real world, and the importance of being personally and financially independent. Equally important, NFTE teaches young people to think like entrepreneurs - to take risks, to be open to learning, and to be empowered to take control of their lives.

**For information regarding NFTE programs and products, contact**
**(212) 232-3333 or (800) FOR-NFTE; fax: (212) 232-2244; www.nfte.com**

# Student Textbook At-a-Glance

Every one of the 50 chapters in the student textbook is consistently organized for predictability and ease-of-use. It is strongly recommended that students be led through an exploratory "tour" of an early chapter so they can become familiar with a typical chapter's structure:

## TEXTBOOK CHAPTER ORGANIZATION

- **Chapter Title, Opening Photo.** The page opener of each chapter is visually friendly and invites the student to anticipate the content. Photos are selected from NFTE's collections and many depict actual NFTE students and alumni engaged in business activities. A deliberate attempt has been made to represent the diversity and multicultural richness of a typical NFTE classroom.

- **Epigraph.** Every chapter opens with an inspirational quotation, business- or chapter-related, or more open-ended. The quotation and its author may be discussed with students as a preamble to beginning work on the chapter.

- **Key Objectives.** The Objectives, stated in terms of knowledge outcomes and performance expectations, briefly and broadly set out the goals of the chapter. Whenever possible, the Key Objectives are stated in this student-directed format:

*This chapter will enable you to:*

- Describe the differences between employees and entrepreneurs.
- Discuss how entrepreneurs create value from "scarce" resources.
- Explain why entrepreneurs like change.
- Evaluate the pros and cons of owning your own business.

- **Chapter Sections and Subsections.** The content of each chapter in the textbook is organized into "chunks" of learning, signaled to the reader by section and subsection headings. Information within those subtopics is often presented using numbered or bulleted lists, charts, tables, examples, formulas, or other visual organizers where appropriate for learning, but NFTE also expects students to read brief prose sections — as they will need to do in their academic studies and in the "real world." The authors have written the textbook at a reading level that will facilitate access to the content and reduce frustration for less capable readers, while still providing sufficient challenge and engagement.

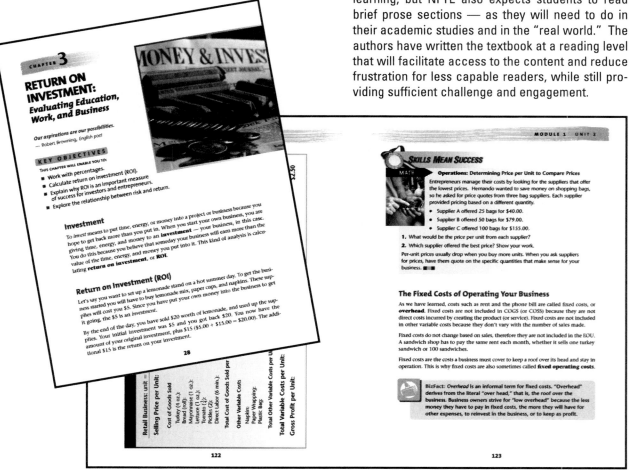

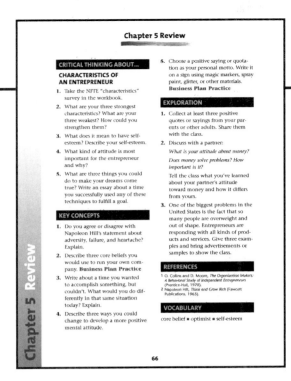

**Chapter 5 Review**

CRITICAL THINKING ABOUT...

**CHARACTERISTICS OF AN ENTREPRENEUR**

1. Take the NFTE "characteristics" survey in the workbook.
2. What are your three strongest characteristics? What are your three weakest? How could you strengthen them?
3. What does it mean to have self-esteem? Describe your self-esteem.
4. What kind of attitude is most important for the entrepreneur and why?
5. What are three things you could do to make your dreams come true? Write an essay about a time you successfully used any of these techniques to fulfill a goal.

KEY CONCEPTS

1. Do you agree or disagree with Napoleon Hill's statement about adversity, failure, and heartache? Explain.
2. Describe three core beliefs you would use to run your own company. **Business Plan Practice**
3. Write about a time you wanted to accomplish something, but couldn't. What would you do differently in that same situation today? Explain.
4. Describe three ways you could change to develop a more positive mental attitude.

5. Choose a positive saying or quotation as your personal motto. Write it on a sign using magic markers, spray paint, glitter, or other materials. **Business Plan Practice**

EXPLORATION

1. Collect at least three positive quotes or sayings from your parents or other adults. Share them with the class.
2. Discuss with a partner:
   *What is your attitude about money?*
   *Does money solve problems? How important is it?*
   Tell the class what you've learned about your partner's attitude toward money and how it differs from yours.
3. One of the biggest problems in the United States is the fact that so many people are overweight and out of shape. Entrepreneurs are responding with all kinds of products and services. Give three examples and bring advertisements or samples to show the class.

REFERENCES

1 O. Collins and D. Moore, *The Organization Makers: A Behavioral Study of Independent Entrepreneurs* (Prentice-Hall, 1970).
2 Napoleon Hill, *Think and Grow Rich* (Fawcett Publications, 1963).

VOCABULARY

core belief ■ optimist ■ self-esteem

66

---

- **Vocabulary.** New, key terms are introduced in bold-face type at the point of first use. A listing of Vocabulary for each chapter also appears at the end of that chapter. However, to keep the Vocabulary section from being unwieldy, not every word or term that should be known will be in boldface. Certain words or terms are important in more than one chapter, but are not duplicated as "Vocabulary" except in a very few instances.

- **Features of Interest.** Visually easy-to-identify features - quotes, tips, and business facts related to the core content — are strategically posted as boxed inserts throughout many chapters to engage interest and provide extensions to or reinforce the content. Teachers can explore and leverage these brief "asides" as desired. *Skills Mean Success* features also appear throughout the textbook, usually two or three per chapter. See **Build Academic and Life-Skill Proficiencies** and **Addressing State Standards through NFTE's Entrepreneurship Curriculum**.

- **Chapter Review.** The end-of-chapter activities provided in the textbook (and, in close parallel, in the student workbook) are a collection of exploration, consolidation, review, and extension opportunities that teachers can use as appropriate, with all or part of the class, before, during, and after the completion of the chapter content.

  ○ **Key Concepts.** Although comprehensive "recall" questions are provided — primarily in the Key Concepts questions — to help students consolidate learning and teachers to assess students' understanding of the chapter content, the end-of-chapter apparatus goes well beyond straightforward review.

○ **Critical Thinking About...** activities ask students to engage in higher-order analysis and interpretation, including applying new knowledge and understanding to their own business plans through *Business Plan Practice* activities.

○ **Exploration** problems and other activities suggested in the textbook and Teacher's Edition require students to conduct research or investigations beyond the textbook based on the chapter topics. Many of the Exploration activities invite students to go into their communities to conduct research and interview business professionals. *These activities should only be conducted with permission from parents/guardians or in accordance with your school or organization's policies.*

○ **Chapter Summary.** This reference reviews the key content and concepts of each chapter.

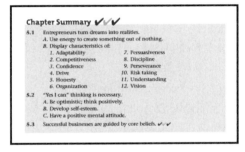

Chapter Summary ✔✔✔
5.1 Entrepreneurs turn dreams into realities.
   A. Use energy to create something out of nothing.
   B. Display characteristics of:
      1. Adaptability          7. Persuasiveness
      2. Competitiveness       8. Discipline
      3. Confidence            9. Perseverance
      4. Drive                10. Risk taking
      5. Honesty              11. Understanding
      6. Organization         12. Vision
5.2 "Yes I can" thinking is necessary.
   A. Be optimistic; think positively.
   B. Develop self-esteem.
   C. Have a positive mental attitude.
5.3 Successful businesses are guided by core beliefs. ✔✔

○ **A Business for the Young Entrepreneur** is a relevant and engaging case study that invites students to learn about and draw conclusions from a real-life young entrepreneur, usually a NFTE graduate, and frequently from a minority. These case studies also provide opportunities for literacy development, critical thinking, and cooperative learning.

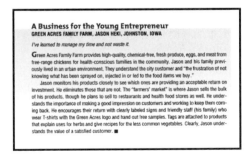

**A Business for the Young Entrepreneur**
GREEN ACRES FAMILY FARM, JASON HEKI, JOHNSTON, IOWA

*I've learned to manage my time and not waste it.*

Green Acres Family Farm provides high-quality, chemical-free, fresh produce, eggs, and meat from free-range chickens for health-conscious families in the community. Jason and his family previously lived in an urban environment. They understand the city customer and "the frustration of not knowing what has been sprayed on, injected in or fed to the food items we buy."
   Jason monitors his products closely to see which ones are providing an acceptable return on investment. He eliminates those that are not. The "farmers' market" is where Jason sells the bulk of his products, though he plans to sell to restaurants and health food stores as well. He understands the importance of making a good impression on customers and working to keep them coming back. He encourages their return with clearly labeled signs and friendly staff (his family) who wear T-shirts with the Green Acres logo and hand out free samples. Tags are attached to products that explain uses for herbs and give recipes for the less common vegetables. Clearly, Jason understands the value of a satisfied customer. ■

○ **References.** Key documents referenced in the chapter and other acknowledgements are included for interest and follow-up.

○ **Vocabulary.** Key terms from the chapter are listed for easy reference and are also defined in the Glossary at the back of the textbook.

## CHAPTER-BY-CHAPTER TEACHING NOTES ORGANIZATION

Extensive but well-organized teaching notes, answers to activities and exercises, and a wealth of instructional suggestions are provided for each chapter of the textbook. In response to feedback from NFTE educators, a more comprehensive — but still customizable — collection of teaching suggestions has been developed for this 10th Edition. As the teacher, you can and should choose from the wide variety of options provided to suit your own style, needs, and goals. The suggestions supplied are intended to support you without overly defining your teaching style or instructional options. In fact, NFTE welcomes suggestions and comments that will enrich and improve the teaching notes.

For ease-of-reference and use, the teaching suggestions to accompany each chapter are consistently ordered and organized in the following schema:

1. Organize the Learning

2. Key Question

3. Prepare for Learning

4. Set a Context for Learning

5. Develop and Close the Learning

6. Assess the Learning

7. Extend the Learning

8. Build Academic and Life-Skill Proficiencies

You can and should treat the suggestions as sources of ideas and instructional aids, picking and choosing those that are best suited to the class, your own teaching style, the time and resources available, and the learning outcomes intended. While NFTE recommends an approach to each chapter that essentially opens, develops, closes, assesses, and extends the learning experience, you should adapt that sequence to your own classroom needs.

- **Organize the Learning.** This convenient, at-a-glance visual organizer summarizes the content, focus, and resources for each chapter to assist you in anticipating the chapter content.

- **Key Question.** Every chapter in this book follows an inquiry approach because most students are engaged by a clearly stated purpose for learning. Accordingly, each Chapter Notes section will suggest a Key Question that, essentially, can be used with students to set a foundation for learning and form a basis of inquiry for the corresponding chapter in the student textbook. Each Summary activity in the Develop and Close the Learning section of each

chapter's teaching notes and the Chapter Summary at the end of each textbook chapter will help draw the students back to the Key Question.

Before beginning a chapter, give the students a chance to flip through that section in their textbooks. Point out the elements — chapter number and title, the epigraph (opening quote), Key Objectives, topic headings, and the end-of-chapter features — to build an overall familiarity with the book's structure. Demonstrate how to "pre-read" a chapter, noticing the essential ideas, observing the graphics and illustrations and, as appropriate, taking notes. It is highly recommended that students preview and/or read each chapter prior to classroom discussion.

- **Prepare for Learning.** This section of each chapter's teaching notes anticipates and provides pre-emptive "ticklers" regarding activities suggested in the teaching notes or textbook that may require planning or pre-work.

- **Set a Context for Learning.** These sections provide suggested (frequently discussion-starter or reflection style) activities designed to engage the students, review prior concepts, and help the class make connections — and for you to assess students' prior knowledge — with a view to establishing a basis for teaching the elements in the Develop and Close the Learning section. This "warm-up" to learning will be critical to helping the class grasp the objectives of the chapter by placing those goals in the context of what students already know or want to know.

*Most activities are of two kinds:*

- **Focus** — often but not always for individuals.

- **Discussion Launcher** — often for small groups, pairs, or other peer-group units.

Some ideas will tie into parallel activities in that section and in the Extend the Learning segment. Teachers should select the most promising or relevant activities as time and interest permit. Answers and possible answers are provided as appropriate.

- **Develop and Close the Learning.** Continuing the instructional model, this section of the teaching notes for each chapter will guide student learning and discovery though a series of "let's find out" activities. Some of the activities suggested are investigative in nature; some involve discussion and problem solving; some require modeling. Most involve team and collaborative learning. All are designed to address key concepts in the chapter. Teachers should pick and choose — or substitute their own ideas — as time, interest, and objectives dictate. Each Develop and Close the Learning section ends with a Summary activity that relates the learning back to the chapter's Key Question, hopefully with some attempt at resolution and closure for the students. Answers and possible answers are provided as appropriate.

- **Assess the Learning.** This section will provide suggestions — some related to the textbook and/or workbook — that can be used to help the teacher to determine how well students have achieved the objectives of the learning and the follow-up learning needs in regard to content: practice, reflection, consolidation, re-teaching, review, concepts not mastered, and readiness to proceed with extension activities and subsequent chapters. A variety of assessment tools in varying degrees of complexity and formality are provided, from the standard chapter quizzes provided in the workbook, to vocabulary review, to more holistic and authentic assessment activities, such as writing or making presentations. Assessing student achievement of the intended learning outcomes and the resolution of the inquiry goal stated in the Chapter Objectives and Key Question, respectively, is an essential step to "closing the loop" in the learning and teaching process.

- Detailed "suggested answers" for the end-of-chapter activities provided in the textbook and in the workbook or blackline masters are provided in each set of Key Concepts and Critical Thinking notes.

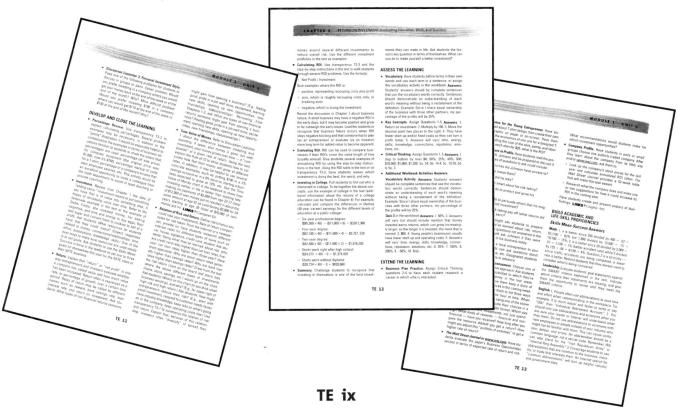

○ Answers for Workbook activities such as Chapter Quiz and Vocabulary not included in the textbook are included in Additional Workbook Activities Answers notes.

Additional assessment activities for each chapter are provided in the electronic "Exam View" test bank, available on CD-ROM. These flexible chapter tests are a mix of True/False, Multiple Choice, Matching, Sentence Completion, and Short Answer test items.

- **Extend the Learning.** Teachers can use the suggestions from this section as time and interest allow, but should always assign business plan-related activities, which are clearly identified.

The activities in Extend the Learning will frequently refer to specific assignments, features, and activities in the textbook, the workbook, and in other supplemental — but highly recommended — NFTE publications, such as *Entrepreneurs in Profile*, a handy anthology of brief, readable, and engaging biographies of well-known entrepreneurs. As with some of the activities in Assess the Learning, those extension activities specifically related to Key Concepts and Critical Thinking activities in the textbook are identified by heading and number. Again, Business Plan Practice activities should be prioritized.

Other activities in this section will invite students to explore beyond the curriculum and to share, network, reflect, and to conduct research on key topics and interests — to reinforce learning and to explore topics of particular individual interest. Activities in this section will frequently involve team and cooperative learning. Most activities are open-ended and cater to a wide range of student interests and abilities. These "enrichment" activities should not be restricted to only the most capable students. Answers and possible answers are provided as appropriate.

- **Build Academic and Life-Skill Proficiencies.** The *Skills Mean Success* features that are provided throughout the textbook (one to four per chapter) are designed to reinforce and extend proficiencies related to key national and state academic standards in English/language arts and math, as well as technology and "leadership" skills. Leadership skills reflect NFTE's Theory of Change, as well as research carried out by Harvard University on NFTE students, regarding important competencies and attitudes displayed by entrepreneurs and by successful adults in general.

The *Skills Mean Success* features are actually informal interventions that complement and reinforce the core entrepreneurship content of the NFTE curriculum. They provide opportunities for learning, and for reviewing and practicing key academic (and other) proficiencies — in context. Many students learn most effectively when they perceive the subject as relevant. Entrepreneurship students in particular will benefit from the opportunity of practicing academic competencies via "real-world" scenarios.

You should employ the *Skills Mean Success* features to complement your own instructional plans with the students as needed — just as you should use selectively the other activities suggested in the textbook, this Teacher's Edition, and other components of the curriculum. You may choose to assign a single *Skills Mean Success* activity to the whole class, to groups, or to individual students, as appropriate. They are important and enabling — but optional — tools for instructional use.

These features are also rich in their potential for shared teaching with colleagues, for cooperative and collaborative learning, for student leadership and peer tutoring, for project-based learning, for integrating applied or contextual academics, for test-taking preparation (or "test prep") activities, as well as offering:

○ to "teach the whole student";

○ to demonstrate how elective courses can reinforce core academic skills and address state standards;

○ to help drive the school's overall mission of increasing academic proficiency for all students;

○ to showcase the entrepreneurship program as an important contributor to providing alternative but supportive pathways to student academic success.

Answers and easy-to-use notes to complement the textbook's *Skills Mean Success* features are included for each chapter in this section. The *Skills Mean Success* features that are found in every chapter of the textbook address academic standards and benchmarks in English and mathematics, as well as technology and "leadership"/life skills, that all students will need to develop and that some students will need to review and reinforce. The academic proficiencies addressed will help students not just "pass the test," but to achieve mastery of these subjects as they continue their education and prepare for post-high-school adult roles. The *Skills Mean*

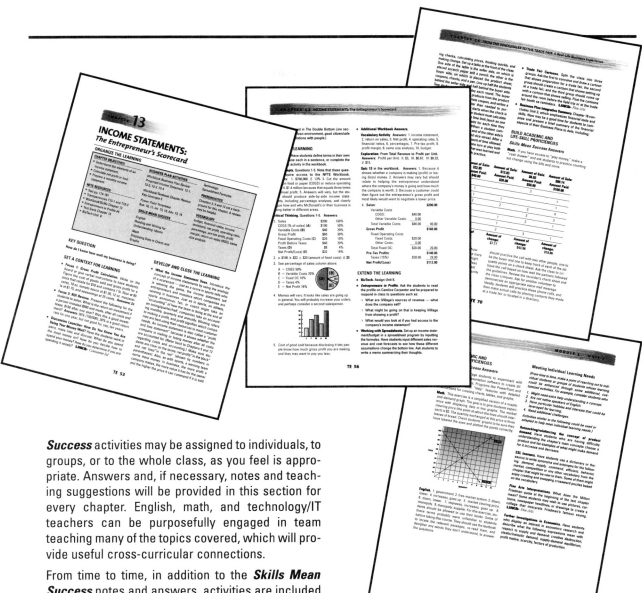

*Success* activities may be assigned to individuals, to groups, or to the whole class, as you feel is appropriate. Answers and, if necessary, notes and teaching suggestions will be provided in this section for every chapter. English, math, and technology/IT teachers can be purposefully engaged in team teaching many of the topics covered, which will provide useful cross-curricular connections.

From time to time, in addition to the *Skills Mean Success* notes and answers, activities are included in this section to remind busy teachers to be mindful of individual student learning needs when possible: ESL, special education, gifted and talented, alternative learning styles, and so on. The suggestions are reminders to find ways to address individual student needs.

- **Integrate Learning and Address Learner Interests.** The NFTE curriculum provides many opportunities to engage students in cross-curriculum learning and to leverage the interests of individual students or groups of students to make learning more personal and meaningful. Some suggested activities outlined in the teaching notes are identified as examples of these types of enhanced learning opportunities. Look for the "**LINKS»»:**" indicators throughout the teaching notes for examples of some — but by no means all — activities that lend themselves to explorations in such areas as:

*Economics; Social Studies; Government; History; Media Literacy; Graphic Arts; Dramatic Arts; Business Ethics; Music; Character Education; Consumer Education* and more.

Be aware of these and the numerous additional potential "learning moments" afforded by the NFTE curriculum that can be used to:

- ○ enhance understanding across disciplines;

- ○ leverage and showcase the interests and talents of individual students;

- ○ help address academic and other standards of learning through Entrepreneurship.

# Pacing Suggestions

**P**acing hints are provided here for one-, two-, and four-semester courses that provide coverage of combinations of the Basic and Intermediate modules or the Basic, Intermediate, and Advanced modules. These are the most common course lengths and configurations for the NFTE curriculum. All course estimates and pacing guides assume three to five 45-to-55-minute classes or instructional blocks per week, nine or ten weeks per quarter, 18 to 20 weeks per semester, and 36 to 40 weeks per year. Pacing will vary depending on number of hours of instructional time per week, on the teacher's individual teaching style, on the school's own event schedules, and on the depth with which topics and extended-learning opportunities are explored — and therefore teachers should adjust accordingly. Teachers who follow block- or modified-block schedules will need to adapt the pacing suggestions to suit their particular time allotments per week or cycle.

## ONE-YEAR, TWO-SEMESTER COURSE (BASIC AND INTERMEDIATE MODULES)

| Semester 1 | | | Semester 2 | | |
|---|---|---|---|---|---|
| | Week 1 | Chapter 1 | | Week 1 | Chapter 17 |
| | Week 2 | Chapter 2 | | Week 2 | Chapter 18 |
| | Week 3 | Chapter 3 | | Week 3 | Chapter 19 |
| | Week 4 | Chapter 4 | | Week 4 | Chapter 20 |
| | Week 5 | Chapter 5 | | Week 5 | Chapter 21 |
| | Week 6 | Chapter 6 | | Week 6 | Chapter 22 |
| | Week 7 | Chapter 7 | | Week 7 | Chapter 23 |
| | Week 8 | Chapters 8 | | Week 8 | Chapter 24 |
| | Week 9 | Chapters 9 | | Week 9 | Chapter 25 |
| | Week 10 | Chapter 10 | | Week 10 | Chapter 26 |
| | Week 11 | Chapter 11 | | Week 11 | Chapter 27 |
| | Week 12 | Chapter 12 | | Week 12 | Chapter 28 |
| | Week 13 | Chapter 13 | | Week 13 | Chapter 29 |
| | Week 14 | Chapter 14 | | Week 14 | Chapter 30 |
| | Week 15 | Chapter 15 | | Week 15 | Review or as Needed |
| | Week 16 | Chapter 16 | | Week 16 | Review or as Needed |
| | Week 17-18 | Trade Fair Visit, as Needed, or Review | | Week 17-18 | Review or as Needed |
| | Week 19-20 | Trade Fair Visit, as Needed, or Review | | Week 19-20 | Review or as Needed |

*Total approx. 40 weeks*

## ONE-SEMESTER COURSE (BASIC AND INTERMEDIATE MODULES)

| Term 1 | | | Term 2 | | |
|---|---|---|---|---|---|
| | Week 1 | Chapters 1 | | Week 1 | Chapter 17 |
| | Week 2 | Chapters 2 | | Week 2 | Chapters 18-19 |
| | Week 3 | Chapters 3 | | Week 3 | Chapter 20 |
| | Week 4 | Chapters 4-6 | | Week 4 | Chapters 21 |
| | Week 5 | Chapters 7-9 | | Week 5 | Chapters 22 |
| | Week 6 | Chapters 10-11 | | Week 6 | Chapters 23-24 |
| | Week 7 | Chapters 12 | | Week 7 | Chapters 25 |
| | Week 8 | Chapters 13 | | Week 8 | Chapters 26-27 |
| | Week 9-10 | Chapters 14-16 | | Week 9-10 | Chapters 28-30 |

*Total approx. 20 weeks*

## ONE-YEAR, TWO-SEMESTER COURSE (BASIC, INTERMEDIATE, AND ADVANCED)

| *Semester 1* | | | | *Semester 2* | | |
|---|---|---|---|---|---|---|
| **Term 1** | Week 1 | Chapters 1 | | **Term 1** | Week 1 | Chapter 31 |
| | Week 2 | Chapters 2 | | | Week 2 | Chapter 32 |
| | Week 3 | Chapters 3 | | | Week 3 | Chapter 33 |
| | Week 4 | Chapters 4-6 | | | Week 4 | Chapter 34 |
| | Week 5 | Chapters 7-9 | | | Week 5 | Chapter 35 |
| | Week 6 | Chapters 10-11 | | | Week 6 | Chapter 36 |
| | Week 7 | Chapters 12 | | | Week 7 | Chapter 37 |
| | Week 8 | Chapters 13 | | | Week 8 | Chapter 38 |
| | Week 9-10 | Chapters 14-16 | | | Week 9 | Chapter 39 |
| **Term 2** | Week 11 | Chapter 17 | | | Week 10 | Chapter 40 |
| | Week 12 | Chapters 18-19 | | **Term 2** | Week 11 | Chapter 41 |
| | Week 13 | Chapter 20 | | | Week 12 | Chapter 42 |
| | Week 14 | Chapters 21 | | | Week 13 | Chapter 43 |
| | Week 15 | Chapters 22 | | | Week 14 | Chapter 44 |
| | Week 16 | Chapters 23-24 | | | Week 15 | Chapter 45 |
| | Week 17 | Chapters 25 | | | Week 16 | Chapter 46 |
| | Week 18 | Chapters 26-27 | | | Week 17 | Chapter 47 |
| | Week 19-20 | Chapters 28-30 | | | Week 18 | Chapter 48 |
| | | | | | Week 19 | Chapter 49 |
| | | | | | Week 20 | Chapter 50 |

*Total approx. 40 weeks*

## TWO-YEAR, FOUR-SEMESTER COURSE (BASIC, INTERMEDIATE, AND ADVANCED MODULES)

| *Semester 1* | Week 1-20 | Chapters 1-16* |
|---|---|---|
| *Semester 2* | Week 1-20 | Chapters 17-30* |
| *Semester 3* | Week 1-20 | Chapters 31-40 |
| *Semester 4* | Week 1-20 | Chapters 41-50 |

*Total approx. 80 weeks*

*\* See One-Year, Two-Semester Course (Basic and Intermediate Modules)*

*For other course lengths and configurations, please contact NFTE. If you have alternative suggested pacing guides that other teaching professionals could benefit from, please feel invited to share them with NFTE.*

# Integrating the Student Textbook/Workbook
# with NFTE Business Plan Activities and BizTech

| Chapter | Objectives | Business Plan Activities | Biz Tech Unit |
|---|---|---|---|
| **Chapter 1:** What is Entrepreneurship? | • Describe the difference between employees and entrepreneurs.<br>• Discuss how entrepreneurs create value from "scarce" resources.<br>• Explain why entrepreneurs like change.<br>• Evaluate the pros and cons of owning your own business. | *Workbook Business Plan Review*<br>Your Business Idea 1-1, 1-2, 1-3, 1-4, 1-5<br>*Workbook/Textbook Chapter Review*<br>Critical Thinking 4<br>*Power Point Templates*<br>Bas. 2; Int. 2; Adv. 2 | |
| **Chapter 2:** The Building Block of Business | • Define a unit of sale for a business.<br>• Describe the four types of business.<br>• Analyze the economics of one unit for each type of business, and calculate gross profit per unit. | *Workbook Business Plan Review*<br>Economics of One Unit 2-1, 2-2, 2-3<br>*Workbook/Textbook Chapter Review*<br>Key Concepts 3-4<br>*Power Point Templates*<br>Bas. 2, 5; Int. 2, 6; Adv. 2, 6 | |
| **Chapter 3:** Return on Investment | • Work with percentages<br>• Calculate return on investment (ROI).<br>• Explain why ROI is an important measure of success for investors and entrepreneurs.<br>• Explore the relationship between risk and return. | *Workbook Business Plan Review*<br>Return on Investment; Business Goals: 3-1, 3-2; Personal Goals: 3-1, 3-2<br>*Workbook/Textbook Chapter Review*<br>Critical Thinking 2-4<br>*Power Point Templates*<br>Bas. 14; Int. 17, Adv. 16 | |
| **Chapter 4:** Opportunity Recognition | • Distinguish between an idea and an opportunity.<br>• Recognize and evaluate business opportunities.<br>• Apply cost/benefit analysis that includes opportunity cost to personal and business decisions.<br>• Perform a SWOT analysis of a business opportunity.<br>• Find business-formation opportunities among people you know. | *Workbook Business Plan Review*<br>Opportunity Recognition 4-1, 4-2<br>*Workbook/Textbook Chapter Review*<br>Critical Thinking 4-5 (and 2-3)<br>*Power Point Templates*<br>Bas. 3; Int. 3; Adv. 3 | |
| **Chapter 5:** Characteristics of the Successful Entrepreneur | • Describe the characteristics of successful entrepreneurs.<br>• Identify your own characteristics.<br>• Develop characteristics that will help you in business.<br>• Train yourself to think positively. | *Workbook Business Plan Review*<br>Core Beliefs 5-1, 5-2<br>*Workbook/Textbook Chapter Review*<br>Key Concepts 2, 5 | 1 |
| **Chapter 6:** Supply and Demand | • Compare and contrast free-market with command economies.<br>• Explain the relationship between supply, demand, and price.<br>• Describe how competition keeps prices down and quality high.<br>• Discuss monopoly's effect on price and quality.<br>• Use a supply-and-demand graph. | *Workbook Business Plan Review*<br>Supply and Demand 6-1, 6-2<br>*Workbook/Textbook Chapter Review*<br>Critical Thinking 2 | |
| **Chapter 7:** Inventions and Product Development | • Develop your creativity.<br>• Practice lateral thinking.<br>• Use "practical daydreaming" to invent new products.<br>• Describe the five steps of developing a product.<br>• Explore the contributions of minority and women inventors. | *Workbook Business Plan Review*<br>Product Development 7-1<br>*Workbook/Textbook Chapter Review*<br>Critical Thinking 4 | |
| **Chapter 8:** Selecting Your Business | • Describe the four types of businesses and the difference between products and services.<br>• Identify your skills and hobbies.<br>• Explore your competitive advantage.<br>• Select your own business and name it.<br>• Define how your business can help your community. | *Workbook Business Plan Review*<br>Competitive Advantage 8-1, 8-2<br>*Workbook/Textbook Chapter Review*<br>Critical Thinking 2, 5<br>*Power Point Templates*<br>Bas. 6; Int. 8; Adv. 8 | 2 |

| Chapter | Objectives | Business Plan Activities | Biz Tech Unit |
|---|---|---|---|
| **Chapter 9:** Costs of Running a Business | • Define your unit of sale.<br>• Explain the difference between costs of goods sold and other variable costs.<br>• Calculate gross profit, including variable costs.<br>• Determine costs of operating your business.<br>• Use depreciation to spread the cost of equipment over several years. | *Workbook Business Plan Review*<br>Operating Costs 9-1, 9-2, 9-3, 9-4<br>*Workbook/Textbook Chapter Review*<br>Critical Thinking; Key Concepts 2<br>*Power Point Templates*<br>Bas. 4, 9; Int. 5, 12; Adv. 5, 11 | 3 |
| **Chapter 10:** What is Marketing? | • Explain why marketing is the business function that identifies customer needs.<br>• Use marketing to establish your brand.<br>• Apply the four elements of a marketing plan.<br>• Create a marketing plan for your business. | *Workbook Business Plan Review*<br>Marketing 10-1, 10-2, 10-3<br>*Workbook/Textbook Chapter Review*<br>Key Concepts 2-3<br>*Power Point Templates*<br>Bas. 7, 8; Int. 9, 10; Adv. 9, 10 | 6 |
| **Chapter 11:** Market Research | • Describe the different types of market research.<br>• Develop an effective market survey for your company.<br>• Use market research to understand your customers' needs.<br>• Analyze your industry. | *Workbook Business Plan Review*<br>Market Research 11-1, 11-2<br>*Workbook/Textbook Chapter Review*<br>Critical Thinking 2-3 (and 1) | 4 |
| **Chapter 12:** Keeping Good Records | • Develop the valuable habit of keeping good records.<br>• Use receipts and invoices correctly.<br>• Open a bank account.<br>• Create an accounting system for your business.<br>• Use your records to analyze and improve your business.<br>• Create financial statements from accounting records. | *Workbook Business Plan Review*<br>Record Keeping 12-1, 12-2<br>*Workbook/Textbook Chapter Review*<br>Key Concepts 1, 4 and Exploration | 15 |
| **Chapter 13:** Income Statements | • Understand the elements of an income statement.<br>• Calculate net profit or loss.<br>• Prepare a monthly income statement. | *Workbook Business Plan Review*<br>Projected Income Statement 13-1, 13-2, 13-3, 13-4<br>*Workbook/Textbook Chapter Review*<br>Key Concepts 5<br>*Power Point Templates*<br>Bas. 10, 11; Int. 13, 14; Adv. 13, 14 | 8 |
| **Chapter 14:** Financing Strategy | • Compare debt and equity financing.<br>• Discuss the three basic legal business structures: sole proprietorship, partnership, and corporation.<br>• Choose alternative forms of financing, such as micro-loans and "bootstrapping."<br>• Calculate debt and debt-to-equity ratios. | *Workbook Business Plan Review*<br>Financing Strategy 14-1, 14-2, 14-3, 14-4, 14-5, 14-6, 14-7<br>*Workbook/Textbook Chapter Review*<br>Key Concepts 1, 2, 5 (and 3-4)<br>*Power Point Templates*<br>Bas. 12-15; Int. 15-19; Adv. 15-17, 20, 21 | 7 |
| **Chapter 15:** Negotiation | • Handle a negotiation.<br>• Practice the art of compromise.<br>• Seek a "Yes" or "No" instead of a "Maybe." | *Workbook Business Plan Review*<br>Negotiation 15-1 | |
| **Chapter 16:** From the Wholesaler to the Trade Fair | • Locate wholesalers and trade fairs (flea markets) in your area.<br>• Sell your merchandise at a trade fair.<br>• Prepare an income statement from a trade fair field trip.<br>• Use an inventory sheet.<br>• Calculate net profit and ROI for the field trip. | *Workbook Business Plan Review*<br>Buying Wholesale 16-1, 16-2 | |

# Integrating the Student Textbook/Workbook
# with NFTE Business Plan Activities and BizTech *(cont'd)*

| Chapter | Objectives | Business Plan Activities | Biz Tech Unit |
|---|---|---|---|
| **Chapter 17:** Competitive Strategy | • Define a competitive strategy. <br> • Explain "business definition." <br> • Identify sources of competitive advantage. <br> • Create a mission statement. <br> • Develop tactics to use in implementing a strategy. | *Workbook Business Plan Review* <br> Your Competitive Strategy; Business Definition Questions: 17-1, 17-2, 17-3; Competitive Advantage Questions: 17-1, 17-2, 17-3; Tactical Question Issues: 17-1, 17-2, 17-3, 17-4 <br> *Workbook/Textbook Chapter Review* <br> Critical Thinking 8, Key Concepts 2, 3, and Exploration | 11 |
| **Chapter 18:** Developing Your Marketing Mix | • Understand the four steps of a marketing plan. <br> • Learn how to develop a successful marketing mix for your business venture. <br> • Learn the basic principles of pricing strategy. | *Workbook Business Plan Review* <br> Your Marketing Mix; Step 1: Consumer Analysis, Step 2: Market Analysis, Step 3: The Marketing Mix <br> *Workbook/Textbook Chapter Review* <br> Marketing Mix Chart, Key Concepts 1, 2, and Exploration 2, 3 <br> *Power Point Templates* <br> Int. 8; Adv. 8 | 10 |
| **Chapter 19:** Advertising and Publicity | • Explain the difference between advertising and publicity. <br> • Generate publicity for your business. <br> • Use promotion to communicate effectively with your market. <br> • Choose ways to promote your business — online and in the media. | *Workbook Business Plan Review* <br> Advertising and Publicity 19-1, 19-2, 19-3, 19-4, 19-5 <br> *Workbook/Textbook Chapter Review* <br> Critical Thinking 3, 4, 5; Key Concepts 2, 4, 5; Exploration 1, 2 | 5 |
| **Chapter 20:** Break-Even Analysis | • Know what break-even means to a business. <br> • Figure how many units your business must sell to "break even." <br> • Use break-even analysis to evaluate your marketing plan. | *Workbook Business Plan Review* <br> Break-Even Analysis 20-1 <br> *Workbook/Textbook Chapter Review* <br> Critical Thinking 1 <br> *Power Point Templates* <br> Int. 19; Adv. 21 | 24 |
| **Chapter 21:** Principles of Successful Selling | • Turn product features into customer benefits. <br> • Turn customer objections into sales advantages. <br> • Pre-qualify a sales call. <br> • Make an effective sales call. <br> • Build good relationships with customers that will lead to more sales prospects. | *Workbook Business Plan Review* <br> Selling 21-1, 21-2, 21-3, 21-4 <br> *Workbook/Textbook Chapter Review* <br> Key Concepts 2, 3; Critical Thinking 1, 2 | 17 <br> 18 |
| **Chapter 22:** Customer Service | • Explain why customer service is an investment with a very high return. <br> • Turn your sales into repeat business. <br> • Handle customer complaints and criticism in positive ways that will be good for your business. <br> • Create a customer database and establish other ongoing market research efforts. | *Workbook Business Plan Review* <br> Customer Service 22-1 <br> *Workbook/Textbook Chapter Review* <br> Critical Thinking 2, 4 | |
| **Chapter 23:** Math Tips to Help You Sell and Negotiate | • Do business math in your head so you can think on your feet. <br> • Convert bulk prices to per-unit costs quickly during negotiations. <br> • Be able to calculate how many years it will take for an investment to double. | *Workbook Business Plan Review* <br> Business Math 23-1 <br> *Workbook/Textbook Chapter Review* <br> Key Concepts 1 | |
| **Chapter 24:** Business Communication | • Write a business memo. <br> • Write a business letter. <br> • Know when to use "cc:" on copies of memos or letters. <br> • Proofread business correspondence. | *Workbook Business Plan Review* <br> Business Communication 24-1, 24-2 <br> *Workbook/Textbook Chapter Review* <br> Key Concepts 4, Critical Thinking 3 | 14 |

| Chapter | Objectives | Business Plan Activities | Biz Tech Unit |
|---|---|---|---|
| **Chapter 25:** Sole Proprietorships and Partnerships | • Explain the pros and cons of sole proprietorships and partnerships.<br>• Register a sole proprietorship.<br>• Research business permits and licenses.<br>• Obtain a sales-tax identification number. | *Workbook Business Plan Review*<br>Legal Structure 25-1, 25-2, 25-3, 25-4, 25-5<br>*Workbook/Textbook Chapter Review*<br>Key Concepts 2, Critical Thinking 4, Exploration<br>*Power Point Templates*<br>Int. 2; Adv. 2 | 9 |
| **Chapter 26:** Manufacturing | • Explain the manufacturing process.<br>• Locate manufacturers in your community.<br>• Have a prototype made.<br>• Investigate zoning laws that might affect your business. | *Workbook Business Plan Review*<br>Manufacturing<br>*Workbook/Textbook Chapter Review*<br>Critical Thinking 4, 5; Exploration | |
| **Chapter 27:** The Production/ Distribution Chain | • Understand the manufacturer-to-consumer chain.<br>• Calculate markup percentages.<br>• Calculate gross profit margin.<br>• Calculate net profit margin. | *Workbook Business Plan Review*<br>Production/Distribution Chain 27-1, 27-2, 27-3<br>*Workbook/Textbook Chapter Review*<br>Key Concepts 1, 3<br>*Power Point Templates*<br>Int. 11; Adv. 11 | 12 |
| **Chapter 28:** Quality | • Explain why quality leads to profit.<br>• Discuss W. Edwards Deming's ideas about quality and profit.<br>• List ten ways to improve quality.<br>• Apply the Japanese concept of *kaizen* to your life. | *Workbook Business Plan Review*<br>Quality 28-1, 28-2<br>*Workbook/Textbook Chapter Review*<br>Critical Thinking 1, 6 | |
| **Chapter 29:** Effective Leadership | • Develop leadership qualities.<br>• Manage your time more efficiently.<br>• Hire employees.<br>• Build a management team. | *Workbook Business Plan Review*<br>Human Resources 29-1, 29-2, 29-3, 29-4, 29-5<br>*Workbook/Textbook Chapter Review*<br>Critical Thinking 4, 6; Key Concepts 4<br>*Power Point Templates*<br>Adv. 23 | 21 |
| **Chapter 30:** Technology | • Explore how entrepreneurs use technology.<br>• Expand your business on the Internet. | *Workbook Business Plan Review*<br>Technology 30-1, 30-2<br>*Workbook/Textbook Chapter Review*<br>Key Concepts 1; Critical Thinking 2<br>*Power Point Templates*<br>Adv. 24 | 16 |
| **Chapter 31:** Finding Sources of Capital | • Identify new sources of capital.<br>• Use sale of equity to finance your business.<br>• Network with other entrepreneurs to find business financing.<br>• Use vendor financing. | *Workbook Business Plan Review*<br>Raising Capital 31-1, 31-2<br>*Workbook/Textbook Chapter Review*<br>Critical Thinking 2, 3 | |
| **Chapter 32:** Corporations | • Understand corporations and limited liability companies (LLC).<br>• Decide whether you should form a corporation or LLC.<br>• Explain how a corporation is treated under tax and business laws.<br>• Evaluate the pros and cons of different business structures. | *Workbook Business Plan Review*<br>Corporations 32-1, 32-2, 32-3, 32-4<br>*Workbook/Textbook Chapter Review*<br>Key Concepts 2-7 | |
| **Chapter 33:** Stocks | • Explain why stocks are traded.<br>• Read a daily stock table.<br>• Calculate a stock's price/earnings ratio.<br>• Calculate a stock's yield. | *Workbook Business Plan Review*<br>Stocks 33-1, 33-2<br>*Workbook/Textbook Chapter Review*<br>Critical Thinking 2, 3 | 19 |

| Chapter | Objectives | Business Plan Activities | Biz Tech Unit |
|---|---|---|---|
| **Chapter 34:** Bonds | • Explain how bonds differ from stocks.<br>• Summarize how bonds work.<br>• Discuss the effect inflation has on the value of a dollar.<br>• Read a bond table. | *Workbook Business Plan Review*<br>Bonds 34-1, 34-2<br>*Workbook/Textbook Chapter Review*<br>Critical Thinking 2, 3 | |
| **Chapter 35:** The Balance Sheet | • Read a simple corporate balance sheet.<br>• Create a balance sheet for your business from the financial records.<br>• Analyze a balance sheet using financial ratios.<br>• Use a balance sheet to tell if a company has been successful over time. | *Workbook Business Plan Review*<br>Your Balance Sheet 35-1, 35-2, 35-3, 35-4<br>*Workbook/Textbook Chapter Review*<br>Key Concepts 3, 4<br>*Power Point Templates*<br>Adv. 18, 21 | 25 |
| **Chapter 36:** Venture Capital | • Explain how and why venture capitalists invest in a business.<br>• Describe the differences between venture capitalists and bankers.<br>• Explain how venture capitalists "harvest" their investments.<br>• Determine a company's total value.<br>• List the elements of a business plan. | *Workbook Business Plan Review*<br>Venture Capital 36-1<br>*Workbook/Textbook Chapter Review*<br>Critical Thinking 5 | |
| **Chapter 37:** Contracts | • Understand the importance of written agreements in running a business.<br>• Use contracts effectively to strengthen your business.<br>• Understand "The Four A's" of a successful contract.<br>• Understand the remedies available in case of breach of contract. | *Workbook Business Plan Review*<br>Contracts 37-1, 37-2, 37-3<br>*Workbook/Textbook Chapter Review*<br>Critical Thinking 1, 2, 3, 4, 5;<br>Key Concepts 4 | |
| **Chapter 38:** Socially Responsible Business and Philanthropy | • Develop a socially responsible business.<br>• Determine how to use your business to help people in the community.<br>• Develop cause-related marketing for your business that will support your competitive advantage. | *Workbook Business Plan Review*<br>Socially Responsible Business 38-1, 38-2<br>*Workbook/Textbook Chapter Review*<br>Key Concepts 4, 5 | |
| **Chapter 39:** Small Business and Government | • Understand the economic definition of efficiency.<br>• Define GDP and GNP.<br>• Understand how government regulations impact small business.<br>• Analyze global business opportunities. | *Workbook Business Plan Review*<br>Small Business and Government 39-1<br>*Workbook/Textbook Chapter Review*<br>Critical Thinking 5 | |
| **Chapter 40:** Building Good Personal and Business Credit | • Explain the difference between good credit and no credit.<br>• Establish a personal credit history.<br>• Define the "Four C's" of business credit.<br>• Know your rights in dealing with credit-reporting agencies.<br>• Befriend your banker. | *Workbook Business Plan Review*<br>Building Good Personal and Business Credit 40-1, 40-2<br>*Workbook/Textbook Chapter Review*<br>Critical Thinking 1; Key Concepts 3, 4 | 22 |
| **Chapter 41:** Cash Flow | • Keep track of your cash on a daily basis.<br>• Use a monthly cash flow statement.<br>• Avoid getting caught without enough cash to pay your bills.<br>• Understand the cyclical nature of cash flow.<br>• Calculate your burn rate. | *Workbook Business Plan Review*<br>Cash Flow 41-1, 41-2, 41-3<br>*Workbook/Textbook Chapter Review*<br>Key Concepts 3; Critical Thinking 1, 2<br>*Power Point Templates*<br>Adv. 19, 24 | 15 |
| **Chapter 42:** Protecting Intellectual Property | • Recognize that your ideas and their expression can have value for your business.<br>• Create and protect your intellectual property.<br>• Apply for patents, copyrights, and trademarks.<br>• Legally obtain and use intellectual property owned by others. | *Workbook Business Plan Review*<br>Intellectual Property 42-1, 42-2<br>*Workbook/Textbook Chapter Review*<br>Critical Thinking 1, 2<br>*Power Point Templates*<br>Adv. 22 | 13 |

| Chapter | Objectives | Business Plan Activities | Biz Tech Unit |
|---|---|---|---|
| **Chapter 43:** Ethical Business Behavior | • Explain the difference between illegal and unethical behavior. <br>• Develop repeat business. <br>• Motivate your employees. <br>• Practice ethical business behavior. | *Workbook Business Plan Review* <br> Ethical Business Behavior 43-1, 43-2 <br> *Workbook/Textbook Chapter Review* <br> Critical Thinking 5, 6; Key Concepts 2, 3 | |
| **Chapter 44:** Taxation and the Entrepreneur | • Understand how to meet your legal tax obligation as a small business owner. <br>• Identify the taxes that support city, state, and federal government. <br>• Find appropriate tax forms and assistance in filling them out. | *Workbook Business Plan Review* <br> Taxation 44-1 <br> *Workbook/Textbook Chapter Review* <br> Key Concepts 3 | 20 |
| **Chapter 45:** Insurance | • Explain how insurance protects businesses. <br>• Determine when a business needs liability insurance. <br>• Explain how insurance companies make money. <br>• Choose coverage for your small business. | *Workbook Business Plan Review* <br> Insurance 45-1, 45-2 <br> *Workbook/Textbook Chapter Review* <br> Critical Thinking 3, 4; Business Plan Interactive Summary | 23 |
| **Chapter 46:** Franchising and Licensing | • Imagine new ways to profit from your brand. <br>• Contrast licensing with franchising. <br>• Explore the benefits and drawbacks of franchising. <br>• Avoid agreements that could tarnish your brand's image. | *Workbook Business Plan Review* <br> Franchising and Licensing <br> *Workbook/Textbook Chapter Review* <br> Critical Thinking 3 | |
| **Chapter 47:** International Opportunities | • Cultivate an understanding of other cultures. <br>• Explore exporting and importing opportunities. <br>• Research customers and competition internationally. <br>• Conduct trade in foreign currencies. | *Workbook Business Plan Review* <br> International Opportunities 47-1, 47-2 <br> *Workbook/Textbook Chapter Review* <br> Critical Thinking 4, 5 | |
| **Chapter 48:** Investment Goals and Risk Tolerance | • Establish the habit of saving ten percent of your income. <br>• Explain the concepts of present and future value. <br>• Discover your investment risk tolerance. <br>• Set financial goals. | *Workbook Business Plan Review* <br> Investment Goals And Risk Tolerance 48-1, 48-2, 48-3 <br> *Workbook/Textbook Chapter Review* <br> Critical Thinking 5 | |
| **Chapter 49:** Investing For a Secure Future | • Choose investments in line with your risk tolerance and goals. <br>• Create an investment portfolio and project its return. | *Workbook Business Plan Review* <br> Investing For A Secure Future 49-1, 49-2, 49-3 <br> *Workbook/Textbook Chapter Review* <br> Critical Thinking 5 | |
| **Chapter 50:** Exit Strategies | • Think about how you want to exit your business one day. <br>• Explore various exit strategies that will "harvest" the wealth created by your business. <br>• Choose exit strategies that will make your business more attractive to investors. <br>• Make a wise decision about when to harvest your business. | *Workbook Business Plan Review* <br> Exit Strategy 50-1, 50-2 <br> *Workbook/Textbook Chapter Review* <br> Critical Thinking 4; Business Plan Integrative Summary | |

# Addressing State Academic Standards and Lifelong Learning Skills through the NFTE Curriculum

The No Child Left Behind (NCLB) Act of 2002, and especially that federal legislation's Adequate Yearly Progress (AYP) provisions, have brought unprecedented attention to students' academic proficiency as well as accountability from districts, schools, and teachers. State-mandated testing requirements in core academic subjects increasingly drive curriculum and instruction in K-12.

Career-technical pathways to student engagement and achievement, such as the NFTE entrepreneurship curriculum, can and *must* contribute to student success in reaching these overarching academic goals. In fact, career-focused programs such as the NFTE curriculum have a special role to play in supporting the attainment of basic academic proficiency for all students — since they provide an applied, real-world context in which academic skills and other enabling proficiencies can be used and enhanced. Learning in context and "by doing" is critically important for many of our students, especially those who are "at-risk" and who have not experienced complete success in traditional "core four" coursework. In short, academic proficiency may not be the primary goal of the NFTE curriculum, but the NFTE curriculum is uniquely suited to contribute to the academic success of many students — through its differentiated approach to learning and achievement, and its emphasis on real-world application and motivating context. Students who struggle to connect with a particular standard or benchmark in an academic classroom may find an empowering entrypoint to taking ownership of that same academic skill in the process of seeing its utility and use in a small business management context.

Additionally, it is important for NFTE teachers and other career-technical educators to demonstrate — and be able to demonstrate — the continuing value of their programs to so many students. Unfortunately, the relevance of some career technical programs in K-12 are questioned by standards-focused stakeholders who challenge how much such curricula take away time and attention from the achievement of academic proficiencies. NFTE teachers are encouraged, therefore, not just to continue to address the needs of the total student, but also to demonstrate the value of the NFTE curriculum in helping students to achieve academic success, as well as core business and life-skill competencies. NFTE teachers, as well, can point out the importance of student-engaging career-pathway programs, such as the NFTE curriculum, to other measures of school and student success, such as the No Child Left Behind mandates: dropout prevention, graduation rates, college continuance, and positive attitudes toward school and learning.

The NFTE curriculum has always provided many opportunities for students to develop academic skills in the context of an entrepreneurship program. Business math and business-related English skills, as well as technology skills and life-long learning, have been part of the curriculum for several past revisions. However, in response to NFTE user feedback, in the fall of 2003, NFTE surveyed a variety of NFTE educators and other teaching professionals to determine the degree of perceived value and interest in having access to an enhanced academic and life skills strand in the planned Tenth Edition of the core curriculum text. A clear consensus emerged:

- Expand the academic proficiencies and life-skills content of the curriculum, but keep that "secondary" content optional and supportive of the core entrepreneurship content.

- Tie academic skills more directly to state and national standards in English and math.

- Do not assume student mastery of state and national standards and benchmarks included at levels prior to grade 9, or even earlier; many students have not mastered pre-high school proficiencies and need reinforcement of so-called elementary and middle school competencies.

- Highlight the visibility of such content so students and teachers could make better and more effective (but optional) use of such features as needed.

It was also clearly recognized that, while only a limited range of academic skills can be "taught" and developed in the context of entrepreneurship, attention to relevant, high-utility academic skills within the framework of the NFTE entrepreneurship curriculum would be a very effective way to help students master certain state standards and benchmarks.

This Tenth Edition of the NFTE curriculum reflects that valuable input and advice from teachers and educators. Every chapter in the text contains new, highlighted features titled "Skills Mean Success," a label that reflects NFTE's approach to personal growth — both in small business ownership and in lifelong learning: young people, like successful adults, need to master essential skills and understandings to realize dreams and aspirations — in education, in careers, and in other adult roles. *Skills Mean Success* activities address, review, and provide student-engaging opportunities to apply key academic skills in the context of a small business ownership curriculum. Although every

*Skills Mean Success* feature provides some form of problem to solve, activity to carry out, or skill to practice, they are not intended to be tutorial or comprehensive in nature. You — or the students — may choose to use or not use that particular *Skills Mean Success* activity as time, interest, and learning needs dictate. They may be assigned as whole-class, group, or individual "time outs" and can easily be expanded to allow delving more deeply into the specific proficiency(ies) and topic(s) addressed.

The topics selected for the *Skills Mean Success* features, which are strategically placed throughout the text — usually two or three per chapter — address one or more core skills areas:

- English and language arts: reading, writing, speaking, listening, presenting, viewing.

- Mathematics: numeracy, arithmetic, geometry, measurement, algebra, data analysis, reasoning, problem solving.

- Technology skills: desktop applications, business technology, Internet use, online research, and communications.

- "Leadership" skills: attitudinal, interpersonal, management, goal setting, team, employment readiness, and other competencies identified in NFTE's "Theory of Change" framework (see below).

*Skills Mean Success* features are designed to reinforce core academic and other enabling proficiencies in the context of real-world business applications and so they are often interdisciplinary — involving more than one subject area; for example, both English and technology — and frequently include several aspects of a core skill area (e.g., mathematical operations, as well as mathematical modeling and data analysis). The intentionally brief subtitles provided in the text may indicate only the primary focus of the activity.

The English and mathematics skills selected were, rather than being based on any one state's standards and benchmarks — an impracticality given NFTE's broad user base — compiled through an analysis of national standards prepared by The National Council for Teachers of English (NCTE) and The National Council of Teachers of Mathematics (NCTM). These frameworks were then compared with the Grade 8 and high school state standards of several states, including New York, Pennsylvania, Massachusetts, Florida, Illinois, and California and a sampling of major school districts, including the Boston and Pittsburgh Public Schools. Many commonalities were revealed. Key standards and benchmarks that were relevant to the context of entrepreneurship were then highlighted and these skills were compared to The International Center for Leadership in Education's Essential Skills Survey (ESS), a study of 20,000-plus educators, parents, business leaders, and other community stakeholders, which force-ranked skills deemed to be *most* critical for students' future success.

It is important to realize that no attempt was made — or should have been — to address all or most state English or mathematics standards and benchmarks. Relevance and natural "fit" with applications within the context of entrepreneurship were the principal criteria for selecting which academic skills to address. Accordingly, many important standards and benchmarks are not included and *Skills Mean Success* should not be equated with or measured against even the most basic curriculum in English or mathematics. For example, "Reading for Interpretation, Analysis, and Literary Appreciation: Conventions of Poetic Expression" (or its equivalent wording) is an important and widely benchmarked (and tested) state standard in Grade K-12 English. However, this proficiency is not addressed in any *Skills Mean Success* activities because literary analysis of poetry is not a commonly occurring application in small business ownership or in an entrepreneurship curriculum.

As a teacher, you are encouraged to correlate the academic proficiencies addressed in the *Skills Mean Success* features — especially the English and math topics — to your own state's academic standards and benchmarks and to share the crosswalks with your colleagues in the English and math departments, along with any of your school's test-prep, remedial/developmental, or ESL teachers or tutors who may be both interested and/or supportive. Doing so may also afford opportunities for collaboration, team teaching, and attention to the learning needs of individual students. Sharing may also allow NFTE teachers to "fine tune" their own use of *Skills Mean Success* to more closely match local academic curricula and instructional preferences or, conversely, sharing may invite academic teachers to draw upon the engaging applications from the world of entrepreneurship and business in their own curriculum.

Technology Skills and Leadership Skills included in the *Skills Mean Success* features were selected by analyzing current practice and sample curricula and frameworks in business technology applications, including the National Business Education Association (NBEA) Standards and the Consortium for Entrepreneurship Education (CEE) Standards, and from NFTE's Theory of Change study.

# Addressing State Academic Standards and Lifelong Learning Skills through the NFTE Curriculum *(cont'd)*

The *Skills Mean Success* features are easy to identify throughout the text. Look for the gold medal-plus-photo icons. Answers and suggestions are provided in the teaching notes by chapter in this Teacher's Edition. The following list identifies, by chapter, the standards and benchmarks addressed. You may want to cross-reference the English, math, and possibly the other standards and benchmarks to your own state's standards. The generic standards shown will readily correlate to equivalent benchmarks in most individual states. Following are the *Skills Mean Success* features by chapter:

| Chapter | Subject Area | Standard/Benchmark/Proficiency Addressed | Your Corresponding State Standard* |
|---|---|---|---|
| 1 | Leadership | Seeing Yourself as an Entrepreneur | |
| | English | Reading for Information and Understanding: Gathering and Interpreting Information | |
| | English | Reading for Information and Understanding: Following Directions, Interpreting, and Analyzing | |
| | Math | Mathematical Reasoning and Number Operations: Multiples, Parts, Increases, Decreases | |
| 2 | Math | Mathematical Reasoning and Operations: Average | |
| 3 | Math | Number and Numeration: Calculating Percentages; Fraction, Decimal and Percentage Equivalents | |
| | Leadership | Goal Setting: Measureable Goals | |
| | English | Writing for Information and Understanding Language Conventions: Abbreviations and Acronyms | |
| 4 | Leadership | Thinking Skills: Problem Solving Process | |
| | Technology | New Technologies and Trends | |
| | Math | Mathematical Modeling: Data Analysis: Pie Charts | |
| 5 | Leadership | Recognizing Strengths: Self-Confidence: Reflecting on Interests, Talents, Self-Improvement | |
| | English | Writing for Social Interaction: Using Appropriate Language and Style | |
| | English | Reading for Information and Understanding: Selecting Relevant Information | |
| 6 | Math | Mathematical Modeling: Data Analysis: Displaying Data in Line Graphs | |
| | Technology | Multimedia Presentations: Using Graphics | |
| | English | Reading for Information and Understanding: Getting Meaning | |
| 7 | English | Writing for Information and Understanding: Completing Forms | |
| | Leadership | Understanding Diversity | |
| | English/Technology | Reading and Writing for Information: Using Text Features and Online Research; Letters and E-mail | |
| 8 | English | Listening and Speaking for Social Interaction: Asking Questions to Clarify Meaning | |
| | Leadership | Responsible and Ethical Behavior | |
| | Math | Mathematical Operations and Reasoning: Calculating Percentages; Problem Solving | |
| 9 | Math | Mathematical Operations: Determining Price per Unit to Compare Prices | |
| | English | Reading for Information: Reasoning and Understanding | |
| | Math | Mathematical Reasoning: Devising Formulas | |
| 10 | English | Listening and Speaking: Listening Attentively; Expressing Ideas Respectfully; Using Non-Verbal Communication | |
| | Technology | Internet Resources and Business Card Design | |

| Chapter | Subject Area | Standard/Benchmark/Proficiency Addressed | Your Corresponding State Standard* |
|---|---|---|---|
| 10 (con'd) | Math | Mathematical Modeling: Representing Numerical Relationships in Graphs; Using Graphics in Presentations | |
| | English | Writing and Speaking to Persuade: Persuasive Strategies | |
| 11 | Math | Mathematical Reasoning and Operations: Using Statistics | |
| | English | Listening and Speaking for Social Interaction: Dealing with Criticism | |
| | English | Writing and Speaking for Social Interaction: Using Open-Ended Questions | |
| 12 | English | Writing to Persuade: Supporting Arguments with Details and Evidence | |
| | Leadership | Presentation Skills | |
| | Math | Performing Operations Using Formulas | |
| 13 | English | Reading and Writing for Understanding: Idioms | |
| | Math | Displaying Data in Charts and Graphs | |
| | Technology | Spreadsheet Formulas | |
| 14 | Math | Math Formulas and Operations: Simple Interest | |
| | English | Reading for Understanding: Reading for Critical Analysis | |
| | Leadership | Interviewing | |
| 15 | English | Listening for Critical Analysis: Communication Skills | |
| | Leadership | Using Nonverbal Communication Skills | |
| 16 | Math | Numeration and Operations: Using Mental Math | |
| | Leadership | Self-Confidence: Learning Self-Improvement | |
| | English | Speaking and Listening for Social Interaction: Telephone Etiquette | |
| 17 | English | Listening and Writing for Information and Analysis: Clarifying Information | |
| | Math | Interpreting Graphs and Charts: Using Diagrams to Develop Strategies | |
| 18 | English | Reading for Understanding: The Main Idea | |
| | Leadership | Market Research | |
| 19 | Math | Estimation and Approximation: Solving Problems that Don't Require Exact Answers | |
| | English/Technology | Writing for Social Interaction: E-mail | |
| 20 | Math | Number and Numeration: Understanding Percentage Mathematical Reasoning: Devising Formulas | |
| | English | Writing for Information and Understanding: Using Standard English - Hyphenation | |
| | Leadership | Why Math Is Important Networking and Communication: Finding Contacts, Listening, Interviewing | |
| 21 | Math | Measurement and Reasoning: Understanding Length and Area | |
| | English | Writing for Information: Cause and Effect | |
| | Leadership | Understanding Customer Needs: Sales Interviews | |
| 22 | English | Listening: Critical Listening Strategies | |
| | Math | Mathematical Operations and Approximation: Percentage and Rounding Numbers | |
| | English | Writing for Information: Creating Tables and Forms | |
| 23 | Technology | Online Research and Devising Spreadsheet Formulas | |
| | Math | Mathematical Reasoning: Rounding Numbers and Proportional Reasoning | |
| | English | Reading for Information: Fact vs. Opinion | |

| Chapter | Subject Area | Standard/Benchmark/Proficiency Addressed | Your Corresponding State Standard* |
|---|---|---|---|
| 24 | English | Reading and Writing for Understanding: Using Appropriate Language and Style in Memos; Deciphering Unfamiliar Words Using Context Clues | |
| | English | Speaking for Information: Presenting Information Clearly | |
| 25 | Leadership | Practicing Risk-taking | |
| | Math | Solving Problems: Using Percentages, Formulas and Substitution | |
| 26 | Math | Measurement and Data: Interpreting Graphs | |
| | Math | Mathematical Reasoning: Making Conjectures to Solve Problems | |
| | Leadership | Negotiation and Thinking Skills: Persistence, Resilience, Innovative Solutions | |
| | English | Reading for Understanding: Analyzing, Interpreting, Evaluating Text | |
| 27 | English | Reading for Understanding: Interpreting Information; Fact vs. Opinion | |
| | Math | Mathematical Operations and Reasoning: Calculating Percentage, Formulas, Patterns | |
| 28 | Math | Mathematical Reasoning: Devising Formulas | |
| | English | Reading and Writing for Interpretation: Using Images to Express Ideas | |
| 29 | Leadership/English | Interviewing Skills; Writing Interview Questions | |
| | Math | Mathematical Reasoning and Data Analysis: Determining Mean, Median, Mode | |
| | Leadership | Recognizing the Need for Math, English, and Computer Skills | |
| 30 | Leadership/ Technology | Locating Computer and Technology Resources | |
| | Math | Mathematical Reasoning: Writing and Using Formulas | |
| | Technology/English | Writing and Speaking: Technology Etiquette: Cell Phones, Voice Mail, E-mail | |
| | English | Speaking and Listening for Understanding: Idioms | |
| 31 | English | Reading for Literary Response: Using Literary Elements to Convey Meaning | |
| | English | Writing for Information and Understanding: Sentence Combining | |
| | Technology | Online Research and Evaluating Web Sites | |
| 32 | Math | Numeration and Solving Problems: Understanding Percentages and Exponents | |
| | English | Reading for Understanding: Questioning Strategies in Reading | |
| | English/Leadership | Preparing, Organizing, and Delivering a Presentation | |
| 33 | Math | Numeration: Place Value | |
| | Technology/English | Reading and Evaluating Web Sites | |
| 34 | Math | Mathematical Reasoning: Estimating and Predicting | |
| | English | Writing and Reading for Information: Using Standard English; Proofreading | |
| | Leadership/English | Understand Customer Needs | |
| 35 | Technology | Online Research | |
| | Math | Mathematical Reasoning: Understanding Ratio, Proportion, and Percentage | |

| Chapter | Subject Area | Standard/Benchmark/Proficiency Addressed | Your Corresponding State Standard* |
|---|---|---|---|
| 35 | English | Writing for Understanding: Test Preparation; Presenting Information Clearly | |
| 36 | Math | Numeration and Operations: Calculating Percentage Change | |
| | English | Writing for Information: Tips for Effective Editing | |
| 37 | Math | Estimation: Rounding Numbers | |
| | English | Writing for Information: Clarifying Information through Details | |
| | English | Writing for Information: Business Letters | |
| 38 | Math | Operations: Percentages of Purchases | |
| | Leadership | Networking: Finding a Mentor | |
| 39 | Technology | Internet Research Skills: Locating Data Online | |
| | English | Reading for Information: Vocabulary | |
| 40 | English | Listening and Writing: Strategies for Note Taking | |
| | Math | Operations and Problem Solving: Interest Charges | |
| | | Measurement and Comparing Data: Graphs | |
| | English | Reading for Understanding: Finding Details | |
| 41 | English | Writing for Information: Using Cause and Effect | |
| | Leadership | Recognizing Why Math Is Important: Solving Real-World Problems | |
| | Math | Mathematical Reasoning: Reading Tables, Identifying Patterns, Solving Problems | |
| 42 | English | Writing for Understanding: Descriptive Writing; Using Details | |
| | Technology | Using a Spell-Checker | |
| | English | Understanding Vocabulary | |
| 43 | English | Observing Rules and Conventions of Grammar | |
| | Math | Measurement: Understanding Length and Area | |
| | Leadership | Connecting to Real World Examples: Reading Skills Used in Business | |
| 44 | Math | Operations: Income Tax Rates | |
| | Technology | Online Research | |
| | English | Presenting Information Clearly | |
| 45 | Math | Probability: Comparing Data and Uncertainty | |
| | English | Speaking: Diction | |
| 46 | Math | Mathematical Reasoning: Substituting a Number to Solve a Problem | |
| | English | Writing for Information: Presenting Clear Instructions | |
| | Technology/English | Writing for Information: Summarizing Web-Site Information | |
| 47 | Leadership | Understanding Cultural Differences | |
| | Math | Mathematical Operations and Reasoning: Calculating Percentage Change in Currency Exchange Rates | |
| 48 | English | Writing for Information and to Persuade: Word Choice | |
| | Math | Mathematical Representation and Data: Interpreting Tables | |
| | Leadership | Entrepreneurial Skills and Attitudes | |
| 49 | Leadership | Preparing and Making a Presentation | |
| 50 | English | Reading for Meaning: Deciphering Unfamiliar Words | |
| | Math | Math Reasoning and Operations: Mental Math, Approximation | |

# Addressing the NBEA National Standards for Entrepreneurship through the NFTE 10th Edition Curriculum

## NATIONAL BUSINESS EDUCATION ASSOCIATION (NBEA) NATIONAL STANDARDS FOR ENTREPRENEURSHIP

| Content Standards and Performance Expectations | Corresponding NFTE Chapters |
| --- | --- |
| **I. Entrepreneurs and Entrepreneurial Opportunities:** *Achievement Standard: Recognize that entrepreneurs possess unique characteristics and evaluate the degree to which one possesses those characteristics.* | |
| A. Characteristics of an Entrepreneur | 1, 3, 4, 5, 15, 17, 21 |
| B. Role of the Entrepreneur in Business | 1, 5, 8, 29 |
| C. Opportunity Recognition and Pursuit | 4, 7, 8, 30, 35, 41, 46 |
| D. Problem Identification and Solutions | 2, 4, 7 |
| **II. Marketing:** *Achievement Standard: Analyze customer groups and develop a plan to identify, reach, and keep customers in a specific target market.* | |
| A. Identifying the Market | 9, 10, 11, 17, 18, 21 |
| B. Reaching the Market | 7, 8, 9, 10, 11, 16, 17, 18, 19, 21, 26, 27, 30 |
| C. Keeping/Increasing the Market | 8, 8, 10, 11, 17, 18, 22, 38, 43 |
| **III. Economics:** *Achievement Standard: Apply economic concepts when making decisions for an entrepreneurial venture.* | |
| A. Economic Concepts | 2, 3, 4, 9 |
| B. Market Economy Characteristics | 1, 6, 17, 28 |
| C. Function of Price | 2, 3, 4, 6, 8, 9, 16, 18, 20, 26 |
| D. Role of Profit and Risk | 1, 3, 4, 7, 9, 12, 16, 20, 27 |
| E. Role of Government | 6, 11, 39 |
| **IV. Finance:** *Achievement Standard: Use the financial competencies needed by an entrepreneur.* | |
| A. Determining Cash Needs | 14, 27, 41 |
| B. Identifying Sources and Types of Funding | 14, 15, 31, 33, 34, 36, 48, 49, 50 |
| C. Interpreting Financial Statements | 12, 13, 16, 20, 27, 35, 41, 43, 44 |
| **V. Accounting:** *Achievement Standard: Recognize that entrepreneurs must establish, maintain, and analyze appropriate records to make business decisions.* | |
| A. Keeping Business Records | 12, 13, 30, 35, 41, 44 |
| B. Identifying Types of Business Records | 12, 13, 16, 22, 35, 41, 43, 44 |
| C. Establishing and Using Business Records | 12, 13, 16, 21, 30, 31, 35, 41 |
| D. Interpreting Business Records | 12, 13, 16, 35, 41 |

| Content Standards and Performance Expectations | Corresponding NFTE Chapters |
|---|---|
| **VI. Management:** | |
| *Achievement Standard: Develop a management plan for an entrepreneurial venture.* | |
| A. Establishing a Vision | 3, 17, 28, 29, 50 |
| B. Hiring Employees | 1, 2, 4, 5, 9, 21, 26, 29, 43 |
| C. Building Teams | 14, 17, 21, 24, 28, 29, 43 |
| D. Monitoring Achievement | 3, 5, 8, 28, 29 |
| E. Managing Risks | 32, 33, 34, 37, 41, 45, 46, 48, 49 |
| **VII. Global Markets:** | |
| *Achievement Standard: Analyze the effect of cultural differences, export/import opportunities, and trends on an entrepreneurial venture in the global marketplace.* | |
| A. Cultural Differences | 7, 28, 30, 39, 47 |
| B. Import/Export Opportunities | 30, 39, 47 |
| C. Global Trends | 28, 30, 47 |
| **VIII. Legal:** | |
| *Achievement Standard: Analyze how forms of business ownership, government regulations, and business ethics affect entrepreneurial ventures.* | |
| A. Forms of Business Ownership | 14, 25, 32, 46, 47 |
| B. Government Regulations | 7, 25, 26, 29, 32, 37, 42, 43, 44, 46, 48 |
| C. Business Ethics | 8, 13, 37, 42, 43 |
| **IX. Business Plans:** | |
| *Achievement Standard: Develop a Business Plan.* | |
| Business Plans | Every chapter 1-50, plus Basic, Intermediate, and Advanced Business Plan Reviews, and sample Business Plans. |

# Best Practices for Using and Teaching the NFTE Curriculum

## LEARNING STYLES AND THE NFTE CURRICULUM

There are many theories of intelligence, cognition, and learning; and many models of predominant learning styles — although no learner uses any single capacity or style exclusively.

- Robert J. Sternberg of Yale University investigated the nature of what he termed "practical" intelligence.

  | Type of Intelligence | Related Occupations |
  | --- | --- |
  | ○ Practical | Entrepreneurs, business executives, workers in skilled and technical trades |
  | ○ Analytical | Scientists, lawyers, doctors, teachers |
  | ○ Creative | Writers, artists |

- Harvard's Howard Gardner outlined seven "Multiple Intelligences," stating that everyone has capacities in all these areas, but each person's configuration is different. Gardner suggested that education should provide experiences that develop all intelligences.

  - ○ Mathematical/logical: reasoning, logical thinking, mathematics — the type of intelligence often measured in "I.Q." tests.

  - ○ Linguistic: language ability — learning languages, writing and speaking well.

  - ○ Bodily/kinesthetic (or body movement): such as dancing and athletic skills.

  - ○ Spatial: navigation, visualizing objects from different angles, architecture and sculpture.

  - ○ Musical: singing, playing instruments, conducting and composing.

  - ○ Interpersonal: getting along with people well — sales, teaching, politics.

  - ○ Intrapersonal: understanding one's own feelings, the ability to reflect and discriminate - artists and writers.

- Kathleen Butler with Anthony Gregorc, developed a useful model of learning styles - based on how information is perceived and processed by learners.

  - ○ Concrete Sequential
  - ○ Abstract Random
  - ○ Abstract Sequential
  - ○ Concrete Random

Educators are naturally pre-disposed to "teach to" — and learners to learn by — their own predominant learning style, whichever combination(s) they might be. Teachers should rely on their own insights into learning styles, but the Butler model can effectively be used to help teachers position and vary instruction in content area subjects such as NFTE's Entrepreneurship curriculum.

Teachers should design their instructional methods to value, address, and embrace *all* learning styles, using various combinations of experience, reflection, conceptualization, and experimentation. Instructors should introduce a wide variety of experiential elements into the classroom, such as sound, music, visuals, tactile-physical models, dance and movement, art, technology, viewing, listening, representing, dramatizing, demonstrating, experimenting, story-telling, game-playing, and dialoguing.

Thanks to lifelong educator Dr. Larry Bond for his insights and assistance.

| Predominant Learning Style | Corresponding Learner Preferences | Related Learner Strengths | Implications for Student Success with the NFTE Curriculum |
|---|---|---|---|
| Concrete Sequential | Factual<br>Practical<br>Structured<br>Detailed<br>Realistic<br>Hands-on | ○ Consistency<br>○ Efficiency<br>○ Logic<br>○ Follows directions and steps<br>○ Planning/organizing<br>○ Deals well with structure<br>○ Accuracy, precision<br>○ Fact-getting and checking<br>○ Results- and detail-focused<br>○ Creating real products | ○ Provide structured, logical, sequential lessons.<br>○ Adhere to regular procedures and standards.<br>○ Give detailed directions and instructions.<br>○ Use realistic examples.<br>○ Allow hands-on activities.<br>○ Explain the value of the learning.<br>○ Assign purpose and deadlines.<br>○ Use demos, modeling, experimenting, direct instruction.<br>○ Provide compensatory support to help students to deal with choosing from several options, lack of detailed directions, coping with abstraction, and opposing viewpoints.<br>○ Encourage students to be patient, reflective, imaginative and empathetic. |
| Abstract Random | Personal<br>Flexible<br>Relating<br>Feeling<br>Interpretive<br>Imaginative | ○ Reflective<br>○ Flexible, adaptable<br>○ Social<br>○ Emotive<br>○ Sensitive to others and to their surroundings<br>○ Holistic; they see the bigger picture<br>○ Imaginative<br>○ Artistic | ○ Use cooperative learning.<br>○ Encourage creativity, role playing.<br>○ Emphasize themes.<br>○ Illustrate with relevant stories and anecdotes.<br>○ Encourage them to use their sensitivity and creativity to develop insights.<br>○ Provide compensatory support to help students to deal with detail, specificity, planning and organizing, deadlines, and concentrating.<br>○ Help students to deal with competing ideas and non-collaborative personalities. |
| Abstract Sequential | Reading<br>Logical<br>Referencing<br>Analytical<br>Conceptual<br>Debating | ○ Debating points of view<br>○ Organizing ideas logically<br>○ Information gathering<br>○ Analysis<br>○ Persistence<br>○ Evaluating of theories<br>○ Confidence<br>○ Writing skills | ○ Assign reading and research.<br>○ Use lecture; emphasize listening skills.<br>○ Provide detailed notes and source data.<br>○ Use guided instruction.<br>○ Encourage discussion and debate.<br>○ Seek structured response and analysis.<br>○ Ask "why?" and "what if?" questions.<br>○ Give independent and individual assignments.<br>○ Allow time for detailed analysis.<br>○ Praise academic achievement.<br>○ Provide compensatory support to help students to appreciate emotion and creativity and to be accepting of disagreement and constructive criticism from others.<br>○ Help students to deal with simulations, role playing, making things, risk taking, cooperative learning, diplomacy. |

# Best Practices for Using and Teaching the NFTE Curriculum (cont'd)

| Predominant Learning Style | Corresponding Learner Preferences | Related Learner Strengths | Implications for Student Success with the NFTE Curriculum |
|---|---|---|---|
| Concrete Random | Divergent Problem-solving Open-ended Experiential Investigative Inventive | ○ Experimentation<br>○ Risk-taking<br>○ Curious<br>○ Independent<br>○ Lateral thinking<br>○ Problem solving<br>○ Competitive<br>○ Self-directed | ○ Use brainstorming, experimentation, critical thinking, and trial and error activities.<br>○ Require real, but imaginative solutions.<br>○ Provide options and choice.<br>○ Assign independent activities.<br>○ Use hands-on learning.<br>○ Allow for alternative and multiple solutions.<br>○ Use open-ended activities and divergent thinking.<br>○ Provide compensatory support to help students to deal with deadlines, focus, specific requirements of formal assignments, and record keeping.<br>○ Engage the students; avoid lectures, controlled environments, and passive learning situations. |

NFTE recommends that teachers make every attempt to address different learning styles.

For example, the use of overhead transparencies to teach a concept appeals to the visual and auditory learner simultaneously. Since the teacher is explaining or having students explain the meaning of the overheads, students with reading skills far below the level of the text can still learn and apply the basic NFTE curriculum topics.

Another visual tool NFTE provides is the Curriculum Student Checklist. This is a wall chart with room for entering each student's name and keeping track of whether or not he or she has completed the fundamental assignments that define the course. These will include: "Played Negotiation Game," "Prepared Marketing Plan," "Opened a Bank Account," "Completed a Sales Call," and the like. The wall chart will allow you to see at a glance if the class is getting through the course at an appropriate pace and to motivate students to complete the assignments.

## CLASS LEARNING STRUCTURES

- **The "At the Door" Lesson.** Modeling the behavior you want from students is extremely important. Instead of waiting inside the room, before class begins, consider the following:

  ○ Illustrate Business Manners: Shake hands with students, and greet them with a businesslike "Good Morning," calling each by name and making eye contact as they enter the classroom.

(You are simulating a business situation, teaching students by example. Discuss with the class what you are doing and how they are responding — keeping all suggestions constructive.)

○ Stress Punctuality: You can show the importance of punctuality by thanking the students who arrive on time. Once class has started, politely point out to any tardy students that they are late and try to get them to commit to coming on time in the future.

○ Remembering Names: Calling students by name shows your personal interest. It is important to learn each student's name as quickly as possible.

○ The "Do Now": Get class started with an assignment as students come into the room. Each chapter's teaching notes includes Set a Context for Learning activities that tie into previous topics, review skills, or lead into new topics. Use these suggestions or make up your own. Avoid "busy work" however; students know when an assignment is just meant to fill time.

○ The Record-Book Look: Check students' record keeping as soon as you have introduced the topic — while they are working on warm-up activities is a good opportunity to do this. Any time they are engaged in group or individual work at their desks, try to check a few students' work. Frequent checking is the only way to insure that students build up good record-keeping habits.

- **Cooperative Learning.** Many of the student activities in the curriculum use cooperative learning to promote discussion and reduce fear of failure. Cooperative group work increases student-to-student interaction and shifts the orientation from teacher-directed instruction. It gives students more opportunity for self-expression and active learning. What goes on in the groups, however, will need to be carefully prepared and monitored to make sure that everyone is constructively participating. In the NFTE curriculum, the structure of each activity is usually explained. The following are examples of ways to organize cooperative groups:

  - Peer Tutor Partners: Pair students who complement each other. For example, pair someone who loves to speak publicly and perform but isn't a good reader with a quiet student who reads and writes well. Each will support and model the other's needs.

  - Jigsaw or Independent Groups: Each member of the group is responsible for the answer to a specific question or problem, but can get help in preparing the answer. The evaluation is given to the group.

  - Shared Responsibility Groups: Each student is responsible for one answer and "teaches" the group. Any group member can then be called upon to answer any question, and the evaluation is given to the group.

  - Spokesperson Groups: All members discuss the questions, but a spokesperson and/or a reporter is responsible for presenting the group's conclusions to the whole class.

  - Reporting from Small Groups: It is important that the work done in the small groups ultimately has an audience and receives some immediate feedback. If you do not use a spokesperson, find some way to have each group share some of its work with the class.

- **Pacing: The Key to Holding Student Interest**

  Experienced teachers know that changing the pace or varying an activity is crucial to keeping students interested. Effective teachers sense, almost before it happens, when their students are becoming bored or restless, and are turning off.

  - Variety within One Class Period: NFTE offers teachers a set of pace-changing activities with which to build relevant skills and reinforce knowledge. These activities may be used to change pace whenever you sense this is needed. NFTE recommends that a pace-changing activity be used at least three times a week.

  - Rapid Pacing: The structure of a typical NFTE lesson is designed to keep instruction moving along quickly with a variety of activities, fitting in with the prescribed time period. NFTE is a high-energy program.

- **Repetition and Reinforcement through Activity Centers**

  In order to ensure that all students are learning the necessary concepts and are improving their skills, you may want to organize class periods in which small groups of students work on different skills in different locations in the room. The following are some possibilities:

  - Mental Math Group: in which four students work together. One student reads problems — or makes them up — while the others try to solve them mentally. Then they rotate so that each student has a turn at reading or making up the problems.

  - Memo Writing Center: in which you outline situations on task cards and four students write memos. They each work on different topics or the same one. Then they compare and contrast their memos, providing each other with constructive criticism.

  - Job Interview Center: in which two pairs of students role-play job interviews. One pair will play the interviewer and the job candidate. The other pair will watch and give feedback at the conclusion of the interview. Then they reverse the scenario. The scenarios can be written on cards using ads cut out from a newspaper.

  - Business Reading Center: in which four to six students read from their copies of *Entrepreneurs in Profile*, newspaper articles, magazines, or books from the library.

  - Word Game Center: in which students match vocabulary cards to definition cards. The definition cards can be displayed on a desk, face up with the word cards drawn in turn. Other alternatives can include word puzzles; students can solve puzzles you have created or make up their own to be used by other students later.

  - Business Advice Center: in which you or a student poses a business problem (case study), and the students discuss which decisions or actions should be taken.

○ Tutoring Center: in which you work individually with students or assign a student expert to tutor those who need help with a particular skill (such as figuring ROI).

● **Organizing Activity Centers**

Setting up the centers will require some extra time for thinking about the procedures and preparing the materials for students to use.

○ Start small: Begin with the reading center and the memo writing center. Assign students to those centers while you work with the rest of the class. Gradually phase in other centers.

○ Rules: Be clear about the rules for using the centers: how many students, how the choices are made, how materials are taken out and put back. You will probably want to assign students at first. Then phase in choices for which centers they will use.

○ Insist on routines: Once routines are established, you will find that the centers are well worth the extra work in terms of learning and how well the students take responsibility for their own progress.

○ Enjoy the change: Being a facilitator at the centers will also give you a break from being "the sage on stage" and directing the whole class. You will have a chance to work with individuals and get to know the strengths and needs of your students in a more in-depth way.

## ROLE OF EXPERIENTIAL ACTIVITIES

The NFTE curriculum supports the concept of "learning by doing," first advanced by John Dewey, one of the most influential philosophers of 19th and early 20th century America. He wrote over two dozen books and scores of articles in many different fields. His influence on education brought about major changes in teaching.

One of Dewey's most important tenets was that children learn most effectively through performing carefully thought-out activities that engage their interest and require them to seek information, synthesize it, and make their own decisions. Educators who followed Dewey's ideas tried to plan learning based, to a large extent, on student participation. The NFTE program supports this methodology, by providing projects and suggestions that enable teachers to create or modify curricula in order to capitalize on students' interests.

NFTE provides a variety of hands-on activities that every student will be expected to complete. These activities relate directly to the information taught. For example, if the students are learning that part of an entrepreneur's budget is used for advertising, they make flyers and business cards for their own businesses. When they learn the formula for figuring return on investment, they use it to complete their own ROI on the items they purchased at a wholesaler's and sold at a trade fair.

## HELPING STUDENTS TO CHALLENGE THEMSELVES

Entrepreneurship requires a competitive spirit and willingness to take calculated risks. Some students in the program may exhibit negative ways of competing or risk avoidance. Such behavior could reveal a lack of knowledge or academic skills. You will need to think of tasks that encourage students with concrete rewards for taking risks, such as answering a question that they are not sure of, going first in a demonstration or presentation, or explaining an idea to the class. The NFTE program is based on encouraging students to break through their fears and insecurities and take positive risks to enhance confidence and self-esteem. Success rests, of course, not just on the individual student, but also on the creation of a classroom climate that shows respect for all individuals, recognizes differences as the norm, tolerates diversity, is mutually supportive, does not punish failure, and encourages second effort.

## DEVELOPING CRITICAL THINKING SKILLS

Every chapter contains critical thinking activities designed to help students build such critical thinking skills as evaluating and analyzing a business situation, comparing and contrasting, solving problems, and making decisions. These are exercises that, by definition, don't have one single correct answer; however the students' answers should reflect an understanding of the chapter concepts and indicate that they used these concepts in answering the critical thinking exercise(s). These exercises will help students begin to think like entrepreneurs, who tend to see opportunities when presented with problems. Encourage students to share their creative solutions with each other and the class, so they can see that a problem can be successfully solved in many different ways. This type of activity helps to build not only critical thinking skills, but self-esteem and positive mental attitude.

## NFTE TEACHER ORGANIZATIONAL CHECKLIST

*Check when completed.*

| Date | | | | | | |
|---|---|---|---|---|---|---|
| The Stock Market Contest | | | | | | |
| The ROI Relay Race | | | | | | |
| The Negotiation Game | | | | | | |
| The Invention Contest | | | | | | |
| The Quick-Change Coupon Game | | | | | | |
| The Trading Game | | | | | | |
| Other | | | | | | |

### The Stock Market Contest

Conduct a Stock Market Contest. Each student will start with a hypothetical sum of money, such as $200. They then make the decisions of investors in the market. They may sell their chosen stocks and buy others. They may also "sell short" (after you cover this subject in class). Each transaction should be recorded and the results announced whenever *The Wall Street Journal* is used in class. The winner will be the student who has made the greatest profit over the period of the contest — weekly, monthly, for the semester, or all three. Use the Stock Market Contest every day that the class reads *The Wall Street Journal*.

### The ROI Relay Race

Divide the chalkboard into several distinct areas, and divide the class into teams, each with a captain. Each team captain writes three to six ROI problems composed by his or her team on the chalkboard, after which the teacher assigns each set of problems to another team. The teacher signals the beginning of the game, and then a team member solves one problem and passes the chalk to the next team member. When all the teams have finished, the one with all the correct answers and best finishing time wins.

### The Negotiation Game

- Objective of Game: To learn negotiating skills and build confidence in negotiating prices by mock sales/purchasing sessions between paired-off classmates.

- When Played: Can be played more than once during the course to sharpen skills: before the Negotiation chapter, and again when the participants are armed with the skills learned from it.

- How Played: The teacher divides the class into equal numbers of "sellers" and "buyers" by alternate count-off. The teacher alternately takes each group (sellers and buyers) into the hall separately and provides instructions:

For sellers: Sell the specific product (that you have chosen in advance, such as a winter coat) for no less than a minimum price you set; e.g. — "You must each try to sell this coat for the highest price you can get, but you cannot sell it for less than $100."

For buyers: Buy the item from the seller as inexpensively as possible but for no more than a maximum amount you set; e.g. — "You must each try to buy this coat for the lowest price you can, but you can't spend more than $125."

Make sure that there is overlap between the buyers' maximum price and the sellers' minimum one to allow for successful negotiation. Also, tell everyone they *must* come to an agreement within the given time limit.

After returning to the class, pair off students into buyers and sellers, and give them a set time (three to five minutes) to reach an agreement. Have pairs write up the agreement they have reached in a contract (the item, price agreed upon, and both signatures).

- Evaluate Results: The negotiators' names, and prices can be written on the board. Note the highest and lowest prices, and discuss with the seller who got highest price and buyer who bought for the lowest what tactics they used. Then discuss tactics used by others.

  Don't overemphasize winners and losers based solely on price. Identify and recognize other important business concepts as they come up, such as customer service. Applaud the seller who does something unique to benefit the buyer when he/she makes the sale (such as selling one unit cheaply to gain more sales later).

- **Business friendships:** Recognize the pairs who seem to have developed a good business relationship based on trust and friendship.

- **Negotiation Techniques**
  - Expect to hear "No." It's usually the opening stance.
  - Persist. Stick to your guns. Sit back and wait.
  - Use the power of silence. Most people can't stand a vacuum.
  - Plan. Research your opponent before the negotiation.
  - Define both the "Least Acceptable Settlement" and "Maximum Supportable Position" in your mind in advance.
  - Seek help. This can make for beneficial relationships.
  - Avoid "overkill."

○ Learn. Evaluate the negotiation afterwards — what could have gone better?

○ Welcome the opportunity to negotiate.

### The Invention Contest

Every student has the potential for inventing a new product. The Invention Contest should be an ongoing project after the first chapter involving inventions has been covered. Allow time for students to present ideas and working models behind their inventions to the class at least once a week, with students signing up, say, a week ahead of time.

### The Quick-Change Coupon Game

- Objective of Game: To reinforce basic math ability and sharpen skill in making change on sales.

- When Played: At your discretion throughout the program. Students should already have the knowledge and skills needed for this game; its purpose is mainly to enhance accuracy and speed.

- Material Needed: Assorted product coupons identifying either percentage reductions or amount reductions (i.e., coupon for $1.00 off a six-pack of soda), and a timer with alarm/bell. Create a "product sheet" with items for which you have coupons and prices.

- How Played: Choose one student to sell and one to buy. Have the "buying" student ask for one of the products from the product sheet and present the appropriate coupon and a paper with an amount greater than needed to purchase the product. The "selling" student must then take the coupon and sheet with the amount tendered and calculate the correct change in a time limit set on the timer (e.g., one minute). Students win by making accurate change before the timer rings. Repeat with different pairs of students while adjusting the time allowed — to make the game both challenging and winnable.

- Evaluating Results: Discuss with students the importance of math, "thinking on one's feet," and providing customer service. After repeated performances of the game, hold a class discussion on how improvement is achieved with practice.

### The Trading Game

If you have a materials budget for your program, or can collect donated materials, you can play the Trading Game.

- Materials: Brown paper "lunch" bag for each student; three "items"(candy, toothpaste, pencils, different foods, etc.) to be placed in each bag.

Make sure each bag has the same number of items.

- To Play: Pass out an already stuffed and sealed paper bag to each student.

- Round 1:
  ○ Students open bag, examine contents, and close it without showing the contents.
  ○ Teacher has students rate their level of happiness by having students raise their hands to indicate where their bag rates on a scale from 1 to 5 (1 being very unhappy and 5 being very happy). Record this information on the board and sum up the total "happiness rating" of the class.

- Round 2:
  ○ Students take the items out of their bag and display them on their desks. Then they should walk around looking at others' items.
  ○ Have students return to their seats and then ask them to re-rate their level of happiness on the same scale of 1 to 5. Record this information on the board and sum up the total happiness of the class.

- Round 3:
  ○ Divide the students into groups and allow them to trade within their group, using negotiating tactics.
  ○ Have them return to their seats after 3-5 minutes of trading and then ask again about their level of happiness on the scale of 1 to 5. Record this information on the board and sum up the total class happiness.

- Round 4:
  ○ Allow students to trade with everyone.
  ○ Have students return to their seats after 5 minutes of trading, and then ask them to rate their level of happiness on the scale of 1 to 5. Record these scores on the board and sum up the total happiness of the class.

The total happiness of the group will probably vary as students compare the items they received with those of other students, and as they were able to participate in voluntary trade with the rest of the class. (If a student who doesn't like chocolate received a candy bar, she or he would be happier if she or he could exchange it for something else.)

- Lesson Learned: The level of happiness of a group will increase when members of a group are allowed to trade freely. This microcosm of "free enterprise" could be contrasted with an alternative one in which the teacher or a team of students arranges and approves all trades that take place or, conversely, allows no trading but assigns items arbitrarily.

# Harvard University Research on the NFTE Curriculum

The time-tested NFTE curriculum has proven itself to be a reliable and effective — even authoritative — approach to and course of studies in entrepreneurship and small business management for young people. As a learning tool, the NFTE curriculum has shown consistently positive results in developing the attitudes, understanding, and skills related to youth entrepreneurship, and also in enhancing students' academic, leadership and technology skills related to business, employment, education, and lifelong learning.

**Two-Year Study.** Following a pilot study in 2000-2001, researchers from Harvard University's Graduate School of Education conducted formal research inquiries — an initial study during the 2001-2002 academic year (at two schools) and an expanded study during the 2002-2003 year (at six schools) — to determine the impact of the NFTE curriculum on student skills, behaviors, and attitudes, when delivered by a NFTE-trained teacher.

**Questions.** Some of the questions that researchers sought answers for included:

- What are examples of entrepreneurial behavior inside and outside the business domain, especially by young people, and how does participation in NFTE influence the development of such behavior?

- How are entrepreneurial behavior and participation in NFTE related to academic achievement and educational outcomes, such as grades, graduation rates, and attendance?

- How are entrepreneurial behavior and participation in NFTE related to psychosocial and intellectual development? In particular, how do achievement motivation, future orientation, self-efficacy, connectedness, and critical thinking interact to form dispositions toward entrepreneurship?

- How do NFTE program implementation variations (different program types, teacher engagement and methods, regional settings, student demographics, etc.) affect NFTE's impact on educational, psychosocial, and intellectual development?

- In what ways does the NFTE program increase leadership-related attitudes such as initiative and locus of control (sense of being more in charge of outcomes through effort and attitude)?

**Findings.** Although further research is warranted, the results were described in the Phase Two Executive Summary as being "highly encouraging" because they suggested a clear connection between student involvement in the NFTE program (in comparison to control groups who were *not* participants in NFTE programs) and heightened, positive attitudes toward:

- attending college and confidence in a successful post-secondary experience;

- higher levels of career aspiration;

- interest in occupations that require post-secondary training;

- engagement in and enjoyment of independent reading;

- goal setting, attainment, and personal achievement;

- inner agency, taking initiative, and control;

- originality, curiosity, industriousness, hopefulness and other indicators of leadership;

- connectedness to the teachers, especially a well-trained NFTE teacher, involved.

There was also some indication in the Phase One studies that Latino students, in particular, may benefit attitudinally from experiencing the NFTE curriculum.

**Conclusions.** Given NFTE's mission of supporting and encouraging urban, minority, and at-risk youth, such results — especially from an esteemed, independent research source such as the Harvard — are both very encouraging to the NFTE organization and a credit to the dedicated, NFTE-trained professional educators and their students who use and enjoy, and obviously derive great benefit from, the NFTE curriculum.

*Initiating, Leading, and Feeling in Control of One's Fate: Executive Summary. Project IF: Inventing the Future,* Harvard Graduate School of Education. Michael Nakkula, Ed.D., Principal Investigator; Miranda Lutyens, Project Coordinator. June, 2004

*Executive Summary. Project IF: Inventing the Future,* Harvard Graduate School of Education. Michael Nakkula, Ed.D., Principal Investigator; Miranda Lutyens, Project Coordinator. September, 2003

# Koch Foundation Evaluation of the NFTE Curriculum

## NEW YORK CITY

In 1998, the David H. Koch Charitable Foundation sponsored one of the most comprehensive studies ever completed on the impact of youth entrepreneurship training in America. The New York-based Research & Evaluation for Philanthropy aggressively tracked a statistically significant random sample of 253 young adults ages 18-28 who had completed the NFTE New York Metro program in junior or senior high school, and compared them with a group of 252 young adults who never participated in NFTE. The young adults surveyed were from low-income neighborhoods in New York, and over half were 21 or older. Some of the highlights from the report include:

- Eighty-three percent of the NFTE alumni wanted to start their own businesses compared with 57% of the comparison group and 50% nationally.

- NFTE New York Metro alumni were more likely to be current part-time business owners than other New York City young adults (8% vs. 6%). In fact, business formation for the alumni was substantially higher than the estimated 1-3% national rate for minority adults.

- Thirty-six percent of the alumni had started a business of their own vs. 9% for the comparison group.

- Of those who had started a business, nearly six in ten of the alumni (58%) were the first in their family to start a business.

- Seventy-six percent of the NFTE alumni thought that starting and owning a small business was a realistic way out of poverty, against 46% of the comparison group.

- NFTE increased high school exposure to business and entrepreneurship training four-fold, and 80% of the alumni thought about going into business for themselves after taking the NFTE course.

- Ninety-five percent of alumni indicated that NFTE gave them a more positive view of business and they were nearly twice as likely to predict that they would support themselves by owning a business in five years.

- Fifty-six percent of the NFTE alumni believed that most businesses are overtaxed, compared with 48% of the American public, 48% of high school seniors, and 41% of the comparison group.

- Nearly all alumni (95%) reported that NFTE improved their business skills and knowledge and 99% of the alumni will recommend the program to others.

## WASHINGTON, DC

The same study was carried out in Washington, D.C., with 120 young adults ages 18-28 who had completed the NFTE Greater Washington program in junior or senior high school, compared to a group of 152 people of equivalent age who had never participated in a NFTE program. The young adults surveyed were from low-income neighborhoods in DC, and more than half were over 20. Some of the report's highlights include:

- Ninety-one percent of the NFTE DC alumni wanted to start their own businesses, compared with 75% of the comparison group and 50% of the American public.

- NFTE DC alumni were two times more likely to be current business owners than other DC area young adults (12% vs. 5%). In fact, business formation for NFTE DC was substantially higher than the estimated 1-3% national rate for minority adults.

- NFTE participation increased the likelihood of wanting to start a business sometime in the future four-fold.

- NFTE increased high school exposure to business and entrepreneurship training fourteen-fold, and nearly nine in ten alumni (88%) thought about going into business for themselves after taking NFTE.

- Ninety-nine percent of the alumni indicated that NFTE gave them a more positive view of business and they were twice as likely to predict that they would support themselves by owning a business in five years.

- Nearly seven in ten NFTE alumni (68%) were the first in their family to start a business.

- Nearly all alumni (97%) reported that NFTE improved their business skills and knowledge and 100% of the alumni would recommend the program to others.

- The comparison group was twice as likely to prefer government employment over business ownership and corporate management than were the NFTE alumni.

- Alumni were more likely to believe that business was overregulated and overtaxed than the comparison group.

# "NFTE University" Teacher Education Programs

**N**FTE University offers an entrepreneurship training program for youth-work professionals and teachers of economics, business, marketing, entrepreneurship, math, and social studies, who are planning school-based and out-of-school entrepreneurship programs. This program provides the essential tools and methodology for teaching all the business concepts covered by NFTE's curriculum, *How to Start and Operate a Small Business*.

After graduating from a NFTE University program, an instructor becomes a NFTE CET (Certified Entrepreneurship Teacher), and can access ongoing resources, professional development opportunities, international awards, and alumni services for their students.

NFTE provides three and five-day NFTE University programs.

- During the school year, NFTE will host three-day programs at its headquarters in New York City, and at select program offices.

- During the summer, NFTE holds five-day programs, hosted at university partner campuses nationwide (such as Columbia, Stanford, Georgetown, and Carnegie Mellon).

- Applications for these programs are managed by the NFTE program offices and the Office of Program Partnerships. Contact your local NFTE divisional office for more information, or visit www.nfte.com.

## NFTE UNIVERSITY BENEFITS

- Receive guidance in NFTE program development and implementation from NFTE staff.

- Learn development strategies to help secure additional resources and funding for your NFTE program.

- Gain eligibility for prestigious teacher awards.

- Enjoy guest lectures by prominent business leaders and academic experts in entrepreneurship education.

- Enhance teaching skills through professional development.

- Network with colleagues.

- Share best practices.

# Theory of Change and the NFTE Curriculum

**A** "Theory of Change" is a detailed overview of an organization's mission that is created by identifying and "mapping" a blueprint of the building blocks and pre-conditions required to achieve that mission. In short, the Theory of Change process and model works "backwards" by first picturing the desired outcomes or improved state and then identifying the pre-conditions needed (or that must be eliminated) to allow the organization to arrive at the desired outcome. A Theory of Change provides a clear roadmap to help an organization identify interim outcomes and the transitional steps necessary to effect the necessary changes, and typically.

- describes a particular set of beliefs to guide an improvement initiative;

- provides a mechanism for communicating those beliefs throughout the organization before, during, and as an ongoing means to assess successful attainment of the mission's goals.

The NFTE Mission statement:

*NFTE teaches entrepreneurship to young people from low income communities to enhance their economic productivity by improving their business, academic, and life skills*

is supported by an organizational assessment based on a Theory of Change. That process and the blueprint/roadmap that was developed as part of the initiative form the core of the outcomes-based NFTE curriculum that includes:

- ABCs of Entrepreneurship: core understandings, skills, and attitudes related to small business ownership.

- Life and leadership skills: generic, workplace-readiness skills and attitudes that owners (and employees) need.

- Academic attitudes: recognition and appreciation of the value of academic skills and educational attainment.

- Engagement in lifelong learning and connections to broader life interests and concerns: realizing every student's full potential to become a caring, concerned, and contributing adult citizen.

These broad-based competencies — cognitive and attitudinal — are reflected in "interventions" throughout the NFTE curriculum, including the "Leadership" and "Technology" skills topics found in many of the *Skills Mean Success* features. These activities focus on key pre-conditions and proficiencies that were identified in NFTE's Theory of Change process as mission-supportive enablers, especially with respect to:

- engaging students in learning;

- helping students to develop career aspirations and interest in post-secondary education;

- allowing students to make connections between entrepreneurship and larger life interests and concerns;

- nurturing students' appreciation of high school achievement as a means to further career and college opportunities.

These enabling and empowerment tools, which address the "total student" and pave the way toward educational, business, and career success, include:

## Academic Attitudes

- Recognizing why and how English, reading, and math are important in school and life.

- Valuing computer literacy and information technology skills as means of achieving academic and business goals.

## Life Skills

- Self-Confidence
- Communication Skills
- Decision-Making and Critical Thinking Skills
- Goal-Setting Skills

NFTE teachers — and ultimately NFTE students — should actively communicate and support the enhancement of these skills and attitudes whenever possible and whenever learning opportunities to address them present themselves during class and throughout the school day. Ideally, the NFTE classroom should nurture a shared, supportive culture that reflects these goals.

# Role of Technology in the Curriculum

### BIZTECH™

BizTech™ 2.0 is an entrepreneurship program that teaches business, information technology, and life skills to young people via the Internet in a teacher-led interactive environment. BizTech™ is flexible, user-friendly, and utilizes the latest technology. Its 25 units are divided into three levels — Basic, Intermediate, and Advanced. BizTech™ 2.0 meets school-to-career, SCANS, and many national and state standards, while reinforcing math, reading, and critical thinking skills. It is appropriate for students ages 13 and above.

| For 10th Edition Textbook Chapter... | Use BizTech™ 2.0 Unit: | |
|---|---|---|
| 5 | 1 | Set your personal and business goals. |
| 8 | 2 | Recognize your business opportunity. |
| 9 | 3 | Define your unit of sale. |
| 10 | 6 | Create your marketing plan. |
| 11 | 4 | Conduct market research. |
| 12 | 15 | Keep good records and project your cash flow statement. |
| 13 | 8 | Forecast your 6-month income statement and calculate your operating costs. |
| 14 | 7 | Develop your financing and networking strategy. |
| 17 | 11 | State your business mission and identify your competitive advantage. |
| 18 | 10 | Develop your marketing mix. |
| 19 | 5. | Develop your advertising/promotion plan and logo. |
| 20 | 24 | Perform your break-even analysis and calculate your financial ratios. |
| 21 | 17 & 18 | Get ready to sell and sell successfully. |
| 24 | 14 | Your business communication strategy. |
| 25 | 9 | Select your legal structure. |
| 27 | 12 | Identify your production /distribution chain. |
| 29 | 21 | Grow your business and hire the right team. |
| 30 | 16 | Your business technology strategy. |
| 33 | 19 | Develop your stock portfolio and identify your competition. |
| 35 | 25 | Create your balance sheet. |
| 40 | 22 | Select your banking partner. |
| 41 | 15 | Keep good records and project your cash flow statement. |
| 42 | 13 | Protect your ideas. |
| 44 | 20 | Organize your taxes and other administrative tasks. |
| 45 | 23 | Forecast your 12-month income statement. |

- **Educational Features**

  ○ **Teacher-facilitated.** BizTech™ 2.0 is designed to be teacher-led. Lesson plans and teaching materials are available for each unit. You track real-time student progress online and quizzes are automatically graded. Pre/post-testing measures business concepts learned in each level.

  ○ **Choose from "Full Curriculum Mode" or "BizPlan Only Mode."** The system will allow you to choose the mode that will work best for the class or individual student. Both modes result in each student completing a concise, feasible business plan.

  ○ **Customize the order of the units.** You will have the ability to organize the 25 units in the order that suits your class or schedule, and add your own materials, if desired.

  ○ **Ongoing support.** The BizTech Help Desk provides customer service and consultation on program implementation (M-F, 10 AM - 6 PM EST, or contact bizhelp@nfte.com).

- **Student Benefits**
  - ○ Program completion results in a finished business plan. The Table of Contents and you, the teacher, will guide students through the three levels of the program: Basic, Intermediate, and Advanced. Business plan activities are completed in each unit and then compiled in the "BizPlan to Date."
  - ○ Interactive graphics reflect student progress through each level.
  - ○ "Trade fair" environment for Basic level, "neighborhood store" for Intermediate, and "corporate office" for Advanced.
  - ○ Student's choice of type of business, business name, and logo are also displayed.
  - ○ Students can create business cards, advertising flyers, and a presentation for their business all within the system.
  - ○ The program also includes case studies of successful entrepreneurs, a business glossary, formula calculator, and personal and business ledgers.
  - ○ You and the students can communicate through a built-in messaging system. Students can send messages to the teacher at any time. Teachers can send messages to individual students or to the entire class at once.

The development of BizTech™ 2.0 was generously funded by The Coleman Foundation, The Goldman Sachs Foundation, Microsoft Corporation, and The Zimmerman Foundation.

For a demo, visit http://biztech.nfte.com then click on BizTech demo.

To order, go to http://biztech.store.nfte.com

For the Help Desk, call 1-800-FOR-NFTE (1-800-367-6383) Ext. 316 or bizhelp@nfte.com

For more info regarding BizTech™ 2.0, contact NFTE.

## INTERNET ACTIVITIES

Included in many lesson plans are Internet activities designed to be used in conjunction with the print curriculum and/or BizTech™. These activities will help students become comfortable with the Internet as a research and business tool while furthering critical thinking, literacy, analytical and problem-solving skills.

## COMPUTERS-AS-TOOLS FOCUS

Throughout the curriculum, students are encouraged to recognize the value and everyday use of (but are not compelled to use or have ready access to) everyday desktop applications, such as word processing, spreadsheet, database, presentation software and e-mail, as business, communication, and study tools.

Activities and examples in the core content, in end-of-chapter exercises, and in the *Skills Mean Success* features emphasize the value of computers in the workplace and lifelong learning. The curriculum also affords many opportunities for available experts - guest computer teachers and computer-adept students — to provide extra insights, demonstrations, and explorations with computer applications for the class.

## SUPPLEMENTARY UNIT: Health and Wellness for Young Entrepreneurs

Health and wellness are increasingly important issues for teenagers and the NFTE curriculum aims to teach the "whole student." Use this supplementary unit on "Vitality" as an extension of Chapter 5 or at any other appropriate point in the curriculum to help students develop awareness of physical well-being and its impact on success in business and in entrepreneurship. The unit could be effectively team-taught with health or physical education teachers or coaches.

## KEY QUESTION

*A company needs resources to operate profitably. How do I make sure my #1 resources — my own body, mind and relationships — are "ready for opportunity"?*

## PREPARE FOR LEARNING

- **Guest Speaker/Panel.** If you plan to invite guest speakers to visit the class — an Extend the Learning activity — remember to make arrangements in advance.
- **Health Assessment.** If you choose to do some or all of these assessments, you may need to distribute parental permission forms and/or make arrangements with physical education or health professionals.

## DEVELOP AND CLOSE THE LEARNING

- **Vitality.** Challenge the students to define this term. (The capacity to grow; physical or intellectual vigor; energy; healthful enthusiasm.) Ask why vitality is important to both entrepreneurs and students. (When a person has vitality, s/he has the physical, mental, emotional resources and energy to complete the tasks that need to be done and to pursue his/her goals.) Have students brainstorm ways that people can increase their vitality. Create an idea "bubble" or "fishbone" chart of their suggestions on the board (where the students' ideas branch off the word "vitality" in the center of the diagram). If students have trouble coming up with ideas, perhaps jump-start them: healthy body, clear-thinking mind, good social network, etc. Establish that entrepreneurial ventures start with vitality; entrepreneurs need to make sure that their bodies and relationships are healthy so that these resources can be used effectively to build a profitable company. Health and vitality create a "readiness for opportunity." Determine

through discussion that entrepreneurs do not want to use sub-standard materials to create their products or services. Likewise, an individual should not ingest sub-par "materials" to run their bodies and minds. Bodies and relationships require the right "inputs" or "raw materials" to function well.

- **Body Health/Nutrition.** Allow students to conduct a Web- or library search to locate information on nutrition, sleep, and exercise, using reputable nutrition authorities (e.g. www.nutrition.gov or www.USDA.gov) to establish general guidelines for eating properly, such as the food pyramid guidelines for number of servings of protein, fruits and vegetables, grains, and dairy; amount of calories needed for bodily functions; the basics of food metabolism; why fats and sugars should be eaten sparingly, etc.. One group might research and report on why fats should be eaten sparingly, another on the benefits of fruits and vegetables, and another on what vitamins do in the body. Other sources include:

  www.nal.usda.gov/fnic, www.navigator.tufts.edu, www.nutrition.org, www.eatright.org/Public

- **Body Health/Sleep and Exercise.** Conduct a poll of students using a show of hands: How many hours of sleep per night do you get? 6? 7? 8? 9? How many hours do you think someone your age should get? How many minutes of exercise do you engage in each week? 15? 30? 60? 120? Convey to students the importance of both relaxation and movement. The body (and mind) need at least 8 hours of sleep per night. Some scientists think teenagers need more. Some students might think that if they short themselves on sleep one night, they can make it up on the weekend. Explain that the body and brain do not work that way. The body works in daily cycles: it needs the same amount of sleep each day. Lack of sleep causes problems with catching infections (colds, flu, etc.), lack of concentration, poorer memory, emotional crankiness, safety concerns (driving drowsy), lethargy, etc. For additional information to share with students (or for students to research and report), visit www.sleepfoundation.org. Brainstorm a list of simple exercises that they can incorporate into their busy schedules: walking rather than driving, taking the stairs rather than the elevator, going for a walk after school, learning a sport (which can also provide social interaction), dancing, stretching, yoga, aerobics, etc. Also brainstorm the benefits of exercise. (Weight control, strength, mental clarity, stress reduction, meet people, feelings of happiness and well-being, long-term health benefits such as reduced heart disease.) For additional information, see:

www.acefitness.org, www.kidshealth.org, www.nlm.nih.gov/medlineplus/exerciseandphysicalfitness.html

- **Relationship Health.** Challenge students: our own physical health depends on our interactions with others. We are not isolated beings. We are connected. One of the best ways to stay healthy is to develop healthy relationships with others. On the board, make two lists: one that lists what students consider are characteristics of good friendships, and one that lists characteristics of bad friendships. In small groups, have students brainstorm: 1) how they can be a better friend to others; 2) how they can involve their friends in their lives in a healthy way to solve problems, share their feelings, etc.; 3) what they can do to work through conflict that occasionally arises in friendship. Allow time for groups to share their ideas. Discuss patterns in the ideas students came up with. Some topics that might be considered: What are difficulties that young adults occasionally face in making healthy friendships? What are skills that youth need to develop to be a good friend and to attract good friends? What should a youth do if s/he is having friendship difficulties? One possible source of additional information: www.caps.unc.edu/relationship.htm

- **Positive Health Cartoon or Comic Strip.** Have students draw a cartoon or comic strip that exemplifies a health-promoting situation. Students who lack confidence in their own drawing skills could perform the activity on a computer using clip art and speech balloons. Display the cartoons around the room.

- **Summary.** Have each student write one specific goal for how s/he will improve a specific behavior within each of the following health areas:
  - Eating/nutrition
  - Sleep/rest
  - Exercise
  - Coping (handling stress)
  - Interpersonal relationships

## ASSESS THE LEARNING

- **Health Diaries.** Have each student start and maintain for at least one week (preferably longer) a health diary. Each daily entry should include the following:
  - **Food:** list all foods eaten, amount or serving size, and time of day.
  - **Sleep:** enter "to bed" and "wake up" times for each day.
  - **Exercise:** list the type of movement (including walking) and duration in minutes for all activities that day. Include walking to/from school, housework, sports teams, dancing, etc.
  - **Stressors:** list any event or activity (with time noted) that created increased stress.
  - **Connections:** list any social interactions (with friends, family, teachers, etc. and with times noted) that created a sense of feeling supported.
  - **Stress level:** at the end of each day, indicate the "stress level" for the day: very stressful, somewhat stressful, somewhat relaxed, very relaxed.
  - **Happiness level:** at the end of the day, indicate the "happiness level" for the day: very happy, somewhat happy, somewhat unhappy, very unhappy.

- **Assessing the Diaries.** Being sure to respect the students' privacy, let volunteers share their diaries after a given period of time. Challenge the students to use the information to find patterns in their lives and perhaps provide constructive suggestions for how they might improve their interactions, habits, etc.

- **Health Assessment.** Parental permission may be needed to conduct this assessment. Check with your principal. It would also be helpful to collaborate with a school coach or health or physical education teacher. Depending on the equipment available at your school and the time available, have each student conduct a series of performance activities to determine his or her fitness level. Rather than conducting one-point-in-time assessments, start them near the beginning of the year, then use some of the continuing health improvement activities to allow students to become more fit; then assess again at mid-year or the end of the year to see how far students have improved.

Performance activities may include:

- An evaluation of the food diary they keep after 1st week then again after a longer period: how many calories per day? fat/carbohydrate/protein balance? how many servings of fruits, vegetables, dairy, protein? etc.

- An evaluation of the exercise diary: how many steps did they take each day? how many minutes of exercise each day? how many calories did they burn?

- An evaluation of the stressor diary: are there any patterns in the types of events, time of day, day of the week, etc. that tend to cause more or less stress? what strategies could be used to avoid, alleviate, or confront these stressors?

- An evaluation of the connections diary: are there any patterns in the types of people, time of day, day of the week, types of situations, etc. that tend to make you feel more or less supported? what strategies might increase these types of interactions?

- An evaluation of their goals (see Health Goals activity above): how far did the student come in reaching his/her self-set health goals? What further strategies can be taken either to still reach the goal(s) or to pursue even higher goal(s)?

- A body-mass index assessment.

- How many sit-ups/push-ups can students do in one minute?

- How far can they run in two minutes?

- Psychosocial adjustment inventories that are self-report measures about interpersonal relationships (your school's guidance counselor may have samples).

## EXTEND THE LEARNING

- **Exploring Your Community.** Ask students to use the phone book or explore their neighborhood (or a supermarket for specific products) to find health-supportive types of businesses or products. (e.g. health-supportive businesses might be workout clubs or gyms, massage or yoga studios, counseling practices, health food stores, restaurants that serve fresh or organic or high-nutrient foods and/or provide gathering places for friends, etc.)

- **Health Role Model.** Ask each student to choose someone in their lives that they think lives a healthy lifestyle. Each student should write a one-page portrait of the person's lifestyle and explain how and why it is healthy. If students are willing, ask them to ask their chosen person to be a "health coach" for the student during the next two months and provide encouragement, information and feedback for the student to improve his/her health habits.

- **Guest Speaker/Panel.** Invite one or more of the following professionals to provide health tips to your class: exercise instructor (from a gym), nutritionist, physician or nurse, yoga instructor, counselor, interpersonal skills or stress reduction trainer. Note that many of these roles can also be entrepreneurs. Try to match the demographic characteristics of the panel to your class (e.g., women, African-Americans, Hispanics, Asians, etc.) and to include entrepreneurs from different age groups. Prep the panel members to be able to give a brief overview of their respective businesses (what products/services they provide, fees they charge, etc.) as well as health tips for a teen population (and perhaps tailored to the gender and ethnic composition of your class, if there are particular teen health issues for those populations). Have students compile lists of additional questions before the speakers arrives.

- **Health Fair.** As an entrepreneurial class project, have the class host a health fair for the school. Divide the class "company" into teams to invite health professionals to booths on different health topics, hold a "dance-a-thon," healthy recipes cooking/prep demonstrations, CPR training, and other ideas the students brainstorm. Health and physical education teachers and coaches may be more than willing to help students organize the fair.

### CHAPTER 1

# WHAT IS ENTREPRENEURSHIP?

---

## ORGANIZE THE LEARNING

### CHAPTER OBJECTIVES

- Describe the difference between employees and entrepreneurs.
- Discuss how entrepreneurs create value from "scarce" resources.
- Explain why entrepreneurs like change.
- Evaluate the pros and cons of owning your own business.

### NFTE RESOURCES

- Textbook pp. 2-15
- Transparencies T1-1 to T1-3
- Workbook/BLMs Chapter 1
- Test Bank Chapter 1

### BUSINESS PLAN ACTIVITIES

*Workbook Business Plan Review*
Your Business Idea 1-1, 1-2, 1-3, 1-4, 1-5

*Workbook/Textbook Chapter Review*
Critical Thinking 4

*Power Point Templates*
Bas. 2; Int. 2; Adv. 2

### SKILLS MEAN SUCCESS

*Leadership*
Seeing Yourself as an Entrepreneur

*English*
Reading for Information: Gathering and Interpreting Information; Reading for Information and Understanding: Following Directions, Interpreting, and Analyzing

*Math*
Mathematical Reasoning and Number Operations: Multiples, Parts, Increases, Decreases

### PREREQUISITES

- Lead the students through a review of Chapter 1 in the textbook. See *Prepare for Learning.*
- Use the Key Question below to set a purpose for their reading.

### VOCABULARY

business, capital, capitalism, economy, employee, entrepreneur, free enterprise system, profit, resource, voluntary exchange

---

## KEY QUESTION

**What is the role of the entrepreneur within a free-enterprise economy?**

*(Every chapter in this book will suggest a **Key Question** that, essentially, can be used to set a foundation for learning and form a basis of inquiry for the corresponding chapter in the student text. Each **Develop and Close the Learning** section here will mirror the "Summary" at the end of each textbook chapter, which will draw the students back to the **Key Question**.)*

## PREPARE FOR LEARNING

- **Textbook Tour.** Before beginning the chapter, give the students a chance to flip through it in their textbooks. Point out the elements — chapter number and title, the epigraph (opening quote), Key Objectives, topic headings, and the end-of-chapter features — to build an overall familiarity with the book's structure. Demonstrate how to "pre-read" a chapter, noticing the essential ideas, observing the graphics and illustrations and, as appropriate, tak-

ing notes. It is highly recommended that, as a useful study habit to develop, students preview and/or read each chapter prior to classroom discussion.

- **Assemble Materials for Trading Game (optional).** If you decide to have the class play the Trading Game, you will need one brown-paper lunch bag for each student, plus three small, inexpensive objects (candy, school supplies, etc.) to be placed in each bag. Make sure each bag contains the same number of objects, but not in identical groupings. To play the game, refer to the **Develop and Close the Learning** section below. *(Look over the **Prepare for Learning** sections in other chapters to alert you to activities, field trips, ideas for guest speakers, necessary materials, etc., that will require advanced planning.)*

- ***Entrepreneurs in Profile.*** If you plan to use this resource, have copies available for students to use in class.

- ***Wall Street Journal.*** Have available copies of the newspaper for students to use during class.

## SET A CONTEXT FOR LEARNING

*(The **Set a Context for Learning** sections provide suggested — frequently discussion-style — activities designed to engage the students and help you assess prior knowledge with a view to establishing a basis for teaching the elements in the **Develop and Close the Learning** section. Some ideas will tie into extension activities in the **Extend the Learning** segment.)*

- **Focus 1: "Can Do."** Write on the board or pose aloud the following: What are three things you think others would say that you "can do" particularly well?

- **Focus 2: Vision of the Future.** Ask the students to visualize: What kind of life do I want? How can I make my community a better place?

- **Discussion Launcher 1: Initiative.** Write on the board or project on an overhead the following quote and ask the students to rewrite or explain it in their own words, and/or give an example of it: "The people who get on in this world are those who get out and look for the circumstances they want and, if they can't find them, make them."

- **Discussion Launcher 2: Who Are Entrepreneurs?** Inform the students that "entrepreneur" is not a social or financial category but a state of mind that focuses on seeking out opportunities, taking action, and finding ways to solve other people's problems in a profitable way. Ask students to think about and name entrepreneurs they know, such as small businesspeople in the neighborhood. Can they think of ways these local entrepreneurs saw problems as opportunities and that they solved the problems in a profitable way? Can any students think of a time when *they* were entrepreneurial in this way?

## DEVELOP AND CLOSE THE LEARNING

- **Free Enterprise.** Elicit from students meanings of the word *free*. Stress that, in the case of the term "free enterprise," it means that anyone may start, own, or sell a business ("enterprise"), may sell goods and services for whatever price they can get for them, and may spend their money and invest their assets as they choose. For example, Juan could open a T-shirt company, buy T-shirts from a supplier of his choosing and pay, say, $4.50 each, mark up the T-shirts by 100% and sell them at $9, because his customers were willing to pay that price. Invite students to share opinions about a free-enterprise economy, both the advantages (such as freedom to succeed, reward for initiative, no interference from others) and disadvantages (such as financial risk and personal responsibility). **LINKS** *»Economics*

- **Defining Entrepreneurship.** Ask students to list the differences between an entrepreneur and an employee. Show transparency T1-1 and compare it to the students' suggestions. Discuss the importance of small businesses, new businesses, and entrepreneurs in our society using transparency T1-2, perhaps after allowing students to predict some of the numbers provided on that list of business facts. Note that many new and small businesses have employees and that entrepreneurs also create jobs for others. Discuss the importance of small businesses, job creation, and minority and female business ownership. Ask students to give reasons why they would rather work for themselves or be an employee in someone else's company. Write student responses on the board. Show transparency T1-3 and compare and/or categorize student responses with the pros and cons of being an entrepreneur listed on the transparency.

- **Entrepreneurship is "COOL."** Use transparency T1-3 as an overview to discuss the four key benefits of entrepreneurship. It may be helpful to chart student responses on the board using the acronym C.O.O.L.:

  - **Control.** Ask what an employee has control over in his/her job. (Not much, not even his/her workspace is private.) Ask what an entrepreneur has control over - or *more* control over. (Time, compensation, working conditions, finances.)

  - **Opportunity.** Ask what opportunities an employee generally has. (Training, promotion, raises — but all decided by someone else.) Ask what opportunities an entrepreneur has. (Growing the business, learning skills, meeting new people, creating wealth based on his/her own and the market's goals and needs.)

  - **Ownership.** Ask what an employee owns in his/her job. (Possibly nothing, unless he or she owns company stock [See Chapter 33.]; certainly not what s/he produces on the job.) Ask what an entrepreneur owns. (Company assets and products, profits, equipment, patents [See Chapter 42.].)

  - **Lifestyle.** Ask students to describe the lifestyle of an employee. (Relatively stable — work times set by someone else, often repetitive work that may be boring, possibly fulfilling, work balanced with outside pursuits.) Ask students to describe the lifestyle of an entrepreneur. (Work is often central, s/he is passionate about the business, always "on the go.")

To orient students to *Entrepreneurs in Profile* or *The Wall Street Journal*, have them skim through the stories of entrepreneurs to find and list examples of the benefits discussed above. Allow them time to share their findings. Ask students to rank these benefits in order of personal importance: which are the most appealing? the least? Poll the class, then list and display the results as a tally or graph.

- **Ownership.** Ask students to define and give examples of "owner" and "tenant." Discuss the definitions brought up. (Ownership is the legal right to possess a thing, which allows you to control and transfer that possession. Tenancy is the legal right to use a thing, which usually does not allow for transfer or include complete control.) Summarize the differences as ownership implies something belongs to you, whereas tenancy implies you can use something belonging to others with their permission. Use examples to make this difference more concrete. Make a two-column chart on the board comparing different aspects of home ownership vs. renting and business ownership vs. employment. See below for sample charts. Emphasize the point that ownership often means that you delay reward further into the future (e.g., you don't get paid for your efforts right away like you do with employment) but that the rewards are often bigger (e.g., you can sell the company for a lot more money than you could've earned in wages as an employee).

| Home ownership | Home renting | Business ownership | Employment |
| --- | --- | --- | --- |
| Down payment | First/last months rent plus damage deposit | Invest capital at start | Just start working |
| Monthly mortgage payment (principal, interest, taxes) | Monthly rent | Other pros/cons listed in Chapters 1-2 | Other pros/cons listed in Chapters 1-2 |
| Do own maintenance on your timeframe | Landlord does maintenance on his/her timeframe | You can keep re-investing in the business as desired | Employer decides; Paid for any maintenance job requires |
| Can improve the property (i.e. add a room); Can later sell it and get money back | Cannot improve the property; When leave, only money you get back is damage deposit | Can sell business and get a lot of money | When leave, may or may not get severance pay |

- **Profit and Value.** Ask: How is an egg a resource? What kind of need(s) can it fulfill? How can it be used to make something else? (Answers will probably relate to satisfying hunger, and use in such food items as omelets and baked goods.) How does turning a raw egg into an omelet *add value*? (Answers will refer to making the egg "taste better," converting it from a raw state by cooking, etc.) Challenge students to think about the following: Two eggs would cost about 40 cents; the cheese in an omelet and cost of a stove to cook it can be figured to cost another 40 cents, yet an omelet in a restaurant costs around $3. Why will people pay $3 for a prepared omelet? (Answers will probably include the needs met and how the omelet ends up being more valuable than the individual components.) Repeat this discussion with different resources — paper, computers, a college education — until students understand that resources fill needs and can be transformed into products (both tangible and intangible) that people will pay for to fill needs. Alternatively or in addition, you could start with a finished product and ask the students to separate it into its component resources — a house into lumber and sheetrock, etc., or a videogame into a story/plot, computer disk, etc., and then explain how value was added. Reinforce that this extra value creates the profit an entrepreneur earns. **LINKS**»*Economics*

- **Opportunity.** Ask students for their definitions of *opportunity*. How is an opportunity different from a problem? (An opportunity is viewed more positively than a problem and considered a situation an individual can do something about. Opportunity is more a matter of attitude toward potential problems than the scenario itself.) Direct students individually or in small groups to brainstorm problems they see in society, their neighborhoods, the school, and their own lives. After a few minutes, ask each student or group to choose one problem. How could it be turned into an opportunity — a product or service that might help solve the problem? How might "can-do" skills brainstormed in Focus 1 be used in relation to this opportunity? Have students/groups present their ideas to the class.

- **Voluntary Exchange/Trading Game (optional).** The purpose of this activity is to demonstrate how participants in an economy tend to be happier when they can freely trade among themselves.

  ○ Assemble paper bags in advance (see page TE 1).

  ○ Give one bag to each student. Allow students to open their bags and examine the contents without showing the others. Ask students to indicate, by a show of hands, how happy they are with the contents of their bags: 1 is very unsatisfied, 3 is neutral, 5 is very satisfied. Ask: How many – raise your hands – are "1 – very unsatisfied?"; "3 – neutral?"; "5 – very satisfied?"; somewhere in between? Record this information on the board and sum up the total satisfaction of the class.

  ○ Allow students to compare their contents. Tally satisfaction again.

  ○ Divide students into groups and allow them to trade within their groups. Tally satisfaction again.

  ○ Allow students to trade class-wide. Tally satisfaction again.

  ○ Discuss the satisfaction scores on the board. Total satisfaction score should go up as students are allowed to trade. **LINKS**)»*Economics*

- **Summary.** Ask students to consider the chapter's key question: What is the role of the entrepreneur in a free-enterprise economy? (Answers should relate to meeting people's needs, taking initiative, introducing or taking advantage of opportunities, using scarce (limited) resources efficiently and profitably, creating jobs for others.) Leave students with the concept of asking themselves this question over the course of the semester: How could *they* play this role?

## ASSESS THE LEARNING

*(This section will provides suggestions — some related to the textbook and/or workbook — that can be used to help the teacher determine follow-up learning needs by chapter in regard to content: practice, reflection, consolidation, re-teaching, review, concepts not mastered, and readiness to proceed with extension activities and subsequent chapters. A variety of assessment tools in varying degrees of complexity are provided, from the standard chapter quizzes provided in the workbook, to vocabulary review, to more holistic and authentic assessment activities, such as writing or making presentations.)*

- **Vocabulary.** Have students define in their own words the terms listed, and then use each term in a sentence. Students who use the accompanying workbook, which is highly recommended, can complete the vocabulary activity provided for each chapter.

- **Key Concepts.** Assign Questions 1 – 4, 6. **Answers:** 1. They work for someone else. 2. Small businesses are defined as having fewer than 100 employees and selling less than $1 million in goods or services per year. 3. Answers may vary but will probably include: learn about an industry or customer needs, provide jobs for self and others for a period of time, cultivate taking initiative in one's life, engage in voluntary exchange with both suppliers and customers, further develop one's business skills, be an active participant in the free-enterprise economy, develop stronger character in the face of adversity. 4. Profit lets entrepreneurs know they are adding value, in an efficient way, to the resources they use in producing their products or services; it also tells entrepreneurs they are meeting a customer need efficiently. 6. Answers will vary but probably will include: capitalism is a type of economic system; anyone can start a business; money used to start a business is capital, capitalism involves competition among companies; capitalism rewards companies who use resources efficiently.

- **Critical Thinking.** Assign Questions 1-3, 6, 9. **Answers:** 1. Answers will vary but should reflect some of the eight advantages mentioned in the textbook: control over time and compensation and working conditions, fulfilling life, wealth, self-evaluation, community, helping others. 2. Answers will vary but should reflect some of the five disadvantages mentioned in the textbook: potential to fail, obstacles, loneliness, financial insecurity, long hours. 3. Answers will vary but should provide an understanding of the difference between an employee (works for others) and an entrepreneur (works for self) and reasons for one's preference. 6. Answers will vary, but probably will focus on ideas such as: Employees get what they deserve because they are paid the wages or salary that their skills merit and that they agree to work for. Entrepreneurs have no such guarantees, despite the effort and risks involved. 9. $195,000; $369,000; $3,300,525.

- **Writing Practice.** Assign Critical Thinking question 7. The written responses received from individual students could be used to initiate a "get acquaint-ed" discussion with each student or with the class as a whole.

- **Additional Workbook Activities Answers.**

  **Vocabulary Activity.** Every chapter in the workbook will include a vocabulary activity, word puzzle, or some other device that students can use to review vocabulary and other key terms in the chapter. Solutions and answers to these puzzles and activi-ties are provided in this section in every chapter. **Answers:** Students' answers should be complete sentences that use the vocabulary words correctly. Sentences should demonstrate an understanding of each word's meaning without being a restatement of the definition. *Example:* Ms. Lopez started her flower shop with $1,000 of capital from her savings and gifts from family members.

  **Quiz 1** *(A "Quiz" for every chapter is provided in the Workbook.)* These tools use a combination of simple factual-recall and inferential-thinking questions to help students (and you) assess their understanding of the chapter's key content and concepts. **Answers:** 1. Employees work for others and entre-preneurs work for themselves. 2. D, in that the work could feel exhausting; but also A, in that the entre-preneur is often doing something s/he loves to do. 3. A. 4. D. 5. A. 6. A. 7. B. 8. No, because failure can pro-vide the experience to start over again from a stronger position.

## EXTEND THE LEARNING

*(You can use the suggestions from this section as time and interests allow, but you should always assign Business Plan-related activities, which are clearly iden-tified. The activities will frequently refer to specific assignments, features, and activities in the textbook, the workbook and in the supplemental — but highly recom-mended — NFTE publication* Entrepreneurs in Profile, *a handy anthology of brief, readable, and engaging biog-raphies of well-known entrepreneurs. Other activities in this section will invite students to explore beyond the curriculum and to share, network, reflect, and conduct research on key topics and interests.)*

- ***Entrepreneurs in Profile.*** Assign Critical Thinking question 8.
- **Time to Succeed.** Use Key Concepts question 5 to have the students discuss in groups how long it would or should take for a business to start making a profit. As needed, use specific hypothetical exam-ples such as the following: a retail T-shirt business

that does not make a profit after 12 months; a pet-sitting service business that does not make a profit for two years; an office cleaning business that does not make a profit for its first 18 months; an whole-sale business that imports handcrafts from Guatemala that has not made a profit in two months of operation. Group students. Allow students time to discuss, then present their key points (e.g. a hand-craft import business would not be expected to have made a profit after just two months because there may have been one-time start-up costs or the inven-tory may not have even arrived from Guatemala yet, etc.). After each group has presented, discuss the similarities and differences among the reasons given. Can students think of examples of types of businesses that earned a profit quickly vs. those that took more time? (e.g., businesses with low start-up costs or that provided a unique, new prod-uct or service and generated immediate sales might be more likely to make a profit sooner.)

- **Internet Exploration.** Assign Critical Thinking ques-tion 5 for homework or during classroom computer time. Have students create posters of what they found that includes the following: the Web address of their favorite site, how the site defines entrepre-neurship, a summary of the information on the site the student found most valuable, and a brief evalua-tion of why that information is important.
- **Business Plan Practice.** Assign Critical Thinking question 4.
- **Jobs to Entrepreneurial Opportunity.** Ask each stu-dent to come up with one profession or occupation s/he is considering as a career. Group students based on jobs that are in a similar interest grouping or in a comparable industry: for example, working with numbers (accounting, insurance), or entertain-ment (actor, musician), or artistic. Give each group a few minutes to brainstorm ways to turn the career into a business opportunity so that students could work for themselves. How might they think about their interests in terms of entrepreneurship? Have each group briefly share its ideas.

  **LINKS** )»*Career Ed*

- **Exploring Your Community.** Have students interview local small businesspeople, as described in the text.

## BUILD ACADEMIC AND LIFE-SKILL PROFICIENCIES

*Note: The Skills Mean Success features that are pro-vided throughout the textbook (two to four per chapter) are designed to reinforce and extend proficiencies related to key national and state academic standards in English-language arts and math, as well as technology and "leadership" skills. Leadership skills reflect NFTE's Theory or Change, as well as research carried out at Harvard, on important competencies and attitudes used by entrepreneurs and by successful adults in general.*

*These features are actually "interventions" that complement and reinforce the core entrepreneurship content of the NFTE curriculum. They provide opportunities for learning, and for reviewing and practicing key academic (and other) proficiencies — in context. Many students learn most effectively when they perceive the subject as relevant. Entrepreneurship students in particular will benefit from the opportunity of achieving academic competencies via "real-world" scenarios.*

*Employ the Skills Mean Success features to complement your own instructional plans with the students only as needed — just as you should use selectively the other activities suggested in the textbook and other components of the curriculum. You may choose to assign a single Skills Mean Success activity to the whole class, to groups, or to individual students, as appropriate. They are important and enabling — but optional — tools for your use.*

*The features are also rich in their potential for shared teaching with colleagues, for cooperative and collaborative learning, for student leadership and peer tutoring, for project-based learning, for test-taking preparation, or "test prep," activities, as well as offering the opportunity*

- *to "teach the whole student".*
- *to demonstrate how elective courses can reinforce core academic skills.*
- *to help drive the school's overall mission.*
- *to showcase the Entrepreneurship program as an important contributor to providing alternate but supportive pathways to student success.*

*Answers and easy-to-use notes to complement the textbook's Skills Mean Success features are included in for each chapter in this section.)*

### *Skills Mean Success* Answers

**Leadership.** Encourage students to write in their "Idea Journals" regularly. Remind them that brainstorming rules apply — there are no *bad* ideas! Encourage students to jot down their thoughts even if they seem farfetched or impractical. The goal is to get into the practice of thinking like an entrepreneur and capturing ideas. These may be developed in the future and will perhaps help trigger new and better ideas. Allow a few minutes at the end of class for journal writing, if needed.

**English.** Assign students who researched the entrepreneurs to a round-table discussion group. Have them take turns sharing their findings. Note how each of the entrepreneurs addressed a cultural change or societal need in developing a product or business:

- Lane Bryant was a seamstress who created the first maternity fashions in the early 1900s. Before this time, it was not considered proper for pregnant women to be seen in public.

- John H. Johnson is a prominent publisher and founder of such magazines as *Ebony* and *Jet*. During the mid-twentieth century, when African Americans were fighting for civil rights and social equality, Johnson created the first magazines that focused on their needs, wants, and achievements.

- In 1906, Sarah Breedlove Walker (Madam C. J. Walker) created a successful business by selling hair-care and beauty products made especially for African-American women. No such products had existed before.

- Russell Simmons is the founder of Def Jam Records. He was one of the first promoters of rap music and hip-hop culture and has been a major force in the genre's commercial success.

- In recent years, experts discovered that children develop critical intellectual ability before the age of three. As a result, Julie Aigner-Clark began selling innovative, educational videos and toys that she had developed for her baby daughter. Her success led to founding a company, Baby Einstein, which she later sold to Disney.

**English.** 1. Answers will and should vary, but, for example: 1. A: a, c, i; B: d, i; C: a, d, i; D: a, d, h, i; E: a, b, e, f, g, i; F: a, b, c, d, h, i; G: b, e, g; H: c, f, i; I: b, e, f, g. 2 and 3. Answers will vary. Look for changes in the students' attitudes that reflect maturing understanding and expectations.

**Math.** This activity asks students to use their powers of mathematical reasoning and their understanding of very basic number operations to reflect on the concepts of multiples, parts, and increases/decreases, in the context of solving business problems. Answers: a. multiply; b. subtract; c. divide; d. multiply or add; e. add; f. multiply; g. divide; h. multiply or add.

### CHAPTER 2

# THE BUILDING BLOCK OF BUSINESS:
## *The Economics of One Unit of Sale*

## ORGANIZE THE LEARNING

### CHAPTER OBJECTIVES

- Define a unit of sale for a business.
- Describe the four types of business.
- Analyze the economics of one unit for each type of business, and calculate gross profit per unit.

### NFTE RESOURCES

- Text pp. 16-27
- Transparencies T2-1 to T2-5
- Workbook/BLMs Chapter 2
- Test Bank Chapter 2
- A Business for the Young Entrepreneur: *Web Design and Hosting*

### BUSINESS PLAN ACTIVITIES

*Workbook Business Plan Review*
Economics of One Unit  2-1, 2-2, 2-3

*Workbook/Textbook Chapter Review*
Key Concepts 3-4

*Power Point Templates*
Bas. 2, 5; Int. 2, 6; Adv. 2, 6

### SKILLS MEAN SUCCESS

*Math*
Mathematical Reasoning and
Operations: Averages

### PREREQUISITES

Students should preview Chapter 2 in the textbook.

### VOCABULARY

cost of goods sold, economics of one unit of sale (EOU), gross profit, unit of sale

## KEY QUESTION

**What are the costs and profit of selling one unit?**

## SET A CONTEXT FOR LEARNING

- **Focus 1: Business Types.** Present this problem: Name two companies you can think of that fit each of the following business types: manufacturing, wholesale, retail, service. For which business type was it easiest and hardest to think of companies?

- **Focus 2: Economics of One Hour of Your Time.** Help students to start realizing that one hour may not always be "worth" the same value—it depends on how a person spends it. Ask students to brainstorm different ways they could spend one hour of time. Have them pick three of the ways and think about how much money this activity might bring in (e.g., a job would bring in a certain wage, going to the movies brings in nothing) and how much money this activity might cost (e.g., going to the movies costs $10).

- **Discussion Launcher: Leadership vs. Labor.** Ask students to discuss the advantages of becoming a

business leader (and not having one's own labor included in the cost of a product or service) as discussed in the text.

## DEVELOP AND CLOSE THE LEARNING

- **Four Types of Businesses.** Use transparency T2-1 to define the four types of businesses (manufacturing, wholesale, retail, service). Ask students to consider what each "does" — make a product, buy and resell products, make the products available to consumers, or "do something for" (provide a service to) consumers. Ask student to brainstorm how each adds value. Divide students into four small groups and assign each group one type of business. Group members should come up with as many examples of that type of business in their community and the country as they can think of in a few minutes. (If you used the Discussion Launcher Focus 1, these companies can be included in students' lists.) Ask: Which types of business are easier or harder to think of? Why might some types of business not be as familiar as others? Which type of business would be most appealing to own? Why?

- **Unit of Sale.** Define "unit of sale" from the textbook. Use transparency T2-2 to outline the primary ways in which the unit of sale is determined. In groups, ask students to pick two or three companies they listed previously and determine what their units of sale would be. (With the Gap, it might be one pair of blue jeans; at a barber shop, it could be one haircut.) Ask students to share any difficulties they ran into in trying to determine the unit of sale. (For example, a clothing store sells a variety of items, a restaurant has a varied menu, an accountant doesn't have a "product," etc.) **LINKS** ⟩⟩*Economics*

- **Gross Profit per Unit.** Discuss how the *sale price* (what a customer pays for one unit) is not the amount of money the entrepreneur actually makes. Businesses incur costs to buy raw materials and in the process of adding value. These costs must be subtracted to determine what's left over for the entrepreneur to use elsewhere. Call this "left over" gross profit. Use transparency T2-3 to explain how gross profit per unit is calculated. Provide several examples (sets of numbers to "plug in") from the text or elsewhere so students can use and become familiar with the formulas. Summarize by stating that using these formulas is called "calculating the economics of one unit." Ask students to speculate why knowing the economics of one unit is so important to an entrepreneur. (Answers should involve how knowing this information provides a snapshot of the whole business — whether it is profitable or not. If one unit is profitable, the business as a whole can be profitable; but if one unit isn't profitable, it doesn't matter how many units the business sells, it won't be profitable. Knowing the economics of one unit also helps the entrepreneur determine what s/he can hire other people to do—the entrepreneur should try to not be part of the labor in economics of one unit.)

- **Cost of Goods/Services Sold.** Once students grasp the formulas, ask them to focus on costs. Use transparency T2-4 and the examples in the textbook (or other examples) to make clear what *is* and *is not* included in cost of goods sold. Be particularly careful to explain what types of labor are figured into COGS (any work that goes directly into making the product or service) and which are not included (any work involved in selling the product or service). Make sure students understand that their own labor must be calculated if they are personally involved in making the product or service. Use the example of Janet in the textbook to clarify what might happen if an entrepreneur does not include his/her own time and labor (s/he will overestimate gross profit).

- **How Entrepreneurs Make Money.** Use transparency T2-5 to recall from Chapter 1 the five main ways an entrepreneur makes money. Differentiate that, whereas employees earn money through a regular paycheck (salary or wage), entrepreneurs have a variety of ways of making money. In pairs, ask students to brainstorm responses to the question posed on the transparency (Why is it better for the entrepreneur to be paid by salary, dividend or sale of company (as a leader) than by wage (as labor)? (Answers should involve that the entrepreneur will make more money with less individual effort by delegating labor tasks to others and taking a "cut" than by trying to do all the work him/herself; entrepreneurs can hire others who might do the labor faster or cheaper or better; entrepreneurs only have so much time and using it on growing the business itself rather than on making the product/service is a more profitable use of time in the long run.) Have a few students share their ideas. Ask students in pairs or groups to brainstorm "exit strategies" for taking themselves out of the economics of one unit for their businesses. You may have to give them an example to start: a service provider such as a T-shirt designer may have to train someone else in her technique; a manufacturer may have to provide equipment/tools for someone else. Have a few students share their ideas. Summarize how this process leads to overall economic growth for the community and the nation by providing jobs for other people.

- **Summary.** Ask students to consider: Which is the best deal for them? A regular job at $10 an hour, an independent contract to provide services with a gross profit of $10 per hour, or opening one's own business that won't make any money for a month but then has the potential to make $5 gross profit per product with expected growth projections of 4% per year. What makes the selected option appealing to the student?

## ASSESS THE LEARNING

- **Vocabulary.** Have students define terms in their own words and use each term in a sentence, or assign the vocabulary activity in the workbook.

- **Key Concepts.** Assign Questions 1, 3, 4. **Answers:** 1. Gross profit is the amount left from revenues after costs of goods sold are subtracted and before fixed/operating costs are subtracted. 3. Unit of sale is 1 hour; gross profit is $30 per hour (40 − 10). 4. Unit of sale equals one sandwich plus one soda; gross profit = 1,000/100 − 5 = $5 per unit of sale.

- **Critical Thinking.** Assign Questions 1-2. **Answers:** 1. Answers will vary. The options are provided in Chapter 1 (salary, wage, dividend, commission). 2. Answers will vary.

- **Writing Practice.** The Explore Your Community activity in Extend the Learning may be used as a writing assessment.

- **Additional Workbook Activities Answers.**

  **Vocabulary Activity.** Answers: 1. d, 2. a, 3. b, 4. c

  **Quiz 2** in the workbook. **Answers:** 1. It provides a snapshot of an entrepreneur's whole business: if one unit of sale is profitable then the business can be profitable too; with this information, an entrepreneur can make better decisions. 2. Any of the following: salary, dividend, selling the company (student should *not* list "wage"). 3. Calculate the unit of sale; determine the economics of one unit; substitute someone else's labor; trying to sell in volume; creating jobs and operating at a profit. 4. Materials and supplies, plus labor used to make the product. 5. The price at which the entrepreneur bought the product from the wholesaler. 6. The entrepreneur's cost of goods sold is too low and incomplete, which overestimates gross profit. 7. Usually one haircut. 8. $15 "average meal" per customer. 9. $10 $(20 - 3 - 7)$. 10. $45 $(3 - 1/3 \times 15 = \$50$ in time, $100 \times .02 = \$2$ in materials, so COGS $= 50 + 3 + 2 = 55$, $100 - 55 = 45)$.

## EXTEND THE LEARNING

- **Business Plan Practice.** Assign Key Concepts question 2. The activity can be made more challenging by also asking students to calculate the average gross profit per unit. **Answers:** 2a. Average unit of sale = $600/60 = \$10$; average gross profit = $5. 2b. Average unit of sale = $1,000/40 = \$25$; average gross profit = $12.50.

- **A Business for the Young Entrepreneur.** Have students read about Tonya Groover and WebElegance at the end of the chapter in the textbook. Before assigning this and the other end-of-chapter readings throughout the book, consider outlining the context. For example, in this chapter ask the students to think about — as they read — how Tonya determined a need, turned that need into an opportunity, added value, engaged in voluntary exchange, and earned a profit.

- **Exploration.** Assign the activity in the textbook. After students have conducted and analyzed their own interviews, have several share their findings with the rest of the class so that the whole group can look for patterns across a larger sample of entrepreneurs.

- **Business Buddy.** In tandem with or independently of the Exploration activity in the textbook, ask students to find one entrepreneur in the community who would be willing to mentor a student (or students) through the NFTE curriculum. This "Business Buddy" would be available by phone or e-mail to help his/her assigned student with a business plan (but not with homework or other assignments). Business Buddies could also be invited to special class functions, such as a networking party, "way out" party, an entrepreneurial world's fair, wholesale trip, and other extension activities suggested in later chapters. Some of the Business Buddies might be willing to act as chaperones on field trips to a bank, a stock brokerage, manufacturing facilities, or to other sites, as well as assist with other activities that will be described from time to time in this book. Ideally, these mentors would be small-business owners, but often employees in larger companies are willing to serve in such mentoring roles.

## BUILD ACADEMIC AND LIFE-SKILL PROFICIENCIES

### *Skills Mean Success* Answers

**Math.** 1. a. 55; b. $24.71; c. 82.7; d. $2.86. 2. a. $48.67; b. $14.25. 3. $18.18. Help students to recognize the difference between 2.b. (what was the average cost to Nicki's of the items sold in the average sale of $48.67?) and 3. (what is the average cost to Nicki's of the six types of items the store sells, i.e. the average of $8.35 + 45.00 + 20 + 10 + 19.00 + 6.75).

# RETURN ON INVESTMENT:
## *Evaluating Education, Work, and Business*

## ORGANIZE THE LEARNING

### CHAPTER OBJECTIVES

- Work with percentages
- Calculate return on investment (ROI).
- Explain why ROI is an important measure of success for investors and entrepreneurs.
- Explore the relationship between risk and return.

### NFTE RESOURCES

- Text pp. 28-41
- Transparencies T3-1 toT3-3
- Workbook/BLMs Chapter 3
- *Entrepreneurs in Profile* #10
- Test Bank Chapter 3
- A Business for the Young Entrepreneur: *T-Shirts*

### BUSINESS PLAN ACTIVITIES

*Workbook Business Plan Review*
Return on Investment
Business Goals: 3-1, 3-2;
Personal Goals: 3-1, 3-2

*Workbook/Textbook Chapter Review*
Critical Thinking 2-4

*Power Point Templates*
Bas. 14; Int. 17, Adv. 16

### SKILLS MEAN SUCCESS

*Math*
Number and Numeration: Calculating Percentages, Representing Fraction, Decimal, and Percentage Equivalents

*Leadership*
Goal Setting: Measurable Goals

*English*
Writing for Information and Understanding: Observing Language Conventions

### PREREQUISITES

Students should have read textbook Chapter 3.

### VOCABULARY

goal, interest rate, investment, percentage, rate of return, return on investment (ROI), risk, Rule of 72, sweat equity

## KEY QUESTION

**Is an investment worth the risk?**

## PREPARE FOR LEARNING

- **Guest Speaker:** If you plan to invite a guest entrepreneur to visit the class — as suggested in Extend the Learning — remember to make arrangements in advance. Providing visitors with a copy of the textbook prior to their visit will help them to focus on the intended learning outcomes. Visitors also provide an opportunity for students to write letters of invitation, make follow-up phone calls, prepare directions and contact information, prepare interview or discussion questions, be a greeter and escort for the visitors in the school, or conduct school tours, and write thank-you letters or e-mails.

## SET A CONTEXT FOR LEARNING

- **Focus 1: In Your Opinion.** Have students jot down ideas for the In Your Opinion questions in the text.

- **Focus 2: Life Goals.** Have students answer Critical Thinking question 6: create a one-sentence "vision statement" that describes personal goals for the next five years.

- **Focus 3: Good Investment Opportunity?** Present this problem: If friends offer to give you $8 in a month if you give them $8 today, would you do it? Why or why not? How much would they have to give you back for you to give them the $8 today? Why?

- **Discussion Launcher 1: Wilcox Quote.** Show the Frederick B. Wilcox quote at the bottom of transparency T3-1 and ask the students to explain what it means. Alternatively, you could write the quote on the board or share it verbally: "Progress always involves risk. You can't steal second base if you keep your foot on first." (Responses should be along the lines of: you won't get ahead if you never move out of your safety or comfort zone; no pain, no gain)

- **Discussion Launcher 2: Invest vs. Spend.** Ask the students to think about and discuss in pairs: What is the difference between *spending* one dollar or one hour of time, and *investing* the same amount?

- **Discussion Launcher 3: Personal Investment Style.** Pose one of the following problems for students to discuss in groups or pairs. *Easier problem:* Would you prefer investing in a company where you would get your money back at the end of the week or at the end of the month? Why? *More difficult problem*: Would you prefer investing $100 in a company where you would get $110 at the end of the week or $150 at the end of the month? Why?

## DEVELOP AND CLOSE THE LEARNING

- **Percentage Review.** Use transparency T3-2 to explain calculating percentages. Several problem examples may be necessary, in addition to the "penny" illustration. It would be especially helpful to contextualize the examples in terms of business situations familiar to students to show the extent that percentages are used: percentage-off sale prices for computer equipment (the original price was $1,000, now it's $750), percentage markup of costs for a T-shirt, percentage of a company's income that pays employee salaries, etc. This activity would be an excellent opportunity to invite a colleague from the math department to assist in team teaching or provide coaching.

- **Investment.** Review from Chapter 1 the idea of "adding value." Investment means to put something you have that is of value into something else, in hopes of increasing value over time. Refer to the lemonade example in the text or the example of Debbi Fields: she invested money, her baking expertise, and time and energy to buy eggs, flour and sugar and convert them to cookies to sell at a profit. Ask students: What resources do students have that they could invest? (Expect responses related to money, connections/relationships, time, effort, possessions, knowledge, skills.) One of the best ways to make sure resources are used wisely is to set goals. Ask students to use the Skills Mean Success criteria in the textbook to set one to three goals for themselves this year for the NFTE class or their NFTE business.

- **Return.** Explain that "return" or "net profit" is one way entrepreneurs and investors evaluate whether a company has added value and how much value has been increased. Return often is expressed as a rate, or percentage of growth, over a certain time period. Rates of return may be called by different names such as reward, bank savings rate, loan interest rate, and return on investment. Ask students: What types of non-financial returns someone

might gain from opening a business? (E.g., feeling good, pride in a job well done, excitement, learning new skills, opening up new opportunities, new friendships, status/prestige). Reviewing from Chapters 1-2, ask: What are types of non-financial returns someone might gain from opening a business? (Feeling good, pride in a job well done, excitement, learning new skills, opening up new opportunities, new friendships, status/prestige.)

- **Time Value of Money.** Refer to Discussion Launcher 1 about the difference between investing and spending: if spent, your money is gone, but with investment, your money grows over time — it "compounds" at a given rate of return. Using the text, explain the Rule of 72 to show students how to calculate how fast their money will grow at different rates. In addition, it may be helpful to use several concrete examples, such as: putting $100 in a 2% savings account vs. in a 9% stock vs. starting a business expected to grow at 10%, etc. Use the Time Value of Money chart in the textbook to show how investing earlier in life is better than starting late: making six payments of $2,000 from age 22-27 (total of $12,000 of own money put in) resulted in about the same amount at age 62 as contributing $2,000 for 34 years starting at age 28 (total of $70,000 of own money put in). **LINKS**»*Consumer Ed*

- **Relation of Risk and Return.** Define risk (chance you could lose your investment). Rate of return compensates for risk taken. From the Internet or a newspaper, provide (or have students research) different interest rates for different types of loans such as car, house, signature, credit card, student. Ask students: Using what they've learned about risk, why are credit card rates higher than car loan rates, five-year car loan rates higher than three-year? Have them speculate: Why are stock return rates generally higher than savings rates? Why are bank loan rates higher than savings rates? Draw from the text the risk-return chart on the board and place dots where the above different types of investments (loans, stock, savings, etc.) would go on the chart. Ask students: Where on this chart do you think small business would go, and why? (E.g., far upper right of high risk and high return.) Ask students: How might entrepreneurs reduce their risk? (E.g., start with small investment, respond to customer needs faster, have industry knowledge, keep tabs on what's going on in the company, keep operating costs low.) Use transparency T3-1 to summarize the relation of risk and return. Explain that, because of this relationship, investors often "diversify" or spread their money around several different investments to reduce overall risk. Use the different investment portfolios in the text as examples.

- **Calculating ROI.** Use transparency T3-3 and the step-by-step instructions in the text to walk students through several ROI problems. Use the formula:

  ○ Net Profit / Investment

  Give examples where the ROI is:

  ○ positive, representing recouping costs plus profit

  ○ zero, which is roughly recouping costs only, or breaking even

  ○ negative, which is losing the investment

  Revisit the discussion in Chapter 1 about business failure. A small business may have a negative ROI in the early days, but it may become positive and grow to far outweigh the early losses. Lead the students to recognize that business failure occurs when ROI stays negative too long and that someone has to plan (as an entrepreneur) or evaluate (as an investor) more long term for added value to become apparent.

- **Evaluating ROI.** ROI can be used to compare businesses if their ROI's cover the same length of time (usually annual). Give students several examples of annualizing ROI by using the step-by-step instructions in the text. Using the ROI table in the text or on transparency T3-2, have students reason which investment is doing the best, the worst, and why.

- **Investing in College.** Poll students to find out who is interested in college. To tie together the above concepts, use the example of college in the text (additional information about the returns of a college education can be found in Chapter 4). For example, calculate and compare the differences in lifetime (40-year career) earnings for the different levels of education at a public college:

  ○ Six-year professional degree:
  ($95,309 × 40) − ($11,000 × 6) = $3,812,360

  ○ Four-year degree:
  ($62,188 × 40) − ($11,000 × 4) = $2,727, 520

  ○ Two-year degree:
  ($42,500 x 40) − ($11,000 × 2) = $1,678,200

  ○ Starts work right after high school:
  ($34,373 × 40) − 0 = $1,374,920

  ○ Starts work without diploma:
  ($20,724 × 40) − 0 = $828,960

- **Summary.** Challenge students to recognize that investing in themselves is one of the best invest-

ments they can make in life. Ask students the lesson's key question in terms of themselves: What can you do to make yourself a better investment?

## ASSESS THE LEARNING

- **Vocabulary.** Have students define terms in their own words and use each term in a sentence. or assign the vocabulary activity in the workbook. **Answers:** Students' answers should be complete sentences that use the vocabulary words correctly. Sentences should demonstrate an understanding of each word's meaning without being a restatement of the definition. *Example:* Since I share equal ownership of the business with three other partners, my percentage of the profits will be 25%.

- **Key Concepts.** Assign Questions 1-5. **Answers:** 1. Return on investment. 2. Multiply by 100. 3. Move the decimal point two places to the right. 4. They have fewer start-up and/or fixed costs so they can turn a profit faster. 5. Answers will vary: time, energy, skills, knowledge, connections, reputation, emotions, etc.

- **Critical Thinking.** Assign Questions 1, 5. **Answers:** 1. (top to bottom by line) $4; 50%; 25%; 40%; $30; $10,000; $1,000; $1,200. 5a. 24; 5b. 14.4; 5c. 10.29; 5d. 4; 5e. 3.

- **Additional Workbook Activities Answers.**

  **Vocabulary Activity Answers:** Students' answers should be complete sentences that use the vocabulary words correctly. Sentences should demonstrate an understanding of each word's meaning without being a restatement of the definition. Example: Since I share equal ownership of the business with three other partners, my percentage of the profits will be 25%.

  **Quiz 3** *in the workbook.* **Answers:** 1. 50%. 2. Answers will vary but should include mention that money invested earns returns, which can grow increasingly larger; so the longer it is invested, the more that is earned. 3. $60. 4. Young people's businesses usually have lower start-up and operating costs. 5. Answers will vary: time, energy, skills, knowledge, connections, reputation, emotions, etc. 6. 25%. 7. 100%. 8. 200%. 9. −50%. 10. Risk.

## EXTEND THE LEARNING

- **Business Plan Practice.** Assign Critical Thinking questions 2-4 to have each student research a career in which s/he is interested.

- **A Business for the Young Entrepreneur.** Have students read about T-shirt design, then create their own T-shirt graphic on paper or on-screen. Have them research the economics of one unit for a designed T-shirt, including the cost of the shirt, paints, and labor. If they sell each shirt for $25, what is the ROI?

- *Entrepreneurs in Profile.* Have students read the profile of John H. Johnson and be prepared to discuss it in class. Types of questions to ask could include:

  ○ What resources did Johnson have access to?

  ○ How did he invest them?

  ○ What risks did he take?

  ○ How was he smart about his risk-taking?

  ○ What did he do to protect and grow his investments?

  ○ What did he do to persuade others that his magazine was a good investment?

  ○ How did his risk-taking pay off (what returns did his investments earn)?

  Alternatively, you might ask students to prepare (based on what they've learned about risk, return, ROI, etc.) one or two questions not answered in the profile that they would ask Johnson if they were considering investing in his business today.

- **Guest Speaker.** Invite a local entrepreneur to your class so your students can ask questions about risks, returns, time value, etc. Designated students should prepare questions in advance.

- **Spend vs. Invest Self-Assessment**. Choose one of the following: Retrospective approach: Ask students to list all the items and activities to which they've given time, effort, or money in the last week. Prospective approach: Have them keep a diary of how they invest their resources in the coming week. Hypothetical approach: Ask them to list three ways they would spend $20 or one hour of time. When students have collected data using one of the above approaches, have them evaluate their choices in a brief essay or presentation slide format: Which pay you back (which are investments, not just spending)? What kinds of rewards — financial and non-financial — have you received? How long after you gave the resource did/will you get a return? How might you adjust this "portfolio of activities" to get a higher rate of return?

- *The Wall Street Journal* or **www.wsj.com**. Have students evaluate the paper's Business Opportunities section in terms of expected rate of return and risk.

What recommendations would students make for which investment opportunities?

- **Company Profile.** Have students in pairs or small groups choose one publicly traded company. After they learn about the company from its Web site and/or **www.wsj.com**, ask them to:

  ○ Look up the company's stock prices for the last year and calculate annualized ROI (often *The Wall Street Journal* provides a 52-week table that will make this task easier)

  ○ Research what the company does and make one or two suggestions for how it could increase its ROI in the coming year.

Have students create and present posters of their findings. **LINKS**»*Graphic Arts*

## BUILD ACADEMIC AND LIFE-SKILL PROFICIENCIES

### *Skills Mean Success* Answers

**Math.** 1. *a* is better since 250 divided by 400 = .62 = 62./100 = 62% but 1,500 divided by 10,000 = .15 = 15/100 = 15%; 2. *a* is better since 20 divided by 2,000 = .01 = 1/100 = 1% (better accident rate) while 5 divided by 125 = .04 = 4/100 = 4%. Question 2 is a bit tricky — since traffic accidents are being compared, a *lower* rate is better. Remind students that they always need to consider *what* is being compared.

**Leadership.** Evaluate students' goal statements against the SMART criteria explained in the text. Indicate which criteria their statements are missing, and give them the opportunity to revise until they meet the SMART criteria.

**English.** 1. People often use abbreviations to save time and effort when communicating in the workplace. For example, it is much easier and faster to write or say "IRA" than "Individual Retirement Account." 2. You should only use abbreviations and acronyms when you are sure your reader or listener will understand what they mean. Do not use abbreviations or acronyms with new employees or people outside of your industry who might not be familiar with them. This can cause confusion, delays, and errors. An abbreviation should be a common language, not a secret code. Remember, IRA can also stand for the "Irish Republican Army" or "Internal Ring Assembly." 3. Encourage students to use abbreviations that are common to the business, industry, or trade that interests them. An Internet search for "common abbreviations" will turn up helpful industry and government sites.

# OPPORTUNITY RECOGNITION

---

## ORGANIZE THE LEARNING

### CHAPTER OBJECTIVES

- Distinguish between an idea and an opportunity.
- Recognize and evaluate business opportunities.
- Apply cost/benefit analysis that includes opportunity cost to personal and business decisions.
- Perform a SWOT analysis of a business opportunity.
- Find business-formation opportunities among people you know.

### NFTE RESOURCES

- Text pp. 42-55
- Transparencies T4-1 to T4-2
- Workbook/BLMs Chapter 4
- Entrepreneurs in Profile #20
- Test Bank Chapter 4
- A Business for the Young Entrepreneur: *Home Baked Goods*

### BUSINESS PLAN ACTIVITIES

*Workbook Business Plan Review*
Opportunity Recognition  4-1, 4-2

*Workbook/Textbook Chapter Review*
Critical Thinking 4-5 (and 2-3)

*Power Point Templates*
Bas. 3; Int. 3; Adv. 3

### SKILLS MEAN SUCCESS

*Leadership*
Thinking Skills: Problem Solving

*Technology*
New Technology and Trends

*Math*
Showing Percentages in a Pie Chart

### PREREQUISITES

- Have the students preview Chapter 4 in the textbook.
- This chapter draws upon the content of Chapters 1-3.

### VOCABULARY

benefit, cost/benefit analysis, opportunity, opportunity cost, SWOT analysis

---

## KEY QUESTION

**How do I find and evaluate opportunities for investing my time, money, and other resources?**

## SET A CONTEXT FOR LEARNING

- **Focus 1: In Your Opinion.** Ask students to jot down ideas for the In Your Opinion questions that appear in the textbook. If they need clarification, say you want them to list other ways they could spend a resource (money, time, etc.) in addition to the one given.

- **Focus 2: What If?** Pose these questions on the board or orally and ask students to respond and discuss. What really annoys you? What product or service might help?

- **Focus 3: ROI Review Problems.** Write on the board or hand out a worksheet with the following problems. It may be helpful to also write the ROI equation on the board.

| Investment | Return | ROI in % |
|---|---|---|
| $50 | $100 | ? |
| $150 | $200 | ? |
| $50 | $25 | ? |

**Answers:** 100%, 33%, -100%

- **Discussion Launcher 1: Decision about Time Use.** Describe or distribute a handout with the scenario below. Ask class to make suggestions about how Zachary should go about deciding (but *not* suggest what he should do).

  *Zachary wants to go to college. He gets good grades so he has a chance at a scholarship. Lately, however, his grades have been going down. He is invited to a party the night before a social studies test. How should he go about assessing these two alternative ways to use his time?*

- **Discussion Launcher 2: Decision about Money Use.** Remind students to consider the differences between spending and investing, as well as goal-setting, as discussed in Chapter 2. Describe or distribute a handout with the scenario below. Ask students to make suggestions about how they would go about making this decision and what choice they would make.

*You have $300. What should you do with it? Options: A. Put it in a savings account for college. B. Spend it on a new television set. C. Spend it on a class to learn computer repair. D. Buy materials for your cookie business. E. Throw a party for all your friends.*

## DEVELOP AND CLOSE THE LEARNING

- **Where Business Ideas Come From.** Challenge students with the notion that *Opportunity is the first rule of entrepreneurship. Opportunities stem from ideas. Ideas result from applying your imagination to events going on around you.* Go over the "roots of opportunity" in the textbook and ask students to provide examples of each. Choose some of the students' suggestions and brainstorm companies that have tried to address that problem, trend, etc. Referring to the Broaden Your Mind section of the text, ask students how they might increase their abilities to perceive and imagine. Invite students to share a particular personal example in which they recently have used their imagination.

- **Converting Ideas into Opportunities.** Emphasize that all ideas do not make good opportunities. Additional criteria must be met: satisfying customer needs at an affordable and profitable price, good timing, and sufficient resources/skills. Discuss transparency T4-1. Drawing upon students' suggestions above, focus on Discussion Launcher responses above, ideas in the text, or current events, choose one or two ideas to evaluate. Use the questions at the bottom of T4-1 For those ideas that seem most promising, invite students to brainstorm possible ways to convert the idea into a product or service.

- **Evaluating Opportunities: Cost/Benefit Analysis.** Use transparency T4-2 to discuss how decision-making usually involves listing and comparing the costs and benefits of each option before making a choice. Write on the board: Decision = Benefits - Costs. If benefits minus costs is a positive number, then the decision is probably a good one; if it is a negative number, then you may want to reconsider and find ways to increase benefits or reduce costs before taking action. Use several decision-making examples to make the point more concrete: present a potential decision and

have students as a whole class or in small groups brainstorm benefits and costs, then weigh them against each other. For example, buying a new outfit (benefits: look fashionable, have fun shopping, etc.; costs: $50, opportunity cost of saving or investing that $50, etc.); going to college; studying for a test; lying to a friend. You also might consider making the examples more complex, such as introducing comparative decisions: going shopping vs. studying for a test that afternoon, etc.

- **Evaluating Opportunities: Opportunity Cost.** Explain that one type of cost people often overlook is opportunity cost. Give several examples of opportunity costs for types of choices that students are likely to be faced with (for example, refer back to Focus 1 or one of the Discussion Launchers above). Emphasize that decisions should not be made in isolation, but in relation to other possibilities. **LINKS**»*Career Ed*

- **Evaluating Opportunities: SWOT Analysis.** Discuss the meanings of strength, weakness, opportunity, as discussed in the textbook. Take the example of the DJ business in the text or find other examples to illustrate the concepts. Pick one of the student business opportunity suggestions from one of the teaching activities listed above and conduct a SWOT analysis. It might be useful to construct a table on the chalkboard like the table in the text. A blank table is available in the workbook. Alternatively, you could break students into groups and have each group fill in one column of the table.

  - ○ Given the findings in this table, is the opportunity a good one?

  - ○ Should the class invest in it?

  - ○ What might be done to make the opportunity better?

- **Post-High School Opportunities Example.** To bring the ideas of the chapter together, analyze the opportunities open to students after they graduate from high school, such as joining the military, getting married, getting a job, going to college, opening a business. Use information from the textbook or other sources. Point out that each of these choices is an opportunity cost affecting the others (i.e., if you choose one, you do not choose the others). Break students into groups. Have each group do a cost/benefit and/or SWOT analysis of one of the options. Allow time for groups to present their analyses and them compare them.

- **Summary.** Return to one of the Discussion Launchers described previously and ask students to reevaluate what they thought, based on what they have learned in this lesson. Alternatively, have them brainstorm ideas for the BizTip in the Apply Cost/Benefit Analysis to Personal Decisions section in the textbook.

## ASSESS THE LEARNING

- **Vocabulary.** Have students define terms in their own words and use each term in a sentence. or assign the vocabulary activity in the workbook.

- **Key Concepts.** Questions 1-6. **Answers:** Answers will vary for all questions but could include the following: 1. Electric cars, commuter shuttle service, consulting with companies to teach them how to transfer some of their jobs to work-at-home options. 2. Grocery store, farmers market, brokering retail store fixtures, commercial real estate/leasing. 3. Airport shuttle service, earplugs, cafe or newsstand in airport. 4. Childcare, women's business clothing, convenience foods, home catering service. 5. Garbage collection service, recycling-bin manufacturing, providing recyclable packaging to other companies. 6. Private school, tutoring service, books, educational software, educational experiences such as camp or Outward Bound or arts field trips.

- **Critical Thinking.** Questions 1-2, 6. **Answers:** 1. A business opportunity is a business idea *that meets a customer need.* 2. Answers will vary but should include a description of a specific change (such as a condo building deteriorating, or people becoming afraid of burglars, or the birth of a lot of babies, etc.), a recognition of a new consumer need this change may create (such as home repair, security, or help with the baby), and at least one idea for a product or service to fill that need (such as painting services, alarm systems, or security guard service, babysitting or diapers). 6. Answers will vary but most should include a "yes" since almost everyone does at least one chore; as with Question 2, answers should display understanding of translating a skill into a customer need and then a business opportunity.

- **Additional Workbook Activities Answers.**

  **Vocabulary Activity Answers:** 1. benefits, 2. opportunity cost, 3. cost/benefit analysis, 4. SWOT analysis, 5. opportunity

  **Quiz 4** in the workbook **Answers:** 1. Answers will vary but should mention that often opportunities are hidden in problems, adversity, and challenge, and they usually require effort to bring them to fruition. 2. Answers will vary but should state a consumer need

(such as thirst or self-expression) and at least one product or service that might fill that need (such as a beverage cart or art-materials exchange service). 3. Answers will vary; better answers recognize that there would be business opportunities all along the way — from those that help build exploration vehicles and space ships early on, to oxygen-creation and lower-gravity construction later. 4. Problems your business could solve; changes in laws, situations, or trends; inventions of new products or services; beating the competition on an existing product or service; taking advantage of technological advances; or unique knowledge of people, situations or tasks. 5. Answers will vary but should include such things as meeting new people, traveling, learning something new, reading outside current interests, developing new hobbies, conversations with others, internships, etc. 6. Because the idea must satisfy a customer need, work within the current business environment, and be timely. 7. A window of opportunity closes when another business beats you to your customers. 8. He recognized a changing trend in cultural and musical tastes before others did, based on the idea that if you know ten people who are eager to buy something, there are probably ten million who would buy it if they knew about it. 9. Any of the following: recognize an opportunity; evaluate it with critical thinking; write a business plan; build a team; gather resources; decide ownership; keep satisfying consumer needs; create wealth. 10. Answers will vary but might include such concepts as keeping an idea file, journal, or other system of writing down and organizing thoughts. 11. Opportunity cost is the lost benefit of doing something else with one's time, money or other resources.

## EXTEND THE LEARNING

- **Talents into Opportunities.** Assign Critical Thinking question 3. To include students who do not believe they have artistic talent, have them return to the "can do" list they made in Focus 1 of Chapter 1 and brainstorm ways they could expand those talents into business opportunities.

- **Business Plan Practice.** Assign Critical Thinking questions 4 and/or 5.

- *Entrepreneurs in Profile.* Have students read the chapter on Jerry Yang and be prepared to discuss in class. Provide questions such as the following in advance to guide and set a purpose for reading:

○ What was Jerry's initial idea?

○ What was the customer need he sought to fill?

○ How did he connect his idea to this need?

Conduct a SWOT analysis of Jerry's situation and business idea. As a further extension, invite students to visit yahoo.com and google.com and conduct a comparative SWOT analysis of the two search engine competitors. Which should the class invest in? Why?

- **Exploring Your Community.** Have students interview an adult they know in the neighborhood as a source of information about local problems. Instruct them to follow the steps in the textbook assignment. Use the business opportunities worksheet in the workbook or ask students to answer the following questions about each idea they come up with: Is it attractive to customers? Will it work in your business environment? Is there a reasonable window of opportunity? Do you have the skills and resources to create this business? If you do not have the skills or resources, do you know someone who does and might want to help you? Do you think you can supply the product or service at a price that customers can pay and that will earn you a profit? Give students time to share what they consider their best idea with the class.

- **A Business for the Young Entrepreneur.** Have students research the types of foods available around your school. What snacks or baked goods might be a good opportunity to see at your school? Have students research online the requirements for food handling and food service in your city.

- **Internet Idea Search.** Split students into teams. Instruct each to use Internet search engines, such aswsj.com, or other online business or news magazines, to look for ideas related to one of the following: problems; new laws; trends; inventions; technological advances; new knowledge. Instruct each team to pick one of the ideas and brainstorm ways to turn it into a business opportunity. Have each team create a poster or slide presentation to share its creation with the class.

- **Comparison of ROI, Cost/Benefit Analysis, and SWOT Analysis.** Briefly review ROI from Chapter 3. Discuss with students how these three concepts are ways of evaluating businesses and business opportunities. As a class, make a list of ways in which they are both similar and different, and what each analysis method's strengths and weaknesses are. For example, ROI usually focuses on initial investment or start-up costs, whereas cost/benefit analysis often includes operating and opportunity costs; ROI seems the most financially/quantitatively oriented whereas SWOT seems the most descriptively/qualitatively oriented and includes more non-financial information; SWOT includes the most information about environmental (outside factors) such as competitors and the general business environment. **LINKS** ))·*Critical Thinking*

## BUILD ACADEMIC AND LIFE-SKILL PROFICIENCIES

### *Skills Mean Success* Answers

**Leadership.** Help students to select a problem that is practical and realistic. Allow them to work in groups for brainstorming. If the problem is outside the scope of what can be implemented in the classroom, allow the class to stop at Step 4, as long as plans have been written for how solutions will be implemented. Emphasize that action plans should

○ Take no more than one page.

○ Include an explanation of the problem and rationale for the solution.

○ Indicate the resources, tools, or people that will be needed to implement the solution.

○ Identify any issues or barriers that will need to be considered and how they can be managed.

○ Provide a schedule/timeline of events.

○ Identify the steps (contingency plans) to be taken if the solution does not work.

**Technology.** 1.d. 2.a. 3.b. 4.c. For an extension activity, have the students list "Advantages/Disadvantages" for each innovation. Encourage students to research one of these advancements and write a short profile of how it led to the development of other products and innovations.

**Math.** 1. $12,500 (25,000 × .50) 2. $6,250 (25,000 × .25) 3. $5,000 (25,000 × .20) 4. $1,250 (25,000 × .05) To figure the percentage of the profits, convert the percentage of ownership to a decimal and multiply it by total profit. Students' pie charts should look like the following:

# CHARACTERISTICS OF THE SUCCESSFUL ENTREPRENEUR

## ORGANIZE THE LEARNING

### CHAPTER OBJECTIVES

- Describe the characteristics of successful entrepreneurs.
- Identify your own characteristics.
- Develop characteristics that will help you in business.
- Train yourself to think positively.

### NFTE RESOURCES

- Vocabulary
- Text pp. 56-67
- Transparencies T5-1 to T5-3
- Workbook/BLMs Chapter 5
- Entrepreneurs in Profile #18
- Test Bank Chapter 5
- BizTech Unit 1
- A Business for the Young Entrepreneur: *Green Acres Family Farm, Jason Heki, Johnston, Iowa*

### BUSINESS PLAN ACTIVITIES

*Workbook Business Plan Review*
Core Beliefs 5-1, 5-2

*Workbook/Textbook Chapter Review*
Key Concepts 2, 5

### SKILLS MEAN SUCCESS

*Leadership*
Recognizing Strengths: Reflecting on Interests and Talents;
Self-Confidence: Learning Self-Improvement

*English*
Writing for Social Interaction:
Using Appropriate Language and Style

*English*
Reading for Information and Understanding: Selecting Relevant Information

### PREREQUISITES

- Preview Chapter 5 in the textbook.
- This chapter assumes that the class has completed Chapter 1.

### VOCABULARY

core belief, optimist, self-esteem

## KEY QUESTION

**What do I need to develop in myself to be more successful?**

## PREPARE FOR LEARNING

- **Guest Speaker:** If you plan to invite guest entrepreneurs to visit the class — an Extend the Learning activity — remember to make arrangements in advance.

## SET A CONTEXT FOR LEARNING

- **Focus 1: First Thoughts.** Pose this question to the class: When something in your life does not go the way you would like, what is the first thought that crosses your mind?
- **Focus 2: Entrepreneurs You Know.** Have students list people they know who own their own businesses, or have in the past.
- **Discussion Launcher: Korda Quote.** Show the Michael Korda quote at the bottom of transparency

T5-1 and ask students to describe how this idea could apply to them and their success in life. Alternatively, write the quote on the board or read it aloud: "In order to succeed we must first believe that we can." To extend the discussion, ask if students agree or disagree with this statement. Have students who agree (or disagree) work together to present their reasons.

## DEVELOP AND CLOSE THE LEARNING

- **Characteristics of a Successful Entrepreneur.** Discuss the characteristics on transparency T5-2. Have students suggest concrete examples or situations in which a person might express each characteristic. Ask students individually to rank the three characteristics they believe are most important for entrepreneurial success. Take a poll to determine which seem to be the most important to the class collectively. As an extension, have them self-assess themselves in class using transparency T5-3 (also see below in Assess the Learning) and compare their answers in small groups. Ask them to determine how their groups might combine their members' characteristics to be even more successful as a team than each student might be alone.

- **Positive Mental Attitude.** Discuss transparency T5-1. Ask students what they should do when things aren't going their way. Divide the class and the list of quotes in the textbook into roughly five groups. Assign a quote group to each student group. Each group's goal is to choose three quotes and come up with a situation or example in a teenager's life that illustrates the quote. **LINKS**»*Health*

- **The Role of Adversity and Challenge.** Review from Chapters 1 and 3 how entrepreneurs turn problems into opportunities. In this way, past adversities or challenges can be turned into strengths and positive character traits. Ask students to brainstorm problems they, their friends or their families have encountered that they choose to share, or situations they've heard about. It may be helpful to give a few examples first. (Expect answers to vary widely: bad grades, body-image problems, immigration, living in a tough neighborhood, teen pregnancy, poverty, hurt feelings, betrayal by a friend, boy/girlfriend breakup, drug use, violence, abuse, learning disabilities.) How might these adversities and challenges be turned into positive characteristics? (Answers should relate to increasing coping/resilience, building skills and confidence through facing and overcoming these obstacles, drive and perseverance to get through hard times, learning about oneself, becoming more understanding or empathic towards others, creating a vision of better times/situations.) Challenge class: So why is it good not to give up on yourself when times are hard?

- **Weight Problem Example.** Use the situation in Exploring Your Community question 3 as an in-class example. How might each of the entrepreneurial characteristics, as well as positive mental attitude, help a person lose unwanted weight? How might this national weight/obesity problem translate into opportunity for an entrepreneur? What types of businesses have been opened to help solve this problem? What other types of businesses might be tried?

- **Company Core Beliefs.** Explain that individuals are not the only ones that live by core beliefs, mottos, or inspiring statements; businesses do too. Often these core beliefs are found in corporate mission statements. Have students research online for mission statements from well-known companies such as Disney, McDonald's, etc. Also, they might ask local business owners for their mission statements. From

these mission statements, discuss what students think the companies' core beliefs are.

- **Summary.** Invite students to share how they think entrepreneurial characteristics, positive mental attitude, optimism, high self-esteem, and success go together and reinforce each other.

## ASSESS THE LEARNING

- **Vocabulary.** Have students define terms in their own words and use each in a sentence. In addition or alternatively, students could give examples from their own lives when they exemplify "optimist" and "self-esteem." If you are using the workbook, assign the vocabulary activity provided.

- **Key Concepts.** Questions 1 and/or 4. **Answers:** 1. Answers will vary but should show understanding of the meaning of Hill's statement, make a clear statement of agreement or disagreement, and provide clear reasons from the student's own life, the text, or other sources. 4. Answers will vary but should involve describing tips, tasks, activities, or challenges that would improve the students' view of themselves, increase optimism about the future, and self-regulate their thoughts to keep away negativity.

- **Critical Thinking.** Questions 2-4. **Answers:** 2. Answers will vary but should show a critical self-awareness. 3. Self-esteem involves how a person values him/herself; high self-esteem goes with a positive mental attitude; students should also include an evaluation of their own self-esteem. 4. A positive mental attitude because it fosters optimism and finding opportunities where others see only problems or threats.

- **Writing Practice.** Assign Key Concepts question 3 or Critical Thinking question 5.

- **Additional Workbook Activities Answers.**

  **Vocabulary Activity Answers:** Students' answers should be complete sentences that use the vocabulary words correctly. Sentences should demonstrate an understanding and correct usage of the terms. Example: Leaving a steady job to start my own business was a risky thing to do, but with courage, optimism, and perseverance, I was able to conquer my fears and stay focused on success.

  **Quiz 5** in the workbook. **Answers:** 1. b. 2. c. 3. d. 4. a. 5. Answers will vary but should incorporate the idea that business ownership/leadership involves problems, setbacks, and even failures; entrepreneurs must be able to see the bright side of these challenges to persevere and succeed. 6. Answers will vary but should include the importance of gaining the trust of customers and suppliers so they will continue to do business with you; the free enterprise and the free-market system depend on honest communication between buyer and seller to maintain market efficiency. 7-11. Any but "b" could be included. 12. He made up self-motivating phrases and repeated these phrases to himself, and he set aside "creative thinking time." 13. They can make you feel powerless and depressed, sap energy, increase stress, and affect your heart. 14. Answers will vary but should focus on the role of thinking positively to build success and high self-esteem.

- **Entrepreneur Characteristics Self-Assessment.** Assign Critical Thinking question 1 or the workbook as homework, or use transparency T5-3 as an in-class assessment. Students could also take the quiz (Chapter 21) in *Entrepreneurs in Profile*.

## EXTEND THE LEARNING

- **Personal Motto.** Assign Key Concepts question 5. Students may choose a quote from the list in the text or from another source, or make one up themselves. Make sure that, if they quote someone else, they give proper credit. Hold a poster party so students can share their. Alternatively, compile the quotes on a sheet that can be posted or distributed school wide to encourage other students to think positively. This activity also could be combined with Exploring Your Community question 1.

- *Entrepreneurs in Profile.* Have students read the chapter on Oprah Winfrey and be prepared to discuss in class. Types of questions to include: What successful entrepreneurial characteristics apply to Oprah? How did she demonstrate positive mental attitude? What role did adversity/challenge play? How has her personal attitude been translated into her company's core beliefs?

- **Business Plan Practice.** Assign Key Concepts question 2.

- **BizTech.** Assign Unit 1.

- **A Business for the Young Entrepreneur.** Have students read about Green Acres Family Farm. Ask: How does Jason think like a successful entrepreneur? What opportunities did he recognize?

- **Directing Your Energy.** Review goal setting and emphasize that a key part of success in life involves directing your energy and strengths toward worth-

while goals. How might the ideas on goal setting from previous chapters (rate of return and goal-setting, cost-benefit analysis and SWOT analysis) be used to develop entrepreneurial characteristics toward better reaching those goals? If students created goal sheets in Chapter 3, have them revisit these goals, pick one, and write a short essay or slide presentation explaining how one or more of the entrepreneurial characteristics would be helpful in attaining that goal.

- **Exploration.** Assign as appropriate to individual student's needs and interests Questions 1 (research and presentation), 2 (cooperative learning and interviewing), or 3 (advertising research).

- **Positive Cartoon or Comic Strip.** Have students draw a cartoon or comic strip that exemplifies a situation in which one of the entrepreneurial characteristics, or positive mental attitude, plays a central role. Students who lack confidence in their own drawing skills could perform the activity on a computer using clip art and speech balloons. Hang these cartoons around the room.

- **Quotation Search Race.** See which pairs or small groups of students can most quickly locate all the quotes in the textbook that:
  - recognize taking advantage of opportunity.
  - deal with dreams or aspirations.
  - deal with overcoming adversity.

  *An alternative format might be to see which group can find the most in each category in a given time frame (for example, 3-5 minutes).*

- **Mental Attitude Journal.** Tell students to notice and record times over the next week in which they think either optimistically or pessimistically. They should record the date, time, situation and what they thought. At the end of the week, they will tally the number of optimistic vs. pessimistic situations—which is higher? In addition, do they see any patterns in the timing or types of situations in which they tend to think optimistically vs. pessimistically? What might they do to turn around their pessimistic thinking to be more positive? They could create a short essay, poster, or slide presentation to present their findings. **LINKS**»*Health*

- **Guest Speaker Panel.** Invite several local entrepreneurs to serve as panel members for a discussion of the benefits and challenges of being an entrepreneur. Consider inviting an entrepreneur from each type of business (manufacturing, wholesale, retail, service). Try to match the demographic characteristics of the panel to your class (e.g., women, African-Americans, Hispanics, Asians, etc.) and to include entrepreneurs from different age groups. Prep the panel members to be able to give a brief overview of their respective businesses (product/service description, type of business, when started, annual sales, etc.) and discuss why they became entrepreneurs, what they see as the main benefits of entrepreneurship, what their greatest challenges have been, what their goals are, etc. Have students come up with lists of additional questions before the speakers arrive.

## BUILD ACADEMIC AND LIFE-SKILL PROFICIENCIES

### *Skills Mean Success* Answers

**Leadership.** Remind students that no one possesses all these characteristics. Everyone needs to develop and improve certain traits. The purpose of this activity is to help students recognize their strengths and identify areas for self-improvement. The activity requires an honest evaluation of self. For that reason, students should work independently and not be required to share their work with classmates.

This process will also provide an opportunity to draw a classmate's name out of a hat and fill out the same question grid — or at least the "strengths" portion — for the name drawn. For this to be a useful activity and in order to protect feelings, only students who choose to participate should have their names put into the draw, no one should share the drawn name, and the filled-out question grid should be turned in to the teacher, who will give it back to the individual. While the rating is only one person's opinion, it may be interesting for students to see how others perceive them.

**English (Writing).** Encourage the students to be creative and allow them to use any context for their hypothetical encouragement — school, sports, hobbies, work, etc. Their responses should focus on positive thoughts, abilities, optimism, and genuinely felt and tactful suggestions for improvement. Responses should *not* be boastful or critical of others. If necessary, remind students that arrogance, egotism, and aggressiveness are not positive characteristics.

**English (Reading).** Students should recognize that even extremely successful people have had to draw on the power of positive thinking to achieve their goals and overcome hardships. After all, Michael Jordan was cut from his high school basketball team! If time allows, encourage students to pose the three questions from the text to successful people in your community — either in brief informational interviews or in business letters. Alternatively, invite a local businessperson to your class to speak about the importance of optimism, positive attitude, and core beliefs.
**LINKS**》·*Health/Wellness*

*("LINKS" icons appear throughout the Teacher's Edition to indicate opportunities for intergrating the NFTE curriculum with other specific subjects, as time and interest permit. These optional "invitations" are, by no means, the only opportunities for cross-curricular learning in the program, but are examples of the many ways that the NFTE curriculum can be leveraged to enhance students' learning experiences and to make connections across the curriculum. "LINKS" may also provide opportunities to address individual students' talents and interests to personalize the learning and enhance students' self-esteem.)*

CHAPTER **6**

# SUPPLY AND DEMAND:
## *How Free Enterprise Works*

## ORGANIZE THE LEARNING

### CHAPTER OBJECTIVES

- Compare and contrast free-market with command economies.
- Explain the relationship between supply, demand, and price.
- Describe how competition keeps prices down and quality high.
- Discuss monopoly's effect on price and quality.
- Use a supply-and-demand graph.

### NFTE RESOURCES

- Text pp. 68-79
- Transparencies T6-1 to T6-3
- Workbook/BLMs Chapter 6
- Entrepreneurs in Profile #1
- Test Bank Chapter 6
- A Business for the Young Entrepreneur: *Frank Reginald Melchor: Frank's Fruit Baskets and Snacks*

### BUSINESS PLAN ACTIVITIES

*Workbook Business Plan Review*
Supply and Demand  6-1, 6-2

*Workbook/Textbook Chapter Review*
Critical Thinking 2

### SKILLS MEAN SUCCESS

*Math*
Measurement and Data: Displaying Data in Line Graphs

*Technology*
Multimedia Presentations: Using Graphics

*English*
Reading for Information and Understanding: Getting Meaning

### PREREQUISITES

- Students should preview Chapter 6 in the textbook.
- Chapters 1-3 will be important background for this chapter.

### VOCABULARY

capitalism, command economy, competition, demand, free enterprise system, market clearing price, monopoly, supply

## KEY QUESTION

**How do entrepreneurs decide what prices to charge?**

## SET A CONTEXT FOR LEARNING

- **Focus 1: Who Decides What We Pay?** Pose the question: Who decides what price you pay for: bus or subway fare? a movie ticket? CDs? bananas? (Or make your own list.) Have students share and compare their answers.

- **Focus 2: How Much Would You Pay?** Have the students consider and discuss the following. What is the *maximum* (in whole dollars) you would you pay for: a CD? a winter coat? a lipstick? a basketball? a year of college? (Or make your own list.) Have students share and compare their answers and keep track of them on the board or on an overhead.

- **Discussion Launcher: Free Enterprise.** Review from Chapter 1 the expression "free enterprise." Does free means "anything goes"? Can a person charge

whatever s/he wants for her product or service? Why or why not? Steer students toward realizing that the buyer, as well as the seller, has a say in pricing. **LINKS**»*Economics*

## DEVELOP AND CLOSE THE LEARNING

- **Price Variability.** Using newspapers or magazines, let students find examples of prices in different product categories: computers, cell phone service, clothing, etc. Ask them to speculate why prices among companies that sell similar products can be so different. (Answers should relate to differences in the products themselves, sales/promotions, focus on different types of customers, etc.) Ask: If you were going to open a business in one of these product categories, how would you go about deciding how to set the initial price?

- **Command vs. Free-Market Economy.** Contrast a command economy (government or some other group owns or controls all businesses, sets prices, decides who works and at what jobs and wages) with a free-market economic structure. Give examples of countries with each type of system. Explain that no economy is purely command or free market: China and Cuba allow some private trading, and U.S. prices are affected by such government decisions as interest rates, industry regulation (airlines, agriculture, broadcasting), and monopoly laws. Describe how a free-market economy is considered more efficient because it better uses the resources available to meet buyers' needs. Why might a command economy be less efficient? (Answers should relate to lack of feedback from buyers to tell sellers what they want/need; corruption; fewer incentives for independent business owners to work hard, be efficient and get ahead; government — or other single, all-powerful decision-maker — simply might make bad choices.)

- **Monopoly vs. Competition.** Ask students to brainstorm industries or products where there is only *one* supplier. (Answers might include postage stamps, currency, city transit authorities, utilities, really innovative products; manufacturers of parts for old machines.) Students may need a clue or two, since outright monopolies are rare in the U.S. Have students work alone or in pairs to make a list of which products/industries listed are really monopolies and to decide why there are few monopolies in a free market. (Answers should relate to government regulations against it, competition develops, consumer demand for lower prices or better quality.) Present examples of monopoly vs. competitive situation. For example, let's say only one grocer in town sells apples and sets her price at 50 cents. What happens when another grocer opens and sells apples at 45 cents? Or 35 cents? Or a third grocer enters the apple market at 45 cents but the apples are organic? What if the first grocer has to pay 37 cents for each apple? Allow students to arrive at the concept of competition—businesses entering and leaving a particular market and trying to persuade buyers to buy from them instead of from others. Competition might be thought of as how suppliers "talk" to each other about setting prices in a product category. Why does an entrepreneur need to watch what competitors are doing? (Probably answers will relate to the fact that *buyers* are paying attention to competitors to get the best price/quality/value.) As a summary, show transparency T6-1. **LINKS** *Economics*

- **Supply & Demand Concepts.** Discuss transparency T6-2. Ask students for factors that might affect supply, emphasizing that *supply* is a decision made collectively by *sellers*. (Answers should relate to

monopoly, competitors' prices, cost of raw materials or processing, seasonality of product, government regulations.) Ask students for factors that might affect demand, emphasizing that *demand* is a decision made collectively by *buyers*. (e.g., changing tastes, changing ability to pay, more people becoming aware of the product). Remind students (as they read in Chapter 4) about the need for entrepreneurs to consider customer needs in starting a business — "demand" is a more formal business concept for thinking about this idea.

- **Supply & Demand Graphs.** Use the examples in the text—or other examples to suit—to show how prices relate to quantity. Several examples may be necessary. Use the information from Focus 2 above to build supply and demand graphs for one or more of the products. For example, poll the class to see how many students would buy a CD for $15, $12, $9, etc. and how many would sell a CD for those same prices. Draw the graph on the board. Use the graph to show how demand goes down (the slope is negative) because people usually buy less at higher prices, and how supply goes up (the slope is positive) because people usually sell more at higher prices. As a summary, show transparency T6-3 and discuss the laws of supply and demand. Note: this would be an excellent opportunity to invite a colleague from the math department to assist in team teaching or to provide coaching.

- **Market Clearing Price.** Use the textbook examples or the student data generated in the previous activity to solicit what happens at the point where the demand and supply lines intersect. The "market clearing price" is the price at which buyers collectively want and sellers collectively are willing to produce the same quantity of product. Ask students why this is the price at which an industry both aspires to be (if it's not there) and settles at (in the long term) — e.g., 1. If the price is too low, buyers want more than sellers can produce and get frustrated. 2. If the price is too high, buyers won't buy enough product and there may be a lot left over that will go to waste. Give examples of each non-ideal case, such as long lines for the latest Game Boy release, or sold-out toys during the first sale of the holiday season, for too-low a price, and the rotting fruit or "bargain bin" books for too-high a price. Ask: If you opened a business, how would you get clues about what the market clearing price is? (Answers should relate to looking at competitors' prices, government regulations for the industry, trial-and-error price setting, to see how many buyers buy at different prices.) **LINKS** *Economics*

- **Summary.** Have the students work in pairs and make lists of factors that might cause prices to go up (higher demand, shortages/lower supply, monopoly sets higher prices) or go down (lower demand, higher supply, competition, monopoly lowers prices).

## ASSESS THE LEARNING

- **Vocabulary.** Have students define and use each term in a sentence.

- **Key Concepts.** Questions 1-4. **Answers:** 1. Price would decline due to low demand because it's colder. 2. Price would go down because no one would need gasoline. 3. Fewer people would sell gasoline because the lack of demand would mean prices were too low for some suppliers to make a profit. 4. With no competition, supply can be limited so prices can be raised; no one can set a lower price because s/he cannot sell the product or service under a monopoly system. Monopolies are allowed in the U.S. only in rare circumstances; the government and customer demand encourage competition. Groups of competing companies, however, may try to agree to keep prices artificially high, which is illegal if discovered.

- **Critical Thinking.** Questions 1-2 combined. **Answers:** 1 & 2. Answers will vary but should include that the quantity students will buy depends on the price, but price is more important for some types of products (such as those that have many competitors) and less important for others (such as necessities: heat, gasoline, transportation, utilities, food). More sophisticated answers might notice that the demand-curve slope for the product where price makes a big difference should be flatter and the demand curve slope for the product where the price makes less difference should be steeper.

- **Writing Practice.** Assign Critical Thinking question 3.

- **Additional Workbook Activities Answers.**

  **Vocabulary Activity Answers:** 1. demand, 2. supply, 3. market clearing price, 4. monopoly, 5. free enterprise system; capitalism, 6. command economy, 7. competition.

  **Quiz 6** in the workbook. **Answers:** 1. Amount of a product or service made available by sellers at different prices. 2. Amount of a product or service buyers are willing and able to buy. 3. Answers will vary but should include reference to most people being less likely to invest because there would be lower demand for ice cream in such a cold climate. 4. The price at which supply quantity equals demand quan-

tity. 5. More. 6. More. 7. Refer to the supply and demand graph on the following page. The market clearing price is where the lines intersect. 8. Price will be lowered; they will go on sale. 9. a.

- **Math Word Problem.** Provide a handout or give verbal instructions to have students solve this problem: T-shirt vendors at the school fair will sell 50 T-shirts at $20, 40 at $17, 30 at $14, 20 at $11. Students are willing and have the funds to buy 10 T-shirts at $20, 20 at $17, 30 at $14, 40 at $11, and 50 at $8. Have students build a supply-and-demand graph to determine the market clearing price and how many T-shirts will be bought and sold at the fair. **Answer:** 30 T-shirts will be sold at $14 each.

## EXTEND THE LEARNING

- **A Business for the Young Entrepreneur.** Assign Key Concepts question 5 to give students practice in applying supply and demand concepts. **Answer:** Frank finds out what products students want so he can monitor demand; he also buys at low prices to keep his costs down so he can charge competitively lower prices than the vending machines so that students will buy from him.

- ***Entrepreneurs in Profile.*** Have students read the chapter about Jeff Bezos and Amazon.com. If possible, visit the Web site. Provide this question to guide their reading:

  ○ In what ways did Jeff use the concepts of supply and demand to start and build his business?

- **Business Plan Practice.** Assign Critical Thinking question 2. **Answer:** Responses will vary but should include reference to "buyer factors" for demand (tastes, disposable income, number of buyers, how many of a product each buyer buys/uses in a given time period, seasonality, etc.) and "seller factors" for supply (cost and availability of raw materials, weather or seasonality, number of competitors, etc.) as discussed in class.

- **Exploration.** Have students research a product's prices across retail outlets as described in the text.

- **Monopoly in the U.S.** Have students individually or in pairs or groups research via the Internet and report (poster, slide show, etc.) on the U.S. government's investigation of Microsoft. Explain the argument the government gave that Microsoft was a monopoly? What was the argument Microsoft gave that it wasn't? Was the decision a good or bad one? Why?

## BUILD ACADEMIC AND LIFE-SKILL PROFICIENCIES

### *Skills Mean Success* Answers

**Technology.** Encourage students to experiment with spreadsheet and presentation software to create different types of graphs. Programs like PowerPoint and Excel contain useful "Help" features with detailed instructions for creating charts, tables, and graphs.

**Math.** This exercise is a simplified version of a supply-and-demand graph. The goal is to give students experience with displaying data in line graphs. The market clearing price (the point at which the lines should intersect) is $3. The quantity exchanged at this price is three loaves of bread. Check students' graphs to be sure they have labeled the axes and plotted the points correctly.

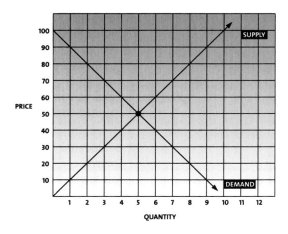

**English.** 1. government. 2. free-market system. 3. down, lower. 4. increases, goes up. 5. market clearing price. 6. down, lower. 7. improves, increases, goes up. 8. monopoly. 9. monopoly; supplier. For this exercise, students should be allowed to use their books. Some of these terms probably were unfamiliar to students before taking this course. They should use the textbook to locate the relevant passages, re-read them, and decipher any words they don't understand, to answer the questions.

## Meeting Individual Learning Needs

*(From time to time, make a point of reaching out to individual students or groups of students whose learning could be enhanced through some additional, customized activities. For example, consider students who*

1. *Might need extra help understanding a concept.*
2. *Are not native speakers of English.*
3. *Have particular hobbies and interests that could be leveraged for learning.*
4. *Need additional challenges.*

*Activities similar to the following could be used or adapted to help meet individual learning needs.)*

**Reteaching/reinforcing the concept of product demand.** Have students who are having difficulty understanding the chapter's main concepts choose a product and list examples of what might make demand for it increase and decrease.

**ESL learners.** Have students use a dictionary or thesaurus to write synonyms and antonyms for the following: *demand, supply, command, efficient, behavior, market, competition* or any other vocabulary from the chapter that might be new to them. Some of them might enjoy creating and swapping crossword puzzles based on the vocabulary.

**Fine Arts Interpretations.** What does the Milton Friedman quote at the beginning of the text chapter mean? Some students may wish to use pictures, cartoons, newspaper headlines, or drawings to create a collage that interprets Friedman's famous saying. **LINKS**»*Fine Arts*

**Further Investigations in Economics.** Have students who display an interest in economics research and describe what the following expressions mean with respect to supply and demand: creative destruction, elastic/inelastic demand, supply-demand equilibrium, profit motive, scarcity, factors of production.

### CHAPTER 7

# INVENTIONS AND PRODUCT DEVELOPMENT

## ORGANIZE THE LEARNING

### CHAPTER OBJECTIVES

- Develop your creativity.
- Practice lateral thinking.
- Use "practical daydreaming" to invent new products.
- Describe the five steps of developing a product.
- Explore the contributions of minority and women inventors.

### NFTE RESOURCES

- Text pp. 80-93
- Transparencies T7-1 to T7-3, T42-1
- Workbook/BLMs Chapter 7
- Entrepreneurs in Profile #8
- Test Bank Chapter 7

### BUSINESS PLAN ACTIVITIES

*Workbook Business Plan Review*
Product Development 7-1

*Workbook/Textbook Chapter Review*
Critical Thinking 4

### SKILLS MEAN SUCCESS

*English*
Writing for Information and Understanding: Completing Forms

*Leadership*
Understanding Diversity

*English and Technology*
Reading and Writing for Information: Using Text Features and Online Research. Writing for Social Interaction: Communicating via Letters and E-mail.

### PREREQUISITES

- Students should have read Chapter 7 in the textbook.
- Chapter 4 informs this chapter.

### VOCABULARY

creativity, invention, lateral thinking, patent, prototype, vertical thinking

*Other suggested words to know:*
assumption, model

## KEY QUESTION

**How does an innovative idea become a new product?**

## PREPARE FOR LEARNING

- **Solicit Prizes for the Invention Contest.** If you will be conducting the Invention Contest in Assess (or Extend) the Learning, create or buy certificates, or ask local businesses to donate small items to be given as prizes, such as movie tickets, cash, CDs, video games, food coupons, etc.

- **Guest Inventor.** If you plan to invite a guest inventor to speak with the class during Extend the Learning, make arrangements now – perhaps through a local invention membership organization.

## SET A CONTEXT FOR LEARNING

- **Focus 1: Interests to Inventions.** Have students in pairs discuss In Your Opinion question 1.

- **Focus 2: Invention Recognition.** Ask students individually to make lists of all the inventions they have used in the last two days that have made their lives easier or better.

- **Discussion Launcher 1: I Wish....** Write this sentence on the board or overhead and ask students to fill in the blanks: "I wish someone would make a _____ that _____ ."

- **Discussion Launcher 2: Who Are Inventors?** Ask students to work in pairs to brainstorm all the inventors they can think of and what they invented.

## DEVELOP AND CLOSE THE LEARNING

- **Creativity.** Ask the class to define "creativity." (Answers will relate to using your imagination, making something new, artists.) How is creativity used in entrepreneurship, especially compared to other fields, such as fine art? (Answers will relate that entrepreneurs must keep customers in mind since their new products must fill a need; their creativity is less about self-expression and more about solving problems in a practical and clever way.) Refer to Discussion Launcher 1 above for examples of identifying potential needs that entrepreneurs could meet; if enough people wish for the same thing, a market is created. Ask: What are ways to improve your creativity? Encourage them to share real-life examples of each way. (Answers could include making new associations between ideas and things that are usually thought of as separate, challenging beliefs, learning something new, talking to people different from us, reading materials outside our current interests, brainstorming/free thinking.) Encouraging students to think back across the chapters you've covered so far, ask: *Why* be creative? (Expect answers to include staying ahead of competitors, because the world changes, people like new things, innovative products often can be sold at higher prices, it stimulates the economy.) **Note:** If you use the nine-dot puzzle in the textbook as an example or activity, the correct answer will be: *Start at the upper left corner and draw a vertical line down through all three points; but go beyond the third point until you can draw a 45 degree line up through the middle point in the bottom row and the last point in the second row and draw that line beyond the point until you can draw a horizontal line left through the top row of points; when your pencil is on the upper left point again, draw a 45 degree line down through the puzzle's middle point and the last point in the bottom row.* (The assumption challenged is that you have to stay within the "boundary" of the points.)

- **Inventions.** The outcome of creativity is invention. Discuss the invention process using transparencies T7-1 and T7-2 as well as the step-by-step product development description in the textbook. Using the examples in the textbook or from *Entrepreneurs in Profile*, relate stories about how inventions came about. Other examples you might use:

  ○ *Toothpick.* Invented in 1869 by Charles Forster, who noticed while traveling in Brazil that Brazilians picked their teeth with slivers of wood whittled from orange trees. Foster invented a machine to produce wooden toothpicks but no one was interested. So he hired fashionable and successful young men to ask loudly for disposable toothpicks in expensive Boston restaurants. Soon embarrassed restaurant owners were calling in with orders.

  ○ *Potato chip.* Invented in 1853 by George Crum, a Native American cook at a restaurant in Saratoga Springs, New York. A customer kept complaining that the fried potatoes were too thick. Crum finally cut an order so thin that they couldn't even be eaten with a fork. Crum eventually sold the recipe to Herman Lay, who started Lay's Potato Chips.

  ○ Other famous inventions that are easy to research online include the Slinky, Silly Putty, Post-It Notes, Band-Aids, the Yo-Yo, and the Frisbee.

- **Patents.** Challenge students: If you show someone your wonderful product idea, what's to stop them from stealing it and producing it themselves? Discuss how the U.S. has laws to prevent one person profiting from another's idea, but the inventor must register the invention with the government. Discuss transparency T42-1 about the patent process.

- **Inventors.** Emphasize that *anyone* can become an inventor. Many people from all walks of life have invented important products. Mention how often invention has been a path to economic opportunity and success for people who were denied more common paths, such as women and minorities. Discuss transparency T7-3 for examples. Have each student pick one inventor from the text that s/he found particularly interesting and share with other students in small groups: Why did you find that inventor/invention particularly interesting? What difference did this person make in the lives of others? What else would you like to know if you could ask the inventor a question? **LINKS**»*History*

- **Summary.** Have students write in their notebook or on a piece of paper to keep and refer to later: How are you creative? List three ways you could develop that creativity further.

## ASSESS THE LEARNING

- **Vocabulary.** Have students define the key terms and use each in a sentence, or complete the vocabulary activity in the workbook.

- **Key Concepts.** Questions 1-3. **Answers:** 1. A prototype is an exact model of an invention made by the actual manufacturing process; it is useful as a "reality check" to help refine the product, work out problems in the design or manufacturing, make sure it can be built profitably, and to get feedback from others. To find a manufacturer, check the Thomas Register. 2. Because they are creative and bring to people's attention new perspectives and products, like artists do; but unlike artists, their products must consider the consumer's perspective as well as their own. 3. Creativity can be developed through lateral thinking, challenging assumptions, learning new skills, learning from and observing others different from you, practical daydreaming, changing perspective, not accepting the "typical" way to solve a problem as the "only" way to solve it.

- **Critical Thinking.** Question 3. **Answer:** 3. Answers will vary but should be positive: everyone has creativity that can be developed. Answers should include a clear description of how students are creative, plus ideas from the chapter — such as lateral thinking, challenging assumptions, learning something new — that could be used to enhance creativity. See also notes for Critical Thinking question 4 in Extend the Learning.

- **Additional Workbook Activities Answers.**

   **Vocabulary Activity Answers:** 1. a, 2. b, 3. c, 4. b, 5. b, 6. c.

   **Quiz 7** in the workbook. **Answers:** 1. Answers will vary but should clearly agree or disagree and provide solid reasons. For example, "agreement" reasoning might include that dreaming provides motivation and energy to keep developing; "disagreement" reasons point out that many people give up their dreams and still live, work, raise a family and are happy. 2. A patent legally protects an inventor's exclusive rights to make, promote, and profit from the invention for a prescribed period of time. 3. Answers will vary but should correspond to the stories given in class. 4-6. Answers will vary. 7. Answers will vary but should come from the text, class discussion, or other known sources. 8. The inventor can lose the right to exclusively profit from the invention because other people can legally produce or make use of it. 9. By applying to the U.S. Patent Office with a drawing and detailed description of the invention, a completed Declaration for Patent Application, a statement that the applicant is the original inventor, and a filing fee. 10. Answers will vary, but should include some of the methods given in the text, such as lateral thinking, challenging assumptions, learning new skills, learning from and observing others different from you, practical daydreaming, changing perspective, not accepting the "typical" way to solve a problem as the "only" way to solve it.

- **Research and Writing Practice.** Assign In Your Opinion question 4 or Critical Thinking question 2. Alternatively, students could create a slide presentation or poster of their findings.

- **Invention Contest.** See full description below in Extend the Learning. This activity could be used as a performance appraisal of how well students not only understand but can apply the key ideas of the chapter. In addition, you could print from the U.S. Patent Office Web site (www.uspto.gov/web/forms) a copy of the patent application cover sheet (or create a simplified version of it) to have students partially complete as practice for filling out forms. The assessment, then, will consist of a mock patent application including the cover sheet, description/specification, and drawing.

## EXTEND THE LEARNING

- **Prototyping Debate.** Use In Your Opinion question 3 to stage a debate about the pros and cons of prototyping an invention. Divide the class in half, with each team taking one side of the argument. Give students time to develop their arguments from the text or other sources. Have each side present, then give teams additional time to develop a rebuttal to the other team's argument and present again. Hold a reflective discussion on the debate. Make sure students brought out the key points of the chapter. For example, the main advantages of prototyping are that it helps work out the kinks of the product and manufacturing process, and it can be tested on potential customers before the full costs of setting up manufacturing facilities and systems are realized — before the product goes to market. The main disadvantages are that it is an expensive up-front cost and other people might steal your idea if you don't protect it — so prototyping entails risk.

- **Invention Contest.** Invite students to create their own inventions. Assign Critical Thinking question 1. Students should write a brief but clear description of the invention that includes: a name, how it works, what it's made of (materials, processes, etc.), whom it would help, and the consumer need it fills. In addition, students should either draw a sketch or create a small model of the invention. Stress to students that an invention will not be judged on the artistic merit of the illustration or model but that any illustrations provided should be as clear as possible in showing what the invention is and does. Hold an Invention Fair, with inventions placed on desks for other students to see. Students might vote for the inventions they think are the best. Invite other teachers and administrators to view and vote as well. (Doing so would have the useful and strategic added benefit of showcasing and gaining support for the NFTE curriculum.) Aim to have one winner for, say, every ten students. **LINKS**»*Fine Arts*

- ***Entrepreneurs in Profile.*** Ask students to read the chapter on King Gillette and be prepared to discuss in class. Types of questions to consider as they read should include: What processes did Gillette go through to make money from his idea? What need(s) did his razor fill? What were obstacles along the way to success and how did he overcome them (or not)? Who or which events helped him along the way, and how?

- **Business Plan Practice.** Before assigning, Critical Thinking question 4, have students discuss and research the concepts of copyright and trademark, which they will be introduced to formally in Chapter 42.

- **Guest Speaker.** Look up inventors through a local invention membership organization and invite one to your class to demonstrate how s/he comes up with ideas for products, decides which ones to develop or sell to manufacturers, and how to work with manufacturers. Encourage the speaker to bring sketches, models, prototypes, and other show-and-tell items to augment the presentation.

- **Invention-in-Use Story.** Have students individually or in pairs choose an invention that has had an important effect on the lives of teenagers today. Instruct them to write a brief story relating how a teen uses the invention, how it makes a difference in his/her life, and what the individual would have to do if the invention didn't exist. Tell them they will get points for drama and cleverness, so they should be creative! **LINKS**»*History*

## BUILD ACADEMIC AND LIFE-SKILL PROFICIENCIES

### *Skills Mean Success* Answers

**English. (Writing).** If students do not have access to the Internet, provide copies of a patent application, or any other common type of business form, such as a bank account application, medical insurance form, or job application. Evaluate forms to be sure they are filled out completely, neatly, and without errors. Note that patent applications will be discussed in greater detail in Chapter 42.

**Leadership.** This activity is highly personal and suitable for independent journal writing. Do not require students to share their responses, but encourage an open and respectful discussion of diversity issues in class, which may include sharing experiences.

**English and Technology (Reading and Writing).** If students don't feel comfortable sending a real letter or e-mail to a business, allow them to "send" these communications to you. If they are actually sending out correspondence, make sure you see each document before it is sent. Review for proper letter or e-mail format and offer feedback on writing style and usage. If necessary, have students make revisions and corrections before sending or mailing their documents.

### CHAPTER 8

# SELECTING YOUR BUSINESS:
## *What's Your Competitive Advantage?*

## ORGANIZE THE LEARNING

### CHAPTER OBJECTIVES

- Describe the four types of businesses and the difference between products and services.
- Identify your skills and hobbies.
- Explore your competitive advantage.
- Select your own business and name it.
- Define how your business can help your community.

### NFTE RESOURCES

- Text pp. 94-115
- Transparency T8-1
- Workbook/BLMs Chapter 8
- Entrepreneurs in Profile #9
- Test Bank Chapter 8
- BizTech Unit 2
- A Business for the Young Entrepreneur: *Break Yo Neck Kicks, Andre Randle McCain*

### BUSINESS PLAN ACTIVITIES

*Workbook Business Plan Review*
Competitive Advantage 8-1, 8-2

*Workbook/Textbook Chapter Review*
Critical Thinking 2, 5

*Power Point Templates*
Bas. 6; Int. 8; Adv. 8

### SKILLS MEAN SUCCESS

*English and Leadership*
Listening and Speaking for Social Interaction: Asking Questions to Clarify Meaning

*Leadership*
Responsible and Ethical Behavior

*Math*
Mathmatical Operations and Reasoning: Calculating Percentages, Problem Solving

### PREREQUISITES

Chapters 1, 2, 4, 5 and 6 inform the content of this chapter.

### VOCABULARY

competitive advantage, foundation, manufacturing, philanthropy, product, retail, service, wholesale

Other suggested words to know: ethic

## KEY QUESTION

**What's your competitive advantage?**

## SET A CONTEXT FOR LEARNING

- **Focus 1: Interests.** Poll the students or initiate a class discussion around the following: What do you like to do in your spare time? What do you do well?
- **Focus 2: Value of Your Time.** Present the students with the following: If you started your own business, what other uses of your time would be given up? List three opportunity costs. For each, estimate how much return you would get for the investment of your time; what do these activities give you back?
- **Discussion Launcher 1: Disney Quote.** Write on the board or overhead or share verbally the Walt Disney quote in the text and ask students to interpret what he means: "I don't make movies to make money; I make money to make movies."

- **Discussion Launcher 2: Philanthropy.** Ask students to copy the following and fill in the blanks: "If I could solve any problem in the world, it would be _____ by doing _____ ."

## DEVELOP AND CLOSE THE LEARNING

- **Integrative Review of Business Opportunity.** Review from Chapters 4, 6, and 7 the emphasis on recognizing and understanding customer needs and demand to determine a successful business opportunity. These are external factors. Review from Chapters 5, 6 and 7 how the entrepreneur's characteristics, mental attitude, resources, and creativity also contribute to a successful business opportunity. These are internal factors. Set the stage for the lesson with these additional variables: Another important internal factor is interests. Another external factor is knowing the competition.

- **Business Types Review.** Review from Chapter 2 the four types of businesses (manufacturing, wholesale, retail, service). Give examples of each (such as Gillette or Nike for manufacturing; a local flower or produce wholesaler; Wal-Mart or a local grocery store for retail; and lawyer, dog walker, or editor for service). Categorize the business types in terms of whether they provide a product or service. (E.g., manufacturing, wholesale and retail are product oriented; service is separate.) Focus on the differences in tangibility between products and services: products you can touch, services you can't. Ask students to speculate why there are three business types for products but only one for services. (E.g., you can't really "pass along" a service through a distribution chain—the service provider usually has to perform the service directly to the customer.) Note how some businesses provide both a product and a service (Domino's provides both pizza *and* delivery; Microsoft provides software *and* technical support.) Ask students to categorize their business ideas from the "interests" activity above and share them with the class.

- **Interests as Opportunity Sources.** Have students share their responses to Discussion Launcher 1 above. Reinforce the idea that it is not the desire to make money but rather the desire to realize a powerful dream that fuels most entrepreneurs. Give examples from the textbook, *Entrepreneurs in Profile*, or news stories such as Apple founder Steve Jobs' dream of computers being easy to use, or King Gillette's dream of an easy-to-use and painless razor, or Russell Simmons' love of rap). Use responses from Focus 1 above or have students complete the table in the text or workbook assessing their interests. Group students by similar interests to look through business suggestions listed in the text to find one or two that fit their shared interest. Have them evaluate these chosen opportunities in terms of local customer needs. Then move students around so groups comprise varied interests. Ask them to consider: How might the group members' interests be combined into a creative business idea? They could refer to the list in the textbook. Again, evaluate these ideas in light of customer needs, etc.

- **Doing Good.** One interest that a lot of entrepreneurs have in common is going beyond profit to helping others and doing what's right. Outline the three ways an entrepreneur can "do good": 1) focusing on customer needs and adding value; 2) being ethical in all business situations; 3) doing philanthropic work. Define "ethic." Ask students to come up with ways they think or have heard of business people behaving unethically. Have students brainstorm ways that the business person could have acted in a more ethical way. Tell the story of Anita Roddick and The Body Shop using information from *Entrepreneurs in Profile* or the company Web site. Discuss the many ways Roddick built "giving back to the community" into her business operations. (Responses could include using products created by local communities, not using products tested on animals, recycling, giving money to environmental causes, allowing causes to use Body Shop stores to promote a message, starting a foundation, helping indigenous peoples.) From Discussion Launcher 2 above, have students share what kinds of causes they would like their businesses to support.

- **Competitive Advantage.** Even though personal interests are a key part of business opportunity, entrepreneurs always have to keep the interests and needs of *others* in mind. In addition to customers, they need to understand what their competitors are doing. Ask students to speculate why. (Answers will probably include that competitors can steal your customers, to see what their products can do, etc.). Introduce the idea of competitive advantage: Whatever competitors are doing, how can you do it better? Pick a product category that students are familiar with (such as hamburgers), list several companies (such as McDonald's, Burger King, Wendy's, a local burger restaurant that is not part of a chain), and itemize each company's strengths and weaknesses. Encourage students to think along several lines: food quality and variety, price, store atmosphere, service, etc. Ask them to summarize: What is each company's competitive advantage in relation to the others? Repeat with different product categories and different types of businesses (manufacturing, retail, service) until they understand the concept and how it applies in different circumstances. **LINKS**»*Marketing*

- **Business Names.** One simple way to show your competitive advantage is through your name. Ask: What should a business name *do*? What makes a good business name? What makes a *bad* business name? Why? (Answers will probably relate to the name as the identity of the business; how the name should clearly describe what the company does and, preferably, its benefit or its target customers; it should not use the entrepreneur's family name or be hard to understand or pronounce, and it should not make a joke that might be misinterpreted.) Have students come up with examples of good and bad business names (such as Krispy Kreme or Dunkin Donuts for good, and Smith's High-Carb Buns for bad).

- **Summary.** Emphasize from the textbook the principles of personal interest, customer need, competitive advantage, and social good to help teens choose a business. Show transparency T8-1. Select a few businesses from this transparency and describe how they could satisfy all the criteria of a good business opportunity. Ask students to think about and rate (on a scale of 1-5) how their business ideas measure up in terms of the above principles.

## ASSESS THE LEARNING

- **Vocabulary.** Have students who use the workbook complete the vocabulary activity. Others might create vocabulary flash cards, then work in pairs to drill one another on terms and meanings.

- **Key Concepts.** Assign Question 1 so students work with a partner. Assign Question 2 individually.

- **Additional Workbook Activities Answers.**

  **Vocabulary Activity Answers:** Students' answers should be complete sentences that use the vocabulary words correctly. Sentences should demonstrate an understanding and correct usage of the terms. 1. A product is tangible, whereas a service is intangible. 2. A business is based on a product if it sells something that exists in nature or is made by human beings. A business is based on a service if it provides time, skills, or expertise in exchange for money. 3. My competitive advantage is my strategy for beating my competition. I will attract more customers to my business by offering superior quality at a reasonable price. 4. The four types of businesses are wholesale, retail, manufacturing, and service. A wholesale business buys products from a manufacturer and sells them to retailers. A retail business sells products directly to consumers. A manufacturing business makes a tangible product, and a service business sells an intangible service to the consumer. 5. Entrepreneurs use philanthropy to solve problems and help people in their communities. Many philanthropic foundations in the United States were established by entrepreneurs.

  **Quiz 8** in the workbook. **Answers:** 1. Answers will vary but should agree that a simpler idea has a greater chance for success because fewer things could go wrong, and it is a good way to gain experience to handle more complexity later if the business grows. 2. Answers will vary. 3. Your name should make a good

first impression, be simple, tell the customer what you do/sell/make, but probably shouldn't include your family name. 4. You make money doing something you love; you can learn more about an interest; your enthusiasm for this interest will carry over into business operations. 5.a. Party planning service or making party decorations. 5.b. Typing, editing or word processing services. 5.c. Translation services. 5.d. Dog walking, pet day care, pet training services. 6. Something you can do better than the competition that attracts customers to your business. 7. Answers will vary but should show that the student is thinking about the businesses in relation to their competitors.

- **Research and Writing Practice.** Assign Exploration Question 1. Alternatively, students could create a slide presentation or poster.

## EXTEND THE LEARNING

- **Production Chain.** Break students into groups and have each choose a familiar product category found in a grocery or department store (such as cereal, macaroni and cheese, clothing, electronics). Using the Internet or interviewing local manufacturers or retailers, have groups research how the product is made and distributed to the customer — from raw materials to arrival at someone's home. It may be helpful for students to choose one brand, such as Cheerios. Invite students to share their findings in class. Discuss how the different types of businesses are related: from raw-materials suppliers to manufacturers to wholesalers to retailers to customers. Ask students to speculate how this chain applies or does not apply to service businesses.
  **LINKS** )»*Research*

- ***Entrepreneurs in Profile.*** Have students read the chapter on Berry Gordy and be prepared to discuss in class. Types of questions could be pre-assigned to guide the reading: How did Gordy turn his passion for music into Motown Records? Where did his company name come from? Is it a good name? What was his competitive advantage? What customer need did Motown fill? Tying together concepts from this and past chapters: What entrepreneurial characteristics did Gordy have? What trends, problems, and/or technological advances did he address or take advantage of? How was he creative? What was his ROI over 30 years, from his sister's loan of $700 to his sale of the company for $61 million?
  **LINKS** )»*Music*

- **Business Plan Practice.** Assign Critical Thinking questions 1-5.
- **BizTech.** Assign Unit 2.

## BUILD ACADEMIC AND LIFE-SKILL PROFICIENCIES

### *Skills Mean Success* Answers

**English.** Students' questions should focus on customer needs and request examples, clarification, and additional information. Questions should be clear and specific. They should have a polite and respectful tone, such as:

1. When do you need your order?

2. What types of trees and shrubs were you looking for?

3. I'm not familiar with the XZ1-2000. Could you tell me more about it?

4. When would you like the products to be delivered?

5. How many copies do you need? When will you need them? How many pages are involved? What is your budget?

**Leadership.** There should be no wrong answers to this exercise. If students make a reasonable attempt to answer the questions seriously and honestly, they will be well on their way to creating a sound code of ethics. For additional assistance, encourage them to go online to www.sba.gov or use an online search engine to locate examples of business codes of ethics and conduct. Also, ask students to think about local businesses and businesspeople they perceive as productive, positive members of the community. What characteristics give this positive impression? If practical, encourage students to contact these businesses for a copy of their codes of ethics.

Every year, several popular publications list the 50 or 100 "Best Companies to Work For." As an extension activity, some students might want to find one of these lists and try to identify four or five common elements among the companies selected.

**Math.** 1. a. Salary = $3,000 × 12 months = $36,000 per year; b. Hourly Wages = $20 × 40 hours × 52 weeks = $41,600 per year; c. Commission = $225,000 × .20 = $45,000 per year. In this case, the highest compensation is: c. Commission. 2. Students may select any method, but should justify their decisions using arguments such as the following.

### Pros and Cons

○ Salary offers a steady income, but if you work a lot of extra hours (as entrepreneurs often do!), you may eventually feel that you're not being compensated fairly for your time.

○ An hourly wage offers both a steady income and compensation for your extra time. However, if you are extremely busy, you may find yourself working more than 40 hours per week. In that case, you might not be able to afford to pay yourself for every hour worked.

○ Commissions offer the greatest potential income but also the greatest risk. Your income will be completely dependent on the company's revenue. If the business has a bad year, you won't earn much money.

Help students to see the complex factors that will need to be considered when determining compensation.

### CHAPTER 9

# COSTS OF RUNNING A BUSINESS:
## *Variable and Fixed*

## ORGANIZE THE LEARNING

### CHAPTER OBJECTIVES

- Define your unit of sale.
- Explain the difference between costs of goods sold and other variable costs.
- Calculate gross profit, including variable costs.
- Determine costs of operating your business.
- Use depreciation to spread the cost of equipment over several years.

### NFTE RESOURCES

- Text pp. 116-131
- Transparencies T9 -1 to T9 -3 Workbook/BLMs Chapter 9
- Entrepreneurs in Profile #17
- Test Bank Chapter 9
- BizTech Unit 3
- A Business for the Young Entrepreneur: *Mother's Helper*

### BUSINESS PLAN ACTIVITIES

*Workbook Business Plan Review* Operating Costs 9-1, 9-2, 9-3, 9-4

*Workbook/Textbook Chapter Review* Critical Thinking; Key Concepts 2 (and 3)

*Power Point Templates* Bas. 4, 9; Int. 5, 12; Adv. 5, 11

### SKILLS MEAN SUCCESS

*Math* Operations: Determining Price per Unit to Compare Prices

*English* Reading for Information: Reasoning and Understanding

*Math* Mathematical Reasoning: Devising Formulas

### PREREQUISITES

Chapters 1, 2, 3, and 5 are important foundations for this chapter.

### VOCABULARY

cost of goods sold, cost of services sold, depreciation, direct cost, fixed costs, fixed operating costs, gross profit, net profit, overhead, variable costs

*Other terms to know:* allocate, cash reserve, economies of scale, revenue, volume, USAIIRD, gross profit per unit

## KEY QUESTION

**What will I need to invest in to run my business successfully?**

## PREPARE FOR LEARNING

- **Purchase or Bring Props.** Some students learn better when concrete examples are presented to represent abstract concepts. If you use the sandwich-demonstration activity in Extend the Learning, you will need to purchase and bring to class the ingredients. These items could include: a loaf of bread, a package of deli meat, one tomato, one onion, one head of lettuce, jar of pickle chips, jars of mayonnaise and/or mustard, package of sliced cheese. Be sure to bring the receipt for these items. If you use the exchange simulation activity in Extend the Learning, bring a deck of playing cards and play money or pennies.

## SET A CONTEXT FOR LEARNING

- **Focus 1: Better Deal?** Write on the board or ask:: Which is a better deal: a 10-ounce candy bar for $1 or a 5-ounce bar for 60 cents? a 10-piece chicken bucket for $8 or a 20-piece bucket for $15? a 12-flower bouquet for $6 or a 20-flower bouquet for $9? Why? **LINKS)**»*Consumer Ed*

- **Focus 2: Ups and Downs of Costs.** Write on the board or ask: Which of the following costs do you think would go up if you made and sold more bicycles — wheels? brakes? salespersons' commissions? heating costs for the plant? interest on the money you borrowed to start your company? shipping the bikes to stores?

- **Discussion Launcher 1: Hobby Costs.** Using the hobbies students discussed in Chapter 7, ask them to list the materials they use for the hobby and the approximate cost of these. (For example, painting would include the costs of paper/canvas, paints, brushes, thinner, and perhaps frames; dance would include the costs of lessons, shoes, leotards, etc.; sports would include the costs of gear.)

## DEVELOP AND CLOSE THE LEARNING

- **Unit of Sale.** Review unit of sale from Chapter 2. Give examples from different businesses to figure unit of sale. Start with easier product examples, such as a pizza parlor (one pizza), computer store (one computer), Starbucks (one cup of coffee), etc. Discuss how services usually have a unit of sale based on time — "per hour" — and give examples (accountant, lawyer, writer). Even service businesses that have standard rates — for example, a haircut for $15 — the unit of sale is still usually based on time, because the barber/hairdresser has learned s/he can do one haircut every half hour. Then move to harder examples, to businesses that sell differently priced items, such as a discount store or restaurant. Show the average unit-of-sale equation and give examples. Close by explaining that the unit of sale is important to know so you can control costs and make a profit.

- **Costs.** Challenge students: When you resell a T-shirt for $20, is all that money profit? When you buy a CD for $15 at a music store, is all that money profit? Use other examples as needed to lead students to realize that the answer is no, because you/stores incur costs. Costs are money you have to pay out: 1) to get raw materials to make and sell your product, and 2) to run the operations of your business. As an overview, show transparency T9-1 and discuss the different types of costs. Emphasize that costs are different than investment discussed in Chapter 3. Note: you may need to clarify that "good" is a synonym for "product"; and that *revenue* is price times the number of customers who bought a product in a specified time period.

- **Cost of Goods Sold and Cost of Services Sold.** Recall from Chapter 2 that the first cost that is subtracted from price is *cost of goods sold* (COGS) for products and *cost of services sold* (COSS) for services. Define COGS as the cost of the raw materials that go into making a product (in manufacturing), or the price at which you bought an item to resell (in wholesale or retail businesses). Define COSS as the costs you incur in providing one hour of service. To be counted as COGS/COSS, the cost must be attributable to a particular item sold or unit of sale. Give examples of different types of businesses and ask

students to speculate what some of the costs that go into COGS or COSS for that product are (for example, a bike manufacturer, a jewelry store, a hairdresser). Use the candy example in the text to show how to calculate average COGS/COSS if a business sells more than one type of product/service. Ask: What are the advantages of using an average? (E.g., Easier and quicker to calculate.) What are the disadvantages? (E.g., Entrepreneur must make sure the average will be accurate to be helpful.)

- **Variable Costs.** Introduce that a business may incur other costs that vary with sales but cannot be attributed specifically to a unit of sale as COGS/COSS can be. Give several examples: sales commissions, shipping costs, packaging costs (e.g., plate, napkin, utensils for food; a box for computers). These costs are different from COGS/COSS because they aren't the costs of materials or labor for the product/service that fulfills the customer need (that is, people don't buy a computer for the box or the shipping). Yet these costs still are assessed per unit of sale and included in the Economics of One Unit.

- **Gross Profit.** Introduce the concept of gross profit by discussing transparency T9-2. Gross profit is how much is left over after you have paid all the costs directly associated with making or selling your product or service. Walk students through several examples of calculating gross profit using examples in the book on watches, sandwiches, writing, and t-shirts, or other common items familiar to students. Ask them to speculate why gross profit is a helpful figure to know. (Answers will probably relate to having a better idea about how much money you are really making, how much is left over after you've "paid your bills" for the goods, etc.)

- **Fixed Costs.** Challenge students: But COGS/COSS and variable costs are not the only costs an entrepreneur incurs. Review the idea of adding value from Chapter 1 and explain that adding value often incurs costs beyond those that can be directly attributable to each product/service. Return to the example of Debbi Fields and her cookies: she also had to pay for oven heat, mixing equipment, bakers, and store fixtures. These costs are not easily attributed to a particular unit of sale. They are called fixed costs, operating costs, or overhead. Explain the main categories of fixed costs using USAIIRD: utilities, salaries, advertising, insurance, interest, rent, depreciation.

- **Comparison of Variable and Fixed Costs.** Return to transparency T9-1 and discuss fixed vs. variable costs. Note: Specify a time period and give several concrete examples. For example, continue the Debbi Fields example or one of the examples from the text and create a chart on the board like the one below so students can see the differences in fixed vs. variable costs. (Costs 5 and 6 are variable, listed after COGS before gross profit; 8 through 12 are fixed, note how they don't change regardless of the number of cookies made/sold.)

|  | | Mth 1 | Mth 2 | Mth 3 |
|---|---|---|---|---|
| 1. | Number of cookies sold | 10,000 | 20,000 | 15,000 |
| 2. | Price per cookie | $2 | $2 | $2 |
| 3. | Revenue (1 × 2) | $20,000 | $40,000 | $30,000 |
| 4. | COGS | $5,000 | $10,000 | $7,500 |
| 5. | Cookie bags | $100 | $200 | $150 |
| 5. | Sales people bonuses | $200 | $400 | $300 |
| 7. | Gross profit | $15,000 | $30,000 | $22,500 |
| 8. | Store rent | $5,000 | $5,000 | $5,000 |
| 9. | Mixing equipment rental or depreciation | $1,000 | $1,000 | $1,000 |
| 10. | Baker salary | $2,000 | $2,000 | $2,000 |
| 11. | Oven heat (it runs continuously 8 hours a day) | $300 | $300 | $300 |
| 12. | Electricity | $200 | $200 | $200 |

Ask: Why might variable costs be considered less risky than fixed costs? (fixed costs don't change regardless of sales so they still have to be paid, even if there is no income). If students need help, return to the cookie example above: What happens if you don't sell any cookies one month, or only a hundred? The riskiness of fixed costs demonstrates why it's a good idea for entrepreneurs to have a cash reserve in the bank equal to three months of fixed costs. Ask: So what would that reserve amount equal for the Debbi Fields' store above? Discuss how keeping fixed costs low can also be helpful because once fixed costs are covered, additional sales revenue goes directly to the bottom line. This principle also applies to economies of scale: it's why companies often give discounts for people who buy in bulk, like at Costco. The higher volume product that fixed costs can be spread across, the lower overall cost per unit, so sometimes the savings are passed on to the customer. Make sure that students are clear that cost of goods sold varies by sales but *can be attributed directly to a particular item* (a wheel for a bicycle, etc.); variable costs help run the business and *vary by sales*; and fixed costs are often stable but *do not vary by sales* — they occa-

sionally vary but are usually due to something else, such as a supplier raising prices or an entrepreneur making a business decision.

- **Net Profit.** Use transparency T9-3 to show the equation for net profit (Net Profit = Gross Profit − Fixed Costs) and take students through the example, or Bob's Furniture example in the text. Also calculate net profit per month for the Mrs. Fields Cookies example above, or other examples. **Answers:** Month 1 = $6,200, month 2 = $20,900, month 3 = $13,550. Allocate the fixed costs each month across the number of cookies sold to get a total cost per unit. **Answers:** Month 1 = $1.36, month 2 = 95 cents, month 3 = $1.08. Figure the net profit per cookie for each month. **Answers:** Month 1 = 64 cents, month 2 = $1.05, month 3 = 92 cents. Discuss why the total cost per unit is lower and the net profit is higher when more cookies are sold. (E.g., the fixed costs, which are the same very month, are allocated across more cookies, which results in lower costs — economies of scale — and higher net profits.)

- **Summary.** Write the full equations on the board:
  - Price per unit of sale × Number of units of sale sold = Revenue
  - Revenue − Cost of goods/service sold − Variable costs = Gross profit − Fixed costs = Net profit

## ASSESS THE LEARNING

- **Vocabulary.** Have students define the terms in their own words and use each term in a sentence.

- **Key Concepts.** Activity 1. **Answers:** 1. Depreciation spreads out the cost of an expensive piece of equipment over time; it helps reduce taxes over several years rather than just the year of purchase; 4,000/4 = 1,000 so you would depreciate $1,000 per year for four years.

- **Critical Thinking. Answers:** a. EOU = $1,000/50 = $20 average per customer. b. Monthly fixed costs = $6,250 (add up list). c. Annual fixed costs = $6,250 × 12 = $75,000. d. Daily gross profit = $1,000 − (50 × 5) − ($6,250/30) = $1,000 − 250 − 208 = $542 (assuming the store is open 30 days a month).

- **Additional Workbook Activities Answers.**

  **Vocabulary Activity Answers. Across:** 1. cash reserve, 6. overhead, 7. USAIIRD, 10. fixed operating costs, 11. gross profit, 12. variable costs, 13. fixed costs, 14. direct cost. **Down:** 1. cost of goods sold,

2. economies of scale, 3. cost of services sold, 4. volume, 5. gross profit per unit, 8. depreciation, 9. net profit.

**Quiz 9** in the workbook. **Answers:** 1. Fixed costs occur every month and are usually the same amount; variable costs may not occur every month and their amounts may vary widely based on the number of units sold. 2. Any five from USAIIRD: utilities, salaries, advertising, insurance, interest, rent and depreciation. 3. $4 \times 12 \times 5 = \$240$. 4. Fixed costs or overhead. 5. Net profit $= (10 - 5) \times 48 = 240 - 10 - 20 = \$210$. 6. Variable cost. 7. $3 assuming no other variable costs. 8. $3 \times 100 = 300 - 50 = 250/100 = \$2.50$.

## EXTEND THE LEARNING

- **Business Plan Practice.** Key Concepts 2 and/or Critical Thinking.

- *Entrepreneurs in Profile.* Have students read about Sam Walton guided by this question: How does the concept of economy of scale apply to Wal-Mart? Discuss how Walton used his knowledge of the psychology of buyers to repackage products at a price at which they would buy more but his costs would remain low. How can keeping costs low in an intelligent way be good for everybody (entrepreneur, customers, employees/managers, investors)? Speculate what the variable and fixed operating costs of a Wal-Mart store might be. **LINKS**»*Economics*

- **BizTech.** Assign Unit 3.

- **A Business for the Young Entrepreneur**: Have students read about a Mother's Helper business and work in pairs to create two lists of 5-10 questions each:

  ○ Questions a parent should ask a prospective mother's helper prior to hiring her or him.

  ○ Questions a candidate should ask before accepting a job as a mother's helper.

  Ask for a mix of questions about employment terms, working conditions and childcare issues.

- **Sandwich Demonstration**. Make the example of the sandwich in the text more concrete by bringing to class the ingredients for a sandwich and actually making one while discussing its costs. Bring in the grocery store receipt to show actual prices of the ingredients purchased. Step students through dividing the bulk ingredients into ingredients-per-sandwich (and their associated costs). Once you have figured all the costs, ask how a similar sandwich would be priced at Subway. What is Subway's approximate gross profit per sandwich? What kinds of fixed and variable costs might Subway incur in running a store and making sandwiches? What is the amount called after these operating costs are deducted? (Net profit.)

- **Card Exchange Simulation**. Assign the roles of entrepreneur, wholesaler, radio station, and two or more customers to students. Distribute play money to the entrepreneur and customers. Give an opened deck of cards to the wholesaler. Have the wholesaler sell the whole deck to the entrepreneur in exchange for a negotiated sum of money. Record on the board the number of cards (52) and the dollar amount exchanged. Have the entrepreneur buy an ad from the radio station to advertise the cards at an agreed-upon price. Record the dollar amount exchanged. Have the customers buy cards from the entrepreneur for a price set by the entrepreneur. Record the number of cards and dollar amount purchased by each customer. Have students calculate the entrepreneur's revenue, COGS, variable costs, gross profit, fixed costs, and net profit for the transactions.

## BUILD ACADEMIC AND LIFE-SKILL PROFICIENCIES

### *Skills Mean Success* Answers

**Math (Price per Unit).** 1. A: $\$40/25 = \$1.60$ per bag; B: $\$79/50 = \$1.58$ per bag; C: $\$155/100 = \$1.55$ per bag. 2. Supplier C is offering the best price. To determine the price per unit, divide the price by the quantity. Determining price per unit is an important skill because it is the only way to compare prices on different quantities. This is also a skill that can be useful in daily life. Encourage students to practice this skill at the grocery store. If a store is offering one brand of macaroni and cheese at 3 boxes for $1 and another brand at $0.40 per box, which is the better deal?

**English.** 1. Fixed. 2. Fixed. 3. Fixed. 4. Variable. 5. Variable. 6. Fixed. 7. Variable. 8. Fixed. 9. Variable. 10. Fixed. 11. Variable. 12. Fixed. Expenses that must be paid no matter how many cakes are sold are **fixed costs**. Other types of costs will vary with the number of cakes sold. These are **variable costs.**

**Math. (Devising Formulas)** 1. d. 2. g. 3. e. 4. b. 5. f. 6. c. 7. a.

### CHAPTER 10

# WHAT IS MARKETING?

## ORGANIZE THE LEARNING

### CHAPTER OBJECTIVES

- Explain why marketing is the business function that identifies customer needs.
- Use marketing to establish your brand.
- Apply the four elements of a marketing plan.
- Create a marketing plan for your business.

### NFTE RESOURCES

- Text pp. 132-143
- Transparencies T 10-1, T10-2
- Workbook/BLMs Chapter 10
- Entrepreneurs in Profile #12
- Test Bank Chapter 10
- BizTech Unit 6
- A Business for the Young Entrepreneur: *Cheep Bird Feeders, Shawn Blakely, Wichita, Kansas*

### BUSINESS PLAN ACTIVITIES

*Workbook Business Plan Review*
Marketing 10-1, 10-2, 10-3

*Workbook/Textbook Chapter Review*
Key Concepts 2-3

*Power Point Templates*
Bas. 7, 8; Int. 9, 10; Adv. 9, 10

### SKILLS MEAN SUCCESS

*English*
Listening and Speaking for Social Interaction: Listening Attentively, Expressing Ideas Respectfully in Conversation, Using Nonverbal Communication

*Technology*
Internet Resources and Business Card Design

*Math*
Mathmatical Modeling: Representing Numerical Relationships in Graphs; Using Graphics in Presentations

*English*
Persuasive Strategies

### PREREQUISITES

The contents of Chapters 1, 4, and 6-8 are important background for this chapter.

### VOCABULARY

brand, business card, cause-related marketing, logo, marketing, market share, mind share, publicity

*Other suggested terms to know:*
marketing vision, marketing plan

## KEY QUESTION

**How do I persuade customers to buy my product or service?**

## PREPARE FOR LEARNING

- **Pizza Pizzazz.** You will need one poster board and markers for each group for the optional Develop and Close the Learning activity.

## SET A CONTEXT FOR LEARNING

- **Focus 1: Well-Known Brands.** Challenge individual students to try to list ten brand-name products in 30 seconds.
- **Focus 2: "Good" Marketers.** Ask students to brainstorm lists: Think of companies that do good works in their respective communities.

- **Discussion Launcher 1: Marketing All Around.** Individually or in pairs, have students answer: In the past 24 hours, how have companies tried to market to you? Try to think of at least five examples. Which efforts do you think were most effective and least effective? Why?

## DEVELOP AND CLOSE THE LEARNING

- **Review of Benefits and Customer Needs.** From Chapters 4 and 8, review the importance of understanding customer needs. Using the examples of drills and makeup from the text, or other examples, discuss how to "think marketing" by converting product features (such as drill bits, car-engine power, eye-shadow colors, mascara being waterproof) into product benefits (making holes, ease of use, prestige, beauty, "worry-free"). Remind the students that the benefits they come up with will depend on the target market, or "targeting," because different types of customers have different types of needs. For example, the benefit of foundation makeup may be different for a teen, who wants to look more mature or hide blemishes, vs. a 40-year-old woman, who wants to fill in wrinkles and look younger, vs. an actor, who wants to avoid looking pale onstage under stage lighting or to be certain the makeup will last under the hot lights. Give or ask students for other examples of products: What are their potential benefits? Define marketing vision as product benefit. Pick a product (such as Apple iPods, oranges, sunglasses, shoes). Divide students into small groups and assign each a potential market (such as elementary school children, teenage boys, businesspeople, grandparents) and have them brainstorm product benefits for their respective markets. Allow each group to share, then compare the benefits for the different markets.

- **What Is Marketing For?** In small groups, have students look through the textbook to find descriptions of what marketing does for a company — the function it fulfills. List findings on the board. (Responses should include: explaining benefits/satisfying customer needs; bringing customers to the product; building a strong brand; increasing demand; strengthening competitive advantage; turning mind share into market share). Ask groups to come up with a clever way to describe why entrepreneurs should engage in marketing — such as writing a radio ad or jingle. Groups may focus on one or all of the functions listed. Have students present their ads/jingles in class.

- **Brand Building.** Use the responses from Focus 1 on the previous page, or ask students to brainstorm all the brands they can think of. Most likely to come to mind are strong brands, such as Coca-Cola, McDonald's, Gatorade, Nike, Dunkin Donuts, Cheerios, Hershey's, etc. Ask: Why do you think you can recall these companies or products so quickly and easily? (Answers will relate to advertising, they've been around a long time, they are seen in the neighborhood, they use the product). Relate the list generated by the students to the brand-building ideas presented in the chapter. Pick one brand and ask students to speculate what else the company could do to continue to build its brand. Ask students to speculate where the company's weaknesses are: If you were an entrepreneur that was going to compete with this company, how would you go about building your brand in relation to this one? (If they need hints, say: Start by defining the customer needs and benefits you would provide — name, personality, etc.)

- **Mind Share and Market Share.** Create (or, better still, have volunteer students create) a pie chart as a visual to show the concepts of market, mind share, and market share. The whole pie represents the market (those people who need and have the ability to pay for the product); 2/3, or 240 degrees, of the pie represents mind share (those people who are aware of the product); and within the 2/3 a smaller slice is the market share (those people who actually purchase the product). Using the list of brands generated above, ask students to indicate by a show of hands how many have heard of the brand and know what it is used for. Write the number on the board. Ask how many actually use the company's product(s) on a regular basis. Write that number on the board. Calculate the percentage of the class that was aware of the product and the percentage that had bought it. Ask: Pretending that the class is composed of everyone that is in the market for the product, which percentage represents mind share and which market share? Ask students to consider why it is important for entrepreneurs to take into consideration both mind share and market share. (Answers will probably relate to how increasing mind share calls for advertising but increasing market share calls for other tactics; because an entrepreneur wants to build both, and convert mind share into market share).

- **Marketing Planning.** Use transparency T10-1 to define and discuss the Four P's of marketing. Using one of the brands discussed above or other examples, have students discuss the brand's current product, price, place, and promotion decisions. Alternatively, bring in advertisements from magazines or newspapers and have students in small groups analyze the ads to describe the company's current Four P's. Ask students to evaluate the ads: do they think it is effective marketing? Why or why not? Allow time for students to present their ideas. Ask: What are ways a business can check to see if its marketing decisions are good ones? (E.g., customer surveys.)

- **Cause-Related Marketing.** Have students look through magazines or newspapers to find examples of companies engaging in cause-related marketing. Instruct each to write a brief paragraph that describes how the ad or article s/he found is an example of cause-related marketing, whether it is effective, and why.

- **Pizza Pizzazz.** You will need one poster board and markers for each group. Divide students into groups. Each group represents an entrepreneurial team that is going to open a pizza restaurant in the neighborhood. The teams' task is to build a brand and write a brief marketing plan for their restaurant. This includes coming up with a name, a logo, descriptions of the product (their "signature" pizza), place/location, price, and promotional ideas to open the business; and a slogan and visuals that will give the brand a distinct personality and competitive advantage. Each group should make these decisions then display them on their poster board to present to the class. Option: Once groups have presented and students see what their competitors are doing, give them a few more minutes to discuss how they might alter their branding ideas based in this new information. They can either create a new poster on the back side of the original or present their revised ideas verbally.

- **Summary.** Use transparency T10-2 to summarize marketing's primary value for an entrepreneur entering a market. It may be helpful to tie the transparency's statements back to the Four P's, market share, and customer benefit.

## ASSESS THE LEARNING

- **Vocabulary.** Have students define the terms in their own words and use each term in a sentence; or complete the workbook activity.

- **Key Concepts.** Question 1. **Answers:** Answers will vary but should not just describe the features of the product or service, but rather emphasize what the customer would get out of using the product or service (for example: holes, not drills; beauty, not eye shadow).

- **Critical Thinking.** Give students a product or service as an example (such as diapers or cell phones or security alarms), then assign Questions 1-2. **Answers:** Answers will vary but should be appropriate for the product or service assigned. Consider giving extra points for students who are creative in determining their market: for example, students who recognize that elderly adults might also be a market for diapers because..., or that adult women and elderly adults are both markets for security alarms but for different reasons, etc.

- **Additional Workbook Activities Answers.**

  **Vocabulary Activity Answers:** 1. publicity. 2. marketing. 3. business card. 4. logo. 5. brand. 6. mind share. 7. market share. 8. cause-related marketing.

  **Quiz 10 Answers:** 1. A product feature is part of what the product *is*; a product benefit is what the product

or feature *does* for the customer; examples will vary. 2. It differentiates your product from that of your competitors; it gives your product a personality and competitive advantage. 3. Answers will vary but should reflect ideas from the chapter: good business name, logo, excellent reputation, personality that entices your target market, business cards, advertising, high quality product/service, high ethical standards, community involvement. 4. Product, price, place, promotion. 5. So it's convenient for customers to find and obtain your product/service. 6. So that potential customers learn about your product/service and are persuaded to try it. 7. They are an inexpensive and convenient way to let people know about you; promotion. 8. *Mind share* is how aware a customer is of your product or service; *market share* is what percentage of those people who need your product and have the ability to pay for it actually purchases your product. 9. Associate with a charity, start a foundation, cause-related marketing, donate profits to a cause, provide goods/services to a cause, etc. 10. That you should be truthful in your marketing: don't lie about your product's features or benefits because you could get in legal trouble; plus, if the product doesn't work as you promised, customers will be annoyed and you will lose market share.

## EXTEND THE LEARNING

- **Business Plan Practice.** Key Concept questions 2-3.

- **A Business for the Young Entrepreneur.** Assign the reading of Cheep Bird Feeders and, as a purpose for reading, ask the students to consider what questions Shawn could ask to pre-qualify a sales call.

- ***Entrepreneurs in Profile.*** Have students read the selection about Ray Kroc and be prepared to discuss in class. Some suggested questions to set a purpose for reading include: What is the McDonald's marketing vision? What is their competitive advantage? Fill in the Four P's for McDonald's. Evaluate the company's brand in terms of the criteria in the text (such as the name, logo, reputation, personality, advertising, quality of product/service, ethical standards, clear product definition, active in the community, associated with charities and causes).

- **BizTech.** Assign Unit 6.

- **Exploration.** Assign Activities 1-2. Consider hanging the flyers around the room or outside the classroom for other students to see.

- **Business Cards.** Let the students design and print business cards for their businesses. They could either create them individually for the ventures they are developing in their business plans, or they could create them in teams based on the above Pizza Pizzazz activity. Additional information is provided in *Skills Mean Success* — Technology (Internet Resources and Business Card Design) in text. You will need access to a computer with Microsoft Word software or Internet access, an inkjet or laser printer, and business card printing sheets available at most office supply stores (such as sheet product type Avery 5371 or 8371). To make more efficient use of computer time, students first should hand draw a sketch of what they want their card to look like. Give each student a set time on the computer to input their information and print out one sheet of cards. Give the following instructions: Use the Avery 5371 or 8371 template. Design your card, add graphics, and type in your business information. Check your card for spelling errors. Print on plain paper to recheck for spelling errors and to hold the sheet against the business card sheet to check for proper alignment with the grid. Adjust as needed to make sure the information fits correctly. Print one sheet of business cards and separate cards at the perforations.

- **Marketing Successes and Failures**. Use the Edsel and Mustang examples in the textbook (or other past examples, such as Coke and New Coke; Big Mac and McDLT that students can research). As a class, compare what Ford did right and wrong with the Mustang and right and wrong with the Edsel. What marketing tips can be learned? Note that it is easy to determine right/wrong in hindsight, once the market "has spoken." Ask students to speculate: How can entrepreneurs assess how well they're doing with foresight to make better decisions? **LINKS**》*History*

- **Loyalty and Demand**. Review supply and demand graphs from Chapter 6. Customer loyalty means that customers will continue to buy about the same quantity of your product even if your price fluctuates a little (especially if it goes up). Ask students to speculate: How would this be represented on the graph? What does loyalty do to the demand curve? (Answere should include: It moves the curve up if the price goes up for a certain quantity, but more importantly it also, in the long term, makes the slope steeper (more vertical) so that price fluctuations will not affect quantity as much). Ask: Why is this a good thing for an entrepreneur? (It reduces risk; there will be fluctuations in business, so it is helpful that customers will stick with you through that volatility).

## BUILD ACADEMIC AND LIFE-SKILL PROFICIENCIES

### *Skills Mean Success* Answers

**English. (Listening and Speaking for Social Interaction: Listening Attentively and Respectfully)** Observe the pairs to be sure they are following the guidelines for resolving customer conflicts. Offer feedback for how they can improve their communication. Alternatively, group students into teams of three and have one serve as an observer to offer feedback as the other two role-play. Have members of the team take turns in the different roles.

**Technology.** Encourage students to be creative and to experiment with different fonts and graphics. Students with graphic or visual arts skills could be used as advisors. Designers advise that no more than three fonts should be used on a business card. Ultimately the designs should be professional, legible, and reflect individual personality and creativity. Allow students to make up any information they don't have, but keep it realistic. If students do not have access to the Internet, allow them to (neatly) design a business card by hand, or to visit a local office supply or stationery store and ask if they can make a design. Have students exchange and critique each others' cards for completeness, accuracy, creativity, and attractiveness.

**Math (plus English, Technology).** 1.a. Dell 18.6%; b. 34.2%; c. 2.5%; d. 0.527%. 2. If students do not have access to computers, allow them to neatly draw and colorize a pie chart by hand. They should still follow the guidelines above, although their pie sections can be approximate. Note that the A-One Taxi section should be the top, right section.

**English (Persuasive Strategies).** Answers will vary. Have students evaluate each others' examples, referencing specific strategies listed.

### CHAPTER 11

# MARKET RESEARCH

## ORGANIZE THE LEARNING

### CHAPTER OBJECTIVES

- Describe the different types of market research.
- Develop an effective market survey for your company.
- Use market research to understand your customers' needs.
- Analyze your industry.

### NFTE RESOURCES

- Text pp. 144-153
- Transparency T11-1
- Workbook/BLMs Chapter 11
- Entrepreneurs in Profile #11
- Test Bank Chapter 11
- BizTech Unit 4

### BUSINESS PLAN ACTIVITIES

*Workbook Business Plan Review*
Market Research  11-1, 11-2

*Workbook/Textbook Chapter Review*
Critical Thinking 2-3 (and 1)

### SKILLS MEAN SUCCESS

*Math*
Mathematical Reasoning and Operations: Using Statistics

*English*
Listening and Speaking for Social Interaction: Dealing with Criticism

Writing and Speaking for Social Interaction: Using Open-Ended Questions

### PREREQUISITES

Chapters 9 and 10 are important lead-ins to this chapter.

### VOCABULARY

demographics, market research, market segment, statistics, survey

## KEY QUESTION

**How do I learn who my customers are and what they need?**

## PREPARE FOR LEARNING

- **Collect.** Bring in magazines or newspapers with surveys or statistics samples (optional).

## SET A CONTEXT FOR LEARNING

- **Focus 1: What People *Don't* Like.** Pose this challenge to the students: If someone is telling you about what they don't like about your product, list three questions you might ask to help you find out how to make the situation better.

- **Focus 2: Birthday Gift.** Ask the class how the following problem could be solved: Your best friend's birthday party is coming up and you want to get a gift s/he would really like but you're not sure what to get. What do you do?

## DEVELOP AND CLOSE THE LEARNING

- **Why Conduct Research?** Refer to either Focus activity above and challenge the students that it was an example of market research: you were trying to find out something about other people that would help you make a good decision. Ask students to recall from the textbook or brainstorm reasons why market research is a good idea. (So you will know more, make better decisions, avoid costly mistakes.) Emphasize how research can never make a decision for you — there's no way to get absolute certainty — but it can reduce the risk of making a bad decision by providing more information. Use the example of Russell Simmons and Def Jam from the text or another example from *Entrepreneurs in Profile* or current events to show that research should be conducted before you open a business and also ongoing while it's in operation.

- **Market Research Types.** Ask students to think of the last time they purchased a snack:

  ○ For what reason did you buy the product?

  ○ How much did you pay?

  ○ How much would you have been willing to pay?

○ Where did you buy it?

○ How would you improve it?

○ What other similar products did you consider before choosing this one?

○ Why didn't you choose another option?

Collect and tally responses on the board. Ask students how they might use this information if they were a snack company. Point out that you just conducted a *survey*, one of the most common ways of collecting market information. Collect and bring in samples of surveys in magazines for students to compare in small groups: which are good (easy to use, easy to understand, ask specific questions) and which are less well done? Discuss the types of market research listed in the text: survey, already available research, statistical research, industry research. Bring in newspapers and magazines (*American Demographics* and *Consumer Reports* are particularly good sources; or use the Internet) and have students find samples of articles or ads that use statistical information. Alternatively, you could print out a few pages of a census report from www.census.gov. Have students share their findings and speculate about ways an entrepreneur could use the statistics. Recall from Chapter 8 the idea of competitive advantage. Ask: How could research help find or reinforce a company's competitive advantage? In addition to information about customers, what types of information should be collected about competitors? (E.g., Research could help you understand what customers think about your competitors so you can make a unique appeal, not an appeal that a competitor has already made; types of information might include number and location of competitors' stores, types of products they sell, pricing, advertising messages, etc.)

- **What Customers Think and Do.** Discuss transparency T11-1, determining how these questions roughly coincide with the Four P's of marketing learned in Chapter 10: product (Questions 1 & 4), price (2), place (3). Ask: What would be a good question to ask about promotion? These questions ask about the customer's relationship to the product. Other questions find out about the characteristics of the customer, how s/he thinks or feels, how and in what situations s/he might use the product. When combined to describe a whole population of customers, the findings are called demographics. Questions may also be asked about competitors. Give students a product or service to work with as a concrete example. Have class, in small groups, brainstorm

questions to ask current and potential customers of the product/service. Put four columns on the board: Internet/library (already existing data), survey (new research), observation of customers or competitors, other. As students share their questions, have the class categorize them in terms of how/where they could get the answer. To use time wisely, ask groups to only share questions that another group hasn't already presented.

- **Market Segmentation.** Recall the definition of "market" from Chapter 10: it comprises all the people who have a potential need for your product/service and the ability to pay for it. Ask students to describe the market of people who go to movie theaters — e.g., teens, children, families, couples. Point out that a market is rarely composed of only one type of person. These different *segments* of people have different needs and derive different benefits from going to the movie. Ask students to speculate what the needs and benefits are for the groups they listed. It may be helpful to create a chart on the board to organize the information. Explain how sometimes businesses don't try to appeal to everyone; instead, they target only one type of customer — one segment. From the chart, note how segmentation is often based more on benefits than by customer characteristics alone. Ask: What would be the advantage of creating a movie theater focused only on teens or on couples? (Answers will probably relate to better satisfying their needs, better use of resources). Use the example of a sandwich shop and have the class brainstorm how to segment the market for sandwiches. First, come up with benefits (such as low fat/lose weight, fresh/organic, quick/convenient, easy to eat on the go, taste, cheap). Next, brainstorm what types of people would most likely be interested in each benefit (such as dieters and women for low fat, businesspeople for convenience, etc.). Divide class into groups and have each write a 30-second radio ad to appeal to one segment. Allow time for groups to share their ads, then compare them: How was the same basic product — a sandwich — portrayed differently, depending on the benefit emphasized and the customer type targeted?

- **Summary.** Ask the students to refer to the business they are planning in their business plan and to list ten people they know who might be interested in the product or service. What further information would they need to know (about the product, pricing, promotion, or location) to market effectively to these people?

## ASSESS THE LEARNING

- **Vocabulary.** Ask students who are familiar with another language to pair (or group) with students who speak only English. Have the students with another language skill say and spell each term in translation and use it in a sentence in that language, then translate back into English. Students who complete the vocabulary activity in the workbook could then ask the second-language expert to help create an equivalent activity in the second language.

- **Key Concepts.** Questions 1-2. **Answers:** 1. Because you will better know what your customers need before you invest money in producing and marketing your product, and you will learn how to invest your money more wisely to create a product with the right benefits and competitive advantage. 2. Surveys, statistical, general and industry. a. Any of the following: customer age, income, background, gender, location, interests, occupation, home ownership, frequency of purchase; competitor sales, number of stores, etc. b. Interview him/her and find out why.

- **Additional Workbook Activities Answers.**

  **Vocabulary Activity. Answers:** 1. c. 2. a. 3. c. 4. b. 5. c.

  **Quiz 11** in the workbook. **Answers:** 1. c; 2. a; 3. b; 4. To learn more about potential customers, how they might benefit from your product, what their needs are, etc., so you can better tailor your product and marketing to meet their needs. 5-7. Answers will vary but should refer to the product (size, style, performance, benefits, etc.), price, how the customer would get it, comparison to other cars, car "personalities," etc. 8. Answers will vary but should reflect such concerns as the number and strengths of competing stores, number and description of consumers who actively participate in training and athletics (or who are sports fans) in the area, any laws or regulations for retail or sporting goods, etc. 9. Answers will vary: age, income level, ethnicity, religious affiliation, gender, geographic location, interests, occupation, home owner or renter, products the person uses and how often, stores the person shops in, reactions to advertising or promotions, how much the person would pay for something. 10. Answers will vary.

- **Unit 2 Business Plan Integrative Summary.** See Extend the Learning for a full description.

## EXTEND THE LEARNING

- **Business Plan Practice.** Assign Critical Thinking questions 1-3 for students to complete in relation to their own businesses. See Exploration.

- **Exploration.** Assign Questions 1-3. This activity also could be combined with Business Plan Practice.

- **Entrepreneurs in Profile.** Have students read the chapter on Robert Johnson and be prepared to discuss in class. Types of questions you might ask: How did Johnson profit from satisfying a need for market segments that were previously underserved? What customer need(s) did his cable channels fulfill? What benefits did they provide? Are there other market segments of the TV viewing public he might target? Why? In what way?

- **BizTech.** Assign Unit 4.

- **Class Survey Project.** As a class, create a market research survey for a product or service for which teens would be a target market (such as in music, entertainment, education, or food). Alternatively, to integrate ethics and philanthropy, ask students to brainstorm and choose a cause about which teens might be concerned (such as pregnancy, environmental concerns, poverty, violence, war). As a class, create a brief survey (five or six questions) with a four-point scale for responses like the sample in Critical Thinking in the text. Type the survey on a computer and make copies. Have each student ask five friends to complete the survey. Break students into groups and have each analyze the results of one question by determining what percentage of the whole number of students surveyed answered 1, 2, 3 or 4. After students present findings, discuss what they mean to an entrepreneur interested in the product category or cause.

- **Business Plan Integrative Summary.** Since Chapter 11 concludes Unit 2, which is rich with tools for the business plan, it may be a good time for students to compose and present a brief summary of their Business Plans to date, including:

  ○ A business name.

  ○ Description of customers the business is expected to address, an estimate of how many customers might exist (demand), how much they would pay for the product/service, and the customer need(s) met.

  ○ A list of a few competitors and a description of the competitive advantage relative to these competitors.

○ A preliminary marketing mix/plan for the business.

○ A preliminary estimate of the expected cost of goods/services sold and operating costs for one month.

○ Expected risks and opportunity costs associated with the business.

## BUILD ACADEMIC AND LIFE-SKILL PROFICIENCIES

### *Skills Mean Success* Answers

**Math.**
1. Number of dog-owning households:
   80,000 ÷ 2.67 = 29,963 households
   29,963 × .361 = 10,817 dog-owning households in your community
2. Number of dogs: 29,963 × 0.578 = 17,319
   or: 1.6 × 10,817 = 17,307

You may wish to allow students to use calculators for this exercise. If students need additional practice with multiplication and division of decimals, have them work out the problems by hand.

**English.** Students should ask clarifying, probing questions and paraphrase comments. With this feedback, a business owner could consider improvements to packaging, ingredients, refrigeration, cost management, signs, and advertising. If time allows, ask students to write additional critique scenarios, and practice role-playing both critic and business owner.

**English.** Accept any questions that meet the criteria for being open-ended (that allow hypothetical respondents to answer in their own words, forming questions that can not be answered by a simple yes or no). The following are examples:
1. What shape do you think would be best for this packaging? Why?
2. Which color(s) on the packaging grabbed your attention?
3. Which words on the package did you notice first?
4. What do you like best/least about living downtown?
5. How would you describe this product to a friend?
6. Which features of this product are better or not as good as the competitor's?

### CHAPTER 12

# KEEPING GOOD RECORDS

## ORGANIZE THE LEARNING

### CHAPTER OBJECTIVES

- Develop the valuable habit of keeping good records.
- Use receipts and invoices correctly.
- Open a bank account.
- Create an accounting system for your business.
- Use your records to analyze and improve your business.
- Create financial statements from accounting records.

### NFTE RESOURCES

- Text pp. 154-173
- Transparencies T12-1 to T12-10, T44-2A and 2B
- Workbook/BLMs Chapter 12
- Test Bank Chapter 12
- BizTech Unit 15
- A Business for the Young Entrepreneur: *Party DJ*

### BUSINESS PLAN ACTIVITIES

*Workbook Business Plan Review* Record Keeping 12-1, 12-2

*Workbook/Textbook Chapter Review* Key Concepts 1, 4 and Exploration

### SKILLS MEAN SUCCESS

*English* Writing to Persuade: Supporting Arguments with Details and Evidence

*Leadership* Presentation Skills

*Math* Performing Operations Using Formulas

### PREREQUISITES

Chapters 3 and 9 should have been studied prior to this chapter.

### VOCABULARY

audit, deduction, invoice, packing slip, purchase order, receipt, taxes, transaction

*Other suggested terms to know:* balance sheet, reconcile, return on sales (ROS)

## KEY QUESTION

**How do I keep track of the money flowing through my business?**

## PREPARE FOR LEARNING

- **Timing.** This chapter is one of the more challenging in the curriculum for many students. The content is critical to understanding later topics and developing skills, so it is worth extra instructional time to make sure students grasp the concepts and are given time to practice the topic before moving on.

- **Accounting Teacher(s).** The emphasis on business record keeping throughout this chapter would lend itself very effectively to cooperative (or guest) teaching by a colleague who teaches Accounting, Business Math, Business Finance or Record Keeping. Additionally, determine which students have taken these courses and invite them to partici-

pate as experts and teaching assistants in helping other students to grasp the concepts and processes.

- **NFTE Journals.** Order and have available one NFTE Journal to distribute to each student in your class, especially for the activities suggested in Extend the Learning.

- **Accounting Materials.** For the Accounting Game and other activities in Develop and Close the Learning: make copies of the following items to create accounting packages for student pairs: three sheets of checks (three checks per page), one check register sheet, one NFTE Journal or a copy of one Journal page, one sheet of receipts (three per page), two invoice sheets, two purchase orders.

- **Checking-Account Materials.** If you plan to use the Bank Account Opening Simulation activity in Develop and Close the Learning below (that is, you are not taking your students on a bank field trip), before class you will need to collect or make the materials needed. Ask a local bank to give you enough checking account applications for each student to have one. If you ask, some local banks may give you empty check registers as well. Alternatively, make a simplified version of an application and check register page on a computer from an actual model. Also make on the computer a receipt form and a page with three or four sample checks on it. Print enough copies so that each student will be able to have one application, one check register page, and a few checks. Also have play money available (optional).

- **Make Field Trip Arrangements.** If you choose the Field Trip activity in Extend the Learning (TE 51), contact a neighborhood bank branch and arrange to tour their facilities. It is best to do this a couple weeks before the date of the class, as you will need to secure signed permission forms from parents, arrange adult chaperones, and make transportation arrangements through the school administration. If transportation funds are not available, an alternative is to have a bank representative or stock broker visit the class as a guest speaker.

## SET A CONTEXT FOR LEARNING

- **Focus 1: Spending.** Ask the students to reflect and make lists:  List everything you bought and what you paid for each item in the last three days. Checkmark those items for which you still have the receipt.

- **Focus 2: How Much Do You Have Left?** Present this problem for students to calculate: Yesterday you cashed your paycheck for $60, spent $10 for a movie and $3 for popcorn last night, and another $8 for lunch today. You need to buy a new dress shirt this afternoon for an event this weekend, which will cost $30 plus 5% tax. How much money will you have left at day's end? **Answers:** $7.50.

- **Discussion Launcher: Bank Transactions.** Ask students to think about times they've visited the bank (including with their parents) and what they did there (open an account, cash a check, etc.). You can use this activity to assess student familiarity with bank transactions in general.

## DEVELOP AND CLOSE THE LEARNING

- **Importance of Record Keeping.** Using the textbook and transparency T12-1, discuss why it is critical for entrepreneurs to keep accurate records of money coming into and going out of their businesses. Introduce and define the following terms so that stu-

dents understand them and how they relate to each other:

- ○ Money coming into the business may be called "sales," "revenue," or "receipts" for money inflow that result from the business's purpose (retail sales, manufacturing, service-providing, etc.); "investment" or "paid-in capital" for money that is put into the business through financing strategies by investors (including the entrepreneur); "interest earned" for money that is kept in a savings or interest-bearing checking account (so the money earns money on itself through *compounding*, as discussed in Chapter 3); "deposit" for money/cash that is put into the business's main checking account (and most money that comes in will be through this account); "accounts receivable" if someone has bought something from you but not yet paid for it. "Income" is a general term that is used for any money coming in.

- ○ Money going out may be called "cost"; "cost of goods/services sold" if it can be attributed to a particular product/service; "expense" if it is an operating cost; "tax" if it pays for taxes owed on profit; and "liability" or "accounts payable" if it is owed to somebody outside the business but has not yet been paid.

- **Banking Relationship.** Ask students to brainstorm independently, in a few minutes, as many services that a bank might provide to an entrepreneur. (Examples might include: checking account, loan, business credit card, line of credit.) Have students share their ideas. Explain that setting up a banking relationship is key to business success. Emphasize that one of the key components of keeping good records is to open a bank account so the entrepreneur can keep track of money inflows and outflows better than s/he can by paying cash.

- **Checking Account Simulation.** See above for preparation needed. This activity is a way to make opening a bank account more concrete and experiential for those students who may not be familiar with banking procedures or for classes that cannot take a field trip to a bank (see below). Give each student various amounts of play money and a checking account application. Step students through completing the form. You are the bank. While students work on another independent extension activity to keep them busy, invite each student individually up to your desk (as the bank officer) to go over his/her application for completeness; ask the student if s/he has any questions, take the student's cash and write a receipt for it, and have the student enter the deposit transaction in his/her register. Alternatively, to speed up the process, you could have the first five students you process also become bank officers and process other students' applications. Once all the students have opened accounts, discuss the process: How did they feel? What questions did it bring up? What was surprising? What could go wrong that you would need to prepare for in the real world? Why open a bank account vs. keeping money in a jar at home? Use transparency T12-2 to show students how to write checks. Present the following scenarios and allow time to enter a deposit or write a check and balance their registers:

❍ You bought a scarf for your friend as a birthday gift from Nellie's Knits for $22.99.

❍ You earned $55 mowing lawns this weekend.

❍ Your account is an interest-bearing checking account at .05% per month. Calculate the interest you earned. (Do this one repeatedly.)

❍ If your balance ever goes below $30, you must pay a finance fee of $1. Check to see if you have gone below the minimum balance and subtract $1 for each time.

❍ You received $50 from your grandmother for your birthday.

❍ You need to pay back your friend the $20 she lent you at the movies the other night.

Tie the need for a checking account back to the idea of good record keeping: it helps track money flowing through the business.

● **Basic Business Accounting System.** Define "accounting" as a record of financial events occurring in the business. This record will provide explanations and justifications for income and expenses; it involves bookkeeping and the preparation of statements concerning the assets, liabilities, and operating results of a business. More common or colloquial terms for accounting that students may relate to are: keeping "the books" and "the paper trail." To keep business operations fair, the business world and the government have agreed on a set of rules or principles — called "Generally Accepted Accounting Practices" (GAAP) — that govern how a business keeps its accounting books. This set of rules makes sure investors can compare companies, and entrepreneurs can know how their businesses are doing in relation to the competition. Use the text and transparencies to show and explain the terms for the documents that comprise a basic business accounting system:

❍ T12-6: Check and check register.

❍ T12-3 and T12-4 Cash Receipts Journal (1 and 2): explain each column heading and how this document keeps a running chronological tally of all money coming into and out of the company.

❍ T12-7: Receipt/packing slip: explain each element and how this document: 1) is both given to a customer and also received from suppliers, and 2) can be given or received at time of sale or with shipping of the product (if ordered).

❍ T12-8: Purchase order: explain each element and how this document is received from a customer or given by the entrepreneur to a supplier when an order is made for later delivery; a purchase order is a promise to pay at a later date but does not represent a cash outlay or receipt.

❍ T12-9: Invoice: explain each element and how this document is sent by the entrepreneur to the customer or by the supplier to the entrepreneur after a purchase order is received to tell the buyer it is time to pay and how much to pay.

❍ T12-5: Income statement: remind students that they first saw this "running equation" in Chapter 9; explain the basic elements (sales/revenue, cost of good sold, operating costs, profit) and how this document provides a summary of events from the journal to show the operations of the business (from a financial perspective) over a set period of time (monthly, quarterly, and annually) to help entrepreneurs and investors make decisions.

❍ T12-10: Balance sheet: explain briefly what an asset, a liability, and owner's equity are, and how this document provides a "snapshot" of the business (from a financial perspective) at a given point in time in terms of what the company owns and owes.

❍ T44-2A, T44-2B: Tax return: there is probably no need to go over all parts of this document in this chapter, but it would be helpful to explain that each year an entrepreneur must complete this form and pay taxes on his/her profits, and that the information will be provided from the other elements of his/her accounting system. This would be an excellent opportunity to invite the school's Accounting teacher to provide an overview of business finance and record keeping.

● **Accounting Process.** Using the text's three basic accounting principles and NFTE Journal categories, plus the information below, walk students through the basic process of using the above documents:

○ When you start a business, enter the initial amount of investment in the check register (as a deposit) and in the journal. Be specific about the event in the explanation column.

○ When you buy anything (materials, inventory, services, utilities, rent), pay by check and enter the cost/expense in the check register and journal, or pay by a purchase order (if the item will be delivered later) and enter the item and amount in the check register and journal when you pay the invoice you will receive from your supplier.

○ When you make a sale: if the customer pays on the spot, give him/her a receipt and enter the sale and amount in the journal the day of the sale and the check register the day you deposit the money into your account. If the customer pays by purchase order, send him/her an invoice and do not enter the sale or amount until you receive the money.

○ Summarize your journal entries by reconciling your journal, creating financial statements on a monthly and annual basis, and calculating ROI

from the income statement. Some formulas are provided in the text after the Chapter Summary.

Use the example in the text (Hernando's T-shirts) or other examples to show the actual use of these documents. That is, re-create the process for each line on the journal provided in the text and create summary documents for the month.

● **Accounting Game.** Divide the class into pairs. Distribute accounting materials package (prepared before class) to each pair. This game can be played step by step if you read each transaction one at a time and allow a few minutes for pairs to do the task. Or the game can be played as a race if you show all the transactions at once on the board or a handout. In both cases, pairs get points for being the first to complete each or all steps accurately. Student pairs are to complete the accounting process for each transaction, including writing checks, entering journal entries, and creating invoices, receipts and purchase orders where appropriate. What students should do for each step is provided in the Answers column.

| Transaction | Answer |
|---|---|
| 4/1: You and a friend start a babysitter-training business by each investing $400 to sell two-hour sessions for $50 per session. | Enter investment in journal and check register, balance. |
| 4/2: You buy some computer equipment from PC Zone for $600 because you plan to deliver the training over a Web site; you write a purchase order. | Write purchase order. |
| 4/3: You hire another friend to help sell training sessions on 10% commission, to be paid at the end of every month. | Nothing. |
| 4/4: You print and distribute $100 worth of flyers and e-mails to young people to publicize your new business. | Write check, enter transaction in journal, balance. |
| 4/6: Two people sign up for your training on purchase order. | Nothing (or accept purchase order) |
| 4/7: You invoice the two customers who signed up. | Write invoices. |
| 4/8: An invoice comes from PC Zone for your computer equipment and you pay half of it on a two-payment installment plan. | Write check for $300, enter transaction in journal, balance. |
| 4/10: Your salesman friend brings you a check for 15 customers to take your training. | Deposit money in account, enter transaction in journal (15 × $50 = $750), balance. |
| 4/11: You buy 50 certificates at $1 each to send to customers who complete your training. | Write check for $50, enter transaction in journal, balance. |
| 4/15: You receive a check for $50 from one of the customers you invoiced. | Deposit money in account, enter transaction in journal, balance. |
| 4/17: You receive a check for $50 from one of the customers you invoiced. | Deposit money in account, enter transaction in journal, balance. |

TE 49

| Transaction | Answer |
|---|---|
| 4/25: Three more people sign up, pay for and take your training. | Deposit money in account, enter transactions separately in journal, balance. |
| 4/26: You pay your electricity bill for $16. | Write check, enter transaction in journal, balance. |
| 4/27: You pay your internet service provider monthly fee of $50. | Write check, enter transaction in journal, balance. |
| 4/30: You pay 60 cents in postage for mailing a certificate to each customer who took your training this month. | Write check for $12 (.60 × 20 students), enter transaction in journal, balance. |
| 4/30: You calculate and write a commission check to your salesman. | Write check for $7 (15 × $50 × .10), enter transaction in journal, balance. |
| 4/30: You determine your monthly profit. | $397 ($1,000 income − $603 expenses). |
| 4/30: You pay 25% tax on your profit. | $99 (.25 × $397). |
| 4/30: You determine your after-tax profit. | $298 ($397 − $99). |

- **Assessing Accounting Game.** Go over each transaction and the journal entries students should have made. Clarify any points they misunderstand. Using their documents, ask the following questions: How is the business doing? (Pretty well, since it turned a profit the first month; but it has plenty of room to grow.) How much money does it have left? ($1173, which should be the ending cash balance.) What is the business's ROI on its initial investment? (e.g., 298/800 = 37%.) What is its return on sales (ROS)? (298/1000 = 30%.) What might the two entrepreneurs do to grow or improve the business? (Answers will vary, but most likely will focus on increase marketing, expand services, keep costs low, etc.)

- **Personal Record Keeping.** Challenge students: Is business ownership the only time when you should keep good records? Steer students to understand that good record keeping is something *everyone* should do, even with personal income and spending. Have students put information listed in Focus 1 in journal form. Ask how this record keeping might help in their personal life. (They can make smarter choices, not go broke, better understand the costs of living.) **LINKS**»·*Consumer Ed*

- **Summary.** Discuss John D. Rockefeller's habit of accounting for every penny he spent. In addition or alternatively, you might refer to the cliché, "Take care of your pennies and the dollars will take care of themselves." What does Rockefeller's habit or this quote mean? Have students complete the In Your Opinion activity in the text and present their ideas to the class.

## ASSESS THE LEARNING

- **Vocabulary.** Have students define terms in their own words and use each in a sentence. Students who use the workbook can complete the Vocabulary Activity.

- **Key Concepts.** Questions 2-3. **Answers:** 2. Particular banks offer different interest rates and balance requirements to appeal to different customer needs. For example, a student checking account may have a low minimum balance, such as $100, and no fees, but also it provides no interest and fewer services. A premier checking account, on the other hand, may require a minimum balance of $2,500 and charge a fee when it goes below that amount, but provide interest on the deposited money, unlimited check writing, and other services. However, banks cannot discriminate in their rates based on gender, race, ethnicity, etc. 3. Any of the following reasons: safer than cash, ease in creating financial statements, documenting payments and deposits made, create a "paper trail" of your money, cancelled checks provide proof a bill/invoice was paid.

- **Critical Thinking.** Create a handout of the transactions for the Accounting Game activity *or direct students to Chapter 12 in the workbook.* **Answers:** 1. See activity listing.

2. Income statement:
   Revenue (20 customers x $50) . . . . . . . . . . . $1,000
   COSS (certificates and mailing) . . . . . . . . . . $62
   Variable Costs (commission) . . . . . . . . . . . . . $75
   Gross Profit . . . . . . . . . . . . . . . . . . . . . . . . . $963
   Fixed Operating Costs (flyers, electricity, ISP) $166
   Other Costs (computer) . . . . . . . . . . . . . . . . $300
   Pre-tax Profit . . . . . . . . . . . . . . . . . . . . . . . $397
   Taxes . . . . . . . . . . . . . . . . . . . . . . . . . . . . . $99
   Net Profit . . . . . . . . . . . . . . . . . . . . . . . . . . . $298

3. Ending balance sheet:
   Assets
   Cash .............................. $1,173
   Inventory (not an inventory business) .. $0
   Capital Equipment (computer) ........ $600
   Other Assets ...................... $0
   Total Assets ....................... $1,773
   Liabilities
   Short-term (still owed on computer) .... $300
   Owner's Equity ...................... $1,473
   Liabilities + OE ...................... $1,773

4. 298/1,000 × 30%.

5. Monthly ROI = 298/800 = 37%. Annualized ROI = 444% (37 × 12).

- **Writing Practice.** Assign In Your Opinion in the text.
- **Additional Workbook Activities Answers.**

   **Vocabulary Activities. Answers:** 1. d, 2. g, 3. e, 4. c, 5. f, 6. h, 7. a, 8. b.

   **Quiz 12** in the workbook. **Answers:** 1. Any of the following reasons: tax deductions, determining profit, analyzing where the money comes from and goes, creating financial statements, documenting payments made. 2. Answers will vary, but the best should be positive and explain that keeping track of money helps people use their money more wisely, which usually leads to success. 3. Answers will vary, but should include: for double-checking, to ensure accuracy, to show what money was for and to categorize it. 4-9. See below. 10. $135, $89.50.

| Date | To/From | For (Explanation) | Deposit | Payment | Balance Fwd. |
|------|---------|-------------------|---------|---------|--------------|
| 3/29 | Boss | Paycheck for part-time job | $60.00 | | $60.00 |
| 3/30 | Movie Theater | Movie | | $7.00 | $53.00 |
| 3/30 | Movie Theater | Popcorn | | $3.00 | $50.00 |
| 3/31 | Flea Market | Table | | $10.00 | $40.00 |
| 3/31 | Subway | Fare | | $3.00 | $37.00 |
| 3/31 | Flea Market Customers | Sales | $75.00 | | $112.00 |
| 4/1 | Wholesaler | Buy inventory | | $35.00 | $77.00 |
| 4/1 | Subway | Fare | | $3.00 | $74.00 |
| 4/1 | Music Store | Tape | | $5.00 | $69.00 |
| 4/3 | Printer | Business cards | | $20.00 | $49.00 |
| 4/3 | Restaurant | Food | | $3.50 | $45.50 |

## EXTEND THE LEARNING

- **Business Plan Practice.** Key Concepts questions 1 and 4.
- **BizTech.** Assign Unit 15 (Note: the cash flow part of the unit will be addressed in Chapter 41.)
- **Bank Field Trip.** This activity is an alternative to the Checking Account Simulation activity above. Before going to the bank, use the text to explain the advantages of opening a savings or checking account, and the differences between these types of accounts. Take a tour of a nearby bank branch to see what services a bank provides to individuals and small businesses, and to learn how savings and checking accounts work. If possible, have students bring $10 or $20 from home to open their own savings accounts. Make sure you have made arrangements with the bank beforehand so they will be able to process so many applications. Also check with the bank and state laws to make sure minors may open accounts (for example, some states require

parental signatures). If you can raise funds from local businesses or personal contacts, it may help motivate students to provide matching funds for whatever amount they deposit. To save time, have the bank send you the application forms so students can complete them in class beforehand. Each month, after students receive their account statements, hold an "interest earned alert" to highlight how their money is making money —- and they don't have to do anything!

- **Exploration.** Assign the activity in the textbook. Alternatively, have each student visit one bank (assign banks so they don't all go to the same one), then compare the bank offerings as a class. A third alternative is to have students research banks and rates on-line. Ask students to choose which bank they personally prefer and why, then give them time to share with the class. See if students can be grouped by similar needs or benefits. Note how the different costs and benefits affect different people in different ways: some are most interested in convenient location, others in friendly tellers, others in computerized banking, others in higher-interest savings rates, etc. Refer back to why it is important for entrepreneurs to understand their customers and consider market segmentation. How might the segments of the class be described (such as "low-cost seekers" for students who want low fees and "high-return seekers" for students who think the interest rate on savings accounts is most important, etc.).

- **A Business for the Young Entrepreneur.** Have students read about the Party DJ business in the textbook. Have them research (on-line or by making phone calls) in your community: the costs of the equipment and materials listed, going rates for DJ services, and other costs that the students think this type of business might incur (equipment, music, prizes, advertising, travel expenses).

- **Personal Record Keeping Follow-up.** Assign students to keep track of all of their income and expenses in journal format for the next week or month. At the end of the time period, have them create a personal income statement and analyze it: how might they get better at spending their money? It might be helpful to distribute NFTE Journals to each student.

- **Recordkeeping Software.** Individually or in teams, have students research on-line accounting or money management software packages. For example, you might assign one software package to each student or team to research its features and benefits. Or you could assign each team to research three packages and determine their strengths and weaknesses relative to each other. Or you could have students make a more open-ended search for what packages are available and make a list. Students or teams could report their findings to the class either verbally or on posters. Then, individually, students could use this information to write a brief report or essay naming the software they would most likely use for their NFTE businesses and why. Once again, the school's Accounting teacher would be a valuable resource.

- **Ongoing Accounting Game.** At the beginning or end of each future class period, add one more transaction to the Accounting Game to keep students in the habit of daily record keeping. These transactions may, but need not, relate to that class period's lesson topic. For example, create transactions while studying Chapter 19 related to advertising or publicity expenses, such as buying airtime for a TV commercial or the printing costs for a flyer; or during

Chapter 21 for customer service training or having to give a refund to an unhappy customer; or during Chapter 26 for purchase of new manufacturing equipment (and reinforcing the idea of depreciation); or during Chapter 30 for new computer hardware, software, or Web-site production.

## BUILD ACADEMIC AND LIFE-SKILL PROFICIENCIES

### *Skills Mean Success* Answers

**English.** Students may write about either method as long as their paragraphs follow the guidelines for being persuasive. They must state a position clearly, explain the advantages of the method selected, support the position with detailed examples, and conclude with the strongest argument. If students have trouble thinking of business examples to support their arguments, allow them to make up the details, as long as their reasoning is logical.

**Leadership.** Assign students to work in groups of three or four to plan, prepare, and deliver their presentations. If practical, encourage them to use PowerPoint slides to accompany the talk. Evaluate the presentations based on planning, organization, content, delivery, and group participation. Students should note that without regular, ongoing, accurate record keeping, business owners would be at risk for

- Failure to reconcile bank statements on a regular basis.
- Lost or missing cash.
- Poor cash flow.
- Theft and ethical problems.
- High costs or declining revenue.
- Lost customers.
- Declined loans.
- Tax penalties.
- Bankruptcy.

Without good records, a business owner will lack control. S/he will not be aware of the business's weaknesses (or strengths) and thus be unable to respond to problems or plan for the future.

**Math.** 1. Monthly ROI = 150%; 2. Annual ROI = 1,800%.

### CHAPTER 13

# INCOME STATEMENTS:
## *The Entrepreneur's Scorecard*

## ORGANIZE THE LEARNING

### CHAPTER OBJECTIVES

- Understand the elements of an income statement.
- Calculate net profit or loss.
- Prepare a monthly income statement.

### NFTE RESOURCES

- Text pp. 174-191
- Transparencies T13-1 and T13-2
- Workbook/BLMs Chapter 13
- Entrepreneurs in Profile #4
- Test Bank Chapter 13
- BizTech Unit 8

### BUSINESS PLAN ACTIVITIES

*Workbook Business Plan Review*
Projected Income Statement 13-1, 13-2, 13-3, 13-4

*Workbook/Textbook Chapter Review*
Key Concepts 5

*Power Point Templates*
Bas. 10, 11; Int. 13, 14; Adv. 13, 14

### SKILLS MEAN SUCCESS

*English*
Reading and Writing for Understanding: Idioms

*Math*
Displaying Data in Charts and Graphs

*Technology*
Spreadsheet Formulas

### PREREQUISITES

Chapters 3, 9 and 12 set a background for this chapter. A review may be helpful.

### VOCABULARY

budget, financial ratios, income statement, net profit, operating ratio, percentage, pre-tax profit, profit margin, return on sales (ROS), same size analysis

## KEY QUESTION

**How do I know how well my business is doing?**

## SET A CONTEXT FOR LEARNING

- **Focus 1: Gross Profit Calculation.** Write on the board or give verbal instructions to have students: Figure the cost of goods sold and gross profit for a pizza that retails for $10 and contains 1 lb. flour at 80 cents, 10 oz. tomato sauce at $1.20, 12 oz. mozzarella at $1.75, and seasonings at 25 cents. **Answers:** $4.

- **Focus 2: ROI Review.** Present the following for the students to solve: What is the return on investment if a person invested $500 and made, after all costs and taxes, $150 after one year? Was this a good investment? **Answers:** 30% (150/500); 30% is a good return rate for one year, but not good for, say, ten years.

- **Discussion Launcher: How Do You Know You Are Using Your Money Well?** Have the students work in pairs, make lists and discuss: What do you spend the most money on? How do you decide how to spend your money? How do you determine if you are spending it wisely? **LINKS**»*Consumer Ed*

## DEVELOP AND CLOSE THE LEARNING

- **What the Income Statement Does.** Introduce the concept of income statements by using the analogy of a scorecard — just as a score in sports tells who is winning the game, the income statement tell entrepreneurs and investors which companies are winning in business. Just as in sports, an athlete, sports announcer, fan, or coach might take an "accounting" of how the team is doing at the end of an inning/quarter/half, companies take an accounting monthly, quarterly and annually. Winning refers to making a profit, and profit signifies which companies are best using their resources to meet customer needs. An income statement is also called a "profit and loss statement" because it shows whether the company is making or losing money after all costs are accounted for. (Refer back to Chapters 9 and 12 regarding costs and accounting.) Make sure students are clear on the terms: net profit/"in the black" and net loss/"in the red" (shown by numbers in parentheses). Also, as with sports, a winning team earns more money. In business, the more profit a company makes, the more value it has for the owner and the higher the price it can command if it is sold.

One general rule (experts differ on this depending on other variables) is that a company is worth three times its net profit. So an income statement tells an entrepreneur: 1) how well the company is doing, 2) how much the company is worth, and 3) indicators of possible ways to improve profitability.

- **Parts of an Income Statement.** Use the Dave's Ties example in the text and transparency T13-1 to make sure students are clear about the terms used in the income statement and where the information comes from (i.e., journal, receipts, etc.). Much of this information is review from Chapters 9 and 12, but is presented in this chapter in a more succinct, summary format. Tie income statements back to the economics of one unit by showing how to fully allocate all costs — COGS/COSS, variable costs, fixed costs — across the number of units sold, as shown in the text: the income statement provides the information needed to fully allocate costs.

- **Bottom-Line Analysis.** Challenge the students: How well is Dave's company doing? How do you know? Explain that a key use of an income statement is to analyze company operations. Entrepreneurs and investors analyze these statements in three ways: focus on the bottom line, use charts/graphs/percentages, and calculate financial ratios. First thing to check is: Is the company making a profit or suffering a loss? Point to the last line on the transparency and explain this line is referred to as "the bottom line." Calculate net profit per unit ($200/1,000 = $2). Let's say this is a monthly income statement. Someone is interested in buying this business: How would Dave decide the selling price and what would the price be? (Multiply net profit by 12 months × 3 = $7,200.)

- **Percentage Analysis.** Remind the students that the bottom line does not tell *how* the business came to make or lose money. Solicit from the students or show them how to transform the raw dollar figures into percentages. Explain that when you convert dollar figures into percentages, you are putting the numbers on "equal footing" — then you can compare across time periods or against your competitors. Define this process as same-size analysis. Use the "same size" income statement examples in the textbook (i.e., Rocket Roller Skate) and ask students: What does it tell us? What might they do to improve net profit? What is their biggest cost? Use transparency T13-2 to calculate all costs as percentage of sales. Then show how these percentages can be represented graphically in a pie chart to give a quick

look at how Dave's sales revenue is used. Ask students: What is Dave's largest expense? (Cost of goods sold.) What might this chart suggest Dave should do to try to get net profit to become a larger slice of the pie? (Reduce the size of the other slices by negotiating with wholesaler for lower COGS, for instance, or reducing sales commissions.) Be clear about what is being shown in a chart — a pie chart can be used to represent how any "whole" or "total" is split. The chart on the transparency represents a "whole" of sales revenue, but pie charts could also be used to analyze fixed costs (what percentage goes to salaries vs. advertising vs. insurance, etc.), variable costs or costs of goods sold for a manufacturer (raw materials, direct labor, etc.). Explain that such percentage/cost analysis is what led to the innovation of the assembly line by Henry Ford — he looked closely at how cars were made and figured out a way to do it at a lower cost, sell at a lower price than his competitors, and make a profit.

Put the following information on the board for students — individually or in teams — to conduct a percentage analysis, create a pie chart, and calculate ROS. Check answers and discuss whether this company is winning (profitable) or not. **Answer:**

| | | | |
|---|---|---|---|
| Sales | $100.00 | 100% | |
| Gross Profit (A) | $50.00 | 50% | |
| Fixed Operating | | | |
| Costs (B) | $20.00 | 20% |  |
| Pre-tax Profit | $30.00 | 30% | |
| Taxes (C) | $5.00 | 5% | |
| Net Profit (D) | $25.00 | 25% | |

ROS = 25/100 = 25%

- **Ratio Analysis.** To continue the discussion, remind students: the bottom line provides a single number signifying "winning" or "losing," and percentage analysis/charts help show us where the bottom line came from. A third way to analyze income statements is by calculating a few financial ratios: operating ratio, ROI and ROS. They are called "ratios" is because they involve division of one number on the income statement or balance sheet by a different number on one of these financial statements. Review the ROI formula from Chapter 3 and give the operating ratio and ROS formulas:

ROI = net profit ÷ investment

ROS = net profit ÷ sales

Operating ratio = a chosen fixed cost ÷ revenue

Continue the example of Dave's Ties: calculate Dave's ROI if he initially invested $200, and his ROS (e.g., ROI = 100%, ROS = 20%). Ask students to speculate: Why is it a good idea to calculate *both* of these return ratios? (An excellent answer would be: ROI tells you how efficiently you are using money that comes from the "outside" — financing — and ROS tells you how efficiently you are using money that comes from the "inside" — sales, business operations.) Ask students to select a fixed cost and calculate its operating ratio: for example, the operating ratio for advertising would be 50/1,000 = 5%, or 5% of the amount of money coming in is going out to pay advertising costs. Ask students: Why would an entrepreneur want to know this information? (to compare it to the industry standard or competitors; to see if it's going up or down over time.)

- **Trend Analysis.** To show how this analysis is related to the others, explain that bottom line, percentage/chart and financial-ratio analyses are often done on one income statement. Ask students to speculate: However, what if you wanted to know how your business is doing over months or years? Explain how a bar chart can be used to show trends. Using the bar chart on transparency T13-2, ask students:

  ○ What is the trend for Dave's sales?

  ○ What might this chart suggest he do? (He was growing, but then leveled off; the sharp drop in May might signal trouble or seasonality of demand and is something he should look at more closely by analyzing the May income statement, sales records, etc.)

  ○ What other information might it be helpful to see in bar charts? (Net profit, operating costs, COGS.)

Using the statements below, draw bar charts on the board for COGS and fixed operating costs:

| Month | Monthly Sales | COGS Costs | Fixed Operating Profit | Net |
|-------|------|------|------|------|
| Jan | $100 | $50 | $24 | $20 |
| Feb | $150 | $75 | $40 | $27 |
| Mar | $200 | $125 | $50 | $19.25 |
| Apr | $200 | $125 | $55 | $15.40 |
| May | $75 | $47 | $55 | $(20.79) |

Ask: ○ What are the trends in COGS, operating costs, COGS relative to sales, etc.?

○ What do these charts suggest Dave might do to improve his business? (Better control operating costs (especially fixed), find a new wholesaler or renegotiate with current one.)

Divide students into teams — one team for each month — and have each team create an income statement for the month using the above figures and calculate net profit. Assume a tax rate of 23%. As a class, draw a bar chart for net profit and discuss what this chart tells you.

- **Competitor/Industry Analysis.** Ask students to consider how these financial ratios — ROI, ROS, operating ratios — as well as same size analysis can be used to determine how well an entrepreneur's business is doing relative to his/her competitors or the industry average. Recreate on the board the following table and ask students to analyze the numbers. Which company is doing the best? The worst? What strategies might each company try to improve its position in the tie industry? Discuss how sometimes such comparisons may not be straightforward — one company might have a great ROS but another has a higher ROI. How do the students interpret these seeming inconsistencies? (A high ROS means a company is using its income from sales well but it may have had high start-up costs and hence a high initial investment, so it's ROI might be lower than a different company that has fewer start-up costs/lower initial investment but does not have as high revenue.)

| Company | ROI | ROS | OR* | OR** |
|---------|-----|-----|-----|------|
| Dave's Ties | 100% | 20% | 5% | 8% |
| Natalie Neckwear | 50% | 60% | 7% | 8% |
| Neck-n-Neck | 80% | 80% | 5% | 6% |
| Tie One On | 60% | 75% | 8% | 4% |

*\* advertising,  \*\* salaries*

- **Budgeting.** Discuss how record keeping not only shows what financial events have happened in the past, but can also be used for planning how to disburse money in future. This future-oriented use of financial information is called "budgeting" and the document is called a "budget" or "pro-forma statement." Budgeting basically uses information from the past (from the journal and past income statements) to project what will happen in the future. Based on the information collected in the Personal Record-Keeping activity above, have students create personal budgets. Alternatively or in addition, have students in teams discuss what is likely to happen in May for the business in the Accounting Game above and create a monthly budget for the business.

- **Summary.** Challenge the students: The income statement focuses on "winning" financially in a business. But there are other ways of winning besides money. What other benefits does an entrepreneur receive besides making a profit? (Answers could include benefits discussed in The Double Bottom Line section of the text: clean environment, good citizen/safe society, good relations with people.)

## ASSESS THE LEARNING

- **Vocabulary.** Have students define terms in their own words and use each in a sentence, or complete the Vocabulary activity in the workbook.

- **Key Concepts.** Questions 1-5. Note that these questions require access to the NFTE Workbook. **Answers:** 1. $708,000. 2. 13% 3. Cut the amount spent on food or paper (COGS) or reduce operating costs. 4. $1.4 million because that equals three times its annual profit. 5. Answers will vary, but the student should produce side-by-side income statements, including percentage analyses, and clearly argue how and why McDonald's or their business is doing better in different areas.

- **Critical Thinking.** Questions 1-5. **Answers:**

  1. | | | |
     |---|---|---|
     | Sales | $200 | 100% |
     | COGS (% of sales) **(A)** | $100 | 50% |
     | Variable Costs **(B)** | $40 | 20% |
     | Gross Profit | $60 | 30% |
     | Fixed Operating Costs **(C)** | $20 | 10% |
     | Profit Before Taxes | $40 | 20% |
     | Taxes **(D)** | $8 | 4% |
     | Net Profit/(Loss) **(E)** | $32 | 16% |

  2. a. $100. b. $32. c. $20 (amount of fixed costs). d. $8.

  3. See percentage of sales column above.

     A = COGS 50%
     B = Variable Costs 20%
     C = Fixed OC 10%
     D = Taxes 4%
     E = Net Profit 16%

  4. Memos will vary. It looks like sales are going up in general. You will probably increase your orders and perhaps consider a second salesperson.

     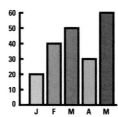

  5. *Cost of good sold* because disclosing it lets people know how much gross profit you are making and they may want to pay you less.

- **Additional Workbook Answers.**

  **Vocabulary Activity Answers:** 1. income statement, 2. return on sales, 3. Net profit, 4. operating ratio, 5. financial ratios, 6. percentages, 7. Pre-tax profit, 8. profit margin, 9. same size analysis, 10. budget.

  **Quiz 13** in the workbook. **Answers:** 1. Because it shows whether a company is making (profit) or losing (loss) money. 2. Answers may vary but should relate to helping the entrepreneur understand where the company's money is going and how much the company is worth. 3. Because a customer could then figure out the entrepreneur's gross profit and most likely would want to negotiate a lower price.

  4. | **Sales:** | | **$200.00** |
     |---|---|---|
     | Variable Costs | | |
     |    COGS: | $40.00 | |
     |    Other Variable Costs: | 0.00 | |
     |    Total Variable Costs: | $40.00 | 40.00 |
     | **Gross Profit** | | **$160.00** |
     | Fixed Operating Costs | | |
     |    Fixed Costs: | $20.00 | |
     |    Other Costs: | 0.00 | |
     |    Total Fixed OC: | $20.00 | 20.00 |
     | **Pre-Tax Profits:** | | **$140.00** |
     |    Taxes (15%) | $28.00 | 28.00 |
     | **Net Profit/(Loss)** | | **$112.00** |

## EXTEND THE LEARNING

- **BizTech.** Assign Unit 8.

- *Entrepreneurs in Profile.* Ask the students to read the profile on Candice Carpenter and be prepared to respond in class to questions such as:

  ○ What are iVillage's sources of revenue — what does the company sell?

  ○ What might be going on that is keeping iVillage from showing a profit?

  ○ What would you look at if you had access to the company's income statement?

- **Working with Spreadsheets.** Set up an income statement/budget in a spreadsheet program by inputting the formulas. Have students input different sales revenue and cost forecasts to see how these different assumptions change the bottom line. Ask students to write a memo summarizing their thoughts.

- **"Selling a Business" Negotiating Game.** Divide the class into pairs. Using Dave's Ties or any of the other income statement examples in the text, have one student be the business owner and the other an entrepreneur who wants to buy the business. Using the "three-times-net-profit" rule and percentages and financial ratio analyses, have the students negotiate a selling price. For example, analyses might be used by the seller to show that operations are efficient and s/he tries to negotiate above the three-times amount, or the buyer might point out that fixed costs are high and ask for a discount, etc. After students have completed their negotiations, discuss the issues that surfaced and how they were dealt with.

- **Income Statement Card Game.** Create three decks of index cards: a "sales" deck, a "COGS" deck, and an "expenses" deck. For each deck, create several cards. The sales deck cards each should include a different selling price and number of units sold (e.g., $1, 10; $3, 5, etc.). The COGS deck should include cards with different wholesale purchase prices. (These should be a lower range than the sale prices). The expenses deck should include cards with fixed operating cost amounts and variable operating costs-per-unit. The game makes two assumptions: product bought equals product sold, and the tax rate is figured at 10%. Divide the class into small groups. Shuffle each deck separately and give each group one card from each. The groups will then create income statements using the card information. Track who finishes first with accurate figures and which group's "company" made the most money. Note that some combinations of cards will result in net losses. Continue as long as student interest and time permit.

## BUILD ACADEMIC AND LIFE-SKILL PROFICIENCIES

### *Skills Mean Success* Answers

**English.** Accept any wording that incorporates the meanings below:

a. "to give the green light" — The manager gave permission to proceed with the project.

b. "out of the blue" — The computer crashed unexpectedly, without warning.

c. "red tape" — These excessive procedures and formalities are slowing my work.

d. "rolled out the red carpet" — He was our biggest client, so we welcomed him with great hospitality and ceremony.

e. "tickled pink" — The customer was delighted with our new product.

f. "with flying colors" — He passed the training course with great success.

Idioms are useful when your communication is brief and informal and with friends or colleagues. However, be aware that idiomatic English can be confusing, especially for people whose first language is not English. Idioms should be used only when you are certain your readers (or listeners) will understand them. As an extension activity, ask students to work in pairs to think of other idiomatic expressions and rewrite them in standard English.

Note: If students struggle with this exercise, allow them to research idioms to try to locate their origins. The following web sites are comprehensive sources for idioms and their meanings.

www.idiomconnection.com
www.idiomsite.com

**Math.** Students' bar graphs should show the tallest bars at June and July and the shortest ones at January and December. Students should note that the bar graph shows Dave's revenue as being seasonal. His revenue is highest in the spring and summer months, when landscaping needs are more common. His revenue is lowest in the winter months when landscaping needs are fewer. This phenomenon is commonly referred to as cash flow, and students will meet it later in the curriculum.

**Technology.** In this activity, students will learn some basic spreadsheet terminology and formula symbols. If possible, demonstrate this spreadsheet on a computer in your classroom (or invite the Computer Ed teacher or a spreadsheet-knowledgeable student to do so) and encourage students to set up their own spreadsheets to see the calculations in action.

| Answers (student text page 189): | Cell | | Formula |
|---|---|---|---|
| | F7 | = | E7/E3 |
| | E8 | = | E6−E7 |
| | F8 | = | E8/E3 |
| | E9 | = | E8*0.2 |
| | F9 | = | E9/E3 |
| | E10 | = | E8−E9 |
| | F10 | = | E10/E3 |

### CHAPTER 14

# FINANCING STRATEGY:
## *Debt or Equity?*

## ORGANIZE THE LEARNING

### CHAPTER OBJECTIVES

- Compare debt and equity financing.
- Discuss the three basic legal business structures: sole proprietorship, partnership, and corporation.
- Choose alternative forms of financing, such as micro-loans and "bootstrapping."
- Calculate debt and debt-to-equity ratios.

### NFTE RESOURCES

- Text pp. 192-203
- Transparency T14-1
- Workbook/BLMs Chapter 14
- Entrepreneurs in Profile #14
- Test Bank Chapter 14
- BizTech Unit 7

### BUSINESS PLAN ACTIVITIES

*Workbook Business Plan Review*
Financing Strategy 14-1, 14-2, 14-3, 14-4, 14-5, 14-6, 14-7

*Workbook/Textbook Chapter Review*
Key Concepts 1, 2, 5 (and 3-4)

*Power Point Templates*
Bas. 12-15; Int. 15-19; Adv. 15-17, 20, 21

### SKILLS MEAN SUCCESS

*Math*
Formulas and Operations: Simple Interest

*English*
Reading for Understanding: Reading for Critical Analysis

*Leadership*
Interviewing

### PREREQUISITES

Students should be familiar with the content of Chapters 3, 4, and 13.

### VOCABULARY

debt, debt ratio, debt-to-equity ratio, equity, financing, promissory note, start-up capital

*Other terms to be be familiar with:*
asset, bankruptcy, bond, cooperative, corporation, leverage, nonprofit, partnership, payback, sole proprietorship, stock

## KEY QUESTION

**How do I get the money needed to start my business?**

## PREPARE FOR LEARNING

- **Make Arrangements for Field Trips.** If you choose to complete the field trip described in Extend the Learning on TE 61, contact a neighborhood bank branch or local brokerage firm and arrange to tour their facilities. It is best to do this a couple weeks before the date of the class as you will need to secure signed permission forms from parents, arrange adult chaperones, and make transportation arrangements through your school administration. As an alternative, have a bank representative or stock broker visit the class as a guest speaker.

## SET A CONTEXT FOR LEARNING

- **Focus 1: ROI Practice.** Provide the chart below and have students complete it: Calculate the return and

decide which option you would prefer to invest in. Why?

| Investment | Annual rate of return | Return |
|---|---|---|
| $1000 loan | 3% guaranteed | $30 |
| $1000 equity | 6% of profit earned | $60 |

- **Focus 2: Where Can You Get the Money?** Pose this question: You need $500 to start your business. Where might you get all or part of this money? Be creative!

- **Discussion Launcher 1: Borrow vs. Sell vs. Save.** Write on the board, distribute a handout, or give verbal instructions to have students discuss with a partner: You need $500 to start your business. If you borrow the money from the bank, you will have to pay back $550 in a year even if your business fails. If you sell equity in the company, your investor wants to tell you how to run the company. If you save the money by working other jobs, you won't be able to open your business for a year and a competitor might do it first. Which option do you prefer and why?

## DEVELOP AND CLOSE THE LEARNING

- **Start-up Capital.** Recall from Chapter 3 the ROI equation: net profit/investment. Investment is also called start-up capital or seed money, when it is received before the business opens. Besides COGS/COSS, variable and fixed operating costs, a business also incurs one-time costs—often substantial—just to open. Ask students: What kinds of things does a business need to start—before it can even make its first sale? (A shop/place, equipment, inventory, employee training.) Besides these one-time costs, fixed costs have to be paid (insurance, advertising to get your first customers to come in, etc.) Introduce the concept of cash reserve: an entrepreneur should have enough in the bank (through initial investment) to cover three months of fixed costs because there is a time-lag between opening and when money starts to come in from operations.

- **Payback.** Explain that start-up costs are recouped after business operations costs have paid for costs of goods sold and operating costs. That is, the net profit shown on the income statement is used to pay back the entrepreneur for his/her initial investment; once this investment is paid back, then real money-making begins. Use the payback example in the textbook or another example to calculate how long it will take to recoup start-up costs. Ask students to speculate: Why is it important to know payback? (Answers should establish that, once start-up costs are recouped and paid back, then the company is finally truly making money and growing; the entrepreneur and investors want to know when they'll get their investment back because the time needed to recoup an investment is related to how risky it is.)

- **Additional Investment after Start-Up.** Extend the idea of capital beyond start-up capital. Ask the students to brainstorm times and instances during a company's operations when it might need more money than the operations themselves or the owner's wealth can provide. When a company needs outside sources of funds after start-up, the capital raised is called "additional paid-in capital." Examples could include: when the company wants to open a new store, when it wants to open an overseas operation, when it needs new major equipment or machinery, when the business is going well but the company is temporarily short of cash flowing in. Emphasize that companies use financing strategies at other times, not just when they first open.

- **Financing.** Financing involves using outside sources of funds — money that is not generated by business operations but from investment. Have the students recall examples from past chapters or from *Entrepreneurs in Profile*: Where does investment money comes from? The most obvious source is from oneself: savings or selling personal property (refer to the Wozniak & Jobs selection in *Entrepreneurs in Profile* as an example). But entrepreneurs can also use "other people's money" (OPM), in several ways: debt and equity. This financing may come from both traditional sources, such as banks and regular investors, or from alternative sources such as those listed in the text. Both debt and equity financing infuse cash into the company but their effects on the company differ. Discuss the differences between debt and equity using transparency T14-1. (Equity involves effectively "selling" part ownership of the company for money. Debt involves borrowing money, but with no sharing of ownership.)

- **Business Legal Structures.** The ways an entrepreneur might finance a business depend in part on how the business is set up. Describe the different types of business legal structures from the text, focusing on sole proprietorships and partnerships, since they are the most likely structures that students will choose. Ask: How does the legal structure of a business affect financing decisions? (Answers could include that sole proprietors and partners are personally responsible for debts so they can not only lose company assets but their own as well, so there is more risk with debt financing; sole proprietorships and partnerships usually take on debt by getting a bank loan, but corporations can offer bonds to investors). **LINKS** *Business Law*

- **Debt.** Use an example to make the advantages and disadvantages of debt more concrete and understandable. You may have to provide more than one example. For example: Roberto borrowed $1,000 at 10% from the bank to open a yoga studio. As long as he made the monthly payments of $92 on time (for the next 12 months), the bank did not care how Roberto ran his studio. He spent the money by renting a studio ($200 per month), printing and distributing coupons for half-off a customer's first visit ($500), and yoga mats ($300). What happens if Roberto doesn't make at least $92 the first month? Encourage students to draw from the example the pros/cons of debt. As real-life examples, use the Berry Gordy and Robert Johnson chapters in *Entrepreneurs in Profile*. Ask students: What are the most common sources of debt — from where do you get loans? (A bank, friends, family, special government loan programs.)

- **Equity.** Use an example to make the advantages and disadvantages of equity more concrete and understandable. You may have to provide more than one example. For instance: Instead of borrowing, Roberto received $1,000 from his uncle to open the yoga studio. In return, his uncle wanted Roberto to check with him before making any purchase decisions. His uncle said he should hold a big grand-opening event to bring potential customers to his studio, which would cost $800. Roberto was concerned that, if it didn't work, he'd only be able to pay the first month's rent of $200 for the space. What would happen if the event is successful and Roberto earns $500 the first month? What happens if the event doesn't work? Encourage students to draw from the example the pros/cons of equity. As real-life examples, use the Anita Roddick, Carol Carpenter, King Gillette, and/or Jerry Yang profiles in *Entrepreneurs in Profile*. Ask: What are the most common sources of equity — who are most likely to be your investors? (Friends, family, "angel" investors, venture capitalists; when you "go public" then anyone can be an investor.)

- **Risk.** Pose these questions to the students:

  ○ Which is riskier for the entrepreneur: debt or equity?

  ○ Which is riskier for the investor?

  Lead students to discuss how business risk is assumed by *someone* (there is never a "free ride"). Equity is riskier for investors than debt because they could lose all their entire investment or not recover it for a very long period of time, whereas a loan must legally be repaid in full. Debt is often the riskier choice for the entrepreneur because the loan must be repaid regardless of whether the company succeeds or fails. Discuss why. Observe that bankruptcy does not automatically free the declarer from all debt obligations nor does a loan guarantee an investor repayment if the borrower goes bankrupt. Both have risks for both parties. Explain that most businesses use a combination of equity and debt financing. Sole proprietorships and partnerships can take out loans (debt) or give away ownership (equity). Corporations can take out loans or issue bonds (debt) or sell stock (equity). If a company goes bankrupt and assets must be sold, debt holders are repaid before equity holders. For this reason, equity holders want to know how much debt a company takes on because debt lowers the value of their stock (shares of ownership).

- **Ratios.** Step students through examples of debt-to-equity and debt-ratio calculations. As a running example, return to the case of Roberto introduced above, who is opening a yoga studio. Assume Roberto took both the $1,000 loan and his uncle's investment of $1,000. What is his debt-to-equity ratio? (1:1.) If his assets are the yoga mats he bought ($300) and the money he has in the bank after paying rent and coupon expenses ($1,000 = $2,000 he received from loan and uncle's investment minus $500 for coupons minus $200 for rent minus $300 for mats), what is his debt-to-assets ratio at the end of the first month? (1:1.3, or about 76%). Using the table in the text, what level of risk does Roberto's business represent? (Answer: "high.") Sometimes when new businesses are considered a high risk, it is hard to find traditional investors and lenders to work with. Use the textbook to discuss alternative sources of financing. In small groups, have students brainstorm bootstrapping tactics beyond those listed in the text.

- **Summary.** Return to the Roberto example and ask the students to discuss or write up as a point-form summary: If you were Roberto, which financing option would you choose and why? Allow a few minutes for students to discuss their responses with a partner.

## ASSESS THE LEARNING

- **Vocabulary.** Have students define the key terms in their own words and use each in a sentence. Assign the vocabulary activity in the workbook.

- **Key Concepts.** Questions 3-4. **Answers:** Answers will vary as these questions ask for personal reflection and self-assessment regarding how much of different types of risks students are willing to take. 3. Answers should reflect understanding that giving up more than 50% equity means losing control of the company. 4. Answers should reflect that the debt financing amount and its interest rate should not be too high or the profits earned may not be able to cover making the interest payments, a situation that could force the entrepreneur into bankruptcy. Furthermore, if the entrepreneur cannot repay the principal balance, the amount s/he pays in interest charges grows and takes away resources from operating and expanding the business.

- **Critical Thinking.** Questions 1-2. **Answer:** 1. Preferences will vary; debt's advantage is that lenders have no say in business operations, and its disadvantage is that repayment is required and must be made on a schedule, regardless of how the business is doing. Equity's advantage is that entrepreneurs only have to repay investors when the company makes a profit, and its disadvantage is that the entrepreneur may have to give investor(s) some say in how the business is run. 2. 10%, $50, $80, $100.

- **Additional Workbook Activities Answers.**

  **Vocabulary Activity Answers: Across:** 2. debt ratio, 6. nonprofit, 9. debt-to-equity ratio, 11. start-up capital, 12. sole proprietorship, 13. financing, 14. equity, 15. bankruptcy, 16. payback, 17. cooperative, 18. leveraged; **Down:** 1. debt, 3. asset, 4. bootstrap financing, 5. partnership, 7. promissory note, 8. corporation, 10. angel.

  **Quiz 14** in the workbook. **Answers:** 1. Sole proprietorship advantages are that it's easy and inexpensive to open and you get to keep all the profit; the disadvantage is that you are personally liable for all the debt. A partnership advantage is that you share liability for the debt: disadvantages are that you also must split the profits, plus partnerships usually require more start-up costs to pay for a lawyer to draw up an agreement. 2. Equity is selling ownership in the company through issuing stock; stockholders share in control of company policy as well as company profits and losses. 3. The business owner does not give up control of the company and does not have to share profits with lenders. 4. The debt must be paid back with interest, regardless of how much money the business is making. 5. A stock investor takes a greater risk because s/he may lose all of the investment. 6. b (leveraged). 7. 2:1. 8. 0.25 or 25% or 1:4. 9. Answers will vary but could include: sell equity to friends or family, take out micro-loans, "angel" financing, bootstrap financing, business incubators. 10. 10 months.

## EXTEND THE LEARNING

- *Entrepreneurs in Profile.* Have students read the chapter on Anita Roddick and be prepared to discuss in class the following: What methods did Roddick use to finance her business when she started it and as it was growing? What were the advantages and disadvantages (or risks) of her decisions? What troubles did she run into or mistakes did she make? How does The Body Shop help fund other entrepreneurs, especially in foreign countries?

- **Business Plan Practice.** Key Concepts 1-2, 5.

- **BizTech.** Assign Unit 7.

- **Business Incubators.** Have students look in the phone book or other sources to determine if there are business incubators locally. As a class, create a brief survey asking what kinds of services incubators provide, what types of businesses they support, what types of financing they may offer, etc. Have students call some of the incubators to find out the information and compile findings in a report about which incubators might be good resources for young entrepreneurs: Do they support simple businesses that teens might open? How do they work with people under age 21? Are they conveniently located? Have students brainstorm what kinds of businesses (perhaps using the list in Chapter 8 in the textbook) might be best supported by local incubators. You might consider sending, with a thank-you cover letter, the class's report to the incubator people the students interviewed. **LINKS**»*Economics*

- **Exploring Your Community.** Assign the bank research activity in Chapter 12 in the textbook if you did not use it previously

- **Scan *Entrepreneurs in Profile* for Debt vs. Equity Financing.** Have students individually or in small groups scan *Entrepreneurs in Profile* chapters for examples of debt and equity financing. Establish the notion that a business could make financing decisions at several points over the course of its business's growth — so each chapter in *Entrepreneurs in Profile* might include more than one financing decision. Remind students to keep careful track of their research and to note: name of the company, type of business (manufacturing, retail, etc.), type of financing (debt, equity), how much, timing (before or after the business opened), circumstances (why was the money needed?). It may be helpful to make a table/worksheet for students to complete. Alternatively, assign certain chapters to groups to research. Compile some of the findings on the board and ask students to look for patterns. For example:

  ○ Do manufacturers more often use debt or equity financing?

  ○ Is that trend the same for retailers or service providers?

  ○ Are there differences between the men and women entrepreneurs?

  ○ Are there differences in timing (such as that either debt or equity is used more than the other at start-up and the other is used more once the business is established)?

- **Brokerage Firm Field Trip.** This activity provides an experience of how ownership/equity is bought and sold. If you live in a city with a stock exchange (such as the New York Stock Exchange, the Chicago Board of Trade, NASDAQ), arrange a visit through its education department. Alternatively, visit a stock brokerage firm to have students learn about what a stock broker does, see a stock ticker, and observe traders at work. When you contact the brokerage firm, emphasize that the tour will take no more than an hour. If an actual field trip is not possible, a cyber-field trip to a stock exchange is an option: www.nyse.com, www.nasdaq.com, www.cbot.com, www.schwab.com or another online trading company.

- **Guest Speaker.** Invite a bank representative, stock broker, or incubator manager to make a presentation to your class about opening a bank account or stock account or an incubator-supported business. It may be a good idea to send a copy of the textbook to the guest speaker so s/he can see what the students will have learned and to make sure the presentation is not too complex with formulas or detailed concepts. Suggest that the speaker bring samples of account applications or statements for students to see and analyze. Have students think of and make lists of questions before the speaker arrives. See also the *Skills Mean Success* — Leadership activity.

## BUILD ACADEMIC AND LIFE-SKILL PROFICIENCIES

### *Skills Mean Success* Answers

**Math.**

| Interest | Amount to Be Paid Back |
|---|---|
| 1. $500 × .05 × 1 = $25 | $500 + $25 = $525 |
| 2. $1,000 × .05 × 1.5 = $75 | $1,000 + $75 = $1,075 |
| 3. $2,500 × .125 × 2 = $625 | $2,500 + $625 = $3,125 |
| 4. $5,000 × .10 × 2.5 = $1,250 | $5,000 + $1,250 = $6,250 |
| 5. $10,000 × .07 × 3 = $2,100 | $10,000 + $2,100 = $12,100 |

Make sure that students understand the relationship between principal, time, and interest rate. The three factors that affect the total amount due to the lender will always include the amount of the loan, the term (length of time) of the loan, and the interest rate charged. The higher that any of these are, the larger the amount you will have to repay. For this reason, it is important to borrow only what is needed, to "shop around" for low interest rates, and to pay back loans as quickly as possible.

Note that in Questions 2 and 5, students must remember to convert the time frame into years.

**English.** 1. c; 2. d; 3. a; 4. e; 5. b. Note that, in reality, these businesses could take on other legal structures than those suggested. The goal of this activity is for students to recognize the different structures from a critical reading of the passage and to identify the logical matches.

**Leadership.** Observe students' role-plays and encourage them to display an appropriate attitude. Remind them to answer questions completely — using formal, standard English. If students have trouble thinking of appropriate questions, they can search the Internet under "business loan interview" to find sites that can provide helpful interview information and questions.

If possible, invite a loan officer from a local bank to talk to the class about the types of questions asked and what the bank looks for in a loan candidate.

### CHAPTER 15

# NEGOTIATION:
## *Achieving Goals through Compromise*

## ORGANIZE THE LEARNING

| CHAPTER OBJECTIVES | BUSINESS PLAN ACTIVITIES | PREREQUISITES |
|---|---|---|
| • Handle a negotiation. | *Workbook Business Plan Review* | None |
| • Practice the art of compromise. | Negotiation 15-1 | **VOCABULARY** |
| • Seek a "Yes" or "No" instead of a "Maybe." | **SKILLS MEAN SUCCESS** | compromise, negotiation |
| **NFTE RESOURCES** | *English* | |
| • Text pp. 204-209 | Listening for Critical Analysis: Communication Skills | |
| • Transparencies T15-1 to T15-3 | *Leadership* | |
| • Workbook/BLMs Chapter 15 | Using Nonverbal Communication Skills | |
| • Entrepreneurs in Profile #15 | | |
| • Test Bank Chapter 15 | | |

## KEY QUESTION

**How can I achieve my goals by working with others?**

## PREPARE FOR LEARNING

• **Choose Product and Price Ranges for Negotiation Game.** Before starting the optional activities in Develop and Close the Learning that begin with Preparing to Negotiate, choose a specific product students would be interested in having, such as an amusement park ticket, movie passes, or a backpack. Set a maximum price for the buyer and a minimum price for the seller (make sure there is overlap).

## SET A CONTEXT FOR LEARNING

• **Focus 1: Negotiation Opportunities.** Ask students to list things they want or activities they want to do in the next week that will need to involve others (such as deciding on a movie to see with a friend).

• **Focus 2: Negotiation Situation.** Provide this scenario for students to answer and discuss: Kevin is negotiating with a wholesaler to buy posters of athletes. The first price the wholesaler mentions is $5 per poster with a minimum purchase of $25. What should Kevin do next?

• **Discussion Launcher 1: Karrass Quote.** Show or share the Chester L. Karrass quote at the bottom of transparency T15-1 and ask students to explain

what it means. Alternatively, write the quote on the board or share it aloud: "You don't get what you deserve, you get what you negotiate."

• **Discussion Launcher 2: Listening Practice.** With the class divided into pairs, have one partner share with the other a brief story of his/her own choosing. The other student then repeats back, in his/her own words, what s/he heard and understood. Then partners switch roles. Ask students to rate their partners and themselves from 1-5 on how well they listened.

## DEVELOP AND CLOSE THE LEARNING

• **Why Negotiate?** Define negotiation from the textbook. Ask students to share types of situations in their lives in which negotiation would have been helpful (perhaps referring to Focus 1 above). Have students speculate: Why might negotiation be better than other tactics, such as arguing/fighting, forcing someone to do something, or giving in to the other person without discussion? (In negotiation both parties can get something they want, even if they don't get everything; negotiation is useful in maintaining long-term relationships; negotiation is more honest and open about expressing needs and goals.) What might make it difficult for some people to negotiate? (Answers will probably relate to not knowing how, being shy, being intimidated by the other person, not knowing what they really want (undefined goals), not knowing what they are willing and not willing to compromise on, low self-confidence, they want something so much they allow no room for negotiation.) In small groups, have students brainstorm situations in which an entrepreneur might need to negotiate. See which group comes up with the most ideas in a set amount of time, or which groups come up with relevant situations no other group thought of. (Answers will probably include: with suppliers, with employees, with investors, with loan officers, with customers who have problems with the product/service, with partners, with union leaders, with the media regarding publicity.) Emphasize that negotiation is a fundamental business skill.

- **Preparing to Negotiate.** Alert students that they will be engaging in negotiations as buyers and sellers of a product you have chosen beforehand. Use this buyer/seller scenario as a running example throughout the lesson. Have students divide a sheet of paper in half vertically to make three columns. Label the first "Tip," the second "Buyer" and the third "Seller." Emphasize that the art of negotiation starts well before you meet the other party. Discuss transparency T15-2. For each point, have students write the "tip" for the buyer and the seller and make notes on their papers. Example: for "set goals," students might come up with "get the highest price possible" for the seller and "get the lowest price possible" for the buyer; for "decide boundaries," the seller column might note "between $_____ and $_____" and that of the buyer "between $_____ and $_____ ." Also, ask students to think about non-financial considerations. For example, the seller also may think it is important that the buyer believes the product is of high quality or that s/he is an honest person, etc.

- **During Negotiation.** Discuss transparency T15-3. For these tips, ask students to brainstorm ideas for accomplishing them.

- **Negotiation Game.** The purpose of this activity is to practice and build confidence in negotiating skills. Divide the class into buyers and sellers. First, take the sellers into the hall and tell them: Your goal is to sell the product for the highest price you can get but you cannot sell it for less than $_____ (a price you set beforehand). Then take the buyers into the hall and tell them: Your goal is to buy the product for the lowest price you can get but you cannot buy it for more than $_____ (a price you set beforehand). Return to the classroom, pair up buyers and sellers, and give everyone specific rules such as the following:

*You must come to an agreement within the*

*set time (for example, 5 minutes). Each pair should have a piece of paper to serve as the contract, which will need to be completed when the bargain is struck with the name of the item, the agreed-upon price, and both negotiators' signatures.*

When all pairs have come to an agreement, have them share their negotiated prices. Write these on the board, and note the highest and lowest ones. Ask the seller who got the highest price and the buyer who got the lowest price what their tactics were. Discuss tactics other students used. In addition to price, recognize other important tactics and concepts, such as the seller who did something unique to benefit the buyer (customer service), or the pair(s) that did a good job of establishing trust, or the negotiator(s) who seemed most oriented toward long-term relationship-building, or the negotiator(s) who did something creative. Alternatively, students could be assigned to research information through the Internet for each side to better understand potential issues before negotiating. For example:

- ○ Employee/employer negotiating for a salary raise.

- ○ Union leader/management negotiating for health-care benefits.

- ○ Two countries negotiating a trade agreement.

- **Summary.** Use transparency T15-1 and ask students to summarize the main points of negotiation. Return to Discussion Launcher 1 above regarding the Karrass quote: How is it true or not true?

## ASSESS THE LEARNING

- **Vocabulary.** Have students define terms in their own words and use each in a sentence.

- **Key Concepts.** Questions 1-5. **Answers:** 1. In a game, the goal is for one person to win and the other to lose; in negotiation, the goal is for all parties to win something. 2. If both negotiators leave the negotiation satisfied, they are more likely to work together and help each other in the future. 3. Answers will vary but should include some of the following: set goals and boundaries, write them down, consider the other person's perspective, think of potential pitfalls and ways to avoid them. 4. Your boundaries, such as minimum and maximum price or other things that are important to you. 5. Silence, extremes, let the other person name a price first.

- **Critical Thinking/Writing Practice.** Question 1.

**Answer:** Answers will vary; some tactics they might include are: throwing out an extreme figure, silence, and waiting for the other person to make the first offer.

- **Additional Workbook Activities Answers.**

  **Vocabulary Activity  Answers:** 1. c, 2. a.

  **Quiz 15** in the workbook. **Answers:** 1. Set goals and boundaries, consider the other person's perspective, think of potential pitfalls and ways to avoid them. 2. Reveal his/her position. 3. No, because a "maybe" is inconclusive and could stop her from moving on to new deals with other people. 4. No, because Mike may have "won" this negotiation but Barry is unlikely to work with him in the future, so Mike lost in the long term. 5. Compromise. 6. Negotiation. 7. Try to negotiate a longer payback period. 8. Any price between $2 and $4 and/or any quantity between 2 and 4 dozen. 9. To make a long-term friend of the other negotiator. 10. Answers will vary but should demonstrate understanding of setting goals and boundaries, taking the other person's perspective, trying to get the other person to reveal his/her position first, always asking for a better deal, and not settling for "maybe."

- **Negotiation Practice.** Critical Thinking question 2.

## EXTEND THE LEARNING

- **In Your Opinion.** Assign the essay question in the text. Alternatively, students could create a slide presentation or poster. Divide the class into those who favor winning and those who favor compromise as a goal of negotiation. Hold a brief debate between the two perspectives.

- ***Entrepreneurs in Profile.*** Ask the students to read about Russell Simmons and be prepared to discuss it in class. Questions to pre-assign to guide the reading include:

  ○ With whom did he negotiate? (His partner Rick, CBS Records, clubs to get his singles played, Sony, Frank Price/Columbia Pictures, HBO, TV director Stan Lathan, employees.)

  ○ For each situation, what were or might have been Simmons' goals and boundaries?

  ○ What negotiation tactics did he use? Note that some answers may not be presented in the chapter but could still be speculated about and discussed.

- **Hi Tech Negotiations.** Individually or in pairs, ask students to brainstorm or research how computers might improve or detract from negotiations (includ-

ing preparing for negotiations) in comparison to face-to-face negotiations.

- **Negotiations in the News.** In class or as homework, have students watch the news on TV and make notes, or look through the newspaper to cut out articles about — or that include — negotiations. **LINKS )**·*Current Events*

## BUILD ACADEMIC AND LIFE-SKILL PROFICIENCIES

### *Skills Mean Success* Answers

**English.** Students' answers will vary, but should demonstrate an understanding of the different purposes of the two listening strategies. In a negotiation, you must use active listening to gain the information needed to arrive at a win/win situation. If the other party tries to convince you of a different position, you must use critical listening to evaluate the speaker's arguments and evidence, and determine what you think about them. Elsewhere in the chapter, students are asked to participate in a negotiation. Remind them to put these listening strategies into practice.

**Leadership.** Invite students to demonstrate the non-verbal communication examples from their lists. Ask the class to identify what messages they think the gestures send. If there were contradictions between the gestures and what was actually being said, ask the student how he/she dealt with the situation. Remind the students about classroom-appropriate vs. inappropriate non-verbal language.

### CHAPTER 16

# FROM THE WHOLESALER TO THE TRADE FAIR: *A Real-Life Business Experience*

## ORGANIZE THE LEARNING

### CHAPTER OBJECTIVES

- Locate wholesalers and trade fairs (flea markets) in your area.
- Sell your merchandise at a trade fair.
- Prepare an income statement from a trade fair field trip.
- Use an inventory sheet.
- Calculate net profit and ROI for the field trip.

### NFTE RESOURCES

- Text pp. 210-221
- Transparencies T16-1 to T16-2, T43-1, T21-2, T15-1, to T15-3
- Transparencies from several other chapters may be useful to help prepare for the field trip.
- Workbook/BLMs Chapter 16
- Test Bank Chapter 16
- A Business for the Young Entrepreneur: *Photo Albums*

### BUSINESS PLAN ACTIVITIES

*Workbook Business Plan Review*
Buying Wholesale 16-1, 16-2

### SKILLS MEAN SUCCESS

*Math*
Numeration and Operations: Using Mental Math

*Leadership*
Self Confidence: Learning Self-Improvement

*English*
Speaking and Listening for Social Interaction: Telephone Etiquette

### PREREQUISITES

The content of Chapters 2, 3, 6-10, 12, 13 and 14 should have been covered in class before starting this chapter.

### VOCABULARY

inventory sheet, trade fair

*Other terms to recognize:*
inventory, making change, markup, retail price, sales receipt, wholesale price

## KEY QUESTION

**What is it like to be a retailer?**

## PREPARE FOR LEARNING

- **Have Cash To Purchase Inventory.** This valuable but involved activity requires some outlay of cash to purchase inventory. There are several options: 1. Use your own money or school petty cash as investment funds. 2. Find an investor who will front the class the money (often this will be a parent, parent group, or neighborhood business). 3. Have each student bring $20 from home and pool the money to buy an inventory of one or two products, rather than have students individually select items. 4. Have the class raise money by selling something else (such as cookies at school or holding a fundraising event, like a car wash). 5. Find a wholesaler who will provide inventory on credit or donate products (but you will still need

to know the wholesale price to be able to calculate the income statement). 6. Make it an assignment for each student to raise a particular dollar figure. Obviously, this and all of the following preparatory activities will need to be planned well in advance.

- **Make Arrangements For The Trade Fair Field Trip.** If you choose the field trip option in Develop and Close the Learning on the next page, contact a neighborhood trade fair or flea market to find out how to set up a booth. It is best to do this several weeks before starting the chapter, since you will need to secure signed permission forms from parents, arrange adult chaperones, and make transportation arrangements through your school administration. If transportation funds are not available, an alternative would be to have a mini-trade fair at school.

- **Assemble Materials for the Quick-Change Coupon Game (optional).** If you intend to use this optional activity in Extend the Learning, collect assorted product coupons that show either percentage reductions (10% off) or amount reductions ($1 off). Also make sure you have a timer, preferably with a bell. Create a product sheet that lists the items for which you have coupons and prices. Print check sheets and cut them into individual checks.

## SET A CONTEXT FOR LEARNING

- **Focus 1: Which Is The Best Price?** Provide the following for students to calculate: Which of the prices below for the same product is the best deal?
  - ○ $10 per dozen
  - ○ $30 for four dozen
  - ○ 80 cents each if you by at least ten
  - ○ $24 for three dozen

  **Answer:** $30 for four dozen (62 cents per unit).

- **Focus 2: Bargain Hunter.** Write on the board or give verbal instructions to have students answer: You sell baseball hats at $10 a piece. A customer comes into your store and wants to buy 20 for $150. Refer to the chapter on negotiation. What should you do now?

- **Focus 3: Making Change.** Challenge the class to solve the following in their heads: You sell candy bars for $1.29 each. One person buys five and gives you a $10 bill. How much change should you give her? **Answer:** $3.45.

- **Discussion Launcher: Pleasant Shopping Experience.** Ask students to discuss with a partner a time when they purchased something and thought the experience was enjoyable or positive. What was it about the salesperson, store environment, or situation that made it pleasant? **LINKS**》*Consumer Ed*

## DEVELOP AND CLOSE THE LEARNING

- **Overview of Content.** This chapter will likely involve several class periods. Because it involves many details, giving students an overview of what will happen could be productive:
  - ○ Preparing to go to the trade fair: students will find/raise initial investment funds (or start-up capital), decide on product(s) to sell, find a wholesaler to buy from; negotiate with the wholesaler to get the best deal, set a price range for negotiating with customers; set up record-keeping books; design and prepare materials for a booth; sign up for tasks to do at the trade fair; and practice selling, negotiation, and making change.

- ○ At the trade fair: students will set up the booth, make sales, keep accurate records, and clean up afterward.

- ○ After the trade fair: students will compile information from their records into an income statement, assess what went well and what they could improve about the process, and repay their investors.

## BEFORE GOING TO THE TRADE FAIR

- **Preliminary Decisions.** Students will need to decide on a product to sell. The class may choose to sell a few products as a group, or each student could select his/her own product. Criteria to consider include: Who will be at the trade fair? What kinds of items sell well at your local trade fairs? What can we afford to buy? What is available locally? What is easy to carry and display? It may be helpful for students to go to a trade fair to observe, or ask students who have been to trade fairs previously to describe them to the class, so everyone knows what to expect.

- **Find a Wholesaler.** Using the text, discuss the role of the wholesaler in connecting manufacturers with retailers, and how they make money. Once the product is determined, discuss how students should research and contact local wholesalers. Ask: What criteria should we consider when deciding which wholesaler to purchase products from? (Answers should relate to price, quality of the product, nearness to school, credit terms, delivery arrangements, and other factors the students think are important based on prior NFTE lessons.) Assign Critical Thinking question 1, and/or Exploration question 2, and/or divide students into teams to research relevant websites such as those listed in the text. Encourage students to use the resources listed in the textbook, the local phone directory, personal contacts, and information from teachers, friends or family. Have students present whom they decided to go with and why. Review negotiation strategies from Chapter 15 and give students a chance to practice their negotiations in pairs before they call wholesalers. **LINKS**》*Economics*

- **Set a Price Range.** Review from Chapters 2, 6 and 9 the concepts of *economics of one unit, demand* and *cost*. Explain how these are the two bases of determining price. Demand takes the customers' point-of-view primarily and determines a price based on what customers are willing to pay. Cost starts with the supplier and determines price based on how much the entrepreneur had to pay the supplier for inventory. Have students refer to their wholesale receipts to determine cost per unit of sale as the lowest cost-based price. In small groups, have students brainstorm and/or research what is known about customers at trade fairs (or the school): What are the benefits of the product? What do they think is most important? For example, flea market (trade fair) shoppers are looking for bargains, so price may be more important than quality or convenience. In particular, what is the maximum price that a customer would pay for one item? One way to do this is to research prices for the relevant products on the Internet through stores/Web sites. Or visit a trade fair to see who the competitors will be and what their prices are. For a trade fair, students do not need to set one price, since price is frequently negotiated customer by customer. However, students should have a price range in mind. Based on the information they have about supplier cost (or wholesale price) and customer demand, ask students to consider: What is the minimum price you should accept for the product? What is the maximum price you are likely to get? What do you think would be a fair or ideal price? (Answers will probably include: the minimum price should at least equal the supplier cost; the maximum price equals the customer demand for different quantities; a fair price should be somewhere in between, as it should not only cover the supplier cost but also — through a markup — cover their costs, such as the booth, marketing materials, and starting cash to make change from the cash drawer, as well as providing some profit; the ideal price should be as close to the highest demand price as possible.) Summarize the economics of one unit (price, COGS, variable costs, gross profit) for each product you will be selling.

- **Customer Interaction.** Coach the students about how to interact with customers. Topics to discuss may include general principles of selling and customer service, such as maintaining a helpful and pleasant demeanor (transparencies T43-1 and T21-2 may help here), negotiation (transparencies T15-1 to T15-3 may be useful), and math tips for calculating tax and making change using examples in the textbook. In addition, you may want to use the Quick Change Coupon Game below in Extend the Learning if students particularly need practice in calculating quickly.

- **Record Keeping.** Emphasize good record keeping: each sale should include a sales receipt and should be reflected on the inventory sheet and sales sheet. Distribute copies of an inventory sheet, sales sheet, and sales receipts for students to practice complet-

ing (or do this in the workbook). You may need to walk students through several simulated transactions: one lady buys 10 for $_____ ; a man buys 25 for $_____ , etc. Discuss the top part of transparency T16-3 (what you should have).

- **Trade Fair Dry Run.** Discuss transparency T16-2 and assign each line to a student or student team (such as booth set-up, making business cards and flyers, making and displaying posters, assembling and protecting the cash box, booth take-down and clean-up). Alternatively, you may assign each student to make a separate flyer for his/her product. Inform students that each of them will be responsible for personal inventory tracking, sales and sales receipts. Allow class or homework time for students or teams to complete their assigned tasks. In addition, set and agree to class safety rules, such as no horseplay in the booth, students may not leave the booth area, students must go to the restroom in pairs, etc. The day before the field trip, have the class do a dry run of how the field trip will go so everyone will be ready. Discuss and affect any solutions or adjustments needed.

## AT THE TRADE FAIR

- **Double-Check Your Materials List.** Before leaving for the trade fair, make sure the class has everything it needs for the booth: tables, chairs, cash box with sufficient change (record how much change you start with), plenty of sales receipts, inventory sheets, inventory, business cards, flyers, booth decorations, and other items the class thought of.

- **Execute Your Plan.** Create a checklist of all the tasks that are to be done and which student or team is in charge. Distribute a copy of this sheet to each adult chaperone. Oversee that all tasks are accomplished. Troubleshoot as needed. In particular, protect the cash box and student safety, and make sure students are keeping accurate records (sales receipts for each transaction, inventory control sheet). As an option, conduct a performance evaluation of students' skills (see below in Assess the Learning).

## AFTER THE TRADE FAIR

- **Prepare and Analyze Financial Reports.** Discuss transparency T16-1. As a class, use the textbook's step-by-step instructions and wristwatch example to prepare an income statement and cash flow statement, and calculate net profit, ROS, operating ratios, and ROI. Assuming the role of the entrepreneur who sells watches, ask students to use these reports to evaluate the watch business: Did you negotiate well with the wholesaler? (For example, "No because our cost of goods sold is too high.") Did you price well for customers? Why or why not? (For example, "Yes, because we sold our entire inventory.") Did you lose any watches? Was your booth profitable? What was your average gross and net profit per unit of sale? Invite the students to come up with other questions that could be answered by analyzing the income statement.

- **Summary.** Have students evaluate the experience of planning and selling at a trade fair: What went well? What would you do differently next time? What tips would you give next year's class before they took this field trip? What lessons did you learn for your own business plans?

## ASSESS THE LEARNING

- **Vocabulary.** Have students define terms in their own words, use each in a sentence and/or have them list and share new business-related terms and expressions learned during the trade fair experience.

- **Performance Assessment.** Take a class list with you to jot down your ratings and notes. At the trade fair, observe students to assess how well they:

  ○ make sales: interact with customers, sell, negotiate.

  ○ handle money: calculate amounts, make change, keep good records.

  ○ run the booth: contribute to overall operations and coordination of tasks.

  For each of these three tasks, rate students using a scale like the following:

  ○ 4: a leader in entrepreneurial skill and attitude.

  ○ 3: successful, systematic.

  ○ 2: sufficient but could use a little more attention.

  ○ 1: minimal effort or significant mistakes or missteps.

- **Critical Thinking Essay.** Assign Question 2 after students have purchased their products from wholesalers.

- **Income Statement.** Assign Critical Thinking question 3 after students have completed the field trip. Students will need to turn in their inventory sheets and sales receipts with their income statements so you can check their math.

- **Additional Workbook Activities Answers.**

  **Vocabulary Activity   Answers:** 1. d, 2. b.

  **Quiz 16** in the workbook.  **Answers:** 1. Answers will vary but should include items such as flyers, business cards, change, sales receipts, inventory sheets, posters, pens and pencils, etc. 2. Sales receipt. 3. Keep the numbers on an inventory sheet or keep a record of the items you start out with and the items you have left. 4. $(50 \times .01) + (20 \times .05) + (20 \times .25) + (70 \times 1) + (60 \times 5) + (10 \times 10) + (4 \times 20) = \$556.50$. 5. $(1 \times 10) + (10 \times 5) + (10 \times 1) + (20 \times .25) + (20 \times .05) + (50 \times .01) = \$76.50$. 6. $80 \times 6 = \$480$. 7. Yes $(\$556.50 = 76.50 + 480)$. 8. Yes, 5 belts $(100 - 80 - 15)$. 9. $80 \times 2 = \$160$.

  | 10. | Revenue (or total sales) | $480.00 |
  |---|---|---|
  | | COGS | 160.00 |
  | | Gross profit | 320.00 |
  | | Operating costs | 15.00 |
  | | Profit before taxes | 305.00 |
  | | Taxes | 30.50 |
  | | Net profit | $274.50 |

- **Basic Module Business Plan.** When this chapter, which concludes the NFTE Basic module, is complete, review the Basic Business Plan. Students may integrate information they have accumulated from past chapters' business plan practice exercises as well as the optional Business Plan Integrative Summaries.

## EXTEND THE LEARNING

- **Exploration.** Have the students research trade fairs or flea markets by assigning Question 1 and reporting back to the class. **LINKS**⟩⟩*Social Studies*

- **A Business for the Young Entrepreneur.** Let students read about Genevieve Johnson and BlueMedia Photo Albums in the text and reflect on what obstacles (like Genevieve's shyness) they have had to overcome to consider opening a business.

- **Technology Transactions.** Ask the students to brainstorm in groups ways the different technologies might aid their trade fair productivity (for example, a computer spreadsheet to automate receipts, updating inventory, etc.). Also, students might be interested in examining different e-market places (like electronic trade fairs) such as eBay and others. Ask students to speculate how they might go about selling their products online.

- **Quick-Change Coupon Game.** The purpose of this activity is to give students additional practice in writing checks, calculating prices, thinking quickly, and making change. Set up a table at the front of the class. One side of the table is the seller side, on which is placed scratch paper and a pencil; the other is the buyer side, on which is placed the product sheet, coupons, checks, and a pen. Line up half the students behind the seller side and half behind the buyer side. Two students step up to play each round. The buyer student asks for one of the products from the product sheet, presents the appropriate coupon, and writes a check for an amount greater than needed to purchase the product. The timer starts when the check is handed to the seller. The seller student must calculate the correct change within the time limit (such as one minute). Students earn one point for each time they make a correct calculation. When a student completes a round, s/he goes to the end of the other side's line (seller goes to buyer line and vice versa). After a couple of rounds, reduce the amount of time allowed. After everyone has had at least one turn at play both as a buyer and a seller, discuss what was learned and how improvement is achieved with practice.

- **Trade Fair Cartoons.** Split the class into three groups. Ask the first to conceive and draw a cartoon that shows preparation for a trade fair, the second group should create a cartoon that shows setting up at a trade fair; and the third group should come up with a cartoon that shows selling. Post the cartoons around the room before the field trip or at the trade fair booth as reminders. **LINKS)**»*Fine Arts*

- **Business Plan Integrative Summary.** Chapter 16 concludes Unit 3, which emphasizes financial tools and skills. Now may be a good time for students to compose and present a brief summary of the financial aspects of their Business Plans to date, including:

## BUILD ACADEMIC AND LIFE-SKILL PROFICIENCIES

### Skills Mean Success Answers

**Math.** If you have access to "play money," make a "cash drawer" and ask students to practice counting out change using the bills and coins.

| | Amount of Sale: $35.28 Amount Paid: $100.00 | Amount of Sale: $22.85 Amount Paid: $40.00 | Amount of Sale: $12.83 Amount Paid: $20.00 | Amount of Sale: $6.02 Amount Paid: $50.00 | Amount of Sale: $80.14 Amount Paid: $100.00 |
|---|---|---|---|---|---|
| $20 bills | 3 | | | 2 | |
| $10 bills | | 1 | | | 1 |
| $5 bills | | 1 | 1 | | 1 |
| $1 bills | 4 | 2 | 2 | 3 | 4 |
| Quarters | 2 | | | 3 | 3 |
| Dimes | 2 | 1 | 1 | 2 | 1 |
| Nickels | | 1 | 1 | | |
| Pennies | 2 | | 2 | 3 | 1 |
| | Amount of change: $64.72 | Amount of change: $17.15 | Amount of change: $7.17 | Amount of change: $43.98 | Amount of change: $19.86 |

**Leadership.** Challenge students to think about how they could build their self-confidence to become more effective in selling, and in other situations that might be unfamiliar or stressful. Invite them to share ideas or practices they already use or can think of to feel more self-confident. This would be a good opportunity for self-reflection in journals.

**English.** Ask for volunteers to demonstrate their phone-conversation techniques for the class. They should practice the call with two other people, one to be the buyer and one to keep track of each of the etiquette points on a check sheet. Ask the class to critique the call based on how well the partners followed the guidelines. Review the recorder's check sheet and the class critiques. Ask for another volunteer to demonstrate an appropriate voice-mail message. Ideally, students will practice these phone calls, and then make actual calls by phoning contacts they made at a trade fair or located in a directory.

**CHAPTER 17**

# COMPETITIVE STRATEGY:
## *Define Your Business, Mission, and Tactics*

## ORGANIZE THE LEARNING

### CHAPTER OBJECTIVES
- Define a competitive strategy.
- Explain "business definition."
- Identify sources of competitive advantage.
- Create a mission statement.
- Develop tactics to use in implementing a strategy.

### NFTE RESOURCES
- Text pp. 230-241
- Transparencies T17-1 to T17-4
- Workbook/BLMs Chapter 17
- Entrepreneurs in Profile #2
- Test Bank Chapter 17
- BizTech Unit 11

### BUSINESS PLAN ACTIVITIES
*Workbook Business Plan Review*
Your Competitive Strategy
Business Definition Questions: 17-1, 17-2, 17-3; Competitive Advantage Questions: 17-1, 17-2, 17-3; Tactical Question Issues: 17-1, 17-2, 17-3, 17-4

*Workbook/Textbook Chapter Review*
Critical Thinking 8, Key Concepts 2, 3, and Exploration

### SKILLS MEAN SUCCESS

*English*
Listening and Writing for Information and Analysis: Clarifying Information

*Math*
Interpreting Graphs and Charts: Using Diagrams to Develop Strategies

### PREREQUISITES
- Students should preview Chapter 17 in the textbook.
- The content of Chapter 8 is important to understanding this chapter.

### VOCABULARY
business definition, competitive advantage, mission, mission statement, strategy, tactics, unique selling proposition

*Other suggested terms to know:*
cost structure, offer, sustainable

## KEY QUESTION

**How do I focus my business on a promising opportunity in the market?**

## SET A CONTEXT FOR LEARNING

- **Focus 1: Comparison.** Ask the students to consider the following: What tasks, tricks, activities, etc., do you do better than your friends? What do your friends do better than you?

- **Focus 2: Games.** Write on the board or give verbal instructions to have students answer the following: Think of a board, card, sports, or video game you like to play. What are things you do when playing that game that help you to win? List at least three "strategic moves" that give you an edge in playing.

- **Discussion Launcher: Lincoln Quote**. Point out the epigraph (chapter-opening quote) from Abraham Lincoln in the textbook and ask students to interpret what he means: "If I had eight hours to chop down a tree, I'd spend six sharpening my ax."

## DEVELOP AND CLOSE THE LEARNING

- **Strategy.** Have students brainstorm around the following questions: In what areas of your lives do you compete? (At school for grades, test scores; in sports or cheerleading; in the band or choir; for dates; for course or college admission.) With whom do you compete? (Other students, themselves [to improve], other teams.) How do you decide what to do to improve your chances of success? Explain that the decisions they make on how to compete effectively comprise their strategy. What they do after they make the decisions and develop a plan are tactics. Use the analogy of a blueprint: it's like building a house and the strategy is the blueprint, whereas the tactics are the workmen's tasks in construction. Or, in business, a strategy might be to grow sales with new products. Tactics would then be researching, designing, developing, manufacturing, and selling the new products. Strategy is also used in business to help companies gain market share, become more efficient, add value, meet customer needs, and make a profit. Give students an overview of the lesson: in business, strategy comprises two elements—business definition and com-

**TE 71**

petitive advantage. A mission statement communicates your strategy, and tactics are actions to carry out your strategy. Throughout this lesson, use a running example of The Most Chocolate Cake Company in the textbook, or another example from *Entrepreneurs in Profile* or elsewhere to help clarify abstract concepts. **LINKS)** *Economics*

- **Business Definition.** Use the text and transparency T17-1 to discuss the elements of a business definition. Have students answer each question on the transparency for the cake company or other example.

- **Competitive Advantage.** Use the text and transparency T17-2 to discuss the elements and sources of competitive advantage. Have students think of potential real-world competitors for the cake company or other examples used, and answer each question on the transparency. Ask: How is the cake company different from its competitors? What are the cake company's and each of its competitor's USPs (unique selling propositions)? Discuss under what conditions students think cooperation might be a competitive advantage. Have students brainstorm, or look up on www.wsj.com or the Internet, partnerships among competitors.

- **Mission Statement.** Define a mission statement as the summary of a business's strategy to use competitive advantage to satisfy customer needs. Use the text and transparency T17-3 to discuss the criteria of a mission statement. In small groups, have students use the mission statement for the cake company in the textbook as a model to create mission statements for other companies (e.g., other examples used in class or from the newspaper, www.wsj.com, *Entrepreneurs in Profile*, or *A Business for the Young Entrepreneur* from different chapters). Have groups share their statements and compare what aspects of strategy different groups chose to focus on. Evaluate the different statements against the criteria on the transparency.

- **Tactics.** Define tactics as the detailed actions you take to run your business and execute your strategy. Use the text and transparency T17-4 to discuss the tactical components of a business plan. Ask students: Why is it a good idea to work out these details before you open your business (i.e., in the planning stages)? (Answers could include: to plan and prepare for what might happen, to better organize your resources, to make sure your tactics fit your strategy.) Have students think through tactics for the cake company or other examples used by answering each question on the transparency. In small groups,

have students double check that the tactics they come up with support the company's strategy.

- **Applying the Concepts.** Pick a familiar product category (such as hamburgers) and list several companies (McDonald's, Burger King, Wendy's, a local "burger joint"). Break students into small groups and assign one company to each. Encourage students to think in several dimensions: food quality and variety, price, store atmosphere, service, etc. Have each group create a strategy (business definition, competitive advantage), mission statement, and tactical plan for its company. Instruct them to summarize this information on a poster or presentation slide. Display the results around the room and have the class compare and evaluate against the criteria for good strategy. Also have students evaluate the companies based on Timmons' criteria in the textbook that assess how strong each company's competitive advantage is.

- **Summary.** Have students think about goals they have set. You might want them to use the goal sheet they created in Chapter 3 and choose one. Have them jot down ideas for implementing a strategy for reaching that goal, using the three components discussed in this lesson.

## ASSESS THE LEARNING

- **Vocabulary.** Have students work in pairs to create flash cards with sentences that demonstrate the meanings of the words on one side, with the definitions on the back.

- **Key Concepts.** Assign Question 1. **Answer:** 1. Not necessarily because it might create a competitive advantage with some attribute other than price, such as product quality, service, delivery time, convenient location, etc.

- **Critical Thinking.** Assign Questions 1-7. **Answers:** 1. Strategy is the plan/blueprint for outperforming your competition, and tactics are the actions you take to carry out your strategy. 2. Offer, target market, and production/delivery capability. 3. They are the source of competitive advantage. 4. Your strategy, including your business definition and competitive advantage, presented in a clear, concise format that can be easily communicated to customers and employees. 5. Answers may vary, but should follow the criteria specified in the lesson. 6. Answers may vary, but most likely will include references to comfort with technology, familiarity with the latest fashions, young people have less fear, etc. 7. Answers will vary.

- **Writing Practice.** Assign Key Concepts questions 2 and 3.
- **Additional Workbook Activities Answers.**

  **Vocabulary Activity Answers:** competitive advantage, strategy, business definition, mission statement, Tactics, unique selling proposition, mission.

  **Quiz 17** in the workbook. **Answers:** 1. A competitive advantage is the reason you expect to succeed in the marketplace because it describes what makes your offer different from what customers can get from your competitors. 2. Answers will vary; an example is McDonald's food consistency and inexpensiveness. 3. Sustainable. 4. A unique selling proposition is the one thing about your business that distinguishes you from your competitors and around which you can build a sustainable competitive advantage. 5. A strategy is a plan to outperform the competition, and tactics are the actions taken to carry out the strategy; examples will vary (e.g., McDonald's strategy is to offer the same food quality worldwide at a low price, and a tactic they use is to carefully time cooking and serving). 6. A mission statement clearly and briefly communicates the business's strategy. 7. Answers will vary (e.g., I am a talented artist; I read a lot; I have a lot of friends). 8. Research online, read trade magazines, go to competitors' stores, talk to competitors' customers. 9. Understand customer needs; understand competitors' offers; determine a unique selling proposition; deliver a product/service at a fair price by controlling costs.

## EXTEND THE LEARNING

- **Business Plan Practice.** Assign Critical Thinking question 8.
- **BizTech.** Assign Unit 11.
- ***Entrepreneurs in Profile.*** Have students read the profile on Richard Branson and be able to discuss in class the following: What business(es) was Branson in (business definition)? Who was his competition? What were his strengths and weaknesses relative to his competition (competitive advantage, unique selling proposition)? Write a potential mission statement for his business(es). What tactics did he use to realize his strategy? What could he have done better?
- **Exploration.** Assign the Internet activity in the text. In addition, you might also assign students to make a competitive advantage analysis of the five businesses they find.

- **Mission Statement Analysis.** Using the Internet, have students collect several samples of mission statements from the Web sites of national or local companies. If possible, they should collect at least three from companies in the same product category (e.g., McDonald's, Burger King, Wendy's; or Wal-Mart, Target, Costco; or Starbucks, Dunkin Donuts, and a local cafe). Using the questions and criteria presented in the textbook and transparencies, have students in small groups determine the business definitions and competitive advantages from the mission statements, and evaluate the mission statements in terms of their ability to clearly communicate strategy.

## BUILD ACADEMIC AND LIFE-SKILL PROFICIENCIES

### *Skills Mean Success* Answers

**English.** 1. For example: a) … that people in a hurry rent from this store to get served faster b) … can honestly say "If it is in video, we have it" c) … serves the true sports fan d) … has mostly "family friendly" videos. 2. Students may want to look for companies in their own areas of interest in the directory. Review alphabetical listing as needed. Insist on complete sentence descriptions in the form "$X$ is the company that…" and remind the students to write slogans' meanings in their own words.

**Math.** Graph 1 — Parents: a) For example, the title explains that the graph shows how many people of which age groups use day care for the children they are responsible for. b) Almost half are between 30 and 40. Very few are over 50, etc. c) Yes, if you want to start a business near where many people in the 20-40 age group live. Graph 2 — Dinner: a) For example, *about* how much do two people spend to have dinner out on average? b) Examples: More than half the time 60% of customers spend $10-20. No customers spend more than $30. c) New restaurants should aim for the average/high price range to match current users' spending habits. But is there a need for a more expensive restaurant, too? Many interpretations and extensions are possible if the data are read accurately.

### CHAPTER 18

# DEVELOPING YOUR MARKETING MIX

---

## ORGANIZE THE LEARNING

### CHAPTER OBJECTIVES

- Understand the four steps of a marketing plan.
- Learn how to develop a successful marketing mix for your business venture.
- Learn the basic principles of pricing strategy.

### NFTE RESOURCES

- Text pp. 242-249
- Transparencies T18-1 to T18-3, T11-1
- Workbook/BLMs Chapter 18
- Entrepreneurs in Profile #14
- Test Bank Chapter 18
- BizTech Unit 10
- A Business for the Young Entrepreneur: *John's Four Season Care, John Steele*

### BUSINESS PLAN ACTIVITIES

*Workbook Business Plan Review*
Your Marketing Mix
Step 1: Consumer Analysis, Step 2: Market Analysis, Step 3: The Marketing Mix

*Workbook/Textbook Chapter Review*
Marketing Mix Chart, Key Concepts 1, 2, and Exploration 2, 3

*Power Point Templates*
Int. 8; Adv. 8

### SKILLS MEAN SUCCESS

*English*
Reading for Understanding: The Main Idea

*Leadership*
Market Research

### PREREQUISITES

- Help the students preview Chapter 18 in the textbook.
- Key foundation concepts for this chapter appear in Chapters 4, 6, 10, 11 and 17.

### VOCABULARY

marketing mix, market segment, value pricing

*Other key terms to know:*
consumer analysis, market analysis, keystoning, cost-plus pricing, penetration pricing, skimming strategy, meet or beat the competition pricing

---

## KEY QUESTION

**What's the best way to match my product/services with customer needs?**

## PREPARE FOR LEARNING

- **Ad Transparency.** If you use Focus 2, find an ad in a magazine or newspaper that effectively conveys the company's or product's Four P's. Make a transparency of it.

- **Women's Magazines Collection.** Collect beauty magazines that seem to target different segments of the women's market (e.g., older women, teens, minority women, health-conscious women, single women, married women).

## SET A CONTEXT FOR LEARNING

- **Focus 1: Marketing Analysis.** Ask students to list advertisements from TV, the radio, the Internet, or magazines that they think do a particularly good job of getting the observer's attention and describe what makes them so good.

- **Focus 2: Four P's Analysis.** Show a transparency of a magazine or newspaper ad that effectively conveys the company's or the product's Four P's. Record students' responses on the board to the question: What is this company's marketing mix?

- **Focus 3: Marketing Manager.** In groups, have the students brainstorm: You are in charge of marketing a new DVD player. What are some initial ideas about the Four P's?

- **Discussion Launcher 1: Better Value.** Have students discuss in pairs: Which is a better value: a. Organically grown apples for $3 a bag or conventional apples for $2? B. A car with a ten-year warranty that gets 30 miles per gallon for $35,000, or a car with a five-year warranty that gets 20 miles per gallon for $22,000? C. A frozen pizza for $3 or a fresh-made pizza for $7? d. The latest, hottest fashion jeans for $40, or last year's fashion style for $20?

- **Discussion Launcher 2: Baked Goods Market Segmentation.** Have students discuss with a partner: You are planning a business to sell homemade baked goods at school. How might you segment the student population by location, population, personality, behavior or income? Which segmentation strategy do you think would work best?

## DEVELOP AND CLOSE THE LEARNING

- **Marketing Overview/Terms Review.** Define marketing and what it means to be market driven from the textbook (a business's plan for highlighting the competitive advantage of the product/service for meeting the customer's needs). Use transparency T18-1 to explain the steps in marketing planning. It may be helpful to start this lesson with a basic review of the marketing related terms presented in Chapters 1-17. To keep students active in learning, divide the class into teams of two or three. Write the terms below on the board in columns (the same number of columns as there are student teams). Hold a race to see which team can find and define the terms in their column in the least amount of time with the fewest errors (teams earn one point for each correctly defined term plus two points if they finish first with all terms correct). For added interest, allow one team to "challenge" another team's definition by asking for an example of the term in use. If the "defining" team cannot give an example and the "challenge" team can, the challenge team gets a point. Either you may check answers or you can have teams check each other's answers. The same term may be included on several teams' lists. Terms to include: customer need, product feature, product benefit, competitive advantage, brand, market, market share, mind share, demographics, market segment, strategy, market research, opportunity, SWOT, demand, market-clearing price, mission statement, USP.

- **Market Segmentation.** Use transparency T18-2 to describe the key ways markets can be segmented, referencing the examples in the text to make the ideas more concrete. It may also be helpful to have students brainstorm products for which each segmentation method may be most appropriate or useful (e.g., location for a laundromat, supermarket, hair salon, or gym; population [age, education, gender, income] for books, movies, or cars; personality for travel/tour services, clothing, cosmetics, or "hangout" restaurants; and behavior for sporting goods, foods, fashion accessories, or video games). Suggest how using more than one method may be advanta-

geous (to better understand the typical customer, to clarify which segment might be most profitable, to improve your chances of making better marketing decisions because you'll gain more information).

- **Consumer Analysis.** Bring in a variety of teen's and women's beauty or fashion magazines. Group students and give each group one magazine.

1. Ask students to flip through the magazine and notice photos, article titles, types of products/services advertised, etc. Based on this information, have groups create a character profile of the "typical" woman or teen who reads this magazine by location, population, personality and behavior categories: How old is she? Does she work? What type of work does she do (e.g., professional, secretarial, blue-collar)? How much money does she make (a lot, not much)? What race or ethnicity is she? Is she married or single? Does she have children? How educated is she? What does she seem most interested in? What seems to be her biggest challenges? Tie this profile back to marketing terms used in the text by suggesting that this typical woman describes the magazine's target market segment.

2. Have students find and tear out a few ads for a specific kind of beauty product found in all of the magazines (mascara, eye shadow, perfume, shampoo). Display ads at the front of the classroom and discuss differences in how the same basic product (e.g., mascara) is marketed across the ads. Which emphasize price, convenience, quality or other benefits? Which are available widely at drug or discount stores vs. only in "finer department stores"? Which give a price and which don't? What benefits do the ads describe? How are the models in the ads similar and different? Are there differences in how many words are in the ad, or the difficulty or "slang" of the language?

3. Give groups a few minutes to make suggestions, based on the discussion of profiles and differences, which ad came from which magazine (i.e., which ad targets which type of woman). Take a poll of what the groups thought. Use this poll, especially discrepancies, to discuss the thinking behind the groups' choices: How did they determine which magazine was most likely to be the ad's source? Why did they think the ad would appeal to the magazine's profile? How do the product's Four P's (as apparent in the ad) seem to appeal to the magazine's profile/market segment? Conclude by emphasizing that marketing

focuses on benefits, not product features, and that the same basic product can emphasize different benefits depending on the needs of the customer (market segment) that the business focuses on. **LINKS**)»*Consumer Ed*

- **Market Analysis/Market Size Estimation.** Continuing from the Consumer Analysis activity, ask students:

  ○ Which form of market segmentation (location, population, personality, behavior, income) seems most important for the beauty product (e.g., mascara)?

  ○ How might the other segmentation methods be used for this beauty product?

  ○ If the students decided to launch a new brand, are there opportunities for using a different market segmentation method? What might that be? For example, what new benefit might a new brand emphasize, or what segment of the market seems underserved?

As a class, create a new profile for a typical woman in this segment; then, in groups, have students brainstorm ways they might go about determining how many women in their neighborhood might fit the profile and be interested in this new brand. (Conduct a survey, observe women in the cosmetics aisle of the drug store, distribute samples and ask for reactions, tally prices of competing brands in cosmetic aisles as an indicator of how much women might pay).

Ask: Once this research is conducted, what findings would suggest that it would be worthwhile to launch this brand? (Market is large enough, women in this segment buy the product often, the market segment/niche is being targeted by none or only a few competitors, you see a lot of women in this segment in the aisles, women in this segment say they want a product like yours.)

- **Marketing Mix.** Use transparency T11-1 to review the Four P's of a marketing plan: product, price, place and promotion. Have each group select one beauty product ad from the Consumer Analysis activity and outline the Four P's for that brand. Ask them to analyze: Do the Four P's reinforce or conflict with each other? How so? Instruct each group to create a new ad for the product that reflects a marketing mix for a different segment of women (e.g., rewrite a teen-oriented ad to appeal to a 30-something mother). Summarize how a company's marketing mix needs to consider both the market segment targeted *and* the marketing mixes of competitors targeting the same segment, so that competitive advantage is emphasized.

- **Pricing.** Emphasize how pricing is a very important P because it not only affects marketing but also directly impacts income and profit: if a company does not price effectively, it may be difficult to be profitable. Use transparency T18-3 to discuss the different pricing strategies given in the text and either provide examples or have students suggest some examples (e.g., keystoning is a cost-plus strategy; a 20% markup on a printing order is cost-plus; new discount airlines that provide deep discounts for new routes is market penetration; prescription drugs, computers and other technology products such as plasma TVs use skimming; pizza parlor discount wars or "match any price" promotions or "we accept competitors' coupons" policies are beat-the-competition). You may also want to remind students of demand-based pricing (market-clearing price) as discussed previously, which focuses on the maximum that customers will pay for a product/service. **LINKS**)»*Economics*

As a class, categorize pricing strategies into three groups:

1. focused on costs (keystoning, cost-plus, value)

2. focused on the competition (penetration, beat-the-competition)

3. focused on customer demand (skimming, market-clearing)

Ask students: If price is so important, why does an entrepreneur also need to pay attention to the other three P's? (Competing only on price is a short-term strategy that is hard to sustain, price must work in tandem with other P's, other P's might allow the entrepreneur to charge a higher price that the basic product warrants because it builds a brand personality for the product.)

- **Summary.** As was anticipated in Discussion Launcher 1, make the point that value depends not on pricing alone, but on the marketing mix in relation to the needs of the customer. Ask students to brainstorm products that are not cheap but that many people think provide good value. (Answers might include America Online, Levi's, good medical care, sunscreen that stays on, Carnival cruises, Disney vacations, satellite TV, tooth braces, organic cotton clothes, gourmet/specialty foods, buffet restaurants, purebred dog, SAT tutoring, trained child care professionals).

## ASSESS THE LEARNING

- **Vocabulary.** Have students define terms in their own words and use each in a sentence.

- **Key Concepts.** Assign Questions 3-5. **Answers:** 3. Cost-plus pricing does not consider the marketing plan or marketing mix (product, place and promotion decisions) that may create competitive advantages for which the entrepreneur could charge more. 4. Penetration pricing occurs when a company introduces a product to a market with a "for a limited time only" low price to gain market share quickly; recent examples include new airline routes and Internet music downloading. 5. Ads and explanations will vary but should show clearly the price and reflect one of the pricing strategies discussed in the text.

- **Critical Thinking.** Assign Questions 1-3. **Answers:** 1. "Market driven" means that every business decision is based on customer demands and is designed to strengthen the customer's perception that the entrepreneur's product/service is the best provider of the benefit the customer seeks; a market-driven approach helps entrepreneurs make better business decisions. 2. Answers will vary but examples should show how the lowest price is not a short-term promotional *tactic* but derives from a sustainable lower cost based on supplier discounts or manufacturing/service efficiencies. 3. Answers will vary but examples should demonstrate a competitive advantage in one of the other three P's (such as a strong brand image through effective promotion [e.g., McDonald's], a convenient location or place of business [e.g., veterinarians that make house calls], or an innovative product [e.g. a new technology or a product with added features or services, such as first-class airline service]).

- **Writing Practice.** Assign Exploration questions 2 and/or 3.

- **Additional Workbook Activities Answers.**

  **Vocabulary Activity Answers:** 1. b, 2. b, 3. d.

  **Quiz 18** in the workbook. **Answers:** 1. Market-driven entrepreneurs use market research to better understand their potential customers. Research improves their marketing decisions because they can discover the benefits the customer seeks. 2. A marketing mix is the combination of decisions regarding the Four P's that communicates competitive advantage; it is important because product, price, promotion, and place decisions reinforce each other to build a strong brand image and customer loyalty. 3. Consumer analysis, market analysis, development of a marketing mix, break-even analysis. 4. A market segment is a group of consumers who respond similarly to a certain marketing mix. 5. By location, population, personality, or behavior. 6. Product, price, place, and promotion. 7. $18. 8. Any two of the following: cost-plus, penetration, skimming, beat-the-competition, demand-based. 9. Price is the amount of money a customer must pay to obtain your product; value is the combination of price, quality, brand personality and other marketing-mix decisions that induce customers to buy your product.

## EXTEND THE LEARNING

- **Business Plan Practice.** Assign Key Concepts question 1-2, Critical Thinking question 4, and/or the Marketing Mix Chart in the text.

- **BizTech.** Assign Unit 10.

- **Exploration.** Assign Question 1 in the text. Alternatively, have pairs of students visit one restaurant (assign locations so students don't all go to the same one). Then compare the restaurants' offerings as a class. Ask students to choose which restaurant they personally prefer and why, then give them time to share with the class. Ask the class to suggest how or if its students can be grouped into market segments based on their preferences.

- **Entrepreneurs in Profile.** Have students analyze the section on Anita Roddick and suggest how she

  ○ determined her target market segment.

  ○ chose the Four P's for The Body Shop.

  Alternatively or in addition, assign students to look up The Body Shop's Web site and complete the Marketing Mix Chart in the text for a particular Body Shop product.

- **High School Cliques.** If students are having difficulty grasping the idea of segmentation, relate the concept to their everyday world of high school. In many ways, cliques are market segments: athletes, honors students, rich students, etc. As an alternative or additional example, ask class to suggest TV shows or movies that portray these different segments. Have students suggest profiles and a list of most-likely-to-buy products for some of these cliques. Discuss how a business might market (using the Four P's) to each of these student market segments.

- **What Doesn't Fit?** To help students further analyze how the Four P's need to work together, share the following table and ask students to determine which marketing decision doesn't fit the other P's in each line/row and why. Add or ask students to add other examples. (Each misfit is indicated.)

| Segment | Product | Price | Place | Promotion |
|---|---|---|---|---|
| *Teen boys* | Jaguar | $35,000 | Luxury dealer | New Yorker ads |
| Mothers | Diapers | $15 | *Upscale dept. store* | Parenting magazine |
| Young entrepreneur | Accountant | *$500/hr.* | Neighborhood office | Word-of-mouth |
| Newlywed couple | *Dating service* | $25/mo. | Internet site | Google ad |
| Teacher | School supplies | $10 | Discount store | Ad on MTV |

- **A Business for the Young Entrepreneur.** Have students read about John Steele and John's Four Season Care in the text. Assign Key Concepts 6. Alternatively or in addition, ask students to outline John's marketing mix. Encourage students to provide other marketing suggestions John might try to further build his business (e.g., selecting a second market segment, devising a new form of promotion, adding a new service).

## BUILD ACADEMIC AND LIFE-SKILL PROFICIENCIES

### *Skills Mean Success* Answers

**English.** 1.a. Ask students to explain why they chose this answer (e.g., was the most accurate; the other choices didn't express the main idea as well, etc.).

**Leadership.** Make sure students understand the chart format and the headings. If they have difficulty arranging interviews, have them speculate about who shops there and whether the store caters to the local neighborhood or a broader area. They could also select a store they know well and make some assumptions about "who" shops there. They can follow that up by a visit to the store and record the approximate ages/genders of those actually going in, perhaps getting the manager's permission in advance. Encourage students to anticipate and ask about other factors that might define the store's segment appeal and customer base, such as price. If appropriate, have a computer-savvy student demonstrate or review how to construct a simple table in a word-processing application. Students could also create a simple pie chart/graph in Excel.

### CHAPTER 19

# ADVERTISING AND PUBLICITY

---

## ORGANIZE THE LEARNING

### CHAPTER OBJECTIVES

- Explain the difference between advertising and publicity.
- Generate publicity for your business.
- Use promotion to communicate effectively with your market.
- Choose ways to promote your business — online and in the media.

### NFTE RESOURCES

- Text pp. 250-263
- Transparencies T19-1, T42-2
- Workbook/BLMs Chapter 19
- Entrepreneurs in Profile #10
- Test Bank Chapter 19
- BizTech Unit 5

- A Business for the Young Entrepreneur: *Bed Stuy's Project Regeneration, Inc. (Non-profit), Marvin "Barnabas Shakur" Scarborough*

### BUSINESS PLAN ACTIVITIES

*Workbook Business Plan Review*
Advertising and Publicity  19-1, 19-2, 19-3, 19-4, 19-5

*Workbook/Textbook Chapter Review*
Critical Thinking 3, 4, 5
Key Concepts 2, 4, 5
Exploration 1, 2

### SKILLS MEAN SUCCESS

*Math*
Solving Problems That Don't Require Exact Answers

*English (plus Technology)*
Writing for Social Interaction: E-mail

### PREREQUISITES

- Students should preview Chapter 19 in the textbook.
- Chapters 8, 10, 11, 17 and 18 are important background.

### VOCABULARY

advertisement, advertising, institutional advertising, media, pitch letter, press release, promotion, publicity

---

## KEY QUESTION

**How do I tell potential customers about my product/service's benefits?**

## PREPARE FOR LEARNING

- **Collect Samples.** Collect samples of magazine ads, newspaper ads, promotional samples (and/or record TV ads) for a variety of products and companies. Try to include a variety of product/service, institutional, and cause-related/sponsored ads.

- **Guest Speaker.** If you plan to use this activity in Extend the Learning, line up the speaker in advance.

## SET A CONTEXT FOR LEARNING

- **Focus 1: Logo-mania.** Ask the students to think of two or three well-known companies, draw their logos, and write their slogans.

- **Focus 2: Ad-ventures.** Ask the students to name the two best commercials they've seen on TV or heard on the radio lately. What makes them so effective?

How might they improve on them?

- **Discussion Launcher 1: Ideal Customer.** Group the students in pairs and give them this task: You sell chocolate syrup that comes in a variety of bright colors (green, purple, etc.). Create a profile or picture of your ideal "end-user" (customer). Some perceptive students may suggest that young children are the most likely end-users but that their parents would be the actual buyers.

- **Discussion Launcher 3: Twain Quote.** Write on the board or share verbally the Mark Twain quote in the text and ask students to interpret what he meant: "Many a small thing has been made large by the right kind of advertising." **LINKS**»*Literature*

## DEVELOP AND CLOSE THE LEARNING

- **Publicity vs. Advertising vs. Online Marketing.** Compare and contrast the advantages and disadvantages of these three marketing venues. It may be helpful to create a chart on the board, similar to the one below, to summarize student comments. Providing examples of product/service categories that tend to use one tactic vs. another may also increase their understanding — car dealers tend to use advertising and promotions, nonprofits use publicity, and books and second-hand items are effectively sold through online marketing [amazon.com, eBay], household cleaners use advertising and coupons and direct mail samples, utility companies use publicity).

### ADVANTAGES

| Publicity | Advertising | Online |
|---|---|---|
| No cost for space | More control over content | Easy to set up |
| May be able to tell longer message | Many media outlets | Often inexpensive |
| | | Easy to change |
| | | Can target audience |

### DISADVANTAGES

| Publicity | Advertising | Online |
|---|---|---|
| Little control over content or timing | Often expensive | Not everyone has a computer |
| Must be "newsy" | Requires multiple exposures | Customer must find your Web page |

- **Publicity Tactics.** Using the textbook, discuss the differences between a pitch letter and a press release. (A pitch letter can be more "sales-oriented" and persuasive regarding why the reader should be interested, whereas a press release gives the facts of the story; a pitch letter explains the relevance of the press release.) Read the sample pitch letter and press release in the text and discuss their elements and structure. Distribute newspaper sections to students and instruct them to find articles that were probably written from a press release. Signs to look for include: quotes from company spokespeople, announcements of new products or company changes, positive/good news, event announcements. As a class:

  ○ Assess how much of our news is influenced by publicity information.

  ○ Analyze the different topics that publicity might cover (e.g., event, charity partnership, new product, product problem/recall).

  ○ Examine how the companies turned these topics into "stories" in the articles (their "angles").

- **Media Advertising/Promotion Tactics.** Discuss transparency T19-1 about advertising media outlets. If pos-

sible, show samples of different types of promotions (coupons, flyers, free samples, direct mail). Group students and assign one media type to each group:

○ Electronic (TV, radio)

○ Print (newspaper, magazine)

○ Phone (telemarketing, 800 number)

○ Printed material (catalog, direct mail, brochure, flyer, coupon, business card)

○ Items (gifts, clothing)

○ Events (special events, sponsorships, partnerships)

Instruct groups to create a 30-second radio or TV commercial that emphasizes the competitive advantage of that media type (e.g., why consumer products companies should advertise in newspapers/magazines). Allow time for groups to perform their commercials. **LINKS**››*Drama*

Distribute copies of newspaper and magazine ads with instructions to label the five parts of each ad. Ask students to label their ad as primarily product/service, institutional, or cause-related. Use transparency T42-2 to discuss the difference between logos and trademarks (a trademark has been registered with the U.S. Patent Office and is legally protected; many corporate logos are trademarked). Help students notice that, even though each ad may be read or seen by many people, it is written like a letter — as if the company is talking to one (usually "ideal" or "typical") customer at a time.

- **Online Marketing Tactics.** Discuss how Internet marketing is one of the fastest-growing media for companies to inform customers about their products. Ask students to brainstorm the most popular or well-known ways the Internet is used to market.

- **Summary.** Ask students: How does a company inform potential customers about its product/service's benefits? Emphasize that these tactics are not "either-or" choices, but are often combined to form a promotional strategy whose total effect equals more than the sum of its parts.

## ASSESS THE LEARNING

- **Vocabulary.** Have students define terms in their own words and use each in a sentence. If the students use the workbook, have them complete the vocabulary activity.

- **Key Concepts.** Assign Questions 1, 3, 4. **Answers:** 1. Visualize your ideal customer so you can personalize the ad. 3. About nine weeks, because for every three times a potential customer sees your ad, s/he will probably ignore it; it takes nine or so "contacts" for a potential customer to grasp a message. 4. Direct mail involves sending the message directly to the postal or e-mail address of your potential customers; answers will vary regarding whether students will use direct mail for their businesses.

- **Critical Thinking.** Assign Questions 1-2. **Answers:** 1. See page 259 for the five parts of a print ad; this ad focuses on the boots' look, feel, and craftsmanship. (Alternatively, distribute a copy of a recent ad for students to label.) 2. Ads will vary, but should focus on the company itself rather than a provided product or service.

- **Writing Practice.** Assign Key Concepts question 5.

- **Additional Workbook Activities Answers.**

  **Vocabulary Activity  Answers:** ACROSS: 1. copy, 3. press release, 4. publicity, 6. headline, 7. advertising, 12. deck, 13. institutional advertising, 14. direct mail; DOWN: 1. cause-related marketing, 2. media, 5. advertisement, 8. graphics, 9. promotion, 10. pitch letter, 11. newsgroup.

  **Quiz 19** in the workbook. **Answers:** 1. Headline or title, deck or subtitle, copy or text, graphics (photos and/or drawings), and logo or trademark. 2. Any three of the following: newspaper, magazine, radio, or Yellow Pages, if there is a reasonable rationale; most likely television would be too expensive unless the student gives a good explanation. 3. A trademark is a logo that has been legally registered with the government and cannot be used by another company. 4. A neighborhood newspaper reaches the local market most likely to buy a young entrepreneur's product/service, and these ads cost considerably less than other media.

## EXTEND THE LEARNING

- **Business Plan Practice.** Assign Key Concepts question 2 with Critical Thinking questions 3-5.

- **BizTech.** Assign Unit 5.

- **Exploration.** Assign Questions 1-2 in the text. Alternatively or in addition, have students visit amazon.com, e-bay, and other electronic stores to familiarize themselves with online marketing venues.

- *Entrepreneurs in Profile.* Have students analyze the chapter on John Johnson and be prepared to discuss it in class. How did Johnson's magazines fill a media niche? What types of products or services might be advertised in *Ebony* or *Jet*? What types of publicity stories might appeal to these magazines' editors?

- **A Business for the Young Entrepreneur.** Have students read about Marvin Scarborough and Bed Stuy's Project Re-Generation, Inc. in the text. Assign Key Concepts question 6.

- **Guest Speaker.** Invite a local entrepreneur, media rep, or advertising agency account executive to make a presentation to your class about a specific marketing campaign s/he was involved in recently.

## BUILD ACADEMIC AND LIFE-SKILL PROFICIENCIES

### Skills Mean Success Answers

**Math.** i. b., ii. c., iii. a., iv. e., v. d.

**English.** 1. and 2. Assess the quality of their e-mail messages against a scale or rubric such as the following.

| | | | | | | | |
|---|---|---|---|---|---|---|---|
| Is the message conveyed clearly? | Very Effective | 5 | 4 | 3 | 2 | 1 | Ineffective |
| Are the length and tone appropriate? | Very Effective | 5 | 4 | 3 | 2 | 1 | Ineffective |
| Is the message polite? | Very Effective | 5 | 4 | 3 | 2 | 1 | Ineffective |
| Are the language and spelling accurate? | Very Effective | 5 | 4 | 3 | 2 | 1 | Ineffective |
| Does the message "pop"? Is it easy to read? | Very Effective | 5 | 4 | 3 | 2 | 1 | Ineffective |
| Does the message clearly explain what to do? | Very Effective | 5 | 4 | 3 | 2 | 1 | Ineffective |
| Does the e-mail allow readers to unsubscribe? | Very Effective | 5 | 4 | 3 | 2 | 1 | Ineffective |
| Is the subject line interesting enough to make a reader open the e-mail? | Very Effective | 5 | 4 | 3 | 2 | 1 | Ineffective |

*Note: Most e-mail programs can be set to check spelling and grammar prior to sending.*

### CHAPTER 20

# BREAK-EVEN ANALYSIS:
## *Can You Afford Your Marketing Plan?*

## ORGANIZE THE LEARNING

### CHAPTER OBJECTIVES

- Know what break-even means to a business.
- Figure how many units your business must sell to "break even."
- Use break-even analysis to evaluate your marketing plan.

### NFTE RESOURCES

- Text pp. 264-271
- Transparencies T13-1; T9-1; T20-1, T20-2
- Workbook/BLMs Chapter 20
- Test Bank Chapter 20
- BizTech Unit 24

### BUSINESS PLAN ACTIVITIES

*Workbook Business Plan Review*
Break-Even Analysis 20-1

*Workbook/Textbook Chapter Review*
Critical Thinking 1

*Power Point Templates*
Int. 19; Adv. 21

### SKILLS MEAN SUCCESS

*Math*
Number and Numeration:
Understanding Percentage
Mathematical Reasoning:
Devising Formulas

*English*
Writing for Information and Understanding: Using Standard English - Hyphenation

*Leadership*
Why Math Is Important:
Identifying Math Resources

Networking and Communication:
Finding Contacts and Listening

### PREREQUISITES

- Students should preview Chapter 20 in the textbook.
- This chapter assumes knowledge of content from Chapters 2, 9, 13 and 18.

### VOCABULARY

break-even analysis, break-even point, break-even units

## KEY QUESTION

**How many units do I need to sell to cover my costs?**

## SET A CONTEXT FOR LEARNING

- **Focus: ROI & Gross Profit.** Pose this question to the class: Lourdes sells perfume. She buys a dozen bottles for $36 and sells them at $9 a bottle. How many bottles does she have to sell to get her investment back? If she sells all the bottles, what is her gross profit? **Answer:** four bottles = $72.

- **Discussion Launcher: Is It Worth It?** Have the students discuss in pairs: You sell custom decorated sweatshirts for $20 a piece. You buy them plain from a wholesaler at $120 for a dozen, then use $2 worth of fabric paint and three hours of your time to design and decorate each sweatshirt. You tie a colorful 50-cent ribbon around each sweatshirt when you sell it. You advertise in the school paper and distribute flyers, which costs $25 per month, and you rent a booth at the school fair each month for $50. Is this business worth your time and effort? Why or why

not? How many sweatshirts would you have to sell to make it worth your while? How would you find out? **Answer:** Student responses will vary, but the math works out as follows: selling price per unit = $20, COGS = $12, variable cost = $0.50, fixed costs = $75; so gross profit = $8 and the student would have to sell $75/ (8 - 0.5) =10 sweatshirts a month to begin to make it profitable (although students may disagree about the value of the 30 hours they would need to spend to make these shirts, which is not being compensated for yet if only ten are sold).

## DEVELOP AND CLOSE THE LEARNING

- **Why Analyze Costs?** Ask: Why do entrepreneurs need to watch their businesses' costs? (To adjust decisions to changing conditions, to make better decisions, to make a profit and avoid a loss, to improve the running of the business, to keep track of where money is going.) Some students may emphasize a "looking back" mentality of seeing where the business has been. Challenge them to think about how understanding costs might be used proactively — "looking forward." If they need a hint, tell them to think about the lessons learned in Chapters 18 and 19 — marketing takes money. (Before launching a marketing plan, you have to see if you can afford it, to see if what you need to sell to cover your costs is realistic.)

- **Income Statement Review.** Remind students that most entrepreneurs do this kind of reflecting on monthly costs by using information from their income statements. Discuss transparency 13-1 to review the parts of the income statement (sales, cost of goods/services sold, variable costs, gross profit, fixed operating costs, profit before taxes, taxes, net profit/(loss)).

- **Costs Review.** Use the following example to remind students about the three different kinds of costs: Ally sells hand-knit scarves. She places each scarf in a box, provides free shipping within the U.S., and sometimes pays her sister a commission if she helps sell scarves during the holiday season. In addition, Ally promotes her scarves on the Internet, through direct mail, and charity partnerships. Which of these are: costs of good sold, variable costs, and fixed operating costs? **Answer:** Yarn is cost of goods sold; box, shipping and sales commission are variable costs; promotion is a fixed cost.

Have students summarize their understanding of the difference between cost of goods/services sold and variable costs, and fixed operating costs and variable costs. Discuss transparency T9-1 ("Three Kinds of Costs") to focus students on fixed operating costs (USAIIRD), which are costs that must be paid whether there are any sales or not. Ask students to recall why it is better if an entrepreneur can keep these fixed operating costs as low as possible (it provides more flexibility in running the business, it is less of a drain on cash resources). Discuss how advertising/marketing can be expensive: "It takes money to make money." Advertising/marketing spending is one of the few fixed operating costs that entrepreneurs can control (often utilities, insurance, rent, etc. are set by someone else). A key question, then, is: Is the money spent on advertising and marketing affordable?

- **Break-Even Point.** Define break-even point from the text: when sales and total costs are equal and the income statement shows neither net profit nor loss. Usually a break-even point is given in break-even units. Review the definition of unit of sale from Chapter 2. Give several examples from the text or elsewhere: 2000 T-shirts, 100 pairs of earrings, 120 meals, 50 hours of accounting service, 25 hours of babysitting, etc. Ask: Why is the break-even point

important to know? (It's the minimum number of units the business must sell to cover fixed operating costs; it indicates that units sold above this point will create profit; it helps entrepreneurs plan their time and resources by giving them a minimum sales goal; it helps "red flag" a problem if costs are too high or prices too low.) Write the break-even point formula on the board:

Monthly Fixed Operating Costs / Gross Profit Per Unit

Explain to students why we use fixed operating costs and gross profit per unit, rather than sales revenue and a sum of COGS/COSS, variable costs and fixed operating costs in this equation: Because it is simpler. The gross profit per unit amount already accounts for sales revenue and COGSS/COSS and variable costs paid. This formula focuses on how much an entrepreneur needs to bring in above and beyond the costs of each sale, as described in the economics of one unit (Chapter 2), to contribute to the general operations of the business.

- **Break-Even Analysis.** Use the text and transparency T20-1 to step students through finding the figures in an income statement needed for break-even analysis. Using the example in the textbook, go through calculating David's break-even point, if necessary, reminding them of the order of operations; do calculations within brackets first. As an option to help students think about how break-even point is affected by different business situations, present the following scenarios:

  ○ Change David's variable costs to $25: "Suppose David hired a commissioned salesperson..." and ask students to figure variable costs per unit and recalculate David's break-even point.

  ○ Increase fixed operating costs: "Suppose David's rent and utilities went up..." and ask students to recalculate break-even point. Continue this process of changing certain figures on the income statement — such as: "Suppose David held a sale and reduced his price to $3.50 per tie for one month..." or: "Suppose David switched wholesalers to get the better deal of $1.75 per tie..."— and recalculating the break-even point to see how the scenario changes.

Look for patterns across the different scenarios:

  ○ Which factors made his break-even point higher or lower?

  ○ Can some general rules be derived for lowering any break-even point? If so, what are they?

To summarize, go through the example of Jersey Mike's from the text. Show transparency T20-2 and ask students to recalculate break-even with the new figures. Ask students individually or in pairs to answer the question on the bottom of the transparency and be able to explain their answer. **Answer**: 94 (rounding up to a whole customer).

- **Break-even Analysis and Economics of One Unit.** Put on the board the equations for EOU and for break-even point:

EOU: Gross Profit Per Unit =
Selling Price Per Unit − COGS/COSS Per Unit

Break-even Point =
Monthly Fixed Costs/Gross Profit Per Unit

Ask students to consider how they are related and how they are different. (Related: both assess how to be profitable — EOU by determining how much money per unit can go toward business operations (fixed operating costs), and break-even point by determining how many units need to be sold to cover fixed operating costs. Differences: EOU is in dollars, break-even point is in units of sale; EOU does not directly include fixed operating costs, although at the end of the term/month fixed costs can be allocated into EOU and then EOU serves also to assess break-even.) Ask students: Why should an entrepreneur do both calculations? (EOU makes sure the business can at least cover the costs of providing the good/service; break-even also makes sure the business can cover the costs of doing business itself.)

- **Summary.** Encourage students to think about how break-even analysis might be used in situations other than their NFTE businesses. Have them list all the things they spent money on in the last two or three days. Ask students: How many hours will you need to work at $5 an hour to cover your expenses? Are those items or experiences worth that much of your working time? **LINKS** »*Life Skills*

## ASSESS THE LEARNING

- **Vocabulary.** Have students define terms in their own words and use each in a sentence.
- **Key Concepts.** Assign Questions 1-3. **Answers:** 1. Break-even analysis indicates whether an entrepreneur can afford the cost of the marketing plan. 2. Monthly Fixed Costs / Gross Profit per Unit. 3. comb $0.40; tie $6.75; watch $10.

- **Critical Thinking.** Assign Question 2, plus Problems and Can You Afford Your Business Plan questions. **Answers:** 2. An income statement and a definition of unit of sale. Problem 1. Technically, this problem is unsolvable as it requires division by zero; however, practically, the meaning of the problem is that the business is operating at a loss as the company's price only covers COGS/COSS and does not contribute any money to covering fixed costs. Problem 2. 60. Problem 3. 250. Can You Afford 1. 75 units (600/8). Can You Afford 2. Yes, 100 units is more than the 75 units needed to cover $600 in fixed operating costs. Can You Afford 3. $200 (100 × 8 − 600).

- **Writing Practice.** Assign Critical Thinking question 3. **Answer:** 3. Memos will vary, but should show understanding that the business is operating at a loss since it sold only 300 units and needs 400 units to break even (the math is: gross profit = 10 − 5 = 5, break-even = 2000/5 = 400 units); strategies students might suggest include: increasing price, trying to negotiate a better deal from the wholesaler, lowering fixed costs, and increasing the number of units sold.

- **Additional Workbook Activities Answers.**

**Vocabulary Activity** in the workbook. **Answers:** 1. c, 2. b, 3. c.

**Quiz 20** in the workbook. **Answers:** 1. $5. 2. 6 bottles. 3. 12 bottles. 4. $75. 5. $0.75 6. $4,800. 7. $6 8. 4800/6 = 800 meals. 9. Answers will vary but students might notice that the trend is toward a loss, so Jorge's business may not be doing well; or they might notice that he has at least broken even two of the three months so maybe he just had a bad March. 10. Answers will vary but should give specific and practical decisions, such as cut costs, improve the product, increase advertising/promotion, find new markets, negotiate better arrangements with suppliers, and perhaps raising prices.

## EXTEND THE LEARNING

- **Business Plan Practice.** Assign Critical Thinking question 1.

- **BizTech.** Assign Unit 24.

- **Break-Even Problems.** Have each student create two break-even problems in the format used above in the lesson. Instruct them to define the unit of sale and include monthly fixed operating costs, variable costs (if any), number of units sold in a month, cost of goods/services sold, and sales price. Then redistribute these problems and have students solve them individually or in pairs.

- **Business Plan Integrative Summary.** Chapter 20 concludes Unit 4, which emphasizes marketing. It may be a good time for students to compose and present a brief summary of the marketing aspects of their Business Plans to date, including:

1. a brief statement of the company's competitive advantage.
2. a description of the marketing mix — the Four P's — and how they work together.
3. a sample advertisement, press release, and/or promotion idea.
4. an estimate of how much they think the marketing plan might cost.
5. an estimate of the break-even point for this marketing plan.

## BUILD ACADEMIC AND LIFE-SKILL PROFICIENCIES

### *Skills Mean Success* Answers

**Math.** 1 and 2

| Fixed-Cost Expenses | Monthly Cost | % of Revenues | % of Total Fixed costs |
|---|---|---|---|
| Utilities | $1,000 | 4.16 % | 8.33% |
| Salaries | $3,000 | 12.5% | 25% |
| Advertising | $4,000 | 16.6% | 33.33% |
| Interest | $0 | 0% | 0% |
| Insurance | $1,500 | 6.25% | 12.5% |
| Rent | $2,000 | 8.333% | 16.6% |
| Depreciation | $500 | 2.08% | 2.08% |
| Total Fixed Costs | $12,000 | 50% | 100% |

3.  a. the percentage of revenue of any expense line in fixed cost = (fixed cost divided by revenue) × 100.

   b. the percentage of total fixed costs of an individual expense item for any business = (individual fixed cost divided by total fixed cost) × 100.

**English.** 1. Some students may select words that have been hyphenated to show line breaks. Encourage them also to find hyphenated compound nouns and adjectives, such as check-in, time-out, co-marketing, self-employed, single-entry, patent-pending, not-for-profit, e-mail, mid-range, short-term, one-time, cost-based, etc. 2. Hyphenation is used a. for line breaks to show that a word has been split at the end of a line, and b. to connect words that are brought together to make new, compound words. Not all compound words are hyphenated, however. Some have become joined as one word and some are "open" compounds: markup, markdown, interest rate, needs analysis, service business, joint venture, goodwill, newsletter.

**Leadership.** Expect answers such as daily, weekly, monthly, quarterly, and annual financial reports; expense reports, purchasing, markup, banking, calculating ad rates, calculating taxes, billing, making change, etc. Math skills used might include calculator and spreadsheet use, estimation, rounding off figures, basic operations, percentages; using graphs, forms, charts and data tables, using formulas, finding patterns, measurement, proportion, etc. Many business owners and managers use math every day.

### CHAPTER 21

# PRINCIPLES OF SUCCESSFUL SELLING

## ORGANIZE THE LEARNING

### CHAPTER OBJECTIVES

- Turn product features into customer benefits.
- Turn customer objections into sales advantages.
- Pre-qualify a sales call.
- Make an effective sales call.
- Build good relationships with customers that will lead to more sales prospects.

### NFTE RESOURCES

- Text pp. 272-281
- Transparencies T21-1 to T21-5
- Workbook/BLMs Chapter 21
- Entrepreneurs in Profile #16
- Test Bank Chapter 21
- BizTech Units 17 & 18

### BUSINESS PLAN ACTIVITIES

*Workbook Business Plan Review*
Selling 21-1, 21-2, 21-3, 21-4

*Workbook/Textbook Chapter Review*
Key Concepts 2, 3;
Critical Thinking 1, 2

### SKILLS MEAN SUCCESS

*Math*
Measurement: Understanding Length and Area

*English*
Writing for Information: Cause and Effect

*Leadership*
Understanding Customer Needs: Sales Interviews

### PREREQUISITES

- Students should have read textbook Chapter 21.
- This chapter builds on Chapters 17 and 18.

### VOCABULARY

commission, sales call

*Other terms to know:*
cold calling, receipt, sales pitch

## KEY QUESTION

**How do I make a sale in a professional way?**

## PREPARE FOR LEARNING

- **Record Television Commercials.** If you use the Sales Ad Analysis extension activity below, record several television commercials that use a spokesperson talking directly to the audience.

## SET A CONTEXT FOR LEARNING

- **Focus 1: Product Features.** Ask the students to list as many features of their NFTE textbook as they can.
- **Focus 2: Features and Needs.** For each of the product features listed below for a portable music system, what customer need might be addressed? 1. Auto-reverse. 2. Earbud headphones. 3. Programmable station settings. 4. Strap-on armband or belt clip. 5. Battery power saver mode.
- **Focus 3: Persuasion.** Have students reflect on this scenario: Think of a time when you persuaded someone to do something you wanted. How did you convince the other person?

- **Discussion Launcher 1: Stone Quote.** Share the W. Clement Stone quote in the textbook and have students discuss in pairs how it applies to their lives: "When there's nothing to lose and much to gain by trying, try."

## DEVELOP AND CLOSE THE LEARNING

- **Marketing vs. Selling.** Ask students: How are marketing and selling alike? (Both focus on customer needs, both bring customer and product together, both emphasize learning about the customer.) How are they different? (Marketing brings the customer to the product, but selling brings the product to the customer; marketing uses mostly impersonal and indirect communication vehicles, but selling uses mostly personal and direct interaction.) Use transparency T21-1 to summarize the differences between marketing and personal selling. Discuss the principles of selling on transparency T21-2 by using a running example in which you try to sell the students some item in the classroom, such as your desk, using each principle. Ask students in groups to rank the principles, based on which they feel are most important in making a sale. Compare group rankings. Ask groups to share their thinking about principles whose rankings widely vary between groups.

- **Needs, Features, and Benefits.** Use transparency T21-3 to guide students through the process of turning product features into benefits. Ask them to list other features of a T-shirt — and their potential benefits — that could be added to the list. Recall the concept of market segments from Chapter 18. Have students consider how benefits might change depending on which market segment is targeted (differences in T-shirt benefits between the parent who washes the family laundry, and the children who wear the shirts, and entrepreneurs who might resell the shirts). Remind students that benefits depend on understanding the individual customers and groups of customers and their needs: customer needs underpin which features of a product are emphasized in marketing and sales.

- **The Sales Call.** Define *sales call*. Discuss transparency T21-4 as an overview of the goals of a sales call. Ask: When is a sales call needed? In what situations is a sales call *not* needed? (Responses might include that a sales call is more likely when the product requires demonstration, is unfamiliar, is expensive, or when the salesperson has to go to the customer, and is less likely for a common product or a retail store environment.) Ask students how technology might help at each step of the sales call. Go over the steps of a sales call in the text. As appropriate, use a running example, such as trying to sell a T-shirt, NFTE textbook, or other classroom item.

- **Closing the Deal.** Challenge the students: Once the customer has agreed to buy your product or service, is your job as a salesperson done? Have students raise their hands if they think "no" and call on a few to give their reasons. Solicit from the students that, in most cases, follow-up to a sales call is required. Continuing your running example, assume that a student has purchased the item you are selling. On the board, write a sample sales receipt for the transaction, calculate the 10% commission, and model good "after-sales" customer service (shaking hands, arranging delivery, asking if the customer is satisfied, adding information into a customer database). Ask the students to suggest additional after-sales follow-up ideas based on this chapter (and to anticipate Chapter 22).

- **Mock Sales Call.** This activity will give students an opportunity to practice the principles of this lesson. Based on the chapter's principles and steps and your running example in class, have each student prepare a two-minute sales pitch to sell the kind of shirt s/he is wearing to a fellow student. Pair up students and provide time for each partner to make a sales pitch and receive feedback. Allow a few more minutes for revising the sales pitches based on the critiques. Ask a few students to volunteer to make pitches to the whole class. If a video camera is available, videotape the sales pitches to allow students to analyze their own and each other's performance using the evaluation questions in the textbook. **LINKS**»*Drama*

- **Summary.** Use transparency T21-5 to describe several famous entrepreneurs who started out in sales. Establish that sales is a great stepping stone for entrepreneurship and ask students why that might be the case (salespeople interact directly with customers, understand their needs and complaints, and may be more likely to see underserved needs or market segments).

## ASSESS THE LEARNING

- **Vocabulary.** Students who use the workbook should complete the Vocabulary activity. Otherwise, have them define the terms in their own words and use each in a sentence.

- **Key Concepts.** Assign Questions 1, 4, 5. **Answers:** 1. Salespeople often become successful entrepreneurs because they are well practiced in listening to customers, are in touch with what consumers want and need, tend to have positive attitudes, and understand that people buy *benefits* of products. 4. Answers will vary, but some suggestions are:

| Product | Features | Benefits |
|---|---|---|
| Diet soda | Comes in can | Easy to carry |
|  | Has one calorie | Stay slim |
|  | Can is recyclable | Good for environment |
|  | Flavoring | Tastes good |
| Earrings | Gold | Stylish |
|  | Clip-on | No piercing needed |
| Necktie | Black | Goes with anything |
|  | Silk | Soft, stylish |
| Delivery service | 24-hour | Convenient |
|  | Insured | Peace of mind |
|  | Friendly drivers | Pleasant experience |

| Product | Features | Benefits |
|---------|----------|----------|
| T-shirt | Cotton | Comfortable |
| | Lightweight | Good in summer |
| | Popular band logo | Hip |

5. Examples will vary but student should emphasize the direction of motion: with marketing, you get the customer to come to you or your product; with sales, you go (or get the product) to the customer. In addition, students might mention that marketing tends to be indirect through media venues, whereas sales tend to be direct through social interaction.

- **Critical Thinking.** Assign Question 1. **Answers:** 1. Answers will vary, but students should show awareness of what a sales call is and take a critical stance in terms of whether it is the best venue for selling a particular product (sales calls are less likely to be used for retail ready-to-wear clothing or inexpensive items such as food, but are more likely for custom clothing such as wedding gowns or expensive suits, or professional services such as those provided by lawyers, accountants, or financial managers.

- **Writing Practice.** Assign Critical Thinking question 2.

- **Performance Assessment.** Use the Mock Sales Call or Let's Make a Sale! activities to assess students' sales performance in class. Evaluation criteria could include: number of selling principles used, demonstrated understanding of selling principles, poise/good attitude, customer benefit focused rather than product feature-focused, and clear/organized presentation.

- **Additional Workbook Activities Answers.**

- **Vocabulary Activity Answers:** Students' sentences should demonstrate an understanding and correct usage of the terms related to selling and the sales call.

- **Quiz 21** in the workbook. **Answers:** 1. Any of the following: make a good impression, view selling as teaching, believe in your product or service, know your competition, know your customers' needs, prepare your presentation, think positively, keep accurate records, make an appointment, don't accept "maybe" but press for a definite answer. 2. Feature: 100% cotton (benefit: soft, breathable, comfortable); double-knit neck (won't stretch, better-looking fit); original design (stands out); customized printing (makes T-shirt unique). 3. Referrals lead to potential customers and more sales opportunities. 4. Listen carefully and try to turn objections into reasons to buy the product. 5. c. 6. Date of sale, item sold, quantity/amount, price. 7. a. preparation d. listen to the customer e. answer objections h. ask for referrals.

## EXTEND THE LEARNING

- **Business Plan Practice.** Assign Key Concepts questions 2-3.

- **BizTech.** Assign Units 17 and/or 18.

- **Exploration.** Assign the activity in the text. The students should also make observations about what the salesperson did well.

- ***Entrepreneurs in Profile.*** Have students read and be prepared to discuss in class the chapter on Madame C.J. Walker. Questions to set the purpose for reading or for follow-up might include: How did Walker create a specific product or service to meet an unserved customer need? Which selling principles did she use? How was her sales approach innovative for the time? If you were a sales-training consultant to Walker, what suggestions might you make for improving her sales pitch?

- **Sales Ad Analysis.** This activity can be done in class if you pre-record a videotape of several television commercials that feature spokespeople, or it can be done by assigning students to watch at least three television commercials that use spokespeople. Ask them to note the principles of selling used by each spokesperson. Which principles seem the most used and which are missing?

- **Sales Principles and Steps Cartoons.** Have students create cartoon scenarios that illustrate each of the principles of selling and/or each of the steps in a sales call. Post the cartoons around the room to remind class of this chapter's key points.
**LINKS** )·*Graphic Arts*

- **Let's Make a Sale!** Hold a "game show"-style competition to help students think on their feet in selling situations. Randomly select students (draw names off the class list by number or out of a bag) to be contestants. When called, the student will have two minutes to sell an object commonly found in a classroom (stapler, chalk, chalkboard, desk, textbook) to the other students. Contestants get points for using selling principles from the chapter, maintaining poise and focus, and for imaginative approaches. This activity could also be used as a performance assessment. **LINKS** )·*Drama*

# BUILD ACADEMIC AND LIFE-SKILL PROFICIENCIES

## *Skills Mean Success* Answers

**Math.**

| Booth # | Length | Width | Price/ Square Foot | Area | Total Price |
|---------|--------|-------|--------------------|------|-------------|
| 233 | 20′ | 12′ | $17 | 240 sq.ft. | $4,080 |
| 415 | 45′ | 12′ | $17 | 540 sq.ft. | $9,180 |
| 418 | 30′ | 17′ | $17 | 510 sq.ft. | $8,670 |
| 536 | 25′ | 32′ | $17 | 800 sq.ft. | $13,600 |

If necessary, review the formula for area (length $\times$ width), and remind students to express their answers in square feet (sq. ft.). Booth 415 is the largest area available for under $10,000. Check for reasonability: $45' \times 12'$ is close to $50 \times 10 =$ approx. 500 sq. ft. @ about $20/sq. ft. = approximately $10,000. The answer is reasonable.

**English.** Needs might include: safety, space for several passengers, cargo space, economical operation, handles well in city or highway driving, reliability, "kid-proof." Make sure that features match needs. Encourage students to name benefits that connect a feature back to needs, so that Need-Feature-Benefit relates. For example, if a prospect's need is safety, the feature of airbags would provide the benefit of protection during a head-on collision.

**Leadership.** 1. Students could use the tips reasearched in #2 (or brainstorm their own lists) to create a checklist to evaluate the sales calls in #1. Share the interview results during class and ask the other students to listen and make notes of key points. Look for skills such as: salesperson listens more than he speaks; no "feature dumping" (listing features) before customer needs are expressed; courtesy and friendliness is shown; salesperson should try to secure a commitment for some action on the part of the customer. The customer should always be thanked for his/her time and interest. 2. Hints collected might include some of the following: be courteous and friendly; be interested in the customer; ask questions about needs; listen attentively; let the customer talk; act professionally; know your product; know your competition; be honest; ask questions to clarify; don't interrupt; sell *your* product, but don't criticize your competitors; don't oversell or overpromise; listen for "buying signals"; ask for the business; thank the customer; invite any after-sales questions, etc.

### CHAPTER 22

# CUSTOMER SERVICE

## ORGANIZE THE LEARNING

### CHAPTER OBJECTIVES

- Explain why customer service is an investment with a very high return.
- Turn your sales into repeat business.
- Handle customer complaints and criticism in positive ways that will be good for your business.
- Create a customer database and establish other ongoing market research efforts.

### NFTE RESOURCES

- Text pp. 282–287
- Transparencies T22-1 and T22-2
- Workbook/BLMs Chapter 22
- Test Bank Chapter 22

### BUSINESS PLAN ACTIVITIES

*Workbook Business Plan Review*
Customer Service  22-1

*Workbook/Textbook Chapter Review*
Critical Thinking 2, 4

### SKILLS MEAN SUCCESS

*English*
Critical Listening Strategies

*Math*
Mathematical Operations and Approximation: Percentage and Rounding Numbers

*English (plus Technology)*
Writing for Information: Creating Tables and Forms

### PREREQUISITES

Students should pre-read textbook Chapter 22.

### VOCABULARY

customer service, repeat business

*Other  terms to know:*
database

## KEY QUESTION

**How do I keep customers coming back?**

## SET A CONTEXT FOR LEARNING

- **Focus 1: Customer Service Experiences.** Invite the students to share personal experiences: Think of a time when you purchased something and thought the customer service was excellent. What made it so? How did you feel? Think of a time when you thought the customer service was awful. What made it so? How did you feel? Get the students to generalize an observation from each example and record these on the board.

- **Focus 2: Customer Information.** Elicit student responses to this problem: You own a bookstore. What types of information about your customers would it be helpful for you to collect to tailor your products and services?

- **Discussion Launcher 1: Marcus Quote.** Use the Bernie Marcus epigraph at the beginning of the chapter. Ask students what he means by "it": "It's not the bottom line. It's an almost blind, passionate

commitment to taking care of customers." (the notion of being successful in business by attending to the satisfaction of customers).

- **Discussion Launcher 2: The Customer Is Always Right.** Have students work in pairs to discuss how a business might show it believes in the expression: "The customer is always right"?

## DEVELOP AND CLOSE THE LEARNING

- **Customer Service Defined.** Refer to the examples shared in Focus 1. Ask students what patterns they see in excellent vs. poor customer service. Build on the board with the class a list of characteristics of good service. Use transparency T22-1 to define customer service, what it entails, and how it affects a business.

- **Customer Service as Interaction.** Ask: List the types of situations in which customer service plays an important role (at point of sale, when a customer calls, product returns, warranty claims, product-liability claims, requests for information, use of your Web site, etc.). Help students realize that just about everything a company does should consider customer service as a component: any time you interact with a customer (or even influence an interaction "behind the scenes," such as setting up a return policy) is a "moment of truth" or choice point for improving or hurting relationships with customers.

- **Customer Service as Marketing.** Elicit from the students that each choice point will not only affect your business's interaction with a particular customer, but hundreds of other people as well. Use the textbook to point out Joe Girard's "Law of 250" and how the power of word-of-mouth can be used to a business's benefit (if you make customers happy and they share that knowledge) or downfall (if you make customers unhappy). Use transparency T22-2 to discuss how to turn an unhappy customer into a happy one.

- **Customer Service as Research.** Elicit from the class or explain that customer service involves listening to customers every time a business interacts with them; it is a form of market research. Ask students to review their responses to Focus 2. Ask:

  - ○ How could the company collect this information?

  - ○ How might a company organize this information to be useful?

  - ○ How might the company use the information?

- **Customer Service Scenarios**. Have pairs of students think of and write a brief description of one entrepreneurial situation in which customer service could be important, without specifying what should be done or the outcome (that is, they just "set the scene").

  Each pair should write its scenario on a sheet of paper, then fold the paper in quarters and identify it as theirs on the outside. Collect the papers, then redistribute them, one each to a different pair. Tell them that they will role-play the people in the situation and try to create a favorable customer service outcome. As students prepare for their roles, instruct them to consider: What should the business owner do in the moment? What should she do in the long term? Students may also refer to the textbook for customer service tips. Give the groups time to think about and discuss the issues and plan their role play, then invite each pair to the front of the room to play out the situation in character. Have the class evaluate the role-plays. What was realistic? What was done well? What could have been done differently? Why? **LINKS》》Drama**

- **Summary.** Return to the list of excellent customer service characteristics collected earlier in the chapter. Have each student or pair create a cartoon exemplifying one of the customer service characteristics. Display the responses around the room. **LINKS》》Fine Arts**

## ASSESS THE LEARNING

- **Vocabulary.** Have students define terms in their own words and use each in a sentence, or assign the activity in the workbook.

- **Key Concepts.** Assign Questions 1-3. **Answers:** 1. Wording and examples will vary but should address the notion that the Law of 250 addresses how information and opinions about a business can spread quickly, so unless you want word to get around that your business is not up to customer expectations, you should turn an unhappy customer into a happy one. 2. Marketing is about bringing customers to your business; customer service focuses on bringing existing customers *back* (repeat business); customer service should reinforce your business's competitive advantage. 3. Answers will vary but could include: to tailor products and services to individual customer needs (preference information); to send further marketing information to existing customers (contact information); to continually improve your business (feedback/evaluation information); to stay abreast of changes in customer needs, customers' perceptions of competitors, etc.; to build friendships with customers.

- **Critical Thinking.** Assign Questions 1, 3. **Answers:** 1. The answer somewhat depends on the type of business and more is often better, but in some businesses it is better to have fewer customers that spend more than more customers that spend less, because costs will be lower and it is easier to track the needs and maintain a competitive advantage. 3. Answers will vary.

- **Writing Assessment.** Use the Exploration memo as a writing assessment. Add a question about suggestions the student might make for improving the customer service encountered. Also encourage the students to point out what impressed them. Share the writing evaluation criteria with the students in advance — clarity of the writing in general and of the description of the experience in particular, organization of memo, relevance to the topic of customer service and usefulness of ideas.

- **Performance Assessment.** Use the Customer Service Scenarios activity to assess students' behavior and performance in class. Share the evaluation criteria to be used: number of customer service characteristics used, a demonstrated understanding of service characteristics, pleasant attitude, proper body language (stand tall, smile, a pleasant and helpful tone of voice), customer satisfaction oriented, listened and understood customer complaint and need, resolved the problem satisfactorily, learned from the experience what to do better the next time.

- **Additional Workbook Activities Answers.**

  **Vocabulary Activity: Answers:** Students' sentences should demonstrate correct usage of the terms and an understanding of the importance of customer service.

  **Quiz 22** in the workbook. **Answers:** 1-3. Specific answers may vary but should include benefits such as repeat business, satisfied customers, long-term relationships with customers, good word-of-mouth advertising, new customer referrals from existing customers, good business reputation. 4. A general guideline suggesting that one customer interaction has implications for making or losing hundreds of other customers because everyone knows 250 other people that s/he can tell about his/her good or bad experience with your company. 5. Answers will vary but could include updating contact information, evaluation of products or services provided, requests of how the company could improve, whether they would like to try samples of other products you provide, etc. 6. This is an opinion question so answers will vary; check that the student's opinions are clear and reflect understanding of lesson material, and that the reasoning is sound. 7. Answers will vary but should refer to or resemble the situations discussed in class. 8-10. Answers will vary but should reflect the characteristics and guidelines of good customer service discussed in class and the textbook, such as resolving the problem, listening, gathering information, pleasant attitude, etc.

## EXTEND THE LEARNING

- **Business Plan Practice.** Assign Critical Thinking question 2.

- **Exploration.** Augment the activity in the text by asking the class to share their experiences with stores they have visited in the past. What impressed the students? What did they find lacking?

- ***Entrepreneurs in Profile.*** Have the students skim the chapters of the anthology to find customer-service principles and strategies that the profiled entrepreneurs used. Ask: In what types of situations did these principles or strategies arise? Which strategies seemed most effective and which less so, and why? What other strategies might a particular entrepreneur have used in a given situation that might have been better? This activity might be combined with the Customer Service Defined or Summary activities in determining characteristics of good customer service.

- **Database Comparison.** Instruct students to go online and find available database software packages (e.g., FileMaker Pro, Microsoft Access, GoldMine). Individually, in pairs, or in small groups, have students compare these programs on criteria the class chooses (e.g., price, ease of use, complexity of features, flexibility/ability to be tailored to a specific type of business, scalability, etc.). Have students discuss which program they think might be best for their own NFTE businesses and why.

- **Classroom Database.** Let students devise a survey about teen or young adult buying habits and preferences. Have each student in the class complete one survey and input their information into the database.

## BUILD ACADEMIC AND LIFE-SKILL PROFICIENCIES

### *Skills Mean Success* Answers

**English.** Typical complaints might include products that don't work, poor or slow or rude service, price complaints, wrong item delivered, personnel couldn't find the item, etc. Responses should generally: acknowledge and confirm the exact nature of the customer's grievance, sympathize with the problem, apologize for the bad experience, confirm the information, and offer to correct the situation or take the matter to someone who can. Listening politely to the issue and repeating it for clarification pleasantly is key.

**Math.** a. $1.30; b. $1.16; c. $29.80; d. $2.50; e. $3.55.

**English and Technology.** Invite the computer applications teacher or expert students to do a lesson on creating word processing tables, charts and, if appropriate, database applications.

### CHAPTER 23

# MATH TIPS TO HELP YOU SELL AND NEGOTIATE

## ORGANIZE THE LEARNING

### CHAPTER OBJECTIVES

- Do business math in your head so you can think on your feet.
- Convert bulk prices to per-unit costs quickly during negotiations.
- Be able to calculate how many years it will take for an investment to double.

### NFTE RESOURCES

- Text pp. 288-293
- Transparency T23-1
- Workbook/BLMs Chapter 23
- Test Bank Chapter 23

### BUSINESS PLAN ACTIVITIES

*Workbook Business Plan Review*
Business Math 23-1

*Workbook/Textbook Chapter Review*
Key Concepts 1

### SKILLS MEAN SUCCESS

*Technology*
Online Research and Devising Spreadsheet Formulas

*Math*
Rounding Numbers and Proportional Reasoning

*English*
Reading for Information: Fact vs. Opinion

### PREREQUISITES

- Students should preview Chapter 23 in their textbook.
- This chapter builds on Chapters 15, 21 and 22.

### VOCABULARY

None

*Other terms to know:*
approximation, keystoning, Rule of 72

## KEY QUESTION

**How can I use mental math to make better business decisions?**

## SET A CONTEXT FOR LEARNING

- **Focus 1: Math Problems.** As a warm-up, use transparency T23-1. Note: Many students will do the calculations "the long way" so this warm-up may take a few minutes. This Focus activity will set up and anticipate a later activity, in which the class will revisit these problems with easier methods. **Answers:** 1. 10 cents; make money; 15 cents. 2. $6 per hour (assuming 50 weeks per year, 40 hours per week). 3. 12 years.

- **Focus 2: Quick Thinking.** Present this scenario: A wholesaler will sell you candy bars for $3.60 per dozen. How much money would you make on each bar if the retail price was 45 cents? Should you buy from the wholesaler at this price? Why or why not? **Answer:** 15 cents per bar.

- **Focus 3: Changing-Units Problems.** Share the following chart on the board or on a worksheet, or give verbal instructions, to have students convert the following amounts to the specified units:

| Amount & Old Unit | New Unit | Answer |
| --- | --- | --- |
| $3,200 per month (full time) | Per hour | $20 (3,200 divided by 40 hours divided by 4 weeks) |
| $15 per hour (full time) | Per month | $2400 (15 × 40 × 4) |
| $200 per month | Per year | $24,000 (200 × 12 months) |
| $10 per hour (full time) | Per day | $80 (10 × 8 hours) |
| $9 per day (half time) | Per day | $45 (9 × 4 hours) |
| $300 per week (w/2 weeks vacation) | Per year | $15,000 (300 × 50 weeks) |

## DEVELOP AND CLOSE THE LEARNING

- **Why Math Is Important.** This activity can also serve as a mini-review (through a mathematical lens) of the NFTE curriculum. In pairs, have students conduct a "scavenger hunt" through the textbook to find and list situations in which an entrepreneur uses math. Emphasize that it is not only important to have math skills, but to be able to think mathematically "on your feet" — there may not be paper/pencil, a calculator, a palm pilot or a computer around when you need to figure a price. To impress customers, suppliers, employees, investors, etc., students will need to know how to calculate or estimate quickly or make unit conversions without tools.

- **Math Tips.** Use the text to describe general tips entrepreneurs use to make calculating easier and quicker. Give scenario examples from the text or elsewhere to show the tips in use during common entrepreneurial activities. To summarize, return to Focus 1 and/or 2 above and ask students which tips might make these problems easier to solve.

- **"Discount Given at Register" Game.** This activity will sharpen and quicken students' abilities to calculate in sales situations. On the board, re-create the first three columns of the table below; the last two columns are answer columns for you). The scenario is a retail sales encounter in which students are salespeople/cashiers to whom a customer has brought a product on sale and a sum of money to pay for the product. There is no calculator and the cash register will not automatically figure in the discount. So students must calculate the discount dollar amount and how much change they should give.

  Encourage students to use the math tips learned in this chapter. Write one row of figures on the board (see below), then allow students one minute to solve the problem. After a few rows, reduce the time allotment to 45 seconds, then 30 seconds, then 20. Have students figure the percentage of problems they answered correctly.

| Price | Discount | Payment | Discount Amount | Change Given |
|---|---|---|---|---|
| $10 | 10% | $10 | $1 | $1 |
| $18 | 15% | $20 | $2.70 | $17.30 |
| $5 | 22% | $10 | $1.10 | $8.90 |
| $29.99 | 50% | $20 | $15 | $5 |
| $150 | 12% | $140 | $18 | $8 |
| $425 | 10% | $400 | $42.50 | $17.50 |
| $1.99 | 33% | $1.50 | $0.66 | $0.17 |

| Price | Discount | Payment | Discount Amount | Change Given |
|---|---|---|---|---|
| $799 | 25% | $600 | $200 or $199.99 | $1 or $1.01 |
| $9 | 2% | $10 | $1.80 | $2.80 |
| $4,795 | 20% | $3,640 | $959 | $4 |
| $9.95 | 5% | $10 | $0.50 | $0.55 |
| $14 | 25% | $10.50 | $3.50 | $0 |

*BONUS QUESTION:*

| Price | Discount | Payment | Discount Amount | Change Given |
|---|---|---|---|---|
| $100 | 25% plus another 10% off the sale price | $80 | $25 plus another $7.50 | $12.50 |

- **Summary.** As a class or in pairs brainstorm how math skills are related to good customer service, marketing strategy, profitability, positive mental attitude, negotiation, opportunity evaluation, competitive advantage, and sales. Relate these ideas to the quote by Henry J. Kaiser: "Problems are only opportunities in work clothes." (Expected student responses: with a little effort invested, math problems are just opportunities for entrepreneurs to lower costs, raise profitability, negotiate a better deal, etc.)

## ASSESS THE LEARNING

- **Key Concepts.** Assign Questions 1-3. **Answers:** 1. Answers will vary but should be specific and clearly include calculation, approximation, etc. 2. Chips 66 cents, 33 cents; trail mix $1.36, 68 cents. 3. 46 cents, 40 cents, 23 cents (rounding up).

- **Critical Thinking.** If you did not do Focus 1 in class, assign Questions 1-4. **Answers:** 1a. 10 cents. 1b. make money. 1c. 15 cents. 2. $12 ($12,000 divided by 1,000 hours). Tell students to assume 50 work weeks per year. 3. 12 years (72 divided by 6 percent). 4. Soda $0.25. Additional workbook answers: Ties $1.00, Socks $0.50, Watches $2.00, Shoes $10.00.

- **Additional Workbook Activities Answers.**

  **Quiz 23** in the workbook. Note: This quiz has been designed so that items 2 through 8 can be solved mentally. It is recommended that the questions be read aloud and that students write down only the answers. As each problem is completed, it should be checked immediately. If students are proficient, Problems 2 through 8 may be given as a speed test. **Answers:** 1. Answers will vary (see Why Math Is

Important activity above for some examples). 2. $10,000; 3.a. 6 years; b. 12 years; c. 7.2 years; d. 9 years; e. 2 years. 4. $1, $5, $3, $1.50, $0.75. 5. $0.25, $1, $0.10, $0.50, $0.10. 6. $3, $1.50; $15, $7.50; $0.50, $0.25; $2.50, $1.25; $6, $3. 7. $1.50. 8. 0.

## EXTEND THE LEARNING

- **Shopping Trip.** Convey the following scenario to the students either verbally in class or on paper as an assignment. Instruct students to keep a running tab of their shopping totals in their heads as they shop. Students should not use paper and pencil or other calculation tools. Answers are given in parentheses within the scenario.

  You enter the grocery store and turn right into the produce department. You buy three pounds of bananas for $0.50 a pound ($1.50), a bag of potatoes for $4.99 ($6.50), three cucumbers at 3-for-$1 ($7.50), two avocados for $0.75 each ($9), and a bag of lettuce for $2.99 ($12). In the meat department, you buy 1 pound of hamburger at $2.99 per pound ($15) and a rotisserie chicken for $5.99 ($21). Finally, you enter the frozen foods section and buy a pint of ice cream for $3.49 ($24.50) and some chocolate syrup for $2.49 ($27). If sales tax is 5% and you have $30 in your pocket, will you have enough money to cover your food bill? (Tax = about $1.30, so yes, you will have enough). **LINKS**»*Consumer Ed*

- **"Bargain Bin" Calculation Relay.** The corresponding real-world scenario for this activity is how the price of an item in a department store might change on its way from being new inventory to the deeply discounted bargain bin. Divide the class into teams of five or six students each and arrange them into lines. Write a starting price on the board, with a discount percentage. The first student calculates the new sale price and whispers it to the second student, who applies the discount percentage to the first student's whispered price and whispers the further discounted price to the third student, etc. The first team to calculate the correct bargain-bin price earns a point.

  If time permits, it may be helpful to do both discount percentage and investment growth and allow students to discuss similarities and differences in calculating "down" (discounts) vs. "up" (growth).

- **Problem Pairs.** This activity not only allows students to hone their problem-solving skills but also to think of scenarios in which need for math expertise may arise. In pairs, have students create problems for each other that can be solved using one of the math tips in this chapter without paper/pencil, etc.

## BUILD ACADEMIC AND LIFE-SKILL PROFICIENCIES

### *Skills Mean Success* Answers

**Technology.** To find additional examples of business math, appoint some students to conduct a Web search under "consumer math."

Some students may want to investigate the formula $FV = PV (1 + i)^N$ (FV = Future Value; PV = Present Value; i = Interest rate; N = Number of periods).

Invite an expert student or teacher to demonstrate how to create mathematical formulas for sums, percentages, products, or quotients ( $+$, %, $\times$, or $\div$) in a spreadsheet. Create a spreadsheet that a sales representative could use to calculate travel expenses on an expense account. Headings for the expenses report might include: Hotel, Meals, Parking, Mileage Allowance, Car Rental, Tips, Airfare, and Miscellaneous.

**Math.** 1. I, b; II, e; III, d; IV, a; V, c. 2.a. $1,200; b. $2.50 $\times$ 50 = $125; c. 3 $\times$ 50 weeks $\times$ 15 min = 2,250 min. (37h and 30 minutes); d. $0.15 per week $\times$ 50 weeks $\times$ 200 = $1,500; e. 50 copies $\times$ $0.05 $\times$ 4 times/yr. = $10.00.

**English.** 1. F; 2. F; 3. O; 4. O; 5. O; 6. F.

### CHAPTER 24

# BUSINESS COMMUNICATION

## ORGANIZE THE LEARNING

### CHAPTER OBJECTIVES

- Write a business memo.
- Write a business letter.
- Know when to use "cc:" on copies of memos or letters.
- Proofread business correspondence.

### NFTE RESOURCES

- Text pp. 294-303
- Transparencies T24-1 to T24-3
- Workbook/BLMs Chapter 24
- Test Bank Chapter 24
- BizTech Unit 14
- A Business for the Young Entrepreneur: *Designs Á La Mode*

### BUSINESS PLAN ACTIVITIES

*Workbook Business Plan Review*
Business Communication 24-1, 24-2

*Workbook/Textbook Chapter Review*
Key Concepts 4, Critical Thinking 3

### SKILLS MEAN SUCCESS

*English*
Reading and Writing for Understanding: Memos

*English*
Presenting Information Clearly

### PREREQUISITES

Preview Chapter 24 in the textbook.

### VOCABULARY

fax, letterhead, memo

*Other suggested terms to know:*
c.c.:, re:, encl.:, heading, interoffice, motto, networking, proofread

## KEY QUESTION

**What common forms of written communication are used in business?**

## PREPARE FOR LEARNING

- **Guest Speaker.** If you plan to use this Extension activity, arrange for the guest speaker in advance.

## SET A CONTEXT FOR LEARNING

- **Focus: Different Communication Forms.** Ask students to consider and discuss the following: Think of people to whom you have written e-mails, letters, or notes. What differences were there in the way you wrote to your grandmother vs. your dad vs. your best friend vs. a teacher vs. a stranger?

- **Discussion Launcher: Sharing Your Idea.** Have students work in pairs regarding the following scenario (or another scenario you create): You are partners in a computer company. One of you has a great idea for developing a new product that provides satellite radio from stations around with world with no commercials. Take a few minutes to communicate your idea to your partner. Then both of you think about

the conversation you just held. What things that were said would be best to write down and why?

## DEVELOP AND CLOSE THE LEARNING

- **Drawbacks of Oral Communication/Rumor Game.** This is a variation of the classic game of "Telephone." Write a sentence of about 12 to 15 words on a sheet of paper that the class cannot see. Whisper the sentence into the ear of a student and instruct him/her to repeat/whisper the sentence to an adjacent student. Students should not be allowed to ask for clarification. Continue until the sentence has been passed on to everyone. Ask the last student that heard the message to say it aloud, and write what s/he says on the board. Share the original sentence as written on the paper. Ask students to compare the sentences (they almost always are different) and think about how it was transformed. Repeat the activity as time permits, perhaps instructing students to be more careful with repeating and listening the next time around. (The point is that inaccuracies will almost always occur). Ask students to draw some general conclusions about the disadvantages of oral communication (It changes with repetition, people hear different things, there is no record).

- **Forms of Written Communication in Business.** Given the unreliability of oral communication, as established by the above activity, have students brainstorm potential advantages of writing things down in business. (Having a clear record and proof of the "what/when/who" of a conversation, finding and clearing up misunderstandings, aiding memory for later, reducing confusion.) Introduce the main types of written communication: memo, letter, e-mail, business card.

- **Business Memo.** Use transparency T24-1 to describe the elements of a business memo. Discuss situations when a memo is appropriate (to signify urgency, as interoffice communication, need to get the information out quickly, to document a conversation, to introduce an idea to someone you already know well, to verify understanding of information received from someone else).

- **Business Letter.** Use transparency T24-2 to describe the elements of a business letter. Compare the letter format to the memo format and differentiate clearly between the two forms. Discuss situations in which a letter may be more appropriate than a memo (formal situations, first contact, serious situations such as legal proceedings, requesting or sharing information with a stranger).

- **Communication Distribution.** Outline the ways a person can send/deliver a memo, letter or other written document — messenger, mail, fax, text messaging, etc. Discuss the pros and cons of using e-mail as a distribution method compared to these other methods. (Pros: fast, cheap, proof of sending time/date, blanket distribution of e-mail using address book feature. Cons: less control over formatting, message can be changed easily and re-sent by someone else, security problems, considered less formal.) Remind students always to keep a copy of every correspondence.

- **Proofreading.** Show transparency T24-3 and have students individually look for and note grammar and spelling mistakes. Pair up students to compare their lists and discuss any differences, then ask the pairs to share their combined findings with the class. Highlight on the transparency where the mistakes are and ask students how to correct them. Discuss strategies they may have to ensure error-free communications. You may need to start the conversation with a few examples, such as using a spell checker on the computer. (Other strategies might include: use a dictionary, have another person read the letter/memo, refer to a grammar book or reference handbook, check for common mistakes such as

subject/verb agreement). As an additional exploration, students may be interested in learning common proofreader marks, which can often be found in many dictionaries and most journalism textbooks.

- **Networking Party.** Discuss how business cards are a form of written communication: What information do they usually provide? (Name, contact information, business name, slogan, logo.) When are they appropriate to distribute? (Business functions, one-on-one, with a mailed letter). If you had students create business cards in Chapter 10, then make sure they have printed about ten business cards. If not, allow time for students to design and print cards for their NFTE business (for instructions, refer to the Chapter 10 Extension activity). Tell students that you are hosting a party to introduce their businesses to the others. Give them class time (or assign as homework) to develop a two-minute description of their businesses and to make sure they have sufficient business cards printed or photocopied. On the day of the activity, if possible (these enhancements are optional but add to the "real world" business ambience of the activity), ask students to dress in business attire, and move desks so there is room to stand in groups as at a business function. Arrange students in groups of three. Each will introduce him/herself to the other two by smiling, shaking hands, giving his/her name, describing the business, and handing out business cards. After ten minutes or so, have them circulate and find two new students, repeating the introductions and continuing the activity as time permits. Bring the class back together and ask students to reflect on their experience:

  ○ How did it feel to "network"?

  ○ What tips did they learn from the others' introductions?

  ○ Did they refine their introductions over the course of the activity?

  ○ What recommendations would they make to a new entrepreneur in regards to networking?

  ○ When are good times/situations to network?

  Try to make the point that an entrepreneur should always carry some business cards because you never know when a networking opportunity might arise.

- **Summary.** Have students write a brief memo to you (using the format on transparency T24-1) outlining the three most important tips they learned from this lesson.

## ASSESS THE LEARNING

- **Vocabulary.** Have students define terms in their own words and use each in a sentence or complete the vocabulary activity in the workbook.

- **Key Concepts.** Assign Questions 1-3, 5. **Answers:** 1. A memo provides proof of communication. 2. A letter, because the customer is an external audience and is probably a stranger, plus a complaint is a serious matter. 3. A memo if the message is an informal or friendly reminder to emphasize customer service; a letter if the message is a warning or other formal type of documentation. 5. Any of the following: from whom sent, to whom sent, date, clear language, "encl." or "cc:" (if appropriate).

- **Critical Thinking.** Assign Question 3. **Answers:** 3. Name, title, business name, address, phone, fax, e-mail, slogan, logo.

- **Writing Practice.** Assign Critical Thinking questions 1-2. As an alternative, use Critical Thinking question 1, memo 1 as the scenario, but in addition to the memo to the teacher, have students write:

  - a letter to the admissions committee of the college to which they applied explaining the situation.

  - an e-mail to a friend describing the situation.

- **Performance Assessment.** The Networking Party activity may be used as an assessment of the following skills: clarity in business communication, portraying a positive attitude, informal public speaking, professional dress and demeanor.

- **Additional Workbook Activities Answers.**

  **Vocabulary Activity Answers:** memo, fax, letterhead.

  **Quiz 24** in the workbook. **Answers:** 1. To verify what was said in conversation, to document decisions, etc. 2. Answer should include: to, from, date, re: 3. Answers will vary but should include one or more of the following: brief, to the point, easily understood, error-free. 4. Errors can be corrected more easily, copies can be made quickly, correspondence can be stored electronically, etc. 5. Via computers with data transmitted over phone or DSL lines. 6. "Profreadd" should be "Proofread"; "corect" should be "correct"; "senence" should be "sentence"; and semi-colon should be a period. 7. Answers may vary but should be a variation of Sincerely, Yours truly, etc. with signature and printed name and title below. 8. Proofread it and make a copy for your files. 9. Letter. 10. Answers may vary but should explain that errors in spelling or grammar, unclear writing, and poor formatting indicate that your business is poorly run, whereas a clear, error-free and properly formatted document indicates a business with which most people would want to interact.

## EXTEND THE LEARNING

- **Business Plan Practice.** Assign Key Concepts question 4. Alternatively or in addition, have students write: 1) a memo to a current investor updating him/her on their business plans, and 2) a letter to a potential investor outlining their business plan.

- **BizTech.** Assign Unit 14.

- **A Business for the Young Entrepreneur.** Have students read about Lapria Deshauna Kelly and Webster Lincoln and their company, Designs À La Mode in the text. Tell students that Lapria and Webster have been invited by a local youth group to talk to them about entrepreneurship. Ask students to write a business letter to the youth group president agreeing to visit and outlining a few ideas they would share about entrepreneurship.

- **Exploration.** Assign students to play the activity in the text with their friends (the same activity played in the lesson). Ask them to write a memo about what the statement was when the game started, what it was when the game ended, and how/why it changed.

- **Business Letter Analysis.** Either collect or have students collect (such as by saving direct mail pieces you or they have received) at least one business letter. As a class, create a checklist, based on the text, of criteria for a good business letter. Have students individually or in groups evaluate one business letter based on these criteria. Have students pretend to be the Communications Director for the company that sent the letter. They should write a memo to the company president evaluating — and providing suggestions for improving — the letter. Alternatively, students may present orally or create a poster or slide presentation.

- **Revision.** The point of this activity is to show students that allowing time away from a document can improve their communications skills and that there is always room for continually improvement. A day or so after students have completed the Writing Practice activity or the Business Letter Analysis activity, have them evaluate and rewrite the document to be even briefer and clearer than their first versions. In class, ask students what "bothered" them about their first versions that they changed in the second, and why.

- **Guest Speaker.** This guest speaker can tie in not only with this lesson but also with Chapter 19 regarding publicity. Invite a copy editor from a local newspaper to make a presentation to your class about how s/he edits and proofreads stories for publication. It may be a good idea to encourage the guest speaker to bring in marked-up versions of stories to show students the details of the editing process. If the newspaper makes available a "proofreader's marks checklist," perhaps s/he could bring copies. An English teacher with a good background in writing might be a productive alternative.

- **Business Plan Integrative Summary.** Chapter 24 concludes Unit 5, which emphasizes communication, so it may be a good time for students to compose and present a brief summary of the communication aspects of their Business Plans to date, including:

  1. a memo describing their customer service strategy to potential employees.
  2. a business letter outlining their business idea to a potential investor.
  3. a business card.
  4. a "script" of their basic sales pitch.

# BUILD ACADEMIC AND LIFE-SKILL PROFICIENCIES

## *Skills Mean Success* Answers

**English (Memos).** 1. Establish the concept of measuring (evaluating) against specific criteria anything that would normally be difficult to judge objectively — such as written work or employee performance. Students will, of course, mark the memo differently. The idea is to review and note the qualities of an effective memo using specific criteria. 2. Review how language "around" or "near" difficult or unknown terms can frequently be used to help a reader or listener figure out their meaning. For example: The *herpotologist* enjoyed learning as much as she could about all varieties of large and small reptiles. One could guess from the context that a herpatologist is a scientist who studies reptiles. Students should be able to provide some interesting additional examples, based on their current "informal" vocabularies. **venture loan:** The sentence suggests it is money lent to start a business; **registering:** the sentence suggests that it is a process of filing official forms for a new business with a government office; **inventory:** since the proposed new business is called "Darnell's Candy," one might expect that candy is the product that will be bought, stored, and sold — i.e., the inventory; **business financing:** since the memo deals with getting money — in this case a loan — to pay for the start-up of a business, the context of the memo might be used to determine the general meaning, although there are several types of business financing. A loan is one type. Context may not be sufficient in this case to understand the specific meaning of the term.

**English (Presenting).** Allowing students to record their messages and hear their own voices will be very helpful. Remind them that the most effective messages are planned in advance. Students should have fun with #3, but remind them about appropriate language for school and the work place.

### CHAPTER 25

# SOLE PROPRIETORSHIPS AND PARTNERSHIPS

## ORGANIZE THE LEARNING

### CHAPTER OBJECTIVES

- Explain the pros and cons of sole proprietorships and partnerships.
- Register a sole proprietorship.
- Research business permits and licenses.
- Obtain a sales-tax identification number.

### NFTE RESOURCES

- Text pp. 304-311
- Transparencies T25-1 and T25-2
- Workbook/BLMs Chapter 25
- Test Bank Chapter 25
- BizTech Unit 9

### BUSINESS PLAN ACTIVITIES

*Workbook Business Plan Review*
Legal Structure  25-1, 25-2, 25-3, 25-4, 25-5

*Workbook/Textbook Chapter Review*
Key Concepts 2, Critical Thinking 4, Exploration

*Power Point Templates*
Int. 2; Adv. 2

### SKILLS MEAN SUCCESS

*Leadership*
Practicing Risk Taking

*Math*
Solving Problems Using Percentages, Formulas and Substitution

### PREREQUISITES

Give the students time to preview Chapter 25 in the textbook.

### VOCABULARY

limited partnership, partnership, permit, sole proprietorship

*Other terms to know:*
assign, certificate, contract, debt, liable, license, regulation, notarized, zoning

## KEY QUESTION

**How do I legally set up my business?**

## PREPARE FOR LEARNING

- **Forms**. If you plan to do the business registration activity in Develop the Learning, it might be helpful to pick up or have sent to you in advance pertinent business-registration and tax-ID forms that students can practice completing.

- **Guest Speaker.** If you plan to invite a guest speaker from a local government business regulatory agency or the Chamber of Commerce (or plan to take the class to one of these locations) as one of the Extend the Learning activities, make contact and arrangements well in advance. Alternatively, these agencies may have informational videos or print material they will share ahead of time.

## SET A CONTEXT FOR LEARNING

- **Focus 1: Permission.** Ask the students to list five activities (such as driving) that they need to get

permission for. Ask why they think permission is necessary. **LINKS**›*Character Ed*

- **Focus 2: Personal Partnerships.** Have the class consider the following: Think of a time when you did something jointly with a friend. What did you like or dislike about the arrangement?

- **Discussion Launcher: Disraeli Quote.** Examine the Benjamin Disraeli quote in the text and ask students to interpret what "be ready" entails: "The secret of success in life is for a man to be ready for his opportunity when it comes."

## DEVELOP AND CLOSE THE LEARNING

- **Risk Review.** Set up the following scenario: Suppose you own a company that makes skateboards. Someone has an accident while using one of your boards. The customer claims the skateboard was defective and this caused the accident. You are sued for $100,000. What can happen if the customer wins? (You might lose everything — not just your initial investment but personal belongings and resources too.) Recall from Chapter 3 the concepts of risk and return. Different legal structures allow entrepreneurs several ways to set up businesses that affect risk and return. Challenge the class: Why might the government allow these different forms of legal structures? (Answers will vary, but should include: different businesses are opened under different circumstances and for different reasons [for example, some businesses require a lot of start-up financing, are started by individuals who work as partners, or are types of businesses that are more vulnerable to lawsuits by customers]; the free enterprise system allows owners freedom of choice within the law so they can set up businesses as they wish; businesses serve different purposes; they require different kinds of investment, operation and ownership.) **LINKS**»*Economics*

- **Types of Legal Structures.** Use transparency T25-1 to discuss the different business legal structures, focusing particularly on the two used most often by young entrepreneurs:

  ○ sole proprietorship

  ○ partnership

  Divide the class into four groups. Each group should research in the textbook and/or brainstorm one of the following: potential returns of sole proprietorship, risks of sole proprietorship, potential returns of partnership, risks of partnership. In addition, ask the groups to rank these risks or returns in terms of personal importance. Allow the groups to present their ideas and discuss as a class the overlaps and disagreements in ranking. Ask students to think of national or local businesses that started as sole proprietorships or partnerships (using the textbook, *Entrepreneurs in Profile, The Wall Street Journal,* the Internet, or other sources of information). Ask:

  ○ What are things entrepreneurs might do to protect themselves from these risks? (Incorporate, get insurance, have customers sign a release.)

  ○ What is likely to be the effect on returns? (Lowering risk usually also lowers the expected return, but makes it more secure.)

  Point out that sole proprietorships should only be used for products or services that are unlikely to injure someone. Corporations (covered more in Chapter 32) aim to limit the liability of the entrepreneur (and other company employees) but in return the entrepreneur gives up some control and potential for personal return on investment to outsiders.

- **Registration and Sales Tax ID Number.** Use the textbook to step students through registering their businesses as sole proprietorships or partnerships (get-ting a general business license). Show the sample business certificate on transparency T25-2. It may be helpful to pick up or have sent to you registration and tax ID forms from your city or state that students can practice completing. As an option, you could assign students to do an Internet search for the business name they were planning to use to see if it is already in use. Ask: Why should you register your businesses? What's the benefit? (Legal requirements, help with entering contracts and obtaining funding, prevent another business from using your name.)

- **Licenses and Permits.** Ask students to define and distinguish between permits, licenses and certificates, as defined in the textbook. Why are these regulatory mechanisms required? (To protect the safety, health and well-being of others.) As a class, brainstorm the types of permits or licenses that might be required for the following types of businesses (or others you can think of): dry cleaner (zoning, environmental/use of hazardous chemicals), restaurant (zoning, liquor license, food permits, employment permits), school (zoning, safety, food preparation, employment permits), accounting (educational credentials, professional license). Ask students to speculate about what types of businesses might require the most regulations (manufacturing, food service, professional services, and other businesses where liability and the possibility of injury may be high). **LINKS**»*Business Law*

- **Agreements.** Discuss with students the need for contracts/agreements when an entrepreneur involves others — individuals or businesses. Define a contract as a legal agreement that specifies, in writing, the contributions, duties, obligations, rights and benefits of each person or *entity* signing the contract. Contracts protect the interests of everyone involved under the law of the land. Ask students to list examples of relationships in which a contract might be helpful (among partners — who might have future disagreements, with suppliers, with employees, with customers for work done over time, with insurance companies.)

- **Summary.** Point out that a business's risk and return need to be considered not only from the perspective of the entrepreneur, but of society in general.

## ASSESS THE LEARNING

- **Vocabulary.** Have students define terms in their own words and use each in a sentence or assign the Vocabulary activity in the workbook.

- **Key Concepts.** Questions 1 and 3. **Answers:** 1. Any two of the following: select a business name and do a name search, research local and state regulations for your business/industry, obtain necessary licenses and permits, and/or obtain a sales-tax ID number. 3. To verify identification or prove that the person signing the form is qualified to sign it.

- **Critical Thinking.** Questions 4-5. **Answers:** 4. Answers may vary but the memo should include topics such as incorporating, getting insurance, making sure s/he is following all regulations and has the necessary permits, making customers sign a liability release form. 5. A certificate; it is a document that proves the business is registered as a sole proprietorship.

- **Writing Practice.** Assign Critical Thinking question 1.

- **Additional Workbook Activities Answers.**

  **Vocabulary Activity Answers:** 1. c., 2. d., 3. a., 4. b.

  **Quiz 25** in the workbook. **Answers:** 1. A sole proprietorship is one individual's business venture whereas a partnership has two or more people involved. 2. Liability means legal responsibility; a person's business can be sued for accidents, defective merchandise, unpaid bills or debt, etc. 3. Any three from the following: easy to start, lower personal income tax rate on earnings, fewer government regulations, quicker decision-making, one person keeps all the profits. 4. Any three from the following list: combined assets for greater resource pool, sharing of long hours, more diverse skills and contacts to help business grow, sharing of risks and liabilities. 5. Any reasonable answer that explains the problems of getting along, being clear about responsibilities, how to come to a decision if partners don't agree, etc. 6. Answers will vary.

## EXTEND THE LEARNING

- **Business Plan Practice.** Assign Key Concepts question 2 and Critical Thinking question 2.

- **BizTech.** Assign Unit 9.

- **Exploration.** Assign the activity in the textbook. As an option, have students create posters that outline these regulations and display them so the class can compare them. Ask students to find patterns and draw conclusions among the different business types. **LINKS**»*Fine Arts*

- **Internet Exploration.** Instruct students to use an Internet search engine to find self-help law libraries that provide information about forming a business (Green and Green Self-Help Law Library). Each student or group might choose one type of business and creates a poster or presentation slide that summarizes the most helpful advice from the Web site.

- ***Entrepreneurs in Profile.*** Have students analyze the chapter on Stephen Wozniak and Steve Jobs to discover how the legal structure of Apple Computer changed over its history.

- **Partnership Agreement.** Assign Critical Thinking question 3. Have students in pairs draw up an agreement that outlines who is responsible for what duties, rights, and benefits for any project in which they may be involved. Have pairs present their agreements for comparison. Ask students to create a summary list of what a partnership agreement should include.

- **Guest Speaker.** Invite a local government regulator (such as someone from the business registration or business tax office) to discuss the specific local regulations, permits, and licenses required for businesses that young entrepreneurs are likely to open (e.g., home office, zoning, employee, food preparation or handling). Suggest bringing samples of forms or pamphlets for class to look at and/or complete. Have students prepare a list of interview questions in advance.

- **Field Trip to the Chamber of Commerce.** Arrange an outing to your local chamber of commerce or have a representative visit your class to discuss this organization's interface between the business community and government.

## BUILD ACADEMIC AND LIFE-SKILL PROFICIENCIES

### *Skills Mean Success* Answers

**Leadership.** For any students who keep a writing journal for English class or for personal use, this reflection activity is a natural fit. Otherwise, students can just jot down notes, but ask them to commit their thoughts to paper. Respect their musings as private, but allow any student who wishes to share with the class to do so.

**Math.** 1. below, 2. p = $50

| State | Sales Tax Rate | Tax on a $25 Sale | Tax on a $1,340 Sale |
|-------|----------------|-------------------|----------------------|
| CT | 6% | $1.50 | $80.40 |
| GA | 4% | $1.00 | $53.60 |
| TX | 6-1/4 % | $1.56 | $ 83.75 |
| VA | 4-1/2 % | $1.13 | $ 60.30 |
| CA | 7-1/4 % | $1.81 | $ 97.15 |
| NM | 5% | $1.25 | $ 67.00 |

### CHAPTER 26

# MANUFACTURING:
## *From Idea to Product*

## ORGANIZE THE LEARNING

### CHAPTER OBJECTIVES

- Explain the manufacturing process.
- Locate manufacturers in your community.
- Have a prototype made.
- Investigate zoning laws that might affect your business.

### NFTE RESOURCES

- Text pp. 312-321
- Transparencies T26-1, T7-2
- Workbook/BLMs Chapter 26
- Test Bank Chapter 26
- A Business for the Young Entrepreneur: *Button Manufacturing*

### BUSINESS PLAN ACTIVITIES

*Workbook Business Plan Review*
Manufacturing

*Workbook/Textbook Chapter Review*
Critical Thinking 4, 5; Exploration

### SKILLS MEAN SUCCESS

*Math*
Measurement and Data: Interpreting Graphs

Mathematical Reasoning: Making Conjectures to Solve Problems

*Leadership*
Negotiation and Thinking Skills
Persistence, Resilience, Innovative Solutions

*English*
Reading for Understanding
Analyzing, Interpreting, Evaluating Text

### PREREQUISITES

- Ask students to work in pairs and skim Chapter 26 to compile a list of five to ten key ideas.
- Chapters 2, 7 and 8 will be useful background.

### VOCABULARY

job shop, manufacturing plants, moving assembly line, setup costs, tooling costs

*Other related terms to know:*
batch/lot , blueprint, consumer products, efficiency, government contract, industrial products, inventory, prototype, specifications

## KEY QUESTION

**How do I make my product efficiently?**

## PREPARE FOR LEARNING

- **Raw Materials.** For the Assembly Line activity in Develop and Close the Learning, bring to class inexpensive materials for the students to use. Options might be: flowers and ribbon to make boutonnières; 8 x 10 cardboard and fabric to make picture frames; or candy, cellophane and ribbon to make goody bags. Some businesses may give away old/outdated materials to work with. The activity's aim is not to make something complex, but to be able to set up an assembly line so that 20-30 items can be made relatively quickly and efficiently.

- **Instruction Sheets.** For the product(s) you choose to have students manufacture, divide the instructions into "spec sheets" for each assembly line station.

## SET A CONTEXT FOR LEARNING

- **Focus 1: Keystoning.** Present this problem to the class: You visit a pet store to buy a birdcage. The store bought the cage from a wholesaler, who bought it from the manufacturer. If the price was keystoned at every step and you paid $80, how much did the manufacturer pay to his supplier for raw materials? **Answer:** $10 (which was doubled to $20 when the manufacturer sold to the wholesaler, doubled again to $40 for the retailer, and doubled again to $80 for you, the consumer).
**LINKS)**·*Consumer Ed*

- **Focus 2: Products Brainstorm.** Challenge students to work in groups to list as many types of manufactured products as they can think of in two minutes. As a follow-up, invite them to suggest multi-layered ways of sorting items in the brainstormed lists, such as: machines, vehicles, consumer vehicles, cars, SUVs.

## DEVELOP AND CLOSE THE LEARNING

- **What Is Manufacturing?** On the board, draw a three-column table. Label the first column "manufacturer," the second "retailer," and the third "service provider." Ask students to brainstorm ideas to complete the table based on the following prompts:

Row 1: What does this type of business do? (Manufacturer transforms raw materials into finished products to meet customer needs; retailer assembles manufactured products in a location that makes it easy for customers to acquire; service provider does some task for or on behalf of the customer.)

Row 2: What is an example of this kind of business? (Manufacturer: Proctor & Gamble, General Motors, Apple Computer, Sony; retailer: Old Navy, Macy's, Wal-Mart; service provider: dry cleaner, hairdresser, accountant, doctor.)

Row 3: What subtypes of this type of business are there? (E.g., manufacturer: consumer products [dish detergent, DVD player], industrial products [tools, machinery], government contracts [weapons, space vehicles]; retailer: department stores [Macy's], discount stores [Wal-Mart], pharmacies [Walgreen's], specialty boutiques [Payless Shoes, People's Florist]; service provider: professional service [doctor, dentist], personal service [massage therapist, hairdresser], repair/maintenance [maids, laundry, dry cleaning, trades]).

Row 4: What are the advantages of this type of business? (Manufacturer: originate products, can get patents; retailer: lower fixed costs and flexibility; service provider: often based on education/knowledge that can't be lost, flexibility.)

Row 5: What are the disadvantages of this type of business? (Manufacturer: high investment and operating costs, often need employees, high risk of product failure; retailer: investment costs for inventory and retail space; often need employees; service provider: often has to do the work him/herself or hire educated/skilled workers with a strong work ethic.)

Row 6: What are some costs associated with this type of business? (Manufacturer: high investment costs for equipment/factory, raw materials cost, tooling costs, set-up costs per batch; retailer: cost of goods purchased; service provider: may have equipment costs [such as a dry cleaner] education/training costs (if professional service), often lower investment costs.)

When the table is filled in, hold a conversation about the patterns students see — similarities and differences among the types of businesses, which types of businesses they see most often in their neighborhoods and why they think that may be the case; which types they think are most important for the local and/or national economy and why.
**LINKS**》*Economics*

- **Product Development Process Review.** Use transparency T26-1 to discuss the steps in product development (additional information is available on transparency T7-2 from Chapter 7). Define "model" (a rough version of a product) and "prototype" (a finished product using the actual manufacturing specs) and discuss similarities and differences between them.

- **Manufacturing Process.** On the board, build a new "transparency" that continues the product development process through manufacturing. Students may use their textbooks as an aid. Examples might include the following, although the students may wish to create a slightly different order:

Step 4: Create a blueprint and/or specifications that employees or a job shop can use as instructions for making the product.

Step 5: Compare the costs and benefits of doing your own manufacturing vs. subcontracting.

Step 6a: If you do your own manufacturing, research zoning laws and permit requirements.

Step 6b: If you subcontract, research job shops.

Step 7: Calculate costs and make sure you can make the product at a profit. If not, consider a different manufacturing process, renegotiate price of raw materials, etc.

Step 8: Buy equipment, train workers, etc.

Step 9: Set up quality-control checks.

Step 10: Determine batch size and inventory.

Step 11: Sell product to distributors.

- **Assembly Line.** Give students the opportunity to experience manufacturing by organizing them into assembly lines to make a small product. Distribute specification sheets and materials, and give students time to manufacture the product (preferably enough time so that each person in the class can have one as a take-away). Instruct students to pay attention during the activity to:

  ○ how long it takes to do their part of the process and how they get faster at it.

○ when the process flows smoothly.

○ what types of snags are encountered.

○ how they might change the process to be more efficient.

After the activity, ask students to share their observations and ask them to speculate about how much the sale price to wholesalers should be, based on the materials costs and labor. Have students calculate the economics of one unit. This discussion will lead into the next activity and may be used as a running example for examining costs specific to manufacturing — a key concept.

- **Manufacturing Costs.** Review from Chapter 9 the main types of costs in a business: costs of goods/services sold, variable costs, and fixed operating costs. Ask students to provide examples of each kind for a manufacturing plant. (Costs of goods sold: raw materials and labor on assembly line; fixed costs: utilities, manager/administrative/support salaries, advertising/sales costs to wholesalers, insurance, depreciation on equipment, inventory and shipping costs. Ask: Where do setup costs fit in these categories? (If the manufacturing plant is "just-in-time," which means it doesn't manufacture goods until they are needed—and thus dependent on sales—setup costs might be categorized as variable costs; however, most companies tend to categorize setup costs as fixed costs.)

- **Manufacturing Investment.** Emphasize that because of the product development, prototyping, and manufacturing processes, a manufacturing business usually requires a high initial investment. Review from Chapter 3 the concepts of investment and return on investment. Ask: What must a manufacturing entrepreneur pay for before a single product is ever produced (that is, what are some things s/he must invest in)? (Leasing/building factory, prototype costs, engineering and manufacturing-process design costs, machinery leasing/purchase; tooling costs). Have students brainstorm ways that a young entrepreneur might reduce the riskiness of a manufacturing venture. (Manufacture an easy-to-make product; subcontract to a job shop; make sure there is a market for the product before manufacturing, etc.)

- **Summary.** Return to Focus 1 and the birdcage. Ask students to pretend they are a job shop that the birdcage designer has asked to manufacture her product. Ask them to list the factors they should consider in deciding whether to do the job: delivery schedule, how complicated the birdcage is, price negotiation, if they have the right equipment, and so on.

## ASSESS THE LEARNING

- **Vocabulary.** Have students define terms in their own words and use each in a sentence.

- **Key Concepts.** Questions 1-3. **Answers:** 1-2. Answers will vary. 3. Answers will vary but should address how the manufacturing process can become more efficient over time, or raw materials may become less expensive, or research and development costs are finally covered.

- **Critical Thinking.** Questions 1-3. **Answers:** 1. Answers will vary; advantages may include quality control and cost control to keep prices low; disadvantages may include limiting growth potential to the local level and zoning law restrictions. 2. Answers will vary. 3. Answers will vary but may include: customer/market research to make sure there is a market for the product; checking out companies that make similar products based on SIC codes or The Thomas Register; visiting job shops.

- **Additional Workbook Activities Answers.**

  **Vocabulary Activity  Answers:** Answers will vary. Explanations should use complete sentences and demonstrate an understanding of the terminology and Ford's impact on the manufacturing process.

  **Quiz 26** in the workbook. **Answers:** 1. Make sure there are interested customers who can pay the price you plan to sell the product for. 2. He developed assembly line production, which made manufacturing much cheaper. 3. A prototype is an exact model of the product made by the manufacturing process that would be used in actual production. 4. Look in the Thomas Register or in the classified ads of trade publications. 5. Answers will vary but should consider zoning restrictions (a job shop is probably already located in a proper area), efficiency (a job shop already has machinery set up), cost (a job shop may be less expensive than setting up one's own operation), or the ability for the entrepreneur to focus energy on sales, distribution, and marketing.

## EXTEND THE LEARNING

- **Business Plan Practice.** Assign Critical Thinking questions 4-5.

- **Exploration.** Assign the activity in the text, then allow students to compare memos.

- **Internet Exploration.** Have students look up local manufacturers in the Thomas Register (www.thomasregister.com or www.thomasregional.com), then look up each company's SIC code

(www.sec.gov/info/edgar/siccodes.htm) and address (phone book and map). Assign them to create a poster that summarizes the main types of manufacturing in your town and in what parts of town these manufacturers seem to be located.
**LINKS**»·*Fine Arts*

- ***Entrepreneurs in Profile.*** Ask the students to compare the manufacturing processes of the businesses started by Henry Ford, Debbi Fields, King C. Gillette, Anita Roddick, Madame C.J. Walker, and Stephen Wozniak and Steve Jobs. Types of questions to ask include: What is each company's SIC code? How/where did each start manufacturing? What problems did each encounter? Did each create their own product or find a more efficient way to make an already existing product? What were some of each company's costs? Does each do its own manufacturing or subcontract? What is a key lesson you take away from each business's manufacturing experience?

- **A Business for the Young Entrepreneur.** Have students read about Daniel Trainor and Button Manufacturing in the textbook. Assign Key Concepts question 4.

- **Technology and Manufacturing.** Let the students research how new technologies have influenced the way certain products — such as cars, computers, sports shoes, cosmetics — are made. Focus students on technology that affected how the product is made, not the product itself.

- **Field Trip to a Factory.** Set up a tour of a local factory and ask a manager to give a presentation on the manufacturing process. Before going to the factory, have students create a checklist of things to look for (e.g., flow of materials through assembly line, batch size) and/or ask about (e.g., costs, potential problems that stop work flow).

## BUILD ACADEMIC AND LIFE-SKILL PROFICIENCIES
### *Skills Mean Success* Answers

**Math (Data).** 1. Ford Motor Co. 2. $161.41B 3. They are $15.88B less. 4. They are $40.6B more. 5. Wal-Mart's revenues are $42.55B more.

**Math (Reasoning).** There are several ways to solve the problem. For example:

- 1,500 $x$ (.05 minus .02) = $2,200.00, where $x$ equals the number of weeks needed to recover the cost of the machine. Since $x$ = 48.88 weeks or, effectively 49 weeks, the machine would pay for itself in 4 years and 1 week.

- Or: 1,500 (number needed per week) per week, times .03 (.05 minus .02) = $45.00 (saving per week); and $2,200 (cost of the machine) divided by $45 = 48.88888 weeks, which is just under 49 weeks.

Have the students speculate as to whether purchasing the machine would be a good investment for Express Dry Cleaning. (If the machine would last four years, how much maintenance and repair would it need; the cost of borrowing the money to buy it, etc.)

**Leadership.** Ask the students if accepting the initial offer would make sense financially ($1,000 over your total cost but only a one-dollar margin over your unit cost) or as a negotiation strategy. Should a first offer ever be accepted? Would this distributor compete with your company if it buys at a low price and resells to your customers? Answers will vary, but look for responses that show a willingness to "negotiate" over price by asking for more per unit, especially since the unit cost is $8. Some students may also creatively propose a sliding scale: lower prices for guaranteed purchases of higher quantities.

**English.** 1. The opening sentence describes Daniel's age and his serious illness. 2. Paragraphs 2 and 4 give examples of Daniel's mathematical thinking. 3. For example: diagnosed with a brain tumor > got a laptop > decided to take BizTech™ > created business plan for buttons > saw an ad for a machine > first button manufactured > took orders at the hospital > helped take his mind off the side effects of his cancer treatments > future plans to set up Web site. 4. No evidence of self-pity; Daniel is optimistic; sees himself as a regular person; gives advice to others. 5. The writer holds Daniel up as an example of a creative, brave, and risk-taking entrepreneur who doesn't let obstacles stop him from achieving his goals.

### CHAPTER 27

# THE PRODUCTION/DISTRIBUTION CHAIN

---

## ORGANIZE THE LEARNING

### CHAPTER OBJECTIVES

- Understand the manufacturer-to-consumer chain.
- Calculate markup percentages.
- Calculate gross profit margin.
- Calculate net profit margin.

### NFTE RESOURCES

- Text pp. 322-329
- Transparency T27-1
- Workbook/BLMs Chapter 27
- Test Bank Chapter 27
- BizTech Unit 12
- A Business for the Young Entrepreneur: *Michelle Lee Araujo and À La Mode*

### BUSINESS PLAN ACTIVITIES

*Workbook Business Plan Review*
Production/Distribution Chain
27-1, 27-2, 27-3

*Workbook/Textbook Chapter Review*
Key Concepts 1, 3

*Power Point Templates*
Int. 11; Adv. 11

### SKILLS MEAN SUCCESS

*English*
Reading for Understanding: Interpreting Information: Fact vs. Opinion

*Math*
Mathematical Operations and Reasoning: Calculating Percentage, Formulas, Patterns

### PREREQUISITES

This chapter builds on Chapter 26.

### VOCABULARY

gross profit margin, markup, production/distribution chain, profit margin

---

## KEY QUESTION

**How does a product get from the manufacturer to the consumer?**

## PREPARE FOR LEARNING

- **Retailer Interview.** If a retailer interview is planned for Extend the Learning, make arrangements in advance.

## SET A CONTEXT FOR LEARNING

- **Focus 1: Price Increases.** Have students calculate how much the following price increased from wholesale to retail:

| Wholesale | Retail |
|-----------|--------|
| $5 | $11 |
| $8 | $16 |
| $12 | $25 |
| $50 | $120 |

**Answers:** $6, $8, $13, $70.

- **Focus 2: Final Price.** Similarly, pose this question: If a hat cost the manufacturer $1 in fabric and $3 in labor to sew it, the manufacturer sells it to a wholesaler, who sells it to a retailer, who sells it to you, and each member of the distribution chain keystones, what is the final price at which you bought the hat? **Answer:** $32 ($4 doubled to $8 doubled to $16 doubled to $32).

- **Discussion Launcher: Relay Race.** Challenge the students to work in pairs or separately to list similarities between a relay race and how a product gets from manufacturer to consumer. In a relay race, one runner passes a baton to another runner, who takes over running toward the finish line. As needed, prompt the students to see how the relay team hand-off concept is analogous to the distribution chain. What do the students think are some advantages of a relay race versus one runner running the whole distance? What are some disadvantages?

## DEVELOP AND CLOSE THE LEARNING

- **The Production/Distribution Chain.** Use transparency T27-1 to discuss how a product travels from a manufacturer's factory (or other facility) into a consumer's hands. Explain that this is a basic diagram, which may be slightly different for various industries: some industries may not use wholesalers, whereas others may have several intermediaries, or middlemen. Ask students to speculate: What is the advantage to the economy of having a distribution channel? What value do "middlemen" add? Why not just have manufacturers sell directly to consumers? (Middlemen take on the costs and responsibilities of warehousing, trucking, and shipping; manufacturers have to negotiate with a smaller group of wholesalers than if they had to sell directly to retailers or consumers; manufacturers know how to manufacture, but may be less knowledgeable about getting their products to the right places to serve customers.) Ask students to speculate: What does the distribution chain look like for a service provider? (It usually has no middlemen, only service provider and consumer [hairdresser, lawyer, massage therapist, maid]; but some do have a retail outlet, such as a dry cleaner with a storefront, which then sends clothes to a larger facility.) Ask: How does having a distribution chain affect a business? (It affects how and how fast your product will get to market [speed] and it affects what the business and its customers pay [price].) **LINKS**»*Economics*

- **Markups.** Stress that every distribution channel member adds value, incurs expenses, and tries to generate a profit. As a result, the price of the product increases at every step. Keystoning is a type of markup. However, not all distribution chain members in all industries use 100% markup. It depends on how much value they add and how price-sensitive consumers are (recall from Chapter 6 the idea of demand). Use the examples in the text or other examples to calculate different markup percentages. The formula given in the book emphases the point of the view of the retailer, as most students will open retail or service businesses. This formula is:

Markup % = (Retail Price − Wholesale Cost)/Wholesale Cost × 100

However, this formula can also be generalized and applied across the production/distribution chain (from manufacturer to wholesaler, wholesaler to retailer, retailer to consumer). The generalized formula is:

Markup % = (Price − Cost)/Cost × 100

It may be helpful to use this formula through the whole production/distribution chain: for example, show the markup percentage of a dozen flowers from the gardener/nursery through the wholesaler and florist to the consumer:

Nursery cost $5, price $7.50. **Answer:** 50%
Wholesaler cost $7.50, price $10. **Answer:** 33%
Retail florist cost $10, price $18. **Answer:** 80%

- **Gross Profit Margin.** Explain that the markup amount in dollars (price − cost) — which is the numerator in the markup % formula — is also called the *gross profit margin*. Review from Chapter 13 that gross profit is the amount of sales revenue left after cost of goods/services sold has been subtracted, and it is used to cover the business's fixed operating expenses as well as — eventually and hopefully — provide a profit. Use the examples in the textbook or other examples to calculate different gross profit margin per unit percentages. The formula in the textbook is:

Gross Profit Margin per Unit % = (Retail Price − Wholesale Cost)/Retail Price × 100

Again, this formula may be generalized and used across the production/distribution chain:

Gross Profit Margin per Unit % = (Price − Cost)/Price × 100

Continuing the above flower example:

Nursery cost $5, price $7.50. **Answer:** 33%
Wholesaler cost $7.50, price $10. **Answer:** 25%
Retail florist cost $10, price $18. **Answer:** 44%

Point out that the main difference between the gross profit margin and the markup equations is the denominator, or the "base" for the percentage. Ask students to speculate: Why does an entrepreneur need to keep track of both percentages? (They give entrepreneurs different information: the markup helps them determine the price to charge, the gross profit margin tells them how much of the price is helping to cover fixed operating costs — and hopefully contributing to profits.)

- **Net Profit Margin.** Use the examples in the text or other examples to calculate different net profit margin — often just called profit margin — per unit percentages. The formula in the textbook is:

Net Profit Margin % = Profit/Sales × 100 [if taken from income statement]

However, if your students are sufficiently skilled in math, this formula can be unpacked so you can calculate profit margin if you have price, cost, units sold, and fixed costs figures but not the final profit figure:

Net Profit Margin % =

$$\frac{(\text{Price} - \text{Cost}) \times \text{Units Sold} - \text{Fixed Costs}}{\text{Price} \times \text{Units Sold}} \times 100$$

Continuing the above flower example:

Nursery cost $5, price $7.50, 100 sold, fixed costs of $100. **Answer:** 20%

Wholesaler cost $7.50, price $10, 50 sold, fixed costs of $100. **Answer:** 5%

Retail florist cost $10, price $18, 25 sold, fixed costs of $100. **Answer:** 22%

Ask: Based on the markup, gross profit margin and net profit margin calculations, which member of this flower distribution chain seems to be doing the best and why? (The retailer has the largest net profit margin.)

- **Summary.** Ask students to discuss why the expressions "Wholesale to the public" or "I can get it for you wholesale" might not be accurate, since wholesalers don't sell to consumers. What message are these companies trying to convey? (They are trying to give the impression that they are less expensive than their competitors because they are cutting out a middleman or two. However, they are still taking a "cut" — they have a markup and profit margin or they would go out of business.) How do students feel about this marketing tactic?

## ASSESS THE LEARNING

- **Vocabulary.** Have students create a crossword puzzle using the new vocabulary.

- **Key Concepts.** Question 2. **Answer:** 2. The suggestion is that the person making the offer can get the item at the wholesaler's price, without the retailer's markup.

- **Critical Thinking.** Questions 1-4. Instruct students to research a product, or give them a table of product information, such as is provided in the textbook. **Answers:** 1. If they research products independently, answers will vary; if you use the workbook table: pencil 50 cents, 200%; pen 40 cents, 100%; hat $6, 300%; sunglasses $1.25, 167%; tennis shoes $25, 100%; flannel shirt $20, 200%; Walkman $10, 200%. 2. Profitability should be measured by markup per-

centage, not markup dollar amount; answers will vary if students research their own product; in the workbook table, the hat is the most profitable item because it has the highest markup percentage. 3. If they research products independently, answers will vary; if you use the workbook table: pencil 25 cents, 50%; pen 60 cents, 60%; hat $14, 88%; sunglasses 25 cents, 25%; tennis shoes $35, 58%; flannel shirt $15, 60%; walkman $5, 50%. 4. The best way to measure profitability is gross profit margin per unit; answers will vary if students research their own product; in the workbook table, the hat is the most profitable.

- **Additional Workbook Activities Answers.**

  **Vocabulary Activity  Answers:** 1. a, 2. b, 3. d, 4. a.

  **Quiz 27** in the workbook.  **Answers:** 1. Markup is the difference between what the entrepreneur pays and the price at which s/he sells. 2. 100%. 3. Manufacturer to wholesaler to retailer to consumer. 4. Wholesaler. 5. Subtract the cost from the selling price and divide by the number of units sold: Gross Profit per Unit − (Price − Cost)/Number of Units. 6. 100%. 7. 50%. 8. Operating costs. 9. 40%.

## EXTEND THE LEARNING

- **Business Plan Practice.** Assign Key Concepts questions 1 and 3.

- **BizTech.** Assign Unit 12.

- **A Business for the Young Entrepreneur.** Have students read about Michelle Lee Araujo and À La Mode in the textbook. Assign Key Concepts question 4.

- **Retailer Interview.** Have students interview a specialty retailer (i.e., a retailer who only sells shoes or clothes — not a general retailer with a great many products). Have students make lists of questions to ask the retailer related to the store's distribution chain and how s/he calculates markups and profit margins. The class then might compare the different product categories or industries based on the information students assemble. For example, do florists or clothing stores tend to have higher markups, and why might that be?

- **Distribution Relay.** Divide the class into teams of three students each. Arrange them in lines, with the first student as the manufacturer, the second as the wholesaler, and the last as the retailer. Copy the table below on the board, with time allowed between writing rows for students to solve each problem. The manufacturer calculates his/her sale price (by keystoning), markup amount and gross profit margin, then passes the sheet of paper to the next person in the distribution chain, who calculates the same based on the given markup percentage and passes it on, etc. The team to finish first with the correct answers (rounded to the nearest whole numbers) earns a point. (M) = Manufacturer, (W) = Wholesaler, and (R) = Retailer.

| (M) Cost | (W) Markup % | (R) Markup % |
|----------|--------------|--------------|
| $10 | 30% | 50% |
| $55 | 80% | 100% |
| $150 | 33% | 50% |
| $2 | 50% | 50% |
| $99 | 40% | 60% |

**Answers:**

| | Sale Price | | | Markup Amt. | | | Gross Profit Margin | | |
|---|------|------|------|------|------|------|-----|-----|-----|
| | (M) | (W) | (R) | (M) | (W) | (R) | (M) | (W) | (R) |
| 1 | $20 | $26 | $39 | $10 | $6 | $13 | 50% | 23% | 33% |
| 2 | $110 | $198 | $396 | $55 | $88 | $198 | 50% | 44% | 50% |
| 3 | $300 | $399 | $599 | $150 | $99 | $200 | 50% | 25% | 33% |
| 4 | $4 | $6 | $9 | $2 | $2 | $3 | 50% | 33% | 33% |
| 5 | $198 | $277 | $443 | $99 | $79 | $166 | 50% | 29% | 37% |

## BUILD ACADEMIC AND LIFE-SKILL PROFICIENCIES

### *Skills Mean Success* Answers

**English.** 1.a. For example: We are both the manufacturer and the seller, so you can get this product for less money. b. We don't trust other people to find the best products for us. c. No one else marks up the price. d. The products we sell are fresh because we get them directly from the farmer, they don't sit in a truck or warehouse. e. There is no wholesaler or distributor between us and the manufacturer to mark up the price. 2. Students could use the newspaper, Yellow Pages, or the Internet. Answers will vary. Challenge students to point out any claims that seem exaggerated or unrealistic.

**Math.** 1.

| Item | (R) Price | (W) Cost | Mark-up $ | Mark-up % |
|------|-----------|----------|-----------|-----------|
| Current Hit DVDs | $29.95 | $16.00 | 13.95 | 87.1% |
| Blank VHS Tape | $7.99 | $5.00 | 2.99 | 59.8% |
| Blank CDs | $24.95 | $9.00 | 15.95 | 177.2% |
| Current Hit Videos | $19.45 | $12.00 | 7.45 | 62% |
| 3 _" Diskettes | $11.05 | $5.50 | 5.55 | 100.9% |

2. The markup range is 59.8% to 177.2%.

3. (Retail Price − Wholesale Price) divided by Wholesale Cost = Markup.

e.g., $24.95 − $9.00 = $15.95 divided by $9.00 = 177.2%.

or

Markup = Retail Price − Unit or Wholesale Cost;

Markup % =

$$\frac{(\text{Retail Price} - \text{Unit or Wholesale Cost})}{\text{Unit or Wholesale Cost}} \times 100$$

4. Retail Price = Unit or Wholesale Cost + $\frac{\% \text{ Markup}}{100}$ × Unit or Wholesle Price

5. Various reasons, including customer demand, competition pricing, use of an item as a "loss leader," item is/is not on sale, rebates from suppliers for higher volume of sales.

### CHAPTER 28

# QUALITY:
## *The Source of Profit*

## ORGANIZE THE LEARNING

### CHAPTER OBJECTIVES

- Explain why quality leads to profit.
- Discuss W. Edwards Deming's ideas about quality and profit.
- List ten ways to improve quality.
- Apply the Japanese concept of *kaizen* to your life.

### NFTE RESOURCES

- Text pp. 330-337
- Transparency T28-1
- Workbook/BLMs Chapter 28
- Entrepreneurs in Profile #4
- Test Bank Chapter 28
- A Business for the Young Entrepreneur: *Al Mezze & Rasha Ayoub*

### BUSINESS PLAN ACTIVITIES

*Workbook Business Plan Review*
Quality 28-1, 28-2

*Workbook/Textbook Chapter Review*
Critical Thinking 1, 6

### SKILLS MEAN SUCCESS

*Math*
Mathematical Reasoning: Devising Formulas

*English*
Reading and Writing for Interpretation: Using Images to Express Ideas

### PREREQUISITES

Have students preview Chapter 28 in their textbook.

### VOCABULARY

continuous improvement, *kaizen*, quality, quality control

## KEY QUESTION

**How do I make sure my product/service is the best it can be?**

## PREPARE FOR LEARNING

- **Product Samples.** Collect different brands of chocolate bars, cellophane tape, sheets of paper, cereal, flowers, or other products among which students would be able to distinguish features and differences.

## SET A CONTEXT FOR LEARNING

- **Focus 1: Defective Merchandise.** Pose the following: Think of a time when a product you purchased broke or did not live up to your expectations. How did you feel? What did you think? What did you do?

- **Focus 2: Fair Treatment.** Present this scenario: Think of a time when you felt you were treated unfairly. How did you feel? What did you think? What did you do?

- **Focus 3: Quality Winners.** Have the students brainstorm: What brand do you consider to have the highest quality in the following product categories: hamburger, pizza, fashion clothes, TV, computer, breakfast cereal, sports car. On what criteria did you base your choices?

- **Discussion Launcher: Wozniak Quote.** Ask if anyone knows the business acronym: DIRTFT — Do it right the first time — and have students suggest what it might mean. Share the Stephen Wozniak quote from the textbook and ask the students to discuss in pairs what he means: "…that doing something with the highest quality, doing it right the first time, would really be cheaper than having to go back and do it again." Challenge each student to cite an example of having to do something over because it wasn't done well the first time.

## DEVELOP AND CLOSE THE LEARNING

- **Defining Quality.** Challenge the students: How do you know when a product or service is of high quality? List their ideas on the board. Try to get students to find patterns in the ideas listed on the board, such as combining them into criteria for "quality" categories (for example, industry specifications and customer needs). Suggest several product categories and have students brainstorm what *quality*

means for that type of product. Use the categories in Focus 3 or other categories, such as colas, recording artists, pizzas, movies, Mexican food, etc. To help students become even more sensitive to distinguishing quality in products, bring in a few different brands of a category — such as chocolate bars — and have a panel of students rank the brands by quality. Have students think about the criteria they used in deciding what was important. Discuss how quality is both a general term (it satisfies customer needs in a major way) but is also specific to product categories and markets (taste and smoothness for chocolate bars). Encourage the students to arrive at the notion that quality is, to some degree, in the eye of the beholder — i.e., not the same for everyone, since needs and expectations differ (a high-quality sound system may be important to a music lover but not a talk-radio listener). Ask: If you have never bought a type of product before, what would you look for to assess quality? (Brand name/image, price in that a higher price is often equated with higher quality, friends' recommendations, etc.)
**LINKS**〉〉*Consumer Ed*

- **The Quality Perspective.** Poll the class: Where is quality located? In the product? In the customer's mind? In the industry specifications?

  Return to (or do) the Focus 3 activity and poll students about which brands they considered highest quality. Ask: What are these companies doing that companies with lower-quality products aren't? Help students realize that quality is an attitude, or perspective, of the manufacturer or user, not just the inherent characteristics of a product. Quality involves a long-term perspective beyond the entrepreneur's own point-of-view that emphasizes meeting customer needs. Quality is cheaper from the long-term perspective. Ask students to speculate why.

- **Ten Ways to Improve Quality.** Use transparency T28-1 to discuss ways entrepreneurs can improve quality in general. Ask students to give a specific example for each principle. Pair up the students and have each twosome create a cartoon or skit to demonstrate one principle of quality. Allow time for the students to perform skits, or display cartoons around the room for other students to see.

- **Quality in Relationships.** Ask students to define ethics. (Rules that govern how we treat each other.) Have them brainstorm how ethics relates to quality. (Ethics might be considered how to maintain high quality in relationships—personal or business.) Discuss the Golden Rule—"Do unto others as you would have others do unto you"—and what it means in business. Ask students to think of business situations in which honesty, fairness, loyalty and other ethical behaviors are critical to business success.

- **Threats to Quality.** Tell, or ask a student to tell, the story of W. Edwards Deming and his success in Japan. What was his main point? (Profit comes from quality.) Give examples of companies with poor quality that became successful by applying Deming's principles. Ask: Should a company wait until customers are complaining or even until it is losing sales/market share to improve quality? (No.) When should quality control be considered and implemented? (From the very beginning of the company.) Emphasize that there is no time like the present to improve quality. Ask students to brainstorm threats to quality or areas of business operation that might need to be addressed. (Poor materials, inexperienced workers, cutting corners in manufacturing, lack of knowledge, unfriendly service, inattention to details, not tracking costs carefully.) In small groups, have students brainstorm kaizen — or continuous improvement — strategies an entrepreneur might take to deal with these threats. Ask students to list how Debbi Fields (in the text or in *Entrepreneurs in Profile*) uses quality and kaizen principles.

- **Summary.** Challenge the students: How might they apply a quality or continuous-improvement perspective to school work (i.e., what might students do to improve the quality of their current "enterprise" of being a student)?

## ASSESS THE LEARNING

- **Vocabulary.** Have students define terms in their own words and use each in a sentence.

- **Key Concepts.** Questions 1-5. **Answers:** 1. The Deming Prize, named for W. Edwards Deming, whose ideas revolutionized the way Japanese products were manufactured by focusing on quality. 2. The quality level of Japanese products rose and they became very successful in America, taking market share from American companies; American businesspeople then wanted to learn "Japanese" strategies. 3. Continually seeking to improve quality will improve profits; answers will vary on how students will apply this concept in their own businesses. 4. Any of the following: quality makes customers more satisfied, decreases replacement/repair costs, increases customer loyalty, generates good word-of-mouth advertising, or lowers costs in the long term. 5. She would not substitute lower quality ingredients; she repeatedly asked customers how she could improve her cookies and was willing to change her cookies to please them; student preferences will vary.

- **Critical Thinking.** Questions 2-4. **Answers:** 2. Answers may include: trust the company, more satisfying product/service/experience, less hassle, and the product will last longer. 3. Deming argued that profits follow quality, so if a company focuses on continuous improvement it will make more money; it was proved correct when Japanese businesses became successful by using Deming's ideas. 4. Answers will vary.

- **Writing Practice.** Critical Thinking Question 5.

- **Additional Workbook Activities Answers.**

  **Vocabulary Activity Answers:** Paragraphs should demonstrate an understanding of the principles of quality from the chapter. All terms should be included and used correctly in complete sentences.

  **Quiz 28** in the workbook. **Answers:** 1. Any reasonable answer; better answers will address that quality products build customer loyalty. 2. Any reasonable answer; better answers will address the perceived trade-off between quality and price; however, price is not always a good proxy for quality. 3. Any reasonable answer based on the in-class discussions. 4. c. 5. b. 6. It improved the reputation and success of Japanese companies. 7. c. 8. Yes; because employees interact with products and customers in the workplace everyday, so they may have great ideas for improving the product, work processes, or workplace atmosphere. 9. Because it's free and people are more likely to believe their friends than a more impersonal advertisement. 10. Any ideas that show there is always room for improvement, being consistent, doing it right the first time, developing long-term relationships, focusing on quality in production and customer service, having a training program, not asking for "perfect" performance, focusing on quality over quantity, asking for suggestions.

## EXTEND THE LEARNING

- **Business Plan Practice.** Assign Critical Thinking questions 1 and 6.

- **Exploration.** Tell students to watch TV and keep a "commercials log." Assign the activity in the textbook. As a variation, ask students to also note the products or types of products being positioned as quality vs. price.

- **Quality Self-Improvement.** Ask students to focus on one aspect of their lives they might want to improve, such as social skills, business skills, making friends, resisting peer pressure, etc. Have each student create a personal quality improvement plan for the chosen aspect that incorporates principles of this chapter. **LINKS**»*Character Ed*

- **A Business for the Young Entrepreneur.** Select a student or two to read aloud the profile about Rasha Ayoub and Al Mezze in the text. Ask class to discuss how even young entrepreneurs with fewer resources than big companies can focus on quality.

## BUILD ACADEMIC AND LIFE-SKILL PROFICIENCIES

### *Skills Mean Success* Answers

**Math.** 1. 6.72 Canadian Dollars; 14.528 Reals; 2.797 Pounds. Note: Foreign exchange is difficult for many adults so this may be a challenging activity for a number of students. It might be effective to have students work in pairs. Remind them how to work backwards from an answer: e.g., if 6 is an answer and the other numbers given are 8 and 4, what happened to 8 and 4 to get 12? Think: $(4 \bullet 8)$ times 2 = 24. What does $\bullet$ mean? (plus) Have students explain in words before attempting to devise a formula. 2. Possible answer: divide 1 by the exchange rate to determine how much one U.S. dollar is worth. Then multiply by 5 (the number of U.S. dollars to be determined). 3. Possible answer: Value of any amount of C (currency) in $ U.S. = 1 ÷ Value Compared to $1 U.S. × number of $U.S. = $ U.S. To calculate the value of $7 U.S. in Brazilian Reals (for example) 1 ÷ 0.34416 = 2.9056 × 7 = $20.339, or about $20.34.

**English.** 1. I, c; II, e; III, b; IV, f; V, a; VI, d. Note, too, the image of "launch" in the last paragraph of the Ayoub article. 2. Look for ideas that involve scoring, teamwork, coaching, star performances, quality of work, and so on. Some students might enjoy illustrating the most creative sports-image phrases.

### CHAPTER 29

# EFFECTIVE LEADERSHIP:
## *Managing Yourself and Your Employees*

## ORGANIZE THE LEARNING

### CHAPTER OBJECTIVES

- Develop leadership qualities.
- Manage your time more efficiently.
- Hire employees.
- Build a management team.

### NFTE RESOURCES

- Text pp. 338-353
- Workbook/BLMs Chapter 29
- Test Bank Chapter 29
- Biz Tech Unit 21
- A Business for the Young Entrepreneur: *Baby-sitting Service*

### BUSINESS PLAN ACTIVITIES

*Workbook Business Plan Review*
Human Resources 29-1, 29-2, 29-3, 29-4, 29-5

*Workbook/Textbook Chapter Review*
Critical Thinking 4, 6; Key Concepts 4

*Power Point Templates*
Adv. 23

### SKILLS MEAN SUCCESS

*Leadership/English*
Interviewing Skills

*Math*
Data Analysis: Determining Mean, Median, Mode

*Leadership*
Recognizing the Need for Math, English, and Computer Skills

### PREREQUISITES

Have students skim Chapter 29 in the textbook to find and list three key ideas for each of the four chapter objectives.

### VOCABULARY

recruitment, resume

*Other terms to know:*
employment-at-will, human resources, layoff, payroll, PERT chart, severance package

## KEY QUESTION

**How do I involve other people to help grow my business?**

## SET A CONTEXT FOR LEARNING

- **Focus 1: "Ran Out of Time."** Ask the students to relate an example from their personal experiences and/or share something from yours: Think of a time when you didn't get everything done you needed to. If you could do it over again, what would you change? How would you use your time differently?

- **Focus 2: Leadership.** Ask the students collectively or individually to brainstorm and share words or phrases about feelings that come to mind when they are asked this question: How do you feel about taking on leadership roles?

- **Discussion Launcher 1: Teamwork.** Write on the board or give verbal instructions to have students discuss in pairs: What does "teamwork" mean to you? How can you tell when teamwork is taking place?

- **Discussion Launcher 2: Help Wanted.** Write on the board or give verbal instructions to have students discuss in pairs: If money were not an issue, what

one task in your life right now would you like to hire someone to help you with? What are the skills, experience, education and other characteristics this person would need? How would you go about trying to find and hire this person?

## DEVELOP AND CLOSE THE LEARNING

- **Growing Your Business.** Challenge students with the following scenario: You have started your company. It is going well — growing, prospering. You are gaining customers and sales. In fact, you have grown so much that you can hardly handle the work. Now what should you do? Allow students to provide gut-reaction answers. Try to steer them toward realizing that growing a business usually means eventually including others in the company's operations. Define "human resources" from the text. Create a chart on the board that shows three basic levels of human resources in a company (owner or executive, management, employees): (M) = Manager; (E) = Employee.

**Owner/Entrepreneur**

| | (M) | | (M) | | (M) | |
|---|---|---|---|---|---|---|
| (E) | (E) | (E) | (E) | (E) | (E) |

- **Level 1: The Entrepreneur.** Ask students: Who is the first "employee" of your company that you should consider? (Yourself, the entrepreneur, the leader.) Remind students, or have them look up in the textbook and review, the characteristics of successful entrepreneurs from Chapter 5. Ask: If you were looking at resumes for entrepreneur/leaders, what types of characteristics would you look for? (Optimism, positive attitude, confidence, energy, persuasiveness, vision, adaptability, risk-taking, honesty/believability, perseverance, inspirational, good communicator, business knowledge, etc.) Write the students' answers on the board. Have students rank these characteristics in importance. Discuss differences among student rankings as well as their reasoning. Ask: What is an entrepreneur/leader's most important asset? (His/her time.) How can a person get the highest ROI possible on this asset? (Time management, prioritizing.) Using the example in the textbook, discuss the use of PERT charts as a tool for time management. Have students share other tools or tricks they use to manage their time well. It may be helpful for some students to first think of threats or challenges they face in managing time (Expectations or demands of others, the draw of the TV or chatting online, friends, etc.). Determine specific ways to overcome these challenges, then generalize these ways into overall time-management tips. (Make a "To Do" list, set aside time each morning to think about what you have to do and how long it will take, reflect on the previous day's accomplishments, etc.) Show how these tips might be grouped and generalized into a "Daily Plan." Review how an entrepreneur gets paid for his/her time. (Commission, salary, wage, dividend.) Explain how tracking time is important for making sure the entrepreneur is using his/her time profitably.

- **Level 2: Employees.** Ask students: When is it time to hire employees? (When you can't get it all done yourself, when you need specialized skills, when you want to focus on one part of the business and think others with more knowledge/experience can do better or at least as well with other parts.) With the students' help, list the ways an entrepreneur can bring people into the business as well as the advantages/disadvantages of each option. (Partner [shares risks but also shares decision-making], consultant [advantage of expert knowledge but can't control his/her work process and often higher hourly rate than employee], employee [can direct work process but also must provide space and resources and pay payroll taxes]). Divide the class into two

teams—one to argue why it is a good idea for entrepreneurs to hire family and friends and the other to argue against this claim. Explain how hiring makes a company more complex in operation and legally. Review the laws and taxes that apply to employers. Using the textbook, step students through the processes involved in employment: understanding employment laws, defining tasks and organizing them into jobs, recruitment, screening resumes, interviewing and checking references, negotiating pay, hiring and orientation, working with people to get their best performance, firing and layoffs. Once you give an overview of the process, divide the class into teams and have each research and create a two-minute "orientation" to one of these processes. As a summary, ask students to share their preferences for business expansion: partnership, independent contractors or employees, and why

- **Level 3: Management.** Continue the scenario: You have hired several employees and your business continues to grow at a rapid pace. It is becoming difficult to keep track of what and how everyone is doing. Now what do you do? Try to steer students beyond just hiring more employees to focus on the middle level of the organization chart: management. Define how managers are specialists in running a business. Ask students to brainstorm titles that managers may go by (manager, director, vice president, supervisor). Note that there may be many levels of management depending on how large the company is. Use the text to describe the ten main management functions. In groups or pairs, have students provide a concrete example/scenario of each function. Alternatively, you might state a concrete scenario and ask students to choose which management function it falls under. (E.g., a coordinating example might be holding a meeting.)

- **Performance Reviews.** Continue the scenario: Now that you have employees and managers, how do you keep track of how well everyone is doing toward achieving your business goals? Introduce the concept of performance reviews and their purpose in keeping employees aligned with the business's mission as well as helping the entrepreneur or managers make decisions about promotion, raises, and firings. Have students evaluate their own performance in two ways. First, have them complete the Sample Employee Performance Plan and Appraisal form in the textbook for their performance in the NFTE class during the past two weeks. Give them objectives to which they must list observed achievements and ratings. Second, ask students to think about how they interact with classmates and friends; then rank order which managerial styles they use — from most to least used. Where do they see areas of their behavior they could improve?

- **Employment Ethics.** Recall from Chapter 28 the definition of "ethics" (rules governing how we treat each other). Ask students to speculate how ethics applies to leadership, management, and employment (e.g., treating employees fairly, being honest with employers). In small groups, have students discuss and answer In Your Opinion in the text. Note that ethics covers more than just what's legal (that is, a person can do something that is legal, but it may still not be ethical — such as hiring a friend or relative over a much more qualified person). In the same or new groupings, have students devise an ethical dilemma that an entrepreneur might face relating to employees or management. As time permits, students can try to solve the dilemmas.
**LINKS》**Character Ed

- **Summary.** Challenge students: What is your time worth? Are you using it wisely? How might you improve your ROI on the time you invest in different activities? How can involving others increase the value and ROI of your time? How can you make sure you are using other people's time in an ethical way?

## ASSESS THE LEARNING

- **Vocabulary.** Have students define the key terms in their own words and use each in a sentence.

- **Key Concepts.** Questions 1-3, 5. **Answers:** 1. 16. 2. Payroll taxes (e.g., Social Security, unemployment). 3. After incorporation, the entrepreneur can sell stock and use the capital raised to hire good managers. 5. An entrepreneur starts an enterprise and often is a "big picture" thinker; a manager maintains an already established enterprise and often is detail oriented; student preferences will vary.

- **Critical Thinking.** Assign Questions 1, 3, 5. **Answers:** 1. Answers will vary but should address the characteristics of leaders described in the text (Chapters 5 and 29), such as optimism, positive attitude, confidence, energy, persuasiveness, vision, adaptability, risk-taking, honesty/believability, etc. 3. Charts will vary but should be in the PERT-chart format. 5. Answers will vary.

- **Writing Practice.** Assign Critical Thinking question 2 and/or Key Concepts question 4.

- **Additional Workbook Answers.**

**Inventories:** Encourage students to complete the Leadership Inventory and Interest/Experience Inventory in the workbook. They should record information and evaluate their skills honestly in order to identify areas they need to develop.

**Vocabulary Activity. Answers:** Recruitment is hiring employees. Perhaps the most important thing a leader/business owner can do is to bring other capable, motivated people into the business. A resume is a one-page summary of work and education experience. During the recruitment process, leaders should carefully screen resumes from job applicants.

**Quiz 29** in the workbook. **Answers:** 1. His/her time. 2. You can't hire anyone under age 16 full time, and you must pay all employees at least minimum wage. 3. Any three of the following: put the right people in the right jobs, provide a fair salary and good working conditions, share your company's vision, give incentives, give employees control over their work. 4. Document what employees are not doing correctly, inform the employee in writing about these issues, keep a file of all communications with the employee; if you don't take these steps, you may get sued. 5. Any three of the following: planning, organizing, leading, directing, staffing, controlling, coordinating, representing, innovating, motivating. 6. Any two of the following: college job fairs, through current employees, executive search, help wanted ads, use an employment agency. 7. Education and work experience. 8. Salary, commission, hourly wage. 9. Tracking how you use your time and planning to use your time more wisely.

## EXTEND THE LEARNING

- **Business Plan Practice.** Assign Critical Thinking questions 4, 6.

- **BizTech.** Assign Unit 12.

- *Entrepreneurs in Profile.* Have students compare how different entrepreneurs grew their human resources team. Chapters that deal with employees, work organization, and management issues include those on Richard Branson, Henry Ford, Berry Gordy, John Johnson, Ray Kroc, Russell Simmons, Madame C.J. Walker, Sam Walton, and Stephen Wozniak & Steve Jobs. Types of questions to ask could include:

  ○ What recruitment and retention strategies did they use for employees?

  ○ How did they treat their employees?

  ○ How did they set up their management teams?

○ What struggles or challenges did they face in growing their business organizations?

○ What management advice would you give them to improve their leadership?

- **A Business for the Young Entrepreneur.** Have students read about a baby-sitting service in the textbook and ask, as they read, to decide how an entrepreneur might go about recruiting, hiring, and managing baby-sitters.

- **Resume Writing.** Using a business-communication or resume-writing book, create a transparency that depicts a basic resume, including contact information (name, address, phone number, e-mail address); education (dates, school, main areas of study, special skills learned, honors); work experience (dates, companies, main duties, awards); after-school organized activities (dates, organizations, title/duties, awards); and references (name, address, phone number). Discuss a resume's purpose (to provide a snapshot of what a person has done and can do), elements (as listed above), and requirements (clarity, succinctness, nice formatting, no typos). Assign students to create or update their own one-page resumes.

- **Employment Role Play.** On index cards, write or type the leadership/management/ employment scenarios below, or create your own. Divide the class into pairs and have each pair draw one card. Allow them a few minutes to prepare to role-play the scenario, then present it to the class. Have the class discuss what happened in the scenario, what went well or not so well, what could be learned from it, and what advice the class would give to the characters to improve the situation. In addition, students could compare how an entrepreneur or employee behaved differently, depending on the situation. Continue with role-plays as time and student interest permits. Sample scenarios:

○ An employee asks an entrepreneur for a raise.

○ An entrepreneur interviews a potential employee for a job opening.

○ An entrepreneur talks with a company manager about what should be done regarding a slow-down in production.

○ An entrepreneur discusses with his/her partner about bringing in a new partner.

○ An entrepreneur discusses with his lawyer the legal implications or restrictions involved in hiring and firing employees.

○ An entrepreneur talks with a college student at a job fair about his/her company's employment opportunities.

○ A manager talks with a potential new employee's former boss to get a reference.

○ A training manager orients a new employee to the company.

○ Two partners discuss ways to keep employees from leaving the company for that of a competitor.

○ A manager talks with an employee about his/her recent poor performance on the job.
**LINKS**›› *Performing Arts*

## BUILD ACADEMIC AND LIFE-SKILL PROFICIENCIES

### *Skills Mean Success* Answers

**Leadership/English.** Questions will vary, but should cover topics such as current position, past employment, interests (particularly career-related), related experience, education, wage requirements, working condition expectations, and why the applicant wants this job and feels qualified for it. Ideally, students will list the easiest, introductory questions first. Make certain they know that they may not ask personal questions of an interviewee. Some students might also want to comment on how the interviewer should put the applicant at ease by asking simple "get to know you" questions that would not be perceived as prying or personal ("Did you have any trouble finding our office?" "Have you heard of our company previously?").

**Math.** 1. b. 2. 316 mi. @ 0.365 = $115.34  Point out that the *mean* isn't one of the actual amounts, but rather the calculated average. 3. 117 mi. or $42.71; the median amount is the middle figure, two are higher, two are lower. 4. Based on October, $600 × 12 = $7,200. 5. Smith and Williams, assuming that sales reps would do the most driving.

**Leadership.** Answers will vary. Depending on the amount of detail the students collect, they could compare and compile results in chart or graph form to show "most frequently used skills" or create a collage of "School Stuff You've Got to Know to Succeed in Business" for the bulletin board.

### CHAPTER 30

# TECHNOLOGY:
## Science Applied to Business

---

## ORGANIZE THE LEARNING

### CHAPTER OBJECTIVES

- Explore how entrepreneurs use technology.
- Expand your business on the Internet.

### NFTE RESOURCES

- Text pp. 354-363
- Transparencies T30-1, T30-2
- Workbook/BLMs Chapter 30
- Entrepreneurs in Profile #7
- Test Bank Chapter 30
- BizTech Unit 16
- A Business for the Young Entrepreneur: *Strategic Resources International*

### BUSINESS PLAN ACTIVITIES

*Workbook Business Plan Review*
Technology  30-1, 30-2

*Workbook/Textbook Chapter Review*
Key Concepts 1; Critical Thinking 2

*Power Point Templates*
Adv. 24

### SKILLS MEAN SUCCESS

*Leadership*
Locating Computer and Technology Resources

*Math*
Reasoning: Writing and Using Formulas

*Technology*
Technology Etiquette, Cell Phones, Voice Mail, E-mail

*English*
Speaking and Listening for Understanding: Idioms

### PREREQUISITES

Students could preview textbook Chapter 30 to compile lists of technology-related terms found in the chapter.

### VOCABULARY

data, e-mail, hyperlink, Internet, ISP, modem, newsgroup, shareware, technology, Web site

*Other terms to know:*
intellectual property

---

## KEY QUESTION

**How can using computer technology aid my business?**

## PREPARE FOR LEARNING

- **Guest Speaker.** If you plan to use this Extend the Learning activity, make arrangements for the guest speaker in advance.

## SET A CONTEXT FOR LEARNING

- **Focus 1: Daily Technology.** As a class, brainstorm the computer-based technologies that students use on any given day. Rank these technologies in order of their impact (good and bad) on their quality of life.

- **Focus 2: Computers and Business.** Have students list as many entrepreneurial/business tasks that they think a computer can do. Are there tasks that a computer *can't* and probably won't *ever* be able to do?

- **Focus 3: Technology-Based Businesses.** Have students work individually or in pairs: List at least five companies that have been started based on a digi-

tal technology. (Microsoft, Apple, Hewlett-Packard, IBM, Dell, eBay, amazon.com, security alarm companies, "smart" credit cards.)

- **Discussion Launcher 1: Information Revolution.** Have students discuss in pairs: What do you think might be the next big technological breakthrough? How will this invention help people? How might it help entrepreneurs?

- **Discussion Launcher 2: Kennedy Quote.** Refer to the John F. Kennedy quote in the text: "Man is still the most extraordinary computer of all." What do students think President Kennedy meant?

## DEVELOP AND CLOSE THE LEARNING

- **What Is Technology?** Do or refer back to Focus 1 to give students an opportunity to explore how extensively technology is used in daily life. On the board, create three columns labeled "hardware", "software", and "connectivity." Allow students to share their lists from Focus 1, and have them categorize each item in one of the three columns. If one of the columns is under-represented (connectivity, perhaps), start class thinking about cell phones, wireless communications, the Internet, etc.

- **Uses of Technology in Business.** Do or refer back to Focus 2. Ask students to find patterns in how businesses use computers. For example, some patterns/categories might be: recordkeeping, communications, marketing, sales/storefronts. Point out how what is considered "high tech" changes over time — a car engine, landline phone, typewriter, and refrigerator used to be "cutting edge" technology but are now passé. Discuss how some jobs and work functions have been automated by technology. In small groups, have students speculate about other business tasks that aren't currently, but someday might be, automated, and tasks they think are less likely to be.

- **Technology-Based Businesses.** Challenge students: Not only is technology used in business, but sometimes businesses are based on technology. Do or refer back to Focus 3. Lead them to focus on the Internet as a key technology on which many new businesses have been founded recently. Use transparencies T30-1 and T30-2 to describe the Internet and its functions. Ask class to brainstorm businesses that can be operated over the Internet. Divide students into teams to debate the following issues, and/or others you can think of. Allow time for rebuttal after each side has presented its case. Issues:

  ○ Does the Internet help or hurt small business? Why? How?

  ○ Is government regulation of the Internet necessary? Why or why not?

- **Technology Costs, Risks, and ROI.** Review the concepts of cost, risk, return and ROI from Chapters 3 and 9. Ask students: What are the costs related to buying and using technology? On the board, list the costs that students think of. (The computer itself, maintenance, hardware updates, insurance, software, software updates, software support, peripherals such as a printer, ISP monthly fee, Web site design, Web site hosting fee, software training.) What returns do businesses gain from using technology? (Faster data processing, potential competitive advantage, tools for running the business, additional communication channel for reaching customers and/or suppliers, more up-to-date records, potential sales vehicle.) What are the risks of using computer technology? (Lost data or unproductive down time due to power surges, computer viruses, disk failure, etc.)  How can we determine if our investment in computer technology has paid off (has a positive return)? (Use the standard ROI formula for dollars invested vs. profit returned, consider the increased productivity/output from computer technology, consider increases in the number of customers reached.)

- **Protecting Your Technology Investment.** Have students brainstorm what can go wrong with:

  ○ A computer (e.g., power surge, hard drive crashes, it becomes obsolete for the software)

  ○ A Web site (e.g., it crashes, the data users transfer is stolen [identity theft], the software doesn't work right)

  ○ Data files (e.g., they become corrupted by a virus, the media on which they are stored goes bad, magnetism/heat destroy them)

  In pairs of small groups, ask students to brainstorm "contingency plans" for the problems they come up with.

- **Summary.** Challenge the students:

  ○ Why is it important for entrepreneurs to keep up with the latest technological developments?

  ○ Why is it important for *you*, whatever career you end up choosing, to be technologically literate?

## ASSESS THE LEARNING

- **Vocabulary.** Have students design an activity that uses at least eight of the vocabulary terms in this chapter.

- **Key Concepts.** Questions 3-4. **Answers:** 3. Answers will vary. 4. Internet service provider (ISP), modem, phone line or DSL line.

- **Critical Thinking.** Questions 1, 3-5. **Answers:** 1. Business uses might include: to research customers/markets, to sell goods (electronic storefront), to keep records (Quicken, QuickBooks, TurboTax), to communicate with customers (e-mail), to create marketing materials (Word, PageMaker), to advertise, to create a Web site, to provide a service (such as resume writing, Web site design, typing, accounting, etc.). 3. Answers will vary. 4. Answers will vary, but evaluate whether the student's chosen market can be reached via the Internet and are tech-savvy, and whether the student's product or service might be advertised or distributed effectively online; home page contents will vary but should include business name, contact information, basic description of product/service. 5.

Power surges (use surge protector), computer virus (use virus protection software and update it often), and disk failure (back up all files).

- **Writing Practice.** Assign Exploration question 2 or Key Concepts question 2. The school's computer education teachers could probably recommend safe shareware sites.

- **Additional Workbook Activities Answers.**

  **Vocabulary Activity Answers:** ACROSS: 2. Internet, 6. shareware, 7. e-mail, 8. ISP, 9. virus, 11. Information Revolution, 14. hyperlink, 17. spam, 18. flames; DOWN: 1. Web browser, 3. URL, 4. data, 5. newsgroup, 10. Moore's Law, 12. modem, 13. technology, 15. license, 16. Web site.

  **Quiz 30** in the workbook. **Answers:** 1. Any reasonable answer including cell phones, Internet, Palm Pilots, etc. 2. Any reasonable answer. 3. Answers will vary but student should take a side and present a case; pros may include: hands-on interaction and increased computer knowledge; cons may include: lack of encouragement or social interaction. 4. Answers will vary. 5. Answers will vary; arguments *for* might include: protection against pornography or protection of children; arguments *against* might include: unnecessary interference with free enterprise or free speech. 6. Any of the following: bookkeeping, inventory records, lists of suppliers or business prospects, scheduling, interfacing with similar companies, Web storefront, e-mailing customers. 7. Any of the following: save time, keep more accurate records, be more productive, make marketing materials in-house, accessing the Internet for research or marketing. 8. The Internet makes great amounts of information available, entrepreneurs can do things that previously a specialist had to be hired to do (e.g., a designer or printer for marketing materials). 9. A web browser, an ISP. 10. Netscape, Internet Explorer, etc.

- **Intermediate Module Business Plan.** This lesson concludes the NFTE Intermediate module. Assign students the Intermediate Business Plan. They may integrate information accumulated from past business plan practice exercises, as well as the optional business plan integrative summaries in Chapters 20, 24 and 30.

## EXTEND THE LEARNING

- **Business Plan Practice.** Assign Key Concepts question 1. Critical Thinking question 2 could be used to enhance or extend the Key Concepts activity.

- **BizTech.** Assign Unit 16.

- **A Business for the Young Entrepreneur.** Have students read about Karthik Mohan, Bharath Sreerangam and Strategic Resources International in the textbook. Assign Key Concepts question 5.

- **Entrepreneurs in Profile.** Have students read Chapter 9 on Bill Gates and be prepared to discuss it in class. Provide questions to guide the reading:

  ○ How did Gates' vision of the role of computers in business help entrepreneurs?

  ○ How does his experience compare and contrast with Wozniak and Job's (Apple Computer) and Yang's (Yahoo!)?

  ○ How did Gates stay in touch with computer users' needs?

  ○ How did he stay abreast of hardware and other developments that could affect his business?

- **Exploration.** Assign Questions 1, 3. Be watchful of the sites visited.

- **Cyber Trip.** Have students pick a business-related topic or an industry, then search for and visit five Web sites related to the topic/industry and create a "tour guide" brochure (similar to a tour brochure for a trip to Italy, say — featuring Rome, Florence, Venice, Milan, and Siena). The brochure should consist of one sheet of paper folded into three panels, and provide the following information for each site: name, address, purpose (provide information, storefront, allow member interactions, etc.), brief description, best features, areas that need to be improved, a "star" rating (one/two/three stars). As a class, devise this "star" rating code (decide what one-star, two-star, etc. means) so that all students use the same criteria. Display the brochures around the classroom so students can see what everyone's cyber-destinations were. **LINKS** ›› *Fine Arts*

- **Web site Creation.** Have students create a simple Web page for their NFTE businesses by either converting a Word document to HTML or using a software package such as Home Page. Encourage them to use graphics and be creative. This activity would be a good opportunity to partner with a computer teacher or technology specialist student.

- **Guest Speaker.** Invite a software engineer, Web site designer, video game programmer, or other "techie" (especially if the person is also an entrepreneur) to make a presentation to your class about what s/he does, how s/he got started in business, what entrepreneurial opportunities exist that are related to technology, what skills a techie-entrepreneur needs, etc. Have students create a list of questions before the speaker arrives.

- **Business Plan Integrative Summary.** Since Chapter 30 concludes Unit 6, which emphasizes aspects of business operations, it might be a good time for students to compose and present a brief summary of the operational aspects of their Business Plans to date, including:

  ○ A decision about legal structure.

  ○ What link in the production/distribution chain the business is (manufacturer, retailer, etc.).

  ○ A memo about how quality will be assessed and kept high.

  ○ An organization chart to use as the business grows.

  ○ What kinds of technology the business will use and how they will be used.

## BUILD ACADEMIC AND LIFE-SKILL PROFICIENCIES

### *Skills Mean Success* Answers

**Leadership.** 1. Answers should include IT management and systems design, computer programmers, computer maintenance, IT trainers, desktop hardware installers, computer troubleshooters and service technicians, "hot line" staff, hiring specialists for both hardware and software, Web designers, Web masters, and Internet maintenance staff. Encourage students to understand that the IT group must support every department in the company — finance, sales, marketing, customer service, order processing and fulfillment, distribution, manufacturing, and so on. Some students may want to present their information in the form of an organization chart, possibly showing connections with other corporate functions. 2. Orders could be lost, inventory could be misplaced or depleted without any record of it, company financial records would be lost, there would be no e-mail, no Web site, no business documents, the company would have to perform thousands of calculations by hand, payroll couldn't be calculated so employees wouldn't be paid, and so on. Try to bring out the idea that information management supports businesses by providing content for decision-making, as well as crucial daily operations.

**Math.** a. $40 + $20 + 0.15 (total minutes used − 200); b. $19.99 + $20 + 0.10 (total minutes used − 100) c. $24.49 + 0.35 (total minutes used − 500).

**Technology (Do's and Don'ts).** Lists will vary but "Do's" might include: Use normal telephone courtesy; use a headset when driving. Don'ts might include caveats about talking so loudly so that you annoy people around you.; or be distracted and careless when talking on the phone while driving.

**English (Idioms).** Answers will vary, but help students to appreciate the differences between the literal meanings of words and phrases and what idioms and slang expressions mean in informal English. Decide why idioms would be difficult for non-proficient English speakers. Invite users of languages other than English to share and explain

○ idioms used in those languages.

○ English idioms they have found challenging.

Solicit from the students why many authors, and even advertisers, use idioms (to be "real," or up to date, or to have impact) and why idiomatic and slang expressions might not be appropriate in business communication (they can seem disrespectul, not serious, or not to the point, and could be confusing).

### CHAPTER 31

# FINDING SOURCES OF CAPITAL

---

## ORGANIZE THE LEARNING

### CHAPTER OBJECTIVES

- Identify new sources of capital.
- Use sale of equity to finance your business.
- Network with other entrepreneurs to find business financing.
- Use vendor financing.

### NFTE RESOURCES

- Text pp. 374-385
- Transparency T31-1
- Workbook/BLMs Chapter 31
- Test Bank Chapter 31
- A Business for the Young Entrepreneur: *2nd Gear Bicycles, Jason Upshaw*

### BUSINESS PLAN ACTIVITIES

*Workbook Business Plan Review*
Raising Capital  31-1, 31-2

*Workbook/Textbook Chapter Review*
Critical Thinking 2, 3

### SKILLS MEAN SUCCESS

*English*
Reading for Literary Response: Using Literary Elements to Convey Meaning

Writing for Information and Understanding: Sentence Combining

*Technology*
Online Research and Evaluating Web Sites

### PREREQUISITES

Students should have studied Chapter 14.

### VOCABULARY

"angel", collateral, co-signer, credit union, line of credit, Minority Enterprise Small Business Investment Company (MESBIC), networking, Small Business Administration (SBA), Small Business Investment Company (SBIC), Securities and Exchange Commission (SEC), venture capital

---

## KEY QUESTION

**From where could I get money to start and grow my business?**

## SET A CONTEXT FOR LEARNING

- **Focus 1: Sources of Money.** Present and discuss the following: When you have no cash and need something, like new clothes or to see a movie, to whom do you turn? List three people you might consider asking for money. Why do you think they give it to you or decide not to give it to you? Whom do you have to pay back and from whom is the money a gift?

- **Focus 2: Personal Network.** Give the following instruction to have students work independently: List a dozen or more people you know. Beside the name of each, note how s/he might be able to help you with the launch or growth of your business — loan, investor, expertise, employee, contacts, etc.

- **Discussion Launcher 1: "Angels."** Discuss in pairs: If you had $1 million to invest to help small entrepreneurs grow, what types of businesses or products would you be most interested in supporting? Why?

- **Discussion Launcher 2: Personal Preference.** How much money would you feel comfortable borrowing from friends or family for your new business? Would you rather pay interest or give equity in exchange for business capital? What is your reasoning?

## DEVELOP AND CLOSE THE LEARNING

- **Financing Review.** Recall from Chapter 14 the basic concepts of *financing* (outside sources of funds — money that is not generated by business operations but from investment) and its two main forms: *debt* (you pay a loan back with interest, usually on a set time schedule) and *equity* (you don't directly pay it back but investors recoup or lose their investment by sharing in the profits/losses and value of the business).

- **Sources of Capital.** Use transparency T31-1 to provide a quick overview of the types of financing that might be available to young entrepreneurs. Split the class into small groups and assign one source to each group: friends, family, angels, banks/credit unions, SBA, venture capital firm, Small Business Investment Companies, awards/competitions. Each group can use the textbook or other references to research, brainstorm, and present the following information to the rest of the class:

○ Whether this source is debt, equity or neither.

○ Advantages of this source to the entrepreneur.

○ Disadvantages of this source to the entrepreneur.

After groups have presented their ideas, be sure that they have covered all the main points in the chapter. See below for a sample chart of advantages and disadvantages. Ask students to rank the different sources of capital in terms of personal preferences: as entrepreneurs, which source would be their first, second, etc., choice to turn to and why. Conclude with a summary of individual differences among resources, risk tolerances, types of businesses to be funded, and what the money will be used for, as possible influencing factors.

**Sample Answers:**

| Source | Type | Advantages | Disadvantages |
|---|---|---|---|
| Friends | E or D | You know them | They might lose their money if you fail |
| Family | E or D | You know them | They might lose their money if you fail |
| Angels | E | They believe in you | You may give up some control |
| Bank/CU | D | Lines of credit flexible  No equity control | Need collateral or co-signer  Must repay and have credit history |
| SBA | D | Often low interest and more flexible terms | Must repay |
| Venture Capital | E | No need to repay | Need to make large return |
| SBIC | E or D | Often good terms  May qualify for special programs | May have to repay  May need to meet special requirements |
| Awards/ Competitions | n/a | "Free" — no repayment or loss of control | Many competitors |

● **Summary.** Ask students to sum up: What are the advantages of using your own money for your business vs. other people's money?

## ASSESS THE LEARNING

● **Vocabulary.** Have students use each term in a sentence.

● **Key Concepts.** Question 1. **Answers:** 1. Debt advantage: no decision-making authority in the company; debt disadvantage: must pay it back regardless of income; equity advantage: don't have to pay it back if company does not make money (return is indexed to profits); equity disadvantage: must share the wealth generated by the business, which could exceed the amount originally invested.

● **Critical Thinking.** Questions 1-2, 5. **Answers:** 1. Answers will vary. 2. Answers will vary but ideas for meeting angels could involve participating in NFTE events, speaking with friends and family, locating clubs for young people, bringing in business speakers, talking to lawyers and accountants, or contacting the SBA or Chamber of Commerce. 5. $600; $1,240; $1,500; $2,030; $1,850; $3,500. 5. a. Year 3. 5. b. $5,220. 5. c. 536%.

● **Writing Practice.** Assign Critical Thinking question 4.

● **Additional Workbook Activities Answers.**

**Vocabulary Activity.** Assign Chapter 31. **Answers:** 1. j. 2. a. 3. g. 4. c. 5. b. 6. d. 7. h. 8. e. 9. k. 10. f. 11. i.

**Quiz 31** in the workbook. **Answers:** 1. Any of the following: to get a loan, general business advice, assistance in meeting possible investors. 2. c. 3. By delaying payment until the payment due date, you have a chance to use the money more profitably in the short term or keep it in your bank account and earn interest. 4. Debt and equity. 5. Any reasonable answer (such as up to 49%), but the entrepreneur should not offer more than 50% equity or s/he could lose control of the company. 6. Any reasonable answer that includes the potential for the investor to receive greater returns on the investment if the business is successful. 7. Any of the following: participating in NFTE events, speaking with friends and family, locating clubs for young people, bringing in business speakers, talking to lawyers and accountants, or contacting the SBA or Chamber of Commerce. 8. A good business plan. 9. Any of the following: family, friends, angels, venture capitalists, banks, credit unions, SBA, SBIC, MESBIC, business plan competitions or awards. 10. Any reasonable answer; the best answers will include the idea that, without money of your own, you will need a really good business idea backed by a solid business plan with convincing indications that you will succeed; then other people will invest in your enterprise.

## EXTEND THE LEARNING

- **Business Plan Practice.** Assign Critical Thinking questions 2 and 3.

- **Community Activity.** Have students find and try to attend one of the following — a Chamber of Commerce event, an SBA meeting or workshop, a meeting of a business networking club — and report to the class on the experience. The students might want to make contact in advance to arrange an invitation or permission to attend, possibly with a letter of introduction from you. Topics the students might address include: What is the mission of the sponsoring organization? How often are these events held? Who should attend? Whom did you meet? What did you learn? How might the experience be helpful to a young entrepreneur? **LINKS**》*Civics*

- **Internet Activity.** Instruct students to use an Internet search engine to find sources of capital/investors that particularly focus on helping young entrepreneurs, women, or minorities.

- *Entrepreneurs in Profile*. Have students pick an entrepreneur profile and outline the sources of capital s/he used, when in the business's life cycle the different sources were tapped, which sources the entrepreneur intentionally decided *not* to use, etc. Ask volunteers to share what they found. Are there any patterns in terms of sources or timing? Why?

- **A Business for the Young Entrepreneur.** Have students read about Jason Upshaw and $2^{nd}$ Gear Bicycles in the textbook. In addition to Key Concepts question 2, ask what other sources he might approach to grow his business.

- **Youth Business Plan Competitions.** Have students research online, using the information provided in the textbook, the various business plan competitions, entrepreneurial awards, or scholarships for young people. **LINKS**》*Research*

## BUILD ACADEMIC AND LIFE-SKILL PROFICIENCIES
### *Skills Mean Success* Answers

**English (Literary Response).** 1. For example: traditionally, "heavenly" angels appear unexpectedly to help people. Similarly, the help of investor "angels" often seems to come from "out of the blue." 2. a. Students will find their own images, but *floating* means to be suspended for a time in air or water. "Floating" a bill means keeping it "in the air" before paying it. b. Runners and vehicles need *traction* (firm contact with a hard surface) to get going. Without an established customer base or a self-selling product, new businesses can have trouble making contact with the marketplace — "getting traction." c. Clothes in a dryer, puddles of water in the sun, and even bone mass in the elderly all *shrink* — get smaller — over time. Shrinkage suggests an uncontrolled, steadily diminishing quantity as, for example, food supplies in the kitchen of a restaurant if employees are sneaking it to eat or stealing it. In fact, shrinkage is a polite way to say "stealing." Students with an interest in visual arts may want to illustrate some of these figurative terms humorously. **LINKS**》*Fine Arts*

**English (Sentence Combining).** Students will use different ways to combine the sentences, but, as necessary, review the concept of *coordinate* clauses (independent complete thoughts) combined by words such as *and, or, but, although, yet, however,* and *subordinate* clauses, which explain an idea in the main (principal) clause of a sentence by using words such as *who, that, which, when, after, before,* and so on.

**Technology.** Criteria could also include: who runs the site — the government, an individual, a business, or some other organization? Is it "selling something" or does it exist strictly for information? Is the information objective and fairly balanced? Does it allow the visitor to ask questions or make comments?

### CHAPTER 32

# CORPORATIONS:
## *Limiting Liability*

## ORGANIZE THE LEARNING

### CHAPTER OBJECTIVES

- Understand corporations and limited liability companies (LLC).
- Decide whether you should form a corporation or LLC.
- Explain how a corporation is treated under tax and business laws.
- Evaluate the pros and cons of different business structures.

### NFTE RESOURCES

- Text pp. 386-397
- Transparencies T32-1 to T32-3, T25-1
- Workbook/BLMs Chapter 32
- Entrepreneurs in Profile #19
- Test Bank Chapter 32
- A Business for the Young Entrepreneur: *Consignment Shop*

### BUSINESS PLAN ACTIVITIES

*Workbook Business Plan Review*
Corporations 32-1, 32-2, 32-3, 32-4

*Workbook/Textbook Chapter Review*
Key Concepts 2-7

### SKILLS MEAN SUCCESS

*Math*
Numeration and Solving Problems: Understanding Percentages and Exponents

*English*
Reading for Understanding
Questioning Strategies in Reading

Preparing, Organizing, and Delivering a Presentation

### PREREQUISITES

- Have the students pre-read Chapter 32 in the textbook and to generate three questions they want answered in class.
- Chapters 3, 14 and 25 will inform the content of this chapter.

### VOCABULARY

board of directors, corporation, dividend, donation, limited liability company, stockholder, tax-exempt

## KEY QUESTION

**As a business owner, how can I protect my personal assets?**

## PREPARE FOR LEARNING

- **Legal guest.** If you plan to invite a guest speaker for the Extend the Learning activity, make arrangements well in advance. Your local NFTE office may have some contacts and suggestions.

## SET A CONTEXT FOR LEARNING

- **Focus: Protection.** Ask the students to list two activities they do that entail risk, such as playing sports, hiking, riding a bike, or driving a car. In what ways do they protect themselves from potential harm while engaged in these activities?

- **Discussion Launcher: Lawsuits.** Have students consider the following: If a sole-proprietor car inventor is sued because her model is judged to be danger-

ous or defective, can she lose her home, money and other property? (Yes.) Can the president of a major car manufacturing company? (Not if the business is incorporated.) What can the sole proprietor and corporate president each do to protect themselves?

## DEVELOP AND CLOSE THE LEARNING

- **Risk Review.** Recall from Chapter 3 the concepts of risk and return. Recall from Chapter 25 two ways that entrepreneurs can legally structure their businesses: sole proprietorship and partnership. Remind students how neither of these structures protect the entrepreneur from losing personal as well as business assets in the case of a lawsuit.

- **Corporation Definition.** Use transparency T32-1 to describe what a corporation is and how it differs from sole proprietorships and partnerships. Be sure to define all terms, such as stock, stockholder, board of directors, and dividends. Ask students to brainstorm corporations they know. (McDonald's, Microsoft, Nike, etc.) Point out that most large, well-known companies are corporations but that many small companies also choose to "incorporate" or become a corporation.

- **Advantages and Disadvantages.** Use the text and transparency T32-2 to discuss the advantages and disadvantages of incorporation. It may be helpful to provide examples of each bullet point.

  ○ Limited legal liability: refer back to Discussion Launcher activity.

  ○ Money raised through stock: relay stories of recent initial public offerings (IPO's) described in *The Wall Street Journal*.

  ○ Ownership easily transferred: describe how people buy and sell stock every day, which is the buying and selling of ownership in different companies.

  ○ Buy/sell/contracts: recall recent mergers in the news.

  ○ More heavily taxed: explain that the corporation must pay business income taxes on the profit it makes and the stockholders must pay personal income taxes on the dividends they receive. If possible, look up on the internet a concrete example of a dividend-paying company (McDonald's) to provide real numbers.

  ○ Founder can lose control to board of directors: tell the story in the text or *Entrepreneurs in Profile* of how Steve Jobs was fired from Apple.

  ○ Expensive to start: explain that the incorporation process involves lawyers and filing a lot of paperwork, such as Articles of Incorporation; if feasible, ask a local entrepreneurial corporation to provide you with a copy of their articles as a show-and-tell prop.

  ○ Subject to many government regulations: explain that corporations are closely watched regarding their accounting practices, disclosure of information, how stock is offered, who may or may not hold stock, etc. Some students may be familiar with and want to share what they know about — or be able to investigate and report on — corporate scandals such as Enron, Adelphia, or WorldCom.

- **Types of Corporations.** Use the text and transparency T32-3 (which is also reproduced in the textbook) to explain the four types of corporations. Explain the name suffixes (Inc., Ltd., PC, LLC) by which people can determine what kind of corporation a company may be.

- **Summary.** Use transparency T25-1 from Chapter 25 as a summary of the different business legal structures. Ask students to summarize the differences among the structures.

## ASSESS THE LEARNING

- **Vocabulary.** Have students define terms in their own words and use each in a sentence or complete the Vocabulary activity in the workbook.

- **Critical Thinking.** Questions 1-5. **Answers:** 1. Sole proprietorship — s/he doesn't need a partner for skills or equipment and doesn't need to incorporate because product is unlikely to cause injury and s/he is probably is not looking to expand the business nationally. 2. Partnership — if s/he could find a partner willing to invest money. 3. Corporation — since it looks like this business could become a national or international company. 4. Nonprofit—this business's mission could qualify for nonprofit, tax-exempt status. 5. LLC—combines the benefits of partnerships and corporations.

- **Writing Practice.** Assign Key Concept question 1.

- **Additional Workbook Activities Answers.**

  **Vocabulary Activity. Answers:** 1. d. 2. c. 3. g. 4. b. 5. a. 6. e. 7. f.

  **Quiz 32** in the workbook. **Answers:** 1. Answers may vary, but the top two advantages are limiting legal liability, which protects the entrepreneur's personal assets, and the ability to sell stock, which aids in raising money to run the business. 2. Answers may vary but the top drawback is double taxation; however, losing control of the company, increased government regulation, and higher start-up costs may also be mentioned. 3. Nonprofit 501(c) (3) corporation. 4. The corporation is taxed on its profits (first taxation), which are partially distributed to stockholders as dividends, which must be reported on personal income tax returns (second taxation). 5. a. 6. b. 7. c. 8. c. 9. C-corporation. 10. Yes, because motorcycles can be dangerous and Kevin would want to protect his personal assets if sued.

## EXTEND THE LEARNING

- **Business Plan Practice.** Assign Key Concepts questions 2-7.

- **Community Activity.** Have students read about Raúl Hernandez and the Mission Economic and Cultural Association in the text. Assign students to look up

**TE 126**

(in the phone book, through the Chamber of Commerce, or through the Internet) associations or organizations that provide economic development assistance to women, Latinos, African-Americans, immigrants, or other minority groups. As an additional assignment, have the class create a standard interview sheet of questions and have students call these groups to find out what types of services they provide to entrepreneurs.

- **Entrepreneurs in Profile.** Have class analyze the chapter on Stephen Wozniak and Steve Jobs. In addition, it may be helpful for students to look at the Apple Web site regarding its financial history. Types of questions to ask: Why do founding entrepreneurs like Jobs hire professional managers like Sculley? How did Jobs lose control of his company? When is a good time in a business's life for the entrepreneur to incorporate? What are some good reasons to incorporate?

- **A Business for the Young Entrepreneur.** Have students read about the Consignment Shop business opportunity in the text. After the reading, ask students to discuss in small groups what the risks might be for this type of business, and the pros and cons for the different legal structures. Have each group decide what legal structure it would choose if opening a consignment shop, and why that structure would be the best. Then assign Key Concepts question 8 for students to consider setting up a nonprofit clothing exchange.

- **Lawsuits.** Instruct students to use the library or Internet to find lawsuit cases brought against major companies (tobacco companies, McDonald's "hot coffee" spill, and obesity cases, Securities and Exchange Commission financial misconduct cases, the pollution case featured in the Erin Brockovich movie, etc.). Have students list the types of issues that can lead to a lawsuit, discuss how a company can protect itself from lawsuits, and the types of consequences that ensue from a lawsuit (payouts, changes in procedure or products, effect on stock price, etc.). Invite the students to distinguish between legitimate and frivolous consumer lawsuits and discuss the concept of tort reform to limit legal liability. **LINKS**»*Law*

- **Guest Speaker.** Invite a local incorporated entrepreneur to share his/her story of incorporation (challenges, benefits, etc.), or a corporate lawyer to describe the basic process and documents of incorporation.

## BUILD ACADEMIC AND LIFE-SKILL PROFICIENCIES

### *Skills Mean Success* Answers

**Math.** 1a.

| Year | Number of Chapters | % Increase from Previous Year Listed |
|------|------|------|
| 1980 | 2 | N/A |
| 1981 | 11 | 450% |
| 1982 | 70 | 536.36% |
| 1983 | 192 | 174.28% |
| 1984 | 350 | 82.29% |
| 1991 | 407 | 16.28% |
| 2004 | 600 | 47.42% |

b. From 1980 to 1981 there was a 450% increase, although the actual number of chapters increased by only nine.

c. Between 1991 and 2004, the actual number of chapters increased by 193, although that percentage was not the highest.

2. a. F; b. T; c. F; d.; T; e. T. A graphing calculator to show the calculations would be helpful.

**English.** Questions will vary, but examples for C-corporation might include:

For additional information: If a corporation is a legal entity, can its directors or managers be sued as individuals if the company does something irresponsible or illegal? (generally, no, but the individuals involved can be charged criminally.). For clarification: "Legal entity" does not mean that a corporation cannot break the law, but that a corporation is *recognized* by the law as an individual "thing." Explain that businesspeople frequently use this question-asking technique after reading reports, business plans, or other forms of communication.

**English/Leadership.** 1. I, c ; II, e; III, a; IV, b; V, d. 2. It cites growth in operating budget from $3,200 to $1.2M and it gives Raul's age (29) when he began his not-for-profit company. 3. For example: growth chart to show dramatic operating budget growth; map showing the Hispanic cultures represented in the annual events; and pics or video of the three annual events.

# STOCKS:
## Selling Ownership to Raise Capital

---

## ORGANIZE THE LEARNING

| CHAPTER OBJECTIVES | NFTE RESOURCES | SKILLS MEAN SUCCESS |
|---|---|---|
| • Explain why stocks are traded.<br>• Read a daily stock table.<br>• Calculate a stock's price/earnings ratio.<br>• Calculate a stock's yield. | • Text pp. 398-405<br>• Transparencies T33-1 to T33-3<br>• Workbook/BLMs Chapter 33<br>• Test Bank Chapter 33<br>• BizTech Unit 19<br>• A Business for the Young Entrepreneur: *Clarence Ross III, The Doughnut Kid* | *Math*<br>Numeration: Place Value<br><br>*Technology*<br>Reading and Evaluating Web Sites |

**BUSINESS PLAN ACTIVITIES**

*Workbook Business Plan Review*
Stocks  33-1, 33-2

*Workbook/Textbook Chapter Review*
Critical Thinking 2, 3

**PREREQUISITES**

Chapters 14, 31 and 32 provide important background information for this chapter.

**VOCABULARY**

share, stock, stockbroker, stock market

---

## KEY QUESTION

**How can I make money by owning part of other people's businesses?**

## PREPARE FOR LEARNING

- ***The Wall Street Journal.*** Bring in copies of *The Wall Street Journal* for the Stock Contest activity. Aim to have at least one copy per three students. If possible, have at least a few copies per week for the last three weeks (say, every Monday's edition). Or, better yet, order a Classroom Edition subscription, which is tailored specifically for high school students. This subscription includes copies of the newspaper, a teacher's guide, a daily copy for the teacher, and access to an interactive teacher Web site. Call 1-800-544-0522 or visit www.wsjclassroomedition.com.

- **Copy Stock Certificate Master.** Make, copy and cut apart 25 pages of the mini stock certificates so that there are 100 shares available for the class.

- **Field Trip Arrangements.** If you did not visit a local brokerage firm in Chapter 14, during this chapter would also be a good time to do that. Contact a local brokerage firm and arrange to tour their facilities.

An alternative is to have a stockbroker visit the class as a guest speaker.

## SET A CONTEXT FOR LEARNING

- **Focus: What Is This Business Worth?** Have students write a monthly income statement based on the following information, then calculate how much the business is worth using the three-times-net-profit rule, assuming Julio's profits are stable.

Julio bought two dozen T-shirts at $9 per dozen. He bought two dozen iron-on designs for $5 per dozen. He ironed on the designs and sold the shirts for $10 each. He spent $15 on flyers. He pays taxes at 10%. Round to the nearest dollar. **Answer:**

| | | |
|---|---|---|
| Sales/Revenue | $240 | |
| Cost of Goods Sold | $28 | (9 × 2) + (5 × 2) |
| Gross Profit | $212 | |
| Fixed Costs | $15 | |
| Profit Before Taxes | $197 | |
| Taxes | $20 | |
| Net Profit | $177 | |

Julio's company would be worth
$177 × 12 months × 3 = $6,372.

- **Discussion Launcher: Risk Preference.** Ask the students to first answer individually, then discuss in pairs or small groups: A stock you bought at $60 is now valued at $55. Would you sell, hold, or buy more? Why? Ask students to think about why their individual answers might be different.

## DEVELOP AND CLOSE THE LEARNING

- **Stocks and Entrepreneurship.** Review the difference between equity and debt financing from Chapters 14 and 31. Explain that, as an entrepreneur, you issue stock through an initial public offering (IPO). When people buy your stock, they are giving you their money to use to grow your business with the expectation that the value of your company will increase and they will make a profit on their investment. The stockholders actually own a portion of your business assets and profits. You do not have to repay the money if your business does not grow, but you have to keep your investors informed of what's going on — through financial reports — and you have to follow strict government regulations to make sure you are using their money appropriately. The Securities and Exchange Commission (SEC) oversees these regulations. After your stock has been issued and is listed on a stock exchange, such as NYSE or NASDAQ, it is out of your control and can be bought and sold without your knowledge or consent, although occasionally a company may try to buy back all its stock and go "private" again. Few high-school-age entrepreneurs issue stock because it is a complicated process. However, anyone can make money *owning* stock. This chapter will help students learn what it means to own parts of other people's companies via stock purchase.

- **Stocks, Ownership, and Stock Markets.** To make the abstract idea of stock ownership and exchange more concrete, ask students to think of a recent time when they and their friends bought a product to share — such as a pizza or video game. Explain that they each had a "stake" in what toppings to add to the pizza or which video game to buy. They had to take into account the whole product, even though each of them would only eat a slice or two of the pizza or play the game for a few hours a week. They shared ownership in one product. The same thing is true with stock ownership — many people own companies that issue stock. For example, Julio from the Focus activity above could sell 100 shares of his company, each for about $63, based on current market value (although he would not want to sell *all* of

his company or even most of it. He would probably sell less than 50% so as to retain a "controlling interest" — in other words, he would sell 49 or fewer of the 100 shares). Use the textbook and the top of transparency T33-1 to describe:

- ○ how stock shares represent owning a portion of a company.

- ○ how stock allows a wider number of people to have a stake in a company and provide financing for a company (i.e., the company becomes "public").

- ○ how — once a company issues stock — it often loses control and track of who owns part of the company. Sometimes even competitor companies can own a stake in it.

- **Stocks and Making Money.** Explain that a stockholder can make money in two ways: price changes and dividends.

- ○ If an individual buys a stock at one price and then sells it at a higher price, s/he is "buying long" and makes a profit. If an individual "borrows" a stock at one price for a specified period of time, finds a buyer for it at that price, then buys it later at a lower price and returns it to the lender, s/he is "selling short" and makes a profit. Although some investors buy and hold stocks for long periods of time, others buy and sell them frequently to make quicker profits.

- ○ If a company shares its profits with stockholders as a *dividend* at the end of the quarter or year, the stockholders make a profit by just holding on to the stock (neither buying nor selling). Of course, stockholders can also lose money, too, because they are not guaranteed repayment of their investment if the price goes down or the company goes bankrupt. Establish that stock investment carries risk.

- **Stock Prices.** Review from Chapter 6 the concepts of market, supply, demand, and market-clearing price. Like other products, stocks are exchanged through a "market" of buyers and sellers. Buyers are investors that want to own part of a certain company in order to make money. Sellers are either the company itself or other investors that no longer want a stake in that company, because they either want to buy stock in another company or they want cash. A stock's price reflects what buyers and sellers agree is the right value at that moment in time. Stock prices change by the day, by the hour, and by the minute. Ask students to speculate: What kind of information goes into a person's decision to buy or sell a stock? What would *you* like to know about a company before you invested in it? (Its profitability, stability, what its assets are, is there confidence in its management, how well the public likes its products, what new products it (or its competitors) are working on, the opportunities for new markets, how important its products are to people's well-being (e.g., mindshare, government regulations, market share, etc.) Where can you find this information? **LINKS**»*Economics*

- **Uncertainty.** Continue the discussion: How reliable do you know this information to be? Write students' ideas on the board. Many answers may relate to speculating about the future (information that is uncertain): what the company *will* do or *will* get in the days, weeks, or months ahead. Explain how a person who expects a lot of opportunities for a company is usually willing to pay more for its stock than a person who expects fewer opportunities. Investors have to *anticipate* what will happen to a company over the time period they plan to hold on to that company's stock. Stock-buying is like playing a game: you have to think ahead, consider what the other players (friends and foes alike) might do, and decide what to do before the moment of choice arises. Then, when the moment of choice does arrive, you have to act decisively. Set up the following scenario:

You buy stock anticipating its price will go up so you can sell it for a profit.

  ○ If the stock goes up, what will you do? (Sell and make a profit now, or hold it because you think the price might go higher.)

  ○ If the stock price goes down, what will you do? (Sell it to avoid further loss if you think the price will keep going down, or hold it because you think the price will go back up, or buy more shares because you think the price will go up and then you can make even more money.)

Use the bottom part of transparency T33-1 to summarize.

- **Buying and Selling Stocks.** Have ready the "stock certificates" you copied prior to class. Create a market in the classroom to make the abstract concept of a stock exchange more concrete. Each student will need one sheet of notebook paper to keep track of transactions. Tell students they each have $200 to invest. You are an entrepreneur that owns a video game design firm. You are currently developing your first game that incorporates virtual reality

technology so players can actually feel the action, not just see and hear it, as with traditional games. The helmet that is required for your video game to provide this additional sensory information is in development by another company and is not yet available to players. You anticipate that it will be ready in three months, the same time your game will be released, and the two companies will jointly market the products.

  ○ You need to raise money to buy additional computer equipment. You are making an initial public offering of 100 shares of stock at $50 per share to raise $5,000. By raise of hands ask: Who would like to invest in your company? How many shares do you want to buy (from 1-4)? Sell to students based on who raises their hands first, second, etc. until all shares are sold or no further students want to purchase. Have students record the transactions.

  ○ Tell students that your company had a setback and the game will not be released for six months, which lowers the stock price to $30. Ask student stockholders: Who wants to sell their stock? Ask students who have cash: Who wants to buy? Have students record the transactions.

  ○ Tell students you have released the video game, it is selling well, and you have only begun to tap the full market for the game; the stock price has risen to $65. Ask student stockholders: Who wants to sell their stock? Ask students who have cash: Who wants to buy? Have students record the transactions.

Continue as long as time permits and students grasp the concept. Other events you may want to use:

  ○ You negotiate to sell your product through a worldwide distributor, which opens up new markets; stock price increases to $100.

  ○ You do your year-end financial statements and show a profit beyond your projections: $200,000; you issue a dividend of 25 cents per share.

  ○ Your partner company runs into trouble with the helmets, which can sometimes short out; they are being sued and have to recall some helmets; your stock price falls to $70.

  ○ Your lead designer leaves in the middle of your company creating a second video game; stock price drops to $50.

At the end of the activity, have students calculate their individual ROIs. Ask students to share how they felt during the activity. (Many will feel uneasy or uncertain, some will feel exhilarated.) What risks did they choose to take or not take? At each event, what further information would they have liked to know? What might they have done in the real world to protect the investment and reduce risk? How many of you think you would like to invest in the stock market? Why or why not? Summarize this activity by explaining that this type of exchange — millions of them — occur every day around the world. But it is mostly electronic; often investors don't get certificates but their shares are held in a computer under their name. Also, stock trading is now conducted online.

- **Stock Tables/Evaluating Companies.** Recall from Chapter 6 that the efficiency of a market depends on the sharing of information between buyers and sellers. With stocks, this information is available through stock tables published daily in the newspaper or online. Use the text and transparency T33-2 to show a stock table, define all terms, and walk students through reading the information the table contains. Have them answer the questions on the transparency. **Answers:** MayDeptStrs; MayDeptStrs; MayDeptStrs; MayDeptStrs; Mattel; MayDeptStrs. Distribute copies of *The Wall Street Journal* and give the class practice in looking up a few stocks, such as GM, Intel, Nike, or other well-known corporations. Look up several together, and then allow students to work independently or in pairs. After a few have shared stock information for these companies, ask students to decide on the companies they would invest in and why.

- **Summary.** Ask: What are the advantages and disadvantages of investing in stock versus putting your money elsewhere (such as in a bank savings account, spending it, opening your own business)? (Advantages would include the opportunity to make higher returns and to be part of the growing economy as an equity owner; disadvantages would include the higher risk compared to savings.)

## ASSESS THE LEARNING

- **Vocabulary.** Have students complete the workbook activity or define terms in their own words and use each in a sentence.

- **Key Concepts.** Questions 1-4. **Answers:** 1. Because different investors have different opinions about the value of a stock and different risk preferences. 2. One ROI of a stock is called the yield, which is calculated by dividing the dividend paid by the stock's closing price and multiplying by 100. 3. Answers will vary. 4a. $600. 4b. $500 − 300 = $200 profit. 4c. 500/300 × 100 = 167%. Key Concepts question 5 appears in the workbook only and requires students to track a stock in the S&P 500 over five days. The workbook contains a chart for recording changes. Answers will vary.

- **Critical Thinking.** Question 1. **Answers:** 1. Answers will vary depending on the date stocks are looked up; check the *Wall Street Journal* for answers or require students to photocopy or cut out the relevant stock table so you can check their answers.

- **Writing Practice.** Assign the Discuss with a Group activity on page 404 in the textbook (Key Concepts).

- **Additional Workbook Activities Answers.**

  **Vocabulary Activity.  Answers:** 1. stock markets. 2. stockbrokers. 3. share. 4. stock.

  **Quiz 33** in the workbook. **Answers:** 1. Stock represents shares of ownership in a company. 2. Corporations sell stock to raise money (capital). 3. Answers may vary but should address making money through dividends received, increases in stock price, or selling short. 4. Avon. 5. AT&T. 6. BellAtl (Bell Atlantic). 7. AT&T. 8. Selling short or the idea of borrowing at one price and paying back at a lower one. 9. Yield tells the investor about one form of ROI on a stock (its dividend); companies that issue a dividend are often stable and profitable, which makes them a quality investment. 10. Answers will vary, but students should include in their reasoning the concept of risk and return.

## EXTEND THE LEARNING

- **Business Plan Practice.** Assign Critical Thinking questions 2-3.

- **BizTech.** Assign Unit 19.

- **Stock Contest.** This activity gives students the opportunity to track stocks as if they were stockholders. First, use transparency T33-3 for a "dry run" of the process of tracking stocks. Have each student pick one stock from the *Journal* and answer the transparency's questions. Instruct each student to copy the question prompts as column headings on a separate piece of paper:

Stock, Date Purchased, Today's Date, Price, Date Sold, Profit/Loss Per Share, ROI

Tell students they each have $500 to invest in stocks. Discuss how they can find good companies to invest in by identifying products or services they think are particularly needed, desirable, or of high quality — then identifying the corporation that makes them. Have students individually or in pairs research companies they might want to invest in, then purchase shares of those companies within their budget. Once a week for the next month (or, even better, through the end of the course, if feasible), students are to check their stocks in *The Wall Street Journal* (or other daily paper that carries stock tables) and enter a new line with the date, current price, and what the profit/loss and ROI would be if the stock were to be sold at that time. Then students will need to decide to hold, sell and buy a different stock, or buy more of the same stock (if they have sufficient cash or by selling a stock). Students may buy and sell stocks as they see fit. It is also helpful to have a jointly agreed-upon class stock that the whole class chooses in the beginning and can track weekly on the board. You might occasionally take a few moments at the beginning of future classes to discuss news affecting the performance of a student stock, as time and appropriateness permit. At the end of the month (or course), identify:

1. the overall performance of the class stock;
2. the top performing student-based on the overall ROI of his/her portfolio;
3. the top performing stock, among all stocks purchased by students.

Recognize the three most successful investors with awards. Note that this activity could be assigned as homework or a project rather than using in-class time, but record sheets should be checked periodically to make sure students are keeping up.

- **Internet Stock Research.** Let students research more about the companies they hold in their Stock Context portfolios, as well as the competitors of those companies, by investigating the companies' Web sites. Most large corporations will have an "investor relations" link on their sites that will provide financial information. Assign students to choose one company and write a brief memo or create a poster that summarizes its strengths, weaknesses, opportunities and threats that might affect its stock price in the future.

- **Exploring Online/Stock Trading.** Have students visit an online trading site, such as www.etrade.com, www.schwab.com, or www.scottrade.com and write a memo about trading stocks online.

- **A Business for the Young Entrepreneur.** Have students read about Clarence Cross, III, The Doughnut Kid in the text. Assign Critical Thinking question 4 as a writing activity.

- **Brokerage Firm Field Trip.** This activity provides an experience of how ownership/equity is bought and sold. If you live in a city with a stock exchange (such as New York and Chicago), arrange a visit to the NYSE, NASDAQ, or Chicago's Board of Trade. Alternatively, visit a stock brokerage firm to have students learn about what a stock broker does, see a stock ticker, and observe traders at work. When you contact the firm, emphasize that the tour will take no more than an hour. If an actual field trip is not possible, a cyber-field trip to a stock exchange is an option: www.nyse.com, www.nasdaq.com, www.cbot.com, www.schwab.com or an online trading company.

- **Guest Speaker.** Invite a stockbroker to make a presentation to your class about opening an account, trading stocks, and the role of the broker. It may be a good idea to send a copy of the textbook to the guest speaker so s/he can see what the students will have learned and to make sure the presentation is appropriate. Suggest that the speaker bring samples of documents for students to see and analyze. Have students prepare questions before the speaker arrives.

## BUILD ACADEMIC AND LIFE-SKILL PROFICIENCIES

### *Skills Mean Success* Answers

**Math.** 1. $582,000, $450,000, $624,500, $735,000. 2. $5,820,000, $4,500,000, $6,245,000, $7,350,000. If necessary, remind students to use the proper number of zeros and to put commas in the correct places.

**Technology/English.** 1. If students do not have access to computers, make arrangements to demonstrate the Web sites on a computer in class, or print out pertinent pages and allow them to evaluate the printouts. 2. The goal is to understand that, when they consult Web sites for information, they must examine them with a critical eye. They should evaluate sites based on credibility, usability, readability, accuracy, attractiveness, and how current they are. Alternatively, assign evaluating specific sites to small groups. The following sites contain detailed stock quotes and information:

- *USA Today* www.usatoday.com
- *CBS Market Watch* www.cbs.marketwatch.com
- *Yahoo! Finance* www.finance.yahoo.com
- *MSN* www.moneycentral.msn.com
- *CNN Money* www.money.cnn.com
- New York Stock Exchange www.nyse.com
- Nasdaq Stock Market www.nasdaq.com
- Dow Jones Indexes www.djindexes.com

### CHAPTER 34

# BONDS:
## *Issuing Debt to Raise Capital*

---

## ORGANIZE THE LEARNING

| | | |
|---|---|---|
| **CHAPTER OBJECTIVES** | **BUSINESS PLAN ACTIVITIES** | **PREREQUISITES** |

**CHAPTER OBJECTIVES**
- Explain how bonds differ from stocks.
- Summarize how bonds work.
- Discuss the effect inflation has on the value of a dollar.
- Read a bond table.

**NFTE RESOURCES**
- Text pp. 406-411
- Transparencies T34-1, T34-2
- Workbook/BLMs Chapter 34
- Test Bank Chapter 34
- A Business for the Young Entrepreneur: *Pet Care*

**BUSINESS PLAN ACTIVITIES**
*Workbook Business Plan Review*
Bonds 34-1, 34-2

*Workbook/Textbook Chapter Review*
Critical Thinking 2, 3

**SKILLS MEAN SUCCESS**

*Math*
Mathematical Reasoning: Estimating and Predicting

*English*
Writing and Reading for Information: Using Standard English; Proofreading

*Leadership*
Understanding Customer Needs

**PREREQUISITES**
Chapters 14, 31, 32 and 33 inform the content of this chapter.

**VOCABULARY**
bond, discount, face value, inflation, maturity, par, premium, principal, securities

---

## KEY QUESTION

**How can I make a profit by loaning money to other people's businesses or to the government?**

## PREPARE FOR LEARNING

- **Wall Street Journal.** Bring in copies of the *Wall Street Journal*.

## SET A CONTEXT FOR LEARNING

- **Focus 1: Rule of 72.** Challenge the students to solve in their heads: Use the Rule of 72 to figure how long it would take your investment to double at each of the following rates: 3%, 4%, 6%, 8%, 9%, 10%. **Answers:** 24 years, 18, 12, 9, 8, 7.2.

- **Focus 2: Inflation.** Ask: If a soda costs $1 today and inflation climbs to 5% in a year, how much will a soda cost in a year? **Answer:** $1.05.

- **Discussion Launcher: Lending to a Friend.** Have students discuss in pairs: Your friend wants to borrow $100 and pay you back in a year, at 5% interest. Inflation is at 3%. Is this investment worth it?

## DEVELOP AND CLOSE THE LEARNING

- **Stocks and Bonds.** Use transparency T34-1 to discuss the similarities and differences of stocks and bonds. (Both are forms of *securities*; both are investments that provide the potential to make money; both incur risk; both are exchanged in an open market; some differences are shown on the transparency; other differences are that stocks are usually considered riskier; bonds are particularly affected by inflation; bonds have a maturity date or time limit and stocks don't; bond interest must be paid every year whereas stock dividend payments are optional to the company.) Point out the parallel terms: stockholder and bondholder.

- **Bond Prices.** Discuss how bonds are also bought and sold like stocks, and bond prices can fluctuate just as stock prices do because a bondholder does not have to keep the bond until maturity. Define *face value, par, discount* and *premium*. Ask students to speculate: Why might an investor buy a bond for $102 if its face value is $100? (Its price is expected to go higher and the bondholder is not planning to hold it to maturity.) Explain that many of the same events that affect stock price also affect bond value (new markets, competitors' activity, mergers, government regulations).

- **Inflation.** Explain that *inflation* particularly affects a bond's price and its attraction as an investment because bonds have time limits. Define inflation as the gradual increase in prices over time, which erodes the purchasing power of money. The higher the inflation rate, the less $1 will buy. (Ten years ago, $1 bought two hamburgers, say, and now it barely buys one.) So, with inflation, a consumer needs more money to buy the same amount of product at a future date. Give the students a few examples: If the inflation rate equals the interest rate on a bond, the investor breaks even; if the inflation rate is lower than the interest rate, then the investor will make money but not as much as the interest rate would suggest; if the inflation rate is higher than the interest rate, then the investor will lose money. Inflation tends to drive interest rates higher because investors need a higher rate of return to offset the inflation.
**LINKS**》*Economics*

- **Bond Tables.** Ask: Companies issue stocks; what types of organizations issue bonds? (Companies, governments.) Use the text and transparency T34-2 to show a bond table, define all terms, and walk class through reading the information the table contains. Ask students to evaluate the bonds: Which is the most expensive? Which will mature first? Which has the highest yield? If Merck's yield rises to 8, has the price of the bond gone up or down? **Answers:** Hewlett-Packard; Bank of America in 2007; General Motors; down — it would be selling at a discount.

  Discuss how the yield is calculated (interest divided by price for bonds; dividend divided by price for stocks). Yield is a ratio, so yield has an inverse relationship with price: if yield goes up, price goes down (discounted) and if yield goes down, price goes up (premium). Ask students: Why is this helpful for investors to know? (It's related to ROI since a high yield means you are getting a better return for the price you pay.) Distribute copies of the *Journal* and give students practice looking up a few bonds. Do a few together as a class, then allow students to work independently or in pairs. After a few students have shared information for these companies, ask them to decide which company they would buy bonds from and why.

- **Summary.** Ask students to consider: Do they prefer to invest in stocks or bonds? Why? Plant the idea that perhaps they should consider investing in both — a variety of stocks and a variety of bonds. This is called *diversification* and helps reduce risk by spreading it across a number of investments. Professional investors, such as Warren Buffett, and mutual fund managers (a mutual fund is where many people pool their money to buy a variety of stocks or bonds) use diversification to improve returns and reduce risk.

## ASSESS THE LEARNING

- **Vocabulary.** Have students define terms in their own words and use each term in a sentence or complete the Workbook activity.

- **Critical Thinking.** Questions 1-4. **Answers:** 1. General Motors. 2. General Motors. 3. Merck. 4. Merck.

- **Additional Workbook Activities Answers.**

  **Vocabulary Activity. Answers:** 1. face value. 2. maturity. 3. discount. 4. par. 5. premium. 6. principal. 7. inflation. 8. bond. 9. securities.

  **Quiz 34** in the workbook. **Answers:** 1. Bonds. 2. Stocks. 3. Stocks. 4. The amount written on the bond or the amount of principal to be paid at maturity. 5. The bondholder is paid the face value. 6. GM. 7. Bank of America. 8. Hewlett-Packard. 9. Answers will vary but should take into consideration risk and return.

## EXTEND THE LEARNING

- **Business Plan Practice.** Assign Key Concepts questions 1-2.

- **A Business for the Young Entrepreneur.** Have students read about Pet Care in the text. Ask them to consider: For which of these pet care business ideas would it be good to incorporate and why?

- **Stock Contest Expansion.** Instruct students to consider bonds they might incorporate into their investment portfolios. Have them research possible bond issues to invest in and give a rationale for why they did or did not buy bonds as part of their portfolio. If they buy a bond, they should track it over time as they are doing for their stocks.

## BUILD ACADEMIC AND LIFE-SKILL PROFICIENCIES

### *Skills Mean Success* Answers

**Math.** 1. a. Think: 24.2% is nearly 25%, which is one-fourth. So, if $1.24 goes up by about one fourth, it will be $1.24 plus $1.24 divided by 4. $1.20 divided by 4 is 30 cents. So the price in 2013 will be about $1.24 plus 30 cents, or about $1.54.  b. Using the same form of estimation, the price in 2023 will be $1.54 plus about one fourth of $1.54. One fourth of $1.60 is 40 cents, so the cost will be approximately $1.54 plus about 40 cents, or about $1.94, just under $2.00. 2. 24.2% divided by ten will show the average (mean) is 2.42% or just under 2.5%. 3. $1.95 is just under $2.00. 5% of $2.00 is ten cents. From 2006 to 2011 is five years. Five times ten cents is 50 cents. So the price of gas in 2011 would be more than $2.50 if the price inflated according to the long-term average rate. What is the price of gas today? How accurate was the estimate?

Use the students' responses to reinforce the notion that inflation forecasts are "best estimates" and cannot be predicted with 100% accuracy. Ask for reasons why estimating rather than calculating exact future costs and inflation rates makes sense. Invite the students to speculate on how rising prices will impact them:

- as business owners.
- as consumers.

A Web search on "consumer price index" will yield some interesting results, including several online calculators of year-to-year changes in the CPI.

**English.** Line 1: interest-bearing, issue; Line 2: capital, even; Line 3: use, to; Line 5: form; Line 6: is, affected, continuous; Line 7: When; Line 8: isn't, period after much, rises; Line 9: one dollar, half, loaf; Line 10. reduces.

**Leadership and English.** Questioning technique is a critical skill for the workplace, for school, and for lifelong learning. Students with a different venture in mind could design surveys for their own business market. As needed, review commonly used types of survey questions.

- Open-ended (guided choice): How many of each kind of pet do you currently have?

  | | |
  |---|---|
  | Dog | _____ |
  | Cat | _____ |
  | Fish | _____ |
  | Bird | _____ |
  | Reptile | _____ |
  | Rodent | _____ |
  | Other | _____ |

- Open-ended (open): What pet care needs do you have that could be filled by a reasonably priced pet service?

- Yes-No: e.g., Do you currently use a pet service? If a pet service such as X were available at a good price, would you use it?

- Multiple choice: If a dog walking service were available for $3 per dog per hour, would you use it: a. once a month b. once per week c. more than once a week.

### CHAPTER 35

# THE BALANCE SHEET:
## *A Snapshot of Your Financial Strategy*

## ORGANIZE THE LEARNING

### CHAPTER OBJECTIVES

- Read a simple corporate balance sheet.
- Create a balance sheet for your business from the financial records.
- Analyze a balance sheet using financial ratios.
- Use a balance sheet to tell if a company has been successful over time.

### NFTE RESOURCES

- Text pp. 412-425
- Transparency T35-1 to T35-4
- Workbook/BLMs Chapter 35
- Test Bank Chapter 35
- BizTech Unit 25

### BUSINESS PLAN ACTIVITIES

*Workbook Business Plan Review*
Your Balance Sheet 35-1, 35-2, 35-3, 35-4

*Workbook/Textbook Chapter Review*
Key Concepts 3, 4

*Power Point Templates*
Adv. 18, 21

### SKILLS MEAN SUCCESS

*Technology*
Online Research

*Math*
Mathematical Reasoning: Ratio, Proportion, and Percentage

*English*
Writing for Understanding: Test Prep; Presenting Information Clearly

### PREREQUISITES

- Have the students read Chapter 35 in the textbook. The balance sheet is a challenging topic so reading in pairs may facilitate understanding.
- Chapters 12, 13, 14 and 31 are important lead-ups to this chapter. It may be prudent to review the key concepts from those chapters.

### VOCABULARY

asset, balance sheet, current ratio, debt ratio, debt-to-equity ratio, fiscal year, liability, liquidity, owner's equity, quick ratio

## KEY QUESTION

**How can I keep track of what my business owns and owes, and how it is financed?**

## PREPARE FOR LEARNING

- **NFTE Journals.** Instruct students to bring to class their NFTE Journals, started in Chapter 12.

- **Materials Preparation.** If you plan to do the Ratio Scramble activity in Extend the Learning, write on four sheets the following headings: debt ratio, debt-to-equity ratio, quick ratio, and current ratio. Then make enough copies of each sheet so there will be at least one four-sheet set per team.

## SET A CONTEXT FOR LEARNING

- **Focus 1: Debt vs. Equity Financing.** Ask the students to discuss this scenario: Zane's and Joey's two businesses each have $1,000 in assets. Zane took out a $400 loan from her dad to start her business. Joey

offered a friend a 40% equity stake in his business in return for $400. Which business do you think is in better financial shape and why?

- **Focus 2: How Much Are You Worth?** Have the students individually complete their own calculation of "net worth": List all the cash and savings you have and estimate the value of your belongings. Add them up. List the value of everything you owe to others (e.g., a friend who loaned you money, something you have on layaway). Add them up. Which total is higher?

## DEVELOP AND CLOSE THE LEARNING

- **Accounting Review.** Recall from Chapters 12 and 13 the roles of the journal and the income statement in tracking and summarizing financial information and performance. (The journal is used daily and provides a chronological accounting of the details of income and expenses, including source/recipient, how much, what for, etc.; the income statement is usually prepared monthly and annually, and provides a summary of sales and the expenses associated with sales or business operations over a given time period). Both of these documents give entrepreneurs and investors an idea about how efficiently the business is operating. But they do not show directly what the business owns and owes, how much it is worth to stockholders, and its sources of capital/financing — which is the purpose of the balance sheet. Show transparency T35-2. Review the format and terminology (assets, liabilities, equity) of the balance sheet as an overview of the rest of the lesson.

- **Assets: What a Business Owns.** Define and explain types of assets: cash, accounts receivable, inventory, marketable securities, equipment, other. Explain that accounts receivable are what customers owe the entrepreneur — recall from Chapter 12 (record-keeping) how sometimes an entrepreneur might sell a product/service to a customer then invoice them and receive payment later; accounts receivable is where this amount goes between when the entrepreneur invoices but before the customer pays. Explain that marketable securities are investments — such as holding stock in another company — that a company may make with its extra cash so that spare cash is earning money.

- **Depreciation: How Assets Fall in Value over Time.** Recall the concept of *depreciation* from Chapter 9 (it spreads the cost of an asset — such as equipment — over a number of years). Note where depreciation shows up on the balance sheet—under assets. It is usually a negative number that increases over the years as more of the asset is depreciated (devalued). In other words, it is subtracted from asset values to get the current total assets valuation.

- **Liabilities: What a Business Owes.** Define and explain types of liabilities: *current* (accounts payable, credit card purchases, short-term loans) and *long-term* (mortgages, long-term loans). Explain that accounts payable is similar to accounts receivable — accounts payable are what the entrepreneur owes suppliers — invoices the entrepreneur has received but not yet paid. Summarize that liabilities represent the amount of assets that were funded by debt financing (i.e., loans).

- **Equity: Net Worth.** Summarize that owner's equity represents the amount of assets that were funded by equity financing. It equals what is left over after debt has been accounted for. Also, owner's equity represents the value or net worth of the business — that is, the value of the assets "net" (or minus) what the business must pay back to others for acquiring some of those assets (or liabilities). Optional, if you

would like to go into more depth: Define and explain types of owner's equity: start-up capital (what the entrepreneur and the investors first put into the business) and additional, paid-in capital (further equity investment the entrepreneur secured after the business was up and running, such as finding more investors or going public).

- **Determining How a Business Is Financed.** Use transparency T35-1 to discuss the balance sheet equation: Total Assets = Total Liabilities + Owner's Equity. Emphasize that this equation must add up — the assets of the business have to be paid for either by debt or equity financing. That is, the two sides must "balance," which is what gives the balance sheet its name. Have students determine the missing numbers on the transparency. **Answers:** 5; 0; 0; 90; 190; 200; 0; 180; 490; 500. Familiarize students with the balance sheets in the textbook.

- **Financing Ratios.** Use transparency T35-3 to show the two financing percentage ratios: debt and debt-to-equity. Discuss what each ratio tells you: the debt ratio shows how much of your assets are owed to pay off creditors (you want it relatively low); the debt-to equity ratio tells you which style of financing is more prevalent (if it is below 1 then equity is stronger; above 1, debt reigns). Return to transparency T35-1 and have students calculate the debt ratio and debt-to-equity ratio for each line. **Answers:** 50%, 100%; 0%, 0%; 100%, undefined division by 0; 10%, 11%; 5%, 5%; 33.3%, 50%; 0%, 0%; 10%, 11%; 2%, 2%; 50%, 100%. Ask: If each line represents a business, which line would you say is doing the best? Why? (Responses may vary; some may choose the business with the most assets [1,000]; others the business with no debt and 0% ratios [line 7 or 2]).

- **Liquidity Ratios.** Transition by explaining that, in addition to assessing how much debt a company has, two other ratios can be useful to determine how well a company is doing. Use transparency T35-4 to define *liquidity* and show the two liquidity ratios: quick and current. Explain what they tell an entrepreneur: the quick ratio tells you if you have enough cash on hand to pay your current bills (you want it to be over 1); the current ratio tells you if you have enough assets that can be converted to cash to pay your current bills (you want it to be over 1 as well.). Use the "same size" balance sheet in the textbook to show how an entrepreneur can assess both the state of his/her business at a point in time and change over time: is a company in better or worse shape now than it was last year? Use one or more of the other balance sheet examples in the textbook to calculate asset value, net worth, and all four ratios for the years given, then determine whether the business has improved its financial standing in the last year.

- **Creating a Balance Sheet.** Use transparency T35-2 up as a model. Have students use the records from their NFTE businesses, or ongoing transactions from their NFTE Journal (see Chapter 12), or transactions you or they devise, to create a balance sheet.

- **Summary.** Have students compare the formats, information provided, and respective purposes of the balance sheet and income statement. Show transparencies T12-5 from Chapter 12 and T35-2. Ask: Why are both needed? What might happen if an entrepreneur calculated only income statements? What might happen if only balance sheets were used?

## ASSESS THE LEARNING

- **Vocabulary.** Have students define terms in their own words and use each in a sentence. Assign the Vocabulary activity in the workbook.

- **Key Concepts.** Questions 1-2. Note that students cannot answer these questions without first completing Critical Thinking questions 4 and 5. Answers: 1. Assets = Liabilities + Owner's Equity: 300 = 100 + 200. 2. $200.

- **Critical Thinking.** Questions 1-2, 4-5. Answers: 1. a. Beginning is 69% (9,000/13,000); end is 29% (5,000/17,000); yes it has improved by 40%. b. Not necessarily, because it still has enough cash to pay off its current liabilities and part of the cash may have been used to pay down liabilities, which is a good thing. c. Yes, at the start of 2007 it had $10,000 in cash and $4,000 in current liabilities. d. $22,270 (17,000 × 1.31). e. It seemed to have paid cash as liabilities did not go up. 2. Quick ratio = 1.33 or 133% ((1,000 + 1,000)/1,500); current ratio = 2 or 200% (3,000/1,500); debt ratio = .3 or 30% (3,000/10,000); debt-to-equity ratio = .43 or 43% (3,000/7,000). 4.

### Balance Sheet (Date)

| Assets | | Liabilities | |
|---|---|---|---|
| Cash | 75 | Loans | 100 |
| Equipment | 200 | Owner's Equity | 200 |
| Inventory | 25 | | |
| Other | 0 | | |
| Total Assets | 300 | Total Liabilities +OE | 300 |

5.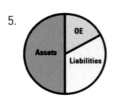

- **Writing Practice.** Critical Thinking question 3. Answers: 3. Answers may vary, but should address the following. Note that ratios given are for the end of August. Her assets have gone up, and her debt financing has gone down (she paid off short-term loans and paid down long-term liabilities) as well as a relatively low amount of debt financing (debt ratio = 18.2%; debt-to-equity ratio = 22.2%), all of which make her a more appealing investment opportunity. However, her cash has gone down and her inventory has increased, which may not be good. If she has higher inventory because of a big order in September, it may be okay, but if she is selling her inventory more slowly, that is not good (she needs to check the income statement). Her liquidity is okay (quick ratio = 1.3; current ratio = 2.7), as she has $2,000 in easily convertible current assets and only $1,000 in accounts payable due within the year.

- **Additional Workbook Activities Answers.**

**Vocabulary Activity.** Answers: ACROSS: 4. depreciation. 11. current liabilities. 12. current assets. 13. assets. 14. liquidity. 15. same size analysis; DOWN: 1. marketable securities. 2 quick ratio. 3 debt-to-equity ratio. 5. owner's equity. 6. fiscal year. 7. balance sheet. 8. current ratio. 9. liabilities. 10. debt ratio.

**Quiz 35** in the workbook. Answers: 1. c. 2. Assets (e.g., cash, marketable securities, inventory, accounts receivable). 3. Because its assets must balance with its liabilities + owner's equity. 4. Its total assets. 5. Current; current; long-term; long-term. 6. See below. 7. .43 or 43%. 8. $700. 9. $300. 10. .75 or 75%.

### Balance Sheet (Date)

| Assets | | Liabilities | |
|---|---|---|---|
| Cash | 500 | Loans | 300 |
| Inventory | 200 | Owner's Equity | 400 |
| Other | 0 | | |
| Total Assets | 700 | Total Liabilities +OE | 700 |

**Exploration and Internet Activity.** Assign these workbook activities to give students additional practice with research and preparing balance sheets. Answers will vary.

## EXTEND THE LEARNING

- **Business Plan Practice.** Key Concepts questions 3-4. **Answers:** 3. 33% (100/300). 4. 50% (100/200).

- **BizTech.** Assign Unit 25.

- **Internet Activity.** Search online for the balance sheets of three publicly traded companies, which are often found in annual reports on company web sites, usually in "investor relations" links. Or students may write to companies to have copies of annual reports sent to them by mail. Use ratio equations to analyze their balance sheets. How are they doing financially relative to each other?

- **Ratio Scramble.** This activity allows students to gain practice in calculating the different types of balance-sheet ratios. Divide the class into teams of four students each. Each student should have a pencil. In the center of each team, put four folded sheets of paper: one each for debt ratio, debt-to-equity ratio, quick ratio, and current ratio. Instruct students to write their answers neatly on these sheets. Write a basic balance sheet format on the board, or use transparency T35-2 and a felt-tip pen. On the board/transparency, write figures into the balance sheet categories then say: "Go!" Students must (politely) grab for one of the sheets, calculate the appropriate ratio using the information you provided, and raise their hands when done. The team that completes all calculations accurately in the shortest time wins a point. Sheets are refolded, placed in the center again and "scrambled." Continue with different balance sheet figures as long as time and interest permit.

## BUILD ACADEMIC AND LIFE-SKILL PROFICIENCIES

### *Skills Mean Success* Answers

**Technology.** Findings, answers, and definitions will vary. Encourage the students to explore the Web sites, definitions, and features and to provide "proof of research" with URLs of sites visited and written definitions and features lists. Many sites invite questions from visitors and can be used to resolve any differences in definitions the students discover.

**Math.** 1. a. +20%. b. +20%. c. +33%. d. N/C. e. +23.1%. 2. a. 1:3; was 2:5. b. 4:5; was 9:13. 3. Thinking "proportionately" is a key business and mathematical skill. Remind the students that ratios, like percentages, show a relationship between two or more numbers or quantities for the purpose of comparing them. Ratios are not numbers. (Batting averages might be helpful analogies. A batting average of .400 describes the relationship between times at bat and hits or that the batter gets hits at a rate of 4 every 10 at bats, or 40% of the time, or 4 out of 10 tries, or four-tenths of the attempts, or 4:10 or 2:5.) Ratios can be converted to percentages, to decimals, to common fractions. Ratio of liabilities to assets in 2005 was 4:13 or 30.7%, but in 2006 it improved to 1:5 or 20% (i.e. liabilities were a lower percentage of assets) The liabilities to assets ratio has improved so, based on that measure, investors would find it more appealing in 2006.

**English.** Explain how multiple-choice questions on a test usually contain four possibilities: the correct answer, an answer that makes sense and is close to the answer but is incorrect, a clearly wrong answer, and a silly answer. True-false items have less latitude, but can be close enough to correct to make the question more challenging. The key for both types is reading (or writing) the items carefully.

### CHAPTER 36

# VENTURE CAPITAL

## ORGANIZE THE LEARNING

### CHAPTER OBJECTIVES

- Explain how and why venture capitalists invest in a business.
- Describe the differences between venture capitalists and bankers.
- Explain how venture capitalists "harvest" their investments.
- Determine a company's total value.
- List the elements of a business plan.

### NFTE RESOURCES

- Text pp. 426-431
- Transparency T36-1
- Workbook/BLMs Chapter 36
- Entrepreneurs in Profile #6, #14
- Test Bank Chapter 36
- A Business for the Young Entrepreneur: *Used CDs*

### BUSINESS PLAN ACTIVITIES

*Workbook Business Plan Review*
Venture Capital 36-1

*Workbook/Textbook Chapter Review*
Critical Thinking 5

### SKILLS MEAN SUCCESS

*Math*
Numeration and Operations: Calculating Percentage Change

*English*
Writing for Information: Tips for Effective Editing

### PREREQUISITES

Chapters 14 and 31 inform this chapter's contents.

### VOCABULARY

majority interest, venture capitalist

## KEY QUESTION

**If I can't borrow money from banks or friends, how else might I finance my business?**

## PREPARE FOR LEARNING

- **Business Plans in Progress.** If you plan to do the Role Play activity in Develop and Close the Learning, advise the students to bring their Basic and Intermediate business plans to class.

## SET A CONTEXT FOR LEARNING

- **Focus: Giving Up the Driver's Seat.** Challenge the students to ponder this problem: You really want a car. Your parents are willing to pay 60% of the price of a used car if you pay 40%, but they will have final say in when, where, and how you can drive, can revoke your driving privileges at any time, or could even sell the car without your consent. Would you take the deal? Why or why not?

- **Discussion Launcher: Not Getting Discouraged.** Have students discuss in small groups and report back to the class: Often entrepreneurs must find people who will finance their dreams and buy their products. Many people will say no. What are some ways that entrepreneurs can keep optimism high and not get discouraged?

## DEVELOP AND CLOSE THE LEARNING

- **Review of Capital Forms and Defining Venture Capital.** Building on their prior knowledge, ask students: What are the similarities and differences between raising money through bank loans, bonds, stocks, and venture capital? (Bank loans and bonds both earn interest and are considered *debt*; bonds and stocks are both traded on an open market; stocks and venture capital are both equity financing; venture capital and bank loans usually stem from one-on-one relationships; venture capitalists are willing to assume more risk than banks, etc.) Ask: Why is venture capital riskier for an entrepreneur than issuing stock or taking on debt? (Because the entrepreneur can lose control of the company and venture capitalists put pressure on companies to grow quickly.) Ask: Then why do entrepreneurs consider venture capital? (e.g., they have nowhere else to go, all other financing options have turned them down, they couldn't raise enough by other means, they think their businesses have the potential to satisfy venture a capitalist's expectations, etc.) Use transparency T36-1 to explain how venture capitalists work and how they use their investments to make money.

- **How a Venture Capitalist Evaluates Businesses.** Explain that venture capitalists judge opportunities through reading a business plan and, secondarily, the entrepreneur's ability to carry out that plan. Use the textbook to discuss the elements of a business plan that venture capitalists would be most interested in. Review from Chapter 14 how a business might be valued at three times its net profit. Another way a company might be valued is by how much money a venture capitalist is willing to pay for a certain percentage of equity:

Total Market Value = Amount of Venture Capital Received/Percentage of Company Sold

Use the Henry Ford example in the text or the other examples below to illustrate this formula:

What is the value of the company if someone will pay:

- ○ $35,000 for 50% equity?
- ○ $100,000 for 1/3 equity?
- ○ $2,500 for 25% equity?
- ○ $250,000 for 80% equity?

**Answers:** $70,000; $300,000; $10,000; $312,500.

- **Role Play.** Instruct students in advance to bring their completed NFTE Business Plans (Basic and Intermediate) to class to use in this activity, or provide a mock business plan. Pair students. One student will play the role of the entrepreneur seeking financing for his/her NFTE Business Plan business. The other will play the role of the venture capitalist seeking a good investment opportunity. Bring all the entrepreneurs together and the venture capitalists together in two groups and have them prepare for their roles. The venture capitalists should make a list of questions to ask about the businesses; the entrepreneurs should create a 1-2 minute presentation that makes their businesses appealing, and try to anticipate questions and have answers ready. Allow the entrepreneurs and the venture capitalists to talk among themselves and help each other prepare. Students will then return to their capitalist/entrepreneur pairs to negotiate financing opportunities. Allow a minute or so after discussion stops for the venture capitalists to decide which businesses they will invest in, sharing their decisions and rationales. As a class, discuss additional questions that could have been asked and answers that could have been given.

- **Summary.** Give students a few minutes to jot down notes (from this chapter and from the role-play activ-

ity in particular) regarding how they might improve their business plans to better seek financing. As a follow-up, have them write their ideas in a memo.

## ASSESS THE LEARNING

- **Vocabulary.** Have students define terms in their own words, and use each in a sentence. Assign the Vocabulary activity in the workbook.

- **Key Concepts.** Questions 1-5. **Answers:** 1. Venture capitalists want equity, often a majority interest, and a high ROI. 2. A well-thought-through business plan that shows the business expects to generate sales of at least $25 million over the next five years. 3. Holding more than 50% of the equity in a company and thus having final say in management decisions; answers regarding willingness will vary. 4. Answers will vary depending on the business chosen; answers for the Workbook table are: $30,000; $1,515; $2 million. 5. a. ROI = (800,000 − 250,000)/250,000 = 220%. b. 40% per year or six times the initial investment after five years. c. The ROI is high, but the return is not six times the initial investment.

- **Critical Thinking.** Questions 1-4. **Answers:** 1. Venture capitalists want growth in equity, whereas bankers want interest earned on loans; venture capitalists are willing to accept high risk, whereas bankers keep risks as low as possible. 2. $30 million (six times the initial investment over five years). 3. The shares can be sold to another investor, or converted into stock after the company goes public then sold on the open market. 4. Answers will vary.

- **Writing Practice.** Have students write a memo to a venture capitalist to interest him/her in investing in their business.

- **Additional Workbook Activities Answers.**

**Vocabulary Activity.** **Answers:** Some investors, called *venture capitalists*, focus on financing new small business ventures that have the potential to earn a great deal of money. They want equity — a piece of the company — in return for their capital. They are willing to take the risk that the venture might fail in order to earn very high returns if it succeeds. *Venture capitalists* will sometimes seek a *majority interest* in a business in order to have the final word in management decisions.

**Quiz 36** in the workbook. **Answers:** 1. 40%. 2. 5 million/.25 = $20 million. 3. c. 4. $4 million. 5. By selling equity to another investor or selling shares of stock after the company goes public. 6. (600 × 100) − 10,000

= $50,000. 7. (60,000-10,000)/10,000 = 500%. 8. 80,000/160,000 = 50%. 9. Any of the following: business idea, long- and short-term goals, market research, competitive advantage, marketing plan, philanthropic plan, start-up and operating costs, management, legal structure, time management, financing plan, break-even analysis, accounting system, projected monthly and annual income statements, financial ratio analysis, balance sheet. 10. Answers will vary but should discuss the tradeoff between giving up control and equity in order to grow the business.

## EXTEND THE LEARNING

- **Business Plan Practice.** Assign Critical Thinking question 5.

- **Entrepreneurs in Profile.** Have students review the chapters on Henry Ford and Anita Roddick and be prepared to discuss the In Your Opinion questions in the text.

- **A Business for the Young Entrepreneur.** Have students read about the Used CD business in the textbook. Assign Critical Thinking question 6.

- **Internet Activity.** Let students use a search engine to find out which local venture capitalists and/or angels might be interested in their businesses. Students whose businesses are similar might work together in groups. Have them create posters describing the most promising venture capitalist/angel they found and why that investor might be best for them.

- **Guest Speaker.** Invite a local venture capitalist to discuss with the class what s/he looks for in a company and in a good business plan — what the criteria are for investing in a young entrepreneur's business. Have students prepare questions before the speaker arrives.

- **Business Plan Integrative Summary.** Chapter 36 concludes Unit 7, which emphasizes business financing. Have the students compose and present a brief summary of the financing aspects of their Business Plans to date, including:

  ○ sources of equity financing they are considering and what percentage of company ownership they would be willing to give up.

  ○ sources of debt financing they are considering and what interest rate they would be willing to pay.

  ○ additional sources of financing, such as angels, venture capitalists, business plan competitions, etc., and how they plan, if need be, to reward these investors.

  ○ a preliminary or pro-forma (anticipated) balance sheet.

## BUILD ACADEMIC AND LIFE-SKILL PROFICIENCIES

### Skills Mean Success Answers

**Math.** 1. a. The equity went from $7,500 to **$16,000**. b. If a value doubles, it is a **100%** increase. c. So, if the worth had gone from $7,500 to **$15,000**, the percentage increase would be 100%. d. Therefore, you could reasonably guess that an increase from $7,500 to $16,000 will be close to **110%**.

2. $\dfrac{16,000 - 7,500}{7,500} \times 100 =$ an increase of **113.33%**

For additional practice with this concept, ask students to determine the percentage *decrease* if the original equity had been $16,000 and the new equity had been $7,500.

$\dfrac{7,500 - 16,000}{16,000} \times 100 =$ a decrease of **53.13%**

If the change in quantity is a *negative* number, then the result will be a percentage *decrease*.

**English.** 1. If students are writing at the computer, encourage them to print out their business plans and edit the printouts. (It is easier to overlook errors when you edit on-screen.) Encourage students to swap business plans with a partner and edit each other's work. 2. Most writers tend to repeat certain types of errors. Being aware of your writing weaknesses, and going back to check for them, is an important part of good editing. 3. A poorly written business plan that has mistakes of any kind can send the message that you are careless and do not pay attention to details. If your business plan contains errors, a potential investor might believe that you would not be a qualified businessperson, and you could lose a valuable opportunity.

### CHAPTER 37

# CONTRACTS:
## *The Building Blocks of Business*

## ORGANIZE THE LEARNING

### CHAPTER OBJECTIVES

- Understand the importance of written agreements in running a business.
- Use contracts effectively to strengthen your business.
- Understand "The Four A's" of a successful contract.
- Understand the remedies available in case of breach of contract.

### NFTE RESOURCES

- Text pp. 432-441
- Transparency T37-1
- Workbook/BLMs Chapter 37
- Test Bank Chapter 37

### BUSINESS PLAN ACTIVITIES

*Workbook Business Plan Review*
Contracts 37-1, 37-2, 37-3

*Workbook/Textbook Chapter Review*
Critical Thinking 1, 2, 3, 4, 5;
Key Concepts 4

### SKILLS MEAN SUCCESS

*Math*
Estimation: Rounding Numbers

*English*
Writing for Information: Clarifying Information through Details

Writing for Information: Business Letters

### PREREQUISITES

Preview Chapter 37 in the textbook.

### VOCABULARY

arbitration, breach of contract, contingency, contract, draft, lawsuit, letter of agreement, signatory, small claims court, statute of limitations

## KEY QUESTION

**How can I protect my interests when working with others?**

## PREPARE FOR LEARNING

- **Guest Speaker.** If you plan to invite a local lawyer, paralegal, or Business Law teacher to discuss contract law as an Extend the Learning activity, make arrangements well in advance.

## SET A CONTEXT FOR LEARNING

- **Focus 1: Keeping Promises.** Challenge the students to list as many strategies as they can think of that:
  - help them keep promises they have made to other people.
  - help ensure that others keep promises made to the students.
- **Focus 2: Contractual Relationships.** Take a poll. How many students have ever entered into *contractual* (formal, legal, written) relationships? Such relationships might include: opened a bank account, signed up for Internet service, bought something on

layaway, rented a car or bicycle, flown on a plane and checked luggage? What other everyday activities do students take part in that involve contractual relationships?

- **Discussion Launcher: Agreements.** Have students discuss in pairs. Kevin agrees over the phone to buy a lawnmower from Andy and take over his lawn-cutting business. Kevin will pay Andy 10% of the money he earns from the business. What could go wrong with this agreement?

## DEVELOP AND CLOSE THE LEARNING

- **Memory Test.** Instruct students to put their pens/pencils down and not take notes. Relate the following story: Alicia and Maria decide to go into business together. Maria can sew and Alicia can paint. They want to make custom-designed T-shirts and scarves. Maria has $500 in savings and Alicia has $300 but is willing to borrow another $200 from her parents. Maria can start sewing T-shirts immediately. Alicia has to finish a school project, so she can't start painting on the T-shirts until the following month. Maria agrees to go ahead and buy materials and start sewing as long as Alicia will set up the business checking account and secure her loan. Then, in the second month, Maria agrees to try to find a sales outlet for the T-shirts while Alicia paints. The girls agree to split the profits equally after Alicia's parents are paid back. Ask students to summarize the story using as many details as possible. Tell students you will revisit this scenario later.

- **Why Contracts Are Needed.** Define what a contract is. Contracts legally protect the interests and rights of everyone involved through a formal agreement. Refer to Focus 2 on the previous page and find out through a show of hands how many students have done which of the activities that were listed. Explain that even though most companies will not enter into contracts with individuals under 18, people enter into implied contracts all the time. For example, with every plane ticket, there is an explanation of the contractual limits and obligations airlines have for taking care of passenger luggage up to a certain value, or to put up passengers overnight in a hotel if a late night flight is cancelled. Discuss the need for formal, written agreements — contracts — when an entrepreneur involves others in his/her business.

- **Memory Test Revisited.** Recall the case of Maria and Alicia. Ask: What did Maria agree to? What did Alicia agree to? Most likely, some students will get some of the details wrong. Determine with the class that people's memories are limited. Establish that "not writing things down" can lead to misunderstanding, the omission of details, and disagreements.

- **Elements of Successful Contracts.** Use the text and transparency T37-1 to discuss the Four A's of a successful contract. Pair students in same gender pairs to role play Maria and Alicia from the Memory Test activity, or Kevin and Andy from the Discussion Launcher activity. Have them negotiate and write up a simple contract that satisfies the Four A's. Then have two sets of pairs review each other's contracts and make suggestions for improvement (using the two questions given in the textbook). Have a few volunteers read their contracts aloud. Ask pairs to look at their contracts again and make a list of ways it could be breached by either party. **LINKS** »*Law*

- **Summary.** Remind students that written contracts do not replace trust or trustworthiness. They should always keep their word even without a contract, because trustworthiness will make them a better friend and a more respected businessperson. But contracts will help ensure that promises made are kept.

## ASSESS THE LEARNING

- **Vocabulary.** Have students make up "word scramble" puzzles based on the chapter's vocabulary, and trade with partners to solve. For example, "arbitration" becomes "inoabtarrti."

- **Key Concepts.** Questions 1-3. **Answers:** 1. Read it carefully and make sure you understand and agree with all the points; have a lawyer look it over to make sure it covers all your rights and interests. 2. Renegotiate the contract if parties are on friendly terms; small claims court if the amount in dispute is less than $2,500; arbitration. 3. It means you have read, understood, and agreed to the contents of the contract.

- **Critical Thinking.** Question 5. **Answers:** 5. Answers will vary but look for details that could serve as the basis of a more formal contract.

- **Writing Practice.** Assign students to write a letter of agreement for providing entrepreneurial tutoring lessons to fellow students. Remind them that the agreement should clearly specify what the tutor and the student should do and not do, any limitations, and contingencies. The business letter shown in Skills Mean Success could be used as a model.

- **Additional Workbook Activities Answers.**

  **Vocabulary Activity. Answers:** 1. g. 2. c. 3. i. 4. b. 5. a. 6. j. 7. h. 8. e. 9. d. 10. f.

  **Quiz 37** in the workbook. **Answers:** 1. Answers will vary but should address how parties may not remember details or may disagree about what was said in the past. 2. No; the law holds parties to an agreement if they signed it, even if they didn't understand what it meant. 3. Have a lawyer review it and explain it to you. 4. No; contracts should provide as much detail as possible, including descriptions of color, size, etc. 5. Answers will vary but should include such specifics as when, how much, penalties for late payment, etc. 6. Including phrasing in the contract that addresses "acts of God" or natural disasters or "circumstances beyond our control." 7. c. 8. Breach of contract (b), signatories (c), statute of limitations (a). 9. Students should disagree because 1) a contract does not substitute for trust, and 2) you shouldn't sign a contract you don't agree with, regardless of whether you have a good attorney. 10. For breach-of-contract lawsuits where relatively small sums of money (such as less than $2,500) are involved.

## EXTEND THE LEARNING

- **Business Plan Practice.** Assign Critical Thinking questions 1-5 and/or Key Concepts question 4. For Critical Thinking question 5, remind students that they should be more specific in their answers than just "partnership agreement." Rather, they should tailor their ideas to their specific businesses (e.g., "partnership agreement with Maria to provide $500 start-up capital, sew 20 T-shirts a month, handle the sales to retail outlets, and receive 50% of the profit after loans are repaid").

- **Contract Scavenger Hunt.** Have students look for examples of contracts or contractual terms in their lives.

- **Community Activity.** Assign Key Concepts question 5 to help students better understand small claims court. **LINKS**»*Government*

- **Internet Activity.** Instruct students to use an Internet search engine to find breach-of-contract lawsuit cases. Have them find and bring to class one lawsuit to share, then have the class list the types of breaches that can lead to a lawsuit, discuss how a person/company can protect itself from lawsuits through better contracts, and examine the effects of lawsuits on the people/companies (tarnished reputation, payouts, changes in procedure or products, effect on stock prices, etc.).

- ***Entrepreneurs in Profile.*** Have students pick a chapter in *Entrepreneurs in Profile* and compile lists of potential contracts the entrepreneur has already signed or might enter into. This assignment may require students to research the industry online to better understand how it works. (For example, Bill Gates might have employment and non-compete contracts with his software designers, contracts with his big customers regarding how many copies of Windows they will purchase, contracts with hardware manufacturers regarding installing Windows on their machines. Berry Gordy would have contracts with his musical artists and recording studios, etc.)

- **Guest Speaker.** Invite a local lawyer, paralegal, or Business Law teacher to discuss contract law with your class. Have students prepare questions before the speaker arrives.

## BUILD ACADEMIC AND LIFE-SKILL PROFICIENCIES

### *Skills Mean Success* Answers

| Math. | Time Billed | Total Fee |
|---|---|---|
| 1.a. | .7 hr. | $70 |
| b. | .75 hr. | $75 |
| 2.a. | .3 hr. | $60 |
| b. | .25 hr. | $50 |
| 3.a. | .5 hr. | $150 |
| b. | .5 hr. | $150 |
| 4.a. | .6 hr. | $240 |
| b. | .75 hr. | $300 |
| 5.a. | 1.8 hrs. | $180 |
| b. | 1.75 hrs. | $175 |

Note that different billing methods can result in different fees. Over time, these differences can add up. It is important to compare the billing rates of different lawyers and to ask them to estimate the amount of time it will to take to handle your legal issues.

**English (Clarifying).** Answers will vary. The sentences are intentionally vague, and students may need to create a context for them. Encourage them to be creative and to invent facts, events, quotes, and examples as necessary. Accept any details that are specific, relevant, creative, and written without errors. As an example, #1 could be rewritten as "According to the manufacturer, Part 37-X for the bicycle was three inches too short for the height of the handlebars."

If necessary, initiate a discussion about the proper level of detail. The goal is to supply sufficient and meaningful details that clarify the sentences. Including *too many* details can make a piece of writing cluttered and incoherent.

**English (Business Letter).** 1. b; 2. d; 3. f; 4. c; 5. a; 6. e. If necessary, review the parts of a business letter. The sample letter of agreement can also be used as a model for the end-of-chapter activities in which students write their own letters of agreement.

### CHAPTER 38

# SOCIALLY RESPONSIBLE BUSINESS AND PHILANTHROPY

## ORGANIZE THE LEARNING

### CHAPTER OBJECTIVES

- Develop a socially responsible business.
- Determine how to use your business to help people in the community.
- Develop cause-related marketing for your business that will support your competitive advantage.

### NFTE RESOURCES

- Text pp. 442-449
- Transparency T38-1
- Workbook/BLMs Chapter 38
- Test Bank Chapter 38
- A Business for the Young Entrepreneur: *Sporting Goods Store*

### BUSINESS PLAN ACTIVITIES

*Workbook Business Plan Review* Socially Responsible Business 38-1, 38-2

*Workbook/Textbook Chapter Review* Key Concepts 4, 5

### SKILLS MEAN SUCCESS

*Math*
Operations: Percentages of Purchases

*Leadership*
Networking: Finding a Mentor

### PREREQUISITES

Chapters 8, 17 and 32 will provide helpful background for this chapter.

### VOCABULARY

cause-related marketing, goodwill, socially responsible business

*Other terms to know:*
foundation, mentor, volunteerism

## KEY QUESTION

**How can my business help the world be a better place?**

## PREPARE FOR LEARNING

- **Newspapers and Magazines.** Gather copies of newspapers and magazines for the Cause-Related Marketing activity in Develop and Close the Learning.
- **Field Trip Arrangements.** If you choose the Field Trip activity in Extend the Learning below, contact a local nonprofit organization to tour. As an alternative, have a nonprofit's community relations officer visit the class as a guest speaker.
- **Guest Speaker.** If you plan to invite a nonprofit/social entrepreneur to discuss contract law with your class as an Extend the Learning activity, make arrangements well in advance.

## SET A CONTEXT FOR LEARNING

- **Focus 1: Good Corporate Citizens.** Let students brainstorm: Think of as many examples of companies that have contributed to charitable causes or supported socially responsible and positive efforts in your community. (Ronald McDonald House, local small businesses who sponsor a fun run to raise money for a children's hospital, local companies that donate money to advertise in the school yearbook or sports program, companies that support Big Brothers/Big Sisters, etc.)

- **Focus 2: Social Issues.** Ask the students to work in pairs or small groups to discuss three social problems, issues, or concerns that they think are important to address. How might a business support efforts to alleviate these problems?
**LINKS**»*Citizenship*

- **Focus 3: Personal Values.** Pose this problem: If your business made a net profit of $10,000 this year, how much would you consider giving to a good cause, and to *which* of these causes would you give, and why? Community garden, local art club, cancer research lab, environmental protection group, animal rights group, after-school tutoring group, political action committee, religious organization.

- **Discussion Launcher 1: Mead Quote.** Discuss the Margaret Mead epigraph for the chapter.

- **Discussion Launcher 2: Goodwill.** Discuss in pairs or small groups: How does goodwill help a company? How might it be reflected in a company's income statement or balance sheet? (Goodwill is not usually shown directly as a line item, although a strong reputation can be considered an asset in assigning a value to a company; and it *can* increase sales.)

## DEVELOP AND CLOSE THE LEARNING

- **The Body Shop.** Using information from the textbook, from *Entrepreneurs in Profile*, Chapter 14, or the company Web site, tell the story of Anita Roddick and The Body Shop's socially responsible business practices. Ask: In what ways did Roddick build "giving back to the community" into her business operations? (Using products created by local communities, not using products tested on animals, recycling, giving money to environmental causes, allowing causes to use her stores to promote a message, starting a foundation, helping indigenous communities.) Ask: What did The Body Shop gain from these activities? What did these activities cost The Body Shop (financially, in time, etc.)? Was it worth it? Why or why not?

- **Types of Community Involvement.** Ask students to give examples, perhaps from the Focus 1 activity on the previous page, of socially responsible acts by businesses. List the student's ideas on the board and ask them to look for patterns and group them (by type of *issue* such as education or health; type of *donation*, such as money or donated services; by type of *activity*, like cause-related marketing or starting a foundation). Have students summarize by brainstorming general ways an entrepreneur might be socially responsible (give money, give employees time, let a charity use the company's name or reputation, donate product, donate services, donate use of facilities). Use transparency T38-1 and the textbook to summarize the main ways a business can get involved. Ask students to share, from Focus 2 above, the social issues they'd like to see businesses address. Ask: What could your NFTE businesses contribute to a cause or nonprofit organization?

- **Cause-Related Marketing.** Divide the class into groups and distribute newspapers and magazines. Ask students to find examples and "dog-ear" pages that show advertisements that include a cause-related marketing element (i.e., seem to support a social, environmental, political, or cultural cause

outside the company itself or its products). For each example, have students speculate why they think the company chose the particular cause to support.

- **Cause-Related Ad.** In small groups, have students choose a social issue mentioned in Focus 2 and a local, neighborhood small business. Instruct groups to create a one-minute commercial from the small business that addresses the social issue or that supports a nonprofit organization that addresses the social issue. Have groups perform their commercials. **LINKS**»*Dramatic Arts*

- **Social Entrepreneurs.** Assemble examples of entrepreneurs that have set up organizations to address social problems from the textbook (Teach for America, UPromise), or from a local newspaper or the Internet (under "social entrepreneurship"), etc. Have groups create posters of social entrepreneurs they researched, which could then be displayed around the classroom or in the hallway to educate and inspire others about the good work entrepreneurs do. **LINKS**»*Graphic Arts*

- **Philanthropy.** Explain that entrepreneurs have been providing financial support to good causes and social organizations for a long time. The Carnegie Foundation, for example, was set up by Andrew Carnegie in 1901, with the profits from selling his steel company. The Ford Foundation and the Rockefeller Foundation, two other premier philanthropic organizations, were established from fortunes made in the automotive and oil industries, respectively. The Bill & Melinda Gates Foundation is an example of a more recent major charitable organization. Divide students into groups and have each research one foundation named in the text to find out how much money it gives away each year and what causes it supports.

- **Summary.** Ask students: What are the benefits to the entrepreneur and the benefits to society of socially responsible business? (e.g., for entrepreneur: goodwill, good reputation, his/her own life or well-being improved; for society: a stronger community, hope, improved well-being for everyone.)

## ASSESS THE LEARNING

- **Vocabulary.** Have students define terms in their own words and use each term in a sentence or complete the Vocabulary activity in the workbook.

- **Key Concepts.** Assign questions 1-3. **Answers:** 1. Philanthropy involves giving money to charities or foundations; socially responsible business involves running your business consistent with your ethics and values. 2. Answers will vary but should take a critical, analytical stance toward the company and ad. 3. Answers will vary.

- **Critical Thinking.** Questions 1-2, 4-6. **Answers:** 1, 2, 4, 5. Answers will vary. 6. Answers will vary but should include differences in financial versus non-financial incentives in starting an enterprise: both for-profit and social entrepreneurs usually focus on helping others and meeting customer needs, but for-profit entrepreneurs can make a profit, issue stock, etc., whereas social entrepreneurs are usually funded through donations and tend to make less money. 7. (Workbook only) Answers will vary.

- **Writing Practice.** Assign Critical Thinking question 3 and/or Exploration question 2.

- **Additional Workbook Activities Answers.**

  **Vocabulary Activity. Answers:** Answers will vary. Paragraphs should use complete sentences and demonstrate an understanding of the terminology and concepts related to socially responsible business.

  **Quiz 38** in the workbook. **Answers:** 1. Running a business in a way that is consistent with the entrepreneur's core values and ethics. 2. Answers will vary but could include: hanging posters in stores to educate customers about Greenpeace, letter-writing campaigns for political prisoners, raising awareness of Brazilian rainforest destruction by partnering with indigenous tribes to supply products. 3. Marketing that focuses customers' attention on an important issue or problem, not directly on the company or its products, but that positions the company as supporting efforts to alleviate the problem. 4. Answers will vary. 5. An intangible asset composed of positive customer associations with a company that improves a company's reputation and can give it a competitive advantage. 6. A corporation that aims to contribute to the greater good of society and not to make a profit; they do not pay federal or state taxes on their operations because they don't make a profit. 7. The expression of concern for social issues through providing money, time or advice to charities; many businesses have a philanthropic arm or foundation. 8. Answers will vary but could include: discounted or free products or services, host fundraising events, cause-related marketing, advice or mentoring, networking/contacts, volunteer employee time, use of the company name or reputation. 9. Answers will vary but could include: personal satisfaction, living according to one's values, a personal connection to the problem

(e.g., knowing someone with muscular dystrophy), religious values.

## EXTEND THE LEARNING

- **Business Plan Practice.** Assign Key Concepts questions 4-5.

- **Exploration.** Assign Question 1 in the text.

- **A Business for the Young Entrepreneur.** Have students read about Sporting Goods Store: Frank Alameda and East Side Sports in the textbook and answer the question at the end of the vignette.

- **Class Philanthropy Project.** Have students research nonprofit organizations and causes in the school's neighborhood. As a class, choose one to partner with. Have students use the entrepreneurial and business skills learned in the NFTE curriculum to write to the organization and offer their skills or time to support the cause. **LINKS** »·*Community Service*

- **Nonprofit Organization Field Trip.** Arrange a visit to a local nonprofit organization. It would be especially instructive to visit one that was started recently. Have students tour the program to understand how it fulfills its mission. Depending on the type of organization you visit, perhaps students could serve as volunteers, actually working at the organization for a few hours — all of which could be arranged in advance.

- **Guest Speaker.** Invite a social entrepreneur to make a presentation to your class about starting a nonprofit organization: the strengths, challenges, opportunities, etc., involved.

## BUILD ACADEMIC AND LIFE-SKILL PROFICIENCIES
### *Skills Mean Success* Answers

**Math.** 1. $3.54. 2. $4.56. 3. $2.88. 4. $1.65. 5. $28.96.

For more detailed information and membership details, visit www.upromise.com. While these amounts may seem small, note that they could add up if more participating offers were used.

**Leadership.** 1-7. Accept any sincere attempt to identify personal traits and the ideal traits of an appropriate mentor. In 7. b., a successful mentoring relationship requires such skills and attitudes as: open and honest communication (including positive reinforcement and constructive criticism); availability and a willingness to devote time to the relationship; trust and loyalty; a focus on goal setting; an ability to solve problems and think critically about decisions; a level-headed approach to risk taking.

# SMALL BUSINESS AND GOVERNMENT

## ORGANIZE THE LEARNING

### CHAPTER OBJECTIVES

- Understand the economic definition of efficiency.
- Define GDP and GNP.
- Understand how government regulations impact small business.
- Analyze global business opportunities.

### NFTE RESOURCES

- Text pp. 450-457
- Transparency T39-1
- Workbook/BLMs Chapter 39
- Test Bank Chapter 39
- A Business for the Young Entrepreneur: *Mexican Fine Arts , Crafts, and Original Designs, Xochitl Guzman*

### BUSINESS PLAN ACTIVITIES

*Workbook Business Plan Review*
Small Business and Government 39-1

*Workbook/Textbook Chapter Review*
Critical Thinking 5

### SKILLS MEAN SUCCESS

*Technology*
Internet Research Skills: Locating Data Online

*English*
Reading for Information: Vocabulary

### PREREQUISITES

Students should be familiar with the content of Chapters 1, 25, and 32.

### VOCABULARY

Consumer Price Index (CPI), currency, Gross Domestic Product, Gross National Product, recession, tariff, trade balance

*Other terms to know:*
exporting, importing

## KEY QUESTION

**How might government policies and regulations affect my business?**

## PREPARE FOR LEARNING

- ***Wall Street Journal.*** Bring in copies of *The Wall Street Journal* to use during the lesson.

## SET A CONTEXT FOR LEARNING

- **Focus: Imports.** Write on the board or give verbal instructions to have students list as many imported brands of cars as they can think of, and note where they think each company is headquartered. **Answers:** Toyota, Nissan, Honda, Suzuki (Japan); Saab, Volvo (Sweden); Mercedes, Volkswagen, BMW (Germany); Aston Martin, Bentley (Britain); Lamborghini, Ferrari (Italy), etc. Invite students to suggest other examples.

- **Discussion Launcher: Government Regulations.** Discuss as a class examples of how government regulations impact business (emissions controls on automobiles, accounting and reporting requirements,

truth-in-advertising regulations, broadcast-content censorship, mandatory warnings printed on food and medicine containers, etc.). Have students discuss in small groups: Do you think businesses should be regulated more or less than they are today? How? Why?

## DEVELOP AND CLOSE THE LEARNING

- **Government's Role in a Free-Enterprise Economy.** Review from Chapter 1 the meaning of a free-enterprise economy and how the U.S. has such an economic structure. Overview this lesson by explaining that, just because people are free to start or close businesses as markets grow or decline, a free-enterprise economy does not mean the government has no role. Discuss how the government affects business in three important ways: 1) maintaining stability within the national and global economy; 2) regulating business practices to ensure fairness and to protect consumers; 3) collecting taxes and providing services for the common good, such as building roads and highways, which all businesses benefit from (taxes will be discussed in Chapter 44). **LINKS**»*Economics*

- **GNP and GDP.** Use transparency T39-1 to define Gross National Product and Gross Domestic Product. Have students look up (in *The Wall Street Journal*, www.wsj.com, or government sites on the Internet) the GNP and GDP for the past few years. Create a graph on the board of these two statistics and ask students to analyze what it means: Have they been rising or falling? Is the economy in recession or recovery? What recent events might have led to this trend? What do students forecast for next year? Is GDP becoming a higher or lower percentage of the GNP? What will that mean for American companies and their employees?

- **The Global Economy.** Establish that the U.S. economy is part of a larger global economy. Most small business entrepreneurs are not affected by this global economy directly. However, they could feel the influence in three ways: 1) if a competitor from a foreign country enters their market; 2) if they import a foreign-made product into the U.S.; 3) if they export their products/services to a foreign country. Discuss the concepts of trade balance and tariffs. Look up on a government Web site (or have students look up) America's current trade balances with various foreign countries, such as Japan, Germany, England, China, or India. Ask: Are these trade balances good or bad for America? How? What should American business do? Ask: Why do you think governments impose tariffs on imported goods? (To protect domestic producers of the same product.) Split the class into two groups. Have one group take the "pro" arguments (advantages) for tariffs, and the other one take the "con" (disadvantages) position. Students may need time to research ideas before constructing and presenting their arguments. Point out that it depends on whose perspective they take (American workers, American corporations, foreign corporations, foreign workers of American companies, American consumers) on whether a tariff may seem to be a good or a bad thing.

- **Money/Currency.** In groups, have students look up in *The Wall Street Journal* or online the day's value of the US dollar versus the Japanese yen, euro, British pound, Canadian dollar, and other currencies, versus last month's value. Ask: Would one dollar buy more or less today than it would have last month in the country you looked up? If an entrepreneur exported products to that country, would they be more or less expensive there this month? If an entrepreneur from the other country imported his/her products to America, would they be more or less expensive this month? What generalizations can we

draw about the impact of currency fluctuations on business? (If the dollar is stronger compared to a foreign currency, then it will buy *more* in that country than it would if, say, there was a 1:1 correspondence; so prices of American goods in that market would go up and be less attractive to foreign consumers, and the prices of goods from that country would be lower and more attractive to Americans.)

- **Government Regulations.** Recall from Chapter 25 some of the governmental requirements when someone opens a business (permits, licenses). Explain that the government plays a role in business operations as well, primarily to collect taxes to pay for common community services (such as fire, police, garbage collection, printing money, national security, etc.), and ensure fair treatment (safety, environmental regulations). Divide the class into small groups and have each take one category of government regulation: environmental protection, employee age/wage laws, anti-discrimination laws, employee safety laws, product safety laws, fairness-in-advertising laws, contract/tort laws, zoning laws. Each group should use the Internet to look up laws in that category that might affect a young entrepreneur. It might be helpful to determine first whether the laws involved are local, state, or federal. Have each group create a poster summarizing the results of their research. After each group talks about its poster for a few minutes, hang the posters around the room. Note that students need not read the actual law (which would be difficult and time-consuming), but find descriptive summaries.
**LINKS** *Government*

- **Summary.** Ask students to consider: If you were running for president this year, what would you suggest as an economic policy platform to improve the American economy?

## ASSESS THE LEARNING

- **Vocabulary.** Have students complete the Vocabulary activity in the workbook, or define the terms in their own words and use each in a sentence.

- **Key Concepts.** Questions 1-4. **Answers:** 1. Because a stable currency helps consumers and businesses make long-term decisions; it decreases uncertainty and anxiety; and it helps with budgeting. 2. GNP includes all of a country's products and services produced within the country or abroad; GDP includes only products and services produced within the country, not exports. 3. Small businesses are legally obligated to follow government regulations, such as tax laws, occupational and product safety regulations, employment anti-discrimination laws, and contract enforcement. 4. Because cultures vary widely in their business customs and an entrepreneur wants to be sensitive to cultural differences and not insult customers, suppliers, or business partners from a different country.

- **Critical Thinking.** In class, tally students' earnings from jobs or allowances. Assign Questions 1-3. **Answers:** 1-3. Answers will vary depending on the class's characteristics.

- **Additional Workbook Activities Answers.**

    **Vocabulary Activity. Answers:** 1. a. 2. c. 3. b. 4. a. 5. a. 6. b. 7. c.

    **Quiz 39** in the workbook. **Answers:** 1. Because stable currency helps consumers and businesses make long-term decisions; it decreases uncertainty and anxiety, and it helps with budgeting. 2. GNP is the market value of all products and services produced by a country's resources; GDP is part of GNP, but includes only products and services produced within a country and excludes exports or products produced by American companies located abroad. 3. Changes in price caused by currency instability affect the affordability of products, which can affect sales and also purchases of items from other companies. 4. Answers will vary but could include: employee age or safety regulations, product safety regulations, licensing requirements for professional services, anti-discrimination laws, zoning regulations regarding business. 5. A trade balance is the difference between the value of a country's imports and exports. 6. An entrepreneur can import new products from other countries; gain insights about sales, marketing, product ideas; export and open new markets for his/her current products/services. 7. A tax imposed by the government on imports, usually to make them more expensive and protect the domestic producers of the same product.

- **Writing Practice.** Assign Critical Thinking question 4.

## EXTEND THE LEARNING

- **Business Plan Practice.** Assign Critical Thinking question 5.

- **A Business for the Young Entrepreneur.** Have students read about Xochitl Guzman and Mexican Fine Arts, Crafts & Original Designs in the text. Assign Key Concepts question 5.

- **Business Traditions in Other Cultures.** Assign Critical Thinking question 6. Students could also create posters summarizing their findings about how an entrepreneur should act and what s/he should know when doing business in that culture. Instruct students to use the Internet, the *Journal*, or other resources.

- **Guest Speaker.** Invite an importer or exporter to make a presentation to the class about experiences interacting with government entities while entering foreign markets, or while bringing manufactured goods from foreign markets into the United States. Suggest that the speaker bring samples of documents for the class to see and analyze. Have students prepare questions in advance.

## BUILD ACADEMIC AND LIFE-SKILL PROFICIENCIES

### *Skills Mean Success* Answers

**Technology.** If students do not have access to computers, print out the appropriate tables; have them identify the correct GDP and GSP from the charts. Ask them to write out the entire number by adding the appropriate number of zeros.

**English.** 1. importing. 2. exporting. 3. exporting. 4. importing. 5. importing.

Remind students that "importing" involves bringing goods from another country into your country to sell them. "Exporting" involves selling products made in your country to customers abroad.

# 40

# BUILDING GOOD PERSONAL AND BUSINESS CREDIT

## ORGANIZE THE LEARNING

### CHAPTER OBJECTIVES

- Explain the difference between good credit and no credit.
- Establish a personal credit history.
- Define the "Four C's" of business credit.
- Know your rights in dealing with credit-reporting agencies.
- Befriend your banker.

### NFTE RESOURCES

- Text pp. 458-469
- Transparency T40-1
- Workbook/BLMs Chapter 40
- Test Bank Chapter 40
- BizTech Unit 22
- A Business for the Young Entrepreneur: *LAVT, Laima A. Tazmin*

### BUSINESS PLAN ACTIVITIES

*Workbook Business Plan Review*
YBuilding Good Personal and Business Credit  40-1, 40-2

*Workbook/Textbook Chapter Review*
Critical Thinking 1; Key Concepts 3, 4

### SKILLS MEAN SUCCESS

*English*
Writing and Listening: Strategies for Note Taking

*Math*
Operations and Problem Solving: Interest Charges

Measurement and Comparing Data: Graphs

*English*
Reading for Understanding: Finding Details

### PREREQUISITES

Chapters 14 and 31 provide background information for this chapter.

### VOCABULARY

charge account, collateral, credit, finance charge, installment, layaway plan, mortgage

*Other suggested terms to know:*
credit history, principal

## KEY QUESTION

**What is credit and how do I get it?**

## PREPARE FOR LEARNING

- **Make Field Trip Arrangements.** If you did not visit a local bank in Chapter 14, this could be a good time to do so. Contact a neighborhood bank branch and arrange to tour their facilities and talk with a loan officer.

## SET A CONTEXT FOR LEARNING

- **Focus 1: Loan Example.** Let the students work in pairs to discuss, record their comments, and be prepared to share findings with the rest of the class: Joe and Michelle each earn $6,000 a year from part-time jobs. Each has $500 in savings accounts. Each wants to borrow $1,000 to start a business. Michelle has a charge account with a local department store and has made regular, on-time payments for two years. She currently owes $300. Joe has always paid

cash for his purchases. Who is more likely to get a loan? Why? What should each of them do to become a more attractive loan customer to a banker?

- **Focus 2: Collateral.** Elicit suggestions from the class: When you buy a car or a house, the bank that gives you the loan holds on to the *title* (a sheet of paper that shows ownership the house) as "collateral." Why do you think they do this?

- **Discussion Launcher: Trust.** Ask the students to discuss the following in pairs or small groups and report their findings: Think of a current friendship. What was it like when you first met that person? Did you share secrets right away? Did you lend them anything? How long did it take for you to feel comfortable doing these things? Why did you wait that long?

## DEVELOP AND CLOSE THE LEARNING

- **Credit Is a Type of Financing.** Review financing categories from Chapter 14. Determine that credit is a type of debt. Define credit. Refer to the Discussion Launcher above and explain how credit is like establishing a long-term friendship with different types of companies. Discuss the tips given in the chapter for creating a good relationship with a banker.

- **Establishing Credit and Credit History.** Using the textbook and your — and perhaps some of the students' — personal experience, explain how an individual establishes credit, starting with eligibility requirements (at least 18 years of age, having a sustained source of income, etc.), and why establishing credit is important as an individual and as an entrepreneur. Discuss what a credit history is (a record of past performance in managing debt), how it is maintained (by banks and credit agencies), who has access to it (potential lenders), how to check it (online credit history data or check with your bank), and what to do if there are inaccuracies on it (report them to a credit agency).

- **The Four C's of Credit.** Use transparency T40-1 and the textbook to discuss what creditors look for in deciding whether to extend credit. Have students in small groups compare the following entrepreneurs and decide who is the better credit candidate based on the Four C's:

  - Juanita is asking the bank for a loan of $3,000 to buy high-end computer equipment to host personal Web sites for teens. She started the business six months ago with an older, slower computer and $200 of her own money, to create advertisements. She already generates $300 a month profit. She wants the new computer to be able to have more storage space and faster processing. Because she is 16, she does not have a credit history. But she has placed items on layaway and paid them off on time.

  - Antoine is asking the bank for an "unsecured" line of credit of $1,000 to pay for general operating expenses (advertising, insurance, supplies) while he gets his clown-for-hire business up and running. He is investing $1,200 of his own money in the business. Antoine has been involved in theater and juggling for years. His older sister encouraged him to turn this talent into a business. Antoine is 18 and has a credit card co-signed by his sister. He has paid his credit card bill each month for six months.

- **The Pros and Cons of Credit.** Divide the class into two groups.

  - One group discusses and builds an argument about the advantages of using credit.

  - The other group discusses and builds an argument around the disadvantages of using credit.

  Allow time for the two sides to present their arguments, then form and share rebuttals to the other group's points.

- **Summary.** Emphasize that credit is not "free money" and that often people get into financial trouble by overusing credit cards, agreeing to high mortgage rates, and incurring other sources of debt. Credit requires paying back what is borrowed, plus interest. Yet it is worth using credit and establishing a credit history. Ask the class to summarize: What steps can you take or tips do you have to make sure you and your friends use credit wisely?
  **LINKS)**»*Consumer Ed*

## ASSESS THE LEARNING

- **Vocabulary.** Have students define terms in their own words and use each in a sentence. Students who use the workbook can complete the Vocabulary activity.

- **Critical Thinking.** Assign Questions 3-5 (Question 5 requires having a mortgage calculator; many large bank Web sites provide these online). **Answers:** 3. Answers will vary but should reflect the concepts in the text. 4. Cash price is $2,100. Credit cost is $1,100 cash payment plus loan of $1,000 plus finance charge of $150 (15%), making the total credit cost $2,250. 5. $579. $270,000, $1,289; $67,500, $374.

- **Additional Workbook Activities Answers.**

  **Vocabulary Activity. Answers:** 1. e. 2. f. 3. g. 4. b. 5. a. 6. c. 7. d.

  **Quiz 40** in the workbook. **Answers:** 1. Credit history is a record of how you have paid your debts in the past. 2. A good credit record is necessary before a bank will lend money to start a business or for another reason. 3. Opening a department store charge account and paying on time or putting something on layaway. 4. More, as you often pay a finance charge or interest. 5. Request records from a credit rating company. 6. Credit history collection, databasing, and reporting on individuals and businesses. 7. Collateral is something of value used to "secure" a loan, such as a car or house, that the bank or creditor can take if the loan is not repaid. 8. Collateral (second choice); cash flow (fourth choice); commitment (first choice); credit history (third choice). 9. It will be difficult or impossible to obtain credit in the future, limiting what you can buy.

- **Writing Practice.** Assign Key Concepts questions 1-2.

## EXTEND THE LEARNING

- **Business Plan Practice.** Assign Critical Thinking question 1 or Key Concepts questions 3-4.

- **BizTech.** Assign Unit 22.

- **The National Debt.** Have students — especially any who are interested in government and economics — research articles about the national debt online. How large is it now? Has it gone up or down in the last few years? What effect does it have on the national economy? What effect does it have in the world markets? Where does the U.S. government get the money to pay its bills (that is, who is lending us the money)? Relate the national debt to the concepts in the chapter: how it represents using credit on a large scale, and whether the U.S. is considered a good credit risk based on the Four C's. Have students discuss and/or report back and debate whether national-debt financing is a good or bad idea for America, what the U.S. government should do instead, etc. **LINKS** ⟩⟩ *Economics*

- **Complete a Credit Application.** Obtain a credit application from a bank or credit card company. Create a transparency of it and use a felt-tip pen to walk students through completing one, highlighting what types of information are required, where that information comes from, what the terms of the agreement are, etc. Assign Key Concepts questions 1-2. **LINKS** ⟩⟩ *Consumer Ed*

- **Credit Interview Role-Play.** It may be helpful for the students to complete Critical Thinking question 2 before doing this activity. Divide the class into pairs or select pairs to role-play for the class. Have one student play an entrepreneur applying for a line of credit and the other will play the role of the banker. Then students should switch roles. After the role-play, ask students to discuss their experiences: What did or did not go well? What would they improve? Who got the loan based on what factors? **LINKS** ⟩⟩ *Dramatic Arts*

- **Bank Field Trip.** This activity will provide experience about how a loan is acquired. Take a tour of a nearby bank branch to learn how loans or credit cards are granted.

- **Business Plan Integrative Summary.** Since this chapter concludes Unit 8, which emphasizes business relationship-building, it may be a good time for students to compose and present a brief summary of the relational aspects of their Business Plans to date, including:

  ○ with whom and for what reasons they may need to sign contracts.

  ○ how they plan to be a socially responsible business and to contribute to the wider community.

  ○ which government regulations and agencies might affect their businesses.

  ○ a plan for using credit effectively.

## BUILD ACADEMIC AND LIFE-SKILL PROFICIENCIES

### *Skills Mean Success* Answers

**English.** If possible, provide a video presentation about credit, banking, or loans officers; the key objective is to help students master the skill of effective listening and note taking so any type of lecture, lesson, presentation — live or taped — will work. Encourage students to list three questions they would like to ask the presenter.

**Math (Interest Charges).** 1. $41.30. 2. $324.50. 3. $76.70. 4. $19.47. 5. $377.60. Reinforce the concept that purchasing an item on credit costs more than paying cash. If the credit card holder had paid only a minimum balance and left the full balance on the card for a longer period, s/he would be paying even more for these items.

**Math (Graphs).** 1. Students can create charts by hand or use spreadsheet software with graph-making capabilities. There has been a great deal of consolidation in the banking industry over the past several years, with larger banks buying smaller ones. The list of the largest banks would change accordingly. 2. Some banks "failed" (went out of business), some merged, and some were purchased by other banks. Students will need to determine what kind of graph to use.

**English (Reading).** a. For example; Past: she taught herself how to build Web sites at age seven; she built sites for the Girls Club, etc. Current or recent: she created LAVT. Future: she plans to major in computer science and maintain her business. b. Quote from a LAVT customer. c. Wants to make her Web site engage customers senses; wants to help teenagers develop positive attitudes. d. Always been interested in computers; taught herself how to design Web sites at seven.

### CHAPTER 41

# CASH FLOW:
## *The Lifeblood of a Business*

## ORGANIZE THE LEARNING

### CHAPTER OBJECTIVES
- Keep track of your cash on a daily basis.
- Use a monthly cash flow statement.
- Avoid getting caught without enough cash to pay your bills.
- Understand the cyclical nature of cash flow.
- Calculate your burn rate.

### NFTE RESOURCES
- Text pp. 470-479
- Transparencies T41-1 to T41-2
- Workbook/BLMs Chapter 41
- Entrepreneurs in Profile: All
- Test Bank Chapter 41
- BizTech Unit 15

### BUSINESS PLAN ACTIVITIES
*Workbook Business Plan Review*
Cash Flow 41-1, 41-2, 41-3

*Workbook/Textbook Chapter Review*
Key Concepts 3; Critical Thinking 1, 2

*Power Point Templates*
Adv. 19, 24

### SKILLS MEAN SUCCESS

*English*
Writing for Information: Using Cause and Effect

*Leadership*
Recognizing Why Math Is Important: Solving Real-World Problems

*Math*
Mathematical Reasoning: Reading Tables, Identifying Patterns, Problem Solving

### PREREQUISITES
Chapters 9, 12, 13 and 35 inform the content of this chapter.

### VOCABULARY
burn rate, cash flow statement, pilferage, projection, shrinkage

*Other terms to know:*
credit

## KEY QUESTION

**How do I make sure I can pay my bills?**

## PREPARE FOR LEARNING

- **NFTE Journal.** Instruct students when to bring their NFTE Journals to class (which the students started in Chapter 12).

## SET A CONTEXT FOR LEARNING

- **Focus 1: Lunch Budget.** Present this mental math problem: If your parents give you $20 a week to pay for your lunches, how long will it last if you spend $7 a day? $5 a day? $2 a day? How much per day can you spend if you want to make the $20 last for a five-day week? **Answers:** About 3 days, 4 days, 10 days, $4.

- **Focus 2: Staying "Afloat."** Have students answer and discuss: Maya's business sells 500 muffins every week for a total of $500. Eighty percent of her customers pay cash on the spot. But she also has a customer who orders them for sales meetings and whom Maya bills $100 per month. This customer pays by check, about ten days after the bill arrives. If Maya's cost of goods sold and fixed costs equal $350 a month, will she be able to pay her bills? What if one month her costs go up to $450 because of a bad batch of muffins she had to throw away? **Answer:** Yes, if her expenses are $350; no if they are $450.

## DEVELOP AND CLOSE THE LEARNING

- **Financial Statements Review.** Divide the class into four small groups. Assign each group one of the following accounting documents to research in the NFTE textbook: NFTE Journal (Chapter 12), bank account register (Chapters 12, 14), income statement (Chapter 13), balance statement (Chapter 35). Questions each group should address:

  ○ what information does the document provide to the entrepreneur?

  ○ why is this document necessary?

  ○ from what other documents or statements does the entrepreneur get the information s/he needs to compile this document (e.g., the income statement draws from the Journal)?

Allow time for each group to present its findings. Use transparencies from Chapters 12, 13, 35 to show samples of each document as the group is discussing it, and to compare and summarize them. **Answers:** The Journal is used daily and provides a chronological accounting of the details of income and expenses including source/recipient, how much, what for, etc. The bank account register is used every time you make a deposit or write a check (often daily); it provides information about who, when, for what you pay for things by check, or receive income. The income statement is usually done monthly and annually but also sometimes quarterly; it provides a summary of sales and the expenses associated with sales or business operations over a given time period (the information is usually taken from the Journal). The balance sheet is done annually; it provides a snapshot at one point in time of what the business owns (assets), what it owes (liabilities) and how much the owner's stake is worth (equity); this information is usually derived from the Journal. The Journal and check register are necessary to provide transaction details, the income statement to determine how efficiently a business is operating and whether or not it is making a profit, and the balance sheet to determine debt and equity financing balances, and what a company owns and how much it is worth at a given point in time.

- **The Concept of Cash Flow.** Define *cash* as money that is easily accessible, that could be used right away. Cash is kept in a checking or savings account; remind students that entrepreneurs always pay with a check to keep a record, they don't "pay cash" like we do at McDonald's. Convey the following scenario to the class: You do Web site design work for a variety of customers. Let's say it's the middle of the month. Your last month's balance sheet shows you have $1,000 in cash as an asset. Your last month's income statement shows an income of $1,500, but you invoice your customers at the end of each month and don't receive their payments until a month after that. Your monthly expenses run $500 a month. This month, you have a $2,000 payment for the computer equipment you bought when you started your company. Will you have enough cash to pay this bill? As students give their answers, make sure they include their reasoning. Explain the answer by focusing on the *timing* of when cash comes in and goes out. It may be helpful to create a table or other visual on the board:

| | Last month | This month | Next month |
|---|---|---|---|
| Cash on hand | | $1,000 (from balance sheet) | |
| Cash in | Did design work | Invoiced | $1,500 (one month after billed) |
| Monthly expenses | ($500) | ($500) | ($500) |
| Computer | | ($2,000) | |

**Answer:** No, not unless some of your customers pay early or you get more financing (i.e., a loan or another investor). You will actually be short by about $1,500.

As a follow-up question, you might ask: Even if you didn't have the computer payment, how many months could you go with the cash you have on hand this month given your monthly expenses? Use the burn rate equation in the text to calculate: Cash on hand/Cash outflow per month. **Answer:** 2 months (1,000/500).

- **Cash Problems.** Let students brainstorm how a business might run out of cash. (Credit squeeze, cyclicality of business, customers pay late, fixed expenses go up, big bills come due, too much or slow moving inventory.) These expenses are part of the "burn rate." Put the burn-rate formula on the board and go through a few scenario problems:

*Cash on Hand/Negative Cash Outflow per Month*
*Scenarios:*

| Cash on hand | Monthly expenses | **Answer** |
|---|---|---|
| $10,000 | $2,000 | 5 months |
| $12,000 | $3,000 | 4 months |
| $25,000 | $2,500 | 10 months |

Explain how an entrepreneur needs to watch business cash carefully — not just how much s/he has, but also the timing of when it flows into and out of the business. Explain or solicit from the students that timing is important because 1) customers often do not pay immediately when they receive an invoice (often it is 30 days, and some may pay late); 2) there may be seasonality or business cycles where costs and cash payments may not coincide (e.g., a nursery incurs year-round overhead relating to uncut Christmas trees but only takes in cash in late November and December). If the entrepreneur runs out of cash, the business is in trouble and s/he either has to find quick sources of financing (loans, investors) or go bankrupt. Clearly define all terms: inflows/receipts for "cash in," outflows/disbursements for "cash out." Use transparency T41-1 to summarize the concepts of positive and negative net cash flow. It may be helpful to give a few examples: when receipts are $500 and disbursements are $300, $500 and $600, etc.

- **Reading a Cash Flow Statement.** In addition to the income statement and balance sheet, entrepreneurs prepare a cash flow statement monthly and annually to summarize their cash situation. Use transparency T41-2 and the textbook to show the items included in the cash flow statement. Ask students to analyze the statement: How is the business doing? (Fine, it has a positive cash flow.) If its supplier doubled the price for the T-shirts, how would the business be doing? (Not good, as its cost of good sold would be $1,920, and cash flow would be negative; the entrepreneur would need to look for a new supplier or additional financing.) It may also be helpful to use the running example of Hernando's T-shirts: Put on the board the income statement from text Chapter 13 and the cash flow statement from this chapter to compare the numbers and how they are calculated.

- **Creating a Cash Flow Statement.** Use transparency T41-2 as a model. Have students use their records from their NFTE businesses, or transactions from their ongoing NFTE Journal recordkeeping activity (see Chapter 12) — or transactions you devise — to create an income statement and cash flow statement for a specified period of time (monthly, quarterly). Discuss any problems that students encounter. Explain or get them to suggest that sometimes entrepreneurs have to estimate their cash flows in advance to better plan how to pay their bills. Define forecasting and projection as the process of accomplishing this task.

- **Summary.** Note that entrepreneurs can also create forecasts or projections of cash flows for budgeting purposes.

## ASSESS THE LEARNING

- **Vocabulary.** Have students define terms in a word puzzle they create that they then swap with a partner to solve.

- **Key Concepts.** Questions 1-2, 4. **Answers:** 1. No customers buying the inventory at a profitable price; pil-

ferage/shrinkage, or the inventory disappearing; being short of cash to pay suppliers because customers haven't paid yet. 2. Estimate receipts from all possible sources; estimate and subtract expenses to be paid that period. 4. (for July 2006 or problem A, information in textbook) Working capital = current assets − current liabilities = 3,000 − 1,500 = $1,500; it's positive so there is money left over to build the business and add value.

- **Critical Thinking.** Questions 1-4. **Answers:** 1. Because an income statement may show sales for which you have not been paid and would therefore give an inaccurate picture of the resources you have to pay your bills; answers will vary regarding the NFTE business example. 2. Answers will vary, but should address that cash outflows tend to be high the first year of a business's operations, which is why entrepreneurs need to get investors to provide a cash reserve to cover expenses. 3. Any of the following: collect cash as soon as possible; pay bills on time but not early; check your cash balance daily; lease rather than buy equipment; avoid inventory that does not sell quickly. 4. Answers will vary; an example would be: if an entrepreneur borrows money to buy supplies to fill a large order and the customer cancels the order, the entrepreneur could have a negative cash flow and eventually may be forced to go out of business.

- **Additional Workbook Activities Answers.**

  **Vocabulary Activity. Answers:** 1. cash flow statement. 2. projection. 3. pilferage. 4. burn rate. 5. shrinkage.

  **Quiz 41** in the workbook. **Answers:** 1. Income statement, balance sheet, and cash flow statement. 2. Cash flow is the difference between cash a business takes in and the cash it spends. 3. The income statement does not show the actual amount of cash held by a business; it counts sales as revenue even when the customer hasn't paid yet, meaning that the business could run out of cash even as it shows a profit. 4. Any of the following: collect cash as soon as possible; pay bills on time but not early; check your cash balance daily; lease rather than buy equipment; avoid inventory that does not sell quickly. 5. Answers will vary; some examples are: air conditioning business (cash flow higher in summer), flower business (cash flow higher in spring and holiday months), coat business (cash flow higher in winter), school supplies (cash flow higher in August/September). 6. Project cash receipts from all possible sources; subtract expenses you expect to have related to these projected receipts. 7. Any of the following: inventory will not sell at a profit, cost of storage, pilferage/shrinkage, getting caught between suppliers needing to be paid and when the customers pay. 8. Five months.

## EXTEND THE LEARNING

- **Business Plan Practice.** Assign Key Concepts question 3.

- **BizTech.** Assign Unit 15.

- *Entrepreneurs in Profile.* Have students work in pairs to skim the chapters in the anthology to find ways that these entrepreneurs found new sources of cash when they were close to running out. Have students create a list of "ways to get cash" for young entrepreneurs.

- **Financial Statements Analysis.** Have students write to major corporations requesting copies of their most recent annual reports, or search for annual reports or actual company financial statements online. Have students in groups compare and contrast the information shown on the balance sheet, income statement, and cash flow statement of each company. Have groups compare financial statements across companies in the same industry using criteria such as: Which is doing better regarding assets or equity or low debt? Which is doing better regarding income or lower expenses? Which is doing better regarding cash flow? Have students read the introduction ("front matter") of an annual report to find out what the management thinks is the most important financial data in terms of how the business is doing. Ask students: Would you buy this company's stock right now? Why or why not?

## BUILD ACADEMIC AND LIFE-SKILL PROFICIENCIES

### Skills Mean Success Answers

**English.** Encourage creative ways of combining the sentences but ensure that the correct meanings are conveyed and that all necessary changes to order and wording have been made. Possible answers may include: a. If someone doesn't pay the phone bill, the phone company will cut off service. b. Since you want to keep that cash a little longer in your own account, pay your bills by the due date, not before. c. Hernando was taking a risk by tying up his cash in inventory because he bought a lot of T-shirts. d. You aren't using a cash flow statement to keep track of your cash, so you could get caught in a squeeze between your suppliers and your customers.

**Leadership.** Follow up with a discussion of which math skills are most important for the entrepreneur, or business leader in general. The results of this sharing could be the creation of a chart or handout-style checklist of "Top 10 Math Skills for Businesses" that could be prominently posted for display. A representative of the math department could be engaged to review the list and compare it with the current math curriculum. Don't be surprised to see that business math topics are essential but not sufficient for high school graduation, or preparation for college. Students intending post-high school studies in business (or other subjects) will see how extensive the preparatory core of foundation high school math is, since college-level business students may be required to study much more math in their undergrad programs.

**Math.** 1. September, Year 3. 2. September, with average of $152, December, with average of $143, January, with average of $113. 3. June; it is the end of the school year. 4. September: it begins a new school year; new students; back to school shopping; December: holiday gifts; January: kids spend holiday gift money; start of a new semester. 5. The inventories should be lowest from May through July because there is the least demand. 6. Perhaps in late June for late August delivery; or in October for early December delivery. Some students may point out the merits of ordering more frequently, if tying up cash and economical order quantities/minimum-order size/unit cost are factors.

**CHAPTER 42**

# PROTECTING INTELLECTUAL PROPERTY:
## *Your Ideas Have Value*

## ORGANIZE THE LEARNING

### CHAPTER OBJECTIVES
- Recognize that your ideas and their expression can have value for your business.
- Create and protect your intellectual property.
- Apply for patents, copyrights, and trademarks.
- Legally obtain and use intellectual property owned by others.

### NFTE RESOURCES
- Text pp. 480-491
- Transparencies T42-1 to T42-3
- Workbook/BLMs Chapter 42
- Entrepreneurs in Profile #13
- Test Bank Chapter 42
- BizTech Unit 13
- A Business for the Young Entrepreneur: *Handmade Crafts*

### BUSINESS PLAN ACTIVITIES
*Workbook Business Plan Review*
Intellectual Property  42-1, 42-2

*Workbook/Textbook Chapter Review*
Critical Thinking 1, 2

*Power Point Templates*
Adv. 22

### SKILLS MEAN SUCCESS
*English*
Writing for Understanding
Descriptive Writing; Using Details

*Technology*
Using a Spell-Checker

*English*
Understanding Vocabulary

### PREREQUISITES
Chapters 4, 9 and 17 inform this chapter.

### VOCABULARY
copyright, electronic rights, infringement, intellectual property, patent, public domain, service mark, trademark, trade secret

*Other suggested terms to recognize:*
confidentiality agreement, fair use

## KEY QUESTION

**How do I protect my ideas to maintain competitive advantage?**

## PREPARE FOR LEARNING

- **Student Logos.** Have students bring to class the logos they designed for their NFTE businesses in Chapter 10 for the marketing plan activity in Develop and Close the Learning.

- **Document Samples.** It may be helpful to download from the Internet samples of patent, copyright and trademark applications to show students. Make transparencies and/or circulate the documents. These documents can be found at www.uspto.gov and www.copyright.gov.

- **Guest Speaker.** If the guest speaker activity in Extend the Learning will be used, issue the invitation as soon as possible and brief the guest in advance.

## SET A CONTEXT FOR LEARNING

- **Focus 1: Uniqueness.** Challenge the students with this instruction: List the parts of your business that are unique, unlike any other. Think about your name, products, business operations, marketing materials, etc. Which of these assets could be protected by patent, copyright, or trademark? Discuss the results and list examples on the board.

- **Focus 2: Infringement.** Present and ask the students to discuss the following scenario: You and your friend are discussing the upcoming school dance. You have been thinking a lot about what to wear. You show your outfit to your friend. When you walk into the dance, you see your friend dressed in the exact same way. How do you feel? What do you do?

- **Discussion Launcher 1: Lincoln Quote.** Refer to the Abraham Lincoln epigraph at the beginning of the chapter and ask students to discuss in pairs what it means: "The Patent System added the fuel of interest to the fire of genius." Help them to see that Lincoln was crediting the formal, legal protection of intellectual (or artistic) property (ideas, inventions, company names, manufacturing formulas, unique processes, company logos and emblems, works of art, published written work, and so on) — through patents, copyrights, and trademarks — with encouraging inventors, artists, and entrepreneurs to invest their time and talent in being creative and productive, secure in the knowledge that they had sole rights to what they created.

- **Discussion Launcher 2: Copycats.** Have students discuss the following in pairs or small groups: Think of products that "copycat" others — e.g., most computers are copies of IBM PCs. Why do companies imitate instead of creating something original? What can the companies being copied do to protect themselves? What is beyond their control?

## DEVELOP AND CLOSE THE LEARNING

- **Logos.** Have students hold up their business logos or display them so everyone can see them. Ask class what aspects of these logos are original. (Design, color combination, motto, the way the name is depicted/displayed.) Pretend to like one logo in particular and decide that you are going to copy it for your own business. Ask the student to whom the logo belongs: What should you do? Transition into a discussion that defines intellectual property and the three main ways the government protects different forms of intellectual property: patents, trademarks, and copyrights. Establish that "intellectual or artistic property" is an end-product that gives form to an idea; it has value for its creator or inventor. For example, book pages by themselves are not intellectual property but the ideas and the arrangement of the words on them are. A CD is not artistic property, but the music and lyrics contained on it are. How, and in what proportions, the individual ingredients are combined to make a new shampoo (chemicals, herbs, oils, scents) is a formula that can be the intellectual property of the inventor, even though s/he buys the individual ingredients from others. Elicit other examples from the students—such as a car-engine design, a company slogan or logo, the seasoning recipe for KFC, a T-shirt design, a movie (what's on the DVD, not the DVD itself), a new digital process for making movies, etc.

- **Patents.** Use transparency T42-1 to discuss the purposes and processes of applying for a patent. Also outline the three types of patents described in the textbook: utility, design, and plant. Ask students to give examples of things that can be patented. (It

must be a novel product or process such as the GUI interface on a computer, iPod, PalmPilot, virtual reality, streaming video technology, Todd Oldham-designed furniture, a new hybrid species of corn.) Show students a copy of a patent application (optional). Ask them to think about their NFTE businesses: Have they created something that is patentable? Does it meet the criteria of useful, new, and non-obvious?

- **Copyright.** Use transparency T42-3 to discuss the purposes and processes of registering a copyright. Ask students to give examples of things that can be copyrighted. (Artwork, novel, textbook, music recording, musical score, dance performance on video, movie, movie script, written play, software program, video game, manual, or their textbook.) It also may be helpful as a class to brainstorm what *can't* be copyrighted. (An idea itself, words that are considered in "common use" such as "team jersey," or family recipes, etc.). Ask: What happens if someone pays you a fee to write a book? Who owns the copyright? What if you don't register your copyright and someone sells unauthorized copies of your music? (The copyright must be negotiated in a work-for-hire situation, but usually it goes to the person who pays for the writing; your copyright is still protected even if it isn't registered, although it may be harder to prove you were the originator of the music.) Show students a copyright registration application (optional). Ask them to think about their NFTE businesses: Have they created something that can be copyrighted? Does it meet the "tangibility" criterion? **LINKS**⟩*Law*

- **Trademarks.** Use transparency T42-2 to discuss the purposes and processes of registering a trademark or service mark. Ask students to give examples of things that can be trademarked. (Logos such as the Nike swoosh, McDonald's Golden Arches, the Coca-Cola ribbon and typeface, the Disney logo/typeface, Intel's "do-do-do-do" sound logo.) Show class a copy of a trademark registration application (optional). Ask students to think about their NFTE businesses: Have they created something that can be trademarked?

- **Trade Secrets.** Use the textbook to define trade secrets and ask students to give examples. (The formula for Coke, recipes for Mrs. Fields cookies, processes for making prescription drugs, special steps an advertising firm might take in developing marketing ideas.) Ask: How do you protect trade secrets? (There is no registration or form; company policy/procedure and people in the company must take reasonable steps to maintain security and not share the trade secret outside of work; confidentiality agreements; limiting employee access to trade secrets; keeping formulas in a vault, etc.) Ask students to think about their NFTE businesses: Do they have any trade secrets?

- **Using Protected Property.** Do not require a show of hands, but ask students if they know about anyone who has copied a friend's software program, movie video, CD, or homework assignment. Challenge them by saying that these things are either breaking the law or (in the case of homework) unethical. It's stealing. Start a discussion by asking if it's okay to download music or games from "free" sites on the Internet. Why or why not? Expect a lengthy discussion and ask if downloading free music is fair to the music publisher, songwriter, and composer, who earn royalties only from actual sales.

Ask the students to discuss when a person legally may use the intellectual property created by others. For example:

- ○ when s/he gets explicit permission from the creator.
- ○ when the item is a work-for-hire and ownership has been negotiated.
- ○ when the work's protection has lapsed and it is now in the public domain.
- ○ when s/he is using only a small part of it for teaching, scholarship, news reporting, review, or research and will not make money from it (fair use).
- ○ when the work is in the public domain.

Emphasize that anything patented, trademarked, or copyrighted cannot be used without permission. Ask: How might an entrepreneur get into trouble regarding intellectual property? (Answers could include not having enough copies of software for the number of computers in the business, buying and selling counterfeit knock-offs of protected goods, downloading information from the Internet illegally, etc.)

**LINKS**» *Business Ethics*

- **Summary.** Reiterate to students that what they—and others—create has value. It is worth protecting that value. Conversely, it is unethical to infringe on the value of the creations of others.

## ASSESS THE LEARNING

- **Vocabulary.** Have students use each term in a sentence.

- **Key Concepts.** Questions 1-6. **Answers:** 1. Since the software is a creation of an original expression that exists physically, both in electronic form and possibly with print documentation and code, you would protect it with a copyright. 2. You would protect it with a patent, which protects inventions. 3. Register it with the U.S. government. 4. For example, any new products, formulas, recipes or processes you create (trade secrets), your Web site, logo, company slogan or trademark, any written or artistic works created or commissioned as part of the business. 5. Information on markets or customers published in print or on the Internet; tools, devices, software and manufactured goods purchased from vendors; trademarks or processes licensed for your use from other owners — for example, in a franchise business 6. Copyrights.

- **Critical Thinking.** Assign Questions 3-5. **Answers:** 3-5. Answers will vary.

- **Writing Practice.** Assign Critical Thinking question 6.

- **Additional Workbook Answers**

  **Vocabulary Puzzle.** Assign Chapter 42. **Answers:** ACROSS: 1. intellectual property. 5. public domain. 6. patent. 8. service mark. 10. trade secret. 12. confidentiality agreement. 13. copyright. 14. assign; DOWN: 1. infringement. 2. plant patent. 3. utility patent. 4. electronic rights. 7. design patent. 9. trademark. 11. fair use.

  **Quiz 42** in the workbook. **Answers:** 1. Tangible manifestation of a person's idea, such as an invention, book, video game, etc. 2. You can apply for a patent once you have a tangible form such as a prototype and you intend to market your product. 3. Public domain encompasses all inventions and works that are not protected by intellectual property laws and so may be used, manufactured or sold by anyone. 4. A company uses a trademark to identify itself and its products and distinguish them from competitors; it helps facilitate "instant recognition" of the company or brand; examples of trademarks will vary (McDonald's golden arches, Nike swoosh, Intel sound, Apple logo). 5. A copyright legally protects the author of a literary, musical, or artistic work and lasts for the life of the author plus 70 years. 6. Electronic rights protect you from your intellectual property being used, reproduced, or distributed over the Internet; companies use encryption, antipiracy software, require licensing and fees to be paid, and make Internet service providers remove copyrighted materials from Web sites.

## EXTEND THE LEARNING

- **Business Plan Practice.** Assign Critical Thinking questions 1-2.

- **BizTech.** Assign Unit 13.

- *Entrepreneurs in Profile.* Have students read the chapter on Spike Lee and be prepared to discuss the following two questions: What types of products does Lee produce? What types of infringement must Lee watch out for? What types of protection would fit Lee's products?

- **Internet Activity.** Have one portion of the class research, individually or in small groups, examples of recent patents, copyrights, trademarks, or cases of infringement. Have the rest look up the penalties associated with infringement. Assign each group the task of writing memos, or creating handouts, posters, or slide presentations to summarize their findings.

- **A Business for the Young Entrepreneur.** As a class, read about Handmade Crafts in the textbook. Have students discuss or write a memo about how such a business might benefit from intellectual property protection, which particular kinds, and why.

- **Napster Lawsuit.** Have students research the recent Napster case regarding illegal downloading of music from the Internet. Divide the class into three teams; have one present the case for Napster, another take the position of the record companies, and the third present the case for the recording artists. Allow time for rebuttal and discussion. Ask the students to research specifically the following: What intellectual property rights were infringed? How were they protected? What were the damages caused by the infringement to the different parties involved? What did each side claim was the right thing to do? What did the courts decide? How has Napster changed as a result of this case?

- **Guest Speaker.** Invite a local inventor, artist, or corporate lawyer to discuss with your class the purposes and processes of protecting intellectual property from his/her point of view. Alternatively, assemble a panel of people with different points of view on a common topic: for example, the designer, the inventor, the licensed manufacturer, and the intellectual property lawyer for a particular product. Suggest that the speaker bring samples of relevant documents for students to see and analyze. Have class prepare questions before the speaker arrives.

## BUILD ACADEMIC AND LIFE-SKILL PROFICIENCIES

### *Skills Mean Success* Answers

**English(Writing).** Encourage students to appeal to as many senses as possible in their writing. The goal is to create a clear and vivid picture of the product in the reader's mind. Have them swap descriptions with a partner for evaluation, based on the on the ability to picture what is being described. Invite partners to then ask questions that will help the writer revise the description to make it more clear. Alternatively, ask students *not* to include a topic sentence or identify what is being described. When students review their partners' descriptions, they should see if they can identify (or draw a picture of) the item without further clues. Have students to revise their work as necessary, adding additional descriptive details until their partners can identify the item.

**Technology.** 1. Ask students to share and compare their results, and then make a comprehensive list. If they do not have access to computers, do this activity as a classroom demonstration with a document you have prepared in advance. For maximum benefit, make sure the document contains planted errors that a spell checker would not catch, along with typos and misspellings that it would. 2. Spelling and grammar checkers are helpful features that can help you identify common errors and "typos" very quickly. Its primary benefit is speed. However, a spell-checker must be used *carefully*. Spelling and grammar checkers sometimes suggest words you don't want, and they won't catch a wrong word that is correct in itself, such as "form" instead of "from," or "your" instead of "you're." Because of these types of errors, it is important to always check your own spelling, using a dictionary if necessary.

**English(Vocabulary).** 1. c. 2. d. 3. a. 4. b. 5. Examples should be fairly easy to locate, including the NFTE textbook. Most published works contain a copyright notice, usually on a left-hand page near the front of a book; many common product packages and labels contain trademark symbols and patent notices. It may be difficult for students to find an example of a service mark. Allow them to search the Internet, and remind them to look for service businesses, such as law firms, medical practices, computer programmers, accountants, etc.

# ETHICAL BUSINESS BEHAVIOR

---

## ORGANIZE THE LEARNING

### CHAPTER OBJECTIVES

- Explain the difference between illegal and unethical behavior.
- Develop repeat business.
- Motivate your employees.
- Practice ethical business behavior.

### NFTE RESOURCES

- Text pp. 492-499
- Transparency T43-1
- Workbook/BLMs Chapter 43
- Test Bank Chapter 43
- A Business for the Young Entrepreneur: *Home and Office Plant Care*

### BUSINESS PLAN ACTIVITIES

*Workbook Business Plan Review*
Ethical Business Behavior 43-1, 43-2

*Workbook/Textbook Chapter Review*
Critical Thinking 5, 6;
Key Concepts 2, 3

### SKILLS MEAN SUCCESS

*English*
Observing Rules and Conventions of Grammar

*Math*
Measurement: Understanding Length and Area

### Leadership
Connecting to Real World Examples
Reading Skills Used in Business

### PREREQUISITES

Chapter 38 provides background information for this topic.

### VOCABULARY

Better Business Bureau, corporate governance, ethics, repeat business

---

## KEY QUESTION

**How do I determine what is the right thing to do?**

## PREPARE FOR LEARNING

- **Codes of Ethics.** Look up — or have a research-adept student look up — on the Internet or from other sources examples of codes of ethics. These might be professional codes of ethics, such as for accountants or doctors, or corporate codes of conduct.

- **Guest Speaker.** If you plan to invite a representative from the Better Business Bureau to class, make arrangements in advance.

## SET A CONTEXT FOR LEARNING

- **Focus 1: Felt Cheated.** Ask the students to consider a time when they bought something and felt cheated. What happened? How did you react? How did the store or company react? Do you still do business there?

- **Focus 2: Ethical Decision.** Pose this scenario for the students to discuss in pairs and report to the class later: Tyrone discovers that the products he bought from the wholesaler are defective. What could hap-

pen if he tries to return them? What could happen if he tries to sell them to the public? What should he do and why?

- **Focus 3: Ethical and Unethical Businesspeople.** Have students consider the following: List 2-3 people you know or who are in the news that you think are good examples of ethical businesspeople. List 2-3 that you think are examples of unethical businesspeople. Discuss the results as a class.
  **LINKS**»*Business Ethics*

- **Discussion Launcher: Ethical Dilemma.** Let students consider (first individually, then in pairs or small groups): A man lost his job and health insurance. His wife is very ill and needs expensive medicine. The man went to a pharmacy, but did not have enough money. The pharmacist does not want to give the man the medicine because he had to buy it from the pharmaceutical company, and the pharmaceutical company would not provide it for free because it needs to recoup its research and development costs. What should the pharmacist do? The pharmaceutical company? The man's former employer? Why?

## DEVELOP AND CLOSE THE LEARNING

- **Ethics Is Good Business.** Ask the students to define ethics (principled behavior; doing the right thing; "doing unto others...," etc.) and determine that ethics in business is particularly concerned with building good relationships. Ask: How is ethics similar to and different from the law? How is doing something ethical similar to and different from doing something legal? (Both have to do with rules that control behavior; the law has to do with criminal and civil infractions and their penalties; ethics is concerned with doing what is right for the common good. Often the "penalties" for unethical behavior are social, through other people's reactions, such as avoidance or not doing business — rather than punitive measures such as fines or imprisonment.)

- **Ethical Relationships.** Divide the class into small groups. Have some groups brainstorm the benefits of acting ethically toward customers (repeat business, good word-of-mouth publicity). Have other groups talk about the advantages of acting ethically toward employees (motivated employees work better, less employee turnover). Are there other people toward which entrepreneurs should behave ethically? (Suppliers, the government, their fellow citizens around the world.)

- **Personal Ethical Business Behavior.** Use transparency T43-1 to discuss the ten aspects of ethical business behavior. Divide the class into ten groups and have each group create a skit that models one aspect. After each performance, ask class if other behaviors were also shown in the skit besides the targeted one (*respect* was included in the skit focused on courtesy, for example). Summarize that ethical business behavior should be practiced so that it becomes a habit.

- **Corporate Ethical Business Behavior.** Share with the class the codes of ethics collected as described in Prepare for Learning. Discuss what issues they address and what function they serve in a company or profession. (Guide behavior, reassure the public or customers about the organization's ethics.) Recall recent corporate ethics cases in the news such as Enron and WorldCom-MCI, and discuss the following: What lessons do these cases teach entrepreneurs about ethical behavior? How can you, as a business owner, protect yourself and your company from ethical wrongdoing? (The four ideas mentioned in the textbook — separate business profits from personal spending, keep accurate records, use financial controls, create an advisory board — plus

other ideas students come up with, such as having a written code of ethics that everyone must adhere to.)

- **Summary.** Ask students to write their own personal code of business ethics.

## ASSESS THE LEARNING

- **Vocabulary.** Have students define terms in their own words and use each in a sentence. Assign the Vocabulary activity to students who use the workbook.

- **Key Concepts.** Questions 1-2. **Answers:** 1-2. Answers will vary.

- **Critical Thinking.** Questions 1, 2, 4. **Answers:** 1-2. Answers will vary, but look for indications that the student has tried to define, understand, and determine the reasons for the behaviors. 4. Answers will vary.

- **Writing Practice.** Assign Key Concepts question 3 and/or Critical Thinking question 3.

- **Additional Workbook Answers**

  **Vocabulary Activity.** **Answers:** When you go into business for yourself, you must decide if you will be guided by good work *ethics*. *Ethics* are standards of behavior that help determine right from wrong. If you treat customers well and exhibit good *ethics*, they will probably come back. This is called *repeat business*. On the other hand, if a customer feels cheated by a business, he or she may report it to the *Better Business Bureau*, a nonprofit organization that publishes reports about the reliability, honesty, and performance of businesses. To avoid scandals and ethical dilemmas, businesses must use *corporate governance* and have safeguards in place to prevent executives from lying and stealing.

  **Quiz 43** in the workbook. **Answers:** 1. Any reasonable answer that discusses treating customers fairly. 2. Answers will vary but should address the idea that it is rude to use other people's time unwisely, since time is money, and being late shows disrespect to the other person. 3. a. Answers may vary; examples include: keeping your word, being there for a customer, keeping appointments. b. Answers may vary; will probably include: using a pleasant tone of voice and demeanor with a customer, listening to the customer's needs. c. Answers may vary; examples include: not using slang or profanity, enunciating clearly, listening. d. Answers may vary; examples should include: wearing clean clothes that are pressed and wrinkle-free, wearing attire appropriate to the occasion, wearing relatively conservative clothing (nothing outrageously colorful or sexy). e. Answers may vary, but include: being clean and neat, having nice penmanship, being organized. 4. It will help you gain repeat business and a good reputation. 5. No, businesses need repeat customers to be successful.

## EXTEND THE LEARNING

- **Business Plan Practice.** Critical Thinking questions 5-6.

- **A Business for the Young Entrepreneur.** Have students read about the opportunities of home and office plant care in the textbook. Have them consider: How do the ten aspects of ethical business behavior apply in this type of business? What ethical situations might arise?

- **Ethical "Gray Areas."** Use the previous Discussion Launcher activity or a current ethical violations case in the news to explore the complications of ethical dilemmas. Sometimes the "right" or "good" answer is not so clear-cut. Have individuals or groups represent and role-play different characters (say, the scenario above with the man going to the pharmacy for medicine: man, pharmacist, pharmaceutical company executive, wife, and others that the students may think should be included). Players should provide their characters' point-of-view, motivations, and options for how to proceed. Have each character present a personal perspective, and then discuss potential contingencies, how his/her position might change depending on what another character decides to do. **LINKS**»*Dramatic Arts*

- **Ethical/Legal Debate.** Given the high profile cases in the news of ethical violations by large corporations (Enron, WorldCom-MCI, etc.) that became legal battles, ask students to take sides and debate the question: Should ethical violations by corporations be punishable through the legal system (civil or criminal penalties) or through industry ethical standards boards? **LINKS**»*Law*

- **Guest Speaker.** Invite a local representative of the Better Business Bureau to discuss with your class what services the BBB provides, the number and types of complaints most often made against different types of businesses, and what businesses can do to keep their BBB record clean.

- **Exploration.** Assign the activity in the workbook.

## BUILD ACADEMIC AND LIFE-SKILL PROFICIENCIES
### *Skills Mean Success* Answers

**English.** 1. Thank you for taking the time to meet with Fred and *me*. "Me" is the object of the preposition "with." **Tip**: You wouldn't say "Thank you for meeting with I," so you know "me" is the correct pronoun. 2. A manager should try to help *his or her* employees succeed. The singular "manager" requires a singular pronoun. This sentence could also be written correctly with plurals: "Managers should try to help their employees succeed." 3. *It's* a shame the store lost *its* best sales associate. "It's" is the contraction of "it is"; "its" is the possessive. 4. All our *employees'* records are kept in the Human Resources Department. A plural possessive takes an apostrophe after the "s." 5. *Whom* should I promote to store manager? "Whom" is the object in the sentence. **Tip**: If you can reword a sentence and substitute "him" or "her," then "whom" is correct. In this case, you could say, "I should promote *her* to store manager." If you can reword the sentence and substitute "he" or "she," then "who" would be correct. Increasingly, however, the use of whom is becoming less common, even in more formal uses of English.

**Math.** 1. $8 \times 8 = 64$ sq. ft.; $12.5 \times 10 = 125$ sq. ft.; $16 \times 9 = 144$ sq. ft. 2. $64 + 125 + 144 = 333$ sq. ft. 3. $333 \times \$.65 = \$216.45$ 4. $372 \times \$.65 = \$241.80 - \$216.45 = \$25.35$. $\$25.35$ is the amount of the overcharge. Students may suggest that you should offer a larger refund or additional discount to make up for your mistake, generate goodwill with the customer, and avoid the appearance of any intentional wrongdoing.

**Leadership.** The Top Ten lists could include any of the following: reading business plans; reading loan and credit applications; reading market research reports; reading competitors' ads and Web site information; reviewing copy for your own ads and brochures; understanding contracts; applying for licenses, trademarks, patents, and copyrights; reading financial statements; screening job applications; completing employee records; understanding letters from customers and vendors; proofreading letters and memos you send; reading newspapers, journals and magazines to keep on top of events that could effect your market or industry; and so on. Reading ability could help a manager or entrepreneur to avoid unethical business behavior by, for example, enabling him or her to better understand contractual obligations and terms, to avoid making false claims in advertising, to keep on top of current business ethics issues in the news, and to "read between the lines" of written communications from customers and employees.

### CHAPTER 44

# TAXATION AND THE ENTREPRENEUR

---

## ORGANIZE THE LEARNING

### CHAPTER OBJECTIVES

- Understand how to meet your legal tax obligation as a small business owner.
- Identify the taxes that support city, state, and federal government.
- Find appropriate tax forms and assistance in filling them out.

### NFTE RESOURCES

- Text pp. 500-513
- Transparencies T44-1 to T44-4
- Workbook/BLMs Chapter 44
- Test Bank Chapter 44
- BizTech Unit 20

### BUSINESS PLAN ACTIVITIES

*Workbook Business Plan Review*
Taxation  44-1

*Workbook/Textbook Chapter Review*
Key Concepts 3

### SKILLS MEAN SUCCESS

*Math*
Operations: Income Tax Rates

*Technology*
Online Research

*English*
Presenting Information Clearly

### PREREQUISITES

The class should have covered the content of Chapters 12, 13, 38, and 43.

### VOCABULARY

audit, Internal Revenue Service (IRS), sales tax, self-employment tax, Social Security, tax , tax evasion

---

## KEY QUESTION

**Why do I have to pay taxes, and how much will they be?**

## PREPARE FOR LEARNING

- **Current Tax Rates and Forms (Optional).** Determine what the current income and sales-tax rates are so you can use them as examples. Get copies of tax forms both for individuals and small business, including sales-tax-reporting forms (or download these documents from the appropriate Web sites).

- **Receipts.** To show sales tax, gather receipts for things you have purchased.

- **Guest Speaker.** If a guest is planned for Extend the Learning, make arrangements in advance.

## SET A CONTEXT FOR LEARNING

- **Focus: "Plus Tax."** Present the following and have students calculate the final price a customer must pay:

| Base price | Sales tax rate | Answer |
|-----------|---------------|--------|
| $25 | 8.25% | $27.06 |
| $30 | 7% | $32.10 |
| $10 | 6% | $10.60 |

| Base price | Sales tax rate | Answer |
|-----------|---------------|--------|
| $76 | 4% | $79.04 |
| $100 | 3% | $103.00 |

- **Focus: Paycheck.** Challenge the students to calculate the following: You make $6 an hour at a part-time job, working 20 hours a week. You get paid every two weeks. Your employer deducts the following taxes from your earnings to send to the IRS: Federal income tax 15%, state income tax 5%, Social Security tax 7.65%. How much will your actual paycheck total be (what you will deposit into your bank account)? **Answer:** $173.64 (6 × 20 × 2 = $240 as your gross amount; Federal tax = 240 × .15 = $36; state tax = 240 × .05 = $12; Social Security = 240 × .075 = $18; 240 − 36 − 12 − 18 = $174).

- **Discussion Launcher: Government Spending.** Discuss: How do you feel about the issues, projects, and programs your local government is spending money on? What do you think they should be spending more on? Less on? Why?

## DEVELOP AND CLOSE THE LEARNING

- **Scenario/Running Example.** Convey the following story to the class for use in calculations throughout this chapter: Chris sells skateboards for $40 each. His business has stabilized and he tends to sell 25 a month. He buys skateboards from a wholesaler for $25 each. His monthly operating expenses are $300. Create an annual income statement on the board for Chris's business up to the Profit Before Taxes line. **Answer:**

| | | |
|---|---|---|
| Sales | $12,000 | (40×25×12 mths) |
| Cost of goods sold | $7,500 | (25×25×12) |
| Gross profit | $4,500 | |
| Operating expenses | $3,600 | (300×12) |
| Profit before taxes | $ 900 | |

- **Types of Taxes.** Use transparency T44-1 to describe the types of taxes involved in business:

  ○ Sales tax: Explain what sales tax is (a tax on purchases), who pays it (retailers or people who sell to the final consumer) and who doesn't (manufacturers and wholesalers who sell to other businesses for resale). Show students store receipts on which sales tax was included (optional). Show a sales-tax-reporting form for your city/state. Have students calculate the sales tax on a skateboard (see Scenario above) at 5.8% to find what a customer would have to pay. **Answer:** Sales tax $2.32, final amount $42.32.

  ○ Personal income tax: Explain what income tax is (a tax on earnings), who pays it (everyone that makes more than $5,500), and the different "graduated" tax rates — depending on how much a person makes in a year (available at www.irs.gov). Show the personal income tax forms for your state. Have students calculate the personal income tax if Chris, the skateboard seller, is a sole proprietor and takes all his profit as personal income. What would his tax rate be? How much will he have to pay? **Answer:** 10% (his income is between $0 and $7,000); $90 (900 × .10).

  ○ Self-employment tax is income tax paid by people who work for themselves. They have no other employer to pay their Social Security taxes. Show students a Schedule SE. Ask: Does Chris have to pay self-employment tax? If so, how much will it be? Then, what is the final amount Chris gets to take home after income and SE taxes? **Answer:** Yes, because he is a sole proprietor and earned more than $400; $137.70 (900 × .153); $672.30 (900 − 90 − 137.70).

  ○ Corporate income tax: Review that a corporation is viewed as an independent "entity" and its profits are taxed separately from the personal income

tax of its owners and employees. The corporation pays taxes on its profits. Stockholders also pay personal income tax on dividends. If Chris, the skateboard seller, was incorporated and the corporate tax rate was 20%, how much tax would the company owe? If the company paid 20% of its after-tax profits to its one stockholder, what would the amount of the stockholder's dividend be? If the stockholder's personal tax rate was 28%, how much personal income tax would s/he owe on the dividend amount? **Answer:** $180 (900 × .20); $144 ((900 − 180) × .20); $40.32.

- **Figuring Taxes.** Use transparency T44-2 and complete this form as a class (as an option, include a Schedule C and Schedule SE) for Chris. Discuss from what business documents the information is drawn (such as the Journal and income statement) and the importance of keeping good records. Or bring in a sample/mock W-2 and use the information to complete this form for an employee. You may want to start by completing a form 1040-EZ first, so students can get a better grasp of the concepts. Then introduce form 1040 to show how tax figuring can become more complicated through self-employment, capital gains/losses (tying into Chapters 33 and 34), home ownership, and other income and expenses (student, medical, etc.).
  **LINKS**»*Citizenship*

- **What Taxes Are Used For.** Use transparency T44-3 to introduce the programs that taxes fund. Have students brainstorm specific projects in their town, state and nationally that taxes pay for. (The Army, printing money, police, fire, garbage collection, road building and repair, welfare, environmental protection, worker safety.) Explain that not all tax dollars go directly to benefits but also are used to pay government employees for the administration of programs, etc. Divide students into groups to address the questions on transparency T44-4. Have each group create and present an argument yes/no for whether taxes are fair given the current type and level of benefits received. **LINKS**»*Government*

- **Summary.** Have students consider and discuss: How do you feel about how the taxes you and your family pay are being spent?

## ASSESS THE LEARNING

- **Vocabulary.** Have students use each word in a sentence.

- **Key Concepts.** Question 2. Note: You will need to provide the forms for students to complete. **Answer:**

2. If students use their own personal income information for themselves or their NFTE businesses, answers will vary. If you are creating a scenario that students will use to complete the forms, create a master of the form, so you can check answers.

- **Critical Thinking.** Questions 1-4. **Answers:** 1. Self-employment tax basically replaces Social Security tax; self-employed people must pay both halves (employer and employee) of this approximately 15% tax since they play both roles and don't have an employer who would contribute to Social Security for them. 2. Answers will vary on whether students earn money from self-employment: they do have to pay self-employment tax if they earn more than $400; they must file a Schedule SE. 3. Keep good records and files of invoices and receipts so that, if you are audited, you can back up your tax return. 4. $16,250, $30,000.

- **Additional Workbook Answers**

  **Vocabulary.** Assign Chapter 44. **Answers:** 1. b. 2. b. 3. c. 4. b. 5. a. 6. c. 7. c.

  **Quiz 44** in the workbook. **Answers:** 1. $8. 2. c. 3. c. 4. a. 5. c. 6. False. 7. True. 8. b. 9. Answers will vary; examples are: Where are my tax dollars going? Are my tax dollars supporting services that will benefit me and my community? Are there better, more efficient ways of providing these services?

## EXTEND THE LEARNING

- **Business Plan Practice.** Assign Key Concepts question 3.

- **BizTech.** Assign Unit 20.

- **Internet Activity.** Have students visit and explore the Internal Revenue Service Web site (www.irs.gov) for information related to self-employment. Ask them to write a memo or create a handout describing the most interesting information they found relevant to entrepreneurship.

- **Improving Public Services.** Assign Key Concepts question 1 to discuss in small groups.

- **Local Taxes.** Have students research online or by phone what the current tax rates are for sales tax (and what is and is not considered taxable) and state personal income tax.

- **Tax-Return Process.** Have students interview someone they know who filed a tax return last year. This individual may be a parent or family friend. As a class, come up with a list of questions to ask regarding what it's like to file a tax return. For example:

How do they organize their paperwork? What aids or sources of information do they find most helpful in completing the return? What do they find most frustrating about the process? Have volunteers share their findings. Break students into two groups: the first could write memos to the IRS describing how the organization might improve the tax-return process based on the (anonymous) information students collected; the second group might write brochure information to taxpayers, with tips to help them to complete their tax returns based on the information collected. **LINKS**》*Citizenship*

- **Guest Speaker.** Invite a local accountant or IRS representative to discuss how income taxes would affect students who work as part-time employees, and as young entrepreneurs.

## BUILD ACADEMIC AND LIFE-SKILL PROFICIENCIES

### *Skills Mean Success* Answers

**Math.** 1. a. Maria — $2,125 (10% of the first $7,000 plus 15% of the remaining $9,500). b. Marvin — $3,655. c. Mac — $4,610. d. Marissa — $15,746.

**Technology.** Pros given may include: ease of use and access, speed, accuracy (most online services check responses for exclusions and omissions), avoids reentering data, customer is more in control, status of order or filing can be easily checked (for example, many sites immediately confirm receipt of data sent), Internet transmission is as safe as hard-copy mailing, etc. Cons may include security (is the information you send safe? can hackers get at and use your personal data?), some people are uncomfortable with technology, not as satisfying as interacting with a "real" person, you may not easily be able to keep copies of forms filed or orders sent, people feel more secure with "paper" records, etc. Discuss with students how a site can be evaluated for its security: Is it a reputable organization or company, are guarantees offered, is a confirmation notice sent, is it possible to check the status of the filing or order?

**English.** Answers will vary, but encourage students to keep the activity practical and realistic, to observe rules of punctuation, and to keep the message direct and concise (but friendly). For models, check any number of existing Web sites with Q&A pages, such as www.irs.gov — or use this example: Q. *If a product I purchase from your store doesn't work properly, what can I do? A. Our company is dedicated to 100% customer satisfaction. If you are not completely satisfied with your purchase, a refund will be cheerfully provided.*

### CHAPTER 45

# INSURANCE:
## Protection from the Unexpected

## ORGANIZE THE LEARNING

### CHAPTER OBJECTIVES

- Explain how insurance protects businesses.
- Determine when a business needs liability insurance.
- Explain how insurance companies make money.
- Choose coverage for your small business.

### NFTE RESOURCES

- Text pp. 514-519
- Transparency T45-1
- Workbook/BLMs Chapter 45
- Test Bank Chapter 45
- BizTech Unit 23
- A Business for the Young Entrepreneur: *Photography*

### BUSINESS PLAN ACTIVITIES

*Workbook Business Plan Review* Insurance 45-1, 45-2

*Workbook/Textbook Chapter Review* Critical Thinking 3, 4; Business Plan Interactive Summary

### SKILLS MEAN SUCCESS

*Math*
Probability: Comparing Data and Uncertainty

*English*
Speaking: Diction

### PREREQUISITES

Students could preview Chapter 45 in the textbook.

### VOCABULARY

deductible, fraud, insurance, insurance agent, insurance policy, liability insurance, premium

## KEY QUESTION

**How can I protect my business from the effects of disaster?**

## SET A CONTEXT FOR LEARNING

- **Focus 1: Fire.** Challenge the students to consider and share what they would do in the following situations:

  ❍ You wake up one morning to a phone call. The fire department tells you your store burned down. No one was hurt, but all of your fixtures, inventory, records, everything was destroyed.

  ❍ You get a phone call from a lawyer. Her client — one of your customers — says he slipped on the wet floor in your store and has broken his arm. She wants you to pay for the medical expenses, plus a penalty for your "carelessness."

- **Focus 2: What Is Your Stuff Worth?** Ask the students to list their personal belongings at home and estimate how much it would cost to replace them — new — if they were stolen or destroyed.

## DEVELOP AND CLOSE THE LEARNING

- **Disasters Happen.** Have a few students share their responses to one of the Focus activities above. Ask what other kinds of disasters might befall a business. (Theft, floods, hurricanes, being sued for a variety of things, product malfunction, product being used in a crime.) Establish that disasters do not happen often, but they can and do happen. Perhaps share examples of product liability cases that made the news: the woman who spilled McDonald's coffee on herself and sued because it was too hot, the suits against the tobacco industry, etc. Buying insurance prevents a disaster from being as devastating as it could have been because insurance helps replace property that was lost or may cover loss of income, etc. Stress that it is always better to try to *avoid* bad things from happening. Ask students for ways of avoiding disasters in business. (Not producing potentially dangerous products, keeping good records, keeping a backup copy of records at an outside location, providing careful instructions to consumers concerning how to use your product, providing quality workmanship, taking security measures.)

- **What Insurance Protects.** Use Transparency 45-1 to discuss what insurance is and does. Using the textbook, describe the types of insurance a business might need. Below are some examples (you can ask the students for others):

  ○ **Liability:** A customer falling because your floor was wet; a customer getting sick after eating your cookies; a person walking by your store is hit on the head by your sign falling off the wall. Note that an entrepreneur should never lie about or hide the dangers of his/her product or service; this would be fraud, a criminal offense.

  ○ **Property:** A fire destroyed your equipment or store.

  ○ **Crime:** Your business was a victim of a theft; a mugging occurred on your property.

  ○ **Worker's Compensation:** One of your employees fell off a ladder while hanging decorations in the store; an employee got carpal tunnel syndrome from working on your computer.

  ○ **Disability:** You or an employee is injured in a car accident and can't work for a period of time.

  ○ **Health:** You or an employee need an operation; one of your employees is pregnant.

  ○ **Life:** Someone dies, so relatives will need money for funeral expenses and to live on after they are no longer being provided for.

Divide the class into three groups. The first group comprises entrepreneurs who are opening businesses to sell homemade snacks at school. The second group is composed of entrepreneurs who are opening skateboard-training businesses. The third group includes entrepreneurs who are opening Web site design and hosting companies. Have each group list examples of the following kind of risks for their business:

  ○ **Liability:** How might your product or service cause injury to someone?

  ○ **Property:** What types of property need to be protected (equipment, inventory)?

  ○ **Worker's Compensation:** How might your employees get hurt while working?

Allow time for groups to share their ideas or ask questions. Ask students to notice both similarities and differences among the different types of businesses and how they would translate into different insurance needs and costs. For example, a pet-sitting service might need liability insurance (in case something happened to an animal) and worker's compensation insurance (in case a sitter got bitten) but probably not much property insurance (because a pet-sitting business wouldn't own much inventory or equipment).

- **How Insurance Works.** Get the students to consider and then explain that insurance basically pools money from many people so that when misfortune strikes a few people, there is money to cover the damage. Each person or business pays a premium each month, quarter, or year based on the value of what is being insured, the type of event being insured against, and the likelihood of that event occurring. Insurance premiums vary depending on many things, including where you or the property to be insured is located (higher crime area, building made of flammable materials) because these factors affect how likely an event is to happen. Demonstrate these principles by continuing the three business scenarios above. Pretend that you represent the All-Safe Insurance Company that specializes in protecting the businesses of young entrepreneurs. Your company's analysts (*actuaries*) have figured out that the annual premium rates for these three businesses are as follows:

|  | Liability | Property | Worker's Comp |
|---|---|---|---|
| Homemade Snacks | $300 | $500 | $500 |
| Skateboard | $1,500 | $200 | $1,000 |
| Web-Site | $200 | $700 | $100 |

Ask students to speculate, given their discussions in the previous activity, why these amounts vary across businesses. (Someone is more likely to get hurt while skateboarding; Web site design and hosting requires costly equipment that would need to be replaced; an employee who helped bake snacks might get burned.) Say: Get out a blank sheet of paper, tear it in horizontal thirds, and write three checks for the different types of insurance. Collect the checks in three piles and have students calculate the value of the pools of money (300 x 1/3 class size and 1,500 x 1/3 class size and 200 x 1/3 class size = liability amounts). Choose one student for each of the following examples:

  ○ **Liability:** A customer's private credit card information was stolen through a Web site that (name of student)'s company hosts and is suing you for $2,000.

  ○ **Property:** One of (name of student)'s employees starts a fire in the kitchen and ruins one oven, several baking pans and a mixer. The replacement cost is $900.

For each of these events, walk the students through the process of checking to see if there is enough money in the pool to cover the disaster. Introduce the concept of *deductible* (what a person thinks s/he can cover without filing an insurance claim). Suppose that the deductible for each of the above businesses was $250. Ask students to figure how much the insurance company should pay for their claims ($1,750 for liability, $650 for property). Then write checks to the two "claimant" students. Re-emphasize the concept of pooling resources so that the relatively few people who suffer disastrous losses are cushioned from the full impact by the money paid from the others insured who did *not* experience any loss. That way, no one person carries the whole cost of an unforeseen event.

- **Insurance Costs.** Use the textbook and suggestions elicited from students to summarize the costs of insurance for a small business:

  ○ When you buy insurance, you are entering into a *contract.* The insurance policy spells out the terms of the contract. You promise to pay the insurance company and in return they promise to pay for any disastrous events that might occur in the future.

  ○ Insurance is a *fixed operating cost* (overhead): its amount is stable and does not vary with sales.

  ○ The amount you pay to the insurance company each month, quarter, or year is called the *premium.* Even if you never incur a disaster or use the insurance, you must still pay the premiums.

  ○ When a disaster happens, you make a *claim* on your insurance policy and provide documentation showing what was lost.

  ○ Another cost is the *deductible*, which is the amount of the cost of unforeseen event you will have to pay out of your own pocket and that will not be covered by the claim. The business owner decides how much deductible s/he is willing and able to pay.

  ○ The relationship between premium and deductible is: the higher the deductible, the lower the premium and vice versa. In the long run, it's probably best to have the highest deductible you can afford.

- **Summary.** Have students write down three reasons for a small business to buy insurance. Allow a few minutes to share ideas and make a master list on the board.

## ASSESS THE LEARNING

- **Vocabulary.** Have students define terms in their own words and use each in a sentence, or assign the Vocabulary activity in the workbook.

- **Key Concepts.** Questions 1-3. **Answers:** 1-2. Answers will vary. 3. Answers may vary; some options are: she can raise her deductible, which would lower her premium; she should shop other insurance companies because rates can vary; she could carry less insurance (only liability and not comprehensive); she could deliver flowers using a bicycle or wagon; she could hire a delivery service to deliver; she could not offer delivery.

- **Critical Thinking.** Questions 1, 2, 4. **Answers:** 1. Fire, liability, worker's compensation, disability. 2. Insurance companies hire analysts (actuaries) to figure out the likelihood of an event such as fire or theft; the analysts then determine how much to charge for premiums to guarantee that, even if the event occurs, the cost of insurance paid out to one policyholder has been covered by the premiums paid by many other policyholders. 4. Answers will vary; it would be best if the student also could print out the Web site page showing the information so you can check their understanding.

- **Writing Practice.** Pretend that a disaster has befallen your NFTE business. Write a formal letter to an insurance company explaining the situation, clearly describing the dollar amount you are claiming, and listing the items to be replaced or how the money will be used.

- **Additional Workbook Activities Answers.**

  **Vocabulary Activity. Answers:** 1. fraud. 2. premium. 3. insurance agent. 4. deductible. 5. liability insurance. 6. insurance. 7. insurance policy.

  **Quiz 45** in the workbook. **Answers:** 1. Insurance protects the policyholder and pays for damages caused by fire, robbery, liability lawsuits, etc. 2. Premium. 3. Deductible. 4. Selecting a product or service that is less likely to harm anyone. 5. To protect themselves from a liability lawsuit; to inform customers of the proper way to use the product; to fairly warn customers about what they are buying because not doing so is fraud. 6. Also need auto insurance. 7. Any of the following: fire, theft, liability, property. 8. Worker's Compensation, disability. 9. Figuring out the likelihood of a disaster occurring and calculating premiums so that the premium payments of many policyholders would pay for the insurance claim of one policyholder, plus the fixed operating costs of the insurance company, plus profit.   10. A higher deductible usually means paying a lower premium.

## EXTEND THE LEARNING

- **Business Plan Practice.** Critical Thinking question 3.
- **BizTech.** Assign Unit 23.
- **A Business for the Young Entrepreneur.** Have students read in the textbook about photography as a business opportunity. Ask students to prepare an insurance-needs assessment for this type of business: what kinds of coverage should it carry?
- **Exploration.** Assign the activity in the textbook. It may also be interesting for students to ask if the business owner has ever made a claim on the insurance and how that process was experienced.
- **Insurance Policy Analysis.** Review the criteria of good contracts from Chapter 37. Bring in a copy of an insurance policy (an insurance agent may be willing to provide copies if you ask). Have students in small groups read the policy carefully and outline the terms of the agreement: who will do what, "exclusions" (what is *not* covered), etc. Ask them to rate how good a contract the policy is for the insurance company and for the policyholder. Emphasize that it is important to always read an insurance policy carefully.
- **Personal Insurance.** Extend the discussion of business insurance needs to explore the insurance needs of individuals and families. For example, repeat the discussion about what insurance protects, but ask the students to provide personal examples (e.g., if someone falls down the stairs in the hallway of an apartment building, if a car or bike was burglarized from a parking area). As a follow-up school-home connection activity, have students interview parents, other adult friends, or family members about the types of insurance they carry. Have students create a personal insurance plan for when they go to college or enter the work world. What types of unforeseen disasters should they protect themselves from? **LINKS**»*Consumer Ed*
- **Catastrophes.** Direct the students to research online news stories about catastrophes, such as hurricanes, floods, wars, 9/11, etc. Hold a discussion about the limits of insurance. What happens when a disaster affects so many people that the "pool" may not be large enough to cover all claims (the money to be paid out to policyholders by the insurance companies)? As an extension, divide the class into groups to represent parties to the catastrophe: the policyholders, the insurance company, the government, and others. Allow time for each group to present its perspective and for the others to respond.

- **Business Plan Integrative Summary.** Since Chapter 45 concludes Unit 9, which emphasizes protecting your business, it may be a good time for students to compose and present a brief summary of the protective aspects of their Business Plans to date, including:
  - ○ a projected cash flow statement.
  - ○ strategies for protecting the company's intellectual property.
  - ○ a company code of ethics.
  - ○ a plan for figuring and paying taxes.
  - ○ a list of expected insurance needs.

## BUILD ACADEMIC AND LIFE-SKILL PROFICIENCIES

### *Skills Mean Success* Answers

**Math.** 1. 1:2 or 0.5 or 50%.  2. 1:52 or 0.019 or 1.9%.  3. 4:52 or 0.76923 or 7.7%.  4. The experiential results will probably — but not necessarily — differ from the theoretical probability. The more times the action is repeated, the greater the odds that the results will approach the theoretical probability. But remind students that the odds of the results on any given repetition are still theoretically the same as the first attempt. 5. For weather: location, season, weather history of the dates, long range weather forecasts, etc.; for a store catching fire: history of fires in the area, location of closest hydrants and fire station, crime statistics, type of building, proximity to other buildings, etc.. Help the students to recognize the complexity of collecting and analyzing such kinds of data.

**English.** Taping the pronunciations may help some students to correct their own and others' mispronunciations. Point out the differences between dialect or accent and mispronunciation. The former are colorful and cultural; the latter is due to lack of skill or effort that customers and business contacts will notice and use, rightly or wrongly, to form opinions about an entrepreneur's ability in other areas.

### CHAPTER 46

# FRANCHISING AND LICENSING:
## *The Power of the Brand*

## ORGANIZE THE LEARNING

### CHAPTER OBJECTIVES

- Imagine new ways to profit from your brand.
- Contrast licensing with franchising.
- Explore the benefits and draw-backs of franchising.
- Avoid agreements that could tarnish your brand's image.

### NFTE RESOURCES

- Text pp. 520-527
- Transparencies T46-1 to T46-3
- Workbook/BLMs Chapter 46
- Entrepreneurs in Profile #5 and #12
- Test Bank Chapter 46

### BUSINESS PLAN ACTIVITIES

*Workbook Business Plan Review*
Franchising and Licensing

*Workbook/Textbook Chapter Review*
Critical Thinking 3

### SKILLS MEAN SUCCESS

*Math*
Mathematical Reasoning:
Substituting a Number to Solve a Problem

*English*
Writing for Information:
Presenting Clear Instructions

*Technology/English*
Writing for Information: Summarizing Web-Site Information

### PREREQUISITES

The content of Chapters 17, 18 and 37 inform this topic.

### VOCABULARY

franchise, franchisee, franchisor, licensing, licensee, licensor, royalty

## KEY QUESTION

**How can I extend my business/brand through strategic partnering?**

## PREPARE FOR LEARNING

- **Field Trip Arrangements.** If you use the Field Trip activity suggested in Extend the Learning, contact the franchisee a couple of weeks before the date of the class.

## SET A CONTEXT FOR LEARNING

- **Focus 1: "I See Them Everywhere!"** Ask the students to list as many fast food restaurants as they can think of that have multiple locations around town (e.g., McDonald's, Burger King, Wendy's, Taco Bell, Subway, etc.). How do they think one company or one owner could afford to have that many stores?
- **Focus 1: Consistency.** Discuss with the students why a _____ (choose a franchised fast-food product) is always the same, no matter where in the world you eat? Establish that the company sets standards for its products and requires all branches — even if they are not directly owned by the parent company — to serve the same menu and quality, size of portions, etc. They do this to make sure that the quality is consistent, so customers know what to expect, wherever they are.
- **Discussion Launcher: Brand Extension.** Ask the students to discuss, in pairs or small groups, the following: You have created and manufactured mascaras in hot colors, like lime green, hot pink, fuchsia, and yellow, under the brand name "Eye Love It!" They have sold very well to teenage girls. Other businesses have asked you for permission to manufacture and sell the same kind of mascara in return for a fee. What types of issues should you consider before you decide whether to allow the manufacturer to move forward?

## DEVELOP AND CLOSE THE LEARNING

- **Brands, Franchises, Licenses.** Elicit definitions of the following: brand, franchise, and license. Have students brainstorm real-world examples of each as you explain them. (Brands: Disney, Coca-Cola, Harvard, Dallas Cowboys, Britney Spears, Cheerios, Jell-O, Reese's; franchises: McDonald's, Dunkin' Donuts, Baskin-Robbins, Maaco, The UPS Store, Big-O Tires, Merry Maids, Minuteman Press, Supercuts, 7-Eleven; licensing: Disney character dolls, Harvard T-shirts, Dallas Cowboy clothing or calendars, Reese's cookie mixes, LL Bean SUVs licensed to Ford for the Ford Explorer.) Use transparency T46-1 to summarize franchising and transparency T46-3 to summarize the difference between franchising and licensing.

- **The Benefits of Franchising and Licensing.** Brainstorm why it might be a good idea to franchise or license a brand. (Sharing the risks and rewards; expanding your brand using capital/investment by others [franchisor/licensor].) Use transparency T46-2 to discuss the pros and cons of franchising. Divide the class into four groups and have each brainstorm the same for licensing — pros/licensor, cons/licensor, pros/licensee, cons/licensee — and share their findings with the class. Discuss how franchisors and licensors get paid through fees or royalties (a percentage of sales or profits). Discuss and summarize how franchising and licensing create valuable relationships that help both parties to be more profitable than they would be separately.

- **Buying a Franchise or License.** Ask: As an entrepreneur, when you purchase a McDonald's franchise, what exactly are you buying? (The brand name and its reputation, a business concept that has already proven successful, training, operating and accounting procedures, quality standards, perhaps incentive programs, a protected market territory into which no other franchisee from this company can do business.) Ask: When you buy a license (such as to use a famous person's image or name) to make a line of clothing, what exactly are you buying? (The brand name and its reputation only.) Review the importance of contracts from Chapter 37. Explain the elements of a basic franchise agreement. In small groups, have students create a basic licensing agreement. Ask: Why would buying a franchise, or licensing an existing product, be a good path to entrepreneurship for women and minorities? (These individuals often have difficulty accessing traditional capital markets; they might run into less discrimination than if they started from scratch because the franchise/license gives them a solid brand image; it's good for franchisors/licensors because they will be expanding the diversity of their ownership and perhaps their customer base.)

- **Issuing a Franchise or License.** Say: Now switch roles. You are the CEO of a company and are considering issuing a franchise. What kinds of things do you need to take into consideration before you issue a franchise? Hint: Think of this like a hiring interview. (Look for the person's commitment to your brand, business experience and track record of success, amount of money s/he has to invest, criminal record, etc.) Ask: You are a recording artist and are considering issuing a license to someone to create a fashion line. What kinds of things do you need to take into consideration before you issue it? Hint: Think of this as similar to researching potential manufacturers. (Look for a commitment to your brand, business experience and track record of success, the quality of the product your name will be associated with, etc.) Ask: What can happen if you don't consider these things in advance? (Your brand's reputation can be tarnished.)

- **Summary.** List the different ways a company can grow that have been discussed in the textbook: reinvesting profits and growing through "bootstrapping"; adding new products or services to increase market share; seeking new investors or going public by issuing stock; franchising; licensing; and other ways students think of. Ask: Which form of growth most appeals to you as an entrepreneur? Why?

## ASSESS THE LEARNING

- **Vocabulary.** Have students define terms in their own words and use each in a sentence, or complete the Vocabulary activity in the workbook.

- **Key Concepts.** Questions 1-3. **Answers:** 1. To make sure the franchisee does not also sell your competitors' products or represent their brands (that is, s/he can't own both a Pizza Hut and a Domino's). 2. A brand is a successful business/product/service that the public recognizes by its name, logo, and slogan; brands can be extended through licensing or franchising; with licensing only the brand's name and reputation are used; with franchising, the brand name/reputation and a standard operating procedure are provided to the franchisee. 3. McDonald's was the first franchisor to provide in-depth training to franchisees in everything from how to make perfect French fries to how employees should dress and greet customers. The entire system of cooking and serving food was timed. These innovations guaranteed that food in McDonald's would taste the same everywhere.

- **Critical Thinking.** Assign Question 1-2, 4. **Answers:** 1. Answers will vary; franchisee advantages include: less risk than starting a business from scratch, help with management and training, the benefit of national advertising campaigns; franchisee disadvantages include: giving up some control, franchisor may not live up to promises, franchisor business practices may adversely affect your business. 2. Answers will vary; license strengths include: name recognition of licensor to boost sales; weaknesses are the additional royalty payment; the licensor's bad behavior may adversely affect your product. 4. McDonald's — $125,000; Arby's — $40,000; GNC — $60,000; Tastee-Freez — $40,000.

- **Writing Practice.** Students could write a memo from the perspective of a particular franchisor/licensor (McDonald's or Disney) to a potential franchisee (a young entrepreneur) to gain experience in persuasive writing that still includes both sides of an issue.

- **Additional Workbook Activities Answers.**

  **Vocabulary Activity. Answers:** 1. a. 2. c. 3. e. 4. b. 5. d. 6. g. 7. f.

  **Quiz 46** in the workbook. **Answers:** 1. Answers will vary but should address that both parties benefit more than if they had tried to accomplish something on their own. 2. Because mutually beneficial relationships usually are more productive and last longer. 3. McDonald's. 4. Examples: Burger King, Pizza Hut, Taco Bell, KFC, Baskin-Robbins, others brought up through class activities. 5. Control: franchisors keep control over the business operations of its franchisees, whereas licensors do not. 6. Any wording that stops a franchisee from starting an additional or subsequent business of the same type for a specified period of time. 7. A predetermined percentage of the franchisee's income that is paid to the franchisor. 8. Any of the following: help with management and training, less risk because the business concept has already proven successful, national or regional advertising support. 9. Any of the following: franchisee may not operate the business as agreed, it may be hard to find qualified or trustworthy franchisees, franchisee may sue if the business loses money, the many government regulations related to franchising. 10. Any of the following: franchisee gives up control over operations, franchisor may not keep to the agreement, franchisor may engage in poor business practices that affect the franchisee.

## EXTEND THE LEARNING

- **Business Plan Practice.** Assign Critical Thinking question 3.

- *Entrepreneurs in Profile*. Have students read the chapter on Ray Kroc and McDonald's, and also Debbi Fields, to be able to answer these questions: Why do you think Kroc decided to franchise whereas Fields decided not to? What do you think might have changed Fields' mind? Discuss the benefits and limitations of their respective decisions?

- **Community Activity.** Have students interview a franchisee in your neighborhood about his/her experience with franchising. Types of questions students might include: What went well? What didn't? In what ways do you wish the franchisor provided more support? What do you wish you knew when you started that you know now? How well is the franchise agreement working?

- **Internet Activity.** Have students research franchising tips and opportunities at www.franchise.org. In addition, ask them to look up one franchising corporation to find out what is provided with a franchise, what the company requires of its franchisees, how the company supports women/minorities, and other information an entrepreneur might be interested in. For example, McDonald's has a "franchising opportunities" page through its Web site, as does Dunkin' Donuts/Baskin-Robbins, through www.dunkin-baskin-togos.com. Instruct students to create a memo or poster summarizing their findings.

- **Franchise/License Agreement Negotiation.** Divide class into groups of four. Two students in each group should think of a company and product, while the other two students figure out ways for franchising or licensing from that company. The two pairs negotiate (review negotiation principles from Chapter 15) and write up an agreement. Bring the groups together as a class and let the students evaluate these agreements against the criteria given in the textbook.

- **Field Trip to a Local McDonald's.** Contact the community relations person for a local McDonald's (or another franchise) and ask if your class might tour the restaurant to see the operations. The purpose of this visit would be to show students standardized procedures. Have students prepare questions beforehand.

## BUILD ACADEMIC AND LIFE-SKILL PROFICIENCIES

### *Skills Mean Success* Answers

**Math.** The answer is d. This is a tricky problem, but one that is common in achievement tests. Because no revenue figures are provided, the problem will require students to pick a number that they will use to solve it.If students have trouble getting started, tell them to choose "100" as the revenue for 2002. Remind them that, whenever they have to figure percentages, and numbers are not provided, they should *always* choose "100" as it will be the easiest to work with.

Solve the problem using the following steps:

2002 revenue = $100
2003 revenue = (100 × .2) + 100 = $120
2004 revenue = (120 × .2) + 120 = $144
144 − 100 = 44

2004 revenue was 44% greater than that of 2002.

**English.** If students don't have a business task, allow them to choose any operation for their instructions, such as baking a cake, listening to a CD player, or even tying shoes. If practical, have them swap papers and try to follow the instructions. They should evaluate each other's work for clarity, completeness, and accuracy. If possible, try to have someone unfamiliar with the task read and try to follow the instructions. People tend to "phantom read" instructions that may not actually be present, because they think they know what is to be done.

**Technology/English.** Evaluate students' summaries for brevity, clarity, and how well they maintained the thrust of the original work. The following sentences are examples.

○ Look for a franchisor that is focused on high-quality products and services.

○ Look for a franchisor that is dedicated to franchising as its main distribution channel.

○ Look for a franchisor that has an established market demand for its products and services.

○ Look for a franchisor that has an established trademark.

○ Look for a franchisor that has a sound business plan and a marketing system in place.

○ Look for a franchisor that has good rapport with its franchisees and a well-organized franchising association.

○ Require a franchisor to provide sales and earnings projections, and look for an adequate ROI.

○ Look for a franchisor that upholds the AAFD's Franchisee Bill of Rights.

If students do not have easy access to computers, you can find the article at the following URL:

http://www.aafd.org. Click on "Buying a Franchise", then select "8 Things to Look for in a Franchise." With the proper permission, print the article and distribute to the class as necessary.

### CHAPTER 47

# INTERNATIONAL OPPORTUNITIES

---

## ORGANIZE THE LEARNING

| | | |
|---|---|---|
| **CHAPTER OBJECTIVES** | **BUSINESS PLAN ACTIVITIES** | **PREREQUISITES** |
| • Cultivate an understanding of other cultures. | *Workbook Business Plan Review* International Opportunities  47-1, 47-2 | Chapters 4 and 39 may provide help-ful background. |
| • Explore exporting and importing opportunities. | *Workbook/Textbook Chapter Review* Critical Thinking 4, 5 | **VOCABULARY** export, foreign exchange rate, import, quota, tariff, trade barrier |
| • Research customers and competi-tion internationally. | **SKILLS MEAN SUCCESS** | |
| • Conduct trade in foreign currencies. | *Leadership* Understanding Cultural Differences | |
| **NFTE RESOURCES** | *Math* Mathematical Operations and Reasoning: Calculating Percentage Change in Currency Exchange Rates | |
| • Text pp. 528-533 | | |
| • Transparencies T47-1 to T47-2 | | |
| • Workbook/BLMs Chapter 47 | | |
| • Test Bank Chapter 47 | | |

---

## KEY QUESTION

**How might I discover and plan for business opportuni-ties abroad?**

## PREPARE FOR LEARNING

• ***Wall Street Journal.*** Collect copies of *The Wall Street Journal* for the Currency Exchange activity.

## SET A CONTEXT FOR LEARNING

• **Focus 1: Exports.** Ask the students to consider the following: What would you guess are the most well-known American exports? **Answer:** Expect the fol-lowing: fast food (McDonald's, KFC, etc.), entertain-ment (movies, music, etc.), soft drinks (Coke, Pepsi), jeans (Levi's), aircraft (Boeing), computers (Intel, Microsoft, IBM), cars (Ford, GM).

• **Focus 2: Cultural Crossroads.** Challenge the class with this scenario: Think of a time when you met someone from a different culture. This person could be from another country or speak a foreign language or even be from another part of the U.S., or the situation could go back to when you first came to the U.S. if you are an immigrant. What misunderstandings arose when you were trying to communicate with this person?

• **Discussion Launcher: Anonymous Quote.** Ask stu-dents to explain: "Where goods cross borders, armies don't." (Trading partners tend to avoid war-fare with each other because they have too much to lose if trade is disrupted. Give the American-Canadian relationship as an example. Although the countries don't always agree on foreign policy, etc., the last actual war between the two neighbors and important trading partners was in 1812, when Canada was still a colony of Great Britain.)

## DEVELOP AND CLOSE THE LEARNING

• **Overview of International Trade.** Refer to Chapter 39 and how the American economy is not isolated but intricately intertwined with the economies of other countries with different cultures. Invite the students to speculate about how international opportunities abound for entrepreneurs —but that there are addi-tional issues that must be considered in business ven-tures that cross borders, such as language, cultures, governmental policies, and currency differences.

• **Importing and Exporting.** Use transparency T47-1 to define importing and exporting. Ask students who are immigrants or those who have traveled to other countries to think of and share any foreign products that they liked but that are not available here.

Categories to consider might include food, clothing, entertainment, modes of transportation, beauty products (or "looks"), etc. Ask students:

○ Would the American public like these products?

○ Might they be good candidates for importing?

○ Are there products you use in America that you couldn't find in the other country?

○ Which products might be good candidates for exporting?

Choose one potential import and one potential export from the discussion. Break class into small groups; assign groups to brainstorm or research (using the textbook or the Internet) a list of questions that would need to be addressed to pursue this importing or exporting opportunity. **LINKS**»*Economics*

- **Cultural Differences.** Explain that not everyone in the world conducts business in the same way — there are different customs and accepted ways of behaving. Have students role-play some common cultural-difference business scenarios. Examples of situations:

  ○ One believes that being direct and getting right to business in a meeting shows respect for the other person's time. The other believes that it is correct and polite to chat, exchange pleasantries, and get to know the person as an individual before starting the business part of the meeting.

  ○ One believes that it is proper to maintain three feet of space between individuals to show respect for the other person's personal space. The other believes that it is proper to greet the other person with a hug and to stand within 18 inches to show friendliness.

  ○ One believes that it is best to give a gift at the beginning of the meeting to pave the way for a smooth negotiation. The other believes that giving/receiving gifts comes at the end of the meeting to solidify the agreement.

  ○ One person comes from a place where it is illegal to give bribes (or any additional payments to individuals involved in a deal) to smooth the negotiation. The other person is used to not doing business that does not include an extra payment for his/her personal attention to the matter.

  ○ One believes that women belong in business. The other does not.

Brainstorm some tips for an entrepreneur entering that particular foreign country to do business. What general areas of behavior might they want to pay attention to (greetings, the giving of gifts, the pace of events in a business meeting, the amount of personal space people need, finalizing contracts, etc.). Challenge students to define "culture" (the behaviors and beliefs of a social group). **LINKS**»*Sociology*

- **Currency Exchange.** Use transparency T47-2 to explain currency exchange and exchange rates. Ask: How might currency exchange affect your record-keeping? (It adds the additional requirement of converting foreign sales or purchases into your home country's currency.) Have students look up the current exchange rates for the yen, euro, British pound, Australian dollar, Canadian dollar, South African rand, Mexican peso, Indian rupee, etc. What would US $10 equal in these foreign currencies?

- **Summary.** Refer to the Discussion Launcher. Discuss how international trade contributes to a more peaceful world by creating friendly and cooperative, rather than antagonistic, relations among people across national and cultural borders.

## ASSESS THE LEARNING

- **Vocabulary.** Have students define the terms in their own words and use each in a sentence, or use the Vocabulary activity in the workbook.

- **Key Concepts.** Questions 1, 4. **Answers:** 1. Answers will vary; it may be helpful to direct students to do some research online to gain insight into wages in foreign countries. 4. Answers will vary; you may want to extend this question to have students consider what country they might want to visit and why.

- **Critical Thinking.** Questions 1-3. **Answers:** 1. 2,380 yen (119 × 20). 2. 1,893.5 yen (189.35 × 10). 3. a. 6 euro. b. $3. c. $3 is less than the $5 the label owner would've made selling in the States, but if the $10 covers costs, the additional sales in the new market, even at $3, add up to additional profit. d. It would be a better deal if the store owner keeps the same price because the label owner's profit will be worth more in U.S. dollars ($6 instead of $3).

- **Writing Practice.** Assign Key Concepts question 3.

- **Additional Workbook Activities Answers.**

  **Vocabulary Activity. Answers:** Answers will vary but should demonstrate an understanding of international opportunities and issues in entrepreneurship along with a correct usage of the terminology. Answers should explore *exporting* and *importing* opportunities and globalization. Issues include cultural differences, *trade barriers*, such as *tariffs* and *quotas*, and calculating *foreign exchange rates*.

**Quiz 47** in the workbook. **Answers:** 1. The way the product travels: importing involves bringing a product *into* a country, whereas exporting involves shipping a product *out* of a country. 2. Tariffs (a tax on imports) and quotas (a limit to the number of products that can be imported). 3. Any of the following: North American Free Trade Agreement (NAFTA); General Agreement on Tariffs and Trade (GATT); Economic Union (EU); the Internet. 4. $30.75; $49.50; $144.00; $145.60; $145. 5. Answers will vary but should describe a specific difference, such as those roles played in class or those described in student posters in the Entrepreneurial World's Fair activity below, and should provide specific tips for how to research and address the differences. 6. Answers will vary; examples: Toyota, Honda, BMW, BBC World news, Who Wants to Be a Millionaire and other British TV show concepts, Cadbury or Lindt chocolate. 7. Answers will vary; examples: Ford, McDonald's, Disney movies, Coca-Cola, Reebok, Levi's.

## EXTEND THE LEARNING

- **Business Plan Practice.** Critical Thinking questions 4-5.

- **Community Activity.** Assign Key Concepts question 5. You may want to instruct students to interview anyone they know who comes from a foreign country, as not all students will have foreign-born relatives. Have them share their findings through presentations, memos or posters.

- **Internet Activity.** Have class look up information online regarding NAFTA and the Economic Union as free trade zones. Ask: Why were these zones created? How well are they working? Who (i.e., groups of people or countries) has benefited the most? The least? What issues are the free trade zones facing? What are the arguments for and against these zones? Assign Key Concepts question 2.

- **Entrepreneurial World's Fair.** Have each student choose a different country to research through the Internet or by using other reference materials, and create a poster or brochure that includes: population, imports, exports, cultural differences that might affect business, amount of trade it does with the U.S., trade barriers found (tariffs or quotas), the currency and its current exchange rate with the U.S. dollar, and any other information the student thinks may be pertinent to potential entrepreneurs. Display

their work around the room and give the class (and visitors) time to view and to learn about different cultures. Students may also ask questions of each other regarding their findings. **LINKS** ↠ *Geography*

- **Tracking Global Business.** Have students track the value of the U.S. dollar relative to other currencies and the U.S. trade balance in the last year. Instruct them to create a graph of the value of the dollar or the U.S. trade balance and interpret what the graph means. Is the U.S. economy stronger or weaker on a global scale than it was a year ago? Ask what they would forecast for the next year.

## BUILD ACADEMIC AND LIFE-SKILL PROFICIENCIES

### *Skills Mean Success* Answers

**Leadership.** Answers will vary based on research. One example is the approach to meetings. For instance, in America, the approach to business meetings is practical and efficient. Attendees will get right to the business at hand after spending only a few minutes on introductions. In Japan, it is considered rude to start a meeting without spending time on relationship-building and pleasantries. Some students may want to discuss why dress may be an important factor in cross-cultural business dealings.

Two helpful online resources are www.traderscity.com and www.culturalsavvy.com.

**Math.** 1. Australia: 25.6% gain in value vs. one U.S. dollar. (In 1990 it took 0.78 $A to equal $1US, but it took only 0.58 $A in 2000.) Canada: loss of 25.86%; Japan: 25.5% gain; Mexico: 236.3% loss; United Kingdom: 14.6% gain 2. Australia 3. Mexico 4. Mexico and Canada, because their goods were cheaper to buy due to their currencies being lower compared to the U.S. dollar. 5. Australia, Japan, and the UK, because the higher value of their currencies compared to the US dollar made U.S. goods cheaper and more affordable for people there to buy. Explain that currency exchange can be tricky. Always check to see how the exchange rate is given: what does one unit of that currency "cost" in U.S. dollars vs. what is $1U.S. worth in the other currency. Some students may want to compare current exchange rates with those from 1990 and 2000.

# INVESTMENT GOALS AND RISK TOLERANCE

## ORGANIZE THE LEARNING

### CHAPTER OBJECTIVES

- Establish the habit of saving ten percent of your income.
- Explain the concepts of present and future value.
- Discover your investment risk tolerance.
- Set financial goals.

### NFTE RESOURCES

- Text pp. 534-547
- Transparencies T48-1 and T48-2
- Workbook/BLMs Chapter 48
- Test Bank Chapter 48
- A Business for the Young Entrepreneur: *Party Clown*

### BUSINESS PLAN ACTIVITIES

*Workbook Business Plan Review*
Investment Goals And Risk Tolerance 48-1, 48-2, 48-3

*Workbook/Textbook Chapter Review*
Critical Thinking 5

### SKILLS MEAN SUCCESS

*English*
Writing for Information and to Persuade: Word Choice

*Math*
Mathematical Representation and Data: Interpreting Tables

### Leadership
Entrepreneurial Skills and Attitudes

### PREREQUISITES

The content of Chapters 3, 33, and 34 will be helpful for understanding this chapter.

### VOCABULARY

diversification, index fund, interest, investment, mutual fund

## KEY QUESTION

**How can I make my money work harder?**

## SET A CONTEXT FOR LEARNING

- **Focus 1: Risk.** Ask the students to consider what "risk" means and how they feel about it. For example, what are activities they consider risky?

- **Focus 2: Risk Survey.** Have students complete the risk survey in the textbook.

- **Discussion Launcher 1: How Much Do You Want to Be Worth?** Ask the students to write down an amount they think would be sufficient to retire on, if they retired in 45 years. Have them discuss in pairs how they might go about accumulating that sum.

- **Discussion Launcher 2: Saying.** Ask students to interpret and discuss: "A bird in the hand is worth two in the bush." The discussion should arrive at the concept of the relative value of being safe and satisfied with a "sure thing" (the bird in the hand), even if that holding is potentially less valuable than what one *could* have (two [birds] in the bush) — i.e., safety and security vs. opportunity with risk.

## DEVELOP AND CLOSE THE LEARNING

- **Investment Review.** Remind students that investing is related to the flow of money through the economy: an investor is letting someone else use his/her money for a time in exchange for (hopefully) getting more money back. For example, putting money in a savings account gives the bank the funds to loan out money to other people at a higher rate; or buying stocks or bonds gives a company the funds to buy equipment, operate, etc. Divide the class into small groups and assign each group one of the following concept groupings:

  ○ Risk, return, ROI, time value of money

  ○ Stock, stock market/trading, dividend

  ○ Bond, maturity, interest, savings account, inflation

  Have each group research and briefly report to the class from an *investor* — as opposed to an entrepreneur — point-of-view: what each term means, why each term is important to an investor. Groups should refer to the following chapters for further information: 3 (ROI), 33 (Stocks) and 34 (Bonds).

- **Savings Challenge.** Use the textbook to discuss the importance of "paying yourself first." Have students brainstorm ways they could save $2 each week from a $10 allowance. Emphasize that such a practice would only mean giving up, say, one soft drink a week or one movie a month; the benefit would be having money when you need it because of unexpected situations that might occur later on. Have students calculate how much that savings account would be worth in six months at $2 a week and .03% interest compounded monthly. Ask students to sign a contract that specifies how much money they will save over the next three months (at 10% of their income?). After three months (say, over the summer), they might send you their most recent bank statement to compete for a prize — for example, a business book — for the students who have met their contract obligation. Emphasize that it is a good idea to keep an amount (about three months' worth of their typical monthly expenses) in a saving account for emergencies before investing money in riskier options.

- **Ways Money Can Grow.** Summarize the groups' presentations by outlining the ways money can make more money:

  ○ Compound interest (savings and bonds) — remind class of the Rule of 72 (amount invested divided by interest rate equals number of periods it will take the investment to double), which is a "short cut" for calculating compound interest.

  ○ Buy low, sell high (stocks and bonds).

  ○ Occasional payouts (stock dividends reinvested).

Ask students, in contrast, to list ways money *doesn't* grow (spending it, putting it "under a mattress"). Use several examples to demonstrate how these growth opportunities work. For example, show on the board (see table below) the growth of these investments over ten years:

  ○ Compound interest: $100 in a savings account that pays 2% a year.

  ○ Stocks: a stock bought for $100 and sold for $500.

  ○ Stock dividends: a stock bought for $100 that pays a quarterly dividend of $1 (table only shows the value of the dividends adding up, without interest, and does not take into account changes in the value of the stock itself).

| Year | Savings interest | Stock price | Stock dividend |
|---|---|---|---|
| 1 | $2.00 | $100 | $4 |
| 2 | $4.04 | $80 | $8 |
| 3 | $6.12 | $145 | $12 |
| 4 | $8.24 | $233 | $16 |
| 5 | $10.41 | $200 | $20 |
| 6 | $12.62 | $300 | $24 |
| 7 | $14.87 | $420 | $28 |
| 8 | $17.17 | $390 | $32 |
| 9 | $19.51 | $450 | $39 |
| 10 | $21.90 | $500 | $40 |

Points to elicit from a class discussion of this table might include: recognition of the *volatility* (tendency to fluctuate in value) of the stock, including losing part of the initial investment amount in Year 2; how the stock dividend (bonus paid to stockholders by a company) is money made *in addition to* changes in stock price; how the principal for the savings account is insured by the federal government and so can't be lost, as stock investments can be; emphasizing the point that compounding only works when an investor keeps the interest earned in the account — so it can earn more interest; the direct relationship between risk and return (higher risk usually means higher return).

- **$1 Now Does Not Equal $1 Later.** Set up the scenario: You have $100 to invest and three opportunities before you:

  ○ A bond that will mature in five years with an interest rate of 5% per year.

  ○ A stock whose rate of return has averaged 6% a year and is expected — but not guaranteed — to remain stable.

  ○ A savings account that pays 2% a year reliably for an unlimited time period.

Whereas the activity above required calculation of compounding, this time introduce the look-up table for the future value of money on transparency T48-2. Show students how to look up how much these investments will be worth in five years. **Answers:** bond — $127.63, stock — $133.82, savings account — $110.41. Another way to look at these situations is from a future point in time backwards toward the present. This is to calculate the present value of money you expect to receive in the future. For example, how much would you need to invest in each of the above investments if you wanted your value at the end to be $100? Use transparency T48-1 to look up the answers. **Answers:** bond $70.36, stock $74.73, savings account $90.57. Return to Discussion Launcher 1. As an example, if a student wanted to be worth $1 million dollars in 45 years, how much would s/he need in savings after 30 years if the interest rate were 7%? After 15 years? Now? **Answers:** Permit the students to use calculators. For example, take $1 million x .36245 to get $362,450, then multiply the new figure by .36245 to get an approximation of $131,370, then multiply the new figure by .36245 to get an approximation of $47,615; that is, if a person invested $47,615 today s/he'd end up with around $1 million in 45 years. Have students similarly figure the present value for their "worth" goals.

- **Types of Risks.** Ask the students to speculate: Are the different future values of the different investments the only thing you should consider? (No, because they are not equal in risk, a factor that is actually reflected in the different rates of return; investors have a higher chance of losing money with stocks than other investments.) Elicit from the class or explain the two main types of risk:

  ○ *time* (when you lay out money now and get a return later).

  ○ *liquidity* (when you give money that is converted into something else that may or may not be sold or converted back to cash easily).

  Discuss why a longer time period or lower liquidity is riskier: what could happen? (You could lose the money: uncertainty about what will happen, the business that has your money closes, etc.) Risks related to time can also be broken down into further categories: the effect of inflation; not getting your money back later; and the lost opportunity of using your money elsewhere, such as to purchase a different investment. Ask students to work in small groups to list concrete examples of each type of risk. (Not getting a sufficient interest rate on a bond to counteract the effect of inflation, a company going bankrupt when you are a stockholder, buying stock in a small business that uses the money to buy specialized equipment that can't be resold easily [low liquidity]). Other examples of investment choices you may want to share: putting money into savings (highly liquid) vs. into building a house (less liquid but can be sold and converted into cash) vs. investing in a hair salon (which may have no assets to sell and thus less liquid). Have students evaluate several investments in terms of their time and liquidity risk. For example, a business with lots of equipment vs. just materials and effort, a business that will show a profit in one year vs. three: which would an investor consider more risky? Why?

- **Investing.** Create a continuum on the board with "least risky" at one end, "most risky" at the other, and "average risk" in the middle. Elicit from the class where to place cash, bonds and stocks on the continuum and ask why they think the three are arranged in this way. (Cash accounts are almost always FDIC-insured, have high liquidity, have low but stable rates of return, so are less risky; bonds are debt and paid back before owner's equity is taken out if a company goes bankrupt, but are not insured and investors could lose principal, so are medium risky; stocks are not insured, highly volatile, and stockholders are the last to get their money in case of bankruptcy, so are more risky.) Ask students to brainstorm the time and liquidity risks of each investment. (Cash accounts have low time and low liquidity risks because you could get your money back at any time; bonds are higher in time but still have relatively low liquidity risks; stocks can be high on both types of risks — because of volatility it's best to buy stocks only when you can stay in the market for ten years or so.) Invite students to share other types of investments: home ownership, other real estate, whole life savings-insurance hybrids, works of art, etc. Return to the results of the earlier Focus activities and the importance of the *subjective* (personal, emotional, "feel good") evaluation of risk. By show of hands, have students share which type of investment they feel most comfortable with. Stress that there are no "wrong" answers. Everyone's situation can be slightly different. Introduce the concept of *diversification* as a way to "have your cake and eat it too." That is, by spreading investment money over several types of investments, you can end up with higher returns for lower risk. Discuss two ways to diversify: either independently buying individual investments of different types to balance them, or buying into mutual funds where you own a share of a wider portfolio of investments. **LINKS**»*Consumer Ed*

- **Summary.** Use transparency T48-2 for reference. Present the following scenario for students to answer individually, then discuss as a class: A friend asks you to lend her $200. If the current market interest rate is 3%, what is the least amount that would be acceptable for her to pay you back at the end of the year? What other factors should you consider in your decision? Would you loan her the money? Why or why not? **Answers:** $206; other factors include risks such as how trustworthy or reliable she may be, or what she will be using the money for, or other opportunities you have for using that same money.

## ASSESS THE LEARNING

- **Vocabulary.** Have students define terms in their own words and use each in a sentence, or assign the Vocabulary activity in the workbook.

- **Key Concepts.** Questions 1-2. **Answers:** 1. Answers will vary. 2. Answers will vary.

- **Critical Thinking.** Questions 1-5. **Answers:** 1. $45; $20. 2. Answers will vary; focus on checking the math. 3-5. Answers will vary.

- **Additional Workbook Activities Answers.**

  **Vocabulary Activity Answers:** 1. interest. 2. diversification. 3. index fund. 4. investment. 5. mutual fund.

  **Quiz 48** in the workbook. **Answers:** 1. $1,060. 2. c. 3. 6 periods using the Rule of 72. 4. Inflation will make the money worth less in the future, there is a risk of not receiving the money back, and you may have lost opportunities to invest it at a better rate elsewhere. 5. $127.63. 6. $3.11. 7. $1,898.30. 8. 82 cents. 9. $50.84. 10. $164.77.

## EXTEND THE LEARNING

- **A Business for the Young Entrepreneur.** As a class, read about party clown businesses. Ask student to determine what other information investors would want to know to help them decide whether this type of business is a good opportunity or not. How risky is this type of business? How liquid? How long would it take to start making money?

- **Internet Activity.** Have students use an Internet search engine to look up the current Federal Reserve interest rate as well as the interest rates on different types of products (savings account, money market account, car loan, mortgage, etc.) at different banks (e.g., Bank of America, Citibank, a local bank). Have them analyze the risks involved for the bank and how they are reflected in the interest rates. Have students discuss in class or write a memo explaining how the Federal Reserve and banks set interest rates. **LINKS**》·*Government*

- **Compounding Relay Race.** Divide the class into groups of five or six. Write on the board: a starting dollar amount, and an interest rate. Each team has one sheet of paper. The first student multiplies the two to determine the new principal amount then hands the paper to the second student to calculate, etc. After the teams are done, they can check their math by calculating the original dollar amount by the multiplier on transparency T48-2 for the interest rate

given and number of students on the team (who represent the "periods of compounding"). For example, $200, 3%, 5 students: first calculation is $206, then 212.18, 218.55, 225.10, 231.85; check by multiplying 200 by 1.1593, which equals 231.86. Continue presenting problems until students seem comfortable with both the compounding calculation and using the chart to check their answers.

- **News Affecting Stocks.** Have students find three news stories that illustrate how current events affect stock prices. For each case, ask students to create a memo or slide that explains how and why.
  **LINKS**》·*Economics*

## BUILD ACADEMIC AND LIFE-SKILL PROFICIENCIES

### *Skills Mean Success* Answers

**English and Technology.** Encourage students who find words and phrases used in humorous, unusual, or memorable ways that will attract readers' attention. Challenge them to use "imagistic" expressions, such as *similes* (a comparison using "like" or "as") and references to popular culture. Invite students who are familiar with the thesaurus (and dictionary) features in word processing software to demonstrate its use to the others. Answers will vary, but, for example: 1. a. promising, exciting, not for the timid, something to celebrate, as exciting as time travel; b. beyond all expectations, richly deserved, encouraging; c. savage, intense, suicidal, like a demolition derby; d. completely satisfied, like an uncle after a Thanksgiving dinner, 102% satisfied; e. foundational, rock solid, how we judge ourselves, our Super Bowl, a buffet of satisfied needs. 2. Make a "Word Power" collage or display of examples collected by the students. Help them appreciate the creativity of the copywriters and communications specialists who developed the ads.

**Math.** 1. a. $45; b. $50.36; c. $ 938.60; d. $ 4,344.40. 2. No; $1,770.59, because the table is based on the value of the investment increasing.

**Leadership.** Answers will vary, but the attitudes and skills for success listed — some of which are suggested by the physically-challenged skier — could include optimism, positive thinking, "can do" attitude, courage, desire to push oneself to achieve, and the ability to think quickly, adaptability, problem solving, and goal setting.

# INVESTING FOR A SECURE FUTURE

---

## ORGANIZE THE LEARNING

### CHAPTER OBJECTIVES
- Choose investments in line with your risk tolerance and goals.
- Create an investment portfolio and project its return.

### NFTE RESOURCES
- Text pp. 548-553
- Transparencies T49-1 to T49-3 and T48-2 from Chapter 48
- Workbook/BLMs Chapter 49
- Test Bank Chapter 49

### BUSINESS PLAN ACTIVITIES
*Workbook Business Plan Review*
Investing For A Secure Future 49-1, 49-2, 49-3

*Workbook/Textbook Chapter Review*
Critical Thinking 5

### SKILLS MEAN SUCCESS
*Leadership*
Preparing and Making a Presentation

### PREREQUISITES
Students should pre- read Chapter 48 in the textbook.

### VOCABULARY
annuity, portfolio

---

## KEY QUESTION

**How can I invest intelligently to achieve my financial goals?**

## SET A CONTEXT FOR LEARNING

- **Focus 1: Security vs. Growth.** Ask the students to decide: What percentage of $100 are you willing to lose to make a 5% return? 10%? 100%?

- **Focus 2: Present Value of Money.** Show transparency T48-1. Ask students to calculate how much they should invest now if they want their investments to equal $10,000 after 10 years at the following annual interest rates: 5%, 8%, 12%.

- **Discussion Launcher: Proverb.** Discuss the English proverb at the beginning of the chapter: "'Tis money that begets money." (If you have money and use it wisely, it will get you more money.)

## DEVELOP AND CLOSE THE LEARNING

- **Chapter 48 Review.** Ask volunteers to summarize the main concepts developed in Chapter 48: the importance of saving; types of investment risks; differences in risk and return between cash, bonds, and stocks; diversification; and the present and future values of money. Chapter 49 will put the concepts of Chapter 48 into action.

- **What Should You Invest In?** Using the textbook and transparency T49-1, define *portfolio* and the criteria for selecting which investments to include. Use the 16-year-old example in the textbook or other examples, to show how different answers to the criteria will result in different allocations of money to various investments. Other examples could include:

  - A 45 year old, who is relatively risk-averse, investing for retirement at age 65.

  - A 25 year old, who has moderate risk tolerance, investing for her five-year-old's college education.

  - A 30 year old investing to be a millionaire by 50.

- **Portfolio Analysis.** Use transparency T49-2 that shows different pie charts of portfolio balances. Divide the class into small groups. Have each analyze one chart and create a profile of the individual who might have such a profile.

- **Annuities.** Recall from Chapter 48 the examples of calculating future value of an investment if *all* of the money was invested at once. Elicit from the students or explain that, however, most people invest a small sum every month, so the principal in their portfolios increases little by little. Explain that this changes the multiplier used to calculate how much the investment will grow over time. Use transparencies T48-2 and T49-3 to have class compare differences and general patterns between the two charts. (In general, an annuity grows faster). Use transparency T49-3 to calculate the future value of several annuities:

- $1,000 for 20 years at 15%.
- $500 for 30 years at 5%.
- $1,200 for 10 years at 3%.

Ask for volunteers to explain IRAs (Individual Retirement Accounts). Explain that many IRAs work like annuities: working people put $2,000 or $3,000 into their IRAs each year and let it grow into a retirement "nest egg." If the interest rate averaged 10% and students put $2,000 into an IRA each year from the first year they started working at age 25, until age 65, how much money would they have to retire on? **Answer:** $885,185. **LINKS )**»*Consumer Ed*

- **Summary.** Have students answer for themselves the three criteria for investment selection: investment goals, risk tolerance, amount of time to reach goals. (This activity will help them prepare to answer the Critical Thinking questions in the textbook.)

## ASSESS THE LEARNING

- **Vocabulary.** Have students define terms in their own words and use each in a sentence, or assign the Vocabulary activity in the workbook.

- **Key Concepts.** Questions 1-2. These questions should be answered after students have done the Critical Thinking questions below. **Answers:** 1-2. Answers will vary.

- **Critical Thinking.** Questions 1-5. **Answers:** 1. Answers will vary; check that figures add up to $10,000. 2. Answers will vary; check that math is correct given students' answers to question 1. 3-5. Answers will vary.

- **Additional Workbook Activities Answers.**

  **Vocabulary Activity Answers:** 1. a. 2. c.

  **Quiz 49** in the workbook. **Answers:** 4. Any of the following: your balance is out of line with your goals or risk tolerance, or your goals or risk tolerance change, or your life circumstances change. 5. $171,825. 6. $57,507. 7. $407,469.

## EXTEND THE LEARNING

- **Stock Contest.** If your class has been doing the stock contest and/or stocks-and-bonds contest introduced in Chapters 33 and 34, this would be a good time to bring their tracking sheets to class. They can use the information, in addition to the cash in their checking accounts, to create pie charts depicting the composition of their portfolios and analyze how diversified their investment holdings are.

- **Mutual Fund Analysis.** Mutual funds are good examples of diversified portfolios that you pay a small fee for someone else to manage for you. Download a prospectus for a mutual fund or two from investment firm Web sites, such as Putnam, Merrill Lynch, etc. As a class, analyze how well balanced their portfolios are or are not (if they are invested in one market or type of stock). **LINKS )**»*Consumer Ed*

- **Investment Consultant.** Divide the class into small groups, each which will be an investment consulting firm. They are competing for the business of the 16 year old (the example in the textbook). This client has provided these firms with the pie chart information in the textbook regarding how she is currently investing her money. The firms' tasks are:

  1. Evaluate her current portfolio based on her present investment goals: Do you think she will reach her goals? What might you help her reach them faster or in a better way?

  2. Help her build a 20-year financial plan. She plans to go to college and become a lawyer, which will take an additional three years of schooling after college. She gets good grades in high school and so may get a scholarship. She plans on working part time during college and also continuing her NFTE flower arranging business. She hopes to get married around the age of 30, after her law career has stabilized, and have children in her early-to-mid thirties.

  Allow time for groups to present their "pitches" for the 16 year old's business.

## BUILD ACADEMIC AND LIFE-SKILL PROFICIENCIES

### *Skills Mean Success* Answers

**Leadership.** This activity can be as complex or as simple as the time available and level of student interest. Encourage the presenters to do some mathematical comparisons of money invested over time, versus savings realized from reinvestment of the same amount in the business, or in lifestyle improvements. Discuss practical purchases vs. frills and self-indulgence; rate of return on investment vs. interest rates being paid out on current debt; risk vs. retention and financial security, and what opportunities might be lost if someone's savings are tied up in either investments or assets.

### CHAPTER 50

# EXIT STRATEGIES:
## *Creating Wealth*

## ORGANIZE THE LEARNING

### CHAPTER OBJECTIVES

- Think about how you want to exit your business one day.
- Explore various exit strategies that will "harvest" the wealth created by your business.
- Choose exit strategies that will make your business more attractive to investors.
- Make a wise decision about when to harvest your business.

### NFTE RESOURCES

- Text pp. 554-563
- Transparencies T48-1, T50-1 to T50-3
- Workbook/BLMs Chapter 50
- Test Bank Chapter 50

### BUSINESS PLAN ACTIVITIES

*Workbook Business Plan Review*
Exit Strategy 50-1, 50-2

*Workbook/Textbook Chapter Review*
Critical Thinking 4;
Business Plan Integrative Summary

### SKILLS MEAN SUCCESS

*English*
Reading for Meaning: Deciphering Unfamiliar Words

*Math*
Mental Math: Reasoning and Operations, Approximation

### PREREQUISITES

The content of Chapter 48 is helpful for understanding this material.

### VOCABULARY

exit strategy, harvesting, liquidation, merger, net present value

## KEY QUESTION

**How can I turn my business into wealth in the future?**

## PREPARE FOR LEARNING

- *Wall Street Journal.* Have available copies of the newspaper for students to use during class.

- **Guest Speaker.** If you plan to invite a speaker as described in Extend the Learning, make arrangements in advance.

## SET A CONTEXT FOR LEARNING

- **Focus: Vision of Future.** Ask the students to dream: What kind of life do I want? How can I make my community a better place?

- **Focus 2: Net Present Value of Money.** Show transparency T48-1. Ask students to calculate how much you should pay for a stock today if it is in an industry averaging 9% growth and the stock is expected to be valued at $100 per share according to its plan to merge in five years. **Answer:** About $65 (look at period 5 and the 9% cell and multiply by $100).

- **Discussion Launcher: Lord Quote.** Ask students to interpret: "What really matters is what you do with what you have." (Anyone successful has made the best use of whatever talents and opportunities s/he was given.)

## DEVELOP AND CLOSE THE LEARNING

- **Exit Strategies for the Entrepreneur.** Use transparency T50-1 to define and describe liquidation and the various harvesting strategies. Explain that liquidation is what entrepreneurs want to avoid — it is like a farmer "losing the crop" — and harvesting is what entrepreneurs aim for. Ask students to ponder what events or factors might lead to liquidation and what, if anything, entrepreneurs might do to prevent them. (Lawsuit, changing consumer tastes, poor management, industry becoming obsolete, personal problems, etc.) Divide the class into small groups and have each take one harvesting strategy (e.g., selling, reducing reinvestment, IPO, merger). Have the groups try to find concrete examples of these strategies in action. Discussion questions might include:

  ○ Which strategy seems to be the least intimidating or stressful, or be the most ambitious (biggest potential reward but also higher risk)?

  ○ What are the steps involved in the various strategies, and how do they differ?

○ Which strategies require more advance planning?

○ Which strategies seem to be used more? Why do you think that is?

- **Exit Strategies for Investors.** Ask: Who besides you, the entrepreneur, is most interested in and likely to be affected by exit strategies? (Your current investors.) Why? (Because they also want to get more money out of your business than they put in; they want to make a high ROI.) Using transparency T50-2, discuss how investors might harvest their investment from your business. Divide the class into five groups and have each create a concrete scenario (e.g., write a story, prepare a skit, record an imaginary meeting) of a company that used one of the strategies. **LINKS**»*Dramatic Arts*

- **Business Valuation.** Explain that exit strategies depend on how much your business is worth to others. Elicit from the students that when a person spends money (rather than investing it) s/he doesn't usually expect the value of the purchase (a car, furniture, a computer, a vacation) to grow or to increase in value or create future earnings; on the other hand, investing means you do expect some future value. A business generates profit and is expected to continue to do so in the future — an investor is counting on that future revenue and it has a *discounted* (or net present) value today.

- **The Present Value of a Business's Future Earnings.** A business's future earnings stream can be converted into present value, using the same present-value-of-money tables as discussed in Chapter 48. However, there are also "short cut" methods of business valuation. Using transparency T50-3, discuss these methods. Ask students to brainstorm what types of businesses might be good for using each method of valuation. (Retail outlets, fast food, and other common businesses for a comparative method; manufacturing, oil, and other long-standing, well-organized or key industries for benchmarks; service businesses or retail businesses for multiple of earnings; book value for companies with assets that are easy to value [mostly not service businesses].) Summarize that, in the end, the value of a business is what a buyer or investor is willing to pay for it.

- **Summary.** Reinforce the notions, which run throughout this curriculum, that the keys to wealth-building are *ownership* and *smart risk-taking*. Explain that many people think renting or employment is less risky than holding a mortgage or starting a business. Elicit from the class some hidden opportunity costs associated with the former:

○ A person can get fired, laid off or evicted and have nothing.

○ The only exit strategy for renting a place to live (as opposed to home ownership) or working for someone else (as opposed to entrepreneurship) is to leave—all the money and time consumed is lost; there is no payout at the end.

○ A steady paycheck or no mortgage may seem safer, but may not be in the long run.

Ask students to brainstorm things they would like to own (e.g., house, college education, car, business, boat, etc.), how much they anticipate these items will cost, whether these purchases are expenses (when you buy them your money is gone/consumed or the items depreciate in value) or investments (these items can generate future cash streams), and how they plan to finance the purchases.

## ASSESS THE LEARNING

- **Vocabulary.** Have students define terms in their own words, or assign the workbook activity.

- **Key Concepts.** Questions 1-3. **Answers:** 1. 1. $12,000; $3,000; $22,500; $90,000. 2-3. Answers will vary.

- **Critical Thinking.** Questions 1-3. **Answers:** 1. With replication (franchising and licensing), an entrepreneur is usually still involved with business operations; with harvesting, s/he is not. 2. Answers will vary; it would probably be most helpful to comment on how well thought through the plans are, and whether the choices made are more oriented toward investing or spending. 3. Answers will vary; check to make sure students applied the three-times-net-profit rule, an industry benchmark, or a comparative approach to valuing the businesses.

- **Writing Practice.** Let the students choose one company from *Entrepreneurs in Profile* and familiarize themselves with the early stages of the business (before they went public). Ask students to write a formal letter to that company's early investors explaining how they will most likely get their money out of the enterprise.

- **Additional Workbook Activities Answers.**

**Vocabulary Activity** Answers: Answers should demonstrate an understanding of potential exit strategies and correct usage of terminology.

**Quiz 50** in the workbook. **Answers:** 1. How the entrepreneur plans to turn his/her investment into wealth when leaving the business. 2. Any of the following:

selling the business (acquisition, ESOP, or MBO), taking it public (IPO), or merger. 3. Because liquidation means the business is not expected to generate a future income stream, so only the assets are sold at the present depreciated value; the entrepreneur gets very little money in this situation, whereas with harvesting, buyers are not only purchasing the business's assets but also its potential to make more money, so the entrepreneur can earn a premium. 4. Answers will vary, but rationales should incorporate the advantages and disadvantages listed in the textbook. 5. They want to know what will affect their investment and how they will be able to get their money out of your enterprise when the right time comes.

- **Advanced Module Business Plan.** This chapter concludes the NFTE Advanced Module.

## EXTEND THE LEARNING

- **Business Plan Practice.** Critical Thinking question 4.
- **Business Auction.** Use simplified versions of real-world companies' annual reports (usually available from their Web sites) or create your own financial statements based on models throughout the textbook. You (or another teacher who agrees to participate) will serve as an auctioneer for these companies whose owners want to sell them. Divide the class into pairs, with each pair role-playing business partners who are interested in purchasing a company. Distribute one index card to each pair. For each business to be auctioned, create handout packets of the financial statements, and present basic background information on the business verbally. Ask the pairs to value the business — using the various methods discussed in the chapter — and decide on a price they would be willing to pay for the company. Each pair writes its price down. The auctioneer starts the bidding by asking one student to give an opening bid (as needed, remind the students about the rules of negotiation and starting low). Then ask for a second bid, etc., until a high bidder is found. No pair may go over their written price. After each auction, ask pairs to share how they came to their prices, why they stopped bidding when they did, what the risks and rewards were that they foresaw with the business, etc. Continue with additional businesses as long as student interest and time permit.
- **Guest Speaker.** Invite a local business broker (or entrepreneur who recently sold his/her company) to make a presentation: how the business was valued, what the process was, etc.

- **"Way Out" Party & Course Evaluation.** Since this is the final chapter in the NFTE curriculum, and it focuses on exit strategies, celebrate the class's accomplishments with a party. Have students plan to share their "parting thoughts" about the NFTE experience with you and the other students. Use this venue for students to present their most recent thoughts on their NFTE business plans, or to create posters outlining their businesses to display around the room, so they can support each other's efforts. Emphasize the idea that every ending brings new beginnings — exits are also entrances into new venues of adventure, learning, growth, and success. As they exit the classroom on the final day of class, shake everyone's hand and wish each student well in his/her future business and academic ventures.

- **Business Plan Integrative Summary.** Chapter 50 concludes Unit 10, which emphasizes creating wealth. Review the wealth-building opportunities of their Business Plans, including franchising and licensing considerations; international import/export possibilities; plan for building good credit; investment plan; business harvesting.

- **End-of-the-Course Ideas:** As the close of the semester or school year approaches, consider the following as possible "extras" to assign to students as "end-of-course" or "takeaway" projects, as appropriate:
  ○ assess needs and costs required to improve an existing business site
  ○ devise a plan to evaluate the cost effectiveness of a company's promotional efforts
  ○ devise a quality control plan and procedures
  ○ estimate personnel and purchasing needs for a future time period based on current and past sales data
  ○ plan and create procedures for handling employee suggestions and complaints
  ○ investigate needs and options for personnel estate planning.

Students could use their own existing business, a business they are planning, or an imaginary business.

## BUILD ACADEMIC AND LIFE-SKILL PROFICIENCIES
### *Skills Mean Success* Answers

**English.** As needed, review the rules and set-ups for crosswords and word-search games.

**Math.** Based on the guidelines given of three times net annual profit: a. Accept. b. Decline. c. Perhaps accept. d. Accept. e. Perhaps accept.

# ENTREPRENEURSHIP

## —How to—
# Start & Operate
# a Small Business

**A Guide for**
THE YOUNG ENTREPRENEUR

*Semester 1:*
**Basic and Intermediate Modules**

*Semester 2:*
**Advanced Module**

**STEVE MARIOTTI,**
*President and Founder of
the National Foundation for Teaching Entrepreneurship, Inc.
(NFTE)*

**with Tony Towle**

**Tenth Revised Edition**

For information regarding NFTE programs and products, contact (212) 232-3333 or (800-FOR-NFTE);  fax: (212) 232-2244;  www.nfte.com.

Copyright © 1987, 1994, 1997, 2001, 2003 & 2006 by
**The National Foundation for Teaching Entrepreneurship, Inc. (NFTE)**
120 Wall Street, 29th Floor, New York, NY  10005.

ISBN 1-890859-18-4

# Dedications & Credits

**This book is dedicated to:**

Raymond Chambers; Elizabeth, Charles G., and David H. Koch; and the Honorable John C. Whitehead

**Special dedication to:**

Diana Davis Spencer, Art Samberg, Mary Myers Kauppila, and the late Bernard A. Goldhirsh

**Special thanks to:**

Joanne Beyer of the Scaife Family Foundation; Barbara Bell Coleman of the Newark Boys and Girls Clubs; Chris Podoll of the William Zimmerman Foundation; Stephanie Bell-Rose of The Goldman Sachs Foundation; The Shelby Cullom Davis Foundation; Tom Hartocollis, Jeff Raikes, and the Microsoft Corporation; The NASDAQ Educational Foundation; Ronald McDonald House Children's Charities; Dr. Kathleen R. Allen, University of Southern California; and from NFTE: Michael J. Caslin, III, Julie Silard Kantor, Leslie Pechman Koch, Michael Simmons, Sheena Lindahl, Dave Nelson, Gary Giscombe, and Chris Brown.

Thanks to special reviewers, Katerina Zacharia, Howie Buffet, Jr., Julie Wineinger, and Joyce Macek. Thanks also to Gudmundur Asmundsson for the use of six photographs.

**Curriculum development assistance from:**

Seana Moran, Chris Meenan, and Nancy Rosenbaum

**Development of the financial and strategy chapters for the 10th Edition:**

John Harris and Peter Patch

**Edited by:**

Debra DeSalvo

**Publishing Consultants and Contributors:**

Peter D. McBride, pete mcbride & associates, and Laurie Wendell

**Design and Composition:**

JWR Design Interaction, LLC

**Photography by:**

Bill Foley, Mike Kuczera, and Krasner & Trebitz

**Illustrations by:**

JWR Design Interaction, LLC, and Maija Wilder (Some illustrations were based on previous work by Jeff Faria, Meryl Hurwich, Al Stern, and Daryl Joseph Moore.)

**Coordinator of the 10th Edition:**

Jean Mahoney

# Consultants & Reviewers

**Alaire Mitchell**
*Former Assistant Director of Curriculum Research New York City Board of Education*

**Elaine Allen**
*National Director Not-for-Profit Services Group Ernst & Young*

**Sunne Brandmeyer**
*Retired Lecturer/Advisor Center for Economic Education University of South Florida*

**Stanlee Brimberg**
*Teacher Bank Street School for Children*

**Howard W. Buffett, Jr.**

**Alan Dlugash, CPA**
*Partner Dlugash & Kevelson*

**Alex Dontoh**
*New York University*

**Thomas Emrick, Ed.D.**

**Deborah Hoffman**
*Audit Manager Ernst & Young*

**Sanford Krieger, Esq.**
*Partner Fried, Frank, Harris, Shriver & Jacobson*

**Dr. Jawanza Kunjufu**
*President, African American Images*

**Corey Kupfer, Esq.**
*Founding Partner, Kupfer, Rosen & Herz, LLP*

**Eric Mulkowsky**
*Engagement Manager McKinsey and Company, Inc.*

**Raffiq Nathoo**
*Senior Managing Director The Blackstone Group, LLP*

**Ray E. Newton, III**
*Managing Director Perseus Capital, LLC*

**William H. Painter**
*Retired Professor of Law George Washington University*

**Peter Patch**
*Patch and Associates*

**Alan Patricof**
*Founder and Chairman Apax Partners*

**Christopher P. Puto**
*Dean and Professor of Marketing Georgetown University, McDonough School of Business*

**Ira Sacks, Esq.**
*Partner Fried, Frank, Harris, Shriver & Jacobson*

**Dr. William Sahlman**
*Professor of Business Administration Harvard Business School*

**Dr. Arnold Scheibel**
*Professor of Neurobiology University of California at Los Angeles*

**Sandra Sowell-Scott**
*State Director, Youth Entrepreneurship Education Fox School of Business & Management Temple University*

**Liza Vertinsky, J.D., Ph.D.**
*Attorney Hill & Barlow*

**Peter Walker**
*Managing Director McKinsey and Company, Inc.*

**Dr. Donald Wells**
*Professor of Economics University of Arizona*

# Acknowledgments

I would like to thank my writing partners, Tony Towle, who from NFTE's very beginning has helped me organize my thoughts and experiences, and Debra DeSalvo, without whose gift for organization and rewriting, this book would never have been possible. I would also like to acknowledge the significant contributions of NFTE executives Del Daniels, Margaret Dunn, Jean Mahoney, Christine Poorman, Jane Walsh, and Joel Warren, all of whom made numerous helpful suggestions. In addition, I would like to thank my brother, Jack, the best CPA I know, and my father, John, for financing much of NFTE's early work, and for their continuing love and guidance.

I must express my gratitude to Jenny Rosenbaum for helping me write many of the entrepreneurial profiles included in the text (which are adapted from NFTE's *Entrepreneurs in Profile*). Thanks also to Howard Stevenson, Jeffry Timmons, William Bygrave, and NFTE Board Member Stephen Spinelli, for their academic and business expertise; my first three students: Vincent Wilkins, Josephine Reneau, and Howard Stubbs; Tom Hartocollis of Microsoft, Richard Fink of Koch Industries, and Carl Schramm, Bob Rogers, and Michael Herman of the Ewing Marion Kauffman Foundation, and Mike Hennessy and John Hughes of the Coleman Foundation — and the many other philanthropists, who have all been crucial to NFTE's development over the years.

I would also like to recognize the efforts and contributions of members of NFTE's National Board of Directors: Albert Abney, Bart Breighner, Michele Courton Brown, Jay W. Christopher, Michael L. Fetters, John Fullerton, Thomas P. Hartocollis, Landon Hilliard, James Holden, Robert Hurst, Loida N. Lewis, James Lyle (Board Chair), Alan J. Patricof, Arthur Samberg, Diana Davis Spencer, Kenneth I. Starr, Peter B. Walker, Lulu C. Wang, and Thomas (Tucker) York.

And I would like to acknowledge the inspired guidance provided by our National Executive Committee: Stephen Brenninkmeyer, Kathryn Davis, Lewis M. Eisenberg, Theodore J. Forstmann, Robert J. Hurst, Elizabeth B. Koch, Abby Moffat, Jeffrey S. Raikes, and John C. Whitehead, and our Regional and International Advisory Board Chairs: Clint Coghill (Chicago), Kimberly Davis & Duncan Hennes ("Fairchester"), Sidney Smith (Greater Washington DC), Peter Cowie (New England), Phyllis Schless (New York), Bradley DeFoor & Joanna Gallanter (Northern California), Linda Dickerson (Pennsylvania), Remi Vermeir (Belgium), Stephen Brenninkmeyer (Germany and the United Kingdom), and Theo Pustjens (The Netherlands).

Further, I would like to thank Steve Alcock, Harsh and Aruna Bhargava, Lena Bondue, Dawn Bowlus, Camy Calve, Shelly Chenoweth, Janet McKinstry Cort, Erik Dauwen, Clara Del Villar, Christine Chambers Gilfillan, Andrew Hahn, Dolores Hirschmann, Kathleen Kirkwood, Dianna Maeurer, Cynthia Miree, David J. Nelson, Helene Robbins, Victor Salama, Henry To, Carol Tully, Dilia Wood, and Elizabeth Wright, as well as Joseph Dominic, Paul DeF. Hicks, Jr., Ann Mahoney, and David Roodberg, who have provided countless insights into providing entrepreneurial opportunities for young people.

Finally, I want to thank my mother, Nancy, a wonderful special-education instructor who showed me that one great teacher can affect eternity; Siena, Nina, Jackson, and Spencer Mariotti; my friends and mentors, Ray Chambers and John Whitehead; the late Bernard Goldhirsh, for twelve years of friendship and who helped put entrepreneurship on the map with the founding of Inc.; and the late Gloria Appel of the Price Institute for Entrepreneurial Studies, for funding NFTE teacher education and being a good friend.

*Steve Mariotti*

# About the Authors

**Steve Mariotti** received his undergraduate and M.B.A. degrees from the University of Michigan, Ann Arbor, and has studied at Harvard University, Stanford University, and Brooklyn College. He began his professional career as a Treasury Analyst for Ford Motor Company. He then moved to New York and founded Mason Import/Export Services.

He made a significant career change in 1982 and became a business teacher in the New York City public school system. It was at Jane Addams Vocational High School in the Bronx that he developed the insight and inspiration for bringing entrepreneurial education to at-risk youth. This led to the founding of the nonprofit National Foundation for Teaching Entrepreneurship (NFTE) in 1987.

Since then, NFTE has become a major force in promoting and teaching entrepreneurial literacy and basic academic and business skills to youth, both in the United States and abroad. As of the end of 2004, NFTE has served over 100,000 young people and trained more than 3,200 teachers and youth workers in 45 states and 14 countries.

Steve has received many honors and awards for his work in the field of youth entrepreneurship, including: Best Economics Teacher in New York State (1988); National Award for Teaching Economics, The Joint Council of Economic Education (1988); Best High School Teacher of the Year, National Federation of Independent Businesses (1988); Honorary Doctorate in Business and Entrepreneurship, Johnson & Wales University (1990); Entrepreneur of the Year Award, *Inc.* Magazine, with Ernst & Young and Merrill Lynch (1992); The Appel Award, Price Institute for Entrepreneurial Studies (1994); The University of Michigan Business School Entrepreneurship Award (1999); the Harold W. Price Lifetime Achievement Award In Entrepreneurship Education, 2004; and the Ernst & Young Entrepreneur of the Year for 2004, Supporter of Entrepreneurship Category.

He has co-authored 16 books — including *Entrepreneurs in Profile*, with Jenny Rosenbaum, and the present volume, *How to Start & Operate a Small Business*, with Tony Towle. A version of this textbook for the general public was published by Times Books, a division of Random House, in 1996. Now in its 10th edition, *The Young Entrepreneur's Guide to Starting and Running a Business* has sold more than 100,000 copies.

**Tony Towle** has worked with Steve Mariotti and NFTE since its inception. In addition, he has written about art, and is a poet whose books include *North, Autobiography, Some Musical Episodes,* and most recently, *A History of the Invitation (New & Selected Poems 1963–2000)*, and *Memoir 1960–1963*. He has received a National Endowment for the Arts Fellowship and a New York State Council on the Arts Fellowship, among other awards.

**The National Foundation for Teaching Entrepreneurship, Inc.** (NFTE, pronounced "Nifty") is a nonprofit organization founded in 1987 to introduce young people to the world of business. NFTE teaches entrepreneurship to young people from low-income communities to enhance their economic productivity by improving their business, academic and life skills.

NFTE believes that many young people have extraordinary potential for business achievement and possess the qualities of the successful entrepreneur, such as a willingness to take risks and resilience in adversity. By making business both interesting and comprehensible, NFTE seeks to encourage its students to participate in their respective local economies and become productive members of the society at large.

NFTE's goal is to strengthen local communities through youth training, teacher education, curriculum research and development, as well as public education and information forums. For more information, please refer to contact information at the front of the book, or on page viii.

# Preface

*How to Start & Operate a Small Business: A Guide for the Young Entrepreneur* is a flexible 80-to-160-hour, one- or two-semester high school course in entrepreneurship and basic business principles. In its ideal usage, this comprehensive material will fill a 160-hour, full-year course. Also, the text is easily adaptable and can be modified and condensed to work with other courses and schedules. It may be broken into three modules — Basic, Intermediate, and Advanced — that can be interwoven into other curricula, or used as an after-school or summer program. This course meets many academic standards, including the U.S. Department of Labor Secretary's Commission on Achieving Necessary Skills (SCANS), the National Council for the Teaching of Mathematics (NCTM) Curriculum and Evaluation Standards, NCSS Curriculum Standards for Social Studies, and the standards for the National Business Education Association (NBEA) and the Consortium for Entrepreneurship Education (CEE).

## Semester One:
## Starting and Operating a Small Business
### (40 to 80 hours)

### Basic Module: Starting Your Business (20 to 40 hours)
*Includes: Chapters 1–16 and Basic Business Plan*
*Field Trips: Wholesaler to purchase goods, with subsequent selling experience at trade fair*

The Basic Module shows how to start a simple small business. Students will explore economic basics, such as supply and demand, cost/benefit analysis, competitive advantage, and opportunity recognition. They will practice such business skills as preparing an income statement, keeping records, and negotiating. Upon completion of Chapter 16, they will prepare a Basic Business Plan.

*These 16 chapters also comprise a stand-alone, 20-to-40-hour course in entrepreneurship for after-school programs, or a supplement to economics or business courses.*

### Intermediate Module: Operating Your Business
### (20 to 40 hours)
*Includes: Chapters 17–30 and Intermediate Business Plan*
*Field Trip: Registration of sole proprietorship*

The Intermediate Module shows how to run a small business successfully. Students will learn about marketing, selling, customer service, and business communication, and will explore such topics as quality as the source of profit, the production/distribution chain, human resources, and business technology. Upon completion of Chapter 30, students will prepare an Intermediate Business Plan.

*Together, the Basic and Intermediate Modules comprise a 40-to-80-hour, one-semester course.*

# Semester Two: Developing a Small Business

## Advanced Module: What You Need to Know to Grow
### (40 to 80 hours)
*Includes: Chapters 31–50 and Advanced Business Plan*
*Field Trips: Stock exchange or brokerage house; opening bank accounts*

The Advanced Module shows how to expand a small business venture. Students will explore such topics as incorporating, venture capital, contracts, intellectual property, insurance, franchising and licensing, philanthropy and socially responsible business, global opportunities, taxation, personal finance, and exit strategies. Upon completing Chapter 50, students will prepare the Advanced Business Plan.

*The Advanced Module is a 40-to-80-hour, one-semester course. Together, the Basic, Intermediate, and Advanced Modules comprise an 80-to-160-hour, two-semester course.*

The three Modules are meant for use in conjunction with the Student Workbook, which contains a review of the Basic, Intermediate, and Advanced Business Plans, as well as the plans themselves. There is also a Teacher's Edition, which includes comprehensive teaching and assessment suggestions for each chapter and other instructional aids. The Modules correlate with NFTE's online learning program, BizTech™, available at http://biztech.nfte.com.

At NFTE we believe that teaching entrepreneurship to young people will give them a hands-on understanding of the business world that will help them create fulfilling careers and be valuable employees in any field, as well as improve their general academic performance by engaging them in hands-on experiences that show the ability to earn a living is directly linked to a grasp of reading, writing, math, critical thinking, and other academic skills.

This course emphasizes business ethics and appropriate business behavior. It also stresses that the characteristics of the successful entrepreneur — a positive mental attitude, the ability to recognize opportunities where others only see problems, and openness to creative solutions — are qualities worth developing. This will help students perform better in any situation they encounter.

Because entrepreneurship draws from a wide variety of disciplines, some of the topics touched on in this course — such as economics and accounting — could not be explored in depth. We hope that students will be inspired to study in greater detail subjects that we can only introduce. Our purpose here is to provide the fundamentals of entrepreneurship as part of NFTE's mission to help young people become economically productive members of society by improving their academic, business, technological, and life skills.

**The National Foundation for Teaching Entrepreneurship, Inc. (NFTE)**
120 Wall Street, 29th Floor, New York, NY  10005
(800) FOR-NFTE  www.nfte.com

# Attention Students

This course can show you how to start and run your own small business! Even if you don't become a lifelong entrepreneur, learning to operate a business will make you a valuable employee and will help you create a fulfilling career for yourself. We believe studying entrepreneurship will help you achieve financial independence and personal satisfaction, and become a positive force in your community.

The characteristics of the successful entrepreneur — a positive mental attitude, the ability to recognize opportunities where others only see problems, and openness to creative solutions — are qualities worth developing. They will help you perform better in any career situation you encounter.

NFTE is proud that this textbook won a very important award in 2002 called the Golden Lamp Award for Books, given by the Association of Educational Publishers (AEP). The book is divided into three Modules — Basic, Intermediate, and Advanced. Upon completion of each module you will write a business plan you could use to start your own real business!

The Basic chapters show you how to start a simple business. You will learn to recognize and evaluate business opportunities, to calculate return on investment, and to utilize an income statement. You will explore your unique skills and talents and choose a business you would like to start. At the end of each chapter, you will complete Business Plan Practice exercises to get you ready to prepare your Basic Business Plan.

The Intermediate Module concentrates on managing your business. Once you have completed these chapters, you will be able to create a marketing plan, register your business, and hire employees. After Chapter 30, you will build on your Basic Business Plan to create an Intermediate Business Plan.

The Advanced Module explores ways to grow a small business venture, including franchising and licensing, international business, and philanthropy. After Chapter 50, you will tackle the Advanced Business Plan.

Good luck!

# Table of Contents

# BASIC MODULE

# Starting Your Business

*The Basic Chapters of NFTE Semester 1 will teach you what you need to know to start a simple business. Once you have completed these chapters, you will be able to prepare an income statement, understand marketing basics, perform cost and benefit analysis, and calculate return on investment. You will also learn what it means to be an entrepreneur and how you can use your unique skills and talents to start a small business venture.*

*After you have finished Chapter 16, you will be ready to apply what you have learned by preparing your Basic Business Plan. A complete version of the Basic Business Plan can be found in your NFTE Workbook.*

# WHAT IS ENTREPRENEURSHIP?

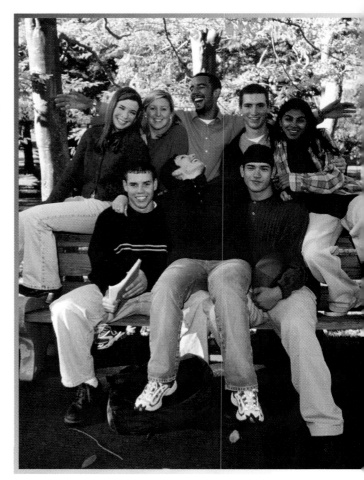

*Everyone lives by selling something.*

— Robert Louis Stevenson, *Scottish author*

**KEY OBJECTIVES**

THIS CHAPTER WILL ENABLE YOU TO:

- Describe the difference between employees and entrepreneurs.
- Discuss how entrepreneurs create value from "scarce" resources.
- Explain why entrepreneurs like change.
- Evaluate the pros and cons of owning your own business.

## Differences between Employees and Entrepreneurs

Most Americans earn money by working in **business**. Business is the buying and selling of products or services in order to make a **profit**. Someone who earns a living by working for someone else's business is an **employee** of that business.

There are many different kinds of employees. At Ford Motor Company, for instance, some employees build the cars, some sell the cars, and some manage the company. But employees all have one thing in common — they do not own a business, they work for others, who do.

Some people start their own businesses and work for themselves. They are called **entrepreneurs**. Entrepreneurs are often both owners and employees. Profit is the money a company has left after expenses and taxes have been paid. As owners, entrepreneurs are in control of the profit made by their businesses.

An entrepreneur is responsible for the success or failure of his or her business. *A successful business sells products or services that customers need, at prices they are willing to pay.* Of course, the prices must also be high enough for the entrepreneur to be able to cover all the costs of running the business, and have money left over as profit.

# Think Like an Entrepreneur

Entrepreneurship is so much more than just learning to run your own business. It is an approach to life that involves thinking of yourself as a "can-do" person. After all, if you can start your own business, you can do just about anything!

When you work for others, you can still think like an entrepreneur. Let this motivate you to do your best on the job:

- Always look for opportunities to learn new skills and take on new responsibilities.
- Show your employer that you understand business and are working to improve the profitability of the company.

Employers notice (and often promote) employees who think entrepreneurially. Remember, every skill learned is yours to take to another job, or to your own business. Never stop learning.

To quote Jeffry Timmons: "Entrepreneurship is a way of thinking, reasoning, and acting that is opportunity-obsessed, holistic in approach, and leadership balanced."[1] People who think like entrepreneurs are excited about what they can accomplish. They feel in control of their lives, even if working for others.

Do *you* feel in control of your life, or do you feel controlled *by* it? If you give starting a business a try, you will learn valuable skills that will make you more successful, no matter what career you may eventually choose. You will also learn how to take charge of your own destiny.

**Entrepreneurs do three important things:**

1. **They listen.** By listening to others, entrepreneurs get ideas about improving a business or creating a new one.

2. **They observe.** By constantly keeping their eyes open, entrepreneurs get ideas about how to help society, about businesses to start, and about what people need.

3. **They think.** When entrepreneurs analyze a problem, they think about solutions. What product or service could solve it?

## *SKILLS MEAN SUCCESS*

**LEADERSHIP**  ▶  **Seeing Yourself as an Entrepreneur**

Nobel Prize-winning scientist Linus Pauling wrote: *The best way to get good ideas is to have lots of them.* Successful entrepreneurs know it is important to capture creative ideas and thoughts. To get into this practice, start an "Idea Journal":

- Carry a pocket-sized notebook with you at all times.

- As you use your listening, observing, and thinking skills, make a habit of writing down any entrepreneurial ideas you have for meeting consumer needs or solving business problems.

- Describe briefly every positive encounter you have with a business.

## Big and Small Business

The public often thinks of business only in terms of "big" business — companies such as Ford, Microsoft, McDonald's, and Nike. A *big* business is defined by the Small Business Administration as having more than 100 employees and selling more than $1 million worth of products or services in a year.

Most of the world's businesses are small businesses. A baby-sitting service and a neighborhood restaurant are examples of small businesses.

Surprisingly, the principles involved in running a large company and a small one are basically the same. In fact, most multimillion-dollar businesses in this country started out as small, entrepreneurial ventures. Many of the largest corporations, such as Microsoft or McDonald's, began as an idea thought up by one or two entrepreneurs.

> **"**   *America's small business owners and their employees represent more than half of the private workforce. These entrepreneurs, who create more than 75 percent of net new jobs nationwide and generate more than 50 percent of the nation's gross domestic product, and the employees who work in small businesses, deserve our thanks. We salute them.*
>
> **— President George W. Bush,**
> from speech celebrating Small Business Week

## A Business Must Make a Profit to Stay in Business

No matter how big or small, a business must make a profit to stay "in business." The amount of money coming in must be greater than the amount of money required to pay the bills. Many ventures do lose money after start-up because they have had to lay out cash to set up operations, and on advertising to attract customers. If the business *continues* not to be profitable, however, the entrepreneur will be unable to pay the bills and will eventually have to close.

 **Rule of Thumb:** When starting a business, it's realistic to expect to lose money for at least the first three months. It can often take that long for a business to start selling enough to earn a profit.

Closing a business is nothing to be ashamed of; in fact, most successful entrepreneurs open and close more than one business in their careers. If your venture is not making a profit after you've gotten it up and running, it could be a signal that you are in the wrong business. Closing it might be the smartest decision.

An entrepreneur may change businesses many times over the years, in response to changing competition and consumer needs. The great economist Joseph Schumpeter called the process of constantly changing businesses, "creative destruction."[2]

## Profit Is the Sign that the Entrepreneur Is Adding Value

If your business is making a profit, you are clearly doing something right. Profit is a sign that an entrepreneur has added value to the "scarce" (limited) **resources** he or she is using. A resource is something of value that can be used to make something else or to fill a need. Oil is a resource because it is used as fuel. Wood is a resource, too, because it can be used to make a house or a table or paper. All resources are limited.

Debbi Fields, the founder of Mrs. Fields Original Cookies, took resources — eggs, butter, flour, sugar, chocolate chips, and labor — and turned them into cookies. People liked what she did with those resources enough that they were willing to pay her more for the cookies than it cost her to buy the ingredients. In other words, she earned a profit. The profit was her signal that she was doing something right — she was *adding value* to the resources she was using.

Debbi Fields added value to resources by using them to create something that people were willing to buy for a price that gave her a profit. This is how entrepreneurs create value.

By the same token, losing money is a sign that the entrepreneur is not using resources well and is not adding value to them.

## The Economic Questions

Since time began, people have had to answer the same basic questions:

- What should be produced?
- How will it be produced?
- Who gets to have what is produced?

Families and individuals, as well as businesspeople, charities, corporations, and governments, have all had to answer these questions. The system that a group of people creates through making these decisions is called an **economy**. The study of how different groups answer these questions is called *economics*.

An economy is a country's financial structure. It is the system that produces and distributes wealth. The United States economy is a **free enterprise system**, because anyone is free to start a business. You do not have to get permission from the government to start a business, although you do have to obey laws and follow regulations.

This economic system is also called **capitalism**, because the money used to start a business is called **capital**. Anyone who can raise the necessary capital is free to start a business. *You* can start a business!

## Voluntary Exchange

The free enterprise system is also sometimes referred to as a "free-trade system" because it is based on **voluntary exchange**. Voluntary exchange is a transaction between two parties who agree to trade money for a product or service. No one is *forced* to trade. Everyone is *free* to trade. Trading only takes place when both parties believe they will benefit. In contrast, robbery would be an example of *involuntary* trade.

## Benefits of Free Enterprise

We all benefit from living in a free enterprise system because it discourages entrepreneurs who waste resources — by driving them out of business. It encourages entrepreneurs who use resources efficiently to satisfy consumer needs — by rewarding them with profit.

We also benefit because free enterprise encourages competition between entrepreneurs. Someone who can make cookies that taste as good as Mrs. Fields Original Cookies, and sell them at a lower price, will eventually attract their customers. This will force Mrs. Fields Original Cookies to lower its prices to stay competitive. Consumers will benefit because they will pay lower prices.

Entrepreneurs are motivated by competition to find ways to use resources more efficiently, so that they can lower prices but still make a profit.

## Entrepreneurs View Change as Opportunity

In the 1970s, the countries that sold oil raised the price dramatically. American automobile manufacturers had to begin making smaller cars because consumers didn't want to buy big ones, which used the now more expensive gasoline.

Giant corporations such as automobile manufacturers can find it difficult to respond to sudden change. They tend to move slowly because so many people and so much money is involved in any change they make. Entrepreneurs, in contrast, understand that change creates opportunities.

Debbi Fields is a millionaire today not because she had a great chocolate chip cookie recipe, but because she had noticed that families were changing. Fifty years ago women generally did not work full time outside the house. They stayed home and cooked and cleaned for their families. But in the 1970s more women entered the workforce. Few now had time to bake. Mrs. Fields took advantage of this change. She created cookies that tasted home-baked. The name "Mrs. Fields Original Cookies" reminded the consumer of coming home to Mom and a plate of freshly baked cookies. Debbi Fields's business probably would not have succeeded if women had not begun working away from home.

 **The number of women-owned and minority-owned small businesses is increasing every year.**

## SKILLS MEAN SUCCESS

**ENGLISH**

### Reading for Information and Understanding: Gathering and Interpreting Information

Locate an article about one of the following entrepreneurs in your library or on the Internet:

- Lane Bryant
- John H. Johnson
- Sarah Breedlove Walker
- Russell Simmons
- Julie Aigner-Clark

Read the article to determine how the entrepreneur created a business opportunity by taking advantage of a change, trend, or consumer need. Write a paragraph about how this took place, and be prepared to share your findings with the class. ■■■

## Why Be an Entrepreneur?

There are both pros and cons of being an entrepreneur:

### Some Disadvantages

Entrepreneurs often put more time into launching their own businesses than many people put into their jobs. While establishing a business, an entrepreneur may also invest a lot of money in the business. He or she may not be able to buy new clothes or a fancy car, or go on vacation. Other disadvantages are:

1. **Business failure** — Many small businesses fail. You risk losing not only your own money but also that of investors.

2. **Obstacles** — You will run into unexpected problems that you will have to solve. In addition, you may face discouragement from family and friends.

3. **Loneliness** — It can be lonely and even a little scary to be completely responsible for the success or failure of a business.

4. **Financial insecurity** — Your earnings may rise or fall depending on how the business is doing. You may not always have enough money to pay yourself.

5. **Long hours/hard work** — You will have to work long hours to get your business off the ground. Some entrepreneurs work six, or even seven, days a week.

### Some Advantages

If so much work and sacrifice and uncertainty are involved, why be an entrepreneur? The entrepreneur works for the following rewards:

1. **Control over time** — Entrepreneurs do not have to operate on anyone else's clock. If you start your own business, you can work flexible hours. You can also hire other people to perform tasks that you don't want to do or aren't good at, so you can focus on what you do best. Bill Gates, who started Microsoft, likes to investigate future uses of technology. He hires others to manage the company and sell Microsoft products.

2. **A creative, fulfilling life** — Successful entrepreneurs are passionate about their businesses. Entrepreneurs are almost never bored. They enjoy both the freedom and the responsibility of being "the boss."

3. **The opportunity to create great wealth** — Ownership is the key to wealth. If you work for someone else, you are selling your time and effort in exchange for money. You are paid only for the work you do. If your work helps to make the company successful, the owner, not you, will receive the greatest rewards. Owners benefit from both higher profits earned and also from the increasing value of the business as it grows. Ownership is how great fortunes are made.

4. **Control over compensation** — Entrepreneurs get to decide how they are paid. As owner of your company you can decide to:
   - Pay yourself a *salary* — a fixed payment made at regular intervals, such as every week or month.
   - Pay yourself a *wage* — a fixed payment per hour.
   - Take a *dividend* — As the owner, you can choose to be paid as if you were an employee (salary or wage) or you can simply pay yourself a share of the business's profits. This kind of payment is called a dividend.
   - Take a *commission* — A commission is a percentage of the value of a sale. If you decide to pay yourself 10% commission and you sell an item for $1000, your commission on the sale would be $100.

5. **Control over working conditions** — As an entrepreneur you can create a working environment that reflects your values. You can make sure your company recycles, for example.

6. **Self-evaluation** — Entrepreneurs evaluate their own performances. If you own your own company, no one else can hire or fire you. Some of the greatest entrepreneurs in the world might not have been able to succeed if they hadn't started working for themselves. Richard Branson had such severe dyslexia that he dropped out of high school. He became an extremely successful entrepreneur, however, creating Virgin Airlines and Virgin Records, among many other companies.

7. **Participation in an international community** — The Internet allows entrepreneurs to compete and make deals all over the world. Institutions like the

World Entrepreneurs' Organization (WEO) help young businesspeople get in touch with each other.

8. **The opportunity to help one's community** — Entrepreneurs create jobs for people in their communities. In addition, many of the world's great museums, libraries, hospitals, and other important institutions and facilities have been founded and supported by entrepreneurs. Entrepreneurs give away many millions of dollars each year to help others and support the arts. Even if your business never earns millions, you can still donate money and time to make your community a better place.

## SKILLS MEAN SUCCESS

**ENGLISH**

**Reading for Information and Understanding:**
**Following Directions, Interpreting, and Analyzing**

People start their own businesses for different reasons.

1. Read the lists below carefully and match each condition in column A with an advantage of starting your own business in Column B. Some advantages will fit more than one condition or reason. Do it like this:
A: c, a, f, g, i

| Reason or Attitude | Advantage |
|---|---|
| **A.** Wants to invent a new piece of medical software. | **a.** Owners can make their own decisions. |
| **B.** Disagrees with company policy on hiring minorities or older people. | **b.** Owners trust their own instincts to build wealth and gain career satisfaction. |
| **C.** Wants to do more to protect environment. | **c.** Owners can pursue their own dreams. |
| **D.** Doesn't like working "nine to five." | **d.** Owners can set their own rules. |
| **E.** Sees a customer need that no business is addressing. | **e.** Owners have opportunity to make — or lose — money. |
| **F.** Has no control over his/her own job. | **f.** Owners find excitement and stimulation in running their own businesses. |
| **G.** Feels he/she can't earn enough money. | **g.** Owners can pursue opportunities as they wish. |
| **H.** Has no interest in his/her own job. | **h.** Owners can set their own hours. |
| **I.** Likes taking risks to earn rewards. | **i.** Owners can set their own priorities. |

2. Describe the three top reasons or attitudes why *you* might want to start a business.

3. Which reasons have changed from what you would have listed

    **a.** a month ago?     **b.** a year ago? ■■■

## Ownership Is the Key to Wealth

Entrepreneurs make money from the profits their businesses earn — hopefully, every year. An entrepreneur can also become very wealthy if the business succeeds and grows and then someone buys it. Let's say your company earns a profit of $20,000 per year. Someone might be willing to buy it for several times that amount, because they will expect it to keep earning at least that much. As the original owner, you not only kept a share of the profits from the yearly earnings, but you would now also make a profit on your investment by selling the business. The new owner would hope to do the same. In the meantime, you can take the money from the sale and use it to start a new business. This is how entrepreneurs can create great fortunes.

Ownership is the key to wealth. Top executives at large corporations may make millions of dollars, but that money is not just salary. They have negotiated payment packages that include stock in the company. In other words, they have become part-owners. Even if you decide not to start your own business, think like an entrepreneur throughout your career — work hard, show your employer that you are key to the company's profitability, and try to become an owner. Once you are an owner, you will be entitled to a share of the profits.

## SKILLS MEAN SUCCESS

**MATH** ▶ **Mathematical Reasoning and Number Operations:**
**Multiples, Parts, Increases, Decreases**

Business owners use math to solve business problems. They may use paper and pencil, calculators, or computers, or sometimes they solve a problem by doing the math in their head. Whatever the method, solving a math problem starts with understanding the problem.

For each statement, decide which mathematical operation would be used to find the answer.

**a.** The buyer offered Anna a price of three times annual sales to buy her business.

**b.** His sales were down by $240 last month.

**c.** One half of her selling price was profit.

**d.** In three years, his sales doubled.

**e.** Manuel's expenses increased by $25,000.

**f.** Rena sold her T-shirt business for ten times what it cost her to start it.

**g.** The cost of rent was only a fifth of Franklin's profits.

**h.** Profits increased 400% in one year. ■ ■ ■

## Living a Life You Will Love

More important than money, however, is having a career you truly enjoy. What do you love to do? What interests you most?

Russell Simmons was a young man in Hollis, Queens, who loved hip-hop. He turned his passion for hip-hop culture into Def Jam Records. Today, he owns a multimillion-dollar enterprise that includes all the Def Jam businesses, Phat Farm clothing, and Rush Management. Becoming an entrepreneur has provided Simmons with:

1.  Wealth — His enterprises are worth over $60 million.

2.  Influence — Simmons has become a force in politics, promoting voter registration drives among young adults.

3.  Control — Simmons is in charge of his money and his time. As the owner of his companies, he chooses how much of the profits to keep for himself, how he spends his time, and what he does with his wealth.

## Profit Is the Reward for Satisfying a Customer Need

Simmons poured his time, money, and energy into starting Def Jam. He postponed immediate pleasures to create a business that would provide rewards in the future.

 *Real estate tycoon Donald Trump was asked, on his TV show* The Apprentice, *if he ran his many ventures for the money. He replied, "No, I do it for the challenge."*

# Chapter 1 Review

## CRITICAL THINKING ABOUT...

### ENTREPRENEURSHIP

1. What would be the best thing about owning your own business?

2. What would be the worst?

3. Would you rather be an employee or an entrepreneur? Why?

4. Describe an idea for a business. Explain how it could satisfy a consumer need.
   **Business Plan Practice**

5. Go on the Internet and research "entrepreneurship." Write briefly about the most interesting site you found.

6. "Employees get paid what they deserve, but entrepreneurs don't." Explain this statement.

7. Identity three non-financial benefits of entrepreneurship that might be important to you. Write a paragraph on each explaining why.

8. Anita Roddick (The Body Shop), John Johnson (BET Holdings), Berry Gordy (Motown Records), Oprah Winfrey (Harpo), and Debbie Fields (Mrs. Fields Original Cookies) are all famous entrepreneurs. Make a list of the obstacles each of them faced in becoming the CEO of a major corporation. (Refer to *Entrepreneurs in Profile* to learn about them.)

9. Figure the selling price for the following businesses, assuming each could be sold for three times yearly net profit.

| Business | Yearly Net Profit |
|---|---|
| Sal's Pizzeria: | $65,000 |
| Books 'n' Things: | $123,000 |
| Office Plantcare: | $1,100,175 |

## KEY CONCEPTS

1. What is one thing all employees have in common?

2. Give a definition of "small business."

3. Even if your enterprise fails, what will you have gained?

4. Explain how profit works as a signal to the entrepreneur.

5. Do you agree that it will probably take about three months for your business to start earning a profit? Why or why not?

6. Describe three things you've learned about capitalism.

## VOCABULARY

business ■ capital ■ capitalism ■ economy ■ employee ■ entrepreneur ■ free enterprise system ■ profit ■ resource ■ voluntary exchange

## REFERENCES

1 Jeffry A. Timmons, *New Venture Creation: Entrepreneurship for the 21st Century* (Irwin McGraw-Hill, 1999).
2 Joseph A. Schumpeter, *Capitalism, Socialism and Democracy* (Harper & Row, 1942).

**Chapter 1 Review**

# Chapter Summary ✔✔✔

**1.1**    Businesses buy and sell goods and services to make a profit.
   A. People who work for someone else's business to earn wages are employees.
   B. People who start their own businesses and work for themselves are entrepreneurs.
   C. Profit is the money a company has left after expenses and taxes are paid.
   D. Successful businesses sell products and services:
      1. That customers need
      2. At prices customers are willing to pay
      3. To earn a profit.

**1.2**    Entrepreneurship is a way of thinking that includes:
   A. Seeking opportunities to learn new skills and take on new responsibilities
   B. Showing a desire to make a business more profitable — even as an employee
   C. Listening to new ideas
   D. Observing opportunities and needs
   E. Thinking about solutions to problems that people would pay for
   F. Recognizing that business principles are basically the same for large and small businesses.

**1.3**    Every business must make a profit.
   A. To earn a profit, a business must take in more money than it spends.
   B. Start-up costs often delay a new business from earning a profit.
   C. Some new businesses remain unprofitable and must close.
   D. Closing a business doesn't mean the entrepreneur has failed.
   E. Successful entrepreneurs often close a failing business, then start a new one.
   F. Profit measures how much value an entrepreneur has added to the scarce (limited) resources being used.

**1.4**    Our economy is a capitalist, free enterprise system.
   A. An economy is the financial system and structure created when decisions are made to answer three basic economic questions:
      1. What should be produced?
      2. How will it be produced?
      3. Who gets to have what is produced?
   B. Free enterprise means that anyone can start a business.
   C. Capitalism relies on capital (money) to start new businesses.

D. Voluntary exchange is the freedom to trade money for a product or service:
1. No one is forced to trade
2. Everyone is free to trade
3. Trading only happens when both parties feel they will benefit.

E. Free enterprise:
1. Discourages the waste of resources
2. Encourages the efficient use of resources (adding value) through the rewards of profit
3. Encourages competition, which helps keep prices lower and quality higher.

F. Being an entrepreneur in a free enterprise system has advantages:
1. Control over time
2. A creative, fulfilling life
3. Opportunity to create wealth
4. Control over compensation
5. Control over working conditions
6. Self-evaluation
7. Participation in an international community
8. Opportunities to help one's community.

G. Being an entrepreneur has disadvantages:
1. Risk of failure
2. Obstacles, unexpected problems, discouragement
3. Loneliness
4. Financial insecurity
5. Long hours, hard work.

H. Owning a successful business rewards an entrepreneur through:
1. Earning profits
2. Increasing the value of the business, which might eventually be sold for a profit
3. Providing an enjoyable career. ✔✔✔

### CHAPTER 2

# THE BUILDING BLOCK OF BUSINESS:
## *The Economics of One Unit of Sale*

*All our records had to be hits because we couldn't afford any flops.*

— Berry Gordy, *founder, Motown Record Company*

### KEY OBJECTIVES

THIS CHAPTER WILL ENABLE YOU TO:

- Define a unit of sale for a business.
- Describe the four types of business.
- Analyze the economics of one unit for each type of business, and calculate gross profit per unit.

## Economics of One Unit of Sale[1]

Entrepreneurs use profits:

1. To pay themselves.
2. To expand their businesses.
3. To start other businesses.

Every entrepreneur, therefore, needs to know how much **gross profit**[2] (price minus cost of goods sold) the business will earn on everything it sells. To do this, entrepreneurs study the **economics of one unit of sale (EOU)**.

Let's begin with the **unit of sale**, which is one unit of the product or service a business sells. Entrepreneurs usually define their unit of sale, depending on the type of business, in the following ways:

- **Retail:** One unit or item (i.e., one watch)
- **Manufacturing:** One order (any quantity)
- **Service:** One hour of service time or a standard block of time devoted to a task (i.e., one hour of lawn-mowing service)
- **Wholesale:** A dozen of an item (i.e., 12 watches)

**16**

- **Combination:** A combination of different items expressed as the average sale per customer (minus the average cost of goods sold per customer). See equation on page 19.

## Cost of Goods Sold for One Unit

The **cost of goods sold** (COGS) can be thought of as the cost of selling "one additional unit." If you buy watches and then resell them, your cost of goods sold per unit is the price you paid for one watch. Once you know your cost of goods sold, you can calculate gross profit by subtracting the COGS from your revenue:

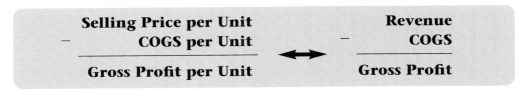

Let's say you can buy watches for $3 each at a wholesaler who will give you that price if you buy at least a dozen at a time. Your unit of sale is one watch. Your cost of goods sold is $3 per unit.

If you are able to sell ten watches at $10 each, your gross profit per unit will be $7. Here's how you would calculate your total gross profit.

| | | |
|---|---|---|
| Total Revenue = 10 watches × $10 selling price | = | $100.00 |
| Total Cost of Goods Sold = 10 watches × $3 COGS | = | − $30.00 |
| Total Gross Profit = $100 revenue − $30 COGS | = | $70.00 |

**Total Revenue − Total Cost of Goods Sold = Total Gross Profit**

*The Economics of One Unit of Sale* is a way to examine a snapshot, or model, of your whole business. If one unit of sale is profitable, the whole business can be profitable, too. On the other hand, if one unit of sale is not profitable, then no matter how many units you sell, your business will never be profitable. The economics of one unit of sale (commonly referred to as the "economics of one unit") is the price of the unit, minus the cost of goods or services sold. This number is equal to gross profit per unit. Total gross profit equals the number of units sold times the gross profit per unit.[3]

| | Economics of One Unit (EOU) | Total Gross Profit for 10 Units (@$10 per Unit Sold) |
|---|---|---|
| Price/Revenue | $10 | $100 ($10 × 10) |
| − Cost of Goods Sold | − $5 | $50 ($5 × 10) |
| Gross Profit | $5 | $50 ($5 × 10) |

## SKILLS MEAN SUCCESS

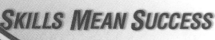

**MATH** ▸   **Mathematical Reasoning and Operations:** Average

*Average* (sometimes called the *mean* or *arithmetic mean*) is a useful way to describe, in simple terms, what a whole group or set of different numbers is like. Averages are used every day. For example, weather is described using "average temperature." Cars on long trips travel at an average speed per hour.

Janelle scored different numbers of points — 11, 8, 15, and 6 — in four different basketball games. Her coach wanted to find out how she was doing over several games, so he calculated her average points per game.

To calculate average, add the numbers in the list, or set, then divide by how many numbers were added. Therefore, Janelle's average points per game would be

$$\frac{(11 + 8 + 15 + 6)}{4} = \frac{40}{4} = 10 \text{ points}$$

Notice that Janelle never actually scored 10 points in any of the games, but 10 is still a useful way to describe "about" or "approximately" how many points she typically scores in one game.

**1.** Calculate the average of each of the following.

  **a.** Speed per hour during a three-hour trip: 65 MPH, 55 MPH, 45 MPH

  **b.** Long-distance telephone costs per month: Sept. $11.00, Oct. $23.50, Nov. $7.25, Dec. $57.10

  **c.** Average high temperature (in Fahrenheit) for a week: 88, 86, 81, 80, 72, 82, 90

  **d.** Average cost of school lunches for one week: $2.50, $3.10, $2.75, $3.60, $2.35

**2.** The amounts customers spent at Nicki's clothing store one morning and the cost of the items they purchased are shown below. What was Nicki's

  **a.** Average total dollar sale per customer?

  **b.** Average cost of those sales?

| Nicki's Sales | Cost of Items in Each Sale |
|---|---|
| *Customer 1:* $17.00 for one belt | $8.35 |
| *Customer 2:* $106.15 for one jacket, one pair of gloves, one scarf | $45.00 + $20 + $10 |
| *Customer 3:* $27.75 for one hooded sweatshirt | $19.00 |
| *Customer 4:* $34.45 for three T-shirts | $6.75 per T-shirt |
| *Customer 5:* $58.00 for one belt, one T-shirt, one hooded sweatshirt | See above. |
| **Average Sale per Customer  $ _____** | **Average Cost per Sale $ _____** |

**3.** What was the average cost of one item? ■■■

## Selling Multiple Units

*If the business sells a combination of differently priced items* (such as in a restaurant), the unit of sale is more complicated. The entrepreneur can use the average sale per customer, minus the average cost of goods sold per customer, to find the economics of one unit of sale. The formula would be:

$$
\begin{array}{r}
\textbf{Average sale per customer} \\
- \quad \textbf{Average cost of sale per customer} \\
\hline
\textbf{Average gross profit per customer}
\end{array}
$$

| UNIT OF SALE & ECONOMICS OF ONE UNIT OF SALE | | | |
|---|---|---|---|
| **Type of Business** | **Unit of Sale** | **Economics of One Unit of Sale** | **Gross Profit per Unit** |
| **1.** Retail & Manufacturing | One item (i.e., one tie) | $7 − $3 = $4 | $4 |
| **2.** Service | One hour (i.e., one hour of mowing a lawn) | $20 − $10 = $10 | $10 |
| **3.** Wholesale | Multiple of same item (i.e., one dozen roses) | $240 − $120 = $120 | $120 |
| **4.** Combination | Average sale per customer minus average cost of goods sold per customer (i.e., restaurant meals) | $20 − $10 = $10 | $10 average gross profit |

## Your Business and the Economics of One Unit

Later, you will learn about the principles of competitive advantage, unique selling proposition, and marketing and advertising. These concepts will be more meaningful if your thinking is based on the full understanding of your economics of one unit of sale.

## The Four Types of Business

There are four types of business, and each has a slightly different way of figuring its economics of one unit:

1.  **manufacturing** — makes a *tangible* product (you can literally touch it). A sneaker manufacturer makes sneakers but does not necessarily sell them to individual consumers.

2. **wholesale** — buys the sneakers in large quantities from the manufacturer and then sells smaller quantities (typically in dozens) to shoe stores.

3. **retail** — retail shoe stores sell the sneakers one pair at a time to consumers.

4. **service** — a service business sells *intangible* products (you can't actually touch them). A personal trainer, for example, sells his or her expertise to help people exercise.

For a manufacturing business, one unit might be one pair of sneakers. The costs would include the money paid to the people who make the sneakers (the labor) and the supplies — such as fabric, rubber, and leather.

---

### ECONOMICS OF ONE UNIT (EOU)

**Manufacturing Business:** unit = 1 pair of sneakers

| | | | |
|---|---|---|---|
| **Selling Price per Unit:** | | | **$15.00** |
| Labor Cost per Hour: | $4.00 | | |
| No. of Hours per Unit: | 2 hours | $8.00 | |
| Materials per Unit: | | 4.00 | |
| **Cost of Goods Sold per Unit:** | | **$12.00** | 12.00 |
| **Gross Profit per Unit:** | | | **$3.00** |

---

The manufacturer makes a gross profit of $3.00 for every pair of sneakers sold. That may not seem like much, but manufacturers sell in *bulk*. In other words, a manufacturer might sell several million pairs of sneakers per year.

The economics of one unit also applies to wholesale, retail, and service businesses.

Let's say the wholesaler buys each set of one dozen pairs of sneakers from the manufacturer for $180 and can sell them to the retailer for $240.

---

### ECONOMICS OF ONE UNIT (EOU)

**Wholesale Business:** unit = 1 dozen pairs of sneakers

| | |
|---|---|
| **Selling Price per Unit:** | **$240.00** |
| **Cost of Goods Sold per Unit:** | 180.00 |
| **Gross Profit per Unit:** | **$60.00** |

---

The retailer pays the wholesaler $240.00 for one dozen pairs of sneakers. The retailer's COGS, therefore, is $20 ($240 ÷ 12). The store sells each pair to its customers for $35.

| ECONOMICS OF ONE UNIT (EOU) | |
|---|---|
| **Retail Business:** unit = 1 pair of sneakers | |
| **Selling Price per Unit:** | **$35.00** |
| **Cost of Goods Sold per Unit:** | **20.00** |
| **Gross Profit per Unit:** | **$15.00** |

Let's look at the economics of one unit for a hair stylist who charges $50 per cut.

| ECONOMICS OF ONE UNIT (EOU) | | |
|---|---|---|
| **Service Business:** unit = 1 hour | | |
| **Selling Price per Unit:** | | **$50.00** |
| Supplies per Unit (hair gel, etc.): | $2.00 | |
| Labor Costs per Hour: | 25.00 | |
| **Cost of Goods Sold per Unit:** | **$27.00** | **27.00** |
| **Gross Profit per Unit:** | | **$23.00** |

## The Cost of Labor in the EOU

Janet is a 10th grade student in an entrepreneurship class. She has a business making greeting cards and her unit of sale is one card. Below is additional information about the business:

- She sells ten cards per week to people in her neighborhood.
- Her selling price is $4.50 each, including an envelope.
- Her costs are 80¢ per card for materials (construction paper, glue, and paint) and 20¢ each for the envelopes.
- On average, it takes her 15 minutes to make each card.
- Janet wants to pay herself $6 an hour. It takes her one hour to complete four cards. So the labor for each card is $1.50 ($6 ÷ 4). Janet wisely realizes

that she must include the cost of her labor in the economics of one unit. See how she did this in the chart below:

| ECONOMICS OF ONE UNIT (EOU) | | |
| --- | --- | --- |
| **Manufacturing Business:** unit = 1 card | | |
| **Selling Price per Unit:** | | **$4.50** |
| Materials: | $1.00 | |
| Labor: | 1.50 | |
| **Cost of Goods Sold per Unit:** | **$2.50** | 2.50 |
| **Gross Profit per Unit:** | | **$2.00** |

*Note: Janet receives $3.50 per card after paying for materials. Her compensation includes $1.50 per unit for her labor and $2.00 for her gross profit per unit. The wage of $1.50 is a reward for her labor. The $2.00 is the profit for being an entrepreneur.*

## Hiring Others to Make the Unit of Sale

Janet realizes that, if more people start buying cards, she will not have enough time to make them all herself. To solve this issue, she hires a friend to make the cards at the rate of $6 an hour. Although the EOU stays the same, Janet is no longer being paid to create cards. Her income from the business will come from the gross profit.

## Going for Volume

Janet meets a greeting card wholesaler. He offers to buy 2,000 cards if Janet can deliver them in one month and sell them at $3.50, $1 less than she had been getting for them. Three questions immediately came to her mind:

1.  Can I produce the 2,000-unit order in the required time frame?

    After doing some calculations, Janet realized that if she hired ten people each to work 50 hours a month, she could deliver the order in time. Janet convinced ten people to take on the one-month, 50-hour commitment.

2.  If I lower the price to $3.50 for each card (instead of $4.50), will I still make an acceptable gross profit per unit?

    To answer this question, Janet created the following chart and realized that her new gross profit per unit would be $1.00. Let's look at the EOU if Janet factors in her labor at $6.00 per hour (she can do four cards an hour).

**ECONOMICS OF ONE UNIT (EOU)**

**Manufacturing Business: unit = 1 card**

| | | |
|---|---:|---:|
| **Selling Price per Unit:** | | **$3.50** |
| Materials: | $1.00 | |
| Labor: | 1.50 | |
| **Cost of Goods Sold per Unit:** | **$2.50** | 2.50 |
| **Gross Profit per Unit:** | | **$1.00** |

**3.** How much in total gross profit will I make from the order?

To answer this question, Janet creates the following chart and realizes that her total gross profit will be $2,000:

**GROSS PROFIT PROJECTION (BASED ON EOU)**

**Janet's Total Gross Profit**

| | | |
|---|---:|---:|
| **Revenue ($3.50 × 2,000 Cards):** | | **$7,000.00** |
| Materials ($1 × 2,000): | $2,000.00 | |
| Labor ($1.50 × 2,000): | 3,000.00 | |
| **Cost of Goods Sold:** | **$5,000.00** | 5,000.00 |
| **Gross Profit:** | | **$2,000.00** |

## Lessons to Be Learned

Janet concluded that $2,000 in one payment was much better than earning $20 a week in gross profit and $15 a week for her labor — based on a volume of ten cards a week at a selling price of $4.50. When Janet realized that she could deliver the order in the required time and make $2,000, she accepted the offer.

Five breakthrough steps entrepreneurs can take are:

1. Calculating the unit of sale.

2. Determining the economics of one unit of sale.

3. Substituting someone else's labor.

**4.** Trying to sell in volume.

**5.** Creating jobs and operating at a profit.

## Becoming a Business Leader

By taking these steps, the entrepreneur is "promoting" him/herself to being a *leader* of a business — the chief executive officer. The compensation could be a salary and a part of the profit. Janet "promoted herself" and, instead of making $2.00 a card and not having much free time, she was able to make $1.00 for every card that her employees made, and enjoy being a leader.

Janet discovered how entrepreneurship leads to wealth. When the entrepreneur figures out how to make something for a profit, she/he can hire others to do the labor. Janet created part-time jobs for ten people to each make 200 cards per month (10 people × 200 units = 2,000 units). By creating jobs for others, Janet is making far more money than she ever could have made alone. She is fulfilling the entrepreneur's role as the driving force for job- and wealth-creation.

At first, an entrepreneur can be part of his or her own economics of one unit. If you start making (manufacturing) computers in your garage, like Steven Jobs and Stephen Wozniak did when they started Apple Computer, you should include your labor on the EOU worksheet. Over time, though, Jobs and Wozniak made enough profit to hire others to manufacture the computers. This left them free to develop creative new ideas for Apple Computer that brought more business and profit to the company. Jobs and Wozniak took themselves out of the economics of one unit so they could be the creative leaders of the company. And, by lowering prices, they were able to sell millions of units.

 **BizTip:** Keep in mind that, if you enjoy making your product yourself, you don't have to substitute someone else's labor. Don't give up what you love to do!

# Chapter 2 Review

## CRITICAL THINKING ABOUT...

### THE BUILDING BLOCK OF BUSINESS

1. If you start a successful business, how will you spend your time? How would you want to be paid? (Hint: Choose one of the four options described in the chapter.) Explain.

2. What are your personal goals for the next five years? What do you hope to accomplish? Write a one-sentence "vision statement" that describes what you would like to achieve over the next five years.

## KEY CONCEPTS

1. Gross profit is a business's profit before which other costs are subtracted?

2. What is the average unit of sale for the following businesses:

   a. A restaurant that serves $600 per day in meals to 60 customers (the average cost of goods sold per unit is $5.00)?

   b. A record store that sells $1,000 worth of CDs per day to 40 customers (the average cost of goods sold per unit is $12.50)?

For the following businesses, define the unit of sale and determine the gross profit per unit.

**Business Plan Practice**

3. Pete, the owner of The Funky DJ, provides DJ services to parties and other social events in his neighborhood. He charges $40 per hour. He rents a double turntable from his older brother at $10 per hour every time he works.

4. Sue, of Sue's Sandwich Shoppe, sells sandwiches and soda from a sidewalk cart in a popular park near her house. She sets up her cart in the summers to raise money for college. Last month she sold $1,000 worth of *product* (sandwiches and sodas) to 100 customers. Her unit is one sandwich (COGS $4) plus one soda (COGS $1). Total COGS = $5.00.

## EXPLORATION

Locate and interview three entrepreneurs in your community. Ask each the questions below. Make up your own questions, too. Do you see anything these entrepreneurs have in common? Create a report or chart summarizing how they compare to one another.

1. Tell me what your business is about. [This will help you get context to understand the other answers better.]

2. What do you value most about being an entrepreneur?

3. Do you think your business will continue to grow?

4. Do you travel for your business? If so, where have you gone, and why? Did you enjoy it?

5. Do you think other people appreciate what you do? If so, what kinds of people, and why? [They don't have to be identified by name.]

**6.** What are your views about business failure? Have you ever experienced failure? What happened?

**7.** If you could "live life over," would you choose to be an entrepreneur again, or would you choose something else?

## REFERENCES

1 Special thanks to John Harris and Michael Simmons for their many ideas for this chapter.
2 Gross profit will be discussed in greater detail later.
3 In Chapter 9 we will include other variable costs to get a complete picture of gross profit.

## VOCABULARY

cost of goods sold ■ economics of one unit of sale (EOU) ■ gross profit ■ unit of sale

## Chapter Summary ✔✔✔

**2.1** The Economics of One Unit of Sale (EOU) is the basis of business profit.
  A. Entrepreneurs use profits to:
      *1.* Pay themselves
      *2.* Expand the business
      *3.* Start new businesses.
  B. A unit of sale can be one item, one hour, one dozen of an item, or one combination of goods or service sold.
  C. Average Gross Profit per Transaction = Average Sale per Transaction ÷ Average Cost of Sale per Transaction.
  D. Unit cost of goods sold (COGS) = cost of selling one additional unit.
  E. Revenue − COGS = Gross profit.
  F. Selling Price per Unit − COGS per Unit = Gross Profit per Unit.
  G. Total Revenue − Total COGS = Total Gross Profit.

**2.2** There are four types of businesses:
  A. Manufacturing — making products
  B. Wholesale — selling products to retailers
  C. Retail — selling products to individual consumers
  D. Service — selling an intangible product.

**2.3** The Economics of One Unit can be calculated for each type of business.
  A. Manufacturing: Gross Profit per Unit = Selling Price per Unit − COGS per Unit (labor cost per unit [labor cost per hr. × no. of hours per unit to manufacture] + supplies cost per unit).
  B. Wholesale: GP per Unit = Selling Price per Unit − COGS per Unit.
  C. Retail: GP per Unit = Selling Price per Unit − COGS per Unit.
  D. Service: GP per Unit = Selling Price per Unit − COGS per Unit (supplies cost per unit + labor cost per unit).

*E.* The unit cost of labor is part of COGS.

    *1.* Start-up entrepreneurs have to add the cost of their own labor to COGS.

    *2.* Eventually entrepreneurs have enough business volume and gross profit to replace their own labor with employees' labor. ✔✔✔

## A Business for the Young Entrepreneur
### WEB DESIGN AND HOSTING

Tonya Groover took the first step toward realizing her dream of being an entrepreneur when she decided to leave her high school clique. As she put it, "My biggest challenge has been learning to be an individual rather than part of a crowd, moving out of my comfort zone." When Tonya began thinking like an entrepreneur, the world opened. Suddenly, there was so much more than her high school acquaintances.

When Tonya started teaching family and friends how to use the computer, she realized that she had the beginnings of a business. She created WebElegance, a Web-site design and hosting company.

Socially responsible business is important to Tonya. WebElegance not only provides a service, but also educates others. Addressing computer illiteracy is one of the business's long-term goals. Tonya is a designated peer mentor at her school, and she teaches fellow students to use the computer and explore the Internet.

Tonya has her sights set on college and will continue to operate her business as she earns a degree. If she meets her business plan projections, by the time she begins graduate school, she will be able to open an office and hire employees to support a growing clientele.

*Describe three decisions Tonya made that contributed to her success.* ■

### CHAPTER 3

# RETURN ON INVESTMENT:
## *Evaluating Education, Work, and Business*

*Our aspirations are our possibilities.*
— Robert Browning, *English poet*

THIS CHAPTER WILL ENABLE YOU TO:

- Work with percentages.
- Calculate return on investment (ROI).
- Explain why ROI is an important measure of success for investors and entrepreneurs.
- Explore the relationship between risk and return.

## Investment

To *invest* means to put time, energy, or money into a project or business because you hope to get back more than you put in. When you start your own business, you are giving time, energy, and money to an **investment** — your business, in this case. You do this because you believe that someday your business will earn more than the value of the time, energy, and money you put into it. This kind of analysis is calculating **return on investment**, or **ROI**.

## Return on Investment (ROI)

Let's say you want to set up a lemonade stand on a hot summer day. To get the business started you will have to buy lemonade mix, paper cups, and napkins. These supplies will cost you $5. Since you have put your own money into the business to get it going, the $5 is an *investment*.

By the end of the day, you have sold $20 worth of lemonade, and used up the supplies. Your initial investment was $5 and you got back $20. You now have the amount of your original investment, plus $15 ($5.00 + $15.00 = $20.00). The additional $15 is the return on your investment.

# Percentage Means "Out of a Hundred"

You can talk about ROI in dollar amounts, as we just did with the lemonade example, but entrepreneurs generally use **percentages**.

*Percentage* literally means "a given part of every hundred." Percentages express numbers as part of a whole, with the whole represented as 100%. Let's say you have 100 pennies. Because percentage means "out of a hundred," if you take 18 pennies out, you have removed eighteen percent of the pennies.

You could also express 18 out of 100 pennies like this: $\frac{18}{100}$. Eighteen divided by 100 is: 0.18.

- $\frac{18}{100}$ is a *fraction*
- 0.18 is a *decimal*

Expressing ROI as a percentage lets you more easily compare different returns on investment when the dollar amounts are not the same.

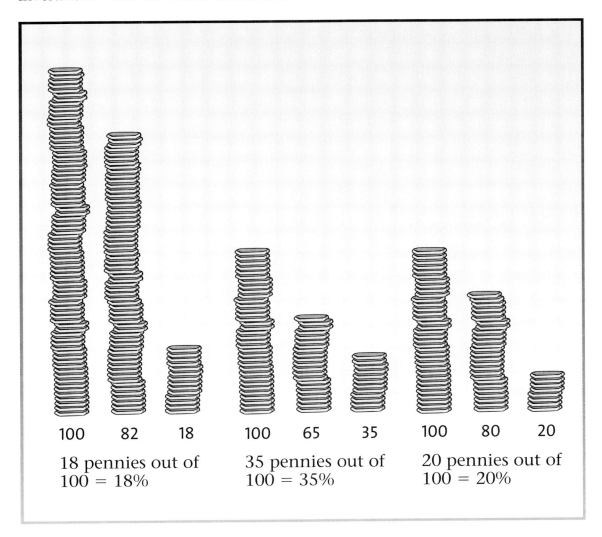

100    82    18      100    65    35      100    80    20

18 pennies out of 100 = 18%     35 pennies out of 100 = 35%     20 pennies out of 100 = 20%

## SKILLS MEAN SUCCESS

**MATH** ▶ **Number and Numeration:** Calculating Percentages; Representing Fraction, Decimal, and Percentage Equivalents

Using percentages is a helpful way to compare numbers based on different parts of a whole. Compare the field-goal shooting of 14 baskets out of 28 shots and field-goal shooting of 6 baskets out of 8 shots, for example. How can you tell which is better? First, divide the numbers to calculate a decimal. Then express it as a fraction with 100 as the numerator. This allows you to compare the numbers more easily because they are both expressed as a percentage: "out of a hundred."

14 divided by 28 = .50 = $\frac{50}{100}$ = 50%

6 divided by 8 = .75 = $\frac{75}{100}$ = 75% (better field-goal rate)

**1.** Which is better:

   **a.** Profits of $250 on an investment of $400?

   **b.** Profits of $1,500 on an investment of $10,000?

**2.** Which is a better record:

   **a.** 20 traffic accidents out of 2,000 deliveries?

   **b.** 5 traffic accidents out of 125 deliveries? ■ ■ ■

## Expressing ROI as a Percentage

In the lemonade example, you started out with $5 and earned a $15 profit. How would you express that ROI as a percentage?

**Step One:  Apply the ROI formula.**

First, you'll need to express ROI as a fraction:     $\dfrac{\text{Net Profit}}{\text{Investment}} = \text{ROI}$

**Rule of Thumb:** In business formulas, "on" means "divided by." Return on Investment means Return (Net Profit) divided by investment.

You invested $5 and earned $15 more than you started with. That was your "return."

$$\frac{\$15.00 \text{ (Net Profit)}}{\$5.00 \text{ (Investment)}} = \text{ROI}$$

**30**

**Step Two:  Express the fraction as a decimal.** To express the fraction as a decimal, divide the bottom number (denominator) into the top number (numerator).

$$\$15.00 \div \$5.00 = 3 = ROI$$

Your ROI expressed as a decimal is 3.00, or three times your investment.

**Step Three: Convert the decimal to a percentage.** Remember, to convert a decimal to a percentage, simply multiply it by 100.

$$3.0 \times 100 = 300\% \; ROI$$

Your ROI expressed as a percentage is 300%, or three times your investment.

Quick method: You can also convert a decimal number to a percentage by moving the decimal point two places to the right.

*3.00*

*300.*

*300%*

The following table shows a number of ROI calculations. Try using the formula and see if you get the same answers.

| RETURN ON INVESTMENT (ROI) | | |
|---|---|---|
| **Net Profit** | **Investment** | **ROI** |
| $1 | $2 | 50% |
| 20 | 30 | 67% |
| 30 | 90 | 33% |
| 9 | 10 | 90% |
| (60) | 120 | (50)% |
| 10,000 | 18,000 | 56% |
| 2,000 | 1,000 | 200% |
| 10,000 | 150,000 | 7% |

## Risk Is the Chance of Losing Your Money

Unfortunately, some investments lose money. **Risk** means the chance of losing your investment. When you buy $50 worth of assorted jewelry wholesale to resell at $100, you *risk* not being able to sell it. You could lose your $50, plus the time and energy you invested.

## Risk/Return Relationship

Riskier investments should earn a higher **rate of return**. A savings account in a bank is safe, but it has a low **interest rate** (return). The savings account can't lose value because the bank guarantees it. If you invest your money in a small business, in contrast, the risk of losing it is higher than it would be if you put the money in a savings account. On the other hand, the small business could earn a higher return.

You can picture the risk/return relationship as a graph. Risk increases left to right, and return increases bottom to top. As the diagonal line shows, the higher the risk, the higher the potential return. The lower the risk, the lower the potential return. The risk/return relationship is not a "law," but it is a useful guideline.

**Risk/Return Relationship**

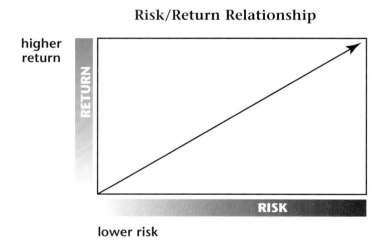

## Risk *and* Returns Are High in Small Business

The rate of return on a small business can be very high, if the business takes off and does well. Unfortunately, the risk of failure for most small businesses is also very high. Remember, the higher the risk of the investment, the higher the required rate of return that investors will expect.

Good business planning and adequate financing (with little debt) help reduce risk for a small business. Other factors that can make a small business less risky for the entrepreneur are:

1. **Small scale:** When the amount invested is small, you won't need as much profit to get a good ROI.

2. **Quick decision making:** Small businesses can solve problems and meet customer needs faster than larger ones.

3. **Industry knowledge:** If the entrepreneur is an expert (or becomes one) in the business, he/she is in a better position to spot warning signs and stay out of trouble.

4. **Lower operating costs:** Entrepreneurs often work to build their businesses without hiring many people, or without paying themselves. Doing so lowers costs. Investing your own time and money in an enterprise for little or no pay is called **sweat equity**.

Depending on a variety of factors, including the skill and knowledge of the entrepreneur and the quality of the business itself, a small business may not be as risky as it looks.

Businesses that young people may start face a lower risk of failure than those started by adults. The young entrepreneur usually has fewer fixed costs, which makes it easier to earn a profit. A young person can often start a small business without a large investment. The smaller the investment, the less return required to earn a good ROI.

## Going to College Is the *Best* Investment You Can Make

The best investment you can make as a young person is to go to college. Getting a college degree will increase your earning power by at least *three* times. Here are average salaries for different education levels:[1]

*No high school diploma —* $20,724
*High school diploma —* $34,373
*Two-year associate's degree —* $42,500
*Four-year college degree —* $62,188
*Professional degree (master's or lawyer or doctor) —* $95,309

Attending college is a big investment. The average private college currently costs about $25,000 per year. The average state college costs about $11,000. You also give up four years of earning money when you decide to go to college. On the other hand, the ROI is very high, when you consider that it covers your entire career. You will earn your investment back many times over because you will make much more money as a college graduate than you would as a high school graduate.

**BizFact: A person with a bachelor's degree will earn about a million dollars more over a lifetime than someone who has only a high school diploma. (The Employment and Training Administration)**

# Goal Setting

Deciding to go to college is an example of a **goal**. A goal is something you wish to accomplish in the future. You might not know how you are going to reach a goal — to pay for college, for example. That doesn't matter. What matters is that you choose your goals carefully and then focus on them. That is how to make things happen. You invest time, money, and energy now in order to achieve a return on the investment in the future.

Write your goals down to stay focused. What would you like to accomplish this week, this month, this year, or during your lifetime? Writing out your goals will program your brain to work on them. Once you have established a goal, you can take small steps every day toward achieving it. Goal setting can help you reach any objective you wish.

## SKILLS MEAN SUCCESS

**LEADERSHIP**

**Goal Setting:** Measurable Goals

To track your goals and know when you are achieving them, make sure your goal statements are "SMART":

**Specific:**       The goal statement is precise and explains what you hope to achieve in detail.

**Measurable:**   The goal statement is clear and can be evaluated.

**Attainable:**    The goal statement is realistic, yet offers a challenge.

**Relevant:**      The goal is meaningful and important to your business or personal life.

**Time-Bound:**  The goal has a time frame and includes a completion date.

To say, "I will network to make more business contacts," is not a SMART goal because it is not specific and has no time frame. A SMART statement for this goal might be: "By April 30, I will make five new banking contacts and get their written comments on my business plan."

Using the examples above, write down three SMART statements for personal or business goals you would like to accomplish over the next six months. ■■■

# The Time Value of Money

If you start saving now, you will have money for such goals as buying a house or retiring comfortably. Investing the money you save will help you, too. Safer investments usually grow slowly; riskier ones often grow faster, as we saw in the section on risk/return relationship.

Invested money grows by *compounding*, which means that you earn interest on your interest. The younger you are when you start saving, the more compound interest will help your money grow.

## SKILLS MEAN SUCCESS

**ENGLISH**  **Writing for Information and Understanding:**
**Observing Language Conventions**

*ROI* and *IRA* are two *abbreviations* used in this chapter. An abbreviation is a shortened form of a word or phrase, such as "Ave." for Avenue or "USA" for United States of America. We use them as "codes" in speech and in writing. Some abbreviations — called *acronyms* — use the first letter of each word in a name or phrase to form a new word, such as "NATO" for "North Atlantic Treaty Organization" or "PR" for "public relations."

1. Why do people, especially in the workplace, use abbreviations and acronyms?
2. When should you *not* use an abbreviation or acronym?
3. Think of ten abbreviations or acronyms and make a crossword puzzle or *Jeopardy*-style game to test your classmates. ■ ■

The **Rule of 72** is a quick way to figure how long it will take to double your money at a given return rate. Divide 72 by the return (or interest) rate to find the number of years needed to increase it by 100% — to "double your money." If you invest money at twelve percent, it will take, then, six years $\left(\frac{72}{12}\right)$ to double. At eight percent, it will take nine years $\left(\frac{72}{8}\right)$.

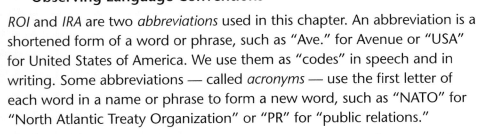

| THE RULE OF 72 | |
| --- | --- |
| **Growth Rate** | **Years to "Double"** |
| 4% | 18 Yrs. |
| 6% | 12 Yrs. |
| 8% | 9 Yrs. |
| 10% | 7.2 Yrs. |
| 12% | 6 Yrs. |

The government allows you to set up tax-free retirement accounts, called IRAs (Individual Retirement Accounts). "Tax-free" means you won't have to pay taxes on your money until you retire. If you withdraw from an IRA before retirement, you will have to pay a penalty *and* current-year income tax.

One type of retirement account, the Roth IRA, can be a good choice for a young person, because it will allow you to make a one-time withdrawal of money to buy a house. So, with the Roth, you can save not only for your retirement, but for buying a house as well! There is a maximum amount of money you are allowed to invest in an IRA each year. To encourage people to save, the government has been increasing that limit.

Let's look at two people who have invested money in IRAs. Let's assume that they both receive 12% per year.

**Person A:**    Invests $2,000 a year for six years at a rate of return of 12%, then stops.

**Person B:**    Spends $2,000 a year on him/herself for six years, then invests $2,000 a year for the next 35 years at a rate of return of 12%.

**Person A:**    Invested a total of $12,000: $2,000 per year × 6 years = $12,000.

**Person B:**    Invested a total of $70,000: $2,000 per year × 35 years = $70,000.

The chart on the next page shows how each person's investment would grow over time.

At "age 62": Person A, who only invested $12,000, has earned nearly as much return on the investment as Person B, who invested $70,000!

> **Start investing early. Let time work for you!**

## TIME VALUE OF MONEY CHART

| | PERSON A | | PERSON B | |
|---|---|---|---|---|
| Age | Payment | Growth at End of Year | Payment | Growth at End of Year |
| 22 | $ 2,000 | $  2,240* | $    0 | $    0 |
| 23 | 2,000 | 4,479 | 0 | 0 |
| 24 | 2,000 | 7,559 | 0 | 0 |
| 25 | 2,000 | 10,706 | 0 | 0 |
| 26 | 2,000 | 14,230 | 0 | 0 |
| 27 | 2,000 | 18,178 | 0 | 0 |
| 28 | 0 | 20,359 | 2,000 | 2,240* |
| 29 | 0 | 22,803 | 2,000 | 4,749 |
| 30 | 0 | 25,539 | 2,000 | 7,559 |
| 31 | 0 | 28,603 | 2,000 | 10,706 |
| 32 | 0 | 32,036 | 2,000 | 14,230 |
| 33 | 0 | 35,880 | 2,000 | 18,178 |
| 34 | 0 | 40,186 | 2,000 | 22,559 |
| 35 | 0 | 45,008 | 2,000 | 27,551 |
| 36 | 0 | 50,409 | 2,000 | 33,097 |
| 37 | 0 | 56,458 | 2,000 | 39,309 |
| 38 | 0 | 63,233 | 2,000 | 46,266 |
| 39 | 0 | 70,821 | 2,000 | 54,058 |
| 40 | 0 | 79,320 | 2,000 | 62,785 |
| 41 | 0 | 88,838 | 2,000 | 72,559 |
| 42 | 0 | 99,499 | 2,000 | 83,507 |
| 43 | 0 | 111,438 | 2,000 | 95,767 |
| 44 | 0 | 124,811 | 2,000 | 109,499 |
| 45 | 0 | 139,788 | 2,000 | 124,879 |
| 46 | 0 | 156,563 | 2,000 | 142,105 |
| 47 | 0 | 175,351 | 2,000 | 161,397 |
| 48 | 0 | 196,393 | 2,000 | 183,005 |
| 49 | 0 | 219,960 | 2,000 | 207,206 |
| 50 | 0 | 246,355 | 2,000 | 234,310 |
| 51 | 0 | 275,917 | 2,000 | 264,668 |
| 52 | 0 | 309,028 | 2,000 | 298,668 |
| 53 | 0 | 346,111 | 2,000 | 336,748 |
| 54 | 0 | 387,644 | 2,000 | 379,398 |
| 55 | 0 | 434,161 | 2,000 | 427,166 |
| 56 | 0 | 486,261 | 2,000 | 480,665 |
| 57 | 0 | 544,612 | 2,000 | 540,585 |
| 58 | 0 | 609,966 | 2,000 | 607,695 |
| 59 | 0 | 683,162 | 2,000 | 682,859 |
| 60 | 0 | 765,141 | 2,000 | 787,042 |
| 61 | 0 | 856,958 | 2,000 | 861,327 |
| 62 | 0 | 959,793 | 2,000 | 966,926 |

| Total Contributions: | $12,000 | | $70,000 | |
|---|---|---|---|---|
| Total at age 62: | | $959,793 | | $966,926 |

* assuming a 12% interest rate

## CRITICAL THINKING ABOUT...

### ROI

1. Complete the chart below. Assume a one-year investment period.

| RETURN ON INVESTMENT (ROI) | | |
|---|---|---|
| **Net Profit** | **Investment** | **ROI** |
| $4 | $ _____ | 100% |
| 30 | 60 | _____ % |
| 25 | 100 | _____ % |
| 4 | 10 | _____ % |
| 10 | _____ | 33% |
| 4,000 | _____ | 40% |
| 2,000 | _____ | 200% |
| _____ | 20,000 | 6% |

2. Describe a business you would like to start. What would your short-term goals be? (Short-term goals are returns on investment you would hope to see in one year.) What would your long-term goals be for the business? (These are goals that would take from one to five years to reach.)
**Business Plan Practice**

3. What is your overall career goal? How much money do you expect to earn each year from your career?
**Business Plan Practice**

4. How much education will you need to achieve your career goal? (Hint: Ask teacher or parents, or do research online.)
**Business Plan Practice**

5. Use the "Rule of 72" to find the number of years needed to double your money at the following rates of growth:

   **a.** 3%    **b.** 5%    **c.** 7%
   **d.** 18%    **e.** 24%

### KEY CONCEPTS

1. What is another term for "rate of return"?

2. How do you convert a decimal into a percentage?

3. What is the "quick way" to convert a decimal into a percentage?

4. Why can businesses started by young people face a lower risk of failure than adult businesses?

**5.** What else can be invested besides money?

## IN YOUR OPINION

What would be the acceptable return to you for investing your time, energy, or money in the following? (Note: Your return does not have to be financial.)

**1.** Baby-sit a neighbor's child for two hours.

**2.** Help your mother with the laundry.

**3.** Do an hour of volunteer work at a hospital.

**4.** Loan a friend $20 to start a candy business.

## VOCABULARY

goal ■ interest rate ■ investment ■ percentage ■ rate of return ■ return on investment (ROI) ■ risk ■ Rule of 72 ■ sweat equity

## REFERENCES

1 Data from the National Endowment for Financial Education.

# Chapter Summary ✔✔✔

**3.1**    Investors want to get more out of a project or business than they put in.
   A. The "extra" earned is profit.
   B. Time, energy, or money put into a business is investment.

**3.2**    Investors use net profit and investment to calculate return on investment.

**3.3**    Entrepreneurs usually calculate ROI as a percentage.
   A. Percentage means "part of every hundred."
   B. Example: 88% = 88 out of 100, or $\frac{88}{100}$ , or 0.81
   C. Percentage as fraction: net profit/investment: $\frac{\$12}{\$20} = \frac{3}{5}$
   D. Convert fraction to decimal by dividing:  $3 \div 5 = 0.6$
   E. Multiply decimal by 100 to convert it to percentage: $0.6 \times 100 = 60\%$
   F. Quick method: move decimal point two places to right: $0.6 = 60.0\%$

**3.4**    Investment involves risk.
   A. Time, energy, or money invested can be lost.
   B. Risk/return relationship: higher risk should mean higher return.
   C. Risk and returns can be high in small business.
   D. Entrepreneurs can reduce risk with:
      1. Smaller investments
      2. Quick decision making
      3. Business knowledge
      4. Keeping costs low, e.g., with sweat equity.

**3.5**    Entrepreneurs set ROI goals.
   A. College education has high ROI.
   B. Goals give entrepreneurs financial and personal targets to aim for.
   C. Rule of 72: 72 ÷ return (or interest) rate = years needed to double an investment: e.g., 72 ÷ 12% interest = 6 years to double a sum. ✔✔✔

# A Business for the Young Entrepreneur
## T-SHIRTS

How many T-shirts do you own with something printed or painted on them? What about your friends? Decorated T-shirts are very popular. It's easy and fun to make colorful T-shirts that other people will want to buy from you.

There are two easy ways to turn a plain T-shirt into a profitable creation:

- Silkscreening
- Fabric painting

## SILKSCREENING

Silkscreening is a *stencil* method of printing. Place the silkscreen, which has your design cut into it, on top of the T-shirt. Next, use a wedge to push the ink through the screen. The ink only comes through where your design has been cut into it.

| Supplies | Where to Find Them |
| --- | --- |
| silkscreen | arts & crafts store |
| wedge | arts & crafts store |
| ink | arts & crafts store |
| plain T-shirts | wholesaler |

## FABRIC PAINTING

Fabric painting is a good method to use if you want each of your T-shirts to have a unique design. You paint directly onto each shirt. Experiment with gluing decorative jewelry to shirts, too.

| Supplies | Where to Find Them |
| --- | --- |
| fabric paint | arts & crafts store |
| plain T-shirts | wholesaler |

## MARKET RESEARCH

Before making your T-shirts, conduct some market research. Ask your friends and other potential customers what size they wear. Ask them what designs they might like. Ask what price they might be willing to pay.

### TIPS

- Wear one of your creations to school to promote your business.
- Offer to silkscreen T-shirts for a school sports team or a local rock band to sell at concerts. They supply the design, you make the shirts.

*What's something creative that you enjoy doing that you could turn into a business?* ■

### CHAPTER 4

# OPPORTUNITY RECOGNITION

*Inch by inch, anything's a cinch.*

— Dr. Robert H. Schuller, *best-selling author*

THIS CHAPTER WILL ENABLE YOU TO:

■ Distinguish between an idea and an opportunity.

■ Recognize and evaluate business opportunities.

■ Apply cost/benefit analysis that includes opportunity cost to personal and business decisions.

■ Perform a SWOT analysis of a business opportunity.

■ Find business-formation opportunities among people you know.

## Where Others See Problems, Entrepreneurs Recognize Opportunities

Many famous companies have been started because an entrepreneur wanted to solve a problem. Entrepreneurs recognize that a problem can be a business opportunity.

Georgette Klinger founded her world-famous skin-care company because she had acne. Anita Roddick started The Body Shop — a cosmetics company that uses natural ingredients and recycles its bottles and jars — because she was tired of paying for expensive fancy packaging when she bought makeup.

Bill Gates was another problem solver. Before he started Microsoft, most software was too complicated and confusing for the average person to use. Gates solved this problem by creating software that was fun and easy to use. In the process, he became one of the richest people in the world.

Entrepreneurs love change because it presents them with new opportunities. Consider the Internet. Most experts believed that telephone companies were going to dominate this new technology, but entrepreneurs like Jerry Yang, who started Yahoo!, and Steve Case, who founded AOL, quickly took over. The phone companies were too big and slow to adapt to the new technology.

It can take a large corporation six years to create a new business. Entrepreneurs are leaner and faster. Small, entrepreneurial companies like Earthlink beat giants like AT&T and signed up millions of customers for Internet services.

## Look at Problems to See Opportunities

To become an entrepreneur who can recognize business opportunities, ask yourself such questions as:

- What would I like to buy that I can never find?
- What product or service would improve my life?
- What really annoys me? What product or service would help?

## SKILLS MEAN SUCCESS

**LEADERSHIP**

**Thinking Skills: Problem Solving**

Think of a problem that you would like to solve in order to create a business opportunity. Use the following six-step problem-solving process to write an action plan.

**1.** Identify the problem. Define it clearly and honestly.

**2.** Brainstorm as many ideas as possible for solutions.

**3.** Evaluate the solutions. Consider the pros and cons of each idea.

**4.** Select the best solution and develop a plan for how you will carry it out.

**5.** Carry out the solution, but be ready to change your plan if necessary.

**6.** Evaluate the results of your decision honestly. If the solution is not working, begin the process again to develop a new one. ■■■

## Use Your Imagination to Create Opportunities

Businesses are also created when entrepreneurs imagine products or services they wish existed. You can jump-start your imagination by asking yourself (and your friends) questions like:

- What is one thing you would like to have more than anything else?
- What does it look like?

- What does it taste like?
- What does it do?

## An Idea Is Not Necessarily an Opportunity[1]

There is one important difference, however, between an idea and an **opportunity**. An opportunity is based on what *consumers* want — not necessarily on what *you* want. You can have a very interesting idea for a business, but if what you're selling doesn't meet anyone else's needs, the business will fail.

You will also need to be able to get your business up and running in your "window of opportu-

nity." This is the amount of time you have before someone else beats you to the customers. You might have a great idea, but if competitors have had the same idea and get it to the marketplace first, your window of opportunity will have been closed.

A business idea may be a good opportunity if:

- It meets a consumer need.
- You have the resources and skills to create the business, or you know someone who does and who could start it with you.
- You can supply the product or service at a price that will be attractive to customers yet will be high enough to earn a profit.
- The business will work in your community. Do you actually know customers who can afford your product or service? Who will want it?
- You can get it up and running before the window of opportunity closes.
- It is *sustainable*, meaning you can keep it going for some time.

# Changing Trends Are also Opportunities

Problems are just one example of opportunities that entrepreneurs need to be able to recognize. Changing trends are also opportunities.

In the late 1980s, for example, Russell Simmons was promoting rap concerts at the City College of New York. At the time, rap was considered a passing fad. Rock music dominated radio and record sales. Simmons believed in rap, though. He formed Def Jam Records with fellow student Rick Rubin for $5,000. They produced hit records by Run DMC and LL Cool J.

Simmons came to be worth over $400 million.[2] He has started many businesses based on opportunities he saw in the hip-hop culture he loves — including not just Def Jam Records, but also television shows like Def Comedy Jam and the Phat Farm clothing line.

Simmons applied one simple principle: If you personally know ten people who are eager to buy a product or service, there are probably ten million who would buy it if they knew about it.

---

### The Ten Rules of Building a Successful Business

1. **Recognize an opportunity** — Simmons believed rap music was a growing trend and therefore a business opportunity.

2. **Evaluate it with critical thinking** — Simmons tested his idea by promoting concerts and observing consumer reaction.

3. **Write a business plan** — Simmons planned his operations.

4. **Build a team** — He partnered with Rick Rubin.

5. **Gather resources** — He and Rubin got $5,000 together.

6. **Decide ownership** — Simmons and Rubin formed their business as a partnership.

7. **Keep good financial records.**

8. **Stay aware** of your economics of one unit and your unique selling proposition.

9. **Keep satisfying consumer needs** — Simmons understood his hip-hop customers and he used this knowledge to create new products — television shows, clothing, Broadway plays, etc.

10. **Create wealth** — As of 2003, Simmons was worth over $400 million.

## The Six Roots of Opportunity[3]

There are six roots of opportunity in the marketplace:

1. **PROBLEMS** that your business could solve.

2. **CHANGES** in laws, situations, or trends.

3. **INVENTIONS** of totally new products or services.

4. **COMPETITION** — If you can find a way to beat the competition based on price, location, quality, reputation, reliability, or hours, you can operate a very successful business with an already existing product or service.

5. **TECHNOLOGICAL ADVANCES** — Scientists may invent new technology, but entrepreneurs must figure out how to market it.

6. **UNIQUE KNOWLEDGE** — You have unique knowledge of your neighborhood, your friends, and your community. When Simmons began promoting rap, he knew it was very popular in his neighborhood. That gave him an edge over record company executives who didn't live in urban areas and weren't aware of rap's potential.

### SKILLS MEAN SUCCESS

**TECHNOLOGY** ▶ **New Technology and Trends**

Technological change often leads to new products, new businesses, or even new industries. Match the technological advancement below to the product or industry it started.

| Advancement | Product/Industry |
|---|---|
| **1.** The Internet | **a.** cell phone |
| **2.** Wireless technology | **b.** OnStar |
| **3.** Global positioning systems | **c.** personal computer |
| **4.** Silicon chip | **d.** e-commerce |

## Business-Formation Opportunities — Your Friends!

Simmons and Rubin turned Def Jam into a huge success because they made a good team. Alone, neither of them had enough money to launch a record label, but together they were able to do it. Their business was also helped by the fact that they each knew different artists and had different contacts in the recording industry.

Everyone you know is a potential opportunity to form a business. Your friends or family members may have skills, equipment, or contacts that would make them valuable business partners.

Let's say you would like to start a T-shirt business, but you're not an artist. If you have a friend who is, the two of you could start the venture together. Or maybe you would like to form a DJ business, but you only have one turntable. If you formed the business with a friend, you could share equipment and records.

> **BizTip:** When putting together a business team, organize it so that everyone involved shares in the ownership and profits. People work harder when they know they will share in the business's success.

## SKILLS MEAN SUCCESS

**MATH** ▶ **Showing Percentages in a Pie Chart**

When a business has multiple owners, they generally share the profits according to *percentages* of ownership. If a company has $25,000 in total profits, what amount would go to each of the following owners?

**1.** Owner #1:  *50% ownership*
**2.** Owner #2:  *25% ownership*
**3.** Owner #3:  *20% ownership*
**4.** Owner #4:  *5% ownership*

Show your work, and then create a pie chart to show the percentages of ownership.

*Hint: A pie chart is a circle divided into slices, like a pizza. The whole circle represents 100%. The slices are drawn to represent percentages of the whole. If you have spreadsheet experience, use a spreadsheet to create your pie chart.* ■■■

## Cost/Benefit Analysis

Every opportunity will require an *investment*. As we have learned, an investment is something into which you put money, time, or energy, because you hope to earn a *return*. Your return could be profit, personal satisfaction, or something else that is important to you.

Simmons and Rubin invested $5,000 when they started Def Jam Records. They also put in a lot of time and effort. How can you decide if you want to invest your time, energy, or money? **Cost/benefit analysis** is the tool for doing just that.

Before making any investment, look carefully at two factors:

**Costs** — money and time you will have to invest, and

**Benefits** — the rate of return on your money or the advancement of your business or career.

If the **benefits** outweigh the costs, the investment will probably be worthwhile. This is cost/benefit analysis. You should use this tool when considering any opportunity.

## Opportunity Cost

Cost/benefit analysis can be inaccurate, however, without a close look at **opportunity cost**. This is the cost of your next-best investment. Opportunity cost is the value of what must be given up in order to obtain something else.

People often make decisions without considering the opportunity costs, and then wonder why they are not happy with their decisions. Each time you add up the costs of an investment, include the cost of the opportunities you are giving up.

If you want to go into the Army for four years, for example, you could gain these benefits:

- Training and work experience.
- Travel.
- Money for college.

To make the right decision, though, compare these benefits to the opportunities you will be losing, such as:

- The opportunity to go to college immediately.
- The opportunity to make money working, or to start a business.

If you choose the Army, make sure the training and skills will be worth postponing college, or work/business experience and income.

## The Value of Your Time

If you were to start a business, what would your opportunity cost be? In other words, what would be the next-best use of your time? How much money could you make working, instead? The answer to this question will give you a rough idea of how to value your time when you start a business and decide how much to pay yourself.

## Apply Cost/Benefit Analyis to Personal Decisions

You should also apply cost/benefit analysis to your personal life. People often make decisions with their emotions, not their reasoning. Strong emotions can overwhelm you, however, to the point where you see only the benefits and not the costs of an action (or vice versa). A good example of this would be the decision to put a major purchase, such as a stereo, on a credit card. The powerful desire for the stereo may make you lose sight of the costs — a major debt. If you train yourself to use cost/benefit analysis, and to consider opportunity costs, you will make good decisions.

**BizTip:** Sit down and make a list — in dollars and cents — of all the costs and benefits of a purchase you are thinking of making (before you make it).

## Education Only *Seems* Expensive

Sometimes getting an education can seem like a waste of time and money. You could be out in the real world earning cash, but instead you are sitting in a classroom. However, for every year of education you get, the earning potential of the rest of your life will rise tremendously. In other words, the opportunity cost of education is not nearly as high as the increase in potential income you will gain.[4] If you add ownership of a business to your career, you can earn even more!

| | | |
|---|---|---|
| $5.15 to $9.46 per hour | → | *Minimum wage* |
| $9.47 to $12.49 per hour | → | *Less than a high school diploma* |
| $12.50 to $14.60 per hour | → | *High school graduate* |
| $14.61 to $15.23 per hour | → | *Vocational or trade school, no degree* |
| $15.24 to $19.27 per hour | → | *Associate's degree (2 years)* |
| $19.28 to $24.03 per hour | → | *Bachelor's degree* |
| $24.04 to $29.99 per hour | → | *Master's degree* |
| $30.00 to $34.94 per hour | → | *Doctoral degree* |
| $34.95 and above per hour | → | *Professional degree* |

These are approximate figures and will vary on the profession chosen and where you live. The point is that every year you spend in school will more than pay for itself, by turning you into an individual who can earn more money during the rest of your life.

## SWOT Analysis

Another way to evaluate a business opportunity is to explore its:

Strengths — Your entrepreneurial ability and contacts.

Weaknesses — What you will face, from lack of money or training to lack of time or experience.

Opportunities — Lucky breaks or creative advantages you can use to get ahead of the competition.

Threats — Anything that might be bad for the business, from competitors to legal problems.

This tool can also be used to evaluate your business every few months once you have it up and running. To perform a **SWOT analysis**, set up a chart and make a list of everything you can think of under each category.

Below, is a SWOT Analysis of an opportunity to start a DJ business with a friend.

| Strengths | Weaknesses | Opportunities | Threats |
|---|---|---|---|
| I've worked in a dance record store and know what kind of music people want.<br><br>My partner and I each have good turntables, headphones and mixers. Together we could create a good system. | I'm not sure my friend will make a good business partner; he's often late.<br><br>We need money to join a record pool so we can get the latest records.<br><br>We don't have transportation for our equipment. | My cousin has already asked me to DJ at a party.<br><br>My partner knows a DJ who says we can sub for him sometimes. | Some parties we might be asked to work at might be in illegal spaces.<br><br>There are a lot of good DJs in the neighborhood already. |

# Broaden Your Mind

Successful entrepreneurs are constantly coming up with business ideas and evaluating them as opportunities. The best way to train your mind to think like an entrepreneur is to broaden it with many new experiences. Practice staying alert for problems and consumer needs, no matter what you are doing.

Effective ways to broaden your mind include:

- Travel.
- Making new friends.
- Learning a new language.
- Reading outside your current interests.
- Listening to others.
- Developing new hobbies.
- Watching the news, reading newspapers and magazines.
- Discussing current events with friends and mentors.
- Internships (working for free in the type of business you would like to start, or work for, in the future).

Remember, not every idea is an opportunity. For an idea also to be an opportunity, it must lead to the development of a product or service that would be of value to consumers.

## CRITICAL THINKING ABOUT...

### RECOGNIZING OPPORTUNITIES

1. Explain how a business opportunity differs from a business idea.

2. Give an example of a change that has occurred or is about to occur in your neighborhood. Discuss any business opportunities this change might create.

3. Do you have artistic ability? How might you turn your talent into a business?

4. List your hobbies, skills, resources, and interests, and those of a friend. Describe three businesses you or he/she could start alone or together. **Business Plan Practice**

5. Choose a business you would like to start, and perform a SWOT analysis. **Business Plan Practice**

6. Do you have a part-time job or do you work around the house to earn money? Describe how you could apply entrepreneurial thinking to your work to earn more money.

## KEY CONCEPTS

Given these hypothetical situations, which business would you consider starting or investing in?

1. A 100% increase in the price of gasoline.

2. A going-out-of-business sign in the window of a local grocery store.

3. A new airport being built near your home.

4. An increase in the percentage of women entering the workforce.

5. Local government decides to privatize garbage collection and impose recycling on households.

6. The state government allows parents to receive a sum of money that they can spend as they wish on education for their children.

## EXPLORATION

Have a conversation with a parent or other adult relative. Ask this person to tell you about which things he or she finds frustrating in the neighborhood. Write down these complaints.

**Step 1:** Generate at least three business opportunities from this conversation.

**Step 2:** Evaluate each of these using the "Business Opportunities" questions in the Workbook.

**Step 3:** Choose one of these business opportunities and write a SWOT analysis.

## IN YOUR OPINION

For each situation listed below, describe your greatest opportunity cost (that is, your next-best investment).

1. You spend $20 on a new shirt.

2. You watch TV for five hours.

3. You invest $10 in your brother's lemonade stand at a guaranteed 100% ROI.

4. You put $10 in your savings account, where it will earn 3% interest.

## REFERENCES

1 Special thanks to Jeffry Timmons, Howard Stevenson, and William Bygrave for ideas they contributed to this chapter.
2 *Black Enterprise* Top 100 List for 2003.
3 Adapted from *Master Curriculum Guide: Economics and Entrepreneurship*. Edited by John Clow, et al., Joint Council on Economic Education, 1991.
4 From Jump$tart Coalition for Personal Finance Literacy, as cited in *Teen Money Tips*, by Sanyika Calloway Boyce, p. 70.

## VOCABULARY

benefit ▪ cost/benefit analysis ▪ opportunity ▪ opportunity cost ▪ SWOT analysis

# Chapter Summary ✔✔✔

**4.1** Entrepreneurs look for opportunities to solve consumer problems.
    *A.* Look at problems as opportunities:
        *1.* Unserved consumer needs
        *2.* Products or services to improve people's lives
        *3.* Annoying problems people have.
    *B.* Imagine new products and services that could be solutions.

**4.2** Not every idea is an opportunity.
    *A.* The idea must match a consumer need.
    *B.* The entrepreneur must act on the idea quickly.
        *1.* The "window of opportunity" can close.
        *2.* Competitors can seize an opportunity first.
    *C.* Entrepreneurs need resources and skills to create a product or service.
    *D.* The price charged must be:
        *1.* Affordable for consumers
        *2.* Profitable for the business.
    *E.* The product or service should be sustainable over time.

**4.3** Opportunities are created by:
    *A.* Solving consumer problems
    *B.* Changes in laws, new situations or trends
    *C.* Inventing totally new products or services
    *D.* Beating the competition on:
        *1.* Price
        *2.* Location
        *3.* Quality
        *4.* Reputation
        *5.* Service.

**4.4**    Entrepreneurs make investment decisions based on analysis, not emotion.
    *A.* Cost/benefit analysis: do benefits outweigh costs?
    *B.* Opportunity-cost analysis: what other (better) investments are available?
    *C.* Value-of-time analysis: could the investor use time more profitably?
    *D.* Consider the potential long-term value of:
        *1.* Getting more education
        *2.* Owning a business.
    *E.* SWOT analysis:
        *1.* Strengths
        *2.* Weaknesses
        *3.* Opportunities
        *4.* Threats.
    *F.* Establish the habit of lifelong learning. ✔✔✔

# A Business for the Young Entrepreneur

## HOME-BAKED GOODS

Debbi Fields, of Mrs. Fields Original Cookies, built a multimillion-dollar business from the chocolate chip cookies she had started baking at the age of thirteen. Do you bake anything really well? Cookies? Banana bread? You can sell home-baked goods at flea markets, garage sales, or school events.

Make your baked goods extra-irresistible by packaging them attractively. Tie a yellow ribbon around the banana bread, or sell cookies in colorful boxes. Make up batches of special items around holidays — green cookies for St. Patrick's Day, or heart-shaped cakes for St. Valentine's Day.

This approach also works for homemade soups, jams and jellies, or any other food item you make that people really like.

### TIPS

- Don't get too elaborate. Stick to one or two products that you can consistently make really well.
- Figure out your "cost of goods sold"; that is, the cost of making "one additional unit" (each cookie or cake). Set your price high enough to cover the cost of goods sold and your time and labor.
- Offer a baking service to busy families. Make up a flyer that advertises your service. Perhaps you could supply, say, a hundred cookies per week.
- Buy ingredients in bulk at a warehouse or grocery club store. Bulk purchases are cheaper and will lower your costs.

Find out if there are food-handling classes in your area. Take the class and apply for a food handler's permit.

Find a business in your neighborhood that sells home-baked goods. Describe what it sells and estimate what you think the cost of goods sold is for the item. ■

### CHAPTER 5

# CHARACTERISTICS OF THE SUCCESSFUL ENTREPRENEUR

*Our greatest glory is not in never falling, but rising every time we fall.*

— Confucius, *Chinese philosopher*

## KEY OBJECTIVES

**THIS CHAPTER WILL ENABLE YOU TO:**

- Describe the characteristics of successful entrepreneurs.
- Identify your own characteristics.
- Develop characteristics that will help you in business.
- Train yourself to think positively.

## What Kind of People Become Entrepreneurs?

Many successful entrepreneurs start life with very little money or education. Growing up in a difficult environment can make them tough-minded and competitive. They often come from families that have little financial wealth but are rich in the ability to dream and turn dreams into reality. These are some of the *characteristics* of successful entrepreneurs. A characteristic is an individual quality that may make someone different from someone else.

## The Entrepreneur Needs Energy

An entrepreneur can be defined as "a person who has created — out of nothing — an ongoing enterprise." To imagine your business, set it up, and make it succeed will take a tremendous amount of energy.

Young people have lots of energy naturally but often don't know what to do with it. Try directing some of your youthful energy toward something positive — like starting a business! Many students who have completed this course have started their own companies. Some have been very successful.

**BizTip:** Your diet can greatly affect your energy level. Candy, soda, and other high-sugar and "junk" foods make you hyperactive at first, but tired and depressed later. If you are moody because of the food you eat, it will show in your business behavior. Drink juice or water instead of soda. Eat fruit, vegetables, nuts, or yogurt instead of candy or potato chips.

# Characteristics of the Successful Entrepreneur[1]

Many successful entrepreneurs started small business ventures when they were children. At an early age they showed some of the characteristics entrepreneurs need to be successful.

But no one is born with *all* the characteristics needed for success. If you have drive and perseverance, though, the other traits can be developed. Take a look at the list below. Notice the characteristics you already possess, as well as those you think you could develop.

**Adaptability** — the ability to cope with new situations and find creative solutions to problems.

**Competitiveness** — a willingness to compete with and test yourself against others.

**Confidence** — the belief that you can accomplish what you set out to do.

**Drive** — the desire to work hard to achieve one's goals.

**Honesty** — a commitment to refrain from lying; to be truthful and sincere in dealings with others.

**Organization** — the ability to structure your life and keep tasks and information in order.

**Persuasiveness** — the knack for convincing people to see your point of view and to get them interested in your ideas.

**Discipline** — the ability to stay focused and adhere to a schedule and deadlines.

**Perseverance** — the refusal to quit; willingness to keep goals in sight and work toward them, despite obstacles.

**Risk taking** — the courage to expose yourself to possible losses.

**Understanding** — an ability to listen to and empathize with other people.

**Vision** — the ability to see the end results of your goals while working to achieve them.

## SKILLS MEAN SUCCESS

**LEADERSHIP** ▶ **Recognizing Strengths:** Reflecting on Interests and Talents
**Self-Confidence:** Learning Self-Improvement

Do you have the traits (characteristics) of a successful entrepreneur? For each of the following, assess yourself on a scale of 1 to 5 (1 = I do not possess this trait; 5 = I am very strong in this trait). Think carefully about your own strengths and weakness, and be truthful in your answers.

| | | | | | |
|---|---|---|---|---|---|
| Energy | 1 | 2 | 3 | 4 | 5 |
| Optimism | 1 | 2 | 3 | 4 | 5 |
| Self-Esteem and Confidence | 1 | 2 | 3 | 4 | 5 |
| Adaptability | 1 | 2 | 3 | 4 | 5 |
| Competitiveness | 1 | 2 | 3 | 4 | 5 |
| Drive and Perseverance | 1 | 2 | 3 | 4 | 5 |
| Honesty | 1 | 2 | 3 | 4 | 5 |
| Organization and Discipline | 1 | 2 | 3 | 4 | 5 |
| Persuasiveness | 1 | 2 | 3 | 4 | 5 |
| Understanding | 1 | 2 | 3 | 4 | 5 |
| Vision | 1 | 2 | 3 | 4 | 5 |

Make a list of the traits on which you gave yourself a "3" or lower. These are the characteristics you can try to develop.

- Write a goal statement for how you will develop each of these qualities.
- Involve others. Ask for support from family, friends, co-workers, and mentors.
- Make a strong effort to use these characteristics in your daily activities.
- At the end of each day think about the improvements you've made and write about them in a journal.
- Recognize your successes and reward yourself for improvements! ■■■

## Entrepreneurs Are Optimists

You may have noticed that your day goes better when you feel good about yourself and the world. This is an *optimistic*, or positive, attitude. Entrepreneurs tend to be **optimists**. They have to be in order to see opportunities where others only see problems. Entrepreneurs view problems as opportunities.

No one is born optimistic, however, and most optimists are that way because they have decided to be so. They know that a *positive mental attitude* is the key to success.

# Positive Thinking Is Powerful

Start paying attention to your own thoughts. Are they mostly negative? Positive? Are you critical of yourself and of others?

Try this: Observe your thoughts and notice how they affect you. You will probably find that negative thinking makes you feel powerless and depressed. Positive thoughts make you feel happy and full of energy.

When you catch yourself thinking a negative thought, such as: "I'm really dumb," make an effort to replace it with a positive one, like "I'm smart and talented." Negativity can turn into a bad habit but, like any habit, it can be changed through a little effort.

Your thoughts affect your body. Scientific devices used to monitor functions such as heartbeat or sweating have proved that negative thoughts can definitely harm your health.

## SKILLS MEAN SUCCESS

**ENGLISH**

**Writing for Social Interaction:**
**Using Appropriate Language and Style**

Studies in education, business, and athletics have shown that words of encouragement and support — both from oneself and from others — can have a positive effect on performance and self-esteem. Rewrite the following phrases to create a positive statement.

**1.** I can't do…

**2.** I'm not good at…

**3.** I'm too shy to…

**4.** I'm not going to be successful at…

**5.** I just don't have time to…

Imagine that you heard someone *else* using this negative way of speaking. Write an encouraging, positive statement to respond to each of the negative phrases. ■■■

## Self-Esteem: A Positive Attitude about Yourself

To feel **self-esteem** is to have a positive attitude about oneself. Many successful entrepreneurs have described a positive mental attitude and high self-esteem as crucial to success. The common thread running through the history of entrepreneurship is the idea that thoughts have power. Who you decide you are can determine who you will become.

A positive mental attitude is easy to maintain when it's a warm sunny day and you have money in your pocket. It's harder to maintain when your life becomes difficult.

Think of it this way: To improve your body's appearance and strength, you have to *stress* it — by running, or weightlifting, or some other exercise. Your mind improves and strengthens in the same way — when you think positively in spite of the stress in your life.

 **BizFact:** Napoleon Hill, who interviewed some 500 wealthy people for *Think and Grow Rich*, wrote: "Every adversity, every failure and every heartache carries with it the seed of an equivalent or a greater benefit."[2]

## The Father of Positive Mental Attitude

The father of "Positive Mental Attitude" was Clement Stone. Stone was only 15 years old when he began going from door to door selling insurance policies in office buildings for his mother's small insurance firm in Detroit.

The first day on the job, Stone was so scared that he ran from office to office to keep his fear of rejection from overwhelming him. He made up self-motivating phrases, such as "Do It Now," and "When there's nothing to lose and much to gain by trying, try."

Stone repeated his phrases to himself over and over. Soon his sales and his confidence improved dramatically. Stone became a master salesman using his method, which he called Positive Mental Attitude.

By the age of 28, Clement Stone was a multimillionaire and had a thousand salespeople working for him selling insurance. He taught them that the key ingredient of the successful sales call was the positive attitude of the salesperson.

Stone believed the mind could be trained to think positively and creatively. He recommended that people "set aside a half-hour each day for creative thinking time." Stone liked to say, "Thought is a power that grows with use."

**BizFact:** Clement Stone wrote two books on the subject of positive mental attitude:

- *The Success System That Never Fails*
- *Success Through a Positive Mental Attitude*

Both books are two of the all-time best sellers in the field of business.

# 50 Positive Quotes to Help You Develop a Positive Mental Attitude

### Wealth Is Thoughts, Not Things... You Are What You Think

1. *Nothing in the world can take the place of persistence. Talent will not; nothing is more common than unsuccessful men with talent. Genius will not; the world is full of educated derelicts. Persistence and determination alone are omnipotent. The slogan "press on" has solved and always will solve the problems of the human race.* — Calvin Coolidge

2. *All virtue lies in individual action, in inward energy, in self-determination. There is no moral worth in being swept away by a crowd, even toward the best objective.* — William Channing

3. *There are two ways of meeting difficulties. You alter the difficulties or you alter yourself to meet them.* — Phyllis Bottome

4. *The world turns aside to let any man pass who knows whither he is going.* — David S. Jordan

5. *Our aspirations are our possibilities.* — Robert Browning

6. *The secret of getting ahead is getting started.* — Sally Berger

7. *A minute's success pays the failure of years.* — Robert Browning

8. *Let him who wants to move and convince others be first moved and convinced himself.* — Thomas Carlyle

9. *Do unto others as you would have them do unto you.* — The Golden Rule

10. *Keep away from people who try to belittle your ambition. Small people always do that, but the really great make you feel that you, too, can become great.* — Mark Twain

**11.** *Success seems to be largely a matter of hanging on after others have let go.*
— William Feather

**12.** *There is a tide in the affairs of men, which, taken at the flood, leads on to fortune; omitted, all the voyage of their life is bound in shallows and in miseries.*
— William Shakespeare

**13.** *There's no such thing as a self-made man. I've had much help and have found that if you are willing to work, many people are willing to help you.*
— O. Wayne Rollins

**14.** *Just don't give up trying to do what you really want to do. Where there is love and inspiration, I don't think you can go wrong.* — Ella Fitzgerald

**15.** *Leadership is knowing what you want and making it happen.* — Miriam Colon

**16.** *History records the successes of men with objectives and a sense of direction. Oblivion is the position of small men overwhelmed by obstacles.*
— William H. Danforth

**17.** *It is not the critic who counts; not the man who points out how the strong man stumbled, or where the doer of deeds could have done them better. The credit belongs to the man who is actually in the arena, whose face is marred by dust and sweat and blood; who strives valiantly; who errs and comes short again and again; who knows the great enthusiasms, the great devotions; who spends himself in a worthy cause; who, at the best, knows in the end the triumph of high achievement, and who, at the worst, if he fails, at least fails while daring greatly, so that his place shall never be with those timid souls who know neither victory nor defeat.*
— Theodore Roosevelt

**18.** *Sometimes I think creativity is magic; it's not a matter of finding an idea, but allowing the idea to find you.* — Maya Lin

**19.** *Someday I hope to enjoy enough of what the world calls success so that someone will ask me, "What's the secret of it?" I shall say simply this: "I get up when I fall down."* — Paul Harvey

**20.** *Don't let the opinions of the average man sway you. Dream, and he thinks you're crazy. Succeed, and he thinks you're lucky. Acquire wealth, and he thinks you're greedy. Pay no attention. He simply doesn't understand.* — Robert G. Allen

**21.** *Courage is resistance to fear, mastery of fear — not absence of fear.* — Mark Twain

**22.** *Wealth is when small efforts produce big results. Poverty is when big efforts produce small results.* — George David

**23.** *Service is the very purpose of life. It is the rent we pay for living on this planet.*
— Marian Wright Edelman

**24.** *The winners in life think constantly in terms of I can, I will and I am. Losers, on the other hand, concentrate their waking thoughts on what they should have or would have done, or what they can't do.* — Dennis Waitley

**25.** *The more you do of what you've done, the more you'll have of what you've got.* — Anonymous

**26.** *The life which is unexamined is not worth living.* — Plato

**27.** *One man with courage makes a majority.* — Andrew Jackson

**28.** *Money is the seed of money and the first franc is sometimes more difficult to acquire than the second million.* — Jean-Jacques Rousseau

**29.** *Ultimately we know deeply that the other side of every fear is freedom.* — Marilyn Ferguson

**30.** *Progress always involves risk. You can't steal second base and keep your foot on first.* — Frederick B. Wilcox

**31.** *I shall be telling this with a sigh, somewhere ages and ages hence: Two roads diverged in a wood, and I — I took the one less traveled by, and that has made all the difference.* — Robert Frost

**32.** *I always test the limits of my abilities and do the best job I can while remaining true to myself.* — Mae C. Jemison

**33.** *If money is your hope for independence you will never have it. The only real security that a man can have in this world is a reserve of knowledge, experience and ability.* — Emile Coué

**34.** *My life seems like one long obstacle course, with me as the chief obstacle.* — Jack Paar

**35.** *You must do the thing you think you cannot do.* — Eleanor Roosevelt

36. *I would rather see a crooked furrow than a field unplowed.*  — Paul Jewkes

37. *The way to develop decisiveness is to start right where you are, with the very next question you face.*  — Napoleon Hill

38. *Have the courage and the daring to think that you can make a difference. That's what being young is all about.*  — Ruby Dee

39. *No person is your friend who demands your silence, or denies your right to grow.* — Alice Walker

40. *You can get everything in life that you want . . . if you'll just help enough other people get what they want.*  — Zig Ziglar

41. *We know too much, and are convinced of too little.*  — T. S. Eliot

42. *Do not follow where the path may lead. Go instead where there is no path and leave a trail.*  — Muriel Strode

43. *No man is free who is not master of himself.*  — Epictetus

44. *Some men have thousands of reasons why they cannot do what they want to, when all they need is one reason why they can.*  — Willis R. Whitney

45. *Nothing in life is to be feared. It is only to be understood.*  — Marie Curie

46. *Goals are as essential to success as air is to life.*  — David Schwartz

47. *Come to the edge, he said. They said, we are afraid. Come to the edge, he said. They came. He pushed them ...and they flew.*  — Guillaume Apollinaire

48. *Unjust criticism is usually a disguised compliment. It often means that you have aroused jealousy and envy. Remember that no one ever kicks a dead dog.* — Dale Carnegie

49. *The man who does not work for the love of work but only for money is not likely to make money or to find much fun in life.*  — Charles M. Schwab

50. *If you have knowledge, let others light their candles in it.*  — Margaret Fuller

## A Company's Core Beliefs

This chapter has explored your beliefs about yourself. When you start your own company, what principles will you use to guide it? These will be the **core beliefs** of your business.

Examples of core beliefs in business might be:

- "At Superior Printing we believe in business practices that will affect the environment as little as possible."

- "At Sheila's Restaurant we believe in supporting our local organic farmers."

- "At David's Wallets, we believe in sharing our financial success with our employees."

Core beliefs can affect your business decisions. The owner of Superior Printing, for example, will choose an ink that is less harmful to the environment. Superior Printing may also have a paper recycling program to minimize its paper use. The owner of Sheila's Restaurant will only buy organic fruits and vegetables from local farmers.

## SKILLS MEAN SUCCESS

**ENGLISH**

### Reading for Information and Understanding: Selecting Relevant Information

Read an article about a successful scientist, athlete, businessperson, entertainer, politician, or leader, and then answer the following:

**1.** How did positive thinking and optimism help this person achieve a goal, or overcome an obstacle or hardship?

**2.** Did the person ever experience problems with depression, negative thoughts, or lack of self-confidence? If so, what was the effect, and how did he or she overcome these problems?

**3.** What lesson did you learn from reading the article? How could you apply it to your own life? ■■■

**BizFact:** Tom Watson Jr. built his father's company, IBM, into a huge international success with these three core beliefs: respect for the individual, unparalleled customer service, and the pursuit of superiority in all that the company undertakes.

# Chapter 5 Review

## CRITICAL THINKING ABOUT...

### CHARACTERISTICS OF AN ENTREPRENEUR

1. Take the NFTE "characteristics" survey in the workbook.

2. What are your three strongest characteristics? What are your three weakest? How could you strengthen them?

3. What does it mean to have self-esteem? Describe your self-esteem.

4. What kind of attitude is most important for the entrepreneur and why?

5. What are three things you could do to make your dreams come true? Write an essay about a time you successfully used any of these techniques to fulfill a goal.

## KEY CONCEPTS

1. Do you agree or disagree with Napoleon Hill's statement about adversity, failure, and heartache? Explain.

2. Describe three core beliefs you would use to run your own company. **Business Plan Practice**

3. Write about a time you wanted to accomplish something, but couldn't. What would you do differently in that same situation today? Explain.

4. Describe three ways you could change to develop a more positive mental attitude.

5. Choose a positive saying or quotation as your personal motto. Write it on a sign using magic markers, spray paint, glitter, or other materials. **Business Plan Practice**

## EXPLORATION

1. Collect at least three positive quotes or sayings from your parents or other adults. Share them with the class.

2. Discuss with a partner:

   *What is your attitude about money?*

   *Does money solve problems? How important is it?*

   Tell the class what you've learned about your partner's attitude toward money and how it differs from yours.

3. One of the biggest problems in the United States is the fact that so many people are overweight and out of shape. Entrepreneurs are responding with all kinds of products and services. Give three examples and bring advertisements or samples to show the class.

## REFERENCES

[1] O. Collins and D. Moore, *The Organization Makers: A Behavioral Study of Independent Entrepreneurs* (Prentice-Hall, 1970).

[2] Napoleon Hill, *Think and Grow Rich* (Fawcett Publications, 1965).

## VOCABULARY

core belief ■ optimist ■ self-esteem

## Chapter Summary ✔✔✔

**5.1** Entrepreneurs turn dreams into realities.
    *A.* Use energy to create something out of nothing.
    *B.* Display characteristics of:

| | |
|---|---|
| *1.* Adaptability | *7.* Persuasiveness |
| *2.* Competitiveness | *8.* Discipline |
| *3.* Confidence | *9.* Perseverance |
| *4.* Drive | *10.* Risk taking |
| *5.* Honesty | *11.* Understanding |
| *6.* Organization | *12.* Vision |

**5.2** "Yes I can" thinking is necessary.
    *A.* Be optimistic; think positively.
    *B.* Develop self-esteem.
    *C.* Have a positive mental attitude.

**5.3** Successful businesses are guided by core beliefs. ✔✔✔

## A Business for the Young Entrepreneur
**GREEN ACRES FAMILY FARM, JASON HEKI, JOHNSTON, IOWA**

*I've learned to manage my time and not waste it.*

Green Acres Family Farm provides high-quality, chemical-free, fresh produce, eggs, and meat from free-range chickens for health-conscious families in the community. Jason and his family previously lived in an urban environment. They understand the city customer and "the frustration of not knowing what has been sprayed on, injected in or fed to the food items we buy."

Jason monitors his products closely to see which ones are providing an acceptable return on investment. He eliminates those that are not. The "farmers' market" is where Jason sells the bulk of his products, though he plans to sell to restaurants and health food stores as well. He understands the importance of making a good impression on customers and working to keep them coming back. He encourages their return with clearly labeled signs and friendly staff (his family) who wear T-shirts with the Green Acres logo and hand out free samples. Tags are attached to products that explain uses for herbs and give recipes for the less common vegetables. Clearly, Jason understands the value of a satisfied customer. ∎

### CHAPTER 6

# SUPPLY AND DEMAND:
## *How Free Enterprise Works*

*There's no such thing as a free lunch.*

— Milton Friedman, *American economist*

THIS CHAPTER WILL ENABLE YOU TO:

■ Compare and contrast free market and command economies.

■ Explain the relationship between supply, demand, and price.

■ Describe how competition keeps prices down and quality high.

■ Discuss monopoly's effect on price and quality.

■ Use a supply-and-demand graph.

## Free Market vs. Command Economy

A **free enterprise system** is an economy in which anyone is free to start a business. This type of economy is also called **capitalism**, because people are free to use their *capital* (money) however they choose.

Did you ever wonder who decides how much gasoline costs? Or bread? In a free market economy, what is produced, the price, and the quantity bought and sold are determined by the daily decisions of everyone in the economy.

In a **command economy**, by contrast, the government sets prices, and tells people where they can work and how much they can earn. Cuba is an example of a country with a command economy.

## A Free Market Is More Efficient Than a Command Economy

In a free market economy, millions of entrepreneurs and consumers make millions of economic decisions every day. When an individual makes a decision, it is in response to prices. Let's say you want to buy a CD. You hear that the new music store in town is having a sale. You choose to go there because you are responding to price information.

In a free market system, the result of all these people making economic decisions every day is *efficiency*. Efficiency is how desired results are obtained with limited resources in an uncertain world. The desired result of an economic system is for consumers to get their needs met. Free market systems are considered more efficient than command economies.

In a command economy, the government looks at consumer needs and tries to meet them. The government sets prices and decides what is best for its citizens. Historically, command economies have not been very efficient. They have often failed to meet the most basic needs of food and shelter. People get frustrated because they can't start their own businesses and create better lives for themselves and their families. For these reasons, many people have risked their lives escaping from command economies, such as Cuba and the former Soviet Union, to immigrate to Western Europe and the United States.

## Most Economies Are a Mix

No country has a purely free market or purely command economy. Governments always control *some* economic decisions. In the United States, the government controls the postal service. There are also many government regulations business owners must follow.

Freedom of choice, of speech, and ownership are protected by law in the United States, though. Most citizens here have more economic and political freedom than people in many other countries. As a result, many Americans enjoy a high standard of living.

Some countries, such as the former Soviet Union and China, have tried command-type economies. These systems failed to keep people happy. Typically, the government ends up using force to make people obey its economic decisions. The Soviet Union finally collapsed and China has been slowly moving toward a more free-market-style system.

## Ownership Is Powerful

When you live in a country that protects free enterprise, you can own any business you create. You can keep all the profit from the business, or you can give some away to help others. It's your choice.

At some point you could decide to sell your business to someone else. Or you could sell pieces — "shares" — of the business to others. You could sell ten percent of the business to a friend, for example. That person would then own ten percent of the company and get ten percent of the profits.

In a capitalist society, you can sell shares of your business to anyone. Some people believe that, if you care about your community, you should consider keeping ownership local. They argue that if the owners were from the community, they would be more likely to make business decisions that would benefit the area.

When Ben & Jerry's ice cream sold shares for the first time, the company only allowed people who lived in Vermont to buy them — because part of the company's mission was to improve the quality of life for Vermonters. Bennett Cohen and Jerry Greenfield, the entrepreneurs who started Ben & Jerry's, made this choice.

## Price Communicates Information

An economic system is "efficient" when consumer needs are met with very little waste of resources or labor. Entrepreneurs who succeed in meeting consumer needs efficiently are rewarded by profit. Profit shows that they have made smart economic decisions. But how do they make them?

*In a free market, changes in prices send signals to entrepreneurs.* If the price of a pair of sneakers rises from $45 to $55 (and other economic factors stay the same), more entrepreneurs will start making and selling sneakers, because they can make a profit. A rise in price will attract producers and lead to increased production.

The entrepreneur knows quickly when the price of a product is too high, because most consumers will refuse to buy it. The entrepreneur knows when the price is too low when the product sells out quickly and consumers want more. Price relays information between the consumer and the entrepreneur.

**70**

## The Laws of Supply and Demand Determine Prices

The price of a product is generally determined by the laws of **supply** and **demand**.

If you are making and selling dresses, you will probably be more motivated to supply them if you can sell them for $50 than if you can sell them for $15. *Supply* is a schedule of the quantities that a business would make available to consumers at various prices.

On the other hand, customers will probably want to buy a lot more of your dresses if you sold them for $15 than if you sold them for $50. *Demand* is a schedule of the quantities that consumers would be willing to buy at various prices.

These two forces — supply and demand — interact in a free market to determine prices.

## Law of Demand[1]

According to the law of demand, as a price goes up, the quantity demanded by consumers will go down.

Let's say you get permission to sell soda at a Little League game. During the first half of the game, you charge $2 per can and sell two dozen. During the second half, you lower your price to $1 per can. You sell five dozen cans of soda. The people attending the game have "obeyed" the law of demand.

*Law of Demand: If everything else remains the same, people will demand more of something at a lower price than they will at a higher one.*

## Law of Supply

On the other side of every market is a supplier. The supplier also reacts to price changes. If your business is baking and selling cookies, how many would you be willing to make if you thought they would sell for 25 cents each? What if people were willing to pay $1.00? You would probably work harder to bake and sell more cookies at the higher price.

The entrepreneur who acts in this way is following the law of supply.

*Law of Supply: If everything else remains the same, businesses will supply more of a product or service at a higher price than they will at a lower one.*

## Using the Laws of Supply and Demand to Predict Market Behavior

Understanding the laws of supply and demand will help you predict market behavior. What would you expect to happen to the demand for air conditioners in the summer? What will most likely happen to the *price* of air conditioners in the summer?

The demand for air conditioners will rise in the summer because more people will want them. Suppliers of air conditioners will be able to raise their prices in late spring because people will be "demanding" this product then. As summer draws to a close, and those who wanted air conditioners have already bought them, the price will probably come down.

## Supply and Demand Schedules

George goes to the grocery store to buy apples. How many he will buy depends on the price. If apples cost 90 cents each, George might only be willing to buy one. At ten cents, he might be willing to buy nine.

The owner of the grocery store might be willing to sell (supply) ten apples if he could sell them at $1.00. At ten cents, he only wants to supply one.

A list of how many units of a product consumers are willing to buy at different prices is called a "demand schedule." Below is a demand schedule for George.

You can see, as the price of apples goes down, George is willing to buy more.

A list of how much of a product producers are willing to supply at different prices is called a "supply schedule." Below is also a supply schedule for the grocer.

| Price of one apple | Number of apples George is willing to buy at the price | Price of one apple | Number of apples grocer is willing to supply at the price |
|---|---|---|---|
| $1.00 | 0 | $0.10 | 1 |
| $0.90 | 1 | $0.20 | 2 |
| $0.80 | 2 | $0.30 | 3 |
| $0.70 | 3 | $0.40 | 4 |
| $0.60 | 4 | $0.50 | 5 |
| $0.50 | 5 | $0.60 | 6 |
| $0.40 | 6 | $0.70 | 7 |
| $0.30 | 7 | $0.80 | 8 |
| $0.20 | 8 | $0.90 | 9 |
| $0.10 | 9 | $1.00 | 10 |

You can see from the supply schedule that, as the price of apples rises, the grocer is willing to supply more.

## The Market Clearing Price

The point at which the supply and demand lines cross is the **market clearing price**. This is the price at which the number of apples George is willing to buy and the grocer is willing to supply are the same. The trade will take place at this point.

According to the graph, the market clearing price is fifty cents. At this price George will buy five apples and the grocer will sell (supply) five.

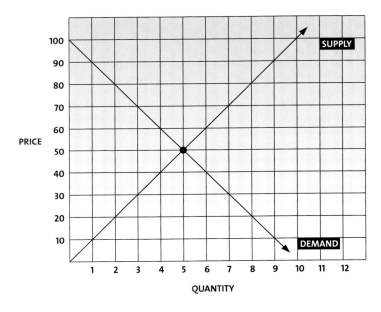

1.   What is the market clearing price of apples?

2.   How many apples is the grocer willing to sell at $0.20?

3.   How many apples is George willing to buy at $0.20?

Together, demand and supply determine how much will be bought and sold and what the price will be in any given market. Remember, a market is a group of people buying and selling a product or service. Businesses would like to charge high prices for their products and services. Consumers seek low prices. The market clearing price occurs when what the buyer wants to pay is the same as what the entrepreneur wants to charge.

Supply, demand, and price information are communicated quickly and clearly between consumers and entrepreneurs in a free market system. Learning to forecast supply and demand in your market will be a key to your success.

## SKILLS MEAN SUCCESS

**MATH**    **Displaying Data in Line Graphs**

A supply-and-demand graph is a line graph. A line graph shows lines rising and falling on X- and Y-*axes* to demonstrate how one thing is affected by another — in this case, price and quantity. A line graph is a helpful way to visually show supply and demand data. It may seem complex, but by following these instructions, you can draw your own supply and demand graph.

- Use graph paper or prepare your own blank graph with a vertical and a horizontal axis.
- Label the vertical (left) axis "Price" and the horizontal (bottom) axis "Quantity."
- On the vertical axis, mark prices from $1 to $5. Start at the bottom.
- On the horizontal axis, mark quantities from 1 through 5. Start at the left.
- Using the data from the demand and supply schedules, draw dots on your graph to represent the quantities demanded and supplied at each price.

| Price of one loaf of bread | Number of loaves shopper is willing to buy at this price |
|---|---|
| $5.00 | 1 |
| $4.00 | 2 |
| $3.00 | 3 |
| $2.00 | 4 |
| $1.00 | 5 |

| Price of one loaf of bread | Number of loaves bakery is willing to supply at this price |
|---|---|
| $1.00 | 1 |
| $2.00 | 2 |
| $3.00 | 3 |
| $4.00 | 4 |
| $5.00 | 5 |

- Draw lines connecting the dots and note where they intersect. Identify the market clearing price and the quantity that will be exchanged at that price. ■ ■ ■

## Competition Keeps Prices Down and Quality High

The laws of supply and demand work when businesses are free to compete with each other. Businesses try to attract consumers by lowering prices, improving quality, and developing new products and services. In your neighborhood, for example, there may be two grocery stores. Each will *compete* for your business by:

- Lowering prices.
- Improving the quality of the food they offer.
- Offering new products or services to attract you.

Each store will try to make smart decisions in order to get your business and make a profit. You, the consumer, benefit from this **competition**. Competition encourages lower prices and higher quality.

# Monopoly Is the Opposite of Competition

When there is only one supplier of a product or service in a market, that supplier has a **monopoly**. The word monopoly comes from two Greek words — *monos*, which means "single," and *polien*, which means "to sell."

A monopoly is the opposite of competition, and has the opposite effect. In a monopoly the supplier doesn't have to compete to attract customers. Customers have no choice but to go to that supplier. Monopolies generally keep prices high and have no incentive to improve quality.

In a free market, a monopoly seldom lasts long. Other entrepreneurs will be attracted by the high prices and will enter the market. They will compete for the customers by offering lower prices and perhaps higher quality.

Some years ago, a flood in Louisiana made it difficult to bring milk into the state. The supply of milk was cut off. The only distributor who had milk started charging very high prices for it. Because the price of milk rose so high, however, it attracted other suppliers, who rushed more milk to the location. As the supply of milk increased, the price dropped immediately in response.

## SKILLS MEAN SUCCESS

**TECHNOLOGY** ▶ **Multimedia Presentations: Using Graphics**

You can add interest to multimedia presentations by adding *graphics* (pictures), such as line graphs, and other charts. Charts and graphs are helpful for presenting complex information in easy-to-understand visuals. You can create some types of charts directly from your presentation software, such as PowerPoint. You can also import charts created in a spreadsheet program, like Excel. Use the following tips when creating graphics in multimedia presentations:

- Use only one graphic per slide.
- Make sure titles and labels are clearly identified.
- Use one clearly legible, large-sized font, such as Arial or Times Roman. Use the same-size type on all graphics.
- Use thick, solid lines, and a different, contrasting color for each line or chart element.
- Include a "legend" (key that explains what each color represents); for instance, Red = Supply and Blue = Demand.
- Avoid shadows, textures, and patterns that can make readability from a distance difficult.
- Acknowledge the dates and sources of your data. ■■■

# Use Supply and Demand as Guides

It may seem, when you start a business, that you will never know what prices to charge or how much product to supply. Each time you make a choice regarding your business, however, the laws of supply and demand will provide you with valuable feedback from your market.

- If the demand falls, the market may be telling you to change your product or service, or lower your price.

- If the supply of your product or service rises, due to other entrepreneurs entering the market, the price may start to fall. You might find that you can't sell enough to make a profit.

- If the demand rises or the supply falls, you may be able to raise your price.

Sometimes it may seem that you've tried everything and paid close attention to the market, but you still can't make a profit. Listen to that signal, too. Perhaps it's the market pushing you to a new and different business!

## SKILLS MEAN SUCCESS

**ENGLISH**

### Reading for Information and Understanding: Getting Meaning

Review the vocabulary and concepts in this chapter and use them to help you locate the best word or phrase to complete the following statements.

Remember to use headings and boldface terms to help you locate the information you need.

1. In a command economy the _____ sets prices.

2. Efficiency is the result of people making economic decisions in a _____ .

3. As price goes up, the quantity demanded by consumers goes _____ .

4. As price goes up, the quantity businesses are willing to supply _____ .

5. The point at which the supply and demand lines cross is the _____ .

6. As competition increases, prices go _____ .

7. As competition increases, quality _____ .

8. The opposite of competition is _____ .

9. _____ means there is only one _____ of a product or service in a market.

## CRITICAL THINKING ABOUT...

### SUPPLY AND DEMAND

1. Is there a product that you stop buying when its price goes up, even a little? Is there another product that you would keep buying even if its price rose considerably? Explain.

2. Choose a product you would like to sell. What factors would affect the demand for it? What factors would affect its supply?

**Business Plan Practice**

3. In the two situations below, what signals are being sent to the business owners? Describe them in a brief essay on each.

   **#1:** You are a dairy and soybean farmer in Wisconsin. You spend half the time farming soybeans and the other half taking care of the cows. The price of milk has just gone up 50 cents a gallon. What signal is the market sending?

   **#2:** You own a nightclub with a "1960s" theme that plays rock and roll from that decade. Your club has been very successful for the last few years, but lately it has not been full. People are going instead to the new club down the street that has a "1970s" theme and plays disco music. You've tried lowering the cover charge, but you are still losing money every night. What signal is the market sending you? What are some ways you could respond?

## KEY CONCEPTS

1. What is likely to happen to the price of air conditioners in December? Why?

2. What would you expect to happen to the demand for gasoline if everyone began using electric cars?

3. How would you expect the use of electric cars to affect the availability of gasoline and its price?

4. Explain why a monopoly can charge any price for the products it sells. Can monopolies develop in a free market system? Why or why not?

5. After reading A Business for a Young Entrepreneur, explain how Franklin is using the laws of supply and demand to make his business profitable.

## EXPLORATION

Choose a product, such as a can of beans, that you know you can find in several different stores in your neighborhood. List the price in each store. Are the stores charging different prices? Why do you think that might be? What other factors, besides price, do you think might affect the supply or demand of a product?

## REFERENCES

1 For an excellent discussion of supply and demand, see *Master Curriculum Guide in Economics, Part II, Strategies for Teaching Economics*, edited by Ronald A. Banaszak and Elmer U. Clawson (The Joint Council on Economic Education, 1981).

**Chapter 6 Review**

## VOCABULARY

capitalism ■ command economy ■
competition ■ demand ■ free
enterprise system ■ market clearing
price ■ monopoly ■ supply

# Chapter Summary ✔✔✔

**6.1**    Free enterprise systems are capitalist economies.
    *A.* People are free to:
       *1.* Start a business
       *2.* Use their capital (money) as they choose.
    *B.* All of the people in the economy, not the government, make decisions on:
       *1.* What products are needed
       *2.* What prices will be paid
       *3.* How much will be bought and sold.
    *C.* Letting everyone in an economy make economic decisions results in efficiency:
       *1.* Less waste of resources
       *2.* Usually produces desired results with prices and products.

**6.2**    Governments make decisions in command economies.
    *A.* Governments decide:
       *1.* What people want and need
       *2.* What will be produced
       *3.* What prices will be charged
       *4.* Who will start what kinds of businesses.
    *B.* Leaving decisions to the government is often not efficient and leads to:
       *1.* Artificially measured resources
       *2.* Unsatisfactory results.

**6.3**    Most economies are mixed.
    *A.* No economy is purely free or purely command.
    *B.* Ownership of a business allows freedom and choice:
       *1.* Owning the whole business
       *2.* Owning shares (pieces) of a business.
    *C.* Efficient economies use labor and resources wisely by:
       *1.* Meeting consumer needs
       *2.* Rewarding entrepreneurs with profits
       *3.* Sending price and purchasing-pattern signals to entrepreneurs.

**6.4**   Law of Supply and Demand determines prices.

    *A.* Law of Demand: People will demand more of something if the price is lower than if it is higher.

    *B.* Law of Supply: Businesses will produce more of a product or service if they can charge a higher price rather than a lower one.

    *C.* Supply and demand determine the market clearing price.

    *D.* The market clearing price can be graphed to show the point at which:

        *1.* The buyer is ready to buy a specific quantity at a specific price, and

        *2.* The seller is ready to supply a specific quantity at a specific price.

    *E.* Competition keeps prices lower and quality higher.

    *F.* Monopolies tend to keep prices higher, quality lower.

    *G.* Entrepreneurs use the Law of Supply and Demand to make decisions on products, pricing, and profit. ✔✔✔

# A Business for the Young Entrepreneur

**FRANK'S FRUIT BASKETS AND SNACKS, FRANKLIN REGINALD MELCHOR**

*One lesson that I have learned from this experience is that it takes time and effort to be a successful businessperson.*

Since the first day of class, Franklin's NFTE teacher was impressed with his eagerness to learn as much as he could about business. Franklin applied this curiosity to his own business, Frank's Fruit Baskets and Snacks. He asked many questions to figure out which snacks would be successful and meet the demand of his market. Then he began meeting that demand, providing fruit baskets and snacks at the school and to people in his neighborhood.

Franklin works hard to make his business a success, shopping on weekends at bulk retailers like the Price Club. He supplies his product at prices lower than the vending machines found in his school, thereby cutting out his direct competitor. Franklin watches buying patterns, establishes regular supply areas, and advertises his business as much as he can. He wears a headband with his company name and has become known around school as the "Candy Man."

Running his own business has taught Franklin the importance of hard work. His efforts have given him greater independence and first-hand knowledge of what it takes to be successful. He runs a profitable business and plans to continue it when he enters college.

If the vending machines were taken out of Franklin's school, what effect might it have on the prices that Franklin could charge? Include terms, such as supply and demand, that you learned in this chapter. ■

### CHAPTER 7

# INVENTIONS AND PRODUCT DEVELOPMENT

*The greatest achievement was at first and for a time (only) a dream.*

— James Allen, *American author*

## KEY OBJECTIVES

THIS CHAPTER WILL ENABLE YOU TO:

- Develop your creativity.
- Practice lateral thinking.
- Use "practical daydreaming" to invent new products.
- Describe the five steps of developing a product.
- Explore the contributions of minority and women inventors.

## Do You Use Your Creativity?

**Creativity** is the ability to invent or make something using your imagination. Everybody has this potential. Children are naturally creative, but as we get older many of us stop using our creativity.

The secret of being creative is the willingness to explore new ideas and change or discard old ones. This is called being "open-minded."

Creative people are not afraid to make mistakes or to be different. Henry Ford worked on a "horseless carriage" in his backyard during the 1890s, even though neighbors made fun of him. Most people believed that, anyway, only the rich would be able to own such machines. Ford's neighbors considered him a daydreaming mechanic.

By the time Ford was 50, however, he was rich and famous. He had created Ford Motor Company, which had become one of the largest automakers in the world.

In the early 1960s, Andy Warhol silkscreened images of Campbell's soup cans and other "popular" images, on large canvases. At first, people thought his paintings were not art, but Warhol, too, become rich and famous. Today, his paintings are prized by collectors and museums.

## The Entrepreneur Is a Market-Minded Artist

The difference between an artist and an entrepreneur is not creativity — both are creative. The difference lies in how that creativity is used:

- Artists create in response to an inner need to express themselves. Andy Warhol painted Campbell's soup cans because he wanted to paint Campbell's soup cans!

- The entrepreneur, in contrast, tries to create something consumers will want to buy at a price that creates a profit. Ford was determined to make a car that the average person could afford because he believed millions of people would want to buy one. Apple co-founder Stephen Wozniak believed millions of people would want to have computers in their homes.[1]

Entrepreneurs can be thought of as the "artists" of the economy. They create businesses from ideas, visions, or dreams — but always with a market in mind.

 **BizFact:** Many artists are also successful entrepreneurs. Missy Elliott is a rapper, but she also owns a record company, Goldmine, Inc. Oprah Winfrey is a talented actress and talk-show host who also owns a film and television production company, Harpo, Inc.

## Lateral Thinking Increases Creativity

Creativity expert Edward de Bono[2] has written that creativity can be increased through **lateral thinking**. Most of us have been trained to use **vertical thinking**, which "stacks" one idea on top of the next. In math, for instance, you learn how to add, then you learn how to multiply.

The problem with vertical thinking, de Bono says, is that it builds "concept prisons of old ideas." Vertical thinking encourages you to try to fit new information into patterns you've already learned. You may even unconsciously ignore new information because it doesn't fit into those patterns.

This is how people hang onto racist or sexist stereotypes. They ignore anything good they see or hear about people different from themselves. They focus instead on negative images that fit into their "concept prisons."

Vertical thinking encourages us to believe that the only way to solve a problem is to go from one logical step to the next, until we reach the one "right" solution. Lateral thinkers look for alternative ways of thinking about a problem or obstacle. They approach problems "sideways."

## Challenge Assumptions to Solve Problems

You can develop lateral thinking by challenging *assumptions*. An assumption is anything you assume or believe to be true. Challenging an assumption can lead to a creative solution to a problem. To experience this yourself, use lateral thinking to solve this puzzle. On a separate sheet of paper, link up the nine dots using only four straight lines and without raising the pencil from the paper.

## Research Suggests Intelligence Can Be Improved

Not only can you become more creative, you can become smarter!

Scientists used to believe that everyone was born with a level of intelligence that never changed. They believed that physical exercise could help muscles grow, but that nothing helped the brain grow.

Research shows, though, that exercising the mind causes brain cells called *neurons* to send out branches of *dendrites*. Dendrites connect brain cells. More dendrites means more brain cells can be used.

Dendrites can be encouraged to grow by doing many things that you probably enjoy. Dr. Arnold Scheibel, Professor of Neurobiology at the University of California-Los Angeles School of Medicine, suggests the following:

- Solving puzzles.
- Playing a musical instrument.
- Fixing something — learning to repair cars or electrical equipment.
- Making art — painting, sculpting, writing poetry.
- Dancing.

- Making friends with people who challenge you to think about new things.

- Having conversations about new subjects.

- Reading books, magazines, and newspapers. An entrepreneur can get great ideas by reading about many different subjects, including current events.

You can always improve your intelligence and use your creativity, so you should never feel that you are not creative or smart enough to succeed. There are many types of intelligence that are not measured well by standardized tests or school grades. In fact, some of the greatest entrepreneurs did poorly in school:

- Richard Branson, founder of Virgin Atlantic Airways (and Virgin Records, Virgin Mobile, and Virgin Radio), has a learning disorder called dyslexia. He found it so hard to keep up with his studies that he dropped out of high school.

- Fred Smith got a "gentleman's C" for his business plan from his professor at Yale. The business, which he started anyway, was Federal Express, one of the most successful companies in the world.

**BizTip:** Artists often start their careers copying great paintings of the past. Musicians learn to play other people's music before they write their own. Likewise, an entrepreneur should read biographies of successful entrepreneurs.

## You Have Unique Knowledge[3]

You have unique knowledge possessed by no one else. You know your neighborhood better than someone from another neighborhood would. You have had life experiences that no one else has had.

These experiences make up your knowledge of the world. You can use that knowledge, along with your creativity and intelligence, to become a successful entrepreneur.

## Your Market

As we have explained, the difference between an artist and an entrepreneur is that artists create for themselves, while entrepreneurs create for a *market*. A market is a group of people who might buy a product or service. Think of your neighborhood and school as your market. Think creatively about your classmates and neighbors. What might they want to buy? What kind of service would save them time? Are there problems you could solve for them by creating a business?

# Practical Daydreaming... about Inventions!

Everyone daydreams, but entrepreneurs daydream with practical ends in mind. Some entrepreneurial daydreams have become **inventions** that have changed the world.

An *invention* is a new creation that can be used for some practical purpose. If you invent something, you can apply for a **patent** from the U.S. government. A patent will give you the exclusive right to produce, use, and sell an invention. The invention becomes your "intellectual property." You own it. No one else can legally use it for commerical purposes.

## SKILLS MEAN SUCCESS

### ENGLISH

### Writing for Information and Understanding: Completing Forms

A patent application is just one example of a business form. In the workplace, people have to use many different kinds of forms to provide and request information. Some common ones are used to:

- Apply for jobs, vacations, benefits.
- Report accidents and other incidents.
- Record daily work: hours, rates, and billing.
- Order supplies.
- Prepare tax returns.
- Apply for loans and bank accounts.
- Provide information for medical records and insurance.

When filling out a form:

- Make a copy of the form *before* you fill it out.
- When filling out a form by hand (as opposed to online), use your neatest printing.
- Provide adequate and complete information.
- Use only standard English — no slang, jargon, or unfamiliar terms.
- Be as brief as possible. Use standard abbreviations, numerals, and symbols, as appropriate.
- Proofread what you wrote for errors, misspellings, or missing information. Correct any problems you find.

Patent applications can be found online at http://www.uspto.gov/web/forms. Select one of the forms and print it out. Complete the form using the guidelines above. ■■■

Computer scientist and entrepreneur An Wang patented 40 inventions in his lifetime. He said his best ideas were "presented to me by my subconscious, almost as a gift."

Wang immigrated to the United States from China in 1945 when he was 25. While at the Harvard Computation Laboratory, he invented the "magnetic memory core." This invention, which Wang patented, made computer memory possible. At 28, Wang left his job and, with a few hundred dollars, started Wang Laboratories in a small loft above a garage.

Sometimes Wang and his wife were treated badly because they were Asian. Wang said this made him more determined to succeed: "A small part of the reason I founded Wang Laboratories," he said, "was to show that Chinese could excel at things other than running laundries and restaurants."

Eventually, IBM purchased the rights to Wang's magnetic core. Wang used the money from the sale to start selling his new inventions, including desk-top calculators. The calculators led to a growth in sales for Wang Laboratories to $39 million by 1972. By 1984, Wang was the fifth richest American, with a net worth of $1.6 billion.

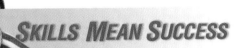

## SKILLS MEAN SUCCESS

**LEADERSHIP** ▶ **Understanding Diversity**

An Wang and his family were treated unfairly because they were "foreign." Holding or sharing oversimplified, misguided beliefs about other cultures and people is *stereotyping*. This kind of prejudice is unfair, inaccurate, and prevents people from working together effectively. In the workplace, stereotyping others and treating them unfairly is known as *discrimination*, and it is *illegal*.

Living and working in a diverse society requires an open mind and a willingness to share and understand cultural experiences. To overcome stereotypes:

- Recognize any stereotypes you may have about others.
- Learn about the people or groups about whom you have stereotypes.
- When appropriate, make an effort to share experiences with these people and to treat them as you would want to be treated.

Have you ever been stereotyped or discriminated against because of your race, gender, age, appearance, or other factor? How did it make you feel? What did you learn from the experience? ■■■

# Product Development

You can use your creativity and the unique knowledge of your market to develop new products (or improve existing ones). Just follow these steps:

**Step 1: Play with possibilities.**[4]

- Ideas don't cost anything. Just write them down.

- To jump-start your imagination, complete this sentence on a separate sheet of paper: "I wish someone would make a _____ that _____."

**Step 2: Think of possible solutions to problems in your neighborhood, community, or even the world!**

- Pretend anything is possible.

- Write down and/or make sketches of your solutions.

**Step 3: Make a model of the product.**

- This model can be rough. Use inexpensive materials such as paper, wood, paint, cloth, or plaster of paris — as you may go through many models.

- Does it work? How could it work better?

- Show the model to your parents, or friends you could trust not to steal your idea. Ask them how you could improve it.

- Revise your design. Don't be afraid to experiment.

**Step 4: Find out who might manufacture your product; have a prototype made.**

- A **prototype** is an exact model of the product made by the manufacturing process that would be used in actual production.

- This can be expensive; prototypes cost many times the final production cost per item.

- Check the *Thomas Register*, which lists all U.S. manufacturers, to find one you might contact about your invention — www.thomasregister.com. You can usually find the *Thomas Register* at your local library, in the business reference section.

The 26 volumes of the *Thomas Register* are broken into three categories:

**GROUP ONE** — Volumes 1-16 provide a list of types of products and services arranged alphabetically. Within each category, you can look up companies alphabetically by state and city. Use Group One to locate manufacturers in your area that make products similar to your invention.

GROUP TWO — Volumes 17 and 18 contain profiles of different companies, listed alphabetically by company name. After you find a manufacturer in Group One that looks interesting, locate its profile in Group Two. This will include the manufacturer's address, telephone numbers, office locations, and the names of company officers.

GROUP THREE — Volumes 19-26 offer catalogs arranged alphabetically by company name. These will include product information, such as drawings, photos, and statistics.

**Step 5: Do a reality check.**

- Does your invention solve a problem that is big enough — that is faced by many people?

- Can you reach your market easily?

- Would the manufacturing cost be too high?

- Is there competition? Is someone else selling a similar product? How is yours better or different?

- Try test marketing. Place a display with the product in a store and see how it sells.

## SKILLS MEAN SUCCESS

**ENGLISH**

**Reading and Writing for Information:
Using Text Features and Online Research; Communicating via Letters and E-mail**

In your library, locate the *Thomas Register* (Volumes 1-16 ). Use the indexes to locate a product category that interests you. Use the state and city headings to locate a manufacturer in your area. Write a brief letter of inquiry to that manufacturer to request more information about the company and its prototype-development capabilities. Inquire if a company tour is available.

Alternatively, go online (http://www.thomasregister.com). Select the "I am searching for a Product or Service" button, and enter the product type in the search box. Click "Find It." Select the appropriate product heading from the list that appears. From the list of companies, select one in your area. E-mail your request to the company. Use the e-mail address provided.

In your letter or e-mail, be polite and specific. Explain what you would like to know and why. Be sure to include your address and contact information. Thank the recipient in advance for taking the time to respond to your request. ■■■

# Patents

Once you have developed a good invention, you can either go into business for yourself or sell the idea to a manufacturer. Before taking either step, however, you must protect your rights as the inventor by patenting the invention. Otherwise someone else can take your invention and use it to start a business — and keep all the profits.

We will discuss the details of filing for a patent in Chapter 42. For now, you will just need to know that a patent application has to include the following:

1. An in-depth description of the invention.

2. A drawing of the invention.

3. A completed "Declaration for Patent Application."

4. A notarized statement verifying that the person applying is the original inventor. ("Notarized" means the statement has been witnessed by a *notary*. Most banks have notaries who will witness statements for a small fee.)

5. The filing fee ($345-$690).

# Early African-American Inventors

Nobody knows how many inventions were thought up by slaves before the Civil War, because the credit was taken by others. There were probably quite a few slave inventors, because ideas for doing a job more easily or quickly often come from those who actually do the work.

In 1895, an African-American Congressman, George Washington Murray, read into the *Congressional Record* a list of 92 patents that had been issued to African Americans. Murray wanted people to know that African Americans had made important contributions to the industrial revolution. Murray himself received eight patents for improvements to farm machinery.

- The first known patent granted to an African American was in 1821 to Thomas L. Jennings of New York for a dry-cleaning device.
- The second went to Henry Blair in 1834, for his improved seed planter.
- In 1842, Norbert Rillieux received a patent for inventing a process for refining sugar.

Elijah McCoy invented a device for the self-oiling of railroad locomotives in 1872. This invention saved a lot of time and money. Before it was available, the train's fireman had to get out of the cab and oil the parts by hand so they would not wear out.

McCoy invented this device because he had performed this job often while working for the Michigan Central Railroad.

Jan E. Matzeliger invented an automatic shoe-stitching device, a "lasting" machine, in 1883. It could stitch 700 pairs of shoes a day, instead of the few pairs that could be sewn by hand. This invention revolutionized the shoe industry and greatly reduced the price of the average pair of shoes.

Almost everyone knows that Thomas Edison invented the electric lamp, but few realize that an African American named Lewis H. Latimer invented the incandescent light bulb. Latimer worked closely with Edison and installed the first city electric-light systems in New York, Philadelphia, London, and Montreal.

## From Inventions to Fame and Fortune

Many early African-American inventors died in poverty because they did not own the patents for their inventions, but there were some fortunate exceptions:

- When Elijah McCoy died in 1929, he was both financially secure and respected by the engineering community.

- Jan Matzeliger died at age 37, but his ten percent ownership of the company that manufactured his shoe-stitching device would have made him very wealthy.

- Although not strictly an inventor, Madam C.J. Walker pioneered the mail-order marketing of beauty products for women of color and became the first African-American millionaire.

Dr. George Washington Carver was an African-American inventor who was internationally known in his lifetime. Born at the end of the Civil War, Carver completely transformed farming in the South by developing new uses for the peanut, the sweet potato, and the soybean. Because of his efforts, the South's dependency on cotton as its only cash crop ended. Although Dr. Carver did not become rich from his work, he did receive honor and fame.

## More Recent Success Stories

In the 1900s, African-American inventors were better able to protect their intellectual property and profit from their inventions.

- When Garret A. Morgan invented a "gas mask" in 1914, he already had a very profitable business based on a hair-straightening cream he had developed. Although his gas mask was meant for use in mines and tunnels, the U.S. Army bought it for the troops in World War I. In 1923, Morgan invented the first three-way traffic signal, the forerunner of today's traffic light. General Electric paid him $40,000 for the rights to his invention, a large sum at the time.

- In the 1960s, Dr. Meredith Gourdine developed a million-dollar company based on inventions in the field of "electrogas dynamics" — converting gas into electricity. Even though Dr. Gourdine became blind in 1973, he remained active in the company he founded.

- Emanuel L. Logan, Jr. invented the bulletproof glass used to protect bank tellers.

- African-American contributors to the United States' space program include Dr. Robert E. Shurney, who designed better tires for the Moon Buggy after the moon landing of 1969, and Dr. George Carruthers, who invented a special ultraviolet camera used aboard Apollo 16's 1972 moon landing.

## Women Inventors

Some of the many inventions by women include:

- solar heating
- the ice cream cone
- windshield wipers
- bras
- dishwashers
- medical syringes
- drip coffee
- rolling pins

Many early women inventors thought up products to help them where they spent most of their time — in the home: cooking, cleaning, and sewing.

- In 1809 Mary Kies became the first woman to receive a patent. She invented a process for weaving straw with silk or cotton thread. When the War of 1812 cut off supplies of hats from Europe, New England hat makers used her process to take over the market.

As women began to work outside the home as secretaries, they invented helpful office products.

- Bette Graham invented Liquid Paper ("whiteout") to save secretaries the trouble of typing over an entire page when they made an error.

As women moved into traditionally male fields, such as medicine and science, their inventions in these areas increased.

- Elizabeth Hazen and Rachel Brown invented Nystatin fungicide in the early 1950s. Hazen and Brown were looking for a cure for the fungus infections that many U.S. soldiers suffered from during World War II. It took six years to convince the government to give them a patent for what turned out to be a very important medicine. The patent generated $13 million in royalties, most of which Hazen and Brown used to establish scholarships for college students studying biology.

- In 1988, Gertrude Elion became the first woman inducted into the inventors' Hall of Fame. During the 39 years she worked for a drug company, Burroughs-Wellcome, Elion patented 45 medical compounds. She shared the 1988 Nobel Prize for medicine with her colleague, George H. Hitchings. They invented a compound that prevents transplant patients' immune systems from rejecting donor organs.

- Ann Moore's invention of the popular child-carrying Snugli™ illustrates that successful inventions often draw on personal experience. Moore got the idea during her service in the Peace Corps in West Africa in the 1960s. In Togo, mothers carried their babies around with them all day in fabric harnesses. Moore developed this concept into a pouch-like child carrier that is comfortable and washable. She began selling the Snugli in 1979. By 1984, annual sales reached $6 million. Moore has used the Snugli technology to develop the Airlift™ — a portable oxygen-tank carrier for people who need a steady supply of oxygen.

## Hispanic-American Inventors

Hispanic-American inventors include Dr. Eloy Rodriguez, who developed important drugs from tropical and desert plants that have been tested on viruses and cancers. He had noticed that monkeys and other primates eat certain plants when they are sick. Dr. Rodriguez established a new field called Zoopharmacognosy — the study of self-medication by primates.

Another medical breakthrough by a Hispanic American is the invention of the process of harvesting insulin from bacterial cells. Dr. Lydia Villa-Komaroff was a key member of the team that developed this process.

These stories illustrate the diverse backgrounds and situations from which great inventors — and new businesses — come.

 **Rule of Thumb:** It's not how smart you are, it's how you are smart.

# Chapter 7 Review

## CRITICAL THINKING ABOUT...

### INVENTIONS

1. Prepare for the class Invention Contest by developing a new invention or a product improvement. Describe your invention briefly and include a drawing. Be sure to describe how your invention will meet a consumer need.

2. Choose an invention that you often use and research it on the Internet. Write a one-page report about the history of this invention.

3. Are you creative? Describe your creativity and come up with three ways you could become a more creative thinker.

4. For your own business, how do you plan to protect your business idea, product, or service: ___ patent, ___ copyright or ___ trademark? Explain your choice.
   **Business Plan Practice**

## KEY CONCEPTS

1. What is a prototype and why is it useful? How can you find a company to make a prototype of your invention?

2. Why can entrepreneurs be called the "artists" of the economy?

3. Do you have to be born with creativity or can you develop it? Explain.

## IN YOUR OPINION

Discuss with a partner:

1. Write a list of businesses you could imagine starting. Ask your partner about his or her interests or hobbies. Now write a list of businesses you could imagine your partner starting, based on what you've learned. Compare and discuss your lists with your partner.

2. Think of a recording artist you and your partner both like. Discuss: Is this person a good entrepreneur? Is he or she setting or following trends? Is this artist aware enough of the market to stay on top? Report your findings to the class.

3. Would you go to the expense of making a prototype for a product that you invented? Why or why not?

4. Write a two-page report about the life of a minority or woman inventor. If you have access to the Internet, research the report online. If not, use library resources, such as an encyclopedia.

## REFERENCES

1 For concise, inspiring biographies of successful entrepreneurs, see *Entrepreneurs In Profile*, available from NFTE.
2 Material in this chapter has been adapted from de Bono's *Lateral Thinking: Creativity Step by Step*, (Harper & Row, 1970).
3 Special thanks to Charles Koch for demonstrating the importance of this concept.
4 Special thanks to Sylvia Stein for the ideas she contributed to this chapter.

**Chapter 7 Review**

## VOCABULARY

creativity ■ invention ■ lateral thinking ■ patent ■ prototype ■ vertical thinking

# Chapter Summary ✔✔✔

**7.1**   Entrepreneurs are the "artists" of the business world.
   A. Artists use creativity to express themselves.
   B. Entrepreneurs use creativity to invent or make something new.
   C. Entrepreneurs seek profits by creating something consumers will want to buy.

**7.2**   Creativity can be developed.
   A. Vertical thinking is based on existing ideas and thought patterns.
   B. Lateral thinking challenges previous assumptions.
   C. Intelligence can be strengthened by exercising the mind.

**7.3**   Some creative ideas become inventions.
   A. Inventors can protect their inventions with patents.
   B. New or improved products are created by:
      1. Playing with possibilities
      2. Thinking of possible solutions to real problems
      3. Making a model of the product
      4. Finding a manufacturer to develop a prototype.
   C. Applying for a patent can protect an inventor's rights.
      1. Describe the invention or process in detail.
      2. Provide a drawing.
      3. Complete a "Declaration for Patent Application".
      4. Sign a notarized statement of ownership of the invention.
      5. File and pay fee.
   D. Many minority and women inventors have been successful. ✔✔

### CHAPTER 8

# SELECTING YOUR BUSINESS:
## *What's Your Competitive Advantage?*

*The propensity to truck, barter, and exchange one thing for another is common to all men.*

— Adam Smith, *Scottish economist*

### KEY OBJECTIVES

THIS CHAPTER WILL ENABLE YOU TO:

- Describe the four types of business and the difference between products and services.
- Identify your skills and hobbies.
- Explore your competitive advantage.
- Select your own business and name it.
- Define how your business can help your community.

Imagine yourself running the business of your choice. Is it a "good fit"? Are you going to stay interested and enthusiastic for a long time?

Consider keeping your business simple. This is probably going to be your first enterprise, so don't bite off more than you can chew. Many successful entrepreneurs create more than one business over the course of a lifetime. Start with something simple that you know you can do well. You will have the rest of your life to move on to greater and more complex challenges.

## Listen to Your Market

The successful entrepreneur listens to what people in the community are saying. What do the people you know like? What do they want? What do they need? Could you fill one of their needs? Remember, you have unique knowledge of your market. Use it to come up with a great business idea that will also serve your community.

## Product or Service?

- A **product** is something that exists in nature or is made by human beings. It is *tangible*, meaning that it can be touched.

- A **service** is work that provides time, skills, or expertise in exchange for money. It is *intangible*. You can't actually touch it.

Your business could sell a product or a service — or both. Are there any products you could make yourself? Are there any products you know that you could buy for less money than you could sell them for to your market?

Is there a service you could perform for your market? Do you have any special skills to offer?

### SKILLS MEAN SUCCESS

**ENGLISH**

**Listening and Speaking for Social Interaction: Asking Questions to Clarify Meaning**

Entrepreneurs must listen to their customers and ask their opinions. Effective listening involves asking questions to make meanings more clear. For each of the following customer comments, write a question you could ask to clarify what was meant, in order to get additional information.

**1.** I wish my order could be ready faster.

**2.** Your store should carry a better selection of flowering trees and shrubs.

**3.** Do you have the new XZ1-2000?

**4.** You should offer quicker delivery services.

**5.** I need my newsletters printed as cheaply as possible. ■■■

## Four Basic Business Types

**1.**   MANUFACTURING — makes a tangible product.

**2.**   WHOLESALE — buys in quantity from the manufacturer and sells to the retailer.

**3.**   RETAIL — sells to the consumer.

**4.**   SERVICE — sells an intangible product to the consumer.

## Turning Hobbies, Skills, and Interests into Businesses

As you will see from the list of ideas in this chapter, the possibilities for young people starting businesses are almost limitless.

What you enjoy doing in your spare time might be turned into a profitable business. Making money through doing what you enjoy is a winning combination.

## Your Strategy for Beating the Competition

For your business to be successful, you will need a **competitive advantage**. Your competitive advantage is your strategy for beating the competition. It's whatever you can do better than the competition that will attract customers to your business.

Competitive advantage comes from one (or a combination) of six factors:

1.  **Quality** — Can you provide higher quality than competing businesses?

2.  **Price** — Can you offer a lower price than your competition?

3.  **Location** — Can you find a more convenient location for customers?

4.  **Selection** — Can you provide a wider range of choices than your competitors?

5.  **Service** — Can you provide better, more personalized customer service?

6.  **Speed/Turnaround** — Can you deliver your product or service more quickly than the competition?

If you are running a video game rental business, perhaps you could deliver the games, so the customers wouldn't have to come to the store. That would be a competitive advantage on service.

To learn which competitive advantages are working in your market, ask your customers (or people you hope to attract as customers) where they shop, and why.

Remember, your education and how you use it can always be a major part of a competitive advantage.

By now you might have several business ideas and can't decide on which. Try writing down some possibilities, and then eliminate them one by one until you end up with the business you like best. During this course you will write a business plan that you will be able to use to start and run this business!

 **BizTip: A youth business should be:  SIMPLE and SAFE. Don't start a business with a product or service that could hurt anyone.**

 **SKILLS MEAN SUCCESS**

 **LEADERSHIP** ▶ **Responsible and Ethical Behavior**

According to the Small Business Administration (http://www.sba.gov), a business ethics policy should look at the big picture. It should consider the business's responsibility to society as a whole. Think of a business that you would like to start and write a code of ethics for it. To get started, write answers to the following:

- What is the primary purpose of your business?
- What is most important to you and to the success of the business?
- What results would make you proud to be the owner of that business?
- What kind of atmosphere and "culture" do you want the business to have?
- What type of behavior and standards will you demand of yourself and of your employees (honesty, loyalty, courtesy, respect, fairness, accountability, dependability)? Give examples.
- What will you do to maintain those standards of behavior?
- How do you want your community to view your business?
- What positive effects will your business have on the community?
- How will you handle ethical and legal dilemmas that may arise?

## The Ethics of Choosing a Business

An *ethic* is a rule for choosing right from wrong. "Do not steal" is an example of an ethic. The Golden Rule — treat other people as you would like to be treated — is a famous ethic.

You've probably seen businesses in action that are not ethical. A business that sells cheap knockoffs of designer goods, for example, is not only unethical but illegal. You may feel that certain businesses are legal but still unethical. If you think cigarettes are harmful, you might feel it would be unethical to make or sell them.

Only you can decide which ethics will guide your personal life and your business. We do, however, recommend the following three basic ethics:[1]

1.  **My business is not illegal (against the law).**

2.  **My business will not hurt others.**

3.  **My business will not spread negative messages or ideas in the marketplace.**

## 100 Business Ideas for Young Entrepreneurs![2]

What kind of business would you like to start? To jump-start your imagination, look through the following 100 business ideas. We've grouped them so you can find your own interests, hobbies, or skills and see what ventures other young people with similar interests have started.

Of course, many business ideas fall into more than one category. Writing skills would be needed for "desktop publishing," "writing a cookbook," and "translation." Consider what your friends, family, and schoolmates want and need. They are your market. In addition, choose a business in which you think you would have a competitive advantage.

You will find the business ideas divided into categories. To help you narrow your choices, we've designed the chart on the next page. To use it, read the descriptions on the right and check "Yes" or "No." Where you've answered "Yes," look under those headings on pages 99–109 for businesses you might be interested in.

| Do You Like to... | Yes | No | Look under: |
|---|---|---|---|
| Work with your hands? | ___ | ___ | Art, Baking, Cleaning, Cooking, Crafts, Gardening |
| Be around animals? | ___ | ___ | Animals, Birds, Fish |
| Work alone? | ___ | ___ | Collecting, Computers, Internet, Woodworking, Writing |
| Work with others? | ___ | ___ | Advertising, Children, Driving, People |
| Speak other languages? | ___ | ___ | Bilingual, Teaching |
| Teach people? | ___ | ___ | Bicycles, Dancing, Music, Teaching |
| Work with machines? | ___ | ___ | Bicycles, Computers, Driving |
| Be creative? | ___ | ___ | Art, Crafts, Dancing, Holidays, Music, Painting, Silkscreening, Woodworking, Writing |
| Entertain people? | ___ | ___ | Entertainment, Dancing, Music |
| Use computers? | ___ | ___ | Computers, Internet |
| Use cameras? | ___ | ___ | Photography, Video |
| Buy clothes? | ___ | ___ | Clothing, Silkscreening |
| Cook? | ___ | ___ | Baking, Cooking |

## Advertising/Publicity

*Are you interested in a career in advertising or publicity? These businesses will give you great experience!*

**Design flyers and posters** — Help a local business create its brand!

**Distribute flyers, posters, and brochures** — Do stores in your neighborhood need people to hand out flyers? These can be distributed on the street, put on car windshields, or given out at social functions. You could offer this service to shopkeepers on a regular basis. (Just make sure you find out where it is legal to put up posters!)

**Publicist** — Get hired to write press releases. Help artists, musicians, or entrepreneurs get publicity by sending out releases, e-mailing, and calling local newspapers and radio stations.

**Image consultant** — Help businesses and entertainers market themselves to young people — like you! Daniel Green (20) and Lukus Eichmann (19) of Saddlelite offer their services as image consultants to celebrities who want to find out how to attract younger fans.

## Animals

*Do you like animals? Read books to learn how to care for them. Ask a neighborhood veterinarian to be your mentor.*

**Cat sitter** — Get hired to care for cats while their owners are out of town. Be sure to have the owner write down the cat's food and water needs, and an emergency number for the vet.

**Dog walker** — Take three or four dogs at a time out for a walk and make money providing a (very) necessary service for your busy neighbors. Don't forget the pooper scooper!

**Pet grooming** — Give a dog a bath today!

**Pet bowls** — Create personalized doggie bowls by painting each dog's name on the bowl in non-toxic paint.

## Art

*Almost any artistic talent can be turned into a business. What can you create that someone else might want?*

**Artist** — Offices decorate with art and so do family members and friends. Create a portfolio of photos of your artwork that you can carry with you to show customers.

**Art gallery** — Do you have talented friends? Show their work in your home or at a youth center or other public space. You can take a commission for every piece you sell.

**Calligraphy** — Learn the art of hand-writing in an elegant or unusual style. Calligraphy is in demand for wedding invitations, menus, birth announcements, etc. You can also hand-letter poems or lyrics on fine paper, frame them, and sell them.

**Pottery** — A hobby like pottery can quickly become a successful business. Sell your pottery at trade fairs. You can put pictures of it online, too. Offer to create special pieces to customers' specifications.

## Baking

*Ideas for selling cakes, cookies, brownies, bread, or other products you can bake at home include:*

**Fresh-baked bread for people in need** — Set up a nonprofit business that delivers baked goods to people who are too old or sick to bake or leave their homes to buy fresh bread.

You could take donations from people and businesses in your neighborhood, and even apply for grants for your business, because it is helping society.

**Bake sales** — Hold a bake sale at a flea market, at your church, in your backyard, or at school (just be sure to get permission first).

**Cookie delivery business** — Sign families up for weekly cookie deliveries. You can deliver a batch of a different type of homemade cookie each week.

## Bicycles

*Just about any skill you have can be turned into a business, if you can find a way to fill a consumer need. Can you ride a bike? Here are some business ideas.*

**Bicycle repair** — Learn to repair flat tires, slipped chains, and worn brakes. You could run a special each spring when people get their bikes out of storage for the warm weather.

**Messenger service** — Have wheels, will deliver! In New York City, businesses depend on the bike messengers who deliver important documents all over town. Perhaps you could provide a similar service in your area.

**Bike design** — A graduate of this course, James MacNeil, started Bulldog Bikes (www.bulldogbikes.com), a company that designs and manufactures BMX bikes for urban streets. Bulldog Bikes even has its own teams!

## Birds

*Are you interested in learning about the birds in your area? Do you have a pet bird? Here are some "bird-brained" ideas:*

**Birdcage service** — Offer to clean cages regularly and stock them with food and water. Bird owners can enjoy their pets while you maintain the cages. How do you find bird owners? Try posting flyers at pet stores.

**Birdwatching guide** — If you teach yourself about the birds in your region, you can organize birdwatching trips to local parks. You can also hire yourself out as a bird guide to people who organize hikes or camping trips.

**Raising birds for sale** — Popular breeds, such as parakeets and finches, are not difficult to raise. Find a mentor to advise you, such as a local veterinarian or pet shop owner.

## Books

*Are you a bookworm? Turn your love of books into a business.*

**Book selling** — Start a business selling books, concentrating on those you like to read yourself. Once you start making money, you can buy in quantity to get lower prices. Although large publishers will only give a discount for large orders, smaller publishers might be willing to sell you small quantities at a discount.

**Used-book selling** — An even cheaper way to get into the book-selling business is to collect used books from friends and family (go through your bookshelf and get rid of books you don't want, too). Set up a table at a flea market or on the street and start selling! (Check local laws before you set up on the street, though.)

**Write a book** — Entrepreneurship student, Michael Simmons, has written *The Student Success Manifesto*, which he sells on his campus at NYU and online at www.successmanifesto.com. What could you write? A novel? A children's book? A book of advice for other students?

## Children

*Do you like kids? Are you reliable and responsible? There are a lot of businesses you can create that involve children. Whenever you work with a child, get a letter of reference from the parent so that other parents will know they can trust you.*

**Baby-sitting service** — Before parents leave their children in your care, make sure they give you phone numbers where they can be reached, the phone number of the nearest relative, and the number for the child's doctor. Be sure to ask about bedtimes, food allergies, television and Internet restrictions, and whether they want you to answer the phone. Then have fun with the kids!

**Mother's helper** — A mother's helper keeps children occupied so busy mothers can relax or devote their attention to something else. The mother will still be in the house, but you take care of the children. This is a safe way to get some baby-sitting/child-care experience.

**Teach activities** — Teach your specialty (such as crafts, cooking, or exercise) to children one or two afternoons a week, or just have a special playtime with puppets, storytelling, or other activities.

**Children's stories** — Create a "story-time" at your house for children in the neighborhood. Parents can drop off their children for an hour or two while you read them stories. You could also make tapes of your readings and sell them.

## Cleaning

*Are you a neatnik? Turn your passion for cleanliness into a business!*

**Car washing** — Washing cars can be a steady source of income if you put some effort into it. Consider working with a team of friends and advertise speedy service for busy people. Learn to wax and detail cars, so you can offer these services, too.

**House/office cleaning** — Houses and offices need to be cleaned. Many people and business owners do not have time to clean and would be happy to hire you.

**Laundry and ironing** — Do you have access to a good washer and dryer? Doing laundry (like dogwalking and house cleaning) is a chore many people can't find time to do.  Both laundry and ironing could be combined with another service, such as child care.

## Clothing

*If you enjoy clothes, there are many businesses you could start. You can sell old fashions, create new ones, or bring the latest trends to the people in your market.*

**Clothing design** — Create your own line and start out selling to local stores. Two of our graduates sold their "skinny jeans" to top stores in New York and Los Angeles.

**Vintage clothing** — Fashions from 20 years ago often become  popular again. Do your parents or other relatives have old clothes that they'd like to get rid of? Collect them and start selling "vintage" clothing!

**Buying wholesale for resale** — A student who took this course, Michele Araujo, traveled regularly from her neighborhood to the wholesale district in the nearest city, where she bought new fashions and resold them locally at her own business, A La Mode Fashions.

## Collecting

*If you collect baseball cards, sports caps, comic books, or other items that are inexpensive now but might gain value in the future, consider a collecting business. You can visit collector fairs to buy and sell your items. Collect things that you genuinely like, because you might have them for a while.*

**Vinyl records** — DJs are always looking for new sounds, so you never know what someone might pay for an old record you bought at a garage sale for 50 cents. Check out *Goldmine* and *Record Collector* magazines for helpful info.

**Comics** — If you have, say, only $200, you might be able to make more money buying and selling comic books than you could in the stock market! Use software like Comic Collector to catalog your collection. *Overstreet Comic Price Review* is another good resource.

## Computers

*Having computer skills will open up many business possibilities.*

**Computer repair/software installation** — Are you the person your friends (or parents) call when they have computer trouble? Become a computer consultant and sell your expertise.

**Word-processing service** — Are you a fast and accurate typist? If you can type well, there are many services you could offer, such as typing papers for other students, or typing a manuscript for a busy author.

**Desktop publishing** — You will need access to a computer, laser printer, and a good word-processing program. You will also need design skills. With these resources, you can create newsletters, menus, and programs, and create and maintain mailing lists.

**Web site design** — If you are computer literate and comfortable on the Internet, assist others in designing their "home pages" on the World Wide Web. Dreamweaver software makes it easy to design Web sites without having to learn HTML.

**Graphic arts** — Learn how to use programs like Adobe Photoshop and Quark and you can provide graphic arts services, including photo retouching, and creation of flyers, posters, brochures, and other promotional materials.

## Cooking

*If you enjoy cooking, you can provide products, services, or both!*

**Catering** — Do you like to cook? A catering business can supply whole menus for parties and other occasions.

**Pasta** — Create a line of fresh pasta and sauces.

**Organic baby food** — Let your creativity soar, but always with the customer in mind. What kind of food do the people in your market like? What is difficult to find?

**Cookbook** — Do you come from a family in which a lot of great recipes have

been handed down over the years? Put them together in a cookbook!

## Crafts

*Do you like to make jewelry, leather goods, or other handicrafts? Sell your own work and perhaps, for a percentage, creations by your friends, as well.*

**Jewelry making** — Start with inexpensive supplies, like wire and beads. Maybe one day you will work with gold and diamonds!

**Greeting-card design** — You can create beautiful greeting cards with rubber stamps, ink, and small silkscreens. If you have a good sense of humor, this is a great place to use it.

**Handbags** — Decorate vintage handbags or make your own out of felt, fabric, or leather.

**Candle making** — A crafts store will have everything you need to make decorative candles. You can buy wax or melt down old candles and crayons. Try using empty milk cartons as molds.

## Dancing

**Dance lessons** — Even if you are a beginner, you probably know enough to teach young children.

**Hip-hop dance troupe** — If you have friends who are also talented dancers, why not get a group together and offer your services to local hip-hop groups?

## Driving

*Do you love to drive? If you start a business using a car or van, make sure you have up-to-date insurance. Do not borrow a car from a parent or friend for your business without being added to the insurance.*

**Errand service** — Offer to run errands and make deliveries for small business-people and others who don't have the time to do so. Make yourself indispensable and you will soon have a growing business.

**Meal delivery** — Are there restaurants in your area that don't offer delivery because they don't want to pay for their own staff? You could offer to make deliveries for three or more restaurants, so that they can share the cost.

**Messenger service** — Do you enjoy running around? Try a small-package delivery service. It is a business with low start-up costs. The service can expand rapidly as you build up a reputation for reliability.

## Entertainment

*Are you a natural performer who enjoys being in front of an audience? Do you know any magic tricks or have theater experience?*

**Clown** — If you love making kids laugh, become a clown and you'll be in demand for birthday parties.

**Magician** — Is there a magic club at your school where you could learn tricks? You can also learn from books and practice on your friends. As a magi-cian, you can entertain at birthday parties and other events.

**Party DJ** — A DJ plays records during a party. You'll need one or two turntables and lots of records. Some DJs form record pools so they can share their records and equipment. Local record labels might give you free records to promote their artists.

**Balloon decorating** — Learn how to make balloon animals and how to tie balloons together to make decorations for parties!

## Fish

*If fish are a hobby of yours, why not turn it into income?*

**Aquarium care** — You will need to know how to care for both fresh and saltwater tanks. Offer your services to local businesses and restaurants, as well as to individuals.

**Fishing** — If you live in an area that has good fishing, become a fishing guide. You can organize day trips to nearby lakes and rivers.

## Gardening

*Chores like mowing the lawn are a lot more fun when you're getting paid. Almost anything you do around the house can be turned into a business.*

**Fresh herbs and flowers** — Is there a room in your house or apartment that gets a lot of sunlight? You can grow fresh herbs and flowers and supply them to restaurants. This can be a good "second" business because plants don't have to be watched every minute of the day.

**Yard work** — Do you like working outdoors? From the street, you can often spot lawns and gardens that are not being kept up by their owners as well as they should be. You could also shovel snow in the winter.

**Plant care** — Offices could hire you to come in once a week to water, clean, and fertilize their plants. As more and more people work outside the home, there is more demand for household plant care, too.

**Window boxes** — Fill wooden window boxes with flowers. You can even make and decorate the boxes yourself.

## Hair

*Do you like to make your friends' hair look great? Before you start a business styling or wrapping hair, however, check out local regulations for any licenses you might need.*

**Hairstyling** — Offer up-dos for special occasions, French braiding, extensions, and other techniques.

**Hair clips** — Create jeweled hair clips by gluing rhinestones onto plain hair clips you can buy wholesale.

**Hair wrapping** — Children especially love temporary colorful hair wrappings.

## Holidays

*Are you one of those people who gets excited about holidays? Each holiday is a business opportunity.*

**Gift baskets** — Every holiday is an opportunity to create a different gift basket that you can sell for a profit. You can also offer customizing and make baskets based on the interests of the persons receiving them.

**Seasonal sales** — Do you have spare time during the holidays? Try selling seasonal specialties, such as Christmas decorations or Valentine's Day candy, which have brief but intense sales seasons. If you are willing to put in the time, you could make a lot of money in a relatively short period.

## Internet

*People come up with creative new businesses using the Internet every day. What will you think of?*

**Genealogy** — Researching genealogy, which is the history of a person's ancestors, is easy online (but you will have to subscribe to some basic sites to access the genealogical information). Teach yourself how to create family trees. Every family is a potential customer.

**Web site** — If you come up with a popular idea for a Web site, you can sell advertising space. Got a great comic character? You could create some fun Quicktime movies. How about electronic greeting cards? What could you put online that others would want to see?

**eBay auctions** — Learn how to bid on eBay and you could offer your services to people who have things to sell but don't have the time or skill to get them online.

## Music

*Do you play music? Or just love being around it? Either way, there are a lot of businesses you could start.*

**Band** — Start a rock band and get hired to play at parties, weddings, and corporate events.

**Music lessons** — Do you play an instrument well enough to teach someone else? Even if you have only intermediate knowledge, you could probably teach young beginners.

**Stickers and buttons** — Rock and rap artists need stickers and buttons imprinted with their logos for promotion. So do stores and sports teams. Why not save them the trouble of contracting with a sticker or button manufacturer? If you establish a relationship with a manufacturer yourself, you can get a good price because you will be bringing new jobs. Turn that price advantage into profit.

**String quartet** — Do you play in the band or orchestra at school? Get some friends together and start a string quartet to get hired for store openings, weddings, parties, etc.

## Painting

*Are you good with a brush?  Advertise your services on grocery store bulletin boards and with flyers at hardware stores.*

**Housepainting** — You will need to learn about types of paints and how to "cut" so your lines look clean. See if you can find someone who is willing to teach you the basics.

**Furniture** — Old furniture can be made to look like new with a nice coat of paint. Shop flea markets for bargains you can refinish and sell, or offer refinishing services.

**Signage** — If you can paint, you can create signs for local businesses.

## People

*Are you a people person? Try businesses that involve getting people together or waking them up!*

**Dating newsletter** — Are you a natural matchmaker? Start an e-mail dating newsletter.

**Wake-up service** — Are you an early riser? Start a wake-up service for your fellow students.

## Photography

*Have you thought about a career in photography? Get experience and earn money at the same time.*

**Wedding photography** — If you are a skilled photographer, offer to shoot a couple of weddings for free to build your portfolio. Wedding photography has to be very professional.

**Photo journalist** — Local newspapers often buy photos of events and parties from freelance photographers.

## Sales

*In Chapter 16, you will learn how to go to a wholesale district and buy items in quantity at a discount that you can then sell at retail. You can sell almost anything: candy, perfume, headbands, jewelry, ties, watches, etc.*

## Silkscreening

*Silkscreening is easy and cheap. All you need are a silkscreen, ink, a wedge to press the ink through the screen, and fabric to silkscreen.*

**T-shirts** — Bands need T-shirts silkscreened with their logos. So do many sports teams.

**Creative clothing** — You can also silkscreen pants, shorts, skirts, and dresses with your own cool designs.

## Teaching

*Are you always explaining school assignments to your friends? Do you like helping people understand things?*

**Tutoring** — Do you know one of your school subjects well enough to teach other students? Giving lessons (tutoring) requires patience, but you will discover the rewards and satisfaction of teaching.

**Give lessons** — Anything you can do, from playing guitar to making clothes, you can teach.

## Translating

*Are you bilingual? Did you grow up speaking another language? Put your language skills to good use!*

**Translation** — Translate ads, flyers, signs, etc., for local shopkeepers who want to reach customers who speak different languages.

**Teach English** as a second language to people in the community who need help.

**Teach your other language** to people who only speak English and want to learn another language.

## Video

*Do you have a good camera or camcorder?*

**Videotape events** — People like to have their weddings, birthdays, parties, and other events videotaped. You'll need samples of your work to show to prospective clients.

**Videotape concerts** — Bands like to have their shows videotaped so they can see how to improve the performances. You'll have to be of legal age, however, to enter a club that serves alcohol.

**Digital moviemaking** — With digital video, anyone with a camera can make a movie without the expense of buying film, which made moviemaking so expensive. Check out Michael Dean's

*$30 Film School* (Muska & Lipman Books).

## Woodworking

*Woodworking skills can be used to create many types of businesses.*

**Carpentry** — If you are skilled at carpentry, sell your services. You can build cabinets, shelves, and help renovate homes.

**Bird cages** — One student who finished this course started a successful business by building bird cages out of wood in his uncle's garage.

**Decorative carving** — If you are artistically talented, try learning scrollwork, which is the decorative woodcarving of screens or other furniture.

**Board games** — Create beautiful versions of board games, such as chess or checkers.

## Writing

*Are you a talented writer?*

**Pennysaver newspaper** — Get local businesses to buy ads in your newspaper that customers can cut out and use as coupons. You can print stories about community businesses and people in the paper, as well.

**Fanzine** — A *fanzine* is a magazine written specifically for fans of just about anything, from genres of music to movie stars.

**Poetry for special occasions** — How about composing poetry for special occasions, like birthdays and graduations? Sell poetry personalized with names, dates and photos, or lace handkerchiefs embroidered with poetry that guests receive as gifts.

## Naming Your Business

What are you going to name your business? This is a very important decision. The name of your business will be the first impression you make on potential customers.

Using your first name to identify your venture — showing the pride you take in it — can be a good idea (Joe's Pizza). Using your last (family) name may not be, as there are risks:

- If the business fails, your name will be associated with the failure. This can hurt you if you decide to start a new business. Potential customers and investors may associate you with the old one.

- If the business succeeds, you might decide to sell it for a profit. But what if you hate what the new owner does with it? What if he or she engages in dishonest business practices? Your actual name is still on the door.

Keep it simple: *The best name is one that tells customers what the company does, sells, or makes.* Here are some examples you probably recognize:

*Federal Express*    *America Online*    *Burger King*    *Microsoft*

As Joe Mancuso says in his best-selling book, *Have You Got What It Takes? How To Tell If You Should Start Your Own Business*, "Naming the company is the first move of many in which you should keep the customer's needs first and foremost in mind."

## Money Alone Is Not a Good Reason to Start a Business

You may not reap the financial benefits of owning your own business until after much hard work. Simply the desire to make money may not be enough to keep you going through a possible difficult early period. *Most successful companies have been founded by an entrepreneur with a powerful dream — not a powerful desire for money.*

Henry Ford dreamed of a "horseless carriage" that the average American could afford. Ford needed this strong vision to sustain him through years of failure. By the time he was nearing 40, Ford had been trying to get his dream off the ground for many years. Several of his attempts to produce and sell cars had failed. He wrote later, "Failure is the chance to begin again more intelligently." Ford Motor Company became hugely successful eventually, but this took tremendous perseverance on Ford's part.

In the 1970s, the founders of Apple Computer, Stephen Wozniak and Steven Jobs, dreamed of a personal computer in every home — even though at the time only universities, some big corporations, and the government had access to computers. They, too, were not an overnight success. The dream is what provides the motivation to succeed.

Entrepreneurs have said they weren't in business for the money so often that it has become a cliché, but, like many clichés, it's based in truth. Entrepreneurs tend to be more excited about realizing their dreams than they are about making money.

## How Could *Your* Dream Help Your Community?[3]

What does your community need that your business could provide? Entrepreneurs have dreamed up businesses that have made a difference in their communities, such as:

- The Detroit Farmers Cooperative, which operated community gardens and neighborhood markets, run by teenagers.
- The Hope Takes Root program, which gave homeless men jobs growing food for local free-meal programs.
- The People's Credit Union, on Manhattan's Lower East Side, which provided affordable banking and loans in a neighborhood that was too poor to attract a commercial bank.
- St. Elmo's Village, a nonprofit artist colony dedicated to teaching art to children from the Los Angeles inner city.

**BizFact:** Walt Disney said, "I don't make movies to make money; I make money to make movies."

## What Is the Value of Your Time?

Starting a business is an opportunity. Like any opportunity it should be evaluated by taking a careful look at the costs and benefits it offers.

Even though a desire for money may not be enough to keep you going over the long run, you should think about the value of your time.

What is the opportunity cost of your time? In other words, what is the next-best thing besides starting and operating a business that you could do? How much would your next-best opportunity pay you? What is the *value* of your time? When you start your business, you will have to think about how you will pay yourself. There are three basic possibilities:

- Salary — Will you pay yourself a flat amount for each week (or month), no matter how many hours you work?
- Hourly wage — Will you pay yourself by the hour?
- Commission — Will you pay yourself a percentage of your sales revenue?

## SKILLS MEAN SUCCESS

**MATH**  ▶  **Mathematical Operations and Reasoning:**
**Calculating Percentages, Problem Solving**

Imagine you own a business with yearly revenue of $225,000. You work 40 hours per week.

**1.** Which form of the compensations below would be greatest? Show how you arrived at your answer.

   **a.** A salary of $3,000 per month?

   **b.** Wages of $20 per hour?

   **c.** Receiving a commission of 20%?

**2.** Which method of compensation would you choose for yourself? Why? What are the pros and cons of each method? ■■■

## Entrepreneurs and Philanthropy

There is a long, proud connection in the United States between entrepreneurship and **philanthropy**. Philanthropy occurs when people express their concern for social issues by giving money, time, or advice. Philanthropists often give their money through **foundations**. A foundation is a nonprofit organization that uses donated money to help others.

Many philanthropic foundations in this country were established by entrepreneurs. The following were all started by entrepreneurs and have helped millions of people worldwide:

- Atlantic Philanthropies USA
- Goldman Sachs Foundation
- Ewing Marion Kauffman Foundation
- John D. and Catherine T. MacArthur Foundation
- Shelby Cullom Davis Foundation
- Pew Charitable Trust
- Robert W. Woodruff Foundation

Use your imagination — if you could solve any problem in the world, what would it be? How could you use your business and the money you make from it to help people in your community?

# Chapter 8 Review

## CRITICAL THINKING ABOUT...

### SELECTING YOUR BUSINESS

1. List your hobbies, interests, and skills.

2. Think of five businesses you could start using your unique knowledge and your hobbies, interests, and skills. Choose a type for each business — retail, wholesale, service, or manufacturing. **Business Plan Practice**

3. Choose one of your business ideas and come up with a name. Explain the reasoning behind your choice.

4. Describe the people who will make up the market for the business you have chosen.

5. What is your competitive advantage? **Business Plan Practice**

## KEY CONCEPTS

1. List five ideas for businesses you would be interested in starting. Discuss them with a partner. Ask him/her to help you evaluate your ideas by asking questions like:

   - Does the idea satisfy a consumer need?

   - Do you have the skills and resources to create this business?

   - What would be your competitive advantage?

   Switch roles and help your partner evaluate his or her ideas. At the end of the discussion, you should each have chosen one business idea to pursue.

2. Write about your business idea. Describe it, and explain how you came up with it. Why do you think your idea will be a success?

3. Read A Business for the Young Entrepreneur on page 115. Write a mission statement for Andre's business.

## EXPLORATION

1. Research one of the foundations listed in this chapter on the Internet and write a one-page report describing who started the foundation, what it does, and how it makes the world a better place.

2. Describe how you plan to pay yourself when you start your own business. Why did you choose this method?

## REFERENCES

1 Special thanks to C.J. Meenan for this material.
2 See Bonnie Drew's *Fast Cash for Kids* (Career Press, 1995) for an excellent source of 101 business ideas for young people.
3 "Community Entrepreneurship," by Michael H. Shuman, NHI Shelterforce Online, Issue #107, September/October 1999.

## VOCABULARY

competitive advantage ■ foundation ■ manufacturing ■ philanthropy ■ product ■ retail ■ service ■ wholesale

## Chapter Summary ✔✔✔

**8.1**    Entrepreneurs need to select the right business to start.
   A. Keep it simple at first.
   B. Decide what a community needs and wants.
   C. Pick a product or service.
   D. Determine the type of business:
       1. Manufacturing, to make a product
       2. Wholesale, to buy in quantity and sell to retailers
       3. Retail, to sell a product to consumers
       4. Service, to sell an intangible product.
   E. Turn a hobby or interest into a business.
   F. Have a competitive-advantage strategy to beat the competition:
       1. Price
       2. Extra benefits
       3. Service and courtesy.
   G. Pick a name that reflects good business sense:
       1. Pride of ownership
       2. Simple and descriptive
       3. Shows concern for customers' needs.
   H. Choose a business that is ethical:
       1. Treats vendors and employees fairly
       2. Legal
       3. Not harmful to others
       4. No negative messages or ideas.

**8.2**    Only wanting to make money isn't a strong reason to start a business.
   A. Have a motivating dream.
   B. Want to make a difference in your community.
   C. Be philanthropic.
   D. Value your time. ✔✔✔

# A Business for the Young Entrepreneur
## BREAK YO NECK KICKS, ANDRE RANDLE MCCAIN

*I plan to use this business to help others realize that just because you're young doesn't mean you can't have a positive impact on others.*

Andre McCain knows that it is important for "children to have somewhere to go as a refuge from the violence and negativity of the streets." He found his refuge with his first computer. "With a computer I spend more time inside and less time getting into trouble." He found his way out of his neighborhood and into a new world.

Andre quickly taught himself HTML, learned how to build Web sites, and began an e-wrestling company online. He wasn't satisfied, though, and wanted to start another business. He thanks his cousin and NFTE for putting him on the path to founding Break Yo Neck Kicks, which sells rare and limited edition Michael Jordan shoes.

The idea came to Andre when he bought a pair of exclusive shoes for himself at a wholesale price. He began to establish relationships with key suppliers, and his company quickly became profitable.

Andre's marketing strategy includes maintaining a Web site from which orders can be filled and shipped, a five-person sales force, a referral program, and distribution through local retail stores. Future plans include opening a mall kiosk and establishing additional retail distributorships.

*Describe Andre's business definition, mission, and tactics.* ■

### CHAPTER 9

# COSTS OF RUNNING A BUSINESS:
## *Variable and Fixed*[1]

*I see something I like, I buy it; then I try to sell it.*
— Lord Grade, *British film and television entrepreneur*

### KEY OBJECTIVES

THIS CHAPTER WILL ENABLE YOU TO:

■ Define your unit of sale.

■ Explain the difference between cost of goods sold and other variable costs.

■ Calculate gross profit, including variable costs.

■ Determine the fixed costs of operating your business.

■ Use depreciation to spread the cost of equipment over several years.

## Define Your Unit of Sale

In Chapter 2, you learned about a key idea in business — the *economics of one unit of sale* (EOU). Now we'll look at the EOU in more depth — as a way to create a financial snapshot of a business's health.

A business earns a profit by selling products or services. Since everything sold has a related cost (or costs), the business can make a profit only if the selling price per unit is greater than the costs per unit. Understanding the economics of one unit of sale tells an entrepreneur if the business is earning a profit.

Before you can get a grip on your costs, however, you must determine your unit of sale. As we have learned in Chapter 2, entrepreneurs commonly define the unit of sale as:

- one item or unit (if the product is sold by the piece), or
- one hour of time (if work is billed by the hour), or
- one job or contract (e.g., mowing one lawn or washing one car), or
- one dozen or more of an item (for wholesale businesses, particularly), or
- different combinations of items expressed as an average sale per customer (say, $25 at a restaurant or $15 at a hardware store).

# Costs: Variable and Fixed

After you have clearly defined your unit of sale, you can begin to calculate the economics of that unit for the product or service. You do that by calculating the costs of one unit of sale.

Costs are divided into two categories: **variable costs** and **fixed costs**.

*Variable costs* vary (change) with sales. They occur in two sub-categories:

1.  **Cost of goods sold** (COGS), (or **cost of services sold** [COSS]), which are the costs associated specifically with each unit of sale, and include:

    -   the cost of materials used to make the product (or deliver the service)
    -   the cost of labor used to make the product (or deliver the service)

2.  **Other variable costs**, including:

    -   commissions (payments to salespeople)
    -   shipping and handling charges, etc.

*Fixed costs* stay constant whether you sell many units, or very few. Examples of fixed costs include: rent, salaries, and insurance.

For any unit of sale, you can study its EOU to figure out what it cost you to make that sale. Below is an example from a business that sells hand-painted vintage T-shirts.

| ECONOMICS OF ONE UNIT (EOU) | | | |
|---|---|---|---|
| **Manufacturing Business:** unit = 1 hand-painted T-shirt | | | |
| **Selling Price per Unit:** | | | **$35.00** |
| Supplies/Materials: | $7.00 | | |
| Labor ($10.00/hour): | 10.00 | | |
| **Cost of Goods Sold per Unit:** | $17.00 | $17.00 | |
| Commission: | $1.00 | | |
| Packaging: | 0.50 | | |
| **Total Other Variable Costs per Unit:** | $1.50 | 1.50 | |
| **Total Variable Costs per Unit:** | | $18.50 | 18.50 |
| **Gross Profit per Unit:*** | | | $16.50 |

\* Technically this is called "contribution margin," but we are using "gross profit" to keep the presentation simple.

# Calculating Gross Profit per Unit

After you know your variable costs per unit of sale, you can calculate your **gross profit** (per unit of sale) by subtracting the COGS and other variable costs per unit of sale from your selling price per unit of sale.

The gross profit of a unit of sale provides a real sense of the profitablity of the business as a whole.

> Selling Price − Cost of Goods Sold − Other Variable Costs = Gross Profit

**Here's another example:**

Let's say you're selling watches at $10 each. Your unit of sale is one watch. You pay a wholesaler $36 for one dozen watches. Your cost of goods sold (or **direct cost**) is $3 per unit, because that's what you are paying for each watch ($36 ÷ 12 watches = $3).

You pay a 20% sales commission to several friends, who sell the watches for you. The commission, therefore, is $2 per watch ($10 watch × .20 = $2 commission). This commission is a variable cost, because it changes with sales. If your friends sell 10 watches, you will pay $20 in commissions. If your friends sell 20 watches, you will pay $40 in commissions.

**Here's how you would calculate your Gross Profit per Unit.**

| | | |
|---|---|---|
| Revenue (money received from sales) | = | $10 per watch |
| − Cost of Goods Sold | = | $3 per watch |
| − Other Variable Costs (commissions) | = | $2 per watch |
| Gross Profit (per unit sold) | = | $5 per watch |

The Economics of One Unit (EOU) analysis for selling one watch is shown below.

| ECONOMICS OF ONE UNIT (EOU) | | |
|---|---|---|
| **Retail Business:** unit = 1 watch | **Date:** 9/25/2006 | |
| **Selling Price per Unit:** | | $10.00 |
| Cost of Goods Sold (1 watch): | $3.00 | |
| Other Variable Costs (commission): | 2.00 | |
| **Total Variable Costs per Unit:** | $5.00 | 5.00 |
| **Gross Profit per Unit:** | | $5.00 |

Note:    **a.** The unit of sale is defined on the EOU.

**b.** The date the analysis was made is shown on the EOU. (Remember that costs change, so you will have to know when the EOU was done.)

## Calculating Gross Profit

You can use the EOU to estimate how much your Total Gross Profit will be.

**Gross Profit per Watch** × **Number of Units Sold** = **Total Gross Profit**

| | | | | |
|---|---|---|---|---|
| $5.00 per watch | × | 10 units sold | = | $50.00 Total Gross Profit |
| $5.00 per watch | × | 50 units sold | = | $250.00 Total Gross Profit |

## Cost of Services Sold (COSS)

For a service business, the cost of selling one additional unit is called cost of services sold. Just as a company that makes a product, a service business uses both labor and materials to deliver the unit of sale. Here's an example:

A writer is selling her labor to write brochures for small businesses, but also uses materials, such as paper and printer ink. Let's assume:

- The writer values her time at $7 per hour.
- It takes 4 hours to complete the average job.
- She uses $1 of paper and ink per job.
- She pays a colleague a 10% commission on each job the colleague brings her.
- The selling price for one job is $50.

| ECONOMICS OF ONE UNIT (EOU) | | | |
|---|---|---|---|
| **Service Business:** unit = 1 writing job | | **Date:** 10/3/2007 | |
| **Selling Price per Unit:** | | | **$50.00** |
| Paper and Printer Ink: | $1.00 | | |
| Direct Labor ($7.00 × 4 hours): | 28.00 | | |
| **Cost of Services Sold per Unit:** | $29.00 | $29.00 | |
| **Other Variable Costs** (commission): | | 5.00 | |
| **Total Variable Costs per Unit:** | | $34.00 | 34.00 |
| **Gross Profit per Unit:** | | | $16.00 |

## Handling EOUs When Selling More than One Product

A business selling different products has to create a separate EOU for each to determine whether each item is profitable. When there are many similar products, a "typical EOU" can be used.

Example: Jimmy sells four brands of candy bars at his school. He sells them all at $1, but pays different wholesale prices. His costs are:

**a)** Snickers      36¢ each      **c)** Butterfinger    42¢ each

**b)** Almond Joy    38¢ each      **d)** Baby Ruth      44¢ each

Rather than make separate EOUs for similar products, Jimmy uses the average gross profit of each transaction as his EOU.

$$36¢ + 38¢ + 42¢ + 44¢ \text{ (prices of the four candy bars)}$$
$$= \$1.60 \div 4$$
$$= 40¢ \text{ (average cost)}$$

| ECONOMICS OF ONE UNIT (EOU) | | |
|---|---|---|
| **Retail Business:** unit = 1 candy bar | **Date:** 11/10/2007 | |
| **Selling Price per Unit:** | | $1.00 |
| Average Cost of Goods Sold (1 candy bar): | $0.40 | |
| Other Average Variable Costs (shipping): | 0.06 | |
| **Total Average Variable Costs per Unit:** | $0.46 | 0.46 |
| **Average Gross Profit per Unit:** | | $0.54 |

Using an average here works as long as the costs are fairly close, and as long as Jimmy sells roughly the same number of each bar. If he can no longer get Snickers and Almond Joy, for example, he would have to change his EOU to reflect the higher average price of the other two.

## An EOU with a Variety of Costs

What if each unit of sale is made up of a complex mix of materials and labor? The economics of one unit can still help you figure the COGS, other variable costs, and gross profit for the product.

Example: Janelle sells turkey sandwiches at $5 each from her deli cart downtown on Saturdays.

The materials and labor that go directly into making each sandwich are the COGS. There are also some other variable costs, such as napkins, paper wrapping for each sandwich, and plastic bags.

Assume the employee making the sandwich earns $7 per hour and can make 10 sandwiches in one hour.

First, make a list of COGS, and any other variable costs:

## COGS

**a)** Turkey costs $2.60 per lb. Each sandwich uses 4 oz. of turkey meat (16 oz. = 1 lb.).

**b)** Bread (large rolls) cost $1.92 per dozen. 1 roll is used per sandwich.

**c)** 1 oz. of mayonnaise is used per sandwich. A 32-oz. jar of mayo costs $1.60.

**d)** Lettuce costs 80 cents per pound and $\frac{1}{16}$ of a pound is used per sandwich.

**e)** Tomatoes cost $1.16 each. Each sandwich uses $\frac{1}{4}$ of a tomato.

**f)** Each sandwich comes with 2 pickles. Pickles cost 5 cents each.

**g)** Employees are paid $7 per hour and can make 10 sandwiches per hour.

## Other Variable Costs

The following supplies are used every time a sandwich is sold:

**a)** Napkins cost $3 per pack of 100. 1 napkin is included with each sale.

**b)** Paper wrapping costs 20 cents per foot (on a roll). Each sandwich uses 2 feet of paper.

**c)** Plastic carryout bags cost $7 per roll of 100. Each sandwich sold uses 1 plastic carryout bag.

The EOU for the turkey sandwich is: *(See chart on page 122.)*

## ECONOMICS OF ONE UNIT (BASIC)

**Retail Business:** unit = 1 turkey sandwich

**Date: 12/1/2008**

**Selling Price per Unit:** $5.00

| Cost of Goods Sold | Price | Units | Quantity Used | Cost Each |
|---|---|---|---|---|
| Turkey (4 oz.): | $2.60 | Per lb. | $\frac{1}{4}$ lb. | $0.65 |
| Bread (roll): | $1.92 | Per dozen | $\frac{1}{12}$ dz. | 0.16 |
| Mayonnaise (1 oz.): | $1.60 | Per 32-oz. jar | $\frac{1}{32}$ jar | 0.05 |
| Lettuce (1 oz.): | $0.80 | Per lb. | $\frac{1}{16}$ lb. | 0.05 |
| Tomato ($\frac{1}{4}$): | $1.16 | Each | $\frac{1}{4}$ each | 0.29 |
| Pickles (2): | $0.05 | Each | 2 pickles | 0.10 |
| Direct Labor (6 min.): | $7.00 | Per hr. | $\frac{1}{10}$ hr. | 0.70 |
| | | | | $2.00 |

**Total Cost of Goods Sold per Unit:** $2.00

| Other Variable Costs | | | | |
|---|---|---|---|---|
| Napkin: | $3.00 | Per 100-pack | $\frac{1}{100}$ pack | 0.03 |
| Paper Wrapping: | $0.20 | Per foot | 2 feet | 0.40 |
| Plastic Bag: | $7.00 | Per roll (100) | $\frac{1}{100}$ roll | 0.07 |
| | | | | $0.50 |

**Total Other Variable Costs per Unit:** $0.50

**Total Variable Costs per Unit:** $2.50    2.50

**Gross Profit per Unit:** $2.50

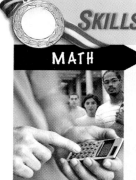

## SKILLS MEAN SUCCESS

**MATH** ▶ **Operations:** Determining Price per Unit to Compare Prices

Entrepreneurs manage their costs by looking for the suppliers that offer the lowest prices. Hernando wanted to save money on shopping bags, so he asked for price quotes from three bag suppliers. Each supplier provided pricing based on a different quantity.

- Supplier A offered 25 bags for $40.00.
- Supplier B offered 50 bags for $79.00.
- Supplier C offered 100 bags for $155.00.

**1.** What would be the price per unit from each supplier?

**2.** Which supplier offered the best price? Show your work.

Per-unit prices usually drop when you buy more units. When you ask suppliers for prices, have them quote on the specific quantities that make sense for your business. ■■■

## The Fixed Costs of Operating Your Business

As we have learned, costs such as rent and the phone bill are called fixed costs, or **overhead**. Fixed costs are not included in COGS (or COSS) because they are not direct costs incurred by creating the product (or service). Fixed costs are not included in other variable costs because they don't vary with the number of sales made.

Fixed costs do not change based on sales, therefore they are not included in the EOU. A sandwich shop has to pay the same rent each month, whether it sells one turkey sandwich or 100 sandwiches.

Fixed costs are the costs a business must cover to keep a roof over its head and stay in operation. This is why fixed costs are also sometimes called **fixed operating costs**.

**BizFact:** *Overhead* is an informal term for fixed costs. "Overhead" derives from the literal "over head," that is, the roof over the business. Business owners strive for "low overhead" because the less money they have to pay in fixed costs, the more they will have for other expenses, to reinvest in the business, or to keep as profit.

An easy way to remember the seven common fixed costs is USAIIRD:

**U**tilities (gas, electric, telephone, Internet service)
**S**alaries
**A**dvertising
**I**nsurance
**I**nterest
**R**ent
**D**epreciation

**Depreciation** is a method used to save the money that will be needed to replace expensive pieces of equipment. Let's say you buy a computer for your business for $2,000, expecting not to have to replace it for five years. To make sure you will have the $2,000 to replace the computer, you should save $400 per year for five years. Saving that amount annually to cover depreciation is a cost of operating your business. Depreciation spreads the cost of items over the period of time during which you actually use them. This will make your income statement more accurate.

## Fixed Costs Do Change — Over Time

If you pay your restaurant manager $1,200 per month in salary, you will have to pay out that same amount whether the restaurant sells one meal or a 1,000 meals. The cost is fixed.

Fixed costs do change over time. At some point you may give your manager a raise, for example. The word "fixed" doesn't mean the cost *never* changes, just that it doesn't change in response to sales. For instance:

Advertising: The cost of advertising will change based on decisions the entrepreneur makes about how much to spend to reach the consumer, not necessarily because of current sales.

Heating costs: The price of heating goes up or down based on the weather and other factors, not on the amount of revenue a business earns.

## Economies of Scale

Check the prices on paper towels at your local supermarket. You will notice that the price of three single rolls is greater than the price of a three-pack.

The quantity of an item you buy (or sell) is called *volume*. The supermarket is offering to give you a lower price if you purchase a higher volume. The price per unit declines as you buy larger amounts.

Similarly, as a business grows, it will begin to get better deals from suppliers because it is purchasing more volume. These advantages of growth are called *economies of scale*. They represent the money a business can save because it can lower costs as it grows. There are two basic concepts:

1. **Spread fixed costs over as much output as possible**, so that the cost per unit decreases. If you are paying $600 per month rent for your glass-blowing studio and are currently selling ten pieces a month at $100 each, you are making $1,000 in revenue and paying $600 in rent. If you can sell 20 pieces per month while still paying $600 in rent, you would now be paying a much lower percentage of your revenue to the landlord.

2. **Get better deals from suppliers.** You can get discounts if you buy in larger amounts. A discount for buying higher quantities is called a "volume" discount. Always ask the supplier where the price breaks for quantity purchases are.

## SKILLS MEAN SUCCESS

**ENGLISH**    **Reading for Information: Reasoning and Understanding**

Identify whether each of the costs below, associated with a specialty cake shop, would be fixed (F) or variable (V). Remember: even if a cost changes from month to month, it is not necessarily a variable cost. Variable costs change based only on the quantity of goods or services sold.

1. Rent
2. Gas, electricity, and water
3. Baking equipment, such as ovens and baking racks
4. Ingredients, such as flour, sugar, fruit, and chocolate
5. Decorating supplies, such as fresh flowers and candy
6. Advertising
7. Cake boxes and packaging
8. Delivery truck
9. Shipping costs
10. Insurance
11. Commissions to sales staff
12. Food-vending license or other permits ■■■

## Make Your Fixed Costs Variable Whenever Possible

Your goal as a business owner is to know, whenever you sell a unit, how much of the revenue will be used to cover the cost of goods sold and other variable costs. Whatever is left over is your gross profit. You will pay your fixed costs out of your gross profit. Whatever is left over after you pay these fixed costs will be your **net profit**.

Fixed costs can be dangerous because they have to be paid whether or not the business makes any gross profit. The entrepreneur should be cautious about taking on fixed costs. An entrepreneur does not have to worry quite so much about variable costs because, if sales are low, variable costs will be low as well.

## Fully Allocating Your Fixed Costs

Here's an example of how to fully allocate your costs, so that you will know, each time you sell a unit, how much of your fixed and variable costs that sale is covering:

Let's say you sell 300 watches in a month at $15 each.

| | | | |
|---|---|---|---|
| **Sales** (300 watches × $15 per watch): | | | $4,500.00 |
| **Total COGS** ($2 per watch × 300 watches): | | $600.00 | |
| Commissions ($1 per watch): | $300.00 | | |
| Shipping ($1 per watch): | 300.00 | | |
| **Total Other Variable Costs** ($2 per watch × 300 watches): | $600.00 | 600.00 | |
| **Total Variable Costs** (COGS + Other Variable Costs): | | $1,200.00 | 1,200.00 |
| **Gross Profit** (Sales − Total Variable Costs): | | | $3,300.00 |

Gross Profit per Unit was $11 ($3,300 divided by 300 watches)

  or

$15.00 − $4.00 per watch = $11.00 per watch

The $11.00 gross profit per watch sold must be used to cover fixed costs before you will make a net profit. Knowing the economics of one unit of sale will help you predict how well you can cover your fixed costs from the gross profit.

**Calculating Total Cost per Unit:**

| | | |
|---|---|---|
| **Total Variable Costs** (COGS + Other Variable Costs): | | **$1,200.00** |
| **Fixed Costs** | | |
| Utilities: | $50.00 | |
| Salaries: | 100.00 | |
| Advertising: | 50.00 | |
| Insurance: | 50.00 | |
| Interest: | 50.00 | |
| Rent: | 100.00 | |
| Depreciation: | 50.00 | |
| **Total Fixed Costs** (per month): | **$450.00** | 450.00 |
| **Total Costs** (Fixed + Variable): | | **$1,650.00** |

**Total Costs per Unit ($1,650 ÷ 300 watches) = $5.50 per watch.**

For every watch you sell, your total costs will be $5.50 ($4.00 in variable, $1.50 in fixed).

# Bob's Discount Furniture: A Smart Cost Decision[2]

Bob Kaufman owns 18 furniture stores in New England. (Bob's Discount Furniture is one of the largest TV advertisers in Connecticut.) When Bob was starting out in the furniture business in 1992, though, he was broke.

He found a store to rent for his furniture business, but the landlord wanted him to sign a one-year lease. Bob understood that rent was a fixed cost. This meant he would have to pay rent every month, whether he could afford to or not, for a full 12 months. He knew that if sales were low he would get into trouble quickly, because he did not have any cash in reserve.

What Bob needed was to change his rent from a fixed to a variable cost. He negotiated with the landlord to pay the rent as a percentage of the monthly sales. That way, if sales were low, the rent would also be low. If sales were high, Bob's rent would go up — but he would be able to pay it. Rent was Bob's largest fixed cost. By changing it to a variable, he cut a lot of the risk out of his new business.

Bob's Discount Furniture became extremely successful. He still pays rent for that first store as a percentage of sales, not as a fixed monthly cost. That deal helped Bob when his business was small, and it still works for him now that it is big. Bob's landlord has been happy with the deal as well and has never asked to change the arrangement. Bob can allocate his rent now to each unit that he sells, using his economics of one unit.

## Keep at Least Three Months of Fixed Costs in Reserve

During the early days of your business, when you are working hard to attract customers and establish your reputation, you may not be selling much of your product or service, but you will still have fixed costs. If you aren't prepared for this, you could be forced out of business.

Try to put enough money in the bank to cover at least three months of fixed costs *before you open your business*. This kind of cushion is called a *cash reserve*. A reserve is money kept for emergencies — such as not being able to sell your handmade swimsuits because it has been raining for a month! A reserve will keep your business going during tough times while you think of new ways to attract customers.

You can build up a reserve by saving, borrowing, or through investors. In later chapters we'll explore in detail how to raise money for your business.

### SKILLS MEAN SUCCESS

**MATH**

**Mathematical Reasoning:** Devising Formulas

To check your understanding of the formulas introduced in this chapter, match the following terms with the correct equations for calculating them.

**1.** Cost of Goods Sold

**a.** Selling Price per Unit − Total Costs per Unit

**2.** Gross Profit per Unit

**b.** Price ÷ Quantity

**3.** Reserve

**c.** Gross Profit per Unit × Number of Units Sold

**4.** Price per Unit

**d.** Cost of Labor + Cost of Materials

**5.** Total Variable Costs

**e.** Monthly Fixed Costs × 3

**6.** Total Gross Profit

**f.** Cost of Goods Sold + Other Variable Costs

**7.** Net Profit per Unit

**g.** Selling Price per Unit − Total Variable Costs per Unit

# Chapter 9 Review

## CRITICAL THINKING ABOUT...

### COSTS OF RUNNING A BUSINESS

For the business below, define the unit of sale and create an EOU to determine the gross profit per unit.

**Business Plan Practice**

Dave opens a retail jewelry store with an $80,000 start-up investment. On average, he sells $1,000 worth of jewelry per day to 50 customers. On average his cost of goods sold per customer is $5. His fixed monthly costs are:

| | | |
|---|---|---|
| Utilities | = | $250 |
| Salary | = | $2,500 |
| Advertising | = | $1,000 |
| Interest | = | $0 |
| Insurance | = | $1,000 |
| Rent | = | $1,000 |
| Depreciation | = | $500 |

a. What is Dave's economics of one unit of sale?

b. What are his total fixed costs per month?

c. What are his total fixed costs annually?

d. What is his total gross profit daily?

## KEY CONCEPTS

1. What is the purpose of depreciation? How would you depreciate a used truck that you bought for your business for $4,000 and expected to have to replace in four years?

2. For a business you would like to start, estimate what you think the fixed and variable costs would be. Choose a category for each from USAIIRD: Utilities, Salaries, Advertising, Interest, Insurance, Rent, and Depreciation.
**Business Plan Practice**

3. Contact a supplier you would like to use for your business and find out how much you would have to buy before getting a volume discount rate. Be sure they know you are a business, not an "end user" (consumer).

## REFERENCES

1, 2 With thanks to John Harris for the story and for reviewing this chapter.

## VOCABULARY

cost of goods sold ▪ cost of services sold ▪ depreciation ▪ direct cost ▪ fixed costs ▪ gross profit ▪ fixed operating costs ▪ overhead ▪ net profit ▪ variable costs

## Chapter Summary ✔✔✔

9.1    Entrepreneurs must earn a profit from every unit of sale and need to understand the economics of one unit (EOU).

   A. Prices charged must be greater than costs in order to create profit.

   *B.* The unit of sale is the basis of a business:
     *1.* One item (or piece) of product
     *2.* One hour of time
     *3.* Completing one job or contract
     *4.* A dozen or more of an item (for wholesale businesses)
     *5.* Different combinations of items as in a restaurant meal (average sale per customer).

**9.2** Costs in a business can be fixed or variable.
   *A.* Variable costs change directly with the number of units sold.
     *1.* Cost of goods or services sold includes the cost of the materials or service provided, and the cost of labor to make the product or provide the service.
     *2.* Other variable costs include commissions paid to sales agents and shipping and handling charges.
   *B.* Fixed costs remain constant and do not vary with how many units are sold.
   *C.* Total Variable Cost per Unit = COGS per Unit + Other Variable Costs per Unit.

**9.3** Subtract Total Variable Costs per Unit from Selling Price per Unit to determine the Gross Profit per Unit of Sale.
   *A.* Selling Price per Unit − Total Variable Cost per Unit (COGS + Other Variable Costs) = Gross Profit per Unit.
   *B.* Gross Profit per Unit × Number of Units Sold = Total Gross Profit.
   *C.* If a company sells several different products or services:
     *1.* Calculate the EOU of each
     *2.* For similar products, average the costs per unit
     *3.* For some products, the variable costs may include several components.

**9.4** Businesses also have fixed costs, not included in the EOU.
   *A.* Fixed costs (overhead) do not vary directly with the number of units sold.
   *B.* Fixed costs are called operating costs — a business needs them to function:
     *1.* Utilities
     *2.* Salaries
     *3.* Advertising
     *4.* Insurance
     *5.* Interest
     *6.* Rent
     *7.* Depreciation (savings to replace expensive equipment in the future).
   *C.* Some fixed costs change over time (e.g., advertising, and heating and air conditioning are seasonal).

**9.5** Growth and size (volume) create economies-of-scale advantages for a business.
   A. Bulk purchasing from suppliers reduces prices and lowers cost per unit.
   B. Volume spreads fixed costs over more units of sale.

**9.6** After fixed costs are covered from gross profit, whatever is left is net profit.
   A. The impact on profit of variable costs is easier to watch: costs vary with the number of units sold.
   B. The impact on profit of fixed costs is more difficult to know: they don't vary with the number of units sold.
   C. Whenever possible, entrepreneurs allocate fixed costs (that is, express them as variable costs) in the EOU to make it easier to check if the EOU is profitable:
      1. Add monthly fixed costs
      2. Add total variable costs for one month's sales
      3. Add them together to find total monthly costs
      4. Divide total monthly costs by the number of units of sale sold in one month
      5. Know the total costs (variable + fixed) per unit sold
      6. Subtract: Selling Price per Unit − Total Costs per Unit = Net Profit per Unit.
   D. Have a cash reserve of at least three months worth of fixed costs. ✔✔✔

# A Business for the Young Entrepreneur
## MOTHER'S HELPER

A mother's helper keeps children occupied so that busy mothers can devote their time and attention to something else. The mother is in the house, but the mother's helper's job will be to take care of the children. This is a good (and safe) way to get baby-sitting and child-care experience.

### SUGGESTIONS

- Bring some games or art supplies. The best way to keep children happy is to keep them interested in something.
- Try not to interrupt the mother with questions. Ask all your questions before she leaves the children with you. Some good ones are:

    *What can I give the children to eat or drink?*
    *Where is the bathroom?*
    *Should I answer the phone?*
    *Can I take the children outside to play?*

- Before you start, discuss how much you will be paid and how long the mother will need you to be there. ■

### CHAPTER 10

# WHAT IS MARKETING?

*Sometimes I think creativity is magic; it's not a matter of finding an idea, but allowing the idea to find you.*

— Maya Lin, *American sculptor*

## KEY OBJECTIVES

THIS CHAPTER WILL ENABLE YOU TO:

- Explain why marketing is the business function that identifies customer needs.
- Use marketing to establish your brand.
- Apply the four elements of a marketing plan.
- Create a marketing plan for your business.

## Identifying and Responding to Customer Needs

**Marketing** is satisfying the customer at a profit.[1] Nike sells sneakers. It puts sneakers in stores where customers can buy them. But Nike also *markets* sneakers. Nike creates advertisements and promotions designed to convince customers that Nike sneakers will inspire them to *Just Do It*. You can choose sneakers from many companies, but Nike hopes you will feel inspired by its marketing to seek out and buy *its* sneakers.

Marketing is the business function that identifies customer needs and responds to them. It is often described as "the art of getting the customer to come to the product." Through marketing, the name of your business should come to mean something clear and concrete in the consumer's mind.

## Meet Your Customers' Needs to Gain Their Loyalty

As an entrepreneur, you should make your current and future customers your top priority.[2] Together, this group of people is your *market*. Marketing is how you will communicate to your customers that you are deeply committed to meeting their needs. By making sure that your product or service meets your customers' needs, you will attract new customers and build a loyal customer base. The more loyal your customers are to your product, the harder it will be for competitors to take them from you. If you need to raise your prices, loyal customers will be more likely to stay with you. Finally, loyal customers talk up your business to their friends — who may become new customers!

## SKILLS MEAN SUCCESS

**ENGLISH**

**Listening and Speaking:** Listening Attentively; **Expressing Ideas Respectfully in Conversation; Using Nonverbal Communication**

It has been said that a satisfied customer will tell five people about his or her experience, but a dissatisfied customer will tell ten. Statistics show that only about four percent of dissatisfied customers actually complain. Because you may not even know if a customer is dissatisfied, you will need to provide excellent service at all times and treat everyone with fairness and respect. If you are faced with a customer complaint, take the following steps to resolve the situation:

- Listen attentively. Let the customer finish without interruption.
- Smile and be pleasant, not confrontational or defensive. Nod to show you are paying attention. (If you're on the phone, say, "I see," or "I understand," to indicate paying attention.)
- Use a confident and relaxed posture and maintain eye contact.
- Ask sincere questions to help you understand the problem and show your concern. Restate the problem to verify that you understood correctly.
- Acknowledge how frustrating the situation is and reassure the customer that you want to help.
- Ask the customer how he or she would like the situation to be resolved.
- Don't blame others. Take responsibility and handle the matter yourself to the best of your ability. If you must defer to someone else or get additional information, be honest with the customer and tell him or her what to expect.
- Follow through with what you said you would do as quickly as possible.

Working with a partner, practice role-playing. Take turns playing an unhappy customer, and follow the guidelines above to resolve the situation. ■■■

## Marketing Explains the *Benefits* of a Product

A customer who goes to a hardware store to buy a drill does not need a drill — he needs a hole. If he could go to the hardware store and buy the hole, he wouldn't bother to buy the drill. So, if you are marketing drills, you should emphasize what good holes your drills make![3]

To "think marketing," figure out what benefit the customers in your market will need to get from your product or service. What are you really selling? Charles Revson, the founder of Revlon cosmetics, famously said, "In the factory we make cosmetics; in the drugstore we sell hope."

## The Marketing Vision Drives All Business Decisions

To market a product or service successfully, ask yourself: Who are my customers? What do they need my product or service to do for them? The answer to those questions will help you form your *marketing vision*. The marketing vision is the benefit you want to show customers that your product or service provides.

Nike's customers want sneakers partly because they know they should exercise. The customers seek out Nike *because they have been convinced by Nike's marketing* that the sneakers will inspire them to get up early in the morning and go for a run. Every business move Nike makes is designed to reinforce its *Just Do It* marketing vision. Nike uses celebrity athletes in its marketing to further reinforce this concept.

Most experts agree that you should develop your marketing vision first; then use it to drive all your business decisions.

## Marketing Establishes Your Brand

All cars do the same job — they get you from Point A to Point B. Why would you buy a particular car? Because its marketing has made you believe that only that car will meet your needs. If safety is your biggest priority, you might buy a Volvo, because its marketing emphasizes that it's the safest car on the road. If you want luxury, you might prefer a Lexus. If you need a car that gets great gas mileage, you might get a Toyota or Honda.

Marketing establishes the **brand** in the customer's mind. A brand is the name that distinguishes a business from its competition. The brand instantly communicates the business's competitive advantage to the consumer. With cars, for example, when you hear Volvo, you think safety. When you hear Lexus, you think luxury. When you hear Toyota, you think good gas mileage. Each brand and its competitive advantage has been established in your mind by television commercials, print ads, and other marketing efforts.

Establishing a brand in the customer's mind can create a fortune. Ray Kroc, who developed McDonald's, did not invent or even improve the hamburger — *he invented a new way of marketing hamburgers.*

Kroc was a saleman; he sold milk-shake machines to restaurants. Through the number of milk-shake machines being ordered and replaced, he noticed that customers were flocking to a small burger restaurant in San Bernardino, California, run by the McDonald brothers.

Kroc realized that these customers were not seeking the ultimate hamburger. They liked the fast, clean service and the low price. These were the benefits that brought them to the product. By marketing those benefits, Kroc made McDonald's the huge success it is today.

## Focus Your Brand

The key to building a successful brand is to focus tightly on the one benefit you want to make sure customers associate with your business. In *Focus: The Future of Your Company Depends on It*, Al Ries explains that the most successful businesses focus their marketing so that they come to own a category in the customer's mind. You want to own a benefit the way Volvo owns "safety" or Federal Express owns "guaranteed overnight delivery."

Even entertainers can become a brand. By developing a consistent image and sound, pop singer Britney Spears became a brand that sold not only millions of records, but also over $50 million worth of dolls, T-shirts, posters, etc., that used her image.

## Ford's Costly Failure — The Edsel

One of the most notorious examples of a product that failed due to lack of focus is a car Ford introduced in 1956, called the Edsel.

Ford tried to cram every kind of gadget and design element it thought consumers might want in a car. Ford also sold more than 20 different models, at different prices. The goal was to try to appeal to everybody, but the company soon learned that a car with something to appeal to everyone, appealed to no one. The Edsel had no outstanding benefit that could be clearly marketed. When it was introduced to the public, it bombed.

Ford spent more money on advertising the Edsel than had ever been spent before on marketing anything. Two years and $350 million later, Ford pulled the plug on the Edsel assembly line. Even millions of dollars of marketing couldn't make consumers buy a product they didn't want.

## Ford's Marketing Success — The Mustang

Ford learned from the Edsel mistake. When Ford introduced the Mustang in the 1960s, it focused very clearly on a target market of people 20 to 30 years old. Everything about the car — from its design to the colors it came in — was made to appeal to young drivers. The marketing described the Mustang as "for the young at heart." Only one model was offered. The Mustang was a huge success.

Interestingly, Ford tried to offer some luxury and four-door versions of the Mustang a few years later. Sales dropped — perhaps because the brand started losing focus. Today, the Mustang remains one of Ford's stronger sellers.

## How to Build Your Brand

You can build your own brand with these steps:

1. **Choose a business name that is easy to remember, describes your business, and establishes "mind share."** **Mind share** is the degree to which *your* business comes to mind when a consumer needs something.

2. **Create a logo that symbolizes your business to the customer.** **Logo** is short for "logotype." A logo is a distinctive company trademark, or sign. The Nike "swoosh" is an example of a logo. So are McDonald's "Golden Arches."

3. **Develop a good reputation.** Make sure your product or service is of the highest quality you can afford to offer. Always treat your customers like gold. You want people to feel good when they think of your brand or hear it mentioned.

4. **Create a brand personality.** Is your brand's "personality" youthful and casual, like the Gap's? Safe and serious, like Volvo's? Customers will respond to brand personality and develop a relationship with it. Personality will reinforce your name and logo.

5. **Communicate your brand personality to your target market.** What type of advertising will best reach your target market? Where should you put flyers? What newspapers or magazines does your target market read?

**BizTip: Computerize Your Visuals** — Your marketing efforts will have a stronger impact if your business materials are tied together with a great logo. Use a computer to create a logo and put it on all your business materials.

- **Business cards**
- **Stationery**
- **Brochures**
- **Posters**
- **Press releases**
- **Flyers**
- **Mailing cards/coupons**

**SKILLS MEAN SUCCESS**

**TECHNOLOGY**

### Internet Resources and Business Card Design

Your business card is an important promotional tool. It should reinforce your brand. The following information should be included: your name and title, company name, address, phone number, fax number, Web site and e-mail address, company logo (or a graphic), and company saying or motto.

Visit one of the following Web sites to design a business card online. Go to the "Business Cards" or "Custom Printing" area of the site and follow the instructions for inserting your own text and logo graphics:

- www.iprint.com
- www.marktheworld.com (Staples)
- www.officedepot.com
- www.vistaprint.com

All of these sites will allow you to design your card, import your own graphics, and print and save a preview copy. When you are ready to print and purchase business cards, these sites offer a variety of services and prices. Before you print anything, however, proofread it carefully to make sure it is error-free. ■■■

## You Represent Your Brand

Always present yourself and your business in such a way that people will have confidence in your product or service. Anything that harms your reputation will damage your sales and profits. Anything that boosts your reputation will have a positive impact on your business.

**Here are eight things you can do to build your brand and its reputation:**

1. Provide a high-quality product or service.

2. Maintain the highest ethical standards.

3. Define your product or service clearly — *focus*!

4. Treat your employees well.

5. Make all your ads positive and informative.

6. Associate your company with a charity.

7. Become actively involved in your community.

8. Make sure your business does not pollute the environment.

**137**

# SKILLS MEAN SUCCESS

**MATH** ▶ **Mathematical Modeling:** Representing Numerical Relationships in Graphs; Using Graphics in Presentations

In the example on the next page, Apple sells about 3% of all personal computers, so its *market share* is 3%. Market share is expressed as a percentage of a whole. In business presentations, market share is often shown as a pie chart.

**1.** Read and interpret the chart at the right.

   **a.** Which single provider has the largest market share? What is the percentage?

**b.** What share do the two largest suppliers have together?

**c.** How much bigger is IBM's share than Apple's?

**d.** If there are approximately 100 "Other" smaller makers of personal computers, about how much market share would each have on average?

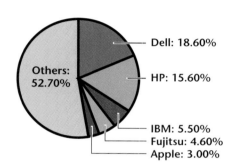

*PC vendors (reported by market research firm, IDC, in April 2004)*

**2.** Create a pie chart for a local taxi cab market using the following data. Use Excel or another software with graphing capability.

| Company | Sales |
|---|---|
| *A-One Taxi* | $250,000 |
| *Going Your Way Taxi* | $150,000 |
| *Ride Fast Taxi* | $50,000 |
| *Airport Taxi and Limo* | $125,000 |
| *All other cab companies* | $175,000 |

When creating pie charts for a business presentation, use these guidelines:

- Give the chart a title, centered at the top of your slide or document.
- Position the chart at the center of the slide or page, and make it as large and easy to see as possible, while leaving sufficient room for labels and margin space.
- The left edge of the most important section of the chart should begin at the top (at the "noon" position, if it were a clock). This may or may not be the *largest* section.
- Use a maximum of six pie segments.
- Make each segment a different color.
- Add labels inside or next to the segments. ■■■

## Mind Share versus Market Share

Advertising builds brand awareness in the mind of the consumer. You generally don't know a brand exists until you see its advertising. By advertising, a company gains *mind share*. But advertising alone usually isn't enough to make a sale.

Apple Computer, for example, has tremendous mind share. Almost everyone is aware of the Apple brand. Yet Apple's **market share** is only 3%. Market share is the portion of the total possible market a company has in relation to its competitors.

After your advertising gains mind share, you will still need marketing to get the consumer to make a purchase. Only then can you take market share from your competitors.[4]

## The Four P's

Marketing is also the term for your plan for bringing your product or service "to market." Every marketing plan has four elements, referred to as *The Four P's*:

- **P**roduct
- **P**lace
- **P**rice
- **P**romotion

1. **Product:** The product (or service) should meet or create a consumer need. The packaging is also part of the product. Your customer might throw away your packaging, but that doesn't mean it's unimportant. Starbucks revolutionized the coffee shop by creating different cup sizes and using Italian names.

2. **Place:** Place your product where customers who need it do their shopping. Selling bathing suits in Alaska in February is not going to fill a customer need. Where should you go to bring your product or service to the attention of your market? If you are selling a luxury item, you will need to place it in stores that are visited by consumers who can afford it. What will it cost to renovate or improve your site to attract the type of consumers you want?

3. **Price:** The product has to be priced low enough so the public will buy it, and high enough for the business to make a profit. Price should also reflect your marketing vision. If you are marketing a luxury item, for example, offering the lowest possible price might not send the right message.

**139**

4.  **Promotion:** Promotion consists of advertising, **publicity**, and promotional items (see below). If a newspaper writes an article about your business, that's publicity. If you buy an ad in that newspaper, you've purchased advertising. Publicity is free, while advertising is purchased.

    Other promotional tools:

    - Your **business card**: This should include the name, address, and contact information (phone and fax numbers, e-mail address and Web site) of your business, as well as your own name and title. A card can also include a short catchy phrase or motto, such as "For Sound Advice" if you are running a stereo-repair business. Carry some cards with you wherever you go, to give to potential clients and contacts.

    - T-shirts or caps bearing the name of your product: These are "walking advertisements."

    - Freebies or discounts: When you open your business you can give away samples of your product to encourage customers to tell their friends about it. You could also offer an initial lower price to attract customers, or give coupons for discounts on future purchases.

As you choose the elements of your marketing plan, always keep your vision in mind: What is the benefit your product or service is providing to customers?

## How Can You Tell If Your Promotions Are Working?

How do you know if your promotions are working? Ask your customers. Get into the habit of asking every new customer who calls or walks through the door: "How did you hear about us?" or "Where did you hear about our sale?"

Another good idea is to request that your customers fill out a card that asks for their address, e-mail, etc. and also: "How did you hear about us?" Online order forms should include that question, with a list of options for customers to check off, such as: the *Yellow Pages*, the Internet, advertisement, etc.

## Philanthropy Can Bring Positive Publicity

As a business owner, you have a responsibilty to help the community you serve. The people and causes you choose to support should be those that matter to you. Helping your community will make you feel good, because it's the right thing to do.

Your philanthropy may also bring positive publicity, because you can choose to promote the giving that you do. For this reason, marketing experts sometimes lump philanthropy with promotion. We prefer to treat it as a separate topic, to emphasize how important philanthropy is to a successful and fulfilling life.

One way to work philanthropy into your business is **cause-related marketing**. This is marketing inspired by a commitment to a social, environmental, or political cause. A business can donate a fixed percentage of its revenue to a particular charity and then publicize this in its marketing.

Another way to help is to donate something your business produces. If you run a sporting goods store, for example, you could donate uniforms to the local Little League baseball team.

These days, customers have access to a lot of information about what companies do with their money. Choose to support causes that are important to you and make sense for your business. Make sure you can always be proud of your choices. Philanthropy will strengthen your relationship with your customers because it goes beyond the sale and into what's important in their lives.

## *SKILLS MEAN SUCCESS*

### ENGLISH ▶ Persuasive Strategies

*Persuasive strategies* are techniques used in writing and speaking to convince readers and listeners to take a certain action or adopt a certain attitude. Imagine that you plan to write a letter or give a speech to convince others to donate money to a charity of your choice. Choose three of the following strategies, and give an example of how you could be persuasive in each.

- Appeal to the audience's emotions.
- Emphasize the benefits to the audience.
- Address audience's potential concerns and counter-arguments.
- Give testimonials from others.
- Provide descriptions and details.
- Present illustrations and graphics.
- State evidence, facts, and examples.
- Share anecdotes and stories. ■■■

# Chapter 10 Review

## CRITICAL THINKING ABOUT...

### FINDING YOUR MARKET

1. Who is in your market?

2. Make a list of the groups below that you think are in your market and describe each in a few sentences.

   - Friends
   - Classmates
   - Relatives
   - Young children
   - Adult women
   - Adult men
   - Elderly adults
   - Local people
   - Businesspeople
   - Other

## KEY CONCEPTS

1. What is the business you hope to start? What is the primary benefit you think will attract customers? In the mind of the potential customer, what need would be fulfilled by your product?

2. Describe "The Four P's" in detail as they apply to your business idea. **Business Plan Practice**

3. Fill out a marketing plan for your business. (See the Workbook for a form.) **Business Plan Practice**

## EXPLORATION

1. Create a logo for your business, either by drawing it on a piece of paper, or with computer software.

2. Create an advertising flyer for your business that includes its logo.

## REFERENCES

1 Adapted from *Principles of Marketing*, Ninth Edition, by Philip Kotler and Gary Armstrong (Prentice-Hall, 2001).
2 See Kotler and Armstrong, *Principles of Marketing.*
3 From *Have You Got What It Takes? How to Tell If You Should Start Your Own Business*, by Joseph Mancuso (Prentice-Hall, 1982).
4 Special thanks to Katerina Zacharia for this and other insights in this chapter, and for the Four P's.

## VOCABULARY

brand ■ business card ■ cause-related marketing ■ logo ■ marketing ■ market share ■ mind share ■ publicity

## Chapter Summary ✔✔✔

10.1 Marketing identifies and profitably meets customer needs.
   A. Current and potential future customers are a company's market.
   B. Marketing is meeting customer needs:
      1. Building the loyalty of current customers
      2. Attracting new — especially competitors' — customers.
   C. Think "customer benefit," not "product" or "product feature."
   D. Start with a marketing vision:
      1. Who are the customers?
      2. What benefits are they looking for?

10.2 Marketing establishes a brand.
   A. Brand is a name and image that distinguish one product from its competitors.
   B. Brand communicates competitive advantage.

C. Brand signals specific perceived benefits.

D. Marketers build brands and brand value.

    1. Business names establish "mind share."

    2. Logos are distinctive symbols that customers recognize.

    3. Reputation for quality makes customers feel good about a brand.

    4. Brands have "personalities" that customers respond to.

    5. Effective advertising reaches the right customers.

E. Businesses should represent their brands through high quality, ethical standards, clear product focus, positive advertising, and responsible behavior.

F. Mind share has to be matched with market share.

**10.3** Marketing Plans describe the Four P's: Product, Place, Price, and Promotion.

A. Marketing is also a plan to bring a product "to market" using the Four P's.

    1. Product, including packaging (or service) must meet a customer need.

    2. Place products where the right customers can find and buy them.

    3. Price must be affordable yet profitable and should reflect the brand's vision.

    4. Promotion consists of (paid-for) advertising and (free) publicity.

B. The effectiveness of advertising and publicity can be measured by:

    1. Asking customers informally

    2. Using surveys. ✔✔✔

# A Business for the Young Entrepreneur

## CHEEP BIRD FEEDERS, SHAWN BLAKELY, WICHITA, KANSAS

Shawn Blakely designs and builds decorative wooden bird feeders. He sells them wholesale to pet stores. A national chain of pet stores has contracted with him to sell his entire line. He carried samples of his feeders everywhere he went, so he could show them to potential customers. Shawn began his business as a 17-year-old student in an entrepreneurship course given by Young Entrepreneurs of Kansas. The demand for his feeders grew so fast that he started making them in his uncle's garage, a few blocks from his home.

Moving into his uncle's garage, though, brought Shawn into violation of local zoning laws. The laws prohibited manufacturing operations in residential areas. Because zoning laws change from town to town, however, Shawn was able to move his business to his grandfather's shed in the next county, where it was not illegal to build his bird feeders.

After placing his product line with the national chain, Shawn had to hire five people to help him fill orders. He used some of his money to buy and maintain snack-vending machines. These machines generated even more profits for this energetic young entrepreneur. ■

# MARKET RESEARCH

*Your most unhappy customers are your greatest
source of learning.*

— Bill Gates, *co-founder of Microsoft*

## KEY OBJECTIVES

**THIS CHAPTER WILL ENABLE YOU TO:**

- Describe the different types of market
  research.
- Develop an effective market survey for
  your company.
- Use market research to understand your
  customers' needs.
- Analyze your industry.

## Listen to the Consumer

Your *market* consists of the potential customers for your product or service. **Market
research** is how you find out who these customers are and what they need.

Through market research, business owners ask consumers questions and listen carefully to their answers. Market research helps entrepreneurs figure out how to market their products and services.

Think of market research as access to other people's thinking. President Woodrow
Wilson once stated proudly, "I not only use all the brains that I have, but all that I
can borrow."

You want to get into your customers' heads and find out what they really think about:

- your product or service
- your logo
- the name of your business
- your prices
- your location
- your promotional efforts

## Target Market Demographics

Find out everything you can about your target market. What do those people eat, drink, listen to, watch on TV? How much do they sleep? Where do they shop? What movies do they like? How much do they earn? How much do they spend?

Facts about groups of people are called **demographics**. Where can you find such information?

- **Internet research.** Search online for reports and statistics about the industry you wish to enter.

- **Magazine articles.** Whenever a major magazine does an article about an industry, the piece usually includes statistics about the size of the target market and its preferences.

- **Business library.** Most large cities have libraries specializing in business. Befriend the reference librarian! He or she can help you find almost anything.

## Types of Market Research

Market research can vary from a simple survey of your classmates that you can finish in one day to detailed **statistics** about a large population. You will also want to research your industry to answer questions like: How large is it? How fast is it growing? Who are the major competitors in the industry?

Some types of market research are:

1.  **Surveys** are sets of questions that you ask consumers — either in interviews or through written questionnaires. Market surveys should ask about:

    - Product use and frequency of purchase.

    - Places where consumers purchase the product (the competition). Ask why consumers like to purchase from these businesses.

    - Business name, logo, letterhead — everything that represents your business in the consumer's mind.

    Make sure your marketing surveys also gather general information about potential customers, such as their:

    - Interests and hobbies

    - Reading and television-watching habits

    - Educational backgrounds

    - Age

    - Annual income

    - Gender

2. **General research**. You can check libraries, city agencies, and other resources for information. If you want to start a sporting-goods shop, you will need to know how many other such stores are already in the area. It would also be helpful to learn which products are selling at the other stores, and what some of their problems are. With such information you can avoid making costly mistakes.

3. **Statistical research**. *Statistics* are facts collected, analyzed, and presented as numbers. An example might be: "Of the 30 students in my class, 40 percent are girls and 60 percent boys."

   Market-research companies are paid by other companies to gather demographic information. The federal government can also provide statistics on consumers in a given area from census data. These sources can provide statistics based on:

   - Age
   - Annual income
   - Ethnic or religious background
   - Gender
   - Geographic location (ZIP Code)
   - Interests
   - Occupation
   - Type of dwelling (house or apartment)

4. **Industry research**. If you want to start a record label, for example, you'll need to know how the record industry is doing. Is it growing? Are people buying more CDs this year, or fewer? Who are the major consumers of CDs? Which age group buys the most? What kind of music is selling?

   To answer such questions, start with the Internet.

   - Look for recent articles on trends in the industry and its major players by using Google or other Internet search engines.

   - Look on your competitors' Web sites to find their annual reports. These are likely to have valuable industry information.

   - Visit the Internet Public Library at http://www.ipl.org/div/subject/browse/bus82.00.00/

   Another source of industry research is interviews. Large (competitor) companies might be willing to arrange for a young entrepreneur to interview one of their executives about the industry and its trends. Don't hesitate to call and ask. If you get an interview, go in with a carefully thought-out list of questions.

   Additional sources of industry information include:

   - Local Small Business Administration (SBA) office
   - Local Chamber of Commerce

- Business schools at local colleges — their libraries and career centers can be great sources.

## SKILLS MEAN SUCCESS

**MATH** ▶ **Mathematical Reasoning and Operations: Using Statistics**

Imagine you are interested in opening a dog-care service, and you have gathered the following facts:

- In 2000, the U.S. Census Bureau estimated that there were 2.67 people per household.

- According to your city's public records, the population of your community is 80,000.

- The *2002 U.S. Pet Ownership & Demographics Sourcebook* estimates that the number of dog-owning households in a community = 0.361 multiplied by the total number of households.

- This Sourcebook also estimates that the number of dogs in a community = 0.578 multiplied by the total number of households — or 1.6 multiplied by the number of dog-owning households.

Determine

**1.** The number of dog-owning households in your community.

**2.** The number of dogs in your community. Round your answers off to the nearest whole number. ■■■

## Your Research Method Is Important

When you design surveys to interview potential customers in your market, bear in mind that *the method you use may affect the answers you get.*

Some people may be less honest when you interview them face to face. They might not want to hurt your feelings by telling you in person that they don't like your business name. Or perhaps they might feel embarrassed admitting to something they feel is a weakness — such as liking junk food.

If you think a direct interview might result in inaccurate answers, consider handing out surveys that people in your market can complete *anonymously* (without signing their names).

## Research Your Market Before You Open Your Business

Large corporations spend a great deal of money on market research before they introduce a product or service. Chrysler spent millions before producing the mini-van. It was worth it, because it was going to cost tens of millions to manufacture it.

You may be impatient to get your business started, but take a lesson from the big companies. Don't begin until you've researched your market thoroughly. Be open to criticism. It is not always pleasant to hear, but it is valuable. Criticism can help you fine-tune your business.

### SKILLS MEAN SUCCESS

**ENGLISH**

**Listening and Speaking for Social Interaction: Dealing with Criticism**

Criticism can be difficult to hear — particularly when it's about your business. Developing a healthy attitude toward criticism is an important skill for entrepreneurs.

- Don't take criticism personally. Remind yourself that the critic is commenting on the business, *not* trying to make you feel badly.

- Keep an open mind. Don't argue or act defensively.

- Use active listening techniques: Ask clarifying questions, and paraphrase the criticism (repeat it back to the critic in different wording) to be sure you have understood it correctly.

- Be open to advice. Ask the critic what the solution should be. He or she may have some good ideas as to how you could improve your product or service.

- Some of the most important lessons and information about your business can come from complaints and criticism. Stay calm and listen for helpful information.

Use the guidelines above to respond to the following criticism. Think of at least one thing you could do as a business owner to address each statement.

**1.** The package is too hard to open.

**2.** The cake doesn't taste fresh.

**3.** Your services are too expensive.

**4.** This store is very difficult to find. ■■■

## Do You Know Ten People Who Love Your Product? You May Have a Winner!

Not everbody has to like your product. What's important is that some people love it — a lot.

Not everybody likes rap, but Russell Simmons loved rap and, more importantly, he knew a lot of other people his age who loved it, too. Simmons started one of the first rap labels, Def Jam Records, and became a multimillionaire. Simmons has said that, if you personally know ten people who love your product, you could have a winner.

What if you conduct your market research and learn that you don't have a winner? Is your business dead? Think positively: This is an opportunity to come up with an even better idea.

## Make Market Research Ongoing

Market research is not something you only do once. Make it an ongoing part of your business. Just as your tastes and desires change as you learn about new ideas and products, so do those of your customers. By continuing to survey them as you operate your business, you will stay current with their needs and how they feel about your product.

## Who Is in Your Market Segment?

Chances are, your product will not be needed by every single consumer in the marketplace. You will need to figure out which segments to target before you conduct your market research.

A **market segment** is composed of consumers who have a similar response to a certain type of marketing. In the cosmetics industry, for instance, one segment responds positively to luxuriously packaged, expensive products. Another segment is most responsive to products that claim to make customers look younger. Another wants low prices. A company that recognizes these segments and chooses one or two to market to will be more successful than one that tries to sell cosmetics to every single woman in the country.

**Step One: What is your market?** Is it everyone in your school? Your friends? Family members? Neighbors? People online?

**Step Two: Which segment of your market should you target?** To figure this out, go back to your overall marketing vision. What is the chief *benefit* you want to show your customers? Which customers in your market would be most interested in this benefit? These are the customers in your market segment. Examples of market segments are:

| Product | Market Segment |
| --- | --- |
| *Hand-decorated T-shirts* | *Girls in my school aged 12 to 14* |
| *Office-cleaning service* | *Offices within walking distance of my home* |
| *Wooden birdcages* | *People within five miles of my home who own birds; also, can sell on the Internet* |

## SKILLS MEAN SUCCESS

**ENGLISH**

### Writing and Speaking for Social Interaction: Using Open-Ended Questions

Open-ended questions are those that cannot be answered with a simple *yes* or *no*. They allow respondents to think about and answer them in their own words. Open-ended questions can reveal what issues are most important to your customers.

When writing survey questions, or asking for feedback in conversations with customers, you can use open-ended questions to:

- Encourage the giving of more information and more detailed answers.
- Ask about complex issues.
- Allow respondents' personalities and feelings to show through in their answers.

Rewrite the following to make limited-answer questions into open-ended ones.

**1.** Do you think our packaging should be round, square, or rectangular?

**2.** Does the color of the packaging grab your attention?

**3.** Is the type on this box easy to read?

**4.** Do you enjoy living downtown?

**5.** Would you recommend this product to a friend?

**6.** Is this product better than our competitor's? ■■■

## Researching Your Market Segment

Once you have chosen your market segment, you can design a survey and begin market research. Collecting data from the people in your market segment can be fun, as well as financially rewarding. Here are a few questions you can adapt to your own product or service:

1. Would you buy this product/service?

2. How much would you be willing to pay for it?

3. Where would you buy it?

4. How would you improve it?

5. Who are my closest competitors?

6. Is my product/service worse or better than those of my competitors?

## Market Research Avoids Costly Mistakes

You can avoid costly mistakes by simply asking your customers what they want. Say you created a design and silkscreened it on five-dozen white T-shirts. After six weeks, you have only sold six. People tell you they would have bought shirts if:

- They came in red or blue.
- You had them in different sizes.
- You had them in different styles.
- The shirts had different designs.
- The price was lower.
- They had known you were selling the shirts at the weekend flea market (flyers would have helped here!).
- You had sold them at school during lunchtime.

With a little market research you could have determined your customers' needs and wishes regarding the Four P's before you made the shirts — and you could probably have sold many more.

 **BizTip: Always listen to the people who bought your product (or used your service) but did not like it. They have valuable feedback.**

# Chapter 11 Review

## CRITICAL THINKING ABOUT...

### MARKET RESEARCH

1. What is your target market? List three things you've found out about it.

2. Describe your market segment.

   - Choose five people from your market segment to research with a survey. Will you ask them questions face to face or give them a survey that they can complete anonymously? Why? What type of market research is this called? What are population statistics called?

   - Research your industry and display the results in a one-page report that includes pie charts and bar or line graphs. **Business Plan Practice**

3. Write ten questions for your market research survey. Ask the survey participants to respond to questions on a scale of one to four, or design your own range. Also ask five open-ended questions (questions that don't have a yes-or-no answer). **Business Plan Practice**

**Sample Survey Questions:**
(*1: not at all;  2: a little;  3: somewhat; 4: very much*)

1. Do you like the name of my business?

2. Would you buy my product?

3. Do you think my product's price is fair?

4. Do you prefer my product to that offered by my competitor?

**Sample Open-Ended Survey Questions**

1. How would you improve my business idea?

2. Where else would you go to buy my product?

3. What price do you think I should charge?

## KEY CONCEPTS

1. How can market research prevent expensive mistakes?

2. What four factors should market research include, and why?

   - What type of statistics do you want to collect as market research for your business? Explain.

   - What's the smartest thing you can do when a customer who bought your product or service says he or she did not like it?

## EXPLORATION

1. Have you found out who else offers your product/service in your area? Create a chart listing the names and:

   a. the prices they charge,

   b. the quality of the product or service (this could include customer complaints or features they really like),

   c. the quality of customer service.

2. Write a brief essay explaining why your product/service is going to outperform the competition.

**Example:**

My DJ service is going to outperform the competition because my DJs always arrive 20 minutes early, in order to have time to get set up. They are also going to have a wider selection of music than my competitors, including lots of hip-hop, which our customers want to hear.

**3.** Would you consider getting a job with one of your competitors? Do you think this would be ethical? Why or why not?

**VOCABULARY**

demographics ■ market research ■ market segment ■ statistics ■ survey

# Chapter Summary ✔✔✔

**11.1** Market research collects information about what customers do, want, and need.

   *A.* Existing statistics about people (demographics) can be researched:

     *1.* Online

     *2.* In the print media

     *3.* In business libraries.

   *B.* Additional data can be gathered through:

     *1.* Surveys: interviews and questionnaires

     *2.* General research

     *3.* Statistical research: market research firms and census data.

   *C.* The research method used affects the answers collected.

**11.2** Businesses need to conduct market surveys.

   *A.* Conduct market research before introducing new products or services.

   *B.* Find "ten people" who love the idea.

   *C.* Make market research ongoing.

   *D.* Market segments are responsive, similar groups in a larger market.

     *1.* Identify your market.

     *2.* Know the segments in that market.

     *3.* Target a segment.

   *E.* Ask the segment specific questions:

     *1.* Do customers want to purchase?

     *2.* At what price?

     *3.* Where and what do they currently purchase?

     *4.* How could it be improved?

     *5.* Who are the competitors?

     *6.* Could a new product offer advantages over the competition?

   *F.* Market research helps prevent mistakes.

     *1.* Ask customers before launching a product.

     *2.* Ask dissatisfied customers why they are. ✔✔✔

### CHAPTER 12

# KEEPING GOOD RECORDS

*The second half of a man's life is made up of nothing but the habits he has acquired during the first half.*

— Fyodor Dostoyevsky, *Russian novelist*

## KEY OBJECTIVES

THIS CHAPTER WILL ENABLE YOU TO:

- Develop the valuable habit of keeping good records.
- Use receipts and invoices correctly.
- Open a bank account.
- Create an accounting system for your business.
- Use your records to analyze and improve your business.
- Create financial statements from accounting records.

## Keep Daily Financial Records

In the 19th century, John D. Rockefeller founded Standard Oil and dominated the oil industry for 50 years. In the process, he became the richest man in the world. He reportedly kept track of every penny he spent from age 16 until his death in 1937, at 98.

Keeping accurate daily financial records is the most important habit an entrepreneur can develop. You will be more successful if you know exactly how much money is coming in and going out of your business — and why.[1]

## Three Reasons to Keep Good Records Every Day[2]

1.  Keeping good records will show you how to make your business more profitable.

    Perhaps you're making less money this month than last month. Did your expenses go up? Maybe you need to try lowering your costs. Did your sales drop? Maybe you're not spending enough on advertising. Use accurate record keeping to constantly improve your business.

2. Keep accurate records to create financial statements and ratios that will show your business is doing well. Keeping good records will *prove* that your business is profitable to potential investors. Remember, you will always need to maintain your

- Income Statement, and
- Balance Sheet

so that you will be up to date on your

- Return on Investment (ROI), and
- Return on Sales (ROS).

3. Keeping good records will prove that payments have been made.

Records help prevent arguments because they will show that you have paid a bill, or that a customer has paid you. Records also prove that you have paid your **taxes** (the percentage of your income due to the government). Sometimes the Internal Revenue Service, which is the federal agency that collects taxes, will visit a business and check its financial records in a process called an **audit**. If you have kept good records, you will have nothing to fear from an audit. (We will discuss taxes in more detail in Chapter 44.)

## The Banking Relationship

As soon as possible, get away from doing business in cash and switch to checks. Checks help you keep good records because they are a written proof of payment. Even though it may be some time before you will be needing "debt financing" for your business, it is never too early to start developing a good relationship with a bank. Start by opening a savings account, and open a checking account when you are ready.

When you have a bank account, you will have a safe place to store your money. People who do not have bank accounts have to carry their money with them or hide it. Both options are risky. Your money is safer in a bank, where it is insured by the Federal Deposit Insurance Corporation (FDIC) up to $100,000. Even if the bank goes out of business, your deposited money will be guaranteed by the government up to $100,000.

## Savings Accounts

When you put money in a savings account, not only is the money safe, but also the bank will pay you interest. It is a low rate of return compared to some other investments, but there is virtually no risk that you will lose your money. A savings account is a "low-risk, low-yield" investment.

Banks make their profit by taking the money of individual depositors and lending it. The banks receive a higher interest rate on the money they lend than on what they pay the depositors.

## Checking Accounts

Paying by check, not cash, is the professional way to do business. When you write a check, you are authorizing the bank to pay someone from your account.

When you pay someone by check, that person deposits the check in his or her bank account. That bank gives the check to your bank, which takes the money out of your account and gives it to the other bank in exchange for the check.

Once your bank has paid the check, it is "cancelled" and given back to you. Cancelled checks provide proof that you paid your bill.

Shop around before you decide where to keep your checking account. Different banks have different fees and requirements. With some accounts it is necessary to maintain a minimum balance. Others require a minimum balance for you to write checks for free — if your balance is lower than the minimum, the bank will charge you for each check you write. Choose the checking account that best suits your needs.

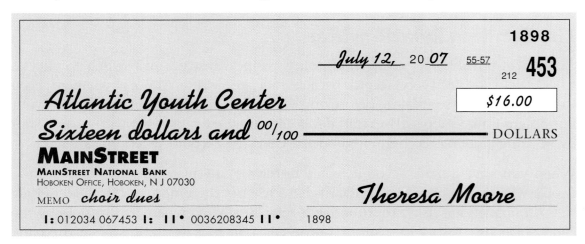

## Technology Tip: 24-Hour Banking and Online Banking

Banks use technology to make themselves available to customers 24 hours a day. You can use your ATM (Automatic Teller Machine) card anytime. Many banks issue "debit cards" that allow you to make purchases from your checking account without writing a check.

Online banking is also easy and convenient. Financial record-keeping software, such as Microsoft Money, lets you input information from your online bank statement directly into the financial records on your computer. You can also arrange to pay monthly bills online.

## A Basic Accounting System

An *accounting system* is a method of keeping track of money. These records help you understand and explain your business better.  The basic parts of your accounting system are:

- Your *business checking account* (including your checks, check register, and monthly bank statements).
- Your NFTE Journal.
- A *place to save your documents* where you can find them. Plastic "check files" with "month" dividers are used by banks. You can get one at an office supply store for about five dollars.
- **Receipts, Invoices, Purchase Orders, and Packing Slips**
    - *When you make a sale*, give the customer a **receipt** and keep a copy for yourself. Write down the date, customer's name, what was bought, and for how much. You can buy a "carbonless" receipt booklet for about two dollars.
    - *If the customer is going to pay later*, send an **invoice**. An invoice (or bill) has the same information a receipt does, except that the money hasn't been received yet. Once the customer pays the bill, the invoice is marked PAID. Your invoice becomes the customer's receipt. Keep a copy of each invoice, in numerical order, or organized by customer name.
    - *When you purchase supplies*, write out a **purchase order**, or PO. PO's record what you ordered, from whom, at what price, and who took the order. PO's are especially important if your order will be shipped to you. When the order comes in, always check the shipment against your purchase order to make sure you received everything in good condition. PO's will need to be dated and numbered. Give the supplier your PO number when you place the order.
    - *When you receive your purchase*, always find and keep the receipt or **packing slip**. If you have a problem with the order, or need to return it, you will use the receipt to prove that you bought it.

**BizTip:** You can make and print your own invoices, purchase orders, and other business documents with your company name and logo, on a computer.

## Save Receipts for Tax Time

U.S. tax law allows business owners to *deduct* certain expenses from their taxes. These **deductions** will save you money, but you must keep all receipts to prove you actually had the expenses. Write the purpose of the expense on the back of the receipt.

## Basic Accounting Principles

1. **Keep Up Your Records Daily.**

   **Keeping good records is simple, *as long as you do it every day.*** When you start skipping days, or trying to remember what your expenses were, maintaining your accounting system (the NFTE Journal) will become impossible.

2. **Support Your Records with Receipts and Invoices.**

   Sometimes you will be too busy to record a purchase or sale in your Journal immediately. If you always use your receipt/invoice book, you can use the copies at the end of the day to bring your records up to date.

3. **Use Business Checks for Business Expenses.**

   Get a checking account and use it only for your business.

   - **Avoid using cash for business.** When you pay with cash, there is often no record of your payment. If you must pay in cash, make sure to get an itemized receipt.

   - **Deposit money from sales right away.** When you make a sale, it will not be complete until the money is in the bank and, if the payment was made by check, until the check has "cleared." You can write the entry in your NFTE Journal when you make the deposit.

**Get Organized!** You can start your business with just a few simple organizing tools:
- File cabinet
- Calendar with day planner
- Accounting software (Quicken, Microsoft Money, etc.)
- Personal Digital Assistant (PDA)

**ENGLISH** ▶ **Writing:** Supporting Arguments with Details and Evidence

In the workplace, record keeping can be *manual* (written and filed on paper by hand) or *electronic* (completed with software and stored on a computer). Write a *persuasive* paragraph in which you argue that either manual or electronic record keeping is better for a small business owner. A persuasive paragraph:

- aims to convince a reader to agree with the writer's position.

- states the writer's position in the topic sentence.

- supports the writer's arguments with valid evidence and factual details and examples.

- concludes with the strongest points of the writer's case. ■ ■

## The NFTE Journal

The NFTE Journal will be the foundation of your accounting system. You will use it to record your income and expenses every day. The NFTE Journal is a set of 12 sheets, one for each month. If you need more than 30 lines over the course of a month, staple a second sheet behind the first one. The NFTE Journal also has an Income Statement (which will be discussed in more detail in the following chapter) and a *balance sheet* on each page. (We will talk in greater detail about the balance sheet in Chapter 35.)

The Journal will help you sort your income and expenses into categories. These will allow you to examine your business and create financial statements.

## The NFTE Journal Is "Cash Only"

The NFTE Journal is a "cash only" accounting system. The only time you will make a Journal entry is when you have paid out or received cash or checks.

## NFTE Journal — Left Side

Every time you pay for something, record it on the left side of the Journal, shown on page 161. Include the check number under "Ck. No." If using a debit card, note "D-Card" in the "Ck No." space. You should be able to transfer this information from your check register.

## NFTE Journal — Right Side

Each column on the right side of the Journal, shown on page 162, has a heading for a category of income or expense. For each entry on the left side of the Journal, make a *matching entry* on the right side. Find the column on the right that describes the entry you made on the left, and enter the same amount in the right-hand column. If you are unsure about an entry, ask your teacher.

## NFTE Journal — Categories

1.   INVESTMENT: Start-up investment plus any money you (or others) have invested in the business. This column is not for loans. This is only for money invested in exchange for part ownership (*equity*).

2.   REVENUE: Money you receive from sales. Whenever you record revenue, declare your COGS in the next column on the same line.

3.   COGS (Cost of Goods Sold): Multiply COGS by the number of units sold to get total COGS. When you receive revenue, write the total COGS in the COGS column. (COGS is not counted in the "balance" of the two sides of your Journal because it is not a "cash" transaction.)

4.   INVENTORY: The cost of goods bought to be resold, all costs of making a product (direct materials and direct labor), as well as the cost of inbound shipping to your place of storage. This includes anything in the sale you either bought or could have bought ahead of time to carry "on hand."

5.   VARIABLE COSTS (VC): Any cost that changes based on the number of units sold. Variable costs include things that cannot be bought ahead of time and carried "on hand" such as labor required to deliver a service, commissions, and the cost of outbound shipping to the customer.

6.   FIXED COSTS (FC): Business expenses that must be paid whether or not sales are made (USAIIRD).

7.   CAPITAL EQUIPMENT: Money spent on business equipment that you expect to last a year or more.

8.   OTHER COSTS: Anything that does not fit into the other expense categories. Include a brief explanation.

# NFTE Journal - 10 ©

Company: _____
Student Name: _____
Class / Section: _____
Teacher: _____

Month / Year: _____

(hint: Write the month and year large so it's easy to see.)

Cash is an **ASSET**

| Ck No. | DATE | TO / FROM | FOR - With Number Details | DEPOSIT $ IN | PAYMENT $ OUT | BALANCE FORWARD - |
|--------|------|-----------|---------------------------|--------------|---------------|-------------------|
| 1 | | | | | | 1 |
| 2 | | | | | | 2 |
| 3 | | | | | | 3 |
| 4 | | | | | | 4 |
| 5 | | | | | | 5 |
| 6 | | | | | | 6 |
| 7 | | | | | | 7 |
| 8 | | | | | | 8 |
| 9 | | | | | | 9 |
| 10 | | | | | | 10 |
| 11 | | | | | | 11 |
| 12 | | | | | | 12 |
| 13 | | | | | | 13 |
| 14 | | | | | | 14 |
| 15 | | | | | | 15 |
| 16 | | | | | | 16 |
| 17 | | | | | | 17 |
| 18 | | | | | | 18 |
| 19 | | | | | | 19 |
| 20 | | | | | | 20 |
| 21 | | | | | | 21 |
| 22 | | | | | | 22 |
| 23 | | | | | | 23 |
| 24 | | | | | | 24 |
| 25 | | | | | | 25 |
| 26 | | | | | | 26 |
| 27 | | | | | | 27 |
| 28 | | | | | | 28 |
| 29 | | | | | | 29 |
| 30 | | | | | | 30 |

1- If sales tax is collected in addition to selling price, it should be included in REVENUE. Sales tax will be calculated by multiplying REVENUE times the imputed sales tax rate for your State.

2- Only income taxes (on profit) are included on this line. Other taxes are included as business expenses.

3- Taxes owed, but not yet paid should be included in the total of Short-term Liabilities. When they are paid, Short-term Liabilities should be reduced by the amount paid.

4- Cost of Goods Sold (COGS) is the same as Cost of Services Sold (COSS) for a service business. Money spent on direct labor and materials (INVENTORY) is not a "cost" until it's sold, when it becomes COGS.

5- SALES is a synonym for (means the same thing as) REVENUE.

6- The dash symbol " - " stands for " 0 " (zero) in Accounting.

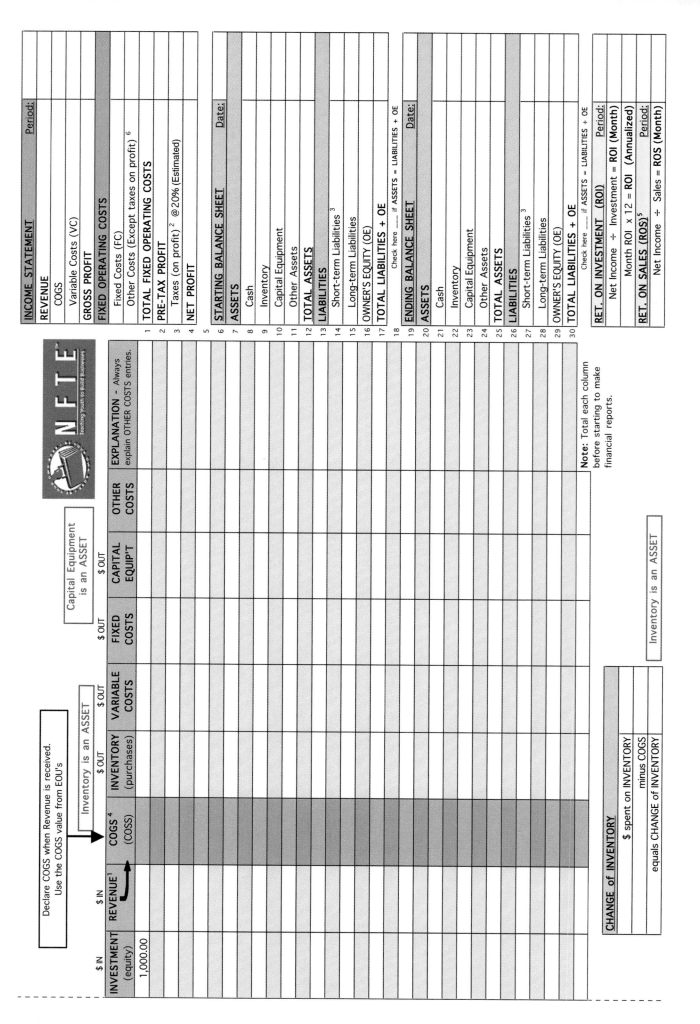

# NFTE
Teaching Youth to Build Businesses!

## INCOME STATEMENT — Period: _____

| | |
|---|---|
| **REVENUE** | |
| COGS | |
| Variable Costs (VC) | |
| **GROSS PROFIT** | |
| **FIXED OPERATING COSTS** | |
| Fixed Costs (FC) | |
| Other Costs (Except taxes on profit) [6] | |
| **TOTAL FIXED OPERATING COSTS** | 1 |
| **PRE-TAX PROFIT** | 2 |
| Taxes (on profit) [2] @ 20% (Estimated) | 3 |
| **NET PROFIT** | 4 |

## STARTING BALANCE SHEET — Date: _____

| | |
|---|---|
| 5 | |
| 6 | **ASSETS** |
| 7 | Cash |
| 8 | Inventory |
| 9 | Capital Equipment |
| 10 | Other Assets |
| 11 | **TOTAL ASSETS** |
| 12 | |
| 13 | **LIABILITIES** |
| 14 | Short-term Liabilities [3] |
| 15 | Long-term Liabilities |
| 16 | OWNER'S EQUITY (OE) |
| 17 | **TOTAL LIABILITIES + OE** |
| 18 | Check here _____ if ASSETS = LIABILITIES + OE |

## ENDING BALANCE SHEET — Date: _____

| | |
|---|---|
| 19 | |
| 20 | **ASSETS** |
| 21 | Cash |
| 22 | Inventory |
| 23 | Capital Equipment |
| 24 | Other Assets |
| 25 | **TOTAL ASSETS** |
| 26 | **LIABILITIES** |
| 27 | Short-term Liabilities [3] |
| 28 | Long-term Liabilities |
| 29 | OWNER'S EQUITY (OE) |
| 30 | **TOTAL LIABILITIES + OE** |
| | Check here _____ if ASSETS = LIABILITIES + OE |

## RET. ON INVESTMENT (ROI) — Period: _____
Net Income ÷ Investment = **ROI (Month)**
Month ROI x 12 = **ROI (Annualized)**

## RET. ON SALES (ROS) [5] — Period: _____
Net Income ÷ Sales = **ROS (Month)**

---

Declare COGS when Revenue is received.
Use the COGS value from EOU's

Inventory is an ASSET

Capital Equipment is an ASSET

| $ IN | INVESTMENT (equity) | REVENUE [1] | COGS [4] (COSS) | INVENTORY (purchases) $ OUT | VARIABLE COSTS $ OUT | FIXED COSTS $ OUT | CAPITAL EQUIP'T $ OUT | OTHER COSTS | EXPLANATION - Always explain OTHER COSTS entries. |
|---|---|---|---|---|---|---|---|---|---|
| | 1,000.00 | | | | | | | | |
| | | | | | | | | | |
| | | | | | | | | | |
| | | | | | | | | | |
| | | | | | | | | | |
| | | | | | | | | | |
| | | | | | | | | | |
| | | | | | | | | | |
| | | | | | | | | | |
| | | | | | | | | | |
| | | | | | | | | | |

**Note:** Total each column before starting to make financial reports.

## CHANGE of INVENTORY

| | |
|---|---|
| $ spent on INVENTORY | |
| minus COGS | |
| equals CHANGE of INVENTORY | |

Inventory is an ASSET

# Using the NFTE Journal (example shown on pages 164 and 165)

- Enter only one **transaction** (payment or deposit) per line.

- Use pencil, so you can erase mistakes. Mechanical pencils are best because they make very thin lines, allowing you to write more in a small space.

- Left- and right-hand entries must match and be on the same line. *The only exception is COGS, which is entered with Revenue on the right side.*

- Describe each transaction. Details like "how many" and "at what price" can be helpful later.

- Figure the "new balance" on the left side. This will tell you how much cash you actually have.

- Take the time to write neatly.

## Sample NFTE Journal

Hernando is starting a business making custom-printed T-shirts and hoodies. His transactions for October 2003 are described below, followed by an example showing how they should be recorded in the NFTE Journal. As you read about the entries, try to find them in the Journal on pages 164 and 165.

**October 1**

1. Hernando invests $1,000.00 of his own money to start his business. On 10/1, he opens his business bank account with a $1,000.00 deposit.

**October 2**

2. Hernando buys a silk-screen printing frame and some equipment for $200.00 from ACME Printing Supply Co. Hernando pays with check number 100.

3. He buys silkscreen inks and supplies from ACE ARTS. He gets enough to make about 100 T-shirts, and pays $100.00 with check number 101.

4. He buys two dozen blank T-shirts from Big Bob's Wholesale. He pays $36.00 per dozen. This means he's paying $3.00 per shirt ($36.00/12). Two dozen shirts cost $72.00. The check number is 102.

**October 5**

5. Hernando pays his friend José Rivera $2.00 each to print two dozen T-shirts. His check number 103 to José is for $48.00 (24 shirts × $2.00 each).

**October 6**

6. Hernando pays the monthly $100 registration fee so he can sell at the Grand Flea Market. Hernando pays with check number 104.

7. Hernando stops in at the Corner Print Shop and buys 500 business cards for $20.00. (Can you figure out what the check number is?)

# NFTE Journal - 10 ©

Company: **Hernando's T-shirts**
Student Name: **Hernando LaHideaway**
Class / Section: **NFTE Entrepreneurship 101**
Teacher: **Mr. Mariotti**

Month / Year: **October, 2003**

(hint: Write the month and year large so it's easy to see.)

Cash is an ASSET

| Ck No. | DATE | TO / FROM | FOR - With Number Details | $ IN DEPOSIT | $ OUT PAYMENT | BALANCE FORWARD – |
|---|---|---|---|---|---|---|
| deposit | 10/1/03 | Hernando | Start-up investment in the business. (Since the account is new, there is no balance to carry forward) | 1,000.00 | | 1,000.00 |
| 100 | 10/2/03 | ACME Printing Supply | Start-up; Silk Screen equipment | | 200.00 | 800.00 |
| 101 | 10/2/03 | ACE ARTS | Start-up; Silk Screen Ink and Supplies - Enough to make 100 printed T-shirts | | 100.00 | 700.00 |
| 102 | 10/2/03 | Big Bob's Wholesale | Buy 2 Dozen blank T-shirts @ $36.00 / doz. ($3.00 each) | | 72.00 | 628.00 |
| 103 | 10/5/03 | Jose Rivera | Pay to have T-shirts printed; Pay Jose $2.00 each for 24 shirts = $48.00 | | 48.00 | 580.00 |
| 104 | 10/6/03 | Grand Flea Market | Monthly Registration Fee | | 100.00 | 480.00 |
| 105 | 10/6/03 | Corner Print Shop | Business Cards, for 500 cards | | 20.00 | 460.00 |
| 106 | 10/8/03 | Corner Print Shop | Flyers | | 10.00 | 450.00 |
| deposit | 10/9/03 | Deposit Checks from Flea Market | Deposit money from sales of 2 Dozen T-shirts @ $12.00 each (COGS of $6.00 each) | 288.00 | | 738.00 |
| 107 | 10/10/03 | Big Bob's Wholesale | Buy 5 Dozen blank T-shirts (60 T-shirts) $36.00 / doz. ($3.00 each) | | 180.00 | 558.00 |
| 108 | 10/12/03 | Jose Rivera | Pay to have T-shirts printed; Pay Jose $2.00 each for 60 shirts = $120.00 | | 120.00 | 438.00 |
| deposit | 10/14/03 | Deposit Checks from Flea Market | Dep.$ from sales- 5 dozen. Shirts sold; 4 dz. @ $12.00 ea., 1 dz. @ $10.00 ea. (COGS of $6.00 each) | 696.00 | | 1,134.00 |
| 109 | 10/16/03 | Big Bob's Wholesale | Buy 5 Dozen blank T-shirts (60 T-shirts) @ $36.00 / doz. ($3.00 each) | | 180.00 | 954.00 |
| 110 | 10/16/03 | ACE ARTS | More silk screen ink and supplies - Enough to make 150 printed T-shirts | | 150.00 | 804.00 |
| 111 | 10/18/03 | Jose Rivera | Pay to have T-shirts printed; Pay Jose $2.00 each for 60 shirts = $120.00 | | 120.00 | 684.00 |
| 112 | 10/19/03 | Corner Print Shop | More Flyers | | 10.00 | 674.00 |
| deposit | 10/21/03 | Deposit Checks from Flea Market | Deposit money from sales; Only 3 doz. @ 12.00 ea. (it rained) (COGS of $6.00 each) | 432.00 | | 1,106.00 |
| 113 | 10/25/03 | Big Bob's Wholesale | Buy 7 Dozen blank T-shirts (84 T-shirts) @ $36.00 / doz. ($3.00 each) | | 252.00 | 854.00 |
| 114 | 10/26/03 | Jose Rivera | Pay to have T-shirts printed; Pay Jose $2.00 each for 7 doz. (84) shirts = $168.00 | | 168.00 | 686.00 |
| deposit | 10/28/03 | Deposit Checks from Giselle's Sales | Deposit money from Sales - 8 doz. @ 12.00 ea. (COGS of $6.00 each) | 1,152.00 | | 1,838.00 |
| 115 | 10/30/03 | Giselle Rivera | Commission @ 25% of Sales; $1,152.00 x 25% = $288.00 | | 288.00 | 1,550.00 |

1- If sales tax is collected in addition to selling price, it should be included in REVENUE. Sales tax will be calculated by multiplying REVENUE times the imputed sales tax rate for your State.

2- Only income taxes (on profit) are included on this line. Other taxes are included as business expenses.

3- Taxes owed, but not yet paid should be included in the total of Short-term Liabilities. When they are paid, Short-term Liabilities should be reduced by the amount paid.

4- Cost of Goods Sold (COGS) is the same as Cost of Services Sold (COSS) for a service business. Money spent on direct labor and materials (INVENTORY) is not a "cost" until it's sold, when it becomes COGS.

5- SALES is a synonym for (means the same thing as) REVENUE.

6- The dash symbol " – " stands for " 0 " (zero) in Accounting.

## INCOME STATEMENT — Period: Oct. 2003

| | |
|---|---|
| **REVENUE** | **2,568.00** |
| COGS | 1,296.00 |
| Variable Costs (VC) | 288.00 |
| **GROSS PROFIT** | **984.00** |
| **FIXED OPERATING COSTS** | |
| Fixed Costs (FC) | 140.00 |
| Other Costs (Except taxes on profit)[6] | 0.00 |
| 1  TOTAL FIXED OPERATING COSTS | 140.00 |
| 2  PRE-TAX PROFIT | 844.00 |
| 3  Taxes (on profit)[2] @ 20% (Estimated) | 168.80 |
| 4  NET PROFIT | 675.20 |
| 5 | |
| 6  **STARTING BALANCE SHEET**  Date: | 10/1/03 |
| 7  ASSETS | |
| 8  Cash | - |
| 9  Inventory | - |
| 10  Capital Equipment | - |
| 11  Other Assets | - |
| 12  TOTAL ASSETS | - |
| 13  LIABILITIES | |
| 14  Short-term Liabilities[3] | - |
| 15  Long-term Liabilities | - |
| 16  OWNER'S EQUITY (OE) | - |
| 17  TOTAL LIABILITIES + OE | - |
| 18  Check here ___ if ASSETS = LIABILITIES + OE | |
| 19  **ENDING BALANCE SHEET**  Date: | 10/31/03 |
| 20  ASSETS | |
| 21  Cash | 1,550.00 |
| 22  Inventory | 94.00 |
| 23  Capital Equipment | 200.00 |
| 24  Other Assets | - |
| 25  TOTAL ASSETS | 1,844.00 |
| 26  LIABILITIES | |
| 27  Short-term Liabilities[3] | 168.80 |
| 28  Long-term Liabilities | - |
| 29  OWNER'S EQUITY (OE) | 1,675.20 |
| 30  TOTAL LIABILITIES + OE | 1,844.00 |
| Check here ___ if ASSETS = LIABILITIES + OE | |

| RET. ON INVESTMENT (ROI) | Period: Oct. 2003 |
|---|---|
| Net Income ÷ Investment = ROI (Month) | 68% |
| Month ROI x 12 = ROI (Annualized) | 810% |
| **RET. ON SALES (ROS)[5]** | Period: Oct. 2003 |
| Net Income ÷ Sales = ROS (Month) | 26% |

---

Declare COGS when Revenue is received.
Use the COGS value from EOU's

Inventory is an ASSET  ($ IN / $ OUT)

Capital Equipment is an ASSET  ($ OUT)

EXPLANATION - Always explain OTHER COSTS entries.

| INVESTMENT (equity) $IN | REVENUE[1] $IN | COGS[4] (COSS) | INVENTORY (purchases) $OUT | VARIABLE COSTS $OUT | FIXED COSTS | CAPITAL EQUIP'T $OUT | OTHER COSTS $OUT | EXPLANATION |
|---|---|---|---|---|---|---|---|---|
| 1,000.00 | | | | | | | | |
| | | | 100.00 | | | | | |
| | | | 72.00 | | | 200.00 | | |
| | | | 48.00 | | | | | |
| | 288.00 | 144.00 | | | 100.00 | | | |
| | | | 180.00 | | 20.00 | | | |
| | | | 120.00 | | 10.00 | | | |
| | 696.00 | 360.00 | 180.00 | | | | | |
| | | | 150.00 | | | | | |
| | | | 120.00 | | 10.00 | | | |
| | 432.00 | 216.00 | | | | | | |
| | | | 252.00 | | | | | |
| | 1,152.00 | 576.00 | 168.00 | 288.00 | | | | |
| **1,000.00** | **2,568.00** | **1,296.00** | **1,390.00** | **288.00** | **140.00** | **200.00** | **0.00** | |

**CHANGE of INVENTORY**

| | |
|---|---|
| $ spent on INVENTORY | 1,390.00 |
| minus COGS | 1,296.00 |
| equals CHANGE of INVENTORY | 94.00 |

Inventory is an ASSET

**Note:** Total each column before starting to make financial reports.

**October 8**

8. Hernando makes flyers at the Corner Print Shop for $10.00.

**October 9**

9. Hernando sells all 24 T-shirts at $12.00 each at the Grand Flea Market. He deposits $288.00 in his bank account. At the same time he "declares" his COGS on the same line as Revenue. His COGS is $6.00 per shirt × 24 shirts = $144.00 ($3 per blank shirt, $2 each printing, $1 each ink).

**October 10**

10. Hernando buys five dozen more T-shirts from Big Bob's Wholesale. They still cost $36.00/dozen ($3.00 each). How much do the five dozen shirts cost all together?

**October 12**

11. Hernando pays José to print the five dozen shirts and pays him $120.00 ($2.00 each).

**October 14**

12. Hernando deposits $696.00 from the flea market sales in the bank. He sold four dozen T-shirts at $12.00 each, and one dozen for $10.00 each. At the same time he declares his COGS, and records that on the same line. COGS is still $6.00 per shirt. He sold 60 units so his COGS is 60 × $6.00 = $360 COGS.

**October 16**

13. Hernando buys five dozen more T-shirts from Big Bob's, at $36.00 per dozen.

**October 8** 

14. Hernando is running out of ink, so he buys enough to print another 150 shirts from ACE ARTS. The ink costs $150.00.

**October 18**

15. Hernando pays José $120.00 for printing the next order of 60 T-shirts.

**October 19**

16. Hernando pays $10.00 for more flyers from the Corner Print Shop.

**October 21**

17. Hernando deposits $432.00 from sales at the Grand Flea Market into the business bank account. Because it rained, he only sold three-dozen T-shirts at $12.00 each (COGS = $36 × 6 = $216).

**October 25**

18. Hernando buys seven dozen T-shirts from Big Bob's Wholesale for $252.00.

**October 26**

19. Hernando pays José $168.00 for printing the seven dozen shirts.

**October 28**

20. Hernando deposits $1,152.00 from sales made by Giselle Rivera, José's little sister. She sold eight dozen T-shirts at $12.00 each the previous week. Total COGS is $576.00 (96 units × $6.00).

**October 30**

21. Hernando pays Giselle Rivera a sales commission of 25%. He writes her a check for $288.00 (.25 × $1,152.00 = $288.00).

## SKILLS MEAN SUCCESS

**LEADERSHIP** ▶ **Presentation Skills**

Working with several classmates, deliver a ten-minute presentation on the effects poor record keeping could have on a business.

- Research the topic and plan your presentation in advance, outlining your main ideas and examples on note cards.

- On each card write down one idea with at least one example, statistic, story, or expert you can cite to support your point.

- Practice your presentation until you have a thorough knowledge of the subject and feel relaxed and confident.

- Use PowerPoint.

- Speak clearly and simply. Don't try to impress your audience with complicated ideas or big words.

- Make eye contact with your audience; speak loudly enough for everyone to hear; and remember to smile. ■■■

## Creating Financial Statements

To create financial statements, simply carry numbers over from the Journal to the blank financial statements on the far right side, as explained below.

Financial statements in the U.S. are prepared according to the Generally Accepted Accounting Principles (GAAP), which are standards set by accounting policy boards that companies voluntarily agree to follow. Be very wary of any financial statements that are not prepared according to GAAP standards.

**Monthly Income Statement:**

1. Put total from REVENUE column on the line marked REVENUE on your Income Statement.

2. Put total from COGS column on the line marked COGS.

3. Put total VARIABLE COSTS on the VC line.

4. Figure GROSS PROFIT by subtracting COGS plus variable costs from REVENUE.

5. Put total FIXED COSTS on the FC line.

6. Put total OTHER COSTS on the OTHER line.

7. Figure Pre-tax PROFIT. Subtract FC and OTHER COSTS from GROSS PROFIT.

**167**

8. Multiply Pre-tax PROFIT by the tax rate (use 20% estimated tax rate). Put it on the TAXES line.

9. Subtract TAXES from Pre-tax PROFIT to get NET PROFIT.

**Monthly Ending Balance Sheet:**  Note: Your Starting Balance Sheet for this month is your Ending Balance Sheet for the previous month.

1. Put current cash balance on the CASH line.

2. Figure how much Inventory you added this month.  Subtract Total COGS from INVENTORY column. Add that to the INVENTORY number from the Starting Balance Sheet for this month to get INVENTORY for the Ending Balance Sheet.

3. Add the CAPITAL EQUIPMENT total to "Capital Equipment" from your Starting Balance Sheet. This will be the Ending for "Capital Equipment."

4. *(Off the Journal...)* If you have "Other Assets," add them to the "Other Assets" number from the Starting Balance Sheet. This will be the Ending for "Other Assets."

5. *(Off the Journal...)* If you have "Short-term Liabilities" at the end of the month, add them to the "Short-term Liabilities" you still owe from the previous month.  Short-term Liabilities are debts you plan to pay in less than a year. Include taxes you owe on this month's profits in "Short-term Liabilities."

6. *(Off the Journal...)* If you have  "Long-term Liabilities" at the end of the month, add them to the "Long-term Liabilities" you owe from the previous month.

7. Calculate Ending OWNER'S EQUITY: Add NET PROFIT from the Income Statement *and* the total of this month's INVESTMENT column *and* the OWNER'S EQUITY number of your Starting Balance Sheet.

8. Add up ASSETS, then LIABILITIES + OWNER'S EQUITY. ASSETS must equal LIABILITIES + OWNER'S EQUITY. If so, your balance sheet "balances" and you are done. If not, you made a mistake somewhere.

Use the NFTE Financial Statements Quick Reference at the end of this chapter to help complete the balance sheet.

# ROI (Return on Investment)

ROI tells you the rate of return on your capital investment in your business. You can calculate it from your Income Statement in the NFTE Journal.

$$\frac{\text{Net Profit}}{\text{Investment}} \ = \ \text{ROI}$$

ROI is normally expressed as an "annual" (yearly) figure. If you used monthly information to calculate it, you can convert to annual ROI by multiplying by 12.

**Monthly ROI% × 12 = Annual ROI%**

ROI is normally expressed as a percentage, not a decimal. See Chapter 3 for information about converting decimals to percentages.

## SKILLS MEAN SUCCESS

**MATH**    **Performing Operations Using Formulas**

In your sewing and alterations business, your financial records for *one month* show the following:

- Investment    $500
- Net Profit     $750

**1.** Determine your monthly ROI%.

**2.** Determine your annual ROI%.

**BizTip:** Always keep a copy of your financial records somewhere other than at your business. If you are using software, back up your data and keep the disc in a different place. At the end of each month, move your new receipts and invoices to this location. If anything happens to your Journal or your business site, you will still have your financial records.

## CRITICAL THINKING ABOUT...

### KEEPING GOOD RECORDS

1. Use the transactions given to you by your teacher to complete your NFTE Journal.

2. Use the entries to create an income statement for the business by writing down all your sales and subtracting all your costs. (In the next chapter, we will learn more about how to do an income statement.)

3. Use the entries to create an ending balance sheet for the business.

4. Using the Journal you created, calculate the return on sales (ROS).

5. Using the Journal information, calculate the business's monthly and annual ROI.

## KEY CONCEPTS

1. What bank accounts do you intend to set up? What bank will you be using? **Business Plan Practice**

2. Are banks required by law to offer all consumers the same rates and balance requirements? Explain.

3. Describe three reasons why it makes more sense to use checks instead of cash when running a business.

4. Describe the record-keeping system you intend to set up for your business. **Business Plan Practice**

## IN YOUR OPINION

*Discuss with a partner:*

Why do you think John D. Rockefeller kept track of every penny he spent? Do you think that was wise? Do you think it was possible? Write a brief essay and present your opinions to the class.

## EXPLORATION

Visit three banks in your neighborhood and collect information about the checking and savings accounts they offer. Write a memo explaining which bank you are going to choose for your accounts.

## REFERENCES

1 A good source on this subject is *Introduction to Financial Accounting*, Sixth Edition, by Charles T. Horngren, Gary L. Sundem, and John A. Elliott (Prentice-Hall, 1996).
2 Special thanks to John Harris for his many ideas for this chapter.

## VOCABULARY

audit ■ deduction ■ invoice ■ packing slip ■ purchase order ■ receipt ■ taxes ■ transaction

# Chapter Summary ✔✔✔

**12.1** Entrepreneurs need to keep accurate business records:
   A. To help make their businesses more profitable
   B. To prove that their businesses are profitable
   C. To prove that payments have been made:
      1. By customers
      2. To suppliers
      3. To the government for taxes.

**12.2** Entrepreneurs need bank services.
   A. Switch from using cash to a checking account:
      1. Safer from theft than cash
      2. Provides paper or electronic record
      3. More professional to pay by check
      4. Shop for the best type of account.
   B. Open a savings account:
      1. Low risk, insured by FDIC
      2. Safe investment that earns interest.
   C. Use ATMs and online banking technology.
   D. Develop a relationship with a bank.

**12.3** An accounting system keeps track of money in a business:
   A. Business checking account
   B. The NFTE Journal
   C. Check and document files
   D. Receipts (proofs of sale), invoices (bills), purchase orders (or PO's; records of orders placed), packing slips (proof of shipment)
   E. Keep receipts from purchases for tax records.

**12.4** Follow accounting principles.
   A. Update records daily.
   B. Support records with receipts and invoices.
   C. Use business checks for business:
      1. Avoid using cash
      2. Deposit receipts from sales immediately.

**12.5** Use the NFTE Journal to record and report income and expenses.
   A. Left side records payments made for expenses.
   B. Right side records income and matching entry expenses:
      1. Investment
      2. Revenue
      3. COGS
      4. Inventory
      5. Variable Costs

6. Fixed Costs
7. Capital Equipment
8. Other (Costs).
C. Enter one transaction per line.
 1. Match left- and right-hand entries, except COGS, which is entered in addition to REVENUE.
 2. Describe each transaction: how many, at what price.
 3. Update balance on left side after every transaction.
 4. Reconcile once per month; put adjustments in Other.
D. Use the Journal to create GAAP-based financial statements:
 1. Monthly Income Statement, including ROI (for month and full year)
 2. Monthly Ending Balance Sheet. ✔✔✔

## INCOME STATEMENT

- **REVENUE** = Total of the REVENUE column this month
- **COGS** = Total of the COGS column this month
- **VARIABLE COSTS (VC)** = Total of the VARIABLE COSTS (VC) column this month
- **GROSS PROFIT** = REVENUE − COGS − VC
- **FIXED COSTS (FC)** = Total of the FIXED COSTS (FC) column this month
- **OTHER COSTS** = Total of the OTHER COSTS column this month (Note that only costs in the "OTHER COSTS" column can be counted)
- **Pre-tax PROFIT** = GROSS PROFIT − FC − OTHER COSTS
- **TAXES** = Pre-tax PROFIT × Tax Rate (estimated 20%)
- **NET PROFIT** = Pre-tax PROFIT − TAXES

## ENDING BALANCE SHEET

Note: "Starting" refers to the "Starting Balance Sheet" numbers. "Ending" refers to the "Ending Balance Sheet" numbers

### ASSETS
- **Ending Cash** = The cash balance at the end of the month
- **Inventory** = Total of the INVENTORY column − total of COGS column + Starting Inventory
- **Capital Equipment** = Total of the CAPITAL EQUIPMENT column this month + Starting Capital Equipment
- **Other Assets** = Starting Other Assets − assets not on the journal sold + assets not on the journal acquired
- **TOTAL ASSETS** = Sum of all assets, above on balance sheet

## LIABILITIES

- **Short-term Liabilities** = Starting Short-term Liabilities − Short-term Liabilities paid off + new Short-term Liabilities (include Taxes owed on NET PROFIT each month as a new Short-term Liability)
- **Long-term Liabilities** = Starting Long-term Liabilities − Long-term Liabilities paid off + new Long-term Liabilities
- **Owner's Equity (OE)** = Net Profit + Investment + Starting balance sheet OE
- **TOTAL LIABILITIES + OWNER'S EQUITY (OE)** = Sum of all Liabilities (ST and LT) and OE, above on balance sheet

**Note:** TOTAL ASSETS must equal TOTAL LIABILITIES + OE

# A Business for the Young Entrepreneur
## PARTY DJ

If you're the kind of person who keeps up with the latest musical trends, you could make a great party DJ. This is a more expensive business to start than some — unless you already own one or two turntables and lots of records.

Some DJs join or form record pools. These are clubs that let the DJs rotate or share records, so they will always have new ones to play. Ask at your local record store about DJ clubs. DJs also get records through the mailing lists of recording labels. Do you know any local labels trying to get attention for their artists? Call and ask about getting free records in return for exposing the artist to a wider audience by playing the records at your parties.

### WHAT YOU'LL NEED TO GET STARTED

- One or two turntables — if you use two turntables, you'll also need a "mixer."
- Speakers and amplifier.
- Records.
- Flyers — advertise your service by handing out flyers at parties and school events.
- Headphones.

Pretend you are starting a business as a party DJ. Make a list of every item you would need to buy, and do some research to find out how much each will cost. ■

# INCOME STATEMENTS:
## *The Entrepreneur's Scorecard*

*You are equal to anyone, but if you think you're not, you're not.*

— Jake Simmons, Jr., *founder of the world's most successful African-American-owned oil business*

THIS CHAPTER WILL ENABLE YOU TO:

- Understand the elements of an income statement.
- Calculate net profit or loss.
- Prepare a monthly income statement.

**A**n entrepreneur uses a monthly **income statement** to track the business's sales and costs.

- *If sales are greater than costs, the income statement balance will show a net profit.*

- *If sales are less than costs, it will show a negative number, which means a net loss.*

The income statement helps the entrepreneur steer the business. If the company is not making a profit, the entrepreneur can examine the income statement to try to figure out why.

If the business is making a profit, the entrepreneur can examine the income statement to see what he or she is doing right! Profit is the reward for using limited ("scarce") resources efficiently to satisfy a consumer need. The power of the income statement is that it tells you whether you are succeeding in meeting customer needs, creating value, and keeping good records.

## The Income Statement Is the Scorecard

The income statement is the "scorecard" of the business. If your venture is successful, the profit you show on your income statements will prove it. Companies typically create income statements to see how they are doing:

- Once a month
- Every three months (quarterly)
- Each year (annually)

You should prepare an income statement at least once a month. Once you have been in business for 12 months, you can create an annual income statement that will show your yearly net profit.

### SKILLS MEAN SUCCESS

**ENGLISH**    **Reading and Writing for Understanding: Idioms**

An *idiom* is a colorful phrase that is used informally. Idioms may not always make sense to people who haven't heard them before. Many idioms are used in business and workplace communication. A business "in the red," for example, is losing money. This idiom comes from the use of red ink to show losses on financial reports. A profitable company, in contrast, is "in the black."

1. Identify the color-based idioms in the following sentences and rewrite them *without* using the idioms. Be sure to express the same meaning.

   **a.** The manager gave the project the green light.

   **b.** The computer just crashed out of the blue.

   **c.** All this red tape is slowing down my work.

   **d.** He was our biggest client so we rolled out the red carpet.

   **e.** The customer was tickled pink with our new product.

   **f.** He passed the training course with flying colors.

2. When is it appropriate to use idioms? When is it *not* appropriate to use them? ■■■

## The Eight Parts of an Income Statement

The income statement is composed of the following parts:

1. **Revenue:** money received from sales of the company's product or service.

2. **COGS (Cost of Goods Sold)/COSS (Cost of Services Sold):** These are the costs of the materials used to make the product (or deliver the service) plus the costs of labor used to make the product (or deliver the service). A monthly income statement reports total COGS for a month. Multiply the COGS from the EOU by the number of units sold during the month.

 **BizTip:** *Never disclose your cost of goods sold.* You will want to keep secret how much you are paying for your product so you can make a profit.

3. **Other Variable Costs:** Costs that vary with sales, such as commissions and shipping.

4. **Gross Profit:** To calculate gross profit, subtract COGS and other variable costs from revenue.

5. **Fixed Costs:** The costs of operating a business that do not vary with sales. The most common fixed costs are Utilities, Salaries, Advertising, Insurance, Interest, Rent, and Depreciation (USAIIRD).

6. **Pre-Tax Profit:** Gross profit minus fixed costs. This is a business's profit after all costs have been deducted, but before taxes have been paid. **Pre-tax profit** is used to calculate how much tax the business owes.

7. **Taxes:** A business must pay taxes on the income it earns.

8. **Net Profit/(Loss):** **Net profit** is the business's profit or loss after taxes have been paid.

## INCOME STATEMENT

**Name of Company:** _____   **Time Period:** _____

**Sales/Revenue:**     $ _____

   **Variable Costs**

      Cost of Goods Sold

         Total Labor/Wage Costs:    $ _____

         Total Supplies:    _____

      Total Cost of Goods Sold:    $ _____

      Other Variable Costs

         Commission:    $ _____

         Shipping:    _____

      Total Other Variable Costs:    $ _____

   **Total Variable Costs:\***    $ _____    _____

**Gross Profit:\*\***     $ _____

   **Fixed Operating Costs**

      **U**tilities:    $ _____

      **S**alary:    _____

      **A**dvertising:    _____

      **I**nsurance:    _____

      **I**nterest:    _____

      **R**ent:    _____

      **D**epreciation:    _____

      **O**ther:    _____

   **Total Fixed Operating Costs:**    $ _____    _____

**Profit:**     $ _____

**Taxes:**     _____

**Net Profit:**     $ _____

\* Also called "total cost of sales."     \*\* Technically this is called "contribution margin," but we are using "gross profit" to keep the presentation simple.

- Total Sales/Revenue = Units Sold × Unit Selling Price
- Total Cost of Goods or Services Sold = Units Sold × Cost of Goods or Services Sold per Unit
- Total Other Variable Costs = Units Sold × Other Variable Costs per Unit
- Total Variable Costs = Total Cost of Goods or Services Sold + Total Other Variable Costs
- Gross Profit = Total Sales − Total Variable Costs
- Total Fixed Costs = Total of USAIIRDO
- Profit/(Loss) = Gross Profit − Total Variable Costs
- Taxes = Profit × .20 (Estimated)
- Net Profit = Profit − Taxes

## SAMPLE INCOME STATEMENT

| For Manufacturing Business | | Date: October, 2007 |
|---|---|---|
| **Revenue:** | | $ _____ |
| **Variable Costs** | | |
| COGS: | $ _____ | |
| Other Variable Costs: | _____ | |
| **Total Variable Costs:** | $ _____ | _____ |
| **Gross Profit:** | | $ _____ |
| **Fixed Operating Costs** | | |
| Utilities: | $ _____ | |
| Salaries: | _____ | |
| Advertising: | _____ | |
| Insurance: | _____ | |
| Interest: | _____ | |
| Rent: | _____ | |
| Depreciation: | _____ | |
| Other Costs: | _____ | |
| **Total Fixed Operating Costs:** | $ _____ | _____ |
| **Pre-Tax Profit:** | | $ _____ |
| Taxes (20%): | | _____ |
| **Net Profit:** | | $ _____ |

**BizTip:** Whenever a number in a financial statement is enclosed in parentheses, it is a negative number. If you see ($100) at the bottom of an income statement, the business had a net loss of $100.

## Dave's Ties

Let's say Dave buys 100 ties at $3 each and sells them all at $10 each:

- His total COGS is $300 ($3 × 100 ties).
- His revenue is $1,000 ($10 × 100 ties).
- Dave pays his salespeople a 20% commission on everything they sell. For this month, therefore, he paid $200 for this variable cost ($1,000 × .20).

Dave's monthly fixed costs (USAIIRD) are:

- $25 for Utilities
- $80 for Salary (his own)
- $50 for Advertising
- $10 for Insurance
- $40 for Interest (on the loan from his father)
- $25 for Rent (storage space)
- $20 for Depreciation.

Dave's monthly income statement shows that he made a profit of $200.

| INCOME STATEMENT | | |
|---|---|---|
| **For Retail Business** | **Date:** October, 2007 | |
| **Revenue:** | | **$1,000.00** |
| **Variable Costs** | | |
| COGS: | $300.00 | |
| Other Variable Costs: | 200.00 | |
| **Total Variable Costs:** | **$500.00** | 500.00 |
| **Gross Profit:** | | **$500.00** |
| **Fixed Operating Costs** | | |
| Utilities: | $25.00 | |
| Salaries: | 80.00 | |
| Advertising: | 50.00 | |
| Insurance: | 10.00 | |
| Interest: | 40.00 | |
| Rent: | 25.00 | |
| Depreciation: | 20.00 | |
| Other Costs: | 0.00 | |
| **Total Fixed Operating Costs:** | **$250.00** | 250.00 |
| **Pre-Tax Profit:** | | **$250.00** |
| Taxes (20%): | | 50.00 |
| **Net Profit:** | | **$200.00** |

**Note:** Fixed Operating Costs are listed in a separate column. The sub-total of that column is repeated in the next column, to be calculated with the other figures.

## Fully Allocated Costs

After you have been in business for a while, you will have enough information to figure out exactly how much of *all* your costs — not just COGS and Other Variable Costs — are covered each time you sell one unit.

Simply add up all your costs — COGS, Other Variable Costs, plus the Fixed Costs — and divide them by the number of units sold. For Dave's Ties:

$750 (COGS $300 + VC $200 + FC $250) ÷ 100 ties = $7.50

For this month, every time Dave sold a tie for $10, $7.50 went to covering the costs of running his business.

## The Double Bottom Line

You have probably heard the expression, "What's the bottom line?" It refers to the last line on an income statement: the net profit. Net profit shows whether a business is profitable or not. *Profitability* is the bottom line.

There is another bottom line to be considered, though, aside from whether or not your business is profitable. Is your business achieving its mission? If your dream is to have the business fill a need for your community, for example, is this goal being realized? Are you able to make a profit and operate your business in a way that makes you proud? Business goals that go beyond profit might be to:

- Protect the environment — Be a good citizen by conducting business in a way that respects the environment: recycling, minimizing waste, looking into energy sources that don't pollute.

- Help the community — Encourage local people to invest in the business and become equity owners.

- Treat employees with respect — Set up profit-sharing so they can participate in the success of the company.

Ideally, you will want to have a positive *double* bottom line — making a profit *and* improving society.

## Pie Charts

Entrepreneurs rely on the data from their monthly income statements to run their businesses. There are some effective ways to show data visually, so that it can be understood quickly. You could take Dave's income statement and show it as a *pie chart*. Imagine you're looking down at a pie. The slices of pie are the *sectors* (segments) of the circle.

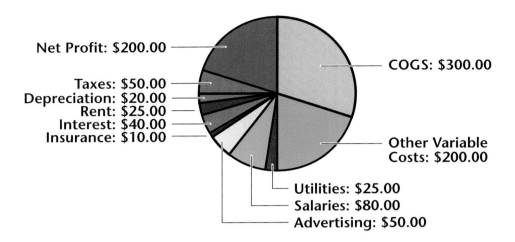

The pie chart is based on **percentages**. Remember, percent means "out of a hundred." The whole pie represents 100%. Each sector represents a part of that whole.

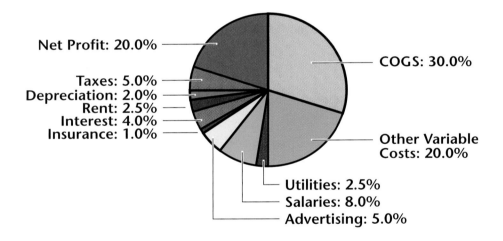

# Bar Graphs

The *bar graph* is another kind of visual display. Here, bars of different heights are used to illustrate data. The higher the bar, the greater the number or amount. For a horizontal bar chart, the longer the bar, the greater the number or amount.

Bar graphs are good at showing trends. Let's say we have six monthly income statements for Dave's Ties. In January, he had zero revenue because he was getting started and hadn't sold anything yet. Fortunately, he had a cash reserve to cover his fixed costs for several months. In February, he sold $150 worth of ties; in March, $250; in April, $400, and in May, $600. What is the trend? Dave's Ties revenue is steadily rising! The bar chart makes that easy to see at a glance.

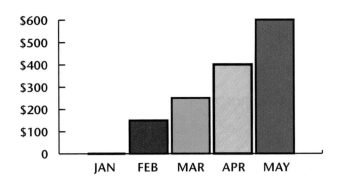

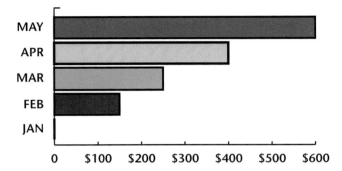

## SKILLS MEAN SUCCESS

**MATH** ► **Displaying Data in Charts and Graphs**

Assume you have a landscaping business. Create a bar graph to show the following monthly revenue from your income statement:

January: $50, February: $100, March: $200, April: $300, May: $400, June: $500, July: $500, August: $400, September: $300, October: $200, November: $100, and December: $50

Analyze your bar chart. What trends are shown? ■■■

## How Entrepreneurs Use Sales Data

The income statement shows the entrepreneur at a glance how much revenue the business is bringing in. This data is important because it tells you how much you can afford to spend on supplies for your next round of sales. It also tells you whether you can afford to hire anyone. You can use your sales data to estimate your *personnel* (hiring) and purchasing needs.

Once your business is up and running, you can use your monthly income statements to forecast your future sales. To do so, plot your sales data with a bar graph. Are sales rising or falling? Is anything coming up, such as a holiday or special event, that will increase or decrease your sales? Use sales data plus knowledge of your industry to forecast sales for the next six months to a year. This will help you in planning your business.

## Financial Ratios Can Help!

You can also create **financial ratios** from your income statement that will help you analyze your business. You already know one financial ratio: return on investment (ROI). To calculate ROI, divide the net profit (or return) by the investment. All financial ratios are created by dividing one number into another.

 **BizTip: In business, "on" usually means "divided by." Return *on* the investment, therefore, is return divided by the investment. Return on sales is the return divided by the number of sales. Remember that your return is what you *made*, or your net profit.**

## Same Size Analysis

Divide sales into each line item and multiply by 100.  In this way, you are expressing each line item as a percentage, or share, of sales.  Expressing each item on the income statement as a percentage of sales will make it easy to see the relationship between items.  In the example below, for every dollar of sales, 40 cents was spent on cost of goods sold.  The gross profit per dollar was 60 cents.  The net profit, after 30 cents were spent on operating costs and 10 cents on taxes, was 20 cents.

| Income statement | Dollars | Math | % of sales |
| --- | --- | --- | --- |
| Sales | $10 | $10 ÷ $10 × 100 = | 100% |
| Less Total COGS | $4 | $4 ÷ $10 × 100 = | 40% |
| Less Variable Costs | $0 | $0 | |
| Gross Profit | $6 | $6 ÷ $10 × 100 = | 60% |
| Less Fixed Operating Costs | $3 | $3 ÷ $10 × 100 = | 30% |
| Profit | $3 | $3 ÷ $10 × 100 = | 30% |
| Taxes | $1 | $1 ÷ $10 × 100 = | 10% |
| Net Profit/(Loss) | $2 | $2 ÷ $10 × 100 = | 20% |

This **same size analysis** makes clear how each item is affecting the business's profit. It will make it easier to experiment with ways to improve the company.

To increase gross profit, you could try cutting the cost of goods sold by 10%. The next time you analyze your monthly income statement, you will be able to see if this cost-cutting increased the gross profit and by how much.

### Example of Same Size Analysis

Financial ratio analysis also allows you to compare the income statements from different months — or years — more easily, even if the sales are different amounts. Same size analysis can be made by changing equivalent figures to percentages and then comparing them.

| INCOME STATEMENT (Short Version) | | | |
|---|---|---|---|
| **Rocket Rollerskate "Same Size"** | | **Date:** January, 2008 | |
| **Revenue:** | **100%** | | **$250,000** |
| **Variable Costs** | | | |
| COGS: | 24% | $60,000 | |
| Other Variable Costs: | 14% | 35,000 | |
| **Total Variable Costs:** | **36%** | **$95,000** | 95,000 |
| **Gross Profit:** | **62%** | | **$155,000** |
| Fixed Operating Costs: | 34% | | 85,000 |
| **Pre-Tax Profit:** | **28%** | | **$70,000** |
| Taxes (20%): | 6% | | 14,000 |
| **Net Profit:** | **22%** | | **$56,000** |
| **Rocket Rollerskate "Same Size"** | | **Date:** February, 2008 | |
| **Revenue:** | **100%** | | **$225,000** |
| **Variable Costs** | | | |
| COGS: | 20% | $45,000 | |
| Other Variable Costs: | 12% | 27,000 | |
| **Total Variable Costs:** | **32%** | **$72,000** | 72,000 |
| **Gross Profit:** | **68%** | | **$153,000** |
| Fixed Operating Costs: | 38% | | 85,000 |
| **Pre-Tax Profit:** | **30%** | | **$68,000** |
| Taxes (20%): | 6% | | 13,600 |
| **Net Profit:** | **24%** | | **$54,400** |

Example: Compare the "same size" income statements on page 184. Rocket Rollerskate didn't have as much revenue or make as much profit in Feburary as it did in January. However, the company was able to lower both its COGS and its other variable costs in February. Which month was better for Rocket? Can you explain why? Do others in the class agree with you?

## Operating Ratio

When you divide sales into one of your fixed costs, you get an **operating ratio**. The operating ratio tells you what percentage of each dollar of revenue is being used to pay the cost.

You can use operating ratios to compare your fixed costs with those incurred by other businesses in your industry. If your rent is $2,000 per month and your sales in a given month are $10,000, your operating ratio for rent is 20%. Is that high or low for your industry? If it's high, you might need to consider changing location to remain competitive.

## ROS (Return On Sales)

The financial ratio created by dividing sales into net profit is called **return on sales (ROS)**. ROS is an important measure of how profitable a business is, because it shows how much of each dollar of sales the business keeps as profit.

ROS is also called **profit margin**. To express this ratio as a percentage, multiply it by 100 (as you would to express ROI as a percentage).

A high ROS ratio can help a company make money more easily. However, the amount of revenue the company has makes a difference. Size of the sale also will make a difference. Hardware stores sell inexpensive items, so they have to have a higher profit margin on each. Car dealers sell expensive items, so they can make money with a smaller ROS on each sale. Rocket Rollerskate's ROS in February was 24%, meaning that, of every dollar of sales, 24 cents was net profit.

| ROS (PROFIT MARGIN) TABLE | | |
|---|---|---|
| **ROS** | **Margin Range** | **Typical Product** |
| Very low | 2 – 5% | Very high volume OR very high price |
| Low | 6 – 10% | High volume OR high price |
| Moderate | 11 – 20% | Moderate volume AND moderate price |
| High | 20 – 30% | Low volume OR low price |
| Very high | 30% – and up | Very low volume OR very low price |

## Projected Monthly Income Statement

As part of a business plan, an entrepreneur will always create a forecast of the annual income statement for the coming year. Below is the forecast that David created for his tie company. David now has a financial plan and will be able to see how the results compare to the plan. A financial plan is also called a **budget**.

| | Jan | Feb | Mar | Apr | May | Jun | Jul | Aug | Sep | Oct | Nov | Dec | Total |
|---|---|---|---|---|---|---|---|---|---|---|---|---|---|
| Units Sold* | 100 | 200 | 200 | 200 | 200 | 200 | 200 | 200 | 200 | 200 | 200 | 200 | 2,300 |
| Unit Selling Price* | 10 | 10 | 10 | 10 | 10 | 10 | 10 | 10 | 10 | 10 | 10 | 10 | 10 |
| Sales/Revenue | 1,000 | 2,000 | 2,000 | 2,000 | 2,000 | 2,000 | 2,000 | 2,000 | 2,000 | 2,000 | 2,000 | 2,000 | 23,000 |
| Total Cost of Goods Sold | 300 | 600 | 600 | 600 | 600 | 600 | 600 | 600 | 600 | 600 | 600 | 600 | 6,900 |
| Total Other Variable Costs | 200 | 400 | 400 | 400 | 400 | 400 | 400 | 400 | 400 | 400 | 400 | 400 | 4,600 |
| Total Variable Costs | 500 | 1,000 | 1,000 | 1,000 | 1,000 | 1,000 | 1,000 | 1,000 | 1,000 | 1,000 | 1,000 | 1,000 | 11,500 |
| Gross Profit | 500 | 1,000 | 1,000 | 1,000 | 1,000 | 1,000 | 1,000 | 1,000 | 1,000 | 1,000 | 1,000 | 1,000 | 11,500 |
| Total Fixed Costs | 250 | 500 | 500 | 500 | 500 | 500 | 500 | 500 | 500 | 500 | 500 | 500 | 5,750 |
| Profit | 250 | 500 | 500 | 500 | 500 | 500 | 500 | 500 | 500 | 500 | 500 | 500 | 5,750 |

| Less Taxes (25%) | 1,437.50 |
|---|---|
| Net Profit | 4,312.50 |

* Units Sold and Unit Selling Price are not part of the Income Statement but when multiplied together give Total Sales/Revenue.

- Total Sales/Revenue = Units Sold × Unit Selling Price
- Total Cost of Goods or Services Sold = Units Sold × Cost of Goods or Services Sold
- Total Other Variable Costs = Units Sold × Other Variable Costs per Unit
- Total Variable Costs = Total Cost of Goods or Services Sold + Total Other Variable Costs
- Gross Profit = Total Sales − Total Variable Costs
- Total Fixed Costs = Total of USAIIRDO
- Profit/(Loss) = Gross Profit − Total Fixed Costs
- Taxes = Profit × .25 (Estimated)
- Net Profit = Profit − Taxes

# SKILLS MEAN SUCCESS

**TECHNOLOGY** ▶ **Spreadsheet Formulas**

An income statement can be calculated using computer spreadsheet software, such as Microsoft Excel. The page of a spreadsheet is divided into rows and columns. Each row has a number, and each column is designated with a letter. The "boxes" created by the rows and columns are called "cells." Each cell is named for the row and column that creates it. For example, the highlighted cell below is called B2. Can you tell why? (Hint: Note that the "2" in the row heading and the "B" in the column heading are in bold. Also the cell name "B2" appears in the "name box" just under where the font — Arial — is shown.)

| | A | B | C |
|---|---|---|---|
| 1 | | | |
| 2 | | ✛ | |
| 3 | | | |
| 4 | | | |
| 5 | | | |
| 6 | | | |
| 7 | | | |

Each cell can hold only one kind of data. The three types of spreadsheet data are:

**1.** Text — words. Use text for labels and other devices that will help people understand the spreadsheet when they read it.

**2.** Numbers, such as 1, 12, 45, $\frac{1}{2}$, .75, etc.

**3.** Formulas — which help to calculate numbers automatically.

For example, if you want the spreadsheet to add the numbers 3 and 6, put them in different cells; then use another cell for the formula that will perform the calculation for you. To write a formula with Excel, put an equals sign (=) in the cell first. This tells the program that you are writing a formula. In the example below, left, can you see how the formula uses the "names" of the cells containing the numerals 3 and 6? The computer will "go get" the numerical values from those cells to do the math, and will show the answer in the cell the formula is in.

| | A | B | C |
|---|---|---|---|
| 1 | | | |
| 2 | | 3 | |
| 3 | | 6 | |
| 4 | | =b2+b3 | |
| 5 | | | |
| 6 | | | |

| | A | B | C |
|---|---|---|---|
| 1 | | | |
| 2 | | 3 | |
| 3 | | 6 | |
| 4 | | 9 | |
| 5 | | | |
| 6 | | | |

**187**

A computer spreadsheet is like a "word processor" for numbers. When you harness the power of the spreadsheet, math becomes a lot less work and a lot more fun!

| ◇ | A | B | C |
|---|---|---|---|
| 1 | | | |
| 2 | | 2,542,875.52 | |
| 3 | | 1,218,362.09 | |
| 4 | | 3,761,237.61 | |
| 5 | | | |

**Computer math:** computers use the addition ( + ) and subtraction ( − ) signs you are already familiar with. However, they don't use the multiplication and division signs you know. Use the following keyboard symbols for basic mathematical calculations.

| SYMBOLS FOR COMPUTER MATH | | | |
|---|---|---|---|
| **Operation** | **Standard** | **Computer** | |
| Addition | + | + | |
| Subtraction | − | − | |
| Multiplication | × | * | (Shift and 8) |
| Division | ÷ | / | |

Can you make the following spreadsheet on a computer, using text, numbers, and formulas? Note that the "green" cells contain numbers, but all other numerals shown, including the percentages, are calculated automatically by the spreadsheet with formulas. (Hint: When using a spreadsheet, do the calculations using formulas. Never just "type in" the right answer, even if you can do it "in your head.")

The formulas for the first four rows (3, 4, 5, and 6) are shown on page 189 to get you started. If you don't have a computer handy, write the formulas out on a piece of paper.

| ◇ | A | B | C | D | E | F |
|---|---|---|---|---|---|---|
| 1 | **Rocket Rollerskate - (simplified) Income Statement** | | | | | |
| 2 | Period: January 2008 | | | | | |
| 3 | **REVENUE** | | | | 250,000 | 100% |
| 4 | Cost of Goods Sold | | | | 60,000 | 24% |
| 5 | Other Variable Costs | | | | 35,000 | 14% |
| 6 | **GROSS PROFIT** | | | | 155,000 | 62% |
| 7 | **FIXED OPERATING COSTS** | | | | 85,000 | 34% |
| 8 | **PRE-TAX PROFIT** | | | | 70,000 | 28% |
| 9 | Taxes | | | 20% | 14,000 | 6% |
| 10 | **NET PROFIT** | | | | 56,000 | 22% |
| 11 | | | | | | |

| | A | B | C | D | E | F |
|---|---|---|---|---|---|---|
| | \multicolumn{6}{l}{**Rocket Rollerskate - (simplified) Income Statement**} |
| 1 | | | | | | |
| 2 | \multicolumn{6}{l}{Period:   January 2008} |
| 3 | REVENUE | | | | 250,000 | =E3/E3 |
| 4 | | Cost of Goods Sold | | | 60,000 | =E4/E3 |
| 5 | | Other Variable Costs | | | 35,000 | =E5/E3 |
| 6 | GROSS PROFIT | | | | =E3-E4-E5 | =E6/E3 |
| 7 | FIXED OPERATING COSTS | | | | 85,000 | 34% |
| 8 | PRE-TAX PROFIT | | | | 70,000 | 28% |
| 9 | | Taxes | | 20% | 14,000 | 6% |
| 10 | NET PROFIT | | | | 56,000 | 22% |
| 11 | | | | | | |

## Henry Ford: Cutting Costs to Make Cars Affordable

The monthly income statement helps the entrepreneur keep track of how costs are affecting net profit. An entrepreneur's ability to find creative ways to cut costs can mean the difference between a struggling business and a thriving one.

In the early 1900s, Henry Ford was determined to create an automobile that most people could afford. To do this, he had to search for ways to cut costs. In those days, cars were made one at a time. It was a slow, expensive process. To cut production costs, Ford invented the "moving assembly line." The cars were *assembled* (built) as they rolled past the workers on a conveyor belt. Ford was able to cut costs enough to be able to offer them at a price that the average American could afford, and still make a profit. He revolutionized the industry by showing the advantages of a moving assembly line and mass production. ■

# Chapter 13 Review

## CRITICAL THINKING ABOUT...

### INCOME STATEMENTS

1. Suppose you have a business selling caps to friends and classmates. This month you bought 20 caps for $5 each and sold them all at $10 each. You paid $40 in commissions to your brother to help sell them, and you spent $20 on posters (FC) as advertising. Your taxes are 20% of your pre-tax profit. Prepare your income statement.

2. After preparing the income statement for the cap business, answer these questions:

   a. What is the cost of goods sold (COGS)?
   b. What is the net profit?
   c. What is the difference between gross profit and profit before taxes?
   d. How much was paid in taxes?

3. Using the income statement for the cap business, prepare a same size analysis and a pie chart.

4. Let's say the cap business earns a net profit of $20 in January; in February, $40; in March, $50; in April, $30, and $60 in May. Show this as a bar graph. Write a brief memo forecasting sales for the business for the rest of the year and describe what purchasing and hiring decisions you would make if you were running the business.

5. Which cost does the wise entrepreneur always keep secret? Why?

## KEY CONCEPTS

Using the McDonald's one-year income statement in your Workbook, answer these questions:

1. What would the profit before taxes be if the owner finds a paper supplier who only charges $100,000 for the year?

2. What would the profit margin for the year be in that case?

3. Suppose you wanted to raise profits by $5,000 a month. What would you do and why?

4. How much do you think the business could be sold for? Why?

5. Do you have a business? If so, compare your income statement with that of McDonald's.

## VOCABULARY

budget ■ financial ratios ■ income statement ■ net profit ■ operating ratio ■ percentage ■ pre-tax profit ■ profit margin ■ return on sales (ROS) ■ same size analysis

# Chapter Summary ✔✔✔

**13.1** Entrepreneurs use income statements to track sales and costs.
  A. If sales are greater than costs, the business has earned a net profit.
  B. If costs are greater than sales, the business has suffered a net loss (negative number).
  C. The income statement is a monthly, quarterly (every three months), or annual scorecard that shows the owner how well the business is doing.

**13.2** Income statements show specific details.
  A. An income statement shows and calculates:
    1. Revenue
    2. COGS
    3. Other Variable Costs
    4. Gross Profit
    5. Fixed Costs
    6. Pre-Tax Profit
    7. Taxes Paid
    8. Net Profit (or Net Loss).
  B. Fully allocated costs include COGS and Other Variable Costs + Fixed Costs.

**13.3** Entrepreneurs analyze their Income Statements.
  A. Is "mission" (the second bottom line) as well as profit being achieved?
  B. Pie charts and bar graphs display sales and expense data visually.
  C. Data can be analyzed to compare (and predict) sales and expenses.
  D. Financial ratios also help an entrepreneur to analyze the business:
    1. ROI (dollars and percentages) = Net Profit ÷ Investment
    2. Percentages allow comparisons of different amounts
    3. Operating Ratio = Expense ÷ Total Revenues (compares one type of fixed cost to revenues; shows the percentage of sales needed to cover that operating expense)
    4. ROS (Return on Sales, or profit margin) = Net Profit ÷ Revenues (shows how much of each dollar of sales is kept as profit). ✔✔✔

# FINANCING STRATEGY:
## *Debt or Equity?*

*In the midst of difficulty lies opportunity.*

— Albert Einstein, *physicist who formulated the Theory of Relativity*

### KEY OBJECTIVES

THIS CHAPTER WILL ENABLE YOU TO:

- Compare debt and equity financing.
- Discuss the three basic legal business structures: sole proprietorship, partnership, and corporation.
- Choose alternative forms of financing, such as micro-loans and "bootstrapping."
- Calculate debt ratios and debt-to-equity ratios.

**R**aising capital for a business is called **financing**. Sometimes you can raise all the money you need for your business yourself, by working and saving. Eventually, however, you will probably need outside cash (capital) to expand the business with new products or marketing.

## Start-Up Capital

How much money will you need to get your business going? **Start-up capital** is the one-time investment of starting a business. Start-up capital is also called "seed money." The seed money to open a restaurant would have to include stoves, food processors, tables, chairs, silverware, and other items that would not be replaced frequently. Also included might be purchasing land and constructing a building, or renovations on an existing space.

For a hot dog stand, the start-up investment might look like this:

- Hot dog cart: $1,500
- License from the city: 200
- Starting supply of hot dogs, buns, sauerkraut, mustard: 300
- Business cards and flyers (advertising): 50
- Telephone answering machine: 100

    **Total start-up investment** **$2,150**

## Keep a Reserve

Start-up capital should include one more thing — *a cash reserve that equals at least half of your start-up costs*. For the hot dog cart, therefore, the reserve would be at least half of $2,150, or $1,075.

Keeping cash in reserve will lower your return on investment (remember, start-up investment is the "denominator" for ROI) but will give you a more realistic handle on your business. The reserve will provide a cushion of protection when you need it. When your computer dies or your biggest supplier raises his prices, you'll be glad you had a reserve.

Having cash in reserve will also let you take advantage of opportunities. Let's say you own a vintage clothing store and you hear from a friend whose great-aunt died and left him clothing and jewelry that is now "vintage." He's willing to sell you the whole lot for $500, which you could resell in your shop for at least $2,000. If you didn't have the extra cash on hand, this opportunity would have been lost.

## Payback

Payback tells you and your investors how long it will take your business to earn enough profit to cover the start-up investment. It is measured in months.

$$\text{Payback} = \frac{\text{Start-up Investment}}{\text{Net Profit per Month}}$$

Example: Business A required a start-up investment of $1,200. The business is projecting net profit per month of $400. How many months will it take to pay back the start-up investment?

$$\text{Payback} = \frac{\$1,200}{\$400} = 3 \text{ months}$$

# Financing Your Business

Where will you get the money to pay for your start-up costs? One way to finance a business is to work at a part-time job and save money, but that can take a long time. A better option may be to use "Other People's Money" (OPM). There are two ways to raise OPM; each will affect a business differently.

1. **Debt** — To finance with **debt**, the entrepreneur borrows money from a person or an institution, signing a **promissory note**. The note is a commitment to make regular payments on the loan, including interest.

2. **Equity** — To finance with **equity**, the entrepreneur trades a percentage of ownership for money. The investor will receive a percentage of future profits.

# Debt Financing: Advantages

One advantage of debt is that the lender has no say in the future or direction of the business as long as the payments are made. When you finance with debt, you don't give up ownership. You will keep all the profits, and no one will be able to tell you how to run your business. Another plus is that the payments are predictable — you'll know exactly what you need every month to pay off the loan.

# Debt Financing: Disadvantages

The disadvantage of debt is that if the loan payments are not made, the lender can force the entrepreneur into *bankruptcy*. To do this, the lender must go to court and prove that the business owner cannot pay the debt. The court can force the owner to close the business and sell its *assets* (anything of value that it owns) to raise the cash to pay the debt. The lender can even try to force the owner of a small business that is not incorporated to sell personal possessions to meet the obligation.

This disadvantage of debt should be considered carefully by the entrepreneur because it often takes time for a new business to show a profit. Failure to make loan payments can destroy a business before it gets the chance to prove itself.

Companies that rely heavily on debt financing are said to be highly *leveraged*. Leveraged means financed through debt. Businesses sometimes find themselves in this position because the business owner is unwilling to give up control by issuing equity.

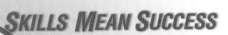

## SKILLS MEAN SUCCESS

**MATH** ▶ **Math Formulas and Operations: Simple Interest**

*Interest* is the fee a bank or other lender will charge to loan you money. It is calculated by this formula:

**Interest** = **Principal** × **Rate** × **Time** (in months or years). If the loan is carried for a term of less than one year, the loan cost (interest) is *annualized* (expressed as an equivalent yearly rate) to be consistent.

This formula is commonly shown as **I = PRT**.

The *principal* is the amount to be borrowed from the bank. The *interest rate* is the percentage the bank or lender uses to calculate your fee. *Time* is how many months or years it will take to pay back the loan. (Time must be expressed in years.)

For example, if $1,000 is borrowed at ten percent to be paid back over one year, the "simple" interest on the loan is $1,000 × .10 × 1 = $100.

The total amount you will have to pay back to the bank is the principal *plus* the interest. In the example, that would be $1,000 + $100 = $1,100.

For each of the following loans, determine the interest and the total amount that will have to be paid back:

|     | Principal | Interest Rate | Time |
|-----|-----------|---------------|------|
| **1.** | $500 | 5% | 1 year |
| **2.** | $1,000 | 5% | 18 months |
| **3.** | $2,500 | 12.5% | 2 years |
| **4.** | $5,000 | 10% | 2.5 years |
| **5.** | $10,000 | 7% | 36 months ■■■ |

# Basic Business Legal Structures

**Sole Proprietorship** — owned by one person, who may also be the only employee. The sole proprietor is personally *liable*, or responsible, for all debt. The sole proprietor keeps all profit from the business. It is easy and inexpensive to register a sole proprietorship with your county courthouse or chamber of commerce. **Example: an artist who makes and sells her own jewelry might choose a sole proprietorship structure.**

**Partnership** — ownership is shared by two or more people. The owners are personally liable for all debt and share the profit from the business. Have a lawyer draw up a partnership agreement before registering this type of business. **Example: two friends who start a house-cleaning business together might choose a partnership structure.**

**Corporation** — an *entity* (legal "person") composed of stockholders, who own pieces of the company. Owners are *not* personally liable; the corporation is liable. It is more expensive and complicated to register and run than a sole proprietorship or partnership. **Example: A clothing designer who hopes to sell her clothes to stores internationally might choose to *incorporate*.**

**Nonprofit corporation** — also called a 501(c)(3); a corporation whose mission is to improve society in some way. Churches, museums, and charities are all examples of nonprofits. The nonprofit structure is appropriate when you want to provide a service to people who can't afford it. Nonprofits accept donations (gifts of money) that they must then use to fulfill their mission. **Example: A woman who wants to provide business clothing for other women who are trying to find jobs but can't afford the right clothes might choose a nonprofit structure. She can then accept gifts of clothing and money and use them to fulfill her mission.**

**Cooperative** — a "co-op" is a business owned and controlled by the customers/members who use its services. Each member has one vote in all decisions, regardless of the number of shares owned. Sometimes small business owners form a co-op so they can purchase services and supplies together. This helps them get cheaper prices than they could as individuals. **Example: a group of DJs might form a co-op so they can purchase and share equipment and records as a group.** ■

## SKILLS MEAN SUCCESS

**ENGLISH**

### Reading for Critical Analysis

Based on the information in the "Basic Business Legal Structures" above, match the following businesses with the most appropriate business legal structure.

1. A manufacturer who plans to sell equipment to industrial sites across the country.

2. A museum for regional pottery and crafts.

3. A writer who produces business newsletters.

4. A group of home-child-care providers who want to purchase and share baby supplies.

5. Two brothers who are starting a landscaping business.

     **a.** Sole proprietorship    **b.** Partnership    **c.** Corporation

     **d.** Cooperative        **e.** Nonprofit corporation

# Equity Financing

An equity investor invests money in a business in exchange for a share of ownership. The share of ownership entitles the investor to a share of the profits.

The equity investor takes a greater risk than the debt lender because, if the business does not make a profit, neither does the investor. The equity investor cannot force the business into bankruptcy and, in fact, may lose the investment. On the other hand, the equity investor may earn a lot more than a debt investor in the long run.

The advantage of equity financing is that the money doesn't have to be paid back unless the business is successful. The disadvantage is that, through giving up ownership, the entrepreneur may lose control of the business to the equity holders if their share of the business is greater than 50 percent.

**Did You Know?** If a business is forced into bankruptcy, debt investors get paid off first from the sale of the business's assets. Equity investors have a claim on whatever is left after the debt investors have been paid.

# Anita Roddick: Using Equity

Anita Roddick didn't expect The Body Shop, which she founded in England, to change the cosmetics industry, be a force for social awareness, and make millions of dollars — but it has. The Body Shop would never have gotten that far, though, if Roddick hadn't sold half the business to her friend Ian McGlinn in exchange for equity financing of £4,000 (around $8,000) that she needed in order to pay her employees. Local banks refused to lend her money because she had only been in business for a few months.

McGlinn's investment came to be worth over £140 million (around $280 million). Roddick says she has no regrets, because without McGlinn's equity financing, she would not have been able to grow her company.

## SKILLS MEAN SUCCESS

### Interviewing

When you apply for a business loan, you will have an interview with a loan officer at the bank. He or she will ask you important questions related to the loan request, the nature and history of your business, your legal organization, the number of your employees and partners, and about your finances — both business and personal. Even if you are incorporated, the interviewer will most likely ask you, as an officer of the corporation, to personally guarantee repayment.

Much as in a job interview, the way you look, act, and speak will probably affect the outcome of the bank's decision:

**DO** wear professional and conservative clothing that is neat and clean.

**DON'T** wear flashy jewelry, unnatural makeup, clothes or buttons having words or phrases on them, sunglasses, or a hat.

**DO** be polite, confident, and prepared. Sit up straight. Shake hands with the interviewer.

**DON'T** slouch, fidget nervously, or look around the room.

**DO** listen carefully. Speak clearly and formally. Answer questions honestly and completely. Ask questions if you have them. Remember the loan officer's name and use it in the conversation. Thank the officer for his/her time. Ask politely when the decision on the loan will be made.

**DON'T** use slang or profanity or interrupt.

Working with a partner, practice role-playing a loan interview. Take turns playing the loan officer and the business owner. A loan officer will be looking to see if you are prepared, enthusiastic and knowledgeable about your business, and clear and realistic about your goals and finances. ■■■

## Debt and Equity

Most companies, from small businesses to large corporations, are financed by both debt and equity. A corporation is a company owned by people who have invested in it. One advantage of incorporating is that, if a corporation goes bankrupt, lenders can only go after the assets of the corporation — not of the owners.

Another advantage of incorporating is that corporations may issue bonds and sell stock:

- A bond is an interest-bearing certificate representing the corporation's promise to pay back the bondholder the amount he or she has lent the corporation, plus interest.

- Corporations sell stock to raise equity financing. A person who buys stock then owns a percentage of the corporation. Stockholders are paid dividends when the corporation is profitable.

We will go into bonds and stocks in more detail in Chapters 33 and 34.

## Ratios

The financial strategy of a company is expressed by its **debt-to-equity ratio**. If a company has a debt-to-equity ratio of one-to-one (expressed as 1:1), it means that for every one dollar of debt there is one dollar of equity.

$$\frac{\text{debt}}{\text{equity}} = \text{debt-to-equity ratio}$$

It is risky for companies to have too high a debt-to-equity ratio. This can hurt an otherwise healthy business. A great deal of debt means the company has heavy monthly loan payments. This extra fixed cost will cut into profits and increase the danger of bankruptcy. Anything over "Moderate" on the following table will make the company less valuable.

| Debt/Equity | Ratio | % of Capital from Debt | Level of Extra Risk |
|---|---|---|---|
| $1/$4 | 1:4 | 20% | Low |
| $\frac{1}{2}$ | 1:2 | 33% | Moderate |
| $\frac{1}{1}$ | 1:1 | 50% | High |
| $\frac{2}{1}$ | 2:1 | 67% | Very High |
| $\frac{4}{1}$ | 4:1 | 80% | Extremely High |

## Debt Ratio

Another ratio that gives an insight into a company's financial strategy is the **debt ratio**. A debt ratio of one means that every one dollar of assets is financed by one dollar of debt and one dollar of equity.

$$\frac{\text{amount of debt}}{\text{amount of assets}} = \text{debt ratio}$$

Example:

$$\frac{0.50}{1.00} = 0.50$$

# Alternative Financing

There are many types of financing for young entrepreneurs.

**Sell equity close to home:** Like Anita Roddick, you can offer an equity stake in your company to friends and family members.

**Micro-loan financing:** The federal government is supporting a growing number of micro-loan programs that make loans ranging from $100 to $25,000. The loan is made based on the entrepreneur's character and business plan. The money can be used to buy machinery, furniture, and supplies, but may not be used to pay existing debt.

**Angel financing:** A small business with a solid business plan might be able to attract "angel" investment. Angels are private investors who are typically worth over $1 million and are interested in backing start-up businesses for a variety of reasons — from friendship to a desire to encourage entrepreneurship in a given field. Bill Gates has been an angel for several biotech start-ups because he has a particular interest in biotechnology. Angel financing typically ranges from $100,000 to $500,000. A good source of angel financing information is ACE-Net. You can learn more at http://acenet.csusb.edu/.

**Bootstrap financing:** Taken from the phrase, "pulling yourself up by the bootstraps," the goal is to get your start-up costs as low as possible. Many successful entrepreneurs get their businesses off the ground with very little money, through such strategies as:

1. Hiring as few employees as possible.

2. Borrowing or renting equipment instead of buying it.
   (Check out local thrift stores for shelves, desks, etc.)

3. Using personal savings.

4. Arranging small loans from friends and relatives.

**Business incubators:** These are organizations that provide office space and equipment, such as fax machines and computers, for entrepreneurs to share while they are getting their businesses off the ground.

*Where there's a will, there's a way!*

# Chapter 14 Review

## CRITICAL THINKING ABOUT...

### FINANCING

1. Which type of financing, debt or equity, would you prefer to use to start your own business? Or would you use a combination? Explain, discussing the advantages and disadvantages of each type.

2. Interest is calculated by multiplying the principal by the interest rate. If $1,200 is borrowed at ten percent to be paid back over one year, the interest on the loan is $1,200 × .10 = $120. Fill in the blanks for the following loans:

| Loan | Interest Rate | Interest Due for One Year |
|---|---|---|
| $1,400 | ____ % | $140 |
| $1,000 | 5% | $____ |
| $400 | 20% | $____ |
| $____ | 10% | $10 |

## KEY CONCEPTS

Answer the following questions to complete a chart like the one below:

1. What are the estimated costs of the items you will need to start your business? List each item and its cost. **Business Plan Practice**

2. How do you plan to finance your business? List your sources of financing, identifying whether each is equity, debt, or a gift. **Businss Plan Practice**

3. What is the maximum percentage of ownership in the business that you would be willing to give up to secure equity financing? Why?

4. If you receive debt financing, what is the maximum interest rate you would be willing to pay? Why?

5. What is your debt/equity ratio and your debt ratio in the scenario given below? Write a memo discussing the pros and cons of the entrepreneur's position. **Business Plan Practice**

| Item | Estimated Cost | Financing Source | % Ownership | Interest Rate |
|---|---|---|---|---|
| Computer | $800 | Equity investment by brother | 20% | N/A |
| Inventory | $1,600 | Personal savings | 100% | N/A |
| Loan | $3,200 | Loan from family | 0% | 7% |

## EXPLORATION

### SHOPPING FOR A BANK

Visit three banks in your neighborhood and ask for information about their savings and checking accounts. Make a presentation to the class describing the costs and benefits of each bank's accounts. Explain which bank you will choose for your savings and which for checking.

## VOCABULARY

debt ▪ debt ratio ▪ debt-to-equity ratio ▪ equity ▪ financing ▪ promissory note ▪ start-up capital

## Chapter Summary ✔✔✔

**14.1** Businesses need financing to pay start-up costs.
   A. Investment to get a business going is called start-up capital or "seed money."
   B. Start-up capital includes:
      1. Cost of equipment, land, construction, and supplies
      2. Cash reserve capital to cushion the business against the unexpected
      3. Cash reserve should equal half of start-up costs.
   C. "Payback" is how many months it will take a business to repay start-up costs from profits.
   D. Payback $= \dfrac{\text{start-up investment}}{\text{net profit per month}}$

**14.2** Financing (raising capital) is done by using debt or equity.
   A. Debt: promissory notes guarantee that loans will be repaid at specific times with interest.
   B. Equity: part ownership of the company is traded for a share of future profits.
   C. Each method has advantages and disadvantages:
      1. Debt Financing

         **Advantages**
         • Financing with debt is called leveraging
         • Lender doesn't get ownership
         • Payments are predictable.

         **Disadvantages**
         • Unpaid lenders can force businesses into bankruptcy
         • Courts can force owners to sell assets to pay debts.

2. Equity Financing

**Advantages**
- More risk for investors
- Investors can't force bankruptcy
- Money doesn't have to be paid back except through profits.

**Disadvantages**
- Less control for owner
- Investors share in all profits
- More profits for investor if business is more profitable.

**14.3** Businesses all have some form of legal structure.
- A. Sole proprietorship: owned by one person who is:
  1. Liable for all debt
  2. Keeps all profit.
- B. Partnership: owned by two or more people, who are liable for debt, but share profits according to a legal partnership agreement.
- C. Corporations: a "person-like" legal entity made up of stockholders. The corporation, not the owners, is liable.
- D. Nonprofit corporation: a corporation that uses donations to improve society in a specified way.
- E. Cooperative: owned by customers or members who use its services and vote on decisions.

**14.4** Businesses use various forms of financing.
- A. Corporations can:
  1. Issue bonds (certificates for repayable loans)
  2. Sell stock (parts of the company's ownership that pay dividends when the company earns a profit).
- B. Financing is measured by ratios.
  1. Debt-to-equity ratio compares how much the company is worth vs. how much it owes:
  $$\frac{debt}{equity} = \text{debt-to-equity ratio}$$
  2. Debt ratio compares debt to assets:
  $$\frac{\text{amount of debt}}{\text{amount of assets}} = \text{debt ratio}$$
- C. Businesses use other financing methods:
  1. Sell equity to family and friends
  2. Government micro-loans
  3. "Angel" or private investor financing
  4. Bootstrap financing
  5. Business incubators. ✔✔✔

### CHAPTER 15

# NEGOTIATION:
## *Achieving Goals through Compromise*

*You don't get what you deserve; you get what you negotiate.*

— Chester L. Karrass, *pioneer of negotiation theory*

### KEY OBJECTIVES

THIS CHAPTER WILL ENABLE YOU TO:

- Handle a negotiation.
- Practice the art of compromise.
- Seek a "Yes" or "No" instead of a "Maybe."

**N**egotiation is the process of achieving one's goals through give-and-take. A classic example of negotiation is a buyer and seller arguing over the price of an item until they finally agree on one that satisfies each of them.

As a small business owner, you will have to negotiate frequently — with suppliers, customers, and employees. How well you negotiate will greatly affect the success of your business.

## Compromise

Negotiation is not about winning, it is about **compromise**. This means sacrificing something you want so that an agreement can be reached that will make both you and the other party happy.

When negotiating, keep in mind that the other person is not your enemy. Ideally, you'll want to do business with this individual again, and vice versa. For this reason, the best negotiations are those in which both parties arrive at a "win/win" agreement. Conduct your negotiations as if you will be dealing with that person again soon.

The best negotiators are tough and resourceful. They are also honest, and careful to make sure the other party is as pleased with the end result as they are. In that way they will expand the circle of people with whom they do business, increasing their opportunities.

# Before the Negotiation

1. **Set your goals and organize your thoughts.** What do you want to achieve in the negotiation? Write down your goals and thoughts on note cards to keep with you during the discussion.

2. **Decide what your boundaries are.** Think about what the best end result for you would be. Then think about the worst. What is the *minimum* you would be willing to accept? What is the *maximum* you are seeking? Knowing this ahead of time will prevent you from getting carried away and giving up too much of one thing in order to get something else. You don't want to win the battle and find you've lost the war.

3. **Put yourself in the other person's shoes.** What does the other party want from the negotiation? Things that aren't important to you could be very important to the other person. Give up something during the negotiation that doesn't mean much to you, but is so important to the other party that he or she will give in on something you really want.

4. **Don't talk dollars until you have to.** When buying or selling, don't begin by mentioning an actual figure. Talk over the situation first. Try to get an idea of what the other party's position is. You might find that he or she is willing to make a better offer than you realized — but you'll never know if you come out with yours right away. The more information you can gather before you name a price, the better.

# During Negotiations

1. **Listen.** *The most important thing you can do during a negotiation is listen.* The greatest negotiators are also the best listeners. Through listening, you will gain the information you need to arrive at a win/win situation.

2. **Let the other person name a dollar amount first.** When discussing the price, let the other party make the first offer. This will reveal his/her position.

3. **Try extremes.** If the party isn't willing to reveal a position, try throwing out an extreme figure — very high or very low (depending on what your own position is). This will force the other person to come forward with some type of response that will help guide you.

4. **Show willingness to bargain.** As negotiations proceed, respond to each counter-offer by giving up something you decided in advance that you could afford to give up.

5. **Silence can be an important tool.** After you state your case, don't say anything for a few moments. This can prompt the other person to say something that you can turn to your advantage.

6. **Always ask for more than has been offered.** When the other person wants you to pay back a loan in ten days, for instance, ask for 15. You may have to settle for 12, but that would be better than the original request.

## Don't Let "Maybe" Waste Your Time [1]

The most frustrating negotiations are not those that end in a firm "No," but those that end with a "Maybe."

If you find that many of your negotiations with customers are ending in "Maybe," you could be seeking the wrong answer. You could be trying too hard to seek a "Yes" from someone who is not really willing to give you one. Spend more time listening to this person to find out how you can solve his or her problem. Be honest if you realize that your product or service may not be right for this customer.

Instead of focusing on getting a sale, focus on listening and getting to know your customer. Selling and negotiating will be less frustrating and much more productive if you keep this concept in mind.

## *SKILLS MEAN SUCCESS*

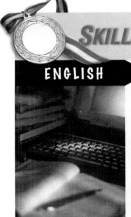

**ENGLISH** ▶ **Listening for Critical Analysis; Communication Skills**

Two strategies that can be used in negotiation are "active" listening and "critical" listening. *Active* listening is used to better understand and remember what you hear. *Critical* listening is used to evaluate and interpret what you hear.

**Active Listening Strategies:**

- Use body language and eye contact to show an interest in what the speaker is saying.

- Demonstrate your interest and encourage the speaker by making such comments as, "Please, go on," "Sure," "I see," "I see your point," etc. But you have to *mean* it.

- Focus on the speaker and maintain an attentive silence.

- Take notes if the situation calls for it.

- Ask occasional questions to clarify information or request more details.

- Restate the speaker's comments to be sure you understood correctly: "So, you're suggesting that we change the business plan?"

- Confirm feelings and meanings, if needed: "It sounds like you're angry that you didn't get a chance to review the business plan earlier."

**Critical Listening Strategies:**

- Try to anticipate what the speaker might say and how she/he will develop the argument.

- Identify the speaker's main point and purpose and assess how well the main points are being supported with evidence.

- Evaluate the evidence the speaker is presenting. Ask yourself: Is it reliable? Is it fact or opinon? Is it *unbiased*?

- Form your own opinion about the speaker's information. Ask youself: "What do I think about this, and why?"

Think up a negotiation scenario and write a paragraph explaining how you could use both active and critical listening strategies. Remember, all negotiations should start with a statement with which both parties can agree. This is called "getting to yes." Never verbally attack the person with whom you are negotiating. Always focus on the concept, or the particular point that is being negotiated. ■■■

# Chapter 15 Review

## CRITICAL THINKING ABOUT...

### NEGOTIATION

1. Play the Negotiating Game with your teacher's guidance. Write a short essay about how you did and how you might improve the next time you play.

2. Use negotiation strategies to get something you want, such as a later curfew, a favor from a friend, time off from work, etc. Write a paragraph describing your negotiation experience.

### KEY CONCEPTS

1. What is the difference between real negotiating and playing a game?

2. Why is it smart to seek a win/win conclusion to a negotiation?

3. Describe how you should get organized before a negotiation.

4. What should you always determine before entering a negotiation?

5. Describe three ways you can try to get the other person to reveal his or her position.

### IN YOUR OPINION

Do you agree that negotiation is about compromise, not winning? Write a short essay giving your opinion and share it with classmates.

### REFERENCES

1 With thanks to Joseph Mancuso, founder of the Center for Entrepreneurial Management.

### VOCABULARY

compromise ■ negotiation

## Chapter Summary ✔✔✔

15.1 Negotiation is using "give-and-take" to achieve business goals.
   A. Neither side wins but both are satisfied.
   B. Both sides compromise:
      1. Give up something to get something
      2. Treat the other party fairly so future deals can take place
      3. Ensure "win-win"
      4. Be tough, resourceful, honest; but know the other party's feelings.
   C. Plan the negotiations:
      1. Set goals
      2. Picture best and worst outcomes
      3. Learn what the other party wants.
      4. Delay talk about money
   D. Conduct the negotiations:
      1. Listen
      2. Let the other party name an amount first
      3. Try extremes to determine the other party's position
      4. Be willing to bargain

5. Try silence
6. Always try for better terms
7. Don't end with "Maybe;" ask more questions to get to "Yes" or "No."
✔✔✔

## SKILLS MEAN SUCCESS

**LEADERSHIP**

### Using Nonverbal Communication Skills

Using nonverbal communication is an important part of negotiating with others. By paying careful attention to body language, you can pick up signals about what the other person is thinking — and whether that matches what he or she is saying.

Gestures that usually show comfort, openness, or enthusiasm:

- Relaxed posture
- Leaning forward
- Smiling, nodding
- Eye contact
- Open palms
- Gesturing warmly or "talking with hands"

Gestures that could show resistance, impatience, or frustration:

- Stiff posture
- Leaning away
- Arms crossed over chest
- Looking away (looking at watch)
- Hands behind the back or neck
- Tapping fingers or fidgeting
- Grasping object tightly (such as chair or pen)
- Placing hand over mouth or chin in hands

Gestures can send warning signs. If someone says, "I'll consider your offer," but he has his arms crossed over his chest and is constantly looking at his watch, he may not mean what he says. It is important to watch and listen for such inconsistencies.

Remember that other people will be watching you, too, so be sure your own body language sends the right signals.

In your interactions with family, friends, and co-workers over the next week, make an extra effort to watch for nonverbal signals. Make a list of the gestures you see and what messages they might be sending. Be sure to note any gestures and signals that seem inconsistent with what the person is saying. ■■■

**209**

### CHAPTER 16

# FROM THE WHOLESALER TO THE TRADE FAIR:
## *A Real-Life Business Experience*

*Courage is doing what you're afraid to do.*
*There can be no courage unless you're scared.*

— Eddie Rickenbacker, *pilot and airline executive*

### KEY OBJECTIVES

THIS CHAPTER WILL ENABLE YOU TO:

■ Locate wholesalers and trade fairs (flea markets) in your area.

■ Sell your merchandise at a trade fair.

■ Prepare an income statement from a trade fair field trip.

■ Use an inventory sheet.

■ Calculate net profit and ROI for the field trip.

## From the Wholesaler to the Trade Fair

This chapter will outline how to buy products from a wholesaler and resell them for a profit at a **trade fair** (flea market). This is a very simple and effective way to learn about business. The experience will allow you to put into practice many concepts you have studied so far, including:

- Evaluating opportunities
- Return on investment
- Marketing

- Keeping good records
- Income statements
- Negotiation

*(Note: Only go to a trade fair to sell your products if you have permission from a parent or guardian.)*

## Getting the Wholesale Price

You may have heard the expression, "I can get it for you wholesale." Wholesalers buy products in large quantities from manufacturers and sell smaller quantities to retailers. Because wholesalers buy large amounts of goods, the manufacturers give them discounts. A wholesaler then sells at the "wholesale price" to retailers. Wholesalers usually won't sell fewer than a dozen pieces of an item at a time, depending on the type of product.

Finally, retailers sell individual items to customers at the "retail price." If someone says he can "get it for you wholesale," he means that he can sell it to you for the wholesale price, without the retail markup.

## Finding Wholesalers

As an entrepreneur, you can visit a wholesaler, buy products at wholesale prices, and resell them to customers at retail. (In most localities you will need to register your business and have a tax ID number to buy wholesale.) You might buy a dozen candy bars for 30 cents each and resell them at 60 cents, for instance.

If you live in a city, there will probably be wholesale outlets you can visit in person. Find them by looking through your local phone company's *Business to Business Guide*. Libraries usually carry these directories.

If you live in a small town or rural area without wholesale suppliers, pick the largest city nearest you and look in its *Business to Business Guide*. You can call wholesalers whose products interest you and order through the mail. You can also find wholesalers on the Internet. Here are a few sources:

**American Science & Surplus**
  http://www.sciplus.com
  *Science, chemistry, and related toys and equipment.*

**Craft Catalog**
  http://www.craftcatalog.com
  *Provides crafts and art supplies, including brushes, paints, and sewing kits.*

**CR's Crafts**
  http://www.crscraft.com
  *Provides crafts, dolls, stuffed animals, and clothing.*

**Golf Discount**
  http://www.golfdiscount.com
  *Golf clubs, balls, and shoes.*

**Johnny's Selected Seeds**
  http://www.johnnyseeds.com
  *Supplier of plant, flower, and herb seeds, and garden accessories.*

**Night Club Items**
  http://www.glowitems.com
  *Provider of nightclub bracelets and glow sticks.*

**OfficeMax Online**

http://www.officemax.com
*Office supplies.*

**OffPrice Clothing**

http://www.offpriceclothing.com
*Provides returned and recycled clothing at low prices.*

**Oriental Trading**

http://www.orientaltrading.com
*Provider of a wide variety of wholesale gift items.*

**Party Pro**

http://www.partypro.com
*Party and paper supplies.*

**Performance Bicycle**

http://www.performancebike.com
*Cycling supplies.*

**St. Louis Wholesale**

http://www.stlouiswholesale.com
*Sunglasses, jewelry, and toys.*

**Sav-On-Closeouts**

http://www.sav-on-closeouts.com/
*Close-out gifts.*

**Superior Snacks Inc.**

http://www.superiorsnacks.com
*Provider of wholesale snacks and candy.*

**WholesaleCentral.com**

http://www.wholesalecentral.com/
*This is undoubtedly the most comprehensive wholesale site on the Internet. It has a large collection of categories and sub-categories, along with a great search feature.*

**Xybermart**

http://www.xybermart.com/
*This site provides wholesale items primarily to retail businesses. It provides a much smaller set of categories than WholesaleCentral.com*

**Yahoo's Wholesaler list**

http://dir.yahoo.com/Business_and_Economy/Business_to_Business/Wholesalers/

You can also look up wholesalers by industry or location in the *American Wholesalers and Distributors Directory.* Your library should have a copy.

Another way to locate wholesalers is through:

**Manufacturers' Agents National Association**
23016 Millcreek Road
P.O. Box 3467
Laguna Hills, CA 92654
1-877-626-2776
http://www.manaonline.org/

## Selling at a Trade Fair

Once you've purchased your products wholesale, you will be ready to sell them at a trade fair. These are open-air markets made up of entrepreneurs who rent space by the day or by the season. Sometimes the space is free, on a first-come, first-served basis. You can get a list of such markets in any community by calling the local chamber of commerce. It is a good way to gain basic business experience.

Consumers shopping at trade fairs are looking for bargains, so try to keep your prices low.

### *SKILLS MEAN SUCCESS*

**MATH**

**Numeration and Operations:** Using Mental Math

Imagine you are selling hand-made purses at a trade fair. Your cash drawer contains coins, and bills in denominations up to $20. Use the chart below to determine the bills and coins you would use to make change for each of the purchases given. (Use the largest-denomination bills and coins possible.) Then write in the correct amount of change. The first column is shown as an example. Do all calculations in your head.

| | Amount of sale: $35.28 Amount given: $100.00 | Amount of sale: $22.85 Amount given: $40.00 | Amount of sale: $12.83 Amount given: $20.00 | Amount of sale: $6.02 Amount given: $50.00 | Amount of sale: $80.14 Amount given: $100.00 |
|---|---|---|---|---|---|
| $20 bills | 3 | | | | |
| $10 bills | | | | | |
| $5 bills | | | | | |
| $1 bills | 4 | | | | |
| Quarters | 2 | | | | |
| Dimes | 2 | | | | |
| Nickels | | | | | |
| Pennies | 2 | | | | |
| | Amount of change: | Amount of change: | Amount of change: | Amount of change: | Amount of change: |
| | $64.72 | _____ | _____ | _____ | _____ |

**Rules of thumb** for selling at trade fairs:

1. Arrive early to get a spot where the most people will see your merchandise.
2. Have plenty of business cards and flyers to give away, even to people who don't buy anything.
3. Display posters or other eye-catching advertisements.
4. Bring plenty of change.
5. Keep track of your merchandise on inventory/record sheets.
6. Write a sales receipt for every sale.
7. Put on your "sales personality." Be outgoing and friendly.
8. Keep your prices low. People come to trade fairs to find bargains.
9. Understand the value your unit of sale will have to the customer.
10. Be prepared with a "sales pitch" for your product.

## SKILLS MEAN SUCCESS

**LEADERSHIP**

### Self-Confidence: Learning Self-Improvement

What does it mean to put on your "sales personality"? It means displaying the self-confidence and positive attitude that effective selling requires. Follow these tips to build a winning sales personality.

- Minimize distractions and negative influences. Focus on building the positive frame of mind that you want others to see.

- Try not to think about past mistakes or concerns. Learn from them but don't dwell on them.

- Praise yourself. Think: "I'm really good at ..." or: "I handled that situation really well."

- Visualize success in your mind.

- Believe in what you are doing and others will, too.

- Increase your energy by getting plenty of rest, exercising regularly, and eating right.

- Dress well. If you look good, you will feel more confident.

- Use successful people as role models and learn from what they do.

- Recall three events in which you succeeded. ■■■

**214**

## Getting Prepared by Knowing Your EOU

Now that you have your products, you must be prepared to sell and keep good records by preparing your EOU's.

**Economics of One Unit:** Before you start selling, figure your economics of one unit, using the method from Chapter 9.

*Example:* Let's say you purchased ten watches for $5 each from the wholesaler. Your beginning inventory is: 10 × $5 = $50.

You will also need to include any variable costs that can be assigned to a unit. Let's say the packaging cost for ten watches is $1.00. That means the packaging cost per watch is 10 cents ($1.00/10). Let's also say you are paying yourself a commission of 50 cents for every watch you sell.

| ECONOMICS OF ONE UNIT (EOU) | | | |
| --- | --- | --- | --- |
| **Retail Business:** unit of sale = 1 watch | | | |
| **Selling Price per Unit:** | | | **$12.00** |
| Cost of Goods Sold per Unit: | | $5.00 | |
| Packaging: | $0.10 | | |
| Commission: | 0.50 | | |
| Total Other Variable Costs per Unit: | $0.60 | 0.60 | |
| **Total Variable Costs per Unit:** | | $5.60 | 5.60 |
| **Gross Profit per Unit:** | | | $6.40 |

## Trade Fair Financials

Now that you've made a trip to a wholesaler and sold your products at a trade fair, you can prepare your economics of one unit and your income statement. You should have:

- The money from your sales
- Your sales receipts
- Your leftover merchandise

1.  **Cash Sales:** First, count your cash. Separate your "personal" money from your "business" money. Subtract the amount of business money you had at the beginning of the trade fair from the amount you have now. This will be the Total Cash Sales.

    **(End of Day Cash) − (Beginning of Day Cash) = (Total Cash Sales)**

2.  **Sales Receipts:** Next, add up your sales receipts. Your total cash sales should exactly match the total of the sales receipts. If it does not, you made a mistake in your transactions during the day, or you simply lost some money. The amount of total cash sales you have on hand is your revenue from the day.

3.  **At the End of the Day:** You will have enough information to create an income statement.

    - You sold five watches for $12 each, so Total Sales is $60.00.
    - Your Total COGS for one unit is $5.00 (see EOU above). For five watches, therefore, your COGS is 5 × $5.00 = $25.00.
    - Your Other Variable Costs per unit are $0.60 (see EOU). For five watches, therefore, your Other Variable Costs are 5 × $0.60 = $3.00.

What about Fixed Costs? Let's say it cost you $2.00 to take the bus to and from the trade fair with your watches; you spent $1.00 photocopying some flyers; and the trade fair provided you with a table for a rental fee of $10. Your fixed costs would be:

| | |
|---|---|
| Bus | $2.00 |
| Photocopying | 1.00 |
| Table rental | 10.00 |
| Total Fixed Costs: | $13.00 |

Now you have everything you need to prepare an income statement. The watch-selling experience would be documented as follows:

## INCOME STATEMENT

| Watch-Selling Business | Period: Date of Flea Market Trip | |
|---|---:|---:|
| **Revenue:** | | **$60.00** |
| COGS: | $25.00 | |
| Other Variable Costs: | 3.00 | |
| **Total Variable Costs:** | **$28.00** | 28.00 |
| **Gross Profit:** | | **$32.00** |
| Bus: | $2.00 | |
| Photocopying: | 1.00 | |
| Table Rental: | 10.00 | |
| **Total Fixed Operating Costs:** | **$13.00** | 13.00 |
| **Pre-Tax Profit:** | | **$19.00** |
| Taxes (20%): | | 3.80 |
| **Net Profit:** | | **$15.20** |

Now prepare a cash flow statement that will show the effect of your inventory investment and trade fair trip on your cash position.

## CASH FLOW STATEMENT

| Beginning Cash Inflow from Operations | | |
|---|---:|---:|
| Investment: | $50.00 | |
| Sales: | 60.00 | |
| **Total Cash Inflow from Operations:** | **$110.00** | **$110.00** |
| **Cash OutFlow from Operations** | | |
| Variable Costs: | $3.00 | |
| Fixed Costs: | 13.00 | |
| Inventory: | 50.00 | |
| **Total Cash Outflow from Operations:** | **$66.00** | (66.00) |
| **Net Cash Flow:** | | **$44.00** |

*Beginning cash = 0, ending cash = $44. Developing a cash flow statement shows that you have a positive cash flow of $44, despite the fact that you made a profit of $15.20. Remember, you have $25 of inventory left over.*

An efficient way to keep track of goods is through the use of an **inventory sheet**. The inventory sheet allows businesspeople to keep track of the goods they are planning to sell, and their prices and markups. It also shows how much profit is being made on each sale. This will make preparation of income statements easier.

### INVENTORY SHEETS

| Product | Wholesale Cost per Unit | Selling Price | Gross Profit per Unit | Markup* Percentage | Quantity | Total Cost of Goods Sold | Total Sales | Total Gross Profit |
|---|---|---|---|---|---|---|---|---|
| Comb | $2.00 | $4.00 | $2.00 | 100% | 100 | $200 | $400 | $200 |
| Brush | 3.50 | 8.75 | 5.25 | 150% | 40 | 140 | 350 | 210 |
| Socks | 1.00 | 3.00 | 2.00 | 200% | 50 | 50 | 150 | 100 |

$$* \text{Markup \%} = \frac{\text{Gross Profit per Unit}}{\text{Wholesale Cost per Unit}} \times 100$$

Inventory sheets also keep track of the markups on each item by expressing the profit both in dollars and as a retail markup percentage.

**Sales Sheets**

During the trade fair, you can keep track of your sales by using a sales sheet:

### TRADE FAIR SALES (SAMPLE)

| Product | A Units Sold (make mark for each sale) | × | B Wholesale Cost Per Unit | = | C Total Cost of Goods Sold | D Selling Price Per Unit | (A × D) Total Sales |
|---|---|---|---|---|---|---|---|
| Comb | IIIII (5) | | $2.00 | | $10.00 | $4.00 | $20.00 |
| Brush | IIIIII (6) | | $3.50 | | $21.50 | $8.75 | $52.50 |
| | | | | | $31.50 | | $72.50 |

*At the end of the day, you can complete your income statement.*

**My Income Statement**

| | | |
|---|---|---|
| My Total Sales are: | | $72.50 |
| My Total Cost of Goods Sold is: | | 31.50 |
| My Gross Profit is: | | $41.00 ($72.50 − $31.50) |
| My Fixed Operating Costs are: | $4.00 | |
| My Total Fixed Operating Costs are: | $4.00 | 4.00 |
| My Net Profit/(Loss) is: | | $37.00 ($41.00 − $4.00) |

## CRITICAL THINKING ABOUT...

### SELLING AT A TRADE FAIR

1. Use your local *Business to Business Guide* telephone directory to call two vendors of a product you would like to buy and resell.

2. After you have purchased inventory at a wholesaler for your trade fair field trip, write a short essay analyzing your experience. What did you buy? How much did you pay? How well do you think you negotiated?

3. Use your inventory sheet to create an income statement after your trade fair (flea market) selling experience.

## EXPLORATION

1. Call your local chamber of commerce and make a list of trade fairs and open markets in your area.

2. Use your local telephone company's *Business to Business Guide* or *The American Wholesalers and Distributors Directory* to locate wholesalers you could visit or from whom you could order products for resale.

## VOCABULARY

inventory sheet ■ trade fair

## Chapter Summary ✔✔✔

16.1 Buying wholesale to sell at a trade fair is a model of how a business works.
   A. Wholesalers buy in large quantities from manufacturers.
   B. Manufacturers give wholesalers large-quantity discounts.
   C. Wholesalers resell to retailers at higher ("wholesale") prices.
   D. Retailers resell to consumers at still higher ("retail") prices.

16.2 Entrepreneurs can set up a trade fair "business."
   A. Entrepreneurs can resell at trade fairs products purchased from wholesalers.
   B. Space for selling is free or low-cost.
   C. Keep and create records of all sales, expenses, and profits earned:
      1. Cash Sales
      2. Sales Receipts
      3. Economics of One Unit (EOU)
      4. Create an Income Statement
      5. Fill in Cash Flow Statement
      6. Keep Inventory Sheets and Sales Sheets. ✔✔✔

## SKILLS MEAN SUCCESS

**ENGLISH**

### Speaking and Listening: Telephone Etiquette

When placing business calls, remember to follow the rules of telephone etiquette.

**When making a call:**

- Concentrate on your purpose. Be prepared and have all necessary information in front of you, along with a pen and paper for taking notes.
- Make sure you are in a quiet environment with no distractions.
- Start with a greeting. Identify yourself. Explain your reason for calling.
- Speak clearly and slowly in a pleasant tone of voice. Use only standard English — no slang. Avoid saying "huh," "okay," or "uhmmm."
- Stay focused on the topic, so you don't waste time.
- Listen attentively and take notes on key information.
- Repeat information for verification, if needed. Be sure to confirm any commitments that either of you have made.
- End the call by thanking the person for his/her time, and close with a pleasant good-bye.

**If you have to leave a voice message:**

- Be sure your message is direct, polite, and businesslike.
- State your name clearly. Spell it and repeat if necessary.
- State your phone number clearly.
- Briefly state the reason for your call.
- Identify the best time to reach you.
- Repeat your name and telephone number.

Working with a classmate, practice role-playing a phone call in which you ask a wholesaler or vendor for information about products you would like to sell. ■■■

# A Business for the Young Entrepreneur
## PHOTO ALBUMS

*The fact that I took a simple idea and turned it into an operating business gives me the confidence that I can do whatever I want. I am grateful for the opportunities I've been given.*

A defining moment for Genevieve Johnson came when she decided she had a right to a future filled with the things most young people desire — college, a career, and a family. Two years later, Genevieve had a thriving business and many long-term goals, including establishing a "Peer-to-Peer Internship Program" to help others who wanted to realize their dreams.

BlueMedia Photo Albums offers albums and scrapbooks for various occasions. The company also provides a custom cover-design service. Genevieve sells the albums at schools and community events. She has a catalog, which is also available digitally. She follows up each customer interaction with a phone call or e-mail, hoping to form a lasting relationship. Customer satisfaction is important and all orders are filled within three days. Future plans include a Web-site launch and product-line expansion.

Genevieve has overcome her natural shyness and become a good speaker and deal-maker. She plans to attend college at the State University of New York at Buffalo. ■

# Resources for Starting Your Business[1]

## BOOKS

### On Starting a Business...

*101 Businesses You Can Start on the Internet*, Daniel S. Janal (International Thomson Publishing, 1996).

*The Art of the Start: The Time-Tested, Battle-Hardened Guide for Anyone Starting Anything*, Guy Kawasaki (Portfolio, 2004).

*Good to Great: Why Some Companies Make the Leap . . . and Others Don't*, Jim Collins (HarperBusiness, 2001).

*Online Success Tactics: 101 Ways to Build Your Small Business*, Jeanette Cates (Twin Towers, 2002).

*The Young Entrepreneur's Guide to Starting and Running a Business*, Steve Mariotti (Three Rivers Press; revised edition, 2000).

### On Thinking Like an Entrepreneur...

*The 48 Laws of Power*, Michael Greene (Penguin Putnam, 2000).

*Focus: The Future of Your Company Depends on It*, Al Reis (HarperBusiness, 1997).

*Secrets of the Young & Successful: How to Get Everything You Want Without Waiting a Lifetime*, Jennifer Kushell and Scott M. Kaufman (Fireside, 2003).

*The 7 Habits of Highly Effective People*, Stephen Covey (Free Press, 1990).

*The Student Success Manifesto: How to Create a Life of Passion, Purpose, and Prosperity*, Michael Simmons (Extreme Entrepreneurship Education Co., 2003).

*Success through a Positive Mental Attitude*, W. Clement Stone (Pocket Books, re-issue, 1991). A classic!

*Think and Grow Rich*, Napoleon Hill (Ballantine Books, re-issue, 1990). Another classic!

*Think and Grow Rich*, Dennis Paul Kimbro (Fawcett Columbine, 1991). An update of Hill's book by an African American.

### On Negotiating...

*Difficult Conversations: How to Discuss What Matters Most*, Douglas Stone, Bruce Patton, Sheila Heen, and Roger Fisher (Penguin Putnam, 2000).

*Getting to Yes: Negotiating Agreement Without Giving In*, Roger Fisher, William Ury, and Bruce Patton (Penguin Books; 2nd/Rep edition, 1991).

*You Can Negotiate Anything*, Herb Cohen (Bantam Books, 1993).

---

[1] Please note that NFTE cannot guarantee that the information in this section will remain current, including possible future changes to the contents of the listed Web sites.

**222**

Basic Resources

## BUYING WHOLESALE...

*The following is a list of sites where you can purchase products wholesale:*

**American Science & Surplus**
http://www.sciplus.com
Science, chemistry, and lab equipment.

**Craft Catalog**
http://www.craftcatalog.com
This site provides crafts and art supplies, including brushes, paints, and sewing supplies.

**CR's Crafts**
www.crscraft.com
Crafts, dolls, stuffed animals, and clothing.

**Golf Discount**
http://www.golfdiscount.com
Golf clubs, balls, and shoes.

**Johnny's Selected Seeds**
http://www.johnnyseeds.com
Supplier of plant, flower, and herb seeds, along with garden accessories.

**Night Club Items**
http://www.glowitems.com
Provider of nightclub bracelets and glow sticks.

**OfficeMax Online**
http://www.officemax.com
Office supplies.

**OffPrice Clothing**
http://www.offpriceclothing.com
Provides returned and recycled clothing at low prices.

**Oriental Trading**
http://www.orientaltrading.com
Large provider of wholesale gifts items.

**Party Pro**
http://www.partypro.com
Party and paper supplies.

**Performance Bicycle**
http://www.performancebike.com
Cycling supplies.

**Sav-On-Closeouts**
http://www.sav-on-closeouts.com/
Close-out gifts.

**St. Louis Wholesale**
http://stlouiswholesale.com
Sunglasses, jewelry, and toys.

**Superior Snacks Inc.**
http://www.superiorsnacks.com
Provider of wholesale snacks and candy.

**WholesaleCentral.com**
http://www.wholesalecentral.com/
This site has a large collection of categories and a great search feature.

**Yahoo's Wholesaler List**
http://dir.yahoo.com/Business_and_Economy/Business_to_Business/Wholesalers/

**Basic Resources**

# Basic Module

## Business Plan Review

*A business plan is the road map that gives a business direction.*
— Joseph Mancuso, *author of How to Write a Winning Business Plan*

## What Is a Business Plan?

A business plan is a document that explains a business idea and how it will be carried out. The plan should include all costs and a marketing plan. It should describe how it will be financed and what the earnings are expected to be.

The number one reason to write a business plan is to organize your thoughts *before* you start your business. Most of the entrepreneurs mentioned in this book wrote a business plan before they made a single sale. A well-written plan will guide you every step of the way as you develop your business. It can also help you raise money from investors.

## Why Do You Need a Business Plan?

Bankers, and other potential investors, will refuse to see an entrepreneur who does not have a business plan. You may have a brilliant idea, but if it is not written out, people will be unlikely to invest in your business.

A well-written plan will show investors that you have carefully thought through what you intend to do to make your business profitable. The more explanation you offer investors about how their money will be used, the more willing they will be to invest. Your plan should be so thoughtful and well written that the only question it raises in an investor's mind is: "How much can I invest?"

## Writing a Business Plan Will Save You Time and Money

As you work on your plan, you will also be figuring out how to make your business work. Before you serve your first customer, you will have answered every question you can. How much should you charge for your product or service? What exactly is your product or service? What is one unit? What are your costs? How are you going to market your product or service? How do you plan to sell it? Figuring all this out in advance will save you time and money.

If you start your business without a plan, these kinds of questions can overwhelm you. By the time you have completed the following pages, though, you will have answers — and you will have a road map for your own business! You will also be able to use these answers to create a PowerPoint presentation that will hit the high points of your business plan.

## Your Business Idea (Chapter 1)

1. Describe your business idea.
2. What is the name of your business?
3. Explain how your idea will satisfy a consumer need.
4. Provide contact information for each owner.
5. If there is more than one owner, describe how the business ownership will be shared.

## Economics of One Unit (Chapter 2)

1. Do you intend to pay yourself a salary, wage, dividend, or commission? Explain.
2. What type of business are you starting?
3. Calculate the Economics of One Unit for your business.

## Return on Investment (Chapter 3)

**Business Goals:**

1. What is your short-term business goal (less than one year)? What do you plan to invest to achieve this goal? What is your expected ROI?
2. What is your long-term business goal (from one to five years)? What do you plan to invest to achieve this goal? What is your expected ROI?

**Personal Goals:**

1. What is your career goal? What do you plan to invest to achieve this goal? What is your expected ROI?
2. How much education will you need for your career?
3. Have you tried to get a part-time job related to your chosen career?

## Opportunity Recognition (Chapter 4)

1. What resources and skills do you (and the other owners of your business) have that will help make your business successful?
2. Perform a SWOT analysis of your business.

## Core Beliefs (Chapter 5)

1. Describe three core beliefs you will use in running your company.
2. Choose a motto for your company. (You can select or adapt from the 50 positive quotes in Chapter 5, find one elsewhere, or make up your own.)

## Supply and Demand (Chapter 6)

1. What factors will influence the demand for your product or service?
2. What factors will influence the supply for your product or service?

## Product Development (Chapter 7)

How do you plan to protect your product/trademark/logo? (Pick one, and explain.)

Patent, copyright, or trademark.

## Competitive Advantage (Chapter 8)

1. What is your competitive advantage?

2. How will your business help others? List all organizations to which you plan to contribute. (Your contribution may be time, money, your product, or something else.)

## Operating Costs (Chapter 9)

1. List and describe your monthly fixed costs.

2. List and describe your monthly variable costs.

3. Re-calculate your economics of one unit, allocating as many variable costs as possible.

4. Add a cash reserve that covers three months of fixed costs.

## Marketing (Chapter 10)

1. Describe the Four P's for your business.

   **Product** — Why will your product meet a consumer need?

   **Place** — Where do you intend to sell your product?

   **Price** — What price do you plan to sell your product for, and why?

   **Promotion** — How do you plan to advertise and promote your product?

2. Fill out a marketing plan for your business.

3. Do you intend to publicize your philanthropy? Why or why not? If you do, explain how you will work your philanthropy into your marketing.

## Market Research (Chapter 11)

1. Research your industry and display the results in a one-page report that includes pie charts and bar or line graphs. Describe your target market within the industry.

2. Describe your market segment and the results of your research on this market segment.

## Record Keeping (Chapter 12)

1. Describe your record-keeping system.

2. List all bank accounts you will open for your business.

## Projected Income Statement (Chapter 13)

1. Complete a monthly projected budget and one-year income statement for your business.

2. Use your projected one-year income statement to calculate:

   Projected ROI for one year:
   _____ %

   Projected ROS for one year:
   _____ %

## Financing Strategy (Chapter 14)

1. What legal structure have you chosen for your business? Why?

2. List the cost of the items you will need to buy to start your business.

3. Add up the items to get your total start-up capital.

4. Add a cash reserve of one-half your total start-up capital.

5. List the sources of financing for your start-up capital. Identify whether each source is equity, debt, or a gift. Indicate the amount and type for each source.

6. What is your debt ratio? What is your debt-to-equity ratio?

7. What is your payback period? In other words, how long will it take you to earn enough profit to cover start-up capital?

## Negotiation (Chapter 15)

Describe any suppliers with whom you will have to negotiate.

## Buying Wholesale (Chapter 16)

1. Where will you purchase the products you plan to sell, or the products you plan to use to manufacture the products you will be selling?

2. Have you applied for a sales-tax ID number?

# INTERMEDIATE MODULE

# Operating Your Business

*The Intermediate Chapters of NFTE Semester 1 will teach you how to successfully manage and run your business. Once you have completed these chapters, you will be able to identify your competitive advantage, and learn the principles of selling and the basics of manufacturing.*

*After you have finished Chapter 30, you will be ready to apply what you have learned by preparing your Intermediate Business Plan. A complete version of the Intermediate Business Plan can be found in your NFTE Workbook.*

### CHAPTER 17

# COMPETITIVE STRATEGY:
## *Define Your Business, Mission, and Tactics*

*If I had eight hours to chop down a tree, I'd spend six sharpening my ax.*

— Abraham Lincoln

THIS CHAPTER WILL ENABLE YOU TO:

- Define a competitive strategy.
- Explain "business definition."
- Identify sources of competitive advantage.
- Create a mission statement.
- Develop tactics to use in implementing a strategy.

Finding a competitive advantage will require understanding your competition. You will have to figure out how to compete successfully for the same customers. (We discussed competitive advantage briefly in Chapter 8.)

Your **competitive advantage** is your **strategy** for beating the competition. It is whatever you can do better, cheaper, or faster than your competitors that will attract customers, satisfy them, and keep them coming back.

A competitive advantage must be *sustainable*, meaning that you can keep it going. If you decide to beat the competition by selling your product at a lower price, your advantage won't last long if you can't afford to continue at that price. Being able to temporarily undercut the competition's prices is not a competitive advantage. Being able to *permanently* sell at a lower price because you have discovered a cheaper supplier *is* a competitive advantage.

## Competitive Strategy [1]

Your competitive strategy is made up of:

1. *The Business Definition:* What your business is about.

2. *The Competitive Advantage:* Why you expect to succeed in a competitive marketplace.

In other words, competitive strategy combines the business definition with competitive advantage. Let's examine these two components of competitive strategy.

The essence of your strategy should be communicated in a **mission statement**. This will briefly but effectively describe what your business is about.

**Tactics** are the specific actions and activities required to carry out your strategy in operating the business. Key tactics will include how the business is presented in the marketplace, and how the product is made and delivered to the consumer.

## Business Definition

A business definition has three elements:

1. *The Offer:* What will you sell to your customers? That is called your *offer*. This will include exactly which products and services you will bring to the marketplace, and how you will price them.

2. *Target Market:* Which segment of the consumer market are you aiming to serve? This will be your *target market*. Defining your target market in a way that helps identify potential customers will be an important factor in achieving success.

3. *Production and Delivery Capability:* How will you provide your offer to your targeted customers? This includes how you will perform all key activities required to produce the product or service, deliver it to your customers, and ensure that they are satisfied.

The business definition answers three questions: What, Who, and How?

a. *Who* will the business serve? In other words, who is the target customer?

b. *What* will the business offer? What are the products (or services) the business will sell?

c. *How* will the business provide the products or services it offers? What are the primary actions and activities required to conduct this business? For example:

- Buying or developing or manufacturing the product.
- Identifying prospective customers and selling the product to them.

- Producing and delivering the product or service.
- Receiving payment.

## Competitive Advantage

To develop a competitive advantage, you must study your leading competitors so you can understand how your business compares. How have they defined their businesses, and what are their respective competitive advantages?

To determine whether you have a competitive advantage, ask yourself the following:

1. *Competitive Offers:* How does your offer compare to those of your leading competitors? What are the key features of each?

2. *Unique Selling Proposition:* Based on that comparison, what is your **unique selling proposition** (USP)? This will require a comparison of offers and the identification of what is unique about yours. What is it about your USP that your competitors cannot or will not match?

3. *Cost Structure:* What is different about your business activities, and "the cost of doing business," from your competitors? Overall, are you at a cost advantage or disadvantage?

To be successful, you must have a unique selling proposition that will attract customers to buy from you.

Second, you must have a cost structure that is sufficiently advantageous so that, when all of your costs are deducted from your revenue, you will have some profit left over. If you can achieve a cost advantage, or at least minimize any cost disadvantage, it will help you achieve a profit. This profit will be your reward for operating a successful business.

A competitive advantage will be the heart of your strategy. It is the reason you will expect to succeed in the marketplace. You must offer something to your target customers that is better or different from other businesses.

## Six Sources of Competitive Advantage

As discussed in Chapter 8, competitive advantage comes from six factors:

| | |
|---|---|
| **1.** Quality | **4.** Selection |
| **2.** Price | **5.** Service |
| **3.** Location | **6.** Speed/Turnaround |

# The Most Chocolate Cake Company

In this example, our entrepreneur makes and sells chocolate cakes. She chose this product because she loves chocolate and enjoys baking cakes. She decided to make the most *chocolate* cakes possible. From this decision, she came up with the concept for her product and the name of her business: The Most Chocolate Cake Company.

Her target market was the segment of the public that loved chocolate cake. Because cakes are usually purchased for special occasions, our entrepreneur believed she could charge a good price — at least as much as a bakery store cake.

She decided she would make the cakes "special" in three ways:

- By using the finest ingredients,
- Through expert custom decorating — personalizing each cake.
- By baking the cakes to order, so they would be fresh for the event.

She baked her cakes at home, which made them literally "homemade" and reduced the costs of making them — she was not renting commercial space or paying a staff.

The chart below shows how our entrepreneur answered the key questions about business definition.

| Business Definition Question | Response |
|---|---|
| 1. *The Offer:* What products and services will be sold by the business? | 1. Chocolate cakes, for special events, at a price competitive with neighborhood stores. |
| 2. *Target Market:* Which consumer segment will the business focus on? | 2. People who love chocolate, and those who would like a special cake for a special event. |
| 3. *Production Capability:* How will that offer be produced and delivered to those customers? | 3. Cakes will be homemade and baked to order to ensure freshness, using high-quality ingredients. |

# Analysis of Competitive Advantage

At this point, our entrepreneur has defined the business in terms of the offer, the target market, and the capability required to produce and deliver that offer to customers. Now she needs to compare her approach to the business to that of her competitors.

One useful exercise is to notice everything you can about particular competitors — especially those that have earned respect in the marketplace. Try to figure out why they do the things they do, and identify the sources of the competitive advantage.

You will also need to keep an eye on the competition *after* you have started your business, because new factors might be undermining your competitive advantage.

Before the Internet, research was both time-consuming and expensive. Today's entrepreneurs, even those starting very small ventures, may face competition from far beyond their neighborhoods because customers can go shopping on the Web. Optimism is a trait that is associated with entrepreneurs — they tend to get excited about the potential customer base on the Web. What they often don't realize is that "The world is already selling to their customers —aggressively and seamlessly."[2] Therefore, get online yourself and conduct a thorough search of your industry. Check out your competition's Web sites.

## SKILLS MEAN SUCCESS

**ENGLISH** → **Listening and Writing for Information and Analysis: Clarifying Information**

An executive of one of the world's largest information publishers once said that you should be able to write your competitive advantage on the back of a business card:

"X is the company/product that...."

For example, "QUICK-NO-PAIN is the low-cost non-addictive headache-reliever medicine that gets rid of a headache fast." This executive was trying to encourage business owners to state the competitive advantage clearly and simply.

1. A *slogan* is a type of concise competitive-advantage statement written for potential customers. Explain what each of the slogans below might be trying to say. Use your own words and complete the statement " _____ is the company that...."

   **a. Quick-Out Video** lets today's technology serve you faster and better.

   **b. VideoMax** is the mega store with the biggest choice — always!

   **c. Eye on Sports Videos** keeps you "in the game" all the time.

   **d. Friendly Corner Video** is where families rent their movies.

2. Look through the phone book business pages or use a Web directory:

   **a.** Find and list three business slogans and the companies that use them to state a competitive advantage.

   **b.** Write a one-sentence description in your own words explaining what each of the slogans is trying to say to potential customers. ■■■

# Is Your Competitive Advantage Strong Enough?

Doing research will help you evaluate your competitive advantage and decide on strategy and tactics. It will also help you get a clearer picture of your market, and of how well your competition is doing in it. According to Jeffry Timmons,[3] a successful company needs to:

- Sell to a market that is large and growing.
- Sell to a market where the competition is able to make a profit.
- Sell to a market where the competition is succeeding but is not so strong as to make it impossible for a new business to enter it.
- Sell a product or service that takes care of issues consumers may have with the competition (such as poor quality or slow delivery).
- Sell at a price that will attract the competition's customers.

If all of these are in place, you should be able to find a way to beat the competition and make a healthy profit, if:

1. You understand the needs of your customers;

2. You have a sustainable competitive advantage, based on a comparison of your offer to that of your competitors, identification of your "unique sales proposition" (USP), an understanding of how your costs compare to your competitors; and

3. You can produce and deliver a product or service that will meet customer needs at a fair price.

Based on these principles, our entrepreneur has determined how she wants to make her offering better and different. These differences will form the basis of her USP.

| Competitive Advantage Question | Competitive Difference (USP) |
|---|---|
| 1. *The Offer:* What will be better or different about the products and services that will be sold by the business? | 1. The Most Chocolate Cake Company will use more and highest-grade chocolate; better ingredients in general, especially in frosting and filling; will have personalized decorations and will be freshly baked to order. |
| 2. *Target Market:* What customers should be the focus of the business, to make it as successful as possible? | 2. People who love chocolate, and those who want a special cake for a special event. |
| 3. *Production and Delivery Capability:* What will be better or different about the way that offer is produced and delivered to those customers? | 3. Cakes will be homemade and baked to order to ensure freshness, using highest-quality ingredients. |

Our entrepreneur is betting that her cakes, with special frosting and decoration, as well as a freshly homemade quality, will be successful in the marketplace. This is her Unique Selling Proposition. She hopes it will be a source of competitive advantage, along with the cost advantage of baking the cakes at home.

## Mission

*Your* **mission** *as an entrepreneur is to use your competitive advantage to satisfy your customers.* Most great entrepreneurs have discovered that the true mission of business is to meet a consumer need better than anyone yet has. A commitment to serve your customers, and to satisfy their needs, is at the heart of a strong mission statement.

The mission of your business, expressed in the *mission statement*, is a concise communication of your strategy, including your business definition and competitive advantage. The function of a mission statement is to clarify what you are trying to do — and it can provide direction and motivation to people who are involved in the business.

A clear mission statement not only tells your customers and employees what your business is about, but also it will be a guide for every decision you make. It should capture your passion for the business and your commitment to satisfying your customers.

Here is an example of a mission statement, based on our business example:

> *The Most Chocolate Cake Company will create the richest, tastiest, most chocolaty cakes in our area. They will be made from the finest and freshest ingredients with our own unique frostings and fillings. Baked to order and individually decorated for that special occasion, they will make any event as wonderful as our cakes!*

The Most Chocolate Cake Company's mission statement defines the business and its competitive advantage, which is the core of its strategy.

## Tactics Carry Out Strategy

Once you have decided how to define your business — the product, the target customers, and how you will produce and deliver your product — you will have a large number of details to work out. These details of operation will be your *tactics*.

There are four tactical issues to address with regard to the implementation of your strategy:

1. Sales Plan
2. Market Communications
3. Operating Plan
4. Budget

Let's look at how our entrepreneur might address these tactical decisions.

| | Tactical Question | Issues | Solutions |
|---|---|---|---|
| 1. | *Sales Plan:* Where and how will you sell to your customers? | How to identify prospects and convert them to sales. | Our entrepreneur will use her network of friends to identify individuals who have a special occasion coming up. |
| 2. | *Market Communications:* How will you communicate with your customers and make them aware of your business offer? | How to make customers aware of your offer; how to attract them to the business. | She will create marketing materials to describe her business and offer an incentive for people to identify prospects. |
| 3. | *Operating Plan:* How will you manage your internal operations? | How to make the business go, and determine who will perform the tasks. | At present volumes, she bakes the cakes at home on order. This gives her an advantage in cost and freshness over stores in the neighborhood. |
| 4. | *Budget:* How do you plan to manage your revenues and expenses? | What are the sources of revenue? What are the items that have to be purchased? | There are two sizes of cakes, priced accordingly. The cost of ingredients is known for each size. The cost of the electricity for baking is estimated. Using a home kitchen is a cost advantage. |

The entrepreneur addressed each question in a way that makes sense for her business. She could have made different tactical decisions, which would have produced a different outcome. Over time, our entrepreneur might decide to change her tactics, to improve performance of the business as it develops.

# Finding Your Own Competitive Advantage

Are you having trouble figuring out what your competitive advantage is? The first place to look is at your hobbies and interests. Do you play an instrument? Take photographs? We tend to develop our individual talents and skills through our hobbies. These skills can be competitive advantages in the marketplace.

Think about your friends, as well. Perhaps you know someone with a special skill who has no business background. With your business knowledge and someone else's skill, you could start a partnership that could lead to a successful business.

## SKILLS MEAN SUCCESS

**MATH**

### Interpreting Graphs and Charts:
### Using Diagrams to Develop Strategies

You can use circle graphs or pie charts to illustrate a market. Visual models are tools that can help you "picture" information, such as your target customers or your competitors. Explain in your own words what the following two graphs are showing:

**a.** What does the graph's title describe about it?

**b.** What does each graph show about the current customers?

**c.** Is there an opportunity to start a new business?

**Total Child Day-Care Service Spending by Parental Age Group**

**Average Cost for a Couple to "Dine Out" in a Local Restaurant**

| Ages of Parents Who Use Day Care | | Average Costs of Dinner for Two | |
|---|---|---|---|
| ■ Under 20: | 5% | ■ Under $10: | 35% |
| ■ 20-30: | 40% | ■ Under $20: | 60% |
| ■ 30-40: | 45% | ■ Under $30: | 5% |
| ■ 40-50: | 9-10% | $30 or more: | 0% |
| ■ Over 50: | 1% | | |

## Cooperate to Compete

Finally, bear in mind that sometimes the best competitive strategy is to cooperate with the competition. Is there another student in the class who wants to start the same business as you do? Perhaps cooperating would be more profitable than competing.

## CRITICAL THINKING ABOUT...

### COMPETITIVE STRATEGY

1. Describe the difference between strategy and tactics.

2. What is included in the definition of a business?

3. Why are these elements important?

4. What key concepts should a business's mission statement contain and why?

5. Write a mission statement for a business in your neighborhood that you have dealt with.

6. Can you think of three competitive advantages for your generation?

7. Imagine you would like to start a business creating T-shirts and stickers for local bands to sell to their fans. Describe your strategy, mission statement, and tactics.

8. Use the following charts to define your own business, analyze your competitive advantage, and determine your tactics.
**Business Plan Practice**

| Business Definition Question | Response |
|---|---|
| 1. *The Offer:* What products and services will be sold by the business? | 1. |
| 2. *Target Market:* Which consumer segment will the business focus on? | 2. |
| 3. *Production Capability:* How will that offer be produced and delivered to those customers? | 3. |

| Competitive Advantage Question | Competitive Difference (USP) |
|---|---|
| 1. *The Offer:* What will be better or different about the products and services that will be sold by the business? | 1. |
| 2. *Target Market:* What customers should be the focus of the business, to make it as successful as possible? | 2. |
| 3. *Production and Delivery Capability:* What will be better or different about the way that offer is produced and delivered to those customers? | 3. |

| | Tactical Question | Issues | Solutions |
|---|---|---|---|
| **1.** | *Sales Plan:* Where and how will you sell to your customers? | How to identify prospects and convert them to sales. | |
| **2.** | *Market Communications:* How will you communicate with your customers and make them aware of your business offer? | How to make customers aware of your offer; how to attract them to the business. | |
| **3.** | *Operating Plan:* How will you manage your internal operations? | How to make the business go, and determine who will perform the tasks. | |
| **4.** | *Budget:* How do you plan to manage your revenues and expenses? | What are the sources of revenue? What are the items that have to be purchased? | |

## KEY CONCEPTS

1. In order to succeed, does a company need to sell a product or service more cheaply than the competition? Explain.

2. Write an essay describing your business's competitive advantage. Discuss the strategy and tactics you intend to use.

3. Write a mission statement for your business.

## EXPLORATION

Use the Internet to research the competition for a business you would like to start. List the Web-site URLs, e-mail addresses, phone and fax numbers, and the addresses of five competitors you located via the Internet.

## REFERENCES

[1] With special thanks to Peter Patch for his contribution to this chapter.
[2] Fred Hapgood, *Inc.* Magazine (June 1997).
[3] Jeffry Timmons, *New Venture Creation: Entrepreneurship for the 21st Century,* 5th Edition (Irwin/McGraw-Hill, 1999).

## VOCABULARY

business definition ■ competitive advantage ■ mission ■ mission statement ■ strategy ■ tactics ■ unique selling proposition

# Chapter Summary ✔✔✔

**17.1** Every business needs a mission or strategy that includes:
  A. The definition of what the business will do — in a written mission statement
  B. The explanation of why the business will succeed against its competition
  C. The plan for how (through the use of tactics) the strategy will be implemented.

**17.2** The definition of a business should answer three questions:
  A. What will be sold (the offer)?
  B. Who are the customers (the target market)?
  C. How will the offer be provided (production and delivery capacity)?

**17.3** The explanation of competitive advantage should answer three questions:
  A. How does the offer compare to those of competitors?
  B. What can't competitors match in the unique selling propositions?
  C. What cost advantages or disadvantages does the business have (cost structure)?
  D. Sources of competitive advantage include:
    1. Quality        4. Selection
    2. Price          5. Service
    3. Location       6. Speed/turnaround
  E. Competitive advantages to consider include:
    1. Large or growing market segment
    2. Profitable competitors already in the market
    3. Room for more competition in the market
    4. Customer-perceived weaknesses in competitors' products
    5. Opportunities to compete based on price
    6. Using talents, hobbies, and interests as well as cooperating with competitors.

**17.4** Mission statements should communicate a strategy:
  A. Briefly and concisely
  B. To both staff and customers
  C. That guides every business decision made
  D. With passionate commitment to serving customers.

**17.5** Tactics based on the mission statement should include detailed action plans for:
  A. Sales
  B. Market Communications
  C. Operations
  D. Budget. ✔✔✔

### CHAPTER 18

# DEVELOPING YOUR MARKETING MIX

*You can't be all things to all people. But I can be all things to the people I select.*

— Donald Neuenschwander, *American banker*

## KEY OBJECTIVES

THIS CHAPTER WILL ENABLE YOU TO:

- Understand the four steps of a marketing plan.
- Learn how to develop a successful marketing mix for your business venture.
- Learn the basic principles of pricing strategy.

## Marketing Communicates with Customers

Once you have figured out your competitive advantage (and your strategy and tactics for carrying it out) how do you communicate it to your customers? How do you convince them to choose you over the competition?

*Marketing* is your plan for bringing your product or service to the consumer in a way that illuminates your competitive advantage, and explains your value proposition.

Successful entrepreneurs are "market driven." Every decision they make is designed to convince the customer that their product or service is the best provider of the benefits the customer is seeking.

## Price: What It Says about Your Product

Remember the Four P's? They are the basic elements of every marketing plan. The Four P's are the ways you communicate information about your business to the consumer.

1. Product
2. Place
3. Price
4. Promotion

You will want to examine each "P" from a marketing perspective. Let's take Price as an example. New entrepreneurs often assume they should simply sell their product or service at the lowest price they can afford. If you are marketing a luxury item, though, offering the lowest possible price might not send the right message to the consumer. Sometimes consumers assume a low price means lesser quality.

BMW's marketing is designed to convince customers that it sells a luxury automobile. If BMW lowered its prices, what would that do to customers' perception? It could damage BMW's competitive advantage as a provider of luxury cars. *Simply selling at a lower price will not necessarily ensure a larger market share.*

You will need to know how the consumers in your market think before you can make good decisions about the Four P's. You will need to develop a carefully researched marketing plan.

 **BizFact:** According to Jay Levinson,[1] a study of consumers in the furniture industry found that price came ninth, when they were asked to list factors affecting the decision to make a purchase.

## The Four Steps of Developing a Marketing Plan

The marketing plan will introduce your product to the market. Developing a plan is a four-step process:

1.  Consumer analysis
2.  Market analysis
3.  Development of a **marketing mix** of the Four P's
4.  Break-even analysis (Break-even analysis will be discussed in Chapter 20.)

## Step One: Consumer Analysis

Before you can develop a marketing plan, you will need to analyze your customers. Who are they? What do they want?

Home Depot sells tools and other items people use to repair and improve their living spaces. But Home Depot *markets* itself as a company that teaches people how to *use* these tools. This is Home Depot's competitive advantage over hardware stores.[2]

Home Depot's tactics include free in-store clinics for developing home-improvement skills, design and decorating consultation, truck and tool rental, home delivery, free plant potting, and other services.

### Market Segments

There is a huge market for home repair that includes professional carpenters and builders. Home Depot's competitive advantage would not be strong in the **market segment** composed of professionals. A market segment is made up of consumers who have a similar response to a certain type of marketing. Home Depot chose to market to the non-professional segment of the market.

It is difficult to target two very different segments of a market at the same time. Volvo, for example, has established a reputation as a safe family car. They target parents with young children. Volvo would have a difficult time trying to market a two-seat convertible sports car to young adults who are concerned more with style and speed than safety.

### Successful Segmenting: The Body Shop

The Body Shop is a good example of the successful targeting of a market segment. Anita Roddick was fed up with paying for expensive packaging and perfumes when she bought cosmetics. Price had become an important part of the image for many brands. One perfume was marketed as the most expensive in the world!

Roddick saw an opportunity to create a different line of cosmetics. She decided to use natural products, packaged inexpensively. Her products appealed to women who didn't care for the hype of the cosmetics industry. Her success proved that selling an honest product straightforwardly can be the most effectively marketing strategy.

## SKILLS MEAN SUCCESS

**ENGLISH**  ▶  **Reading for Understanding: The Main Idea**

Which of the following best expresses the main idea behind The Body Shop?

**a.** Anita Roddick created a business by appealing to those women who wanted a no-nonsense and no-waste approach to cosmetics.
**b.** Women don't want to pay a lot for cosmetics.
**c.** Most women like expensive and expensively packaged cosmetics.
**d.** Men wish their wives would spend less on cosmetics. ■■■

## Step Two: Market Analysis

What if Roddick had found out that there were very few women interested in natural cosmetics? Her business would not have survived because, even though the cosmetics market is very large, her segment would have been too small to support a business.

It is possible to go after a small, "niche" segment, if you can set your price high enough (or your costs are low enough) to make a profit. Jaguar and Rolls-Royce each sell far fewer cars than Honda or Ford, but at *much* higher prices. Jaguar and Rolls-Royce target the luxury segment of the car market.

## There are five basic ways to analyze a market:

**BY LOCATION:** Segmenting consumers according to where they live. You could decide that the market for your home-baked goods would be everyone within five miles of where you live.

**BY POPULATION:** Segmenting consumers based on age or gender or education. You could decide to market your line of cosmetics to women between the ages of 15 to 35.

**BY PERSONALITY:** Segmenting consumers by opinion (conservative or liberal), or lifestyle. You could decide to market your services as a hiking guide to people who go camping.

**BY BEHAVIOR:** Segmenting consumers by observed purchasing patterns, such as brand loyalty or responsiveness to price. If you are making hacky-sacks, you could decide to focus on people who already play Frisbee, because they will show up as consumers interested in outdoor games of skill.

**BY INCOME:** Segmenting consumers by their economic status is another important way markets are analyzed. You could decide to focus on selling your jewelry to people who earn between $30,000 and $60,000 per year.

## Analyzing a Market Segment

Let's say you want to make and sell hacky-sacks at your high school, where there are about 2,000 students. How do you determine which segment of that market to target? You could use one of the above methods. For example:

**BY LOCATION:** You could decide that your market is everyone who lives within two miles of the school.

**BY POPULATION:** You could decide to limit your marketing efforts to juniors and seniors.

**BY PERSONALITY:** You would almost certainly decide to market to students who enjoyed playing games and being outside.

**BY BEHAVIOR:** You could decide to market to people who buy Frisbees because they are likely to buy hacky-sacks too.

"Income" would probably not play a part in this analysis because any student in your school would be able to afford one.

You could research your market by taking a sample survey of 200 students. Show them the product and ask such questions as:

Do you relax by going outside between classes? Do you play Frisbee?

Would you be interested in purchasing this hacky-sack if it were available?

If 50 of the 200 students surveyed seem interested in your hacky-sack, you could expect that roughly 500 of the 2,000 would represent your market. Now you can focus your marketing efforts on those students.

## SKILLS MEAN SUCCESS

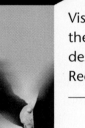

**LEADERSHIP** **Market Research**

Visit a retail business or two in your neighborhood. Get a sense of who the average customers are. Then ask the owners or managers to describe their average customers by age ranges and by where they live. Record your findings using a form like the following:

| Store Visited | Products Sold | Approximate Ages of Typical Customers | Where Typical Customers Live | Comments |
|---|---|---|---|---|
| Kicks | Shoes | 15-30 | All over the city. | Kicks caters to younger people who like brand-name casual shoes. |
| | | | | |

## Step Three: The Marketing Mix

Now that you have chosen your market segment, you are ready to develop a "marketing mix." This is the combination of the Four P's — product, price, place, and promotion — that will communicate your competitive advantage, strategy, and tactics.

If you change one "P" you must pay attention to how it will affect the others. If you raise your price, should you now still sell the product in the same place? Or will you need to move to a location that will better attract consumers willing to pay (and be attracted by) the new price?

# Value Pricing

Most consumers are driven by a strong desire to get value for their money. They want to feel good about spending it. **Value pricing** is not just price-cutting. It means finding the balance between quality and price that will give the customers in your market segment the value they seek. *Value* is not the same as *cheap*. If the quality of a product is superior, consumers will be willing to pay a higher price.

# Retailers' Rule of Thumb: Keystoning

Retailers who buy goods wholesale and resell them to the consumer sometimes use the "keystoning" method, which means doubling the wholesale price to arrive at a retail price. If you buy cell phones for $42 each from a wholesaler, selling them for $84 in your store will probably cover your costs and provide you with an acceptable profit.

Keystoning is a good way to roughly estimate a price — but the entrepreneur must be sensitive to competitive advantage, and to what competitors are charging.

# Other Pricing Strategies

**Cost-Plus:** Figure all your costs and add the desired profit margin. This method fails, however, to consider the marketing plan.

**Penetration Strategy:** This can work well during the early stages of a product's life cycle, as it is based on using an initial low price to gain market share. Japanese companies used this method to dominate the VCR market.

**Skimming Strategy:** The opposite of Penetration Strategy, this method seeks to charge a high price during a product's introductory stage, when it is new and has no or few competitors. RCA used this strategy when it came out with color television.

**Meet or Beat the Competition:** This is a common strategy in service businesses. Periodically, airlines tend to compete intensely by lowering ticket prices. The more you can show that your business is different from your competition, however, the less you will have to compete with your price. When Richard Branson started Virgin Atlantic Airways, he offered massages and individual videos at each seat. His marketing emphasized how much fun it was to fly on Virgin. This marketing strategy was successful, even though Virgin did not always offer the lowest fares.

Pick a price that communicates your competitive advantage to your market segment. The same goes for the rest of the Four P's — make all your business decisions market-driven and you will be successful.

## CRITICAL THINKING ABOUT...

### YOUR MARKETING MIX

1. Why is it important for an entrepreneur to be "market driven"? What does this mean?

2. Give an example of a business in which having the lowest price has been a successful strategy. Explain the strategy.

3. Give an example of a business that successfully uses a different strategy from charging the lowest possible price. Explain that strategy.

4. What do you think is the right market segment for your business? How do you intend to learn more about your target market?

## KEY CONCEPTS

1. What business are you planning to start? Which method will you use to segment your market? Explain.

2. Which pricing strategy do you intend to use for your product (or service)? Explain.

3. What is a drawback of "cost-plus" pricing?

4. What is "penetration" pricing? Can you think of an example of a company that has used penetration pricing to introduce a new product?

5. Bring to class an ad from a newspaper or magazine that illustrates one of the pricing strategies explained in this chapter.

6. Read A Business for the Young Entrepreneur on the following page. Describe John's pricing strategy.

## MARKETING MIX CHART

My Market Segment:

| Marketing Mix | Decision | Explanation |
|---------------|----------|-------------|
| Product       |          |             |
| Price         |          |             |
| Place         |          |             |
| Promotion     |          |             |

**Business Plan Practice**

## EXPLORATION

1. Visit three different fast food restaurants, then answer the following:

   a. What do you think the competitive advantage of each restaurant is?

   b. Did you see any differences in how the employees handled customers' orders? Describe them.

   c. Describe what you think the pricing strategy of each restaurant is.

2. How can the community benefit from your philanthropic activity?

3. How can your business benefit from your philanthropic activity?

## REFERENCES

1 Jay Levinson, *Guerrilla Marketing Attack* (Houghton Mifflin, 1989).

2 B. Marcus and A. Blank, *Built from Scratch: How a Couple of Regular Guys Grew the Home Depot from Nothing to $30 Billion* (Random House, 1989).

## VOCABULARY

marketing mix ■ market segment ■ value pricing

# Chapter Summary ✔✔✔

**18.1**   Marketing is the plan used to communicate a product or service to customers:
A. Shows competitive advantages
B. Explains value proposition (benefits vs. price)
C. Being "market driven" means decisions are based on the market.

**18.2**   Marketing plans use research to address the "Four P's":
A. Product
B. Place
C. Price
D. Promotion.

**18.3**   Develop a marketing plan in steps.
A. Analyze consumers by segment:
  1. A segment is a group of customers who respond similarly
  2. Target similar segments.
B. Analyze:
  1. Markets by location, population, personality, behavior, and income
  2. Segments by location, by population, by personality, and by behavior.
C. Decide on a marketing mix (using and balancing the "Four P's"):
  1. Value pricing: match quality, price, segment
  2. Keystoning (doubling the wholesale price) to establish a retail price
  3. Cost-Plus pricing adds desired profit margin to product costs
  4. Penetration Strategy uses low initial pricing to gain market share
  5. Skimming Strategy is the opposite of Penetration
  6. Meet-or-Beat-the-Competition pricing. ✔✔✔

# A Business for the Young Entrepreneur
## JOHN'S FOUR SEASON CARE, JOHN STEELE

John Steele has about three-dozen customers who depend on him to keep their yards clean. He gets out of bed before dawn to mow lawns in the summer, rake leaves and re-soil in the fall, and shovel snow in the winter. His market segment consists of homes in his neighborhood. He prices himself below the professional landscaping services in the area, but he delivers the same quality of service. His customers appreciate the value he provides.

John started his business when he was 14. "People give me business because they really like to see kids working hard — not just hanging out or doing drugs. Too many kids want to make money illegally. This way you can do it legally and be proud."

John says that a student entrepreneur must be reliable: "People won't ask you back if you show up late or don't do a good job. They won't recommend you to their neighbors, either."

*Describe John's pricing strategy. What else do you think he could do to market his business?* ■

CHAPTER **19**

# ADVERTISING AND PUBLICITY

*Many a small thing has been made large by the right kind of advertising.*

— Mark Twain, *American author*

## KEY OBJECTIVES

THIS CHAPTER WILL ENABLE YOU TO:

- Explain the difference between advertising and publicity.
- Generate publicity for your business.
- Use promotion to communicate effectively with your market.
- Choose ways to promote your business — online and in the media.

**T**he marketing mix of the Four P's communicates competitive advantage, strategy, and tactics to the consumer. But how will you deliver it? Entrepreneurs use **advertising** and **publicity** to convey a marketing mix to their customers.

## Ads Cost Money; Publicity Is Free

An **advertisement** is a paid announcement that a product or service is for sale. Examples of advertising include television commercials, billboards, and magazine ads.

Publicity, in contrast, is free. It is attention paid to a business by the **media** — "print" (magazines, newspapers, etc.) and television and radio. When you buy an ad in a newspaper, it is advertising. When the newspaper publishes an article about your business, it is publicity.

Together, advertising and publicity are called **promotion**. The goal of promotion is to establish a positive image of the business in the mind of the consumer.

## Publicity Provides Credibility for Your Business

Publicity is valuable because customers are more likely to believe it than advertising, since it comes from a third party. Publicity will give your business credibility. On the other hand, you can't control what the media says about you. With advertising, you have the advantage of saying exactly what you want.

Publicity is extremely important for a small business, which typically has a low advertising budget. Save any publicity you receive to show potential customers.

## How to Get Publicity

To get publicity, you will need to mail or fax **pitch letters** and **press releases** to magazines, newspapers, TV, or radio stations you hope to interest in your business.

The letter will "pitch," or *sell*, your story. It tells the person reading the letter why he or she should be interested in your business. A press release consists of several paragraphs of factual information that can be used by a writer as the basis for an article, or a radio or television story. In a press release, you are announcing the who, what, when, where, and why of an event. A pitch letter allows you to explain the story behind the press release, and why it is relevant to the media's readers, listeners, or viewers.[1]

Before mailing or faxing the pitch letter and/or press release, call the media outlet and ask whom you should contact. Say something like, "My name is Jason Hurley and I'm a young entrepreneur with a delivery/messenger service downtown. I'd like to send WKTU a press release about the commitment we have just made to donate ten hours of free delivery service per month to Meals on Wheels for Seniors. To whom should I direct a press release?"

Send out a press release when you get involved with a charity, for example, or when you hold special events. Press releases can generate positive stories about your business in local newspapers and radio stations. Make sure you send the press release well in advance. Follow up with a phone call two weeks later, and another one a week before the date. Be polite but persistent. Don't wait for a call back — call again. The worst that can happen is that you will hear a "No." But a "No" can be the beginning of a productive conversation.

## What's Your Story?

Younger entrepreneurs can have an advantage here because few young people start their own businesses. The print, radio, and television journalists in your town may want to hear about you.

Bear in mind, however, that reporters like *news,* and they want facts. It's fine to send out a press release announcing the opening of your business, but be aware that it would not be a "story" until your business is at least up and running. There is no point to sending a pitch letter and press release until you are actually in business and have a story to tell. What is your story? Try to make it interesting enough so that reporters will want to write about it.

Throughout this text, we have included narratives of young entrepreneurs who have started their own businesses. As you read them, think about your own possibilities.

- What has happened to you, or what have you done, that would make you and your business an interesting story?
- Did you have to overcome any obstacles in order to start your business?
- Is your product/service unique or something your community needs?
- How has your business changed you and helped your community?

Answers to these questions would help reporters determine whether your story might be of interest to their readers or viewers. Reporters are very busy people, so keep your answers to these questions clear and concise. Try to find one focus or "angle" for your story.

 **BizTip:** Avoid using the phrases "hopes to," "plans to," or "expects to" in your press releases. When reporters see those phrases, they know there is no story yet.

## Sample Pitch Letter *(page 253)*

## Sample Press Release *(page 254)*

A press release must provide contact information (name, phone, e-mail, and Web site, if available) and answer these basic questions:

- Who?
- What?
- When?
- Why?
- Where?

January 1, 2005

Dear _____ :

When Malik Armstead opened his soul food take-out restaurant, The Five Spot, on Myrtle Avenue in Brooklyn eight years ago, he was taking a risk. He was putting all his savings into a business in a neighborhood that was far from fashionable. On the other hand, Armstead came from a less-than-fashionable neighborhood himself, but when he was still a teenager, an organization called the National Foundation for Teaching Entrepreneurship (NFTE, pronounced "nifty") believed that he could make it as an entrepreneur and gave him the skills to do so.

"NFTE taught me that you don't necessarily have to have a lot of money to start a business," says Armstead. "I started my first business in high school with only $50."

Today, the restaurant is thriving, based entirely on word-of-mouth advertising, and has become a neighborhood mainstay, providing generous portions of high-quality soul food at reasonable prices.

Other entrepreneurs have followed the 29-year-old Malik's lead. Clinton Hill has been "discovered" by people who cannot find affordable apartments in Manhattan, Brooklyn Heights, or Park Slope. The area is flourishing.

Malik has hired many young people from the neighborhood. For two current employees, The Five Spot was their first job. One of them has been with the restaurant for over three years now and has risen from dishwasher to sous-chef.

On February 1st, Malik plans to expand The Five Spot from its current 800 square feet to 2,500 square feet, including a 60-foot mahogany bar and a 150-foot stage, as well as a second full dining room. He will continue to serve great soul food while providing live music by local artists.

I invite you to meet and interview this young entrepreneur who has helped to transform a neighborhood. You are also invited to join us at The Five Spot for a VIP party on February 1st at 9 pm, where there will be free food, drinks, and entertainment.

Sincerely,

*Brenda G. West*

West Public Relations

JANUARY 1, 2005

**FOR IMMEDIATE RELEASE**

<u>Soul Food Restaurant Expands</u>

Popular Restaurant Revitalized Myrtle Avenue

On February 1st, Malik Armstead plans to begin expanding The Five Spot Restaurant at 459 Myrtle Avenue from its current 800 square feet to 2,500 square feet, including a 60-foot mahogany bar and a 150-foot stage, as well as a second full dining room. To celebrate, Armstead is hosting a VIP party on February 1st at 9 pm, where there will be free food, drinks, and entertainment.

The Five Spot will continue to serve great soul food while providing live entertainment by musicians from the neighborhood and showcasing local artists.

Armstead was a pioneer in bringing his restaurant to Myrtle Avenue eight years ago, before the Clinton Hill area of Brooklyn was "discovered" by people who could not find affordable housing in Manhattan, Brooklyn Heights, or Park Slope.

The restaurant became a success entirely through word-of-mouth advertising, and has become a neighborhood mainstay, providing generous portions of high-quality soul food at reasonable prices.

Other entrepreneurs have followed the 29-year-old Armstead's lead in bringing businesses to Clinton Hill.

The Five Spot has made a policy of hiring people from the neighborhood. For two current employees, The Five Spot was their first job. One has been with the restaurant for over three years and has worked his way up from dishwasher to sous-chef.

For more information, contact:
Malik Armstead (718) 555-7839

## Follow Up a Press Release by Phone

Follow up your press releases with phone calls. Try to reach the journalists directly. Take a whole day to make phone calls pitching your story. Have a one-sentence opener to explain why your story is newsworthy. Try to build friendships. Positive reporting often develops because the reporter comes to care about the entrepreneur.

## The Media

**Print** — Newspapers, magazines, and newsletters are primary examples of print media. Consider running a coupon in a neighborhood newspaper. Send press releases to local publications.

There is a rule of thumb that says a consumer needs to see an advertisement at least nine times before the marketing message penetrates. In addition, for every three times a consumer sees an ad, he/she will ignore it twice. This suggests that a potential customer will have to see your ad 27 times before actually making a purchase.

If you take out a newspaper ad that runs three times a week, therefore, commit to running it for at least nine weeks. A common mistake is to give up too soon. If you aren't sure you want to spend the money on an ad in a particular publication, read a few issues, and see whether your competitors use it regularly. If they do, they are probably seeing a good return on their investment, so you should, too.

Customers looking for a product or service often turn to the *Yellow Pages*, the phone book that lists businesses in a community. Place an ad in the *Yellow Pages* as soon as you can afford to do so.

**Television** — Commercial television advertising rates, as well as the cost of creating TV ads, are extremely high. However, the rates on local cable stations would be lower, and an entrepreneur with a new business and an interesting story might be able to get a free mention (publicity).

**Radio** — University and local stations are often willing to mention a new business venture that has an interesting angle. They might even interview you.

**Banner ads** — These are advertisements that run on Web sites.

**Billboards** — Billboards are usually in highly visible locations and use short, punchy copy and large pictures or photos that drivers can grasp at a glance. Next time you see one, write down the message and try to find the same company's ad in a magazine. How does the billboard presentation differ from the magazine's?

**Brochures** — Place brochures in "Take One" boxes around town. Make sure you put them where your customers would tend to go, and give them out to people you meet. Think carefully about whether you want to put a lot of brochures in a few strong locations, or put a few in many.

**Business cards** — A business card should have your name and title, name of business, all contact information (address, phone/fax numbers, and e-mail and Web site). If possible, include a short motto or statement about the benefit of doing business with your company. Carry business cards with you wherever you go. You can design business cards on your computer or have them made at a local print shop.

**Direct mail** — Whenever you make a sale, get the customer's address, phone and fax numbers, and e-mail address. Once you've developed a mailing list, send out cards or letters regularly, to inform customers of sales and special events. You can also send special discounts for mailing list customers only. You can send e-mail updates. Mailing-list software is easy to use, so you can keep organized (including printing labels).

Always include this statement in the e-mail: *If you wish to be removed from this list, please type REMOVE in the subject line of your response.* This shows you respect the privacy of your customers.

**Catalogs** — By the time you have built up a list of about 10,000 names, you may be able to afford a four-color catalog. Two-color catalogs are less expensive, so look into that possibility sooner.

**Discount coupons** — Give a discount (price break) to first-time customers or for a limited time. This will encourage new consumers to try your product or service. You can also give existing customers discounts to discourage them from going to the competition.

**Flyers** — Flyers are one-page hand-out ads you can draw by hand, or create using computer software.

- Fax your flyer to customers on your mailing list who have agreed to receive faxes (in some states it is illegal to send unrequested faxes).
- Photocopy your flyer and distribute it at community functions, sporting events, under windshield wipers; and post them on bulletin boards, at laundromats, and other community gathering spots, such as local high

schools, colleges, restaurants, community centers — or hand them out on the street. Flyers can also include discount coupons.

**Free gifts** — "Freebies" draw potential customers the way honey draws flies. But don't disappoint with gifts that look and feel cheap. Go to a wholesaler, where you can get good prices on large quantities of calculators, watches, desk pens, or other useful items.

**Partner with another business** — You can try to connect with a business that has a customer base similar to the one you are interested in. If your product is a new health snack, you could join with a juice company and suggest putting a cents-off coupon in the juice package to encourage their customers to try your product.

**Promotional clothing** — T-shirts or caps bearing the name of your business can turn you and your friends into walking advertisements for your business. You can even put the name of your business on shopping bags. Note how many coffee and soda cups carry names of products and services.

**Samples or demonstrations** — Offer samples of your product to potential customers passing by your business. Or take samples to a location where there are many people. If you are selling a service, demonstrate outdoors or in a mall (get permission first!).

**Special events** — Stage contests, throw parties, or organize events to attract attention and customers to your business. Holding contests will gather valuable names for your mailing list, too.

**Special offers** — Offer "Buy three cookies and get a fourth one free!" Or "The tenth person to buy a T-shirt gets a free CD!"

**Team sponsorships** — Sponsoring a local sports team is a great way to involve your business in the community and meet potential customers.

**Web site** — Software such as Dreamweaver makes it easy to create your own business Web site. Or, many Internet service providers and Web-site hosting companies offer the ability to sell goods and services online using e-commerce systems — commonly known as online stores. An online store makes your goods and services accessible to anyone in the world. You can search Google on the Internet for Web-site hosting companies.

**800 Numbers** — Contact your phone company to find out how to set up an 800 number for your business, so your customers can call you for free. Some long-distance providers offer special discounts to small-business owners.

## SKILLS MEAN SUCCESS

**MATH**     **Solving Problems that Don't Require Exact Answers**

**1.** Using *estimation*, predict which cost goes with each advertising activity. Check your answers with a calculator.

| | |
|---|---|
| **i.** Between $2,000 and $3,000 | **a.** printing 9000 flyers at $6 per hundred copies. |
| **ii.** Over $5,000 | **b.** $50 newspaper ad run every day for two months. |
| **iii.** Approximately $550 | **c.** $200 30-second TV ad run twice daily for 2 weeks. |
| **iv.** Approximately $100 | **d.** $20 radio spot run 40 times. |
| **v.** Slightly over $750 | **e.** 30 T-shirt giveaways at $3.30 wholesale. |

**2.** Use the rates listed in #1. Plan a mixed-media advertising campaign for a holiday sale for your own business or for the clothing store where you work. Your budget is approximately $1,100. Try to do the calculations in your head. ■■■

## Visualize the Customers *Before* Placing an Ad

Before placing an ad, visualize your ideal customers. How old are they? What is their average income? What are the benefits of your product or service that an ideal customer would want? Remember, the goal of promotion is to establish your competitive advantage in the customer's mind.

Once you have visualized your ideal customer, you will be able to make sensible advertising decisions. If you were promoting a rap concert, it would be a waste of money to take an ad in a magazine for senior citizens. Don't waste precious advertising dollars on customers who won't need or want your product or service.

Of course, sometimes you'll spend money on an ad and get no response. Use that information to make a better decision next time. John Wanamaker, a department store founder, remarked, "Half the money I spend on advertising is wasted; the trouble is, I don't know which half."

## The Small-Business Ad

Most ads for small businesses are designed to sell the consumer a specific product or service. Small businesses can't usually afford to engage in **institutional advertising**, as large corporations do. This is non-specific promotion designed to keep a company or industry in the mind of the general public. Most small businesses begin their advertising with a simple print ad in a local newspaper or magazine.

An effective small-business ad concentrates on the aspect of the product or service that is most important to the customer. That aspect is usually one of these:

1. Price
2. Product/Service
3. Location

## The Five Parts of a Print Ad

These are the five basic parts of a printed advertisement:

1. Headline (Title)
2. Deck (Subtitle)
3. Copy (Text)
4. Graphics (Photographs or Drawings)
5. Logo/Trademark[2]

## Marketing Online

There are millions of people all over the world who are connected to the Internet. Your marketing message might only appeal to a tiny percentage, but even a fraction of the online market represents a great many people. Better still, the online marketplace is organized into special interest groups, so it's not hard to figure out where to promote your business. There are many ways to market your business online:

**Online services** — Online services offer classified ads, billboards, and Internet shopping malls. Talk to a marketing staff person at your Internet service provider (ISP) about setting up your own storefront in such a mall.

259

**Newsgroups** — A "newsgroup" is an online forum where people leave messages for each other on selected topics. The messages form an ongoing discussion. Although you can't advertise your business in a newsgroup, you can get to know the other participants and conduct informal market research.

**E-mail** — Electronic mail is fast and easy to use, but be careful about how you use it. Most people greatly resent unsolicited e-mail, so only send it to customers who have told you they want to hear from you. Develop a list of customers who want to receive e-mails, but even then resist the urge to send too many. When you do send an e-mail, keep it informative and entertaining, so that customers will be happy to get it.

**Web site** *(See "Web site" on page 257.)*

**Search engines** — You can buy "keywords" from Google, so that when people are looking for a specific category, your Web site will be at the top of the list. You will only be charged if someone clicks on the link and becomes a potential customer.

## SKILLS MEAN SUCCESS

**ENGLISH** ▶ **Writing for Social Interaction: E-mail**

**1.** Write an e-mail to your mailing list offering a discount or free gift on any purchase over $25. Re-read the tips in the Free gifts, Discount coupons, and Direct mail sections earlier in this chapter. Make sure your spelling and grammar are correct for maximum impact.

**2.** Exchange e-mail messages with a partner. Proofread and make two suggestions that will make your partner's e-mail more effective to a prospective customer. ■■■

## Cause-Related Marketing

Cause-related marketing is inspired by a commitment to a social, environmental, or political cause. A business can donate a fixed percentage of its revenue (say, one or two percent) to a particular charity and then publicize this in its marketing.

Which causes matter to you? As a young entrepreneur, you might consider donating one dollar from every hundred sales to a charity that is promoting a cause that is important to you. Getting involved is not only the right thing to do but will also be good for your business. You will meet new customers and contacts. You might even get written up in the local newspaper! Publicity related to charitable giving often results in positive image and increased sales.

## CRITICAL THINKING ABOUT...

### ADVERTISING AND PUBLICITY

1. Label the five parts of the print ad below reproduced in the workbook. On which aspect of the product does the ad focus?

**There Is No Substitute For Martin Cowboy Boots.**

Our cowboy boots are designed by Martin and crafted to Martin's exclusive specifications. They are backed by Martin. Continually refined and enhanced by Martin's extensive research and development program.

Naturally, we believe that there is no substitute for a pair of Martin boots. So we designed Martins to have their own unique look and feel. To be handcrafted to their own high standards of quality and workmanship. To share the Martin tradition of excellence, while being affordable to as many different budgets as possible. Including yours.

Try a pair on at your Martin dealer.

**MARTIN**
In the Martin tradition.

2. Locate an example of "institutional" advertising in a newspaper or magazine and bring it to class. Explain why you think it is or is not effective.

3. Answer the questions below and use them to write a press release for your business.[3]
   **Business Plan Practice**

   a. What was your life like before you began the study of entrepreneurship?

   b. Were you having any problems in school or at home?

   c. What have you learned about business that you didn't know before?

   d. What's the best thing about running your own business? What obstacles have you had to overcome to get your business going?

   e. Has running your own business changed how are you doing in school? Has it changed how you get along with your family?

   f. Are you more involved in your community since you started your business?

   g. How has your business changed your life? What would you be doing if you were not an entrepreneur?

   h. If you could give one piece of advice to students who were thinking about starting a business, what would it be?

   i. What are your dreams for the future?

4. Develop a concept for your own business and use it to create a flyer and a print ad.

5. Create a business card and include a motto or statement.

## KEY CONCEPTS

1. What's the most important thing to do before buying or designing an ad? Explain.

2. Describe three ways you plan to promote your business.
   **Business Plan Practice**

3. If you buy an ad that runs in a newspaper four times per week, what is the rule of thumb for how long you should keep the ad running? Why?

4. What is "direct mail"? Will you use it to promote your business? Explain.

5. What's your "story"? Write a one-page description of yourself and your development as an entrepreneur.

6. After reading A Business for the Young Entrepreneur, write a press release about Marvin's two new initiatives. What angle will you use?

## EXPLORATION

1. Find an online newsgroup that might be a good source of customers for your business.

2. Contact an Internet service provider or hosting service to find out how much it would cost to set up a Web site. Write up your findings.

## REFERENCES

1 Special thanks to Tom Philips for ideas used in this chapter.
2 Trademarks will be discussed in more detail in Chapter 42.
3 Special thanks to Jan Legnitto for this "critical thinking" exercise and for other assistance with this chapter.

## VOCABULARY

advertisement ■ advertising ■ institutional advertising ■ media ■ pitch letter ■ press release ■ promotion ■ publicity

## Chapter Summary ✔✔✔

19.1 Advertising and publicity are forms of promotion.
   A. "Promotion" is building a positive image for consumers.
      1. Advertising is paid-for announcements
      2. Publicity is free attention from the media.

19.2 Publicity can be generated.
   A. Use pitch letters and press releases to provide positive, factual (who, what, when, why, where) information to media writers.
   B. Follow up by phone after sending information to media writers.
   C. Have a "story" about the business or product.

19.3 Decide on which media to use.
   A. Choose from among print, TV, radio, banner ads, billboards, brochures, business cards, direct mail, catalogs, coupons, flyers, gifts, partnering, promotional clothing, samples, demonstrations, offers, sponsorships, Web sites, and "800" phone numbers.
   B. Decide which advertising methods will most effectively reach customers.
   C. Decide what advertising methods the business can afford.
   D. Use small-business ads to emphasize the Four P's: price, product, place, or location.

E. Print ads consist of:
   1. Headline/title
   2. Deck/subtitle
   3. Copy/text
   4. Graphics: photos or drawings
   5. Logo/trademark.
F. Online advertising uses:
   1. Online services
   2. Newsgroups
   3. E-mail
   4. Web sites
   5. Search engine "keywords."
G. Cause-related marketing creates goodwill and publicity. ✔✔✔

## A Business for the Young Entrepreneur

**BED STUY'S PROJECT RE-GENERATION, INC. (NONPROFIT),
MARVIN "BARNABAS SHAKUR" SCARBOROUGH**

Before launching Bed Stuy's Project Re-Generation, Barnabas had no experience in running a non-profit business. That did not stop him. He immersed himself in researching on the Internet and in libraries, and talking to business owners and consultants. His efforts have earned many awards, including first place in NFTE's national Advanced Entrepreneurship Business Plan Competition, and Student Entrepreneur of the Year, Minority Enterprise Development Agency (U.S. Commerce Department). The publicity from these awards has helped his business to attract donors. He also is working toward a degree at New York City Technical College.

Driving these efforts was his goal to establish a nonprofit dedicated to providing urban minority young adults with work and volunteer experience. He is committed to revitalizing the Bedford-Stuyvesant community in Brooklyn by providing clean-up and maintenance services. This meets two vital community needs: increased property values, and opportunities for young adults.

The organization has launched two initiatives to help revitalize the community: Rites of Passage (ROP) and Youth Always Committed to Outstanding Restoration (ACTOR). ROP provides volunteer experience and workshops in job training, professional development, and financial management. ACTOR teaches young people to claim a stake in making their communities safe and clean. ■

### CHAPTER 20

# BREAK-EVEN ANALYSIS:
## Can You Afford Your Marketing Plan?

*Nothing in life is to be feared. It is only to be understood.*

— Marie Curie, *French-Polish scientist*

### KEY OBJECTIVES

THIS CHAPTER WILL ENABLE YOU TO:

■ Know what break-even means to a business.

■ Figure how many units your business must sell to "break even."

■ Use break-even analysis to evaluate your marketing plan.

## The Break-Even Point

Once you've created a marketing plan, you will have to answer one more important question: Can you afford it? Luckily, there is a tool to help you answer this. It is the fourth and final step of the marketing process: **break-even analysis**.

As you've learned, the income statement shows whether or not a business has made a profit. When sales and costs are equal, there is neither profit nor loss. The total at the bottom of the income statement will be "zero." This scenario is called the **break-even point**.

Break-even analysis will help you find the point at which your business will sell enough units to *cover its costs*. This is your break-even point. It will help you figure out how many units you need to sell to be able to afford your marketing plan, as well as your other fixed costs. If you make sales of 2,000 units a month, but your break-even analysis shows that you will need to sell 5,000 units to cover your fixed costs, you will have to rethink the costs in your business plan.

## Break-Even Analysis

Let's look at David's income statement again.

David bought 25 ties at $2 each and sold them all for a total of $100. He was selling each tie for $4, or keystoning ($100/25 ties = $4 per tie).

- David's selling price per unit is $4.

- David's unit of sale is one tie.

- David's cost of goods sold per unit is $2.

$4 (Selling Price per Unit) − $2 (Cost of Goods Sold per Unit) = $2 (Gross Profit per Unit)

David's gross profit per unit is $2.

| INCOME STATEMENT | | |
|---|---:|---:|
| **David's Ties** | | **Date: 10/27/2007** |
| **Revenue: (25 ties × $4)** | | **$100.00** |
| COGS: (25 ties × $2) | $50.00 | |
| Other Variable Costs: | 0.00 | |
| **Total Variable Costs:** | **$50.00** | 50.00 |
| **Gross Profit:** | | **$50.00** |
| **Total Fixed Operating Costs:** | | 24.00 |
| **Pre-Tax Profit:** | | **$26.00** |
| Taxes: | | 6.00 |
| **Net Profit:** | | **$20.00** |

The gross profit per unit is used to pay the fixed operating costs of a business. Marketing costs are fixed because they are not affected by sales. They come about through decisions made by the entrepreneur about such questions as how much advertising to buy.

*Break-even units formula:* $\dfrac{\textbf{Fixed Operating Costs}}{\textbf{Gross Profit per Unit}}$ = **Break-Even Units**

Using gross profit per unit, David can calculate how many units he will have to sell each month to cover his fixed operating costs. The **break-even units** are the number David will have to sell each month to cover fixed operating costs. His fixed operating costs of $24 represent the amount of money he spends each month on flyers to advertise his business.

$$\frac{\text{Fixed Operating Costs}}{\text{Gross Profit per Unit}} = \text{Break-Even Units}$$

$$\frac{24}{2} = \text{Break-Even Units}$$

$$12 = \text{Break-Even Units}$$

David has to sell 12 ties each month to cover his fixed operating costs (the flyers) and stay in business. If he sells fewer than 12 ties, he will suffer a loss. If he sells more than 12, he will earn a profit. If he sells exactly 12, he has covered his costs, but no more. When you "break even," you have neither a profit nor a loss.

When you develop your marketing plan, remember that all fixed operating costs have to be covered. If you can't sell enough units to reach your "break-even point," you may have to reconsider your marketing plan.

Let's figure the break-even units for a shoe store with the following figures. In this analysis, we are figuring the number of units that have to be sold per month for the business to break even:

*Monthly Fixed Operating Costs: $1,200*
*Gross Profit per Unit: $12*

$$\frac{\text{Fixed Operating Costs}}{\text{Gross Profit per Unit}} = \text{Break-Even Units}$$

$$\frac{1,200}{12.00} = \text{Break-Even Units}$$

$$100 = \text{Break-Even Units}$$

The store has to sell 100 shoes per month to cover its fixed operating costs.

Break-even analysis is a good tool for looking at all your costs and should be performed frequently. It is especially important after you've completed your marketing plan and before you open your business, to see if your plan is realistic.

It usually takes time for a new business to increase sales enough to make a profit. Until then, the business has to have enough cash to "burn" to cover losses while the business grows. A break-even analysis and a good forecast of sales growth can estimate about how long it will take for a new busines to become profitable.

## SKILLS MEAN SUCCESS

**MATH** → **Number and Numeration:** Understanding Percentage
**Mathematical Reasoning:** Devising Formulas

1. One way for a business owner to watch fixed operating costs is to compare them to revenue. If the Jersey Mike's store in Newark had average monthly sales of $24,000, calculate the *percentage of revenue* of each fixed cost vs. *total* fixed cost, below. The first one is done for you as an example.

2. Another way that owners can keep track of fixed operating costs is to study *each* cost in relation to the total. How do the individual fixed costs compare to total fixed costs?

| Fixed Operating Costs | Monthly Cost | % of Revenues | % of Total Fixed Operating Costs |
|---|---|---|---|
| Utilities | $1,000 | 4.16% | 8.33% |
| Salaries | $3,000 | | |
| Advertising | $4,000 | | |
| Interest | $0 | | |
| Insurance | $1,500 | | |
| Rent | $2,000 | | |
| Depreciation | $500 | | |
| Total Fixed Operating Costs | $12,000 | | 100% |

3. Check your answers and think about the operations you used in #1 and #2 above. Write a formula in words (or symbols) using the "equals" sign ( = ) that could be used to help an intern at the store:

   **a.** find the percentage of revenue of *any* individual fixed cost
   **b.** find the percentage of total fixed operating costs of an individual fixed cost for any business.

*Remember:* a formula is a general description or rule that is true for all examples. If a formula is correct, you can put any numbers in it, and it will still be true. ■■■

## Break-Even Analysis for Jersey Mike's

The National Foundation for Teaching Entrepreneurship owned a student-operated outlet of a fast-food franchise in Newark called Jersey Mike's. Here is a break-even analysis for the restaurant:

1. A customer at Jersey Mike's typically bought a sandwich for $4 and a drink for $1, so the average sale per customer was $4 + $1 = $5. Therefore, the unit of sale was defined as a "sandwich with drink," which sold for $5.

2. The cost of goods sold (COGS) for each unit was $1.25 for the components of the sandwich, 50¢ for the direct labor to assemble the sandwich, and 25¢ for the drink. The total COGS for the "sandwich with drink" was $2.00 per unit of sale.

3. There were variable costs of 50 cents per unit (25 cents packaging and 25 cents delivery/shipping).

| ECONOMICS OF ONE UNIT (EOU) | | | |
|---|---|---|---|
| **Retail Business:** unit = 1 sandwich with drink | | | |
| **Selling Price per Unit:** | | | **$5.00** |
| Materials: | $1.25 | | |
| Direct Labor: | 0.50 | | |
| Drink: | 0.25 | | |
| **Cost of Goods Sold per Unit:** | $2.00 | $2.00 | |
| **Total Other Variable Costs per Unit:** | | 0.50 | |
| **Total Variable Costs per Unit:** | | $2.50 | 2.50 |
| **Gross Profit per Unit:** | | | $2.50 |

4. The store was open 20 days each month.

5. The monthly fixed operating costs at Jersey Mike's were:

| FIXED OPERATING COSTS (USAIIRD) | |
|---|---|
| Utilities: | $1,000.00 |
| Salaries:* | 3,000.00 |
| Advertising: | 2,000.00 |
| Interest:** | 1,000.00 |
| Insurance: | 1,000.00 |
| Rent: | 1,000.00 |
| Depreciation: | 1,000.00 |
| Total USAIIRD: | $10,000.00 |

\* Not including direct labor counted in COGS.     \*\* 10% interest on $120,000 bank loan.

Apply the formula to figure out how many units they had to sell to break even each month. Then figure how many they had to sell to break even each day.

$$\frac{\textbf{Fixed Operating Costs}}{\textbf{Gross Profit per Unit}} = \textbf{Break-Even Units}$$

$$\frac{\textbf{10,000}}{\textbf{2.50}} = \textbf{Break-Even Units}$$

$$\textbf{4,000} \quad = \textbf{Break-Even Units}$$

The Jersey Mike's outlet had to make sales of 4,000 units a month to break even. Since the store was open 20 days a month, to break even each day the store had to sell:

$$\frac{\textbf{4,000}}{\textbf{20}} = \textbf{Break-Even Units per Day}$$

$$\textbf{200} \quad = \textbf{Break-Even Units per Day}$$

| INCOME STATEMENT | |
| --- | --- |
| Revenue (4,000 × 5): | $20,000.00 |
| Less Variable Costs (4,000 × 2.5): | 10,000.00 |
| Less Fixed Operating Costs: | 10,000.00 |
| Net Profit: | $0.00 |

*The break-even point is 4,000 units.*

## SKILLS MEAN SUCCESS

**ENGLISH** ▶ **Writing for Information and Understanding:**
Using Standard English — Hyphenation

1. Flip through today's newspaper, an online news source, or any magazine, Web site, textbook or other document. Make a list (randomly check any ten pages) of a dozen *hyphenated* words you find, such as "break-even." Don't confuse hyphenated words with thoughts or examples separated from the main sentence by *dashes* — which should be longer.

2. Write a one- or two-sentence rule for business writers about when and why to hyphenate a word. Compare your rule with a partner's and revise as needed. Be prepared to share it with the class. ■■■

## CRITICAL THINKING ABOUT...

### BREAK-EVEN ANALYSIS

1. Describe how finding your business's break-even point would help you operate your business.
   **Business Plan Practice**

2. Before you can find your break-even point, what other financial statement(s) and information would you need?

3. Let's say you have a business selling a product for $10 per unit that you buy from a wholesaler for $5. The business has $2,000 per month in fixed costs. Last month you sold 300 units. Write a memo analyzing this business from the perspective of a break-even point and discuss three strategies for improving the situation.

## KEY CONCEPTS

1. Describe why break-even analysis is the fourth step in the marketing process.

2. What is the formula for calculating break-even units?

3. Figure gross profit per unit:

| Item | Selling Price per Unit | COGS per Unit | VC per Unit | Gross Profit per Unit |
|------|------------------------|---------------|-------------|----------------------|
| Comb | 1.00 | .50 | .10 | _____ |
| Tie | 10.00 | 3.00 | .25 | _____ |
| Watch | 20.00 | 8.00 | 2.00 | _____ |

## PROBLEMS

Apply the break-even formula to find the "break-even" number of units for each problem.

### Problem 1

*Monthly fixed operating costs* = $100
*Gross profit per unit* = $0

### Problem 2

*Monthly fixed operating costs* = $1,200
*Gross profit per unit* = $20

### Problem 3

*Monthly fixed operating costs* = $3,000
*Gross profit per unit* = $12

## CAN YOU AFFORD YOUR BUSINESS PLAN?

1. A business expects to sell 100 units next month. They anticipate $600 of fixed operating costs. How many units would have to be sold to "break even"?

   *Monthly marketing cost* = $400
   *Other monthly fixed operating costs* = $200
   *Gross profit per unit* = $8

2. If they sell 100 units, could the business afford to have $600 in fixed operating costs?

**3.** If yes, how much profit will they make? If no, how much will they stand to lose?

break-even analysis ▪ break-even point ▪ break-even units

## SKILLS MEAN SUCCESS

**LEADERSHIP**

**Why Math Is Important:** Identifying Math Resources
**Networking and Communication:**
**Finding Contacts and Listening**

Interview at least one local business owner or manager to find out how math is used in the business. What kinds of "mathematical" records are kept? What mathematical skills are needed? Which of these are most important? How many times a week/month are these skills used? Write out four or five interview questions in advance and listen closely to the responses. Be prepared to present your findings to the class. ■■■

# Chapter Summary ✔✔✔

**20.1**  Break-even analysis shows how much a business can afford to spend on marketing and other operating costs.

    *A.* When sales and total costs are equal, the business reaches the break-even point: no profit, no loss.

    *B.* The Gross Profit from every unit sold must help pay Fixed Operating Costs.

    *C.* A business must sell enough units of sale to cover its Fixed Operating Costs.

    *D.* That number of units is the Break-Even Units number.

    *E.* $\dfrac{\text{Fixed Operating Costs}}{\text{Gross Profit per Unit}} = \text{Break-Even Units}$

    *F.* New businesses often don't have enough sales to earn a profit. Their total Gross Profit isn't high enough to do more than cover costs. ✔✔

# CHAPTER 21

# PRINCIPLES OF SUCCESSFUL SELLING

*When there's nothing to lose and much to gain by trying, try.*

— W. Clement Stone, *sales expert and advocate of "positive mental attitude"*

## KEY OBJECTIVES

THIS CHAPTER WILL ENABLE YOU TO:

- Turn product features into customer benefits.
- Turn customer objections into sales advantages.
- Pre-qualify a sales call.
- Make an effective sales call.
- Build good relationships with customers that will lead to more sales prospects.

## Business Is Based on Selling

If marketing is the art of bringing the customer to your product or service, *selling* is the art of bringing your product or service to the customer. All business is based on selling products or services for money, but the key to making a sale is to listen to your customers until you figure out what your product or service can do for them. A successful sale matches a product or service with a consumer need.

## Entrepreneurs Are Salespeople

Many of America's great entrepreneurs started out in sales:

Ray Kroc, founder of McDonald's, was selling milkshake machines before he was inspired to turn the McDonald brothers' hamburger restaurant into a national operation.

Aristotle Onassis was a wholesale tobacco salesman before becoming a multimillionaire in the shipping industry.

King C. Gillette was a traveling salesman when he got the idea for the safety razor.

W. Clement Stone started out selling newspapers at the age of six before going on to build a great fortune in the insurance industry.

William C. (Billy) Durant, the founder of General Motors, began his career as a buggy salesman. He liked to say, "The secret of success is to have a self-seller, and if you don't have one, get one."

## Salespeople Learn about Customers

Salespeople often become successful entrepreneurs because they hear what the consumer needs and wants on a daily basis. If a customer is dissatisfied, it is the salesperson who hears the complaint. Successful salespeople work hard at getting to know their customers.

Once you start selling, you will be amazed at how much you can learn about your customers. Selling is a skill you can never improve on enough. It will encourage you to develop a positive attitude, because you will quickly notice how much more willing people are to buy from a positive, upbeat person than from a grouch.

## Sell the Benefits, Not the Features

Inexperienced salespeople make a common mistake: They think telling the customer about the features of the product will sell it. But remember, a customer who buys a drill doesn't need a drill, she needs to make a *hole*. The essence of selling is explaining *why* the outstanding features of your product or service will be beneficial.

Let's say you are selling hats that fold without wrinkling, are washable, and come in a wide range of colors. Don't sell the hat by telling the customer that it folds, doesn't wrinkle, and comes in many colors. Those are the *features*. Instead, explain the *benefits*:

- This hat can be folded up so that it fits into your pocket or bag — you can take it anywhere. Because it doesn't wrinkle, it will always look neat.

- You can toss this hat in the wash, so you will save money on dry cleaning.

- This hat comes in many colors, so you can find one to match your coat.

The features of a product are facts about it. The creative art of selling is teaching the customer how the features will be benefits.

## Ways to Sell

There are many ways to sell, including:

- By appointment (sales call).
- Trade fairs, flea markets, street fairs.
- Direct mail (sending product or service offers through the mail).
- Door to door.
- Through classmates at school.
- Through community, school, or religious functions.
- "Cold calling" (contacting or visiting a prospect without an appointment).
- By telephone.
- Through listings in a catalog.
- From home.
- From your own store.
- From your Web site.
- Through other stores.
- Through outside salespeople on commission.
- Through your own sales team.
- Through newspaper, radio, or television advertising.

Not all of these methods, of course, will be applicable or affordable for a beginning entrepreneur. One or more, however, may be perfect for your business.

### SKILLS MEAN SUCCESS

**MATH**

**Measurement: Understanding Length and Area**

Exhibition space at trade shows is often rented based on the number of square feet. Space at the annual Home and Garden Show at the convention center rents for $17 per square foot. Which of the following available booth-display areas is the biggest one that you could afford if your budget were $10,000? Check your choice by asking yourself if the answer is reasonable.

| Booth Number | Length | Width | Price/ Square Foot | Area | Total Price |
|---|---|---|---|---|---|
| 233 | 20' | 12' | $17 | | |
| 415 | 45' | 12' | $17 | | |
| 418 | 30' | 17' | $17 | | |
| 536 | 25' | 32' | $17 | | |

## Focus on One or Two Products

A good rule for a young entrepreneur is to find one product or service and focus on it until the business is successful. The more you are able to concentrate your time, energy, and resources, the better your chances of success. Also, give each product line you sell its own name. If one name comes to represent too many items, you will run the risk of confusing the public. People will become unsure as to what your name represents.

### SKILLS MEAN SUCCESS

**ENGLISH** ▶ **Writing for Information:** Cause and Effect

Consider car buying. Buyers may tell you they spend a lot of time driving on the highway, which makes their legs tired or lower back sore.

- The prospect's *need* is relief of sore back or tired legs.
- The *product feature* that meets that need is cruise control.
- The customer benefit that cruise control provides is that it allows a driver to remove the foot from the accelerator while driving on a highway. By allowing the driver to move his or her legs around while driving, soreness or tiredness may be reduced or eliminated.

Write a Need/Feature/Customer Benefit chart for a car shopper. List at least five Needs, Features, or Benefits. Use a form like this one:

| Prospect Need | Product Feature | Customer Benefit |
|---|---|---|
| | | |

## The Sales Call

A **sales call** is an appointment with a potential customer to explain or demonstrate a product (or service). The goals of an effective sales call are to:

- Make the customer aware of your product.
- Ask questions to uncover the customer's needs.
- Demonstrate to the customer how the product's features will create benefits to fulfill those needs.

Even if you do not make the sale, you will still have made an effective call if you:

- Ask the customer to refer you to others who might be interested in your product or service. This is a good way to develop new sales prospects.

● Establish a friendly relationship with the customer so that you can make future sales.

## Before Your First Sales Call

Before going on any sales call, take the time to get your marketing materials right. These are brochures, order forms, samples, etc. They should be clear and easy to read and use. All marketing materials for your business should reinforce your competitive advantage in the customer's mind.

Good marketing materials will accomplish three things:

1. Preparing them will make you organize your thoughts.

2. You can use them to teach employees about your business quickly.

3. They will be helpful during a sales call.

## Pre-Qualify Your Sales Call

Before calling to make an appointment for a sales call (also called a sales *pitch*), ask yourself: Is this person in my market? Would he/she need my product? Can he/she afford it?

If the answer to any of these is "No," making the call could be a waste of time. Asking these kinds of questions is called "pre-qualifying" a sales call.

## The Eight-Step Sales Call

1. **Preparation.** First, be neat, clean, and dress appropriately. Prepare yourself mentally. Think in advance about how your product or service could benefit this person. Have the price, discounts, all technical information, and any other details memorized. You don't want to waste time fumbling for information you should know. Be willing to get more information, however, should it be requested. Practice your sales presentation by yourself or with a friend, and remember: think positive thoughts.

2. **Greeting.** Greet the potential customer graciously. Do not plunge immediately into business talk. The first few words you say could be the most important. Keep a two-way conversation going. Maintain eye contact and keep the person's attention.

3.  **Showing the Product/Service.** Good salespeople believe in what they are selling. Understand how your product's features can be of benefit. Try to "personalize" the features by pointing out the benefits for this particular individual. Use props and models (or the real thing) where appropriate.

4.  **Listen to the Customer.** After you pitch your product or service once, listen closely to the reaction. This is when you will get your most valuable information. You will learn what the potential customer needs and wants. Your goal here and throughout the sales call will be to convince the person that you are trying to solve his/her problem — not just make a sale. That's how you establish trust and a real relationship.

5.  **Answering Objections.** During the listening phase, you may hear objections. Always acknowledge these concerns and deal with them. Don't pretend you didn't hear. Don't overreact. Sometimes objections are simply misunderstandings. If you listen carefully, perhaps you can clear these up.  A famous real estate entrepreneur, William Zeckendorf, said, "I never lost money on a sales pitch when I listened to the customer." Do not hesitate to tell the truth about any aspects of your product or service that do not meet the customer's needs. Each time you respond honestly to a concern, you gain trust.

6.  **Asking for a Commitment.** If concerns have come up, point out that, at this price, the product or service would still be an excellent buy. Review the benefits of the product. Narrow the choices. Ask the customer to commit to making the purchase. If it appears that the product does not match the customer's needs, however, do not try to force a sale. Don't overstay your welcome. You may make a sale to this person in the future. If the sale is successful, fill out a receipt to finalize it. Keep a careful record of every sale you make.

7.  **Follow-Up.** Make regular follow-up calls to find out how the customer likes the product or service. Ask if you can be of any further help. If the customer has a complaint, don't ignore it. Keeping customer trust after the sale is extremely important — a successful business is built on repeat customers. Plus, every time you talk to a customer, you are deepening a friendship. Your best sales prospects in the future are people who have already bought something from you. Keep them posted on your business by sending postcards or flyers.

8.  **Ask for References.** Ask customers to refer you to potential customers. Try to set up a system that encourages others to send sales prospects your way. Offer discounts, gift certificates, or other incentives to customers who refer people to you.

**BizFact:** Research has shown that, in successful sales calls, the buyer does most of the talking — not the salesperson!

## Analyze Your Sales Calls to Become a Star Salesperson

Every sales call is an opportunity to improve your selling skills — even if you don't make a sale. The star salesperson analyzes each call by asking him/herself:

- Was I able to get the customer to open up to me? Why or why not? Did I do or say anything that turned the customer off?

- Which of my questions did the best job of helping the customer zero in on the problem?

- Was I able to make an honest case for my product/service being the one that could solve the problem?

- Did I improve my relationship with this person during the call?

## Use Technology to Sell

You can use technology to sell your product and to stay in touch. For example:

- A videotaped demonstration or presentation of your product.

- Web site customers can visit for updates, sales, and other information.

- E-mail and fax to stay in touch with your customers.

- A customer database. This is a list of all actual and potential customers. The database should include each person's name, mailing address, and other contact information (phone, fax, e-mail). Include the date of your last contact and a note about what the person bought and said.

### SKILLS MEAN SUCCESS

**LEADERSHIP**    **Understanding Customer Needs:** Sales Interviews

1. Work in pairs. One partner should be a customer with a need. The other should be a sales professional with a solution. Role-play a sales call; then switch roles. Videotape the scenario so you can decide what was done well and where additional effort is needed.

2. Ask a professional salesperson about his or her top ten hints for successful selling. ■□■

## The Sales Receipt

When you make a sale, you should fill out a receipt for the customer in a carbon-copy receipt book (or use two-part carbonless forms). The original is the proof of income that you will record in your NFTE Journal.

The receipt should include the date of the sale, the item sold, and its price. It can also include the name and address of the purchaser. The copy of the receipt is the customer's proof that the item or service was purchased.

In the example on the right, "Reg. No." (cash register number) and "Clerk" would be applicable to larger stores; #28 is the style number of the T-shirt. This is important to know for purposes of inventory (the amount of a product you have on hand).

### GINA'S T-SHIRT CO.

| | | |
|---|---|---|
| Date | **June 13** | **2005** |

Sold to: **George Braxton**

Address: **123 E. Orange St.**

Reg. No. _____ Clerk _____

| | | | |
|---|---|---|---|
| 1 | **1 red T-shirt (#28) @** | **$10.99** | **$10.99** |
| 2 | | | |
| 3 | | Tax | .61 |
| 4 | | | |
| 5 | | Total | $11.60 |
| 6 | | | |
| 7 | | | |
| 8 | | | |
| 9 | | | |
| 10 | | | |

*Paid in Cash*

Style 1200 **495-1**

## The Sales Commission

When you are ready to hire salespeople for your business, you can encourage them to sell by paying them a **commission**. As you have learned, this means that they will receive a percentage of every sale they make. A car salesman making a ten percent commission, for instance, would get $2,000 if he were to sell a $20,000 car (.10 × $20,000 = $2,000). The owner of the car dealership pays the sales staff a commission to encourage them to sell more cars.

**Rule of Thumb:** If a customer says "No" three times, you still have a shot at making the sale. If the customer says "No" a fourth time, he/she really means it.

## CRITICAL THINKING ABOUT...

### SUCCESSFUL SELLING

1. Do you plan to make sales calls for your business? Why or why not?

2. Have you created any marketing materials? If so, have three friends and a mentor (someone older that you respect who can give you advice about your business) look over your materials and give you feedback. Write a memo listing suggestions and what you plan to do to improve your marketing materials.

## KEY CONCEPTS

1. Explain three reasons why salespeople often become successful entrepreneurs.

2. Choose three ways you plan to sell your product or service. Describe why you have chosen these three and why you think they will work. **Business Plan Practice**

3. Write a sales pitch for the product (or service) your business will be selling. Include the features and benefits. **Business Plan Practice**

4. Develop a list of features and customer benefits for the following:
   a. Diet soda
   b. Earrings
   c. Necktie
   d. Delivery service
   e. T-shirt

5. Using examples from the media, explain the difference between marketing and selling.

## EXPLORATION

Visit a store in your neighborhood and let a salesperson try to sell you a product. After this experience, pretend you are the owner of the store and write a memo to that person evaluating his or her selling techniques (without actually sending it). What criticism would you have? What kinds of suggestions would you make?

## VOCABULARY

commission ▪ sales call

## Chapter Summary ✔✔✔

21.1 All business is based on selling products or services for money.
   A. Marketing brings customers to your product.
   B. Selling brings your product to customers.
   C. Salespeople often become successful entrepreneurs because they:
      1. Constantly listen to customers
      2. Understand customers
      3. Learn from customers
      4. Are positive and upbeat.
   D. Great salespeople sell customer benefits, not just product features.
   E. Many young entrepreneurs focus on selling just one (or two) products.

**21.2**   Sales professionals make sales calls by appointment with potential or existing customers.

A. Effective sales calls:
1. Make customers aware of products or services
2. Determine customer needs
3. Show the connections between product features and related benefits that match customer needs
4. Gather leads on other potential customers
5. Build relationships between seller and customer.

B. Before making a sales call appointment:
1. Get marketing and ordering materials right
2. Pre-qualify prospective customers.

C. Use the eight-step sales call:
1. Prepare and practice in advance
2. Greet the customer
3. Pitch the product or service in a personalized way
4. Listen to customer reactions and needs
5. Answer objections
6. Ask for a commitment
7. Follow up to ensure customer satisfaction
8. Ask for references to other potential customers.

D. Sales superstars analyze their sales calls:
1. Did the customer "open up"?
2. Which questions worked best? Least?
3. Was the feature-benefit-need link honestly established in the customer's mind?
4. Did the call develop the relationship with the customer?

**21.3**   Use the tools of the sales trade.

A. Technology:
1. Video demos of products
2. Web sites for information access
3. E-mail and faxes to stay in touch with customers
4. Customer databases.

B. Sales receipts:
1. For customer records of purchase
2. For business records of sales and cash.

C. Sales commissions:
1. To reward salespeople
2. To encourage them to sell more. ✔✔✔

### CHAPTER 22

# CUSTOMER SERVICE

*It's not the bottom line. It's an almost blind, passionate commitment to taking care of customers.*

— Bernie Marcus, *founder of Home Depot*

## Customer Service Has a Very High ROI

**Customer service** is everything you do to keep your customers happy — especially *after* they've bought something. It includes maintaining and repairing the product or service once it has been sold, and dealing with customer complaints.

Why would you invest time, energy, and money into keeping customers happy *after* they've already bought your product or service? Because the return on this investment can be very high. Successful businesses are not built on single sales but on **repeat business** — customers who buy from the same company over and over again. The management of Home Depot has calculated that one satisfied customer is worth more than $25,000 in sales during his or her lifetime!

Smart entrepreneurs pay close attention to their customers. They constantly ask questions and analyze their needs. They train their employees to look for customer needs that might be going unfulfilled. The most successful entrepreneurs become customer service experts.

## Joe Girard's "Law of 250"

Joe Girard has been called "The World's Greatest Salesman" 12 times by *The Guinness Book of Records.* In his best-seller, *How to Sell Anything to Anybody*, Girard presents his Law of 250 as follows: "Everyone knows 250 people in his or her life important enough to invite to the wedding and to the funeral. This means that if I see 50 people in a week, and only two of them are unhappy with the way I treat them, at the end of the year there will be about 5,000 people influenced by just those two."

Have you heard the expression, "The customer is always right"? There will be times when a customer may get angry at you, complain, or make demands that you believe are unreasonable. At those times, remember Joe Girard's Law of 250. Do you really want to send this person away unhappy? One unhappy customer can keep a great many people away from your business.

Use your self-control to stay polite, even when a customer is getting annoyed. Do your best to find a solution that will send him/her away satisfied. Your effort will protect your business and may even earn you a customer for life.

## Customer Complaints Are Valuable

You may not enjoy hearing a customer complain about your product or service, but a complaint is full of valuable information that no one else will tell you — and you won't have to pay for it! Listen closely to learn what your customers need and want:

- Always acknowledge complaints and criticism and deal with them. Never pretend that you didn't hear a negative comment.

- Don't overreact to negative remarks. And, above all, don't take them personally!

- Always tell the truth about any negative aspect of your product or service. When you admit a negative, you gain a customer's trust.

Remember, a successful business is built on repeat customers. When you listen to a customer you are building a friendship. You are encouraging loyalty to your business.

 **BizTip:** Keeping a customer's trust after the sale is the most important part of the transaction.

## SKILLS MEAN SUCCESS

**ENGLISH** ▶ **Critical Listening Strategies**

1. Write three comments that an angry or dissatisfied customer might make to your staff about a faulty product, or other bad experience he/she has had with your business. Then, for each, write the response that you would want your staff member to make in reply. For example:

   *Complaint:* "I can never get anyone to help me in this store."

   *Response:* "I'm sorry to hear that. We try to make service our top goal. I do know that sometimes we get very busy. If you ever need help in the future, look or ask for me. And now, how may I help you today?"

2. Practice with a partner. Express your "complaint" as a customer might, and invite a verbal response. How did your partner's response compare to what you wrote? Was it better? Why? ■■■

## Customer Service *Is* Marketing

Marketing brings a customer to your business, but it doesn't stop there. Once the customer is inside the door, the treatment should be consistent with your marketing. If your competitive advantage is speedy service, make sure your employees work quickly and efficiently. If your competitive advantage is a cozy, easygoing environment, make sure each customer is warmly welcomed and made to feel at home. Your customer service must reinforce your marketing.

## Customer Service Is a Source of Market Research

Market research should not end once you open your business. Each customer is a valuable source of (free!) market research. Possibilities for collecting market research as part of your customer service:

- Include a short survey on a stamped postcard with every item purchased. Or include a survey that can be redeemed at the store for a 10% discount on the next item purchased.

- Ask selected customers to fill out a longer survey in the store, again, offering a discount as an incentive.

- Always ask (and have your employees ask) standard questions when completing a sale, such as: "Do you have any suggestions on how we could improve our product?" or, "Were you satisfied with the service you received today?" But of course do not pester the customers to the point of being obnoxious.

## SKILLS MEAN SUCCESS

**MATH**   **Percentage and Rounding Numbers**

The Best Animals pet shop is offering ten percent off any customer's next purchase (excluding sales tax) for completing and returning a customer survey. Estimate the discounts given on the following items:

**a.** dog food: $12.99

**b.** dog leash and collar: $11.59

**c.** aquarium, hood with lights, gravel, filter, tubing, motor, heater: $297.95

**d.** gerbil cage: $24.95

**e.** *Teach Your Mynah Bird to Sing* book and CD: $35.49

The best people to market to are those who have already bought or shown interest in your product or service. When a customer makes a purchase or a potential customer asks about your business, ask for an e-mail address. Use this information to set up a simple *database* on your computer. A database is a collection of information stored and organized for easy reference.

Your customer database should include:

- Customer's name
- E-mail address
- Phone and fax numbers
- Mailing address
- Date of last contact
- Comments or notes on last purchase or request.

As your mailing list grows, you can organize it by region or customer interest and send out targeted e-mails. If you sell gourmet sauces, for example, your notes could tell you whether a customer is interested in hot sauces or dessert sauces. When you add a new hot sauce to your product line, you will know whom to target with an e-mail announcement introducing the sauce, possibly with a special offer.

Most word-processing programs will allow you to set up a simple table, like this:

| Name | Address | Phone | Fax | E-mail | Last Purchase | Notes |
|------|---------|-------|-----|--------|---------------|-------|
|      |         |       |     |        |               |       |

## Stay in Touch with Customers

Stay in touch with your customers and potential customers. Build friendships so your customers will be loyal to your business for life.

The first few words you say to a new customer may be the most important. Keep a two-way conversation going. Maintain eye contact and keep the customer's attention. Remember that he/she is first and foremost a human being with whom you are forming a friendship. The more you can learn about family, hobbies, interests — anything to help develop a genuine relationship — the better your chances of eventually securing a sale.

### SKILLS MEAN SUCCESS

**ENGLISH** **Writing for Information:** Creating Tables and Forms

Use the *Table* function in word-processing software to create a customer-contact table like the example shown on page 285, *or* investigate samples and features of "customer management" software that you will find on the Internet (try searching under "*customer management software*"). Present your constructed chart or your findings to the class in a one-page document. ■■■

**BizTip:** Contact your phone company to find out how to set up an 800 number for your business, so customers can call for free. Some long-distance providers offer special discounts to small-business owners. AT&T, for example, currently has a program called Small Business Advantage.

## Ask Customers to Refer You to New Customers

If you did a good job for people who needed your product or service, ask them to refer you to others. Offer discounts, gift certificates, etc., for referrals. Also, offer business cards for customers to pass on to their friends.

## CRITICAL THINKING ABOUT...

### CUSTOMER SERVICE

1. Would it be better to have 25 customers who each spend $1, or 100 customers who each spend 25 cents? Explain.

2. Create a database for your business. Which five questions will you ask every customer?
   **Business Plan Practice**

3. Describe a business that you deal with as a customer. Describe the customer service at this business. What do you like (or dislike) about it? How could the business improve its customer service?

4. List five things you intend to do at your business to offer superior customer service.

## KEY CONCEPTS

1. Explain Joe Girard's "Law of 250" in your own words, with examples from your own life.

2. Why is customer service an extension of marketing?

3. Give three reasons why you think it's important to keep collecting market research even after you have opened your business.

## EXPLORATION

Visit three businesses in your community and note how you are treated. Write a memo comparing the customer service at the three. Include such information as: Were you greeted when you came in? Did anyone offer to help you? If you bought something, were you given a survey?

## VOCABULARY

customer service ■ repeat business

# Chapter Summary ✔✔✔

22.1 Quality customer service generates repeat sales business from loyal, happy customers.
   A. Remember the "Law of 250."
   B. View customer complaints as valuable feedback.
   C. Use customer service as a competitive advantage.

22.2 Customer service can support marketing efforts.
   A. Survey customers — formally and informally — when and after they buy.
   B. Offer rewards for customer feedback, referrals, and ideas.
   C. Gather customer e-mail addresses and other contact information.
   D. Develop a database to store information about customers.
   E. Build personalized relationships with customers. ✔✔✔

### CHAPTER 23

# MATH TIPS TO HELP YOU SELL AND NEGOTIATE

*Problems are only opportunities in work clothes.*

— Henry J. Kaiser, *American industrialist*

## KEY OBJECTIVES

THIS CHAPTER WILL ENABLE YOU TO:

- Do business math in your head so you can think on your feet.
- Convert bulk prices to per-unit costs quickly during negotiations.
- Be able to calculate how many years it will take for an investment to double.

**A**s you become an entrepreneur, you will find that you need math skills to run a business. You must have a solid grasp of basic math to negotiate the best possible deals, calculate your profits, and figure out your expenses. Being able to do math in your head will help you "think on your feet" in business situations.

## SKILLS MEAN SUCCESS

**TECHNOLOGY** ▶ **Online Research and Devising Formulas**

The "Rule of 72" is an easy way to calculate how long it will take an investment to double. Take any fixed annual interest rate, change it into a decimal, and divide it into 72. The result is the number of years it will take for the investment to grow to twice its size.

Search the Internet and ask business contacts, family members, or friends for math tips that you can share with the class. If two people each saved $11 a week, but one saved for five years and the other saved for ten years, and each earned 6% interest calculated annually on the year-end balance, how much more would the second person have?

# Math in Your Head[1]

If you can do simple calculations in your head, you will be able to negotiate prices and quantities with greater success. When you are bargaining with a wholesaler or supplier, you will need to convert the price for large quantities into a per-unit purchase price. This will help you determine quickly whether the deal would be profitable.

Sheila sells lipsticks at $1 each. She buys them wholesale in boxes of five. In her head, she calculates:

**5 sticks per box × $1 per stick = $5**

Sheila can make a profit only if the wholesaler will sell her a box for less than $5. She knows that she must pay less than $1 per lipstick or she won't make a profit. When buying wholesale, the most you can afford to pay per item — your "limit" — is somewhere below your resale price.

## SKILLS MEAN SUCCESS

**MATH** ▶ **Rounding Numbers and Proportional Reasoning**

**1.** Rounding numbers to perform a calculation in your head is a skill many business-people use regularly. For each calculation in the box, match the set of actual numbers (numbered) with the math operation (lettered) that would be the closest "fit" to arrive at an approximate (rounded) answer.

| I.   | 9 × 16        | a. | 20% of 100    |
|------|---------------|----|---------------|
| II.  | 248 × 997     | b. | 10 × 15       |
| III. | 26,154 ÷ 52   | c. | 400 ÷ 100     |
| VI.  | 19% of 105    | d. | 25,000 ÷ 50   |
| V.   | .012 (393)    | e. | 250 × 1000    |

**2.** Estimate the annual cost to a business of each item below.

| | Item | Frequency | Estimated Cost | Estimated Yearly Cost |
|---|---|---|---|---|
| a. | Employee sick days. | 1 per month | $90 per day | $ _____ |
| b. | Employees 15 minutes late. | 1 per week | $2.54 per week | $ _____ |
| c. | Employee personal phone calls. | 3 per week | 14 min. per call | _____ Hours _____ Minutes |
| d. | 191 employees taking office supplies. | 1 per week | 14¢ per week per employee | $ _____ |
| e. | Use of company copier for personal needs. | 45 copies every 3 months | 4.5¢ per copy | $ _____ |

**289**

# Business Math Tips

Here are some other mental math tips that businesspeople use — often!

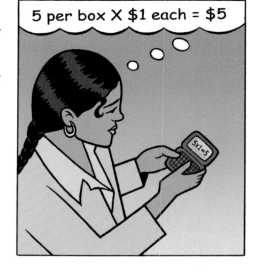

5 per box X $1 each = $5

**1.** Break one big problem into several smaller ones and solve them one at a time.

**Example:** A wholesaler says he can sell you a dozen hats for $60. You know you can sell the hats at $11 each. What profit would you make if you bought two dozen hats at the wholesaler's price and sold every one? Break the problem into steps:

**1:** There are 12 hats in a dozen.

**2:** If a dozen costs $60, each hat would cost $5 ($60 ÷ 12 = $5).

**3:** If you sold each for $11, you would make $6 gross profit per hat ($11 − $5 = $6).

**4:** Two dozen is 24.

**5:** If you sell 24 hats, you will make $144 gross profit (24 × $6 = $144).

**2.** Round off numbers to make it easier to calculate in your head. Adjust for the rounding-off after you have made the first calculation, as shown below.

**Example:** A wholesaler offers you a box of 20 blank videocassette tapes at $49.00. About how much does one cassette cost?

*Round off:* Round up $49.00 to $50.00

*Calculate:* $50.00 ÷ 20 = $2.50

*Adjust:* But you rounded up by $1.00 for 20 cassettes, so you now have to subtract the rounded-up cost per tape.

*Think:* $1 ÷ 20 tapes = $0.05 per tape (the round-up for each tape)

*Subtract:* $2.50 − $0.05 = $2.45

The exact wholesale cost of one blank videocassette tape is $2.45.

**3.** If all you need is an approximation to know whether you are getting a good deal, just round off and calculate. Skip the adjustment.

**Example:** Consider the same offer. A wholesaler offers you a box of 20 blank videocassette tapes for $49.00. You know that you can make a good profit if you can buy videotapes at less than $2.75 each. Can you make a profit if you buy them at $49.00 for a box of 20?

*Round off $49 to an easier number to work with:* $50.00

*Calculate:* $50.00 ÷ 20 = $2.50

*Compare:* Since $2.50 is less than $2.75, you know that you can make a profit buying at that price.

4. Approximation can be helpful in translating between hourly and daily rates.

   **Example:** Someone works for you for $10 per hour. How much will he cost per year?

   *Approximate:* He works about 40 hours per week.

   There are about 50 work weeks in a year.

   40 hours per week × 50 weeks per year = 2,000 hours per year.

   *Calculate:* 2,000 hours per year × $10 per hour = $20,000 per year.

   OR

   *Approximate:* He works about 8 hours a day.

   *Calculate:* 8 hours per day × $10 per hour = $80 per day.

   *Approximate:* There are 250 work days in a year (5 days per week × 50 weeks).

   *Calculate:* $80 per day × 250 days per year = $20,000 per year.

   Or, if necessary, use simpler numbers to calculate:

   In your head, divide $80 by 10 and 250 by 10 to get $8 × 25

   So, $8 × 25 = $200

   Remember to multiply by 10 twice to reverse the two division operations.

   So, $200 × 10 × 10 = $20,000

5. The Rule of 72: 72 divided by ROI = number of years it will take to double an investment.

   **Example 1:** If you invest $10 in a savings account that pays 5% annual interest, how long will it take, at that rate of return, for your $10 to grow to $20?

   *Rule of 72:* 72 ÷ 5 = 14.4

   It will take 14.4 years for your $10 to grow to $20.

**291**

**Example 2:** You purchase a newsstand business that nets 20% per year. You paid $20,000 for the stand. How many years will it take to double your investment?

*Rule of 72:* 72 ÷ 20 = 3.6

In 3.6 years your $20,000 will grow to $40,000.

Practice doing business math in your head whenever you can. Let's say apples at your local supermarket cost $1.10 per dozen. How much would one apple cost? Practicing business math will make you a sharper businessperson.

6.  Keystoning: Many businesspeople "keystone" to decide what price to charge customers. Keystoning means doubling a unit cost to determine a safe selling price that should cover expenses and also provide a profit.

    **Example:** If a store owner buys DVDs from a distributor at $17 each and CDs at $8 each, what should her selling prices be?

    17 × 2 = $34 and $8 × 2 = $16.

    Her selling prices should be $34 per DVD and $16 per CD.

*If you can do simple math in your head, you will be more successful in business.*

## SKILLS MEAN SUCCESS

**ENGLISH** ➤ **Reading for Information: Fact vs. Opinion**

Doing math in your head is an important business skill. Being able to distinguish a fact from an opinion quickly is another. Read the following and decide if each sentence sounds like a fact (F) or an opinion (O).

**1.** The biggest one-day loss in the Dow Jones Industrial Averages was 684.81 points, on Sept. 17, 2001.

**2.** That was the day the New York Stock Exchange reopened after 9/11.

**3.** The drop would have been sharper if the market had been allowed to open on September 12.

**4.** Such a drop is unlikely ever to happen again.

**5.** It's best to sell all your stocks whenever the DJI average drops significantly.

**6.** The New York Stock Exchange was closed for five days after 9/11.

*Source: Guinness World Records 2004* ■■■

## CRITICAL THINKING ABOUT...

### BUSINESS MATH

Try these problems in your head!

1.  A wholesaler offers to sell you pens at $1.20 per dozen. You know you can sell them at school for $.25 each.

    **a.** How much will each pen cost?

    **b.** Would you make or lose money buying and selling these pens?

    **c.** How much would you make or lose on each?

2.  You want to hire someone to help with your business for 20 hours a week. The person you want to hire would like to earn $12,000 per year. How much would you need to offer per hour to equal $12,000 per year?

3.  How long would it take to turn $5,000 into $10,000 if you had an investment that yielded a 6% return, compounded annually?

4.  Figure out the cost of one individual item.

| Item | Cost per Dozen | Individual Item Cost |
|------|------|------|
| Soda | $3.00 | |

## KEY CONCEPTS

1.  Give two examples from your own experience of moments when you either did math in your head or wished that you could.

2.  Use the concept of keystoning to calculate the retail price and gross profit of each item.

| Item | Whole-sale Cost | Retail Price | Gross Profit |
|------|------|------|------|
| Soda | $0.25 | $0.50 | $0.25 |
| Chips | $0.33 | | |
| Trail Mix | $0.68 | | |

3.  Figure out the cost of one unit for each item.

| Item | Cost per Dozen Units | Unit Cost |
|------|------|------|
| Bottles of juice | $6.00 | $0.50 |
| Bags of peanuts | $5.50 | |
| Apples | $4.72 | |
| Bags of sunflower seeds | $2.70 | |

## REFERENCES

1 Special thanks to Jack Mariotti for ideas he contributed to this chapter.

## Chapter Summary ✔✔✔

23.1 Math skills — especially mental math — help make entrepreneurs successful.
   A. Do math "in your head."
   B. Break big problems into steps.
   C. Round off numbers.
   D. Know when and how to use approximations.
   E. Use the Rule of 72.
   F. Use keystoning. ✔✔

### CHAPTER 24

# BUSINESS COMMUNICATION

*Remember that time is money.*

— Benjamin Franklin, *American statesman, inventor, writer, and entrepreneur*

THIS CHAPTER WILL ENABLE YOU TO:

- Write a business memo.
- Write a business letter.
- Know when to use "cc:" on copies of memos or letters.
- Proofread business correspondence.

**E**ntrepreneurs need to move fast — and communicate even faster. If your business is making furniture and the lumber stores in your community decide to compete with each other by cutting prices, you will want to know right away so you can stock up on wood. Are you on the e-mail and **fax** lists for your suppliers, so you can get up-to-the-minute information? Do you have a cell phone and pager so customers and employees can reach you at all times? Entrepreneurs are constantly in contact with the market, ready to adjust to change at any time.

## The Business Memo

The saying "Time is money" is especially true for the entrepreneur. You don't have time to read, or write, long letters when you need to make a point. One of the best ways to save time when writing is through the use of the business **memo**.

The word "memo" is short for *memorandum*, from the Latin, "to be remembered." A memo is a brief, clearly written note from one businessperson to another. It is usually written or typed on plain paper. The purpose of the memo is to inform or remind the reader of an idea, suggestion, observation, or request from the writer.

Memos are sent to business associates, not customers. A memo is most often sent *interoffice*, that is, from one person to another within the same company. Today, it is common practice to send such memos by fax (short for "facsimile," which means copy). Ideally, a memo should be written, sent, and received on the same day.

Why not just telephone the person, instead of going to the trouble of writing a memo? A memo will provide you with proof of the communication. Nobody can remember exactly what was said in a conversation.

Have you ever had someone deny that you told them something when you were sure you did? This can be frustrating in one's personal life, but in business such a misunderstanding could cost you money, a customer, or a job. With a memo, no one will "forget" who said what and when. Memos are a great way to save time and prevent confusion.

Whenever you write a memo, make a copy for your files. Sometimes a copy is sent to others who may be concerned with the subject discussed.

## How to Write a Business Memo

A business memo is usually composed of the following parts:

1.  A heading at the top of the page:

    | | |
    |---|---|
    | **To:** | *(Name of addressee)* |
    | **From:** | *(Name of sender)* |
    | **Date:** | *(Date memo is written)* |
    | **Re:** | *(Briefly states the subject of the memo)* |

    Many businesses have memo stationery with the heading printed on it.

2.  An introduction, which summarizes the topic.

3.  The "body," in which the main points are discussed as concisely as possible.

4.  The conclusion, in which the sender closes the memo with a polite restatement of the main point.

5.  Signature or initials. A memo differs from a business letter in that a full, formal signature, including your title, is not necessary. If you know the person to whom you are sending the memo fairly well, you might just sign your first name or put initials next to it in the heading.

    For more formal memos, write in your full name.

6.  A "cc:" (pronounced "cee-cee") stands for "carbon copy," though now usually a photocopy is made. This is used only when copies of the memo will be sent to others. For example, if you've written a memo to George Louis, but you want your partner, Bill Jones, to see it too, you would write or type (in the lower left-hand corner of the page):

    **cc:** Bill Jones

    *or*

    **cc:** B. Jones (if Mr. Louis knows who Bill Jones is).

This lets Mr. Louis know that you keep your partner informed of business details. After you sign the original memo, photocopy it. Keep one for your files and give one to Bill Jones.

**Here is an example of a memo.**
*(Notice how the first letter of each line begins at the left-hand margin.)*

---

**To:**  C. J. Meenan
**From:**  Darnell Jones  *D. J.*
**Date:**  4/7/05

**Re:**  Request for business financing

I am hereby requesting a venture loan of $200 to start "Darnell's Candy." I would use the money as follows:

1.  Business cards: $22
2.  Advertising (posters and flyers): $20
3.  Registering business at County Clerk's Office: $30
4.  Telephone-answering machine: $50
5.  Candy inventory: $78

Total: $200

I look forward to hearing from you.

**cc:**  S. Mariotti

---

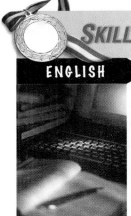

## SKILLS MEAN SUCCESS

**ENGLISH** ▶ **Reading and Writing for Understanding:** Memos

1. Re-read Darnell's memo. Rate its effectiveness as business communication: 5 = Excellent; 1 = Needs Improvement.

2. Explain how someone could try to determine the meanings of *venture loan*, *registering*, *inventory*, and *business financing* from the context of the memo.

| Quality | 5 | 4 | 3 | 2 | 1 |
|---|---|---|---|---|---|
| The topic is stated early and quickly. | | | | | |
| The body of the memo sets out the main points concisely. | | | | | |
| The conclusion is polite and restates the main point. | | | | | |
| The *To, From, Date, Re:* and *cc:* are clearly indicated. | | | | | |

Memos can effectively convey a sense of urgency. Perhaps that is why Prime Minister Winston Churchill sent this memo to the head of the British Navy in 1940, early in World War II.

---

**To:**     The First Lord of the Admiralty
**From:**   Winston Churchill
**Date:**   April 1940

**Re:**     The Preparedness of the Royal Navy

Please send me today, on no more than one sheet of paper, your evaluation of the strengths and weaknesses of the Royal Navy and how the weaknesses may be remedied.

---

This seemingly simple request was made at a time when England was in danger of being invaded by Hitler's Germany. It was not a simple request at all, and Churchill knew it. He wanted his admirals to look accurately and honestly at their resources because the country was in a desperate situation.

## Business Cards

Businesspeople exchange business cards when they meet. This is called *networking*. You can hand out your card to suppliers and others you do business with so they will know how to reach you. You can also give your card to potential customers you meet outside your business. Keep a stack of your cards at your business for customers to take when they leave.

Collect the business cards you receive and keep them in alphabetical order for easy reference. Each contact you make can open up a whole world of opportunity for you.

## The Business Letter

Like the business memo, the business letter should be concise and clear. Its tone is usually more formal, and its form is somewhat different. Business letters are used for first contact or when a serious matter needs to be put into writing.

A business letter should be:

- Typed on **letterhead** (stationery with printed name, address, other contact information, and business logo).

- Mailed in a business envelope. Fold the letter neatly into thirds to fit in the envelope. Make sure, when you address the envelope, that your handwriting is clear and that you use the right postage. All these details will make you and your business look professional.

Always keep a copy of every business letter you send.

There are two basic business-letter formats:

- All addresses, the date, and your signature are flush left (lined up against the left margin).

- A more traditional style is to center your name and address at the top of the page as if on a printed letterhead, have the date flush right, the address of the person you are writing to flush left, and then your signoff and signature flush right.

- Notice how the business letter, unlike the memo, provides full address and title information for both the sender and the receiver. Also, the salutation, or greeting, is followed by a colon ( : ) not a comma ( , ). A comma follows a greeting only in a personal, non-business letter. A personal letter would begin "Dear Chris," for example. The note "encl:" in the lower left indicates that the reader of the letter should look for an enclosure in the envelope; in this case, Darnell's check to Mr. Meenan.

Here is Darnell's letter using the flush-left format:

**Darnell's Candy**
**235 East 13th Street**
**New York, NY 10009**
**(212) 555-3210**

April 7, 2005

Mr. C. J. Meenan, Vice President
Meenan and Associates, Inc.
116 East 59th Street, Suite 3
New York, NY 10021

Dear Mr. Meenan:

I am writing to thank you for approving the venture loan of $200. I have used the money, as we discussed when we met, to start Darnell's Candy.

Business is going very well. I am enclosing my first payment to you of $50 and expect to be able to continue paying you $50 a month for the next three months, which will be payment in full.

Thank you again for giving me the chance to start my own business.

Sincerely,

*Darnell Jones*

Darnell Jones,
President

encl: $50 check
cc: Mike Caslin

Here is the same letter using the traditional format.

**Darnell's Candy**
**235 East 13th Street**
**New York, NY 10009**
**(212) 555-3210**

April 7, 2005

Mr. C. J. Meenan, Vice President
Meenan and Associates, Inc.
116 East 59th Street, Suite 3
New York, NY 10021

Dear Mr. Meenan:

I am writing to thank you for approving the venture loan of $200. I have used the money, as we discussed when we met, to start Darnell's Candy.

Business is going very well. I am enclosing my first payment to you of $50 and expect to be able to continue paying you $50 a month for the next three months, which will be payment in full.

Thank you again for giving me the chance to start my own business.

Sincerely,

*Darnell Jones*

Darnell Jones,
President

encl: $50 check
cc: Mike Caslin

## Proofread Carefully

Grammatical and spelling mistakes can lower the respect the reader of your memo or letter has for you, and will diminish your credibility. Proofread all your business communications carefully before you send them. It's a good idea to have someone else proofread them, too.

## Electronic Communication

Today there are a variety of ways to communicate, including:

- **Voice mail** — a phone system that allows the leaving and receiving of messages through phones that are not on the users' premises.
- **Fax** — machines that send printed material over phone lines.
- **E-mail** — messages sent between computers over phone lines.
- **Text messaging** — typed messages sent between cell phones or between computers and cell phones.

Whether you're leaving a message on an answering machine or a voice-mail system, sending a fax, a text message, or an e-mail, you will still need to use correct grammar and spelling. People are more willing to do business with an entrepreneur who can communicate concisely and clearly.

 *SKILLS MEAN SUCCESS*

 **ENGLISH** ▶ **Presenting Information Clearly**

1. Estimate how long an effective phone voice-mail greeting should be.

2. Write out and say aloud (or record) two phone voice-mail greetings for your own company (or the business where you work):
   - one for customers who call your business
   - and one for vendors, business partners, and staff.

   Make some notes about what you will say in each message before you record it. Decide on your tone of voice, talking speed, length of message, and word choice, as well.

3. You may also want to record the most *ineffective* (or funniest) message you can imagine for a business, such as a restaurant or clothing store. Make it as annoying or funny as you like. ■■■

**301**

## CRITICAL THINKING ABOUT...

### BUSINESS COMMUNICATION

1. Write a memo for each subject.

   **Memo 1:** You received A's on all your exams, but your teacher gave you a B+ for the class because you were late four times — but it wasn't your fault. Write a memo to the teacher about your grade.

   **Memo 2:** Your school is hosting a picnic and you would like to supply the soda because you can buy cans for 25 cents each and sell them at the picnic for 50 cents. Write a memo to an adult relative or mentor requesting a loan of $100.

   **Memo 3:** You have a part-time job but would like to take a day off to attend a track meet. Write a memo to your boss asking permission to miss one day of work.

2. Proofread the memos you have written; then have a friend proofread them too. Did your friend find any errors you had missed?

3. What information would you put on your business card? Do you have a motto or slogan?

## KEY CONCEPTS

1. What advantage does communicating by memo have over using the phone?

2. In the following situation, would you write a memo or a business letter? Explain.

   A customer has written to your business complaining about how

she was treated by an employee at your store.

3. Would you write a memo or a business letter to the employee involved in the situation in #2? What would you say?

4. Describe the types of communication you plan to use in your business.

5. What is one thing that should be included in both memos and business letters?

## EXPLORATION

*The Rumor Game:*

Play this game with the whole class to test the efficiency of verbal communication. Have one person make up a sentence, write it down, and then whisper it into the ear of the student to his/her right. Then have that person pass it on until the message has gone through the whole class. Have the last student who hears the sentence repeat it aloud. Is it the same as the original?

## VOCABULARY

fax ■ letterhead ■ memo

# Chapter Summary ✔✔✔

**24.1**   Entrepreneurs need to communicate effectively.
  A. Memos are brief, clearly written or typed messages that contain:
    1. Ideas
    2. Suggestions
    3. Observations
    4. Requests.

**24.2**   Memos are usually written, sent, and received on the same day.
  A. Memos are often sent interoffice (within the same company) or faxed.
  B. Memos provide a written record for the sender and the receiver.
  C. Memos consist of heading, introduction, body, conclusion, signature, and perhaps a cc:.

**24.3**   Keep and file business cards for networking and contact information.

**24.4**   Business letters are used for more formal correspondence.
  A. Letterhead and envelopes are used.
  B. Business letters follow standard formats: flush-left or traditional.
  C. Proofread business letters (and memos) for both impact and mistakes.

**24.5**   Businesses increasingly use electronic communication.
  A. Voice mail, faxes, e-mail, and text messaging. ✔✔✔

# A Business for the Young Entrepreneur
## DESIGNS Á LA MODE, LAPRIA DESHAUNA KELLY AND WEBSTER LINCOLN

*We are the future, but without guidance how can we get there?*

Designs Á La Mode creates and manufactures fashionable and affordable beaded jewelry. The company backs its products with a repair service. The partners emphasize the importance of maintaining good communication and trust.  The partners sell the jewelry at their high school and at trade fairs. They plan to expand distribution to more schools and to retail stores, as well as sell through a Web site.

Both Lapria and Webster are concerned about the youth in their area.  They decided the best way to help would be by becoming role models. They have focused on expanding their business and sharing what they've learned about entrepreneurship with their peers.

*How does Designs Á La Mode provide customer service?* ■

### CHAPTER 25

# SOLE PROPRIETORSHIPS AND PARTNERSHIPS

*The secret of success in life is for a man to be ready for his opportunity when it comes.*

— Benjamin Disraeli, *English politician and novelist*

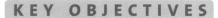

### KEY OBJECTIVES

THIS CHAPTER WILL ENABLE YOU TO:

- Explain the pros and cons of sole proprietorships and partnerships.
- Register a sole proprietorship.
- Research business permits and licenses.
- Obtain a sales-tax identification number.

## What Is a Sole Proprietorship?

When you start a business, you have to choose a legal structure. The most common legal structure is the **sole proprietorship**. This is a business owned by one person, who may also be the only employee. A sole proprietorship is the easiest legal structure to form and maintain.

The owner of a sole proprietorship receives all the profits from the business, but also suffers all losses and bears all the risk. The sole proprietor is personally *liable* (responsible) for any debts incurred by the business and any lawsuits that arise from accidents, faulty merchandise, unpaid bills, or other problems.

This means that, if the business fails to pay a debt, the sole proprietor's personal property — such as a house, car, or money in a personal bank account — could be taken to pay off the debt. Similarly, the sole proprietor will be personally liable if the business is sued. If someone goes to court and claims to have been hurt by a sole proprietor's product or service, and the court awards that person damages, the sole proprietor's personal property could be sold to pay the award.

Since personal assets are at risk, anyone starting a sole proprietorship should make sure the products or services sold are unlikley to cause harm. Stick to simple and safe products and services.  Avoid those that can cause injury, such as driving lessons, fireworks, or horseback riding lessons.

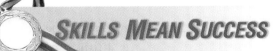

## SKILLS MEAN SUCCESS

**LEADERSHIP** > **Practicing Risk Taking**

Entrepreneurs have to be risk takers. Think about examples in your life when you took a risk. Don't worry if you haven't climbed mountains or parachuted from a plane. Risk taking occurs in everyday life, too. People who tell a joke take a risk: listeners may not find it funny. People who speak out on an issue take a risk: others may strongly disagree. People who volunteer or get elected to office run risks: others may criticize them, sometimes unfairly. Make a list of some risks you have taken in your life. Which risks that you took made you proud of yourself afterwards? ■ ■ ■

## What Is a Partnership?

A **partnership** consists of two or more owners who make decisions for a business together and share the profits and losses. Partners are personally liable for the actions taken by the business, and they (like the sole proprietor) are personally responsible for paying debts or damages. If your partner incurs a debt on behalf of the partnership, you will be jointly responsible for paying it.

Partners bring different strengths and skills to a business. This can help a venture grow and succeed. In addition, partners can support and advise each other. On the other hand, strong partnership disagreements can destroy the business — and friendships.

Despite the advantages of partnerships, be cautious about entering into one, even with a good friend or relative. Have a lawyer draw up a Partnership Agreement that carefully defines all aspects of the business.  The Agreement should include a clear understanding about issues such as:

- The money and intellectual property that each partner is contributing
- The ongoing responsibilities of each partner
- The way in which decisions will be made
- How profits and expenses will be shared
- What happens if the partners decide to add new partners or to *dissolve* (shut down) the partnership.

## Limited Partnership

A **limited partnership** includes both "general" partners, who are personally liable for the actions of the business, and "limited" partners, who have a limited role or no role in managing the business and also have limited liability. There must be at least one "general partner," who is liable for all partnership debts. The "limited partners" make an investment but have no say in daily operations. The partners should draw up a Limited Partnership Agreement that describes the relationship between the partners and the duties, obligations, and benefits that each will receive.

## Registering a Sole Proprietorship

It is easy and inexpensive to register a sole proprietorship. It is important to register because:

- There are city and state regulations requiring you to register, and you may be subject to fines if you don't. The IRS requires that you identify your business and pay taxes on income earned.
- You will need a registered business if you intend to obtain bank loans or enter into contracts.
- You can add having operated a registered business to your resume.

## Registration Usually Takes the Following Steps

1. Choosing a name for your business.

2. Filling out a "Doing Business As" (D.B.A.) form with the name of the business and your name, so the state will know the name of the individual who owns the business. D.B.A.s are registered at the county courthouse.

3. An official may then conduct a name search to make sure the one you have chosen is not already being used. You may even be asked to help research the records yourself.

4. After the name of your business has been established, you will fill out a registration form and pay the required fee.

5. You may be asked to take the form to a notary, have it notarized, and bring it back to the registration office. A notary is a person who has been given the authority by the state to witness the signing of documents. You will have to show the notary identification, such as a school I.D. or driver's license.

## Registering a Partnership

Registering a partnership involves steps similar to those on the previous page. In addition, as discussed, the partners should have a partnership agreement between themselves. If the partnership is going to be based on intellectual property developed by the individual partners (e.g., a trademark, or written materials), each partner will need to *assign* (transfer ownership of) the rights to the partnership.

## Licenses, Permits, and Certificates

Once registered, you will need to research local regulations that may apply to your business at the chamber of commerce.

Zoning regulations often prohibit certain types of businesses from operating in specified areas. There may be other regulations, too, such as restrictions on obtaining a liquor license for a bar or restaurant. If your business involves food, you will need to comply with safety and health regulations, and probably obtain certain **permits** (see below).

Contact the county courthouse or your local chamber of commerce to find out which licenses and permits are necessary.

- *Permit* — an official document that gives you the right to carry on a specific activity, such as holding an outdoor concert.
- *License* — an official document that gives you the right to engage in an activity for as long as the document is valid. For instance, a driver's license gives you the right to operate a motor vehicle for a specified length of time.
- *Certificate* — official document that verifies something. A D.B.A., for example, proves that your business is registered as a sole proprietorship.

## Federal, State, and Local Laws and Regulations

Federal laws and regulations (including employment laws and tax laws) apply everywhere in the country. Every state also has its own laws and regulations governing how companies operate and compete. There will also be local regulations that will vary. If you are an employer, you will need to pay special attention to rules governing the payment and treatment of your employees.

## Sales-Tax Identification Number

In many areas, every business, regardless of its size, must obtain a sales-tax identification number and collect the appropriate taxes on all retail sales.

To find out which sales taxes must be collected in your locality, consult the phone book for your state's sales-tax office, or other relevant government branch.

It is extremely important to follow all federal, state, and local regulations, and to pay all applicable personal and business taxes. As your business expands, your records and dealings must be completely legal.

## SKILLS MEAN SUCCESS

**MATH** ▶ **Solving Problems Using Percentages, Formulas, and Substitution**

1. Sample sales-tax rates for several states are shown below. Calculate the sales tax a business would have to charge its customers for each purchase in each state.

| State | Sales Tax Rate | Tax on a $25 Sale | Tax on a $1340 Sale |
|-------|----------------|-------------------|---------------------|
| CT | 6% | | |
| GA | 4% | | |
| TX | $6\frac{1}{4}$% | | |
| VA | $4\frac{1}{2}$% | | |
| CA | $7\frac{1}{4}$% | | |
| NM | 5% | | |

2. Javier's company ordered a gift box of oranges for a customer from a company in Florida. The total bill (b) was $53, and Javier knew the sales tax (s) was 6%. What was the actual price (p) of the box of oranges?

Find p, if $p + (6 \div 100) p = \$53$ ■ ■ ■

## Advantages of a Sole Proprietorship

- It is relatively easy to start. Registration does not require much paperwork and is less expensive than a partnership or corporation.

- The business owner pays personal income tax on the business's earnings.

- There are fewer government regulations than for the other business structures.

- Sole proprietors can make quick decisions and act without interference from others.

- A sole proprietor keeps all the profits from the business.

## Disadvantages of a Sole Proprietorship

- It can be difficult to raise enough money by oneself to start or expand the business.

- A sole proprietor must often put in long hours, working six or even seven days a week.

- There is unlimited personal legal liability.

- There is often no one to offer encouragement or feedback.

- There is only one stakeholder — you. This limits your ability to share risk and to utilize the talents and energies of others.

## Advantages of a Partnership

- Partners can pool their resources to provide more assets for the business.

- The risks, long hours, and legal liabilities are shared.

- Different skills and contacts are brought to the business.

## Disadvantages of a Partnership

- The profits must be shared.

- Each partner is liable for the actions taken by the business, even for decisions made by another partner.

- Disagreements among the partners can destroy the business.

- Partnerships can be difficult and unpleasant to dissolve.

**BizFact:** Businesses, such as airlines, that sell products or services where the potential for harm is significant: (1) form a corporation, or other limited-liability entity; (2) buy liability insurance; and/or (3) require customers to agree to bear part of the risk (by signing a release, for example).

## CRITICAL THINKING ABOUT...

### SOLE PROPRIETORSHIPS AND PARTNERSHIPS

1. Pretend you are a lawyer asked by a client to explain the differences between a sole proprietorship and a partnership. Write a business letter to this client.

2. Do you think a sole proprietorship, partnership, or limited partnership would be the right legal structure for your own business? Explain. **Business Plan Practice**

3. Pick a friend in class and imagine starting a business together. Draw up a partnership agreement that specifies each partner's duties, and how much money and time each will invest in the business. Detail how the profits will be divided.

4. Your friend wants to start a business making custom skateboards. Write a memo to that friend explaining the risks involved and ways to protect him/herself.

5. Is a D.B.A. form a certificate, a permit, or a license? Explain.

## KEY CONCEPTS

1. In addition to registration, describe two other things you have to do before opening a business.

2. What government identification number must you have before you can sell a product or service? Why? **Business Plan Practice**

3. What is the purpose of having a form notarized?

## EXPLORATION

For the business you plan to start, research the zoning and licensing regulations in your area and describe how they will affect your business.

## VOCABULARY

limited partnership ■ partnership ■ permit ■ sole proprietorship

## Chapter Summary ✔✔✔

25.1 Sole proprietorships and partnerships are the simplest legal structures for a business.
   A. Sole proprietorships are businesses owned by one person who:
      1. May be the only employee
      2. Receives all profits
      3. Suffers all losses and bears all risk personally
      4. Is personally liable for debts and lawsuits.
   B. Partnership businesses have two or more owners who:
      1. Combine their talents and support each other
      2. May be the only employees
      3. Share all profits
      4. Together suffer all losses and bear all risk personally

5. Often sign a partnership agreement that describes the relationship, responsibilities, and dissolution (closing down) procedure.

C. Every limited partnership must have at least one general partner.

1. A general partner directly manages the business and is personally liable for debts.

2. A limited partner is an investor not involved in daily operations.

25.2 Registering a sole proprietorship or partnership is simple and inexpensive.

A. Obey city and state regulations.

B. Choose an unused business name.

C. File a "Doing Business As" (D.B.A.) form.

D. Complete and sign a registration form and pay fees.

E. Use a notary (official witness) if required.

F. If a partnership, sign a partnership agreement, and assign any marks and intellectual property rights to the partnership.

25.3 Every new business must follow government regulations.

A. Obey all taxation, zoning, hiring, and employment laws.

B. Obtain any required permits and licenses (documents permitting certain types of activities) and certificates (documents that prove qualifications or memberships).

C. Obtain sales-tax identification number and collect retail sales tax.

25.4 Sole proprietorships and partnerships have advantages and disadvantages.

A. Sole Proprietorships:

| Advantages: | Disadvantages: |
|---|---|
| 1. Easy to start | 1. Difficult to finance or expand |
| 2. Owner pays only personal income tax on business earnings | 2. Long hours |
| 3. Fewer government regulations | 3. Unlimited personal liability |
| 4. Owner makes independent decisions | 4. No support |
| 5. Owner keeps all profits. | 5. No one to share risk. |

B. Partnerships:

| Advantages: | Disadvantages: |
|---|---|
| 1. Partners can pool resources | 1. Profits must be shared |
| 2. Risks, liabilities and work are shared | 2. Partners are liable for each others' actions |
| 3. Skills and contacts are expanded. | 3. Disagreements can end the business |
| | 4. Dissolving the business can be difficult. ✔✔✔ |

**311**

### CHAPTER 26

# MANUFACTURING:
## *From Idea to Product*

*Your life is a work of art. A craft to be most carefully mastered. For patience has replaced time and you are your own destination.*

— Rick Jarow, *professor and author*

### KEY OBJECTIVES

THIS CHAPTER WILL ENABLE YOU TO:

- Explain the manufacturing process.
- Locate manufacturers in your community.
- Have a prototype made.
- Investigate zoning laws that might affect your business.

## Manufacturing [1]

*Manufacturing* companies make and sell the products that people buy and use every day. Cell phones, cameras, watches, and cars are all examples of manufactured products. Manufacturers benefit society by creating products that make life better.

Some manufacturing companies make products their founders invented. When Thomas Edison developed the light bulb, he started a company to manufacture it. That company became General Electric.

Some companies are formed to improve products, or to make them more efficiently. Henry Ford did not invent the automobile, but he designed a more efficient way to manufacture cars. Ford's **moving assembly line** let him make cars less expensively, so that the average person could afford to buy one.

Before there were manufacturing businesses, people often had to make what they needed, including clothes and furniture. When companies began making clothing, furniture and other necessary consumer goods, people bought them instead of making them. Manufacturing of household goods started to become widespread in the late 1700s and early 1800s and quickly changed the world. This "Industrial Revolution" lasted well into the 20th century, when it was supplanted by the Technological Revolution we are experiencing today.

## The Manufacturing Process

The manufacturing process starts with raw materials, or *parts*, and transforms them into finished products. This process uses labor, machinery, or other tools, including **manufacturing plants** (factories). The process can be very simple or extremely complicated, depending on what is being made. Like other businesses, manufacturing companies must sell their products for more than their costs.

## Advantages

Manufacturing businesses have some unique advantages. They can make a product that isn't already available on the market. They can also fine-tune products or add features to meet consumers' needs and expand a market. Wholesalers and retailers can't do this. Manufacturers also minimize competition by:

- taking out patents on their designs so others can't make identical products,
- being big enough to cover the market better than a new competitor could.

## Disadvantages

It can cost a lot of money to be a manufacturer. The factory equipment and the space needed for operations can be very expensive. It can also be costly to hire and train workers. In addition, manufacturers might need to store more inventory than they need immediately, which is expensive. The more complex the product to be made, the more costly it will probably be to manufacture.

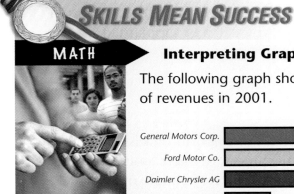

## SKILLS MEAN SUCCESS

**MATH** ▶ **Interpreting Graphs**

The following graph shows the world's largest manufacturers in terms of revenues in 2001.

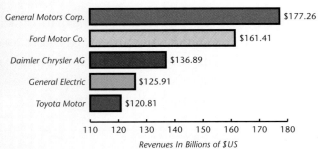

| | |
|---|---|
| General Motors Corp. | $177.26 |
| Ford Motor Co. | $161.41 |
| Daimler Chrysler AG | $136.89 |
| General Electric | $125.91 |
| Toyota Motor | $120.81 |

110 120 130 140 150 160 170 180
*Revenues In Billions of $US*

*Source:* The Top 10 of Everything 2004, *Russell Ash, DK Publishing*

1. Which company is the world's second-largest manufacturer?

2. Approximately what are its revenues?

3. How do its revenues compare to the largest manufacturer's?

4. How do its revenues compare to those of the fifth-largest manufacturer?

5. The world's largest company is Wal-Mart Stores, at $219.81B. How do Wal-Mart's revenues compare to those of the largest manufacturer? ■ ▨ ■

## Types of Manufacturers

There are as many kinds of manufacturers as there are customer needs. Grouping them by the kinds of customers they serve can be helpful.

- Consumer products — used by consumers.
- Industrial products — used by other businesses.
- Government contracts — military equipment, space vehicles, etc.

The U.S. Government has developed Standard Industrial Classification (SIC) codes to group manufacturing businesses. A sample of these are listed below. You can learn more about SIC codes online at http://www.sec.gov/info/edgar/siccodes.htm

| | |
|---|---|
| 2200 | Textile Mill Products |
| 3100 | Leather & Leather Products |
| 3320 | Iron & Steel Foundries |
| 3523 | Farm Machinery & Equipment |
| 3600 | Electronic & Other Electrical Equipment (except computers) |
| 3630 | Household Appliances |

The *Thomas Register* is an extensive catalog that lists almost all the manufacturing companies in the United States (it is composed of about two dozen volumes, each about four inches thick). Their national and regional catalogs can be found in libraries, or at:

- http://www.thomasregister.com/ (national)
- http://www.thomasregional.com/ (regional)

## Make or Buy?

Manufacturing companies can make their own products, have other companies make them, or combine both strategies. Many companies make the most important or complex parts of their products, but sub-contract minor parts to other companies. Manufacturers like Ford and General Motors rely on such sub-contractors for parts that go into their cars. Many companies do the final assembly, regardless of who makes the parts.

## Job Shops

Some manufacturing companies don't actually make "final" products. Instead, these **job shops**, or "jobbers," are sub-contractors for other manufacturers. They use their manufacturing plants and equipment to make parts or even entire products for other companies. Job shops usually work with drawings and specifications provided by the product's manufacturer. They usually get work by submitting and winning a bid. Job shops are useful to manufacturers because they are often able to:

- make a part less expensively
- deliver a part more quickly
- maintain and provide specialized equipment so larger manufacturers don't have to purchase or maintain it themselves
- offer manufacturing facilities to companies that don't have their own.

It doesn't matter whether a company makes its own product or has parts or all of it made by sub-contractors. What counts is that the manufacturer controls the design, formula, or specifications of how the product is to be made.

## Manufacturing and You

If you have an invention, or an idea for a product, you might have what it takes to become a successful manufacturer. You might also be successful if you could make something better, quicker, or less expensively than others can.

The first step in manufacturing is to be certain that there will be customers interested in the product you have in mind and at the price you plan to sell it for. Many companies have created interesting products only to find out that too few customers wanted to buy them. Consider manufacturing only after you have determined that there is a market for the product.

## SKILLS MEAN SUCCESS

**MATH**

### Mathematical Reasoning

Businesses need to decide when it makes sense to buy the manufactured goods they need and when to make the goods themselves. Express Dry Cleaning can buy coat hangers from a supplier for five cents each. The company can buy a machine for $2200 and make its own coat hangers for two cents each. Express uses, on average, 1500 coat hangers a week. In how many weeks would the machine pay for itself? Draw a chart or graph to illustrate your answer. ■■■

## Steps in the Development Process

**Idea to design:** To turn your idea into a product design that can be manufactured and sold will take thought and creativity. You will have to balance how your customers will benefit against how much it will cost you to make it. Knowing the customers' needs and understanding the manufacturing technology or processes involved will help. When you design the product, you will make:

- Drawings and Specifications. This will include written information about the materials, dimensions, formulas, *tolerances* (range of acceptable variations in size or ingredients), and parts or materials to be used. Sketches may be okay at first, but complete and highly accurate drawings or descriptions will eventually be needed.

- Parts and Materials List. This includes all the materials and parts you will need. You must know ahead of time where to get everything and how much it will cost.

**The prototype:** As we learned in Chapter 7, this is a working example of the product. A prototype will allow you to see if the product works correctly. This is especially important for inventions. Prototypes also help manufacturers see ways to improve the product, including ways to make it more cheaply. Because you will be making only one (or a few), prototypes cost much more than one unit of the actual finished product. To find a company that can make your prototype, look in the *Thomas Register*. You will need to give complete and accurate drawings of your product to the company making your prototype.

**Getting ready for production:** Whether you do it yourself or have others do it for you, manufacturing usually involves **tooling** and **setup costs**. These are additional expenses separate from what it will cost to actually manufacture the product. You will have to know these costs ahead of time.

- *Tooling costs* are required to make or adapt the equipment for your product. These are also called "one time" costs because you pay for them when you set up the first time, but not for additional orders. Manufacturers usually do not include these expenses in their "cost each" (cost of goods sold) of the product. Not all products have significant tooling costs.

- *Setup costs* have to be paid each time you make a batch, or a "lot" of the product. They normally are included in the "cost each" of the product. The larger the quantity produced, the lower the setup costs will be per item made. Almost all products have setup costs.

If your product is *easy to make*, you may be able to assemble all or part of it where you live. Most cities and towns have zoning laws, however, that limit what you can do in a residential area. If you can't work in your home you may have to rent space in a commercial location.

If your product is *difficult to make*, or will require expensive plant and equipment, you can work with a job shop that will make the product for you. You can use one shop or many, depending on the product. Or, you may be able to buy the parts but do the final assembly yourself. Many large manufacturers do this.

**Getting help with your design:** You may not have the money to hire a professional engineer, but you can probably get help with your design from people who work in job shops. They are experts in manufacturing and may have helpful ideas. You may or may not have to pay for this. If a jobber gives you advice, though, you should definitely let that company do the work. Relationships with sub-contractors can make or break a small manufacturing business.

## SKILLS MEAN SUCCESS

**LEADERSHIP**          **Negotiation and Thinking Skills**

A distributor wants to buy your product at a discount and then resell it through a catalog. They have offered to buy 1,000 units from you wholesale at $9 per unit. You think they might purchase larger quantities if you give them a good price. Your normal retail price is $15.95. Your unit cost is $8.00. Would you accept their terms? Explain. ■■■

## CRITICAL THINKING ABOUT...

### MANUFACTURING

1. Write an explanation of the advantages and disadvantages of choosing to manufacture your product yourself.

2. Conduct research at the library or online to find an important trade publication or Web site for your industry. Find three advertisements from prototype makers, manufacturers, or distributors who could be helpful to your business. Share the ads with the class.

3. Discuss how you would research a new product you intended to manufacture.

4. Describe any zoning laws in your community that could affect your business.
   **Business Plan Practice**

5. Do you intend to manufacture your product? If so, describe the manufacturing process you will use. If not, describe how your product is to be manufactured.
   **Business Plan Practice**

## KEY CONCEPTS

1. Pick a common product you often use and list the materials you think went into its manufacture.

2. Estimate the cost of each of these materials, and then:

   a. Estimate the total cost of goods sold for one unit of the product.

   b. How much did you pay for it retail?

   c. What do you think the gross profit would be?

3. Think of a product that has dropped significantly in price during your lifetime. Write a brief explanation of why you think this occurred.

4. After reading A Business for the Young Entrepreneur on page 320, research button-making machines on the Internet. What was the best price that you found? In your opinion, which of the machines you saw would make the highest-quality buttons? Why? Was this the cheapest one?

## EXPLORATION

Call your chamber of commerce to find out about manufacturing laws in your area. Write a memo describing these zoning laws and how they could affect your business.

## REFERENCES

1 Special thanks to John Harris for his many contributions to this chapter.

## VOCABULARY

job shop ■ manufacturing plants ■ moving assembly line ■ setup costs ■ tooling costs

# Chapter Summary ✔✔✔

**26.1**   Manufacturers make and sell for a profit products they invented, improved, or bought the rights to.

A. The manufacturing process changes raw materials or parts into finished products using labor, tools, machinery, and manufacturing plants.

B. Manufacturing has advantages over other types of business:

1. Making all-new products that aren't available elsewhere
2. Improving or adding features to existing types of products
3. Protecting their designs with patents
4. Covering the market better than new competitors could.

C. Manufacturing also has disadvantages over other types of business:

1. Cost of equipment, factories, space, labor, inventory
2. More complex products cost more to make.

**26.2**   Manufacturers serve a variety of customers and customer needs.

A. Manufacturers are often grouped by whom they serve:

1. Consumer products
2. Industrial products (used by other businesses)
3. Government contracts (such as military equipment).

B. The government groups manufacturers by Standard Industrial Classification (SIC) codes.

**26.3**   Manufacturers make products or have other companies make them.

A. Some manufacturers make the most important or complex parts they need and assemble the final product, but sub-contract for minor parts.

B. Job shops (jobbers) make parts or entire products for manufacturers inexpensively, quickly, with the latest equipment, or with specialized equipment other manufacturers don't own.

C. Manufacturers always control the product design, formula, or specifications.

**26.4**   Following a development process for manufacturing is important.

A. Turn an idea into a design:

1. Drawings and specifications: describe materials, dimensions, formulas, ranges of variation (tolerances)
2. Parts and materials lists.

B. Develop a prototype or make working examples of the product, which is especially important for inventions.

C. Prepare for production:

1. Tooling: one-time cost to obtain and install the equipment to make the product; not usually included in unit cost
2. Setup: repeated cost to make every batch or "lot" of a product; usually included in unit cost.

D. Self-manufacture a product or sub-contract harder-to-make products or parts to a job shop.
  1. Obey zoning laws that limit where manufacturing can take place.
  2. Get design help from manufacturing experts such as jobbers. ✔✔✔

## A Business for the Young Entrepreneur
### BUTTON MANUFACTURING

Daniel Trainor was diagnosed with a brain tumor when he was 11. He began to miss school due to his cancer treatments, so he was spending a lot of time at home. He had received a laptop computer for his birthday, which led him to BizTech, NFTE's online entrepreneurship course. Using BizTech, Daniel created a business plan for making and selling buttons. He saw an ad for a button machine for $100 in the back of a magazine, and bought it. The first buttons Daniel manufactured said: *PEACE ON EARTH*.

"I had already learned what a business is — getting receipts, keeping records. Once I understood it, it was pretty simple." Daniel sold the buttons for a dollar apiece and took orders from staff members at the hospital where he was being treated.

Starting his own business not only gave Daniel something to do that was worthwhile, it helped take his mind off the side effects of his cancer treatments, which were keeping him out of school for long periods of time.

One of Daniel's plans was to establish a Web site for his business with help from his brother. "I expect to be able to make $40 or $50 a week once it's up and running," he explained. "It only takes 15 seconds to make a button."

Daniel's advice to other kids: "You need to do something that you like doing." ■

## SKILLS MEAN SUCCESS

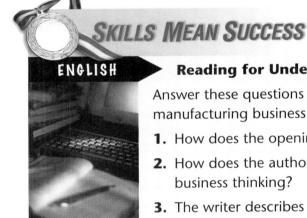

**ENGLISH**

### Reading for Understanding

Answer these questions about Daniel Trainor's button manufacturing business.

**1.** How does the opening sentence try to catch a reader's interest?

**2.** How does the author show that Daniel used math in his business thinking?

**3.** The writer describes several events in Daniel's story in the order of when they happened. This is called *chronological* order. List them in a brief timeline.

**4.** Do you think Daniel is someone who feels sorry for himself? Why or why not?

**5.** What do you think the writer wants readers to learn from Daniel's story? ■■■

# THE PRODUCTION/ DISTRIBUTION CHAIN

*You give birth to that on which you fix your mind.*

— Antoine de Saint-Exupéry, *French author*

**KEY OBJECTIVES**

THIS CHAPTER WILL ENABLE YOU TO:

■ Understand the manufacturer-to-consumer chain.

■ Calculate markup percentages.

■ Calculate gross profit margin.

■ Calculate net profit margin.

## The Production/Distribution Chain

As we learned in Chapter 2, the consumer is the final link in the connections that extend from the manufacturer through the wholesaler and retailer. When a consumer buys a pair of sneakers in a sporting goods store, the chain could be:

1. Manufacturer produces thousands of pairs of sneakers.

2. Wholesaler buys hundreds of sneakers from the manufacturer.

3. Retailer buys a hundred sneakers to stock his/her store.

4. Consumer walks into retailer's store and buys one pair of sneakers.

    **Manufacturer** → **Wholesaler** → **Retailer** → Consumer

This manufacturer-to-consumer process is called the **production/distribution chain**, or "the distribution channel."

There can be other links in this chain besides the four above. A manufacturer may have to buy raw materials or other manufactured goods to make the product. There may be other *middlemen* — agents or brokers or other wholesalers — between manufacturer and wholesaler, or between wholesaler and retailer. On the other hand, there is no middleman in the chain if the retailer is purchasing directly from the manufacturer.

## A Slow Distribution Channel Can Hurt Your Business

Inexperienced entrepreneurs sometimes don't realize how important the distribution channel is to the success of a business. You need to know how long it will take to get each item you want to sell. If your product moves too slowly through the channel, you can lose customers who don't want to wait for it. A clothing store owner can lose business if she is not able to get the latest styles into her store while they are still in fashion. Customers looking for new trends will buy from her competition.

If you are running a business that requires quick delivery, try to find suppliers in your area — in order to cut down on delivery time.

### SKILLS MEAN SUCCESS

**ENGLISH**

**Interpreting Information: Fact vs. Opinion**

Many companies advertise that they eliminate steps in the distribution chain (and therefore extra markups) to save money for consumers.

**1.** Explain what you think each of these statements means:

   **a.** We make our own blinds so you can buy direct from the factory.

   **b.** Our own buyers visit the countries where our products are hand-crafted.

   **c.** No middlemen!

   **d.** Direct from the farm to your table.

   **e.** We deal directly with the manufacturer.

**2.** Find three examples of ads that make similar claims. ■■■

## Markups: Prices Increase at Every Link in the Chain

At every link in the production/distribution chain, the price of a product is increased to cover expenses and to generate a profit for that link. These increases in price are called **markups**. At each step along the way, the price of a product is "marked up," usually anywhere from 25% to 100%.

When you buy a shirt from a store, you are not paying the same price for that shirt that the store owner paid. Let's say the owner purchased ten shirts for $200 from a wholesaler, at a per-unit price of $20. The store owner will "mark up" the shirts to a higher price to sell to his customers — $39.99, for example. This markup will cover the price the owner paid for the shirts, plus his operating costs. The owner will hope to sell at least enough shirts to break even, and hopefully enough to make a profit.

If you are able to purchase a product at a relatively low wholesale price, and customers are willing to pay a retail price that includes a relatively high markup, you will have a very profitable business.

## Percentage Markups

Because most entrepreneurs sell many items at different prices that had different wholesale costs, it would be time-consuming to try to figure an acceptable markup for each item. Instead, retailers use "percentage" markups. Each item in a gift shop might be marked up 50%, regardless of the exact wholesale cost.

$$\textbf{Wholesale Cost} \times \textbf{Markup \%} = \textbf{Markup}$$

If you know the markup and wholesale cost of an item, you can figure the markup percentage using this formula:

$$\textbf{Markup \%} = \frac{\textbf{Markup}}{\textbf{Wholesale Cost}} \times 100 = \textbf{ROI}$$

Let's say the gift shop buys cards at $2.00 each from the wholesaler and sells them for $3.00 each.

$$\textbf{Markup} = \$3.00 - \$2.00 = \$1.00$$

$$\textbf{Markup \%} = \frac{\$1.00}{\$2.00} \times 100 = 50\%$$

If the gift shop owner finds, while doing her monthly income statements, that she is not generating enough profit, she can raise her markup percentage slightly to try to increase revenue. Or she can try to find a cheaper supplier to lower her wholesale costs.

## The Relationship between Price, Gross Profit, and Cost

When consumers purchase a product from a retail store, they are paying the retailer's **gross profit margin** — the markup from the price the retailer paid the wholesaler to the price the retailer is charging the consumer. This markup, related to gross profit per unit, is used to cover operating costs as well as provide a profit for the entrepreneur.

If a shoe store buys a pair of sneakers from the wholesaler at $20 and sells it for $45, the retailer's markup is $25. This $25 markup is also called the gross profit per unit.

$$\text{Gross Profit} \quad = \quad \text{Retail Price} \quad - \quad \text{Wholesale Cost}$$
$$\$25 \quad = \quad \$45 \quad - \quad \$20$$

## Gross Profit Margin per Unit

A business that can't cover its operating costs (USAIIRD) won't stay in business very long, so business owners like to know what percentage of each dollar of revenue is covering operating costs. To calculate this gross profit margin per unit, divide the retail price of an item into its gross profit.

$$\text{Gross Profit Margin per Unit (\%)} = \frac{\text{Gross Profit per Unit}}{\text{Retail Price}} \times 100$$

## Retail Price

In the case of the gift shop owner:

$$\text{Gross Profit Margin per Unit} = \frac{\$1.00}{\$3.00} \times 100 = 33\%$$

For every dollar the gift shop owner receives from selling an item, therefore, 33 cents will be used to pay operating costs and, hopefully, provide a profit.

## Profit Margin

Finally, for the business as a whole, the **profit margin** is calculated by dividing profit by sales and multiplying by 100. This will show how much of each dollar of sales is profit.

$$\text{Profit Margin (\%)} = \frac{\text{Profit}}{\text{Sales}} \times 100$$

**325**

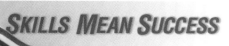

## SKILLS MEAN SUCCESS

**MATH** ▶ **Calculating Percentage, Formulas, Patterns**

Not all items in the same store have the same markup percentage.

**1.** Study the examples below and find the markup and markup rate (percentage) for each item.

**2.** What is the range of markups this store is using?

**3.** Write the formulas for determining *any* markup and markup percentage.

**4.** Write the formula for determining *any* retail price if you know the unit cost and markup rate.

**5.** Why might a store mark up different items at different rates?

| Item | Retail Price | Wholesale Cost | Markup $ | Markup % |
|---|---|---|---|---|
| Current Hit DVDs | $29.95 | $16.00 | | |
| Blank VHS Tape | $7.99 | $5.00 | | |
| Blank CDs | $24.95 | $9.00 | | |
| Current Hit Videos | $19.45 | $12.00 | | |
| $3\frac{1}{2}''$ Diskettes | $11.05 | $5.50 | | |

■■■

**BizFact:** The expression, "I can get it for you wholesale," means the person making the offer can get the item at the wholesaler's price — without the retailer's markup. The tradition of bargaining in certain cultures is carried on with the knowledge that the seller has marked up the cost. The bargainers are really negotiating the seller's profit margin.

# Chapter 27 Review

## THE PRODUCTION/DISTRIBUTION CHAIN

1. Given the retail price and wholesale cost of a product, calculate its markup and markup percentage.

    Formulas:

    **Retail Price − Wholesale Cost = Markup**

    $$\frac{\textbf{Markup}}{\textbf{Wholesale Cost}} \times \textbf{100} = \textbf{Markup \%}$$

    Example:

    | Item | Retail Price | Wholesale Cost | Markup | Markup Percentage |
    |------|--------------|----------------|--------|-------------------|
    | Watch | $20.00 | $12.00 | $8.00 | 66% |

2. Looking at the markup and markup percentage above, which is the best way to measure profitability? Which product is the most profitable? Why?

3. Given the retail price and wholesale cost of a product, figure its markup profit and gross profit margin.

    Formulas:

    **Retail Price − Wholesale Cost = Gross Profit per Unit (Markup)**

    $$\textbf{Gross Profit Margin per Unit \%} = \frac{\textbf{Gross Profit per Unit}}{\textbf{Retail Price}} \times \textbf{100}$$

    Example:

    | Item | Retail Price | Wholesale Cost | Markup | Markup Percentage |
    |------|--------------|----------------|--------|-------------------|
    | Watch | $15.00 | $12.00 | $3.00 | 20% |

4. Looking at the markup and markup percentage above, what would be the best way to measure profitability? Which product is the most profitable? Why?

## KEY CONCEPTS

1. Use this form to show the production/distribution chain for your own business, and the markups at each point along the way. **Business Plan Practice**

    **Manufacturer:**

    Name: _____

    Contact information: _____

    Markup: $ _____   Markup: % _____

**Wholsaler:**

Name: _____

Contact information: _____

Markup: $ _____ Markup: % _____

**Retailer (You):**

Name: _____

Contact information: _____

Markup: $ _____ Markup: % _____

2. What does the expression, "I can get it for you wholesale," mean?

3. Write a memo discussing any concerns you have with the distribution channel you have imagined setting up for your business in question #1.

4. After reading A Business for the Young Entrepreneur, describe a business you could start that would involve bringing a product from another area to your neighborhood. Describe the distribution channel for this business.

**VOCABULARY**

gross profit margin ■ markup ■ production/distribution chain ■ profit margin

# Chapter Summary ✔✔✔

27.1 The production/distribution chain (or channel) is the process by which goods reach consumers from the manufacturer.
   A. Manufacturers produce mass quantities of consumer items.
   B. Wholesalers buy large quantities from manufacturers.
   C. Retailers order shipments from wholesalers.
   D. Consumers buy a single item from a store.
   E. Variations to the chain may involve:
      1. Manufacturers obtaining raw materials or parts
      2. Additional "middlemen" such as agents or brokers
      3. No wholesaler; retailers buy directly from manufacturers.
   F. Entrepreneurs require speedy ordering and delivery through the chain.

27.2 Prices are marked up (increased) at every stage in the chain to generate a gross profit margin (profit plus expenses).
   A. Markups range from 25% to 100%.
   B. Wholesale Cost × Markup % = Markup

C. $\text{Markup \%} = \dfrac{\text{Markup}}{\text{Wholesale Cost}} = \text{ROI} \times 100 = \text{ROI \%}$

D. Gross Profit = Retail Price − Wholesale Cost

E. $\text{Gross Profit Margin \% per Unit} = \dfrac{\text{Gross Profit per Unit}}{\text{Retail Price}} \times 100$

F. $\text{Profit Margin \%} = \dfrac{\text{Profit}}{\text{Sales}} \times 100$ ✔✔✔

# A Business for the Young Entrepreneur
## Á LA MODE, MICHELLE LEE ARAUJO

*Who would ever think a teenage mother living in public housing on public aid with three children could ever own her own business and graduate from college?*

"**M**y dream is not to die in poverty, but to have poverty die in me," says Michelle Lee Araujo. Michelle insists that there is always time to start your own business — even if you're a single mother and a full-time college student. Michelle should know, because at 19 she started her own business while caring for her daughters Angela, 3, Erica, 18 months, and her newborn son, Kristian — while attending college.

Michelle owns a clothing retail company called Á La Mode. She had always loved fashion, so she was excited to be visiting Manhattan's wholesale clothing district with her NFTE class. Michelle knew there was a demand in her hometown for the latest styles, but she hadn't figured out how to satisfy it.

During her trip to New York, Michelle realized she could buy clothes wholesale and mark them up for resale to her neighbors back home. She could even outperform the competition by offering the latest styles at lower prices than the stores in town. Michelle would resell the clothes from her home or on visits to her customers. It turned out that her friends and neighbors were delighted to have an alternative to high local prices. They also enjoyed shopping in a more intimate setting.

Michelle plans to continue with her store when she finishes college. "There are very few clothing boutiques in my town," she explains. Michelle hopes her success will spark a revival of small business in the community. ■

### CHAPTER 28

# QUALITY:
## *The Source of Profit*

*We started off with a very idealistic perspective — that doing something with the highest quality, doing it right the first time, would really be cheaper than having to go back and do it again.*

— Stephen Wozniak, *co-founder of Apple Computer*

### KEY OBJECTIVES

THIS CHAPTER WILL ENABLE YOU TO:

- Explain why quality leads to profit.
- Discuss W. Edwards Deming's ideas about quality and profit.
- List ten ways to improve quality.
- Apply the Japanese concept of *kaizen* to your life.

The **quality** of a product is its degree of excellence. The consumer is usually willing to pay more for quality because:

- A quality product will last longer.
- A quality service will be more satisfying.

"Quality" is the buzzword of American business in the new millennium. "Total quality control" is the subject of many business-magazine articles.

Quality was not always considered such an important concept by American corporations. For many years, American business focused on short-term profits and lowering costs. Less attention was given to quality.

## Profit Comes from Quality

In the early 1950s, though, an American named W. Edwards Deming argued that the quality of the product was the very essence of business. His position was that a business that focused on quality would be more profitable than a business that focused only on lowering costs. Deming insisted that profits came from quality.

This simple notion was actually quite profound: If profits come from quality, then a business that focuses on improving quality should find profits increasing as a result. Deming's theory suggested that a business's goal should be quality, not immediate profit.

## Deming Goes to Japan

Deming's revolutionary concept was ignored by the American business community, so he went to Japan, which was rebuilding its economy after the devastation of World War II.

In those days, Japan was notorious for the poor quality of its manufactured products. The phrase "Made in Japan" was found on cheap gift items and toys, and Americans would use the phrase to refer to anything poorly made.

Deming gave lectures to business leaders in Japan that changed the Japanese philosophy of manufacturing. The Japanese took Deming's advice to heart and focused on making high-quality products, not short-term profits. As a result, the quality of Japanese cars broke the American automakers' control of the American market. Millions of Americans began to buy Japanese cars.

Today, Japanese products are known for their excellent quality, and Japanese companies like Sony and Toyota are very profitable. Deming's *thesis* (argument) that profits follow quality was proven correct. The Japanese government presents annual Deming Prizes to Japanese companies that have demonstrated the very highest standards of quality control. To win one of these awards is a great honor.

American businesspeople traveled to Japan to study why Japanese companies had become so successful. They brought Deming's ideas back home, where they were finally adopted by American business.

## Why Quality Is Actually Cheaper

A high-quality product is actually cheaper than one made by cutting corners, for the following reasons:

1.  You don't have to fix it, or replace it as quickly.

2.  You get the most valuable advertising possible — your satisfied customers tell others how good the product is, bringing new customers to the business.

3.  You earn customer loyalty. Quality builds a base of repeat customers. Repeat customers generate profits.

This vision of quality is expressed as **continuous improvement**. The idea is that continually seeking to improve quality will steadily increase profits. This concept in Japanese is **kaizen** (pronounced KYE-zen). Many American companies now teach continuous improvement to their employees.

## SKILLS MEAN SUCCESS

**MATH**      **Reasoning:** Devising Formulas

Anyone who works with businesses in other countries will need to be able to convert currencies. Most countries have their own currency. The Japanese use the *yen*, Mexico, the *peso*, and many countries in Europe use the *euro*. Currencies aren't worth the same amount one on one. One U.S. dollar might be worth 1,200 yen, for example. This equivalent value is referred to as the "exchange rate." Currencies change in relation to each other every day. You can find today's exchange rates in the newspaper or online.

1. The first three answers in the chart are done for you. Work backward from the answers provided or guess and test to figure how the calculations were made. Then use that method to calculate the next three.

| Country | Currency | Exchange rate compared to one U.S. dollar (on a given day) | What would $5U.S. be equal to? |
|---------|----------|------------------------------------------------------------|--------------------------------|
| Japan | Yen | $0.0092 | 543.478 Yen |
| Many European Countries | Euro | $1.19 | 4.201 Euros |
| Saudi Arabia | Riyal | $0.2666 | 3.75 Riyals |
| Canada | Dollar | $0.7436 | |
| Brazil | Real | $0.34416 | |
| United Kingdom | Pound | $1.7876 | |

2. Use sentences or a formula to explain what you just did: how to calculate the value of $5U.S. in another currency.

3. Use sentences or a formula to explain how to calculate the value of *any* amount of U.S. dollars in another currency. ■■■

## Start with Quality

Build the foundation of your business on quality from the very beginning. When you are estimating your start-up investment, for example, you might be tempted to cut costs by using the cheapest possible materials. If you are running a delivery business and you buy an old van cheaply, however, it might cost you a great deal in repairs in the long run. Start with the best possible quality you can afford.

## Treat Suppliers and Employees Well

Another aspect of *kaizen* is that both the suppliers and employees must be treated *ethically*. Ethics are rules that govern how we treat each other. The Golden Rule is a famous ethic: "Do unto others as you would have others do unto you."

Ethics can be applicable to your business because:

- Suppliers will not be loyal to a company that deals with them unfairly.
- Employees won't focus on continuous improvement unless they feel good about their company.

Smart entrepreneurs try to make employees feel that their interests and the interests of the company are one and the same. American corporations are realizing that this is a good idea and are using the approach to improve relations between workers and management.

## Ten Ways to Improve Quality[1]

1. Adopt a philosophy of continuous improvement. Use a motto to inspire your commitment to improvement.

2. Be consistent. Don't attempt everything in one big effort, but constantly look for small ways to make things better.

3. Do it right the first time. This will be cheaper than having to fix a job or product later and possibly irritate and lose a customer.

4. Develop long-term relationships with suppliers based on loyalty and trust, even if it means not getting the lowest price every time. Some sacrifice of profit in the present can be repaid many times over when you need help or credit, and the supplier helps you because he or she has become your friend.

5. Focus on quality in production and customer service.

6. Develop a training program for yourself and your employees.

7. Eliminate fear. Your employees and customers should not be afraid to point out ways to improve your business.

8. Don't ask for perfect performance from your employees (or yourself). Instead, work a little smarter and better every day.

9. Focus on the *quality* of what your business does, not the quantity.

10. Quality is everybody's job. Ask for comments and suggestions from employees, customers, and suppliers and provide incentives for improvements in quality.

## Quality Control: Debbi Fields

**Quality control** is using standards to make sure your product or service is delivered to the customer at the level you want to provide. Consistency is very important. Customers need to know what to expect when they buy from your business. When you go to McDonald's you expect your Big Mac to taste the way it has before.

Debbi Fields was only 19 when she opened her first cookie store. Fields knew nothing about running a company, but she'd been baking cookies for six years. She believed that, if her cookies were made from quality ingredients and were served with a smile, people would buy them. Fields's commitment to quality and customer service was an excellent business strategy. By the age of 30, she owned more than 500 Mrs. Fields Original Cookies stores in 25 states and five foreign countries.

Fields always put quality before profit. She refused to substitute margarine-butter blends for pure butter, for example, even though the substitution would have saved the company money.

One day, Fields walked into her third store and noticed that the cookies looked flat and overcooked. When she asked the store clerk what he thought of the cookies, he said, "Aw, they're good enough." Fields silently slid each tray of cookies into the garbage — losing about 500 dollars worth of merchandise. She told the clerk: "Good enough never is."

In 1984, Fields began to expand internationally by opening stores in Japan, Hong Kong, and Australia. Instead of hiring consultants to tell her what type of cookies would sell best in these countries, Fields conducted personal, hands-on market research. She simply traveled to each place, opened a store, and began giving away cookies. She would ask customers what they preferred. Fields learned that in some countries people preferred dark-chocolate to milk-chocolate chips, or liked macadamia nuts better than pecans. Her new stores became successful because Fields used quality ingredients to make the cookies people told her they would buy.

## CRITICAL THINKING ABOUT...

### QUALITY

1.  Write a motto for your present business (or one you would like to start) that will remind you to stay focused on quality.
    **Business Plan Practice**

2.  Write a paragraph describing at least two reasons why a customer might be willing to pay more for quality.

3.  Explain W. Edwards Deming's *thesis* (argument). How was it proven correct?

4.  Create your personal ethic and explain what it means to you.

5.  Write an essay discussing these questions:

    **a.** Do you care more about quality or price when you buy?

    **b.** When you buy something, are you willing to pay more for better quality?

6.  Describe the quality-control procedure for your business.
    **Business Plan Practice**

## KEY CONCEPTS

1.  What is the name of the quality prize given out in Japan? Why?

2.  What happened in Japan that convinced American entrepreneurs to pay more attention to quality?

3.  What does the Japanese word *kaizen* mean? How do you intend to apply kaizen to your business?

4.  Give three reasons why entrepreneurs should focus on quality.

5.  Explain how Debbi Fields's competitive strategy used Deming's ideas to succeed. Are there products for which you are willing to pay a higher price for higher quality? Explain.

## EXPLORATION

Count how many commercials use (or imply) the word "quality" during one hour of television. Count how many use (or imply) "price." Report your findings to the class. Explain what you think your observations reveal about Americans' attitudes about quality.

## REFERENCES

1 Adapted from the works of W. Edwards Deming and others.

## VOCABULARY

continuous improvement ■ *kaizen* ■ quality ■ quality control

## Chapter Summary ✔✔✔

28.1   Quality is the key to profit.
  A. Consumers pay more for products and services they feel are high quality:
    1. Quality products last longer
    2. Quality service satisfies customers
    3. American business did not always consider quality to be key.
  B. Deming taught that continuous improvement, not lowering costs, is more profitable:
    1. Quality products last longer and need fewer repairs or replacements
    2. Customers recommend quality products to others
    3. Customers are loyal to quality products
    4. *Kaizen* is the concept of continuous improvement
    5. Treat employees and suppliers ethically to build loyalty and boost quality.
  C. Quality can be improved:
    1. Adopt a philosophy and motto that inspire commitment to quality
    2. Constantly look for small ways to improve
    3. Do it right the first time
    4. Develop long-term supplier relationships
    5. Focus on quality in customer service, production, training, and elsewhere
    6. Encourage constructive criticism without fear
    7. Work smarter and better; emphasize quality over quantity
    8. Use standards to measure quality control and consistency. ✔✔✔

## A Business for the Young Entrepreneur
### AL MEZZE, RASHA AYOUB

*NFTE inspired me to develop the idea that brought me closer to my ethnic background.*

Rasha Ayoub understands that quality is the foundation of her business. She is developing Al Mezze, a Middle Eastern meat store that provides *halal* meat to the Islamic community. Halal meat has been slaughtered according to Islamic rules governing cleanliness and quality.

Presently, customers who want to purchase halal meat have to travel quite far to find it. Rasha hopes that the quality of her products will attract non-Islamic customers, as well.

Rasha grew up in a large family and learned that you have to find your own identity in order to make your mark. At the same time, she feels that it is important to hold on to your heritage. Creating Al Mezze allowed her to combine the business skills she learned at NFTE with the richness of her Middle Eastern background.

Before taking entrepreneurship classes, Rasha was too shy to speak in front of a crowd, and her understanding of business practice was limited. Today, she is working on her undergraduate degree at the University of Connecticut, where she is, among other things, Vice President of the Diverse Student Association.

When she graduates from college, Rasha will launch Al Mezze, and intends to expand her operation to include spices, grains, and other foodstuffs. She hopes one day to open a restaurant featuring Middle Eastern cuisine. ■

## SKILLS MEAN SUCCESS

**ENGLISH**

**Reading and Writing:** Using Images to Express Ideas

Business writing, such as letters, reports, and memos, tends to be more impersonal and concise than notes to friends or casual e-mails. Business communication should use no-nonsense, clear, and simple language. Business writers, however, sometimes use the tools that other authors do. In the profile of Rasha Ayoub, the writer suggests that quality is the foundation of her business. This is writing using an image. It connects an idea that suggests an image, or mental picture, to the reader.

1. Match the sentences below with what the writer was suggesting.

   **I.** As a manager, Sasha was a tiger.

   **II.** His keyboarding was like a snail stuck in mud.

   **III.** He was as friendly as a tree stump.

   **IV.** We've got to hit a home run for the company.

   **V.** Mike was buried under his work.

   **VI.** The financial report was Greek to Jamal.

   **a.** There was a great deal of work to be done.

   **b.** His social skills were so weak they might as well have been dead.

   **c.** The leader was aggressive, maybe even mean.

   **d.** The information was so hard to read, it seemed like another language.

   **e.** He was slow.

   **f.** The business needs something good to happen.

2. Business writers and speakers often use sports images as *metaphors* to describe the world of work. List five examples of sports metaphors that you have seen or heard used in business, or can find in business material. Example: Hernandez just beat the buzzer turning in his report. In other words, he just made the deadline. ■■■

### CHAPTER 29

# EFFECTIVE LEADERSHIP:
## *Managing Yourself and Your Employees*

*You must do the thing you think you cannot do.*

— Eleanor Roosevelt, *American politician and humanitarian*

### KEY OBJECTIVES

THIS CHAPTER WILL ENABLE YOU TO:

- Develop leadership qualities.
- Manage your time more efficiently.
- Hire employees.
- Build a management team.

**A** leader is someone who has the confidence and energy to do things on his or her own, and inspire others as well. Running a business requires leadership. One day you may have employees who will look to you for leadership.

Leadership abilities come from self-esteem. If you believe in yourself, you can do things with confidence. Develop a positive attitude and you will become a leader. Great leaders are optimists — they have trained themselves to think positively, no matter what.

## The "PERT" Chart

Leaders learn how to manage their lives so they can get more done in less time. One of the most important things you can do when you start your first business is to learn how to manage your time more efficiently.

You may not have employees to manage yet but you can probably manage yourself better. Here is a tool called a PERT Chart (**P**rogram **E**valuation and **R**eview **T**echnique) that you can use when you feel overwhelmed by the many things you will need to do when starting up your first business. You can use it to manage a short-term project, or to organize your planning for long-term projects.

| SAMPLE PERT CHART | | | | | | |
|---|---|---|---|---|---|---|
| Task | Week 1 | Week 2 | Week 3 | Week 4 | Week 5 | Week 6 |
| Befriend banker | X | X | X | X | X | X |
| Order letterhead | | X | | | | |
| Select location | X | | | | | |
| Register business | X | | | | | |
| Bulk-mail permit | | | X | | | |
| Select ad agency | X | | | | | |
| Meet with lawyer | | | | X | | |
| Meet with accountant | | | | X | | |
| Meet with suppliers | | | | | X | |
| Utilities deposits | | | | | X | |
| Promotional material | | | | | X | |
| Phone system | | | X | X | X | |
| Web-site design | | | | | | X |
| Set up database | | | | | | X |
| Network computers | | | | | | X |

## Pay Yourself

Before you hire employees for your business, figure out how to pay your first employee — yourself. To help calculate your salary or stipend, keep track of how many hours you actually spend on your business.

Once the business is breaking even, decide how you will distribute the profit. The decisions you make will affect your financial record keeping, so think it through. As we have discussed, there are four possibilities:

1. Pay yourself a *commission* — a percentage of every sale. This is treated as a variable operating cost, because it fluctuates with sales.

2. Pay yourself a *salary*, which is a fixed amount of money paid at set intervals. You could choose to receive your salary once a week or once a month. A salary is a fixed operating cost, because it does not change with sales.

3. If you have a service or manufacturing business, you could pay yourself an *hourly wage*. An hourly wage is considered as a cost of goods sold, because it is factored into the cost of the product or service.

4. Pay yourself a *dividend*, which is a portion of the business's profits.

Entrepreneurs who do not pay themselves regularly tend to overstate their return on investment, because they have not taken their pay out of the net profit as a cost. This can also increase the amount of tax the business will owe. Anything that reduces the net profit reduces the tax on net profit. Of course, you will have to pay income tax on the money you pay yourself, but generally you will come out ahead if you treat some of your business profit as self-payment.

Another reason to pay yourself is that it will enable you to be honest about whether or not your business is really worth the time. Could you be making more money working for someone else? Is to keep working for yourself the best choice? Thinking entrepreneurially includes a realistic consideration of whether you would be happier *not* running a business.

## SKILLS MEAN SUCCESS

**LEADERSHIP** ▶ **Interviewing Skills**

Interviewing is a key skill in hiring talented staff. Write a list of *general* (not job-specific) questions that could be used to interview job applicants.

- Avoid questions that are overly personal.
- Use questions that cannot be answered "yes" or "no."
- Ask questions that would help the interviewer decide if the candidate would be a good employee. ■■■

## Adding Employees to the Mix

As the business grows, you may need to hire people. At first these might just be friends or family members that help you with deliveries or boxing up shipments. But eventually you may have to hire "real" employees. Once you do, you will need to become aware of the laws and tax issues affecting hiring. These include:

- **Payroll taxes.** You will have to deduct payroll taxes from employee earnings. Your accountant can advise you in more detail when you get to this point. For now, it is important to know you will also be responsible for contributing to Social Security on their behalf.

- **Fair Labor Standards Act.** This law, passed in 1938, requires you to pay employees at least minimum wage. It also prohibits you from hiring anyone under 16 full time.

- **Equal Pay Act of 1963.** This law requires employers to pay men and women the same rates for the same work.

- **Anti-discrimination laws.** There are laws that protect employees against discrimination on the basis of age, race, religion, national origin, or because of color, gender, or physical disabilities.

## Human Resources

Human Resources (also called HR, Human Capital, or Personnel) is the department of a business that hires, trains, and develops the company's employees.

For a business just starting out, it may not be practical to have a director of human resources. Instead, the entrepreneur will handle such tasks as hiring. Rarely does a company hire a separate human resources professional until they have a staff of 20 or more.

 **Rule of Thumb:** Many companies will staff their human resources departments with one HR executive per 50 to 200 employees.

## Hiring

Hiring employees is also called **recruitment**. Perhaps the most important thing you can do is to bring other capable, motivated people into your business. In the bestseller *Good to Great*, management expert Jim Collins says great leaders "get the right people on the bus — sometimes even before a company decides exactly what business it will be in."

Here are some ways to bring employees into your business:

- Bring people in as partners. Partners share the risks and rewards of the venture, and will co-own the business with you.

- Hire experts to work on specific tasks on a contract or hourly basis. For example, you might hire a professional accountant to work one day per month on your record keeping.

- Hire someone as a full-time, permanent employee. The most common way to do this is through an "at will" arrangement. Typically, "at will" employment continues for an indefinite amount of time, but can be ended by either party in writing with, say, two weeks notice.

There are specific steps in the recruiting process:

1. **Defining the job.** Think about what you need this employee to do, and what kinds of skills will be needed for the job.

2. **Posting the job.** Will you place an ad in a newspaper? Put up want-ad posters?

3. **Screening resumes.** When you post the opportunity, ask the applicants to mail or fax their **resumes**. A resume is a one-page summary of education and work experience.

4. **Interviewing candidates.** Use the resumes to choose several people to interview. Before an interview, prepare the questions you want to ask about the person's skills and ambitions.

5. **Checking references.** Ask the candidates who interest you to provide at least two references from previous employers or other professional people who could tell you about their character.

6. **Negotiating salary.** You and the candidate you choose will have to negotiate how much you will pay, and any benefits your company will provide, such as health insurance.

7. **Hiring.** Once you decide to hire someone, you will have paperwork to fill out to start creating paychecks.

8. **Orientation.** This is the process of introducing the employee to the company and to the requirements of the job.

Each step of the process will require careful attention, skill, judgment, and fairness.


## Growing Your Team

Ways to find talented employees include:

- **Campus Recruiting.** Companies from all industries visit college campuses every year to meet and offer recent undergraduate- and graduate-level students full-time employment. Established companies in banking, consulting, accounting, consumer products, technology, health care, and many others, are all major recruiters on college campuses. (Another good reason to continue your education past high school!)

- **Staffing and Recruiting.** Companies plan and hire according to staffing plans and budgets, and typically use a combination of internal recruiters (employees of the company), outside recruiters (agencies or contingency firms) and job-board postings (online job listing services like www.careerbuilder.com and www.monster.com).

- **Executive Search.** When companies need to hire a senior executive, either the CEO (chief executive officer), the board of directors, or the director of human resources will engage in an "executive search." These top job openings are usually not advertised, and the process is often managed by an outside search firm.

## What about Family and Friends?

There are compelling reasons for entrepreneurs to hire family members and friends, including:

- Loyalty — Family and friends are more loyal to the entrepreneur than strangers might be.

- Lower costs — Family and friends might be willing to work for less money than strangers.

- Fun — It can be fun to share your workload with friends and family.

There are also disadvantages of hiring family and friends, including:

- Never being able to get away from the business — If you hire family and friends, will you ever have any time when you are not discussing the business, or working on it?

- Disagreements can get very personal.

- Will you really be hiring the best person for each job — or are you being swayed by your feelings for a friend or family member?

Also be aware of the following potential problems:

- Establish clear lines of responsibility — you are still the boss. Make sure you only hire family members and friends who can respect that, and will treat the job like a "real" one.

- Put aside your personal feelings.

- Hire family or friends you get along with, and who will share your vision for the business.

## Getting the Best out of Your Employees

Whoever you hire, treat them fairly and with respect. This approach will get the best results. Many companies make their employees part owners by giving out shares of company profits. Wouldn't you work harder if you knew your efforts would make a difference in your paycheck?

Follow these guidelines for being a boss:

1.  Get the right people. This means getting to know each employee's strengths and weaknesses.

2.  Provide a fair salary and good working conditions.

3.  Share your vision for the company.

4.  Give employees incentives to work hard — start a profit-sharing plan.

5.  Give them control over their work.

6.  Give each employee definite responsibilities and areas of control.

## Corporate Management — Building a Team

If it is successful, a small business may reach a point where the entrepreneur and a few employees cannot handle operations efficiently. At that stage, the business will need *managers*. These are people who specialize in business operations. Many successful entrepreneurs are creative people who tend to get bored with the everyday details of running a large firm. The best entrepreneurs recognize this about themselves and hire specialized professionals.

An entrepreneur with a growing corporation can raise capital by selling stock. Some of this capital can be used to hire managers. This will free the entrepreneur to spend less time managing and more time thinking up new ideas for the business.

A management organizational chart for a small business might look like this ("Fred" is the President):

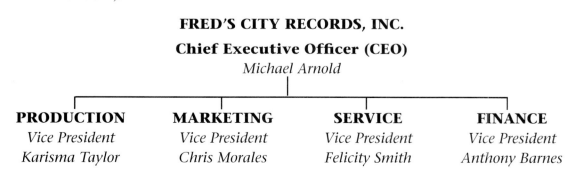

**FRED'S CITY RECORDS, INC.**

**Chief Executive Officer (CEO)**

*Michael Arnold*

| **PRODUCTION** | **MARKETING** | **SERVICE** | **FINANCE** |
| --- | --- | --- | --- |
| *Vice President* | *Vice President* | *Vice President* | *Vice President* |
| *Karisma Taylor* | *Chris Morales* | *Felicity Smith* | *Anthony Barnes* |

## SKILLS MEAN SUCCESS

**MATH**

**Data Analysis:** Determining Mean, Median, Mode

The employees of a company are paid *mileage* whenever they use their own cars on company business. The company pays them $0.365 for every mile driven. Use the following mileage report to answer the questions below.

| Employee | Miles Driven in October | Mileage Rate | Mileage Expenses Paid |
|---|---|---|---|
| Smith | 427 | $0.365 | $155.86 |
| Johnson | 53 | 0.365 | 19.35 |
| Williams | 956 | 0.365 | 348.94 |
| Brown | 117 | 0.365 | 42.71 |
| Jones | 28 | 0.365 | 10.22 |

**1.** Estimate the total mileage paid in October:

    **a.** About $800    **b.** About $600    **c.** About $1000

**2.** Find the *mean* for Mileage Expenses Paid.

**3.** What was the *median* amount paid in October?

**4.** Estimate total mileage paid by the company over one year.

**5.** Which employees might be traveling sales representatives? ■■■

## Management Functions

But what do managers do? Ideally, they perform the functions that will help a small business grow into a large and successful company.

**1. Planning.** This function includes deciding on the company's long-term goals and creating strategies to achieve them.

**2. Organizing.** This includes everything from hiring, to buying or leasing equipment. It includes setting up an organizational chart and defining responsibilities.

**3. Leading.** Managers lead the employees through the carrying out of company strategies.

4. **Directing.** After the entrepreneur has made the plans and organized the employees and resources, managers have to motivate the employees to perform the work that will move the company toward its strategic goals.

5. **Staffing.** This function involves hiring and firing and making sure employees are placed in the positions that best utilize their respective skills and experience.

6. **Controlling.** This step involves measuring the business's performance and figuring out how to improve it. Is the budget actually being followed? Are products achieving the desired level of quality? How about customer service?

7. **Coordinating.** Coordinating includes creating in-house communications (telephone and e-mail systems), and teaching everyone to use them, scheduling regular meetings and updates, and making sure managers are working toward the same goals.

8. **Representing.** Managers represent a company to its people and its people to the company; they also represent the company to the outside world. Managers need to dress and behave in a way that appropriately reflects the "company culture."

9. **Innovating.** Managers should always be thinking about and creating new ways to help the company meet its goals. The entrepreneur may be the guiding, creative force behind the company, but the managers should be problem solvers, as well.

10. **Motivating.** Each decision the managers make will affect how employees feel about working for the company. If managers assume that people need to be pushed to do their jobs, and treat the employees that way, they will incur resentment. A manager who assumes that employees want to do their best will be more successful. Some ways managers can motivate employees include: involving them in decisions, recognizing outstanding contributions, and rewarding achievement.

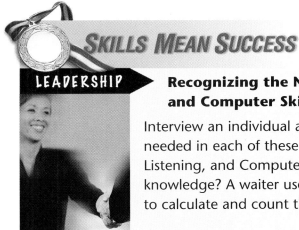

## SKILLS MEAN SUCCESS

**LEADERSHIP**

**Recognizing the Need for Math, English, and Computer Skills**

Interview an individual about her or his job. List the types of expertise needed in each of these areas: Math, Reading, Writing, Speaking, Listening, and Computer Skills. How would this person use each area of knowledge? A waiter uses math to add up the bill, to make change, and to calculate and count tips, for example. ▪▫▪

## Firing and Laying Off Employees

Sometimes you hire someone and it just doesn't work out. Can you fire that person? Yes, but protect yourself by documenting the reasons. You can be sued if an employee thinks he or she was fired for no good reason. If an employee is violating rules, notify him or her in writing (and keep a copy for your records). If things still don't improve and you have to let the employee go, you will have proof that there were problems with job performance.

One good way to have proof is to evaluate your employees periodically — every three to six months, and definitely once a year. Employee appraisal can be simple feedback from you, or it can consist of observations from several different people in the company who interact with that individual. Regardless, having regular appraisals on file will help you make your case should you ever have to let an employee go.

Sometimes you might have to "lay off" employees that you might otherwise keep. They may have performed their jobs well but you either don't need their skills anymore, or can't afford to continue to employ them. When employees are laid off, try to offer a "severance package" (continued salary for a limited time) and/or help them find a new job. Always treat people the way you would like to be treated.

## Sample Employee Performance Plan and Appraisal

Objective #1: _____

Observed achievements: _____

Objective #2: _____

Observed achievements: _____

Objective #3: _____

Observed achievements: _____

**Manager feedback only:**

*General comments:* _____

*Employee strengths:* _____

*Areas for improvement:* _____

Overall Rating (based on numerical scale below): _____

**RATING KEY:**

1.  **Outstanding:** Extraordinary performance, well beyond the expectations or requirements of the position.
2.  **Above Satisfactory:** Excels beyond the basic requirements of the position.
3.  **Satisfactory:** Meets requirements of the position. Displays the work of a fully competent employee (the broadest category of the group).
4.  **Needs Improvement:** At times, performs at a level that is below that of a competent employee. Improvement is necessary.
5.  **Unsatisfactory:** Performance is consistently inferior to the standards set for this position. The employee clearly fails to complete certain tasks that have been deemed critical. A rating at this level may result in demotion or termination.

Date: _____

Employee signature: _____

Manager signature: _____

# Managerial Styles that Work

As your business grows, it will develop its own culture. Companies like Wal-Mart and Home Depot spend significant amounts of time and money to create a work environment that inspires and motivates. How you or your managers treat the employees of your business will have a profound effect on the company culture. Adopt the best managerial style for your business and maintain it consistently. According to expert Daniel Goleman, the main managerial styles and their advantages and drawbacks are:

1.  **Coercive.** To *coerce* means to pressure someone into doing what you want. This "commanding" approach can be effective in a "disaster" situation or with problem employees who need forceful management. In most scenarios, though, a coercive leadership style hurts employee morale and diminishes

the flexibility and effectiveness of the business. Employees stop thinking and acting for themselves.

2. **Authoritative.** An authoritative leader takes a "come with me" approach, stating the overall goal but giving employees freedom to figure out how best to achieve it. This can work well, but not if the leader is not an expert in a field but is "leading" people (a team of scientists, say) who are.

3. **Affiliative.** This is a "people come first" style that is good when the business is in the team-building stage. It can fail when employees become lost and need direction.

4. **Democratic.** This style gives employees a strong voice in how the company is run. This can build morale and work if employees are capable of handling responsibility. It can result, however, in endless meetings and confused employees who feel leaderless.

5. **Pacesetting.** This type of leader sets high performance standards and challenges employees to meet them. This can be good when employees are also motivated, but can overwhelm those who are not as committed to the business.

6. **Coaching.** This style focuses on helping each employee to grow, through training and support. This can be a good approach for starting and growing a business but may not work with those who have been with the company awhile and may be resistant to change.

The key lies in not choosing one strategy that is "best," but in being aware of all of them and selecting the one that will work in a particular case. The most effective leaders apply the right style at the right time.

# Chapter 29 Review

## CRITICAL THINKING ABOUT...

### LEADERSHIP

1. What characteristics do you most admire in a leader? Why? Describe three leaders that have these characteristics.

2. Write a brief essay detailing how you could find five more hours in your weekly schedule to manage your business.

3. Create a weekly time-management schedule for yourself.

4. Fill out a PERT Chart for your business. **Business Plan Practice**

5. Do you have any employees for your business yet? If so, describe how much you pay them and how this is working out. If not, describe your ideal employees, what you would pay them, and what their jobs would be.

6. Create an organizational chart for your business.
**Business Plan Practice**

## KEY CONCEPTS

1. How old does someone have to be before they can work full time?

2. What is one kind of tax employers have to pay for employees?

3. How does incorporating help an entrepreneur put management into place?

4. Write an essay on what you would do to develop teamwork for your management and employees.

5. Describe the trade-offs between being an entrepreneur versus being a manager. Which role would suit your personality and skills better?

## IN YOUR OPINION

Discuss with a group:

Should an employer be able to fire an employee if the employee is very often ill? Before the discussion, prepare by searching the Internet to find out what legal issues exist in firing employees.

## VOCABULARY

recruitment ■ resume

## Chapter Summary ✔✔✔

29.1 Leaders have the energy and confidence to get things done and also to inspire others to succeed.
   A. Leaders manage time and projects efficiently using tools such as PERT Charts.
   B. Leaders pay themselves out of the profits they earn:
      1. Commission: a percentage of sales
      2. Salary: a fixed amount paid regularly
      3. Hourly wage (calculated as a cost of goods sold)
      4. Dividend: a portion of the profits.

C. Paying themselves reduces net profit which reduces taxes.

D. Growing businesses hire employees and must follow tax and labor laws:
1. Deduct employees' payroll taxes and contribute to their Social Security
2. Follow the Fair Labor Standards Act and the Equal Pay Act of 1963
3. Obey anti-discrimination laws.

29.2 The functions of Human Resources in a business include hiring, training, and developing employees.

A. Recruitment includes hiring talented and committed workers as well as experts.

B. Full-time permanent employees are usually hired "at will."

C. Recruiting involves several steps:
1. Defining the job
2. Posting the job
3. Screening resumes from applicants
4. Interviewing candidates
5. Checking references
6. Negotiating salary
7. Hiring
8. Orientation.

D. Recruiting can be done via campus searches, job-posting, recruiters, or executive search.

E. Hiring family members and friends has:
*Advantages:*
1. Loyalty
2. Lower costs
3. Fun
4. Shared visions for the business.
*Disadvantages:*
1. No escape from "work talk"
2. Disagreements can get personal
3. Risk of being swayed by feelings
4. Can be tough to "be the boss."

F. Treating employees fairly and respectfully gets the best results:
1. Get the right people in the right jobs
2. Provide a fair salary and good working conditions
3. Share the company vision
4. Provide incentives for hard work
5. Give employees control over their work and specific responsibilities.

**29.3** Entrepreneurs often want to stay focused on creative growth opportunities so they assign routine management tasks to managers as the company grows.

A. Key management functions include:

1. Planning
2. Organizing
3. Leading
4. Directing
5. Staffing
6. Controlling
7. Coordinating
8. Representing
9. Innovating
10. Motivating.

B. Managing also includes firing and laying off employees.

1. Document in writing all reasons and discuss with the employee in advance to prevent possible legal problems later.
2. Provide regular employee appraisals using written performance plans.
3. Offer severance packages if possible, especially to laid-off employees.

C. Different management styles can be effective, depending on the company, the timing, and the individual scenario:

1. Coercive: effective in a crisis, but demoralizing and inflexible
2. Authoritative: effective for leaders who are experts leading non-experts
3. Affiliative: effective in team settings; may fail if more direction is needed
4. Democratic: builds morale with responsible, self-directed employees, but can be inefficient elsewhere
5. Pacesetting: works with highly motivated employees, but can be overwhelming and create resentment
6. Coaching: effective with growing, start-up companies, but may not work with resistant, long-time employees. ✔✔✔

# A Business for the Young Entrepreneur
## BABY-SITTING SERVICE

*Parents of young children are always searching for responsible baby-sitters. You probably have friends who baby-sit. Why not be a leader and start a baby-sitting service?*

Each week, have the baby-sitters who work for your service call to tell you when they can work. In return for matching sitters with jobs, you will earn a commission (a percentage of each sale). You could charge, say, ten percent.

If the Smith family needs a baby-sitter on Friday night for four hours, you look on your list and see that Sara can work Friday night and lives near the Smiths. Mrs. Smith agrees to pay Sara five dollars per hour. That means Sara will earn:

$5 per hour $\times$ 4 hours = $20

Sara will pay you ten percent of that money because you got her the job. Here's how you figure your commission:

1.  "Percentage" means "out of a hundred." Ten percent (10%), means ten out of a hundred. Divide one hundred into ten.

    $$\frac{10}{100} = 10\%$$

2.  Another way to express percentage as a number is to move the decimal point two places to the left (this is the same as dividing the percentage by 100).

    20% percent becomes .20
    45% becomes .45
    10.5% becomes .105

3.  To figure your commission, multiply the percentage, expressed as a number, by the total sale.

    Commission on Sara's job = $20 $\times$ .10 = $2.00
    Your commission will be two dollars.

*If you owned a baby-sitting service,*
*how would you make sure the baby-sitters you hired*
*were qualified?* ■

### CHAPTER 30

# TECHNOLOGY:
## *Science Applied to Business*

*Man is still the most extraordinary computer of all.*

— John F. Kennedy, *35th President of the United States*

### KEY OBJECTIVES

THIS CHAPTER WILL ENABLE YOU TO:

- Explore how entrepreneurs use technology.
- Expand your business on the Internet.

**T**echnology is scientific knowledge that is applied to business and used by people. You are probably aware of the rapid improvements in computer technology. Every year video games look more real, and you can store more words or music in less space.

This is possible because of the incredible growth in the speed of computing. This phenomenon has been called the Information Revolution — it has become so much easier for data to be communicated around the world by telephone or over the Internet. Smart entrepreneurs take advantage of the latest breakthroughs in technology.[1]

**BizFact:** In 1965, scientist Gordon Moore observed that the speed of microprocessing will double every two years. This is called Moore's Law.

## Computers

The computer can be very important for the entrepreneur. Even the least expensive model can help you:

- Create stationery and business cards.

- Type professional-looking letters and correct spelling before you print them out.

- Create presentations.

- Keep financial records.

- Make flyers and posters.

- Keep a list of customers and print labels for mailing.

- Communicate with customers, employees, and suppliers.

Of course, the computer itself is not the only expense. You will also need to buy a printer, ink cartridges, paper, and CDs for storing data.

If you don't have a computer, ask a teacher or counselor if you could use one at school. The local library might be another place to access a computer. In addition, some communities have nonprofit technology centers that are open to the public. Various organizations provide refurbished computers at low prices.

## SKILLS MEAN SUCCESS

### LEADERSHIP ▶ Locating Computer and Technology Resources

One of the fastest-growing departments in many large companies is the IT (Information Technology) team.

1. Do Internet or library research, or interview a manager in a small or medium-sized company. Gather enough information about corporate jobs in IT to present a ten-minute slide presentation to the class.

2. Make a list of things that could go wrong if a company's technology system breaks down. ■■■

## Computer Software Programs

There are software programs for just about every business need you might have — from typing a report to filing your taxes. Most computers come stocked with basic software, but you may want to buy accounting and inventory tracking programs or other business applications. Office supply and computer stores will carry most of the software you want, but sometimes the best prices can be found elsewhere.

A lot of software is available for free or at a low cost on the Internet. Many software companies offer their programs directly to customers as **shareware**. Although free of charge, shareware usually does not include upgrades or technical support.

Most good anti-virus programs will "monitor" the installation of any software, including shareware. If you install software without an anti-virus program being present, run a virus check as soon as possible.

Several software packages for entrepreneurs are on the market, including:

- Biz Builder — www.bizbuilder.com
- Tim Berry's Business Plan Pro — www.bizplans.com

When you install software, you will be asked to agree not to copy it. This is because you do not really own it. It is "intellectual property" in the same way that inventions or works of art belong to those that created them. You are really buying a *license* to use the software.

## SKILLS MEAN SUCCESS

**MATH**

**Reasoning: Writing and Using Formulas**

The cell phone is another technology that businesses depend on. There are many cell phone payment-plan options, including a flat fee per month plus an additional charge for minutes used.

Write a formula that explains how to calculate the cost of each of the following plans.

**a.** $40 per month plus $20 for the first 200 minutes; then $0.15 per minute.

**b.** $19.99 per month plus $20 for the first 100 minutes; and then $0.10 per additional minute.

**c.** $24.49 per month. The first 500 minutes are free. Additional minutes are $0.35 each. ■■■

## Protect Your Computer Data

Collections of information are called **data**. Important business data on your computer might include mailing lists, invoices, letters, and financial records. If anything happens to your computer, you could lose valuable data that you spent hundreds of hours creating. You will need to protect your computer from:

1.  **Power surges or outages.** A power surge can send too much electricity through your computer and damage it. Plug all your computer equipment into a "power strip" outlet that has a surge protector. Another safety feature, Uninterruptible Power Supply (UPS), may be purchased in computer stores.

2. **Computer viruses.** A *virus* is a computer program that can attach itself to your software files and hard drive and destroy them. Safeguard your computer with virus-protection software programs, such as those available from Norton or McAfee. These companies have Internet update services that you can download to protect yourself from new viruses.

3. **Disk failure.** Hard drives can "crash," destroying valuable data. To prevent this, save everything you do by copying it to backup disks, and be sure to "enable" your word processing program's auto-save feature.

## The Internet

When you go online to check e-mail or look at **Web sites**, your computer is tapping into a vast network called the **Internet**. The Internet began in the 1960s as a much smaller network of government scientists and defense experts who wanted to be able to send data to each other. It became available to the public in the 1970s and presently operates in dozens of countries and is accessed by many millions of people worldwide. It is used daily for sending and receiving e-mail, obtaining information, and maintaining databases, among many other applications.

## Going Online

To access the Internet — "go online" — your computer must have a **modem**. The modem lets your computer send and receive data through:

1. **A phone line.** This is a dial-up connection from your telephone. If you only have one phone line, you will not be able to use your phone when you are online.

2. **A cable line.** This is the same connection that provides you with cable television. You must be a cable TV subscriber to use a cable line.

3. **A DSL line.** This stands for Digital Subscriber Line. It runs along the phone line but does not interfere with the phone; you can use your phone while using a DSL.

You will also need to subscribe (usually for a monthly fee) to an **ISP** (Internet Service Provider). Smaller ISPs will provide you with the software for direct connection to the Internet. Larger ISPs, such as America Online or Microsoft Network (MSN), give access to the Internet plus "extras," such as shopping malls, magazines and newspapers, reference works, chat rooms (where subscribers can "talk" directly with each other), health and fitness advice, classified ads, and other features.

You can also choose the speed of your connection. Dial-up, is less expensive but is also much slower than DSL or cable connections.

**SKILLS MEAN SUCCESS**

**TECHNOLOGY** ▶ **Technology Etiquette: Cell Phones, Voice Mail, E-Mail**

Make a list of Do's and Don'ts for any or all three communications tools. Turn the best one into a slide-show presentation for the class. For example:

| Cell Phone Do's: | Cell Phone Don'ts: |
| --- | --- |
| *Turn your phone off in meetings.* | *Let your phone ring in meetings or when you are in an audience at a concert or other event.* |
| *Use normal telephone courtesy.* | *Talk loudly so that you annoy people around you.* |
| *Use a headset when driving.* | *Be distracted and careless when talking on the phone while driving.* ■ ■ ■ |

## The World Wide Web

The World Wide Web is a subset of the Internet, made up of elements that include not just text, but graphics, too. Web pages are *hypertext* documents, meaning they combine text with graphics. Web pages are also marked with **hyperlinks**. These are areas on the page that, when clicked on, lead somewhere else — another Web site, for example, or other pages, graphics, sounds, or videos within the Web site being visited. To "surf the Web" you will need a Web browser. Most ISPs provide a Web browser with a subscription.

Web pages are the material you look at while surfing the Web. Web pages have addresses called *URLs* (Uniform Resource Locators). Many entrepreneurs maintain Web sites, which are collections of Web pages, for their businesses. Software programs make it possible to create your own Web site. Once you have one, you can reach customers anywhere in the world. The first page of your site will be your "home page." Think about how you want it to look and what it should project. The home page will be your online customer's first impression of your business.[2]

## The Internet as Business Opportunity

There are three types of businesses that can be operated over the Internet:

1.  **Selling goods, services, and information.** Amazon.com is a good example.

2. **Selling advertising space.** If you can create a site that draws lots of visitors, advertisers will want to buy ad space from you.

3. **Charging a subscription fee to those wanting to visit your site.** www.morningstar. com, for instance, offers information on investments to its members.

You can also use the Internet:

- **To find the best deals.** Many Internet businesses offer products at low prices by cutting out the wholesaler and selling directly to the consumer. This could really improve your product/distribution chain. Dell Computer is a good example of a company that decided to sell directly to the consumer, and was therefore able to offer very competitive prices.

- **To market your business.** The Internet will allow you to reach far beyond your immediate geographical area for potential customers. Selling *collectibles* (such as baseball cards or stamps) is a good Internet business because your market of collectors will probably be spread around the country.

- **To buy and sell.** Web sites like eBay offer opportunities to reach potential customers, and to get good prices on equipment and supplies.

**BizTip:** Many online retailers are able to sell their products tax-free over the Internet. This is another reason customers love buying online — and why you should consider selling your products there.

# E-mail

**E-mail** is short for "electronic mail." These are messages sent between computers via the Internet. Most ISPs provide an e-mail account. If you choose AOL as your ISP, for example, and you want your e-mail address to be "Jane," it would be jane@aol.com. If your ISP does not provide e-mail, you can get it free from Yahoo! (http://www.yahoo.com) or at MSN Hotmail (http://www.hotmail.com). Set up an e-mail address for your business. It's a great way for customers to reach you with questions or orders. You can also use e-mail to stay in touch with your suppliers.

Just be careful not to annoy anyone with e-mail promoting your business. Unwanted advertising on the Net is called "spam." Sending spam can result in your e-mail inbox being jammed with "flames," angry e-mails from people who received your spam.

## Newsgroups

**Newsgroups** are public message boards that usually focus on a particular topic. Newsgroups can be local, regional, or international. There may be many different newsgroups for the same topic.

Sending e-mail or posting messages on newsgroups can be used to contact sales prospects and keep in touch with customers you already have, but you must use these methods carefully. In the "real world," you can search for sales prospects by distributing flyers or cold-calling people on a list. But online newsgroups do not appreciate spam, and sending it will be counterproductive.

 **BizTip:** Use "permission marketing" on the Internet. Get people to sign up for your e-mail list so you know you have permission to e-mail them.

Becoming involved in a newsgroup can lead to increased business, if it is handled properly. Let's say you sell photographic supplies and you hear about an interesting newsgroup for photographers. Don't post ads for your business! Instead, before posting any messages, observe the conversation of others in the group for a while. Get a feel for the discussions taking place. Once you feel comfortable, try posting a message such as the following:

> *The discussion this week on the advantages of the new Nikon mini-camera was very interesting. I'm in the photography supply business and I'm looking for new items to add to my Web site. I have already posted articles from Advanced Photography magazine and have received tips from some of my clients. Does anyone have any ideas for other useful information I could post?*
>
> *Thanks!*
>
> *Sandra Bowling*
>
> *PhotoSupply Online  http://www.photosupply.net  e-mail: photosupply@aol.com
> The Photographer's Source for Supplies and Advice*

Because this is not a sales pitch, no one in the newsgroup should take offense, and it could attract customers to your site.

Whether you use e-mail or newsgroups, it is important that you never give out personal information, such as a home phone number or address. Provide a separate e-mail address and business phone number for customers to get in touch with you.

# Chapter 30 Review

## CRITICAL THINKING ABOUT...

### TECHNOLOGY

1. Do you have access to a computer? If so, list five ways you could use it for your business. If you don't have a computer, write up a plan for how you intend to get access to one.

2. Create a budget for the technology you think you will need to start your business.

3. If you have access to the Internet, go online and find a newsgroup that would be a good resource for your business.

4. Do you think it would be a good idea to create a Web site for your business? Why or why not? What would you put on your home page?

5. Describe three things that can threaten computer data. How would you protect your data from being damaged?

## KEY CONCEPTS

1. Make a list of all the technology you would like to use to run your business. Even if you can't afford some of it right now, write a memo explaining how you could get access to the technology you will need. **Business Plan Practice**

2. Go online and find a shareware version of a type of software that you would like. Write a memo describing the differences between the shareware and the purchased version of the software.

3. What is your favorite technology?

4. Describe the three items your computer needs to communicate on the Internet.

5. Read A Business for the Young Entrepreneur on the next page. Describe an experience you had when you were required to do something or go somewhere that was foreign to you.

## EXPLORATION

1. Go online and find five software packages you think would be useful for your business.

2. Write a paragraph describing what you think will be possible with the Internet in 20 years.

3. Do you have any favorite Web sites? If not, explore until you find three you like. Would you order a product over the Internet? What would your concerns be? How would your own business solve a similar customer concern?

## REFERENCES

1 Thanks to Mike Caslin, Nick Gleason, Michael Simmons, and Sheena Lindahl for material in this chapter.
2 E. Tittel, et al., *HTML for Dummies*, 3rd Edition (IDG Books Worldwide, Inc., 1997).

## VOCABULARY

data ■ e-mail ■ hyperlink ■ Internet ■ ISP ■ modem ■ newsgroup ■ shareware ■ technology ■ Web site

## Chapter Summary ✔✔✔

30.1 Entrepreneurs need to use technology wisely.
   A. Technology is science applied to business:
      1. Computers make many business activities easier
      2. Free software called "shareware" can be useful
      3. Protect computer systems from power surges, viruses, disk failure.
   B. The Internet offers business opportunities:
      1. It connects people and businesses
      2. Modems link computers with the Internet via phone, cable, or DSL
      3. Internet Service Providers (ISPs) connect subscribers to the Internet
      4. The World Wide Web (www) contains Web sites, each with its own URL (Uniform Resource Locator) address
      5. A business's Web site provides access to customers.
   C. E-businesses and other companies use the Internet:
      1. Selling goods, services, information, Web site advertising, subscriptions to users
      2. Finding deals and low-priced products a business needs
      3. Reaching new customers, nationwide and international
      4. Using e-mail to connect with customers (but avoid spamming)
      5. Online newsgroups provide information to and about customers
      6. Web sites can be Internet "stores" for customers to shop online.
          ✔✔✔

## A Business for the Young Entrepreneur
### STRATEGIC RESOURCES INTERNATIONAL, KARTHIK MOHAN AND BHARATH SREERANGAM

*We always believed there was a way and that we had to take action. Otherwise it would not have been possible to leave the comfort of home, country, and culture in pursuit of dreams. We are thrilled with the journey and look forward to the future.*

Karthik and Bharath founded Strategic Resources International (SRI), and they presently have a staff of 22. SRI is a consulting business that provides fast, reliable technological assistance to corporations. The company focuses on three areas: consulting, project implementation, and managing information inventory. SRI has a strategic alliance with Netage Consultants, a 200-person ERP consulting firm based in Princeton. Clients include such names as AT&T, DeLoitte Touche, FedEx Kinko's, Aetna, and HSBC.

Karthik and Bharath, both formerly with AT&T Labs, completed the NFTE program through the Prudential Young Entrepreneur Program. Their industry knowledge and experience built a company that had revenues of $400,000 in 2003.

Entrepreneurs face many challenges and obstacles as they build their businesses. Karthik and Bharath faced additional challenges as newcomers to the United States. They adjusted to a foreign culture, improved their English-language skills, and managed this with family far away. They want SRI to be a socially responsible corporation. For that reason, each partner has contributed time and resources to Habitat for Humanity, the Red Cross, and the Sierra Club. ■

## SKILLS MEAN SUCCESS

**ENGLISH**

### Speaking and Listening: Idioms

Karthik and Bharath did not always speak English. They worked hard to learn the language. Some of the most difficult things to learn in any language are *idioms*. These are expressions that don't mean *literally* what the words normally would. For example, "I'll see you" means that I'm sure we will meet again. "He's a champ" means that he is very skilled. "Up the creek without a paddle" means to be in serious trouble (or perhaps danger). Idioms can be very confusing to new speakers of a language. You should avoid them when speaking to those who would probably not understand.

Listen to conversations around you or to the dialogue on a popular TV show, or keep an eye out in books or articles you read. Make a list of *idiomatic* expressions. Decide which ones might be confusing to new learners of English and why. ■ ■ ■

# Malia Mills Swimwear

### Malia Mills' Mission

When 38-year-old Malia Mills decided to launch her own swimwear company, she set out to do much more than just sell high-end bathing suits. Mills wanted to change the way that women felt about themselves.

The slogan of Mills' business is: "Love Thy Differences," because Mills is passionate about encouraging all women — regardless of age, weight, or body type — to celebrate their uniqueness. In Malia Mills' world, if a woman doesn't like the way she looks in a swimsuit, it's the suit that has to change, not the woman. As Mills explains, "We are passionate about inspiring women to look in the mirror and see what is right instead of what is wrong."

A native of Hawaii, Mills saved up money for her startup investment by working as a waitress in New York City for many years. Before starting her company, she gained experience in the fashion industry by working as a designer at established clothing companies. Finally, armed with both start-up capital and experience, she opened Malia Mills Swimwear in 1991.

### The Polaroid Project

If you walk past the Malia Mills Swimwear flagship store in New York City's chic Soho district, the first thing you'll notice are the photographs in the window. Instead of showcasing fashion models, Malia Mills has created a makeshift collage of Polaroid pictures that feature regular customers wearing her signature swimwear. According to Mills' sister, Carol, who manages the store, "We've had so many customers walk in off the street because of those photographs. People are thrilled to see actual women in all colors, shapes, and sizes wearing our suits."

This "Polaroid project" began as a brainstorm by a summer intern on a particularly slow sales day. Mills liked the idea of using photographs of her customers because it resonated with the core mission of her business.

### Place Matters: Setting the Right Tone

As a customer, Mills always hated trying on bathing suits in department stores under the glare of unflattering fluorescent lights. In Malia Mills' boutiques, the lighting is soft, and dressing rooms are located in the back so customers won't feel exposed in front of other shoppers.

To create a comfortable environment for her customers, Mills has designed her stores to feel like cozy lounges. She even provides free bottled water to customers so that they can feel relaxed and at home. Sales associates are always on hand to help customers find the suits that will best fit their body types.

Mills does not believe in one-size-fits-all design. Accordingly, Mills' tops are sized like bras, and bottoms come in sizes 2-16. All pieces are sold as separates, allowing customers to mix and match across different style and fabric options.

### The Price/Production Connection

Malia Mills' suits are priced at the high end of the swimwear market. A bikini top will cost between $88 and $96, bikini bottoms cost $86, and full-piece suits cost an average of $182. Mills' pricing reflects the choices she has made about how her suits are produced. Mills chose to manufacture in New York City, for example, rather than to outsource production to countries where labor costs are lower. Mills says: "It costs us much more per unit to sew our suits locally, but supporting our community is worth it. The mostly women who sew our suits do so with extra care — we visit them often, and they know how important quality is to us."

Mills imports her fabrics from Europe and typically buys fabric in small quantities — which is more costly — so that her suit designs stay fresh. Mills also pays a premium to the fabric mills that custom-dye her materials in unique colors.

## Smart Selling Requires Trial and Error

Early on, Mills sold her suits wholesale to larger department stores, but she found that this sales strategy didn't fit well with her core mission. The department store salespeople didn't understand how to properly answer customers' questions about the unique features of her products, such as why they are sized differently from typical swimsuits. Eventually Mills pulled the plug on the department stores and decided to sell directly to customers. Maintaining control over sales has allowed Mills to stay true to her company's mission of providing women with a fun and empowering experience purchasing swimwear in a comfortable environment.

## Promotions: Getting the Word Out

Mills' mission has drawn the interest of the media, and over the years Mills has generated some terrific PR for her small business. Her company has been profiled in *The New York Times*, *Sports Illustrated*, *Harper's Bazaar*, and other major publications. The company also gets a boost when celebrities such as Madonna are seen and photographed wearing her suits.

Mills recently began purchasing advertising for the first time in local print publications. She is doing this as an experiment to see if it has a noticeable impact on generating new customers.

In the meantime, the growth of Malia Mills Swimwear continues to be propelled by word of mouth and customer loyalty. She sometimes worries that she is undercutting herself in the marketplace by making such high-quality suits. If the average woman owns two to three bathing suits and a Malia Mills suit can last up to several years, then it could take a long time for a customer to purchase a replacement. Each day, however, Mills connects with new passers-by who are drawn into the store by the Polaroids of regular women wearing her bathing suits. Once these women walk in off the street, there's a pretty good chance that they will walk out as customers, shopping bags in hand.

## Questions

1. Describe the unique features of Malia Mills' product.
2. Malia Mills swimwear is not inexpensive. Why do you think customers are willing to pay a premium for her product?
3. The case mentions that Malia Mills Swimwear is currently experimenting with paid advertising. If you were in charge of marketing for Malia Mills Swimwear, what would you do to assess whether or not it was cost effective for the company to continue to purchase advertising?
4. What kind of environment is Malia Mills trying to create in her stores? Why is this important?
5. Besides her own boutiques, specialty stores, and online, what might be some additional sales venues for Malia Mills Swimwear to consider exploring?
6. Why was the "Polaroid project" a successful promotional venture?
7. Imagine a scenario where Malia Mills Swimwear hired you as a media consultant. Answer the following:
   - Brainstorm a cause-related marketing strategy for the company.
   - Describe three strategies for the company to pursue to obtain media coverage.

## Sources

Malia Mills Web site: www.maliamills.com

"Chic to Chic — Turn Style into Sales with a Clothing-Design Company" by Pamela Rohland, *Business Start-Ups* Magazine, December 1999.

Interviews with Malia and Carol Mills

# Intermediate Module
## Business Plan Review

*NOTE: Complete the Intermediate Business Plan Worksheets in your Workbook. Use the Review here to become familiar with the topics covered in the Intermediate Business Plan.*

*I hope that I have convinced you — the only thing that separates successful people from the ones who aren't is the willingness to work very, very hard.*

— Helen Gurley Brown, *author and magazine publisher*

**N**ow you are ready to write a more detailed plan for your intended business. If you are satisfied with your Basic Business Plan, use those worksheets to help you fill out the Intermediate Business Plan. Consider taking this opportunity, however, to improve your Plan or even change it entirely. Maybe you have decided to start a different business, or have done more research on your costs and can be more accurate now. In addition, the Intermediate Plan includes variable costs, more detailed marketing planning, competitive strategy, and strategies for selling and manufacturing.

## Variable Costs

Operating costs such as rent, advertising, salaries, and insurance can be broken into:

- Fixed costs — which do not change with sales. Example: Rent on your store does not increase when you make more sales, or decrease when there are fewer.

- Variable costs — which do change with sales. Example: If you pay a commission on each sale, commissions are a variable cost.

For the Basic Business Plan you may have assumed that your variable costs will be zero, but in fact most businesses do have some variable costs — electricity bills that go up when a store is more active, perhaps. If more customers are visiting your business, they are probably taking more flyers, brochures, and business cards. So your advertising costs do tend to increase with sales, as well.

Even if you don't have obvious variable costs, such as sales commissions, we recommend that you assume variable costs to be a percentage of your revenue and include this in your income statement. A good rule of thumb is to assume variable costs will be one to two percent of the revenue you hope to earn.

## Your Business Idea (Chapter 1)

1. Describe your business idea.
2. What is the name of your business?
3. Explain how your idea will satisfy a consumer need.
4. Provide contact information for each owner.
5. If there is more than one owner, describe how the business ownership will be shared.

## Economics of One Unit (Chapter 2)

1. Do you intend to pay yourself a salary, wage, dividend, or commission? Explain.
2. What type of business are you starting?
3. Calculate the Economics of One Unit for your business.

## Return on Investment (Chapter 3)

### Business Goals:

1. What is your short-term business goal (less than one year)? What do you plan to invest to achieve this goal? What is your expected ROI?
2. What is your long-term business goal (from one to five years)? What do you plan to invest to achieve this goal? What is your expected ROI?

### Personal Goals:

1. What is your career goal? What do you plan to invest to achieve this goal? What is your expected ROI?
2. How much education will you need for your career?

3. Have you tried to get a part-time job related to your chosen career?

## Opportunity Recognition (Chapter 4)

1. What resources and skills do you (and the other owners of your business) have that will help make your business successful?
2. Perform a SWOT analysis of your business.

## Core Beliefs (Chapter 5)

1. Describe three core beliefs you will use in running your company.
2. Choose a motto for your company. (You can select or adapt from the 50 positive quotes in Chapter 5, find one elsewhere, or make up your own.)

## Supply and Demand (Chapter 6)

1. What factors will influence the demand for your product or service?
2. What factors will influence the supply for your product or service?

## Product Development (Chapter 7)

How do you plan to protect your product/trademark/logo? (Pick one, and explain.)

Patent, copyright, or trademark.

## Competitive Advantage (Chapter 8)

1. What is your competitive advantage?

2. How will your business help others? List all organizations to which you plan to contribute. (Your contribution may be time, money, your product, or something else.)

## Operating Costs (Chapter 9)

1. List and describe your monthly fixed costs.

2. List and describe your monthly variable costs.

3. Re-calculate your economics of unit, allocating as many variable costs as possible.

4. Add a cash reserve that covers three months of fixed costs.

## Marketing (Chapter 10)

1. Describe the Four P's for your business.

   **Product** — Why will your product meet a consumer need?

   **Place** — Where do you intend to sell your product?

   **Price** — What price do you plan to sell your product for, and why?

   **Promotion** — How do you plan to advertise and promote your product?

2. Fill out a marketing plan for your business.

3. Do you intend to publicize your philanthropy? Why or why not? If you do, explain how you will work your philanthropy into your marketing.

## Market Research (Chapter 11)

1. Research your industry and display the results in a one-page report that includes pie charts and bar or line graphs. Describe your target market within the industry.

2. Describe your market segment and the results of your research on this market segment.

## Record Keeping (Chapter 12)

1. Describe your record-keeping system.

2. List all bank accounts you will open for your business.

## Projected Income Statement (Chapter 13)

1. Complete a monthly projected budget and one-year income statement for your business.

2. Use your projected one-year income statement to calculate:

   Projected ROI for one year:
   _____ %

   Projected ROS for one year:
   _____ %

## Financing Strategy (Chapter 14)

1. What legal structure have you chosen for your business? Why?

2. List the cost of the items you will need to buy to start your business.

3. Add up the items to get your total start-up capital.

4. Add a cash reserve of one-half your total start-up capital.

5. List the sources of financing for your start-up capital. Identify whether each source is equity, debt, or a gift. Indicate the amount and type for each source.

6. What is your debt ratio? What is your debt-to-equity ratio?

7. What is your payback period? In other words, how long will it take you to earn enough profit to cover start-up capital?

## Negotiation (Chapter 15)

Describe any suppliers with whom you will have to negotiate.

## Buying Wholesale (Chapter 16)

1. Where will you purchase the products you plan to sell, or the products you plan to use to manufacture the products you will be selling?

2. Have you applied for a sales-tax ID number?

# Your Competitive Strategy (Chapter 17)

1. Using the charts on pages 239 and 240 of Chapter 17, define your business, analyze your competitive advantage, and determine your tactics.

2. Describe your strategy for outperforming the competition.

3. What tactics will you use to carry out this strategy?

4. Write a mission statement for your business in less than three sentences that clearly states your competitive advantage, strategy, and tactics.

# Your Marketing Mix (Chapter 18)

### Step One: Consumer Analysis

1. Describe your market segment.

2. Describe your target consumer: age, gender, and income.

### Step Two: Market Analysis

1. How will you look at location, population, personality, and behavior when you analyze your market segment?

2. Use your market analysis method to describe your market segment. Roughly how many consumers are in this segment?

3. Explain how your marketing plan targets your market segment.

4. What percentage of your market do you feel you need to capture for your business to be profitable?

5. Who are the potential customers you plan to approach in the first two months of business?

### Step Three: The Marketing Mix

1. Describe The Four P's for your business.

    **Product** — How will your product meet a consumer need?

    **Price** — Are your prices competitive? Do a comparison. What price do you plan to sell your product for, and why? What is your pricing strategy?

**Place** — Describe your business location and its competitive advantages.

**Promotion** — How do you plan to advertise and promote your product?

2. Fill out a marketing plan for your business.

## Advertising and Publicity (Chapter 19)

1. What is your business slogan?

2. Where do you intend to advertise?

3. How do you plan to get publicity for your business?

4. Are you planning to use cause-related marketing?

5. Write a sample press release for your business.

## Break-Even Analysis (Chapter 20)

Perform a break-even analysis of your business.

## Selling (Chapter 21)

1. Describe the features and benefits of the product (or service) your business will focus on selling.

2. Choose three ways you will sell your product or service. Explain why you think these methods will work.

3. Write a sales pitch for your product (or service).

4. Describe three customers you intend to pitch.

## Customer Service (Chapter 22)

Create a customer database for your business. Include name, e-mail, phone, fax, address, last contact, and/or last purchase. What five questions will you ask every customer?

## Business Math (Chapter 23)

Double-check all of the math and financial information in your business plan to be sure it is accurate.

## Business Communication (Chapter 24)

1. Which of these business communication tools will you use?

Phone, voicemail, fax, e-mail, text messaging, and/or other (describe).

2. Have you designed a letterhead for your business?

## Legal Structure (Chapter 25)

1. What is the legal structure of your business: Sole Proprietorship, Partnership, Limited Partnership, C Corporation, Subchapter-S, Limited Liability Corporation, or Nonprofit Corporation?

2. Why did you choose this structure?

3. Who will be the partners or stock-holders for your company?

4. Have you registered your business?

5. Have you applied for a sales-tax identification number?

# Manufacturing (Chapter 26)

1. What are the zoning laws in your area? Does your business comply?

2. Do you intend to manufacture your product? If so, describe the manufacturing process you will use. If not, describe how your product is manufactured.

# Production/Distribution Chain (Chapter 27)

1. How do you plan to distribute your product to your target market?

2. Use this chart to show the production/distribution channel for your own business, and the markups at each point in the chain.

**Manufacturer**
Name: _____
Contact information: _____
Markup: $ _____ Markup: % _____

**Wholesaler**
Name: _____
Contact information: _____
Markup: $ _____ Markup: % _____

3. What is the estimated time between your placing an order with your supplier and the product's availability to your customers?

# Quality (Chapter 28)

1. How will you deliver a high-quality product (service) to your customers? Describe your quality control procedure.

2. Write a motto for your business that will remind you to stay focused on quality.

# Human Resources (Chapter 29)

1. Fill out a PERT Chart for your business.

2. Will you be hiring employees? If so, describe what their qualifications should be, what you intend to pay them, and how they will help your business.

3. Provide contact information for your accountant, attorney, banker, and insurance agent.

4. What are your policies toward employees? How do you plan to make your business a positive and rewarding place to work?

5. Create an organizational chart for your business.

# Technology (Chapter 30)

1. Which technology tools will you use for your business, and why?

2. Write a memo explaining how you will access this technology.

# ADVANCED MODULE

# What You Need to Know to Grow

*The Advanced Chapters of NFTE Semester 2 will teach you how to grow a small business venture you have already started. Once you have completed these chapters, you will be able to create a balance sheet, understand contracts, and select the best financing strategy for your business and personal assets.*

*After you have finished Chapter 50, you will be ready to apply what you have learned by preparing your Advanced Business Plan. A complete version of the Advanced Business Plan can be found in Appendix F at the back of this book.*

# FINDING SOURCES OF CAPITAL

*One great, strong, unselfish soul in every community could actually redeem the world.*

— Elbert Hubbard, *American lecturer and essayist*

## KEY OBJECTIVES

THIS CHAPTER WILL ENABLE YOU TO:

- Identify new sources of capital.
- Use sale of equity to finance your business.
- Network with other entrepreneurs to find business financing.
- Use vendor financing.

## Financing Your Business

It takes money to operate and expand a business. Businesses may need money to purchase equipment, inventory, advertising, or to renovate a rental space. It often is a challenge for a young entrepreneur to find the money needed to operate or expand a business. This chapter will help you learn about where to get the money for your business needs.

## Sources of Capital

There are many potential sources of capital. Except for gifts, all money will come into your business as either *debt* or *equity*. Sources of capital include:

- Family and friends
- "**Angels**" and **venture capital** (There will be more on venture capital in Chapter 36.)
- **Small Business Investment Companies (SBICs)** and other government programs

- Minority financing sources
- Banks and credit unions/**Small Business Administration (SBA)** guarantee

## Family and Friends

Family and friends are obvious sources for loans. But what about offering them a share of your profits instead? Unless your business is incorporated,[1] you won't have actual shares of stock to sell. But you could sell equity to a limited number of "friends and family" investors as part of a private sale. However, get some legal advice before you take this option.

You can still offer a portion of your profits in exchange for investment, however. You might offer ten percent of the profits, in exchange for the financing you need. You can use the assets of your business to secure a loan, or you can offer a portion of the profits in return for a loan.

Explain that a loan will only earn back the amount of the loan plus interest. If an investor would be willing to give you capital in exchange for *equity*, on the other hand, he or she could earn back much more than the original investment.

Acknowledge that equity is more of a risk than debt, but the potential for reward is much higher. However, be careful not to take money from friends and family that they can't afford to lose, in case your business is not successful.

When deciding how to finance your business, pay attention to the legal regulations that may apply. When you sell equity in a company, for instance, you must follow state and federal laws that control how shares may be sold. The **Securities and Exchange Commission (SEC)** oversees the exchange of *securities* (stocks and bonds) in the United States.

## "Angels"

Angels are private investors, typically worth over $1 million, who look to finance start-up ventures. Like any investors, they want to make a profit, but they may also have additional reasons for investing. An angel investor might be interested in a type of business or might want to support entrepreneurs in his/her community. Sometimes an angel takes an interest in an individual entrepreneur or wants to be involved in something interesting. Bill Gates has funded several biotechnology start-ups. Angel investors generally only invest on an equity basis.

If you have a solid business plan, you might be able to raise angel financing. Their investments are usually in the $10,000 to $500,000 range. Angel investors are one of the best sources of financing.

You can find angel investors through lawyers, accountants, or business clubs for young people in your community that bring in speakers or provide a location for meeting local businesspeople. Some states also have "angel networks." Call your local Small Business Administration (SBA) office or chamber of commerce for details. Regional networks can be helpful because angels tend to invest in businesses they can visit easily.

## SKILLS MEAN SUCCESS

**ENGLISH**

**Reading for Literary Response:**
**Using Literary Elements to Convey Meaning**

People use *figurative* terms like "angel" to create new meanings from familiar words.

1. Explain why "angel" is a good image for a private investor who funds start-up businesses.

2. Consider the following figurative words and phrases used in business. Explain why each is appropriate:

   a. She *floated* the bill for 20 days.

   b. There were so many competitors that his new store couldn't get any *traction* in the marketplace.

   c. The new restaurant had to close, due to inventory *shrinkage*. ■ ■ ■

A famous example of angel investment is the funding obtained by Anita Roddick (which we described earlier), founder of the hugely successful The Body Shop. When she wanted to open a second store, no bank would lend her the money. However her friend Ian McGlinn lent her the equivalent of $8,000 for 50% equity in the company. McGlinn became a multimillionaire from this relatively modest investment, but Roddick did not regret her decision.

As additional funders invest in your company and receive shares, the percentage ownership of the early investors declines. This is called *dilution*. As long as the later investors are adding value to the company, though, the "diluted" stockholders will see their ROIs increase, though with smaller shares of the company.

**BizFact:** Although equity can be an effective way to finance your business, you are essentially inviting investors to be your partners. So, don't sell so much equity that you risk losing control of the business!

## Online Networking

**Networking** is the act of making contact and exchanging valuable information with other businesspeople. The key to successful networking is to identify ways you can meet the needs of the other person, while also helping your own business. The Internet makes networking easy. You can also search for angels and connect with other young entrepreneurs online. Use search engines such as Google, Excite, and Yahoo!, and visit Web sites like http://www.yeo.org (Young Entrepreneurs Organization). Networking can be a good way to locate angel financing.

## Banks and Credit Unions

Banks and **credit unions** make loans and expect to be repaid in cash, not in equity. You will be required to make regular monthly payments to pay back the loan — without fail. Banks and credit unions are also likely to:

1.  Ask for **collateral** against the loan. If you can't pay, they will take and resell the collateral to satisfy the loan.

2.  Ask for a **co-signer**, who will have to repay the loan in case you can't.

3.  Only make loans to businesses that have a good track record.

4.  Credit unions will probably also require that you be a member. Credit unions are nonprofit organizations and charge less interest than banks do. It might be worth it to become a member of a credit union to quality for a loan.

Loans from banks or credit unions *must* be repaid. If you can't make payments, they can and will bring suit against you. You could end up bankrupt and with a ruined personal credit rating.

## SBA Loans

The Small Business Administration is the agency of the government that helps small business. The SBA can guarantee a bank loan. This means that, if you can't repay the bank, the SBA will. An SBA guarantee would make it much more likely to get a loan. You can also visit the SBA online at the following addresses:

- http://www.sba.gov/
- http://www.sba.gov/financing/sbaloan/snapshot.html
- http://www.sbaonline.sba.gov/
- http://www.sba.gov/INV/offices/

## Bank Line of Credit

A **line of credit** is a kind of bank loan that is specifically designed for short-term financing. It's a pre-approved sum of money that will be available for you to draw on when you need to pay operating expenses but don't have the cash. When cash comes in from your business, you put the money back. Advantages of a line of credit include:

1.  You won't have to apply for a loan every time you need money. A line of credit is pre-arranged with your bank.

2.  You only pay interest on the money you've withdrawn, not on the total amount available.

3.  Your monthly payment to the bank is only for the interest on what you've borrowed. You don't pay back the principal (the actual amount you borrowed) until you get cash back from sales.

**BizFact:** It's easier to get the cash you need if you can delay payment of expenses. Most vendors give businesses 30 days after receipt of the shipment to pay the bill. (That could end up being 45 days better than paying cash in advance because the shipping itself can take time.) In some cases, you can get 30/60/90 terms of payment. This means you pay one-third of the bill in 30 days, the next third in 60, and the last third in 90. Low inventory and fast turnover of inventory will also help your cash flow.

## Venture Capital

Venture capital companies invest in start-up businesses. Unlike angel investors, however, venture capitalists have funds that include invested money from other people. Venture capital firms, therefore, are more highly structured and focused on ROI than angel investors might be. They want to buy into businesses they think will do very well and return large profits. Venture capitalists invest in less than one percent of the businesses they consider. Since venture capital investment is a high-risk business, these investors typically seek to earn five to ten times their original investment over five years. Venture capitalists are normally only interested in a percentage of ownership in the business (equity). You can find out more about venture capital by doing research on the Internet.

## Small Business Investment Companies

Small Business Investment Companies (SBICs) are partially financed through guaranteed loans from the government. There are hundreds of SBICs that specialize in equity investments and loans for small businesses. You should investigate the SBICs in your area at: http://www.sba.gov/INV/offices/

## Minority Financing

If you are African American, Hispanic, Asian, or belong to another minority group, or if you are a woman, look into **Minority Enterprise Small Business Investment Companies (MESBICs)**. These are private investment firms, chartered by the SBA, that provide both debt and equity capital to new small businesses. To find a "MESBIC" in your community, try Google, Excite, or Yahoo! on the Internet. Enter MESBIC and your state or city.

The Minority Business Development Centers (MBDCs) are another good resource. You should be able to find a center in your area through http://www.mbda.gov.

## Youth Financing[2]

As a young entrepreneur, you may qualify for grants, scholarships, and awards designed to promote youth entrepreneurship. Such sources of start-up capital include:

**Dollar Diva** Business Plan Competition for teen women —
http://independentmeans.com/imi/dollardiva/bizplan/index.php

### Ernst & Young's Entrepreneur of the Year Program —
http://www.ey.com/global/content.nsf/International/EGC_-_Events_-_EOY

To qualify, you must be an owner/manager primarily responsible for the recent performance of a privately held or public company that has been in existence for at least two years. Eight to ten award recipients are selected in several industry and special award categories.

### Global Student Entrepreneur Awards — http://www.gsea.org/

The Global Student Entrepreneur Awards recognize those outstanding undergraduate student entrepreneurs who are simultaneously balancing course work and cash flows — and succeeding at both! The awards were instituted in 1988 by Saint Louis University's Jefferson Smurfit Center for Entrepreneurial Studies.

### National Association for the Self-Employed Future Entrepreneur of the Year Award —
http://benefits.nase.org/show_benefit.asp?Benefit=FEScholarship

The NASE "Future Entrepreneur of the Year" award and scholarship program is the nation's only major prize supporting the philosophy of entrepreneurship rather than a specific profession. The maximum award of $24,000 is given to a young person who has demonstrated leadership and academic excellence, ingenuity, and entrepreneurial spirit. In addition, NASE gives 22 $4,000 scholarships. Since the program's inception, the organization has provided over $1 million in awards.

### NFIB Free Enterprise Scholars Awards —
http://www.nfib.com/page/educationFoundation.html

Each year the NFIB Young Entrepreneur Foundation grants at least 300 NFIB Free Enterprise Scholars Awards nationwide in the amount of $1,000 each. These are not based on financial need and are non-renewable. The NFIB Free Enterprise Scholars Awards can be applied to educational expenses at any accredited, nonprofit two- or four-year college, university, or vocational/technical school in the United States. A recipient may transfer from one school to another and retain the award.

### NFTE Young Entrepreneur of the Year — http://www.nfte.com

NFTE graduates can win an all-expense-paid trip to New York City for NFTE's annual "Salute to the Entrepreneurial Spirit" Awards Dinner and a grant of $750 (business plan category) or $1,000 (operational business category) to be used for the graduate's college education or business.

**SBA Young Entrepreneur of the Year Award** — http://www.sba.gov

During National Small Business Week, each state, the District of Columbia, Puerto Rico, and Guam select a Small Business Person of the Year. From this group, the SBA chooses the national Small Business Person of the Year.

**Youth In Action Awards** — http://www.youthlink.org/us/awards.php

Youth In Action presents awards to youth leaders and their projects that promote social change and connect to local communities. They support youth-led projects that have clearly defined goals with potential for growth or further replication. Award recipients receive $1,000, which includes funds for a disposable camera to photo-document the project for an online photo gallery. Award recipients will also have the opportunity to take part in an online journal and contribute to a booklet of case studies of young people around the world who are bringing positive change to their communities.

## SKILLS MEAN SUCCESS

### ENGLISH

**Writing for Information and Understanding: Sentence Combining**

Combine the following pairs of sentences to make the meaning clearer:

1. Friends and family might loan you money to start a business. They could also provide money in return for part ownership instead of a loan.

2. You should extend your *accounts payable* terms as long as possible. Accounts payable are the amounts a business owes its supplers.

3. MESBICs are private investment firms that support minority businesses. They provide debt and capital equity to some new, small businesses.

4. Many new businesses take time to become profitable. If a business remains unprofitable for years, it may have to close. ■■■

# Business Plan Competitions

- NFTE Advanced Entrepreneurship Seminar Business Plan Competition
- Carrot Capital — http://www.carrotcapital.com
- Junior Chamber International Best Business Plan (BBP) of the World Competition — http://www.jci.cc/members/info.php?lang_id=1&info_id=2030
- Bank of America Youth Entrepreneur Awards for New York City — http://ccnyc.neighborhoodlink.com/ccnyc/genpage.html?n_id=304302039

## SKILLS MEAN SUCCESS

**TECHNOLOGY** ▶ **Online Research and Evaluating Web Sites**

The Internet can be a great source of useful and important information, including contacts and facts about competitors, to help you start and run your business.

1. Create a Web-site-analysis checklist that rates sites for quality and usefulness in specific categories. How easy is the site to use? Is it well organized? Is the information current? Does it provide interactive tools to use in financial calculations and decision making? — and so on. Score each category 1–5, 5 being "excellent."

2. Work alone or with a partner. Use a Web search engine to find three new sites that provide funding ideas or would be useful to an entrepreneur. Evaluate each using your checklist and be prepared to share your ratings with the class. ■■■

 **BizFact:** You can finance by reinvesting profits in your business. This is called *financing with retained earnings*. These profits are kept (retained) rather than paid out to owners as dividends. If you are willing to build the business as you go, you may be able to avoid seeking help from others — who may want a share of ownership. This lets you keep control of the company without taking on debt. This kind of funding is also called "bootstrap financing" — the entrepreneur pulls him/herself up "by the bootstraps."

# Chapter 31 Review

## CRITICAL THINKING ABOUT...

### SOURCES OF CAPITAL

1. Make a list of friends and family members who might be willing to invest in your business in exchange for equity.

2. Do you know any potential "angels"? How could you meet some?

3. Searching the Internet, find a MES-BIC in your area. Write a memo describing this MESBIC and why you think you (or a real or imaginary friend) would qualify for financing.

4. Describe financing sources that might be willing to invest in your business in exchange for equity.
   **Business Plan Practice**

   *Friends and family*

   _____

   *Angels*

   _____

   *SBICs or MESBICs*

   _____

   *Other*

   _____

5. If you receive $2,000 in equity financing from your uncle to start your business, and agree to pay him 10% of your net profit each year, how much will you owe him in the following years, according to the following figures?

| Net Yearly Profit | Payment Due to Equity Investor |
|---|---|
| Year 1: $6,000 | $ _____ |
| Year 2: $12,400 | $ _____ |
| Year 3: $15,000 | $ _____ |
| Year 4: $20,300 | $ _____ |
| Year 5: $18,500 | $ _____ |
| Year 6: $35,000 | $ _____ |

a. In what year will your uncle have made back his investment?

b. What will your uncle's net profit be in Year 5?

c. What will your uncle's ROI be after the full six-year period?

## KEY CONCEPTS

1. List the advantages and disadvantages of debt vs. equity funding.

2. After reading A Business for the Young Entrepreneur on page 385, describe how Jason financed his business.

## DISCUSS WITH A GROUP

1. How much money would you feel comfortable borrowing from friends or family for your new business?

2. Would you rather pay interest or give equity in exchange for business capital? What are the trade-offs of each approach? Would it make sense to use a combination?

## REFERENCES

1 There will be more about incorporating a business in Chapter 32.
2 Special thanks to the Youth Entrepreneur Web Resources page of New York University's Leonard N. Stern School of Business, and to the *Extreme Entrepreneurship Youth Resource Guide* (Extreme Entrepreneurship Education Corporation).

## VOCABULARY

"angel" ■ collateral ■ co-signer ■ credit union ■ line of credit ■ Minority Enterprise Small Business Investment Company (MESBIC) ■ networking ■ Small Business Administration (SBA) ■ Small Business Investment Company (SBIC) ■ Securities and Exchange Commission (SEC) ■ venture capital

# Chapter Summary ✔✔✔

**31.1** Entrepreneurs find and use debt (loans) and equity (selling shares) sources to finance (start or expand) their businesses.

A. Loans and loan assistance can be obtained from:
　1. Family and friends
　2. Banks and credit unions, which can also provide pre-approved, short-term lines of credit.

B. Loans, loan assistance, and equity can be obtained from:
　1. The Small Business Association (SBA)
　2. Small Business Investment Companies (SBICs)
　3. Minority Enterprise Small Business Investment Companies (MESBICs).

C. Commercial lenders will:
　1. Expect to be repaid in cash
　2. Usually ask for collateral and a co-signer before lending.

D. Grants, awards, and loan assistance can be obtained from:
　1. Youth financing grants
　2. Business plan competitions
　3. Other awards.

E. Equity in incorporated businesses can be sold:
　1. To "angels," venture capitalists, and other investors
　2. Following state laws and rules of the federal Securities and Exchange Commission (SEC).

**31.2** Online networking helps entrepreneurs:

A. To make contacts with possible financing sources
B. To find the best sources of financing for their businesses. ✔✔✔

# A Business for the Young Entrepreneur
## 2nd GEAR BICYCLES, JASON UPSHAW

*When Jason Upshaw was growing up in his low-income neighborhood, he always wondered about the large number of abandoned bicycles lying around.*

When Jason was 12, he learned how to repair bikes at a local shop. Later, with capital funding from the Youth Venture Program, he founded a community-based program called 2nd Gear Bicycles, which taught kids in his neighborhood how to repair and maintain bikes.

In addition to selling new bikes and teaching young people to repair broken ones, 2nd Gear's Earn-a-Bike program gave youngsters the chance to get a used bike in exchange for taking three bike-riding lessons totaling 15 hours, and spending ten hours doing community-service work.

As of 2004, more than 800 young people have been trained to repair bikes at 2nd Gear, and more than 300 have earned free bikes. The business has grossed $100,000. But the biggest reward for Jason was hearing children who had worked with him say that, without 2nd Gear, they didn't know where they would be.

Jason graduated from Babson College in 2003. His plans for 2nd Gear include selling more used bikes to other organizations, and using the profits to create an economic mechanism for social change.

*Describe how Jason financed his business.*
*How could you apply what he did to your own business?* ■

### CHAPTER 32

# CORPORATIONS:
## *Limiting Liability*

*Great works are performed not by strength, but perseverance.*

— Samuel Johnson, *English author*

## KEY OBJECTIVES

THIS CHAPTER WILL ENABLE YOU TO:

- Understand corporations and limited liability companies (LLC).
- Decide whether you should form a corporation or LLC.
- Explain how a corporation is treated under tax and business laws.
- Evaluate the pros and cons of different business structures.

**A corporation** is a business structure that is considered to have its own legal identity. It is owned by **stockholders**, and its daily operations are conducted by officers (including a president, a treasurer, and a corporate secretary). Decision making is controlled by a **board of directors**. A corporation is treated as an individual (*entity*) under business law. It incurs expenses, earns income, and pays taxes.

Whether large or small, corporations:

- Issue stock, representing shares of ownership.
- Elect officers and a board of directors. The board is a group of people chosen by the stockholders to oversee the company.

A corporation may be a "privately held" business or a "publicly held" company, like General Motors or IBM. *Shares* of stock represent ownership in a corporation. If privately held, the shares are sold by the company owner(s) to a limited number of individuals. In a "public" corporation, the stock is offered for sale to the general public. Anyone may purchase a public company's shares at the market price.

Stockholders of a privately held business generally obtain shares of the company by investing money or providing intellectual property or services. There are a number of laws and regulations that need to be understood before an entrepreneur sells stock to the public, even to a small group of investors. Stockholders may be paid **dividends** if the company is profitable. Dividends are part of the stockholders' return on investment in the company, and are determined by the board of directors.

# Corporate Liability: Limited Liability

As we have said, a corporation is a separate and independent legal entity. When the corporation enters into agreements, engages in actions that may result in liability, or incurs debt, the corporation is solely responsible. The individual stockholders, employees, and the board of directors are not responsible for the actions or debts of the corporation, only for their own wrongdoing.

**Example:** If an automobile manufacturer is sued because of a defect in one of its models, the corporation uses its resources to pay any court costs or settlements. The personal assets of the company's owners, employees, and stockholders may not be sold to pay the corporation's debts or settlements, unless they have acted outside the scope of their responsibilities (e.g., committed fraud). The corporation acts like a shield, protecting the assets of the company's managers.

### Advantages of Corporations

- Limited legal liability (the personal assets of the officers or stockholders cannot be used to pay corporate debts).

- Money can be raised through the issuance and sale of stock.

- Ownership can be transferred easily, because the new owner will not be personally responsible for the corporation's existing financial obligations.

- Corporations can buy and sell property and enter into legal contracts.

### Disadvantages of Corporations

- Corporations are subject to "double taxation." Profits earned by a corporation are subject to tax (1) as the income of the corporation, and (2) again, if this income is paid to stockholders as dividends.

- The founder of a corporation (the original entrepreneur) can lose control to the stockholders and board of directors if he or she no longer owns more than half the voting stock.

- It is more expensive to start a corporation. There are also costs associated with operating a corporation (including state filing fees and other maintenance costs).

- Corporations are subject to many government regulations.

**BizFact:** Steve Jobs, the co-founder of Apple Computer, was fired by his own company's board of directors in 1985. He was invited back as interim CEO in 1996, and today he is CEO of both Apple and Pixar, the maker of the *Toy Story* movies.

# Four Kinds of Corporations

### #1: C Corporation

Most big companies, and many smaller ones, are C Corporations. They sell ownership as shares of stock. Stockholders may vote on important company decisions. To raise capital, the C Corporation can sell more stock, or obtain loans from banks or investors.

### #2: Subchapter-S Corporation

To qualify as a Subchapter-S corporation, the company must have fewer than 75 stockholders, no corporate, partnership, or non-resident alien shareholders, and no shareholders who are not U.S. citizens. This corporate structure offers most of the legal protection of a C Corporation, without the double taxation on income. Subchapter-S corporate income is only reported by the stockholders as personal income — it is usually not also taxed as corporate income.

### #3: Professional Corporation

Doctors, lawyers, architects, and other professionals can also incorporate themselves. The initials P.C. ("Professional Corporation") after a doctor or lawyer's name means the individual has incorporated his or her practice, or belongs to a practice with others in the same profession. Professional corporations are subject to special rules relating to the particular profession.

### #4: Nonprofit Corporation

Nonprofit corporations, also called 501(c)(3) corporations (from the title of the tax-code regulation pertaining to them), raise money through charitable contributions in order to accomplish specified public objectives. Churches, museums, charitable foundations, and trade associations are all examples of nonprofit corporations.

If you would like to provide a service to benefit society, consider starting a nonprofit corporation. A nonprofit raises money through **donations** (gifts) of money or through charging dues to members. The nonprofit may also raise part of its funds through selling its own goods and services. A person who contributes to a nonprofit is a *donor*.

**BizFact:** When you make a donation to a nonprofit organization, you may be able to deduct part of it from your income tax. This would, in turn, lower the amount of income tax due, because the amount of tax depends on how much you earn.

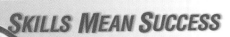
## SKILLS MEAN SUCCESS

**MATH** ▶ **Understanding Percentages and Exponents**

One of the best-known not-for-profit organizations in the U.S. is Mothers Against Drunk Driving, or MADD. It was founded in 1981 by two women whose children were involved in tragic car accidents caused by drunk drivers.

**1.** The number of chapters of MADD increased 450% between 1980 and 1981.

**a.** On that information, complete the chart to the right.

**b.** Which year-to-year increase was the greatest, percentage-wise?

**c.** Which percentage increase represents the greatest actual number of chapters?

| Year | Number of Chapters | % Increase from Previous Year Listed |
|------|--------------------|--------------------------------------|
| 1980 | 2 | N/A |
| 1981 | 11 | 450% |
| 1982 | 70 | _____% |
| 1983 | 192 | _____% |
| 1984 | 350 | _____% |
| 1991 | 407 | _____% |
| 2004 | 600 | _____% |

*Source: http://www.madd.org/aboutus*

**2.** Which of the following statements are true? (Estimate; then check.)

**a.** By 1984, the number of chapters was more than the 1981 number$^3$.

**b.** By 1982, the number of chapters was more than the original 1981 number$^3$.

**c.** The number of chapters in 1982 had increased by 2004 by more than a power of 2.

**d.** By 1984, the original two chapters had increased to more than $2^8$.

**e.** The original number of chapters in 1980 had increased to more than $2^9$ by 2004. ■■■

Nonprofit corporations are **tax-exempt**. They do not pay taxes because their income is used to address public needs and objectives. State and federal governments closely monitor nonprofit corporations to make sure they are really using their donations for the stated purpose.

Nonprofits may not pay dividends or bonuses. Although nonprofit organizations may have members, they cannot issue stock.

Some $123 billion is given annually to nonprofits in the United States, making it a huge market for an entrepreneur interested in using this kind of corporation to help society.

## Limited Liability Companies

The **limited liability company** (LLC) is a good choice for many small businesses because it combines some of the beneficial features of partnerships and corporations.

- As in a partnership, income is taxed only once, as the personal earnings of the members. The LLC can elect to be treated either as a corporation or a partnership for tax purposes.
- As in a corporation, the personal assets of the LLC's members are protected from creditors and lawsuits brought against the LLC itself.

LLCs have a more flexible strcture than other corporations. This is sometimes a benefit (flexibility), and sometimes a cost (they are less well understood by investors).

LLCs are often run according to the terms of an operating agreement. A typical LLC will have members who own percentage interests in the company, and one or more managers, appointed by the members.

## What's in a Name?

**Corporation:** When the abbreviation "Inc." (for "Incorporated") or "Corp." (for "Corporation") appears after a company's name, it suggests that it has been legally incorporated. The name of every corporation must contain the word "Incorporated," "Corporation," "Limited," or "Company," or the abbreviation "Inc.," "Corp.," "Ltd," or "Co."

**Nonprofit Corporation:** The name of every nonprofit corporation must contain the word "Corporation," "Incorporated," or "Company," or the abbreviation "Inc." or "Co." Names of nonprofit corporations may not contain the words "and Company," "and Co.," "& Company," or "& Co."

**Limited Partnership:** The name of every limited partnership must include the word "Limited," or the abbreviation "Ltd."

**Limited Liability Company:** The name of every limited liability company must contain the words "Limited Liability Company" or "Limited Company," or the abbreviations "LLC" or "LC." The word "Limited" may be abbreviated as "Ltd," and the word "Company" may be abbreviated as "Co."

## SKILLS MEAN SUCCESS

**ENGLISH**    **Reading for Understanding**

Asking questions about material you have read is a good way to check and expand your understanding of the content. Re-read the explanations and "What's in a Name?" definitions of the different kinds of corporations. Write two questions that ask for additional information or for a clarification of the information provided. ■■■

## Think Ahead

Think ahead to your long-term goals. If you are starting a small T-shirt design business while you are in high school to make money for college, the cost of incorporating will probably be higher than the benefits. In this case, a sole proprietorship will serve you very well. On the other hand, if your goal is to develop a clothing-design firm that you hope will eventually place your fashions in every department store in the country, you might consider incorporating from the start.

If your business involves selling goods or services that may involve risk of injury, then you should consider incorporating, or forming an LLC. You will need the limited liability offered by a corporation or LLC to protect your personal assets from potential lawsuits.

When it comes time to choose a legal structure for your business, make the decision carefully, with a lot of thought — and advice from an attorney. As your business develops, however, you can reevaluate your decision and change your legal structure. You will be able to change from a sole proprietorship, partnership, or LLC to a corporation — but it is difficult to go the other way.

## COMPARISON OF LEGAL STRUCTURES

| | Sole Proprietorship | General or Limited Partnership | C Corporation | Subchapter-S Corporation | Nonprofit Corporation | Limited Liability Company |
|---|---|---|---|---|---|---|
| **Ownership** | The proprietor | The partners | The stockholders | The stockholders | No one | The members |
| **Liability** | Unlimited | Limited in most cases | Limited | Limited | Limited | Limited |
| **Taxation issues** | Individual* (lowest rate) | Individual* (lowest rate) | Corporate rate; "double taxation" | Individual * (lowest rate) | None | Individual * (lowest rate) |
| **How profits are distributed** | Proprietor receives all | Partners receive profits according to partnership agreement | Earnings paid to stockholders as dividends in proportion to the number of shares owned | Earnings paid to stockholders as dividends in proportion to the number of shares owned | Surplus cannot be distributed | Same as partnership |
| **Voting on policy** | Not necessary | The partners | Common voting stockholders | Common voting stockholders | The board of directors/trustees agreement | Per agreed-on operating procedure |
| **Life of legal structure** | Terminates on death of owner | Terminates on death of partner | Unlimited | Unlimited | Unlimited through trustees | Variable |
| **Capitalization** | Difficult | Easier than sole proprietorship | Excellent — ownership is sold as shares of stock | Good — same as partnership | Difficult because there is no ownership to sell as stock | Same as partnership |

* When the double taxation of corporations is taken into account.

## Raúl Hernández: Nurturing Latino Culture and Hispanic-American Business

**W**hen Hispanic-American Raúl Hernández noticed how nonprofit corporations, such as the YMCA and the Red Cross, raised millions of dollars for their causes, he said to himself, "Why can't Latinos do the same for their causes, their programs?"

In 1985, at the age of 29, Hernández founded the Mission Economic and Cultural Association (MECA) in San Francisco. His first goal was to build an economic base for San Francisco's Spanish-speaking community. He also wanted to promote needed services, such as child care. His third goal for MECA was to help preserve the cultural traditions of people from Mexico and Central and South America.

MECA has held three major festivals each year: a re-creation of Brazil's *Carnaval*; the *Festival de las Américas* (which celebrates the independence of eight Central and South American countries from Spanish rule); and *Cinco de Mayo*, which celebrates Mexico overcoming attempted French occupation in the 1860s. Together, the festivals are attended by millions of people and help Hispanic businesses network, promote, and advertise their products and services. MECA evolved from a $3,200 organization in 1985 to a nonprofit corporation with a budget of $1.2 million by 1990. It supports itself and has stimulated the Hispanic-American economy in many ways. Since 2000, MECA has run the largest Carnaval parade in the United States. The enterprising Hernández realized his dream, which was to have a financially self-sufficient business that would help his community. ■

**BizTip:** Find out which regulations apply to the business structure you are selecting. What tax forms will you need? Are there special records that you will need to keep? Will you need to file forms or pay fees to the local or state government?

## SKILLS MEAN SUCCESS

**ENGLISH** ▶ **Preparing, Organizing, and Delivering a Presentation**

Imagine that you have to prepare a presentation on MECA for Raúl Hernández.

**1.** What information would you put on each presentation slide? Match the slide number with the information.

| Slide | Information |
|---|---|
| **I.** Background | **a.** Description of three major festivals |
| **II.** Mission of MECA | **b.** 1985 vs. 1990 financial statistics |
| **III.** Program | **c.** Hernández's inspiration |
| **IV.** Growth of MECA | **d.** Popularity with people and impact on Hispanic businesses |
| **V.** Impact | **e.** Description of three goals of MECA |

**2.** How does the article use numbers and statistics to emphasize its key points about Raúl's success as a young entrepreneur?

**3.** Other than the slides listed, what other visual aids or techniques could you use to make the presentation on MECA more interesting to listeners or readers? ■■■

# Chapter 32 Review

## CRITICAL THINKING ABOUT...

### LEGAL STRUCTURES

Choose the best legal structure for each business below and explain your choice:

1. A DJ who already owns all the equipment she needs to entertain at parties.

2. Someone who wants to start his own record company and has several artists lined up, but no money.

3. A jewelry designer whose work is sought after by a national department-store chain.

4. A social worker who wants to start a program to bring meals to housebound senior citizens.

5. Several doctors who want to go into practice together.

## KEY CONCEPTS

1. Which business entity should you select? Write a memo to a mentor explaining the advantages and disadvantages of incorporating and how these would apply to your business.

2. Is your business a:

   Sole Proprietorship _____

   Partnership _____

   Limited Partnerhsip _____

   C Corporation _____

   Subchapter-S _____

   Limited Liability Corporation _____

   Nonprofit Corporation? _____

3. Why did you choose this structure?

4. If you were to form a corporation:
   - Who would the stockholders be?
   - Who would your officers be?
   - Who would your board of directors be?

5. Write a letter to an individual, asking him/her to be a member of your board, and explaining why he/she should accept.

6. Research either online or by phoning your local chamber of commerce exactly what steps you will have to take to register your business. Make a list of the places that you contacted.

7. Write a memo explaining the steps and listing what documents and fees you will need in order to create and operate your business.

8. Read A Business for the Young Entrepreneur on page 397. Describe how a used-clothing shop like the one described could be organized as a nonprofit corporation. What would the owners have to do? What benefits would the people who donate clothing receive?

## VOCABULARY

board of directors ■ corporation ■ dividend ■ donation ■ limited liability company ■ stockholder ■ tax-exempt

# Chapter Summary ✔✔✔

**32.1** A corporation is a business structure that is formed as a "legal entity" that earns income, has expenses and pays taxes.

A. The business, not its employees or owners, is liable for debts.

B. Corporations are:

1. Owned by stockholders who have shares and can earn dividends from profits
2. Run by officers elected by stockholders
3. Controlled by elected boards of directors.

C. Shares of ownership in a corporation are sold:

1. To a limited number of people in a "privately held" corporation
2. To the general public in a "public" corporation.

**32.2** Corporate legal structures have advantages and disadvantages.

A. The corporate business structure offers its owners advantages:

1. The officers and stockholders are protected from personal liability for debts
2. Money can be raised by selling stock
3. Ownership can be transferred easily
4. Corporations can buy and sell property and enter into contracts as if they were persons.

B. There are disadvantages to a corporate business structure:

1. Double taxation — the corporation is taxed on profits, and stockholders are taxed on dividends received from those profits
2. Loss of owner control — founders need to own more than half of the voting stock if they want to keep control of the company
3. Cost and government regulations — taxes, filing fees, and other expenses and government rules make running a corporation more expensive and complicated than other forms of business.

C. The government allows different types of corporations:

1. C Corporation (identified as Inc., Corp., or Ltd in its name) — most companies that sell stock or take out loans to raise money
2. Subchapter-S Corporation (identified as Inc. or Co.) — fewer than 75 employees, limits on whom stock can be sold to; corporate income is usually not taxed
3. Professional Corporation (PC) — used by individual or groups of professionals such as doctors or lawyers; subject to rules relating to that profession
4. Nonprofit Corporation [501(c)(3)] — museums and charities that raise money from membership dues, donations, grants, and sales of goods or services for specific purposes that benefit the public; tax-exempt because all profits are used to help the public

5. Limited Liability Company (LLC or LC) — only personal incomes of owners, not the corporation's profits, are taxed; owners have no personal liability for debts or lawsuits; taxed as a limited partnership (Ltd) or corporation as the owners choose; members enter into an operating agreement; more flexible and less expensive to set up than a C-corporation structure. ✔✔✔

# A Business for the Young Entrepreneur
## CONSIGNMENT SHOP

Do you ever throw out clothes because you're tired of them? Maybe someone else would buy the clothes you don't want anymore. Maybe you would like to buy some of the clothes your friends don't want anymore.

This is the idea behind the clothing-resale or "consignment" shop. People bring in clothes they don't need and the shop sells them. The person who brought in the clothes receives a percentage of the sale, usually 30% to 50%. You could run a consignment shop from your house (in your garage or basement) after school or on weekends.

### HOW TO BUY AND SELL CLOTHES ON CONSIGNMENT

- Decide how much commission you will pay on each sale.
- Have each person who brings you clothing fill out a tag with his or her name, address, and phone number. Put in writing how much commission you will pay.
- When you sell a piece of clothing, take the tag and write on it the amount for which you sold the garment.
- At the end of the day, make a list of whose clothes you sold and for how much.
- Let each person know how much money you owe. Let's say Daphne brought you a dress that you sold for $15. If you have agreed to pay a commission of 30%, you will owe Daphne $15.00 × .30 = $4.50. Your profit is $15.00 − $4.50 = $10.50.

### TIPS

- Only take articles of clothing on consignment that you really think you can sell. Don't take clothes that aren't in good condition.
- Wash or dry-clean all garments before selling them, or make a rule that you will only take cleaned clothing.
- Create a fun atmosphere when your shop is open. Play your friends' favorite music. You can even sell lemonade and cookies.

*Let's say you start a consignment shop and it becomes so popular that you are able to start four more shops in other communities. What legal structure would you choose for your business and why?* ■

# STOCKS:
## *Selling Ownership to Raise Capital*

*My life seems like one long obstacle course, with me as the chief obstacle.*

— Jack Paar, *entertainer*

### KEY OBJECTIVES

THIS CHAPTER WILL ENABLE YOU TO:

- Explain why stocks are traded.
- Read a daily stock table.
- Calculate a stock's price/earnings ratio.
- Calculate a stock's yield.

**S**tockholders actually own a corporation. Each **share** of **stock** represents a percentage of ownership, with a stock certificate representing this "piece of the company." How large a piece depends on how many shares of stock are owned.

If Street Scooters, Inc. has sold ten shares of stock, each to a different individual, that would mean there were ten stockholders. Each would own $\frac{1}{10}$ of the company. If Street Scooters sold 100 shares of stock, each to a different individual, there would be 100 stockholders. Each would own $\frac{1}{100}$ of the company.

Public corporations sell their stock to the general public on the open financial markets to raise capital. They use the capital to expand or pay off debts.

## The Stock Market Is Where Stocks Are Traded

Once the stocks are sold, however, a corporation no longer has any control over them. The stock can be bought and sold by anyone. Such trading activity occurs constantly on the **stock market**. The stock market is not in one location. It is made up of a collection of exchanges around the world where stocks are traded. The New York Stock Exchange, on Wall Street in New York City, is probably the most well known.

Stocks are traded by brokers. A **stockbroker** has a license that gives him or her the right to make trades for clients. If you want to buy stock, you usually contact a stockbroker to make the trade for you. You, in turn, will pay a commission to the broker. Look in the *Yellow Pages* or online to find stockbrokers.

## A Stock's Price Reflects Opinions about the Company

The price of a stock reflects opinions about how well the company is going to perform. Both the general public and financial experts will have varying ideas about the future success of a business, however. You might have bought a share in a company for $50. Your friend might have had enough confidence in that company to pay $60. You could sell your share to your friend for $60 and earn a profit of ten dollars ($60 − $50 = $10). That is the principle behind stock trading.

The daily record of trading activity appears in tables published in *The Wall Street Journal* and in the business sections of many other newspapers. These tables allow investors to track the changing value of their investments.

Let's say you own ten shares of a stock you bought at $10 (a total of $100). You see in that day's stock table that the price per share has declined to $8.50. Your $100 investment is now worth only $85 (10 shares × $8.50/share = $85). You have three choices:

1.  Sell the shares before their value declines further.

2.  Keep them, hoping the decline is temporary and the price will go back up.

3.  Buy more shares at the lower price to increase your profit when the price does go back up.

## Reading Stock Tables [1]

At first glance, stock tables appear to be written in a foreign language, but they are not hard to read once you understand the symbols used. In this chapter is a sample stock table from *The Wall Street Journal*. Below are explanations of some of the terms you will see:

**52-Week High Low:** The first figure in the column is the highest price at which the stock traded over the previous year. The second figure is the lowest.

**Stock:** The name of the company. *The Wall Street Journal* gives both the company name and its symbol. Every stock has a symbol, consisting of one to four letters.

**Div (Dividend):** Corporations can pay each stockholder a dividend, which is a sum of money tied to the number of shares the stockholder owns. A dividend is a return on investment (ROI) for the stockholders. Corporations pay dividends out of the company's profits.

A figure of 1.00 in this column means a dividend of $1 per share of stock was paid out to the company's stockholders over the course of the year. A stockholder who owned 100 shares was, therefore, paid $100 ($1 × 100) in dividends.

**Yld (Yield) %:** The rate of return on the stock expressed as a percentage:

$$\frac{\textbf{Dividend Paid}}{\textbf{Closing Price}} \times \ 100$$

The yield on a stock is low compared to the ROI on some other investments. Stock is usually purchased with the expectation that the price will go up. Reselling the stock at a higher price is how an investor's ROI is usually made in the stock market.

**P/E Ratio (Price/Earnings Ratio):** The P/E is the price of one share of a company's stock divided by the earnings per share. If the price of the stock is $28, and the company earned $7 for each share outstanding, the P/E Ratio would be four: 28 ÷ 7 = 4.

A P/E of four is considered low. A low P/E can indicate a stable company. A high P/E is about 20 and above. A P/E of 8 is more or less average.

In general, the higher a P/E, the greater the risk investors are willing to take. They have confidence that the company is going to make more money in the future. A new industry, like genetic engineering, will often have a high P/E because the future earnings are as yet unknown. If the company makes a scientific breakthrough, its stock prices might soar because investors hope the company will earn a great deal of money.

**vol 100s (Volume of Shares Traded):** The number of shares traded (bought and sold) during the previous day's trading period. (The New York Stock Exchange trades Monday through Friday from 9:30 a.m. to 4 p.m. Eastern Time.)

Volume is given in hundreds of shares. Add two zeros to a number in the vol 100s column to get the correct figure. When there is a very high volume of a stock being traded, it means investors are taking an interest in that stock. Volume does not indicate whether the price will go up or down.

**Hi Lo Close:** The highest, lowest, and last price the stock was traded for during the previous day's trading period. Again, the figures are given in fractions of dollars.

**Net Chg (Net Change):** The change in price from the close of the previous day's trading period.[2]

| 52 WKS | | | | | | | | | | | |
| --- | --- | --- | --- | --- | --- | --- | --- | --- | --- | --- | --- |
| **52 WK** | | | | | | | **Vol** | | | | **Net** |
| **Hi** | **Lo** | **Stock** | **Sym** | **Div** | **Yld** | **P/E** | **100s** | **Hi** | **Lo** | **Close** | **Change** |
| 8.44 | 1.79 | RiteAid | RAD | — | — | 19 | 31028 | 4.50 | 4.20 | 4.31 | +0.21 |
| 51.25 | 27.69 | Rockwell | ROK | 1.02 | 2.1 | 14.5 | 6412 | 47.99 | 47.00 | 47.54 | +0.24 |

## SKILLS MEAN SUCCESS

**MATH**

### Numeration: Place Value

Like stock tables, many financial reports present numbers in hundreds or thousands of dollars. To read "100s," you must add two zeros to the number to get the correct figure. To read "1,000s," you must add three zeros to the number.

**1.** In the following table, determine the quarterly sales revenue if the numbers are being presented in 100s.

**2.** Determine the quarterly sales figures if the numbers are presented in 1,000s.

**Yearly Sales Figures**

| Quarter | 1st | 2nd | 3rd | 4th |
| --- | --- | --- | --- | --- |
| Revenue | $5,820 | $4,500 | $6,245 | $7,350 |

## Selling Short

Stock traders make money by buying a stock and then selling it for a profit when the price of the stock rises, or *appreciates*. Traders can also make money when a stock is falling by "selling short."

Selling short is a way to make money when you expect a stock's price to decline. Let's say you "borrow" a $100 share of stock from a broker with an agreement to give it back at the end of three months. Next, you sell the stock for $100 — which is its present market value — to a buyer. At the end of the three months, the price of the share of stock has fallen to $50 in the market. You buy a share for $50 and return it to the broker you borrowed it from. You have made a $50 profit because you sold the borrowed stock for $100 and replaced it for $50 ($100 − $50 = $50).

Like stock trading in general, short selling is *speculative*. This means it is risky. If, in the example above, the price of the stock does not go down, as you thought it would, but rises to, say, $150 at the end of the three months, you will have lost $50 on the transaction. It will cost you $50 more than you paid to return the stock to the broker ($150 − $100 = $50).

Only about five percent of all investors get involved with selling short, and these are usually experts in the financial markets. The point is that there are ways to make money when the economy as a whole is not doing well. Don't think only in terms of making money in an "up" market.

## SKILLS MEAN SUCCESS

**TECHNOLOGY** ▶ **Reading and Evaluating Web Sites**

The Internet can be a great place to locate free stock market information and analysis of stock quotes and charts. Some sites, however, may contain information designed to mislead investors. Using a search engine, such as Google, enter the keyword "stock quotes." Visit three Web sites from your search results.

**1.** Look up a company's stock symbol at each site. Then, enter the symbol to get the stock quote and review the charts.

**2.** Write an evaluation of the sites you used. You may write it in paragraph form or create a table that lists the relevant information for each site. Consider the following questions:

- How easy was it to locate the information you needed?
- How many times did you have to "click" to find the information?
- How quickly did the site generate your results?
- How up-to-date was the information?
- How useful were the graphics on the site?
- How many advertisements did you have to go through to get to the site?

- What links to other helpful sites were available?
- What experts and sources were quoted on the site?
- What "help" features were offered?
- Was the site sponsored by some other business? ■■■

# Chapter 33 Review

## CRITICAL THINKING ABOUT...

### STOCKS

1. Look up the stocks below in *The Wall Street Journal*, and then answer the questions.

   *Ford Motor Co.*
   *J.P. Morgan Chase & Co.*
   *Colgate-Palmolive*
   *Reebok*
   *Disney*

   a. Which stock would cost the most?

   b. Which stock paid the highest dividend?

   c. Which stock has the highest yield?

   d. Which stock has the lowest P/E ratio?

   e. For each stock that has paid a dividend, show the math for figuring out the yield.

2. If you plan to incorporate your business, describe what percentage of your company would be owned by ten shares of stock.
   **Business Plan Practice**

3. Will your corporation's stock be publicly or privately held?
   **Business Plan Practice**

4. In A Business for the Young Entrepreneur on page 405, if you went into business with Clarence as a partner, how would you feel about him donating ten percent of the company profits to an African nation? Write a memo to Clarence describing how you would handle that aspect of the business.

## KEY CONCEPTS

1. Why are investors willing to pay different prices for the same stock?

2. What is the return on investment of a stock called? How is it calculated?

3. Pretend you could buy one share of any stock listed in *The Wall Street Journal* (or the financial section of your local newspaper). Monitor that stock for one week and answer the questions below.

   a. What is the name of your stock?

   b. What is the closing price of your stock?

   c. What is the stock's symbol?

   d. Go online and find the Web site for your stock's company. What is the full name of the company? What does it sell?

   e. If you had bought ten shares of your stock on Monday, how much money would you have had to spend?

   f. If you sold your stock the following Monday, would you have gained or lost money? How much?

   g. Calculate the return on investment (ROI) if you had bought 100 shares and sold them one week later.

4. Let's say you buy 100 shares of Street Scooters, Inc. at $6. Answer the following:

   a. How much did you spend on the investment?

**b.** If the stock price rises to $10 and you sell half your shares, what will your profit be?

**c.** What is your ROI on the sale?

**Discuss with a Group:**
Based on your knowledge of current events and trends, from which of the three companies below would you buy stock? Write a memo explaining your decision and share it with the class.

- Company A makes a vital part for cellular phones.

- *Company B* has just invented a process for cloning cows.

- *Company C* manufactures automobiles.

**Hint:** There is no "right" answer. Like any stockholder, your preference will depend on your opinions about the economy and your feelings about risk.

## REFERENCES

1 Adapted with permission from materials prepared by Dow Jones, Inc.
2 Note: There are additional special symbols that are explained at the bottom of the published stock tables.

## VOCABULARY

share ▪ stock ▪ stockbroker ▪ stock market

# Chapter Summary ✔✔✔

**33.1** Corporations are businesses owned by their stockholders.
   A. Corporations sell shares of stock (portions of ownership of the company) to investors.
   B. Selling shares raises money (capital) for the owner to expand the business or pay expenses.
   C. Each share sold represents a percentage of ownership.
   D. Investors earn profits when shares increase in value.

**33.2** Stocks are bought and sold through stock markets (exchanges) around the world.
   A. Anyone can buy and sell any public corporation's stock.
   B. Licensed stockbrokers earn commissions for trading (buying and selling) stocks for investors.
   C. Prices for stocks rise and fall hourly.
   D. Prices vary according to how profitable people think the companies will be in the future.

**33.3** Prices and other information are reported in published stock tables.
   A. 52-Week Hi/Lo: What are the highest/lowest prices the stock has sold for in the last 12 months?
   B. Stock: What is the company's name and/or (1-4 letter) symbol?
   C. Div (Dividend): How much ROI has the company paid stockholders as a share of profits in $'s?

*D.* Yld (Yield) %: Dividend Paid ÷ Latest (closing) Price × 100 = Yield %

*E.* P/E Ratio (Price/Earnings Ratio): How much did an investor earn per share vs. the price paid per share?

*F.* Vol 100s (Volume of Shares Traded): How many hundreds of shares were traded yesterday?

*G.* Hi Lo Close:  How high/low were prices paid for the stock over the previous day?

*H.* Net Chg (Net Change): How did the price change from the day before?

33.4    Despite the risks, investors can earn profits by trading stocks.

*A.* If the value of the stock goes up (appreciates), the investment is worth more.

*B.* When the value of a stock goes down, investors can still make money by "selling short."

*C.* Buying and selling stocks is speculative (risky). ✔✔✔

# A Business for the Young Entrepreneur
## THE DOUGHNUT KID, CLARENCE CROSS, III

At 11:55 a.m. most of the kids at Woodrow Wilson Senior High School are getting ready to have lunch. But for Clarence Cross it's the beginning of his super-short work day. In just ten minutes, Cross makes about $18.00. That's $108 per hour, or $360 for a little more than three hours of selling each month.

Clarence noticed someone selling Krispy Kreme doughnuts on a bus for a fundraiser. A light went off in his head. "I can do that cheaper," Clarence thought, so he started his business — The Doughnut Kid.

"I believe the best advertising for my business is my mouth," the young entrepreneur has said. He also markets his business name on a T-shirt, so that customers will recognize him and know where to find him. But this young entrepreneur isn't in business just for the money. Over the past four years, Clarence has donated more than 325 hours of service at the VA Medical Center where his father is chaplain and his mother is a doctor. Since starting The Doughnut Kid, he has also given away free doughnuts to many of the patients.

After his father returned from a humanitarian mission to Africa, during which supplies ran short, Clarence made an important decision. This year, he is donating ten percent of his profits from The Doughnut Kid to an African nation he will decide on.

"Being in business, I've learned that the world isn't just my community, but a larger place where I can make a difference in people's lives." ■

### CHAPTER 34

# BONDS:
## *Issuing Debt to Raise Capital*

*Give a man a fish and you feed him for a day. Teach a man to fish and you feed him for a lifetime.*

— Lao Tzu, *founder of the philosophy of Taoism*

### KEY OBJECTIVES

THIS CHAPTER WILL ENABLE YOU TO:

- Explain how bonds differ from stocks.
- Summarize how bonds work.
- Discuss the effect inflation has on the value of a dollar.
- Read a bond table.

**B**onds are interest-bearing certificates that corporations (and governments) issue to raise capital. The federal government, state governments, and city and town governments use bonds to finance roads, bridges, schools, and other public projects.

Bonds are loans. The original amount borrowed, plus interest, must be paid back by the borrower. Bonds are a form of debt financing.

Stockholders never know if they will receive dividends or even if the value of their stocks will increase. They may make or lose money on their investments. The risks, and therefore the rewards, can be high. Bondholders, on the other hand, are guaranteed a specific return on the investment (the interest rate on the bond) and will get their money back after a specified time period. The risks of holding bonds are lower but, typically, so are the returns. Bonds and stocks together are called **securities**.

## How Bonds Work

Bonds are different from other loans because a corporation that issues a bond does not have to pay regular monthly payments on the **principal** (the amount of a debt before the interest is added). A bond pays interest each year to the person who bought it (the bondholder) until **maturity**, when the investor returns the bond to the corporation and it is *redeemed*. The investor gets his/her original investment back on that date.

As we have said, by financing with bonds instead of a bank loan, a company does not have to make payments on the principal, only the interest. However, the company must have the cash available when the bond matures.

If a company stops paying interest on a bond, the bondholders can sue. A court may force the company to sell assets to pay the bondholders not only the interest, but also the full amount of the bond.

Until maturity, bonds may be traded publicly, with the price going above or below **face value**. Face value is the original amount the purchaser paid ("loaned" to the corporation). The face value of a single bond, also referred to as **par**, is usually $100.

When the bond's market value rises above par, it means the bond is being traded for more than $100 — perhaps someone purchased it at $102. A bond trading above par is trading at a **premium** — in this case, the premium is $2. A bond trading below par is trading at a **discount**. If the above bond were trading at $94, the discount would be $6.

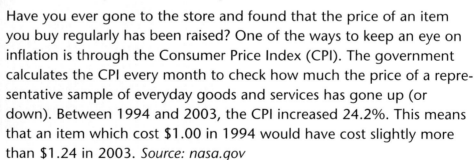

## SKILLS MEAN SUCCESS

**MATH**        **Estimating and Predicting**

Have you ever gone to the store and found that the price of an item you buy regularly has been raised? One of the ways to keep an eye on inflation is through the Consumer Price Index (CPI). The government calculates the CPI every month to check how much the price of a representative sample of everyday goods and services has gone up (or down). Between 1994 and 2003, the CPI increased 24.2%. This means that an item which cost $1.00 in 1994 would have cost slightly more than $1.24 in 2003. *Source: nasa.gov*

1. Assume the rate of inflation will be 3% each year from 2004 to 2023. If an item costs $1.24 in 2004, estimate what it will cost:

   **a.** in 2013

   **b.** in 2023.

2. If the inflation over ten years was 24.2%, estimate the average or *mean* annual inflation rate during that period.

3. If a gallon of gasoline is priced at $1.95 in 2006, about how much will it cost in 2020, if the price continues to increase at the rate of 5% a year (as it has since 1980)? ■□■

## Bonds and Inflation

The value of bonds is affected by **inflation**. Inflation is a gradual, continuous increase in the prices of products and services in an economy. When prices rise, money isn't worth as much. If the cost of a loaf of bread suddenly goes from one dollar to two dollars, the dollar you earn can now only buy half a loaf. Inflation reduces the value of money.

A $100 bond bought today will only pay the bondholder back $100 at maturity. The bond offers no protection against inflation because, no matter what happens to the value of a dollar, the bond will still only be redeemable for $100. When investors hear economic news that makes them worry about inflation, therefore, bond prices usually decline. No investor wants to pay $100 for a bond that may only be worth $85 at maturity.

Until the maturity date, the bonds are traded, like stocks, on the open market. If more people want to buy the bond than sell it, the price will rise.

## Reading Bond Tables

Current bond prices can be found in *The Wall Street Journal* and other newspapers on a daily basis.

| Bond | Coupon | Maturity | Last Price | Last Yield | Vol (000s) |
|------|--------|----------|------------|------------|------------|
| General Motors | 8.375 | 07/15/2033 | 101.31 | 8.25 | 347,275 |
| Bank of America | 5.250 | 02/01/2007 | 103.182 | 3.557 | 49,352 |
| Hewlett-Packard | 6.50 | 07/01/2012 | 113.180 | 4.389 | 50,000 |
| Merck | 4.375 | 02/15/2013 | 98.639 | 4.580 | 47,740 |

Bonds are discussed in lots of $100. In the example above, General Motors has issued bonds that pay $8.37 interest on every $100 each year until maturity. The bond issue becomes due on July 15, 2033, at which time the bonds are redeemed, or turned in, for their face value.

## The Remainder of the Table Explained

**Last Price:** The price in dollars at the end of the last day of trading.

**Last Yield:** The yield is the interest divided by the price you paid for the bond. If the bond price declines, the yield will rise. This means that the bond is trading at a discount. If the bond is trading at a premium, the yield will decline.

**Vol.** (Volume of bonds traded): The numbers are given in thousands. As with stocks, when there is a great deal of volume in a given issue, it means that investors are taking an interest but does not indicate whether the price will go up or down.

## Wal-Mart's 100-Year Bond[1]

In the mid-'90s, Wal-Mart's managers got a clever idea about how to finance growth with debt. Most long-term bonds mature in 20 to 30 years. They decided to sell bonds that would mature in a century.

Wal-Mart's 100-year bonds sold out almost immediately. There were plenty of investors willing to trust the company's ability to pay a loan back so far in the future. Wal-Mart has the incredible advantage of being able to use this money for an entire century. The company is now in the process of opening a network of stores in China.

### SKILLS MEAN SUCCESS

**ENGLISH**

**Writing for Information:
Using Standard English; Proofreading**

Proofread and improve the following business glossary descriptions. Identify the edits you would make in each. Watch for spelling, punctuation, and subject-verb agreement errors.

*Do it like this:*

Line 1: bearing, not baring

1  *Bonds* are interest-baring certificates that corporations (and governments) issues
2  to raise capitol. The federal government, state governments, and ever city and
3  town governments uses bonds too finance roads, bridges, schools, and other
4  public projects. Bonds are loans, so the original amount borrowed, plus interest,
5  must be paid by the borrower. Bonds are a forms of debt financing.

6  The value of bonds are effected by inflation. Inflation is a gradual continuously
7  increase in the prices of products and services in economy. when prices rise,
8  money aren't worth as much  If the cost of a loaf of bread suddenly rise from
9  one dollars to two dollars, the dollar you earn may now only buy have a lofe.
10  Inflation reduce the value of money. ■ ■

# Chapter 34 Review

## CRITICAL THINKING ABOUT...

### BONDS

*Use the bond table in this chapter to answer the following questions:*

1. Which bond has the highest yield?

2. Which bond had the highest volume in trading?

3. Which bond closed at the lowest price?

4. Which bond is selling below par?

## KEY CONCEPTS

1. Do you intend to use debt to finance your business? Explain.
   **Business Plan Practice**

2. Do you think you will ever issue bonds to finance your business?
   **Business Plan Practice**

## REFERENCES

[1] Special thanks to John Harris for the Wal-Mart 100-year bond story.

## VOCABULARY

bond ■ discount ■ face value ■ inflation ■ maturity ■ par ■ premium ■ principal ■ securities

# Chapter Summary ✔✔✔

34.1  Corporations sell bonds to raise capital.
   A. Bonds and stocks together are called securities.
   B. Bonds, unlike stocks, are guaranteed to pay back a specified amount of interest, plus the principal.
   C. Bonds are loans that pay interest every year until maturity.
   D. At maturity, the face value of the bond is redeemed by the investor.

34.2  Bonds are traded among investors.
   A. Face value (par) is the amount the original bond purchaser paid.
   B. If someone buys or sells the bond:
      1. Above face value, the bond is trading at a premium
      2. Below face value, the bond is trading at a discount.

34.3  Inflation affects the value of bonds.
   A. Inflation is the tendency of prices to increase over time.
   B. Inflation reduces the value of what money is worth.
   C. Traders consider the effects of inflation when they buy and sell bonds.

34.4  Bond tables are published daily in newspapers.
   A. Bond prices are valued in "lots" of $100.
   B. Bond tables list:
      1. Last Price — price in $'s at the end of the last day of trading

*2.* Last Yield = Interest ÷ price paid

*3.* Vol. (Volume) — expressed in thousands of units. ✔✔✔

## A Business for the Young Entrepreneur
### PET CARE

If you love animals, there are several money-making services you can offer. Here are some ideas:

**Dog Walking** ♦ Many people are too busy to walk their dogs every day. Is there a dog run in your neighborhood park? Arrange to take several dogs for a run each afternoon. This is also a good way to meet other dog owners who might need your service.

**Cleaning Aquariums** ♦ Fish tanks are beautiful but require regular cleaning and care. This service will require some knowledge about caring for fish. A fish tank is a delicate environment. If there are the wrong chemicals in the water or they are fed too much food, fish can die. This is a good business idea, therefore, only if you understand fish and how to take care of them. You should know how to clean both freshwater and saltwater tanks.

**Pet Sitting** ♦ You can take care of pets for people who are on vacation. Before accepting a job, though, go to the home and meet the pet. Make sure it's an animal you feel comfortable handling and being with. Before the owners leave, ask how to contact them in an emergency. You should also get the phone number and address of the family veterinarian.

**Pet Grooming** ♦ Cats and dogs need regular baths and flea treatments. If you have a good pair of clippers, you can also offer haircuts for dogs. It's a good idea to muzzle dogs before grooming them, however, as they can become nervous and nip you. Veterinarians usually offer free booklets on the care and grooming of pets. A veterinarian or pet store can direct you to the best bath and flea products. ■

### LEADERSHIP ▶ Understanding Customer Needs

Design a one-page questionnaire that you could use to find out if pet owners in your neighborhood would use a new service. Use a combination of "yes-no," open-ended (open and "guided choice"), and multiple-choice questions. First, decide what you want to find out; then create questions that will get the information you need. Make sure your questions are written clearly. Ask a partner to evaluate your questionnaire for effectiveness. ■■■

### CHAPTER 35

# THE BALANCE SHEET:
## *A Snapshot of Your Financial Strategy*

*Money is better than poverty, if only for financial reasons.*

— Woody Allen, *American comic and film maker*

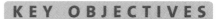

### KEY OBJECTIVES

THIS CHAPTER WILL ENABLE YOU TO:

- Read a simple corporate balance sheet.
- Create a balance sheet for your business from the financial records.
- Analyze a balance sheet using financial ratios.
- Use a balance sheet to tell if a company has been successful over time.

**A balance sheet** is a financial statement that shows how much a company is worth at a particular point in time. This includes cash and everything else the business owns, such as inventory or real estate. The balance sheet shows the **assets**, **liabilities** (debts) and **owner's equity** of a business.

- Assets — things a company owns that are worth money.
- Liabilities — debts a company has that must be paid, including bills.
- Owner's Equity (OE) — the difference between assets and liabilities.

A balance sheet is called a "point in time" financial statement because it shows the state of a business at a specific moment — like a snapshot. It also represents the value of a business that the owners have built up.

## The Fiscal Year

The annual balance sheet is typically prepared at the end of the **fiscal year**. This is the 12-month accounting period chosen by the business. The fiscal year often differs from the calendar year (January 1st to December 31st). A business that used the calendar year would prepare its ending balance sheet on December 31st.

## Assets Are Owned

*Assets* are all items of worth owned by the business — cash, inventory, furniture, machinery, intellectual property, etc.

- *Short-term assets* (also called "current" assets) are those that could be converted to cash within one year — money, inventory, and stocks, for example.

- *Long-term assets* are those that could take more than a year to turn into cash — furnishings, machinery, and other capital equipment.

## Liabilities Are Owed

*Liabilities* are debts owed by the business, such as bank loans, mortgages, credit-card purchases, and loans from family or friends.

- *Short-term liabilities* (also called current liabilities) are those that must be paid within one year.

- *Long-term liabilities* are those that will be paid over a period of longer than a year.

## Owner's Equity[1]

Owner's Equity (OE) represents the *value* of a business. It is what is left after liabilities are subtracted from assets. Owner's equity in a successful venture builds up over time.

> **Assets − Liabilities = Owner's Equity (OE)**

The left and right sides of this equation are always equal. If they aren't, then a mistake has been made in creating the balance sheet.

The balance sheet is divided into two parts. All business assets are listed in one section, and all liabilities and owner's equity are listed in the other. Sometimes the two sections are shown side by side; sometimes they are vertical.

| **BALANCE SHEET ("side by side" layout)** | |
|---|---|
| **Assets** | **Liabilities** |
| Cash:  $ _____ | Short-Term Liabilities:  $ _____ |
| Inventory:  _____ | Long-Term Liabilities:  _____ |
| Capital Equipment:  _____ | |
| Other Assets:  _____ | **Owner's Equity:**  $ _____ |
| **Total Assets:**  $ _____ | **Total Liabilities + OE:**  $ _____ |

> **BALANCE SHEET ("vertical" layout)**
>
> **Assets**
>
> Cash: $ _____
> Inventory: _____
> Capital Equipment: _____
> Other Assets: _____
>
> **Total Assets:** $ _____
>
> **Liabilities**
>
> Short-Term Liabilities: $ _____
> Long-Term Liabilities: _____
>
> **Owner's Equity:** $ _____
> **Total Liabilities + OE:** $ _____

Every item a business owns was obtained through either debt or equity financing. Therefore the total of all assets must equal the total of all liabilities and owner's equity.

- If an item was financed with debt, the loan is a liability.
- If an item was purchased with the owners' own money, it was financed with equity.

Say a restaurant owns its tables and chairs (worth $3,000), a stove (worth $5,000), and has $10,000 in cash. There is also $4,000 in inventory. In other words, the business has a total capital equipment investment of $3,000 + $5,000 = $8,000, plus the $10,000 in cash. The restaurant also took out a $5,000 long-term loan to buy the stove. The total assets are $22,000. However, there are long-term liabilities of $5,000 (the loan for the stove) and a short-term loan of $4,000, which leaves $13,000 of owner's equity (OE).

*On a balance sheet, assets must equal ("balance") liabilities and owner's equity.*

**Total Assets = Total Liabilities + Owner's Equity (OE)**

The OE is $13,000. It is equal to the total of the cash ($10,000) and the tables and chairs ($8,000) and the $4,000 inventory owned by the business, minus the $9,000 in liabilities. Together, the liabilities and the owner's equity have "paid" for the assets of the business.

Assuming the restaurant has no other assets and liabilities, this is how its balance sheet would look:

| BALANCE SHEET | | | |
|---|---|---|---|
| **Restaurant** | | | **Dec. 31, 2006** |
| **Assets** | | **Liabilities** | |
| Cash: | $10,000 | Short-Term Liabilities: | $4,000 |
| Inventory: | 4,000 | Long-Term Liabilities: | 5,000 |
| Capital Equipment: | 8,000 | | |
| Other Assets: | – | **Owner's Equity:** | **$13,000** |
| **Total Assets:** | **$22,000** | **Total Liabilities + OE:** | **$22,000** |

## The Balance Sheet Shows How a Business Is Financed

The balance sheet is an especially good tool for looking at how a business is financed. It clearly shows the relationship between debt and equity financing. Sometimes businesses make the mistake of relying too heavily on either debt or equity.

- An entrepreneur who relies too much on equity can end up losing control of the company because there will be other owners. If the other owners have more than a 50% share of the business, they may insist on making the management decisions.

- An entrepreneur who takes on too much debt can lose the business to a bank or other creditors if he or she becomes unable to meet the loan payments.

All the information you need to analyze a company's financing strategy — total debt, equity, and assets — is in its balance sheet. People who invest in businesses use ratios to quickly grasp a company's financial situation. As an entrepreneur, you will want to understand these ratios to be able to talk intelligently with investors.

## Analyzing a Balance Sheet

A business usually prepares one balance sheet at the beginning of its fiscal year and another at the end. Comparing the beginning balance sheet to the ending one is an excellent way to see whether or not a business is succeeding. If it is, the Owner's Equity (OE) will increase.

Let's look at the restaurant example again. This time, several other assets and liabilities have been included.

The beginning balance sheet was prepared on December 31, 2006. The ending balance sheet was done a year later, on December 31, 2007. Compare the two balance sheets to see what has changed after one year.

| BALANCE SHEET | | |
|---|---|---|
| **Restaurant** | Dec. 31, 2007 | Dec. 31, 2006 |
| **Assets** | | |
| Cash: | $8,000 | $10,000 |
| Inventory: | 5,000 | 4,000 |
| Capital Equipment: | 9,000 | 8,000 |
| Other Assets: | – | – |
| **Total Assets:** | **$22,000** | **$22,000** |
| **Liabilities** | | |
| Short-Term Liabilities: | 1,000 | 4,000 |
| Long-Term Liabilities: | 4,000 | 5,000 |
| **Owner's Equity:** | **$17,000** | **$13,000** |
| **Total Liabilities + OE:** | **$22,000** | **$22,000** |

### ASSETS

- *Cash* has decreased from $10,000 to $8,000. Businesses have cash going in and out all the time, so this isn't necessarily bad — as long as the bills are being paid.

- *Inventory* has risen from $4,000 to $5,000. If more inventory helps the restaurant offer more items on the menu, it could help increase business. In any case, inventory is an asset because it is worth money.

- *Capital Equipment* has risen from $8,000 to $9,000. The restaurant must have bought more equipment during the year. This is another increase in assets.

- *Other Assets* has not changed.

- *Total Assets* has not changed. The business is keeping less cash, but now has more of what it needs to operate (Inventory and Capital Equipment).

There are no more assets at the end of the year than there were at the beginning. Does this mean the restaurant did not have a successful year? *(Hint: The rest of this analysis will help you figure that out.)*

## LIABILITIES

- *Short-Term Liabilities* have declined from $4,000 to $1,000. That's good, because it means the restaurant doesn't owe as much money as it did before.

- *Long-Term Liabilities* have declined from $5,000 (the stove) to $4,000 because the restaurant paid off part of the loan. Part of the payment went for *interest,* and the rest paid off some of the *principal.*

- *Owner's Equity* has increased from $13,000 to $17,000. That's good news because it means the restaurant owners have more "value" than they did at the beginning of the year.

The restaurant doesn't have any more total assets than it had at the beginning of the year, however, and it has less cash. On the other hand, the business has less debt than it did. Because of the balance-sheet equation (Assets = Liabilities + OE), that means the owners have added equity in the business by paying off (paying *down*) some debt. Paying down debt is one of the smartest things a business can do with extra cash.

Here's another look at the balance sheet, with a "percentage change" column added. This represents how much change took place over the year. (Note that any value written in red and set in parentheses is negative.)

| "SAME SIZE" BALANCE SHEET ANALYSIS | | | |
|---|---|---|---|
| **Restaurant** | Dec. 31, 2007 | Dec. 31, 2006 | % Change |
| **Assets** | | | |
| Cash: | $8,000 | $10,000 | (20)% |
| Inventory: | 5,000 | 4,000 | 25% |
| Capital Equipment: | 9,000 | 8,000 | 13% |
| Other Assets: | – | – | |
| **Total Assets:** | **$22,000** | **$22,000** | **0%** |
| **Liabilities** | | | |
| Short-Term Liabilities: | $1,000 | $4,000 | (75)% |
| Long-Term Liabilities: | 4,000 | 5,000 | (20)% |
| **Owner's Equity:** | **17,000** | **13,000** | **31%** |
| **Total Liabilities + OE:** | **$22,000** | **$22,000** | **0%** |

Even though total assets are unchanged, the restaurant's liabilities (debts) are down. Short-Term Liabilities are 75% lower, and Long-Term Liabilities are 20% lower than they had been at the start of the year. Owner's Equity is up 31%.

The restaurant paid off almost 45% of its total debt during the year ($4,000 ÷ $9,000 = about 44%). Paying off debt is a smart strategy that can improve a company's balance sheet.

The growth of owner's equity is a good way to measure company success. The table below shows how investors would view different rates of owner's equity growth.

| Annual Rates of Growth in Owner's Equity of Major U.S. Corporations | |
| --- | --- |
| Annual Growth | Assessment of Annual Growth Rate |
| 3% | Very slow, and unsatisfactory in most cases. |
| 6% | Slow, but acceptable in some cases. |
| 10-11% | Average growth rate. |
| 16% | High growth rate. |
| 24% | Extremely high growth — not many companies can achieve this, much less keep it up. |

How does the growth of owner's equity in the restaurant compare to that of major corporations?

$$\text{Debt Ratio:} \quad \frac{\text{Total Debt}}{\text{Total Assets}}$$

The **debt ratio** describes how many of the total dollars in your business have been provided by creditors. A debt ratio of 55% means your debt equals 55% of total assets.

If the business has a high debt ratio, that means it is using creditors and suppliers to finance the business rather than their own money. This is good because it helps the owners achieve a higher return on their investment. On the other hand, more debt means higher expenses and less cash to run the business with. Companies with lower debt ratios are considered more financially stable, because they have lower payments for loans and are less likely to run out of cash — and perhaps be forced into bankruptcy.

Bankers don't like to lend money to businesses with high debt ratios. If you need to borrow money from a bank or establish credit with a supplier, a low debt ratio will help you.

Whether a ratio is good or bad will depend on the amount of debt considered acceptable in your industry, and on how easily the company can make its loan payments.

$$\text{Debt-to-Equity Ratio:} \quad \frac{\text{Total Debt}}{\text{Owner's Equity}}$$

A **debt-to-equity ratio** of 100% would mean that for every dollar of debt the company has a dollar of equity. Equity is money that is either kept in the business or returned to shareholders, as you have learned, to reward them for their investment. These payments made to shareholders are called dividends.

## SKILLS MEAN SUCCESS

**TECHNOLOGY** ▶ **Online Research**

The balance sheet is an important tool for business owners. However it is one of the more challenging topics in business finance. Conduct a Web search or use the library to find helpful information about balance sheets.

**1.** Make a list of the most helpful sites to present to the class. Give reasons for your choices. Why were they helpful? What unique features do they have? Make a list of the key formulas you find and compare them to those in this chapter.

**2.** Find definitions for the following terms and compare them to the definitions provided in this chapter: current assets, liquidity, fiscal year, long-term liabilities, depreciation, owner's equity. ■■■

## SKILLS MEAN SUCCESS

**MATH**

**Math Reasoning:** Ratio, Proportion, and Percentage

**Jean M's Florida-Style Subs, Inc.:** Balance Sheet Ending Dec. 31st

| Assets | 2006 | 2005 |
|---|---|---|
| Cash: | $10,000 | $10,000 |
| Inventory: | 30,000 | 25,000 |
| Capital Equipment: | $40,000 | $30,000 |
| **Total Assets:** | **$80,000** | **$65,000** |
| **Liabilities** | | |
| Short-Term Liabilities: | $10,000 | $15,000 |
| Long-Term Liabilities : | 6,000 | 5,000 |
| **Owner's Equity:** | 64,000 | 45,000 |
| **Total Liabilities + OE:** | **$80,000** | **$65,000** |

As you can see, Assets = Liabilities + OE.

1. What is the year-to-year percentage change in the value of

   **a.** inventory     **c.** capital equipment     **e.** liabilities + OE

   **b.** long-term liabilities     **d.** cash

2. What is the ratio of

   **a.** cash to inventory in 2006? How has it changed from 2005?

   **b.** owner's equity to total assets in 2006? How has it changed from 2005?

3. Investors and buyers like to put their money into companies that have a low ratio of liabilities to assets. Has that ratio become more or less appealing from 2005 to 2006? ■■■

## "Quick" and "Current" Ratios

The balance sheet also tells you about a business's **liquidity**. This is the ability to convert assets into cash. Businesspeople use two ratios, *quick* and *current*, to understand liquidity. Most entrepreneurs prepare a monthly balance sheet, as well as a balance sheet at the end of the fiscal year, so they can keep an eye on liquidity.

$$\text{Quick Ratio:} \quad \frac{\text{Cash + Marketable Securities}}{\text{Current Liabilities}}$$

Marketable securities are investments, such as stock, that can be converted to cash quickly.

The **quick ratio** tells you whether you have enough cash to cover your current debt. The quick ratio should always be greater than 1. This means that you have enough cash at your disposal to cover all your current short-term debts. If you had to pay all of these (bills, loan payments, and everything else due within a year), you would have enough cash to do so.

$$\text{Current Ratio:} \quad \frac{\text{Current Assets}}{\text{Current Liabilities}}$$

It is also good to try to maintain a **current ratio** greater than 1. This indicates that, if you had to, you could sell some assets to pay off your debts.

## Depreciation

As you learned in Chapter 9, *depreciation* is a portion of an asset that is subtracted each year until the asset's value reaches zero. Depreciation reflects the wear and tear on an asset over time. Time reduces the value of the asset. A used car, for instance, is worth less than a new one.

More complex balance sheets show depreciation as a subtraction from long-term assets. Many youth businesses have minimal or no depreciation and will not need to show it on the balance sheet.

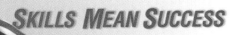

### SKILLS MEAN SUCCESS

**ENGLISH**

**Writing: Presenting Information Clearly**

This chapter explains some complicated — but very important — concepts in business. Create a test or practice test that a teacher could use to review the content and see if the students understand the topic. Write five multiple-choice questions and five true/false questions. Include answers with each. ■■■

## CRITICAL THINKING ABOUT...

### BALANCE SHEETS

1. Using the restaurant balance sheet in the chapter (page 417), answer these questions:

   a. What are the debt-to-equity ratios at the beginning and end of the 2006 fiscal year? Has it improved? If so, by how much?

   b. The restaurant has less cash at the end of the year than it had at the beginning. Is this a bad thing or not? Explain.

   c. Do you think the restaurant will have enough cash to pay its expenses going into 2007?

   d. The restaurant "grew" its OE by 31% during the 2006 fiscal year. At that rate, how much will the business have in owner's equity in two years (on Dec. 31, 2008)?

   e. The restaurant added some Capital Equipment during the year. Do you think it took out another loan for that equipment, or did it pay cash? Explain your thinking.

2. Using the balance sheet of Angelina's Jewelry Company at the end of July, on on page 423 (Problem A), calculate all four financial ratios (quick, current, debt, and debt-to-equity) for the business.

3. Write a memo analyzing the financial strengths and weaknesses of Angelina's venture. Use the same size analysis on page 423 (Problem B). Would you invest in her business? Why or why not?

4. Suppose you have started a small business making and selling silk-screened T-shirts. You used $200 in savings to buy a silk-screening machine to make the shirts. You borrowed $100 from your parents to buy 10 shirts wholesale at $2.50. Call these shirts "inventory," which is an asset. The money used to purchase them is owner's equity. Prepare your balance sheet.

5. Create a pie chart illustrating the balance sheet you made for the T-shirt business above.

## KEY CONCEPTS

1. What is the financial equation for the T-shirt balance sheet?

2. What is the net worth of the T-shirt business?

3. What is the company's debt ratio?
   **Business Plan Practice**

4. What is the company's debt-to-equity ratio?
   **Business Plan Practice**

## REFERENCES

1 Material in this section has been derived from *Introduction to Financial Accounting*, 6th edition, by Charles T. Horngren, Gary L. Sundem, and John A. Elliott (Prentice-Hall, 1996).

## VOCABULARY

asset ■ balance sheet ■ current ratio ■ debt ratio ■ debt-to-equity ratio ■ fiscal year ■ liability ■ liquidity ■ owner's equity ■ quick ratio

## BALANCE SHEET (Problem A)

**Angelina's Jewelry Co.**                                            July 30, 2006

### Assets

**Current Assets**

| | |
|---|---|
| Cash: | $1,000 |
| Inventory: | 1,000 |
| Securities: | 1,000 |
| **Total Current Assets:** | **$3,000** |
| **Long-Term Assets:** | **7,000** |
| **Total Assets:** | **$10,000** |

### Liabilities

**Short-Term Liabilities**

| | |
|---|---|
| Accounts Payable (AP): | $1,000 |
| Short-Term Loans: | 500 |
| **Total Short-Term Liabilities:** | **$1,500** |
| **Total Long-Term Liabilities:** | **1,500** |
| **Owner's Equity:** | **$7,000** |
| **Total Liabilities + OE:** | **$10,000** |

## BALANCE SHEET (Problem B)

| Angelina's Jewelry Co. | Aug. 30, 2006 | July 30, 2006 | % Change |
|---|---|---|---|
| **Assets** | | | |
| **Current Assets** | | | |
| Cash: | $500 | $1,000 | (50)% |
| Inventory: | 2,000 | 1,000 | 100% |
| Securities: | 1,500 | 1,000 | 50% |
| **Total Current Assets:** | **$4,000** | **$3,000** | **33%** |
| **Long-Term Assets:** | **7,000** | **7,000** | **0%** |
| **Total Assets:** | **$11,000** | **$10,000** | **10%** |
| **Liabilities** | | | |
| **Short-Term Liabilities** | | | |
| Accounts Payable (AP): | $1,000 | $1,000 | 0% |
| Short-Term Loans: | – | 500 | (100)% |
| **Total Short-Term Liabilities:** | **$1,500** | **$1,500** | **0%** |
| **Total Long-Term Liabilities:** | **500** | **1,500** | **(67)%** |
| **Owner's Equity:** | **$9,000** | **$7,000** | **29%** |
| **Total Liabilities + OE:** | **$11,000** | **$10,000** | **10%** |

# Chapter Summary ✔✔✔

**35.1**  A balance sheet is a financial statement ("snapshot") that shows how much a company is worth on a specific date, based on:

A. Assets: things the company owns and what they are worth:
   1. Short-term (current) assets could be converted into cash within one year, such as inventory or stocks
   2. Long-term assets would take longer than one year to convert into cash, such as capital equipment.

B. Liabilities: company debts that must be paid, including bills, loans, and mortgages:
   1. Short-term (current) liabilities must be paid within one year
   2. Long-term liabilities will be paid over more than one year.

C. Owner's Equity (OE): the difference between assets and liabilities:
   1. Assets - Liabilities = Owner's Equity (OE)
   2. OE is the value of the business that the owner has created.

D. Balance sheets are typically prepared:
   1. At the beginning and ending of each fiscal year (whatever 12-month accounting period the company decides to use)
   2. Monthly.

**35.2**  The balance sheet provides detailed information about a business.

A. Assets and liabilities are listed in separate sections, side by side or in vertical layouts.

B. Assets must equal (balance) liabilities and OE.

C. Reading a balance sheet shows how much the owner has financed the business using debt compared to equity.
   1. Excessive equity financing indicates that the owner could lose control.
   2. Too much debt indicates that the owner may not be able to repay loans.

D. Comparing beginning-of-year and end-of-year balance sheets shows if the business is succeeding (i.e., if OE is increasing).

E. Items listed under Assets include:
   1. Cash
   2. Inventory
   3. Capital Equipment
   4. Other Assets
   5. Total Assets
   6. Depreciation (allowance for lowering the value of long-term assets over time, usually only in more complex businesses).

*F.* Items listed under Liabilities include:
1. Short-Term and Long-Term Liabilities plus Owner's Equity
2. Paying off debt reduces liabilities and can improve the balance sheet by increasing OE.
3. 10-11% is average annual OE growth rate among major U.S. corporations.

**35.3** A balance sheet can be used to devise key ratios that indicate how well a company is doing:

*A.* Debt Ratio indicates how much of total assets are financed by debt.
1. Debt Ratio = Total Debt ÷ Total Assets
2. High Debt Ratios allow higher ROI, but have higher expenses and less cash.
3. Companies with lower Debt Ratios are considered more stable financially by lenders.
4. The correct Debt Ratio varies according to type of business.

*B.* Debt-to-Equity Ratio indicates how much debt a company has compared to how much equity it creates.
1. Debt-to-Equity Ratio = Total Debt ÷ OE
2. Equity can be rewarded to investors (as dividends) or reinvested in the business.

*C.* Liquidity ratios measure how easily a company could find cash to pay off short-term debts if it had to do so.
1. Quick Ratio indicates if a business has enough "cash" to cover current debts.

$$\textbf{Quick Ratio: } \frac{\textbf{Cash + Marketable Securities*}}{\textbf{Current Liabilities}}$$

*(\*Marketable Securities are highly liquid investments, such as stock.)*

2. Current Ratio indicates if there are enough current assets that could be sold to pay current debts.

$$\textbf{Current Ratio: } \frac{\textbf{Current Assets}}{\textbf{Current Liabilities}}$$

3. The Quick Ratio should always be greater than "1" — i.e., there would be enough "cash" to pay off all short-term debts, if necessary.
4. Good businesses also try to maintain a Current Ratio that is greater than "1" — i.e., there would be sufficient assets that could be sold to pay off debts if necessary. ✔✔✔

### CHAPTER 36

# VENTURE CAPITAL

*We are not permitted to choose the frame of our destiny. But what we put into it is ours.*

— Dag Hammarskjöld, *Secretary-General of the United Nations and recipient of the Nobel Peace Prize*

## KEY OBJECTIVES

THIS CHAPTER WILL ENABLE YOU TO:

- Explain how and why venture capitalists invest in a business.
- Describe the differences between venture capitalists and bankers.
- Explain how venture capitalists "harvest" their investments.
- Determine a company's total value.
- List the elements of a business plan.

## Venture Capital

Some investors and investment companies focus on financing new small business ventures that have the potential to earn a great deal of money. These investors provide start-up capital in exchange for equity and are called **venture capitalists**.

Venture capitalists expect a high rate of return on their investments. The rule of thumb is that they look to get six times their money back over a five-year period. That works out to about a 40 percent ROI. Typically, professional venture capitalists won't invest in a company unless its business plan shows it is likely to generate sales of at least $25 million after five years.

## Venture Capitalists Want Equity

Venture capitalists want *equity* — a piece of the company — in return for their capital. They are willing to take the risk that the venture might fail in order to earn very high returns if it succeeds. Venture capitalists will sometimes seek a **majority interest** in a business, meaning more than 50 percent. A majority stakeholder has the final word in management decisions.

In general, venture capitalists monitor their risks. They often want seats on the board of directors of companies in which they make investments, and can be helpful with business strategy, introduction to customers, and negotiations of contracts.

When he founded the Ford Motor Company in 1903, Henry Ford gave up 75 percent of the business for $28,000 of badly needed capital. Use this formula to determine how much the company was worth at the time:

$$\frac{\text{Amount of Venture Capital Received}}{\text{\% of Company Sold}} = \text{Total Market Value of Company}$$

$$\frac{\$28,000}{.75} = \$37,333 \text{ Total Initial Value of Ford Motor Co.}$$

Ford eventually regained majority control of his company. (Today, Ford Motor employs over 350,000 people worldwide and has annual sales of over $160 billion.)

Small business owners sometimes turn to venture capitalists when they want to grow the business but can't convince banks to lend them money. Venture capitalists can also be useful for additional financing if more capital is needed than a bank is willing to lend.

## SKILLS MEAN SUCCESS

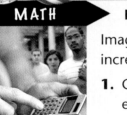

**MATH**    **Numeration and Operations:** Calculating Percentage Change

Imagine that a business owner's equity in her cosmetics business increased from $7,500 to $16,000.

**1.** Complete the following steps for estimating the increase in her equity percentage.

   **a.** We know that the equity went from $7,500 to $_____.

   **b.** If a value doubles, that's a _____ % increase.

   **c.** So, if the worth had gone from $7,500 to $_____, the percentage of increase would have been 100%.

   **d.** Therefore, you could reasonably guess that an increase from $7,500 to $16,000 would be close to _____%.

**2.** Calculate the exact percentage of increase by using the followng formula (*Hint: You must first figure out the "change in quantity."*):

$$\frac{\text{change in quantity}}{\text{original quanitity}} \times 100 = \text{percentage change} \ \blacksquare\square\blacksquare$$

427

## How Venture Capitalists Get Their ROI

Venture capitalists typically "harvest" equity investments in one of three ways:

1. The venture capitalist sells the piece of the business to another investor.

2. The venture capitalist waits until the company "goes public" (starts selling stock in the open market) and converts his/her share of the business into stock. The stock can now be traded. The venture capitalist can sell the stock for cash now or wait and see if the stock *appreciates* (increases in value) over time. The market will decide what a company is worth. The price of a company's stock will be based on the market's opinion of what the company's future earnings will be.

3. The company is sold and the venture capitalist and other equity holders are paid out of the proceeds. In many cases, all or some of the company's management team stays with the firm after the sale.

## The Business Plan

Venture capitalists, bankers, and other investors want to see a business plan before they will even consider lending money. An entrepreneur may have a brilliant idea, but if it is not set out in a well-written business plan, no professional investor will be interested.

A plan must include:

- The business idea
- Long- and short-term goals
- Market research
- The competitive advantage
- Marketing plan
- Philanthropic plan
- Start-up and operating costs
- Management
- Legal structure
- Time management
- Financing plan
- Break-even analysis
- Accounting system
- Projected monthly income statement
- Projected yearly income statement
- Financial ratio analysis
- Balance sheet

The business plan should be no longer than 20 typed pages, about an hour of reading time. Serious investors don't think a good plan has to be longer than that.

In order to ensure that investors understand the key points of your idea, the plan should include an executive summary of about five pages at the beginning, covering the plan's highlights and the key selling points of the investment opportunity.

Most venture capitalists will immediately reject an incomplete or poorly presented plan. They see a large number of plans each year and make very few investments.

## SKILLS MEAN SUCCESS

**ENGLISH**

### Writing for Information: Tips for Effective Editing

*Editing* is the stage of the writing process in which you review your work and correct errors. Editing will be important when you write a business plan. Before you show a business plan to an investor, check your work carefully for mistakes in grammar, spelling, or math.

- Read your written work *several* times — once to focus on meaning and clarity, once to review for spelling, grammar, etc.
- Try reading backwards, one sentence at a time. This will help you concentrate on the words and phrases, rather than the meaning.
- It can be difficult to edit your own work. Ask someone else to read your writing and suggest improvements.
- Make sure all sentences are complete, start with a capital letter, have a subject and verb, and end with a period or question mark.
- Check for correct grammar and punctuation.
- Make sure all proper nouns and the title are capitalized.
- Double-check your math.
- Re-read your work one final time for errors.

1. Follow these tips to edit your current business plan (or another paper you have written recently). Mark any errors you find in color. Go back and correct those errors in your final document.

2. Make a list of the types of errors you found. Keep this list in your notebook and use it as a reminder to watch for these errors in the future.

3. What would be the effect of giving a potential investor a business plan that contained punctuation and spelling errors? ■■■

## CRITICAL THINKING ABOUT...

### VENTURE CAPITAL

1. Describe the differences between venture capitalists and bankers. Which type of investor do you think would be better for your company and why?

2. If a venture capitalist invested $5 million to help you start your business, how much money would he or she hope to earn over the next five years?

3. Discuss two ways that a venture capitalist who invested in your company could attempt to cash in on the investment.

4. Have you written a business plan yet? How many business plan parts do you know how to write (look over the list on page 428)? Which ones do you still need to learn?

5. Have you found any sources of venture capital for young entrepreneurs that you intend to contact? Describe. **Business Plan Practice**

6. Pretend you are starting the business described in A Business for the Young Entrepreneur (on page 431).
   a. How would you raise the capital to start the business?
   b. Can you think of ways to expand such a business that would require venture capital? Use your imagination!

## KEY CONCEPTS

1. What rewards do venture capitalists seek for the risks they take?

2. What will a venture capitalist want to see before investing?

3. What does "majority interest" mean? Would you be willing to give up majority interest in your company for financing? Explain.

4. Calculate the value of a business, given the amount of venture capital invested and the percentage of the company it represents.

| Venture Capital | % of Company Sold | Company's Value |
|---|---|---|
| Example: $1,000 | 20% | $5,000 |

5. Pretend you are a venture capitalist who has invested $250,000 in a robotics company in exchange for a ten percent equity stake. After five years, the company's net worth has increased from $500,000 to $8 million. You decide to sell your equity in the company to another investor for $800,000.
   a. What was your return on investment for the five years?
   b. What is the ROI a typical venture capitalist hopes to see on an investment after five years?
   c. Did your investment meet your expectations as a venture capitalist? Describe.

## IN YOUR OPINION

Discuss with a group:

1. To finance your business, would you be willing to give up as much equity as Henry Ford did?

2. Re-read the example of The Body Shop in Chapter 31 (page 376).

Anita Roddick says she doesn't hold a grudge against the man she made a multimillionaire. Would you feel the same way?

**VOCABULARY**

majority interest ■ venture capitalist

## Chapter Summary ✔✔✔

**36.1** Venture capitalists invest their money in risky start-up businesses.
- A. Venture capitalists hope to earn high ROIs relatively quickly from the equity (ownership) they buy in new businesses.
- B. Venture capitalists may seek majority interest (more than half) ownership — and therefore control — of the businesses they invest in.
- C. Entrepreneurs go to venture capitalists when they can't find other sources of capital.

**36.2** Venture capitalists expect:
- A. To sell their equity to other investors for a profit
- B. To wait until a company "goes public" and then convert their equity into stock that can be sold for a profit
- C. To receive profitable proceeds if a young company is sold
- D. To see a business plan before they invest. ✔✔✔

## A Business for the Young Entrepreneur
### USED CDS

**A**n interesting thing about CDs is that people get tired of listening to them before they wear out. There is a strong market, therefore, for used ones. Your parents, their friends, and your own friends probably have CDs they don't really want anymore. Offer to buy their unwanted CDs for a dollar apiece. You could sell them to people who do want them for as much as they are willing to pay — from two dollars on up! Use part of your profit to buy more CDs to keep your business going.

**TO GET STARTED**
- Make business cards and flyers announcing that you buy and sell used CDs.
- Decorate the boxes you display them in with paint or stickers.
- Make cards to divide your CDs into categories, such as "Rock" or "Rap." This will make it easy for your customers to browse for the ones they might want.

**TIPS**
- Don't just buy CDs you like. Try to stock different types of music.
- If possible, arrange with the school administrators to sell your CDs in the cafeteria during lunch hour, or at school events.
- Sell your CDs at a local trade fair (flea market). ■

### CHAPTER 37

# CONTRACTS:
## *The Building Blocks of Business*

*No legacy is so rich as honesty.*

— William Shakespeare, *English poet and playwright*

### KEY OBJECTIVES

THIS CHAPTER WILL ENABLE YOU TO:

■ Understand the importance of written agreements in running a business.

■ Use contracts effectively to strengthen your business.

■ Understand "The Four A's" of a successful contract.

■ Understand the remedies available in case of breach of contract.

**A contract** is a formal agreement between two or more parties. Contracts are typically put into writing and signed. They can be verbal and, in some cases, *unilateral* (relating only to one of the parties). In some cases, you may take actions that imply a contractual obligation to somebody.

*Example:* When you sign up with an Internet service provider, such as AOL or Earthlink, you are entering into a contract. You are agreeing to pay for the service for a specified number of months, and in return the company agrees to provide you with Internet access, an e-mail account, and probably other features, as well.

*Example:* When you click "I agree" online or while installing software, you are actually "signing" a contract, so be sure to read everything before you make the click!

In some cases you may enter into an employment or consulting contract with people who work for your company. These contracts are critical when the employee or consultant is developing intellectual property or other work that you will want your company to own.

The power of a contract is that, once the individuals involved have signed it, the law will typically require them to perform the agreed-upon obligations. If someone refuses to put a verbal agreement in writing, you might find that you will have difficulty in enforcing the terms.

## Contracts Support Good Business Relationships

Putting the terms of an agreement in writing will allow both you and the other party to have a clear understanding of what you are agreeing to do. A good contract should identify all the important aspects of your working relationship, allowing each of you to have clear expectations. In order to be a valid contract, it must clearly identify key parts of the bargain, such as price, quantity, and delivery terms.

 **BizTip:** When handling an important business agreement, it is a good idea to detail the arrangements in writing and have both parties sign it.

## Contracts Allow Planning

Contracts are the building blocks of business.

*Example:* A department store wants to sell your hammered-silver necklaces. You work out a six-month contract specifying how many necklaces you will supply at what price, and how and when the store will pay you.

With that contract in hand, you can call your wholesaler. Because you have a large order, you will want to get your supplies in bulk. With the contract as written proof of your relationship with the store, a wholesaler may give you credit. You can try to arrange to buy the silver you need now to fill the order, and pay for it after you sell the necklaces to the store. You should have a contract not only with the customer, but also with your wholesaler.

Also, you can plan ahead with your advertisers or work out an advertising plan with the store as part of the contract.

A contract will also allow you to sue the store for **breach of contract** if it does not honor the agreement. If the store fails to buy your necklaces as agreed, and you have satisfied your part of the contract, then you can ask a court to force the store to pay you. In that way, you will be able to honor the contract with your silver supplier.

## See a Lawyer

Never sign a contract that you have not read yourself from top to bottom. Think about whether it covers all aspects of the deal. It may be advisable to have the contract reviewed by a lawyer. But you should still read and understand it, regardless of what the lawyer tells you. Your signature at the bottom tells the court that you read, understood, and agreed to every word. If you are ever taken to court and argue that "I didn't understand that part of the contract," it will not satisfy the judge.

The cost of legal advice adds up quickly, so be as prepared and organized as possible before visiting a lawyer. Read the contract ahead of time and make a copy of it. Circle sections on the copy that you do not agree to or understand. This will help your attorney advise you effectively.

## SKILLS MEAN SUCCESS

**MATH** ▶ **Estimation: Rounding Numbers**

Hourly fees are the most common form of billing used by lawyers. Hourly fees can range from $100 to $400 or more, depending on the lawyer and the type of legal services. Attorneys generally bill by the tenth-of-an-hour (six-minute *increments* of time) or by the quarter-hour (fifteen-minute increments).

When determining the time to be billed, lawyers round up to the nearest increment. For example, a lawyer who bills by tenth hours and spends 23 minutes on your legal services will bill you for 0.4 hours (23 ÷ 60 minutes is .38, rounded up to 0.4 hours). A lawyer who bills by quarter hours would bill you for 0.5 hour (23 minutes rounded up to the nearest quarter hour is two quarters, or .5).

*(Source: "Understanding Legal Fees" by Cynthia Thomas Calvert, 1999, http://www.womenlawyers.com/legalfee.htm)*

Determine the time billed and the total fee in each of the scenarios below:

| | Time Worked | Billing Method | Time Billed | Hourly Fee | Total Fee |
|---|---|---|---|---|---|
| **1.a.** | 42 minutes | tenth hours | _____ | $100 | $ _____ |
| **b.** | 42 minutes | quarter hours | _____ | $100 | $ _____ |
| **2.a.** | 13 minutes | tenth hours | _____ | $200 | $ _____ |
| **b.** | 13 minutes | quarter hours | _____ | $200 | $ _____ |
| **3.a.** | 29 minutes | tenth hours | _____ | $300 | $ _____ |
| **b.** | 29 minutes | quarter hours | _____ | $300 | $ _____ |
| **4.a.** | 31 minutes | tenth hours | _____ | $400 | $ _____ |
| **b.** | 31 minutes | quarter hours | _____ | $400 | $ _____ |
| **5.a.** | 1 hr., 44 min. | tenth hours | _____ | $100 | $ _____ |
| **b.** | 1 hr., 44 min. | quarter hours | _____ | $100 | $ _____ |

# Drafting a Contract

When you make a **draft** of a contract, begin by determining your needs. What do you want from this agreement? What should it say? Make a list. You should also consider the needs of the other party.

**A successful contract should achieve "The Four A's":**

1. **A**void misunderstanding
2. **A**ssure work
3. **A**ssure payment
4. **A**void liability

## Avoid Misunderstanding

When putting together a contract, spell out everything that will be done, even what is obvious. Go into full detail (not just how many shirts you will supply to the store and when, but what types and sizes). If you don't cover all the details, the person with whom you are contracting may add provisions or find "loopholes" you won't like.

## Assure Work

For a contract to be legally binding, both parties must:

- Do something or exchange something of value, or
- Agree not to do something they were legally entitled to do. This is called a *consideration* for entering into the contract. The contract should assure that you or the other person fulfill some kind of obligation. The exact nature of the obligation, and the time frame for accomplishing it, should be clearly specified.

## Assure Payment

A good contract specifies how payment will be made, and when and for what. It should leave no room for misinterpretation.

## Avoid Liability

Because the world is full of surprises, your contract should spell out **contingencies**. A contingency is an unpredictable event that could cause you to fail to fulfill your responsibilities. The contract should list contingencies for which you would not be liable. Common ones are "acts of God" (earthquake, hurricane, etc.), or illness. It should also clearly describe what will happen in the event that the parties agree to walk away from the agreement.

> **When you take the draft of your contract to an attorney, ask these basic questions:**
>
> 1. Will this agreement protect my interests?
> 2. What would you add, drop, or change?
> 3. What will happen if I fail to satisfy the terms of this agreement?
> 4. What can I do if the other party fails to satisfy the terms of this agreement?

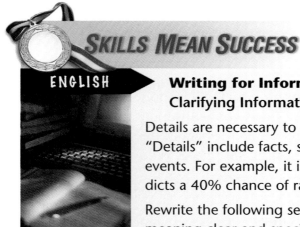

## SKILLS MEAN SUCCESS

**ENGLISH**

**Writing for Information:**
**Clarifying Information through Details**

Details are necessary to add clarity and interest to any type of writing. "Details" include facts, statistics, examples, quotes from experts, and events. For example, it is much clearer to say, "The meteorologist predicts a 40% chance of rain tomorrow," than "It might rain tomorrow."

Rewrite the following sentences by adding details to make the meaning clear and specific.

1. The part was too small.
2. The coat is expensive.
3. The lost dog was brown.
4. That location won't work for my bicycle shop.
5. The patient was hurt but is okay now. ■■■

## Letter of Agreement

Sometimes you won't need a contract, because the relationship is going to be brief or the work and money involved are relatively minor. In such cases, a **letter of agreement** could be enough.

A letter of agreement puts a verbal arrangement in writing, in the form of a business letter. The other party may respond to it in writing, either agreeing to it as is, or suggesting changes.

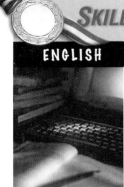

# SKILLS MEAN SUCCESS

**ENGLISH**

## Writing for Information: Business Letters

Every business letter has six essential parts. Read the following letter of agreement and match the names of the parts to the labeled sections of the letter.

**①** XYZ Painting
123 Main Street
Pleasant, NY 10101

**②** March 30, 2005

**③** Mr. Ronald Smith
16 Willow Lane
Pleasant, NY 10101

**④** Dear Mr. Smith:

**⑤** As we discussed, XYZ Painting will paint the front door and ten windows of your home at 16 Willow Lane for $800. This fee will include all supplies and labor. The work will be completed during the week of May 15. We will be unable to work in dangerous weather conditions, such as heavy rain, thunderstorms, or high winds. Any work delayed due to weather conditions will be rescheduled within three weeks.

Thank you for your business.

**⑥** Best regards,

*Susan Jasper*

Susan Jasper,
President, XYZ Painting

____ **a.** body        ____ **d.** date
____ **b.** letterhead   ____ **e.** closing
____ **c.** salutation   ____ **f.** inside address

**437**

## Breach of Contract

A contract is broken, or "breached," when one of the **signatories** (an individual who signed the contract), fails to fulfill it. The person injured by the signatory's failure to comply with the terms may then sue for breach of contract.

For a contract to be breached, it must first be "legally binding." Most states require that all signatories be 18 years of age and that the contract represent an "exchange of value." If a contract is breached, a **lawsuit** must be brought by the injured party within the state's **statute of limitations**, which limits the time period within which legal action may be taken.

A lawsuit is an attempt to recover a right or claim through legal action. Because lawyers are expensive and court cases time-consuming, lawsuits should be avoided whenever possible. Other options are **small claims court** and **arbitration**.

### Small Claims Court

Conflicts involving less than a certain sum of money, which varies by state law, can usually be resolved in a small claims court. In New York State, claims for $2,500 or less can be settled in this manner. In small claims court, each party is allowed to represent him/herself before a court official. The official hears each side's arguments and makes a decision that is legally binding.

### Arbitration

Sometimes contracts specify that conflicts may be settled through arbitration, instead of in court. In such cases an *arbitrator* — someone both sides agree to trust — is chosen to act as judge. All parties agree to abide by the arbitrator's decision.

## A Contract Is No Substitute for Trust

A contract is not a substitute for understanding and communication. If you don't like or trust someone, having a contract will not improve the relationship. It could lead, instead, to a lawsuit. Never sign a contract with someone you don't trust or get along with.

## Renegotiation

Running a small business is challenging and unpredictable. When entering into a contract with someone, you should consider the possibility that you might need to renegotiate with this individual in the future. You should have a good working relationship with the people whom you enter into contracts with.

Using the example from earlier in the chapter, what if, after you get credit from your silver supplier, the department store decides not to buy the necklaces? How will you pay the supplier? If you have a friendly relationship, you should be able to explain the situation and renegotiate a longer term for the contract, to give you time to find another buyer.

**NFTE**
Teaching Youth to Build Businesses

# *CONTRACT FOR SALE OF GOODS*

**A**greement made and entered into this *May 17, 2005*, by and between:

The *National Foundation for Teaching Entrepreneurship, Inc. (NFTE)*, 120 Wall Street, 29th Floor, New York, NY 10005, referred to as *Seller*, and

*John D. Doe*, 33 Mockingbird Lane, Smallville, NY 10562, referred to as *Buyer*.

Seller hereby agrees to transfer and deliver to buyer, on or before May 25, 2005, the following goods: *2 Toshiba laptop computers*.

The agreed upon purchase price is *$1,000* per unit.

Goods shall be deemed received by Buyer when delivered to address of Buyer as described above. Until such time as said Buyer has received goods, all risk of loss from any damage to said goods shall be on Seller.

Buyer has the right to examine the goods on arrival and has 10 days to notify Seller of any claim for damages on account of the condition, grade, or quality of the goods. That said notice must specifically set forth the basis of the claim, and that the failure to either notify Seller within the stipulated period of time or to set forth specifically the basis of the claim will constitute irrevocable acceptance of the goods. This agreement has been executed in duplicate, whereby both Buyer and Seller have retained one copy each, on May 17, 2005.

_____          _____
         *Buyer*                              *Seller*

## CRITICAL THINKING ABOUT...

### CONTRACTS

1. Brainstorm a list of the types of contracts you think you might enter into during the course of doing business over the next five years.

2. What is the most important contract you will need to run your business?

3. Describe any additional contracts you have, or plan to secure. **Business Plan Practice**

4. Create a sample contract between you and a wholesaler for business supplies.

5. Negotiate and write a letter of agreement between you and a fellow student. You could agree to become business partners, for example, or to supply a product or service for his/her business.

## KEY CONCEPTS

1. Which two things should you do before signing a contract?

2. Describe alternatives to settling a breach of contract with a lawsuit.

3. What will your signature at the bottom of a contract mean in a court of law?

4. Find a lawyer who might be willing to help you with your business. The SBA sometimes offers free or low-cost legal services. **Business Plan Practice**

5. Find the small claims court in your community. Call and ask what the minimum fee is for filing a lawsuit. Write a memo describing the experience.

## VOCABULARY

arbitration ■ breach of contract ■ contingency ■ contract ■ draft ■ lawsuit ■ letter of agreement ■ signatory ■ small claims court ■ statute of limitations

## Chapter Summary ✔✔✔

37.1 Contracts are formal, written, signed agreements between two parties that create legal obligations to perform in agreed-upon ways.
   A. Written, signed agreements clarify understanding better than verbal ones and are typically more enforceable by law.
   B. Valid, written contracts identify all aspects of an agreement and establish clear expectations for both parties.
   C. Contracts can be verbal or "unilateral" (relating to only one party).

37.2 Contracts are useful business tools.
   A. Contracts help establish good business relationships by clarifying understanding.

B. Contracts allow for better planning by:
1. Securing relationships with suppliers or customers
2. Providing proof of existing relationships
3. Protecting a business against breach of contract.
C. Any contract should be carefully read and reviewed in advance:
1. By the person who will sign it, before seeking legal advice
2. By that person's lawyer, who will charge for the legal service.

37.3   Drafting a contract involves considering "The Four A's":
A. Avoid Misunderstanding:
1. Spell out all details and avoid "loopholes."
B. Assure Work:
1. Bind both parties either to do or exchange something of value, or not to do something of value they were legally entitled to do
2. Guarantee fulfillment of obligations by both parties
3. Specify the nature and timing of all obligations.
C. Assure Payment: how, when, and for what will payments be made.
D. Avoid Liability:
1. State what happens if unpredictable events (contingencies) prevent responsibilities from being met
2. List contingencies for which parties are not liable
3. Describe what happens if either or both parties "walk away" from the agreement.
E. Use letters of agreement to put simple verbal agreements into writing.

37.4   Breach of contract occurs when one party who has signed a contract (signatory) fails to fulfill its obligations.
A. The injured party can sue the other for breach of contract if:
1. The contract was legally binding and represented an "exchange of value"
2. The signatories were (in most states) 18 or older
3. The state's statute of limitations has not expired.
B. Expensive and time-consuming lawsuits held in a formal court to recover an injured party's rights or claims can be avoided through:
1. Small claims courts: informal self-representation by both parties for smaller amounts of damage before a court official whose decision is legally binding
2. Arbitration: both parties agree to abide by the decision of an arbitrator (someone trusted by both parties, who judges the disagreement outside of court).
C. Contracts should never substitute for understanding and trust.
D. Renegotiation of a contract is possible if a working relationship is good.

**441**

# SOCIALLY RESPONSIBLE BUSINESS AND PHILANTHROPY

*Never doubt that a small group of concerned citizens can change the world — indeed it is the only thing that ever has.*

— Margaret Mead, *American anthropologist*

## KEY OBJECTIVES

THIS CHAPTER WILL ENABLE YOU TO:

- Develop a socially responsible business.
- Determine how to use your business to help people in the community.
- Develop cause-related marketing for your business that will support your competitive advantage.

**A**s you have been learning throughout this course, there are many ways that entrepreneurs can use their businesses to help their communities and contribute to society. As an entrepreneur, you already make an important contribution by providing needed goods or services to consumers in your area. You can also use your business to support important social issues. By running the company in a way that is consistent with your ethics and core values, you will develop a **socially responsible business**.

Anita Roddick, founder of The Body Shop, is a good example of an entrepreneur who has used her company as a force for social change. Her first big campaign came in 1985. Roddick let Greenpeace, an environmental preservation group, put up posters in Body Shop stores to educate people about the dumping of hazardous waste into the North Sea.

In the 1990s, 15 political prisoners were released due to the volume of letters that Body Shop customers wrote. Another Body Shop campaign raised public awareness about the destruction of the Brazilian rainforest.

## "Trade, Not Aid"

While traveling in Brazil, Roddick met with tribal leaders in the Amazon region to figure out how the forest could produce income without cutting down trees. The Body Shop began buying Brazil-nut oil and vegetable-dye beads from some of the tribes. This helped them establish businesses without destroying the rainforest.

## Cause-Related Marketing

Roddick's social and environmental campaigns created tremendous publicity for The Body Shop. Roddick would have had to spend millions of dollars to buy so much exposure for her company.

This kind of success has inspired other companies to get involved in **cause-related marketing**, which demonstrates a commitment to a social, environmental, or political cause. This kind of marketing can really instill loyalty in customers. It's also a good way to differentiate your business from the competition and achieve a *triple bottom line*:

1. a profitable business
2. a business that improves society
3. a business that protects the environment.

Roddick chose causes that she believed in, but they also made sense for her business because they reinforced The Body Shop's competitive advantage. The Body Shop differentiates itself from the competition by offering customers natural products in packaging that is friendlier to the environment. Roddick supported causes that were also important to the kinds of customers The Body Shop tries to attract.

Consider associating your business with a cause that you believe in — but make sure you do research first. Be sure you understand the activities and purpose of any organization you choose to support through your business. If possible, choose a cause that aligns with and supports your competitive advantage.

Encourage your employees to participate, too. *Volunteerism* is a great way to improve morale and make a difference. AT&T pays employees to devote one day a month to community service.

## Gaining Goodwill

Many entrepreneurs try to make a difference in their communities by giving money and time to organizations that help people. Microsoft, for example, made it possible for NFTE to develop an Internet-based curriculum, BizTech (www.nfte.com). Microsoft has donated both money and computer-programming expertise to this project.

Why would Microsoft do this?

- First, the company's founder, Bill Gates, believes in NFTE's mission and wants to help young people learn about business. The Internet-based program makes it easier to teach entrepreneurship to greater numbers of young people around the world.

- Second, supporting this program is an intelligent business move for Microsoft. Microsoft gains publicity and **goodwill**. Goodwill is composed of *intangible* assets, such as reputation, name recognition, and customer relations.

## Nonprofit Organizations

Nonprofit organizations are corporations whose mission is to contribute to the greater good of society. The Internal Revenue Service classifies nonprofits under "501(c)(3)" in the tax code. As discussed in Chapter 32, these are corporations that are tax exempt. This means they do not have to pay federal or state taxes, and they are not privately or publicly owned. Essentially, a board of directors controls the operations of a 501(c)(3) organization.

Such well-known institutions as the Boys and Girls Clubs of America, the YMCA, the Girl Scouts, the Red Cross, and Big Brothers/Big Sisters are all examples of nonprofits. Their founders were social entrepreneurs and, although they did not earn large sums of money personally, and could not sell the organizations for a profit, they received great satisfaction and "made a difference." Wendy Kopp, of Teach for America, and Michael Bronner, of Upromise, are two examples of social entrepreneurs who founded the innovative and successful nonprofits described below.

## Teach for America and Upromise

Founded in 1991, Teach for America recruits recent college graduates to become public school teachers. The organization has trained over 10,000 young teachers, and placed them in two-year positions in schools where teachers were badly needed.

Michael Bronner, a former marketing executive who became a social entrepreneur, started Upromise in 2001. Bronner felt strongly that the cost of sending a child to college had become too expensive for most families. He believed that there needed to be a better way of helping families save money for college.

Bronner came up with the idea that a portion of the money that families already spent on popular goods and services, such as groceries and toys, could go into a college savings account for their children. Upromise works with established corporations, such as AT&T, America Online, and Toys 'R' Us. Every time a registered family makes a purchase from one of these companies, a percentage of their spending automatically goes into a special college savings account.

## SKILLS MEAN SUCCESS

**MATH**

**Operations:** Percentages of Purchases

According to Upromise.com, you can save the following amounts for college on purchases at these retail stores (with proper enrollment and membership). Determine how much you could save if you spent the amounts listed per year at these locations. (Round off to the nearest cent.)

| | Retail Locations | Savings | $ Spent per Year | Amount Saved per Year |
|---|---|---|---|---|
| **1.** | Best Buy.com | 1% on purchases | $353.52 | _____ |
| **2.** | Bed Bath & Beyond | 2% on purchases | $227.82 | _____ |
| **3.** | Exxon Mobil | 1¢ per gallon of gas | 288 gallons | _____ |
| **4.** | Hickory Farms stores | 5% on purchases | $32.99 | _____ |
| **5.** | Back Porch Restaurant | 6% on purchases | $482.64 | _____ |

## What Is Philanthropy?

There is a long, established connection in the United States between entrepreneurs and philanthropy. As you learned from the discussion in Chapter 8, philanthropists express their concern for social issues by giving money, time, and advice to selected charities. Philanthropists often give their money through *foundations*. A foundation is a nonprofit organization that distributes donated money, through grants, to other nonprofits that help people and social causes.

The Bill & Melinda Gates Foundation is one of the world's largest, with over $23 billion in capital. This money comes from the personal wealth that Gates earns from Microsoft. As a private foundation, it is required by the federal government to give away 5% of the fair market value of its assets every year. The Gates Foundation provides a great deal of money annually to other charities. These in turn use the funds to finance social and community programs that the Gates Foundation supports, such as education and health care.

You could give your time to an organization that does work you support. If you know how to paint houses or have carpentry skills, for instance, you could help build homes for an organization such as Habitat for Humanity, which constructs affordable housing for low-income families. If you love animals, volunteer at your local animal shelter.

## What Entrepreneurs Have Built

Many philanthropic organizations in this country were created by entrepreneurs who wanted to give back some of the wealth that they earned. Entrepreneurs have financed great museums, libraries, universities, and other important institutions. Some foundations created by famous entrepreneurs include the Rockefeller Foundation, the Coleman Foundation, the Charles G. Koch Foundation, the Ford Foundation, and the Goldman Sachs Foundation.

Some of the most aggressive entrepreneurs in American history, such as Andrew Carnegie, have also been the most generous. In 1901, after a long and sometimes ruthless business career, Carnegie sold his steel company to J.P. Morgan for $420 million. Overnight, Carnegie became one of the very richest men in the world. After retiring, he spent most of his time giving away his wealth to libraries, colleges, museums, and other worthwhile institutions that still benefit people today. By the time of his death from pneumonia in 1919, Carnegie had donated over $350 million to philanthropic causes.

## You Have Something to Contribute

You may not have millions of dollars to contribute to your community — yet. But there are many ways you could be philanthropic, get your employees excited, and create goodwill:

- Pledge a percentage of your sales to a nonprofit organization you have researched, believe in, and respect. Send out press releases announcing your pledge.

- Become a mentor to a younger entrepreneur. Help that individual by sharing your contacts and expertise.

- Volunteer for an organization that helps your community. Find out how you can serve on its board of directors.

- Sell your product at a discount to a charity that you support. The charity can then resell it at full price to raise money.

- When you give it a little thought, you will realize that you have a lot to give. Remember, making a contribution doesn't necessarily mean giving money.

# Chapter 38 Review

## CRITICAL THINKING ABOUT...

### BEING SOCIALLY RESPONSIBLE[1]

1. If your business made a net profit of $10,000 this year, to which of the charities below would you donate $100? On a separate piece of paper, write a short paragraph explaining your choice.

    a. A community garden

    b. A local arts club

    c. A cancer-research lab

    d. An environmental group

    e. Other (create your own)

2. Find a foundation that might support your choice. (Hint: Check out The Foundation Center at http://fdncenter.org/)

3. Write a business letter to another entrepreneur in your class asking him or her also to donate $10. (Explain the purpose of the organization and how it will benefit from the money. Also, explain how donating benefits your classmate.)

4. If you could create your own foundation, what would it do? Whom would it help? What name would you give it? Write a short mission statement for your foundation.

5. Make a list of social issues you think are important. Find at least five nonprofit organizations that address some of those issues. Conduct research on each. What are their respective mission statements? How do they make a difference?

6. Do you think the founders of tax-exempt 501(c)(3) organizations would have the same incentives as founders of for-profit companies? Discuss and explain.

## KEY CONCEPTS

1. How does philanthropy differ from socially responsible business?

2. Find a company you like that uses cause-related marketing. Describe how it is used and why you think it is effective. If possible, bring in an ad that uses cause-related marketing to show the class.

3. Do you have a mentor? If so, describe your relationship and how it helps you. If not, write up a plan for finding one for your business.

4. Describe three ways you plan to run a socially responsible business. **Business Plan Practice**

5. What cause-related marketing do you intend to use for your business? How will this support and reinforce your competitive advantage? **Business Plan Practice**

## EXPLORATION

1. Find a charity in your community and call or visit to learn how you could get involved. Make a commitment to this organization to give time or money every month. Write a memo to your teacher describing your commitment.

2. Write a short essay describing what you think is the most important social or environmental problem in your community. Discuss how you think entrepreneurship could help solve it.

## REFERENCES

1 Thanks to Vicki Kennedy for the idea behind this exercise.

## VOCABULARY

cause-related marketing ■ goodwill ■ socially responsible business

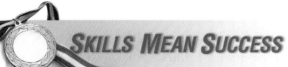

## SKILLS MEAN SUCCESS

**LEADERSHIP** 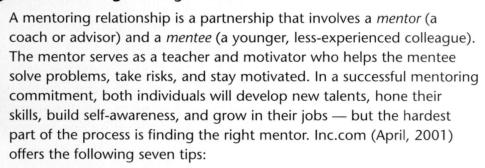 **Networking:** Finding a Mentor

A mentoring relationship is a partnership that involves a *mentor* (a coach or advisor) and a *mentee* (a younger, less-experienced colleague). The mentor serves as a teacher and motivator who helps the mentee solve problems, take risks, and stay motivated. In a successful mentoring commitment, both individuals will develop new talents, hone their skills, build self-awareness, and grow in their jobs — but the hardest part of the process is finding the right mentor. Inc.com (April, 2001) offers the following seven tips:

1. *Know yourself.* Identify your strengths and weaknesses and recognize how a mentor could help you grow.

2. *Be proactive.* Allow mentoring relationships to form naturally, if possible, but make an effort to get to know people whom you think could possibly be mentors.

3. *Ask for referrals.* Ask friends, family members, and colleagues for suggestions.

4. *Keep an open mind.* Look for someone who exemplifies your goals, values, and desired skills. Do not assume that a mentor has to be a supervisor or manager; he or she could be anyone who has the appropriate skills and attitudes.

5. *Identify good sources of mentors.* Don't hesitate to look outside your workplace. Associations, online groups, local business owners, retirees, religious groups, and people with similar hobbies can all be good sources of mentors.

6. *Know what you want to achieve from the relationship.* Be clear about your purpose in finding a mentor and what you hope to get out of the relationship.

7. *Think about past mentors.* Think about people who have taught or positively influenced you in the past. Identify the traits that you appreciated about them, and seek those traits in a potential mentor.

   **a.** Using the steps above, make a list of your own strengths and weaknesses and the traits you look for in a mentor. Identify three possible sources of mentors.

   **b.** In your opinion, what communication skills and attitudes would be important for a successful mentoring relationship? ■■■

# Chapter Summary ✔✔✔

**38.1** Entrepreneurs can choose to run socially responsible businesses.
   A. Socially responsible businesses make profits, but also help their communities or chosen causes.
   B. Cause-related marketing:
      1. Serves social, environmental, or political projects
      2. Wins like-minded customer loyalty and goodwill, which have value to a company
      3. Involves employees as volunteers.

**38.2** Nonprofit corporations contribute to the good of society.
   A. The government classifies them as 501(c)(3) for tax purposes.
   B. Nonprofit organizations don't pay taxes.
   C. Nonprofit organizations:
      1. Are not permitted to make profits
      2. Cannot be "owned" by individuals or stockholders.

**38.3** Philanthropists are entrepreneurs who donate money to help others.
   A. Foundations are nonprofit organizations created by entrepreneurs to distribute donations through grants to charities.
   B. Entrepreneurs donate money and services to worthy charities through:
      1. Volunteer work and time
      2. Lump sums of money or funding for specific purposes
      3. Percentages of sales or profits
      4. Mentoring services. ✔✔✔

# A Business for the Young Entrepreneur
## SPORTING GOODS STORE

Even if your venture is small, you can do a lot that will be beneficial for your business as well as your community. Frank Alameda ran a sporting goods store on Manhattan's Lower East Side, called East Side Sports. He purchased ads in the *Yellow Pages* but believed his most valuable promotion was community service. Each year Frank sponsored 22 local baseball and basketball teams in the area by providing them with uniforms and balls. This filled his store with kids and made him very popular with the parents in the neighborhood, too!

Frank says he knew his business would succeed because of his location in an area full of young people. He made it even more popular by getting personally involved with the community.

Frank found a cause that worked with the competitive advantage of his business, which was a location where sports-minded young people lived. This made more sense than giving his time, and some profits, to a charity that did not relate to his business.

*How did Frank make his business socially responsible and how did his business benefit?* ■

# SMALL BUSINESS AND GOVERNMENT

*This land was made for you and me.*

— Woody Guthrie, *American folksinger*

## KEY OBJECTIVES

THIS CHAPTER WILL ENABLE YOU TO:

- Understand the economic definition of efficiency.
- Define GDP and GNP.
- Understand how government regulations impact small business.
- Analyze global business opportunities.

## Small Business and the Economy [1]

Small business is an important part of the national economy. As an entrepreneur, you will create value that contributes to the country's **Gross Domestic Product (GDP)**. The GDP of the United States includes all value created by businesses operating in the country, even if the company is foreign-based. The cars produced by Toyota (a Japanese company) at its plant in Kentucky, for example, are part of the American GDP. Every sale you make, no matter how small, contributes to the GDP. Each year, GDP increases or decreases (usually by a very small percentage).

A decrease in GDP means businesses are producing fewer goods and services. They have less money to hire people, and some will have to close. This in turn causes unemployment. Since fewer people have jobs, there is less money spent on goods and services, and the economy may go into a **recession**, or economic downturn. An increase in the GDP means that businesses are making profits and entrepreneurs are making good decisions and using resources efficiently.

**BizFact:** Prior to 1991, the market value of production was measured by the **Gross National Product (GNP)**. The GNP of the United States includes all value created by American companies, whether they are operating here or abroad. So, shoes produced by Nike (a U.S. company) at its plant in Taiwan would be part of the GNP. Although GDP is the more common measurement now, GNP is still calculated. GNP is often used to compare the performance of the economies of different countries.

## SKILLS MEAN SUCCESS

**TECHNOLOGY** ▶ **Internet Research Skills:** Locating Data Online

The U.S. Department of Commerce Bureau of Economic Analysis provides GDP statistics, available online at http://www.bea.gov. Visit this site to locate the following information:

**1.** Gross Domestic Product for 2004.

*Hint:* Follow the "National" links to "Gross Domestic Product" and open the file to "Current-dollar and 'real' GDP." In the column, "GDP in billions of current dollars," locate the figure for 2004.

**2.** Gross State Product for New York for 2003.

*Hint:* Follow the "Regional" links to "Gross State Product" and click on the "Interactive Tables." In the appropriate boxes, select "Gross State Product," "New York," "Total Gross State Product," and "2003." ■■■

# Government and Business

The United States has a free-market economy, meaning that anyone can start a business. The government itself does not own or control private businesses, but it does make laws about business practices. In 1970, for example, Congress passed the Occupational Safety and Health Act (OSHA) to protect American workers. The act established the Occupational Safety and Health Administration in the Department of Labor, which enforces laws designed to prevent workers from being injured or killed on the job.

The government also enforces minimum age requirements in the workplace and prohibits discrimination on the basis of gender, race, age, disability, religion, national origin, or sexual orientation. It provides a court system that enforces contracts between businesses and consumers. An entrepreneur who has paid a designer for a Web site, for example, may take that designer to court if he fails to complete the task. The court acts as a neutral judge of the dispute and provides a solution. The designer might be ordered to return the money paid by the entrepreneur, or to complete the work.

In the United States, city, state, and federal government regulations control many elements of business. You should always call your local chamber of commerce and ask about regulations that might apply to your venture. It is your obligation to be fully informed of and to follow all government laws and regulations.

## The Small Business Administration

Small business is so important to the U.S. economy that the government established the Small Business Administration (SBA) in 1953 to help entrepreneurs. In 1964, the SBA began providing Equal Opportunity Loans to entrepreneurs in poor neighborhoods who could not qualify for bank financing.

Since 1953 the SBA has helped nearly 20 million small businesses with financing, advice, and other assistance. From 1991 to 2000 the SBA assisted 435,000 small businesses get $94.6 billion in loans. The SBA continues to branch out to increase business participation by women and minorities with its programs for minority-owned small businesses, microloans, and the publication of Spanish language informational materials. To find out more about how the SBA could help you, visit www.sba.gov.

## Stable Money Is Important [2]

The government plays an important role in a nation's political and economic stability. If the country goes to war, that will have a direct impact on your business; it could make economic conditions unstable. During wartime it can be difficult or impossible to communicate with customers and suppliers overseas, and life will probably be disrupted at home, as well. When you are old enough to vote, be sure to stay informed about politics and choose politicians whom you think will make decisions you can support.

Money that can be exchanged internationally is often referred to as **currency**. The government tries to ensure economic stability by keeping its currency *stable*. Money is stable when a dollar has the same value today that it had in the recent past. If you can buy a loaf of bread with a dollar today, you should be able to buy a loaf of bread with a dollar a few months from now.

When currency values change rapidly, consumers and businesses are harmed because they are unable to make long-term decisions. Instead, these groups must make choices while they are uncertain about the future value of their money.

When the value of a currency goes down, so does the ability of consumers and businesses to buy products and services. An entrepreneur who plans to buy a computer six months from now might choose to buy it today, for fear that it will be more expensive then. Because she is making this purchase out of anxiety about the currency's stability, she is not free to make the most efficient choice for her business.

If an entrepreneur knows that the buying power of a dollar will be worth the same today as it will be next week, she will make more efficient decisions. In the United States, the central bank, called the Federal Reserve, is charged with keeping the value of money stable. Increases and decreases in the prices consumers must pay for the things they buy are measured by the **Consumer Price Index (CPI)**. The CPI is updated monthly by the U.S. Department of Labor, which keeps track of costs of housing, food, transportation, etc.

## Globalization

When you start a business, you will enter not only the national, but also the global, economy. Because of improvements in technology, communication between businesspeople has become worldwide. Airplanes enable rapid travel across vast distances, while the Internet allows customers to place orders reliably and instantly for products manufactured abroad. Today, even a small business can operate in many countries at once.

As an entrepreneur, you should consider international opportunities. These may include:

- **Importing** — you bring products from other countries into your own country to sell.
- **Exporting** — you sell your products to customers in other countries.

When you import or export, you affect your country's **trade balance**, which is the difference between its overall imports and its exports. A trade balance is *positive* when a country's businesses export more than they import.

If you decide to import or export goods, carefully research whether there are special taxes, called **tariffs**, in either of the countries involved, which could make the transaction more expensive.

**453**

For assistance, contact:

- U.S. Export Assistance Centers (http://www.sba.gov/oit) — located in major metropolitan areas throughout the United States. They advise small businesses on setting up import-export operations.

- The Export-Import Bank of the United States (Ex-Im Bank — http://www.exim.gov) — a federal agency that helps small businesses develop import-export business with a variety of insurance, loan, and guarantee programs.

## SKILLS MEAN SUCCESS

**ENGLISH**

**Reading for Information: Vocabulary**

Imagine that you run a multi-location American retail business that sells hard-to-find gourmet foods and fine hand-crafted items. Indicate whether the following activities are examples of *importing* or *exporting*.

**1.** You sell Mexican silver jewelry in your store in Ohio.

**2.** You sell your own hand-crafted light fixtures to customers in Mexico.

**3.** You sell your hand-made candles to a retail chain in Canada.

**4.** You sell French candles in your store in New York.

**5.** You sell vanilla beans from Madagascar to a gourmet food store in Florida. ■■■

## Business and Culture[3]

If you decide to take advantage of opportunities overseas, be aware that business practices in other countries may differ from those in your own. Take the time to find out what is polite, acceptable social and business behavior *before* you approach a new market. In the United States, for example, businesspeople often like to discuss matters right away. In Mali, in Africa, on the other hand, business meetings often begin with long greetings and pleasantries. Sometimes people talk and drink tea for hours before the business at hand is discussed. It would be considered rude to try to get down to business immediately.

Respecting cultural preferences can greatly increase your chances of success. This will help you to create solid relationships with your new customers or suppliers.

# Chapter 39 Review

## CRITICAL THINKING ABOUT...

### SMALL BUSINESS AND GOVERNMENT

With your teacher's guidance, calculate the following statistics for your class.

1. Class GDP for one day.

2. Class GDP for one week.

3. Number of part-time employees.

4. Why do you think some Americans are worried about globalization? Search the Internet for two news articles about anti-globalization protests. Write a short essay giving your opinion about how you think globalization affects entrepreneurs.

5. Which laws — such as minimum wage and age requirements, health and safety regulations, or anti-discrimination laws — will affect your business? **Business Plan Practice**

6. Pick a country and research how people prefer to do business there. Write a memo describing how you would do business with people from that country so as not to offend them.

### KEY CONCEPTS

1. Why is stable money important to entrepreneurs?

2. How is GDP different from GNP?

3. Explain why entrepreneurs should understand government regulations.

4. Why should an entrepreneur research the culture where he or she plans to conduct business?

5. After reading A Business for the Young Entrepreneur on page 456, research the Internet and find three government policies or rules that might have affected Xochitl's importing of essential oils from Mexico.

### EXPLORATION

Visit the Small Business Administration online. Find and describe a program that you think could help you with your business — if not now, then in the future.

### REFERENCES

1 Special thanks to Sue Bartlett of the University of South Florida Economics Department.
2 See *Master Curriculum Guide, Economics: What and When*, edited by June Gilliard, et al. (Joint Council on Economic Education, 1989), for an excellent discussion of money supply.
3 Thanks to Kerri Kennedy for ideas in this chapter.

### VOCABULARY

Consumer Price Index (CPI) ▪ currency ▪ Gross Domestic Product ▪ Gross National Product ▪ recession ▪ tariff ▪ trade balance

## Chapter Summary ✔✔✔

39.1 Small businesses contribute to the national economy.
   A. Entrepreneurs' profits are calculated as part of the country's Gross Domestic Product (GDP).
   B. GDP = Total value-added (profits) of all companies operating in the U.S.

C. The GDP changes:
  1. Increases (profitable economic upturn), or
  2. Decreases (economic downturn, or recession).
D. Recessions reflect lower profits: fewer new jobs are created, and there is less spending by businesses and consumers.

39.2 Even in free-market economies, governments set up rules about how businesses can operate.
A. Laws protect workers' safety on the job.
B. Governments enforce laws to prevent:
  1. Child labor
  2. Gender, racial, age, disability, sexual-orientation, and other discrimination
  3. Violations of legal contracts.
C. The Small Business Administration (SBA) helps small companies.

39.3 Governments create conditions that support business.
A. Keeping currency value stable:
  1. Operating the central banking system (Federal Reserve)
  2. Measuring changes in everyday consumer prices using the Consumer Price Index (CPI).
B. Monitoring international trade by setting rules and taxes for:
  1. Importing (selling foreign goods in your country)
  2. Exporting (selling domestic goods in other countries)
  3. Tariffs (taxes on imports or exports).
C. Helping small businesses to buy and sell in international markets. ✔✔✔

# A Business for the Young Entrepreneur
## MEXICAN FINE ARTS, CRAFTS & ORIGINAL DESIGNS, XOCHITL GUZMAN

From the time she was a young girl, Xochitl Guzman dreamed of becoming an entrepreneur. "My father was an artist. He never went to college, but he was always able to put food on the table by selling jewelry and later doing batik," she remembers, "so I always wanted a business of my own."

When her father put her in charge of a booth at a fair when she was only eight years old, she sold more goods than her whole family put together. But, as Xochitl grew up, fending for herself became a challenge. "Being a person of color and looking young for my age, I didn't get a lot of jobs that I was capable of doing," she remembers. "I was unfocused and had low self-esteem, but I knew I didn't want to work for anyone."

When she graduated from high school, Xochitl's parents couldn't afford to put her through college. So the 19 year old began waitressing to pay her own way. But it was grueling work that didn't leave enough time or energy to focus on her schoolwork.

Remembering the NFTE business training she received in high school, Xochitl went home to Mexico to buy essential oils from her father for one-fourth of the price they sold for in the United States. By importing the oils from Mexico, she was able to increase her profit margin. Setting up shop in a booth on Telegraph Avenue in Berkeley, Xochitl was able to make enough money to support herself while studying theater at San Francisco State.

Later, she tried to get a job with a store that sold henna tattoos. After being rebuffed by the owner, the young entrepreneur vowed to become the store's competition. Xochitl created Henna Tattoos, making $500 a day selling her tattoos on the Avenue.

When the henna tattoo market gave out, Xochitl reinvented herself again — using her language skills to start an interpreting business. As Whole Foods Market's official interpreter, she made $60 an hour. The high pay and flexible schedule left her plenty of time for studying. In 2000, Xochitl switched to importing arts and crafts from her homeland — many of them custom-made from her own designs. ■

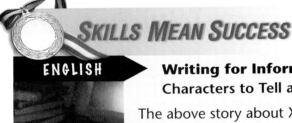

## SKILLS MEAN SUCCESS

**ENGLISH**

### Writing for Information: Using Detail, Tense, Dialogue, and Characters to Tell a Story

The above story about Xochitl Guzman is a *narrative* — a style of writing in which a story is told, events are explained, or facts are related.

1. What background information is presented in the *introductory* (first) paragraph?

2. Identify five main events in the story and put them in the correct chronological sequence.

3. For each main event, identify a supporting detail that helps make the story more interesting.

4. What verb tense is used in the story?

5. Identify two uses of *dialogue* (what is actually said by individuals) in the story.

6. What was the complication or problem that the main character (Xochitl) had to solve?

7. How was the story resolved in the final paragraph? ■■■

### CHAPTER 40

# BUILDING GOOD PERSONAL AND BUSINESS CREDIT

*Industry, thrift, and self-control are not sought because they create wealth, but because they create character.*

— Calvin Coolidge, *30th President of the United States*

## KEY OBJECTIVES

THIS CHAPTER WILL ENABLE YOU TO:

- Explain the difference between good credit and no credit.
- Establish a personal credit history.
- Define the "Four C's" of business credit.
- Know your rights in dealing with credit-reporting agencies.
- Befriend your banker.

**Y**ou will probably need to borrow money to expand your business at some point in your career. To do so, you will need to have good **credit**. Credit can be defined as integrity in financial matters and making payments when due. Great fortunes have been built on good credit. It will be one of your most important intangible assets. A good credit rating will increase your financial options dramatically.[1]

## *No* Credit Is Not *Good* Credit

If you've never borrowed money, you don't have good credit. What you have is *no* credit, meaning that you have no credit history. To establish one, you must show that you can borrow money and make regular payments on time.

Most banks and other lending institutions do not like to lend money to people who have no credit.

> **Rule of Thumb:** Develop the good habit of always depositing 10% of your income into a savings account.

# The "Four C's"

Bankers are concerned with "The Four C's":

1. **C**ollateral
2. **C**ash flow
3. **C**ommitment
4. **C**redit history

If you approach a bank for a loan for your small business, your banker will ask you about:

### Collateral

The banker wants to know what you own that can be pledged against the loan. In other words, what can the bank take if you fail to repay? Examples of such **collateral** include a house, a car, or business assets, such as a silk-screening machine or an oven.

### Cash Flow

Most small-business loans are repaid from cash generated by the business. Your business plan must include a cash-flow statement that proves to the banker that your business will generate enough cash to pay back the loan.

### Commitment

How much of your own money have you invested in your business? Have you gotten friends and family to invest? What about venture capital? The banker wants to see that others have confidence in your business, too.

### Credit History

As we have discussed, your credit history is crucial. A banker will not lend money to someone with bad credit and will almost never lend money to someone with no credit.

## SKILLS MEAN SUCCESS

**ENGLISH**

**Writing and Listening:** Strategies for Note Taking

Use the following strategies to take careful notes during a presentation. Choose an event such as a speech, a lesson or lecture at school; or a TV show or video presentation and practice the skill of taking good notes.

- Sit where you can pay attention.
- Listen attentively.
- Write the date, name of the speaker, and title of the presentation.
- Listen carefully to introductory comments, so you will know what to expect.
- Write your notes neatly, so you will be able to read and understand them later.
- Be brief, writing down only what is important. Use your own words, not the speaker's.
- Listen for "signal" words and cues that tell you what to expect, such as *first, second, next, finally, then, thus, another important…, therefore, on the other hand, remember,* etc.
- Keep listening even if the speaker says something you disagree with.
- Use abbreviations and symbols that you will remember.
- Take note of anything the speaker writes on the board or a transparency.
- If the speaker summarizes the talk, listen carefully and use it as an opportunity to check your notes for accuracy and completeness.
- Jot down questions during the presentation to get answers for later. ■■■

## Use a Charge Account to Establish a Good Credit History

How can you establish a credit history? You will need to show that you can be trusted to borrow money and make regular, on-time payments. You can start with a charge card.

Most department stores are willing to open a **charge account** for customers with no credit history. Charge accounts enable people to buy things without paying cash at the time of purchase. At the end of the month, you will be expected to pay either the balance or a portion of it ("minimum amount due"). Sometimes you will not be charged interest if you pay within a month. Otherwise, you will be charged on the remaining balance. Most stores will require you to be at least 18 years old before they will issue a charge account.

When you are old enough to get your first charge account, make a few small purchases and pay for them right away. This is a good way to establish a credit record. Never miss a payment or pay later than the "date due."

Another option is to buy something on **layaway**. Layaway plans allow you to make a down payment on an item and then pay monthly **installments** until you complete the purchase. Making payments on time will prove that you know how to manage your money.

## Using Credit Costs Money

The most important thing to remember about credit is that it costs money. It costs more to buy on credit than to buy with cash. Whether you are borrowing from a bank, or through a credit card, you will be paying not only the *principal* (original amount borrowed) but a **finance charge** (interest on the original amount) as well.

While credit will make it easier to purchase what you want when you want it, sooner or later you will have to pay back the loan, plus the interest.

Using credit can be risky and expensive. Risky, because once you have a bad credit rating, it can take many years to become creditworthy again. Expensive, because finance charges can add up dramatically over time.

### SKILLS MEAN SUCCESS

**MATH**

**Operations and Problem Solving:** Interest Charges

Imagine you have purchased the following items on your credit card, which has an interest rate of 18% (compounded monthly). If you don't pay the balance on your account for one month, how much will you actually be paying for each of the following?

| | | |
|---|---|---|
| **1.** Dinner at a restaurant: | | $35.00 |
| **2.** Business suit: | | $275.00 |
| **3.** Dress shoes: | | $65.00 |
| **4.** Movie tickets: | | $16.50 |
| **5.** Laser printer for your home office: | | $320.00 |

## Pros and Cons of Credit Cards

Using credit cards if you can't pay them off regularly is a bad idea. Most cards have high interest rates — 16 to 19 percent. Your best bet is to pay off any credit card debt in full each month, to avoid the high interest charges.

Whenever you pay a debt (credit card or otherwise) your monthly payment will include the interest payment and an additional amount that goes toward paying back the principal. On a $2,000 credit card bill with an interest rate of 19%, for example, a monthly payment of $100 would go mostly to paying the interest! It will take a long time to pay off the principal at $100 a month because the interest will keep adding up.

On the other hand, credit cards do offer some excellent benefits for small businesses, including:

- Insurance
- Fraud protection
- Theft protection
- Discounts for small business

Use credit cards only if you have the discipline to pay them off regularly.

## Check Your Credit History Regularly

Before a banker will lend you money or a credit card company will grant you a card, they will investigate your credit history. There are several firms that keep credit reports on individuals and businesses. Personal credit agencies are Equifax, Experian, and TransUnion. Major companies that keep credit reports on businesses are Dun & Bradstreet and NCR Corp.

These companies gather information given to them voluntarily by bankers, suppliers, and other creditors. Credit agencies can make mistakes. They do not always verify the information they receive; they just record it. For this reason, you should run credit checks on yourself at least once a year. Contact the main agencies to see if they have reports on you or your business. Ask them for a copy of your reports, which they are required by law to supply.

## Clearing Up Negative Credit Reports

You may have a negative comment on your report because you failed to pay a bill on time. But the reason may have been legitimate, and you might be able to have it cleared. Perhaps you failed to pay because you moved and the bill did not come to your new address. You can then pay it and have it erased from the report.

You can also have non-payment recorded as "disputed," not as bad credit. If you are refusing to pay for your new refrigerator because it is not working properly, and the store has reported you as a bad credit risk, you can contact the reporting agency and have the debt designated as "disputed" instead of "unpaid."

Finally, you can file reports on yourself with a credit agency. Give them information that will make your credit report stronger.

## Buying a Home Is Smarter than Renting

Probably the largest personal purchase you will ever make will be a home. Owning is better than renting because, when you pay rent, you are giving money to someone else who owns the property where you live. You will never own that property, no matter how much rent you pay.

To buy a home, on the other hand, you must have a down payment, which is typically ten to twenty percent of the cost of the home. Next, you will visit a bank and get a **mortgage**, which is a loan that will pay the rest of the price of the house or apartment you are purchasing. Instead of paying rent, you will make monthly mortgage payments. As you pay back the loan, however, you will gain *equity*, or ownership, of your home. This equity becomes collateral that strengthens your credit rating and makes you a more attractive borrower. Once you have paid the mortgage, you will own your home.

## Business Credit

It is hard for a business to grow without the use of credit. As a small-business owner, you are going to need the help and support of bankers. It is in your long-term interest to learn how to work with them. You will be asking for money for your business, so think of the banker as a potential friend. Be sure to call around to different banks and compare the interest rates they charge.

## Befriend Your Banker

Since, at some point in your entrepreneurial career, you will find yourself sitting in a banker's office asking for a loan, wouldn't it be better if that banker were already your friend? Banks are a major source of business-capital loans, so it is a good idea to establish a relationship with a bank early on.

As soon as you start your first business, introduce yourself to a loan officer at your bank. People are often nice to young entrepreneurs and like to hear about their businesses. Make friends with this banker and show him or her your business plan, asking for suggestions.

As your business grows, keep your banker informed about how you are doing. Take your banker to lunch and talk about your business. If you are involved in social enterprise, involve your banker, too. Perhaps the bank would also be willing to contribute time or money to the charity you are supporting.

By the time your business needs a loan, you will have a friend at the bank. As your business grows, so will your relationship with your banker. Your banker can be a great source not only of loans, but of contacts with other financial institutions, venture capitalists, and advisors. This could become one of your most important friendships, so nurture it carefully.

## SKILLS MEAN SUCCESS

### MATH ▸ Measurement and Comparing Data: Graphs

1. Create a circle graph (pie chart) to show the assets of the top ten banks. Use the list below or conduct a Web search to find a more up-to-date ranking. Why might such a list change from year to year?

2. The number of banks in the U.S. decreased from 15,295 in 1935 to 9,905 in 2000. During the same period, deposits rose from $45.1M to $4,914.8M. Show these data as graphs. Give three reasons why the number of banks may have decreased.

| Rank | Name (city, state) | Consolidated assets (in millions) |
|------|--------------------|-----------------------------------|
| 1. | J. P. Morgan Chase & Company (New York, N.Y.) | $621,696 |
| 2. | Bank of America Corp. (Charlotte, N.C.) | 574,410 |
| 3. | Citigroup (New York, N.Y.) | 514,803 |
| 4. | Wachovia Corp. (Charlotte, N.C.) | 323,783 |
| 5. | Bank One Corp. (Chicago, Ill.) | 226,331 |
| 6. | Wells Fargo & Company (San Francisco, Calif.) | 196,755 |
| 7. | FleetBoston Financial Corp. (Providence, R.I.) | 192,100 |
| 8. | U.S. BC (Cincinnati, Ohio) | 177,979 |
| 9. | Suntrust Banks, Inc. (Atlanta, Ga.) | 118,315 |
| 10. | HSBC North America Inc. (Buffalo, N.Y.) | 85,936 |

*Source:* infoplease.com, World Almanac ■■■

## Reginald F. Lewis: Billion-Dollar Businessman

Reginald F. Lewis was born in Baltimore in 1942. When he died in 1993 at age 50, he was one of the nation's wealthiest entrepreneurs. Much of his fortune was created by his intelligent use of bank financing.

Showing his entrepreneurial drive early on, Lewis grew his first paper route from ten to a hundred subscribers. He acknowledged no racial boundaries as he worked his way through high school and Virginia State University. Lewis was determined to enter Harvard Law School, and he was accepted in 1965.

Being a successful lawyer might have satisfied most people, but Lewis was eager to move into the world of high finance. In 1983 he assembled financing from Wall Street investment banks to buy McCall Pattern for $22.5 million. To motivate McCall's management team, Lewis offered them equity in return for investment. This kept them in the company and highly motivated them to make it succeed. Together, in two years, they doubled the company's revenue. Lewis sold it in 1987 for $65 million. This provided a 90 to 1 return for investors. Next, Lewis bought Beatrice International for $985 million. This deal made him one of the most well-known financiers in the world.

At the time of his death, Lewis was worth $400 million, putting him on the *Forbes* magazine list of the 400 wealthiest Americans. You can read more about Lewis in *"Why Should White Guys Have All the Fun?": How Reginald Lewis Created a Billion-Dollar Business Empire* (John Wiley & Sons, 1995). ■

# Chapter 40 Review

## CRITICAL THINKING ABOUT...

### CREDIT

1. My personal credit history is (check one):

   Bad      _____

   Good      _____

   Not yet established      _____

   Describe how you plan to establish good credit.

### Business Plan Practice

2. Write a memo explaining why you would qualify for a $500 loan for your business. Describe the purpose of the loan and the "Four C's" as they would apply to you.

3. Give an example of a time that you borrowed money (or anything else). Did you handle the situation in a way that established good credit for yourself? Explain. What would you do differently now?

4. Jenny wants to buy the used car in excellent condition that her neighbor has for sale. However, she's $1,000 short of the $2,100 purchase price. Her bank is willing to lend her $1,000 at an annual interest rate of 15%, to be paid back over one year.

   **Calculate the credit price of the car:**

   *Cost of Buying the Car with Cash*
   Cash price of the car:   $_____

   *Cost of Buying the Car with Credit*
   Cash payment:      $_____
   Plus loan:      $_____
   Cost of credit:      $_____
   Cost of car with credit: $_____

5. Use a mortgage calculator to solve the problems below. When you enter the interest rate of the mortgage loan and the number of years it will take to pay it, the mortgage calculator will tell you how much your monthly mortgage payments would be.

| Home Price | Down Payment | Mortgage | Years | Interest Rate | Monthly Mortgage Payment |
|---|---|---|---|---|---|
| $120,000 | $12,000 | $108,000 | 30 | 5% | $ _____ |
| $300,000 | $30,000 | $ _____ | 30 | 4% | $ _____ |
| $75,000 | $7,500 | $ _____ | 20 | 3% | $ _____ |

## KEY CONCEPTS

1. Visit a local bank and ask for a personal loan application.

2. Fill out the application and bring it to class. Write a short essay analyzing whether you think the questions on the application are fair and fully capture a person's credit-worthiness.

3. Write a memo describing your plan for befriending a banker. Think about everything you've learned in this course — any business plans you've written, your commitments to philanthropy, your personal background, and anything else that would make you an interesting young businessperson that a banker might want to meet.

4. Introduce yourself to an officer at the bank you have chosen to do business with. Write a memo to your teacher describing how the meeting went and your plan for developing a relationship with this contact.

## REFERENCES

1 Special thanks to Loida Lewis for ideas used in this chapter.

## VOCABULARY

charge account ■ collateral ■ credit ■ finance charge ■ installment ■ layaway plan ■ mortgage

## Chapter Summary ✔✔✔

**40.1** Entrepreneurs need to understand credit and establish good credit ratings to be able to borrow money.

A. Credit is built by demonstrating financial integrity and responsibility.

B. Having no credit history is not an advantage.

C. Borrowing money and then repaying it when payments are due builds a favorable credit history that lenders value.

D. When considering loan applications, banks and other lenders use "The Four C's":

1. Collateral: what the would-be lender owns that the lender could take if the loan isn't repaid

2. Cash Flow: cash-flow statements that show if the borrower's business generates enough cash to repay the loan

3. Commitment: proof that the borrower and others have already invested in the business

4. Credit History: proof that a borrower can responsibly manage loans and their repayment.

**40.2**   Entrepreneurs should understand and manage credit wisely in their personal affairs and in their businesses.

A. Use charge accounts and layaway plans to make purchases at stores on credit.

1. Pay off the balance every month on every charge account by the due date to build credit history and avoid costly interest charges.

2. After making a down payment, pay the monthly installments on time for any layaway purchases.

B. Paying on credit costs more money than paying by cash.

1. Credit card purchases are really loans.

2. Like loans, credit purchase repayments include the principal (original amount borrowed or spent), but also include finance charges (interest on the principal).

C. Using credit cards has advantages and disadvantages:

1. Many include insurance purchaser protection against fraud and theft, and some offer discounts to small businesses

2. Interest rates on most credit cards are very high. Making only minimum payments can add to debt.

D. Credit agencies compile and maintain credit reports and credit histories of borrowers.

1. Consumers can ensure the accuracy of their own credit records by requesting credit checks on themselves, which agencies must provide.

2. Agency records are sometimes inaccurate, but can be corrected and erased or listed as disputed.

3. Consumers can submit their own reports to credit agencies.

E. Buying a home, even with a mortgage loan, builds equity, which:

1. Becomes collateral that strengthens a personal credit rating

2. Is usually a better investment than renting.

F. Most entrepreneurs need credit to help their businesses survive and grow:

1. Establish relationships with bank loan officers

2. Keep bankers informed about the business's progress

3. Use bankers to network and to meet new advisors and investors.

# A Business for the Young Entrepreneur
## LAVT, LAIMA A. TAZMIN

*Laima has always had a keen interest in computers. At age seven, she taught herself how to build Web sites from her older brother's book on HTML. She built one for the Girls Club, one on Barbie dolls, and others for family and friends.*

**W**ith the encouragement of her NFTE instructor and computer teacher, Laima created LAVT, a Web-site-design business for individuals, families, and entrepreneurs. "Most Web-site companies cater to established businesses and often sacrifice good design and aesthetics for the latest special effects," says Laima. "With my Web designs, I try to give site visitors a sense of the beautiful by combining natural and energetic colors with textures that engage the senses."

One satisfied LAVT customer, who maintains a Web site for selling used books, notes that Laima is "never short of inventiveness and does not let her creativity get in the way of providing customer satisfaction."

Laima plans to major in computer science and business at college as well as grow her company. In the meantime, she hopes to expand her business to offer online games and software. A favorite project would be to develop a life-mentoring, role-playing game for teens to learn how to deal with simulated situations that they face in real life. "I want to help teenagers develop positive mental attitudes about their communities and their lives," she says.

*Write a memo to Laima Tazmin, recommending a strategy for developing good banking relationships, so she can expand her business while in college.* ■

## SKILLS MEAN SUCCESS

**ENGLISH** ▶ **Reading for Understanding:** Finding Details

*Answer these questions about the Laima Tazmin profile:*

**a.** Like many biographical sketches, the article uses *chronological* order (from past to future) to organize the information. List two events from Laima's past, one current or recent, and one future.

**b.** What proof does the writer use to show that others think Laima is a successful entrepreneur?

**c.** How does the writer show that Laima cares about others and has goals beyond profit making?

**d.** What facts does the writer include to show that Laima was an intelligent child? ■■■

### CHAPTER 41

# CASH FLOW:
## *The Lifeblood of a Business*

*The secret to getting ahead is getting started.*

— Sally Berger

### KEY OBJECTIVES

**THIS CHAPTER WILL ENABLE YOU TO:**

- Keep track of your cash on a daily basis.
- Use a monthly cash flow statement.
- Avoid getting caught without enough cash to pay your bills.
- Understand the cyclical nature of cash flow.
- Calculate your burn rate.

## WORKING CAPITAL

Entrepreneurs use three basic financial statements:

1. Income statement
2. Balance sheet
3. Cash flow statement

You've already learned about the income statement and balance sheet. The income statement shows what is going on with sales. It tells you how much revenue is coming in, and how much that revenue is costing you in terms of cost of goods sold and fixed operating costs. The balance sheet is a snapshot of your business. It shows your assets and liabilities and net worth at a moment in time.

The **cash flow statement** records inflows and outflows of cash when they actually occur. If a sale is made in June, but the customer doesn't pay until August, the income statement will show the sale in June. The cash flow statement won't show the sale until August, when the cash "flows" into the business.

You cannot guide your business's daily operation using an income statement alone. You will also need a monthly cash flow statement to track the cash going in and out. Cash flow is the difference between the money you take in and the money you spend.

# SKILLS MEAN SUCCESS

**ENGLISH** ▶ **Writing for Information: Using Cause and Effect**

Writers sometimes combine sentences to show *cause and effect*. They want to show that two separate but complete thoughts are related because one *causes*, or *brings about*, the other. For example:

*A sale is made in June. The income statement will show the sale in June.*

can be combined to show cause and effect as:

*If a sale is made in June, the income statement will show the sale in June.*

The word *if* tells you that one complete thought is a condition (*cause*) of the other.

Combine these sentences using the word in parentheses. Make all changes needed.

**a.** Sometimes people don't pay the phone bill. The phone company will cut off service. (if)

**b.** Pay your bills by the due date, not before. You will have that cash a little longer in your own account. (since)

**c.** Hernando bought 200 T-shirts. He was taking a risk by tying up his cash in inventory. (because)

**d.** You aren't using a cash flow statement to keep track of your cash. You could get caught in a squeeze between your suppliers and your customers. (so) ■■■

# The Income Statement Does Not Show Cash on Hand

Once you start a business, however, you will notice that sometimes, even when the income statement says you are making a profit, you have no money! This can happen because there is often a time lag between making a sale and actually getting paid. If you sell something and the customer promises to pay you in a week, the sale is posted on the income statement, but you don't actually have the cash yet.

*Cash* is the energy that keeps your business flowing, just as electricity keeps the lights burning. Run out of electricity and your lights will go out. Run out of cash and your business will soon be finished. Without cash on hand, you may be unable to pay important bills, even while the income statement says you are earning a profit. This lag can be dangerous. If your phone gets cut off because you didn't pay the bill, it won't matter what the income statement says.

**471**

## Ways to Keep Cash Flowing

In order to avoid getting caught without enough cash to pay your bills:

1.  **Collect cash as soon as possible.** When you make a sale, try to get paid on the spot.

2.  **Pay your bills by the due date, not earlier.** You don't have to pay a bill the day it arrives in your mailbox. Look for the "due date." You will need to mail your payment so it arrives by that date. Never pay a bill after the due date without getting permission from the creditor first.

3.  **Check on your cash balance every day.** Always know how much cash you have on hand. In Chapter 12, you learned to use the NFTE Journal to keep track of the money your business earns and spends each day. One measure of your cash flow, therefore, is the cash balance in your Journal.

4.  **Lease instead of buying equipment where feasible.**

5.  **Avoid buying inventory that doesn't resell quickly.** Unless it's part of your competitive advantage to offer customers a wide selection, minimize the amount of inventory you stock. Inventory ties up cash — the cash you use to purchase inventory and the cash you spend storing it.

Use your Journal to keep track of the money your business earns and spends each day. Keep receipts for every purchase you make. Cash flow will equal the cash receipts less the cash disbursements for a business, over a period of time.

You can calculate your ongoing cash balance by subtracting cash disbursements from cash receipts. Your goal is never to have a negative cash balance.

## Cash Flow Is Cyclical

Cash flow is *cyclical* for many businesses. This means that the amount of cash flowing in may depend on the time of year.

A flower store will have a lot of cash coming in around Mother's Day and Valentine's Day, but may have very few sales in the fall. A college campus bookstore will have to spend a lot of cash before September to buy books to sell to students for the new semester. In contrast, it will have a lot of cash coming in during the following month or two as students buy books for their courses.

The phone company or the bank will not care how much cash you will have coming in over the next three months — they will want their regular monthly payments. When you write your business plan, describe your expectations for cyclical changes in your cash flow.

# Reading a Cash Flow Statement[1]

Below, is a simple cash flow statement for Hernando's T-Shirts, the business from Chapter 12.

The first section of the statement records all sources of income. These are cash inflows, or *receipts*. (Here, the word receipt does not mean the same thing as the slip of paper you get when you buy something — those receipts are proof of purchase.)

| NFTE CASH FLOW STATEMENT | | |
|---|---|---|
| **Hernando's T-Shirts** | **Date:** October, 2007 | |
| **Beginning Cash Balance:** | | $0.00 |
| **Cash Inflow** | | |
| Investment: | $1,000.00 | |
| Sales: | 2,568.00 | |
| **Total Cash Inflow:** | **$3,568.00** | **3,568.00** |
| **Cash Outflow** | | |
| Inventory: | $1,390.00 | |
| Variable Costs: | 288.00 | |
| Fixed Costs: | 140.00 | |
| Equipment: | 200.00 | |
| Other Outflows: | 0.00 | |
| **Total Cash Outflow:** | **$2,018.00** | (2,018.00)* |
| **Net Cash Flow:** | | 1,550.00 |
| **Ending Cash Balance:** | | $1,550.00 |

\* Note that parentheses and red means negative.

The NFTE Journal is a cash only system. Therefore the FC Column will not include depreciation, which is not a cash transaction.

The next section reports cash outflows or disbursements that must be made that month — the phone bill, cost of goods sold, salaries, etc.

The last section shows the net change in cash flow. This tells the entrepreneur whether the business had a positive or negative cash flow that month. You can have a lot of sales and still go out of business if you don't have enough cash coming in to cover your monthly cash outflows.

**The Cash Flow Equation: Cash Flow = Cash Receipts − Cash Disbursements**

## SKILLS MEAN SUCCESS

**LEADERSHIP**

**Recognizing Why Math Is Important:**
Solving Real-World Problems

Review the chapter. Use a chart such as the following to identify cash-flow topics and processes that require math skills and identify those skills.

| Topic | Math Skill |
|---|---|
| Project cash receipts based on history | Read numbers, perform operations, identify patterns, estimate |
|  |  |
|  |  |

## Forecasting Cash Flow

A **projection** is an educated guess, or forecast, of the future. As you get your business off the ground, you will need to prepare monthly cash flow projections to make sure there is enough money coming in to pay your bills. There are two steps to forecasting cash-flow receipts:

1.  Project your cash receipts from all possible sources. Remember, orders are not cash receipts because you cannot guarantee when or if an order will become cash. Some orders may be cancelled, and some customers might not pay. Cash receipts are checks that you know will clear, or credit card orders that have been phoned in, or cash itself.

2.  Subtract cash expenses you expect to have from these projected cash receipts. Cash expenses are only those expenses you will actually have to pay during the projected time period.

How can you be sure that these projections will be accurate? You can't, but create them anyway. Review and update them daily.

## Risking Your Cash on Inventory

The entrepreneur takes a risk every time he or she spends cash. If you buy inventory, you are taking the risk that no one will buy it at a price that will give you a profit. When Hernando bought T-shirts, he was taking a risk by tying up his cash in inventory.

There are two other risks with inventory: storage costs and **shrinkage**. Shrinkage is the unexplained disappearance of inventory due to loss or theft. **Pilferage**, which is the stealing of inventory by employees or customers, is an example of shrinkage. Barney's, the famous New York clothing store, had a 7% pilferage rate. This was one of the reasons the store went bankrupt.

If you have to pay rent to store your inventory somewhere, you will have to make sure you can sell it at a price high enough to cover the storage costs.

## SKILLS MEAN SUCCESS

**MATH**

**Mathematical Reasoning:**
**Reading Tables, Identifying Patterns, Problem Solving**

The Spirit Club at the high school sells T-shirts imprinted with the school logo in the school store. They order their inventory from a wholesaler and sell to parents, teachers, and students. Their sales for the past three years, by month, are as follows.

**Total Sales by Month (in $) for the Past Three Years**

|  | J | F | M | A | M | J | J | A | S | O | N | D |
|---|---|---|---|---|---|---|---|---|---|---|---|---|
| **Year 1** | 100 | 95 | 50 | 30 | 20 | 10 | 0 | 35 | 150 | 100 | 15 | 135 |
| **Year 2** | 115 | 80 | 55 | 25 | 25 | 5 | 0 | 25 | 125 | 110 | 25 | 155 |
| **Year 3** | 125 | 100 | 40 | 30 | 15 | 15 | 0 | 40 | 180 | 105 | 20 | 140 |

1. Which month in which year has the highest monthly sales?

2. What have been, on average, the top three months every year for sales over the past three years?

3. Which month, on average, has the second-lowest sales volume every year over the past three years? Why might that month be the lowest?

4. Explain why sales might be highest in each of the three best months every year.

5. In which three months would you expect the Spirit Club to have the lowest inventory?

6. If you were in charge of ordering new inventory, in which two months might you want it to be checked, your needs forecast, and major new inventory ordered — if it takes two months to place and take delivery? ■■■

## Credit Squeeze

Credit is the ability to buy something without spending actual cash at the time of purchase. Once you have established a good relationship with a supplier, he or she may be willing to let you buy on credit. If you own a store, you might be able to buy Christmas ornaments from your supplier in October with a promise to pay for them in 60 days, after your Christmas sales.

If you aren't using a cash flow statement to keep track of your cash, however, you could get caught in a squeeze between your suppliers and your customers. If the suppliers want you to pay for inventory you have purchased, and you are short on cash because your customers haven't paid you yet, you could get into trouble with your suppliers. They might not want to extend credit to you in the future. If you get into a position where you can't pay your suppliers at all, you could be forced to sell the business.

## The "Burn Rate"

You are likely to spend more than you earn in the beginning stages of your business. That's why you will want to have a good enough business plan so that investors will include money to pay the first few month's bills. We strongly recommend you begin your business with a cash reserve that will cover your operating costs for at least three to six months.

Typically, a new company will spend more money that it earns while it gets off the ground. The question for the entrepreneur is: How long can you afford to lose cash?

The answer will depend on two things:

1. The amount of cash invested as capital in the business.

2. The amount of cash you are generating. Together:

**Beginning Cash + Cash Surplus (or − Cash Deficit) = Ending Cash Balance**

The rate at which your company needs to spend cash to cover overhead costs before you begin to generate a positive cash flow is called the **burn rate**. This is typically expressed in terms of cash spent per month. A burn rate of $10,000 per month means that the company is spending $10,000 each month to cover rent and other operating expenses. If the company has, say, $20,000 in cash and a burn rate of $2,000 a month, how long could it hold out?

$$\frac{\text{Cash on Hand}}{\text{Negative Cash Outflow per Month}} = \text{Number of Months before Cash Runs Out}$$

$$\frac{20,000}{2,000} = 10 \text{ months}$$

## How Much Cash Does the Company Have to Grow?

Once a business is operational, entrepreneurs keep an eye on *working capital*, which is, simply, current assets minus current liabilities.

**Current Assets − Current Liabilities = Working Capital**

Working capital tells you how much cash the company would have if it paid all its short-term debt with the cash it has on hand. What's left over is the cash the company can use to build the business, fund growth, and produce value for the shareholders.

All other things being equal, a company with positive working capital will always outperform a company with negative working capital. A company with negative working capital can't spend as aggressively to bring a product to market. In addition, if a company runs out of working capital and still has bills to pay and products to develop, it may not be able to stay in business.

## CRITICAL THINKING ABOUT...

### CASH FLOW

1. Explain why it would be dangerous to use only a monthly income statement to operate your business. In the explanation, give an example from your own business or one you would like to start.

2. Describe what you think the cash cycle will be for one year for a business you would like to start. Explain how you think the cash flow will be affected during the course of the year.

3. What are three rules for managing your cash?

4. Imagine and describe a situation where a cash flow crunch could develop and force bankruptcy.

## KEY CONCEPTS

1. What are the three risks an entrepreneur takes when buying inventory?

2. What are the two steps to projecting cash flow?

3. Create a six-month projected cash flow statement for your business, or one you would like to create. **Business Plan Practice**

4. Calculate working capital for Angelina's company. (See Chapter 35, page 423.) Describe how her level of working capital might affect her business decisions.

## REFERENCES

1 Remember to add back Depreciation, as it is a non-cash expense.

## VOCABULARY

burn rate ■ cash flow statement ■ pilferage ■ projection ■ shrinkage

# Project Summary ✔✔✔

**41.1**  Keep cash flowing and use Cash Flow Statements to track inflows and outflows of cash — so there will always be enough for expenses.

A. Collect cash as soon as possible.

B. Pay bills by the due date, not before.

C. Check cash balance daily.

D. Lease instead of buying when feasible.

E. Keep inventory as low as needed to run the business.

F. Keep all receipts (proofs of sale or purchase).

G. Cash Receipts − Cash Disbursements = Cash Flow.

H. Understand the annual cycles of cash flow in a business.

I. Learn to use and read Cash Flow Statements:

    *1.* Cash inflows or "receipts"

    *2.* Cash outflows or disbursements

    *3.* Net change in cash flow: positive or negative

    *4.* The Cash Flow Equation:

        Cash Flow = Cash Receipts − Cash Disbursements.

**41.2**  Cash flow projections help a business to have enough cash to pay monthly expenses.

A. Project cash receipts from all sources by month.

B. Subtract expenses due to be paid during each month.

C. Include in expenses amounts bought on credit that will have payments due.

D. Know the "burn rate" to determine how long cash reserves will last — i.e., how long the business can afford to lose cash.

    *1.* Beginning Cash + Cash Surplus (or − Cash Deficit)
        = Ending Cash Balance

    *2.* $\dfrac{\text{Cash on Hand}}{\text{Negative Cash Outflow per Month}}$ = Number of Months before Cash Runs Out

E. Working Capital equals amount of cash a business would have left over if it paid all its short-term debt.

F. Current Assets − Current Liabilities = Working Capital.

G. Positive working capital is a sign of a profitable company and can be used to:

    *1.* Build and grow the business

    *2.* Produce value for owners and shareholders

    *3.* Protect future cash flows

    *4.* Make the company more attractive to potential investors. ✔✔✔

### CHAPTER 42

# PROTECTING INTELLECTUAL PROPERTY:
## *Your Ideas Have Value*

*The Patent System added
the fuel of interest to the fire of genius.*

— Abraham Lincoln, *16th President of the
United States*

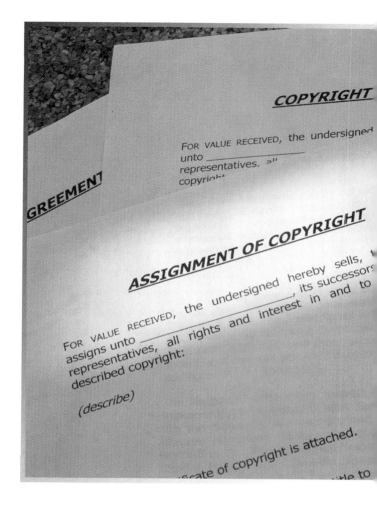

### KEY OBJECTIVES

THIS CHAPTER WILL ENABLE YOU TO:

- Recognize that your ideas and their expression can have value for your business.
- Create and protect your intellectual property.
- Apply for patents, copyright, and trademarks.
- Legally obtain and use intellectual property owned by others.

Every great business started as an idea or collection of ideas — a new kind of product or service; a new way of making or using products or services; a new way of advertising, delivering, or selling products or services; or even a new way of finding and retaining customers or employees.

## Turning Ideas into Intellectual Property

You should explore ways of creating property rights from your ideas. This will allow you to stop others from copying or using your ideas in a competing business without your permission. Once you create such property rights, you will be able to use them to create a competitive advantage in your market, or you can license and sell your **intellectual property**.

# The Four Kinds of Intellectual Property

1.  **Patents**, which protect inventions.

    Let's say your business involves creating and selling a new kind of electronic pen that improves handwriting. Your design for this pen might be an invention that you could protect with a patent.

2.  **Copyrights**, which protect the original expression of ideas fixed in a *tangible* form (something that exists physically, such as a recording, a painting, a photograph, or writing).

    If your business is to write and sell newsletters — both printed and electronic — your work in both forms would be protected by copyright.

3.  **Trademarks**, which protect words, names, symbols, or designs (or combinations of them) that are used to identify the source of a product. The Nike "swoosh" is an example of a trademark. **Service marks** are the equivalent designation to identify the source of a service. The AOL triangle is an example of a service mark.

    *Example:* You develop a line of clothing with your own design label, "Creativa." You could protect "Creativa" as a trademark. If you offer design services using this mark, you could protect "Creativa" as a service mark as well.

4.  **Trade secrets**, which are methods, formulas, or other kinds of information that have commercial value in your business and derive that value from being kept secret.

    *Example:* The formula for making Coca-Cola is a trade secret.

    To protect a trade secret, you must take reasonable steps to maintain the *confidential* nature of the information. Steps for protecting a trade secret include requiring people to sign "confidentiality agreements" that require the signers to keep the secret, and restricting the number of people who have access to the information.

# Three Kinds of Patents

There are three kinds of patents in the United States: *utility, design,* and *plant* patents. Utility patents are the most common.

A *utility patent* may be granted to anyone who invents or discovers any "new and useful process, machine, article of manufacture, or composition of matter, or any new useful improvement thereof." A utility patent generally has a term of 20 years from the date of filing the patent application.

An invention must satisfy certain conditions in order to qualify for a patent. It must be:

- *Useful,* meaning that it has an identifiable use and that it is possible to make or use it for this purpose.

- *New,* meaning that the invention has not already been discovered or invented.

- *Non-obvious,* meaning that your invention would not be obvious to somebody who has ordinary skill in the industry or area of science or technology in which your invention falls.

If you invent a video game that involves taking an existing one and adding new features that are common to similar types of video games, then your invention will probably not qualify for a patent.

A *design patent* may be granted to anyone who invents a "new, original, and ornamental design for an article of manufacture." A design patent protects the way an article *looks,* whereas a utility patent protects the way an article *works* (is used). A design patent is granted for 14 years from the date of the grant of the patent.

*Example:* You design a special ornamental structure for a lamp. This structure is unique because of its design but does not have a function. The design may qualify for a design patent.

A *plant patent* may be granted to anyone who invents or discovers and asexually reproduces any distinct and new variety of plant. A plant patent lasts for 20 years from the date of filing the application.

*Example:* You create a new multi-colored rose.

## Applying for a Patent

A patent application must include the following:

1. An in-depth description of the invention.

2. A drawing of the invention (if appropriate).

3. A completed "Declaration for Patent Application."

4. A notarized statement from the inventor(s) to the effect that he or she is (or they are) the original inventor(s) of the subject of the application.

5. The filing fee (see U.S. Patent and Trademark Office Web site for fees).

Once you have submitted the patent application, it will be examined to determine whether it meets all of the requirements.

Different countries have their own patent offices and their own rules. You will need to obtain foreign patents if you want patent protection overseas.

In the United States, the first person to invent something is entitled to the patent, but in some other parts of the world the first person *to file the patent application* is entitled to the patent — even if he or she was not the first inventor.

**BizTip:** Before deciding whether to apply for a patent:
(1) consider whether your invention is unique;
(2) determine whether obtaining a patent would help your business to make money; and
(3) consider the alternative ways in which you might be able to protect your idea at lower cost and/or greater benefit (e.g., keeping it a trade secret).

## SKILLS MEAN SUCCESS

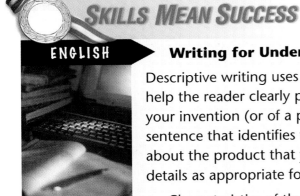

**ENGLISH**

### Writing for Understanding

Descriptive writing uses concrete details and appeals to the senses to help the reader clearly picture what is described. Write a description of your invention (or of a product you use regularly). Start with a topic sentence that identifies what is being described. Then, list every detail about the product that you can see or remember. Include the following details as appropriate for your product:

- Characteristics of the product, such as size, color, shape, material.
- Purpose of the product and how it works.
- Measurements, such as length, width, weight, speed, temperature.
- Analogies (what the product looks like, acts like, or is similar to).
- Location and positioning of parts.
- Sounds it makes; what it tastes like, smells like, etc. ■■■■

## Copyright Protects Art, Music, Plays, Books, Software

*Copyright* protects the original expression of ideas when fixed in a tangible form.  It provides the creators of "original works of authorship" — including books, music, plays and computer software programs — with the exclusive right to do (and authorize other people to do) the following:

1. To *reproduce* the work in copies or by recording.

2. To prepare *derivative* works (works that are based on and incorporate parts of the original).

    *Example:* A translation of a book into a foreign language is a derivative work. A modification of a song by adding a different beat is a derivative work.

3. To *distribute* copies or recordings of the work to the public.

4. To *perform* or *display* the work publicly, in the case of movies, music, sound recordings, and audiovisual materials.

If you purchase a copy of a novel, you own it and can resell that copy to a second-hand bookstore. However, you may not make copies of the novel, and sell them, without permission from the copyright owner.

Authors of works of visual arts (such as sculpture) have additional rights to protect their work, such as the right to have their name associated with the work and to prevent certain modifications of it.

A copyright has a term that lasts from the date it was created to the end of the author's life plus an additional 70 years (or, for anonymous works, 95 years from publication or 120 years from creation, whichever is shorter).

## How to Obtain Copyright Protection

The author of a new work owns the copyright to it as soon as the work is fixed in a tangible form (e.g., recorded, put in writing, or *captured* — as a photograph). If a work is created by two or more people, they will be co-owners.

In the case of a "work made for hire," the employer owns the work that is created by the employee within the scope of his or her employment. Certain kinds of projects that are created by a consultant may also be works for hire that are owned by the employer, including contributions to a book or movie or a translation.  In many cases, however, a consultant will own the copyright to what he or she creates, unless it is stipulated otherwise in writing.

 **BizTip:  If you ask somebody to create designs or other artistic works for your business, make sure you have a written agreement that your business will own the copyright.**

# Registering Copyright in the United States

You don't need to register your work in order to acquire a copyright. You may, however, get some additional benefits if you do. To file, request forms from the U.S. Copyright Office. The forms are easy to fill out. To secure the copyright, send a completed form and two examples of the work with a registration fee. (The detailed requirements can be found on the U.S. Copyright Office Web site.)

Different countries have different rules concerning copyright ownership. A number of countries provide *national treatment* for foreign works, which means that the foreign copyright holder is treated similarly to a national copyright holder.

You can *assign* (transfer) some or all of your rights to a work to another person. You can also *license* some or all of your rights. You could, for example, give someone the exclusive right to make and distribute copies of a translation but keep the exclusive right to make and distribute copies of the work in the original language.

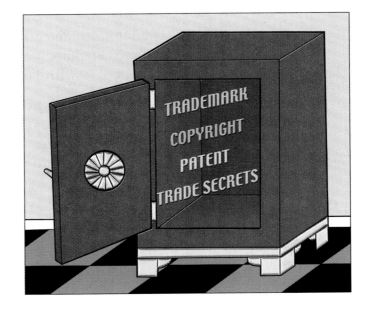

# Electronic Rights and the Digital Millennium Copyright Act

Intellectual property rights apply to the contents of Web sites and the materials and information that can be obtained on the Internet. Entrepreneurs must also protect their intellectual property online. The rights to reproduce someone's work online are called **electronic rights**.

The Digital Millennium Copyright Act (DMCA) was enacted in 1998 to update the U.S. copyright laws for the digital age. The DMCA focuses mainly on technologies that are used to prevent illegal copying and distribution of software and digital recordings. It includes the following:

1. It is a crime to circumvent anti-piracy measures that are built into commercial software.

2. It is a crime to manufacture, sell, or distribute code-cracking devices that illegally copy software (with some limited exceptions for specific purposes, such as testing security in computer systems).

3.  Internet service providers that transmit information over the Internet must remove material from users' Web sites if it appears to be infringing copyright.

4.  Webcasters must pay licensing fees to record companies.

## Trademark Rights

You obtain rights to a trademark by using it in connection with products or services in the marketplace.  You can secure additional protection by obtaining a trademark or service mark registration from the U.S. Patent and Trademark Office.

Once you have registered your trademark, you can put an ® next to your product name. If you are claiming a trademark but have not yet registered it, you can use ™. To indicate a service mark, use ˢᴹ with your service name.

Trademark rights may be used to prevent others from using a similar mark, but not from making or selling the same products or services. The test for determining if there is a violation, or **infringement**, of your rights is whether a trademark is being used that is confusingly similar to yours.

## Applying for a Trademark

A trademark application must include the following:

1.  A completed application form.

2.  A drawing of the trademark.

3.  Three specimens showing the actual use of the mark on or in connection with your product or service.  You can also file an "intent to use" application if you plan to use a mark but have not yet started.

4.  A filing fee (see www.uspto.gov for the current filing fees).

You can also apply online at: www.uspto.gov.

Before you apply for a trademark or service mark you will need to determine whether someone else has obtained rights for the same or a similar mark.  You can do your own searching using the Internet and the database on the U.S. Patent and Trademark Office site, or hire a company that offers search services.

**BizTip:** Trademark and service mark registrations can be continuously renewed provided that you keep using the marks. If you stop, you could lose your rights.

## Using Someone's Intellectual Property

If you want to use other people's intellectual property in your business, you must generally obtain permission.

If you use intellectual property without obtaining permission, you could be infringing on someone's rights.

You may:

   **a.** ask for permission to use the intellectual property for a limited purpose;

   **b.** ask for a license to use the intellectual property;

   **c.** offer to buy the intellectual property; or

   **d.** pay someone to create intellectual property for you as a work for hire.

## What Is "Public Domain"?

The **public domain** consists of ideas and their expression that are not protected as intellectual property.  When copyrights and patents expire, the inventions and creative works they protected become public domain and are thereafter available for anyone to use.

### SKILLS MEAN SUCCESS

**TECHNOLOGY** ▶ **Using a Spell-Checker**

Word processing programs contain spelling and grammar checkers that can search your documents for errors. *But they won't guarantee that your document is free of mistakes.*

**1.** Run a spelling check on a paper that you have recently written and word-processed. Make a list of the types of errors the program corrected and the types of errors it did not catch.

**2.** What are the pros and cons of relying on spelling and grammar checkers to edit your work? ■ ■ ■

## What Is Fair Use?

The *fair use* of a copyrighted work, including for purposes such as review, comment, news reporting, teaching, scholarship, or research, is not an infringement of copyright.

You do not need to obtain the consent of a copyright owner in order to make "fair use" of the work. Similarly, others can make fair use of your work.

The Copyright Act does not define fair use. Instead, it is determined by balancing these factors:

1. The purpose and character of the use.

2. The nature of the copyrighted work.

3. The amount and substantiality of the portion used in relation to the work as a whole.

4. The effect of the use on the potential market for, or value of, the copyrighted work.

Be sure to respect the intellectual property of others. Some rules of thumb to avoid infringing on someone's intellectual property in your business include:

1. Don't sell counterfeit knockoffs of popular brands.

2. Don't take things from the Web without permission and/or payment.

3. Always know the source of the products you are buying to avoid the risk of dealing in stolen goods.

## SKILLS MEAN SUCCESS

**ENGLISH** ▶ **Understanding Vocabulary**

Match the terms to the phrases that best describe them.

1. copyright    **a.** identifies and distinguishes the source of a product

2. patent    **b.** identifies and distinguishes the source of a service

3. trademark    **c.** protects an original artistic or literary work

4. service mark    **d.** protects an original invention

5. Identify an example of a copyright notice, a patent notice, a trademark, and a service mark. Be prepared to share your findings with the class. ■■■

# Chapter 42 Review

## CRITICAL THINKING ABOUT...

### INTELLECTUAL PROPERTY

1. Describe the intellectual property you are developing for your business. **Business Plan Practice**

2. How do you plan to protect your intellectual property? Explain why it qualifies for protection. **Business Plan Practice**

3. Find an invention or artwork that is currently in the public domain. *(Hint: You may want to do some research on the Internet.)*

4. Write a business letter to the United States Patent and Trademark Office or the United States Copyright Office requesting information on how to file for a patent, trademark, or copyright. Or, if you have access to a computer, visit www.uspto.gov or www.copyright.gov and print out the information.

5. Copyright-infringement lawsuits have been brought against some rap artists who "sample" other people's music. Research the current policy of the U.S. Copyright Office regarding sampling and report your findings to the class.

6. Write a confidentiality agreement that you could have employees sign to protect any trade secrets that are important to your business.

## KEY CONCEPTS

1. If you invent a new software program, how should you protect it?

2. What protection should you try to obtain if you invent a new mechanical device?

3. Design a trademark or service mark for your business. How will you protect it?

4. What kinds of intellectual property are likely to be most important for you in your business?

5. What kinds of intellectual property owned by others would you be most likely to use?

6. What rights are being violated by downloading an artist's music without paying for it?

## VOCABULARY

copyright ■ electronic rights ■ infringement ■ intellectual property ■ patent ■ public domain ■ service mark ■ trademark ■ trade secret

## Chapter Summary ✔✔✔

42.1 Ideas and their expression add value to a business.
   A. Intellectual property rights can stop others from copying or using a business's:
      1. Ideas
      2. Expression of ideas.

**42.2** Entrepreneurs can create and protect their intellectual property.
    *A.* Patents protect inventions.
    *B.* Copyrights protect original works (original expressions of ideas fixed in a tangible [physical] form, such as recordings, paintings, books).
    *C.* Trademarks and service marks protect names, symbols, or designs that identify a product's or service's original source.
    *D.* Trade secrets protect methods, formulas, and valuable commercial information:
        *1.* The company needs to keep trade secrets confidential
        *2.* Signed confidentiality agreements require employees and business partners to keep trade secrets private.

**42.3** Patents, copyrights, and trade secrets protect intellectual property.
    *A.* Three kinds of patents protect inventions in the U.S.:
        *1.* Utility patents protect new, non-obvious processes, new types of machines, new manufactured articles or "forms of matter" (or useful improvements to them) for 20 years
        *2.* Design patents protect new, original, and ornamental designs for manufactured products for 14 years (e.g., new lamp design)
        *3.* Plant patents protect the invention or reproduction of any distinct new type of plant (e.g., a new type of rose)
        *4.* Patent applications can be submitted to the U.S. Patent and Trademark Office.
    *B.* Copyrights and electronic rights protect the rights of authors, software developers, recording artists, movie producers, to:
        *1.* Reproduce the work, prepare derivative works, sell copies of the work, or perform or display the work in public or online
        *2.* Register with the U.S. Copyright Office.
    *C.* Using (and then registering) trademarks and service marks protect names, descriptions, and symbols that identify products and services:
        *1.* The U.S. Patent and Trademark Office prevents use by others that confuse consumers
        *2.* Applicants must prove first use.

**42.4** Entrepreneurs may use someone else's intellectual property:
    *A.* By obtaining the owner's permission or license to use it
    *B.* By purchasing or contracting a "work for hire"
    *C.* Under "fair use." ✔✔✔

# A Business for the Young Entrepreneur

## HANDMADE CRAFTS

Do you like to sew or work with wood? If making things comes easy to you, consider making a simple product to sell. People enjoy buying handmade items. Products you could make include:

- decorative pillows
- bird cages
- stuffed animals
- puppets
- jewelry
- candles

Think of something you will enjoy making that people in your market will want to buy.

A great place to sell handmade crafts is at a local trade fair (see Chapter 16). You can get a list of these from the chamber of commerce in your area. Find out how to rent a booth or table. Bring:

- Colorful flyers
- Business cards to hand out to customers and potential customers
- A receipt book; give each customer a receipt
- Lots of change

Describe something you know how to make. Would it qualify for a patent? Why or why not? If yes, for which type of patent might it qualify? ■

## CHAPTER 43

# ETHICAL BUSINESS BEHAVIOR

*All businesses were launched by entrepreneurs, and all were once small.*

— Nat Shulman, *family business owner and columnist*

### KEY OBJECTIVES

THIS CHAPTER WILL ENABLE YOU TO:

- Explain the difference between illegal and unethical behavior.
- Develop repeat business.
- Motivate your employees.
- Practice ethical business behavior.

**Ethics** are standards and rules that help one determine right from wrong. The Golden Rule, "Do unto others as you would have others do unto you," is a well-known ethic. The Golden Rule can help you "do the right thing" in many situations.

A behavior may be legal and still not be ethical. For example, it is not illegal to be rude to your customers and employees, but it is unethical (and not very smart).

Ethical business behavior is not only moral, it makes good sense. Have you ever bought something from a store and felt you were cheated? How did you react? Did you ever go back to that store again? Probably not. You may have even told your friends about the experience. The store lost more than just the one customer.

## Success Is Based on Repeat Business

Business success is not built on drawing in a customer just once and making a sale. Success is based on building a satisfied group of customers who not only buy your product or service again, but also recommend it to their friends and relatives. That is called **repeat business**.

If a customer is angered or feels cheated by a business, he or she may report it to the **Better Business Bureau**. This is a nonprofit organization that publishes reports about the reliability, honesty, and performance of businesses. It bases much of its reporting on complaints submitted by customers. Think about that when you are tempted to ignore a customer's request or to lose your temper. Even if you believe you are right, your reaction could damage your company's reputation.

## Ethical Employer/Employee Relationships

It is important to treat your employees well, too. Aside from the fact that it is morally right to treat people ethically, it is in your best interest to do so. As the entrepreneur, your values will set the ethical tone for your company. If you think it is okay to be rude or cheat a customer, your employees will not only copy your behavior, they will probably try to cheat *you*.

Employees who feel used by their employers will not do their best work. The most successful companies are those in which the employees' interests correspond with what is best for the company.

Many large businesses offer their employees company stock at a discount, or give out generous bonuses at the end of the year, based on how well the company has done. In this way, the employees know that they will profit from the business's success. They will be motivated to care about the company for which they work.

 **BizTip: Treat your employees as you would want to be treated.**

## Ethical Business Behavior

A successful business is like a well-built house. Good ethics represent a solid foundation. Good behavior creates the floor — where everything takes place. To build a strong, successful business, lay the following behavior over an ethical foundation.

1.  **Punctuality.** Be on time for business appointments. If you are late for meetings, you will lose customers and clients — and perhaps eventually even your business. If, for reasons beyond your control, you are late or miss an appointment, apologize immediately and graciously.

2.  **Reliability.** Just as your customers must be able to count on you to arrive on time, they will need to count on your product or service to perform properly. A successful business is built on customers who keep coming back because the product or service is reliable.

3. **Courtesy.** If you are not courteous and polite, you will turn off customers and business contacts. Advice and support from other businesspeople are extremely important to the new business owner, but you will not get them if you are rude.

4. **Respect.** Show respect for your customers and other businesspeople by being punctual, reliable, and courteous.

5. **Communication.** Show respect for others and for yourself by how you speak — and by how you listen. The best entrepreneurs are good listeners. Don't use slang or obscenities.

6. **Clothing.** From the moment they meet you, customers are deciding whether or not they should trust you with their money. Before your product or service can prove itself, you are already being judged by what you are wearing. Choose clothes that project the image you want customers to associate with your business.

7. **Neatness.** Make sure you always look clean and neat. Customers are quick to judge people by appearance. Accept this as part of doing business.

8. **Honesty.** Always tell the truth. You will develop a solid reputation that will draw customers to you.

9. **Empathy.** Get in the habit of putting yourself in other people's shoes. This will help you in both selling and negotiating.

**10. Competence.**  Be efficient and capable in all your dealings with customers and employees.

Without good business behavior, you will alienate customers and employees and your business will suffer. In addition, other entrepreneurs and businesspeople will not share information with someone who is perceived as doing "bad business." This will cut you off from valuable networking.

If you feel you are lacking any of these business principles, don't try to develop them all at once. Choose one and work at it. Changing one's habits takes time — that is why they are called habits. One theory is that you must practice a new habit for about 90 days before it becomes something you will do naturally.

## SKILLS MEAN SUCCESS

**ENGLISH** ▶  **Observing Rules and Conventions of Grammar**

Poor grammar isn't necessarily an ethical issue but, in business writing, it can give the appearance of carelessness and lack of overall knowledge. The following sentences contain some of the most common grammatical errors found in business writing today. Identify the errors and rewrite the sentences correctly.

**1.** Thank you for taking the time to meet with Fred and I.

**2.** A manager should try to help their employees succeed.

**3.** Its a shame the store lost it's best sales associate.

**4.** All our employee's records are kept in the Human Resources department.

**5.** Who should I promote to store manager? ■ ■ ■

## Ethics and Corporate Governance

Business ethics made headlines in 2002, when several huge corporations were found to have published inaccurate financial statements. These false numbers made the companies look so good that they were some of the most highly recommended stock picks on Wall Street.

Top executives at Enron, WorldCom-MCI, and other firms, had inflated their companies' earnings so they could pocket enormous bonuses while misleading shareholders. When the truth came out, public confidence in the stock market dropped, along with stock prices. Investors lost millions.

One of the companies, the energy giant, Enron, had strongly encouraged its own employees to invest their retirement savings in Enron stock — even while top company executives knew the worth of the stock was based on false numbers. These employees had their life savings destroyed by the unethical behavior of these executives.

Enron collapsed, and thousands of employees lost their jobs and saw their pension funds reduced to nothing.

## SKILLS MEAN SUCCESS

**LEADERSHIP** ▶ **Connecting to Real-World Examples**

Make a list of what you consider to be the ten most important reading skills and uses of reading for an entrepreneur or business manager. Consider how reading skills could hinder unethical behavior. Prepare a slide or handout to present to the class.

These scandals were a failure of **corporate governance**, meaning that companies did not have safeguards in place to prevent executives from lying and stealing. Even at this early stage in developing your business, you must think about how you will guarantee that your business remains both ethical and legal as it grows.

1.  **Keep business profits separate from your personal spending.** Disbursing company profits is a *business* decision and should not be casually treated as personal income. Instead, decide on a regular wage or stipend you will pay yourself. Always document this payment, as well as your expenses related to company business.

2.  **Keep accurate records.** As your business grows, have your "books" checked once a year by a reputable accountant. By the time your company grows into a multi-million-dollar corporation, you will have established a reputation for honest financial reporting.

3.  **Use financial controls.** Once you have employees, use simple controls, such as:

    - Always have two people open the mail, so no one can steal checks.
    - Arrange for yourself and one other person to sign all checks sent out by the business. Using a "double signature" will assure that no one person can use company funds for personal expenses.

**4.    Create an advisory board.** Ask businesspeople you respect and other community leaders to be on your *advisory board* — a group of people who will give you advice. Choose people with strong ethics, and listen to them.

## SKILLS MEAN SUCCESS

**MATH**    **Understanding Length and Area**

Pretend that you own a carpet installation company. You find out that on your last job one of your employees figured the square footage of the rooms improperly and you mistakenly overcharged the customer.

Your rate for carpet installation per square foot is sixty-five cents. The three rooms you carpeted were 8' x 8', 12'6" x 10', and 16' x 9'.

**1.** What is the square footage of each room?

**2.** How many square feet in total did you carpet?

**3.** How much should you have charged the customer?

**4.** If your employee figured a total of 372 square feet, how much money would you refund your customer? ■■■

# Chapter 43 Review

## CRITICAL THINKING ABOUT...

### ETHICAL BEHAVIOR

1. Write a paragraph about a time when someone was late, unreliable, or rude to you. How did being treated like that make you feel?

2. Write an essay describing how you would handle the following situations if you were an employer:

   **a.** An employee repeatedly hands in sloppy paperwork.

   **b.** After the introduction of a new office computer system, one employee seems to be avoiding his work because he's unsure of how to use the new equipment.

3. It's important in business to know how to apologize if you offend a client, supplier, or business contact. Write a letter apologizing for something you did or said that you regret. Offer to do something to make amends for your behavior.

4. Think of a behavior that is legal but that you consider unethical. Write a paragraph explaining why you feel it is wrong.

5. Describe the corporate governance plan for your company. It should include five policies (rules) that will be the backbone of your company's ethics.
   **Business Plan Practice**

6. List your planned board of advisors. Describe each potential member. **Business Plan Practice**

## KEY CONCEPTS

1. Choose a corporation that has been involved in an ethical scandal and research that company online. Tell the story of the scandal in a presentation to the class. Describe the lessons you have learned as an entrepreneur from researching this event.

2. Visit the Better Business Bureau at www.bbb.org and research a company you plan to use as a supplier for your business. Write a memo describing why you think this supplier is reputable or not reputable.

3. Review the list of business behaviors in the chapter and write a memo describing your strengths and weaknesses in this area, and how you intend to improve.

## VOCABULARY

Better Business Bureau ■ corporate governance ■ ethics ■ repeat business

# Chapter Summary ✔✔✔

**43.1** Ethical business behavior is not always the same as legal behavior.
    *A.* Ethical standards are used to determine right from wrong (vs. legal from illegal).
    *B.* Doing "the fair and right thing," not just doing what is not illegal:
        *1.* Creates repeat business from customers
        *2.* Earns employee and vendor loyalty.
    *C.* Ethical business behavior includes: punctuality, reliability, courtesy, respect, appropriate forms of communication, dress and neatness, honesty, empathy, and competence.

**43.2** Entrepreneurs should practice ethical corporate governance.
    *A.* Keep business and personal finances separate.
    *B.* Maintain accurate records.
    *C.* Use financial controls.
    *D.* Form an advisory board. ✔✔✔

# A Business for the Young Entrepreneur
## HOME AND OFFICE PLANT CARE

Do your friends say you have a green thumb? People like to have plants in their homes and offices but don't always have time to care for them. Plant care is a business that is inexpensive to start and doesn't require a lot of time. Most plants only need attention once or twice a week, so plant care is a good small business for a busy student.

Make flyers and ask if you can put them up in the lobbies of office buildings near your home or school. To learn how to care for different types of plants, visit a local nursery or store. Ask the owner to recommend some books on the subject.

| SUPPLIES | WHERE TO FIND THEM |
| --- | --- |
| watering can | hardware store or nursery |
| plant food | nursery or flower shop |
| rags for dusting plant leaves | make from old shirts |
| notebook for instructions on how to care for plants | stationery store |
| calendar/appointment book to keep track of visits | stationery store |

### TIPS

- Ask customers for details on how to care for each plant. Write them down!
- Offer customers a discount on your services if they refer you to potential customers. ■

### CHAPTER 44

# TAXATION AND THE ENTREPRENEUR

*You can get everything in life that you want ... if you'll just help enough other people get what they want.*

— Zig Ziglar, *sales expert*

## KEY OBJECTIVES

**THIS CHAPTER WILL ENABLE YOU TO:**

■ Understand how to meet your legal tax obligation as a small business owner.

■ Identify the taxes that support city, state, and federal government.

■ Find appropriate tax forms and assistance in filling them out.

**O**nce you start a small business, you will have to pay **taxes**. A tax is a percentage of your gross profit that is taken by the government. The government uses taxes to build roads, and to support schools, the military, and the police and fire departments. These are called *public* services, because they are provided by the government to everyone.

## States Use Sales Taxes to Raise Money

"The government" exists on federal, state, and local levels.

The federal government is basically composed of the Executive Branch (the President and his Cabinet), the Legislative Branch (Congress), and the Judicial Branch (the Supreme Court and other federal courts). They maintain the armed forces, build highways, and operate many agencies, such as the SBA (Small Business Administration) and OSHA, the Occupational Safety & Health Administration. The federal government is financed by personal and corporate income tax.

State governments, on the other hand, raise money from taxing the sale of goods, and sometimes services. **Sales tax** is a percentage of the cost of an item sold that is added to its price. If a state charges 8% sales tax on a $10 item, the sales tax would be 80 cents. The customer would pay the seller a total of $10.80.

# SKILLS MEAN SUCCESS

## MATH

### Operations: Income Tax Rates

Personal income tax rates depend on how much you earn and whether you are single or married, as well as on other factors. Tax rates are *progressive*, meaning that the percentage of income tax you pay increases the more you earn. For example, the first $7,000 in net income earned are taxed at 10%. The next $21,400 are taxed at 15%, and so on.

Use the table below to determine the federal taxes payable by each individual.

| Name | Taxable Income |
|------|----------------|
| Maria | $16,500 |
| Marvin | $26,700 |
| Mac | $31,200 |
| Marissa | $75,000 |

**Federal Personal Income Tax Rates for 2003:**
*Filing Status and Taxable Income Level*

| Single filers | Tax Rate |
|---------------|----------|
| Up to $7,000 | 10% |
| $7,001 – $28,400 | 15% |
| $28,401 – $68,800 | 25% |
| $68,801 – $143,500 | 28% |
| $143,501 – $311,950 | 33% |
| $311,951 or more | 35% |

If you sell retail, you will have to collect sales tax from your customers and pay it to the state. In the previous example, you would collect $10 from the customer for your business and 80 cents for the state. Businesses are typically required to pay the collected sales tax to the state four times per year (quarterly).

Some (but not all) states also impose an income tax. The services states provide include building and maintaining state highways, state police, and state colleges. City and other local (county) governments are supported primarily by taxes on property, such as land and houses. Local governments provide such public services as police and fire departments, chambers of commerce, and public schools.

## A Sole Proprietor Pays Two Kinds of Taxes to the Federal Government

Like employed people, people who work for themselves pay income tax. They also pay **self-employment tax**.

Entrepreneurs pay self-employment tax because they don't have an employer who contributes to **Social Security** for them. The federal government's Social Security program pays money to retired people and the families of deceased or disabled workers. People who are employees have taxes for Social Security withheld from their paychecks. They get this money back when they retire, essentially, as monthly Social Security checks from the government. People who work for themselves do not have this money withheld from their paychecks, so they must pay it to the government each year as self-employment tax.

## Forms to File

Income-tax returns, which include self-employment tax forms, must be filed by midnight on April 15th of each year. If you file late, you may have to pay penalties and interest. The **Internal Revenue Service (IRS)** is the government bureau in charge of federal taxation. Failure to file taxes is illegal, and the IRS can, in serious cases, put a person in jail for **tax evasion**.

The basic income tax form is the 1040 U.S. Individual Tax Return and Schedule C — Profit or Loss from Business. Self-employment tax is filed using Schedule SE. Tax forms are usually available at your local post office or bank. Forms can also be ordered from the IRS by calling 1-800-829-3676 or online at www.irs.gov. We have included some sample forms later in this chapter.

### SKILLS MEAN SUCCESS

**TECHNOLOGY** ▶ **Online Research**

Visit the IRS Web site at www.irs.gov. Locate and evaluate the online tax filing information. How is your personal information protected when you file your taxes online? What about when you shop online, or apply for a credit card? Make a chart listing the pros and cons of using the Internet for filing, shopping, or sending personal information online.

**Advantages**          **Risks**

## Getting Help from the IRS

The tax code is very complex, so the IRS offers booklets and a telephone service to help answer questions. Help with the 1040 form is available at 1-800-829-1040 or online at www.irs.gov. You can also go to the local IRS office and meet with an agent who will guide you through the forms for free. It is important to get new forms and booklets annually, as rules, rates, and forms change from one year to the next. You may want to have your taxes prepared by a CPA — Certified Public Accountant.

## SKILLS MEAN SUCCESS

**ENGLISH**    **Presenting Information Clearly**

Create a "Q&A" (Question and Answer) document that could be posted on your company Web site or used in a brochure as a service to your customers. Write at least four questions and answers. Don't write questions that can be answered with a simple "yes" or "no." They should require answers at least two sentences long. Write answers that will provide easy-to-understand information or directions. ■■■

## Help Yourself by Keeping Good Records

You will make filing your taxes easier by keeping good records throughout the year. You will have to determine your net income (gross income minus expenses). If you have kept track of income and expenses in your ledger, this should not be too difficult.

If you are in doubt, call the IRS or visit an accountant or tax-preparation office, such as H&R Block. Serious mistakes on your tax return could cause the IRS to **audit** you. That means they will send an agent to your business or home to examine your ledgers and receipts and invoices thoroughly to make sure your taxes were filed correctly. This is another compelling reason to keep good records and file all your invoices and receipts in a safe place.

## Where Are My Tax Dollars Going?

As a taxpayer, you have the right to ask such questions as:

- Where are my tax dollars going?
- Are they supporting services that will benefit me and my community?
- Am I paying taxes to support services that could be better supplied by private industry instead of the government?
- Are the tax rates fair?

Taxpayers demand answers to these questions from the politicians who represent them in city councils, state legislatures, and the Congress. One of the most important jobs politicians do each year is figure out government budgets and then determine how much tax money will be needed to finance them. They also pass laws that change (*amend*) the tax code. On the next few pages are sample tax forms. Note that these may change from year to year. Call the IRS at 1-800-829-3676 or visit www.irs.gov to obtain the most recent forms.

Form **1040**

Department of the Treasury—Internal Revenue Service

**U.S. Individual Income Tax Return** **2004** (99) IRS Use Only—Do not write or staple in this space.

For the year Jan. 1–Dec. 31, 2004, or other tax year beginning , 2004, ending , 20 OMB No. 1545-0074

**Label**

(See instructions on page 16.)

**Use the IRS label.** Otherwise, please print or type.

**Presidential Election Campaign** (See page 16.)

L A B E L H E R E

Your first name and initial | Last name | Your social security number

If a joint return, spouse's first name and initial | Last name | Spouse's social security number

Home address (number and street). If you have a P.O. box, see page 16. | Apt. no.

City, town or post office, state, and ZIP code. If you have a foreign address, see page 16.

▲ **Important!** ▲
You **must** enter your SSN(s) above.

**Note.** Checking "Yes" will not change your tax or reduce your refund.
Do you, or your spouse if filing a joint return, want $3 to go to this fund? . . . ▶

| | You | | Spouse |
| Yes | No | Yes | No |

**Filing Status**

Check only one box.

1 ☐ Single
2 ☐ Married filing jointly (even if only one had income)
3 ☐ Married filing separately. Enter spouse's SSN above and full name here. ▶
4 ☐ Head of household (with qualifying person). (See page 17.) If the qualifying person is a child but not your dependent, enter this child's name here. ▶
5 ☐ Qualifying widow(er) with dependent child (see page 17)

**Exemptions**

If more than four dependents, see page 18.

6a ☐ **Yourself.** If someone can claim you as a dependent, **do not** check box 6a . . . .
b ☐ **Spouse** . . . . . . . . . . . . . . . . . . . . . . . . .
c **Dependents:**

| (1) First name   Last name | (2) Dependent's social security number | (3) Dependent's relationship to you | (4) ✔ if qualifying child for child tax credit (see page 18) |
|---|---|---|---|
| | | | ☐ |
| | | | ☐ |
| | | | ☐ |
| | | | ☐ |

Boxes checked on 6a and 6b ____
No. of children on 6c who:
• lived with you ____
• did not live with you due to divorce or separation (see page 18) ____
Dependents on 6c not entered above ____

d Total number of exemptions claimed . . . . . . . . . . . . . . .

Add numbers on lines above ▶

**Income**

Attach Form(s) W-2 here. Also attach Forms W-2G and 1099-R if tax was withheld.

If you did not get a W-2, see page 19.

Enclose, but do not attach, any payment. Also, please use **Form 1040-V.**

7 Wages, salaries, tips, etc. Attach Form(s) W-2 . . . . . . . . . | 7
8a **Taxable** interest. Attach Schedule B if required . . . . . . . . | 8a
b **Tax-exempt** interest. **Do not** include on line 8a . . . | 8b |
9a Ordinary dividends. Attach Schedule B if required . . . . . . . . | 9a
b Qualified dividends (see page 20) . . . . . . . . | 9b |
10 Taxable refunds, credits, or offsets of state and local income taxes (see page 20) . . | 10
11 Alimony received . . . . . . . . . . . . . . . . . . . . . | 11
12 Business income or (loss). Attach Schedule C or C-EZ . . . . . . | 12
13 Capital gain or (loss). Attach Schedule D if required. If not required, check here ▶ ☐ | 13
14 Other gains or (losses). Attach Form 4797 . . . . . . . . . | 14
15a IRA distributions . . | 15a | b Taxable amount (see page 22) | 15b
16a Pensions and annuities | 16a | b Taxable amount (see page 22) | 16b
17 Rental real estate, royalties, partnerships, S corporations, trusts, etc. Attach Schedule E | 17
18 Farm income or (loss). Attach Schedule F . . . . . . . . . . | 18
19 Unemployment compensation . . . . . . . . . . . . . . | 19
20a Social security benefits . | 20a | b Taxable amount (see page 24) | 20b
21 Other income. List type and amount (see page 24) _____ | 21
22 Add the amounts in the far right column for lines 7 through 21. This is your **total income** ▶ | 22

**Adjusted Gross Income**

23 Educator expenses (see page 26) | 23 |
24 Certain business expenses of reservists, performing artists, and fee-basis government officials. Attach Form 2106 or 2106-EZ | 24 |
25 IRA deduction (see page 26) . . . . . . . . . . | 25 |
26 Student loan interest deduction (see page 28) . . . . | 26 |
27 Tuition and fees deduction (see page 29) . . . . . | 27 |
28 Health savings account deduction. Attach Form 8889 . | 28 |
29 Moving expenses. Attach Form 3903 . . . . . | 29 |
30 One-half of self-employment tax. Attach Schedule SE . . | 30 |
31 Self-employed health insurance deduction (see page 30) | 31 |
32 Self-employed SEP, SIMPLE, and qualified plans . . . | 32 |
33 Penalty on early withdrawal of savings . . . . . . | 33 |
34a Alimony paid b Recipient's SSN ▶ _____ | 34a |
35 Add lines 23 through 34a . . . . . . . . . . . . . . | 35
36 Subtract line 35 from line 22. This is your **adjusted gross income** . . . . . ▶ | 36

For Disclosure, Privacy Act, and Paperwork Reduction Act Notice, see page 75. Cat. No. 11320B Form **1040** (2004)

Form 1040 (2004)                                                                                                           Page **2**

| | | | 37 | |
|---|---|---|---|---|

**Tax and Credits**

**37** Amount from line 36 (adjusted gross income) . . . . . . . . . . . **37**

**38a** Check if: ☐ **You** were born before January 2, 1940, ☐ Blind. / ☐ **Spouse** was born before January 2, 1940, ☐ Blind. } **Total boxes checked ▶ 38a**

**b** If your spouse itemizes on a separate return or you were a dual-status alien, see page 31 and check here ▶ **38b** ☐

**Standard Deduction for—**

- People who checked any box on line 38a or 38b **or** who can be claimed as a dependent, see page 31.
- All others:

Single or Married filing separately, $4,850

Married filing jointly or Qualifying widow(er), $9,700

Head of household, $7,150

**39** **Itemized deductions** (from Schedule A) **or** your **standard deduction** (see left margin) . . **39**

**40** Subtract line 39 from line 37 . . . . . . . . . . . . . . . . **40**

**41** If line 37 is $107,025 or less, multiply $3,100 by the total number of exemptions claimed on line 6d. If line 37 is over $107,025, see the worksheet on page 33 . . . . . . . . **41**

**42** **Taxable income.** Subtract line 41 from line 40. If line 41 is more than line 40, enter -0- **42**

**43** Tax (see page 33). Check if any tax is from: **a** ☐ Form(s) 8814 **b** ☐ Form 4972 . . . **43**

**44** **Alternative minimum tax** (see page 35). Attach Form 6251 . . . . . . . . . **44**

**45** Add lines 43 and 44 . . . . . . . . . . . . . . . . . . . ▶ **45**

**46** Foreign tax credit. Attach Form 1116 if required . . . . | **46** |

**47** Credit for child and dependent care expenses. Attach Form 2441 | **47** |

**48** Credit for the elderly or the disabled. Attach Schedule R . . | **48** |

**49** Education credits. Attach Form 8863 . . . . . . . . | **49** |

**50** Retirement savings contributions credit. Attach Form 8880. | **50** |

**51** Child tax credit (see page 37) . . . . . . . . . . | **51** |

**52** Adoption credit. Attach Form 8839 . . . . . . . . | **52** |

**53** Credits from: **a** ☐ Form 8396 **b** ☐ Form 8859 . . | **53** |

**54** Other credits. Check applicable box(es): **a** ☐ Form 3800 **b** ☐ Form 8801 **c** ☐ Specify _____ | **54** |

**55** Add lines 46 through 54. These are your **total credits** . . . . . . . . . **55**

**56** Subtract line 55 from line 45. If line 55 is more than line 45, enter -0- . . . . . ▶ **56**

**Other Taxes**

**57** Self-employment tax. Attach Schedule SE . . . . . . . . . . . . . **57**

**58** Social security and Medicare tax on tip income not reported to employer. Attach Form 4137 . . **58**

**59** Additional tax on IRAs, other qualified retirement plans, etc. Attach Form 5329 if required . **59**

**60** Advance earned income credit payments from Form(s) W-2 . . . . . . . . . **60**

**61** Household employment taxes. Attach Schedule H . . . . . . . . . . . **61**

**62** Add lines 56 through 61. This is your **total tax** . . . . . . . . . . . ▶ **62**

**Payments**

If you have a qualifying child, attach Schedule EIC.

**63** Federal income tax withheld from Forms W-2 and 1099 . . | **63** |

**64** 2004 estimated tax payments and amount applied from 2003 return | **64** |

**65a** Earned income credit (EIC) . . . . . . . . . . | **65a** |

**b** Nontaxable combat pay election ▶ | **65b** |

**66** Excess social security and tier 1 RRTA tax withheld (see page 54) | **66** |

**67** Additional child tax credit. Attach Form 8812 . . . . . | **67** |

**68** Amount paid with request for extension to file (see page 54) | **68** |

**69** Other payments from: **a** ☐ Form 2439 **b** ☐ Form 4136 **c** ☐ Form 8885 . | **69** |

**70** Add lines 63, 64, 65a, and 66 through 69. These are your **total payments** . . . . ▶ **70**

**Refund**

Direct deposit? See page 54 and fill in 72b, 72c, and 72d.

**71** If line 70 is more than line 62, subtract line 62 from line 70. This is the amount you **overpaid** **71**

**72a** Amount of line 71 you want **refunded to you** . . . . . . . . . . . . **72a**

▶ **b** Routing number _____ ▶ **c** Type: ☐ Checking ☐ Savings

▶ **d** Account number _____

**73** Amount of line 71 you want **applied to your 2005 estimated tax** ▶ | **73** |

**Amount You Owe**

**74** **Amount you owe.** Subtract line 70 from line 62. For details on how to pay, see page 55 ▶ **74**

**75** Estimated tax penalty (see page 55) . . . . . . . . . | **75** |

**Third Party Designee**

Do you want to allow another person to discuss this return with the IRS (see page 56)? ☐ **Yes.** Complete the following. ☐ **No**

Designee's name ▶ _____  Phone no. ▶ ( ) _____  Personal identification number (PIN) ▶ _____

**Sign Here**

Joint return? See page 17. Keep a copy for your records.

Under penalties of perjury, I declare that I have examined this return and accompanying schedules and statements, and to the best of my knowledge and belief, they are true, correct, and complete. Declaration of preparer (other than taxpayer) is based on all information of which preparer has any knowledge.

| Your signature | Date | Your occupation | Daytime phone number ( ) |
| Spouse's signature. If a joint return, **both** must sign. | Date | Spouse's occupation | |

**Paid Preparer's Use Only**

| Preparer's signature ▶ | | Date | Check if self-employed ☐ | Preparer's SSN or PTIN |
| Firm's name (or yours if self-employed), address, and ZIP code ▶ | | | EIN | |
| | | | Phone no. ( ) | |

Form **1040** (2004)

**SCHEDULE C**
**(Form 1040)**

Department of the Treasury
Internal Revenue Service

# Profit or Loss From Business

(Sole Proprietorship)

▶ Partnerships, joint ventures, etc., must file Form 1065 or 1065-B.

▶ Attach to Form 1040 or 1041. ▶ See Instructions for Schedule C (Form 1040).

OMB No. 1545-0074

**2004**

Attachment
Sequence No. 09

Name of proprietor

Social security number (SSN)

**A** Principal business or profession, including product or service (see page C-2 of the instructions)

**B** Enter code from pages C-7, 8, & 9
▶

**C** Business name. If no separate business name, leave blank.

**D** Employer ID number (EIN), if any

**E** Business address (including suite or room no.) ▶ ..........................................................
City, town or post office, state, and ZIP code

**F** Accounting method: **(1)** ☐ Cash **(2)** ☐ Accrual **(3)** ☐ Other (specify) ▶ ....................

**G** Did you "materially participate" in the operation of this business during 2004? If "No," see page C-3 for limit on losses    ☐ Yes ☐ No

**H** If you started or acquired this business during 2004, check here . . . . . . . . . . . . . . . . . ▶ ☐

## Part I    Income

| | | | |
|---|---|---|---|
| 1 | Gross receipts or sales. **Caution.** If this income was reported to you on Form W-2 and the "Statutory employee" box on that form was checked, see page C-3 and check here . . . . . . ▶ ☐ | 1 | |
| 2 | Returns and allowances . . . . . . . . . . . . . . . . . | 2 | |
| 3 | Subtract line 2 from line 1 . . . . . . . . . . . . . . . . | 3 | |
| 4 | Cost of goods sold (from line 42 on page 2) . . . . . . . . . . | 4 | |
| 5 | **Gross profit.** Subtract line 4 from line 3. . . . . . . . . . . | 5 | |
| 6 | Other income, including Federal and state gasoline or fuel tax credit or refund (see page C-3) . . . | 6 | |
| 7 | **Gross income.** Add lines 5 and 6 . . . . . . . . . . . ▶ | 7 | |

## Part II    Expenses. Enter expenses for business use of your home **only** on line 30.

| | | | | | | |
|---|---|---|---|---|---|---|
| 8 | Advertising . . . . . . | 8 | | 19 Pension and profit-sharing plans | 19 | |
| 9 | Car and truck expenses (see page C-3). . . . . . . | 9 | | 20 Rent or lease (see page C-5): | | |
| | | | | a Vehicles, machinery, and equipment . | 20a | |
| 10 | Commissions and fees . . | 10 | | b Other business property. . . | 20b | |
| 11 | Contract labor (see page C-4) | 11 | | 21 Repairs and maintenance . . | 21 | |
| 12 | Depletion . . . . . | 12 | | 22 Supplies (not included in Part III) . | 22 | |
| 13 | Depreciation and section 179 expense deduction (not included in Part III) (see page C-4) . . . . . . | 13 | | 23 Taxes and licenses . . . . | 23 | |
| | | | | 24 Travel, meals, and entertainment: | | |
| | | | | a Travel . . . . . . . . | 24a | |
| 14 | Employee benefit programs (other than on line 19). . | 14 | | b Meals and entertainment | | |
| 15 | Insurance (other than health) . | 15 | | c Enter nondeductible amount included on line 24b (see page C-5) | | |
| 16 | Interest: | | | | | |
| a | Mortgage (paid to banks, etc.) . | 16a | | d Subtract line 24c from line 24b | 24d | |
| b | Other . . . . . . . . | 16b | | 25 Utilities . . . . . . . | 25 | |
| 17 | Legal and professional services . . . . . . | 17 | | 26 Wages (less employment credits) . | 26 | |
| 18 | Office expense . . . . . | 18 | | 27 Other expenses (from line 48 on page 2) . . . . . . . | 27 | |

| | | | |
|---|---|---|---|
| 28 | **Total expenses** before expenses for business use of home. Add lines 8 through 27 in columns . .▶ | 28 | |
| 29 | Tentative profit (loss). Subtract line 28 from line 7 . . . . . . . . . . | 29 | |
| 30 | Expenses for business use of your home. Attach **Form 8829** . . . . . . . . | 30 | |
| 31 | **Net profit or (loss).** Subtract line 30 from line 29. | | |
| | • If a profit, enter on **Form 1040, line 12,** and also on **Schedule SE, line 2** (statutory employees, see page C-6). Estates and trusts, enter on Form 1041, line 3. | 31 | |
| | • If a loss, you **must** go to line 32. | | |
| 32 | If you have a loss, check the box that describes your investment in this activity (see page C-6). | | |
| | • If you checked 32a, enter the loss on **Form 1040, line 12,** and also on **Schedule SE, line 2** (statutory employees, see page C-6). Estates and trusts, enter on Form 1041, line 3. | 32a ☐ All investment is at risk. 32b ☐ Some investment is not at risk. | |
| | • If you checked 32b, you **must** attach **Form 6198.** | | |

For Paperwork Reduction Act Notice, see Form 1040 instructions.    Cat. No. 11334P    Schedule C (Form 1040) 2004

Schedule C (Form 1040) 2004                                                      Page **2**

**Part III**   Cost of Goods Sold (see page C-6)

33   Method(s) used to value closing inventory:   **a** ☐ Cost   **b** ☐ Lower of cost or market   **c** ☐ Other (attach explanation)

34   Was there any change in determining quantities, costs, or valuations between opening and closing inventory? If "Yes," attach explanation . . . . . . . . . . . . . . . . . . . . . . . . ☐ **Yes**   ☐ **No**

| | | |
|---|---|---|
| 35   Inventory at beginning of year. If different from last year's closing inventory, attach explanation | 35 | |
| 36   Purchases less cost of items withdrawn for personal use | 36 | |
| 37   Cost of labor. Do not include any amounts paid to yourself | 37 | |
| 38   Materials and supplies | 38 | |
| 39   Other costs | 39 | |
| 40   Add lines 35 through 39 | 40 | |
| 41   Inventory at end of year | 41 | |
| 42   **Cost of goods sold.** Subtract line 41 from line 40. Enter the result here and on page 1, line 4 | 42 | |

**Part IV**   **Information on Your Vehicle.** Complete this part **only** if you are claiming car or truck expenses on line 9 and are not required to file Form 4562 for this business. See the instructions for line 13 on page C-4 to find out if you must file Form 4562.

43   When did you place your vehicle in service for business purposes? (month, day, year) ▶ ___/___/___

44   Of the total number of miles you drove your vehicle during 2004, enter the number of miles you used your vehicle for:

**a** Business ___   **b** Commuting ___   **c** Other ___

45   Do you (or your spouse) have another vehicle available for personal use? . . . . . . . . . . . ☐ **Yes**   ☐ **No**

46   Was your vehicle available for personal use during off-duty hours? . . . . . . . . . . ☐ **Yes**   ☐ **No**

47a   Do you have evidence to support your deduction? . . . . . . . . . . . . . . . ☐ **Yes**   ☐ **No**

**b**   If "Yes," is the evidence written? . . . . . . . . . . . . . . . . . . . . . ☐ **Yes**   ☐ **No**

**Part V**   Other Expenses. List below business expenses not included on lines 8–26 or line 30.

| | |
|---|---|
| | |
| | |
| | |
| | |
| | |
| | |
| | |
| | |
| 48   **Total other expenses.** Enter here and on page 1, line 27 | 48 |

Schedule C (Form 1040) 2004

This is the form that you would use to report "sales and use tax" to the New York State Department of Taxation and Finance. Every state has its own forms. Contact your State Department of Taxation and Finance or visit your local library to obtain the correct forms for your state.

---

New York State Department of Taxation and Finance

**Quarterly ST-100**

2nd Quarter

**New York State and Local**
**Quarterly Sales and Use Tax Return**

| June | July | August |

Tax period
June 1, 2004 – August 31, 2004

Sales tax identification number ▶

Legal name *(if no label, print legal name as it appears on the Certificate of Authority)*

dba (doing business as) name

Number and street

City, state, ZIP code

September 2004

| S | M | T | W | T | F | S |
| --- | --- | --- | --- | --- | --- | --- |
| | | | 1 | 2 | 3 | 4 |
| 5 | 6 | 7 | 8 | 9 | 10 | 11 |
| 12 | 13 | 14 | 15 | 16 | 17 | 18 |
| 19 | 20 | 21 | 22 | 23 | 24 | 25 |
| 26 | 27 | 28 | 29 | 30 | | |

205

**20** Due date:
Monday,
September 20, 2004
You will be responsible for penalty and interest if your return is not postmarked by this date.

**No tax due?** Check the box to the right and complete Step 1; in Step 3 on page 3, enter *none* in boxes 13, 14, and 15; and complete Step 9. You **must** file by the due date even if no tax is due. **There is a $50 penalty for late filing of a no-tax-due return.** See ❶ in instructions. ☐

**Multiple locations?** If you are reporting sales tax for more than one business location **and** your identification number does not end in *C*, check the box to the right and attach a list of your locations. ☐

**Final return?** Check the box to the right if you are discontinuing your business and this is your final return; complete this return and the back of your *Certificate of Authority.* Attach the *Certificate of Authority* to the return. See ❷ in instructions. ☐

**Has your address or business information changed?** If so, check the box to the right and enter new mailing address on preprinted label above. See ❸ in instructions. ☐

| **Step 1 of 9** Gross sales and services | Enter total **gross sales and services** in box 1 .............................. ➤ | 1 .00 |
| --- | --- | --- |

Do not include sales tax in the gross sales and services amount. See ❹ in instructions.

**Step 2 of 9** Identify required schedules | Check the box(es) on the right below, then complete the schedule(s) if necessary and proceed to Step 3. **Need to obtain schedules?** See *Need help?* on page 4 of this form.

| Quarterly schedule | Description | Check the box for each schedule you are attaching |
| --- | --- | --- |
| SCHEDULE **A** | Use Form ST-100.2, *Quarterly Schedule A,* to report tax and taxable receipts from sales of food and drink (restaurant meals, takeout, etc.) and from hotel/motel room occupancy **in Nassau or Niagara County,** as well as admissions, club dues, and cabaret charges in Niagara County. | ☐ |
| SCHEDULE **B** | Use Form ST-100.3, *Quarterly Schedule B,* to report tax due on **nonresidential utility services** in certain counties where school districts or cities impose tax, and on **residential energy sources and services** subject to local taxes. Reminder: Use Form ST-100.3-ATT, *Quarterly Schedule B-ATT,* to report sales of these nonresidential utility services made to QEZEs. | ☐ |
| SCHEDULE **FR** | Use Form ST-100.10, *Quarterly Schedule FR,* to report **retail sales of motor fuel or diesel motor fuel,** and fuel taken from inventory, as explained in the schedule's instructions. | ☐ |
| SCHEDULE **H** | Use Form ST-100.7, *Quarterly Schedule H,* to report **sales of clothing and footwear eligible for exemption** from New York State and some local sales and use tax on August 31, 2004. | ☐ |
| SCHEDULE **N** | Use Form ST-100.5, *Quarterly Schedule N,* to report taxes due and sales of certain **services in New York City.** Reminder: Use Form ST-100.5-ATT, *Quarterly Schedule N-ATT,* if you are a provider of parking services in New York City. | ☐ |
| SCHEDULE **Q** | Use Form ST-100.9, *Quarterly Schedule Q,* to report **sales of tangible personal property or services to Qualified Empire Zone Enterprises (QEZEs) eligible for exemption** from New York State and some local sales and use tax. | ☐ |
| SCHEDULE **T** | Use Form ST-100.8, *Quarterly Schedule T,* to report taxes due on **telephone services, telephone answering services, and telegraph services** imposed by certain counties, school districts, and cities. Reminder: Use Form ST-100.8-ATT, *Quarterly Schedule T-ATT,* to report sales of these services made to QEZEs. | ☐ |

**Schedules CT and NJ:** For reciprocal tax agreement filing requirements, see ❺ in instructions.

*Refer to instructions (Form ST-100-I) if you have questions or need help. Please be sure to keep a completed copy of your return for your records.*

For office use only

ST-100 (6/04) **Page 1** of 4

Proceed to Step 3, page 2 ▶

---

**Page 2** of 4   ST-100 (6/04)   Sales tax identification number   | 205 | Quarterly

### Step 3 of 9   Calculate sales and use taxes
*Refer to instructions (Form ST-100-I) if you have questions or need help.*

Enter total from Form ST-100.10 (if any) in box 2  FR

Enter totals from:  A + B + B-ATT + H + N + Q + T + T-ATT =

| Column A Taxing jurisdiction | Column B Jurisdiction code | Column C Taxable sales and services | Column D Purchases subject to tax | Column E Tax rate | Column F Sales and use tax (C + D) × E |
|---|---|---|---|---|---|
| | | **3** .00 | **4** .00 | **2** / **5** | |
| New York State only | NE 0011 | .00 | .00 | 4¼% | |
| Albany County | AL 0171 | .00 | .00 | 8¼% | |
| Allegany County | AL 0211 | .00 | .00 | 8¼% | |
| Broome County | BR 0311 | .00 | .00 | 8¼% | |
| Cattaraugus County (outside the following) | CA 0491 | .00 | .00 | 8¼% | |
| Olean (city) | OL 0411 | .00 | .00 | 8¼% | |
| Salamanca (city) | SA 0421 | .00 | .00 | 8¼% | |
| Cayuga County (outside the following) | CA 0501 | .00 | .00 | 8¼% | |
| Auburn (city) | AU 0551 | .00 | .00 | 8¼% | |
| Chautauqua County | CH 0601 | .00 | .00 | 7¼% | |
| Chemung County | CH 0701 | .00 | .00 | 8¼% | |
| Chenango County (outside the following) | CH 0821 | .00 | .00 | 8¼% | |
| Norwich (city) | NO 0841 | .00 | .00 | 8¼% | |
| Clinton County | CL 0901 | .00 | .00 | 8% | |
| Columbia County | CO 1001 | .00 | .00 | 8¼% | |
| Cortland County | CO 1121 | .00 | .00 | 8¼% | |
| Delaware County | DE 1211 | .00 | .00 | 8¼% | |
| Dutchess County | DU 1301 | .00 | .00 | 8¼% | |
| Erie County | ER 1401 | .00 | .00 | 8¼% | |
| Essex County | ES 1501 | .00 | .00 | 7¼% | |
| Franklin County | FR 1601 | .00 | .00 | 7¼% | |
| Fulton County (outside the following) | FU 1701 | .00 | .00 | 7¼% | |
| Gloversville (city) | GL 1761 | .00 | .00 | 7¼% | |
| Johnstown (city) | JO 1771 | .00 | .00 | 7¼% | |
| Genesee County | GE 1801 | .00 | .00 | 8¼% | |
| Greene County | GR 1901 | .00 | .00 | 8¼% | |
| Hamilton County | HA 2001 | .00 | .00 | 7¼% | |
| Herkimer County | HE 2101 | .00 | .00 | 8¼% | |
| Jefferson County | JE 2201 | .00 | .00 | 7¼% | |
| Lewis County | LE 2311 | .00 | .00 | 8% | |
| Livingston County | LI 2401 | .00 | .00 | 8¼% | |
| Madison County (outside the following) | MA 2501 | .00 | .00 | 8¼% | |
| Oneida (city) | ON 2531 | .00 | .00 | 8¼% | |
| Monroe County | MO 2601 | .00 | .00 | 8¼% | |
| Montgomery County | MO 2791 | .00 | .00 | 8¼% | |
| Nassau County | NA 2801 | .00 | .00 | 8¾% | |
| Niagara County | NI 2901 | .00 | .00 | 8¼% | |
| Oneida County (outside the following) | ON 3001 | .00 | .00 | 8¼% | |
| Rome (city) | RO 3021 | .00 | .00 | 8¼% | |
| Sherrill (city) | SH 3041 | .00 | .00 | 8¼% | |
| Utica (city) | UT 3051 | .00 | .00 | 8¼% | |
| Onondaga County | ON 3101 | .00 | .00 | 7¼% | |
| Ontario County (outside the following) | ON 3271 | .00 | .00 | 7¼% | |
| Canandaigua (city) | CA 3231 | .00 | .00 | 7¼% | |
| Geneva (city) | GE 3241 | .00 | .00 | 7¼% | |
| Orange County | OR 3311 | .00 | .00 | 8¼% | |
| Orleans County | OR 3471 | .00 | .00 | 8¼% | |
| Oswego County (outside the following) | OS 3591 | .00 | .00 | 7¼% | |
| Fulton (city) | FU 3531 | .00 | .00 | 8¼% | |
| Oswego (city) | OS 3541 | .00 | .00 | 7¼% | |
| Column subtotals; also enter on page 3, boxes 10, 11, and 12: | | **6** .00 | **7** .00 | **8** | |

| Quarterly | 205 | Sales tax identification number | | | | | ST-100 (6/04) | Page 3 of 4 |

| Column A<br>Taxing jurisdiction | Column B<br>Jurisdiction code | Column C<br>Taxable sales and services | + | Column D<br>Purchases subject to tax | × | Column E<br>Tax rate = | Column F<br>Sales and use tax (C + D) × E |
|---|---|---|---|---|---|---|---|
| Otsego County | OT 3611 | .00 | | .00 | | 8¼% | |
| Putnam County | PU 3701 | .00 | | .00 | | 7½% | |
| Rensselaer County | RE 3871 | .00 | | .00 | | 8¼% | |
| Rockland County | RO 3901 | .00 | | .00 | | 8⅛%* | |
| St. Lawrence County | ST 4081 | .00 | | .00 | | 7¼% | |
| Saratoga County (outside the following) | SA 4101 | .00 | | .00 | | 7¼% | |
| Saratoga Springs (city) | SA 4121 | .00 | | .00 | | 7¼% | |
| Schenectady County | SC 4231 | .00 | | .00 | | 8¼% | |
| Schoharie County | SC 4311 | .00 | | .00 | | 8¼% | |
| Schuyler County | SC 4401 | .00 | | .00 | | 8¼% | |
| Seneca County | SE 4501 | .00 | | .00 | | 8¼% | |
| Steuben County (outside the following) | ST 4681 | .00 | | .00 | | 8¼% | |
| Corning (city) | CO 4601 | .00 | | .00 | | 8¼% | |
| Hornell (city) | HO 4631 | .00 | | .00 | | 8¼% | |
| Suffolk County | SU 4701 | .00 | | .00 | | 8¾% | |
| Sullivan County | SU 4801 | .00 | | .00 | | 7¾% | |
| Tioga County | TI 4911 | .00 | | .00 | | 8¼% | |
| Tompkins County (outside the following) | TO 5091 | .00 | | .00 | | 8¼% | |
| Ithaca (city) | IT 5011 | .00 | | .00 | | 8¼% | |
| Ulster County | UL 5101 | .00 | | .00 | | 8¼% | |
| Warren County (outside the following) | WA 5291 | .00 | | .00 | | 7¼% | |
| Glens Falls (city) | GL 5201 | .00 | | .00 | | 7¼% | |
| Washington County | WA 5301 | .00 | | .00 | | 7¼% | |
| Wayne County | WA 5411 | .00 | | .00 | | 8¼% | |
| Westchester County (outside the following) | WE 5591 | .00 | | .00 | | 7½% | |
| Mount Vernon (city) | MO 5511 | .00 | | .00 | | 8½% | |
| New Rochelle (city) | NE 6851 | .00 | | .00 | | 8½% | |
| White Plains (city) | WH 5551 | .00 | | .00 | | 8% | |
| Yonkers (city) | YO 6501 | .00 | | .00 | | 8½% | |
| Wyoming County | WY 5601 | .00 | | .00 | | 8¼% | |
| Yates County | YA 5711 | .00 | | .00 | | 8¼% | |
| **Taxes in New York City** [includes counties of Bronx, Kings (Brooklyn), New York (Manhattan), Queens, and Richmond (Staten Island)] | | | | | | | |
| New York City/State combined tax | NE 8011 | .00 | | .00 | | 8⅝%* | |
| New York State/MCTD (fuel and utilities) | NE 8041 | .00 | | .00 | | 4½% | |
| New York City - local tax only (enter box 9 amount in Step 7B) | NE 8021 ⑨ | .00 | | .00 | | 4⅛%* | |
| | | .00 | | .00 | | | |
| Column subtotals from page 2, boxes 6, 7, and 8: | | ⑩ .00 | | ⑪ .00 | | | ⑫ |
| (STOP) If the total of box 13 + box 14 = $300,000 or more, see page 1 of instructions. **Column totals:** | | ⑬ .00 | | ⑭ .00 | | | ⑮ |

**Credit summary** — Enter the total amount of credits claimed in Step 3 above, and on any attached schedules (see ⑫c).

| Step 4 of 9 Calculate special taxes | Internal code | Column G<br>Taxable receipts | × | Column H<br>Tax rate = | Column J<br>Special taxes due (G × H) |
|---|---|---|---|---|---|
| Passenger car rentals | PA 0003 | .00 | | 5% | |
| Information & entertainment services furnished via telephony and telegraphy | IN 7009 | .00 | | 5% | |
| | | | | **Total special taxes:** | ⑯ |

| Step 5 of 9 Calculate tax credits and advance payments | | Internal code | Column K<br>Credit amount |
|---|---|---|---|
| Credit for prepaid sales tax on cigarettes | | CR C8888 | |
| Credits against sales or use tax (see ⑯ in instructions) | | C | |
| Advance payments (made with Form ST-330) | | A | |
| Unclaimed vendor collection credit (attach Form TR-912) | | UN 7804 | |
| | | **Total tax credits and advance payments:** | ⑰ |

*8⅛% = 0.08125; 8⅝% = 0.08625; 4⅛% = 0.04125

Proceed to Step 6, page 4 ▶

**Page 4** of 4   **ST-100** (6/04)

Sales tax identification number

| | | | | | | | | | |

**205**   Quarterly

**Step 6 of 9   Calculate taxes due**

Add *Sales and use tax* column total (box 15) to *Total special taxes* (box 16) and subtract *Total tax credits and advance payments* (box 17).

**Taxes due**

Box 15 amount $ _____ + Box 16 amount $ _____ − Box 17 amount $ _____ = | **18** |

**Step 7 of 9   Calculate vendor collection credit or pay penalty and interest**

You are eligible for **vendor collection credit ONLY** if you file by **September 20, 2004, and** you pay the full amount due with the return. If you are not eligible, enter *"0"* in box 19 and go to **7D.**

**7A** If you are not required to file any schedules, start at the asterisk (*) in 7B.

Schedule B, Part 4, box 3 _____
Schedule B-ATT + _____
Schedule H + _____
Schedule N + _____
Schedule Q + _____
Schedule T-ATT + _____

Total adjustment = _____

**7B** Schedule FR, Step 3, box 7 _____
*Form ST-100, page 3, box 13 + _____
**Total adjustment** from **7A** − _____
Form ST-100, page 3, box 9 − _____

**Eligible sales amount** *(move to 7C)* = _____

**7C** | Eligible sales amount from *7B* above | State tax rate | Credit rate |

$ _____ × 4¼% = $ _____ × 3½% = $ _____ **★★**

**Vendor collection credit VE 7704**

| **19** |

**★★** In box 19, enter the amount calculated, but not more than $150

**OR**   **Pay penalty and interest if you are filing late**

**7D** Penalty and interest are calculated on the amount in box 18, *Taxes due.* See ㉒ on page 3 in the instructions.

**Penalty and interest**

| **20** |

**Step 8 of 9   Calculate total amount due**

Make check or money order payable to *New York State Sales Tax.* Write on your check your sales tax ID#, *ST-100,* and *8/31/04.*

**Total amount due**

**Final calculation:** **Taking vendor collection credit?** Subtract box 19 from box 18.
**Paying penalty and interest?** Add box 20 to box 18.

**Step 9 of 9   Sign and mail this return**
*Please be sure to keep a completed copy for your records.*

Must be postmarked by **Monday, September 20, 2004,** to be considered filed on time. See below for complete mailing information.

Please enter NAICS code below *(see instructions).*

Printed name of taxpayer _____ Title _____
Daytime telephone ( )

North American Industry Classification System (NAICS)

Signature of taxpayer _____ Date _____

Printed name of preparer, if other than taxpayer _____

Preparer's address _____

Signature of preparer, if other than taxpayer _____ Daytime telephone ( )

**Where to mail your return and attachments**
*If using a private delivery service rather than the U.S. Postal Service, see* ㉔ *in instructions for the correct address.*

Do you participate in the New Jersey/New York or the Connecticut/New York Reciprocal Tax Agreement?

**No**
**Address envelope to:**
NYS SALES TAX PROCESSING
JAF BUILDING
PO BOX 1205
NEW YORK NY 10116-1205

**Yes**
**Address envelope to:**
NYS SALES TAX PROCESSING
RECIPROCAL TAX AGREEMENT
JAF BUILDING
PO BOX 1209
NEW YORK NY 10116-1209

✓ Make check payable to *New York State Sales Tax.*

2971
David Sample
100 Elm Street
Albany, NY 12203

DATE September 10, 2004

PAY TO THE ORDER OF   New York State Sales Tax   $ 1,050.32

One thousand fifty and 32/100   DOLLARS

**First State Bank**

00-0000000   ST-100   8/31/04

*David Sample*

Don't forget to write your sales tax ID#, *ST-100,* and *8/31/04.*
Don't forget to sign your check

**Need help?**
Internet access: *www.nystax.gov*
(for information, forms, and publications)

**Fax-on-demand forms:** Forms are available 24 hours a day, 7 days a week.   1 800 748-3676

**Telephone assistance** is available from 8:00 A.M. to 5:00 P.M. (eastern time), Monday through Friday.
To order forms and publications:   1 800 462-8100
Business Tax Information Center:   1 800 972-1233
From areas outside the U.S. and outside Canada:   (518) 485-6800

**Hotline for the hearing and speech impaired:**
If you have access to a telecommunications device for the deaf (TDD), contact us at 1 800 634-2110. If you do not own a TDD, check with independent living centers or community action programs to find out where machines are available for public use.

**Persons with disabilities:** In compliance with the Americans with Disabilities Act, we will ensure that our lobbies, offices, meeting rooms, and other facilities are accessible to persons with disabilities. If you have questions about special accommodations for persons with disabilities, please call 1 800 972-1233.

*Refer to the instructions (Form ST-100-I) if you have questions or need further help.*

## CRITICAL THINKING ABOUT...

### TAXES

1. Why does the government ask self-employed people to pay self-employment tax in addition to income tax?

2. Do you earn any money from self-employment? Do you earn enough to pay self-employment tax? What tax form would you use to report self-employment income?

3. How can you help reduce the chance that the IRS will choose to audit your business?

4. How much income tax would you owe given the following tax rates and net incomes?

| Tax Rate | Net Income |
|----------|-----------|
| 25% | $65,000 |
| 30% | $100,000 |

## KEY CONCEPTS

1. In a group, choose a public service you think could be provided more efficiently by private business. Develop an argument for replacing this service with a private business and present it to the class. Have the class vote on your proposal.

2. Fill out tax forms provided by your teacher.

3. Which tax forms will you have to fill out for your business?

_____ 1040 U.S. Individual Tax Return

_____ Schedule C, Profit or Loss from Business

_____ Schedule SE, Self-Employment Tax

_____ Quarterly Sales and Use Tax Return

**Business Plan Practice**

## VOCABULARY

audit ▪ Internal Revenue Service (IRS) ▪ sales tax ▪ self-employment tax ▪ Social Security ▪ tax ▪ tax evasion

# Chapter Summary ✔✔✔

**44.1**   Federal, state, and local governments raise money to support public services from taxes.
   A. The federal government raises money from personal and business income taxes.
   B. State governments raise money from sales taxes (percentage of the price of certain items and services purchased) collected by businesses and, in some states, from state income tax.
   C. Local governments raise money from property taxes.
   D. Social Security taxes support the Social Security program (support paid by the federal government to retired workers and to the families of disabled or deceased workers).
   E. All employers and employees pay Social Security taxes.
   F. Self-employed people who do not have an employer pay self-employment tax to support Social Security.

**44.2**   Federal income taxes are paid to the Internal Revenue Service (IRS).
   A. Income tax evasion is a serious crime.
   B. Penalties and interest are charged for late payments.
   C. Federal income tax returns must be filed by April 15th every year using specific, applicable forms:
      1. Form 1040 U.S. Individual Tax Return — for employees
      2. Schedule C — Profit or Loss from Business — for businesses
      3. Schedule SE — for self-employed workers.
   D. IRS agents and "for hire" tax specialists can assist with tax questions and preparation.
   E. Individual states and local governments create their own tax forms.
   F. Keeping good records makes filing taxes easier and will provide proof of earnings and expenses during an audit (detailed review by an IRS agent).

**44.3.**   Taxpayers have the right and the responsibility to ask their political representatives how and if:
      1. Taxes are being allocated wisely and used efficiently and effectively by the various levels of government
      2. Government services are providing benefits to taxpayers and their communities
      3. Services could be better supplied by private industry, rather than by governments
      4. Tax rates are fair or if the tax codes need amending. ✔✔✔

CHAPTER **45**

# INSURANCE:
## Protection from the Unexpected

*There is a tide in the affairs of men, which, taken at the flood, leads on to fortune; omitted, all the voyage of their life is bound in shallows and in miseries.*

— William Shakespeare, *English poet and playwright*

### KEY OBJECTIVES

THIS CHAPTER WILL ENABLE YOU TO:

- Explain how insurance protects businesses.
- Determine when a business needs liability insurance.
- Explain how insurance companies make money.
- Choose coverage for your small business.

**I**nsurance protects people and businesses from having property or wealth stolen, lost, or destroyed. There are many kinds of insurance, and almost anything can be insured.

Insurance is an operating cost. It is the second "I" in USAIIRD (Utilities, Salaries, Advertising, Interest, Insurance, Rent, Depreciation). If you owned a restaurant, you would need fire insurance. Your insurance agent would help you calculate how much money it would take to replace everything in the restaurant and rebuild if a fire were to destroy it.

## Insurance Protects Your Business from Disaster

Let's say rebuilding your restaurant would cost $150,000. You would need an **insurance policy** that will guarantee you $150,000 in case of fire. An **insurance agent** will figure out how much you must pay for this policy. You might pay $100 per month, for instance. This monthly payment is the **premium**.

As long as you pay the premiums on your fire-insurance policy, you will not have to worry about losing your restaurant to a fire. If it burns down, your insurance company will pay you the money to rebuild and stay in business. Insurance prevents random events from destroying you financially.

## Liability Insurance Protects You and Your Customers

What if someone visiting your store trips on a loose tile and breaks her arm? Who will pay the medical bills? Smart entrepreneurs carry **liability insurance**, which pays the expenses of anyone who is injured while on your property or using your product or service.

Before you decide to sell a product or offer a service, try to imagine how it could cause injury to someone. If you think it *might* cause injury, don't sell it.

## Lying about the Risks of Your Product Is Fraud

Failure to inform a customer of potential danger from your product or service can be seen as **fraud**. The entrepreneur has a moral and legal duty to inform customers of possible danger. The best idea is not to sell a product or service that could be harmful. Even if you're selling something as harmless as ties, make sure they are not made of highly flammable material!

## How Insurance Companies Make Money

By now you may be wondering, "How can an insurance company afford to pay $150,000 to a restaurant owner whose business has just burned down, if the owner has only been paying $100 a month?"

The answer is that insurance companies employ experts who calculate the odds of a particular event actually happening. An insurance company that specializes in fire insurance will have information about fires in restaurants going back many years. Analysts study this information and figure out how often fires tend to occur and how much they will cost.

Analysts decide how much to charge for premiums so that, even if some fires do occur, the cost of insurance paid out to one policyholder has been covered by the premiums paid by the many other policyholders.

## SKILLS MEAN SUCCESS

**MATH** ▶ **Comparing Data and Uncertainty**

Insurance companies employ a useful type of mathematics called *probability* to estimate how likely an event (such as a store burning down) is to happen. You, too, can use math to calculate the *theoretical* probability of an event. Theoretical probability (what should happen mathematically) isn't, however, the same as *experimental* probability (what actually happens).

1. If there are two sides to a coin, what are the chances of it landing heads up?

2. If there are 52 playing cards in a deck in four suits, what are the chances of you selecting the nine of hearts?

3. In the same deck, what are the chances of you selecting any nine?

4. Perform an experiment with a deck of cards or a coin. Draw or flip ten times. Record the results. Compare your answers to the theoretical probabilities you answered in questions 1, 2, or 3. Repeat the experiment another ten times. Compare the results to the first ten.

5. Make a list of the kinds of information you would need to estimate the probability of a much more complex or unlikely event, such as ten days in a row without rain or a particular store burning down. ■■■

## Basic Coverage for Small Business

You won't need insurance if you are simply selling ties on the street or at school, but the moment you move your business into a building, you will need it.

A **deductible** is the amount of loss or damage you agree to cover before the insurance takes over. In the restaurant example, the owner might feel confident that he or she could cover $5,000 in damages from a fire without going bankrupt. The insurance company would have to pay the remaining $145,000. So it would charge a lower premium — say, $90 per month. The policyholder pays a lower premium in return for a higher deductible.

**Rule of Thumb:** When buying insurance, choose the policy with the highest deductible you can afford to cover. This will give you the lowest possible premium.

Lower deductible = Higher premium

Higher deductible = Lower premium

**Although state laws vary, most require business owners who have employees to carry:**

**Workers' Compensation** — covers employees for loss of income and medical expenses due to job-related injuries.

**Disability Insurance** — covers employees for loss of income due to a disabling injury or illness.

**If you have a car or truck, you must carry:**

**Auto Insurance** — covers your liability for personal injuries in an accident, as well as damages to any vehicle involved, and injuries to other people.

**Other Important Types of Insurance:**

**Property Insurance** — replaces any property damaged by fire, flood, vandalism, or other types of damage as specified in the policy.

**Crime Insurance** — protects against robberies as well as theft by employees. The federal government has a program that provides crime insurance for small businesses located in high-crime areas where insurance companies usually won't provide coverage.

*There are other types of insurance that may suit your business. When you are ready to take this step, ask other businesspeople to recommend an insurance agent.*

## SKILLS MEAN SUCCESS

### ENGLISH ▸ Diction

Whether you like it or not, some people will judge you as a business leader by how well you speak. Learn to pronounce problematic words.

**1.** Say each of the following words aloud and tap out the *syllables*. Make sure you see and hear the word clearly. Work with a partner: take turns correctly pronouncing each word. Coach your partner.

| *probability* | *disability* | *deductible* |
|---|---|---|
| *liability* | *compensation* | *theoretically* |

**2.** List some words that you have trouble pronouncing. Let your partner coach you. ■■■

# Chapter 45 Review

## CRITICAL THINKING ABOUT...

### INSURANCE

1. Imagine that a small hardware store with several employees is destroyed by fire. What types of insurance should the store owner have carried, and why?

2. Explain how insurance companies make money, even though they sometimes have to make large payouts.

3. What types of insurance will your business need, and why? What is the highest deductible you feel you can afford?

### Business Plan Practice

4. Pick one type of insurance you would like to have for your business and find a company online that sells it. Describe the premium, deductible, and payout.

## KEY CONCEPTS

1. Some businesses do sell products and services that can injure customers. List three examples and explain how these companies might use insurance to stay in business.

2. Choose one of the companies you listed in number 1 and research news stories about it on the Internet. Find out if the company ever had to pay customers who were injured using its products or services. Report your findings to the class.

3. Mandy is buying an old van from her brother to start her flower-basket delivery service. She planned to buy auto insurance, in case she ever got into an accident. She finds that type of insurance will cost her $3,000 per year, which is more than she can afford. What do you think Mandy should do?

## EXPLORATION

Interview an entrepreneur about insurance policies. Ask how the insurance was decided on. Present a report on your entrepreneur's insurance plan to the class.

## VOCABULARY

deductible ■ fraud ■ insurance ■ insurance agent ■ insurance policy ■ liability insurance ■ premium

## Chapter Summary ✔✔✔

45.1 Insurance protects businesses from potential losses and damages.
   A. Insurance agents sell insurance policies that help clients recover losses.
   B. Insured clients pay a monthly or annual premium to buy insurance protection.

45.2 Liability insurance pays for injuries caused by a product or service or sustained on business property.
   A. Failing to warn customers of potential dangers from a product may be fraud.

*B.* Consider the possible risks in all products and services sold.

**45.3** Insurers earn profits by knowing the odds of loss or damage happening.

    *A.* Not many of the insured will ever suffer major losses or damages.

    *B.* Premiums collected from the insured add up to more than claims paid.

    *C.* Deductibles limit insurers' claims:

        *1.* Lower deductible = Higher premium

        *2.* Higher deductible = Lower premium.

**45.5** Business owners carry other kinds of insurance.

    *A.* Employee-related:

        *1.* Workers' Compensation

        *2.* Disability.

    *B.* Vehicle-related.

    *C.* Loss/damage-related:

        *1.* Property

        *2.* Theft. ✔✔✔

# A Business for the Young Entrepreneur
## PHOTOGRAPHY

Is photography one of your hobbies? You might turn it into a profitable business by taking pictures of groups or special events. Here are some opportunities:

**Musicians:** Rock bands, rappers, and solo artists all need photos to send to clubs, newspapers, music magazines, and record companies. Most artists need many copies of their photos. You can get paid for taking the photo and for supplying the prints, too!

**Sports teams:** Little League teams, high school teams, and adult softball teams all need photos to send to newspapers, put on posters, or give away as souvenirs.

**Other opportunities:** Graduation parties, birthday parties, and weddings.

### TIPS

- Very important: Always insure your photographic equipment. Get insurance that protects it not only in your home but also while you are using it on location.
- Get on the staff of your school yearbook as a photographer. You will gain experience and take photos you can show customers as samples of your work.
- Start a *portfolio.* This is a portable case with pages for mounting photographs and artwork. It also means the work itself. Customers will want to see your "portfolio." Mount your best photos in the portfolio and show it to potential clients. You can also post photos on your Web site.
- Put up flyers advertising your business in music stores, sporting goods stores, and party supply stores.

*Describe the types of insurance a photographer should carry.* ■

### CHAPTER 46

# FRANCHISING AND LICENSING:
## *The Power of the Brand*

*The first and best victory is to conquer self.*
— Plato, *Greek philosopher*

### KEY OBJECTIVES

THIS CHAPTER WILL ENABLE YOU TO:

- Imagine new ways to profit from your brand.
- Contrast licensing with franchising.
- Explore the benefits and drawbacks of franchising.
- Avoid agreements that could tarnish your brand's image.

**A** *brand* identifies the products or services of a company. The brand represents the company's promise to consistently deliver a specific set of benefits to customers.

One entrepreneur can create a business that grows from a sole proprietorship to an international empire. But there is another way to grow a business — selling people the right to use your name. That's the power of a strong brand.

## Franchise Your Business

Once you have developed a strong business and created a brand people recognize, you can use the brand name to grow your business. Selling **franchises** is one option. A franchise is a business that has purchased a license to sell a product or service developed by someone else in a prescribed way.

Instead of laying out the costs of starting up branches of your business, you can sell other entrepreneurs the right to start branches in their localities. In return, you will receive a fee and a **royalty**, a percentage of the revenue earned by the franchise.

## SKILLS MEAN SUCCESS

**MATH** ▶ **Substituting a Number to Solve a Problem**

In 2003, your franchise revenue was 20% higher than in 2002. In 2004, your franchise revenue was 20% more than in 2003. Your revenue was greater by what percentage in 2004 over 2002?

**a.** 20    **b.** 24

**c.** 40    **d.** 44 ▪▫▪

# McDonald's Restaurants Are Franchises

McDonald's restaurants are franchises, owned by individuals who follow the business system designed by Ray Kroc. The original McDonald's was one simple yet highly successful hamburger restaurant in California owned by the McDonald brothers. Ray Kroc was a traveling milkshake machine salesman who persuaded the brothers to let him sell other entrepreneurs the right to start McDonald's restaurants.

# Making the Perfect French Fry

Kroc knew that what made the original McDonald's successful was consistently good food in a clean location, served quickly at a low price. Kroc's breakthrough was his decision to teach **franchisees** — the people who bought McDonald's franchises — how to make the food taste the way it did in the original McDonald's. McDonald's was the first **franchisor** to provide in-depth training to franchisees — in everything from how to make perfect french fries to how employees should dress and greet customers. The entire system of cooking and serving the food was timed so that everything at all McDonald's restaurants would be and taste the same. Customers would know what they were getting.

The first of Kroc's McDonald's opened in Des Plaines, Illinois, in 1955. By 1960 there were 228 McDonald's around the country. A hundred additional restaurants opened each year until 1968. After 1968, over 200 opened annually. By 1983, McDonald's was a $3 billion company with 7,778 restaurants owned by entrepreneurs in 30 countries. Through franchising, Ray Kroc turned a simple idea — the efficient production of inexpensive hamburgers — into an internationally recognized symbol of American enterprise.

The McDonald's franchisee owns the restaurant, but agrees to make and market the food under the McDonald's name and trademark in the fashion developed by Kroc. The franchisee invests his or her capital in a proven, successful business concept.

McDonald's receives a fee and a share of the franchisee's profits. McDonald's provides its trademark, management training, marketing, national advertising, promotional assistance, and standardized operating procedures to the franchisee.

**BizFact:** Exactly how many seconds to cook the french fries is one of many things spelled out in the McDonald's franchising contract. The contract protects the brand, so it continues to mean the same positive things in the mind of the consumer — no matter who owns and operates the business.

## SKILLS MEAN SUCCESS

**ENGLISH** ▶ **Presenting Clear Instructions**

Guaranteeing consistent quality across multiple franchise locations can be difficult. For this reason, it is important to have clear and specific instructions for employees to follow when they carry out specific tasks.

Instructions should be written as a step-by-step explanation of how to do something. Use the following tips to write a set of instructions for a task an employee would have to perform in your business.

- Use simple, direct language.
- List the materials that will be needed to complete the task.
- Identify any tasks that must be completed before beginning the instructions (such as: "Wash hands thoroughly," or "Preheat oven to 350 degrees").
- Number each step in the task and list the steps in the order that they should be completed.
- Start each step with a command verb, such as: "Mix," "Push," "Lift," "Add," "Open," etc.
- Include safety warnings — such as "Be careful when handling the pan; it will be very hot" — *prior* to the step concerned.
- When your instructions are complete, put yourself in the place of the reader and try to follow them!
- Make any necessary revisions. ■■■

## The Franchise Boom

Many different kinds of businesses have been franchised — fast-food restaurants, auto-repair shops, motels, health clubs, insurance agencies, hair salons, and so on.

As an entrepreneur, you could develop a brand and a system that can be reproduced. When that happens, you can franchise your business and reap the rewards of all your hard work. You could also decide to buy a franchise, if you'd like to be an entrepreneur but you don't want to create a business from the ground up. A franchise may be less risky than starting your own business because it is based on a proven operation.

Although franchising has been around since the Singer Sewing Machine Company first developed it in the 1850s, its popularity has exploded in recent years. Over 4,000 companies now offer franchising. The number of individual franchises grew to nearly half a million between 1977 and 1997.

Women and minorities have been especially drawn to franchises as a way to enter the business world. Recognizing this, Burger King, Pizza Hut, Taco Bell, and Baskin-Robbins all offer special financing and other incentives to recruit minority franchise owners. Other franchise programs have focused, with great success, on recruiting women.

## Benefits of Franchising

**Franchisor**

- Growth with minimal capital investment.
- Lower marketing and promotion costs.
- Royalties.

**Franchisee**

- Ownership of a business that has less risk than is involved in starting a business alone.
- Help with management and training.
- Advertising — the franchise chain can afford television ads, etc., that the small-business owner could not.

## Drawbacks of Franchising

**Franchisor**

- The franchisee may disregard the training and fail to operate the business properly, tarnishing the reputation of the franchise and the brand.
- It can be difficult to find qualified or trustworthy franchisees.
- Franchisees who do not experience success may try to sue the franchisor.

Franchisee

- Giving up control — much of the franchise's operations are dictated by the franchisor.

- The franchisor may fail to deliver promised training and support.

- The franchisor may engage in poor business practices that affect the earnings or image of the franchise.

## The Franchise Agreement

The franchise agreement establishes the standards to assure that customers will receive the same product and service at your branch as at any other.

Included in a franchise agreement are:

1. The *term* of the agreement, or length of time the franchisor and franchisee agree to work together.

2. Standards of quality and performance.

3. An agreement on royalties — the percentage of the franchise's sales that is paid to the franchisor.

4. "Non-compete clauses" stating that, for instance, if you own a McDonald's, you cannot also own a Blimpie's.

5. Territory — franchisees are usually assigned areas in which they can do business. Within an assigned area no other franchisee from that company will be allowed to compete.

6. Remember, there are many federal and state regulations in franchising. Before you enter an agreement, make sure that you understand them.

## License Your Brand

**Licensing** is another way to profit from your brand. With franchising, you teach someone how to operate an exact copy of your business. With licensing, you sell someone the right to use your name to sell a product. Let's say you have started a successful clothing line for teenage girls. You could license your brand name to a perfume company that wants to create a perfume targeted to teenage girls. By using your brand, the perfume company doesn't have to start from scratch to establish the perfume's appeal.

The difference between licensing and franchising is one of control.

- The franchisor controls every aspect of how the franchisee runs the franchise. It is all specified in the franchise agreement.

- The **licensor** grants the **licensee** the right to use the former's name on a product or service but exerts less control on how the licensee does business.

- The licensee pays a fee for the license and may pay royalties on sales to the licensor.

Many fashion designers and celebrities have made millions by licensing their familiar names for perfume, athletic shoes, and other products. Licensing is also subject to fewer government regulations than franchising.

## SKILLS MEAN SUCCESS

**TECHNOLOGY** ▶ **Summarizing Web-Site Information**

The American Association of Franchisees and Dealers (AAFD) is a national trade association that represents the rights and interests of franchisees and independent dealers across the country. Visit this association online at http://www.aafd.org to learn more about the resources available to franchisees.

Under "Buying a Franchise," on this site, select "8 Things to Look for in a Franchise."

For each of the eight tips in the article, write a one-sentence *summary* in your own words. A summary is a shortened version of something you have read that covers the important points. The goal is to be brief and clear without changing the main ideas in the material. ■■■

## Respect Your Brand

Like franchising, licensing must be done carefully, with respect for the brand. Many companies have taken popular brands, such as Adidas athletic shoes, and applied them with disastrous results to such products as cologne. It didn't work to apply a brand associated with sneakers to cologne!

Using an established brand to promote different kinds of products is called "line extension." It can work if the brand is strong and the new product the brand is being applied to relates to the original. Kraft Foods successfully applied the Jell-O brand name to a line of puddings, after it had established Jell-O as the preeminent gelatin dessert. In most cases, however, focusing your brand tightly on your product would be a better strategy.

## CRITICAL THINKING ABOUT...

### FRANCHISING[1]

1. Would you be interested in running a franchise? Why or why not? Write a memo analyzing the advantages and disadvantages.

2. Find an item that you wear or use that involves licensing. Write a memo analyzing the licensing strategy's weaknesses and strengths.

3. Do you plan eventually to franchise your business, or license any of your products? Explain.
**Business Plan Practice**

4. For each franchise in the table, use this formula to calculate how much you would owe the franchisor in royalties if you made one million dollars in sales:

**Royalties = Royalty Fee × Sales**

| Franchise | Franchise Fee | Start-Up Costs | Royalty Fee |
|---|---|---|---|
| McDonald's | $45,000 | $489,000 – $1.5 million | 12.5% |
| Arby's LLC | $25,000 – $37,500 | $333,000 – $2 million | 4% |
| GNC Franchising Inc. | $30,000 | $132,000 – $182,000 | 6% |
| Tastee-Freez LLC | $5,000 | $39,000 | 4% |

## KEY CONCEPTS

1. Why do you think a franchising agreement would include a "non-compete" clause?

2. Write a brief description of the differences between branding, franchising, and licensing.

3. What did Ray Kroc do with his franchisees that was unique?

## REFERENCES

1 Figures may not reflect current arrangements.

## VOCABULARY

franchise ■ franchisee ■ franchisor ■ licensing ■ licensee ■ licensor ■ royalty

# Chapter Summary ✔✔✔

**46.1** Franchises are businesses that buy rights to copy a successful operation and its brand.

    *A.* Products and services that become brands:

        *1.* Earn profits for the company that creates them

        *2.* Can be licensed to other businesses to sell under franchise agreements.

    *B.* Franchisees pay a franchise fee plus royalties (percentage of revenues) to franchisors for use of their brand licenses.

**46.2** Franchises have risks, but also benefits.

    *A.* Franchisors provide franchisees with proven trade secrets (recipes, formulas, designs, systems, training, etc.).

    *B.* Franchisees still own their own businesses and assume their own risks, but benefit from:

        *1.* Fewer risks than starting from scratch

        *2.* Rights to proven products/services

        *3.* Help with proven operational know-how

        *4.* Advertising costs that are shared across franchisees.

    *C.* Franchisors benefit from:

        *1.* Growth and profits with less investment and risk

        *2.* Lower marketing and promotion costs

        *3.* Earned franchise fees and royalties.

    *D.* Risks to franchisors include:

        *1.* Inability to control franchisees

        *2.* Franchisees who may tarnish the brand value

        *3.* Legal issues.

    *E.* Risks to franchisees include:

        *1.* Loss of some control to the franchisor

        *2.* Franchisor failure to provide benefits

        *3.* Franchisor failure to protect the brand.

**46.3** Franchising and licensing agreements protect a brand's value.

    *A.* Term (time), standards of quality or performance, royalty rate, non-compete clauses, and territory are all specified in franchise agreements.

    *B.* Licensing agreements grant to licensees only the right to use a brand name, not to copy an existing business model. ✔✔✔

### CHAPTER 47

# INTERNATIONAL OPPORTUNITIES

*"Where goods cross borders, armies don't."*

— Anonymous

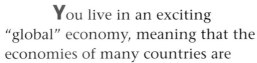

## KEY OBJECTIVES

THIS CHAPTER WILL ENABLE YOU TO:

- Cultivate an understanding of other cultures.
- Explore exporting and importing opportunities.
- Research customers and competition internationally.
- Conduct trade in foreign currencies.

You live in an exciting "global" economy, meaning that the economies of many countries are linked to one another through trade and communication. The world is one huge marketplace and, through the Internet, it is available to everyone. The more you can learn about other cultures, the better entrepreneur and business leader you will become.

Entrepreneurs look for opportunities not just in their own backyards, but around the world. In doing so, they raise the standard of living everywhere.

## Cultivate Tolerance of Others

The best entrepreneurs are tolerant and open-minded. They are curious about other countries, other cultures, and other ways of life, because these are all potential sources of business.

Perhaps there is a product you will discover on a backpacking trip in Europe that you could profitably **import** to the United States. Perhaps there is a consumer need you will find while reading about Panama online that you can meet by **exporting** your product there. Once you realize you are a citizen of the world, the sky is the limit for business opportunities.

- To *import* means to bring a product from another country into your country to sell.

- To *export* means to sell a product from your country to someone in another country.

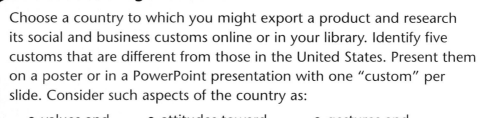

## *SKILLS MEAN SUCCESS*

**LEADERSHIP** ▶ **Understanding Cultural Differences**

Choose a country to which you might export a product and research its social and business customs online or in your library. Identify five customs that are different from those in the United States. Present them on a poster or in a PowerPoint presentation with one "custom" per slide. Consider such aspects of the country as:

- values and attitudes
- manners and etiquette
- gift giving
- greetings
- invitations

- attitudes toward superiors
- differing attitudes toward men and women
- dining in a restaurant
- dining in someone's home

- gestures and body language
- use of time
- humor
- travel
- dress codes
- holidays ■■■

## Freer Trade and Easier Communication

For centuries, trade was often very difficult. To sell products in another country required long and dangerous journeys over land or by ship. Many countries closed themselves off to outside trade.

Governments have sometimes imposed **trade barriers**, such as taxes on selected products, that make foreign goods expensive for their citizens to buy. Taxes placed by a government on imports and exports are called **tariffs**. Governments also use **quotas** to control trade, which are restrictions on how many of a particular import or export may cross the country's borders.

Today, trade barriers are falling all over the world. The North American Free Trade Agreement of 1994 (NAFTA) ended trade barriers between the United States, Mexico, and Canada. This turned the entire continent into a free-trade zone. The General

Agreement on Tariffs and Trade (GATT) cut or eliminated tariffs between 117 countries. Where people are free to trade voluntarily to as large a market as possible, their ability to find someone to buy their goods or services increases. So does their ability to meet consumer needs.

Meanwhile, the Internet has made it much easier for entrepreneurs to find customers all over the globe. Shipping, too, has become much faster and less expensive. It's an exciting time to be in business!

## Research the Competition — Worldwide

The Web greatly increases your potential customer base, but it also increases your competition. Today, small American businesses that used to worry only about local rivals may have competitors from Asia, South America, and Europe — all with sites in English and prices in dollars. Companies in these countries are aware of the fact that four out of every five online dollars are spent by Americans.

What can you do? Get online yourself and conduct a thorough search of your industry, including Web sites from other countries. Learn who your competitors are and you can figure out how to compete with them successfully.

## Using Foreign Exchange

What if a customer from Germany contacts your Web site and wants to buy your product — in euros? As we have learned, *currency* is another word for money —specifically, money that can be exchanged internationally. In the United States, the currency is the dollar. In Japan, the yen. In Europe, it is the euro. In Mexico, the peso.

The **foreign exchange rate** is the relative value between currencies. It describes the "buying power" of a currency relative to the money of another country. The foreign exchange rate, or FX, is expressed as a ratio. If $1 is worth €1.25 (euros),

then the ratio is 1:1.25. To figure out how many euros a certain number of dollars is worth, multiply by 1.25.

$$\$5 = \$5 \times 1.25 = €6.25$$

How would you figure how many dollars €6.25 is worth? Divide €6.25 by 1.25.

$$€6.25 \div 1.25 = \$5.00$$

## SKILLS MEAN SUCCESS

**MATH**

### Calculating Percentage

Values of foreign currencies change, or *fluctuate*, over time, compared to the U.S. dollar.

**1.** Calculate the changes in foreign currency value (gain or loss compared to one American dollar) for the ten-year period shown in the *World Almanac*.

| Country (currency) | How many units of the currency were equal to one U.S. dollar in: | |
|---|---|---|
| | *1990* | *2000* |
| *Australia (dollar)* | 0.78 | 0.58 |
| *Canada (dollar)* | 1.16 | 1.48 |
| *Japan (yen)* | 144.79 | 107.80 |
| *Mexico (peso)* | 2.81 | 9.45 |
| *United Kingdom (pound)* | 1.78 | 1.52 |

**2.** Which currency gained the most value compared to the $U.S. during that period?

**3.** Which currency lost the most compared to the $U.S. during that period?

**4.** If you were an importer, from which countries might you have bought more goods as a result of the ten-year fluctuation?

**5.** If you were an exporter, to which countries might you have sold more? ■■■

**BizFact:** Today, the American dollar is the most important currency in the world. Most business deals are made in American dollars. In the 1800s, the British pound (sometimes referred to as "the pound sterling") was the most important currency, and most international trading was conducted in pounds.

## CRITICAL THINKING ABOUT...

### INTERNATIONAL OPPORTUNITIES

1. If the FX rate between the U.S. dollar and the Japanese yen is 1:119, how many yen will it take to equal $20?

2. If the FX rate between the Japanese yen and the euro is 189.35:1, how many yen will equal €10?

3. You own a small record label. You sell CDs through your Web site for $15, including shipping and handling. You get an e-mail from someone who owns a store in France who would like to sell your CDs. He wants to buy them at $10 each and sell them at €30. He says his profit from each sale would be €12 and he will split it with you.

    Assuming the exchange rate between the dollar and the euro is $1 = €2:

    a. How much profit would you get from the sale of each CD in the French store?

    b. How much is that profit in dollars?

    c. Is this a good business opportunity for you? Why or why not?

    d. If the FX rate between the dollar and the euro fell to $1 = €1, would this be a good business opportunity for you? Why or why not?

4. Do you think there might be customers for your business in other countries? How would you reach them? **Business Plan Practice**

5. Describe any international competitors you have found who may be able to access your customers. How do you intend to compete? **Business Plan Practice**

## KEY CONCEPTS

1. Examine the labels on your shoes, clothing, or household items and note which were made in foreign countries. How many dollars per hour do you think the people earned who made these items? Why do you think the companies that manufactured the products had them made in those countries?

2. Some people argue that free trade is not a good idea because American companies can now move their factories to Mexico, where wages are much lower. Research this issue on the Internet and write a short essay exploring the pros and cons of free trade.

3. Answer the following question in a brief essay: "Some American companies have been pressured by political groups to raise the wages they pay to their workers in other countries. Do you think this pressure is fair or not?"

4. Does your school offer an exchange program that would enable you to go to school in another country for a semester? Research exchange programs or come up with another plan that

would enable you to visit a foreign country.

5. Conduct the interview outlined below with a parent, guardian, grandparent, or other adult family member to find out what kind of currency was used in the country or countries they came from. Add your own questions if you wish.

**Family member interviewed:**

_____

*(Relationship)*

1. Where did you or your parents/grandparents/great grandparents live before moving to this country?

2. What were some of the currencies our ancestors used?

3. Do you have any examples of a currency that I could show my class?

4. Other (make up one or more questions).

## VOCABULARY

export ■ foreign exchange rate ■ import ■ quota ■ tariff ■ trade barrier

# Chapter Summary ✔✔✔

47.1 Entrepreneurs are "global" thinkers.
    A. Countries are increasingly linked by trade and communications.
    B. Understanding and respecting other cultures can increase business opportunities.

47.2 International trade means new customers.
    A. New products are imported into the U.S.
    B. U.S.-made products are exported to other countries.
    C. Trade barriers control some international sales:
        1. Tariffs are taxes charged on some imports or exports
        2. Quotas limit the quantity of some exports or imports
        3. "Free Trade" agreements and the Internet reduce barriers, but also increase competition.

47.3 International businesspeople understand foreign currency exchange.
    A. Different countries use different currencies.
    B. Foreign exchange rates are used to compare and convert money values:
        1. Between currencies
        2. At agreed-upon ratios. ✔✔✔

### CHAPTER 48

# INVESTMENT GOALS AND RISK TOLERANCE

*Where there's a will, there's a way.*

— Anonymous

**S**tarting and running a successful small business is a fine achievement. What you do with your earnings, however, will determine whether you have a secure financial future or whether you will be always struggling to get by.

The key to being able to buy a car and a home, put your children through college, and retire comfortably, is saving money and investing it. Whether you have a career as an entrepreneur or work in some other field, always think like an entrepreneur when it comes to the money you earn. Learn how to invest your money so it earns more money! Even when you work for others, you are still working for yourself — and you should put your money to work for you.

## Always Save Ten Percent of Your Income

When you earn money, what do you do with it? If you're like most people, you will use it to pay bills and buy things. Here's an idea: pay yourself first. Get into the habit of automatically saving ten percent of your income and you will have taken the first step toward building wealth.

If you don't make very much money, this may sound hard, or even impossible. Try it, though, and you will discover ways to get by without that ten percent. Let's say you plan to pay yourself $200 from your small business this month. Without even thinking about it, put $20 into your savings account. You will still have $180 to use for bills and purchases.

**BizFact:** To calculate ten percent of any sum of money, just move the decimal point one place to the left. Ten percent of $50, for example, is $5. Ten percent of $32.00 is $3.20.

## Make Your Money Work for You

When John D. Rockefeller was a teenager (back in the mid-19th century) he lent $50 to a neighboring farmer. A year later the farmer paid him back the $50 plus $3.50 interest on the loan. Around the same time, Rockefeller had made $1.12 for 30 hours of backbreaking work hoeing potatoes for another neighbor. "From that time on," he said in his biography, "I was determined to make money work for me." Rockefeller built a great fortune on that insight.

An **investment** is something you buy with your savings that you hope will earn money. Money grows on its own through wise investing. You are not doing physical labor but mental labor, when you invest, by choosing the best place to put your money.

If you invest $100 at ten percent interest for one year, you will have $110 at the end of that period. If you let the accumulating interest and the original $100 remain in this investment for ten years, it will grow to $259. The **interest** is *compounding*. "Compound" interest is the money you earn on the interest that you earned in a previous period. Money making money like this is the essence of investment.

The concept of compounding interest can be misunderstood. Some people think that $1.00 invested at ten percent over five years will return $1.50. The actual amount would be $1.61.

## The Present Value of Money

Another way to look at investing is embodied in the old saying, "A bird in the hand is worth two in the bush." Your money is worth more to you when you actually have it for three reasons.

1. Possibility of inflation.  (When prices rise, a dollar tomorrow will buy less than a dollar does today.)

2. Risk of the investment not being paid back.

**3.** Loss of the opportunity to use the money for a better investment in the present.

You always want to have your money now. If you can't have it now, you want to be compensated with a return.

**For example:**

A client promises to pay you, three years from now, $100 for services you render today. Your next-best opportunity for investment has a ten percent ROI. Look at the Present Value N-Chart (on page 538) under period 3 (for three years) at ten percent. The present value of $1.00 for three years at ten percent is $0.75. The present value of the promise of $100, therefore, is $75 ($100 × 0.75 = $75).

Your client's promise of $100 is worth only $75 now. Anytime you are asked to wait for payment, you should be compensated. Why? Because money in your hand now is worth more than money promised for the future.

When you sell a business, the price is not just for the business as it exists — you are also selling the future stream of income that the business is expected to generate.

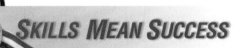

## SKILLS MEAN SUCCESS

**ENGLISH** ▶ **Word Choice**

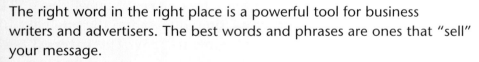

The right word in the right place is a powerful tool for business writers and advertisers. The best words and phrases are ones that "sell" your message.

**1.** Use a *thesaurus* (in book form or online) to improve the power of each statement below. Replace the words indicated with accurate and persuasive words or phrases that will have more impact on a reader or listener.

    **a.** The future of our young company is *very good*.

    **b.** Profits for the last two years have been *nice*.

    **c.** The competition in our market is *bad*.

    **d.** A customer who feels *happy* is our greatest success.

    **e.** Our record of customer service is *really exciting*.

**2.** Find two examples of an effective choice of words in an ad or business report that you can share with the class. ■■■

## Future Value of Money

The *future value* of money is the amount it will *accrue* (gain) over time through investment.

The Future Value N-Chart on page 539 can help you figure out how much one invested dollar will be worth over time at a given interest rate. Look at the chart to find that $1 invested for ten periods at ten percent will grow to $2.59. (So $100 invested at ten percent for ten years becomes $259.)

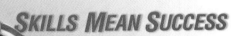

### SKILLS MEAN SUCCESS

**MATH**

### Interpreting Tables

1. Using the Future Value Table, figure the net gain (or loss) of the following investments:

   **a.** $500 invested at 9% for 1 year.

   **b.** $100 invested at 6% for 7 years.

   **c.** $2,000 invested at 8% for 5 years.

   **d.** $2,000 invested at 8% for 15 years.

2. Can you calculate losses using the same table? Would $2,000 invested at an average loss of 3% per year after four years equal $1,749? ■■■

## The Risk-Reward Relationship

There are three types of financial investments (assets): stocks, bonds, and cash. (You learned about stocks and bonds in Chapters 33 and 34, respectively.) *Real estate*, which is land or buildings, can be another important investment.

All investments involve some risk, which is the possibility that you could lose money. As you learned back in Chapter 3, there is a relationship between risk and reward:

**The greater the potential reward of an investment, the more risky it is likely to be.**

**High Reward = High Risk**

This implies that:

**If an investment has little risk, the reward will probably not be high.**

**Low Risk = Low Reward**

# N-CHART

## THE PRESENT VALUE OF MONEY

## Lost Investment Opportunities
## Present Value of $1 after "n" Periods

| Periods (in years) | 1% | 2% | 3% | 4% | 5% | 6% | 7% | 8% | 9% | 10% | 11% | 12% |
|---|---|---|---|---|---|---|---|---|---|---|---|---|
| 1 | .99010 | .98039 | .97087 | .96154 | .96238 | .94340 | .93458 | .92593 | .91743 | .90909 | .90090 | .89286 |
| 2 | .98030 | .96117 | .94260 | .92456* | .90793 | .89000 | .87344 | .85734 | .84168 | .82645 | .81162 | .79719 |
| 3 | .97059 | .94232 | .91514 | .88900 | .86384 | .83962 | .81630 | .79383 | .77218 | .75131 | .73119 | .71178 |
| 4 | .96098 | .92385 | .88849 | .85480 | .82379 | .79209 | .76290 | .73503 | .70843 | .68301 | .65873 | .63552 |
| 5 | .95147 | .90573 | .86261 | .82193 | .70363 | .74726 | .71299 | .68058 | .64993 | .62092 | .59345 | .56743 |
| 6 | .94204 | .88797 | .83748 | .79031 | .74622 | .70496 | .66634 | .63017 | .59627 | .56447 | .53464 | .50663 |
| 7 | .93272 | .87056 | .81309 | .75992 | .71068 | .66506 | .62275 | .58349 | .54703 | .51316 | .48166 | .45235 |
| 8 | .92348 | .85349 | .78941 | .73069 | .67404 | .62741 | .58201 | .54027 | .50187 | .46651 | .43393 | .40388 |
| 9 | .91434 | .83675 | .76642 | .70259 | .64461 | .59190 | .54393 | .50025 | .46043 | .42410 | .39092 | .36061 |
| 10 | .90529 | .82035 | .74409 | .67556 | .61391 | .56839 | .50835 | .46319 | .42241 | .38554 | .35218 | .32197 |
| 11 | .89632 | .80426 | .72242 | .64958 | .58468 | .52679 | .47509 | .42888 | .38753 | .35049 | .31728 | .28748 |
| 12 | .88745 | .78849 | .70138 | .62440 | .56684 | .49697 | .44401 | .39711 | .35553 | .31683 | .28584 | .25667 |
| 13 | .87866 | .77303 | .68095 | .60057 | .53932 | .46884 | .41496 | .36770 | .32618 | .28966 | .25751 | .22917 |
| 14 | .86996 | .75787 | .6612 | .57747 | .50607 | .44230 | .38782 | .34046 | .29925 | .26333 | .23199 | .20462 |
| 15 | .86135 | .74301 | .64186 | .55526 | .48102 | .41726 | .36245 | .31524 | .27454 | .23939 | .20900 | .18270 |

To find the present value, take a given interest rate, go down column to correct number of periods, then multiply by the number you find.

*If it will be two years before you receive the dollar, and you could have invested it at 4%, you are actually receiving 92 cents.

# N-CHART

## THE FUTURE VALUE OF MONEY

## Future Value of $1 after "n" Periods

| Periods (in years) | 1% | 2% | 3% | 4% | 5% | 6% | 7% | 8% | 9% | 10% | 11% | 12% |
|---|---|---|---|---|---|---|---|---|---|---|---|---|
| 1 | 1.0100 | 1.0200 | 1.0300 | 1.0400 | 1.0500 | 1.0600 | 1.0700 | 1.0800 | 1.0900 | 1.1000 | 1.1100 | 1.1200 |
| 2 | 1.0201 | 1.0404 | 1.0609 | 1.0816* | 1.1025 | 1.1236 | 1.1449 | 1.1664 | 1.1881 | 1.2100 | 1.2321 | 1.2544 |
| 3 | 1.0303 | 1.0612 | 1.0927 | 1.1249 | 1.1576 | 1.1910 | 1.2250 | 1.2597 | 1.2950 | 1.3310 | 1.3676 | 1.4049 |
| 4 | 1.0406 | 1.0824 | 1.1255 | 1.1699 | 1.2155 | 1.2625 | 1.3108 | 1.3605 | 1.4116 | 1.4641 | 1.5181 | 1.5735 |
| 5 | 1.0510 | 1.1041 | 1.1593 | 1.2167 | 1.2763 | 1.3382 | 1.4026 | 1.4693 | 1.5386 | 1.6105 | 1.6851 | 1.7623 |
| 6 | 1.0615 | 1.1261 | 1.1941 | 1.2653 | 1.3401 | 1.4185 | 1.5007 | 1.5869 | 1.6771 | 1.7716 | 1.8704 | 1.9738 |
| 7 | 1.0721 | 1.1487 | 1.2299 | 1.3159 | 1.4071 | 1.5036 | 1.6058 | 1.7138 | 1.8280 | 1.9487 | 2.0762 | 2.2107 |
| 8 | 1.0829 | 1.1717 | 1.2668 | 1.3686 | 1.4775 | 1.5939 | 1.7182 | 1.8509 | 1.9926 | 2.1436 | 2.3045 | 2.4760 |
| 9 | 1.0937 | 1.1951 | 1.3048 | 1.4233 | 1.5513 | 1.6895 | 1.8385 | 1.9990 | 2.1719 | 2.3580 | 2.5580 | 2.7731 |
| 10 | 1.1046 | 1.2190 | 1.3439 | 1.4802 | 1.6209 | 1.7909 | 1.9672 | 2.1589 | 2.3674 | 2.5937 | 2.8394 | 3.1059 |
| 11 | 1.1157 | 1.2434 | 1.3842 | 1.5395 | 1.7103 | 1.8983 | 2.1049 | 2.3316 | 2.5084 | 2.8531 | 3.1518 | 3.4786 |
| 12 | 1.1268 | 1.2682 | 1.4258 | 1.6010 | 1.7959 | 2.0122 | 2.2522 | 2.5182 | 2.8127 | 3.1384 | 3.4985 | 3.8960 |
| 13 | 1.1381 | 1.2936 | 1.4685 | 1.6651 | 1.8057 | 2.1329 | 2.4098 | 2.7196 | 3.0658 | 3.4523 | 3.8833 | 4.3635 |
| 14 | 1.1495 | 1.3195 | 1.5126 | 1.7317 | 1.9799 | 2.2609 | 2.5785 | 2.9372 | 3.3417 | 3.7975 | 4.3104 | 4.8871 |
| 15 | 1.1610 | 1.3459 | 1.5580 | 1.8009 | 2.0789 | 2.3966 | 2.7590 | 3.1722 | 3.6425 | 4.1773 | 4.7846 | 5.4736 |

To find the future value, take a given interest rate, go down column to correct number of periods, then multiply by the number you find.

* If you invest $1 at 4% for two years, it will be worth $1.08 at the end of that period.

**BizTip:** If someone tries to sell you an investment by claiming that it is low risk yet offers a high return, be cautious. The investment is probably too good to be true.

## Time and Liquidity Affect Investment Risk

Factors that affect investment risk include *time* and *liquidity*.

**Time:** The longer someone has your money, the greater the chance that your investment could somehow be lost. The longer you have to wait for the payback on your investment, the greater the return should be.

**Liquidity:** Liquidity (as you remember from Chapter 35) refers to the ease of getting cash in and out of an investment. How "liquid" is it? Can you get your money out in 24 hours? Or do you have to commit to keeping your money in for a specified period?

More time equals more risk, therefore less liquid investments are riskier. They should offer higher returns than liquid investments. The easier your money is to retrieve, the lower your return will probably be.

## How Much Risk Can *You* Tolerate?

There is one more factor to consider when deciding on the risk and potential reward an investment offers: How do *you* feel about risk?

Everyone has a different tolerance for risk. Some people love to skydive. Others don't even like roller coasters. People who like to skydive are not *better* than people who prefer to stay on the ground, they are just different.

Similarly, there is no "right" level of tolerance for investment risk. Some people prefer safe investments that offer lower rates of return, because they are not very risky. Some prefer to take greater risks with their money, with hopes of earning higher returns.

It is important to know how *you* feel about risk — before you make a decision. You don't want to enter into investments that keep you awake at night.

Take this survey to find your investment risk-tolerance level.[1]

### Category I: Thinking about Risk

1.  I would be willing to earn less on my investments in order to receive a rate of return I could count on.

2. I am much more concerned with getting solid, consistent results on my investments than high returns that are risky.

3. If my investments *fluctuate* (change value) year by year, I can handle it, if it means I might get higher total returns in the long run.

4. Keeping risk very low is more important for me than taking a chance in order to achieve high investment returns.

5. I am willing to accept some risk in order to get my investments to grow.

6. The final result is more important than how I got there. If I have to risk a bad year to meet my goal, that's okay.

## Category II: Thinking about the Future

1. When it comes to my future, I like to play it safe. I don't want to lose *any* of the capital (money) I invest.

2. I would prefer investments that earn income now. That is more important than keeping all my capital.

3. I am interested in preserving my capital, but I can handle some decrease in value to increase the income I am earning on my investments right now.

## Category III: Thinking about My Capital

1. I am not much of a gambler. I am more concerned with preserving the value of my capital than in making riskier investments that may increase in value later on.

2. The growth of my capital in the future is as important to me as preserving its present value.

3. I am more concerned with providing greater future growth than playing it safe now and preserving my current assets.

## Category IV: Thinking about ROI

Given the choice of the following three investments, I would choose:

1. A 100% chance of a 5% rate of return per year over the next five years.

2. A 75% chance of a 10% rate of return per year, or 25% chance of a 4% rate of return per year over the next five years.

3. A 50% chance of a 20% rate of return per year, or 50% chance of a 5% loss per year over the next five years.

**Your Score:** Add up the numbers next to your check marks. Find your risk level below.

| Point Total | Risk Level |
| --- | --- |
| 3-5 | *Low risk tolerance* |
| 7-9 | *Medium risk tolerance* |
| 12-15 | *High risk tolerance* |

Remember, it is not *better* to have high or low tolerance for risk. All that matters is that you know what it is, so you can choose investments that are right for you!

## Choosing Investments: Stocks, Bonds, or Cash?

Once you have saved some money, and have determined your risk tolerance, you are ready to invest. You can choose from three types of investments:

- **Stocks** represent equity shares of a company. If you own stock in a corporation, you own a piece of the business, however small. Stocks may pay dividends, which are a share of the company's profits. Stocks are *traded* (bought and sold) on the stock market. Stocks tend to be more risky (and potentially more rewarding) than bonds or cash.

- **Bonds** are interest-bearing loans. Corporations use bonds to borrow money that they agree to pay back on a specific date. If you buy a bond, you will be paid interest. When the bond comes due, the money you paid for it will be returned to you. Bonds can also be traded — on the bond market. Bonds are riskier than cash, but less risky (typically) than stocks.

- **Cash** investments can be retrieved in 24 hours. They have low rates of interest because the risk of losing the investment is low. Stocks and bonds can also be turned into cash by selling them, but the price you may get could be lower than what you paid. That is one reason stocks and bonds are riskier than cash.

Your savings account is an example of a cash investment. There is almost no risk that you will lose your money, so a savings account typically pays a very low rate of interest. Treasury bills are another cash investment. Treasury bills are short-term loans issued by the U.S. government. The government pays you a fairly low interest rate and guarantees your money. Both the risk and the return are low. Treasury bills can be sold on the market for cash within 24 hours.

**BizFact:** Treasury bills are called "bills" instead of "bonds" because they mature — come due — in less than a year. The government also issues Treasury bonds, which have longer maturities (from one to ten years, and more).

# Keep an Emergency Fund in Cash

Before you invest in stocks and bonds, make sure you have enough cash saved to cover your personal expenses (food, clothes, rent, transportation, etc.) for at least three months. This is your emergency fund. It will prevent you from having to sell off other investments in the event that an emergency prevents you from being able to earn money for a while. Keep your emergency fund in a savings account, or in other investments that can be turned into cash within 24 hours.

# News Affects Investments

Investments can be affected by news and world events. If war breaks out, stock prices usually fall. When there is uncertainty, people tend to move their money into cash and other low-risk, highly liquid investments, even if means taking a loss. Bad news often drives the stock market down.

A stock's price may change in reaction to news about the company that issued it, economic news, political changes, and world events. Because stock prices change in reaction to information, they are considered to be *volatile* investments. This means they can change frequently and unpredictably.

# Diversification

Protect yourself from volatility by spreading your money over different types of investments. This method of decreasing risk is called **diversification**. It is the opposite of "putting all your eggs in one basket."

If you have $10,000 and you put it all in the stock of one company, you will lose all your money if that company goes out of business. It is wiser to diversify — buy smaller amounts of many different stocks. When you own $1,000 of each of ten stocks, if one company fails, you will only lose a small part of your investment. Because the stock market and the bond market tend to behave differently, it is good to diversify by owning both. When the stock market goes down, bonds usually rise, and vice versa.

# The Stock Market Goes Up over Time

Although stocks can be volatile over short periods, the ups tend to cancel out the downs. The stock market has historically averaged returns of around 11% per year. This is higher than less risky investments, such as Treasury bills. A good rule of thumb is to only invest money in stocks that you can keep invested for over ten years. This lets time work for you to neutralize potential volatility.

# Mutual Funds: Diversification You Can Afford

Unless you have the money and knowledge to buy many individual stocks, consider investing in **mutual funds**. A mutual fund is a company that collects money from thousands of investors. The fund's managers then make investments. You (and the many other investors) are letting the mutual fund managers use your money to pick the investments they think will maximize the ROI of the fund as a whole.

When you buy into a mutual fund, you are buying shares in that fund, which probably owns hundreds of stocks (or bonds). You own these investments, too, even if you only invested 100 dollars. There are many kinds of stock mutual funds. Some invest only in certain industries, such as aerospace technology or precious metals. Others invest widely in the stock market as a whole, to spread out the risk.

**BizTip: Index Funds.** Most mutual funds charge management fees for investing your money. Some, however, are not "managed" because they are designed to buy and hold stocks in the same proportions as an *index* — such as the S&P 500, an index created by Standard & Poor's, that tracks 500 representative stocks. With these index funds, more of your money goes into the actual investment, because you don't pay management fees.

In the next chapter, you will use what you've learned in this chapter to choose investments that meet your financial goals and your tolerance of risk.

## SKILLS MEAN SUCCESS

**LEADERSHIP**

### Entrepreneurial Skills and Attitudes

Understanding tolerance for risk is a skill that is important for any entrepreneur. Create a simple table, and under each heading, list some qualities that you believe are important for success. Be prepared to explain your choices. *(Hint: Does the photo of the skier give you any ideas?)*

| Attitudes | Skills |
| --- | --- |
|  |  |
|  |  |

# Chapter 48 Review

## CRITICAL THINKING ABOUT...

### INVESTMENT GOALS AND RISK TOLERANCE

1. If Gina earns $50 per week babysitting, how much would she have left to spend each week after saving ten percent? How much would she save in a month?

2. Think of an item you would like to buy. Answer the following questions to develop a plan for saving up to buy it.

   **a.** How much does this item cost?

   **b.** How much money do I make each week?

   **c.** If I put ten percent of that money aside, how much would I be saving weekly?

   **d.** How long would it take to save enough money to buy the item?

3. Describe your risk tolerance. What are some of the factors that affect your risk tolerance?

4. What are your financial goals...

   one year from now?
   five years from now?
   ten years from now?
   twenty years from now?

5. I plan to save ___ % of my net income to achieve personal financial goals.

   My primary financial goal is

   _____ .

   My investment risk tolerance is (low, medium, high)

   _____ .

## KEY CONCEPTS

1. Buying a home:

   **a.** How much will you need to save in order to buy a home? You will need a down payment to secure a mortgage, which is a loan from a bank to purchase a home. The down payment is often ten percent of the price. So, with a down payment of $15,000, you could probably buy a $150,000 home.

   **b.** I have ___ years to save for my first home.

   I can invest for my home in (circle the answer that applies):

   **a.** stocks (I have more than ten years to invest for this goal).

   **b.** bonds (I have fewer than ten years to invest for this goal).

   **c.** I plan to save a down payment of $ _____ so that I can buy my first home at age ___ for $ _____ .

2. Saving for college:

   **a.** What do you plan as a career? Fill in the blanks.

   I plan to work toward a career as a _____ with a starting annual salary of $ _____ .

   **b.** Do you know how much education you will need for your chosen career? If not, do research online or ask a teacher, parent, or mentor. Describe the results of your investigation.

**c.** How much money will it take for you to achieve the education you desire? (Again, do research online or get help from a teacher, parent, or mentor.)

**d.** Do you know of any scholarship opportunities you could apply for? If not, how could you find out about some?

### REFERENCES

**1** From the Merrill Lynch financial literacy publication, "Investing Pays Off."

### VOCABULARY

diversification ▪ index fund ▪ interest ▪ investment ▪ mutual fund

## Chapter Summary ✔✔✔

**48.1** Saving and investing part of your profits will earn even more money and build net worth.
A. Follow the "ten percent" rule.
B. Invest, so savings will earn compound interest.
C. Consider the present value of money vs. the future value of the money that will accrue.

**48.2** All investments involve the Risk-Reward Relationship.
A. Greater potential rewards = Greater potential risks.
B. Lower potential risks = Lower potential rewards.
C. The risk of an investment varies with:
  1. Time: how long does the money have to stay invested?
  2. Liquidity: how easy is it to get cash into and out of the investment?
  3. Type of investment: is it possible to lose any, some, or all of it?

**48.3** Cash, stocks, and bonds are common forms of investment.
A. Stocks are shares of ownership of a company that:
  1. May pay dividends (if the company is profitable)
  2. Can be traded (bought and sold) to earn profits
  3. Have more potential risk and reward than bonds or cash.
B. Bonds are guaranteed loans made to a company or government. They:
  1. Are borrowed for a specific length of time to raise cash
  2. Earn guaranteed interest
  3. Are repaid in full on the due date (maturity)
  4. Can be traded (bought and sold) to earn profits
  5. Have more risk and reward than cash but usually less than stock.
C. Cash can be saved in savings accounts and Treasury bills that:
  1. Pay very low rates of interest but have little or no risk
  2. Can be retrieved in 24 hours
  3. Ensure a ready source of current and emergency cash that everyone needs to have.

**48.4** Diversification lowers risk.

    *A.* Stock values are volatile, changing frequently and unpredictably according to business and world events.

    *B.* Investing in a variety of investment "vehicles" reduces risk:

        *1.* When stocks go down in value, bonds often rise, and vice versa

        *2.* Different stocks gain and lose value at different times

        *3.* The average stock market return over time is 11% annually

        *4.* Invest only in stocks that can be held for ten years or longer to avoid market cycles

        *5.* Invest in mutual funds, which pool money from many investors and then buy and sell (manage) a variety of stocks and bonds. ✔✔✔

# A Business for the Young Entrepreneur
## PARTY CLOWN

**D**o you know how to juggle or do magic tricks? Do you enjoy making people laugh? Become a party clown. Parents will hire you to entertain at their children's birthday parties. Hospitals and restaurants also hire clowns.

Make up some short, entertaining clown routines. These might include:
- Mime
- Jokes
- Juggling
- Tumbling
- Balloon tricks
- Silly songs

You will need:
- Clown costume
- Clown make-up
- A bag with whatever you need for your routines (balloons, balls, etc.); bring some games with you, too, like Pin-the-Tail-on-the-Donkey.

Before each job:
- Find out the age of the children at the party so you can practice appropriate routines.
- If there is a birthday boy or girl, or a guest of honor, get his or her name in advance. Have this child pointed out to you.
- Discuss how long you will be expected to entertain at the party and how much you will be paid. ◼

### CHAPTER 49

# INVESTING FOR A SECURE FUTURE

*'Tis money that begets money.*
— English proverb

## KEY OBJECTIVES

**THIS CHAPTER WILL ENABLE YOU TO:**

- Choose investments that are in line with your risk tolerance and goals.
- Create an investment portfolio and project its return.

## Creating Your Portfolio

A collection of investments is called a **portfolio**. The investments you choose to put in your portfolio will depend on:

1. Your investment goals.
2. Your risk tolerance.
3. The amount of time you have to reach your goals.

Let's say you are 16, you have medium risk tolerance, and your goal is to buy a house by age 26. You have ten years to reach your goal. You are comfortable with some risk and you have enough time (ten years) to consider investing in stocks. You have $300 to invest and you decide to put $150 in a stock mutual fund and $150 in a bond mutual fund. Your portfolio would be:

| Current Cash Value | Investment Mix |
|---|---|
| Stocks: $150 | Stocks: 50% |
| Bonds: $150 | Bonds: 50% |
| Cash: $0 | Cash: 0% |
| Total: $300 | Total: 100% |

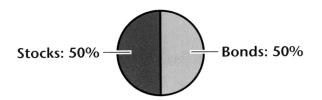

Stocks: 50% — —— Bonds: 50%

You should also keep an emergency fund in cash. Here is what your portfolio would look like if you had $400 and kept $100 in cash:

| Current Cash Value | Investment Mix |
|---|---|
| Stocks: $150 | Stocks: 37.5% |
| Bonds: $150 | Bonds: 37.5% |
| Cash: $100 | Cash: 25% |
| Total: $400 | Total: 100% |

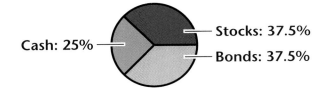

Cash: 25% — —— Stocks: 37.5%
—— Bonds: 37.5%

When you invest, choose stocks, bonds, and cash according to percentages that you set as goals. Pick an amount you can afford to invest every month and invest it in your portfolio. For instance, you can afford $200 per month and you already have your emergency fund set aside. If you decide to invest 50% in stocks and 50% in bonds, you would invest $100 each month in stocks and $100 in bonds.

## Rebalance Your Portfolio Once a Year

Let's say you have a portfolio invested 70% in stocks, 20% in bonds, and 10% in cash. What if your bond investments do well and your stocks don't? Before you know it, your portfolio could be 50% in stocks, 40% in bonds, and 10% in cash.

You will need to rebalance your portfolio because you are now overinvested in bonds. Even though the bonds are doing well, you should sell some and buy stocks instead, until you return to your 70%/20%/10% ratio.

**Rule of Thumb: Once a year, say, on your birthday, check to see if your portfolio needs to be rebalanced.**

## SKILLS MEAN SUCCESS

**LEADERSHIP** **Preparing and Making a Presentation**

Investing is a sound financial decision, but whether you make short- or long-term investments should be measured against what other uses you could be making of the money.

Create a software presentation for the class that shows, with examples, the advantages and disadvantages of using your profits or savings to invest rather than to purchase items you may want or your business may need. Include specific examples of what would happen if, instead of investing $5,000, you used it to buy extra inventory at a bargain price, make a down payment on your own building or condo, pay off a loan or credit card debt, buy a more reliable car, or purchase a new piece of equipment that would save time and lower your operating costs. ■■■

Invest or purchase?

## Future Value of an Annuity

An **annuity** is a fixed sum of money that is paid or invested every year. Use the table on the next page to answer such questions as: "If, beginning one year from now I can invest $3,000 a year for a period of 30 years, and I expect to earn ten percent compound interest during this time, how much will I have at the end of the 30 years?"

Start with the percentage (10%), and go to the number of periods (30). There you will find the factor (164.4940). Multiply the annual annuity ($3,000) by this factor (164.4940) to determine the amount you will have at the end of the period.

$$\$3,000 \times 164.4940 = \$493,482$$

You will have $493,482 at the end of 30 years if you put $3,000 into this investment each year.

## FUTURE VALUE OF AN ANNUITY

| n / i | 3% | 5% | 7% | 10% | 12% | 15% | 20% |
|---|---|---|---|---|---|---|---|
| 1 | 1.0000 | 1.0000 | 1.0000 | 1.0000 | 1.0000 | 1.0000 | 1.0000 |
| 2 | 2.0300 | 2.0500 | 2.0700 | 2.1000 | 2.1200 | 2.1500 | 2.2000 |
| 3 | 3.0909 | 3.1525 | 3.2149 | 3.3100 | 3.3744 | 3.4725 | 3.6400 |
| 4 | 4.1836 | 4.3101 | 4.4399 | 4.6410 | 4.7793 | 4.9934 | 5.3680 |
| 5 | 5.3091 | 5.5256 | 5.7507 | 6.1051 | 6.3528 | 6.7424 | 7.4416 |
| 10 | 11.4639 | 12.5779 | 13.8164 | 15.9374 | 17.5487 | 20.3037 | 25.9587 |
| 15 | 18.5989 | 21.5786 | 25.1290 | 31.7725 | 37.2797 | 47.5804 | 72.0351 |
| 20 | 26.8704 | 33.0660 | 40.9955 | 57.2750 | 72.0524 | 102.4436 | 186.6880 |
| 25 | 36.4593 | 47.7271 | 63.2490 | 98.3471 | 133.3339 | 212.7930 | 471.9811 |
| 30 | 47.5754 | 66.4388 | 94.4608 | 164.4940 | 241.3327 | 434.7451 | 1181.8816 |
| 40 | 75.4013 | 120.7998 | 199.6351 | 442.5926 | 1358.2300 | 1779.0903 | 7343.8578 |
| 50 | 112.7969 | 209.3480 | 406.5289 | 1163.9085 | 2400.0182 | 7217.7163 | 45497.1908 |

# Chapter 49 Review

## CRITICAL THINKING ABOUT...

### INVESTING

1. Pretend you have $10,000 to invest. How would you choose to invest it? From the possibilities below, decide how much you would put into each investment. In other words, how would you diversify? Create your own portfolio, but remember, the total has to add up to $10,000.

   - Savings account (historically, two to three percent ROI): $_____

   - "Blue Chip" stock (a high-quality stock with an ROI of ten percent over the last ten years): $_____

   - New computer company's stock (ROI over the last six months of 25%): $_____

   - Mutual fund that invests in a wide variety of stocks (ROI over last ten years of 11%): $_____

   - S&P Index mutual fund (ROI over last ten years of 11%): $_____

   - Bonds that pay six percent interest and return the principal after 20 years: $_____

   - *Total invested:* $_____

2. Describe your portfolio.

   **Current Cash Value**

   Stocks: _____
   Bonds: _____
   Cash: _____

   **Investment Mix**

   Stocks: _____
   Bonds: _____
   Cash: _____

3. Choose imaginary sums that you would invest in this portfolio each year:

   $_____ in stocks

   $_____ in bonds

   $_____ in cash

4. Rebalancing: I will rebalance my portfolio once a year on (date):

   _____

5. Calculate the value of your portfolio 20 years from now without further investment. To do this you will need to create a *weighted* (average) ROI for your portfolio, because each segment may have a different ROI. Use this formula:

   (ROI on Investment A × Weight of Investment A)

   + (ROI on Investment B × Weight of Investment B)

   + (ROI on Investment C × Weight of Investment C)

   = Weighted Average ROI of All Investments

*Example:*

**A:** S&P Index Mutual Fund
50% of portfolio:
Expected ROI 11%

**B:** Bond Fund
20% of portfolio:
Expected ROI 12%

**C:** Savings Bonds
20% of portfolio:
Expected ROI 6%

**D:** Money Market Fund
10% of portfolio:
Expected ROI 4%

Remember, "%" means "out of 100" so, to express a percentage as a number, divide it by 100 — 50% becomes .50 (50/100 = .50), 100% becomes 1.00, etc.

$(.50 \times .11) + (.20 \times .12) +$
$(.20 \times .06) + (.10 \times .04) =$

$(.0555) + (.024) + (.012) + (.004)$
$= .0955$ or 9.55%

The weighted average annual return for this portfolio is 9.55%.

To find the future value of your portfolio, look up your weighted average return in the Future Value N-Chart in Chapter 48.

### KEY CONCEPTS

1. Use the Future Value of an Annuity chart to figure the future value of the amount you plan to invest each year.

2. Figure the total future value of your portfolio by calculating the future value of the annuity.

### VOCABULARY

annuity ■ portfolio

## Chapter Summary ✔✔✔

**49.1** An investor's mixture of stocks, bonds, and cash is called an investment portfolio.
   A. Match your portfolio with:
       *1.* Financial goals — what do you need to accomplish?
       *2.* Risk tolerance — how safe do you want your investments to be?
       *3.* Timeline — when will you need the money from your investments?
   B. Portfolios should be checked and rebalanced every year.
   C. An annuity is an agreed-to and fixed sum of money paid from (or into) an investment fund every year.
   D. Annuity tables show the future value of an annuity by year. ✔✔✔

# CHAPTER 50

# EXIT STRATEGIES:
## Creating Wealth

*What really matters is what you do with what you have.*

— Shirley Lord, *magazine editor*

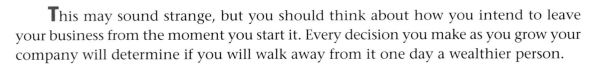

**KEY OBJECTIVES**

THIS CHAPTER WILL ENABLE YOU TO:

- Think about how you want to exit your business one day.
- Explore various exit strategies that will "harvest" the wealth created by your business.
- Choose exit strategies that will make your business more attractive to investors.
- Make a wise decision about when to harvest your business.

This may sound strange, but you should think about how you intend to leave your business from the moment you start it. Every decision you make as you grow your company will determine if you will walk away from it one day a wealthier person.

To leave your business with a chunk of its value in your pocket as cash or stock is called **harvesting**. There are several ways to do this. You could:

- Sell it. The sale would provide you with cash.
- Take it public (sell stock in the stock market). Your share of the business will be turned into stock that you can then trade.
- Join your business with another company. This is called a **merger**. A merger can involve you staying with the business in some role, or being bought out for stock and/or cash.

## Liquidation

Not every business can be harvested. Some, even though they have provided the entrepreneur with a good living, eventually become unprofitable. At that point, the business can be dissolved and the assets sold. This is called **liquidation**. The entrepreneur can use the money from the liquidation sale to pay any debts, keeping what remains.

## SKILLS MEAN SUCCESS

**ENGLISH** ▶ **Deciphering Unfamiliar Words**

Words that appear strange or unfamiliar are sometimes related to words that you already recognize, know, and use. When you encounter a new term, look for a "root" within it. Recognizing the root can often help you figure out the meaning. For example, the root verb for *harvesting* is *harvest*, which means to gather crops or other resources.

Identify the root in each word below. Use the roots to write your own definitions of the words. Create a crossword or word-search puzzle using at least eight of the words. Trade with a partner and solve each other's puzzles.

| | |
|---|---|
| *liquidation* | *exiting* |
| *strategic* | *merger* |
| *emotionally* | *realization* |
| *complementary* | *acquisition* |
| *mandatory* | *diversification* |
| *weighted* | *tolerance* ■■■ |

## The Net Present Value of Money

The **net present value** of money is the value to you today of something that you hope to get in the future. The price of a stock now represents what the market thinks the net present value of the company's future cash flow will be.

A business that is profitable and is likely to be profitable in the future can be sold for a sum that represents its net present value today. This is net present value in action.

## How to Value a Business

There are many ways to estimate the net present value of a business. Value, after all, is subjective, meaning it relates to individual opinion or preferences. One person might be willing to pay a higher price for a business than another would. The first buyer has a higher opinion of the business or may simply want it more than the other buyer.

Here are some methods entrepreneurs use, to estimate the value of a business:

1.  Compare it to similar businesses. If you are looking to sell your dry-cleaning store, check out how much other dry-cleaning businesses in your area are bringing in when they are sold.

2.  In most industries, there are one or two key benchmarks used to help value a business. For gas stations, it might be barrels of gas sold per week. For a dry-cleaner, it might be the number of shirts per week.

3.  Look at a multiple of net earnings. One rule of thumb says a business can sell for around three times its net annual profit. If the business earns $100,000 net profit per year, it could be expected to sell for $300,000.

4.  Book value. The book value method estimates a company's worth as Assets minus Liabilities. This method is the most common one for determining a company's value, and also the simplest.

## The Art of Valuation

Despite the sophistication of these four techniques, they will only be estimates. Each business will have unique characteristics and special circumstances. In the end, it will be the entrepreneur's job to use negotiation to get the highest price possible.

## Choose Your Exit Strategy

In Chapter 46, we discussed replication strategies, such as franchising and licensing. Harvesting differs from replication in that the entrepreneur is typically no longer involved once the business is harvested. This is why harvesting is also referred to as *exiting*.

In William Petty's article on harvesting in *The Portable MBA in Entrepreneurship* (Wiley, 1997), he says: "If the entrepreneur's goal with the venture is only to provide a living, then the exit or harvest strategy is of no concern. But if the goal is to create value for the owners and the other stakeholders in the company, a harvest strategy is absolutely mandatory."

The **exit strategy** is the means by which you will turn your company into wealth on your way out of the business. Offers to buy your business, take it public, or merge it with a bigger company may come as your business develops.  Although you will want to consider all opportunities, it typically takes at least ten years to build a company worth harvesting.

# Ways to Sell Your Business[1]

There are many ways to exit your business, including:

1.  *Harvest cash over time.* For the first seven to ten years, you will want to reinvest as much revenue as possible into the business. Once you are ready to exit, you can begin reducing reinvestment and start collecting revenue as cash. This strategy will require investing only the amount of cash needed to keep the business effective in its current target markets, without attempting to move into new ones.

    **Advantages:**

    - You can retain ownership of the firm with this strategy.
    - You don't have to look for a buyer.

    **Disadvantages:**

    - You will need a good accountant to help avoid major taxes.
    - It can take a long time to execute this strategy.

2.  *Management Buy-Out (MBO).* In this scenario, the entrepreneur sells the firm to the managers, who raise the money to buy it via personal savings and debt.

    **Advantages:**

    - If the business has value, the managers usually do want to buy it.
    - The entrepreneur has the emotional satisfaction of selling to people he knows and has trained.

    **Disadvantages:**

    - If the managers borrow money to buy the company, they may not be able to actually pay the entrepreneur in the end.
    - If the final payment to the entrepreneur depends on the company's earnings during the last few quarters, the managers may be tempted to lower the company's profits.

3.  *Employee Stock Ownership Plan (ESOP).* This strategy both provides an employee retirement plan and allows the entrepreneur and partners to sell their stock and exit the company. The firm establishes a plan that allows employees to buy company stock as part of their retirement. When the owners are ready to exit, the ESOP borrows money and uses the cash to buy their stock. As the loan is paid off, the stock is added to the employee benefit fund.

**Advantages:**

- The ESOP has some special tax advantages — the company can deduct both the principal and the interest payments on the loan, and the dividends paid on any stock held in an ESOP are a tax-deductible expense.

**Disadvantages:**

- This is not a good strategy if the entrepreneur does not want the employees to have control of the company. The ESOP must extend to all employees and requires that the entrepreneur open the company's financial records.

4. *Merger or Acquisition.* If you create a company that another company would like to buy, you can merge with that company or sell the business outright. This can be an exciting exit strategy for an entrepreneur who would like to see the business have an opportunity to continue growing.

**Advantages:**

- This strategy can finance growth that the company would not be able to achieve on its own; the entrepreneur can either exit the company at the time of the merger or acquisition, or be part of the growth and exit later.

**Disadvantages:**

- This can be an emotionally draining strategy with a lot of ups and downs during negotiations; the sale might easily take over a year to finalize.

5. *Initial Public Offering (IPO).* "Going public" means to sell stock in your company on the open market. It requires choosing an investment banker to develop the IPO, making sales presentations to brokers and institutional investors (the "road show") both nationally and internationally.

**Advantages:**

- If your business is "hot," this can be a profitable way to harvest. The market may place a sizeable premium on your company's value.

**Disadvantages:**

- This can be an exciting, but stressful and all-consuming, way to harvest a company and it will require a lot of work from the entrepreneur. In the end, the stock market will determine whether or not it is a success.

 **BizTip: If you decide to sell your business, you can list it with databases such as Inc.com's BizBuySell. Registered users looking to buy businesses will be alerted by e-mail to your sale.**

# Investors Care about Your Exit Strategy, Too

The harvest strategy is important not only to the entrepreneur but also to investors. They want to know how they will one day get a return on their investment. Your business plan should tell them, by describing your eventual exit strategy.

In the business plan, spell out for investors how and when they should be able to get their return on investment. The entrepreneur will need to show financial data that indicate in about how many years the investors could cash out.

Many entrepreneurs think it's enough to simply tell investors that someday the business will "go public" and their share of the business will be worth a lot of money. Of the thousands of new ventures launched every year in the United States, however, only a small percentage actually ever go public. Yet, according to David Newton, in Entrepreneur.com (January 15, 2001), over 70 percent of all formal business plans presented to angel investors and venture capitalists name "going public" as the primary exit strategy. Many estimate that going public will happen within just four years from the launch date.

# Exit Strategy Options

Simply claiming that your business will go public at some point in the future may get a skeptical reaction from potential investors. Investors understand that you cannot guarantee an exit strategy, but you can show you understand the difficulties of small businesses going public. Show that you understand exit strategies by thinking through these four basic possibilities. Choose the one that you think best describes what could happen for your business.

1. **Acquisition:** Do you believe that you could create a business that someone will want to buy (*acquire*) one day? Your exit strategy could be that you intend to create a business that will be valuable for one of your suppliers, or a major competitor, to buy. The plan is that the purchase price will pay you and your equity investors more money than you put into the business. A fair sale price, based on the business's annual net profit, should allow the original investors to realize a good return on their investment. A common rule of thumb says that a business is worth three times its annual net profit. Let's say you have developed a landscaping company that earns about $8,000 per year. That business should be worth at least $24,000.

2. **Earn Out:** To use an earn-out strategy, you will need projected cash flow statements to show that the business will eventually begin to generate a strong positive cash flow. At that point, you can start offering to buy out your

investors' shares at a price greater than they paid for them. The purchase price usually rises over time.

3. **Debt-Equity Exchange:** If your investors will be lending you money, you can offer eventually to trade equity for portions of the debt. This will slowly reduce the interest due over time (as the face value of the loan decreases). In this way, you can decide at what pace — and at what price — to reduce your debt.

4. **Merger:** This strategy is similar to that of acquisition but, with a merger, two companies join together to share their strengths. One company might have an extensive customer base, while the other might have a distribution channel the first company needs. Or perhaps each company is doing well in separate markets, and a merger would open up these *complementary* markets to each other's products and services. Regardless, cash will change hands, and original investors can make their shares available for sale to complete the merger.

## What Would You Do with Wealth?

This chapter has provided an overview of exit strategies. You might want to explore further the one that you think would work best for your business. You might also want to think about your long-term life goals. If you do gain wealth from exiting your business one day, what would you do with it? Many entrepreneurs use this kind of ROI to start a second business. In this way, over time, individuals have built great fortunes. Others use their money to go back to school. Still others become philanthropists and focus on helping others.

The most important lesson entrepreneurship can teach you is that you have the power to think for yourself and create an exciting and fulfilling life. When you use your imagination and skills to grow a small business, you prove to yourself that you can create something real and valuable from an idea.

Whether you become a lifelong entrepreneur, or choose another career entirely, remember that you will always be working for yourself. Never stop asking such questions as:

- What kind of life do I want?
- How can I make my community a better place?
- What makes me happy?
- How can I make others happy?

Use your imagination to grow not only the business of your dreams, but the life of your dreams, as well.

# Chapter 50 Review

## CRITICAL THINKING ABOUT...

### EXIT STRATEGIES

1. How is harvesting different from replication?

2. Describe your hopes for the growth of your business. How much wealth do you imagine you could receive from eventually exiting your business? Why? Imagine you could earn $1 million ten years from now by selling your company. What would you do with the money?

3. About how much money do you expect your business to earn each year? Given this potential, approximately how much do you think your business will be worth after five years?

4. Choose the exit strategy that you will include in your business plan. Write a short paragraph explaining this strategy to your investors. **Business Plan Practice**

## KEY CONCEPTS

1. A rule of thumb is that a business can be sold for about three times its net annual profit. Using that rule, fill in the chart below for the following businesses.

| Business | Average Yearly Profit | Estimated Sale Price |
|----------|----------------------|---------------------|
| Web-site design | $4,000 | $ _____ |
| Aquarium cleaning | $1,000 | $ _____ |
| DJ service | $7,500 | $ _____ |
| Clothing boutique | $30,000 | $ _____ |

2. Describe some of the investors you either have, or hope to have, for your company. What kind of exit strategy do you think would appeal to them most? Explain.

3. Choose an entrepreneur you admire who became wealthy, and answer the following questions (research on the Internet may help).

   - How did this entrepreneur gain his or her wealth?

   - What has he or she done with it?

   - Why do you admire this individual?

## REFERENCES

1 Thanks to *New Venture Creation: Entrepreneurship for the 21st Century*, by Jeffry A. Timmons (McGraw-Hill, 1999).

## VOCABULARY

exit strategy ▪ harvesting ▪ liquidation ▪ merger ▪ net present value

# Chapter Summary ✔✔✔

**50.1**   Every entrepreneur should develop an exit (harvesting) strategy that will provide wealth from the business when the owner decides to leave.

A. Entrepreneurs can harvest cash from a business by:
   1. Selling the business for cash
   2. Taking the company public (selling shares on the stock market)
   3. Merging with another business.

B. If a business cannot be harvested or is unprofitable, the owner can liquidate (sell its assets for cash) and keep what remains after debts are paid.

**50.2**   Net present value is the value something has today, based on its future cash flow.

A. Transactions are really based on net present value — i.e., what the future value may be.

B. Net present value is used to set the worth of a profitable business that is likely to remain profitable in the future.

C. Different people have individual opinions and perceptions of any net present value.

D. Net present value can be estimated using different methods:
   1. Comparisons to the selling prices of other similar businesses
   2. Benchmarking activities, such as sales per week, against similar businesses
   3. Calculating multiples of net earnings (profit).

**50.3**   Various methods used for selling or harvesting a business have advantages and disadvantages for the owner.

A. Harvest cash over time by not reinvesting profits:
   1. Advantages: the owner retains control and doesn't need a buyer
   2. Disadvantages: the owner needs to avoid high taxes; the process takes a long time.

B. Management Buy-Out (MBO):
   1. Advantages: managers are motivated to buy a successful, known business; the owner knows the buyers
   2. Disadvantages: managers may need to borrow money for the purchase and could manipulate profits to lower an "earn-out" purchase price.

C. Employee Stock Ownership Plan (ESOP):
   1. Advantages: attractive tax advantages for the company; retirement savings and investment options for employees
   2. Disadvantages: unattractive if the owner doesn't want employee control or full disclosure of company records.

*D.* Merger or acquisition:
  *1.* Advantages: provides cash for company growth; owner may be able to delay departure
  *2.* Disadvantages: often involves complex, lengthy negotiations.
*E.* Initial Public Offering (IPO):
  *1.* Advantages: can generate a high selling price for the owner
  *2.* Disadvantages: stressful, time consuming, and dependent on how investors value the business.

**50.4** Every entrepreneur should use a business plan to explain his or her chosen exit strategy option to investors.
  *A.* Acquisition: sell the business at a price profitable for the current owner and investors.
  *B.* Earn-out: generate enough cash to offer to buy the owner's and investors' shares at prices higher than they paid for them.
  *C.* Debt-equity exchange: trade equity in the business to lenders over time in exchange for debt reduction and cash.
  *D.* Merger: join with another company in a way that the original owner and investors can sell their shares for a profit.

**50.5** Entrepreneurs also need to know what they want to do after they exit.
  *A.* What kind of lifestyle do they want?
  *B.* What makes them happy?
  *C.* Could they use their wealth to help others or their community? ✔✔✔

## SKILLS MEAN SUCCESS

**MATH** ▶ **Reasoning and Operations Approximation**

People who buy and sell businesses consider "future value." Which of the following purchase offers for your small business would you accept or decline? Use the net earnings (profit) "rule of thumb."

**a.** Your net profit: $3,000 | The offer: $10,000
**b.** Your net profit: $76,500 | The offer: $150,000
**c.** Your net profit: $9,500 | The offer: $25,000
**d.** Your net profit: $71,289.20 | The offer: $213,000
**e.** Your net profit: $27,200 | The offer: $54,400, plus $35,000 if the revenues exceed last year's level for the next two years. ■■■

# Malden Mills

## Malden Mills

In 1906 a Hungarian immigrant named Henry Feuerstein built a textile mill named Malden Mills on the outskirts of Boston. Over the years, the business was passed down to Henry's grandson Aaron. Aaron's father and grandfather taught him that Malden Mills' employees were the foundation of the business. They encouraged him to value the employees and treat them with respect.

Under Aaron Feuerstein's leadership during the 1980s, Malden Mills invented a unique fabric called Polartec or "fleece," made from recycled plastic. Polartec is lightweight, warm, and durable. Malden Mills used Polartec to manufacture jackets, vests, and other outerwear products. In 1999 *Time* Magazine named Polartec one of the top inventions of the century.

During the 1980s and '90s, many American manufacturing businesses relocated to other countries where labor and production costs were cheaper. Malden Mills bucked this trend, however, and kept its operations firmly planted in Massachusetts. As Feuerstein explained: "We have a mission of responsibility to both shareholders and our top asset: our employees. We're not prepared to skip town for cost savings."

## The Fire

In December 1995 a devastating fire broke out at the Malden Mills plant. Within hours, most of the factory had burned to the ground. Feuerstein's 3000 employees feared that their jobs had been destroyed along with the fire. But within a day, Feuerstein announced that "it was not the end" and that he would rebuild the factory buildings exactly where they had stood. He vowed to use the insurance money from the fire to continue paying his employees, with full benefits, until the plant was back in business.

## "We Will Rebuild"

It took Feuerstein months to rebuild, and cost him millions of dollars to fulfill the promise he had made to his employees. Business-minded skeptics questioned Feuerstein's decision making. It would have been cheaper if he had cashed out of his business altogether or rebuilt his plant in Asia. How could he justify paying people who weren't doing any work?

Because Malden Mills was a privately owned family business, Feuerstein did not need to seek approval for his plans from shareholders or board members. He could call his own shots.

"I consider our workers an asset, not an expense," explained Feuerstein. "I have a responsibility to the worker, both blue-collar and white-collar. I have an equal responsibility to the community. It would have been unconscionable to put 3,000 people on the streets and deliver a deathblow to the cities of Lawrence and Methuen. Maybe on paper our company is worth less to Wall Street, but I can tell you it's worth more."

## Corporate Hero

Feuerstein's gestures of corporate goodwill earned him praise from employees, customers, and the public. The media ran countless stories on him, President Clinton invited him to Washington as an honored guest, and he was awarded 12 honorary degrees. People who heard his story wrote him fan letters and sent in donations totaling $10,000. His employees cheered him and worked doubly hard to get the business back off the ground. "Before the fire, that plant produced 130,000 yards a week," Feuerstein said. "A few weeks after the fire, it was up to 230,000 yards. Our people became very creative. They were willing to work 25 hours a day."

## An Uphill Battle

In the wake of the fire, Malden Mills struggled to regain its profitability. Despite the hard work and dedication of its employees, the company was losing money. Feuerstein had secured $100 million dollars in bank loans to finance the rebuilding of the plant and was struggling to pay back his creditors. In 2001 Feuerstein reluctantly filed for Chapter 11 bankruptcy protection. Critics questioned whether Feuerstein was a case study in nice guys finishing last. Feuerstein disagreed: "I don't attribute our financial problems to our employees. We got ourselves over-leveraged after the fire and weren't aggressive or creative enough in marketing. We're going to emerge successfully from this. You'll see: The future will be great."

## Phoenix Rising

In 2003, Malden Mills landed a $19 million dollar contract with the U.S. Department of Defense to manufacture high-performance apparel for the military. The publicity that came from Feurstein's ethical position regarding his employees and their community was recognized by political leaders, and this helped Malden Mills secure this valuable government contract. Within weeks, Malden Mills announced that it was no longer facing bankruptcy.

## Restructuring

In the aftermath of its Chapter 11 filing, Malden Mills was restructured and it now has a corporate board. Because it assumed tremendous debt to rebuild after the fire, different creditors now hold the company's stock. This means that Feuerstein no longer owns his business outright — his creditors do. Feuerstein is trying to obtain a new loan with the U.S. Import/Export Bank so that he can raise the capital to repay his creditors and reassume direct control over Malden Mills.

## Case Analysis

1. List the pros and cons of Feuerstein's decision to spend $25 million dollars to pay his employees in the aftermath of the fire. In what ways did this decision both benefit and harm Malden Mills?
2. Imagine that you are the president of Malden Mills. What would you have done after the fire? Write a paragraph describing your action plan.
3. Write a paragraph describing Feuerstein's philosophy of human resource management.
4. Before the fire, Malden Mills was a privately held company, owned by Feuerstein. After the fire, Feuerstein had to borrow money from different creditors in order to rebuild his business. Please answer the following:
   - What is the difference between a privately owned company and a publicly owned company?
   - What was Feuerstein able to do when he had private ownership over Malden Mills that he couldn't do once he sold equity to creditors?
   - What are the costs of debt financing and what are the benefits?
5. Feuerstein has been described as an ethical businessperson. Explain why Feuerstein has developed this reputation.
6. Brainstorm three concrete ways that Feuerstein's reputation has helped his company.

## Sources

Articles and press releases on Malden Mills' Web site: http://www.polartec.com/about/corporate.php

**Advanced Case Study**

# Advanced Module

## Business Plan Review

*It is necessary to try to surpass oneself always; this occupation ought to last as long as life.*
— Queen Christina of Sweden *(1626-1689)*

**C**ongratulations! If you've made it this far, you have given yourself a thorough entrepreneurial education. You are ready to write a business plan that will impress potential investors and lenders.

If you are satisfied with your Intermediate Business Plan, use those worksheets to help you fill out your Advanced Business Plan. This is an opportunity, however, to improve on your Intermediate Business Plan or even change it entirely. In addition, this Advanced Business Plan includes a projected balance sheet, financing strategy, and exit strategy planning. These features will make your plan a better road map for you to use to run your business, and will make it more attractive to investors.

Before showing a business plan to investors, you may want to hire experts to help you tweak sections. An accountant can help make sure your financial statements are correct, for example.

## Your Business Idea (Chapter 1)

1. Describe your business idea.

2. What is the name of your business?

3. Explain how your idea will satisfy a consumer need.

4. Provide contact information for each owner.

5. If there is more than one owner, describe how the business ownership will be shared.

## Economics of One Unit (Chapter 2)

1. Do you intend to pay yourself a salary, wage, dividend, or commission? Explain.

2. What type of business are you starting?

3. Calculate the Economics of One Unit for your business.

## Return on Investment (Chapter 3)

### Business Goals:

1. What is your short-term business goal (less than one year)? What do you plan to invest to achieve this goal? What is your expected ROI?

2. What is your long-term business goal (from one to five years)? What do you plan to invest to achieve this goal? What is your expected ROI?

### Personal Goals:

1. What is your career goal? What do you plan to invest to achieve this goal? What is your expected ROI?

2. How much education will you need for your career?

3. Have you tried to get a part-time job related to your chosen career?

## Opportunity Recognition (Chapter 4)

1. What resources and skills do you (and the other owners of your business) have that will help make your business successful?

2. Perform a SWOT analysis of your business.

## Core Beliefs (Chapter 5)

1. Describe three core beliefs you will use in running your company.

2. Choose a motto for your company. (You can select or adapt from the 50 positive quotes in Chapter 5, find one elsewhere, or make up your own.)

## Supply and Demand (Chapter 6)

1. What factors will influence the demand for your product or service?

2. What factors will influence the supply for your product or service?

## Product Development (Chapter 7)

How do you plan to protect your product/trademark/logo? (Pick one, and explain.)

Patent, copyright, or trademark.

## Competitive Advantage (Chapter 8)

1. What is your competitive advantage?

2. How will your business help others? List all organizations to which you plan to contribute. (Your contribution may be time, money, your product, or something else.)

## Operating Costs (Chapter 9)

1. List and describe your monthly fixed costs.

2. List and describe your monthly variable costs.

3. Re-calculate your economics of unit, allocating as many variable costs as possible.

4. Add a cash reserve that covers three months of fixed costs.

## Marketing (Chapter 10)

1. Describe the Four P's for your business.

   **Product** — Why will your product meet a consumer need?

   **Place** — Where do you intend to sell your product?

   **Price** — What price do you plan to sell your product for, and why?

   **Promotion** — How do you plan to advertise and promote your product?

2. Fill out a marketing plan for your business.

3. Do you intend to publicize your philanthropy? Why or why not? If you do, explain how you will work your philanthropy into your marketing.

## Market Research (Chapter 11)

1. Research your industry and display the results in a one-page report that includes pie charts and bar or line graphs. Describe your target market within the industry.

2. Describe your market segment and the results of your research on this market segment.

## Record Keeping (Chapter 12)

1. Describe your record-keeping system.

2. List all bank accounts you will open for your business.

## Projected Income Statement (Chapter 13)

1. Complete a monthly projected budget and one-year income statement for your business.

2. Use your projected one-year income statement to calculate:

   Projected ROI for one year: _____ %

   Projected ROS for one year: _____ %

## Financing Strategy (Chapter 14)

1. What legal structure have you chosen for your business? Why?

2. List the cost of the items you will need to buy to start your business.

3. Add up the items to get your total start-up capital.

4. Add a cash reserve of one-half your total start-up capital.

5. List the sources of financing for your start-up capital. Identify whether each source is equity, debt, or a gift. Indicate the amount and type for each source.

6. What is your debt ratio? What is your debt-to-equity ratio?

7. What is your payback period? In other words, how long will it take you to earn enough profit to cover start-up capital?

## Negotiation (Chapter 15)

Describe any suppliers with whom you will have to negotiate.

## Buying Wholesale (Chapter 16)

1. Where will you purchase the products you plan to sell, or the products you plan to use to manufacture the products you will be selling?

2. Have you applied for a sales-tax ID number?

## Your Competitive Strategy (Chapter 17)

1. Using the charts on pages 239 and 240 of Chapter 17, define your business, analyze your competitive advantage, and determine your tactics.

2. Describe your strategy for outperforming the competition.

3. What tactics will you use to carry out this strategy?

4. Write a mission statement for your business in less than three sentences that clearly states your competitive advantage, strategy, and tactics.

## Your Marketing Mix (Chapter 18)

### Step One: Consumer Analysis

1. Describe your market segment.

2. Describe your target consumer: age, gender, and income.

### Step Two: Market Analysis

1. How will you look at location, population, personality, and behavior when you analyze your market segment?

2. Use your market analysis method to describe your market segment. Roughly how many consumers are in this segment?

3. Explain how your marketing plan targets your market segment.

4. What percentage of your market do you feel you need to capture for your business to be profitable?

5. Who are the potential customers you plan to approach in the first two months of business?

### Step Three: The Marketing Mix

1. Describe The Four P's for your business.

   Product — How will your product meet a consumer need?

   Price — Are your prices competitive? Do a comparison. What price do you plan to sell your product for, and why? What is your pricing strategy?

Business Plan Review

**Place** — Describe your business location and its competitive advantages.

**Promotion** — How do you plan to advertise and promote your product?

2. Fill out a marketing plan for your business.

## Advertising and Publicity (Chapter 19)

1. What is your business slogan?

2. Where do you intend to advertise?

3. How do you plan to get publicity for your business?

4. Are you planning to use cause-related marketing?

5. Write a sample press release for your business.

## Break-Even Analysis (Chapter 20)

Perform a break-even analysis of your business.

## Selling (Chapter 21)

1. Describe the features and benefits of the product (or service) your business will focus on selling.

2. Choose three ways you will sell your product or service. Explain why you think these methods will work.

3. Write a sales pitch for your product (or service).

4. Describe three customers you intend to pitch.

## Customer Service (Chapter 22)

Create a customer database for your business. Include name, e-mail, phone, fax, address, last contact, and/or last purchase. What five questions will you ask every customer?

## Business Math (Chapter 23)

Double-check all of the math and financial information in your business plan to be sure it is accurate.

## Business Communication (Chapter 24)

1. Which of these business communication tools will you use?

   Phone, voicemail, fax, e-mail, text messaging, and/or other (describe).

2. Have you designed a letterhead for your business?

## Legal Structure (Chapter 25)

1. What is the legal structure of your business: Sole Proprietorship, Partnership, Limited Partnership, C Corporation, Subchapter-S, Limited Liability Corporation, or Nonprofit Corporation?

2. Why did you choose this structure?

3. Who will be the partners or stockholders for your company?

4. Have you registered your business?

5. Have you applied for a sales-tax identification number?

## Manufacturing (Chapter 26)

1. What are the zoning laws in your area? Does your business comply?

2. Do you intend to manufacture your product? If so, describe the manufacturing process you will use. If not, describe how your product is manufactured.

## Production/Distribution Chain (Chapter 27)

1. How do you plan to distribute your product to your target market?

2. Use this chart to show the production/distribution channel for your own business, and the markups at each point in the chain.

### Manufacturer
Name: _____
Contact information: _____
Markup: $ _____ Markup: % _____

### Wholesaler
Name: _____
Contact information: _____
Markup: $ _____ Markup: % _____

3. What is the estimated time between your placing an order with your supplier and the product's availability to your customers?

## Quality (Chapter 28)

1. How will you deliver a high-quality product (service) to your customers? Describe your quality control procedure.

2. Write a motto for your business that will remind you to stay focused on quality.

## Human Resources (Chapter 29)

1. Fill out a PERT Chart for your business.

2. Will you be hiring employees? If so, describe what their qualifications should be, what you intend to pay them, and how they will help your business.

3. Provide contact information for your accountant, attorney, banker, and insurance agent.

4. What are your policies toward employees? How do you plan to make your business a positive and rewarding place to work?

5. Create an organizational chart for your business.

## Technology (Chapter 30)

1. Which technology tools will you use for your business, and why?

2. Write a memo explaining how you will access this technology.

## Raising Capital (Chapter 31)

Describe financing sources that might be willing to invest in your business in exchange for equity.

Friends and family, "Angels," MESBICs, and other.

## Corporations (Chapter 32)

1. Is your business a: C Corporation, Subchapter-S, Limited Liability Corporation, or Nonprofit Corporation?

2. Why did you choose this corporate structure?

3. Who are the stockholders of your corporation?

4. Who is on your board of directors?

## Stocks (Chapter 33)

1. If your business is incorporated, describe what percentage of your company is represented by one share of stock.

2. Is your corporation's stock publicly or privately held?

## Bonds (Chapter 34)

1. Do you intend to use debt to finance your business? Explain.

2. Would you ever issue bonds to finance your business?

## Your Balance Sheet (Chapter 35)

1. Create a Projected Balance Sheet for your business for one year.

2. Create a pie chart showing your assets, short-term liabilities, long-term liabilities, and owner's equity.

3. What is your debt ratio?

4. What is your debt-to-equity ratio?

## Venture Capital (Chapter 36)

Have you found any sources of venture capital that you intend to contact? Describe.

## Contracts (Chapter 37)

1. What is the most important contract you will need to run your business?

2. Describe any additional contracts you have, or plan to secure.

3. Who is your attorney?

## Socially Responsible Business (Chapter 38)

1. Choose three of the ways below you would use to run a socially responsible business.

   - Recycling paper, glass, and plastic.
   - Donating a portion of profits to a nonprofit.
   - Not using animals to test products.
   - Offering employees incentives to volunteer in the community.
   - Establishing a safe and healthy workplace.
   - Other.

2. What cause-related marketing do you intend to use? How will this support and reinforce your competitive advantage?

## Small Business and Government (Chapter 39)

What laws — such as minimum wage and age requirements, health and safety regulations, or anti-discrimination laws — will affect your business?

## Building Good Personal and Business Credit (Chapter 40)

1. My *personal* credit history is:

   bad, good, not yet established?

   Describe how you plan to establish good personal credit.

2. My *business* credit history is:

   bad, good, not yet established?

   Describe how you plan to establish good business credit.

## Cash Flow (Chapter 41)

1. Use the cash flow chart in your NFTE Workbook to create a projected cash flow statement for your business for one year.

2. Calculate the "burn rate" for your business.

3. Use your projected balance sheet (Chapter 35) to calculate your working capital.

## Intellectual Property (Chapter 42)

1. Describe any intellectual property you are developing for your business.

2. How do you intend to protect your intellectual property? Explain why it qualifies for this protection.

## Ethical Business Behavior (Chapter 43)

1. Describe the corporate governance plan for your business. It should include five policies (rules) that will be the backbone of your company's ethics.

2. Provide information on each of your mentors or advisors. If there will be a board of advisors, list each member and describe his or her commitment to the business.

## Taxation (Chapter 44)

Which tax forms will you have to fill out for your business?

- 1040 U.S. Individual Tax Return
- Schedule C, Profit or Loss from Business
- Schedule SE, Self-Employment Tax
- Quarterly Sales and Use Tax Return

## Insurance (Chapter 45)

1. What types of insurance will your business need? Explain.

2. Describe the premium, deductible, and payout for each policy you plan to carry.

**Business Plan Review**

## Franchising and Licensing (Chapter 46)

Do you plan to franchise your business, or license any of your products? Explain.

## International Opportunities (Chapter 47)

1. Are there customers for your business in other countries? How do you plan to reach them?

2. Describe any international competitors you have found who may be able to access your customers. How do you intend to compete?

## Investment Goals and Risk Tolerance (Chapter 48)

1. I plan to save _____ % of my net income to achieve personal financial goals.

2. My primary financial goal is

   _____ .

3. My investment risk tolerance is

   _____ .

## Investing for a Secure Future (Chapter 49)

1. I will invest my savings as follows:

   **Current Cash Value**
   Stocks $ _____
   Bonds $ _____
   Cash $ _____

   **Investment Mix**
   Stocks _____ %
   Bonds _____ %
   Cash _____ %

2. My weighted average ROI is:

   _____

3. Using the Rule of 72, the number of years it will take my portfolio to double is: _____ years.

## Exit Strategy (Chapter 50)

1. Describe your exit strategy.

2. Why will this exit strategy be attractive to potential investors?

# Appendices

# How to Read *The Wall Street Journal**

*T*he Wall Street Journal is read daily by American business — over two million people a day! But even *The Wall Street Journal* began as a small, entrepreneurial venture.

In 1882, Charles Dow and Edward Jones started a service for people working in New York City's financial district. Their service provided handwritten, up-to-the-minute financial news to subscribers. Dow and Jones's first office was in a room behind a soda fountain, in a building next to the New York Stock Exchange on Wall Street. By 1889, *The Wall Street Journal* was being sold as a newspaper for two cents.

Since then, the *Journal* has become the largest daily newspaper in the United States. When you pick up the *Journal*, you are reading the same paper as the world's most successful entrepreneurs. *The Wall Street Journal* is available on newsstands and by subscription. To have it mailed or delivered to you, call: (800) 975-8609 or visit http://www.wsj.com.

For a more detailed look at *The Wall Street Journal*, see *The Dow Jones-Irwin Guide to Using the Wall Street Journal* by Michael B. Lehmann (Homewood, IL: Dow Jones-Irwin, 1987).

## THE JOURNAL'S THREE SECTIONS

Breaking the paper down into its three main sections, Front Page, The Marketplace, and Money & Investing will make it much easier to read.

### Section A, "Front Page"

1.  **What's News** is a brief description of the major stories of the day.

2.  At the bottom of the front page is **Today's Contents**. This will help you find the page numbers of other features and departments.

3.  Columns 1 (far left) and 6 (far right) are the spots for in-depth articles on a wide range of business topics and for profiles of business and political leaders.

4.  Column 5 is reserved for what the *Journal* calls its "**Newsletter**."

The front page is the first page of Section A. Here is what you'll find in the rest of the section:

1.  On page A2 is the latest economic news.

2.  The middle part of Section A is generally composed of the stories listed in **What's News**.

3.  The daily **Industry Focus** spotlights one company or one industry.

4.  Near the back of Section A are two pages devoted to **International Reports** — business and political news from other countries.

5.  In its **Leisure & Arts** section, the *Journal* reviews books and music and covers sports news.

6.  The two facing pages at the end of Section A are the **editorial pages**.

## Section B, "The Marketplace"

This section contains the important business stories of the day. On the first page of the section, look for:

1. The **lead story**, given the most prominent spot at the top of the page.

2. **"The orphan"** — a short, amusing, true story.

Here is what you will find in the rest of Section B:

1. **Index to Business** (page B2). This is a list, by page number, of the businesses written about in that day's issue.

2. The **Enterprise** feature is about smaller, entrepreneurial companies.

3. **Technology** reports on high-tech businesses.

4. **Marketing & Media** covers advertising and the media.

5. **The Law** reports on legal issues affecting business.

6. **The Mart** appears in Business Opportunities at the end of Section B, and consists of classified pages that list employment opportunities and businesses for sale.

## Section C, "Money & Investing"

Activity on the five major financial markets during the previous 18 months and the previous week is represented through **graphs**. The markets are:

- Stocks
- Bonds
- Interest (rates)
- U.S. Dollar (compared to five foreign currencies)
- Commodities

In the rest of Section C, you will find:

1. An important financial market column, **Heard on the Street**.

2. Reports on how various financial markets, including the stock market, are performing.

Back in 1889, *The Wall Street Journal* started reporting the Dow Jones Industrial Average (DJIA), an average of the prices of 11 major stocks, to indicate how the economy in general is doing. Today, Dow Jones reports price averages for three types of stocks and includes many more companies.

The price movements of these stocks are averaged at the end of each day. These averages are called the "Dow Jones Averages." You've probably heard them announced during the business news on television or on the radio.

Other financial markets covered in Section C of the *Journal* are:

- Mutual Funds
- International Stocks
- Foreign Currencies
- Credit Markets
- Futures & Options

## RESOURCES

For a more detailed look at *The Wall Street Journal, see The Dow Jones-Irwin Guide to Using the Wall Street Journal*, by Michael B. Lehmann (Homewood, Illinois: Dow Jones-Irwin, 1987).

* Adapted with permission from materials prepared by Dow Jones, Inc.

**577**

**Appendix A**

# Not-for-Profit Organizations

## TIPS FOR ENTREPRENEURS WHO WANT TO START NOT-FOR-PROFIT ORGANIZATIONS

There are huge markets where people have needs — for food, shelter, education, and more — but can't afford to pay money out of their own pockets to have their needs met.

In the United States, the government created the 501(c)(3) nonprofit corporation to help address this situation. Technically speaking, a 501(c)(3) is a tax-exempt legal structure that can receive charitable donations from individuals, businesses, government agencies, and philanthropic foundations. Examples of well-known not-for-profits include: the Boys and Girls Clubs, the YMCA, and the Sierra Club. People who donate money to these charitable organizations benefit by deducting the contributions from their taxable income.

In the United States, close to one million organizations qualified for 501(c)(3) status in 2003 compared to 600,000 in 1993. Charitable donations have also risen: in 1993, $148.4 billion dollars were invested in the not-for-profit sector, compared to $240.7 billion in 2003.* While competition for resources has increased, more resources are now available to support the growth of organizations that choose to incorporate as not-for-profits.

Like any business, a not-for-profit needs to generate revenue to cover its expenses. It needs to identify a target market and figure out how it will deliver its products and services to that market. Some key differences and considerations exist, however, and you should be aware of them before you choose this legal structure:

1. **No one can own a not-for-profit organization:** A nonprofit cannot be bought and sold like other businesses. If you decided to dissolve such an organization, you would not be able to sell it for your own financial gain. Nor can you issue stock in the corporation to raise money for the organization. Employees of not-for-profits typically earn money by drawing a salary as a fixed cost of the organization. Not-for-profits are great vehicles for improving society; they are less effective as tools for creating wealth and sharing that wealth with others.

2. **Not-for-profits are mission driven:** Before you can go into business as a not-for-profit, you will need to be crystal clear about your organization's mission. What problem(s) are you trying to solve? Is there a market of donors who will contribute money to your cause?

3. **Not-for-profits have a different perspective on their EOU:** Like any business, not-for-profit organizations need to conduct an Economics of One Unit (EOU) analysis. Your EOU will reveal how the business defines a typical "unit of sale," the amount you plan to charge per

---

\* MBAs at the Crossroads of Corporate and Nonprofit America, Jessica Stannard-Friel, "On Philanthropy" Web site, 12/3/04: http://www.onphilanthropy.com

unit, and how much it costs the business to deliver this unit to an average customer. For-profit businesses pay close attention to their gross profit per unit because this dollar amount sheds light on the potential to become profitable.

Not-for-profit organizations must also assess their EOU, but here the focus is a bit different. Since not-for-profits do not exist to generate a financial gain, the difference between the organizations' cost per unit and their selling price per unit should be modest. Remember that not-for-profits receive charitable contributions from donors who want to make sure that their money is being invested directly into the organizations' programs and services — not their savings accounts. Not-for-profits must strike a delicate balance between charging donors "at cost" and ensuring that they have enough money to pay their overhead and stay afloat. If your donors and the general public suspect that your organization is mismanaging its funds, your reputation will be badly damaged. Many not-for-profits have gone out of business for this reason.

4. **Analyze Your Social Return on Investment (SROI)\*:** With a for-profit business, the return on investment is calculated by looking at the corporation's financial returns. Not-for-profit entrepreneurs need to think about their ROI a little bit differently. Not-for-profits don't exist to make money, so the ultimate measure of success won't be financial in nature. Your SROI will be

based upon how much it costs your organization to provide its services. This must then be analyzed in relationship to the value of the level of change that was brought about as a result of this investment.

5. **Define Your Unit of Change:** As a not-for-profit entrepreneur you will need to set goals regarding the changes you intend to cause in society. How many homeless people will you feed? How many students will graduate as a result of your dropout prevention program? These goals must tie back to your costs and your EOU. What constitutes a unit of service? Is it based on one person, one classroom, or one square mile of the rainforest? How much does it cost you to provide services on a unit-by-unit basis? Given these costs, how many units of change did your organization produce? How can you prove that your not-for-profit caused these changes?

6. **You Can Still Be Your Own Boss — But with a Twist:** Even though the not-for-profit entrepreneurs do not own their organizations, they still get to be their own bosses. They also benefit from the satisfaction of having started something from scratch that improves society in unique and innovative ways. However, unlike a business owner who runs a privately held company, a not-for-profit entrepreneur must answer to its Board of Directors. This scenario mirrors what happens when a private company decides to "go public" and sells shares to the public. Here, the company must

---

\* The term "Social Return on Investment" was developed by the Roberts Enterprise Development Fund. For more information see http://www.redf.org/results-sroi.htm

establish a Corporate Board that will oversee the interests of the company's shareholders. Similarly, a not-for-profit organization's Board of Directors manages the entrepreneur and oversees the organization's finances and operations. All nonprofits are, in a sense, "publicly held" because they cannot, by definition, be privately owned.

7. **Analyze Your Financing Strategy:** Not-for-profit corporations can tap into a large revenue stream that other business structures cannot access. Not-for-profits generate revenue through grants, gifts, and earned income.

The Advanced Business Plan Review includes a section for students to consider corporate structure. If you are starting a nonprofit, please fill out the following section and adjust your business plan accordingly.

If you are starting a not-for-profit business:

1. What is the name of your nonprofit organization?

2. What problem(s) are you trying to solve?

3. Describe your organization's mission.

4. Describe the programs and services you plan to create.

5. How will your organization achieve its mission?

6. What is the "unit of change" (per person, animal, house, etc.)?

7. How will you measure these changes?

8. Who are your competitors?

9. How much will it cost you to deliver a unit of service?

10. Which foundations support your organization's mission? What are their funding guidelines? Make a list of five to ten possible grants for which you could apply.

11. Which individuals will you approach to raise money for your enterprise? How much will you request? Make a list of five to ten prospective donors:

12. Will you have any sources of earned income? What products or services do you plan to sell directly to the public to generate income? List the possible sources of earned income and how much money you expect to earn from each source.

# Resources for the Young Entrepreneur*

## BOOKS

### On Starting a Business and Succeeding...

*101 Businesses You Can Start on the Internet*, Daniel S. Janal (International Thomson Publishing, 1996).

*The Art of the Start: The Time-Tested, Battle-Hardened Guide for Anyone Starting Anything*, Guy Kawasaki (Portfolio, 2004).

*Good to Great: Why Some Companies Make the Leap... and Others Don't*, Jim Collins (HarperBusiness, 2001).

*How to Make 1000 Mistakes in Business and Still Succeed: The Small Business Owner's Guide to Crucial Decisions*, Harold L. Wright (The Wright Track, 1995).

*In Search of Excellence: Lessons from America's Best Run Companies*, Thomas J. Peters and Robert H. Waterman (Warner Books; reissue, 1988).

*Mancuso's Small Business Resource Guide*, Joseph Mancuso (Sourcebooks, 1996).

*Online Success Tactics: 101 Ways to Build Your Small Business*, Jeanette Cates (Twin Towers, 2002).

*The E-Myth Revisited: Why Most Small Businesses Don't Work and What to Do About It*, Michael Gerber (HarperBusiness, 1995).

*The Young Entrepreneur's Guide to Starting and Running a Business*, Steve Mariotti (Three Rivers Press; revised edition, 2000).

### On Thinking Like an Entrepreneur...

*The 48 Laws of Power*, Michael Greene (Penguin Putnam, 2000).

*Focus: The Future of Your Company Depends on It*, Al Reis (HarperBusiness, 1997).

*Secrets of the Young & Successful: How to Get Everything You Want Without Waiting a Lifetime*, Jennifer Kushell and Scott M. Kaufman (Fireside, 2003).

*The 7 Habits of Highly Effective People*, Stephen Covey (Free Press, 1990).

*The Student Success Manifesto: How to Create a Life of Passion, Purpose, and Prosperity*, Michael Simmons (Extreme Entrepreneurship Education Co., 2003).

*Success through a Positive Mental Attitude*, W. Clement Stone (Pocket Books, re-issue, 1991). A classic!

*Think and Grow Rich*, Napoleon Hill (Ballantine Books, re-issue, 1990). Another classic!

*Think and Grow Rich*, Dennis Paul Kimbro (Fawcett Columbine, 1991). An update of Hill's book by an African American.

---

* Please note that NFTE cannot guarantee that the information in this section will remain current, including possible future changes to the contents of the listed Web sites.

**581**

## On How Other Entrepreneurs Succeeded...

*Ben & Jerry's: The Inside Scoop: How Two Real Guys Built a Business with a Social Conscience and a Sense of Humor*, Fred "Chico" Lager (Crown Publishers, Inc., 1994). The former CEO of Ben & Jerry's describes the company's activism and remarkable history.

*Body & Soul*, Anita Roddick Tells the Story of The Body Shop, Inc. (Crown Publishers, 1991).

*Entrepreneurs in Profile: How 20 of the World's Greatest Entrepreneurs Built Their Business Empires — and How You Can Too*, Steve Mariotti and Michael Caslin with Debra DeSalvo (Career Press, 2000).

*Kitchen Table Entrepreneurs: How Eleven Women Escaped Poverty and Became Their Own Bosses*, Martha Shirk, Anna Wadia, Marie Wilson, and Sara Gould (Westview Press, 2004).

*Steve Jobs: Wizard of Apple Computer*, Suzan Willson (Enslow Publishers, 2001).

*Student Entrepreneurs: 14 Undergraduate All-Stars Tell Their Stories*, Michael McMyne and Nicole Amare (Premium Press America, 2003).

*The Men Behind Def Jam: The Radical Rise of Russell Simmons and Rick Rubin*, Alex Ogg (Omnibus Press, 2002).

*Trump: The Way to the Top: The Best Business Advice I Ever Received*, Donald Trump (Crown Business, 2004).

*Upstart Start-Ups!: How 34 Young Entrepreneurs Overcame Youth, Inexperience, and Lack of Money to Create Thriving Businesses*, Ron Lieber (Broadway; 1st edition, 1998).

## On Negotiating...

*Difficult Conversations: How to Discuss What Matters Most*, Douglas Stone, Bruce Patton, Sheila Heen, and Roger Fisher (Penguin Putnam, 2000).

*Getting to Yes: Negotiating Agreement Without Giving In*, Roger Fisher, William Ury, and Bruce Patton (Penguin Books; 2nd/Rep edition, 1991).

*You Can Negotiate Anything*, Herb Cohen (Bantam Books, 1993).

## On Accounting...

*Accounting the Easy Way*, Peter J. Eisen (Barron's Educational Series, 4th Edition, 2003).

*The Guide to Understanding Financial Statements*, S.B. Costales (McGraw-Hill, 1993).

## On Investing, Money Management, and Personal Finance...

*The Motley Fool Investment Guide for Teens: 8 Steps to Having More Money Than Your Parents Ever Dreamed Of*, David Gardner, Tom Gardner, Selena Maranjian (Fireside, 2002).

*Rich Dad, Poor Dad: What the Rich Teach Their Kids About Money — That the Poor and Middle Class Do Not!*, Robert T. Kiyosaki and Sharon L. Lechter (Warner Business Books, 2000).

*The Laws of Money, The Lessons of Life: Keep What You Have and Create What You Deserve*, Suze Orman (Free Press, 2003).

*The Millionaire Next Door*, Thomas Stanley and William Danko (Pocket, 1998).

*Understanding Wall Street*, Jeffrey Little (McGraw Hill, 2004).

**On Marketing...**

*Purple Cow: Transform Your Business by Being Remarkable*, Seth Godin (Portfolio, 2003).

*Social Marketing: Improving the Quality of Life*, Philip Kotler, Ned Roberto, and Nancy Lee, (SAGE Publications; 2nd edition, 2002).

*The 22 Immutable Laws of Branding*, Al Reis and Laura Reis (HarperBusiness, 2002).

*The Tipping Point: How Little Things Can Make a Big Difference*, Malcolm Gladwell (Back Bay Books, 2002).

## MAGAZINES

*BusinessWeek*
1221 Avenue of the Americas
New York, NY  10020
(212) 512-2000
Subscriptions: 1-800-635-1200
www.businessweek.com

*Inc.*
375 Lexington Avenue
New York, NY  10017
Tel: 212-499-2000
Subscriptions: www.inc.com

*Entrepreneur*
Entrepreneur Media Inc.
2445 McCabe Way
Irvine, CA  92614
(949) 261-2325
Subscriptions: (800) 274-6229
www.entrepreneur.com

*Fast Company*
375 Lexington Avenue
New York, NY  10017
Subscriptions: 515-248-7693
www.fastcompany.com

*Forbes*
60 Fifth Avenue
New York, NY  10003
212-620-2200
Subscriptions: www.forbes.com

*Fortune*
1271 Sixth Avenue, 16th Floor
New York, NY  10020
Subscriptions: (800) 621-8000
www.fortune.com

As entrepreneurship has taken hold among minorities, several magazines have sprung up to serve those markets:

*Black Enterprise*
130 Fifth Avenue
New York, NY  10011
(212) 242-8000
www.blackenterprise.com

*Hispanic Business*
425 Pine Avenue
Santa Barbara, CA  93117
(805) 964-4554
www.hispanicbusiness.com

## WEB SITES

BizBuySell, http://www.bizbuysell.com, sends registered users who might want to buy your business e-mails, alerting them that you want to sell.

Business Owners' Idea Café, http://www.businessownersideacafe. com, provides a tool for figuring out how much capital you need to get your business off the ground.

United States Copyright Office, http://www.copyright.gov

CPA Finder at http://www.cpafinder.com can help you locate a certified public accountant.

Download.com, http://www.download.com, has free software. Be sure to run all software through your virus detection program before installing it on your hard drive.

Ecommerce-Guide, http://e-comm.internet.com

Internal Revenue Service, http://www.irs.gov. You can download any tax form you need from the IRS Web site.

The Internet Public Library, http://www.ipl.org, is a good source for industry and market statistics.

InterNIC, http://www.internic.net, is the location for registering your Web site.

Practical Money Skills for Life, http://www.practicalmoneyskills.com

Sell It on the Web, http://www.sellitontheweb.com

The Social Venture Network (SVN) Standards of Corporate Responsibility at http://www.svn.org/initiatives/standards.html provides ideas on how to make your business socially responsible.

The *Thomas Register* is a comprehensive catalog that lists almost all the manufacturing companies in the United States (about 25 volumes, each about four inches thick). There are national and regional versions of this publication. You can find a copy in most public libraries, or you can use the sites below: http://www.thomasnet.com/ http://www.thomasregister.com

## ADDITIONAL RESOURCES

The Small Business Administration (SBA) is a government agency created to support and promote entrepreneurs. The SBA offers free and inexpensive pamphlets on a variety of business subjects. Some local offices offer counseling to small business owners.

***Small Business Administration***
409 Third Street, SW
Washington, DC 20416
(800) 827-5722
http://www.sbaonline.sba.gov/

Call this toll-free number to reach the Small Business Answer Desk, which assists entrepreneurs with their questions and can help you locate an SBA office near you: (800) 827-5722.

The Minority Business Development Agency (MBDA) is the federal agency created to foster the establishment and growth of minority-owned businesses in America. MBDA provides funding for a network of Minority Business Development Centers (MBDCs), Native American Business Development Centers (NABDCs), and Business Resource Centers (BRCs). The Centers provide minority entrepreneurs with one-on-one assistance in writing business plans, marketing, management and technical assistance, and financial planning to assure adequate financing for business ventures. To find a Minority Business Development Center near you, visit http://www.mbda.gov.

The Service Core of Retired Executives (SCORE) is a group of retired businesspeople who volunteer as counselors and mentors to entrepreneurs. To locate an office near you, contact:

*Service Core of Retired Executives*
*(SCORE Association)*
409 3rd Street SW, 6th Floor
Washington, DC  20024
(800) 634-0245
http://www.score.org

The National Association of Women Business Owners helps female entrepreneurs network. You can join a local chapter of female entrepreneurs in your area.

**National Association of Women Business Owners**
8405 Greensboro Drive
McLean, VA  22102
(800) 556-2926
http://www.nawbo.org

The *Small Business Reporter* is a series of more than 100 pamphlets on entrepreneurial subjects, including financial statements. Each pamphlet is available for a small postage and handling charge. For a free index, write to:

**Small Business Reporter**
Bank of America
PO Box 3700, Dept. 36361
San Francisco, CA 94317

The Young Entrepreneurs' Organization provides learning and networking opportunities worldwide for young entrepreneurs through YEO and the World Entrepreneurs' Organization (WEO).

**Young Entrepreneurs' Organization**
1199 Fairfax Street, Suite 200
Alexandria, VA 22314
703-519-6700
http://www.yeo.org

## SCHOLARSHIPS FOR YOUNG ENTREPRENEURS

Most business schools offer scholarships. If you are interested in studying business and entrepreneurship in college, contact the business school at the college you wish to attend.

Having run your own business will be a big plus on your scholarship and college applications!

Here is a sampling of scholarship programs that focus on entrepreneurship:

**FDU Entrepreneurial Studies Scholarship**
http://www.fdu.edu/academic/rothman/scholarship.htm
For New Jersey students seeking to study entrepreneurship.

**Indiana University Kelley School of Business**
http://www.kelley.iu.edu/ugrad/scholarships/index.html

**Johnson Scholarship Foundation, Tribal College Entrepreneurship Scholarship Program** http://www.johnsonscholarships.org/TRJSF_Application.pdf

**The Minority Scholarship Awards Program**
http://www.black-collegian.com/news/ifa402.shtml
Encourages the study of franchising by minority students.

**MIT Entrepreneurship Center, Awards and Scholarships**
http://entrepreneurship.mit.edu/awards_scholarships.php

**Xavier University Williams College of Business, Scholarships in Entrepreneurial Studies**
http://www.xu.edu/management/scholarships.cfm

# Sample Student Business Plan

The following sample business plan is for a greeting card business started by two teenagers. Review the business owners' answers and note how they have created a road map to follow in running their business. After reading this sample business plan, consider how you could improve on your own business plan.

## Your Business Idea (Chapter 1)

**1.** Describe your business idea.

We are twin sisters starting a greeting card business. Together we will design, market, and sell our cards. Our cards will be geared toward young people aged 13-18.

**2.** What is the name of your business?

Teen Greetings

**3.** Explain how your idea will satisfy a consumer need.

Teenagers like to give cards to their friends on different occasions. It's hard to find greeting cards designed for and by teens. Our cards will appeal to people in our age group.

**4.** Provide contact information for each owner.

| Karen Walker | Cynthia Walker |
|---|---|
| 150 Buena Vista Road | 150 Buena Vista Road |
| Austin, Texas 78744 | Austin, Texas 78744 |

**5.** If there is more than one owner, describe how the business ownership will be shared.

Teen Greetings will be owned by both of us, and we will each have a 50% equity stake in the business.

## Economics of One Unit (Chapter 2)

**1.** Do you intend to pay yourself a salary, wage, dividend, or commission? Explain.

We plan to pay ourselves in the following ways:

- Salary: We will each receive a monthly salary of $150. This business cost will compensate us for the work we will be contributing to Teen Greetings as owners and managers.

- Dividend: If we have a net profit at the end of the year, we will divide 10-25% of this amount as dividend income. We will reinvest the remainder in the business so it can continue to grow.

**2.** What type of business are you starting?

Teen Greetings will be a manufacturing business.

**3.** Calculate the Economics of One Unit for your business.

| ECONOMICS OF ONE UNIT (EOU) | | | |
|---|---|---|---|
| **Manufacturing Business:** unit = 1 dozen greeting cards | | | |
| **Selling Price per Unit:** | | | **$12.00** |
| Materials: | $1.50 | | |
| Labor (making the card): | 6.00 | | |
| **Cost of Goods Sold per Unit:** | $7.50 | $7.50 | |
| Packaging: | 0.50 | | |
| **Total Other Variable Costs per Unit:** | $0.50 | 0.50 | |
| **Total Variable Costs per Unit:** | | $8.00 | 8.00 |
| **Gross Profit per Unit:**[*] | | | $4.00 |

We are estimating that it will take one hour to manufacture one unit, or 12 cards.

## Return on Investment (Chapter 3)

Business Goals:

**1.** What is your short-term business goal (less than one year)? What do you plan to invest to achieve this goal? What is your expected ROI?

Our short-term goals are to:

- Position Teen Greetings to generate $18,000 in sales
- Sign distribution contracts with five local retailers
- Have our local newspaper write at least one article about our business
- Earn a net profit of $1,500 before the end of our first year of operations

**2.** What is your long-term business goal (from one to five years)? What do you plan to invest to achieve this goal? What is your expected ROI?

Our long-term goals are to:

- Grow the business by 20% per year while we attend college
- Earn a net profit of at least $4,000 by the end of our fifth year of operations
- Donate 3% of Teen Greetings' yearly net profits to charity

In order to achieve these goals (both short- and long-term) we will need to remain focused. We plan to invest a lot of time and energy in the business. In exchange for this investment, our ROI will be the satisfaction and experience of running a successful venture.

**Personal Goals:**

**1.** What is your career goal? What do you plan to invest to achieve this goal? What is your expected ROI?

Our goals are to:

- Finish college in four years
- Work for an established graphic design firm (Karen) and an accounting firm (Cynthia) for two years after graduation
- Start our own graphic design company within eight years after graduating from college
- Save $10,000 towards start-up investment

**2.** How much education will you need for your career?

Karen plans to attend art school and study graphic communication.
Cynthia intends to major in economics and then earn a Master's in Business Administration.

**3.** Have you tried to get a part-time job related to your chosen career?

Last summer Karen worked as an intern in the art department at an advertising agency. Cynthia currently holds an after-school job at an accounting firm.

## Opportunity Recognition (Chapter 4)

**1.** What resources and skills do you (and the other owners of your business) have that will help make your business successful?

Our skills and resources include:

| Karen | Cynthia |
|---|---|
| • talented artist and designer | • good writer |
| • excellent computer skills | • excellent in math |
| • good "people" skills | • very organized and likes to think strategically |

**2.** Perform a SWOT analysis of your business.

| STRENGTHS | We have the skills and talents to manufacture well-designed greeting cards that will appeal to teenagers. |
|---|---|
| WEAKNESSES | We will be producing our cards in small quantities so manufacturing costs will be higher per card than those of our competitors. Since this is our first business, we expect to make mistakes due to lack of experience. We will learn by trial and error. |
| OPPORTUNITIES | There aren't many (if any) teen-owned and operated greeting card companies in the marketplace. |
| THREATS | This is an easy business to start so other teens may decide to copy our idea. |

## Core Beliefs (Chapter 5)

1. Describe three core beliefs you will use in running your company.

   - Teen Greetings will make quality the first priority.
   - Teen Greetings will deliver the product to the customers on time.
   - Teen Greetings will stay on the cutting edge of teen greeting-card design.

2. Choose a motto for your company. (You can select or adapt from the 50 positive quotes in Chapter 5, find one elsewhere, or make up your own.)

   *"In the pursuit of excellence, leave no stone unturned."*

## Supply and Demand (Chapter 6)

1. What factors will influence the demand for your product or service?

   Demand Factors:

   - Retailers: Retailers are used to dealing with adult manufacturers. They might not take a teen-owned business seriously. (We will prove them wrong!)
   - Price: Large greeting card companies can manufacture their cards at a much lower cost per card than we can. At the same time, we will need to keep our pricing competitive so that our retail clients will want to do business with us.

2. What factors will influence the supply for your product or service?

   Supply Factors:

   Direct Labor: We plan to hire two subcontractors to help us make our cards, at an hourly rate of $6. It is our estimate that it will take a subcontractor one hour to produce one unit of 12 cards. Ultimately our supply will depend on whether these estimates are accurate. We hope that we can find qualified people to hire who will do good work and be willing to accept a modest hourly rate.

## Product Development (Chapter 7)

How do you plan to protect your product/trademark/logo? (Pick one, and explain.)

Patent, copyright, or trademark.

   We will copyright the text of our greeting cards. We will also trademark our logo.

## Competitive Advantage (Chapter 8)

1. What is your competitive advantage?

   Teen Greetings will manufacture uniquely designed greeting cards for teens. We plan to make cards for occasions that are significant to our market. For example:

   - getting a driver's license
   - first after-school job
   - getting braces removed

- getting into college
- winning a sports event or getting on a team
- anniversary with boyfriend or girlfriend

We will keep the retail price low by selling directly to the retailer.

**2.** Who are your primary competitors? Where are they located?

The three largest greeting card companies in the United States are Hallmark, Gibson, and American Greetings. All three companies distribute their cards nationally. None has a line designed specifically for teenagers.

**3.** How will your business help others? List all organizations to which you plan to contribute. (Your contribution may be time, money, your product, or something else.)

Teen Greetings will sponsor a college scholarship award for high school students in Austin, Texas. We will allocate $500 a year for this opportunity. Applicants will need to write an essay on how they have made a difference in their community.

## Operating Costs (Chapter 9)

**1.** List and describe your monthly fixed costs.

| Utilities: | $50.00 |
|---|---|
| Salaries: | $150.00 |
| Advertising: | $30.00 |
| Insurance: | $40.00 |
| Interest: | $0.00 |
| Rent: | $25.00 |
| Depreciation: | $25.00 |
| Other (Unforeseen) | $20.00 |
| **TOTAL FIXED COSTS:** | **$340.00** |

**2.** List and describe your monthly variable costs.

Packaging: .50 per unit. Our packaging consists of a plastic box, packaging paper, and a label. We plan to sell an average of 100 units per month, so our monthly packaging cost will be $50.

## Marketing (Chapter 10)

**1.** Describe the Four P's for your business.

**Product** — Why will your product meet a consumer need?

Teens care about their friends. We like to be recognized for special occasions and accomplishments. Greeting cards are a great way for teens to express their appreciation for their friends.

**Place** — Where do you intend to sell your product?

We will sell our greeting cards wholesale to retailers in downtown Austin. Prospective clients include bookstores and stationery stores. We will also target clothing stores that cater to the teen market.

**Price** — What price do you plan to sell your product for, and why?

Our cards will cost $2.00 each. This will allow us to make a small profit, and it will also be affordable to teens.

**Promotion** — How do you plan to advertise and promote your product?

- We will purchase ads in local newspapers.
- We will register with the Austin Chamber of Commerce.
- We will write press releases for Teen Greetings' annual college scholarship awards and our other cause-related marketing activities.

**2.** Fill out a marketing plan for your business.

| Methods | Description | Target Market | Amount to Be Spent |
|---|---|---|---|
| Brochures | Our brochures will include reproductions of our greeting cards so clients can see samples of our work. | Store owners | $150 |
| Business Cards | High-quality business cards with our business name, e-mail, phone number, and slogan. | Store owners | $50 |
| Special Events | We will organize a promotional event each year when we announce the winner of Teen Greetings' College Scholarship award. | Teens and their parents | $500 for the scholarship |
| Promo Items | For our cause-related marketing, we plan to donate cards to the local teen center during the winter holidays. | Teens | $100 |
| Flyers | We will pass out flyers to raise awareness of our brand. | Teens | $20 |
| E-mail | We will create a mailing list so that we can stay in touch with our customers and inform them about special events, sales, and promotions. | Store owners and teens | No additional cost |

**3.** Do you intend to publicize your philanthropy? Why or why not?
If you do, explain how you will work your philanthropy into your marketing.

Teen Greetings plans to purchase advertising that publicizes our annual teen essay-writing award. The public will associate Teen Greetings with a teen-positive cause. As our business grows, we also plan to donate at least 3% of our annual net profits to a charity.

## Market Research (Chapter 11)

**1.** Research your industry and display the results in a one-page report that includes pie charts and bar or line graphs. Describe your target market within the industry.

According to the Greeting Card Association, over $7 billion are spent each year in the United States on greeting cards. According to Black Enterprise, the three companies that dominate 80-85% of this market share are: Hallmark, American Greetings, and Gibson.* There are over 3,000 companies that compete for the remaining 15-20% of the market. We will be competing against these other companies for a niche market.

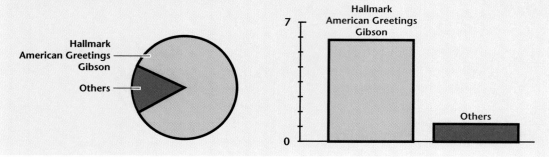

**2.** Describe your market segment and the results of your research on this market segment.

The center city of Austin has a population of 650,000; 15% of the population is made up of teenagers (approximately 100,000 people).

We conducted market research with 40 teenagers from three Austin high schools and learned the following:

- On average, teens buy seven greeting cards for their friends each year.

- Teens would be willing to pay up to $3 per card. They felt that $2 was a "good deal."

- Eight out of ten teens have an after-school job and earn $100 per week after tax.

- Occasions that teens most commonly buy cards for include: graduation, birthdays, and holidays (Valentine's Day, etc.). Five out of ten teens complained that they often can't find cards for particular occasions that are relevant to their lives.

---

* "Boom in Black Greeting Cards" by Marjorie Wingham-Desir, *Black Enterprise* Magazine, December 1995.

## Record Keeping (Chapter 12)

**1.** Describe your record-keeping system.

> We will keep track of orders and inventory using a computerized database program. Cynthia will be in charge of preparing our financial documents. We will sit down together twice a month to review our income statements, balance sheet, and cash flow statements.

**2.** List all bank accounts you will open for your business.

> Once we register our business, we will open a checking and savings account under our business name.

## Projected Income Statement (Chapter 13)

**1.** Complete a monthly projected budget and one-year income statement for your business.

### MONTHLY INCOME STATEMENT

**Teen Greetings**                                          **Date: September, 2007**

|  | # of Units | Unit Price |  |  |
|---|---|---|---|---|
| **Revenue:** | 100 | **$12.00** |  | **$1,200.00** |
| **Cost of Goods Sold** |  |  |  |  |
| Direct Labor: |  | $6.00 | $600.00 |  |
| Materials: |  | 1.50 | 150.00 |  |
| **Other Variable Costs** |  |  |  |  |
| Packaging: |  | 0.50 | 50.00 |  |
| **Total Variable Costs:** |  | **$8.00** | **$800.00** | 800.00 |
| **Gross Profit:** |  |  |  | **$400.00** |
| **Fixed Operating Costs** |  |  |  |  |
| Utilities: |  | $50.00 |  |  |
| Salaries: |  | 150.00 |  |  |
| Advertising: |  | 30.00 |  |  |
| Insurance: |  | 40.00 |  |  |
| Interest: |  | 0.00 |  |  |
| Rent: |  | 25.00 |  |  |
| Depreciation: |  | 25.00 |  |  |
| Other Costs: |  | 20.00 |  |  |
| **Total Fixed Operating Costs:** |  | **$340.00** |  | 340.00 |
| **Pre-Tax Profit:** |  |  |  | **$60.00** |
| Taxes (estimated 20%): |  |  |  | 12.00 |
| **Net Profit:** |  |  |  | **$48.00** |

## YEARLY INCOME STATEMENT

### Teen Greetings

Date: 2007

| | # of Units | Unit Price | |
|---|---|---|---|
| **Revenue:** | 1500 | $12.00 | **$18,000.00** |
| **Cost of Goods Sold** | | | |
| Direct Labor: | | $6.00 | $9,000.00 |
| Materials: | | 1.50 | 2,250.00 |
| **Other Variable Costs** | | | |
| Packaging: | | 0.50 | 750.00 |
| **Total Variable Costs:** | | $8.00 | $12,000.00 | 12,000.00 |
| **Gross Profit:** | | | **$6,000.00** |
| **Fixed Operating Costs** | | | |
| Utilities: | | $50.00 | $600.00 |
| Salaries: | | 150.00 | 1,800.00 |
| Advertising: | | 30.00 | 360.00 |
| Insurance: | | 40.00 | 480.00 |
| Interest: | | 0.00 | 0.00 |
| Rent: | | 25.00 | 300.00 |
| Depreciation: | | 25.00 | 300.00 |
| Other Costs: | | 20.00 | 240.00 |
| **Total Fixed Operating Costs:** | | $340.00 | $4,080.00 | 4,080.00 |
| **Pre-Tax Profit:** | | | **$1,920.00** |
| Taxes (estimated 20%): | | | 384.00 |
| **Net Profit:** | | | **$1,536.00** |

2. Use your projected one-year income statement to calculate:

Projected ROI for one year: _____ %

Projected ROI for one year: (Net Profit ÷ Start-up Investment × 100)
$1,536 ÷ $4,350 × 100 = 35%

Projected ROS for one year: _____ %

Projected ROS for one year: (Net Profit ÷ Sales × 100)
$1,536 ÷ $18,000 × 100 = 8.5%
*Please see Chapter 14 to complete the ROI equation.*

## Financing Strategy (Chapter 14)

1. What legal structure have you chosen for your business? Why?

Teen Greetings is a Limited Liability Company. The business will be co-owned by Karen and Cynthia Walker.

**2.** List the cost of the items you will need to buy to start your business.

| Item | Cost |
| --- | --- |
| Assorted blank greeting cards and envelopes (1,000 of each) and packaging materials | $300.00 |
| Printer/Fax/Copier and Toner | $300.00 |
| Art Supplies (sketchbook, markers, colored pencils) | $100.00 |
| Digital Camera | $200.00 |
| Computer | $1,500.00 |
| Cell Phone | $80.00 |
| Office Supplies (paper, pens, files, filing cabinet, etc.) | $250.00 |
| Chamber of Commerce Registration Fee | $75.00 |
| Trademark, Copyright, and Legal Fees | $475.00 |
| Consultation with Bookkeeper | $50.00 |
| Entrepreneurial Time (Optional) (Hours × Hourly Rate) | We decided not to include our labor in our start-up investment. |
| Cash reserve covering 3 months of fixed costs | $1,020 (3 × $340) |
| **TOTAL START-UP INVESTMENT** | **$4,350.00** |

**3.** List the sources of financing for your start-up capital. Identify whether each source is equity, debt, or a gift. Indicate the amount and type for each source.

| Funding Source | Equity | Debt | Gift | TOTAL |
| --- | --- | --- | --- | --- |
| Cynthia Walker's Personal Savings | $1,750.00 | | | $1,750.00 |
| Karen Walker's Personal Savings | 1,750.00 | | | 1,750.00 |
| Brian Walker (our father) | | | $850.00 | 850.00 |
| **Subtotal** | **$3,500.00** | **$0** | **$850.00** | |
| **TOTAL START-UP INVESTMENT** | | | | **$4,350.00** |

**4.** What is your debt ratio? What is your debt-to-equity ratio?

Our debt ratio is zero and our debt-to-equity ratio is 0:100. We own 100% equity in our business and are carrying no debt.

**5.** What is your payback period? In other words, how long will it take you to earn enough profit to cover start-up capital?

Payback period: (Total Start-up ÷ Yearly Net Profit)
Payback = $4,350 ÷ $1,536 = 2.8 years

## Negotiation (Chapter 15)

Describe any suppliers with whom you will have to negotiate.

> We plan to negotiate with the suppliers of our computer, software, and electronics products. We will be buying a number of expensive items so we would like to negotiate for a discount on the total price.

## Buying Wholesale (Chapter 16)

1. Where will you purchase the products you plan to sell, or the products you plan to use to manufacture the products you will be selling?

> Our computer and electronics equipment and other office equipment and supplies will be purchased online. Our art supplies will be purchased from a local arts and crafts store in downtown Austin.

2. Have you applied for a sales-tax ID number?

> Yes, we submitted our application last week.

## Your Competitive Strategy (Chapter 17)

1. Using the charts on pages 239 and 240 of Chapter 17, define your business, analyze your competitive advantage, and determine your tactics.

| Business Definition Question | Response |
|---|---|
| 1. *The Offer:* What products and services will be sold by the business? | 1. Original greeting cards designed by and for teens. |
| 2. *Target Market:* Which consumer segment will the business focus on? | 2. Retailers that cater to teenagers and also sell greeting cards. |
| 3. *Production Capability:* How will that offer be produced and delivered to those customers? | 3. We will manufacture the cards and sell them at a wholesale price to local retailers. |

| Competitive Advantage Question | Competitive Difference (USP) |
|---|---|
| 1. *The Offer:* What will be better or different about the products and services that will be sold by the business? | 1. Our business is teen-owned and operated. Teens will relate better to our greeting cards. |
| 2. *Target Market:* What customers should be the focus of the business, to make it as successful as possible? | 2. We need to keep our focus on the retailers who will be selling our products. If we deliver a quality product that sells, they will continue to do business with us. |
| 3. *Production and Delivery Capability:* What will be better or different about the way that offer is produced and delivered to those customers? | 3. Teen Greetings will operate in Austin, Texas where our retail customers will also be located. If there are problems, we will be on the spot to address them. |

Appendix D

| Tactical Question | Issues | Solutions |
|---|---|---|
| 1. *Sales Plan:* Where and how will you sell to your customers? | How to identify prospects and convert them to sales. | We will bring samples of our cards to local retailers. |
| 2. *Market Communications:* How will you communicate with your customers and make them aware of your business offer? | How to make customers aware of your offer; how to attract them to the business. | Our communication will be face to face. |
| 3. *Operating Plan:* How will you manage your internal operations? | How to make the business go, and determine who will perform the tasks. | We will divide the key tasks. One of us will focus on design and manufacturing, the other on marketing and finance. |
| 4. *Budget:* How do you plan to manage your revenues and expenses? | What are the sources of revenue? What are the items that have to be purchased? | At the beginning, most of our revenue will go back into the business. As our business grows, we will make joint decisions about how to invest the profits. |

**2.** Describe your strategy for outperforming the competition.

We will provide excellent customer service. We plan to develop personal relationships with the retailers who carry our products. We will keep the price low by manufacturing and selling directly to the retailer.

**3.** What tactics will you use to carry out this strategy?

We will make regular visits to our retailers to see how our products are selling and if we can assist them in any way.

**4.** Write a mission statement for your business in less than three sentences that clearly states your competitive advantage, strategy, and tactics.

*Teen Greetings' mission is to create original high-quality greeting cards made by and for teens. We will devote ourselves to manufacturing an excellent product that commemorates important events in teens' lives that other greeting card companies tend to overlook. Our cards will be sold at retail stores in Austin, Texas where teens like to shop. We will pride ourselves on building outstanding relationships with the retailers who sell our products.*

## Your Marketing Mix (Chapter 18)

**Step One: Consumer Analysis**

**1.** Describe your market segment.

We have two markets to consider.

**#1:** The first market includes **the retail stores** in downtown Austin that are popular with teenagers and also sell greeting cards. These stores are located in the prime shopping areas where teens like to shop.

**#2:** The second market includes the **teenagers** who will buy cards from these retail stores.

2. Describe your target consumer: age, gender, and income.

| | |
|---|---|
| **Market #1:** | Store Owners |
| *Age:* | 30s - 60s |
| *Gender:* | male and female |
| *Income:* | Varies, but all are small businesses so they are concerned about costs. |
| **Market #2:** | Teenagers |
| *Age:* | 13 - 18 |
| *Gender:* | male and female |
| *Income:* | Our target teenaged customer has an after-school or weekend job and earns about $100 per week. |

**Step Two: Market Analysis**

1. How will you look at location, population, personality, and behavior when you analyze your market segment?

We will conduct two rounds of market research. The first will focus on retail stores, and the second will target teens. We want to find out:

- How much revenue are the stores generating from greeting card sales?
- How many greeting card brands do they carry in the store; which cards are the most popular with teens?
- Where do teenagers like to shop (favorite stores)?
- Where do they buy greeting cards currently?
- What trends are popular with teens right now?

2. Use your market analysis method to describe your market segment. Roughly how many consumers are in this segment?

We are estimating that 100,000 teenagers live in Austin. These are the potential consumers of our cards.

Again, since we are a wholesale business, our direct customers will be the stores that sell our cards. There are:

- eight bookstores in downtown Austin
- ten stationery stores
- five clothing stores that also sell greeting cards

3. Explain how your marketing plan targets your market segment.

Here are two specific ways we plan to appeal to both teenagers and the retail stores that will be selling our cards:

We will make effective displays for our cards that catch the attention of teens.

We will work on our sales pitch to convince retailers that we have identified an overlooked niche in the greeting card market.

**4.** What percentage of your market do you feel you need to capture for your business to be profitable?

Since the costs for running our business will be fairly low, we won't need to capture a large percentage of the total market in order to make a profit.

**5.** Who are the potential customers you plan to approach in the first two months of business?

Word Soup Bookstore

Teen Life Apparel

## Advertising and Publicity (Chapter 19)

**1.** What is your business slogan?

Teen Greetings: 100% Original. 100% Made by and for Teens.

*We give you the words to express what's in your heart.*

**2.** Where do you intend to advertise?

We will purchase advertising in our local newspaper.

**3.** Are you planning to use cause-related marketing?

Yes. We plan to hold workshops at the local teen center to help teens who are interested in starting their own businesses. We will publicize our cause-related marketing activities by writing a press release. Hopefully our goodwill can earn us some media coverage, which will strengthen the profile of our business.

**4.** Write a sample press release for your business.

FOR IMMEDIATE RELEASE. AUSTIN, TEXAS. OCTOBER 1, 2006

**TWIN SISTERS FROM AUSTIN START TEEN-THEMED GREETING CARD COMPANY**

Today twin sisters Karen and Cynthia Walker announced the debut of their first entrepreneurial venture, Teen Greetings. According to co-owner Karen Walker, "Teen Greetings is a business that is teen-owned and operated. We will be creating unique greeting cards that teenagers can relate to."

The sisters plan to sell their cards to leading retailers in downtown Austin, such as Word Soup Bookstore and Teen Apparel. Word Soup's owner, Ben Hamilton, spoke enthusiastically about Teen Greetings' products: "We have a lot of teenagers, especially girls, who like to hang out in the store. We already sell greeting cards, but this is the first time that we're stocking a greeting card line that's designed specifically for teens. I think the cards will be a big hit here."

The twins decided to start their business when they couldn't find a card for a friend who had just gotten her braces removed. "We realized that there are events that happen in teenagers' lives that other greeting card companies overlook. We plan to fill that niche."

Each of the sisters brings unique talents to the business. Karen is a talented artist and designer while Cynthia will manage marketing and business operations. Both students are juniors at Los Alamos High School where Karen serves as Vice President of her class.

Teen Greetings plans to sponsor an annual essay writing award for Austin teenagers. The winner will receive a college scholarship equal to 3% of Teen Greetings' net profit. Co-owner Cynthia explained: "A lot of teens need help with paying for college. Our business wants to support young people in achieving their dreams for the future."

## Break-Even Analysis (Chapter 20)

Perform a break-even analysis of your business.

Monthly Fixed Costs ÷ Gross Profit per Unit = $340 ÷ $4

Monthly break-even units = 85

## Selling (Chapter 21)

**1.** Describe the features and benefits of the product (or service) your business will focus on selling.

The features and benefits of our product include:

- Original designs
- Affordable price
- We commemorate occasions that are important to teens and that other greeting card companies overlook.

**2.** Choose three ways you will sell your product or service. Explain why you think these methods will work.

**Direct Sales:** We will go to retailers with samples of our cards. We will pass out flyers at local high schools to teenagers. This will raise awareness of our brand.

**Customer Referrals:** We will ask our loyal customers to request that retailers sell our product.

**Online Sales:** We are building a Web site so that we can sell our products directly to retailers and possibly expand our market beyond Austin, and beyond Texas.

**3.** Write a sales pitch for your product (or service).

Teen Greetings is a teen-themed greeting card company that "is 100% original and 100% for and by teens." Teen Greetings specializes in creating cards for occasions that really matter to teenagers. The business is owned and operated by teenaged twin sisters Karen and Cynthia Walker. Teen Greetings is committed to providing its customers with inspirational cards at affordable prices. "We give teens the words to express what's in their hearts."

**4.** Describe three customers you intend to pitch.

Word Soup Bookstore

Teen Apparel (Clothing Store)

Magical Kingdom (Stationery and Art Supply Store)

## Customer Service (Chapter 22)

Create a customer database for your business. Include name, e-mail, phone, fax, address, last contact, and/or last purchase. What five questions will you ask every customer?

| | |
|---|---|
| **Name:** | Ben Hamilton, owner of Word Soup |
| **E-mail:** | Ben@wordsoupbooks.com |
| **Phone:** | 512-555-4567 |
| **Fax:** | 512-555-4566 |
| **Address:** | 125 Piedmont |
| **Last contact:** | September 15, 2006 |
| **Last purchase:** | September 1, 2006 |
| **Name:** | Ramona Hernandez, owner of Teen Apparel |
| **E-mail:** | Ramona@teensrule.com |
| **Phone:** | 512-555-5678 |
| **Fax:** | 512-555-5677 |
| **Address:** | 349 Modesto Boulevard |
| **Last contact:** | August 1, 2006 |
| **Last purchase:** | Negotiations are still in process. |
| **Name:** | Ian Brooks, owner, Magical Kingdom |
| **E-mail:** | Ianb@magicalkingdom.com |
| **Phone:** | 512-555-4560 |
| **Fax:** | 512-555-4561 |
| **Address:** | 189 Piedmont |
| **Last contact:** | Will call next week. |
| **Last purchase:** | Has not purchased yet. |

These are the questions we would pose to our retailer customers:

**1.** How can Teen Greetings help your business to do better?

**2.** Are you satisfied with the quality of our product?

**3.** What products do teens buy the most in your store?

**4.** How much revenue does your store make each month from teen customers?

**5.** (If they are an existing customer) Which of our cards did you sell the most/least of this month?

## Business Communication (Chapter 24)

**1.** Which business communication tools will you use?

Phone, Voicemail, Fax, and E-mail

**2.** Have you designed a letterhead for your business?

Yes.

## Legal Structure (Chapter 25)

**1.** What is the legal structure of your business?

Limited Liability Company

**2.** Why did you choose this structure?

We chose a Limited Liability Company as our legal structure because it protects our personal savings and assets in the event that the business fails.

**3.** Who will be the partners or stockholders for your company?

The partners/stockholders are: Cynthia Walker and Karen Walker

**4.** Have you registered your business?

Yes. We registered our business at the county courthouse.

**5.** Have you applied for a sales-tax identification number?

Yes.

## Manufacturing (Chapter 26)

**1.** What are the zoning laws in your area? Does your business comply?

This is not relevant to our business.

**2.** Do you intend to manufacture your product? If so, describe the manufacturing process you will use. If not, describe how your product is manufactured.

Our cards will be manufactured in the following steps:

**One:** Karen will be in charge of card design. She will create the art and text for every card that we sell.

**Two:** Once Karen has finalized her card designs, she will print the cards in quantity from her computer.

**Three:** We will hire subcontractors to organize and pack the cards and envelopes.

**Four:** Cynthia will perform quality control. She plans to inspect every card to ensure that it meets our standards of quality.

**Five:** Our subcontractors will package and label each unit (12 cards). The cards will then be ready for distribution.

## Production/Distribution Chain (Chapter 27)

**1.** How do you plan to distribute your product to your target market?

In the beginning we will hand deliver our orders to our customers. As our business grows, we will ship our orders.

**2.** Use this chart to show the production/distribution channel for your own business, and the markups at each point in the chain.

### Manufacturer

| | |
|---|---|
| **Name:** | Karen and Cynthia Walker |
| **Contact information:** | 150 Buena Vista Road, Austin, Texas 78744 |
| **Cost per Unit:** | $8.00 per dozen |
| **Price to Retailer per Unit:** | $12.00 per dozen |
| **Markup:** | $4.00 |
| **Markup Percentage:** | 50% |

### Retailer

| | |
|---|---|
| **Cost per Unit:** | $12.00 per dozen |
| **Retail Price per Unit:** | $24.00 per dozen at $2 per card |
| **Markup:** | $12.00 |
| **Markup Percentage:** | 100% |

**3.** What is the estimated time between your placing an order with your supplier and the product's availability to your customers?

We expect that it will take an average of two weeks to deliver our product to market once an order has been placed. This will depend, in part, on the size of the order.

## Quality (Chapter 28)

**1.** How will you deliver a high-quality product (service) to your customers? Describe your quality control procedure.

Every time we design a new product line we will conduct market research with our target consumers (Austin teens). We want to know how we can improve our cards so that they meet the needs of our customers.

Cynthia will be in charge of quality control. She will check the work produced by our subcontractors to make sure that the cards are colored properly.

**2.** Write a motto for your business that will remind you to stay focused on quality.

*Quality lies in the details.*

## Human Resources (Chapter 29)

**1.** Fill out a PERT Chart for your business.

| Task | Wk 1 | Wk 2 | Wk 3 | Wk 4 | Wk 5 | Wk 6 | Wk 7 | Wk 8 |
|---|---|---|---|---|---|---|---|---|
| **TEEN GREETINGS: PERT CHART** | | | | | | | | |
| Purchase card stock and other start-up supplies | X | | | | | | | |
| Create initial designs for introductory product line | | X | | | | | | |
| Conduct market research | | X | | | | | | |
| Make flyers and business cards | | | X | | | | | |
| Create a filing system to keep track of orders and our financial records | | | X | | | | | |
| Open a bank account | | | | | X | | | |
| Make sales calls to local retailers | | | | | | X | | |
| Hire one or two subcontractors who can hand-color each card | | | | | | | X | |

**2.** Will you be hiring employees? If so, describe what their qualifications should be, what you intend to pay them, and how they will help your business.

We plan to hire two subcontractors who can perform the direct labor of hand-coloring our cards.

**3.** Provide contact information for your accountant, attorney, banker, and insurance agent.

**Accountant:** Joan Sikes, CPA., 512-555-9297

**Attorney:** Sandra Rhodes, Esq., 512-555-5544

**Banker:** Don Flowers, Keystone Bank, 512-555-3243

**Insurance Agent:** Lionel Hastings, 512-555-1212

**4.** What are your policies toward employees? How do you plan to make your business a positive and rewarding place to work?

We will serve as both owners and employees. We have made a commitment to talk through any problems or disagreements that might come up until we reach a compromise. We want our business to be fun as well as profitable.

**5.** Create an organizational chart for your business.

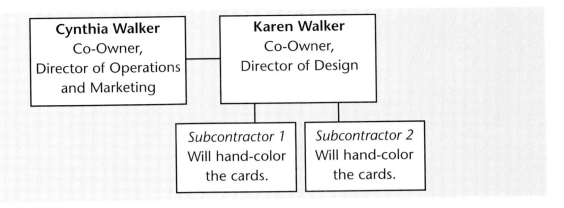

## Technology (Chapter 30)

**1.** Which technology tools will you use for your business, and why?

| Tool | Function |
| --- | --- |
| Cell Phone | Sales calls; Customer care and communication |
| Computer and Printer | Design and print cards; Billing and record keeping |
| E-mail and Internet | Customer care and communication |
| Scanner/Copier/Printer | Tools for greeting card design |

**2.** Explain how you will access this technology.

Teen Greetings plans to purchase our technological equipment from a supplier that can offer us excellent quality at a competitive price. We will conduct research online about different products and prices. If we find a supplier who sells most or all of the things we need, we will negotiate the total sale price. Since we will be buying a large number of items, the supplier might be willing to offer us a discount.

## Raising Capital (Chapter 31)

**1.** Describe financing sources that might be willing to invest in your business in exchange for equity.

This is not relevant to our business at this time.

## Corporations (Chapter 32)

**1.** Is your business a: C Corporation, Subchapter-S, Limited Liability Company, or Nonprofit Corporation?

Limited Liability Company

**2.** Why did you choose this corporate structure?

We chose it for flexibility.

**3.** Who are the stockholders of your corporation?

We are the sole shareholders of Teen Greetings. We each own 50 shares of 100 shares outstanding.

**4.** Who is on your board of directors?

Our Board of Directors will include:

- Brian and Louise Walker (our parents)
- Nancy Rosenbaum (our entrepreneurship teacher)
- Michael Simmons (local entrepreneur who has agreed to be our mentor)

## Stocks (Chapter 33)

**1.** If your business is incorporated, describe what percentage of your company is represented by one share of stock.

1/100

**2.** Is your corporation's stock publicly or privately held?

All of our shares are privately held by the owners.

## Bonds (Chapter 34)

**1.** Do you intend to use debt to finance your business? Explain.

Our start-up investment is being funded by our personal savings and gifts. We might consider debt financing later on, as our business grows.

**2.** Would you ever issue bonds to finance your business?

We don't expect to issue bonds.

## Your Balance Sheet (Chapter 35)

**1.** Create a Projected Balance Sheet for your business for one year.

| TEEN GREETINGS: BALANCE SHEET | | |
|---|---:|---:|
| **After Start-up Costs and Before First Sale** | | |
| **Current Assets** | | |
| Cash: | $1,020.00 | |
| Inventory: | 300.00 | |
| **Total Current Assets:** | $1,320.00 | $1,320.00 |
| **Furniture and Equipment:** | $2,080.00 | |
| Less Depreciation: | 0.00 | |
| **Net Property and Equipment:** | $2,080.00 | 2,080.00 |
| **Total Assets:** | | $3,400.00 |
| **Total Liabilities + Owner's Equity:** | | $3,400.00 |

## TEEN GREETINGS: BALANCE SHEET

### After First Year

**Current Assets**

| | | |
|---|---|---|
| Cash: | $2,856.00 | |
| Inventory: | 300.00 | |
| **Total Current Assets:** | **$3,156.00** | **$3,156.00** |
| **Furniture and Equipment:** | **$2,080.00** | |
| Less Depreciation: | 300.00 | |
| **Net Property and Equipment:** | **$1,780.00** | 1,780.00 |
| **Total Assets:** | | **$4,936.00** |
| **Total Liabilities + Owner's Equity:** | | **$4,936.00** |

**2.** Create a pie chart showing your assets, short-term liabilities, long-term liabilities, and owner's equity.

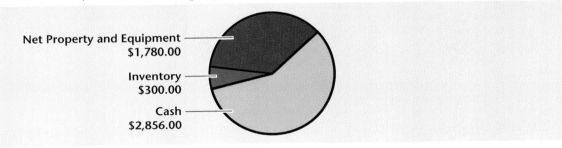

Net Property and Equipment — $1,780.00

Inventory — $300.00

Cash — $2,856.00

**3.** What is your debt-to-equity ratio?

0 (zero)

## Venture Capital (Chapter 36)

Have you found any sources of venture capital that you intend to contact? Describe.

We do not plan to pursue VC capital at this time. As our business grows, we will look into the possibility of VC financing. Before we can seek such investors, we will need to prove that Teen Greetings is a profitable business.

## Contracts (Chapter 37)

**1.** What is the most important contract you will need to run your business?

We will establish contracts with the retailers that buy and sell our products. The contract will outline the quantity of cards the retailer is purchasing from us along with the terms of payment.

**2.** Describe any additional contracts you have, or plan to secure.

We will sign a contract with our insurance agent.

**3.** Who is your attorney?

Sandra Rhodes, Esq. is our attorney. She is a friend of the family and runs her own law firm.

## Socially Responsible Business (Chapter 38)

**1.** Choose three ways you would use to run a socially responsible business.

Recycling paper, glass, and plastic.

Establishing a safe and healthy workplace.

*Other:* Printing our cards on recycled paper.

**2.** What cause-related marketing do you intend to use? How will this support and reinforce your competitive advantage?

We plan to hold workshops at the local teen center to help teens who are interested in starting their own businesses. We will publicize our cause-related marketing activities by writing a press release. This will strengthen our competitive advantage by showing teens that we care about their success in life — not just about selling them greeting cards.

## Small Business and Government (Chapter 39)

What laws — such as minimum wage and age requirements, health and safety regulations, or anti-discrimination laws — will affect your business?

We want to make sure that the suppliers we do business with comply with these laws. Otherwise, our business is at risk of having its reputation damaged by association.

## Building Good Personal and Business Credit (Chapter 40)

**1.** My *personal* credit history is: bad, good, not yet established?

Not yet established.

Describe how you plan to establish good personal credit.

We do not plan to take on debt until we attend college and take out student loans. After we graduate, we will pay off our loans over a period of years. We will make payments on time.

**2.** My *business* credit history is: bad, good, not yet established?

Not yet established.

Describe how you plan to establish good business credit.

Teen Greetings will pay its suppliers in full and on time each month.

# Cash Flow (Chapter 41)

1. Use the cash flow chart in your NFTE Workbook to create a projected cash flow statement for your business for one year.

| | DEC | JAN | FEB | MAR | APR | MAY | JUN | JUL | AUG | SEP | OCT | NOV | DEC |
|---|---|---|---|---|---|---|---|---|---|---|---|---|---|
| **Beginning Cash:** | 0 | 1,020 | 1,093 | 1,486 | 1,559 | 1,632 | 1,705 | 1,778 | 1,851 | 1,924 | 1,997 | 2,070 | 2,463 |
| **Cash Inflows** | | | | | | | | | | | | | |
| Cash Sales: | 0 | 1,200 | 2,400 | 1,200 | 1,200 | 1,200 | 1,200 | 1,200 | 1,200 | 1,200 | 1,200 | 2,400 | 2,400 |
| Cash Investment: | 4,350 | | | | | | | | | | | | |
| **Total Cash Inflows** | 4,350 | 1,200 | 2,400 | 1,200 | 1,200 | 1,200 | 1,200 | 1,200 | 1,200 | 1,200 | 1,200 | 2,400 | 2,400 |
| **Cash Outflows** | | | | | | | | | | | | | |
| **Variable Costs** | | | | | | | | | | | | | |
| COGS/COSS: | | 750 | 1,500 | 750 | 750 | 750 | 750 | 750 | 750 | 750 | 750 | 1,500 | 1,500 |
| Other Variable Costs: | | 50 | 100 | 50 | 50 | 50 | 50 | 50 | 50 | 50 | 50 | 100 | 100 |
| **Total Variable Costs:** | | 800 | 1,600 | 800 | 800 | 800 | 800 | 800 | 800 | 800 | 800 | 1,600 | 1,600 |
| **Fixed Costs** | | | | | | | | | | | | | |
| Utilities: | | 50 | 50 | 50 | 50 | 50 | 50 | 50 | 50 | 50 | 50 | 50 | 50 |
| Salaries: | | 150 | 150 | 150 | 150 | 150 | 150 | 150 | 150 | 150 | 150 | 150 | 150 |
| Advertising: | | 30 | 30 | 30 | 30 | 30 | 30 | 30 | 30 | 30 | 30 | 30 | 30 |
| Insurance: | | 40 | 40 | 40 | 40 | 40 | 40 | 40 | 40 | 40 | 40 | 40 | 40 |
| Interest: | | 0 | 0 | 0 | 0 | 0 | 0 | 0 | 0 | 0 | 0 | 0 | 0 |
| Rent: | | 25 | 25 | 25 | 25 | 25 | 25 | 25 | 25 | 25 | 25 | 25 | 25 |
| Unforeseen: | | 20 | 20 | 20 | 20 | 20 | 20 | 20 | 20 | 20 | 20 | 20 | 20 |
| **Total Fixed Costs:** | | 315 | 315 | 315 | 315 | 315 | 315 | 315 | 315 | 315 | 315 | 315 | 315 |
| Taxes: | | 12 | 92 | 12 | 12 | 12 | 12 | 12 | 12 | 12 | 12 | 92 | 92 |
| **Capital Investment** | | | | | | | | | | | | | |
| Office Supplies: | 350 | | | | | | | | | | | | |
| Inventory: | 300 | | | | | | | | | | | | |
| Computers: | 1,500 | | | | | | | | | | | | |
| Equipment: | 580 | | | | | | | | | | | | |
| Start-up Fees: | 600 | | | | | | | | | | | | |
| **Total Capital Investment:** | 3,330 | 0 | 0 | 0 | 0 | 0 | 0 | 0 | 0 | 0 | 0 | 0 | 0 |
| **Total Cash Outflows** | 3,330 | 1,127 | 2,007 | 1,127 | 1,127 | 1,127 | 1,127 | 1,127 | 1,127 | 1,127 | 1,127 | 2,007 | 2,007 |
| **Net Increase/Decrease in Cash Flows** | 1,020 | 73 | 393 | 73 | 73 | 73 | 73 | 73 | 73 | 73 | 73 | 393 | 393 |
| **Ending Cash** | 1,020 | 1,093 | 1,486 | 1,559 | 1,632 | 1,705 | 1,778 | 1,851 | 1,924 | 1,997 | 2,070 | 2,463 | 2,856 |

## Appendix D

**2.** Calculate the "burn rate" for your business.

Zero. We will make our money back by month #1.

**3.** Use your projected balance sheet (Chapter 35) to calculate your working capital after 1 year.

Current Assets − Current Liabilities = $3,156 − $0 = $3,156

## Intellectual Property (Chapter 42)

**1.** Describe any intellectual property you are developing for your business.

Teen Greetings' original greeting card text and artistic designs will be our intellectual property.

**2.** How do you intend to protect your intellectual property? Explain why it qualifies for this protection.

We plan to copyright the text in our cards and trademark the original artwork we feature on them. These works need to be protected because we have created them from scratch. A competitive advantage of our business is the fact that our cards are 100% original.

## Ethical Business Behavior (Chapter 43)

**1.** Describe the corporate governance plan for your business. It should include five policies (rules) that will be the backbone of your company's ethics.

Teen Greetings will:
- Make full disclosure to our Board of Directors
- Treat all suppliers and customers with professionalism and respect
- Develop and sell a high-quality product
- Keep accurate records
- Pay our suppliers and taxes on time

**2.** Provide information on each of your mentors or advisors. If there will be a board of advisors, list each member and describe his or her commitment to the business.

*Mentor:* Ms. Nancy Rosenbaum, Entrepreneurship Teacher, Los Alamos High School

*Mentor:* Michael Simmons, Owner, Simmons Software

## Taxation (Chapter 44)

Which tax forms will you have to fill out for your business?

1040 U.S. Individual Tax Return

Schedule C, Profit or Loss from Business

Schedule SE, Self-Employment Tax

Quarterly Sales and Use Tax Return

## Insurance (Chapter 45)

**1.** What types of insurance will your business need? Explain.

We plan to purchase general business liability insurance.

**2.** Describe the premium, deductible, and payout for each policy you plan to carry.

The annual cost of the policy will be $480.

## Franchising and Licensing (Chapter 46)

Do you plan to franchise your business, or license any of your products? Explain.

We do not plan to franchise. In the future, as our business grows, we will consider licensing our designs to other companies.

## International Opportunities (Chapter 47)

**1.** Are there customers for your business in other countries? How do you plan to reach them?

There are teenagers all over the world! However, at this time we want to focus our business on the market we know and understand — retailers who sell products to teenagers in Austin, Texas.

**2.** Describe any international competitors you have found who may be able to access your customers. How do you intend to compete?

There are international companies who manufacture greeting cards. Those cards are distributed to stores in Austin, where we will be selling our products. Our advantage is that we know our locality and can communicate with our customers face to face.

## Investment Goals and Risk Tolerance (Chapter 48)

**1.** I plan to save **10%** of my net income to achieve personal financial goals.
**2.** My primary financial goal is **to save money for college**.
**3.** My investment risk tolerance is **high**. The "I" on the form should be read as "we," as we have the same goals and risk tolerance. We have a great advantage in being young. Time is on our side. If our investments don't do well in the short term we can invest in something else or wait to see if our investments yield better results in the future.

## Investing for a Secure Future (Chapter 49)

**1.** I will invest my savings as follows:

| Current Cash Value/Mix | | Expected % ROI | W. Avg. |
|---|---|---|---|
| Stocks | $100 = 40% | 10% | 4.0 |
| Bonds | $100 = 40% | 5% | 2.0 |
| Cash | $50 = 20% | 2% | .4 |
| **TOTAL** | | | **6.4** |

**2.** My weighted average ROI is: 6.4%

**3.** Using the Rule of 72, the number of years it will take my portfolio to double is:

Rule of 72 = (72 ÷ weighted average ROI)

72 ÷ 6.4 = **11.2 years**

## Exit Strategy (Chapter 50)

**1.** Describe your exit strategy.

We plan to run Teen Greetings for the rest of high school and during our college years. After college graduation we both plan to become employees so that we can gain additional experience. We hope to be able to sell our business to another teenager so that we can continue Teen Greetings' mission of being "100% by and for teens."

**2.** Why will this exit strategy be attractive to potential investors?

Many teens would like the chance to own and operate a business so this would be a good opportunity for the right individual. By the time we sell, Teen Greetings will have already established itself as a successful brand in our local marketplace. This should be an attractive feature to a potential investor. We will make sure to choose our successor carefully so that Teen Greetings continues its tradition of quality and customer satisfaction.

**3.** How much would you be willing to sell your business for in three years?

Using the future earnings method, we would be trying to sell the business for around $6,400.

**4.** How would you calculate the valuation of your business?

We would value Teen Greetings using the following calculations:

**Assumptions:**

**1.** Yearly Growth Rate (Assumption): 20%

**2.** Sales Multiple of Future Earnings: 3 — based on similar sale of companies in community.

| Year | Calculation | Net Operating Income |
|---|---|---|
| 1 | Projected Income Statement | $1,488 |
| 2 | $1,488 × 1.2 | $1,785.60 |
| 3 | $1,488 × 1.2 × 1.2 | $2,142.72 |
| **3-Year Valuation** | **$2,142.72 × 3** | **$6,428.16** |

# Math for Entrepreneurs

1. Average Unit of Sale = Total Sales ÷ Number of Customers

2. Revenue − COGS = Gross Profit

3. Total Revenue − Total Cost of Goods Sold = Total Gross Profit

   Gross Profit per Unit × Units Sold = Total Gross Profit

4. Return on Investment = Net Profit ÷ Investment

5. Projected Annual ROI = Monthly ROI × 12

   Quarterly (three months) ROI × 4 = Projected Annual ROI

6. The Rule of 72:

   72 ÷ Annual Interest Rate = # of years it will take for investment to double

   Use the rule of 72 to figure out how long it will take an investment to double. Take any fixed annual interest rate and divide it into 72. The result is the number of years it will take for the investment to double.

7. The seven common operating costs are USAIIRD:

   **U**tilities (gas, electric, telephone, Internet service)
   **S**alaries
   **A**dvertising
   **I**nsurance
   **I**nterest
   **R**ent
   **D**epreciation

8. Return on Sales (ROS) = Net Profit ÷ Sales

9. Payback = Start-Up Investment ÷ Net Profit per Month

10. Debt-to-Equity Ratio: Debt ÷ Equity

11. Debt Ratio: Debt ÷ Assets

12. Break-Even Units = Fixed Costs ÷ Gross Profit per Unit

    To include variable costs:
    Break-Even Units = Fixed Costs ÷ Gross Profit per Unit − Variable Costs per Unit

13. Stock Yield: Dividend ÷ Closing Price × 100

14. Price/Earnings Ratio: P ÷ E = Price per Share ÷ Earnings per Share

15. Bond Yield: Interest ÷ Price of Bond

16. Owner's Equity (OE) = Assets − Liabilities

    Total Assets = Total Liabilities + Owner's Equity (OE)

17. Quick Ratio: Cash + Marketable Securities ÷ Current Liabilities

18. Current Ratio: Current Assets ÷ Current Liabilities

19. Total Market Value of Company = Amount of Venture Capital Received ÷ % of Company Sold

20. Cash Flow = Cash Receipts − Cash Disbursements

    Beginning Cash + Cash Surplus = Ending Cash Balance

21. Burn Rate: Cash on Hand ÷ Negative Cash Outflow per Month

22. Working Capital = Current Assets − Current Liabilities

# Entrepreneur's Skills Toolkit

## Reading Tips

**R**eading skills are essential in today's information-driven workplace. To run a business, you will need to read and understand many different types of workplace documents.

### PURPOSES FOR READING

- To learn something new
- To gather and interpret information
- To apply instructions
- To solve problems
- To understand what employees or customers want or need
- To identify relevant information and details
- To interpret laws, rules, regulations, forms, and contracts

### TYPES OF WORKPLACE DOCUMENTS

- Memos and e-mail
- Letters
- Faxes
- Graphs and charts
- Employee procedures and handbooks
- Instructions and manuals
- Business reports and proposals
- Contracts
- Estimates, bids, and invoices
- Web sites and online information

### STRATEGIES FOR BETTER READING

You'll read faster and understand more if you use the following reading strategies:

- Read at your own pace. It doesn't matter how fast you read or how many times you need to read the information, so long as you get the information you need.
- Know why you're reading and what you want to know.
- Prioritize your reading. Read the most important things first and let other things wait. Throw away "junk" and outdated reading materials.
- Skim the text before you read. Review the table of contents, index, title and headings, and captions to determine where to look and what material you need to read closely.

- Scan lines of text to find a particular word, detail, or fact. Follow the lines of text quickly with your eyes, follow along with your finger, or mark text with a highlighter or Post-it note.
- Make notes of key facts, page numbers, and ideas as needed.
- Read carefully and slowly the sections that contain crucial information.
- Try to read without stopping. If you lose your place, stay focused on the words by following along with your hand. If you keep losing interest, take a short break or read something else for a while.
- Predict the meaning of unfamiliar words by reviewing the surrounding words or analyzing the root word. Confirm the meaning by checking with a dictionary.
- Summarize what you read to make sure you understood it correctly. Would you be able to apply the information to a task? Ask questions, if possible, and go back and re-read sections as needed.
- Read in a comfortable place with good lighting and without distractions.
- Practice! As with any skill, the more reading you do, the more you will improve.

## WATCH OUT FOR MISLEADING AND CONFUSING INFORMATION

- Distinguish facts from opinions.
  - Opinions may be stated as if they were facts.
  - Make sure all statements are supported by data and proof.
- Watch for jargon.
  - Specialized language is common in business, but can be confusing to readers.
  - Look up any terms you don't understand, or ask an expert.
- Think about figures and statistics.
  - Facts and statistics can be manipulated or put into a context to slant their meaning.
  - It sounds a lot better to say "costs will only go up $500" than to say "costs will double," but both could mean the same thing.
- Watch for bias.
  - Be suspicious of any material that seems to be one-sided or supports a bias.
  - Consider alternative viewpoints.
- Read the fine print of important business documents, such as bids and contracts.
  - Read them closely and take notes.
  - Ask questions and read them several times if necessary.
  - Check all numbers and facts and read for common sense and logic.
  - If you have doubts or questions, ask an expert or seek legal counsel.

# Evaluating Web Sites

The Internet can be a great source of useful and important information, including contacts and facts about your industry and competitors. But, when you consult Web sites for information, look at them with a critical eye. Evaluate sites based on credibility, usability, readability, accuracy, attractiveness, and how current they are. The answers to the following questions can help you determine if a Web site is a reliable source of information:

- Is the site easy to use? How easy was it to locate the information you needed?
- Is the site well organized with clearly written information?
- Is the information current and up to date? When was the site last updated?
- Does the site provide interactive tools to use in financial calculations and decision making?
- Is the site "selling something" or strictly for information?
- How many advertisements did you have to go through to get to the site?
- Does the site offer useful links to other sites?
- Does the site allow the visitor to ask questions or make comments?
- What "help" features are offered?
- How quickly did the site generate search results?
- How useful were the site's graphics?
- What experts and sources are quoted?
- Who runs the site:
  - A government agency?
  - An organization?
  - A business?
  - An individual?
- Is the host a reputable organization or company?
- Does it have a bias or is it trying to convince you of something?
- Are opposing opinions and viewpoints presented fairly?
- Are guarantees and protection/security offered?
- If you ordered something, was a confirmation notice sent? Can you check the status of your order?

# Writing Process

**A** writing task becomes less overwhelming if you think about it as a process. Every writer goes about it differently, but they all go through the same stages of the writing process. In fact, writers often move back and forth between the stages.

## PRE-WRITING

This stage involves everything you do *before* you begin to compose your document. During this stage you should:

- Identify your purpose and audience. Determine what your readers know, what they will need to know, and why they need to know it. Knowing your audience will shape your purpose, tone, and presentation.
- Generate ideas by brainstorming — alone or with others.
- Make lists of ideas and group the ones that seem related. Identify main ideas and supporting sub-topics in a list or outline format.
- Ask questions about your topic to generate interesting thoughts and ideas.
- Identify the main idea, narrow the topic until is manageable and audience-focused, and select the most compelling supporting ideas.

## DRAFTING

This stage is your first attempt to get your words on paper or on the computer screen.

- Your goal is to generate rough sentences and paragraphs with a beginning, middle, and end.
- Depending on your pre-writing, your draft may be fairly complete or more loosely organized.
- The goal is to generate a rough draft. Quality is not essential at this stage.

## REVISING

In this stage, evaluate and improve your draft. You may need to go through several drafts before you achieve the right content and the best organization.

- Focus on the organization of your ideas.
- Use clear sentences with strong supporting details and active verbs.
- Revising involves making major changes to a document, such as:
  - Moving paragraphs around to improve organization
  - Changing the order of sentences for better structure and coherence
  - Adding transitions between paragraphs and sentences
  - Adding examples and details
  - Removing irrelevant or wordy material.

## EDITING AND PROOFREADING

At this stage, review your work and correct errors. Focus on fine-tuning sentence structure and style, removing unnecessary words, and improving word choice.

- Carefully read your work word-by-word for errors in spelling, grammar, and punctuation.
- Be sure that all sentences are complete and all proper nouns and titles are capitalized.
- Check facts, math, and figures.
- Ask someone else to read your writing and help you find errors and problems.
- Leave the work for a day or two and then carefully read it again.
- Try reading backwards, one sentence at a time. This will help you concentrate on the words and phrases themselves, rather than thinking about the content.
- Print out documents and edit the printouts. (It is easier to overlook errors on-screen.)
- Don't rely solely on spell-checker programs. They can help you identify some common errors and "typos," but they miss many mistakes.
- Use a dictionary and reference books to correct errors and improve word choice.

## PRESENTING/PUBLISHING

The presentation and format of your writing will depend on your audience and purpose for writing. This stage will involve creating a professional, properly formatted document in the most readable and appropriate form — one-column, two-column, single-spaced, double-spaced, 11-point, 12-point, headers, footers, page numbers, etc.

**Appendix F**

# Business Writing Tips

Businesses today rely on clear, precise communication in a variety of formats. People are more willing to do business with an entrepreneur who can communicate concisely and clearly. How you write even routine documents such as memos and e-mails can have an impact on your success. Errors make a bad impression, and unclear writing can cause confusion and costly mistakes. In business, you will use writing for a variety of purposes.

## PURPOSES FOR WRITING

- To convey information
- To explain directions and procedures
- To request information
- To correspond with others
- To prepare reports, plans, and proposals
- To make or respond to requests
- To persuade others to take a certain action
- To express goodwill or show appreciation
- To create a business plan; to explain how you will succeed in a new business or effectively market your product or service

## TYPICAL DOCUMENTS IN THE WORKPLACE

- Product descriptions
- Press releases
- Memos, e-mail, and business letters
- Sales letters
- Policies, procedures, and handbooks
- Announcements
- Flyers, brochures, and advertising
- Instructions and manuals
- Reports and proposals
- Presentation aids and visuals

## THE FOUR C'S OF COMMUNICATION

Writing should always be complete, concise, clear, and correct.

### Complete

- Include all necessary facts and answers to potential questions.
- Organize your writing:
  - Think about what you want to communicate.
  - Decide on a logical order and flow of ideas.
  - Utilize pre-writing and drafting strategies.

### Concise

- Say what you need to say in as few words as possible.
- Use simple, direct language. Delete unnecessary words. Aim for an average sentence length of 15-20 words or fewer. (But vary sentence length to keep your writing interesting.)
- Avoid long, complicated words when simple words would work just as well.
- Make sure important information stands out by keeping paragraphs short and easy to read.

### Clear

- State your purpose clearly.
- Make your key points in a straightforward way. Organize the paragraphs to support each main idea.
- Support and clarify your ideas with details, but don't clutter your writing with unnecessary information.
- Make sure your writing is focused. Delete any sentences that take the reader off the main message.
- Use effective words. The right word in the right place is a powerful tool for business writers.
- Use the active voice. Use the passive voice sparingly — e.g., "The team adopted new procedures," vs. "New procedures were adopted by the team."
- Use a strong, positive, and businesslike (but courteous) tone suitable for the intended audience. Know when writing should be formal and when informal writing would be more effective.

### Correct

- Make sure the message is correct and all grammar and spelling errors have been corrected.
- Take time to revise your work thoroughly — no one gets it completely right in the very first draft.
- Proofread all your business communications carefully before you send them.

---

### ADDITIONAL STRATEGIES FOR BETTER WRITING

- Have a positive attitude about writing to overcome "writer's block" and anxiety.
- Allow plenty of time to write. Work in a comfortable place that is free from distractions.
- Use a dictionary, thesaurus, and writing handbook to check formats, spelling, and word choice.
- Practice! The more you write, the more you will improve.

# E-mail Tips

---

## DO'S AND DON'TS OF E-MAIL MESSAGES

### Do's

- Always include a brief subject line. Make sure it is relevant enough to make the reader open the message.
- Be courteous, brief, and specific, using one subject and one message per e-mail. If lengthy information is necessary, send it as a file attachment.
- Make sure your message is clear and easy to read. Divide text into short paragraphs or use bullets for readability.
- Use an appropriate salutation and closing.
- Be polite and use an appropriate tone for your reader(s).
- Respond promptly.
- Use correct punctuation, capitalization, and spelling. Always spell-check.
- Use company e-mail for business purposes only. Watch what you send and where you send it. Send e-mails only to those people who need the information.
- Always read your messages for clarity, accuracy, and proper tone before sending.
- Know and respect your company's policies on e-mail transmissions.

### Don'ts

- Don't engage in spamming or flaming.
- Don't use confusing language, such as slang, acronyms, jargon, and sarcasm.
- Don't use "emoticons" in business e-mail.
- Don't send formal thank-yous as e-mail.
- Don't write in all capital letters. This is the on-screen equivalent of yelling.
- Don't open e-mail from unfamiliar sources.
- Don't use e-mail to discuss sensitive subjects that are best resolved in person.
- Don't rush a response to an angry message.
- Don't send private information via e-mail. Employers are entitled by law to monitor employees' e-mail communications.
- Don't use heavy formatting, colors, and images in e-mail. Readers may not be able to open the e-mails or see the formatting.
- Don't rely on a spell-checker to catch errors.
- Don't send jokes, chain letters, or unsolicited personal messages without permission.
- Don't copy people on messages unnecessarily, and be careful not to inadvertently forward or reply to a message.
- Don't send anything that you wouldn't want other people to read. E-mail can be forwarded and retrieved easily.

# Abbreviations

The list below shows some common abbreviations and acronyms — shortened forms of words and phrases used frequently in business communication. There are many, many others, and every organization has its own set of abbreviations and acronyms. Always use a reference manual to look up any abbreviations you don't understand, and only use abbreviations when you are sure your reader will understand what they mean.

| | | | | | |
|---|---|---|---|---|---|
| **a.f.b.** | air freight bill | **CPA** | Certified Public Accountant | **html** | hypertext markup language |
| **a.m.** | before mid-day (*ante meridiem*) | **cr.** | credit or creditor | **i.e.** | that is (*id est*) |
| **A.P.** | Accounts Payable | **DBA** | doing business as | **I.O.U.** | I owe you |
| **A.R.** | Accounts Receivable | **dept.** | department | **Inc.** | Incorporated |
| **a/c** | account | **disc.** | discount | **incl.** | including |
| **acct.** | account | **div.** | division | **int.** | interest |
| **ADA** | Americans with Disabilities Act | **dr.** | debtor | **inv.** | invoice |
| **agcy.** | agency | **Dr.** | doctor | **Jr.** | junior |
| **a.k.a.** | also known as | **e.g.** | for example (*exempli gratia*) | **LLC** | limited liability company |
| **ASAP** | as soon as possible | **e.o.m.** | end of month | **lbs.** | pounds |
| **asst.** | assistant | **encl.** | enclosure | **Ltd.** | Limited |
| **attn.** | attention | **esp.** | especially | **M.B.A.** | Masters of Business Administration |
| **bal.** | balance | **Esq.** | Esquire (*an attorney*) | **max.** | maximum |
| **C.B.D.** | cash before delivery | **est.** | established | **mfr.** | manufacturer |
| **cc** | carbon copy | **et al.** | and others (*et alii*) | **min.** | minimum |
| **C.O.D.** | cash on delivery | **etc.** | and so forth (*et cetera*) | **mortg.** | mortgage |
| **C.O.S.** | cash on shipment | **f.x.** | foreign exchange | **mpg** | miles per gallon |
| **c/o** | care of | **FAQ** | frequently asked questions | **mph** | miles per hour |
| **Co.** | company | **frt.** | freight | **msg.** | message |
| **COB** | close of business | **ft.** | foot or feet | **n/a** | no account, no advice, or not applicable |
| **COLA** | cost of living allowance | **fwd.** | forward | **no.** | number |
| **comm.** | commission | **FYI** | for your information | **NSF** | not sufficient funds |
| **cont.** | continued | **HP** | horsepower | **oz.** | ounces |
| **Corp.** | corporation | **ht.** | height | **p.m.** | after mid-day (*post meridiem*) |

| | | | | | | |
|---|---|---|---|---|---|
| **P.O.** | post office (as in P.O. Box) or purchase order | **pls.** | please | **rpm** | rotations per minute |
| **P.S.** | postscript | **pp.** | pages | **shipt.** | shipment |
| **p/c** | petty cash | **Ppd.** | prepaid | **Sr.** | senior |
| **P/L** | profit and loss | **pref.** | preference | **tel.** | telephone |
| **p.** | page | **pt.** | payment | **tech.** | technician or technology |
| **pat.pend.** | patent pending | **qty.** | quantity | **temp.** | temporary or temperature |
| **PC** | personal computer | **R.S.V.P.** | Please respond (*Répondez s'il vous plaît*) | **URL** | Uniform Resource Locator (WWW address) |
| **PDF** | portable document format | **rec.** | received or receipt | | |
| **Ph.D.** | Doctor of Philosophy | **recd.** | received | **w/** | with |
| | | **ref.** | reference | **w/o** | without |
| **PIN** | personal identification number | **reg.** | registered | **WWW** | World Wide Web |
| | | **Re:** | in regard to | **yd.** | yard |
| | | **retd.** | returned | **yr.** | year |
| **pkg.** | package | **rev.** | revenue | **yrly.** | yearly |
| | | **ROI** | return on investment | | |

Special abbreviations of commonly used phrases are used exclusively in *very informal* e-mail and text messaging. There is a time and place for their use, and they should be used sparingly and only when considered appropriate etiquette for your organization and colleagues (i.e., not in your resume). Below are some typical acronyms you could encounter in online communications.

| | | | | | |
|---|---|---|---|---|---|
| **AFAIK** | As far as I know | **IMHO** | In my humble opinion | **RSN** | Real soon now |
| **BBL** | Be back later | **LOL** | Laughing out loud | **TIA** | Thanks in advance |
| **BFN** | Bye for now | **NBD** | No big deal | **TTFN** | Ta ta for now (goodbye) |
| **BRB** | Be right back | **IC** | I see | | |
| **BTW** | By the way | **NOYB** | None of your business | **TTYL** | Talk to you later |
| **FWIW** | For what it's worth | **OTL** | Out to lunch | **TYVM** | Thank you very much |
| **FYI** | For your information | **OTOH** | On the other hand | **WYSIWYG** | What you see is what you get |
| **IAE** | In any event | **PTB** | Powers that be | | |
| **IMO** | In my opinion | | | | |

# Test-Taking and Study Tips

## BE PREPARED

Many people get nervous before a test. The best cure for test anxiety is preparation.

- Don't wait until the last minute and then cram.
- Instead, study for shorter periods every day, before the test.
- Refer to your textbook, workbook, class notes, and previous tests.
- Plan ahead and use available study time wisely.
- Study in a quiet, comfortable place with good lighting and no distractions.
- Take short breaks during long periods of study — 15 minutes for every two hours of study time is a good rule of thumb.
- Keep a positive attitude and visualize yourself doing well.
- Get plenty of rest and eat healthy food prior to a test.
- Arrive at the test site early with any necessary materials.

## TAKING A TEST

When you sit down to write a test:

- Before you begin, quickly scan the entire test.
- Decide how best to spend your time and efforts in order to complete the entire test.
- Read the directions carefully and ask questions if you don't understand something.
- Write clearly and carefully.
- If you are unsure of an answer, take a guess only if you know there is no penalty for a wrong answer.
- If you can't answer a question or a section, move on and come back to it later. Some test-takers always like to start with the easiest questions.
- After completing a test, check all of your answers. Be sure that you have answered everything.

### True/False Questions

The key to answering true/false questions is careful reading. Look for "clue" words, such as *all, none, only, generally, always, never, probably, seldom,* and so forth. Words like *only, all, never,* and *always* can indicate a false statement. Words like *probably* and *generally* tend to point to a true statement. Remember, if part of the statement is false; the whole statement is false.

### Multiple-Choice Questions

Multiple-choice questions on a test usually contain several choices: the correct answer, an answer that makes sense and is close to the answer but is incorrect, a clearly wrong answer, and a silly answer. The key is to read all of the choices carefully. Read over the questions and all the choices before making a selection. Look to see that the answer you have selected agrees with the grammatical structure and logic of the question e.g., the answer "127" is probably not a correct answer to a "why"-type question.

### Essay and Short-Response Written Questions

Read each essay question carefully. Make sure you understand what it is asking for. On a separate sheet of paper, make a brief outline of your answer to the question. List your main ideas/paragraphs and the supporting details you will include for each. This will help you remember key points as you write. After finishing, reread your essay to be sure you have answered the question posed and addressed all the key points.

## TAKING NOTES

Taking notes is an important part of learning, whether in a classroom or a business meeting. Use the following strategies for effective note taking:

- Write the date, course, and title of the lesson or meeting.
- Be brief; write down only what is important. Use your own words, not the instructor's or presenter's.
- Summarize with a few main words and phrases, and use abbreviations and symbols that you will remember.
- Write your notes neatly, so you will be able to read and understand them later.
- Leave space around your notes and review them later. Fill in any missing explanations, questions, or ideas and rewrite anything that is illegible.
- Highlight or underline the important parts of the notes to simplify studying or to review later.
- Take notes on all definitions, lists, key facts, formulas, or solutions, and write down anything the instructor or presenter puts on the board or on a transparency.
- Listen for "cue" words and phrases, such as *first, second, third, take note of, remember that, for example, on the other hand, finally, therefore,* or *as a result,* which can indicate that the information to follow is important.
- Note the teacher's or speaker's tone of voice and body language, which can also reveal what he or she thinks is important.

## MEMORIZING INFORMATION

Several techniques can help make memorization easier:

- Study in frequent, short periods rather than cramming in long sessions at the last minute.
- Begin memorization early and review the content within 24 hours of your first study session.
- Be sure that you thoroughly understand the material that you need to memorize.

- If you are a "visual" learner, write down what you need to memorize. If you are an "auditory" learner, read the material aloud or listen to a recording.
- Develop memory aids — e.g., ROY G. BIV helps us remember the colors of the rainbow (red, orange, yellow, green, blue, indigo, and violet).
- Visualize the material that you need to memorize. Try to "see" it as if it were a photograph.
- Repeat and review the material frequently. Test and retest yourself.
- Consider starting a study group or find a "study buddy," so members can quiz each other.

## STUDYING A TEXTBOOK

- Scan your book carefully by looking at the table of contents and familiarizing yourself with the subject matter and the parts of the book.
- Prior to reading a new chapter, skim the chapter reviewing the introduction, objectives, sub-headings, bolded terms, summaries, captions, and other highlighted information.
- Read the questions at the end of the chapter so you will know where to focus your attention.
- Carefully read the chapter *without underlining*.
- After the first reading, re-read the chapter and either underline or highlight, or make an outline on a separate sheet of paper, noting the key words and phrases and examples.
- Write down any unfamiliar words, and then look them up in the dictionary.

## STUDYING MATH

- Correctly copy into a notebook all mathematical symbols, theorems, and formulas presented. Memorize them and learn how to use them by working on examples until you can perform them easily.
- Stay current in class. Math concepts build on one another. If you miss a class or do not understand something, you will probably have trouble with later lessons. Get help promptly if something doesn't make sense.
- Review all your solutions carefully, checking to see if the answer is reasonable and makes sense.
- Make sure all required steps in the solution are shown.
- Give answers in the appropriate units — e.g., $, %, miles per hour, cubic yards.

# Listening Tips

One of the most important elements — perhaps the most important — in communication is the ability to listen. Poor listening skills can lead to miscommunication, misunderstandings, damaged work relationships, and poor work performance. To prevent these problems, improve your listening skills by using active listening techniques.

## ACTIVE LISTENING STRATEGIES

- Use a confident and relaxed posture and maintain eye contact.
- Focus your attention on what is being said. Don't anticipate what might be said next or plan your next question or comment.
- Listen attentively. Let the speaker talk without interruption.
- Use receptive language. Show your interest and encourage the speaker by making courteous comments such as, "Please, go on," "Sure," "I see," "I see your point," etc.
- Ask occasional questions to clarify information or request more details.
- Smile and be pleasant, not confrontational or defensive. Nod to show you are paying attention. (If you're on the phone, say, "I see," or "I understand," to show attention.)
- Be ready to give feedback. Listen for hints that the speaker wants a response.
- Watch for and interpret nonverbal signals.
- Take notes if the situation calls for it, but avoid unnecessary note taking that can be distracting.
- Never fake paying attention.

## STRATEGIES FOR LISTENING TO A PRESENTER

- Sit in a location that will allow you to pay close attention and minimize distractions.
- Listen attentively to the speaker.
- Focus on the words and not on the speaker's appearance.
- Listen carefully to the introductory comments, so you will know what to expect.
- Listen for key words and transition words that indicate a new topic, sequence, or importance.
- Take notes if the situation calls for it.
- Keep an open mind and listen attentively, even if the speaker says something you disagree with.
- If the speaker summarizes his/her talk, listen carefully and use it as an opportunity to check your notes for accuracy and completeness.
- Jot down questions that you think of during the presentation and ask them in the designated question-and-answer time. Ask questions to confirm understanding and get additional information. Confirm what you heard by rephrasing or summarizing. This will help the speaker fill in any information that may have been incomplete or misunderstood.

# Body Language Tips

**N**onverbal communication is any meaning conveyed through "body language," through the way the voice is used, and through the way people position themselves in relation to others. How something is said is frequently just as important as what is said. Tone of voice, facial expression, gestures, or haste may determine how we interpret the words used. In fact, nonverbal communication can often tell you more about people than what they say. Likewise, your nonverbal cues send a message about you to others. By paying careful attention to body language, you can pick up signals about what another person is thinking — and whether that matches what he or she is saying.

### Gestures that usually show comfort, openness, or respect:

- Maintaining an open posture
- Leaning forward slightly to show interest
- Smiling
- Nodding to show agreement and understanding
- Maintaining eye contact to show attentiveness
- Gesturing warmly or "talking with hands"
- Respecting personal space. In the U.S., appropriate space between speakers is about three feet.

### Gestures that could show resistance, impatience, or frustration:

- Stiff posture
- Leaning away
- Crossing arms over the chest
- Looking away (looking at watch)
- Hands behind the back or neck
- Tapping fingers or fidgeting
- Grasping object — such as chair or pen — tightly
- Placing hand over mouth or chin in hands
- Standing too close to or too far away from the other person

### When using nonverbal communication, remember:

- Nonverbal communication must *always* be considered along with the words used and the situation. If you try to interpret meaning from just a nonverbal cue, you may well be wrong.
- Nonverbal communication varies greatly from culture to culture. When interacting with people from other cultures, understand and respect their nonverbal customs.
- Nonverbal communication such as closeness or touching may be misinterpreted at work. Even an innocent pat on the back or hand on the arm can be taken the wrong way. These gestures should usually be avoided in the workplace.

Appendix F

# Speaking Tips

**W**hether you like it or not, some people will judge you as a business leader by how well you speak. Learning to improve your speaking skills can help you make a positive impression on others.

### SUGGESTIONS FOR IMPROVING SPOKEN COMMUNICATION

- **Think Before Speaking.** Ask yourself, "What do I want to communicate?" The key to communication is truly understanding what must be communicated. Plan and prepare your communication if necessary.
- **Speak in a Pleasant Voice.** Use a natural, expressive speaking voice. Make sure it is pleasant and appropriate for the situation. Use a professional tone, and match your volume to the situation. Listen to your voice and your message and make adjustments as needed.
- **Use Effective Word Choice.** Correct grammar and pronunciation is important. Develop an ability to use clear, descriptive, and specific language. Avoid idioms, jargon, slang, and other potentially confusing expressions. Try to cut down on saying "like" and "you know." Learn to pronounce unfamiliar words. And, of course, never use profanity or derogatory terms.
- **Use "I" Phrases.** Using "I" phrases, such as "I believe," or "I don't understand," is much more effective than comments such as "You are wrong," or "You are confusing me," which can make other people feel defensive.
- **Get Feedback and Follow Up.** Ask for feedback from listeners to confirm understanding. Follow up your explanations in writing if needed.
- **Be Willing to Speak Up.** Don't worry too much about what others will think. Your ideas and participation may help them to gain understanding. In class or in a meeting, ask precise, appropriate questions to show that you are paying attention and want to contribute.
- **Be Discreet and Truthful.** Know when it's best to remain silent. Respect honesty, confidentiality, and privacy both at work and in personal relationships.

# Presentation Tips

Speaking well is a useful skill in any business, and speaking presentations come in a variety of forms: from product demonstrations to training sessions to staff announcements. People in almost every walk of life have to make a presentation sometime. The following techniques can help you fine-tune your public speaking and presenting skills.

## PLANNING

- Be prepared. Know the size of the room, seating arrangements, lighting, sound, audiovisual equipment, etc.
- Find out everything you can about what your audience knows about your topic. Understand their interests and needs. Don't make assumptions about what they already know.
- Research your topic and plan your presentation in advance, outlining your main ideas and examples on note cards.
- On each note card write down one idea with at least one example, statistic, story, or expert you can cite to support your point. Keep your message short and simple.
- Select appropriate visuals, examples, anecdotes, and analogies.

## PRACTICE

- Rehearse in front of a mirror, another person, or video camera and critique yourself.
- Practice your presentation until you have a thorough knowledge of the subject and feel relaxed and confident.

## ORGANIZATION

- Start with a solid introduction that will interest the audience and make them want to listen to the presentation. Begin with a story, quotation, preview of your topic, current events, or pose a question to the audience to get them to participate.
- Move into the middle (body) of the presentation. Transition smoothly from one point to the next; summarizing as needed and offering details for each main point before moving on to the next.
- End with a strong conclusion. Include a brief summary or refer back to key points.
- Depending on your topic and purpose, your presentation can be outlined in chronological (time) order, by topic, by region/geography, by causes and effects, or by problems and potential solutions.
- Humor can be a great tool in presentations, but use it only if it is natural to you and, of course, be careful in choosing what your audience may/may not find funny. If a joke's content is even the least bit questionable, don't use it.

## DELIVERY

- On the day of the presentation, wear appropriate, professional clothing. Avoid jewelry, loud clothing, or makeup that will divert the audience's attention from your message.
- Be yourself. Use confident, calm body language and posture, and your voice will relax.
- Make eye contact with your audience, speak loudly enough for all to hear, and remember to smile.
- During the first half minute of your presentation, smile, walk confidently to the podium or front of the room, establish eye contact by scanning the group, and thank your host/introducer and audience.
- Begin with a humorous or light remark or just a friendly "Hello, how are you today?"
- Speak clearly and simply. Don't try to impress your audience with complicated ideas or big words. Speak so that they will understand.
- Vary your distance from sections of the audience to stop their talking or to get them to participate.
- Lean forward when asked a question and look at everyone in the group.
- Draw in non-attentive or non-responsive audience members by looking at them or asking them a question directly.
- Engage the audience by establishing common ground and appealing to their interests and beliefs.
- Read audience body language. Fidgeting might show indifference. Watch for confused or concerned expressions.
- Handle questions in a pleasant, professional manner. Repeat the question for all to hear. Listen carefully before answering. If you don't know the answer, tell the person that you will get back to him/her about it or ask other audience members to respond.
- Rephrase negative questions into positive remarks. Politely offer to discuss irrelevant or aggressive questions with the individuals involved after the presentation.

# Interview Tips

In a job interview, the interviewer tries to learn more about a candidate to decide whether he or she is the best person for the job. The interviewee tries to "sell" him/herself, helping the interviewer to find out what he or she can do for the company. In addition, the interview is a time when an interviewee can evaluate the company and learn more about the position that is available. The way that both people look, act, and speak will probably affect the outcome of the interview.

## TIPS FOR THE INTERVIEWEE

### Preparing for an Interview

- Prepare thoughtful, honest answers to common interview questions.
- Prepare some questions you can ask about the company and the position.
- Think about how you can present weaknesses (such as inexperience) in a positive light.
- Verify the time, date, location, and name of interviewer.
- Research as much information about the company as possible.
- Be sure you know how to get to the location.
- Know your salary requirements and local salary ranges.
- Practice with a friend and get honest feedback, or videotape yourself and evaluate your own performance.
- Be organized. Bring a cover letter, resume, letters of recommendation, references, work permit, work samples, diploma or transcripts.

### Tips for Successful Interviews

- Arrive a few minutes early and be on your best behavior from the moment you enter company property. Smile and be pleasant and respectful to everyone you meet.
- Dress appropriately for the position. Wear professional and conservative clothing that is neat and clean. Avoid flashy jewelry, unnatural makeup, clothes or pins with words or phrases, sunglasses, or a hat.
- Do not smoke or chew gum.
- Be polite, confident, relaxed, and prepared. Sit up straight. Shake hands with the interviewer.
- Don't slouch, fidget nervously, or look around the room.
- Listen carefully. Speak in formal, standard English. Answer questions honestly and completely. Ask questions if you have them. Remember the interviewer's name and use it in the conversation. Thank the interviewer for his/her time.
- Never use slang or profanity or interrupt an interviewer.
- Explain how your qualifications make you the best candidate for the position.
- Never speak badly about a previous employer.

- Explain any negative work experiences in an unemotional manner, emphasizing what you learned and how you improved.
- Show interest in the job and the company by asking informed questions.
- Ask for clarification of duties and expectations. Show ambition and desire by asking about opportunities for training and advancement.
- Do not bring up salary first. If asked about salary requirements, discuss appropriate ranges.
- Remain enthusiastic even if you feel the position isn't for you.
- Close by shaking hands, thanking the interviewer (use his/her name). Restate your interest in the job and ask when a decision will be made.
- Be prepared to take pre-employment tests.

### Follow-Up

- Immediately after an interview, write a thank-you note to each of the interviewers you met.
  - Express thanks/appreciation.
  - Emphasize your interest and briefly restate your qualifications.
  - Ask for the job.
  - Make a good impression with a neat, error-free letter.

Keep interview progress charts to help you keep track of and measure your job search progress.

### QUESTIONS AN INTERVIEWER MIGHT ASK

- Tell me about yourself.
- What are your strengths and weaknesses?
- Why should we hire you?
- Describe a time when you were faced with a challenging situation and how you handled it.
- What are you looking for in a job?
- Why did you leave (or why do you want to leave) your current job?
- Why do you want to work for this company?
- What are your long-term career objectives?

### QUESTIONS YOU MIGHT ASK AN INTERVIEWER

- What types of skills are you looking for?
- What type of training program do you have?
- If I perform well, what are the opportunities for promotion?
- What hours would I be working?
- What is the salary range for this position?
- What benefits are available/provided?

## INAPPROPRIATE INTERVIEW QUESTIONS

- Questions related to the following topics are inappropriate (and may be illegal) in an interview:
  - Age
  - Marital status
  - Children
  - Criminal record
  - National origin
  - Religion
  - Disability

- These types of questions usually indicate an inexperienced interviewer, but they may indicate discrimination.
- An interviewee has the right to refuse to answer illegal questions, but the interviewer might view this as an uncooperative attitude.
- If you are the interviewer, avoid such questions. If you are the interviewee, draw the conversation back to your skills and experience, or ask how the information is relevant to the position.

## TIPS FOR THE INTERVIEWER

- Be sure you know what skills, traits, attitudes, etc. you want in the people you hire. Write a complete job description if one doesn't already exist.
- Develop a list of questions related to the candidate's current position, past employment, interests (both personal and career), related experience, education, wage requirements, working-condition expectations, why the applicant wants this job and feels qualified for it.
- Make sure all of your questions are job-related and not personal in nature.
- Prepare a checklist of information you want to share with the candidate about the position and the company.
- Look for a candidate who is prepared, enthusiastic, and knowledgeable about your business, and clear and realistic about your organization's goals and finances.
- Watch for good eye contact and listen for confidence in the interviewee's voice.
- Listen carefully and take notes during or immediately after the interview.
- Be open-minded and put aside any preconceptions or biases.

**Appendix F**

# Negotiation Tips

**A** negotiation is a discussion that is intended to produce an agreement with someone else. Negotiation is the process of achieving one's goals through give-and-take. Being able to negotiate agreeable and fair solutions is an important entrepreneurial skill. How well you negotiate will greatly affect the success of your business. Most experts agree on the following basic steps for "win/win" negotiating:

- Be ready; have a sense of what you can accept as an agreement and what you want to achieve in the negotiation.
- Think about what your best (and worst) end result would be. Identify your next-best alternative, in case your desired outcome isn't possible.
- Put yourself in the other person's shoes and think about what he or she wants from the negotiation.
- Listen carefully and ask questions to learn as much as possible about the other person's needs.
- Don't talk dollars until you have to. Discuss the situation first. Let the other person name a dollar amount first.
- If the other party won't reveal a position or an amount, suggest a very high or very low figure (depending on which side of the negotiation you are on) to see how he or she responds.
- Be flexible; be willing to bargain and to give and take.
- Be honest and respectful, and strive for fairness.
- Be willing to consider creative alternatives if necessary.
- Before closing the deal, be sure you can meet your commitments and that the outcome will support your goals.
- Also, make sure the other party is reasonably satisfied and that you feel confident in her or his willingness and ability to uphold the deal.
- Negotiating business deals is not personal, but good negotiations leave the door open for future dealings with the other party.

# Goal-Setting Tips

**A** goal is the objective, target, or end result expected from the completion of tasks and activities. To accomplish anything in your business or personal life, you will need to set goals. Successful achievement depends on setting effective and challenging goals.

## CHARACTERISTICS OF EFFECTIVE GOALS

**Effective goals are SMART:**

- **Specific.** Writing down goals increases understanding and commitment.
- **Measurable.** Specific goals have criteria for determining if you are achieving them.
- **Achievable.** Goals should be focused on actions that are doable with effort and represent something that you are willing to work hard to achieve. Use positive words to express goals.
- **Realistic.** Challenging but attainable goals provide satisfaction and reduce frustration. Goals should be reasonable expectations of what can be achieved over a given period of time.
- **Time-specific.** Short-term goals are those tasks that must be accomplished immediately or in a short time frame. Long-term goals may take years to accomplish. Break down long-term goals into short-term goals that can be steps for achieving them.

## WORKING TOWARD GOALS

- Set aside time each day or week to do work specifically related to your goals.
- Review and reevaluate your goals frequently to make certain you are still on track toward achieving them. If not, be flexible and willing to adjust your approach. Situations and circumstances may change. If you are not progressing as expected, reevaluate, figure out what went wrong, and adjust your plan.
- Once you have determined your goals, commit yourself. Letting others know about your goals can help. Be sure to say specifically what it is you plan to accomplish, and seek their support.
- Visualize success. Be determined and persistent. Get a mental image of your goal and think when, not if. Make sure goals are both meaningful and achievable.

**Appendix F**

# Business Ethics Tips

**D**ifficult decisions every day require using our sense of what is right or wrong, good or bad, ethical or unethical. Business ethics involves not only distinguishing right from wrong, but also what is fair, good, and proper. Ethical actions in business require the following characteristics:

- **Honesty and truthfulness.** Do not cheat, steal, or deceive others. Remember that stealing includes stealing time — arriving late to work, taking long breaks, doing personal business on the job, or using business equipment for personal tasks.
- **Keep promises.** Keep your word and do not make excuses to get out of commitments.
- **Loyalty.** Be loyal to your organization and its people. Do not disclose secrets or reveal confidential information of any kind. Respect privacy.
- **Respect.** Be considerate, helpful, and respectful of others.
- **Fairness.** Treat people equally and be open to their points of view.
- **Responsibility.** Be accountable for your decisions and actions. Work diligently and meet your commitments. Follow rules and be reliable. Do not blame others for mistakes or take credit for their accomplishments.
- **Thoughtfulness.** Always think through the consequences of your actions on others and on the business.

**When faced with questions of business ethics, ask yourself:**

- What are the consequences of my actions? Who will benefit? Who will suffer? What risks are involved?
- Do I have all the facts? Where can I get more information?
- Can I get help? What trusted experts or resources could help me?
- Is it legal?
- Would I like to see this on TV or on the front page of the newspaper? Would I mind explaining my actions to my family?
- Does this decision support or damage our organization's culture or values?
- Does it cause a knot in my stomach?

# Team Skills

**A** team is a group of people who work together to reach a common goal. In business, teamwork leads to higher productivity, better product quality, and increased job satisfaction. More ideas from more people lead to better and more creative decisions. However, workplace teams can only be successful when team members communicate effectively with one another and share SMART goals that everyone understands.

## TECHNIQUES FOR BEING AN EFFECTIVE TEAM MEMBER

- Be fair, honest, and cooperative. Offer support and accept support from team members.
- Give and receive constructive feedback. Don't take criticism personally.
- Be respectful and open to the ideas and points of view of others.
- Support others; create an open, safe environment for sharing ideas.
- Give other team members encouragement and assist them with their tasks when necessary.
- Share information, ideas, and recognition.
- Show interest, enthusiasm, and loyalty to the team and its goals.
- Assert yourself. Respond to negative or unproductive behavior in a tactful but firm manner.
- Take initiative. Present new ideas and build on the ideas of others.
- Help keep the team on track. Stay focused.
- Listen actively, ask questions, and offer feedback.
- Be flexible. Accept and respect differences, and be willing to try different things and consider different points of view.
- Know your role and the team's goals. Be aware of your strengths and weaknesses and what you can contribute to the team.
- Resolve conflicts fairly and constructively. Some degree of minor conflict is not only normal — it can lead to creativity and new ideas. Too much conflict, however, is destructive. Avoid unproductive arguments.
- Strive for win/win outcomes and encourage open, honest expression.
- Share praise. Do not claim credit for yourself if a team effort was involved.

## TIPS FOR RUNNING A MEETING

Meetings can be some of the biggest time wasters in the workplace. Practicing a few important strategies can help all attendees manage their time and get the most out of the meeting. Try these guidelines for running an effective meeting:

- Hold meetings in places that are comfortable, free from distractions, easily accessible, and private. Or consider using *groupware* — software that facilitates the meeting of virtual teams, when team members are not in the same location.

- Call meetings for specific purposes as needed; decide how often the team needs to hold regular meetings.
- Assign individuals — not the manager or team leader — to act as recorder, facilitator, and time keeper.
- Provide an advance agenda that lists what is to be discussed or accomplished during the meeting. Set time limits on the meeting and topics.
- Invite only those people who are needed or need to know.
- Start and finish on time.
- Set clear goals/purposes for the meeting.
- Prevent hidden agendas or disruptions by strictly adhering to your planned agenda.
- Ideas that the facilitator or members think are worth discussing — but are outside of the agenda — should be listed on a flip chart so they can be revisited later or at another meeting. This list is sometimes called the "parking lot."
- If a member's comments stray off-topic or into too much detail, any member may make that observation aloud. Some team meetings throw "penalty flags" or foam balls, or use a signal word such as "weeds" (meaning the speaker is "in the weeds" — off-course or going into too much detail) as ways to remind the speaker to get back on topic. The facilitator has the final decision.
- Assign and record action items during the meeting — what, who, assisted by whom, by when.
- Distribute brief, point-form meeting minutes within 48 hours after the meeting.
- Schedule an action item follow-up.
- Move quickly, cover all scheduled topics in the shortest possible time, and accomplish the planned meeting objectives.

## BRAINSTORMING

Teams often use brainstorming to generate new ideas or creative solutions to problems or to make shared decisions on important issues. Brainstorming can be kept simple or made more formal. One technique might involve the following:

- Provide team members with a topic or problem.
- A facilitator asks each member in turn to respond, suggesting one idea per turn.
- No ideas can be judged as good or bad by anyone yet.
- A recorder copies down all ideas with the member's name on a flip chart that all can read. If possible, the recorder lists related items on the same sheet. As needed, sheets are taped up around the room.
- The recorder checks and clarifies members' suggestions as needed.
- Team members may only ask questions to clarify the meaning of another member's idea.
- Members continue to take turns sharing an idea on each turn.

- Any member may "pass" when it's his or her turn, but may use his or her later turn.
- The turns continue until all members have passed or the facilitator calls closure.
- The facilitator and recorder invite questions of clarification or explanation only.
- The facilitator and recorder invite the team members to identify duplicate or similar responses that can be regrouped or combined to reduce the number of responses.
- As needed, the recorder recopies or adjusts the lists accordingly so that all of the responses are grouped. Members vote to determine replacements within groups if needed.
- Working through each group of responses in turn, members rank their "top three" (or two, four or five).
- The recorder tallies the members' responses and lists the "final" top three (or four or five).
- Members debate and discuss the selections and, as appropriate, vote to narrow the lists further to the overall most important/critical two or three items.
- The process is repeated — sometimes in a streamlined fashion or in smaller break-out groups of team members — to create SMART goals and action plans for the teams' final choices.
- Action plans are assigned to specific members and recorded for follow-up.

# Glossary

**accounts payable *n.*** money a business owes its suppliers. (381)

**accrue *v.*** to increase or grow because interest is being added periodically. (537)

**acquisition n.** the purchase of one company by another. (559)

**advertisement *n.*** an announcement or broadcast of the sale of a product or service. (250)

**advertising *n.*** putting announcements (advertisements) before the public with the intent of selling a product or service. (250)

**"angel" *n.*** a potential investor who might invest in your business and probably would not demand as high a rate of return as a venture capitalist or a bank. (375)

**annual (annualized) *adj.*** yearly, as in "annual rate of return"; an annualized number is one that has been projected as a yearly rate from data gathered from a shorter period, such as a month. (195)

**annuity *n.*** an amount of money paid out on a regular basis. (550)

**arbitration *n.*** the settlement of a conflict with the help of another person both parties trust, rather than in a court of law. (438)

**asset *n.*** any item of value owned by a business. Cash, inventory, furniture, and machinery are all examples of assets. (194)

**attitude *n.*** a way of acting, thinking or feeling that expresses an opinion or emotion. (272)

**audit *n.*** a formal examination of financial records conducted by the Internal Revenue Service to determine whether the taxpayer being investigated is paying the appropriate amount of taxes. (503)

**average unit of sale *n.*** the unit of sale arrived at when a business sells products at varying prices. (16)

**balance *n.*** 1. the difference between the credit and the debit side of a ledger; also, the difference between the assets and liabilities of a financial statement. 2. **v.** to calculate such differences; to settle an account by paying debts; to keep books properly so credits and debits in an account equal each other. (414)

**balance sheet *n.*** a financial statement summarizing the assets, liabilities, and net worth (or owner's equity) of a business, so called because the sum of the assets equals the total of the liabilities plus the net worth (or owner's equity). (412)

**bankrupt *adj.*** describes a business or person that does not have enough money to pay creditors. (194)

**bar graph *n.*** a chart that uses vertical or horizontal bars to show data; especially good for showing trends in data over time. (181)

**benefit *n.*** an improvement in one's condition; an advantage gained by doing or accepting something. (48)

**board of directors *n.*** a group of persons who manage or control a business. The board of directors of a corporation is chosen by the stockholders. Unincorporated business owners sometimes appoint a board of directors to advise the business. (343)

**bond *n.*** an interest-bearing certificate issued by a government or business that promises to pay the holder interest as well as the value of the bond at maturity. (542)

**brand *n.*** a name (sometimes used with a symbol or trademark) that distinguishes a business from its competition and makes its competitive advantage instantly recognizable to the consumer. (134)

**breach of contract *n.*** failure of a signatory of a contract to comply with its provisions. (433)

**break-even analysis** *n.* an examination of the income statement that helps an entrepreneur find the break-even point for a business. (264)

**break-even point** *n.* the point at which the total at the bottom of the income statement is zero, because the business has sold exactly enough units for profit to cover costs. (264)

**break-even units** *n.* the number of units of sale a business needs to have sold to arrive at the "break-even" point of neither earning a profit nor taking a loss. (265)

**budget** *n.* a plan for spending money in an efficient way. (186)

**burn rate** *n.* negative cash flow; cash on hand divided by monthly operating costs, which is a ratio that indicates how many months a business can cover its overhead without making a profit. (476)

**business** *n.* the buying and selling of goods and services in order to make a profit. (2)

**business card** *n.* a small, rectangular card imprinted with a business's name, logo, and contact information (and, often, a slogan). (137)

**business definition** *n.* a specific description of what a particular business will sell to whom and how it will do it. (115)

---

**capital** *n.* money or property owned or used in business. (6)

**capitalism** *n.* the free-market economic system; anyone with the "capital" is free to start a business. (6)

**cash flow** *n.* cash receipts less cash disbursements over a period of time. Cash flow is represented by the cash balance in an accounting journal or ledger (cash flow statement). (470)

**cause-related marketing** *n.* marketing that is tied to a social, political, or environmental cause that the entrepreneur wants to support. (141)

**charge account** *n.* credit extended by a store, allowing qualified customers to make purchases up to a specified limit. (460)

**checking account** *n.* a bank account against which the account holder can write checks. (156)

**collateral** *n.* property or assets pledged by a borrower to a lender to secure a loan. (377)

**command economy** *n.* an economy in which the government owns most or all businesses, and sets prices and quantities produced. (68)

**commission** *n.* a percentage of a sale given to a salesperson as payment. (279)

**competition** *n.* rivalry in business for customers or markets. Competition in a free market leads to lower prices and produces better quality goods and services for consumers. (74)

**competitive advantage** *n.* a benefit that you can deliver to the consumers in your market better than any of your competitors. (96)

**compound interest** *n.* the money one earns on interest that one earned in a previous time period. (535)

**compromise** *n.* a settlement in which each side in a negotiation has given in on some demands. (204)

**consumer** *n.* a person or business that buys goods and services for its own needs, not for resale. (7)

**Consumer Price Index (CPI)** *n.* statistics kept by the government on the retail cost of representative goods. (453)

**contingency** *n.* an unforeseen or unpredictable event. (435)

**continuous improvement** *n.* constantly improving quality and efficiency within a business (see *kaizen*). (332)

**contract** *n.* a formal written agreement between two or more people legally binding each party to fulfill obligations as specified. (306)

**copyright** *n.* the exclusive legal right to an artistic or scholarly work. (481)

**core belief** *n.* a fundamental principle used in guiding a company. (64)

**core competency** *n.* a fundamental knowledge, ability, or expertise in a particular subject or field that is critical to the success of a business; another term for "competitive advantage." (230)

**corporate governance** *n.* the ethics and rules corporations put in place to regulate themselves. (496)

**corporation** *n.* a legal "person" (or entity), composed of stockholders, that is granted the right to buy, sell, and inherit possessions, and is legally liable for its actions. (196)

**co-signer** *n.* an individual who will sign a loan agreement or other contract with someone else in order to guarantee the loan payments in case the first signer is unable to make those payments. (377)

**cost** *n.* an expense; the amount of money, time, or energy spent on something. (48)

**cost/benefit analysis** *n.* a decision-making process in which the costs of taking an action are compared to the benefits; if the benefits outweigh the costs, action may be taken. (47)

**cost of goods sold** *n.* the cost of selling "one additional unit" for a product-based business. (17)

**cost of services sold** *n.* the cost of selling "one additional unit" for a service-based business. (117)

**creativity** *n.* the ability to invent something using imagination or to perceive an already existing thing or situation in a new way. (80)

**credit** *n.* the ability to buy something without spending actual cash at the time of purchase. (458)

**credit union** *n.* a nonprofit cooperative organization that offers low-interest loans to members. (377)

**currency** *n.* another word for "money," specifically money that can be exchanged internationally. (332)

**current ratio** *n.* the comparison of a business's assets to liabilities at any given moment, with a view to making sure that assets at least equal liabilities. (421)

**customer service** *n.* everything the entrepreneur does after a sale to keep the customer happy, including maintaining and repairing a product or service once it has been sold, and handling customer complaints. (282)

**cyclical** *adj.* occurring in cycles, periods when something occurs again. (472)

---

**data** *n.* information, such as customer addresses, stored in a computer. (356)

**database** *n.* a collection of information stored and organized for easy reference. (285)

**debt** *n.* an obligation to pay back a loan; a liability. (194)

**debt ratio** *n.* the ratio of debt (liabilities) to assets. (199)

**debt-to-equity ratio** *n.* a comparison that expresses financial strategy by showing how much of a company is financed by debt and how much by equity. (199)

**deductible** *n.* the portion of an insured loss or damage not covered by insurance; the higher the deductible, the lower the insurance premium. (516)

**deduction** *n.* expenses incurred during the course of doing business. A business owner may subtract deductible amounts from income when figuring income tax due. (158)

**demand** *n.* the willingness and desire for a commodity together with the ability to pay for it; the amount consumers are ready and willing to buy at the price offered in the market. (Often coupled with *supply* as in the term "supply and demand.") (71)

**demographics** *n.* population statistics. (145)

**depreciation** *n.* the amount of value of an asset subtracted each year until the asset value becomes zero; reflects wear and tear on the asset. (124)

**direct cost** *n.* the cost of selling a product or service; also called cost of goods sold (COGS). (118)

**discount** *n.* (referring to bonds) the difference between a bond's trading price and par when the trading price is below par. (407)

**distributor** *n.* a company that will arrange to have your product sold in stores over a wide geographical area. (75)

**diversification** *n.* the strategy of maintaining a variety of investments to minimize the possibility of losing money. (543)

**dividend** *n.* each stockholder's portion of the profit per share paid out by a corporation to its stockholders. (9)

**donation** *n.* a gift or contribution to a charitable organization. (196)

**draft** *v.* to write a version of a contract or agreement with the understanding that it will probably need to be developed and rewritten further. *n.* a working, as opposed to final, version of a contract or other document. (435)

---

**economics of one unit** *n.* the figuring of markup and profit around a business's unit of sale. (16)

**economy** *n.* the financial structure of a country or other area that determines how resources and wealth are distributed. (6)

**electronic rights** *n.* protection of a creator's intellectual property (writing, art, music, etc.) from being used on a Web site without payment to the creator. (485)

**e-mail** *n.* short for electronic mail; messages sent between computers using the Internet. (359)

**employee** *n.* a person hired by a business to work for wages, salary, or commission. (2)

**enterprise** *n.* a business. (6)

**entrepreneur** *n.* a person who organizes and manages a business, assuming the risk for the sake of the potential return. (2)

**equity** *n.* ownership in a company received in exchange for money invested. In accounting, equity is equal to assets minus liabilities. (194)

**ethics** *n.* a system of morals, or standards of conduct and judgment. (492)

**exit strategy** *n.* the strategy by which you turn your business into wealth when you leave (exit) the business. (556)

**exporting** *n.* the act of selling products in other countries. (528)

---

**face value** *n.* the value printed on a bill or bond; not necessarily its market value. (407)

**fax** *n.* short for *facsimile*, a machine that electronically sends printed material over a telephone line; **v.** to use a fax machine. (295)

**file** *v.* (referring to taxes) to fulfill one's legal obligation by mailing a tax return, with any taxes due, to the Internal Revenue Service or state or local tax authority. (502)

**finance charge** *n.* the cost of credit, calculated as a percentage of the amount borrowed. (461)

**financial ratio** *n.* a fraction created by dividing one financial number into another in order to express the relationship between the two numbers (such as return on investment). Financial ratios are often expressed as percentages. (183)

**financial statement** *n.* a report that contains financial information about a company. (167)

**financing** *n.* the act of raising capital for a business. (192)

**fiscal year** *n.* a twelve-month period between settlement of financial accounts. (412)

**fixed cost** *n.* business expenses that must be paid whether or not any sales are being generated — USAIIRD: utilities, salaries, advertising, insurance, interest, rent, and depreciation. (Also called **fixed operating cost**.) (117)

**float** *n.* the time between a payment transaction and when the cash actually is received into someone's account. (376)

**foreign exchange rate** *n.* the relative value between one currency and another. The "F/X" rate describes the "buying power" of a currency. (530)

**foundation** *n.* an organization that manages donations given by philanthropists. (112)

**franchise** *n.* a business that markets a product or service developed by a franchisor, in the manner specified by the franchisor. (520)

**franchisee** *n.* owner of a franchise unit or units. (521)

**franchisor** *n.* person who develops a franchise or a company that sells franchises. (521)

**fraud** *n.* intentional failure by a business owner to inform a customer that he or she could be hurt in some way by the business's product or service. (515)

**free enterprise system** *n.* economic system in which businesses are privately owned and operate relatively free of government interference. (6)

**future value** *n.* the amount an investment is worth in the future if invested at a specific rate of return in the present. (537)

---

**goal** *n.* something an individual wishes to accomplish in the future. (34)

**goodwill** *n.* an intangible asset generated when a company does something positive that has value — goodwill can include the company's reputation, brand recognition, and relationships with the community and customers. (444)

**Gross Domestic Product (GDP)** *n.* the annual estimated value of all products and services produced within a country. (450)

**Gross National Product (GNP)** *n.* the annual market value of all products and services produced by the resources of a country. (451)

**gross profit** *n.* total sales revenue minus total cost of goods sold. (16)

**gross profit margin** *n.* the difference between a wholesale price and a retail price, before any costs are deducted. (325)

---

**harvest** *v.* to leave a business with a portion of the value of the business converted to cash or stock. (554)

**hyperlink** *n.* a highlighted or underlined word, phrase, or icon on a Web site that, when clicked on, leads to a new document page somewhere on the Internet. (358)

---

**immigrant** *n.* a person who settles in a new country or region, having left his or her country or region of birth. (564)

**importing** *n.* the act of bringing products from one country into another country to sell. (453)

**incentive** *n.* something that motivates a person to take an action — to work, start a business, or study harder, for example. (75)

**income statement** *n.* a financial statement that summarizes income and expense activity over a specified period of time and shows net profit or loss. (174)

**index fund** *n.* a mutual fund designed to buy and hold securities in the same proportions as an index, such as the S&P 500. (544)

**inflation** *n.* a continuous increase in the prices of products and services, usually resulting from an increase in the amount of money in circulation in an economy. (408)

**infringement** *n.* violation of a copyright, trademark, or patent. (486)

**installment** *n.* payment on a loan or debt made at regular intervals. (461)

**institutional advertising** *n.* advertisements placed by large corporations to keep the name of the company in the mind of the public, not as promoting a specific product or service. (258)

**insurance** *n.* a system provided by insurance companies to protect people or businesses financially from having property or wealth lost, damaged, or destroyed. (514)

**insurance agent** *n.* an employee who sells insurance and helps purchasers determine what kind of insurance is needed to protect their assets. (514)

**insurance policy** *n.* contract between an insurance company and an individual or business being insured that describes the premium(s) to be paid and the insurance company's obligations. (514)

**intellectual property** *n.* intangible property created using the intellect, such as an invention, book, painting, or music. (480)

**interest** *n.* payment for using someone else's money; payment received for lending money. (535)

**interest rate** *n.* money paid for the use of money, expressed as a percentage per unit of time. (32)

**Internal Revenue Service** *n.* the federal government bureau in charge of taxation. (502)

**Internet** *n.* the world's largest computer network, connecting many millions of users worldwide. (357)

**interoffice** *adj.* referring to something sent from one person to another in the same office or company, using an office distribution system. (295)

**invention** *n.* a new creation that can be used for some practical purpose. (84)

**inventory** *n.* items on hand to be sold. (160)

**inventory sheet** *n.* sheets of columned paper that make it easy to keep track of which products are being sold at what prices. (218)

**investment** *n.* something into which one puts money, time, or energy with the hope of gaining profit or satisfaction, in spite of risks. (28)

**invoice** *n.* an itemized list of goods delivered or services rendered and the amount due; a bill. (157)

**ISP** *n.* Internet Service Provider; services that provide access to the Internet for subscribers. Some ISPs, such as Microsoft Network or America Online, also provide software for browsing the Internet and chatting with other subscribers, among other services. (357)

---

**job shop** *n.* a business that is hired by other companies to manufacture products or parts of products. (315)

---

**kaizen** *n.* Japanese for "continuous improvement"; the concept that continually seeking to improve quality will steadily increase profits. (332)

---

**lateral thinking** *n.* a way of perceiving that looks for indirect approaches to a problem or obstacle; the opposite of vertical thinking. (81)

**lawsuit** *n.* attempt to recover a right or claim through legal action. (438)

**layaway plan** *n.* store policy allowing a customer to make a down payment on an item to secure it and then make regular monthly payments on the remaining balance (the store keeps the item until it is fully paid for). (461)

**letterhead** *n.* stationery imprinted with the name, address, phone and fax numbers, logo, etc., of a business. (298)

**letter of agreement** *n.* written agreement between parties regarding a business arrangement; less formal and detailed than a contract and usually used for arrangements of brief duration. (436)

**leveraged** *adj.* financed by debt (rather than equity). (194)

**liability** *n.* an entry on a balance sheet showing the debts of a business. (412)

**liability insurance** *n.* insurance that covers the cost of injuries to a customer or damage to property caused by a business's product or service. (515)

**liable** *adj.* to be responsible for lawsuits that arise from accidents, unpaid bills, faulty merchandise, or other problems. (304)

**license** *n.* (1) authorization by law to perform a specified action (2) to grant the right to use a licensor's name on a product or service. (307)

**licensee** *n.* person granted the right to use the licensor's name on a product or service sold by the licensee. (525)

**licensing** *n.* authorizing others to use a brand or product; also, granting permission to do something that would otherwise be illegal. (524)

**licensor** *n.* person who sells the right to use his or her name or company name to a licensee; unlike the franchisor, the licensor does not attempt to dictate exactly how the licensee does business. (525)

**limited liability company (LLC)** *n.* a form of business ownership offering the tax advantages of a partnership as well as limited legal liability; this form is not available in all states. (390)

**limited partnership** *n.* form of partnership in which certain partners have limited investment in a business and therefore limited liability. (306)

**line of credit** *n.* a predetermined amount of money that a customer may borrow from a bank on an as-needed basis. (378)

**liquidation** *n.* the sale of the assets of a business that is closing. (554)

**liquidity** *n.* the ease with which cash can be retrieved from an investment. (420)

**logo** *n.* short for logotype, a distinctive company trademark or sign. (136)

---

**majority interest** *n.* ownership of more stock in a corporation than all other stockholders together. (426)

**manufacturing** *n.* the making or producing of tangible products. (19)

**manufacturing plants** *n.* factories; one or more buildings where the manufacturing of products takes place. (313)

**market** *n.* a group of people potentially interested in buying a given product or service; any scenario or designated location where trade occurs. (83)

**market clearing price** *n.* the price at which the amount of a product or service demanded by consumers equals the amount the supplier is willing to sell at that price; the price at which the supply and demand lines cross. Also called "equilibrium price." (73)

**marketing** *n.* the business function that identifies consumer needs and responds to them in order to satisfy the customer and to make a profit. (132)

**marketing mix** *n.* the combination of four factors — product, price, place, and promotion — that communicate a marketing vision to your consumer. (243)

**market research** *n.* the investigation a business carries out to find out the wants and needs of consumers in order to make its marketing and advertising plans more successful. (144)

**market segment** *n.* a group of consumers who have a similar response to a particular type of marketing. (149)

**market share** *n.* the percentage of the total market for a product that a given company holds. (139)

**markup** *n.* an increase in the price of a product that covers expenses and creates a profit for the seller. (323)

**matching entry** *n.* in double-entry bookkeeping, the entry on the right side that matches the entry made on the left side of the accounting journal. (160)

**maturity** *n.* the date at which a bond must be redeemed by the company that issued it. (406)

**media** *n. pl.* means of communication (newspapers, radio, television, etc.) that reach the general public, usually including advertising. (250)

**memo** *n.* short for *memorandum*, from the Latin word for "to be remembered"; a brief, concise note from one person to another. (294)

**mentor** *n.* a person who agrees to volunteer time and expertise, and provide emotional support to help another individual reach his or her goals. (280)

**merger** *n.* a joining of two or more companies into one. (554)

**mind share** *n.* awareness of a product or company created in the consumer's mind by the company's marketing. (136)

**Minority Enterprise Small Business Investment Company (MESBIC) *n.*** loan organizations partially financed through the government that provide loans to minority small business ventures (see SBIC). (379)

**mission *n.*** the primary objective of a business. (236)

**mission statement *n.*** a short, written declaration that informs customers and employees of a business's goal and a description of the strategy and tactics to be used to meet it. (231)

**modem *n.*** device that connects a computer to a phone or cable line and translates digital information between them. (357)

**monopoly *n.*** a market with only one producer; the control of the pricing and distribution of a product or service in a given market as a result of lack of competition. (75)

**mortgage *n.*** a loan, generally from a bank, that pays the balance of the price of a house (after the buyer contributes a down payment). (463)

**moving assembly line *n.*** continuous moving line in a factory where parts are put together to make a completed product. (312)

**mutual fund *n.*** a company that collects money from investors and invests it for them in diversified securities. (544)

---

**negotiation *n.*** discussion or bargaining in an effort to reach agreement between parties with differing goals. (204)

**net *n.*** final result; in business, the profit or loss remaining after all costs have been subtracted. (126)

**net present value *n.*** the value of something in the future considered in the present, such as a stock price. (555)

**net profit *n.*** the profit left after all costs, including taxes, have been subtracted. (126)

**networking *n.*** the act of exchanging valuable information and contacts with other businesspeople. (298)

**newsgroup *n.*** an online discussion group that focuses on a specific subject. (260)

**nonprofit corporation *n.*** a corporation whose mission is not to make a profit but to benefit society in a specified way; also called not-for-profit corporation. (196)

**operating cost *n.*** each cost necessary to operate a business, not including the cost of goods sold. Operating costs can almost always be covered by USAIIRD: utilities, salaries, advertising, insurance, interest, rent, and depreciation. Operating costs are also called "overhead." (123)

**operating ratio *n.*** the percentage of each dollar of revenue needed to cover costs. (185)

**opportunity *n.*** a chance or occasion that can be turned to one's advantage. (44)

**opportunity cost *n.*** the value of what must be given up in order to obtain something else. (48)

**optimist *n.*** one who consistently looks on the bright side of situations or outcomes. (58)

**overhead *n.*** the continuing fixed costs of running a business; the costs a business has to pay to be able to operate. (123)

**owner's equity *n.*** net worth; the difference between assets and liabilities. (412)

---

**packing slip *n.*** a list of goods accompanying a shipment. (157)

**par *n.*** the face value of a bond. (407)

**partnership *n.*** an association of two or more people in a business enterprise. (305)

**patent *n.*** an exclusive right, granted by the government, to produce, use, and sell an invention or process. (481)

**percentage *n.*** "a given part of a hundred"; a number expressed as part of a whole, with the whole represented as 100 percent. (29)

**permit *n.*** an official document granting the right to carry out an activity. (307)

**philanthropy *n.*** a concern for human and social welfare expressed by giving money to charities and foundations. (112)

**pie chart *n.*** a circular diagram that looks like a pie, with each "slice" representing a portion of the whole. (47)

**pilferage *n.*** the theft by employees or customers of a business's inventory. (475)

**pitch letter *n.*** a press release in the form of a letter sent to individuals in the media for publicity purposes. (251)

**portfolio *n.*** a mix of cash, bond, and stock investments designed to achieve financial goals. (548)

**premium *n.*** the amount above par for which a bond is trading on the open market; the cost of insurance, usually expressed as a monthly or annual payment by the policyholder to an insurance company. (407)

**647**

**present value** *n.* the amount an investment is worth discounted back to the present. (535)

**press release** *n.* an announcement sent to the media to generate publicity. (251)

**pre-tax profit** *n.* a business's profits after all costs have been deducted except taxes. (176)

**principal** *n.* the amount of a debt or loan before interest is added. (406)

**product** *n.* something that exists in nature, or made by human industry, usually to be sold. (95)

**production/distribution structure** *n.* the manufacturer-to-wholesaler-to-retailer-to-consumer chain along which a product progresses. (322)

**profit** *n.* the sum remaining after all costs are deducted from the income of a business. (2)

**profit per unit** *n.* the selling price minus the cost of goods sold of an item. (265)

**profit margin** *n.* the percentage of each dollar of revenue that is profit; profit divided by revenue times 100. (325)

**progressive tax** *n.* taxes that take a greater percentage of higher incomes than of lower ones. (501)

**projection** *n.* a forecast or prediction of financial outcome in the future; business plans include projections of how an entrepreneur expects financial statements to come out. (474)

**promissory note** *n.* a written promise to pay a certain sum of money on a specified date. (194)

**promotion** *n.* the development of the popularity and sales of a product or service through advertising and publicity. (250)

**prototype** *n.* a model or pattern that serves as an example of how a product would look and operate if it were manufactured. (86)

**public domain** *n.* that which is free of copyright or patent restrictions. (487)

**publicity** *n.* free promotion, as opposed to advertising, which is purchased. (251)

**purchase order** *n.* a detailed document recording the ordering of supplies for a business. (157)

**quality** *n.* the degree of excellence of a product or service. (330)

**quality control** *n.* the process of ensuring that the appropriate level of quality is maintained. (334)

**quick ratio** *n.* the comparison of cash to debt, with the idea that a business should have at least enough cash on hand to pay its current debts. (421)

**quota** *n.* a restriction imposed by the government on the amount of a specified product that can be imported into that country. (529)

**rate of return** *n.* the return on an investment, expressed as a percentage of the amount invested. (32)

**real estate** *n.* land or buildings that may be bought and sold. (277)

**receipt** *n.* the detailed written proof of a purchase. (279)

**recession** *n.* an economic downturn, resulting in less employment and business activity. (450)

**recruitment** *n.* the search for and hiring of employees. (341)

**redeem** *v.* to turn in a bond to the issuer at the date of maturity for conversion into cash. (407)

**repeat business** *n.* sales resulting from loyal customers making repeat purchases from the same company. (282)

**reserve** *n.* money kept on hand (typically cash) in the event that enough revenue does not come in to cover fixed costs. (128)

**resource** *n.* a supply of something; a source, either natural or intellectual. (5)

**resume** *n.* a summary of an individual's education and work experience. (342)

**retail** *n.* a business that sells products or services directly to the individual consumer. (20)

**return on investment** *n.* profit on an investment, expressed as a percentage. (28)

**risk** *n.* the chance of loss. (31)

**royalty** *n.* a share of the proceeds of the sale of a product paid to a person who owns a copyright; also refers to the fee paid to a franchisor or licensor. (520)

**Rule of 72** *n.* a formula for finding out how long it will take an investment to double in value. (35)

**sales call** *n.* an appointment made with a potential client with the intention of selling a product or service. (325)

**sales tax** *n.* consumption tax levied on items that are sold by businesses to consumers. States raise revenue through sales tax. (500)

**same size analysis *n.*** a comparison of finanical data made by putting the various figures into percentages. (183)

**savings account *n.*** a bank account in which money is deposited and on which the bank pays interest to the depositor. (155)

**securities *n.*** stocks and bonds. (406)

**Securities and Exchange Commission (SEC) *n.*** the government agency that oversees the trading of stocks and bonds. (375)

**self-employment tax *n.*** a tax people who work for themselves pay in addition to income tax; includes a Social Security tax obligation. (501)

**self-esteem *n.*** a belief in and positive feeling about oneself. (59)

**service *n.*** intangible work providing time, skills, or expertise in exchange for money. (20)

**service mark *n.*** a word, name, symbol, or device used by a manufacturer or merchant to distinguish a service business (equivalent to a trademark for a product-based business). (481)

**setup cost *n.*** the costs a manufacturing business will have before it starts to make a product. (317)

**share *n.*** a single unit of stock. (398)

**shareware *n.*** free software available on the Internet; shareware is usually the "test" or "light" version of the software. (355)

**shrinkage *n.*** the unexplained disappearance of inventory from a store or warehouse. (475)

**signatory *n.*** an individual who signs a contract, thereby making a legal commitment. (438)

**Small Business Administration (SBA) *n.*** the federal agency that assists and looks after the interests of small business. (375)

**Small Business Investment Company (SBIC) *n.*** loan organizations partially financed through the government that provide loans to small businesses. (374)

**small claims court *n.*** state court where disputes for relatively small amounts of money are settled between complainants who are allowed to represent themselves instead of using attorneys. (438)

**socially responsible business *n.*** a business venture that expresses an entrepreneur's ethics and core values. (442)

**Social Security *n.*** a federal program that pays benefits to retired people and the families of dead or disabled workers. (501)

**sole proprietorship *n.*** a business owned by one person. The owner receives all profits and is legally liable for all debts or lawsuits arising from the business. (304)

**speculative *adj.*** uncertain or risky. (401)

**start-up investment *n.*** expenses involved in getting a business going; start-up investment is also called the "original" investment, or start-up capital. (332)

**statistics *n.*** facts (data) collected and presented in numerical fashion. (145)

**statute of limitations *n.*** the time at which a law or regulation ceases to be in effect. (438)

**stereotype *n.*** a predetermined opinion or attitude about something, often regarding a group of people. (85)

**stock *n.*** a share in the ownership of a corporation, based on how much has been invested. (398)

**stockbroker *n.*** a financial services professional who has a license to trade stock for clients. (399)

**stockholder *n.*** the shareholders who own a corporation through its stock. (386)

**stock market *n.*** a collection of exchanges around the world where stocks are traded. (398)

**strategy *n.*** the plan for how a business intends to improve its operations and outperform the competition. (230)

**supply *n.*** a schedule of the quantities that a business will make available to consumers at various prices. (Often coupled with *demand* as in the term "supply and demand.") (71)

**sweat equity *n.*** the time and effort for little or no pay an entrepreneur puts into a venture in the hope of future return. (33)

**SWOT analysis *n.*** a consideration of a situation based on Strengths, Weaknesses, Opportunity, and Threats. (50)

---

**tactics *n.*** the practical ways in which a business carries out its strategy. (231)

**tariff *n.*** a tax imposed by a government on an import to make it more expensive than a similar domestic product and, therefore, less attractive to domestic consumers. (453)

**tax *n.*** a percentage of a business's gross profit or an individual's income levied by a government to support public services. (500)

**tax evasion *n.*** deliberate avoidance of the payment of taxes; can lead to penalties or jail. (502)

**tax-exempt** *adj.* the condition of not having to pay taxes. (390)

**technology** *n.* a way of applying knowledge using technical processes and methods, and those processes and methods themselves. (354)

**test market** *v.* to offer a product or service to a limited, yet representative, segment of consumers in order to receive feedback and improve the product or service, before attempting to place it in a larger market. (87)

**tooling** *n.* the installation of the machinery necessary to manufacture a product. (317)

**trade balance** *n.* the difference between the value of a country's imports and its exports. (453)

**trade barrier** *n.* a government-imposed tax or other effort to discourage citizens from importing or exporting certain products. (529)

**trade fair** *n.* open-air (usually) markets where merchants rent space by the day to sell their products; flea market. (210)

**trademark** *n.* a word, name, symbol, or device used by a manufacturer or merchant to distinguish a product. (259)

**trade-off** *n.* an exchange in which one benefit or advantage is given up in order to gain another. (350)

**trade secret** *n.* the proprietary formulas or other intellectual property of a business that derive value from being kept secret. (481)

**transaction** *n.* in accounting, a payment or deposit written into an accounting journal. (283)

---

**unique selling proposition** *n.* the identification and description of how a business differs from its competitors and makes it unique. (232)

**unit of sale** *n.* the amount of product (or time, in a service business) from which a business figures its operations and profit; considered the "building block" of a business. (16)

---

**value pricing** *n.* a strategy based on finding the balance between price and quality that will attract the most consumers. (247)

**variable cost** *n.* any expense that changes according to the volume of units sold; a term sometimes used instead of "cost of goods sold." (117)

**variable cost per unit** *n.* the identical costs associated with selling "one additional unit" (of sale). (117)

**venture** *n.* a business (or any undertaking that involves risk). (242)

**venture capital** *n.* funds invested in a potentially profitable business enterprise despite risks. (374)

**venture capitalist** *n.* an individual or firm whose business is investing venture capital. (426)

**vertical thinking** *n.* a type of thought process that "stacks" one idea on top of another; vertical thinking can lead to "concept prisons" as new information is fit into existing patterns. (81)

**volatile** *adj.* the state of being subject to frequent and unpredictable change. (543)

**voluntary exchange** *n.* a mutually agreed-on business transaction. (6)

---

**Web site** *n.* an Internet document on the World Wide Web that may contain sound and graphics, as well as text. (357)

**wholesale** *n.* the kind of business that buys from manufacturers or other wholesalers and sells to retail businesses. (20)

**working capital** *n.* the amount of money (assets minus liabilities) that a business has for its operations at any given moment. (477)

**World Wide Web** *n.* referred to as "www" or the "Web"; a subset of the Internet made up of documents that may include text, graphics, and sound. As such, Web pages are *hypertext* documents. (358)

Glossary

# Index

Index

**654**

Index

Index

**Index**

Tyco, 495-496

**Index**